The Oxford Companion to
Modern Poetry

Jeremy Noel-Tod is a Lecturer in Literature and Creative Writing at the University of East Anglia. His published criticism includes articles on a wide range of modern poets, from W. H. Auden to Rae Armantrout. He has reviewed poetry for the *Times Literary Supplement*, the *Daily Telegraph*, the *Guardian*, the *New Statesman*, and the *London Review of Books*.

Ian Hamilton was the editor of *The Oxford Companion to Twentieth-Century Poetry in English*. He was an influential literary critic who wrote extensively on poetry, including *A Gift Imprisoned: The Poetic Life of Matthew Arnold* (1998), and *Against Oblivion: Some Lives of the Twentieth-Century Poets* (2002). He also published studies of the little magazine, the novelist J. D. Salinger, and the footballer Paul Gascoigne. His *Collected Poems* appeared posthumously from Faber and Faber in 2009.

(⊕) SEE WEB LINKS

Some entries in the Companion have recommended web links. When you see the above symbol at the end of an entry go to the dictionary's web page at http://www.oup.com/uk/reference/resources/modernpoetry, click on **Web Links** in the Resources section and locate the entry in the alphabetical list, then click through to the relevant websites. There is also an appendix of recommended general links which can be accessed on the same site.

The Oxford Companion to

Modern Poetry

SECOND EDITION

First edition edited by IAN HAMILTON
Second edition edited by JEREMY NOEL-TOD

OXFORD
UNIVERSITY PRESS

OXFORD
UNIVERSITY PRESS

Great Clarendon Street, Oxford, OX2 6DP,
United Kingdom

Oxford University Press is a department of the University of Oxford.
It furthers the University's objective of excellence in research, scholarship,
and education by publishing worldwide. Oxford is a registered trade mark of
Oxford University Press in the UK and in certain other countries

First Edition published as *The Oxford Companion to Twentieth-Century Poetry
in English* in 1994
First issued as an Oxford University Press paperback 1996
Second Edition published in 2013

Impression: 1

British Library Cataloguing in Publication Data
Data available

Library of Congress Cataloging in Publication Data
Data available

ISBN 978-0-19-964025-6

Printed in Great Britain by
Clays Ltd, St Ives Plc

Contents

Introduction to the Second Edition

The first edition of this unique guide to English-language poets from the last hundred years is itself nearly twenty years old. In the process of bringing it up to date, the final line of a poem by my predecessor, Ian Hamilton, has often come to mind: 'The trellis that needs fixing, that I'll fix' ('The Forties'). Disorderly as a garden, a reference work on living writers and reputations comes with a never-ending 'to do' list. Anthology editors may gather the blooms, but the *Companion* under-gardener has pruning, planting, and fixing to do.

Of the various changes that have been made to this second edition, the most prominent is the title: *The Oxford Companion to Twentieth Century Poetry* is now *The Oxford Companion to Modern Poetry*. Coverage now extends to the first decade of the twenty-first century, while the starting-point for inclusion by publication has been brought forward to 1910: the year when, among other auspicious events for poetic modernity, T. S. Eliot began 'The Love Song of J. Alfred Prufrock', Gertrude Stein wrote her verse-portrait of Picasso, and Thomas Hardy asked a 'crocus root', stirring for spring, 'How do you know?' ('The Year's Awakening').

The majority of the volume remains the 'map of modern poetry' that Ian Hamilton compiled in 1994. The A-Z text, however, is now exclusively a biographical dictionary of poets, supplemented by an appendix on the groups and movements in which they were involved. A handful of entries on versification and other contextual topics has been withdrawn in deference to more comprehensive works. With the remaining text, I have followed a policy of primarily bibliographic revision, augmenting the critical judgements of the original contributors with later publication history: glass extensions to buildings of character. Where I have amended or added to those judgements, this has been indicated by an asterisk after the original author's name.

Another small but comprehensive revision has been the substitution of publisher name for place of publication. The country of a poet's predominant activity may be inferred from the life, but the progress of a career through small presses or large houses is itself a revealing history. There is also a passing poetry to the names of the former (if not the latter) that I hope will appeal to the readers of this *Companion*.

Unlike the first editor, who played a solely commissioning role, I have also written the majority of new entries in this edition, supported by the invaluable expertise of a number of other hands, old and new. The aim has been to expand the map as much as possible, at a time when the cartographic metaphor itself might be considered a historical artefact. The Anglophone poetic cultures covered by this book remain strongly concerned with—and strikingly bound by—national territories. But the international nature of the language they use, and the digital dissemination of their activity, makes the network, rather than the map, seem the most appropriate way to imagine contemporary poets in relation to each other now. Cross-references are one way in which I have attempted to cross borders.

Tracing the nodes of a network is also one way in which I have approached the representation of competing territorial claims. On each national stage, the poets continue their civil wars, and there are undoubtedly too many on all sides for any single-volume work to encompass. One of the most pressing and controversial questions, therefore, in compiling such a guide, is which individuals to single out. Entering the lists, I have been guided by anthologies published since 1994, paying particular attention to two categories that were significantly under-anthologized twenty years ago: female poets and avant-garde poetics. The first edition figure of 13% for women poets was not a statistic that reflected well on the twentieth century. I am pleased to note that among new entries it is nearly 50%.

At the same time, I have tried to maintain the geographic proportions of the first edition. An equal share of new entries for the British Isles and the United States reflects the fact that this remains a companion that comes from Britain (and within it, England). It is also one that continues to investigate the century-long question of the relationship between 'the daily island life' of poetry here—as Stein put it—and the emergence of independent Anglophone literary traditions, especially across the Atlantic. The previous editor, who felt he had lived through the late-century 'divorce' of England and America, evidently viewed the divergence anxiously. If I am allowed my own pious hope it is that the Internet may be a great healer. It has certainly made revising this *Companion* a relatively practical task for one person.

It seems time to declare the judgements I have made in editing 'Hamilton', metonym and man. I echo him in hoping that this second edition 'will be seen as serious and useful', but read for entertainment, too. It is, after all, the high delight of poetry that we are talking about here. At the same time, I have tried to maximize its interest for those readers and students who (like me) consider the last hundred years of Anglophone poetry a major literary epoch. I have, therefore, left in the twentieth century a number of novelists not remembered for their verse; a number of poets whose claim to inclusion seemed pre-dominantly historical (e.g. Second World War combatants); and various one-offs, such as a lone songwriter (Bob Dylan), and a lone place, 'Fitzrovia'—a nod, perhaps, to the literary London where the networks of the first edition were established. I have also removed, replaced, or sought to temper entries which seemed more suited in tone to a bar-room dismissal, and even, in some cases, calculated to start a brawl.

One area of contention that I have largely tried to sidestep is the judgement of quality implicit in the length of an individual entry. Revising original contributions, I have rarely picked up my scissors, though I have sometimes picked up my pen. All new poets have been introduced concisely, within a hundred words of each other, and a handful of entries for poets already in the first edition have been replaced entirely. For the age of the Internet I have tried to devise a compact resource that guides outwards to wider reading. Longer biographies, audio recordings, and poems themselves may be explored via the appendix of web links.

The first edition's partial survey of poetry magazines has now been subsumed, where possible, under the entries for their poet-editors. I have dropped the earlier policy of cross-referencing some names solely to the group or movement with which they are associated. I have also attempted to rationalize the definition of such groups to critically-formulated associations of individuals with a common literary aim. This *Companion* focuses on the art of verse for the page, but other forms that cross over into other media have been given entries for representative poets, chosen according to measures of prestige such as anthologies, publications, prizes, and criticism, as well as that more intangible thing: reputation.

The essential criteria for the inclusion of new poets remains age: over 30, if still living. My own higher bar has been set at the publication of at least three full-length collections or equivalent by 2011. In light of the boom in poetry publishing and creative writing as a career since the 1990s, this seems a reasonable inflation. Inevitably, any number of young, neglected, or simply modest poets have consequently been passed over—many personal enthusiasms among them. All poetry lovers cherish forgotten causes. I have tried to keep in mind an ideal reader who wants to find out about poets they know, poets they have heard of, and poets they may read next.

All oversights are of course entirely my own, but I would like to thank the following people for their assistance, advice, and contributions over the last two years: Fleur Adcock, Paul Batchelor, Marianne Boruch, Beverley Bie Brahic, Vahni Capildeo, Tom Clark, Henri Cole, Eleanor Cook, Emily Critchley, Alison Croggon, Amy De'Ath, Toby Davidson, Carrie Etter, Giles Foden, Mark Ford, Roger Garfitt, Peter Gizzi, Jim Goar, Jonathon Green, Emily Grosholz, Kelly Grovier, Ross Hair, Nathan Hamilton, Allan

Hepburn, Alan Jenkins, Joshua Jones, Daniel Kane, Thomas Karshan, Kate Kilalea, John Kinsella, Nicholas Laughlin, Paddy Lyons, Chris McCabe, Robyn Marsack, Leo Mellor, Rod Mengham, Vanessa Mitchell, Blake Morrison, Fiona Nairn, Vivek Narayan, Pat Norse, Bernard O'Donoghue, Femi Oyebode, Christopher Pollnitz, Rachel Potter, Robert Potts, Richard Price, William H. Pritchard, Graeme Richardson, Sam Riviere, Sophie Robinson, Carol Rumens, Nick Selby, Kelwyn Sole, Thomas Swiss, Patrick Taylor, Toh Hsien Min, Jeff Titon, David Wheatley, Clive Wilmer, and Heather Yeung. I would also like to thank the University of East Anglia for the research leave during which I began this work; the staff of the Saison Poetry Library in London for maintaining a working haven; my research assistant, Iain Rowley, for his bibliographic labours; and my editors at Oxford University Press, Rebecca Lane and Joanna Harris, for patiently guiding me through the reference-work process. My contribution to this *Companion* is dedicated to the memory of my father, who gave me the first edition, and with love to my day-to-day assistants, also known as my family: Beccy, Edie, and Violet.

Jeremy Noel-Tod

Introduction to the First Edition

This *Companion* is offered both as a reference work and as a history, a map of modern poetry in English. It may be thought that the territory has already been well mapped, in anthologies and textbooks, but I can think of no other single-volume publication that runs from 1900 to the present day and covers topics, movements, magazines, and genres as well as individual poets, dead and alive.

Over the five years that I have worked on the *Companion* I have more than once paused to remind myself how speedily such maps can change, how fashions rise and dive. Imagine a similar compilation put together in, say, 1950. Dylan Thomas would have had more space than he gets here, and so too would Nicholas Moore, Karl Shapiro, Sidney Keyes, and other big-name figures of that time. Surrealism would have bulked larger, and there would have been a more tender deference to periodicals like *Poetry Quarterly* and *Poetry London*. The precise contours would of course have depended on who had done the mapping, but the general shape would surely have reflected the epoch's taste for the florid and religiose, its lack of any real interest in technique, its suspicion that the political poets of the 1930s had somewhat let the side down, and so on.

Ten years later, the map would have changed again, with Auden and Empson restored to favour. We would note a new respect for the output of the American academies and for those writers of the 1940s who had kept their wits about them and not turned to God, or Jung. Overall, there would have been more braininess than ecstasy, more common sense than communal subconscious. In covering these bygone decades, I have tried to keep in mind some notion of how things must have seemed *then*, and to balance this against what I take to be history's subsequent or current valuation. At the same time, I have been wary of the passage-of-time school of literary judgement. It isn't true that 'if it's good, it will survive'; someone, somewhere has to keep saying that it's good—or if not good, exactly, then at least worthy of a small piece of the historical jigsaw, the map. There are poets discussed in this *Companion* who would probably not get into any 'up-to-date' anthology of modern verse. Their inclusion, though, should not be viewed as merely archivistic. Who knows how things will look in ten years' time?

Perhaps the first thing to be confessed of this 1994 *Companion* is that it comes from England (or Britain: 'England', in this introduction, should be taken to mean the United Kingdom as a whole). Forty years ago this would not have seemed like much of a confession; after all, the book is meant to be about poetry in *English*, is it not? Indeed, when I imagined a pre-1960 version of it, I automatically did the imagining in terms of poetry in England, with only parenthetical reference to the United States. In spite of all the movable road signs, London was still the metropolis that mattered. Take it on to the mid-Sixties, though, and there is a serious effrontery in this assumption. A *Companion* done in 1965 would have needed to acknowledge Boston or New York or San Francisco—or even Liverpool, alas. Nowadays, London is but one of several capitals, and most people are agreed that 'poetry in English' can no longer be thought of in the singular.

If the *Companion* has a plot, then, it is to do with this shift from 'poetry' to 'poetries'. And in order to make sense of this shift, the plot inevitably centres on the relationship between the poetries of England and America. It tells of a courtship, a marriage, a divorce. In the first third of the century we have a lively interplay between the English and American traditions, each seeming to vitalize the other; in the middle third there is a struggle for control; the final third shows a gradual decline of interest, so that in the end even the rivalry seems to have died.

And if we look beyond England and America to the poetries of Australia, Canada, and the several other English-speaking territories covered in this book, we can see that they too have an involvement in the central romance: they have invariably felt the need to take one side or the other, however determined they have been to establish identities which they can call their own. These identities are already distinctive and describable, as I hope the *Companion*'s coverage makes clear, and can only become more so as the poets of these territories continue to explore the ways in which *their* English differs from the English of England and America. And this is to talk only of language-differences—differences of sensibility we take to be already well-declared. At the moment, it is hard to imagine the poetries of Australia, Canada, and so on, making a complete break with their Anglo-American parentage. There is a wish to make that break, and a wish not to. It is perhaps from this conflict that distinctiveness currently ensues. To which someone will no doubt retort: try telling that one to the Aborigines.

People talk about modern poetry being different from other, earlier poetry. When asked what they mean, they usually reply that it is less accessible, less disciplined in its technique: modern poets, they say, care little for their audience and are contemptuous of tradition. None of these definitions can be made to stick. 'Difficulty' is not a twentieth-century invention, nor is the wish to make innovations in technique. And as for questions of 'audience' and 'tradition', it could be argued that these are topics on which modern poets have worried themselves almost to excess.

It could further be contended that the insistency of such worries was what first marked off modern poetry from the poetry we had before. At no earlier period, it could be said, were the makers of poems required so nakedly to ask themselves: why poems? At no earlier period was the potential audience so thrillingly immense and yet (or therefore) so depressingly neglectful. At no period were the tribal bard's tribe-altering pretensions so cheerfully disdained. For a poet in, say, 1920, there was real, sometimes exquisite anguish in perceiving what the new 'mass literacy' was likely to amount to, in terms of the survival of his art. Edmund Wilson's essay 'Is Verse a Dying Technique?' appeared in 1928. It was all very well for Eliot to extol poetry as civilization's 'highest point of consciousness, its greatest power and its most delicate sensibility', but which 'civilization', exactly, did he have in mind? In his own poems, the consciousness, both powerful and delicate, is one of exclusion and defeat, as if a doctor were prohibited from tending his sick patient—with the prohibition coming from the patient.

But Eliot's cultural idealism (and Pound's too) was American in origin, and when we try to define the differentness of modern poetry this is perhaps where the investigation should begin: at the point when English poetry became Anglo-American. No earlier English poetry took much cognizance of outsiders, unless those outsiders were long dead and came from Greece or Rome. By the 1920s, though, the two most impressive and influential poet-critics in London were writing with at least one eye on their own, far-away backyards—in Massachusetts or Idaho. And from those backyards there was an answering alertness. When William Carlos Williams read *The Waste Land*, he said: 'I had to watch him carry my world with him, the fool, to the enemy.' The enemy was Europe, and 'my world' was 'the local conditions in America'—what Williams called 'the American grain'.

As Ezra Pound saw it, Williams's sense of betrayal sprang from a kind of fake primitivism, from envy and ignorance, the sort of backwardness, or backyardness, that had driven Pound to Europe in the first place. To him, Williams—or 'little Bill', as he liked to call him—was no more than a 'village cutup', the 'most bloody inarticulate animal that ever gargled'. And yet, from their opposing standpoints, both Pound and Williams dreamed of an American Renaissance. For Pound this could only be achieved by treating the United States as medieval, lagging 500 years behind the Europeans. For Williams, America was more than just a cultural condition, it was an actual place, 'a world of great beauty and ripest blossom'. It was also a 'hard, truculent, turbulent mass' that had yet to be properly, open-mindedly explored. Europe and its art had 'painted over, smeared' the mysteries of the New World. The newness of America had never been grasped or understood on its own terms by native artists because the cultural assumptions and ambitions of those artists had not actually been native. The ethnic-American poetries that are so trumpeted today have their roots in Williams's start-afresh polemic. After all, did not Pound also mock Williams as a 'dago immigrant'? Williams's mother, he seemed to recall, came from Santo Domingo.

The quarrel between Williams's nativism and Pound's cosmopolitanism was an American quarrel, and it is chiefly in the history of American poetry that we can see its consequences acted out: in the proudly reactionary attitudinizing of Ransom, Tate, and the Southern Agrarians; in the New Criticism on the one hand and Black Mountain on the other; in the split between a poetry of the academy and a poetry of the soil—the Paleface versus Redskin, cooked versus raw face-offs identified by Robert Lowell—and in the continuing argument between readers and performers, page and stage. The Lowell generation was probably the last on either side of the Atlantic to believe in the continuity of the Anglo-American collaboration, and in *Life Studies* Lowell nobly tried to get the best of 'his' two worlds: to write a European poetry under the influence of William Carlos Williams. When Lowell moved from strict metres to *vers libre* he was deferring not to Pound's Europe but to Williams's America. We can, if we wish, now view *Life Studies* as even more comprehensively elegiac than it seemed in 1959.

There have of course been post-Lowell Americans who looked to England for their models, but they have been marginalized in their own culture or, as with the current New Formalists, they have been obliged to make a stately song-and-dance about their reverence for Tradition or Antiquity. And there are today British poets who cut a dash by imitating Ashbery or Merrill. But English poetry since Auden has, on the whole, tried to make Englishness a virtue. The Amis–Larkin generation chucklingly made a point of declaring its contempt for all things transatlantic—or, come to that, cross-channel. Would they have been more stylistically adventurous, more feelingful and eloquent, if the American irritant had not been there? Has 'being English' in this sense actually been shaped by the wish not to be American? The English native tradition has been kept intact and is seemingly vigorous, but is it not too arrogantly static?

Every so often the English have gone in for a bout of transatlantic yearning—A. Alvarez's 1963 anthology *The New Poetry* more or less told English poets to learn from America or die—in Pound's words—'piecemeal of a sort of emotional anaemia'—and these bouts will now and then recur. There is a solemnly programmatic strain in American letters which will always attract the undriven, the good learners. But the Americans are less impressed than they used to be by English imitations, and their critical rhetoric these days tends to be aggressively home-spun. Helen Vendler introduces her Faber (or Harvard, depending where you are) anthology of *Contemporary American Poetry* with the warning that her book 'will be able to extend its charm only to those who genuinely know the American language—by now a language separate in accent, intonation, discourse and lexicon, from English'. This is not so very different from what Auden said in 1956 when he introduced *his* Faber book of *Modern American Verse*. Speaking of the difference between American and English, Auden called it 'the most subtle difference of all and the hardest to define ... what the secret of the difference is I cannot put my finger on', but he could tell it when he heard it, in Robinson or Frost, and did not in the least feel that it debarred him from responding to those poets' charms.

It is Vendler's tone of 'Keep off, this is now *ours*' that makes one hesitate to suggest a speedy reconciliation. Maybe American poets *need* fifty years of freedom from English constraints. And maybe the English need a break from having to reaffirm their Englishness. We'll see. But the two languages still have much in common, much that the one can borrow from the other; so that I do now and then find myself entertaining the pious hope that this *Companion* might help to rekindle an old spark. It seems to me that each side should at least know what the other side is up to, and have some sense of the ins and outs of the historical relationship.

It will perhaps be thought that I am straining for a narrative that isn't/ wasn't there. If I am, then you can blame it on *my* taste—a taste shaped in the early to mid-1960s, when the examples of Europeanized Americans like Lowell, Snodgrass, Berryman, Roethke, and Plath really did seem to be urging a renegotiated treaty. The 'enemies' in those days were twofold: in America, the academic-experimental, with its theories about breath, pulse, the open field of the white page, and sundry other elaborations or distortions of the Williams line; in England, the Beatlish ingratiators, with their student-union poetry readings, their 'disaffiliate' life-styles, and their wide-eyed insistence that 'most people ignore most poetry because most poetry ignores most people'—a cry both electrifying and anaesthe-tizing, as it proved. These enemies are still abroad, in various new guises, and several of them will be found to feature in this book. They have to; they are on the map.

In other words, this is not a critical anthology; nor is it a textbook I want it to be seen as serious and useful, but I will not at all mind if it is read for fun, as a kind of documentary-entertainment. For those who like making lists, as I do, I here offer a few leads (all figures are approximate, and susceptible to computerized riposte). The *Companion* covers about 1,500 poets, 100 subjects. Of the poets, 550 are British, 550 American. Other territories break down as follows: Australia (120), Canada (110), Africa (60), Asia (40), New Zealand (35), Caribbean (30). There are about 200 women and 100 black writers. Twenty-seven poets had nervous breakdowns, fifteen committed suicide, and fifteen were/are diag-nosed as alcoholic. Nineteen served time in jail, fourteen died in battle, three were murdered, one executed. Zany professions include lumberjack tax inspector, furniture remover, carpet salesman, and policeman, but of course the vast majority of poets earn their living in universities. The most popular off-campus day-job is that of doctor or psychiatrist. Only one poet has played hockey for his country.

Ezra Pound is most often mentioned as an influence on other poets, with Auden, Yeats and Williams runners-up. Eliot is named less often than Lowell and Stevens. Rilke is the most influential foreign poet. More poets died in their seventies than at any other time of life. More lived past the age of 80 than died young (that is, before the age of 40). The most popular year to be born in was 1947, with 1934 not far behind. The dominant poetic star-sign is . . .

Enough, though. To qualify for inclusion in this *Companion*, a poet needs to have lived in the twentieth century, if only for a month or so. Thus, Stephen Crane sneaks in but Hopkins is omitted. A poet also has to be over 30, if still living; the youngest in the book was born in 1963. He or she must have published at least one substantial collection of poetry. There may well be poets who have been unjustly overlooked, and reviewers will no doubt tell me who they are. In some instances, the poets themselves will bear the news. The choice of subjects and contributors, the allocation of space, and the general orienta-tion of the book have been my responsibility. The opinions expressed by individual contributors are not always opinions that I share.

Attempting to cover such a vast field has of course meant soliciting lots of advice, and I am grateful to many of my contributors for their informal guidance. In particular, I would like to acknowledge the help of Douglas Dunn (on Scotland), Peter Porter (Australia), and Mario Relich (Caribbean). For the American coverage I have sought assistance from numerous quarters, and most of my US contributors have at one time or another been conscripted as editorial consultants (unofficial and unpaid): I have appreciated their forbearance even though I have not always followed their advice. On US matters I have also had useful comment from Donald Hall, Richard Howard, Mary Gray Hughes, Stanley Plumly, Mark Strand, and David Wojahn. On Commonwealth poets, Alistair Niven of the Arts Council of Great Britain gave me many useful leads, and I should also mention with gratitude Guy Butler, J. M. Coetzee, Patrick Cullinan, James Curry, C. J. Driver, Lloyd

Fernando, Andrew Gurr, Dennis Lee, Alan Lawson, Leslie Monkman, John Robinson, Elizabeth Richie, and Kelwyn Sole.

The original idea for the *Companion* came from Kim Scott Walwyn of the Oxford University Press, and I am grateful to her for helping to set out the guidelines, so to speak, and for generally getting the thing moving. In the later stages, Frances Whistler and Andrew Lockett have kept it on the rails and Jeff New has made numerous mechanical— and some not-so-mechanical—adjustments; in their different ways each has saved me a few blushes, for which I am most thankful. My chief debt, though, has been to my day-to-day assistant Charis Ryder. She has managed the administration with her customary thoroughness, but her vigilance has extended to all aspects of the undertaking so that she has been, in effect, co-editor.

Ian Hamilton

Selection of Anthologies

Against Expression: An Anthology of Conceptual Writing, ed. Craig Dworkin and Kenneth Goldsmith (Northwestern University Press, 2011).

American Hybrid: A Norton Anthology of New Poetry, ed. Cole Swensen and David St. John (Norton, 2009).

American Poets in the 21st Century: The New Poetics, ed. Claudia Rankine and Lisa Sewell (Wesleyan University Press, 2007).

American Women Poets in the 21st Century: Where Lyric Meets Language, ed. Claudia Rankine and Juliana Spahr (Wesleyan University Press, 2002).

An Anthology of Modern Irish Poetry, ed. Wes Davis (Belknap Press of Harvard University Press, 2010).

An Anthology of New (American) Poets, ed. Lisa Jarnot with Leonard Schwartz and Chris Stroffolino (Talisman House, 1998).

An Anthology of New Zealand Poetry in English, ed. Jenny Bornholdt, Gregory O'Brien, and Mark Williams (Oxford University Press, 1997).

An Anthology of Twentieth-Century New Zealand Poetry, ed. Vincent O'Sullivan (Oxford University Press, 1987).

Anthology of Twentieth-Century British and Irish Poetry, ed. Keith Tuma (Oxford University Press, 2001).

Australian Verse: An Oxford Anthology, ed. John Leonard (Oxford University Press, 1998).

Big Smoke: New Zealand Poems 1960–1975, ed. Alan Brunton, Murray Edmond, and Michele Leggott (Auckland University Press, 2000).

The Bloodaxe Book of Contemporary Indian Poets, ed. Jeet Thayil (Bloodaxe, 2008).

The Blue Wind: Poems in English from Pakistan, introduced by Peter Dent (Interim, 1984).

Breathing Fire: Canada's New Poets, ed. Lorna Crozier and Patrick Lane (Harbour, 1995).

Botsotso: An Anthology of Contemporary South African Poetry, ed. Allan Kolski Horwitz and Ken Edwards (Reality Street, 2009).

Conductors of Chaos: A Poetry Anthology, ed. Iain Sinclair (Picador, 1996).

Contemporary American Poetry, ed. Donald Hall (Penguin, 1962, 1971).

Contemporary American Poetry, ed. A. Poulin Jr. (Houghton Mifflin, 1971, 1975, 1980, 1985, 1991, 1996, 2001, 2006).

Contemporary Australian Poetry, ed. John Leonard (Houghton Mifflin, 1990).

Contemporary Indian Poetry in English, ed. Kaiser Haq (Ohio State University Press, 1990).

Dream State: New Scottish Poets, ed. Donny O'Rourke (Polygon, 1994, 2002).

The Faber Book of Irish Verse, ed. John Montague (Faber, 1974).

The Faber Book of Modern American Verse, ed. W. H. Auden (Faber, 1956).

The Faber Book of Modern Australian Verse, ed. Vincent Buckley (Faber, 1991).

The Faber Book of Modern Verse, ed. Michael Roberts (Faber, 1936, 1951, 1965, 1982).

The Faber Book of Twentieth-Century Scottish Poetry, ed. Douglas Dunn (Faber, 1992).

The Faber Book of Twentieth-Century Women's Poetry, ed. Fleur Adcock (Faber, 1987).

The Fate of Vultures: New Poetry of Africa, ed. M. Zimunya, P. Porter, and K. Anyidoho (Heinemann, 1989).

The Firebox: Poetry in Britain and Ireland after 1945, ed. Sean O'Brien (Picador, 1998).

From Our Yard: Jamaican Poetry since Independence, ed. Pamela Mordecai (Institute of Jamaica, 1987).

From the Other Side of the Century: A New American Poetry 1960–1990, ed. Douglas Messerli (Sun & Moon, 1994).

The Fugitive Poets: Modern Southern Poetry in Perspective, ed. W. C. Pratt (Dutton, 1965).
Furious Flower: African American Poetry from the Black Arts Movement to the Present, ed. Joanne V. Gabbin (University of Virginia Press, 2004).
Gathering Ground: A Reader Celebrating Cave Canem's First Decade, ed. Toi Derricotte and Cornelius Eady (University of Michigan Press, 2006).
The Golden Apples of the Sun: Twentieth Century Australian Poetry, ed. C. Wallace-Crabbe (Melbourne University Press, 1980).
A Group Anthology, ed. E. Lucie-Smith and P. Hobsbaum (Oxford University Press, 1963).
Harper's Anthology of Twentieth-Century Native American Poetry, ed. Duane Niatum (Harper & Row, 1988).
The Harvard Book of Contemporary American Poetry, ed. Helen Vendler (Belknap Press of Harvard University Press, 1985).
The Harvill Book of Twentieth-Century Poetry in English, ed. Michael Schmidt (Harvill, 1999).
The Heinemann Book of African Poetry in English, ed. Adewale Maja-Pearce (Heinemann, 1990).
Hinterland: Caribbean Poets from the West Indies and Britain, ed. E. A. Markham (Bloodaxe, 1989).
Identity Parade: New British and Irish Poets, ed. Roddy Lumsden (Bloodaxe, 2010).
Indivisible: An Anthology of Contemporary South Asian American Poetry, ed. Neelanjana Banerjee, Kaipa Summi, and Sundaralingam Pireeni (University of Arkansas Press, 2010).
Infinite Difference: Other Poetries by U.K. Women Poets, ed. Carrie Etter (Shearsman, 2010).
In the American Tree, ed. Ron Silliman (National Poetry Foundation, 1986, 2002).
Language for a New Century: Contemporary Poetry from the Middle East, Asia and Beyond, ed. Tina Chang, Nathalie Handal, and Ravi Shankar (Norton, 2008).
The Lava of this Land: South African Poetry 1960–1996, ed. Denis Hirson (Northwestern University Press, 1997).
Legitimate Dangers: American Poets of the New Century, ed. Michael Dumanis and Cate Marvin (Sarabande, 2006).
Lyric Postmodernisms, ed. Reginald Shepherd (Counterpath, 2008).
Mambo Book of Zimbabwean Verse in English, ed. C. and O. Style-Gwern (Mambo, 1986).
The Mid-Century: English Poetry 1940–1960, ed. David Wright (Penguin, 1965).
Modern American Poetry, ed. Louis Untermeyer (Harcourt, Brace, 1962, 1969).
Modern Canadian Poets, ed. Todd Swift and Evan Jones (Carcanet, 2010).
Modern Irish Poetry, ed. Patrick Crotty (Blackstaff, 1995).
Modern Poetry from Africa, ed. Ulli Beier and Gerald Moor (Penguin, 1963; revd. as *The Penguin Book of Modern African Poetry*, 1984).
Modern Women Poets, ed. Deryn Rees-Jones (Bloodaxe, 2005).
The New African Poetry: An Anthology, ed. Tanure Ojaide and Tijan M. Sallah (Lynne Rienner, 1999).
The New American Poetry, 1945–1960, ed. Donald M. Allen (Grove, 1960).
The New Australian Poetry, ed. John Tranter (Makar, 1979).
A New Book of South African Verse in English, ed. Guy Butler and Chris Mann (Oxford University Press, 1979).
The New British Poetry, ed. Gillian Allnutt, Fred D'Aguiar, Ken Edwards, and Eric Mottram (Paladin, 1988).
New British Poetry, ed. Don Paterson and Charles Simic (Graywolf, 2004).
The New Canon: An Anthology of Canadian Poetry, ed. Carmine Starnino (Véhicule, 2005).
The New Century of South African Poetry, ed. Michael Chapman (Donker, 2002).
New Impulses in Australian Poetry, ed. T. Shapcott and R. Hall (University of Queensland Press, 1968).

The New Irish Poets, ed. Selina Guinness (Bloodaxe, 2004).
New Music: An Anthology of Contemporary Australian Poetry, ed. John Leonard (Five Islands, 2001).
The New Oxford Book of Australian Verse, ed. Les Murray (Oxford University Press, 1986, 1991).
The New Oxford Book of Canadian Verse in English, ed. Margaret Atwood (Oxford University Press, 1982).
The New Oxford Book of Irish Verse, ed. Thomas Kinsella (Oxford University Press, 1986).
The New Penguin Book of Scottish Verse, ed. Robert Crawford and Mick Imlah (Penguin, 2000).
The New Poetry, ed. A. Alvarez (Penguin, 1962, 1966).
The New Poetry, ed. Michael Hulse, David Kennedy, and David Morley (Bloodaxe, 1993).
The New York Poets II, ed. Mark Ford and Trevor Winkfield (Carcanet, 2006).
The New Young American Poetry, ed. Kevin Prufer (Southern Illinois University Press, 2000).
The Norton Anthology of Modern and Contemporary Poetry, ed. Jahan Ramazini with Richard Ellmann and Robert O'Clair (Norton, 2003).
Open Field: 30 Contemporary Canadian Poets, ed. Sina Queyras (Persea, 2005).
Oral Poetry from Africa, ed. J. Mapanje and L. White (Longman, 1983).
OTHER: British and Irish Poetry Since 1970, ed. Richard Caddell and Peter Quartermain (Wesleyan University Press, 1999).
Out of Everywhere: Linguistically Innovative Poetry by Women in North America & the UK, ed. Maggie O'Sullivan (Reality Street, 1996).
The Oxford Book of American Verse, ed. F. O. Matthiessen (Oxford University Press, 1950).
The Oxford Book of Caribbean Verse, ed. Stewart Brown and Mark McWatt (Oxford University Press, 2005).
The Oxford Book of Contemporary New Zealand Poetry, ed. Fleur Adcock (Oxford University Press, 1982).
The Oxford Book of Scottish Verse, ed. John MacQueen and Tom Scott (Clarendon, 1966).
The Oxford Book of Twentieth-Century English Verse, ed. Philip Larkin (Clarendon, 1973).
The Oxford India Anthology of Twelve Modern Indian Poets, ed. A. K. Mehrotra (Oxford University Press, 1992).
The Penguin Anthology of Australian Poetry, ed. John Kinsella (Penguin, 2008).
The Penguin Anthology of Twentieth-Century American Poetry, ed. Rita Dove (Penguin, 2011).
The Penguin Book of Canadian Verse, ed. Ralph Gustafson (Penguin, 1958, 1967, 1975).
The Penguin Book of Caribbean Verse in English, ed. Paula Burnett (Penguin, 1986).
The Penguin Book of Contemporary British Poetry, ed. Blake Morrison and Andrew Motion (Penguin, 1982).
The Penguin Book of Contemporary New Zealand Verse, ed. I. Wedde and H. McQueen (Penguin, 1985).
The Penguin Book of Contemporary Verse, 1918–1960, ed. Kenneth Allott (Penguin, 1962).
The Penguin Book of Modern Australian Poetry, ed. J. Tranter and P. Mead (Penguin, 1991).
The Penguin Book of New Zealand Verse, ed. Allen Curnow (Penguin, 1960; revd. edn., ed. Douglas Stewart, 1966).
The Penguin Book of Poetry from Britain and Ireland since 1945, ed. Simon Armitage and Robert Crawford (Penguin, 1998).
The Penguin Book of Southern African Verse, ed. Stephen Gray (Penguin, 1989).
Poems for the Millennium Volume Two: From Postwar to Millennium, ed. Jerome Rothenberg and Pierre Joris (University of California Press, 1998).
Poems from East Africa, ed. D. Cook and D. Rubadiri (Heinemann, 1971).

Poems from India, Sri Lanka, Malaysia and Singapore, ed. Y. Gooneratne (Heinemann, 1979).

Poems of Black Africa, ed. Wole Soyinka (Heinemann, 1975).

Poetry by Canadian Women, ed. Rosemary Sullivan (Oxford University Press, 1982).

The Poetry of War, ed. Ian Hamilton (Ross, 1965).

Poets of the New Century, ed. Roger Weingarten and Richard Higgerson (Godine, 2001).

Postmodern American Poetry, ed. Paul Hoover (Norton, 1994).

Reasons for Belonging: Fourteen Contemporary Indian Poets, ed. Ranjit Hoskote (Penguin, 2002).

Rebel Angels: 25 Poets of the New Formalism, ed. Mark Jarman and David Mason (Story Line, 1996).

Red: Contemporary Black British Poetry, ed. Kwame Dawes (Peepal Tree, 2010).

Ten South African Poets, ed. Adam Schwartzman (Carcanet, 1999).

Ten Twentieth-Century Indian Poets, ed. R. Parthasarathy (Oxford University Press, 1976).

Twentieth Century Poetry and Poetics, ed. Gary Geddes (Oxford University Press, 1969, 1973, 1985, 1996, 2006).

Twenty Contemporary New Zealand Poets, ed. Andrew Johnston and Robin Marsack (Carcanet, 2009).

Two Decades of Indian Poetry: 1960–1980, ed. K. N. Daruwalla (Vikas, 1989).

Vanishing Points: New Modernist Poems, ed. Rod Mengham and John Kinsella (Salt, 2004).

A Various Art, ed. Andrew Crozier and Tim Longville (Carcanet, 1987).

The Vintage Book of African American Poetry, ed. Michael S. Harper and Anthony Walton (Vintage, 2000).

The Vintage Book of Contemporary American Poetry, ed. J. D. McClatchy (Vintage, 1990, 2003).

Key to Contributors

MQA	Michael Q. Abraham	LdeS	Lakshmi de Silva
LA	Lionel Abrahams	LD	Laurence Donovan
FKA	**Fleur Adcock**	JD	Jeff Doyle
FA	Fadzilah Amin	DED	Douglas Dunn
RA	Ranjana Ash	**CE**	**Carrie Etter**
CLB	Charles Bainbridge	NE	Nicholas Everett
DBa	Douglas Barbour	GE	Gavin Ewart
JDB	Jonathan Barker	CF	Colin Falck
DRB	Donald R. Bartlett	DWF	D.W. Fenza
PBa	**Paul Batchelor**	GF	Giles Foden
CB	Christopher Benfey	PF	Peter Forbes
BB	Bruce Bennett	**MF**	**Mark Ford**
RB	Reg Berry	EHF	Edward Foster
NB	Neil Besner	EDF	Elaine D. Foster
SPB	Sven Birkerts	RF	Robert Fraser
PB	Peter Bland	AF	Anne French
GB	Gillian Boddy	SPG	Sharmani Patricia Gabriel
JB	James Booth	**RGa**	**Roger Garfitt**
MB	**Marianne Boruch**	GG	Gary Geddes
GHB	George Bowering	RG	Roger Gilbert
MCB	Matthew C. Brennan	**WG**	**William Gillies**
DBr	David Brooks	DG	Dana Gioia
WSB	W. S. Broughton	MG	Michael Gnarowski
SB	Stewart Brown	KG	Kevin Goddard
AB	Alan Brownjohn	NG	Noreen Golfman
EB	Edward Butscher	KGo	Ken Goodwin
RWB	R. W. Butterfield	YG	Yasmine Gooneratne
ALRC	Angus Calder	SEG	Sherrill E. Grace
JC	James Campbell	JG	Jamie Grant
AC	Amit Chaudhuri	RJG	Richard Gray
TC	**Tom Clark**	RGr	Robert Gray
GC	Graham Clarke	SG	Stephen Gray
HC	**Henri Cole**	AG	Arthur Gregor
EC	**Eleanor Cook**	**EG**	**Emily Grosholz**
JTC	Jane Todd Cooper	**KGr**	**Kelly Grovier**
WC	William Corbett	RSG	R. S. Gwynn
NC	Neil Corcoran	RHa	Rachel Hadas
ECr	**Emily Critchley**	JH	John Haffenden
JCr	Julian Croft	**RoH**	**Ross Hair**
ACr	**Alison Croggon**	**NH**	**Nathan Hamilton**
PD	Peter Dale	CHa	Cliff Hanna
TD	**Toby Davidson**	CPH	Claire Harman
DD	Douglas Daymond	TJGH	T. J. G. Harris
ADA	**Amy De'Ath**	KH	Kevin Hart
TDeP	Thomas DePietro	SbinH	Shuaib bin Hasan

AHa	Alamgir Hashmi	LMcM	Lynne McMahon
DHa	Dennis Haskell	IMcM	Ian McMillan
RBH	Ronald B. Hatch	RMcP	Robert McPhillips
HH	Hugh Haughton	HMcQ	Harvey McQueen
DHe	David Headon	WM	Wes Magee
SH	Seamus Heaney	AM-P	Adewale Maja-Pearce
MH	Michael Heller	POM	Pierre Maldive
PDH	Philip Hobsbaum	BM	Bill Manhire
DH	Daniel Hoffman	DM	David Mason
CH	Christopher Hope	GM	Glyn Maxwell
RH	Ron Horning	CM	Clive Meachen
AH	Andrew Hudgins	PM	Philip Mead
EH	Eamonn Hughes	AKM	Arvind Krishna Mehrotra
MHu	Michael Hulse	**LMe**	**Leo Mellor**
MI	Mick Imlah	BMe	Bruce Meyer
KI	Kevin Ireland	**AMl**	**Ange Mlinko**
SMI	S. Manzoorul Islam	JM	John Mole
MacDJ	MacDonald Jackson	**PBM**	**Blake Morrison**
DJ	Dan Jacobson	AM	Andrew Motion
MJ	Mark Jarman	M-HM	Mpalive-Hangson Msiska
AJ	**Alan Jenkins**	LM	Les Murray
NJ	Nicholas Jenkins	**VN**	**Vivek Narayan**
KJ	Kai Jensen	WHN	W. H. New
EJ	Evan Jones	**JNT**	**Jeremy Noel-Tod**
PK	Paul Kavanagh	SO'B	Sean O'Brien
JKK	Janice Kulyk Keefer	**BO'D**	**Bernard O'Donoghue**
SK	Sandra Kemp	KO	Kole Omotoso
DK	David Kennedy	MO'N	Michael O'Neill
KK	**Kate Kilalea**	**FO**	**Femi Oyebode**
BK	Bruce King	MP	Michael Palmer
KBS	Koh Buck Song	JP	Jay Parini
JLa	John Lang	RPa	Rajeev Patke
RL	Richard Lansdown	TP	Tom Paulin
ETL	Edward T. Larrissy	RSP	Robert S. Phillips
NL	**Nicholas Laughlin**	PP	Peter Pierce
ARL	A. Robert Lee	RP	Roben Polito
ML	Michele Leggott	**CP**	**Christopher Pollnitz**
DL	David Lehman	PNFP	Peter Porter
MLe	Marcia Leveson	NP	Neil Powell
LCS	Lim Chee Seng	JPr	John Press
HL	Herbert Lomas	**WHP**	**William Pritchard**
MLo	Mary Lord	WP	Wyatt Prunty
JL	John Lucas	JR	Jonathan Raban
PL	**Paddy Lyons**	DR	David Rampton
GMacB	George MacBeth	JRa	Jarold Ramsey
PMcC	Patricia McCarthy	LR	Liam Rector
PMcD	Peter McDonald	CJR	Christopher Reid
RMcD	Robert McDowell	MR	Mario Relich
FMcK	Frank McKay	CR	Clay Reynolds
WMcK	Wayne McKenna	**GR**	**Graeme Richardson**
SMcK	Susan McKernan	LRi	Lynn Risser
LMacK	Lachlan MacKinnon	**SR**	**Sam Riviere**
EMcM	Elizabeth McMahon	RR	Roger Robinson

SRo	**Sophie Robinson**	RS	Richard Stull
JRo	Judith Rodriguez	**TSw**	**Thomas Swiss**
MLR	M. L. Rosenthal	JGS	Julian Symons
MRu	Mark Rudman	JTFT	James T. F. Tanner
CAR	**Carol Rumens**	AT	Ann Thwaite
DStJ	David StJohn	AST	Anthony Thwaite
PMStP	Paul Matthew St Pierre	**JT**	**Jeff Titon**
PMS	Peter Sanger	**THM**	**Toh Hsien Min**
IES	Ian Sansom	ATT	A. T. Tolley
WS	William Scammell	WT	William Toye
GS	Grace Schulman	LT	Lewis Turco
MS-S	Martin Seymour-Smith	AU	Alan Urquhart
TWS	Tom Shapcott	HV	Helen Vendler
IS	Iain Sharp	AW	Andrew Wallace
WGS	W. G. Shepherd	CW-C	Chris Wallace-Crabbe
KS	Kirpal Singh	RW	Ronald Warwick
DeVS	De Villo Sloan	SW	Stephen Watson
VS	Vivian Smith	IW	Ian Wedde
CS	Colin Smythe	TW	Ted Weiss
SS	Shaista Sonnu	NW	Nigel Wheale
DS	David Staines	**DW**	**David Wheatley**
JHS	Jon Stallworthy	HW	Hugo Williams
DES	Donald E. Stanford	MW	Mark Williams
CKS	C. K. Stead	**CW**	**Clive Wilmer**
JSt	James Steele	TWi	Terence Winch
TS	Timothy Steele	CWo	Catherine Woeber
MS	Meic Stephens	WMY	Wong Ming Yook
AS	Anne Stevenson	MRW	Mark Wormald
PS	Peter Stitt	CMW	Charlotte M. Wright
LS	Leon Stokesbury	**HY**	**Heather Yeung**
JS	Jennifer Strauss	RZ	Robert Zaller

Abercrombie, Lascelles (1881–1938) Born just outside Manchester, at Ashton upon Mersey, Abercrombie was educated at Malvern College and at Victoria (later Manchester) University. He worked as a journalist for several years but at the age of 38 became a lecturer at the University of Liverpool; subsequently, he was professor of English at Leeds (from 1922) and Goldsmith's Reader in English at Oxford (from 1935).

In an essay entitled 'The Function of Poetry in the Drama' (1912), Abercrombie sought to redefine the possibilities of verse drama, but his own attempts at the genre are unhappily innocent of stagecraft. A clue to his more fruitful development as a poet is provided by the publication, also in 1912, of his study of Thomas *Hardy: at his best, he is less a stereotypical *Georgian than a second-class Hardy, fond of combining muscular rural imagery with lyric or ballad forms. This mixture, in poems such as 'The Fear' and 'The Stream's Song', evidently appealed to Yeats, who included eight pages of Abercrombie's work in the *Oxford Book of Modern Verse* (1936).

Though his poetry lacks the distinction of a major talent, it is enjoyable, capably written, and now unjustly neglected. It was collected as *The Poems of Lascelles Abercrombie* (Oxford University Press, 1930), and a supplementary volume, *Lyrics and Unfinished Poems*, appeared in 1940, two years after the author's death.   NP

Abrahams, Lionel (1928–2004) Born in Johannesburg, he studied at Wits University. As a child, he was taught by the short-story writer Herman Charles Bosnan, whose work he posthumously edited. He was an influential critic, publisher, and teacher. In 1956, Abrahams founded a magazine, *The Purple Renoster*. This led in the early 1970s to Renoster Books, a significant publisher during the apartheid period of black South African poets such as Oswald *Mtshali and Mongane *Serote. He also edited the poems of Ruth *Miller.

Abrahams' own published poetry began with *Thresholds of Tolerance* (Bateleur, 1975), which was followed by three further collections: *Journal of a New Man* (1984), *The Writer in the Sand* (1988—both Donker), and *A Dead Tree Full of Live Birds* (Snailpress, 1995). The title poem of his last volume is a characteristically ironic yet passionate reflection on the liberal literary values he espoused in his criticism ('Defection into silence would annul | the inner galaxy.')

Abrahams suffered from a form of cerebral palsy, although he managed for most of his life without a wheelchair. He fictionalized his experiences in two books of prose about the character 'Felix Greenspan'. *Lionel Abrahams: A Reader* (Donker), edited by Patrick *Cullinan, appeared in 1988. His seventieth birthday was celebrated by a festschrift, *A Writer in Stone* (David Philip, 1998).   JNT

Abse, Dannie (Daniel) (1923–   ) Abse is from a Jewish background, is Welsh, and a doctor: biographical facts which feature in his poems. He has an immediately likeable poetic voice, compassionate, humorous, observant. But the poems are not content with likeableness, nor are they satisfied with the merely personal. 'Return to Cardiff', one of his better-known pieces, describes Abse's feelings on revisiting his native city: loss, brief retrievals of the past, a sense of identity's oddness. The writing is conversational; it is also sharp and intelligent. Its rhythms win an unpredictable music from the musing hesitations of Abse's speaking voice.

'Return to Cardiff' was included in his 1962 book, *Poems, Golders Green*. Abse had by then sloughed off an initial weakness for rhetoric. Subsequent volumes blend a keen appetite for the everyday with an appalled, unmelodramatic awareness of suffering. 'A Night Out' revolves round watching a film about Auschwitz. Troubled, resilient, and anchored in the particular, the poem shows Abse's honesty to advantage. 'Hunt the Thimble' illustrates his interest in the riddle or parable; the repeated questions and answers mimic a child's game but generate a potently obscure menace. These two poems were included in *A Small Desperation* (Hutchinson, 1968); as the self-deprecating title suggests, Abse's imagination finds suburbia frustrating yet stimulating territory.

Some of Abse's tonally surest work occurs in his later volumes such as *Way Out in the Centre* (Hutchinson, 1981; in the US, *One-Legged on Ice*, University of Georgia Press, 1983). Both his alertness to the strangeness at the heart of familiarity and his wry grappling with the numinous (especially evident in *Ask the Bloody Horse* (Hutchinson, 1986)) find supple expression here.

New Selected Poems 1949–2009 (2009) marked the sixtieth anniversary of his debut, *After Every Green Thing* (1949—both Hutchinson). *Goodbye, Twentieth Century* (Pimlico, 2001) updates his earlier memoir, *A Poet in the Family* (Hutchinson, 1974) and *The Two Roads Taken* is a selection of his non-fictional prose (Enitharmon, 2003). See Cary Archard, *Dannie Abse: A Sourcebook* (Seren, 2010). In 2012, Abse was awarded a CBE.   MO'N

Achebe, Chinua (1930–2013) One of the foremost literary figures in Africa, Achebe was born in Ogidi, in rural Eastern Nigeria, where, alongside his family's Christianity, he absorbed the still-vigorous traditions of his Igbo people. He was educated at Government College, Umuahia, and University College, Ibadan, and after working for a time as a teacher, joined the Nigerian Broadcasting Company in Lagos. *Things Fall Apart* was the first of four major novels

published between 1958 and 1966. In 1969, during the Civil War, Achebe toured the United States with fellow writers to promote the Biafran cause. He turned to different forms of writing: essays, short stories, and poems. After the war he became professor of literature at Nsukka and editor of the journal *Okike*. A long-awaited fifth novel, *Anthills of the Savannah*, appeared in 1987. In 1990 he was severely paralysed in a road accident. In the same year, he became Charles P. Stevenson Jr. Professor of Languages and Literature at Bard College, New York.

Lucidity and self-possession characterize Achebe's poems as they do his prose. His Igbo conviction that 'nothing is absolute' imparts a wry detachment to his philosophizing. While 'Beware Soul Brother' blends Christian spirituality and Igbo communalism, other poems satirize both religions. 'Lament of the Sacred Python' shows 'cannibal' Christians blasphemously dining on the divine snake, while 'Those Gods are Children' exposes Igbo prudence in sacrificing only the smallest yams to the ancestors. His most moving poems focus on wry or poignant real-life incidents: the struggle of a mango seedling to root itself on a concrete roof, the deadpan stare of a starving child confronted by a rose-cheeked baby in a Christmas crib-scene.

Achebe's *Collected Poems* (Anchor, 2004) includes his first volume, *Beware, Soul-Brother and Other Poems* (Heinemann, 1972; in the US, *Christmas in Biafra and Other Poems*, Doubleday, 1973). See also *Chinua Achebe: Novelist, Poet, Critic*, by David Carroll (2nd edn., Macmillan, 1990).   JB

Ackerman, Diane (1948–) Born in Illinois, and received her doctorate from Cornell University in 1978; she writes regularly for *The New York Times*. Eclectic, witty, and impetuous, her poetry collects its vocabulary from Hollywood and Donne, NASA and Einstein's letters, origami and Egyptian hieroglyphs. *Reverse Thunder* (Lumen, 1988) continues to celebrate the visionary appetites expressed in *Wife of Light* (1978) and the visceral imaginings of *The Planets* (1976—both Morrow). *Jaguar of Sweet Laughter: New and Selected*

Poems was published in 1991. See also *I Praise my Destroyer* (1998—both Random House) and *Origami Bridges* (HarperCollins, 2002). She has also written sixteen prose books, most notably *A Natural History of the Senses* (1990).

Ackerman combines a fascination with human nature and a scientifically informed interest in nature. Her writing thus often seems like the cultivation of opposites. In her poems, the most abstract concepts are hitched to the plumpest, most redolent images: 'An event is such a little piece of time-and-space | you can mail it through the slotted eye of a cat.' God hidden in his universe becomes a soft-shelled crab, and Venus in her atmosphere 'a buxom floozy with a pink boa; | mummy, whose black | sediment desiccates within'. Conversely, her poems of love securely lodged in the body tend to ally themselves with moon and ghost, things bloodless, luminous, atmospheric: 'the popsongs, | the gone-sours, | the setbacks, the blights, | the cartwheel heart | where love careens, | all the little dismals | and the giant dreams.'   EG

Acorn, Milton (1923–86) Born in Charlottetown, Prince Edward Island. Seriously wounded in the Second World War, he returned home and worked as a carpenter until *In Love and Anger*, his first volume of poems, was published privately in 1956. He then quit carpentry and devoted himself to writing. In 1962 he married poet Gwendolyn *MacEwen; the marriage failed the following year. After living in Toronto, Vancouver, and Toronto again, Acorn returned to Charlottetown and spent the remainder of his life there. *The Island Means Minago* (NC Press, 1975) won the Governor General's Award for poetry.

Idealistic and at times angry, this Marxist-Leninist poet occasionally falls into political rhetoric. In his best political poems, however, he is a sincere and passionate denouncer of social injustice. 'I've Tasted My Blood' and 'Knowing I Live in a Dark Age' are masterful poems of this kind. But Acorn is not a poet of a single theme. 'Charlottetown Harbour' and 'November' are superb descriptive lyrics in which the language is evocative and the images precise.

Acorn's many volumes of poetry include *I've Tasted My Blood* (Ryerson, 1969), *More Poems for People* (NC Press, 1972), *Jackpine Sonnets* (Steel Rail Educational, 1977); *Captain Neal MacDougal and the Naked Goddess* (Ragweed, 1982), *Dig Up My Heart: Selected Poems of Milton Acorn 1952–83* (McClelland & Stewart, 1983), and *Whiskey Jack* (HMS Press, 1986), with and edited by James Deahl. Deahl has also edited and published three other volumes of Acorn's poems: *The Uncollected Acorn* (Deneau, 1987), *I Shout Love and Other Poems* (1987), and *Hundred Proof Earth* (1988—both Aya Press).   DRB

Adams, Léonie (1899–1988) Born in New York City and educated at Barnard College. Her second book, *High Falcon* (John Day), was published in 1929 to critical acclaim, but her *Poems: A Selection* (Funk & Wagnalls) did not appear until 1954, with twenty-four new poems. It won the Bollingen Prize in Poetry. Like her friend Louise *Bogan, Adams was a painstaking, severe, and not prolific poet. She was married to William Troy in 1933; in 1935, she and her husband joined the faculty of Bennington College. Adams work might well be called Platonic, for it is a poetry of forms, schematic and elegant, from which the messy details of private life or historical accident have been abstracted. The most successful poems embed their metaphysical reflection in natural forms. Although Adams disdains the particulars of history, she gives her poetry a welcome concreteness in terms of tree, flower, and evening star. 'The moon above the milky field | Gleaning moves her one slant light; | Wind weeps from out its cloud. | Then, weeping wind, unshroud | Pale Cassiopeia.'

This obsessive use of natural emblems creates an odd tension, however, since ultimately Adams poetry is about the weather in her own rather isolated and changeable soul. Agnostic, uncertain of the claims of art, having no reason to suppose a correspondence between nature and self, Adams uses the pathetic fallacy not to expand into the world but to contract into self-reflection. 'The will shall learn itself alone, | For walking by the waters' side.' The only comfort offered by nature is cold, since its recurrences are blind to the human face, deaf to its voice; the most one can ask for is forgetfulness.   EG

Adamson, Robert (1943–) Adamson grew up in Sydney but while a young teenager ran away to live as a fisherman on the Hawkesbury River and spent periods in remand homes and prison.

Adamson first made his mark, in *Canticles on the Skin* (Illumination, 1970), with poems that reflected these experiences but played with the roles that the experiences offered. Adamson's poetry has had three strands: imagistic celebrations of nature, particularly of the Hawkesbury River, its birds and fish; extravagant celebrations of existence as mythological quest; and a modern scepticism which directs irony at this penchant for romantic celebration.

All these elements have been apparent in his work from the beginning. His poems in the prize-winning *The Clean Dark* (Paper Bark, 1989) are perhaps his most serene. Gone are the jumpy rhythms and sardonic rhymes frequent in his poems about drugs and prison. Yet even here a degree of restlessness and self-consciousness is frequent. Adamson's poems are sometimes allusive, and he has acknowledged the influence of the American avant-garde, from Robert *Creeley and Robert *Duncan to *Zukofsky and the *New York poets. For a decade Adamson was influential in contemporary Australian poetry through his editorship of the magazine *New Poetry*. In 1986, he founded Paper Bark Press, and is a brilliant book designer.

After *Waving to Hart Crane* in 1994 (Angus & Robertson), Adamson was awarded the FWA's Christopher Brennan Award for a lifetime's achievement in poetry. *The Language of Oysters* (Craftsman House, 1997) was a collaboration with photographer Juno Gemes. A volume of autobiography, *Inside Out* (Text Publishing), appeared in 2004, and a new collection, *The Goldfinches of Baghdad* (Flood) in 2006. See *Mulberry Leaves: New & Selected Poems 1970–2001* (Paper Bark, 2001), published in the UK as *Reading the River: Selected Poems* (Bloodaxe, 2004).   DHa*

Adcock, Fleur (1934–) Born in Auckland, spent the war years as a child in various parts of England, and in 1947 returned to live in Wellington, where she was educated at Victoria University. For a brief period she taught in the classics departments at Victoria and Otago universities. She then became a librarian. In 1963 she settled in London, working in the library of the Foreign and Commonwealth Office. Since 1979 she has been a freelance writer, with London as her base.

It was in Dunedin and Wellington in the late 1950s and early 1960s that Adcock began publishing poetry. In fact, as she writes in 'In Memoriam: James K. Baxter', she 'married . . . into the art', marrying part-Polynesian poet Alistair *Campbell at the age of 18. She has two sons. Her first collection, *The Eye of the Hurricane*, was published in Wellington in 1964. New Zealand anthologists continue to claim her, and she has acknowledged Ursula *Bethell as an influence. In several of her poems questions of identity are touched on in terms of allegiance to one or the other hemisphere. Adcock's poems range from tightly controlled rhymed structures to relaxed conversational pieces in looser forms. Her characteristic manner is decorous, urbane, and poised, but may also be astringent, and many of her strongest poems are tense with intuited menace, their composure holding nightmare at bay: it is as though the writing of poems were a strategy for maintaining the cool persona who delivers them. She is a shrewd observer of personal, especially sexual, relations.

Poems 1960–2000 (Bloodaxe, 2000) draws on all her volumes to *Looking Back* (Oxford University Press, 1997). She was awarded the Queen's Gold Medal for Poetry in 2006 and made a Companion of the New Zealand Order of Merit in 2008. *Dragon Talk* (Bloodaxe, 2010) continues Adcock's interest in writing her family history. She also edited *The Faber Book of Twentieth Century Women's Poetry* (1987) and has done translations from Romanian and from medieval Latin. She was interviewed for *Landfall*, 143 (1982), and *Thumbscrew*, 17 (2000/1); an autobiographical essay appeared in *Beyond Expectations*, ed. Margaret Clark (Allen & Unwin/Port Nicholson, 1986).   MacDJ*

Adnan, Etel (1925–) Born in Beirut to a Greek mother and Syrian father, Adnan was educated in French convent schools in Lebanon, and studied philosophy at the Sorbonne in Paris. She did postgraduate work at the American universities of Berkeley and Harvard, and taught philosophy in California. Between 1972 and 1976 she worked in Lebanon as a newspaper cultural editor. In 1977, she published her acclaimed novel of the civil war, *Sitt Marie-Rose*, and returned to America.

Also a visual artist, Adnan has written poetry in French and English. These activities combine in her major long poem, *L'Apocalypse Arabe* (Papyrus, 1980), which she translated into English for The Post-Apollo Press as *The Arab Apocalypse* in 1989. In long verse lines interspersed with hieroglyphics, Adnan presents a vision of a violent, hallucinatory landscape under a relentless sun shining on the Middle East, America, and Europe. Other works in English, composed in markedly differing styles, include the lyric sequences of *The Indian Never Had a Horse* (1985), the prose poems of *There: In the Light and the Darkness of the Self and the Other* (1997), and the broken, halting language of *In/ Somnia* (2003—all Post-Apollo). All draw her philosophical interests towards her global political awareness. She has also written essays, plays, documentaries, and an experimental memoir, *In the Heart of the Heart of Another Country* (City Lights, 2005).

See *Etel Adnan: Critical Perspectives on the Arab-American Writer and Artist* (McFarland, 2002), ed. Lisa Suhair Majaj and Amal Amireh.   JNT

Afrika, Tatamkhulu (1920–2002) Born Muhamed Fu'ad Nasif in Egypt, but fostered by a white family in South Africa from 1923. During the Second World War, he spent three years in European prison camps. Afterwards, he worked as a copper miner. In the 1960s he settled in Cape Town District 6, where he became a Muslim and elected to be classed as non-white. An active member of the African National Congress, he was arrested on terrorism charges in 1987. He adopted his ANC codename (which means 'old man of Africa') to get around the subsequent ban on public activity.

Afrika wrote his first novel, *Broken Earth* (Hutchinson, 1940) under his Afrikaans foster name, John Charlton, at the age of 17. His first volume of poetry, *Nine Lives* (Carrefour/Hippogriff), appeared in 1991, and was followed by seven more, ending with *Mad Old Man Under the Morning Star* (Snailpress, 2001). The poems vividly describe incidents from his life, including his violent opposition to apartheid ('Hit Squad'), as well as salutary encounters with the otherworld of nature ('Shaman'). By the end of his life, Afrika had won every major South African literary prize and award, although he continued to live frugally. He was hit by a car—a fate he described befalling another man in 'The Accident'— shortly after the launch of his fourth novel, *Bitter Eden* (Arcadia, 2002). He died in hospital. A book of selected poems, *Nightrider* (Kwela, 2003), and an autobiography, *Mr Chameleon* (Jacana, 2005), were published posthumously.   JNT

Agard, John (1949–) Born in British Guiana (now Guyana). Together with Linton Kwesi *Johnson and Benjamin *Zephaniah, he can be considered a *dub poet, for many of his poems use vernacular and dialect modes and are written to be performed, though they display a hard-edged wit which loses nothing in print. The link with performance and musical accompaniment is emphasized by his own description of himself as a 'poetsonian', and is strongest in *Man to Pan* (1982), which won the Casa de las Américas prize. It contains poems which continually allude to the music of steel bands in an often delightful, occasionally disturbing, but always unpredictable manner. In 1977 he came to England, and has been a prolific author for children. The poems in which a limbo dancer functions as an elusive persona through which Agard probes the pain and alienation bequeathed by history in the Caribbean are among his most effective, and were first published in *Limbo Dancer in Dark Glasses* (Greenheart, 1983). 'Listen Mr. Oxford Don', from the same period, is famous for promising to 'mash up yu grammar'. Since *From the Devil's Pulpit* in 1997, he has been published by Bloodaxe Books: see *We Brits* (2006). *Alternative Anthem* (2009) is a selected poems which comes with a DVD of Agard's performances.   MR*

Agbabi, Patience (1965–) Born in London to Nigerian parents, Agbabi spent part of her childhood in Wales. She studied English Literature at Oxford University and later took an MA at the University of Sussex. She has lectured in Creative Writing at several British universities, and has been poet-in-residence at both a tattoo studio and Eton College.

Agbabi is a popular performer, influenced by *dub poetry and rap, who nevertheless values invention in traditional poetic form. She is also notable for her contemporary use of the dramatic monologue, as in 'The Wife of Bafa', after Chaucer. Her poetry has become well-known to readers through its appearance in a number of anthologies, as well as her own published volumes: *R.A.W.* (Gecko, 1995), which won the 1997 Excelle Award, *Transformatrix* (Payback, 2000), and *Bloodshot Monochrome* (Canongate, 2008). There is a critical discussion of her work in Bruce King, *The Internationalization of English Literature* (Oxford University Press, 2004).   JNT

Ai (1947–2010) Born Florence Anthony in Albany, Texas, of mixed Native American, African-American, Irish, and Japanese heritage (her adopted name means 'love' in Japanese); she studied writing with Galway *Kinnell at the University of California at Irvine. The author of six books of poems— *Cruelty* (1973), *Killing Floor* (1978), *Sin* (1986), *Fate* (1991—all Houghton), *Greed* (1993), and *Dread* (2003—both Norton)—

she taught for many years at Oklahoma State University.

All Ai's work is stark, harsh, and dramatic in style. But as her preoccupations move from personal violence to historic atrocity, her imagination opens out into the public arena; the domestic turns political. Throughout her poetry, a stripped-down diction conveys an underlying, almost biblical indignation—not, at times, without compassion—at human misuses of power and the corrupting energies of various human appetites.

Although virtually all the poems present themselves as spoken by a particular character, Ai makes little attempt to capture individual styles of diction, personal vocabularies; the result, if monotonous, is also striking. A Mexican revolutionary, an old woman with a young lover, the dead Robert Kennedy, a Vietnam veteran—all speak with a sullen, deadpan passion that galvanizes our attention through the voice's intensity rather than by the accumulation of realistic detail. The foreshortened, nearly parodic vividness of Ai's characters makes them closer to types than to historical portraits. *Black Blood* (1997) is a novel. See *Vice: New and Selected Poems* (1999—both Norton).   RHa

Aidoo, Ama Ata (1942–) Ghanaian playwright, short-story writer, and poet, was christened Christina Ama Aidoo, but now uses her African name. She read English at the University of Ghana, Legon, and made an early reputation with her plays, *The Dilemma of a Ghost* (1965) and *Anowa* (1969), which placed her among the most original of modern African dramatists. Her poems and short stories appeared first in the journals *Okyeame*, *Black Orpheus*, and *Presence africaine*. She has pursued a career as writer and university teacher in Ghana, Kenya, Zimbabwe, and the United States, where she was Visiting Professor at Brown University until 2010.

Aidoo's work is strongly influenced by oral tradition, and her writing is intended primarily to be heard. Sometimes, like the traditional *griot*, she makes no clear distinction between prose and verse, and her novel *Our Sister Killjoy: or Reflections from a Black-Eyed Squint* (Longman, 1977) moves constantly between prose and loose free verse. The work takes the form of the indignant tirade of a Ghanaian student on an officially sponsored cultural visit to Germany. She attacks the polite racism of Europe, the corrupt leaders of neo-colonial Africa, educated Africans who waste their skills in First World countries, and the sexism of both western and African societies.

Her first collection, *Someone Talking to Sometime* was published in Harare in 1985, followed by *Birds and Other Poems* (1989—both College Press) and *Angry Letter in January and Other Poems* (Dangaroo, 1992).

See also Anne V. Adams (ed.), *Essays in Honour of Ama Ata Aidoo at 70: A Reader in African Cultural Studies* (Ayebia Clarke, 2012).   JB

Aiken, Conrad (Potter) (1889–1973) Aiken was deeply affected throughout his life by the tragedy in his childhood. He was 11 years old when he heard, from the next room, the sound of the shots with which his father had killed both the boy's mother and himself. The early years in Savannah (to which he returned in old age) were changed to life with an ancient aunt in Massachusetts. He was educated at Concord and Harvard, where he became friendly with T. S. *Eliot. Aiken's finest novel, *Great Circle*, deals directly with his parents' violent deaths, and his interest in psychoanalysis sprang from the need to explain or exorcise the most crucial event of his life.

Aiken's output began with *Earth Triumphant* (1914) and in the next decade he produced almost a book of verse a year. The *Selected Poems*, which excluded almost all of his first, second, and fourth books, appeared in 1933, and was followed by another *Selected* (1961) and a *Collected* (1953; 2nd edn., 1970—both Oxford University Press). Aiken was married three times, and had three children by the first marriage. His autobiographical excursion *Ushant* appeared in 1952. Books about him include Houston Peterson's largely psychoanalytical *The Melody of Chaos*

(1931) and *Conrad Aiken: A Life of his Art*, by Jay Martin (Princeton University Press, 1962).

Writing to Malcolm *Cowley in 1941, Aiken called himself 'an almost unique phenomenon, a poet who has acquired a Reputation, or a Position, or what have you, without ever having been caught in the act': that is, the act of writing anything considered by critics as poetry. It is true that although Aiken was loaded with prizes and awards (the Pulitzer Prize, National Book Award, Gold Medal for Poetry, etc.), much critical writing about him has been dismissive or slighting. This is in part because of a deadly facility, combined with a liking for conventionally musical rhythms, in part because of his tendency to treat historical themes or myths as subjects for dramatic rhetoric. The result was long poems like *Punch: The Immortal Liar* (1921) and *The Kid* (1947), which contain fine passages yet are unmistakably failures taken as a whole. There is some truth in Randall *Jarrell's comment that Aiken was 'a kind of Midas: everything he touches turns to verse', with the corollary that 'everything *blurs* into everything else'.

At least that is true of Aiken's easiest and most nostalgic writing. His finest poetry, however, achieves in places the grandeur he was always looking for, and in others gets beyond the fluent expression of nostalgia to what comes through as genuine anguish. *Preludes for Memnon* (1931), his finest volume, was apparently intended, along with its lesser successor *Time in the Rock* (1936), as a single work attempting to fix many 'fragments of consciousness . . . so that the life which the consciousness reflects may be known and judged'. The idea has a typically Aikenian vagueness, but these preludes are best seen as individual poems, most of them using the forms of Elizabethan and Jacobean dramatic verse as a springboard for wholly original work. Many of the poems deal at one or two removes with aspects of the poet's life and loves, others play with a constant concern for 'the ding-an-sich, | The feeling itself, the round bright dark emotion'. The idea of poetry as a 'thing in itself', outside feeling but still part of it, along with the belief that *words* can never express *things*, never ceased to fascinate Aiken. In *Preludes for Memnon* the expression of these preoccupations is all the more convincing because it is joined to jokes and outrageous puns. The prelude that begins 'Two coffees in the Español, the last | Bright drops of golden Barsac in a goblet, | Fig paste and candied nuts', and goes on to reflections about age, love, and death, is one of the grandest, most successful examples of his rhetoric.

Some of the other late poetry is accomplished and personal without being totally original, but a sizeable selection could still be made of poems that could have been written by nobody else, in particular those where his characteristic nostalgia is laced with irony. 'King Borborigmi' (who is 'King of infinite space in a walnut shell—| But has bad dreams; I fear he has bad dreams'), 'The Wedding', and 'Psychomachia' are three examples of the variety of manners Aiken could command. His talent lost something by being diffused instead of concentrated, but was still remarkable.   JGS

Aldington, Richard (christened Edward Godfree Aldington) (1892–1962) Born in Portsmouth (a town of suffocating dullness, according to his self-pitying poem 'Childhood'), the son of a solicitor, and educated at Dover College and (for one year) London University. In 1911 he met the American poet H. D. (Hilda *Doolittle), six years his senior, and the pair were taken up by Ezra *Pound, who coined the term *Imagistes* (*See* IMAGISM) for them, sent their work to Harriet Monroe for *Poetry* magazine in Chicago, and published them in his own anthology *Des Imagistes* (1914).

Aldington married H. D. in 1913, but they were soon estranged (though the marriage was not annulled until 1938, to enable him to remarry). He stayed a proclaimed Imagist when the group was appropriated by Amy *Lowell (his second and third volumes were *Images of War* and *Images of Desire*), and from 1914 to 1917 he edited the literary pages of the *Egoist*, which became the movement's main organ; T. S. *Eliot replaced him as literary editor when Aldington went to the Western Front. After his experiences in the trenches he was diagnosed neurasthenic,

and through the Twenties, feeling broken and embittered, he scraped a living as a freelance writer and translator (see *Fifty Romance Lyric Poems*, 1931). Publication in 1929 of his angry war novel, *Death of a Hero*, made him famous. Quitting England, he spent the Second World War in America, but eventually settled in Montpelier, where in his last years he wrote controversial biographies of D. H. *Lawrence (whose poems he had edited), Norman Douglas, and T. E. Lawrence.

Only Aldington's very earliest poems, collected in the volume *Images* (1915), are now much regarded. The book is Hellenistic in spirit, and in its yearning vocatives (four consecutive poems begin 'Potnia, Potnia . . . ', 'O you, O you most fair . . . ', 'O Artemis . . . ', 'Pan O Pan . . . ') and the preponderance of colour effects there are unexpected echoes of the Tennyson of 'Oenone'. These lean pieces of imitation marble are offset by a group of contemporary urban poems, 'Cinema Exit', 'In the Tube', 'Hampstead Heath', and others.

Of subsequent volumes, *Images of War* is an unrewarding clash between theory and terror (though 'Blood of the Young Men' is still often anthologized). The poems of *Exile* show a developing interest in the verse paragraph, and *Words for Music* even includes some 'Metrical Exercises'. His most characterful extended work, ridiculed on publication, is the phantasmagoric *Fool i' the Forest* (1925), which owes much to *The Waste Land*. The poem, which presents three figures ('I', the Conjuror, and the fool Mezzetin) as aspects of a single person, is an unstable amalgam of dream, allusion, and Poundian satirical rant at the capitalist system: 'And Helen's married to a Guggenheim. | (Sweet Helen, make me immortal with a kiss).'

See the autobiography, *Life for Life's Sake* (Viking, 1941) and the introduction to *The Complete Poems* (Wingate, 1948). H. D.'s *Bid Me to Live* (Grove, 1960; new edn., University Press of Florida, 2011) contains a vivid portrait of Aldington as 'Rafe Ashton'.   MI

Alexander, Elizabeth (1962–) Born in New York, Alexander grew up in Washington D.C., and attended the universities of Boston, Pennsylvania, and Yale, where she is now Professor of African-American Studies. In 2009 she read a poem at the inauguration of President Obama, 'Praise Song for the Day', included in *Crave Radiance: New and Selected Poems* (Graywolf, 2010). She is a member of the *Cave Canem group.

The Venus Hottentot (University Press of Virginia, 1990; repr. Graywolf, 2004) introduced Alexander's essayistic mix of dramatic and autobiographical poems on the history of 'a strange thing ... "race"', from a description of her first year as a black female student in Boston to the affirmative 'A Poem for Nelson Mandela'. Her later collections are *Body of Life* (Tia Chucha, 1996), *Antebellum Dream Book* (2001), and *American Sublime*, which includes the sequences 'Ars Poetica' and *'Amistad'* (2005). *The Black Interior* (2003—all Graywolf), a collection of her writings on African-American culture, includes essays on Langston *Hughes, Gwendolyn *Brooks, and Michael *Harper. See also *Power and Responsibility* (University of Michigan Press, 2007), and, in the UK, *American Blue* (Bloodaxe, 2006), a selection from her first four volumes.   JNT

Alexander, Meena (1951–) Born in Allahabad, India, Alexander was educated in India, North Africa, and England. She lives in New York where she is a Distinguished Professor of English at Hunter College.

Her first volume, *Stone Roots* (Arnold-Heinemann, 1980), was published in New Delhi, and her second, *House of a Thousand Doors* (Three Continents, 1988) in Washington D.C. Two poem-dramas, published as chapbooks by Red Dust Press— *The Storm* (1989) and *Night-Scene, The Garden* (1992)—concern the history of her family homes in Kerala. *The Shock of Arrival* (Southend, 1996) presented 'reflections on postcolonial experience' through a combination of poems and essays, while the title poem of *Illiterate Heart* (Northwestern University Press, 2002), dedicated to Adrienne *Rich, reflects on a life of imaginative travel between European literature and an Indian childhood. She has also written a critical study, *Women in Romanticism*

(1989), a memoir, *Fault Lines* (1993), and two novels, *Manhattan Music* (1997) and *Nampally Road* (1991). See also *House of a Thousand Doors* (Three Continents, 1988), *River and Bridge* (TSAR, 1996), *Raw Silk* (2004), and *Quietly Flowing River* (2008—both TriQuarterly).   JNT

Alexie, Sherman (1966–) Born and grew up on the Spokane Indian reservation in Wellpinit, Washington. He studied at Washington State University, where he began to write and had his first work published. He also has a successful career as a film-maker and a novelist.

Alexie's debut collection of poems and short fiction, *The Business of Fancydancing* (Hanging Loose, 1992) established his storytelling style and sharply ironic humour, and has been reprinted eight times. A decade later, Alexie wrote and directed a film of the same title. *I Would Steal Horses* (Slipstream), a chapbook of poems, appeared in the same year, and was followed in 1993 by *First Indian on the Moon* (Hanging Loose), a second collection of prose and poetry. The opening lines of Alexie's anecdotes can seem invitingly artless, but their cumulative mood rarely remains so gentle. Their dominant subject is the genocidal history and ongoing inequality of Native Americans in their own country, often finding dark comedy in the split between popular representation and the pathos of reality. 'All of the Indians must have tragic features' begins 'How to Write the Great American Indian Novel': 'tragic noses, eyes, and arms'. Alexie's first novel was *Reservation Blues* (Grove/Atlantic, 1994). He has acknowledged the influence of stand-up comedians such as Bill Hicks on his work, and as a performer he has won several international poetry slams. *Face* (Hanging Loose, 2009) experiments with harnessing the momentum of his free verse to traditional forms.   JNT

Ali, Agha Shahid (1949–2001) Born in Delhi. His father was a professor of education and Ali was educated in American, Indian, and Kashmiri schools and universities. After teaching at Delhi University and in Kashmir, Ali settled in the United States as a professor of English and creative writing. One of the few Indians then from an Islamic family to write poetry in English, Ali blends the traditions of the Urdu *ghazal* with contemporary American verse. His themes are the unrootedness, fears, joys, incongruities, and surprises of exile alongside memories and imagining of a past which has increasingly become distanced and which continues to evolve without his presence. There is also amusement with his life in America and an existential insecurity resulting from having left the protecting comfort of his family.

Ali's first two volumes, published in Calcutta, *Bone-Sculpture* (1972) and *In Memory of Begum Akhtar* (1979—both Writers Workshop) were heavily drenched with the sadness of Urdu poetry and T. S. *Eliot's sense of loss. *The Half-Inch Himalayas* (Wesleyan University Press, 1987) is carefully composed of linked images, allusions, and recurring situations. It expresses the anxieties, fantasies, and discoveries of the continual traveller who imagines lives he and others might have had. *A Walk Through the Yellow Pages* (Sun/Gemini, 1987) uses a highly American idiom, advertising slogans, and parodies of folktales to reveal nightmarish fears hidden by the commonplace. Ali also translated Faiz Ahmed Faiz from Urdu.

A Nostalgist's Map of America (Norton, 1991) was followed by an Indian selected poems, *The Beloved Country* (Viking Penguin, 1992). His next two books, *The Country Without a Post Office* (1997) and *Rooms Are Never Finished* (2001) were highly praised for their extended treatment of the tragic history Ali left behind in Kashmir. *Call Me Ishmael Tonight* (2003), a collection of ghazals, was published posthumously, and his collected poems, *The Veiled Suite*, appeared in 2009 (all Norton). Ali also wrote a scholarly monograph, *T. S. Eliot as Editor* (UMI Research Press, 1986), and edited a book of 'real ghazals in English', *Ravishing Disunities* (University Press of New England, 2000).   BK*

Allen, Dick (1939–   ) Born in Troy, New York, and grew up in Round Lake Village, a rural community north of Albany. At Syracuse University he became editor-in-chief of the college newspaper, before graduating in 1961. He was a graduate student in writing at Brown University in the early Sixties, studying there with *Berryman, and in 1964 went on to teach at Wright State University in Dayton, Ohio, where he co-founded *Mad River Review*. In 1968 he joined the faculty at the University of Bridgeport in Connecticut, where he held the Charles A. Dana Endowed Chair of English until his retirement in 2001. In 2010 he became Connecticut State Poet Laureate.

The influence of science fiction on his poetry has been apparent from his first volume, *Anon and Various Time Machine Poems* (Delacorte, 1971), highlighted by the long 'pop epic' of Anon, an American Everyman of the Sixties making a surreal journey through the contemporary American landscape and, via time travel, backwards and forwards through American culture and history. The shorter 'Time Travel Poems' established the type of lyric that characterizes his subsequent volumes, *Regions with No Proper Names* (St Martin's, 1975), *Overnight in the Guest House of the Mystic* (1984), and *Flight and Pursuit* (1987 —both Louisiana State University Press). They are by turns erotic and mystical, rooted in the matrix of his life in New York State, Ohio, Rhode Island, and Connecticut, as in 'The Poet at Eighteen', 'Visit', and 'Janes Avenue', even as they explore other lives in narratives like 'Cliff Painting', and veer from the quotidian in 'Crossing the Stars on New Year's Eve' and 'Barge Lights on the Hudson'.

Since 1981 Allen has become increasingly associated with the revival of narrative and metre in American poetry, and in 1988 he edited a special issue of *Crosscurrents* containing poems and essays pertaining to the *New Formalism and the *New Narrative. This involvement has given his later poetry a technical polish that tempers the frenetic wildness of his inventive but uneven earlier work. *Ode to the Cold War: New and Selected Poems* appeared in 1997, and has been followed by *The Day Before* (2003) and *Present Vanishing* (2008—all Sarabande).   RMCP

Allen, Fergus (1921–) Born in London and educated at Quaker schools in Dublin and Waterford before taking an engineering degree from Trinity College, Dublin. Returning to England he became a civil servant, working in the Cabinet Office and becoming First Civil Service Commissioner. His first collection, *The Brown Parrots of Providencia* (Faber, 1993) appeared after his retirement. Possessed of the cultural omnivorousness of the anthropologist, Allen rejects the implied centrality of any one perspective. His poems combine revisitings of his Irish childhood with studies of exotic (if not exoticized) elsewheres or 'Foreign Relations', the latter showing affinities with the work of Alan *Ross, an acknowledged influence.

In 'Other', Allen describes himself as feeling 'more than a little extraterrestrial', and questions of distance and obliquity are frequently in evidence. Like the remembered leaf warblers of his youth, Allen exults in his camouflage, preferring to stay 'Directionless, meaning and whereabouts both concealed'. A natural reserve and dryness should not be mistaken for emotional impoverishment, however. With their sensitivity to long historical vistas, Allen's poems feed the glow from the 'radioactive innards' of memory that 'Still lights up today's dark matter'. Subsequent collections are *Who Goes There?* (1996), *Mrs Power Looks Over the Bay* (1999—both Faber), *Gas Light & Coke* (Dedalus, 2006), and *Before Troy* (CB Editions, 2010).   DW

Allison, Drummond (1921–43) Born at Caterham in Surrey, and educated at Bishop's Stortford College and Queen's College, Oxford, where he took a wartime shortened degree in history before joining the army. He served as an Intelligence Officer with the West Surrey Regiment, and was killed in action between Naples and Rome in December 1943.

At Oxford, Allison became a close friend of John *Heath-Stubbs and Sidney *Keyes, both of whom were at Queen's College. The only poems by Allison to appear in his lifetime were those included in *Eight Oxford Poets* (1941), edited by Michael Meyer and Keyes. After his death a collection of his poems, *The Yellow Night*, was published (Fortune Press, 1944), and several appeared in the anthology *Poetry from Oxford in Wartime* (Fortune Press, 1945), ed. William Bell. *The Poems of Drummond Allison* (Whiteknights, 1978), ed. Michael Sharp, added to these twelve further poems from manuscript.

Unlike Heath-Stubbs, Keyes, and the rest of that circle in early wartime Oxford, Allison was an admirer of W. H. *Auden, whose work he had first read at school. This is clear from such poems of 1940/1 as 'Come let us pity Death', 'The Seaside Hotel', 'One finds in leaves his solace', 'The gardener rises restive', and 'For Karl Marx'. But Allison's poems are certainly not just Audenesque pastiche. His work has a tough and yet supple intellectual sinew, and enjoys a vocabulary both wide and apt.

Chaucer, Malory, and Arthurian myth supplied him with some material, but there is also plenty of the ordinary world he knew: the suburbs, Oxford, the army, all treated wittily, wryly, and sometimes with elegiac power of a surprising and authoritative kind, as in 'Dedication', 'My Sister Helen (1917)', and 'The Brass Horse'.   AST

Allnutt, Gillian (1949–) Born in London. She spent much of her childhood in Newcastle upon Tyne, and was educated at Cambridge and Sussex universities. From 1981 to 1983, she was active in the Sheba feminist publishing collective, and later became Poetry Editor of the London-based listings magazine *City Limits* (1983-8). Her first full collection, *Spitting the Pips Out* (Sheba, 1981), was followed by *Beginning the Avocado* (Virago, 1987). In 1988 she co-edited the revisionist anthology *The New British Poetry, 1968–1988* (Paladin).

Blackthorn (1994) marked Allnutt's move to Bloodaxe (who have published all her subsequent poetry collections) and helped to establish her as an original and engaging voice. *Nantucket and the Angel* (1997) and *Lintel* (2001) were both shortlisted for the T. S. Eliot Prize. *Sojourner* (2004) widened her reputation and the 2007 publication of *How the Bicycle Shone: New & Selected Poems* revealed a poet whose always-graceful combination of political and verbal intelligence was increasing in emotional power. While her technique includes an inventive and sometimes playful treatment of assonantal and rhythmic nuance, the focus may be pared down to almost *Imagist spareness, as in the striking sequence 'North: Sketches for a Portrait'. Much of her adult working-life has been in the North-East of England as a creative-writing tutor. Her concern with women's writing is reflected in *Berthing: A Poetry Workbook*, published by Virago with the NEC in 1991. She received a Northern Rock Foundation Writer's Award in 2005.   CAR

Allott, Kenneth (1912–73) Spent his childhood and youth in Cumberland, took First Class Honours in English at Durham University, and emerged as a poet at Oxford, where he was co-editor of the little magazine *Programme*. He made a poetic reputation in the Thirties as one of the principal contributors to *New Verse*, published in collaboration with Stephen Tait a comic novel, *The Rhubarb Tree* (1937), in which the heroine is no more than a voice on the telephone, and then *Poems* (1938), followed by another collection, *The Ventriloquist's Doll* (1943). He later became a professor at Liverpool University, where he edited the standard edition of Matthew Arnold's poems, and also *The Penguin Book of Contemporary Verse* (1950, revised and enlarged 1962). He was twice married. Allott was the most deliberately stylish poet of the Thirties, always verbally witty, at times almost too careful and thoughtful. He used surrealistic effects brilliantly, as in one of his best-known poems, 'Lament for a Cricket Eleven', but with a deliberation alien to a true surrealist. His skilful rhetoric was always under control, so that the indignation expressed in such a poem as 'Exodus' ('From this wet island of birds and chimneys | Who can watch suffering Europe and not be angry?') was genuine but seemed calculated. The general tone of his first collection is elegiac, regretting the past, seeing little hope in the future, and taking conscious refuge in personal happiness. 'The Professor' blends a controlled surrealism in the image of a wild professor meditating on death, with an arbitrary but wonderfully effective final couplet: 'Heaven is full of clocks which strike all day. | It is to music we are put away.' *The Ventriloquist's Doll* does not fail in wit or stylishness, but adds little of importance to *Poems*.

Like almost all other English poets of his generation Allott was influenced by *Auden, but he was one of the few who absorbed the influence and produced, not imitation Auden, but poems individual to himself and unique in the decade during which he was a poet. His *Collected Poems* appeared in 1975 (Secker & Warburg).   JGS

Alurista (1947–) By birth Alberto Baltazar Urista Heredia, Alurista moved with his family from Cuernavaca and Acapulco, Mexico, to San Diego in 1960. Much influenced by the example of César Chávez and his United Farm Workers, in 1967 he helped to found MECHA (Movimiento Estudiantil Chicano de Aztlán), the Chicano Student Movement of Aztlán. If he is indeed the poet laureate of Chicano culture, as he has been dubbed, it rests upon several counts: his celebration of 'Aztlán' as the mythic, south-western homeland of the Chicano people; his creation of an 'interlingual' verse which switches between Spanish (whether Mexican or the *caló* of the barrio), English (mainstream or black), and Amerindian (Náhuatl or Mayan); and his adeptness in the use of pre-Columbian folklore and imagery.

Floricanto en Aztlán (1971), with its amalgams of English and Spanish, set the note in which a poem like 'when raza' typically calls for an end to alienation ('mañana doesn't come | for he who waits'). But Alurista's versatility also extends to the Maya-influenced incantatory verse of *Nationchild Plumaroja, 1969–1972* (1972), the language experiments and puns of *Spik in Glyph* (1980), and the European poems of *Dawn's Eye* (1982). Principal collections include *Floricanto en Aztlán* (1971), *Nationchild Plumaroja* (1972), *Time-space Huracán* (1976), *A'nque* (1979), *Return: Poems Collected and New* (1982), *Et tú…Raza?* (1996—both Bilingual Press), and *As our barrio turns: who the yoke b on?* (Calaca, 2000). In 2011 UCLA Chicano Studies Research Center Press published an illustrated anniversary edition of *Floricanto en Aztlán*, with a preface by the author.   ARL

Alvarez, A. (Alfred) (1929–) Born in London and educated at Oundle School and Corpus Christi College, Oxford. After a brief academic career, which produced *The Shaping Spirit* (1958), a study of modern poetry, and *The School of Donne* (1961—both Chatto & Windus), he became a freelance writer and Poetry Editor of *The Observer*. In his influential Penguin anthology *The New Poetry* (Penguin, 1962) he urged the superiority of such American moderns as *Lowell, *Berryman, and *Plath to *Larkin and British 'gentility'.

As a critic Alvarez identified himself closely with *Confessional Poetry, coming to regard emotional breakdown or extremism as a virtual criterion of seriousness, and arguing that poetry itself was a 'murderous art'. This line of thought culminated in *The Savage God* (Weidenfeld & Nicolson, 1971), a study of suicide among writers and artists, remembered now chiefly for its memoir of the last months of Sylvia Plath. A mixture of perspicacity and dubious special pleading, his criticism is perhaps better at locating intensity than at explaining its workings, or distinguishing between suffering and self-pity. What is lasting in the poetry he endorsed, though, is not its sickness but its health. His critique of British poetry's tendency to slip back into neo-*Georgian cosiness and inhibition was timely and acute, as was his insistence that honesty should take precedence over received good taste.

His own poetry is collected in *Lost* (Turret, 1968) and *Autumn to Autumn* (Macmillan, 1978). Blood and death figure largely: 'God is a cannibal' ('The Killing'). *New and Selected Poems* was published by Waywiser Press in 2002.   ws

Alvi, Moniza (1954–) Born in Lahore, Pakistan, and came to England shortly afterwards. She studied in York and London, and has worked as a schoolteacher and creative-writing tutor.

Alvi's first book, *Peacock Luggage* (Smith/Doorstep, 1991), was shared with Peter Daniels. She has published several collections since, including *The Country at My Shoulder* (1993), *A Bowl of Warm Air* (1996—both Oxford University Press), *Carrying My Wife* (2000), and *Souls* (2002). *Split World: Poetry 1990–2005* appeared in 2008 (all Bloodaxe). In 1994, she was included in the *New Generation group of British poets, sharing its fondness for a conversational manner, surprising imagery, and wry humour (she has cited Edward *Thomas and Stevie *Smith among her influences). Alvi's treatment of the 'split world' of her background, however, pushes towards a more surreal feeling for history, as when a 'Grand Hotel' is 'propelled | into the middle of India, || breathing fire and ice'. *How the Stone Found its Voice* (2005) and *Europa* (2008) develop this mythopoetic vein, retelling stories of origin in modern cross-cultural contexts. Alvi has also published translations of the French poet, Jules Superveille, under the title *Homesick for the Earth* (2011—all Bloodaxe).   JNT

Amis, Kingsley (1922–95) Born in South London and educated at the City of London School and St John's College, Oxford, where Philip *Larkin was a fellow undergraduate and close friend. He served in the army during the Second World War, and was a university teacher at Swansea, Princeton, and Cambridge, becoming a full-time writer in 1963. Publication of two early volumes of poems, *Bright November* (1947) and *A Frame of Mind* (1953), preceded *Lucky Jim* (1954), the first of the many entertaining novels for which he is better known. There followed *A Case of Samples* (1956), a pamphlet, *The Evans Country* (1962), and *A Look Round the Estate* (1967). The *Collected Poems 1944–1979* (Hutchinson, 1979) contains six poems from *Bright November*, almost everything from the later books, and some previously uncollected poems. As editor, Amis compiled the *New Oxford Book of Light Verse* (1978) and the *Faber Popular Reciter* (1978).

Amis's early verse did more than the work of any of the contemporaries with whom his name was linked (Larkin, John

*Wain, D. J. *Enright, Elizabeth *Jennings, and others in Robert *Conquest's *New Lines* anthology of 1956) to set the tone for the 1950s *Movement in poetry. Clear, and assiduously crafted, it upheld traditional forms and devices, debunked intellectual or emotional pretentiousness, and sought to demonstrate that common experience invariably undermines romantic (including erotic) aspiration. At the same time, to write about love and personal disillusionment at all (sometimes movingly, and with unexpected vulnerability in poems like 'Masters' and 'Sources of the Past') is to acknowledge that poetry is still a suitable repository for feeling; and a persisting subromantic note can still be detected in Movement verse. This remains in Amis's poetry even when, from the mid-1950s onwards, he brought his comic talents into play, hinting ruefully at an inability to produce love poems ('A Bookshop Idyll') and envying the sexual conquests of a commercial traveller ('A Song of Experience'). But he was steadily developing his distinctive identity as a poet: that of the no-nonsense, more than averagely sensual man who can curb undue romantic tendencies but will still poignantly register regret and nostalgia ('A Chromatic Passing-Note', 'In Memoriam W.R.A.'), and deplore the disappointments of love ('Sight Unseen', 'A Point of Logic'). By the time he reached *The Evans Country*, a group of bawdy cameos set in a philistine, lower-middle-class South Wales (anticipating his much later novel, *The Old Devils*), this identity was firmly established. The last twenty poems in *Collected Poems* are the work of twenty years; their bluff, abrasive humour and technical adroitness leave his admirers regretting that Amis did not produce more verse in this period.   AB*

Ammons, A. R. (Archie Randolph) (1926–2001) Born and raised in rural North Carolina, Ammons was the youngest of a tobacco farmer's three surviving children. He started writing poetry on board a United States destroyer escort in the South Pacific during the Second World War. Upon his return to civilian life he majored in science at Wake Forest University and later did graduate work in English at the University of California, Berkeley. For a year he was principal of the tiny elementary school in the island village of Cape Hatteras. For the better part of a decade he worked as a sales executive in his father-in-law's biological glass company on the southern New Jersey shore.

Ammons published *Ommateum* (Dorrance), his first book, at his own expense in 1955; sixteen copies were sold in the next five years. In 1964, the year he joined the English faculty at Cornell University in Ithaca, NY, he published his second collection and rather rapidly went from total obscurity to wide acclaim. *Collected Poems 1951–1971* (1972), which won the National Book Award in 1973, capped an astonishingly productive period. Other high honours attended the publication of *Sphere* (1974) and *A Coast of Trees* (1981—all Norton).

Ammons is a maverick talent, utterly distinctive in voice, marked by high poetic ambition yet capable of whimsy. A nature poet, with a highly developed scientific acumen that sets him off from his contemporaries, Ammons often seems intent on making the consciousness of the poet the secret or real subject of the poem. In many cases, meticulous observation of the natural world is put at the service of abstract investigations and themes, such as the question of the one and the many; Ammons is constantly on the search for a unifying principle among minute and divergent particulars. The much-anthologized 'Corsons Inlet' is characteristically peripatetic, chronicling the poet's thoughts as he walks along the shore, where he celebrates fluid forms and disdains artificial enclosures. The critic Harold Bloom has championed Ammons as a transcendentalist, 'the most direct Emersonian in American poetry since Frost'. Like *Frost, Ammons loves nature too deeply to sentimentalize it or flinch in the face of its cruelties. But he is warmer; where Frost is a poet of terror, Ammons would convert fear into praise. He aspires, as he writes in 'The City Limits', to a transcendent 'radiance' that illuminates equally a sublime landscape or the scene of a natural slaughter.

Among his long poems, *Tape for the Turn of the Year* (Cornell University Press, 1965) is a notable experiment in form. The poem's skinny lines are the result of Ammons's decision to type out the poem, without revision, on a long roll of adding-machine paper. The buoyant and discursive *Sphere* (1974), Ammons's masterpiece, displays his formal and prosodic originality. Consisting of 155 sections, each containing four three-line stanzas, *Sphere* enacts 'the form of a motion' (the book's subtitle). The colon is used as an all-purpose punctuation mark, with the effect that closure is continually postponed. The three-line stanzas resemble a species of *terza libre*—a rhymeless version of the stanza unit of Shelley's 'Ode to the West Wind'. Ammons writes in the American idiom, has a 'democratic' bias in favour of lower-case letters, switches rapidly from high to low diction, and in one mood may remind his readers that 'magnificent' in North Carolina comes out 'maggie-went-a-fishing'. But his sly wit doesn't obscure the visionary nature of his poetry, the aim to affirm the magnificence of creation, however lowly in appearance, however dark in design.

Garbage (Norton, 1993)—which won another National Book Award—was widely acclaimed as his late masterpiece, a characteristically garrulous meditation on the 'legit | museums of our desecrations'. He continued to be prolific in his final decade: see *Brink Road* (1996) and his final long poem, *Glare* (1997). *Bosh and Flapdoodle* appeared posthumously in 2005 (all Norton) and an American Poets Project *Selected Poems* in 2006.

See 'A. R. Ammons: The Breaking of the Vessels' in *Figures of Capable Imagination*, by Harold Bloom (Seabury, 1976), 'A. R. Ammons' in *Alone With America*, by Richard Howard (Atheneum, 1980), and *A. R. Ammons and the Poetics of Widening Scope*, by Steven P. Schneider (Fairleigh Dickinson University Press, 1994).   DL*

Anderson, Ethel (1883–1958) Born in England but educated in Sydney, was married to an officer in the Indian Army and hence lived for some time in India, a fact which is reflected in *Indian Tales* (1948), as in some of her poetry. She returned to Australia in 1926, her husband serving on the staff of several governors and with the governor-general at Yarralumla. Her other collections of short stories are *The Little Ghosts* (1959) and the brilliantly idiosyncratic *At Parramatta* (1956); there are two volumes of essays.

Her collections of poetry are *Squatter's Luck* (1942) and *Sunday at Yarralumla* (1947). In the former she develops a distinctively Australian version of pastoral on a loose Virgilian model. Her style is mannered, sometimes a little archaic, and decidedly witty. Although seldom noticed by the literary mainstream, she had an effect on the more substantial work of David *Campbell.

Except for a new edition of *At Parramatta* (Penguin, 1985; with an afterword by Paul Salzman), Anderson's work is out of print. Chris *Wallace-Crabbe discusses her pastoral poetry in *Falling into Language* (Oxford University Press, 1990).   CW-C

Anderson, John (1948–97) Born in Kyabram, Victoria, John Anderson grew up in rural Australia, and his poetry reflects a continuous engagement with his environment. He moved to Melbourne in 1966 to study at the University of Melbourne and after 1975 lived in the city near the Merri Creek, which became the locale for much of his poetry. He travelled in Europe, South-East Asia, New Guinea, and extensively around Australia, and died in 1997 after a short illness.

His first collection of poetry was *the blue-gum smokes a long cigar* (Rigmarole, 1978). This was followed by a silence of more than two decades before his subsequent collections—*the forest set out like the night* (1995) and *the shadow's keep* (1997)—were published by Black Pepper Press. Anderson's deep interest in natural science emerges in a concern with precision and observation. Deeply influenced by the poetry of Francis Ponge, he brought to his poetry a lively awareness of the details of environment, and especially of the cultural frames through which it is experienced. His landscape poems focus on nuance, arguing against the European eye that traditionally dismissed the bush (most famously in A. D.

*Hope's poem *Australia*) as 'A nation of trees, drab green and desolate grey'. His poems integrate European modernist aesthetics with Aboriginal perspectives, creating an original diction remarkable for its delicate precision.   ACr

Anderson, Jon (Victor) (1940–2007) Born in Somerville, Massachusetts, Anderson was associate professor of English at the University of Arizona. Married three times, he wrote, with frequent elegiac turns, about the impermanent boundaries of selfhood, desire, and personal relationships.

Although his badly titled first book *Looking for Jonathan* (1968) misled some reviewers to pigeonhole Anderson as a merely *Confessional poet, the collection included a number of cunning, allegorical inventions; it also established the terse lyricism he was to refine in his later works, *Death & Friends* (1970) and *In Sepia* (1974—all University of Pittsburgh Press). *The Milky Way: Poems 1967–1982* (Ecco, 1983) demonstrated that, overall, he is a resourceful, meditative poet. While Rilke is, perhaps, the strongest influence evident in his poems, Anderson's humanism is lonelier and more secular, and less consoled by any literary aestheticism. Obsessed with defining the mutable limits of the self, Anderson is also, necessarily, obsessed with death. He provides the sting and satisfaction of a life undergoing keen examination and smart prescriptions, as in the poem 'In Autumn': 'We who have changed, & have | No hope of change, must now love | the passage of time.' A later collection, *Day Moon* (Carnegie Mellon University Press), appeared in 2001.   DWF

Anderson, Patrick (John McAlister) (1915–79) Born in Ashtead, Surrey and educated at Sherborne School, Dorset, as well as Oxford and Columbia. He spent ten fruitful and influential years (1940–50) in Canada as a schoolmaster and member of the avant-garde poetry circles of Montreal. After leaving Canada, Anderson travelled widely in Egypt, Malaya, and Greece. He took a position in 1957 with the English Department at Trent Park College of Education, Barnet, Hertfordshire, where he remained until his retirement.

Anderson's Canadian stay is noteworthy for his strong involvement in the little magazine culture of Montreal, his Marxist politics, and his emergence as a poet. His poems appeared in the key anthologies of the period and he published two accomplished collections of verse, *A Tent for April* (First Statement, 1945), and *The White Centre* (Ryerson, 1946), while *The Colour as Naked* (McClelland & Stewart, 1953) appeared after he had left Canada. A skilful if, on occasion, derivative poet with a clear debt to *Auden and *Spender, Anderson made a genuine contribution to Canadian poetry with his energy and creative verve.

In the middle 1950s he turned to prose, and published several works of autobiography and travel. In the 1970s he made a number of return visits to Canada; these rekindled his interest in poetry and resulted in *A Visiting Distance. Poems: New, Revised and Selected* (Borealis, 1976), and *Return to Canada: Selected Poems* (McClelland & Stewart, 1977).   MG

Andrews, Bruce (1948–   ) Born in Chicago and studied at Johns Hopkins and Harvard. Since 1975, he has taught international politics at Fordham University in New York. With Charles *Bernstein, Andrews was a founding editor of *L=A=N=G=U=A=G=E* magazine, which ran from 1978 to 1981. During the same period, he was an editor of the journal *New Political Science*. Andrews is notable even among the *Language poets for the sustained left-wing radicalism of his poetic theory and practice, with its insistence—contra the *Imagism of *Pound—that 'there is no "direct treatment" of the thing possible, except of the "things" of language'.

Andrews' early poetry began to appear through small presses in 1973. Like contemporary work by Clark *Coolidge and Robert *Grenier, it employed an atomized vocabulary in non-referential patterns (early titles include *Edge*, *Corona*, and *Vowels*). Andrews' later writing has moved towards forms of more extended discourse, albeit filled with vigorously subverted meaning, as in the prose poems of *I Don't Have Any Paper So Shut Up (Or, Social Romanticism)* (Sun & Moon, 1992). *Ex*

Why Zee (Roof, 1995) collects improvised performance texts, *Paradise & Method: Poetics and Praxis* (Northwestern University Press, 1996) critical essays. *Lip Service* (Coach House, 2001) is a free, cacophonic translation of Dante's *Paradiso* which continues his advocacy of 'the rigors of formal celebration, a playful infidelity... [and] a wide-open exuberance' (it ends 'let's start all over stars'). *Designated Heartbeat* (Salt, 2006) is a collection of shorter pieces and sequences.   JNT

Angelou, Maya (1928–) Born in St Louis, Missouri, she grew up in Arkansas and California. She toured Europe in *Porgy and Bess* before moving to New York where she worked as a night-club singer and performed in Genet's *The Blacks*. After becoming involved in black struggles in the Sixties she was editor of the *African Review* in Ghana. She has written six books of autobiography and now holds a lifetime appointment as Reynolds Professor of American Studies at Wake University, North Carolina.

Her first collection of poetry, *Just Give Me a Cool Drink of Water 'Fore I Diiie* (1971), was combined with her second, *Oh Pray My Wings Are Gonna Fit Me Well* (1975—both Random House), under the former title for publication by Virago in London in 1988. In the same way *And Still I Rise* (1978) was published with *Shaker, Why Don't You Sing?* (1983—both Random House) under the title of the former collection (Virago, 1986). *I Shall Not Be Moved* appeared in 1990, and *The Complete Collected Poems of Maya Angelou* in 1994 (both Random House and Virago).

The strength of her lyrics, with their unashamed and passionate use of iambic rhythm and full rhyme, lies in the combination of blues and gospel traditions with strong emotional and political insight. She was chosen to read her poem starting 'A Rock, A River, A Tree' and ending 'Very simply, | With hope | Good morning', at President Clinton's inauguration ceremony.   CB

Angira, Jared (1947–) Born in Kenya. He took a degree in commerce at the University of Nairobi and represented Africa on the executive committee of the World University Service. He also served as chairman of the Kenya Organization of Writers Association. Angira has published seven volumes of poetry, including *Silent Voices* (Heinemann, 1972), *Cascades* (Longman, 1979), and *The Years Go By* (Bookwise, 1980). He writes wittily, sometimes cynically, about life in the slums of Nairobi. Several of his poems are included in Wole *Soyinka's *Poems of Black Africa* (Secker & Warburg, 1975). A selected poems, *Tides of Time*, appeared in 1996, and *Lament of the Silent and Other Poems* in 2004 (both East African Educational).   KO

Ansen, Alan (1922–2006) Born in Brooklyn, grew up on Long Island, and took both his BA and MA at Harvard in 1944. Back in New York, Ansen, asked by W. H. *Auden to go over the drafts of *Age of Anxiety*, developed enduring friendships with Auden and Chester *Kallman, as well as with William Burroughs, Allen *Ginsberg, Gregory *Corso, and other figures in the *Beat movement. Ansen moved to Europe in 1954 and lived first in Venice, then in Athens.

The double dedication of Ansen's first book of poems, *Disorderly Houses* (Wesleyan University Press, 1961), shows his twofold heritage from Auden and Burroughs. Pattern and chaos; fervent homage to tradition and a truculent stance towards society—Ansen's idiosyncratic, learned, and gloomily exuberant poetry embraces such oppositions with gusto. Scholarly and critical tones, and an encyclopedic knowledge of Western culture, blend surprisingly with confessional and experimental modes, as in the poem entitled 'Imperfect Tributes: A Shriek, a Song and a Discourse'. A notable influence on such writers as *Kerouac and Corso, Ansen appears in various guises in their work.

Several volumes of Ansen's poetry were privately printed in Athens, but an excellent selection of his work is available in *Contact Highs: Selected Poems* (Dalkey Archive, 1989), which includes a biographical introduction and a bibliography. Ansen collected his memories of conversations with Auden in *The Table Talk of W. H. Auden* (Sea Cliff, 1989; Faber, 1991).   RHa

Antin, David (1932–) Born and grew up in New York City, studying at City College (where he met Jerome *Rothenberg) and New York University. He taught visual arts for many years at the University of California, San Diego, alongside his wife, the artist Eleanor Antin.

The translation of scientific textbooks informed the use of 'found' language in early volumes such as *Definitions* (Caterpillar, 1967) and *Code of Flag Behavior* (Black Sparrow, 1968). Antin is now best-known, however, for the wittily improvisatory 'talk poems' that he has been performing for audiences since the early 1970s. Antin credits his interest in an anecdotal, oral poetics to the experience of being raised by an extended European immigrant family. *Stein, *Cage, and *Olson were also important influences. In *talking at the boundaries* (New Directions, 1976) he speaks of his 'mixed feelings' about being formally defined as a 'poet': '*if robert *lowell is a poet i dont want to be a poet* [. . .] *if socrates is a poet ill consider it*'.

Sun & Moon Press published a selection of Antin's early poetry in 1991. Later transcripts of talk poetry include *tuning* (1984), *what it means to be avant-garde* (1993—both New Directions) and *i never knew what time it was* (University of California Press, 2005). Charles *Bernstein's *A Conversation with David Antin* (Granary) appeared in 2001. Antin's conversational critical prose can be found in *Radical Coherency: Selected Essays on Art and Literature, 1966–2005* (University of Chicago Press, 2011).   JNT

Anyidoho, Kofi (1947–) Born in Ghana, he attended teacher-training college before taking a degree in English at the University of Ghana, and then pursued postgraduate studies in America. He teaches at the University of Ghana in Accra. In spite of his educational background, Anyidoho's development as a poet is almost totally home-grown, drawing on his Ewe background and his reading in Ewe poetry, both modern and traditional. His first volume, *Elegy for the Revolution* (Greenfield Review, 1978) is a lament for Ghana's failed military revolution. His next

collection, *A Harvest of Our Dreams* (Heinemann, 1984), is more personal, although it includes poems from the first book and shares its communal concerns. In 1985 Anyidoho published *Earthchild, with Brain Surgery* (Woeli) and in 1992 *AncestralLogic & CarribeanBlues* (Africa World Press).   KO

Arasanayagam, Jean Solomons (1934–) The daughter of a Dutch burgher family with roots in colonial Sri Lanka, married to a Tamil Hindu, Arasanayagam combines her European and Asian heritages in her poetry. A university-educated teacher, she is also a painter, batik artist, linoprint maker, fiction writer, and poet, whose early verse recorded painterly impressions of Sri Lankan life and landscape (especially of the mountain country of Kandy, her birthplace).

The tranquil surface of Arasanayagam's poetry changed dramatically following Sri Lanka's ethnic disturbances in 1983. Much of her recent work expresses the fear and despair experienced by prisoners, exiles, and refugees from ethnic violence. Honoured by Sri Lanka Arts Council awards for poetry and non-fiction, she has also held writing fellowships at the universities of Iowa and Exeter.

Published in magazines in Sri Lanka and abroad, Arasanayagam's work is included in *Poems from India, Sri Lanka, Malaysia and Singapore* (Heinemann, 1979), ed. Y. Gooneratne. Her own publications include *Kindura* (1973), *Poems of a Season Beginning and a Season Over* (1977), *Apocalypse 83* (1984), *A Colonial Inheritance* (1985), all printed privately in Sri Lanka; and *Trial by Terror: Sri Lankan Poems* (Rimu, 1987). Later volumes include *The Colour of My Mind* (2009) and *The Word Never Dies* (2011—both Godage). There is an extended discussion of the 'fugitive selves' of her writing in Minoli Salgado, *Writing Sri Lanka: Literature, Resistance and the Politics of Place* (Routledge, 2007).   YG

Armantrout, Rae (1947–) Born in California. Armantrout studied at the University of California, Berkeley, where she was taught by Denise *Levertov, and later took a Master's degree in creative writing at San Francisco State University. She is now a professor of creative writing at the University of California, San Diego.

Armantrout's voice has been notably consistent in form and focus since her first books, *Extremities* (The Figures, 1978) and *The Invention of Hunger* (Tuumba, 1979). Working with small fragments of everyday language, she analyses the narratives that structure modern American life, and in particular female identity. To quote 'Anti-Short Story' in full: 'A girl is running. *Don't* tell me | "She's running for her bus." || All that aside!' Sharp enjambments and concrete imagery align Armantrout's free verse with the example of William Carlos *Williams and the *Objectivist tradition. In Armantrout's postmodernist world, however, even apparently innocent observations are implicitly placed in quotation marks. The same quizzical tone informs her prose poems, such as the title piece of *The Pretext* (Green Integer, 2001).

An important member of the West Coast group of *Language poets, Armantrout has collaborated with Ron *Silliman, who wrote the foreword for *Veil: New and Selected Poems* (Wesleyan University Press, 2001). As well as a prose memoir, *True* (Atelos, 1998), she has published more than a dozen volumes of verse. *Versed* (2009) obliquely confronts a cancer diagnosis. It won the 2010 Pulitzer Prize for Poetry and was followed by *Money Shot* (2011—both Wesleyan University Press).   JNT

Armitage, Simon (1963–) Born in Huddersfield, West Yorkshire, where he still lives, Armitage studied geography at Portsmouth Polytechnic and social work at Manchester University. Having worked as a probation officer, he is now a freelance writer and broadcaster, and Professor of Poetry at the University of Sheffield.

Armitage is one of the most popular and widely respected poets to have emerged in Britain since the 1980s. His full-length debut, *Zoom* (Bloodaxe, 1989), employs a distinctively northern and youthful demotic alongside 'official' literary language, often to deadpan effect. It is notable that while he has obvious social and political concerns,

the problems of linguistic status and deracination which vex the older northern-born poet Tony *Harrison do not figure largely in his work.

Armitage's poems are both firmly grounded in place and wide in their imaginative, emotional, and technical range, moving easily between anecdote, larger narrative, art, and politics. The influence of Paul *Muldoon is sometimes apparent, but the strongest impression is of a considerable talent going confidently about its business.

In 1992 Armitage published *Xanadu* (Bloodaxe), the text of a BBC poem-film set in a Rochdale housing estate, and *Kid* (Faber), his second full collection. The latter sustains the narrative and comic elements of *Zoom*, while attending more closely to matters of identity (in a series of poems employing the character of Robinson, originally created by Weldon *Kees), and showing a deepening historical and political interest ('Lines Thought to have been Written on the Eve of the Execution of a Warrant for his Arrest').

Book of Matches (1993) continued to experiment with longer-form writing—the title sequence is a series of free sonnets. *The Dead Sea Poems* (1995) concludes with 'Five Eleven Nine Nine', a *fin-de-siécle* allegory, and 'The Whole of the Sky' in *Cloud Cuckoo Land* (1997) turns the constellations to autobiography. *Killing Time* (1999), a 1000-line poem-film commissioned for the Millennium year, saw Armitage's verbal facility running at its least inventive. His translation of *Sir Gawain and the Green Knight* (2007—all Faber), on the other hand, is notable for its freshness and fluency.

A *Selected Poems* (Faber) appeared in Britain in 2001 and in America as *The Shout* (Harcourt) in 2005. There have been two further collections of verse: *The Universal Home Doctor* (2002) and *Tyrannosaurus Rex versus the Corduroy Kid* (2006). Armitage has a considerable talent for observational prose, first evident in *Moon Country* (1996—all Faber), a revisiting of *Auden and *MacNeice's *Letters from Iceland* written with Glyn *Maxwell. *All Points North* (Viking, 1998), *Gig* (Viking,

2008), and *Walking Home* (Faber, 2012) are memoirs of life in Northern England. He has also written two novels: *The Green Man* (2001) and *The White Stuff* (2004). Fiction and poetry successfully combine in *Seeing Stars* (Faber, 2010), a volume of James *Tate-esque prose poems. See Ian Gregson, *Simon Armitage* (Salt, 2011).   SO'B*

Arrowsmith, William (1924–92) Born in New Jersey and spent his boyhood in Massachusetts and Florida. He graduated from Princeton University, attended Oxford University on a Rhodes Scholarship, and embarked on a career as professor of classics, essayist, translator, editor, and film critic. A teacher of legendary force and the author of widely hailed articles on educational reform, he held many teaching appointments, including at the University of Texas at Austin (1958–70), Yale University, Johns Hopkins University, New York University, Emory University, and Boston University (1986–92).

His learned and racy translations from the classics gained a wide audience. In particular, his version of Petronius's *Satyricon* (University of Michigan Press, 1959; repr. 1961), his many plays of Euripides, and his translations of *The Birds* (University of Michigan Press, 1961; repr. 1962) and *The Clouds* (University of Michigan Press, 1962) of Aristophanes brought classical literature to life for several generations of readers and theatre-goers. In later years Arrowsmith turned to modern Italian literature. His *Hard Labor*, poems by Cesare Pavese (Grossman, 1976; repr. 1985) influenced the development of the hard-bitten, anti-lyrical poetics in the United States in the late Seventies, and by the time of his death he had translated all the books of poems which Eugenio Montale published in his own lifetime.

Arrowsmith was equally influential as an editor and essayist, founding some of the liveliest journals in the United States (*The Chimera, The Hudson Review, Arion*). In his editing, as in his scholarship and translation, he wedded imaginative vigour to erudition. His edition and translations of Nietzsche (*Unmodern Observations*, 1990)

and his essays on T. S. *Eliot and Antonioni show his consistent devotion to the dynamism within the European tradition.

Arrowsmith's many honours include the Landon Translation Prize from the Academy of American Poets for Montale's *The Storm and Other Things* (1986), and the International Montale Prize. His translation of *The Collected Poems of Eugenio Montale* (Norton), ed. Rosanna Warren, appeared posthumously in 2012.   RW

Ash, John (1948–) Born in Manchester, and studied at the University of Birmingham then worked as an elementary-school teacher and research assistant before moving to New York in 1985. He co-wrote a book on the effects of the tourist trade in underdeveloped nations, and has published ten volumes of poetry, the most recent of them *The Parthian Stations* (2007) and *In the Wake of Day* (2010), which contains a series of poems 'After Cavafy'. In addition to his poetry, Ash has written numerous articles and reviews for literary journals, and two travel books about Turkey. A *Selected Poems* (all Carcanet) appeared in 1996, the year that he moved from America to Istanbul, a transition reflected in *The Anatolikon* (Talisman House, 2000).

Ash's chief source of inspiration has come not from his native tradition but from the more experimental strains of French and American poetry. In his earlier work Ash openly evokes the decadent phase of French symbolism; his later writing derives heavily from the *New York School, especially the poetry of his friend and homonymous mentor John *Ashbery. Despite the unmistakeable debts that Ash owes to Ashbery, his poetry has a visual clarity and phonic lushness that distinguish it from that of other New York School writers. Ash's imagination is drawn to culture rather than nature; his poems evoke both the beauty and the fragility of human constructs. This is most clearly evident in his frequent recourse to an imagery of crumbling architecture. Ash is an urban elegist, at once romantic in his sense of the city's pathos and nobility, and postmodern in his concern with surface, ambiguity, and dissolution.   RG*

Ashbery, John (1927–   ) Born in Rochester, New York, and brought up on a farm in Sodus nearby. He attended Harvard College, graduating in 1949, and afterwards enrolled in graduate school at Columbia University, New York, receiving his MA in 1951. His first book, *Some Trees*, was published in 1956 in the Yale Younger Poets series with an introduction by W. H. *Auden. He spent 1955–6 studying in Paris on a Fulbright Scholarship, and returned to Paris in 1958 where he was employed as art critic for the Paris *Herald Tribune*. He returned to New York in 1966, working until 1972 as Executive Editor of *Art News*. In 1974 he was appointed to a teaching post at Brooklyn College.

Ashbery's first volume, *Some Trees*, is influenced by the work of Wallace *Stevens and W. H. Auden, and reflects also Ashbery's reading of avant-garde French poets such as Raymond Roussel, Pierre Reverdy, and Max Jacob. In its most famous poem, 'The Instruction Manual', the poet is supposed to be writing an instruction manual 'on the uses of a new metal', but instead he drifts into a pastel travelogue-style reverie about the Mexican city of Guadalajara. After his move to Paris Ashbery began experimenting with more radical styles of poetic disjunction. His second volume, *The Tennis Court Oath* (Wesleyan University Press, 1962), contains a number of cut-up poems composed out of seemingly arbitrary fragments of language. The long poem 'Europe' is the most extreme of these. Even some of Ashbery's most fervent admirers have been puzzled by this book, and Harold Bloom, one of his earliest champions, has called it 'a fearful disaster'. Ashbery himself has said that in these poems he was 'taking poetry apart to try to understand how it works', while in his next volume, *Rivers and Mountains* (Holt, 1966), he set out 'to fit it back together'. Over half of *Rivers and Mountains* is taken up by the long poem 'The Skaters', in which Ashbery expansively develops a beguiling series of possible fictions for the poetic self, though without ever identifying a su-

preme one. Its long lines and extreme openness have provoked various critics to see this poem as Ashbery's 'Song of Myself'.

In his next collection, *The Double Dream of Spring* (Dutton, 1970)—the title is borrowed from a painting by Giorgio de Chirico, whose work Ashbery greatly admires— he explores more obviously lyrical modes of poetry. In the poem 'Soonest Mended' he characterizes his poetic stance as 'a kind of fence-sitting | Raised to the level of an esthetic ideal'. In this poem in particular, which he has called his 'one-size-fits-all Confessional poem', Ashbery is able to transform his sense of life's ability to escape all imposed formulations into a resonant and fertile uncertainty: 'For this is action, this not being sure, this careless | Preparing, sowing the seeds crooked in the furrow, | Making ready to forget, and always coming back | To the mooring of starting out, that day so long ago.'

Ashbery's willingness to experiment is well illustrated by his following volume, *Three Poems* (Viking, 1972), which is in fact three long prose pieces, with occasional interspersed lyrics. *Self-Portrait in a Convex Mirror* (Viking, 1975; Carcanet, 1976), undoubtedly Ashbery's most popular and successful volume, was awarded three of America's most prestigious literary prizes, including a Pulitzer. Its long title poem is a meditation based on the Mannerist painter Parmigianino's famous self-portrait. Although the poem is not Ashbery's own favourite, most critics see it as his seminal work, and this is probably because it eschews many of the surrealist and disjunctive effects with which so much of his work is inflected. In the poem Ashbery broods on his familiar themes—the relationship between art and life, the instability of any sense of self, the impossibility of a single coherent narrative, the passing of time— with a clarity and directness unusual for him.

Later Ashbery volumes have found new ways of approaching such dilemmas. The enormous, seventy-page poem 'Litany' from *As We Know* (Viking/Carcanet, 1978) is in double columns, 'meant to be read as simultaneous but independent monologues' (Author's Note). *Shadow Train*

(Viking/Carcanet, 1981) consists of fifty sixteen-line poems. In 1985 Ashbery was awarded a five-year MacArthur fellowship, much of which he spent composing his most ambitious poem to date, *Flow Chart* (Knopf/Carcanet, 1991). *Flow Chart* is well over 200 pages long, and includes a virtuoso double sestina that makes use of the end words of Swinburne's double sestina 'The Complaint of Lisa'.

Since the success of *Self-Portrait in a Convex Mirror*, Ashbery's poetry has proved increasingly influential both in America and abroad. Its impact is perhaps best encapsulated by the title of a collection of essays on his work edited by the critic Susan M. Schultz: *The Tribe of John: Ashbery and Contemporary Poetry* (University of Alabama Press, 1995). Ashbery is now one of America's most honoured poets of all time, having received virtually every US poetry award, and many international prizes too. He was the first living poet to be included in the Library of America; their edition of his *Collected Poems* covered the first half of his career, from 1956 to 1987 (2008; revd. edn., Carcanet, 2010), and ran to over 1,000 pages. A second volume covering the latter half of his career is likely to prove even longer, for Ashbery has produced some 13 further collections since 1987. He has also published three volumes of criticism (*Reported Sightings: Art Chronicles 1957-87* (Knopf/Carcanet, 1989), *Other Traditions*, his Charles Eliot Norton lectures (Harvard University Press, 2000), and *Selected Prose* (University of Michigan Press/Carcanet, 2004), ed. Eugene Richie, as well as a volume of plays (*Three Plays*, Z Press, 1978; Carcanet, 1988), a novel, *A Nest of Ninnies*, co-written with James *Schuyler (Dutton, 1969; Carcanet, 1987), and a translation of Rimbaud's *Illuminations* (Norton/Carcanet, 2011). The secondary literature on his oeuvre has grown steadily year by year. In March 2012 he was presented with a National Arts and Humanities Medal by Barack Obama.   MF

Atkins, Tim (1962–   ) Grew up in Toronto, and Worcestershire, England, before studying Buddhism at Kings College, London. A former member of Carla *Harryman's Poets Theatre, San Francisco, Atkins now teaches creative writing at the University of East London, and edits the online poetry journal *Onedit*. He is a practising Buddhist.

Atkins is known for his experimental translations, which depart from literal meaning freely and humorously. He has engaged extensively with the Italian of Petrarch and has also translated Horace and Buddhist texts. Atkins' playful attitude to canonical literature also extends to his use of the sonnet, which follows the experimental example of Ted *Berrigan. Many of the poems in *1000 Sonnets* (if p then q, 2010) engage thematically, historically, and visually with the form whilst breaking most of its traditional elements. Short lines, numerals, ellipses, and other typographical substitutions lead to a minimalistic, Eastern-influenced iteration of the fourteen-line lyric. Atkins' other publications include *To Repel Ghosts* (Like Books, 1998), *Horace* (O Books, 2007), *Folklore* (Salt, 2008)—a prose poem sequence set in Worcestershire—and *Petrarch* (Barque, 2011). There is a selection of his sonnets in *The Reality Street Book of Sonnets*, ed. Jeff Hilson (Reality Street, 2008).   SRO

Atwood, Margaret (Eleanor) (1939–   ) Born in Ottawa, Canada. She grew up in Ottawa and Toronto, but as a child spent the summers with her family in northern Quebec. She received her BA from the University of Toronto in 1961 and her MA from Radcliffe College, Harvard, in 1962. She won a Governor General's Award for her first book of poetry, *The Circle Game* (Contact, 1966), and went on to become one of the finest and most prolific of contemporary writers. She has published poetry, novels, collections of short stories, critical studies of Canadian literature, biographical essays, and has edited other works, including *The New Oxford Book of Canadian Verse in English* (1982). She has been active in such organizations as the Writers' Union of Canada, Amnesty International, and PEN, and has lectured widely around the world. Atwood has won many prizes, including a Guggenheim Fellowship and the Molson Prize (both in 1981), and has received several honorary degrees. She is a Companion of the Order of Canada and an Honorary Member of the American Academy of Arts and Sciences.

Atwood's poetry is characterized by the vivid precision of her language and the power of her imagery. In her short, laconic lyrics she provides sharp insights into the consciousness of the speaker, while in her series of connected poems she develops symbolic and visionary explorations of the ironic dualities of existence. Her interest in the politics of human relationships has led her to explore a wide range of subjects, from the conflicting attitudes towards Canada of the pioneer, Susanna Moodie, in *The Journals of Susanna Moodie* (Oxford University Press, 1970) to the myths and deceptions of romantic love in *Power Politics* (Anansi, 1973); to the ambiguities of myth in *You Are Happy* (1974) and the horrors of torture and repression in *True Stories* (1981—both Oxford University Press).

Eating Fire is a selected poems from the mid-1990s (Virago, 1998). *Morning in the Burned House* appeared in 1995 and *The Door* in 2007 (both McClelland & Stewart/ Houghton/Virago). Two books of lectures—*Strange Things: The Malevolent North in Canadian Literature* (Oxford University Press, 1996) and *Negotiating with the Dead: A Writer on Writing* (Cambridge University Press, 2002)—have been followed by *Writing with Intent,* a collection of later occasional prose (Carroll & Graf, 2005). See *Margaret Atwood: Vision and Forms* (Southern Illinois University Press, 1988), ed. Kathryn Van Spanckeren and Jan Garden Castro, and *The Cambridge Companion to Margaret Atwood* (Cambridge University Press, 2006), ed. Coral Ann Howells.   SEG*

Auden, W. H. (Wystan Hugh) (1907–73) Born on 21 February 1907 into a provincial English world still Tennysonian in outlook. He was the third son of a gentle, cultivated family doctor and a domineering former nurse who had once wanted to go to Africa as a missionary. Auden was by nature a versatile, polymorphous writer, one who felt that, amongst other things, poetry was 'a game of knowledge'. The odd geometry of his parents' marriage seems to have added an intellectual openness and restlessness, even as it left him personally extremely anxious. He boarded at Gresham's School in Norfolk, then in 1925 went up to Christ Church, Oxford, where he soon switched from reading biology to English.

For a collected edition made late in his career, Auden divided his poetry into broad phases; each constituted, he felt, a 'chapter'. The first stretches from 1927 until the end of 1932, and in it Auden emerges from the sacred ground of English Romanticism, the Lake District. The landscape of these guarded, archaic-sounding poems is the same as Wordsworth's, though in Auden the area is desolate and the solitary is numbed by feelings of intense isolation and disappointment. Even the shared resources of English are denied: conjunctions and pronouns have flaked away, leaving a language of glittering, compacted hardness.

A pamphlet, *Poems*, was cranked out on a hand-press by his friend Stephen *Spender in 1928. The same year Auden left Oxford and spent the next nine months in Germany (mainly Berlin), writing, reading widely in psychology, and brothel-crawling. At a moment when Europe's foundations were starting to shudder, he also became concerned about political issues. In September 1930, a few months after Auden had returned to England, T. S. *Eliot at Faber and Faber published Auden's first full-length book, again austerely called *Poems* (1930). Meanwhile, Auden had gone off to teach at a seedy Scottish prep-school.

In *Poems* (1930) there is a dark, autistic vein of love poetry; there is also a kind of admonitory satire, castigating Britain's spiritual torpor. His next book, *The Orators* (1932), is the culmination of both these tendencies and it reads like a surrealist explosion of language. There are hints of a narrative involving a failed insurrection against the governing class, but the real subject of *The Orators* is its own bristling verbal energy.

Despite the obscurity of his early work, Auden was hailed by critics as the leader of a group of young, left-wing, writers that included Louis *MacNeice, Spender, and

C. Day *Lewis. Backed by Eliot, and fuelled by a growing literary confidence, Auden seems to have felt for a while that he could have a role to play in the country's renewal. This belief soon evaporated, and by the end of the decade he was to feel trapped by his sense of responsibility. None the less, the revolutionary 'movement' was an important means of self-definition for these poets as they were crawling out of the shadow of *Yeats and Eliot. It also gave Auden a clearly defined audience to write for and a reason to try and forge an accessible public style.

He soon came to see *The Orators* as a botched effort, and his work, which shows a strong evolutionary urge, began to move forward. In the autumn of 1932 he started teaching at the Downs School in Herefordshire. In that mellow world his poetry opened like a bud, becoming more expansive and much richer in surface detail. This is the start of the second 'chapter', the phase when Auden, drawing on Marx and Freud, was able to make a brilliant stream of connections between individual guilts and pleasures and the crisis that seemed to be eating away at European civilization. Simultaneously, his interest in the possibilities of verse-forms burst out in a profusion of beautifully adroit sonnets, sestinas, and ballads.

Auden was homosexual, but in 1935 he married Thomas Mann's daughter, Erika, a fugitive from Nazi persecution, in order to get her an English passport. The same year he left the Downs. In search of a wider field of vision he joined a documentary film company, where he worked briefly and unhappily. For six years after that he was a freelance writer. A second collection of lyrics, *Look, Stranger!* (1936)—the American edition is *On This Island* (1937)—extended his reputation.

So did his plays. Auden had composed a long charade, *Paid On Both Sides* (1928), and a polemical 'masque', *The Dance of Death* (1933). In the later Thirties he and Christopher Isherwood turned out a string of dramas: *The Dog Beneath the Skin* (1935), *The Ascent of F6* (1936), and *On the Frontier* (1938). Although none of the plays is a fully integrated work, they contain flashes of great poetry. The choruses in *The Dog Beneath the Skin* offer huge panoramas of English life, and *F6* contains an allegory of Auden's early fantasy of himself as a healer and redeemer of society. He later said it was while working on the play that he realized that, for the sake of his artistic growth, he would have to leave England.

Auden's pre-war years were a period of fertility in many media and of almost continuous wandering. In 1936 he went with MacNeice to Iceland (where he liked to believe his ancestors had come from), a trip that resulted in their *Letters from Iceland* (1937). The volume contains Auden's masterpiece of autobiographical light verse, 'Letter to Lord Byron'. Then, in January 1937, he went to observe the Spanish Civil War. Auden was never a member of the Communist Party, and he seems to have been shunted aside by the party bosses in Spain. Immediately after he returned, though, he wrote his most famous call to action, 'Spain', a poem full of local brilliance but one that cannot now be separated from knowledge of the Civil War's tragically convoluted history. Auden hardly ever spoke about his experiences in Barcelona, but in the wake of the visit his poems darkened; many from the later Thirties are bleakly pessimistic, shielding themselves from the historical turmoil behind layers of stylization and irony. In early 1938, after he had hurriedly assembled his *Oxford Book of Light Verse* (1938), Auden went abroad again, this time with Isherwood. They travelled to China to write about the Sino-Japanese War. Their book, *Journey to a War* (1939) became a parable about the difficulty of politically engaged writing: as Isherwood recounts it, they could never find any clearly drawn lines of battle in China. The problem is developed in the volume's sonnet sequence 'In Time of War', which finds the war going on everywhere, all the time. The sonnets show an important broadening of Auden's moral imagination, and throughout, Christian symbolism begins to bubble to the surface.

On their voyage to England in mid-1938 Auden and Isherwood stopped off in New York. In January 1939 they went back there.

Going to America was another turning-point, and Auden began purging himself of a rhetoric that he felt had now been exhausted. The next phase of his career, initiated by a series of elegies and psychological portraits, is a period of much more intimate writing, concerned above all with subjectivity and loneliness. He had fallen in love with a younger American writer, Chester Kallman, and his happiness seems to have released a flood of other feelings, including what were only half-suppressed religious impulses. *Another Time* (1940) contains some of his best work, though, as the title indicates, the poems already seemed to him to belong in a vanished era. The book includes 'September 1, 1939', a lyric written the weekend war was declared, which tries to come to terms with the failure of the 'clever hopes' of a 'low dishonest decade' for social and personal renewal, and attempts a new, modestly heroic, role for the writer. Auden later came to dislike the sanctimoniousness of the piece.

The suggestions of religious and poetic conversion were strengthened in *The Double Man* (1941; published in London the same year under the title *New Year Letter*). Again admitting the failure of the utopian hopes of the Thirties, the volume's main element, a long neo-Augustan verse epistle, is a dissection of man's spiritual predicament and of the dualism in European secular thought which Auden believed had ultimately led to the catastrophe of war. It ends with a petition for aid from a mysterious—though still unnamed—power. Around October 1940, just after he finished the book, Auden began going to church.

Although he remained a Christian for the rest of his life, Auden never became pious or dogmatic, at least in his poems. In fact his faith seems to have increased his intellectual appetite. By inclination his mind was speculative, synthesizing, and eclectic—he was probably the only poet from the earlier half of the century well acquainted with the most advanced

thought of the day—and Christianity allowed him to order this vast store of knowledge from philosophy, history, and theology into a harmonious and poetic world-view.

In the next few years he produced three more long poems. Each addresses the situation created by the 'crisis' of the war and of his conversion to Christianity, and each deals with its implications for his art. It is a retrenchment in the form of an enormous, almost forbidding, flowering: Auden's developing artistry feeds off his complex feelings about literature, and particularly about his own early writing. Two of these poems, 'For the Time Being', a Christmas Oratorio dedicated to his mother who had died in 1941, and 'The Sea and the Mirror', a verse 'commentary' on *The Tempest* that Auden described as his 'Ars Poetica', were published together in *For the Time Being* (1944). His final long poem is *The Age of Anxiety* (1947). This ornate, rather Joycean work, which won the 1948 Pulitzer Prize, is an interior portrait of the average twentieth-century city-dweller, cast in the form of a meeting between four New Yorkers in a bar on All Souls' Night, 1944.

Between 1939 and early 1947 much of his time was taken up with work on these long poems and earning a living as a university lecturer. In 1945, though, he spent a few months in Germany as an observer with the US Air Force's 'Strategic Bombing Survey', studying the effects of aerial bombardment. Amongst the ruins of Darmstadt and Munich his interest in rebuilding cities took on renewed urgency, and some of his most ambitious works of the post-war years open out into an investigation of how to unify the contemporary world. The most important in this respect are the poem 'Memorial for the City' (1949), and a series of anti-Romantic lectures, *The Enchafèd Flood* (1950).

In 1946 Auden became a US citizen. The following year was one of artistic uncertainty, a time when he was again casting around for a new literary direction. Once more a fresh 'chapter' began with a change of air. From 1948 until 1957 Auden summered—and wrote most of his poetry—on Ischia, an island in the Bay of Naples. This period, during which Auden became the first truly rootless, international poet since Byron, was inaugurated by the elegiac syllabics of 'In Praise of Limestone'. The poem appeared in the transitional *Nones* (1951). The Mediterranean breathed a restrained, 'classical' feeling into Auden's work, and renewed his interest in the natural world and in the great movements of human history. The poems are more relaxed, but there is no slackening of artistic authority: his writing is both colloquial and gracefully elevated.

Auden believed that every poem should pose a new technical challenge for the poet. Thus, formal precision is balanced in the Fifties by a great deal of formal experimentation. The main thematic preoccupation is with the humanist task of defining Man through his relations with the world around him, and this culminates in a pair of major sequences from mid-decade: 'Bucolics' and 'Horae Canonicae'. Both were published in *The Shield of Achilles* (1955), along with that book's title poem, a meditation on the West's culture of violence. The final pieces from the period were gathered into *Homage to Clio* (1960).

As his verse became more conversational, Auden found an outlet for his love of the grand style by writing opera libretti. (He had already worked on an operetta, *Paul Bunyan*, with Benjamin Britten in 1939–41.) He and Kallman now produced the words for Stravinsky's *The Rake's Progress* (1951). Later they collaborated on *Elegy for Young Lovers* (1961) and *The Bassarids* (1966), both by Hans Werner Henze, and *Love's Labour's Lost* (1973) by Nicolas Nabokov.

Auden's activities were not confined to poetry and opera, though. He also produced a torrent of critical prose and, with Norman Holmes Pearson, edited a five-volume anthology of verse, *Poets of the English Language* (1950). From 1956 to 1961 he was Professor of Poetry at Oxford, countering the authority of his lectures in the Sheldonian with a stream of baroque occasional verses and academic clerihews.

In 1958 he and Kallman moved again, this time to a summer cottage outside Vienna. Increasingly Auden's poetry came under the influence of Herbert and Dryden, becoming dryer and more sober, though he set even the most apparently parochial of his poems in the sweep of long historical vistas. In fact, Auden was now beginning to produce a subtle, highly crafted poetry of old age, crankier, but also much more topical and political than it had been for several decades. He continued to seek out new formal challenges as well, and his long, chatty meditations are interspersed by showers of brilliantly sharp haiku diary-jottings. Both sides of this Goethean persona are represented in *About the House* (1965), which contains another major sequence, a poem for every room in his home, except—their relations continued to be complicated—Kallman's bedroom.

Auden's final books, *City Without Walls* (1969), *Epistle to a Godson* (1972), and the posthumous *Thank You, Fog* (1974) are the completion of the curve. Each of these books contains important poems: wry, ego-less musings in which extinction—feared, witnessed, and, occasionally, inflicted—is a frequent subject. Auden maintained that poets died once they had finished their historically appointed task. He spent the summer of 1973 in Austria and had planned to fly back to Oxford, where he now spent his winters. However, on 28 September 1973, in the middle of his last night in Vienna, he suffered a fatal heart-attack.

Since his death Auden's polemical aura, whether in its early political or in its later High-Churchy form, has faded. He now seems an extraordinarily comprehensive and various writer; not one voice, but many. He was a master of the sparkling detail who also loved the vast, inhuman overviews of geography and history, a poet of great technical finesse who was ambivalent about the worth of literature, the century's wittiest public versifier who could also sound the note of someone speaking out into an unpeopled silence. Only a major poet could have mingled and brought to perfection so many different styles, and only a great one could have been so ready to throw away his successes and move on.

The bulk of his work is part of its meaning, too. In historical terms, his importance lies in his reaction against Modernism's tortured sense of stasis and restriction. Auden is a self-effacing poet: the nearest he got to an autobiography was *A Certain World* (1970), a vast collection of his favourite texts from other writers. Looked at from one point of view, this distaste for personal revelations and visionary extremity can be traced to the accidents of his psychological make-up. Looked at from another, though, his encyclopaedic intellectual scope, his polyglot linguistic inclusiveness, and his insistence that all forms and subjects are still available to the contemporary poet, look like the dynamic of poetry working itself out through him. Auden is a powerful precursor figure for later poets, and his voice reverberates in writing as different as *Lowell's churning sonnets and *Ashbery's cool, loose webs.

The bibliographical situation is tangled, and no one book can represent all the important facets of Auden's career. The bedrock is the *Collected Poems* (3rd edn., 2007). However, when Auden was trying to discover what sort of poems he wanted to write next, he often looked back sourly on earlier work and even cut out several key poems, notably 'Spain' and 'September 1, 1939'. This means that the *Collected Poems* must be supplemented by two anthologies. The *English Auden: Poems, Essays and Dramatic Writings 1927–1939* (1977—both Faber/Random House) provides a much broader picture of the first decade or so, and includes *The Orators*. For the original version of 'Spain', the reader needs the *Selected Poems* (Vintage/Faber, 1979). All three are edited by Auden's literary executor, Edward Mendelson. A multi-volume, historically oriented edition, *The Complete Works of W. H. Auden*, also under Mendelson's editorship, is under way. A volume of the dramas written with Isherwood, *Plays and Other Dramatic Writings 1929–1938* (Princeton University Press, 1988; Faber, 1989), and a volume of the libretti composed with Kall-

man, *Libretti* (Princeton University Press/Faber, 1993) have appeared. In addition to *The Enchafèd Flood* (see above), there were three collections of fairly late prose: *The Dyer's Hand* (Random House, 1962; Faber, 1963), based on Auden's lectures as Professor of Poetry at Oxford; *Secondary Worlds* (Faber, 1968; Random House, 1969), the 1967 T. S. Eliot Memorial Lectures; and *Forewords and Afterwords* (Random House/Faber, 1973). The *Prose* has now reached four volumes from Princeton University Press, up to 1962, bringing to light a large quantity of valuable occasional material. Auden's 1946/7 *Lectures on Shakespeare* were reconstructed by Arthur C. Kirsch from the notes of Alan *Ansen in 2002, and his 1920s *Juvenilia* was edited by Katherine Bucknell in 2003. Annotated critical editions of the *The Sea and the Mirror* and *The Age of Anxiety* are also available (all Princeton University Press).

Information on work from the final few years of Auden's life and on discoveries made since his death can be found in Mendelson's 'W. H. Auden: A Bibliographical Supplement', in Katherine Bucknell and Nicholas Jenkins (eds.), *W. H. Auden: 'The Map of All My Youth'* (Clarendon, 1990). The best account of Auden's life is Humphrey Carpenter's *W. H. Auden: A Biography* (Allen & Unwin, 1981); Alan Ansen's *The Table Talk of W. H. Auden* (Ontario Review, 1990; Faber, 1991) gives a good impression of his witty, playful intelligence. *The Age of Auden* (Princeton University Press, 2011) by Aidan Wasley surveys his influence on post-war American poetry. The fullest guide to the poems, plays, and libretti is John Fuller's *W. H. Auden: A Commentary* (Princeton University Press/Faber, 1998). Critical works include *The Auden Generation* by Samuel Hynes (Faber, 1976; Viking, 1977), *Early Auden* and *Later Auden* (Farrar, Straus/Faber, 1981 and 1999) by Edward Mendelson, *W. H. Auden* by Stan Smith (Blackwell, 1985), and *W. H. Auden: Towards a Postmodern Poetics* (Palgrave, 2000) by Rainer Emig. Auden left instructions that after his death his friends should burn all letters from him. In fact not much seems to have been destroyed, but until publication of the *Complete Works* is finished no edition of his correspondence will appear.   NJ*

Avison, Margaret (1918–2007) Born in Galt, Ontario, brought up on the Canadian prairie, and educated at the University of Toronto. She worked as a librarian and teacher, but after a profound Christian vision she took up her vocation as a social worker at a church mission in downtown Toronto. As a poet she wrote steadily but did not rush into print over a long career.

Often characterized as 'metaphysical', sometimes 'difficult', Avison's poetry is intensely modern. It is improvised according to the play of sound, and nearly always concerned with the act of seeing. The poems are Christian but not doctrinaire. Avison looks for images among poor people, strangers, and the lonely wanderers of the city. She looks at them carefully, and humanizes them in their singularity. Her sympathy and her skill have won over writers and readers who will never share her faith.

Avison always discouraged the makers of reputation, especially the literary press and the academics. Thus, for a long time, she had a greater following among poets than among critics. Her first two books were published outside Canada, and the next two by a nearly unknown press in Nova Scotia. Yet there is now agreement that she is one of Canada's most accomplished poets.

Avison's first two volumes were gathered as *Winter Sun/The Dumbfounding: Poems 1940–1966* (McClelland & Stewart, 1982). This was followed by *No Time* (Lancelot, 1989; repr. Brick, 1998) and *Selected Poems* (Oxford University Press, 1991). *Concrete and Wild Carrot* (Brick) won the 2003 Griffin Poetry Prize. Her collected poems, *Always Now* (Porcupine's Quill) appeared in 2005, followed by *Momentary Dark* (2006) and *Listening: Last Poems* (2009—both McClelland & Stewart), a posthumous volume. A collection of essays about her work, and a bibliography, can be found in *'Lighting Up the Terrain': The Poetry of Margaret Avison*, ed. David Kent (ECW, 1987).   GHB

Awoonor, Kofi (1935–) (formerly George Awoonor-Williams) Born in Wheta, Ghana, and educated at the famous Achimota School and the University of Ghana at Legon, from which he graduated in 1960. He lectured in English at the School of Administration until 1963, and at the Institute of African Studies until 1967, when he left to take an MA at the University of London. He travelled to the United States the following year on a scholarship from the University of California at Los Angeles and Columbia, and was subsequently appointed chairman of the department of comparative literature at the State University of New York at Stony Brook, where he taught until his return to Ghana in 1975 to take up a post at the University of Cape Coast. In January 1976 he was imprisoned without charge for almost a year for harbouring a fugitive at a time of political uncertainty in the country, an experience which he later recorded in *The Ghana Revolution* (Oases, 1984). After his release he resumed teaching at the University until 1984, when he was appointed Ghanaian ambassador to Brazil and then Cuba. His collected essays, *The African Predicament* (Sub-Saharan), appeared in Ghana in 2006.

An intensely lyrical poet, Awoonor has spoken of the necessity for the writer in contemporary Africa 'to provide . . . a certain articulate vision, which must order his society because otherwise social life would be a very sterile and a very futile exercise'. Although very much a modern poet who has drawn heavily from the poetry of other societies and cultures, he has attempted to incorporate elements from the Ewe oral tradition to give his poetry a more African feel.

In 1971 Awoonor published an influential novel (or 'prose-poem', as he terms it), *This Earth, My Brother* (Doubleday, 1971; Heinemann, 1972), and he has also written on African culture in *The Breast of the Earth* (Anchor, 1975), and on Ewe traditional poetry in *Guardians of the Sacred Word* (Nok, 1974). There are five collections of his verse: *Rediscovery* (Mbari, 1964); *Night of My Blood* (Doubleday, 1971); *Ride Me, Memory* (1973); *The House by the Sea* (1978); and *Until the Morning After: Collected Poems, 1963–1985* (1986—all Greenfield Review). His poetry has appeared in the major anthologies of African poetry. A critical appreciation of his work can be found in Robert Fraser, *West African Poetry: A Critical History* (Cambridge University Press, 1986).   AM-P

Babstock, Ken (1970–) Born in New-foundland, grew up in the Ottawa Valley, and now lives in Toronto. He began as a philosophy student at Concordia University in Montreal, but did not complete his degree, and spent the next decade working as a manual labourer, an experience that informs the richly descriptive tactility of his work. A prize-winning writer since his first appearances in magazines, Babstock has already been called 'the best Canadian poet of his generation'. His four volumes to date, all published by House of Anansi Press (where he has also worked as an editor) have followed a stellar trajectory. *Mean* (1999) won the Milton Acorn People's Poet Award and the Atlantic Poetry Award; *Days into Flatspin* (2001) won the K. M. Hunter Award; *Airstream Land Yacht* (2006) won the Trillium Award; and *Methodist Hatchet* (2011) won the Griffin Poetry Prize. Praised for its originality and realism, Babstock's om-nivorously observant voice—like that of Simon *Armitage in England and John *Kin-sella in Australia—roams the urban, wild, and literary landscapes in shapeshifting verse that returns repeatedly to a fascination with the construction of contemporary life, and what it feels like to be 'organized as Canadians' ('Caledonia').   JNT

Baca, Jimmy Santiago (1952–) Of mixed Chicano and Apache origins, Baca had a disastrous childhood—his mother murdered by her second husband, his father dead of alcoholism. He then absconded from a New Mexico orphanage, drifted into a violent 'street' and drug-affected adolescence, and found himself early in penitentiaries from San Quentin to Arizona. The inmate writing which he turned to in default of any better path he has said 'bridged my divided life of prisoner and free man'. It also found a supporter in Denise *Levertov, then poetry editor for the radical periodical *Mother Jones*. That led on to *Martín & Meditations on the South Valley* (1987), a richly localized journey-poem centred on the south-west. For its 'de-tribalized Apache' narrator, the new-found encounter with land and heritage becomes restorative. A similar sense of self-discovery runs through his *Black Mesa Poems* (1989—both New Directions), whether remem-bered poverty and drift, the different land-scapes of Mexico and Texas, the life of the *pueblo* with its *ristras* and *curanderas*, or even, as in a poem like 'I Am Here', the fevers of prison life. Baca's verse reads much in the tradition of the chronicle, a poetry of witness made the more affecting by his clarity of image. See also the essays in *Working in the Dark: Reflections of a Poet of the Barrio* (Red Crane, 1992) and his memoir, *A Place to Stand* (Grove, 2001).

Since the 1980s, Baca has run communi-ty writing workshops across America, in schools, prisons, and libraries. *Immigrants in Our Own Land & Selected Early Poems* is an expanded edition of his 1979 debut (1990). *Selected Poems/Poemas Selectos* (2009) draws on all his work up to the landscape sequences *Winter Poems Along the Rio Grande* (2004) and *Spring Poems Along the Rio Grande* (2007—all New Directions).   ARL

Bailey, Alfred Goldsworthy (1905–97) Born in Quebec City and studied at the universities of New Brunswick and Toronto, and the London School of Eco-nomics. He worked as a journalist and museum curator before becoming head of History at the University of New Bruns-wick in 1938.

Bailey's first book, *Songs of the Saguenay & Other Poems* (privately printed, 1927), imitated the late nineteenth-century style of the Confederation poets. In the 1930s, however, he came under a wider range of contemporary influences, including T. S. *Eliot and Dylan *Thomas (see 'The Unreturning'), and his friend, Earle *Birney. In 1945 he founded *The Fiddlehead*, one of Canada's most important modern literary magazines. His intermittent later poems—not collected again for another twenty years—pursued a more experimental tendency. *Border River* appeared in 1952 and *Thanks for a Drowned Island* in 1973 (both McClelland & Stewart). Robert Gibbs has written that Bailey's 'central themes are the impingement of one culture on another, the aspirations of explorers and settlers, and the difficulties of maintaining continuity and purpose'. These are themes also of his academic work, but treated in his poems with an imagistic abstraction.

Bailey was made an Officer of the Order of Canada in 1978. *Culture and Nationality* (McClelland & Stewart, 1972) collects some of his most important writings as an ethnohistorian. *Miramichi Lightning: The Collected Poems of Alfred Bailey* (Fiddlehead Poetry) was published in 1981. There is a selection in *Modern Canadian Poetry*, eds. Evan Jones and Todd Swift (Carcanet, 2010).   JNT

Baker, Howard (1905–90) Born in Philadelphia, but educated in the west, receiving his BA in 1927 from Whittier College, California; his MA in 1929 from Stanford; and his PhD in 1937 from the University of California at Berkeley. He studied at the Sorbonne, 1929–31.

At Stanford he became acquainted with Yvor *Winters, and was one of the first members of the *Stanford School, editing, with Winters and Janet *Lewis, *The Gyroscope* (1929–30). He published eight poems in Winters' anthology *Twelve Poets of the Pacific* (1937). In the early Thirties he was an editor of *The Magazine*. He had planned to be a teacher but, discontented with academic life, he settled at Terra Bella, California, and established a successful orange-growing and packing business.

His poems are highly crafted, perceptive, intellectual, and witty. There are frequent references to Greek myths and literature, with which he became increasingly absorbed in his later years. Among his most memorable poems are 'Pont Neuf', 'Ode to the Sea', 'Psyche' (inspired by Robert *Bridges' 'Eros and Psyche'), and 'Letter from the Country', written as 'advice to a young editor', warning him to avoid popular fads in contemporary poetry and to set his standards by the models of Greek literature.

His prose works include the novel *Orange Valley* (Coward-McCann, 1931), his scholarly *Introduction to Tragedy: A Study in the Development of Dramatic Form* (Louisiana State University Press, 1939), and *Persephone's Cave: Cultural Accumulations of the Early Greeks* (University of Georgia Press, 1979). Most of his best poetry is in his *Ode to the Sea and Other Poems* (Swallow, 1966).   DS

Bang, Mary Jo (1946–) Bang grew up in St. Louis, Missouri, where she now directs the Creative Writing programme at Washington University. Formerly poetry co-editor on the *Boston Review*, she attended Northwestern and Columbia universities in the United States, and Westminster University in London, where she studied photography.

Bang's debut, *Apology for Want* (University Press of New England, 1997) was chosen for the Katharine Bakeless Nason Poetry Prize by Edward *Hirsch. Her eye for the fragmentary construction of feminine identity in American popular culture sometimes recalls the ironies of Rae *Armantrout, but Bang's broken images are carried more fully into narratives and voices: see *The Downstream Extremity of the Isle of Swans* (University of Georgia Press, 2001), *Louise in Love* (2001), and *The Eye Like a Strange Balloon* (2004—both Grove), a book of ekphrastic poems. Her fifth collection, *Elegy* (2007), confronts the year after the death of her son in powerful, pared-back free verse that repeatedly searches for a story: 'The narrative begins and we fill in the blanks'. It won the National Book Critics Circle Award. Her latest book is a free, contemporary translation of Dante's *Inferno*, illustrated by Henrik Drescher (2012—both Graywolf).   JNT

Banning, Lex (Arthur Alexander Banning) (1921–65) Born in Sydney. Although more than one of Lex Banning's teachers recognized the boy's intelligence, his formal education was hampered by the cerebral palsy over which he would eventually triumph. Unable to master handwriting, he learned to type and persuaded Sydney University to let him enrol in an arts course, where he won distinction in English and philosophy. An interest in philosophical questions and language is one constant of his poetry, and perhaps reflects the influence of Professor John Anderson, whose libertarian thinking and logical rigour shaped at least two generations of Sydney intellectuals.

From the mid-1940s to the early 1960s Banning was a leading and seminal figure around the Push, as Sydney's Bohemia was then called. His verse is typically formal and succinct, though also strongly experimental within those limits. Fond of learned allusion, archaizing language, and the very simplest stanza forms, he abhorred the merely personal, though it is possible to discern a moving trace of self-portraiture in his poem 'Nursery Rhyme,' which begins 'There was a crooked man | who walked a crooked mile'.

Poetry had a talismanic quality for Banning. When a fellow poet in a public lecture called it 'the wine of literature', he gulped a characteristic throatful of air and interjected 'no! the cognac!' Publishing only two pamphlets and one slim volume in his lifetime, Banning has not been lucky in his immortality. As a nearly apolitical exponent of the Forties *poème bien fait*, and lacking a secure measure of fame when he died, he was quickly eclipsed by the politicizing shift in literary sensibility which occurred soon afterwards. A retrospective collection of all his work, plus a short biography, was brought out by Angus and Robertson in 1987: *There Was a Crooked Man*, by Richard Appleton.   LM

Baraka, Amiri Imamu (1934–) Born Everett LeRoi Jones in Newark, New Jersey, where he attended school and began college at the Newark branch of Rutgers University. He transferred to Howard University subsequently and took his BA there in 1954. He was a member of the US Air Force from 1954 to 1956. He married a white Jewish woman in 1958, a union which was discussed in his first wife's book, *How I Became Hettie Jones* (Dutton, 1990). He was divorced in 1965 and married again the following year. His teaching career included academic positions at the New School for Social Research in New York City from 1961 to 1964 and shorter appointments at Columbia and San Francisco State universities. From 1985 to 2000 he taught at the State University of New York, where he is now professor emeritus.

Preface to a Twenty Volume Suicide Note (Totem, 1961) was LeRoi Jones's first collection of poems; subsequent volumes were *The Dead Lecturer* (Grove, 1964); *Black Art* (Jihad, 1966), *Black Magic: Poetry 1961–1967* (Bobbs-Merrill, 1969), and *It's Nation Time* (Third World, 1970). By the publication of *Spirit Reach* (Jihad, 1972) Jones had changed his name and changed his religion to Black Islam and was well established as the leading poet of the *Black Arts movement. He had also become a playwright, written a novel, a collection of short stories, and edited or written many other titles, most of them on social issues. His *Selected Poetry* (Morrow) was published in 1979.

Although Baraka's is a militant black poetry, his primary influences were the modernist poets *Pound and *Williams, via Charles *Olson and his quondam *Black Mountain school of poetry. Baraka's earliest work was lineated prose, and it remained so, though as his work matured he sometimes used the longer lines of Whitman and *Ginsberg. Jones's sojourn for a summer in the 'Little Black Mountain' of the State University of New York at Buffalo in 1964, where Olson was teaching, enabled him to absorb directly from their source theories of 'open form', and 'breath-pause' lineation. If Baraka had little in common with the formalism of such Afro-American poets as Robert *Hayden, Gwendolyn *Brooks, or even Langston *Hughes, his practice approached those of his older black contemporaries when it came to the influence of jazz forms, for his poems are often a sort of 'scat' for performance.

Baraka has inspired more scholarship since 1973 than any other black poet in America. William J. Harris's *The Poetry and Poetics of Amiri Baraka: The Jazz Aesthetic* (University of Missouri Press, 1985) examines the poet's ethnic literary-musical roots, as does Baraka's own *The Music: Reflections on Blues & Jazz* (Morrow, 1987). His *Autobiography of Le Roi Jones— Amiri Baraka* (Freundlich) was published in 1984. See *Transbluesency: The Selected Poems of Amiri Baraka* (Marsilio, 1995), ed. Paul Vangelisti, *The LeRoi Jones/Amiri Baraka Reader* (Basic, 1999), ed. William J. Harris, and Jerry Gaffo Watts, *Amiri Baraka: The Politics and Art of a Black Intellectual* (New York University Press, 2001). The title poem of Baraka's 2003 volume, *Somebody Blew Up America & Other Poems* (House of Nehesi), written during his tenure as New Jersey Poet Laureate, implied that the Israeli and the US governments were complicit in the attacks of September 11, 2001. The resulting controversy ended in the abolition of the post.   LT*

Barbour, Douglas (1940–) Born in Winnipeg, he has spent all but a decade of his life on the prairies. Resident in Edmonton from 1969, he has become, with Robert *Kroetsch, one of the leading prairie poets, and a distinguished critic of Canadian poetry. He began initially to work in a Poundian open-field poetics expanded by reading *Creeley, *Duncan, and *Levertov. His earlier poems—collected in *Land Fall* (Delta, 1971) and *White* (Fiddlehead, 1972)—announce his investigation of the prairie landscape within this tradition. His long poem, *Visions of My Grandfather* (Golden Dog, 1977), showed the influence of bp *Nichol and Phyllis *Webb.

Collaboration with Stephen Scobie in the sound/performance poetry duo Re:Sounding resulted in *The Pirates of Pen's Chance* (Coach House, 1981), a collection of 'homolinguistic' (English to English) translations produced associatively from source texts. Subsequent works, particularly *Story*

for a *Saskatchewan Night* (rdc, 1990), uncover the open field of both prairie and page, displaying a generative tension between lyric and anti-lyric elements.

Visible Visions (NeWest, 1984) selects from his first eight volumes and adds twenty new poems with a useful introduction by Kroetsch; *Story for a Saskatchewan Night* selects from the later explorations. *Fragmenting Body etc.* (2000), a volume of longer poems, was published in Canada by NeWest Press (which Barbour founded) and in the UK and Australia by Salt. *Continuations* (2006) and *Continuations 2* (2012—both University of Alberta Press) is a collaborative work, created by email with the American poet Sheila E. Murphy. For Barbour's criticism, see *Lyric/Anti-Lyric: Essays on Contemporary Poetry* (NeWest, 2001). He has also written studies of Daphne *Marlatt, Michael *Ondaatje, and Nichol.   RB*

Barker, George (1913–91) Born in Loughton, Essex, Barker was educated at Marlborough Road, Chelsea, and Regent Street Polytechnic, London. For a period in his early life (1939–41) he held an academic post in Japan; but, with a few exceptions (appointments briefly attached to universities in Britain and the United States), he worked as a freelance writer. He has sometimes been seen as 'the last Romantic'—or at any rate the last of the Bohemians.

Barker emerged almost as a boy prodigy, and at about the same moment as two other prodigies, Dylan *Thomas and David *Gascoyne, in the early 1930s. With no advantages except his own talent and wayward charm, he published his first book at the age of 20 (*Thirty Preliminary Poems*, 1933), a novel that same year, and in 1935 both a book of poems and a work of prose fiction with T. S. *Eliot at Faber. In 1936, when W. B. *Yeats published his *Oxford Book of Modern Verse*, Barker was the youngest poet whom Yeats included: 'a lovely subtle mind', wrote Yeats, 'and a rhythmical invention comparable to Gerard Hopkins.'

His career through the 1930s was indeed charmed, and for several years Barker was seen as one of the most important poets of the generation that immediately succeeded

*Auden and *MacNeice. *Poems* (1935) was followed by the long poem *Calamiterror* (1937), *Lament and Triumph* (1940), and, after his return to Britain during the war, *Eros in Dogma* (1944). What characterized all these poems was a fluent, heady, occasionally absurd rhetoric, often imitated and as often parodied: when the reactionary drama critic, James Agate, wanted to make mockery of 'modern poetry', all he needed to do was to quote a few lines of George Barker.

Barker's reputation became most controversial at the moment when part of his *True Confession of George Barker* (1950) was broadcast on the BBC Third Programme: this long, Villonesque work had originally been rejected by Barker's usual publisher, Faber, on grounds of obscenity, and then was the subject of shocked questions in Parliament after some of it had been broadcast. After Dylan Thomas's death in 1953 Barker's standing seemed somehow to diminish, as if the literary public could not cope with two doomed romantics at the same time. Though Barker went on publishing (another ten volumes for adults between 1950 and 1978), he was in eclipse.

The publication, first, of his long poem *Anno Domini* in 1983, and then of his *Collected Poems*, ed. Robert Fraser (Faber), in 1987, helped to build and consolidate his later reputation. He can no longer be conventionally seen as a standard New Romantic, or member of the '*New Apocalypse': his range, from elegiac rhetoric to proverbial plainness, is impressively wide, and his many masks and poses over many years need to be carefully and sympathetically examined. See also *Street Ballads* (Faber, 1992) and *The Chameleon Poet: A Life of George Barker* by Robert Fraser (Cape, 2002).   AST

Baugh, Edward (1936–   ) Born in Port Antonio, Jamaica, Baugh studied English literature at the University College of the West Indies in Mona, Jamaica, followed by postgraduate studies at Queen's University in Kingston, Ontario, and at the University of Manchester. He taught at the University of the West Indies—first at Cave Hill, Barbados, then at Mona—from 1965 until 2001.

Best known as a literary scholar, Baugh is a leading authority on the work of Derek *Walcott. His *Derek Walcott: Memory as Vision* (1978) was followed by editions of the St Lucian poet's *Another Life* (2004), a *Selected Poems* (2007), and a volume on Walcott in the Cambridge Studies in African and Caribbean Literature Series.

Baugh's own poetic oeuvre consists of two slim volumes: *A Tale from the Rainforest* (1988) and *It Was the Singing* (2000—both Sandberry Press), the latter incorporating the full contents of the former. The poems often begin with quiet observation, which Baugh pursues into wry insight. In his best-known poem, 'Nigger Sweat'—inspired by a sign in the US embassy in Kingston—real anger fuels fierce sarcasm, a departure from the characteristic intelligent melancholy.   NL

Baxter, James K. (1926–72) Born at Dunedin, New Zealand. His father was a pacifist farmer of Scottish descent and his mother took degrees in languages at Sydney and Cambridge. Baxter began to write verse at 7 and his elegy-dominated first volume, *Beyond the Palisade*, was published in 1944 when he was 18, manifesting the influence of *Yeats and Dylan *Thomas; the following year Allen *Curnow singled him out for praise in the introduction to his *A Book of New Zealand Verse 1923–45*. He entered the University of Otago in 1944 but soon gave up, largely (by his own admission) because of excessive drinking. From an early age he claimed various mystical experiences which turned Christian in his late teens. He became a fervent Roman Catholic at the age of 32, but this did not lessen the pace of his hard-lived life; his major conflict was with the Calvinism in which he said he had been brought up, claiming that 'New Zealand society (and, indeed, modern Western society in general) carries like strychnine in its bones a strong unconscious residue of the doctrines and ethics of Calvinism'. He remained a self-styled figure of the 'wilderness' who always saw the artist as a tribesman cut off from his tribe, even when he returned to Otago University as Burns Fellow. Latterly he lived in the small Maori settlement of

Jerusalem; he died at the age of 46 while on a visit to Auckland.

Despite his breaches of taste, his repetitiveness, and his excessive output, Baxter is a major figure in twentieth-century English poetry: in New Zealand only Allen Curnow can rival his achievement. Curnow's urbanity and self-consciousness contrast markedly with the more inspirational wildness of Baxter; Baxter attacked Curnow fiercely for being stuck in the politically anxious Thirties, when writers agonized over the imperialist ill-treatment of the Maoris, ignoring the new poets who 'in the late Forties and Fifties . . . seceded from the self-conscious New Zealandism . . . and began to write simply as people who happened to live in a given time and place'. It is an ironic charge for Baxter to level, since his poetry, though founded in personal observation and experience of nature, is always socially aware (he was lastingly affected by the poverty of Japan and India, which he visited on a UNESCO grant in 1958), and his later poetry is suffused with Maori words and themes. Paradoxically, too, his attacks on Calvinism cover a Calvinist contempt for modern culture's shoddy acquisitiveness. His poetry is hectoring, vatic, and often sexist; but it is never dull, because nearly every line has urgency and verbal life. He was a fine critic, and he wrote good pieces on 'Tam O'Shanter' and on Wilde.

Baxter's *Collected Poems* have been excellently edited by J. E. Weir (Oxford University Press, 1980). A useful bibliography is J. E. Weir and B. A. Lyon, *A Preliminary Bibliography of Works By and Works About James K. Baxter* (University of Canterbury, 1979) and there are two good introductory studies: V. G. O'Sullivan, *James K. Baxter* (1976), and J. E. Weir, *The Poetry of James K. Baxter* (1970—all Oxford University Press); as well as a biography, *The Life of James K. Baxter*, by Frank McKay (1990).

See *Selected Poems* (Auckland University Press/Carcanet, 2010), edited with notes and commentary by Paul Millar, who has also edited Baxter's early correspondence, *Spark to a Waiting Fuse* (Victoria University Press, 2001), and his unpublished second

collection from the same period, *Cold Spring* (Oxford University Press, 1996).   BO'D

Beaver, (Victor) Bruce (1928–2004) Born in Manly, New South Wales, Australia. With its arcades, malls and beaches, Manly became the setting for much of his later poetry, which consists largely of meditations and personal explorations of both social and metaphysical concerns.

Like Patrick White, Beaver has a well-developed intuition for the outcasts of society, as well as for the humanizing features of life, even the life of those kicked and trampled by city living. A contemporary of Peter *Porter and Vincent *Buckley, he first came to literary prominence with his fourth collection of poems *Letters to Live Poets* (South Head, 1969), awarded three major prizes. This book-length sequence was the first landmark in the 'new' Australian poetry that found expression in the Vietnam War years, and the volume remains crucial to an understanding of later Australian poetic developments.

His novel, *You Can't Come Back* (Rigny, 1966), was based on Beaver's early experience as a surveyor's linesman. Its tough depiction of working-class life and its laconic recognition of a brutalizing environment implicitly established the context from which the author's own later search for values and spiritual meanings was to strike out. His most important later books include *Lauds and Plaints: Poems 1968–1972* (South Head, 1974), *As It Was* (1979), and *Charmed Lives* (1988—both University of Queensland Press). In these works Beaver's essentially pluralist concept of spiritual striving is most ardently articulated. *As It Was*, which won for him the Patrick White Prize, is in many ways his most accessible book. In two sections, it explores with grace and often playful detail the many-layered levels of childhood and adolescence in the depression years of Manly.

Charmed Lives contains some of the author's most rich and expressive writing and concludes with a major sequence, 'Tiresias Sees', which surveys with raunchy wit the cavalcade of living from the point of view of age and the close-felt presence of death. Dorothy *Porter called it 'one of the most entertaining and imaginatively scintillating sequences of poems I have ever read'.

New and Selected Poems from the University of Queensland Press in 1991 illustrates clearly the significance of his work in the 1980s. His later books included *Anima and Other Poems* (1994), which won the C. J. Dennis Prize for Poetry, and *The Long Game and Other Poems*, published posthumously (2005—both University of Queensland Press). See also 'Bruce Beaver: A Survey', in *Biting The Bullet: A Literary Memoir*, by Thomas Shapcott (Simon & Schuster, 1990).   TWS*

Beckett, Samuel (Barclay) (1906–89) Born in Dublin to a prosperous, Protestant, Anglo-Irish (originally French Huguenot) upper-middle-class family, and educated at Portora Royal School, Enniskillen, and Trinity College, Dublin. During two years (1928–30) he spent as *lecteur d'anglais* at the École Normale Supérieure in Paris he formed close attachments to James *Joyce, Thomas McGreevy, Nancy Cunard, and the circle of writers who contributed to the avant-garde magazine *transition*. Returning to Dublin he was made an MA and resigned a Trinity lectureship in French after teaching for four terms. This abandonment of a promising academic career began a period of great uncertainty, dominated by Beckett's difficult relationship with his mother, his struggle to establish himself as a writer against her determination that he should enter the family business (quantity surveying), bouts of heavy drinking, various ailments and illnesses, probably psychosomatic in origin, solitary travels between Germany, France, and Ireland, and 'two bad years' (1933–5) in London, during which Beckett made several abortive ventures into literary journalism and underwent psychoanalysis. In 1938, the year in which his first novel, *Murphy*, was published (after rejection by forty-two publishers), Beckett settled in Paris where, with Suzanne Deschevaux-Dumesnil, he remained for the rest of his life (apart from an interruption in the Second World War when Beckett, a member of the Resistance, narrowly escaped capture by the Gestapo and went into hiding in unoccupied France); there he wrote, for the most part in French and translating himself, the novels and plays that brought him international renown and (in 1969) the Nobel Prize for Literature.

Like his earliest stories, the free-verse poems Beckett wrote in English before he was 30—with titles like 'Whoroscope' (on the life of René Descartes), 'Echo's Bones', and 'Sanies'—brandish their learned author's admiration for Dante and the extravagantly punning Joyce of *Finnegans Wake*; nevertheless, they anticipate in a harsher manner some of his much more disciplined later prose works. There are echoes of Rimbaud (whom Beckett translated, along with Apollinaire and Eluard), but the phrasing and the frame of reference are Irish (with touches of London and Paris), the idiom strenuously modernist in its disruptions of continuity, and full of a violence not yet subordinated to syntax, veering wildly between throw-away exactness and arch punctilio. In all this there are glimpses of raw—all too raw—material that fuels the novels' and plays' ferocious comedy of 'ignorance and impotence'. Poems in French of the late 1930s and 1940s, some of them translated by the author, achieve a bleaker, barer statement of recognizably Beckettian despairs (but with scarcely Beckettian solemnity), and move inexorably towards the brevity of 'Mirlitonnades' and the translations from the maxims of Sébastien de Chamfort ('how hollow heart and full | of filth thou art'). *Collected Poems in English and French* (Calder and Grove, 1977) contained all the original poems and translations that Beckett wished to preserve. A later volume edited by John Calder, *Samuel Beckett: Poems 1930–1989* (Calder, 2002) was found to be 'peppered with errors' by the critic Christopher Ricks. See, instead, *Collected Poems* (Faber, 2012), a fully annotated edition, ed. Seán Lawlor and John Pilling, and also *Selected Poems, 1930–1989* (Faber, 2009), edited with an introduction by David *Wheatley.   AJ*

Beer, Patricia (1924–99) Born in Exmouth, Devon, of a Plymouth Brethren family. Educated at Exmouth Grammar

School, Exeter University, and Oxford, Beer lived in Italy, lecturing in English, from 1946 to 1953; from 1962 to 1968 she taught at Goldsmith's College, London. In 1964 she married Damien Parsons, an architect, and settled once more in Devon.

Beer's poems bring a wary, observant, wry, and well-read intelligence to bear on a relatively narrow range of themes and subjects: mortality, the workings of good and evil, the mysterious ways of God, and religious belief; love, nature, the passing of time and of generations, small but exalted moments of illumination. Her verse may have grown more casual and comprehensible with each volume, but her approach remained tenaciously modest and domestic. In the introduction to her *Collected Poems* she comments on her first encounter, at university in the 1940s, with modern poetry, and her own early attempts, on her return from Italy in 1953, to write it. 'The poetic scene I stepped into was inevitably a death-trap. It was really the scene of the Forties still . . . The myth-kitty had not been sneered out of existence; to many it was still Aladdin's cave.' She is harsh towards her early poems; but in fact those that survive into the first part of her *Collected* seem less like the 'verbal debauchery' she accuses herself of than a fairly disciplined adumbration of later work. In first-person lyrics and brief historical monologues, Beer wrote about Devon, Italy, literature, landscape, the lives of ancestors, and the death of parents—above all, about death, the insecurity and fearfulness that surround an apparently comfortable existence, and the various ways in which the dead haunt the living.

Her verse often sounds more instinctive than regular (though this conceals considerable artfulness—an enduring attachment to unostentatious syllabics, an equally firm preference for neat stanzaic forms with loose or irregular rhyme), and her tone is resolutely colloquial and informal. She herself remarked that she had 'never been accused of imitating any other poet', and though 'imitation' is certainly not in question, it is possible to detect echoes in Beer of a long tradition of English verse, from medieval charms to nineteenth-century

hymns; of *Hardy; and perhaps of Stevie *Smith, with whom 'There had been friendship, not close, coming late in the day', and with whom Beer shared an element of whimsical, *faux-naïf* surprise and sly, dark humour.

Beer's *Collected Poems* (1988 and 1990) assembled, in chronological order, the pared-down contents of her seven collections (including the 1979 *Selected Poems*), and added fourteen previously uncollected pieces. She also published an autobiography, *Mrs Beer's House* (Macmillan, 1968) and *Moon's Ottery*, a novel (Hutchinson, 1978). Her later volumes of poetry were *Friends of Heraclitus* (1993) and *Autumn* (1997). *As I Was Saying Yesterday* is a posthumous selection of essays and reviews (2002—all Carcanet).   AJ

Belitt, Ben (1911–2003) Born in New York City, where he spent several years in an orphanage before rejoining his mother, an orthodox Jew. He attended the University of Virginia, and in 1938 became a professor of English at Bennington College. During his long career he received relatively little critical attention, in part, no doubt, because of his scanty output, but more centrally because his poetry's mixture of high Romanticism and extreme, uncompromising difficulty has placed it outside the various fashions of the past seven decades. By the same token, however, he attracted a small group of dedicated admirers, among them the poet Howard *Nemerov and the critic Harold Bloom. Belitt's poetry combines an austere, abstract vision of human alienation with a loving and sensuous attention to scene and locality—an unlikely conjunction, and one that may account for the poet's ongoing obsession with duality and doubleness, as evinced in the title of his book *The Double Witness* (Princeton University Press, 1976). Upon his essentially Jewish resignation to a tragic universe he grafts a romantic celebration of nature's beauty and abundance, and the result, while at times elusive in tone and affect, is a rich, densely worked, and strikingly intelligent body of poetry that deserves more praise than it has had. Belitt was also a prolific translator of Spanish, Italian, and French poetry, particularly of Pablo Neruda. See *This Scribe, My Hand: The Complete Poems of Ben Belitt* (Louisiana State University Press, 1998) and *The Forged Feature: Toward a Poetics of Uncertainty: New and Selected Essays* (Fordham University Press, 1995).   RG

Bell, Martin (1918–78) Born in Southampton and educated at Taunton's School and University College, Southampton. He was an exemplar of Thirties poetic enthusiasm, a follower of *Auden, and a member of the Communist Party. But he was also (much more unusually) an intellectual of the working class, an enthusiast for French poetry, especially the Surrealists, and a lover of Italian opera. Later Bell was to write of a Southampton friend killed in the war, that he was 'a pattern of accomplishments, | And joined the Party first, and left it first' ('Letter to a Friend'). He could have been describing himself. Bell's poetry was both late-arrived, as one of Auden's epigoni coming into flower in the age of the *Movement, and prescient of what was to come, in its defence of Leftish humanism against the dismantling of the Welfare State. Bell died in poverty in Leeds in 1978.

Bell's first successful poem was a translation of Gérard de Nerval's celebrated sonnet 'El Desdichado', written while he was serving in the Royal Engineers in Italy. He wrote slowly and rarely on his return to civilian life and work as a schoolteacher in London. His creative time began when he joined The *Group, and encouraged by his reception there, especially the advocacy of Philip *Hobsbaum and Peter *Redgrove, he produced a string of powerful poems in the decade 1955 to 1965. This included 'Headmaster: Modern Style', 'Reasons for Refusal', 'Winter Coming On' (after Laforgue), 'Ode to Himself', 'High Street, Southampton', and 'Ode to Groucho'. In the last decade of his life he produced a substantial number of stylish translations of the French surrealist poets Reverdy, Desnos, Peret, and Max Jacob.

Bell's poetic legacy is contained in the one book he produced during his lifetime, his *Collected Poems* (Macmillan/St Mar-

tin's, 1967). Although a selection of his work appeared in *Penguin Modern Poets, 3* (1962), and his posthumously published *Complete Poems* (Bloodaxe, 1988) gathered together fragments from his later life, all his finest poetry fits into that span of one hundred pages which was both his debut and his apotheosis.   PNFP

Bell, Marvin (Hartley) (1937–) Born in New York City, he was Flannery O'Connor Professor of Letters at the University of Iowa until 2005, having been associated since his debut (*Two Poems*, Hundred Pound Press, 1965) with the Iowa Writers' Workshop. He is an autobiographical, not to say *confessional, poet, writing in the tradition of *Snodgrass and *Lowell, but with a deliberate emphasis on the comic and the trivial in the manner of *Rothenberg, Jonathan *Williams, and other allied poets. *Seques* (Godine, 1983) consists of a correspondence in verse with the poet William *Stafford, in which he can be seen reacting to the often amusing 'probes' of the older poet. His verse is conversational, diffuse, often jokey, much concerned with the intimate details of his family and domestic life, and with many echoes of *Roethke's manner, but without Roethke's regard for traditional form.

Bell's later work includes the ongoing series begun in 1994 with *The Book of the Dead Man* (Copper Canyon), written under the Zen admonition, 'Live as if you were already dead'. A freewheeling departure from Bell's early verse, the 'Dead Man' poems relate the experiences of their hero as he explores the world, employing a long anaphoric line that recalls Whitman and *Ginsberg. *Nightworks: Poems 1962–2000* was published by Copper Canyon Press in 2000, the same year that he became Iowa's first Poet Laureate.   MS-S*

Bellerby, Frances (1899–1977) Née Parker, she was born and brought up in Bristol. Reticent about personal details, she knew much hardship and illness and published her first book of verse, *Plash Mill* (Peter Davies, 1946), when in her forties. Her work was never widely read or anthologized, but had many devotees, such as

Charles *Causley, who edited her *Selected Poems* (Enitharmon, 1970). She wrote a novel, *Hath the Rain a Father?* (Peter Davies, 1946), and three books of stories. The most potent influences on her work are the counties of Cornwall and Devon, in which she lived for much of her life. She was a religious and contemplative nature poet much akin to Ruth *Pitter, but quieter and without the oddities, quirks, and prolificity. At the age of 30 poetry (she wrote) 'seeped away, unregretted'; then, some fifteen years later, it returned 'for no known or surmised reason'. Her taut and disciplined poems almost always depict landscapes—usually with a quiet sense of menace and mystery.

See *The Stuttering Water and Other Poems* (Arc, 1970) and *The First-Known and Other Poems* (Enitharmon, 1974).   MS-S

Belloc, Hilaire (Pierre René) (1870–1953) Born in Paris, the son of a French lawyer and his English wife. He was educated at Oxford. In the Edwardian era—during which he was a Liberal MP—he, Wells, Shaw, and *Chesterton were known as the 'big four'; but his reputation gradually faded, owing in part to the extreme truculence of his Roman Catholic polemic, and to diminishing powers. He wrote two kinds of poetry, serious and light. The serious, included in *Collected Verse* (Penguin, 1958), is melodious and skilfully crafted: 'Tarantella' remains the best-known example. As an author of light verse Belloc is outstanding. He exploited this vein from *The Children's Bad Book of Beasts* (1896) until 1930; all is collected in *Cautionary Verses* (Duckworth, 1939) and in *Hilaire Belloc's Cautionary Verses* (Knopf, 1959). Here he displayed the more relaxed, 'English' side of himself. The mock-solemn, deliberately bathetic manner arose from Belloc's affectionate parodying of the often-moralizing nursery rhymes of Jane and Ann Taylor (*Original Poems for Infant Minds*, 1804). The tone of his tales (do not, for example, play with matches or you will be burned to death) is always light and charmingly inconsequential, rather than satirical of over-strict Victori-

an morality; they act as a counterpart to Belloc's unbridled ferocity in polemic.

See *The Life of Belloc* (Hollis & Carter, 1957), by R. W. Speaight, and *Hilaire Belloc* (Hamilton, 1984), by A. N. Wilson.   MS-S

Bennett, Louise (1919–2006) Jamaican poet and folklorist, born in Kingston. In 1945 she won a British Council Scholarship to study at the Royal Academy of Dramatic Arts in London, and subsequently worked as a comedienne for repertory companies in England, and also for the BBC. She returned to Jamaica in 1955, and from 1959 to 1961 lectured in drama and Jamaican folklore at the University of the West Indies. Among the many honours she received was an MBE.

Bennett was famous in the Caribbean for her performances as 'Miss Lou', and her poems, written in dialect employ various comic personae. They are informed by the oral tradition, making use of such devices as the 'Anancy' tales of the cunning spider, familiar proverbs, and cautionary tales. As a consequence, they have tended to be underrated as the work of an amusing, but not quite 'respectable' entertainer. In fact, Bennett's poems at their best display great mastery of characterization and complex irony, as well as serious social comment. The closest English equivalent might well be *Kipling, also a master of common speech, though perhaps he would not have appreciated 'Colonisation in Reverse'. This poem is a witty, mocking, and buoyantly good-humoured tilt at the irrational fears of many in the 'mother country'.

Some of Bennett's poetry is available in audio recordings, and much of her best in *Selected Poems*, ed. Mervyn Morris (Sangster's Book Stores, 1983). In 2001, Bennett was awarded the Jamaican Order of Merit. She died in Canada. See Denise deCaires Narain, *Contemporary Caribbean's Women's Poetry: Making Style* (Routledge, 2002).   MR

Bentley, E. C. (Edward Clerihew) (1875–1956) English novelist and humourist, was born in London, son of an official in the Lord Chancellor's Department. He went to school with G. K. *Chesterton, a lifelong friend. After a distinguished career at Oxford he was called to the bar (1902), but soon afterwards devoted himself to journalism, working for the *Daily Telegraph* from 1912. Most famous for the superior detective novel, *Trent's Last Case* (1913), Bentley also invented a new (light) verse form, the clerihew (so called from his second name). A collection of these, *Biography for Beginners* (1905), illustrated by Chesterton, was published as by Edward Clerihew. The clerihew, still a frequently attempted form, was defined by Bentley as a 'sort of formless four-line verse'. It consists of two rhyming couplets. The most quoted is: 'The art of Biography | Is different from Geography. | Geography is about maps, | But Biography is about chaps.' *Clerihews Complete* were published in 1951, and reprinted as *The Complete Clerihews* with an introduction by Gavin Ewart (Oxford University Press, 1981).   MS-S

Berg, Stephen (1934–) Born in Philadelphia and educated at the University of Pennsylvania, Boston University (where he was taught by Robert *Lowell), and the University of Iowa (where he attended the Iowa Writers' Workshop). Between 1959 and 1961 he lived in Mexico. He has taught at Princeton and Haverford College, and is currently professor of the humanities at the University of the Arts, Philadelphia. He married Mildred Rutherford Lane in 1975 and has two daughters.

Since 1972 Berg has, as co-founder, been co-editor of *American Poetry Review*. Established in 1971, it immediately distinguished itself from other journals like *Poetry* (Chicago) by means of its tabloid format, which was doubtless intended to counter the image of literary magazines as stodgy and academic. It is perhaps most notorious for publishing large photographs of the poets it prints, a practice that for some epitomizes the aspect of contemporary American poetry known as 'Po Biz'. The practice may also reflect the bias of its editors towards more personal poetic modes, chiefly those that centre on the poet's own reported experience; Berg co-edited the influential anthology *Naked Poetry*, which helped to codify and canonize those modes in the Sixties.

Berg's early poems deal with personal experience without insisting on the biographical facts of the poet's identity. A long immersion in the work of Anna Akhmatova reflected a poetic uncertainty about the self he wanted to present, but led to more than one volume. Subsequently, the prose poems of 'Shaving' and the extended 'Homage to the Afterlife' show, respectively, debts to Lowell and *Ginsberg which are repaid with a more naked and specific examination of personal disquiet.

Berg's poems are generously represented in *New and Selected Poems* (Copper Canyon, 1992). His individual collections include *The Daughters* (Bobbs-Merrill, 1971), *Grief* (Grossman, 1972), *Akhmatova at the Black Gates* (1981), *In It* (1986), *Oblivion* (1995), and *X=* (2002—all University of Illinois Press). He has also published, often in collaboration, translations from the Japanese, Aztec, Eskimo, Greek, and Hungarian. See *The Steel Cricket: Versions 1958–1997* (1997). *Cuckoo's Blood* (Copper Canyon, 2008) is a rewriting of his translations of the Zen poets. See also *The Elegy on Hats* (Sheep Meadow, 2005).   RG/LMaCK*

Bergvall, Caroline (1962–) Born in Germany to French-Norwegian parents. She studied at Paris and Warwick, and has taught performance writing in England and the United States. Bergvall's first language was French, but the main vocabulary of her poetry is English. 'Spitting out the most intimate and most irretrievable, the most naturalized source language, so-called mother tongue', she has said, 'starts a whole process of re-embodying one's language's spaces', and marked the point where she began to see her own writing as a 'public project'.

Her cross-disciplinary work with sound, image, and word has been exhibited and performed in galleries in Europe and America. *Strange Passage: A Choral Poem* (Equipage, 1993) was the voice text of one such project. Another, *Éclat: sites 1–10* (Sound & Language, 1996), began as a live tour of a house. Its verbal disassembly of female identity pays knowing tribute to the domestic cubism of *Stein's *Tender Buttons* ('Your uncle Gertrude doesn know her inside from her outside').

Parts of a longer project titled *Goan Atom* have appeared in various forms: *Goan Atom: Jets-Poupee* (Rem Press, 1999)— which responds to erotic surrealist representations of dolls—*Goan Atom (1. Doll)* (Krupskaya, 2001) and *Fig (Goan Atom 2)* (Salt, 2005). *Meddle English* (Nightboat, 2011), a new and selected volume, includes Bergvall's *conceptual translations of *The Canterbury Tales*, as well as pieces of her critical prose.   JNT

Berkson, Bill (William Craig) (1939–) Poet, art-critic, and curator, Bill Berkson was born in New York, and studied at Lawrenceville, Brown, and Columbia Universities, the New School for Social Research, and the Institute for Fine Arts (New York). Berkson is Professor Emeritus at the San Francisco Art Institute, having taught literary and art history there between 1984 and 2008. He has published over twenty books and pamphlets of poetry and prose, and has won numerous fellowships and awards.

Berkson's poetry demonstrates a concern with the movement away from the object and towards freedom of form and articulation. Just as he sees 'quick specific truths' as central to Frank *O'Hara's poetics, so they are to his: 'You never know what lands to the eye | ... And the nib flows'. See *Portrait and Dream: New and Selected Poems* (Coffee House, 2009). Kenneth *Koch was an early poetic mentor, and introduced him to the poetry of Pierre Reverdy and Henri Michaux as well as to the poets, artists, and musicians of the *New York School with whom he formed many personal and artistic relationships. These led to collaborative work and dedicatory volumes such as *Recent Visitors* with Joe Brainard (Boke, 1971); *Hymns of St Bridget* with Frank O'Hara (Adventures in Poetry, 1975); *Ted Berrigan* with George Schneeman (Cuneiform, 2009).

The Sweet Singer of Modernism (Qua, 2004) collects Berkson's art writing from the last fifty years; *Sudden Address* (Cuneiform, 2007), his lectures; and *For the Ordinary Artist* (BlazeVox, 2010), interviews and various other writings.   HY

Bernstein, Charles (1950–) Born in Manhattan and majored in philosophy at Harvard, where he wrote a thesis on *Stein and Wittgenstein. Bernstein has been a visiting professor at various North American universities and teaches English and Comparative Literature at the University of Pennsylvania. From 1978 to 1981, he edited *L=A=N=G=U=A=G=E* magazine with Bruce *Andrews, and has remained one of America's most editorially active advocates of *Language and other avant-garde poetry. He was a co-founder of the Buffalo Poetics Program, as well as the online archives at PennSound and the Electronic Poetry Center.

Bernstein began to publish poetry in the late 1970s, when he was working as a freelance medical writer. His first book, *Asylums* (Asylum's Press, 1975), presented a sequence of discrete parts, a form which later collections have developed. Like those of John *Ashbery, Bernstein's disjunctive discourses have a mercurial confidence ('I've a pile of memories on my other | drive') which he habitually interrupts with more curiously formal pieces. The voices of Bernstein's poetry and critical prose are frequently interwoven—see *My Way: Speeches and Poems* (1999) and *Attack of the Difficult Poems: Essays and Interventions* (2011— both University of Chicago Press). Bathos and naivety are also provocatively valued, as in 'The Ballad of the Girly Man', a riposte to the machismo of the then-Governor of California, Arnold Schwarzenegger. Bernstein has produced translations of French poetry, libretti, and collaborations with his wife, the artist Susan Bee. His many volumes of poems are selected in *All the Whiskey in Heaven* (Farrar, Straus, 2010).   JNT

Berold, Robert (1948–) Born in Johannesburg, Berold studied at the University of Witwatersrand in South Africa and Cambridge University in England. He lives on a farm in the Eastern Cape, where he has worked in rural development and more recently as a freelance editor. As the editor of the journal *New Coin* from 1989 to 1999, Berold published many important new poets of the post-apartheid era, including Lesego *Rampolokeng, Mxolisi *Nyezwa, and Kelwyn *Sole: see *It All Begins: Poems from Post-Liberation South Africa* (Gecko, 2003). He has also edited many individual poetry collections, and runs his own press, Deep South.

Berold's own volumes of poetry are: *The Door to the River* (Bateleur, 1984), *The Fires of the Dead* (Carrefour, 1989), *Rain Across a Paper Field* (Gecko, 1999), and *All the Days* (Deep South, 2008). As their titles suggest, they are in a contemporary South African tradition of elemental lyricism and landscape, introspective but open to vision, where the veld can be seen 'ablaze with feathery abundance, | of itself, for everyone' ('Two Meditations on Chuang Tsu'). JNT

Berrigan, Daniel (J.) (1921–) Born in Minnesota. He was jailed, along with his brother Philip, for anti-war activities in 1968, and became for a short while an international *cause célèbre* as one of the Catonsville Nine. His play *The Trial of the Catonsville Nine* was produced in Los Angeles in 1970. His early devotional verse, although unconventional in Catholic terms, showed the influence of George Herbert, but dispensed with the English poet's formalism; clearly Berrigan had been affected by the radical American Catholic Dorothy Day, and by Caroline Gordon's sympathetic portrait of her in her novel *The Malefactors*. The poetry written after he had founded Clergy and Laymen Concerned about Vietnam is more direct and programmatic, in keeping with the man who poured blood on, and burned, draft papers; there were later similar poems arising from his imprisonment: *Trial Poems* (Beacon, 1970), *Prison Poems* (Unicorn, 1973). This is the poetry of an activist rather than that of a poet contemplating activism, but it is eloquent none the less. In 2000, Berrigan became poet-in-residence at Fordham University. See *And the Risen Bread: Selected Poems, 1957–1997* (Fordham University Press, 1998). MS-S

Berrigan, Ted (Edmund Joseph Michael Berrigan) (1934–83) Born in Providence, Rhode Island. He served in the army from 1954 to 1957, then attended the University of Tulsa before moving to New York City in the early 1960s. In New York he met poets and painters, published art criticism and book reviews, and wrote, during a three-month period in 1963, a series of short poems, most of them fourteen lines long, which he brought out the following year as *The Sonnets* ('C' Press, 1964). Their themes are the conventional ones of love, friendship, art, and how they play and prey upon each other, but Berrigan explodes the sonnet form's conventions—literally, by repeating, varying, and scrambling lines, many lifted from other poets; and figuratively, by taking perceptions and insights as he finds them rather than where sonnets of the past might have led him to place them.

Although none of Berrigan's later books can touch the luxurious brilliance of *The Sonnets*, all are characterized by an engaging emotional directness and a bracing command of everyday speech. Twice married and the father of four children, he taught at universities across the United States and in England, and died unexpectedly of blood poisoning caused by a perforated ulcer. A *Collected Poems* (2005) and *Selected Poems* (2011—both University of California Press) have been edited by Alice *Notley, his widow, and their sons, Anselm and Edmund Berrigan, also poets. In 2000, Notley published an expanded and annotated edition of *The Sonnets* (Penguin). Berrigan, whose light-hearted self-elegy 'Last Poem' has often been anthologized ('Let none regret my end who called me friend'), has been the subject of several memoirs by friends and collaborators such as Ron *Padgett and Tom *Clark. See also *Nice To See You: Homage to Ted Berrigan* (Coffee House, 1991), ed. Anne Waldman. RH*

Berry, Francis (1915–2006) Born in Malaya, held chairs in English at the University of Sheffield, 1947–70, and at Royal Holloway College, University of London, 1970–80. After retirement he held visiting appointments in the United States, the West Indies, India, Australia, Malawi, and Japan. In addition to criticism, radio plays, and a novel, he published some nine volumes of verse: *Galloping Centaur: Poems 1933–1951* (Methuen, 1952), selected from four earlier volumes, was followed by *Morant Bay and Other Poems* (1961), *Ghosts of Greenland* (1966—both Routledge & Kegan Paul), and *From the Red Fort* (Redcliffe, 1984). He mainly wrote long narrative poems, usually with a historical setting: for example, 'Murdock' is the story of a feud between two brothers, 'Morant Bay' describes a negro uprising in Jamaica in 1865, 'Illnesses and Ghosts at the West Settlement' is set in Greenland in the time of Erik the Red, and 'The Singing Dome' is about Shah Jehan, builder of the Taj Mahal. His *Collected Poems* was published by Redcliffe in 1994. See Philip Hobsbaum, 'Auditory Imagination: The Poetry of Francis Berry', in *PN Review* 82 (1991).   POM

Berry, James (1924–) Born in Boston, a coastal village in Jamaica. He spent his late teens working in America, but moved to 'dislocated' London, as he put it, in 1948, and has been in Britain ever since. After having worked for Post Office International Telegraphs from 1951 to 1977, he went on to become a full-time writer, an opportunity which began with his C. Day Lewis fellowship (1977–8). His poem, 'Fantasy of an African Boy', won first prize in the National Poetry Competition for 1981. He is an accomplished reader of his own work.

Berry's poetry not only reflects both Jamaican and British culture, but also merges them 'to make it new'. He owes something to Louise *Bennett in his use of Jamaican dialect, proverbs, and folk-tales but he also excels in poetry about the experience of being black in Britain, particularly in *Lucy's Letters and Loving* (New Beacon, 1982), in which 'Lucy' is an unlettered immigrant woman. In *Chain of Days* (Oxford University Press, 1985), he occasionally echoes the younger generation of *dub poets like Linton Kwesi *Johnson and Benjamin *Zephaniah. Poems like 'My Father' and 'Faces Around My Father' are clear-eyed in their self-analysis.

Other collections include *Fractured Circles* (New Beacon, 1979) and *When I Dance* (Hamilton, 1988). In 1990, he received an OBE. Berry has also written prolifically for children. His poetry has been selected in *A Story I Am In* (2011) from Bloodaxe Books, who also published *Hot Earth Cold Earth* (1995) and *Windrush Songs* (2007).   MR

Berry, Wendell (1934–) Born and raised on a farm in Kentucky. Having taught for several years in California and New York, Berry returned to the Kentucky River region where he writes and farms seventy-five acres in Henry County with his wife and children. His poems, which often have a quietly meditative aura, are characterized by simplicity of line and a straightforward narrative structure. The poet returns frequently to themes that have interested him from the beginning, such as the power of natural cycles, family responsibility, and the importance of community. His language is always unaffected, finely tuned to the cadences and rhythms of common speech, though he avoids the use of local dialects. A fair number of his poems, such as 'At a Country Funeral', are written in traditional (almost Wordsworthian) blank verse, but he is a versatile poet who has worked in any number of forms, including free verse. A strong conservationist and defender of small-scale farming, he often infuses his poems with political passion, as in 'Dark with Power'. Throughout the years he has written a number of poems that protest against war, industrialism, and the interruption of traditional agriculture in America.

Each of these themes has been taken up separately in books of essays too, such as *The Unsettling of America* (1977) and *Standing by Words* (1983). In his essays, as in the poetry, he is by turns social critic, naturalist, and prophet. A strong religious bent underlies everything Berry has written; as he says in *Standing by Words*: 'The imagination is our way to the Divine imagination, permitting us to see wholly—as whole and holy—what we perceive as scattered, as order what we perceive as random.' In addition to the poems and essays, Berry has also written several novels and volumes of short stories set in the fictitious Kentucky town of Port William.

Since *Selected Poems* (Counterpoint, 1998), Berry's volumes have included

Given: New Poems (Shoemaker & Hoard, 2005), *The Mad Farmer Poems* (2008), and *Leavings* (2009—both Counterpoint). In 2010, he was awarded the National Humanities Medal by President Obama. *New Collected Poems* was published by Counterpoint in 2012.   JP

Berryman, John (1914–72) Born John Smith Jr. in rural Oklahoma, the result of a miserable marriage between a feckless, small-town banker and a schoolteacher who thought she deserved better. His father, John Allyn Smith Sr., drifted toward the Florida land boom when his banking career foundered. The Smiths opened a restaurant in Tampa in 1925, and closed it the following year when the boom collapsed. John Smith Sr. died of a gunshot wound that, despite questionable details, was ruled a suicide. His father's death haunts all of Berryman's books, and biographers have taken it to be a key to his life and work (as, indeed, did the psychoanalytically inclined poet himself). Smith's widow remarried, this time to a dapper Georgian called John Berryman. The couple moved to New York, and John Smith Jr. became John Berryman Jr.

Berryman attended the South Kent School and Columbia, where he came under the courtly influence of the poet and critic Mark *Van Doren. Berryman dressed like a dandy, attended strip shows and speakeasies, and memorized the lyrics of 150 popular songs—a plausible source for the forms and diction of his later lyrics. Upon graduation, he won a Columbia fellowship to spend two years at Cambridge University. He spent an hour with *Yeats, got drunk with Dylan *Thomas, and returned to New York, in 1938, with a beard, fine tweeds, and a clipped British accent.

After false starts in journalism and high-school teaching, Berryman became what he despised, a college professor, with stints through the Fifties and Sixties at Princeton, Harvard, Iowa, and, tenured at last, at Minnesota. He was notorious for his sweating, spitting lecture style and for his capacity for drink, which played havoc with his professional and marital life—he was married

three times. Not until 1969, however, did Berryman admit to himself or his friends that he was an alcoholic; his unfinished novel *Recovery*, published posthumously in 1973, records his struggles with alcoholism.

While his famous contemporaries—Robert *Lowell, Elizabeth *Bishop, Delmore *Schwartz—have begun to settle in the imagination, Berryman has remained, since he leaped to his death from a bridge above the Mississippi River in 1972, elusive, changing shape in the mind as he constantly changed shape during his life. His imaginative life seems, in retrospect, a ventriloquist's search for an appropriate dummy. He was drawn to the great impersonators in literature: Shakespeare (whose biography he tried for twenty years to write), Yeats, and Stephen Crane (whose biography he did write). His interest in the extra-marital affair commemorated in *Sonnets to Chris* (1947, published as *Berryman's Sonnets* in 1966) cooled early, but to give the sonnet sequence the requisite twists he purposefully, like an improvising (and rather heartless) actor, prolonged and complicated the relationship. In his first major poem, *Homage to Mistress Bradstreet* (1953, 1956), Berryman impersonated a seventeenth-century woman poet. Although he despised Ann Bradstreet's poetry ('all this bald | abstract didactic rime I read appalled'), it was her body, not her words, that he appropriated for his seduction fantasy. The centre-piece of the poem is a childbirth scene written with Joycean gusto and lack of punctuation.

What redeemed the disintegration of his own life, Berryman always assured himself, was the poetry. But by the time he began writing his loosely autobiographical *Dream Songs* (1969), the book he is famous for, redemption by art no longer seemed so certain to him. He announced that he was 'down on Rilke and the hieratic boys just now'—especially Yeats—for not mixing with real men and women. Whitman became his model, and, in his last poems, a woman poet whose words he did not despise: Emily Dickinson. But he was coming to seem increasingly unreal to himself—such were the effects of prolonged alcohol abuse—finding himself 'less impressed than I used to be by the universal notion of a continuity of individual personality'. *The Dream Songs* are conceived as a sort of running minstrel show, with its hero sometimes in black face. The book has moments of jaunty brilliance and piercing clarity, especially in the many elegies for Berryman's contemporaries. 'I'm cross with god who has wrecked this generation', he wrote in one song. But occasionally the songs sound like a drunk who stayed too long at the party.

Berryman wrote some of his best poetry during the last years of his life, when he seemed willing, finally, to drop his disguises, letting the circus animals go home. Some of these poems seem almost posthumous in their disillusioned gravity, like the Yeatsian 'He Resigns' of summer 1970. The undertow of his father's death tugs at many of these late poems, as though some reconciliation were at hand.

Berryman's poetry, except for *The Dream Songs* (Farrar, Straus, 1969; Faber, 1990), is collected in Charles Thornbury (ed.), *John Berryman: Collected Poems, 1937–1971* (Farrar, Straus, 1989; Faber, 1990). There are two full-length biographies of Berryman: John Haffenden's *The Life of John Berryman* (Routledge & Kegan Paul, 1982) and Paul Mariani's *Dream Song: The Life of John Berryman* (Morrow, 1990). Notable critical studies include Haffenden's *John Berryman: A Critical Commentary* (Macmillan/New York University Press, 1980) and Joel Conarroe's *John Berryman: An Introduction to the Poetry* (Columbia University Press, 1977). There is a fascinating memoir by Berryman's first wife, Eileen Simpson, *Poets in Their Youth* (Random House, 1982). Berryman's own best critical work is collected in *The Freedom of the Poet* (Farrar, Straus, 1976).

His essays on Shakespeare have been edited by John Haffenden as *Berryman's Shakespeare* (Farrar, Straus, 1999). Berryman's influence on contemporary poets, through the example of the *Dream Songs*, is now widespread: see Stephen Burt, 'My Name is Henri', in *Close Calls With Nonsense* (Graywolf, 2009) and *After Thirty Falls: New Essays on John Berryman*, eds.

Philip Coleman and Philip MacGowan (Rodopi, 2007). Kevin *Young has made a selection from all of Berryman's poems for the Library of America (2004).   CB*

Berssenbrugge, Mei-Mei (1947–)
Born in Beijing to a Chinese mother and a Dutch-American father. She grew up in Massachusetts and then attended Reed College and the School of the Arts at Columbia University. Since then she has lived in New Mexico and in New York.

Berssenbrugge's early poems were imagistic, almost classically Chinese in their bias towards objects and description, but with her second book, *Random Possession*, she began to let her images fan out, expand, and in the process became a philosophical poet, questioning being and language simultaneously. By the time of *Empathy* (Station Hill, 1989), she had developed a long line that breaks the 'normal' horizontal border of the page. Her work is rescued from preciousness by precision, and by a vision which goes beyond the iteration of particulars. She is an experimental writer in the sense that the poems do not have different 'subjects' as such. She is experimenting with getting the language of philosophy into her work, making poems that ask questions about representation, what it means to engage the world with language. As she has said in conversation with Charles *Bernstein, 'I try to make language into a net for my meaning which tends to be emotion in continuum with some perceptual or conceptual slant'.

Her other books include: *The Heat Bird* (Burning Deck, 1984), *Four Year Old Girl* (1998) and *Nest* (2003). She has published two collaborations with the sculptor Kiki Smith: *Endocrinology* (1997) and *Concordance* (2006—all Kelsey Street). *I Love Artists: New and Selected Poems* was published by University of California Press in 2006.   MRU*

Bethell, (Mary) Ursula (1874–1945)
Born in England to wealthy parents who had already made their home in New Zealand and soon returned there. She grew up in the South Island, was educated there and in Europe, and devoted herself to social work in, alternately, Christchurch and

London. After the First World War she went back to New Zealand, built a house in the Cashmere Hills overlooking Christchurch, where she lived with her friend Effie Pollen from 1924 to 1934, and began writing poetry. Her first collection, *From a Garden in the Antipodes* (published under the pseudonym Evelyn Hayes in 1929), is literally about her garden, with detailed descriptions of plants, weather, and seasonal events. The poems are mostly in free verse and have a lively freshness of style, not without irony, humour, and occasional whimsy. Although Bethell felt drawn to England (planting primroses to remind her of the English spring), her poetry is physically rooted in the New Zealand landscape, which she presents as it is and not, like her predecessors, with the eyes of an outsider. The poet D'Arcy Cresswell wrote: 'New Zealand wasn't truly discovered . . . until Ursula Bethell, "very earnestly digging", raised her head to look at the mountains.' Bethell's work stands at the beginning of modern poetry in New Zealand.

Her later books (*Time and Place*, 1936; *Day and Night, Poems 1924–34*, 1939) show an alteration of style which could be viewed as a regression to more stilted *Georgian and Victorian models; the verse is formal, the diction more artificial, the impulse less spontaneous. Bethell was a devout Anglican much exercised by her spiritual struggles and anxious to direct her poetry towards devotional aims. This, and her increasing technical ambition, had the effect of subduing much of what was instinctive in her writing. Nevertheless, there are attractive and successful poems among her uneven later output. After Effie Pollen's death in 1934 Bethell wrote little poetry, apart from the agonized 'Six Memorials' to her friend. *Collected Poems*, ed. Vincent O'Sullivan, was published by Oxford University Press (1985).   FA

Betjeman, Sir John (1906–84) Born in Highgate, the son of a manufacturer of Dutch descent who made luxurious household articles. His childhood was marred by school bullies, a sense of social inferiority, and a sadistic Calvinist nurserymaid who appalled him with tales of eternity and hell:

'I caught her terror then. I have it still.' He was happy at the Dragon School, Oxford, but fear of bullying made his life wretched at Marlborough, although he loved the countryside and numbered among his friends Louis *MacNeice, Bernard *Spencer, Ellis Waterhouse, and Anthony Blunt. At Magdalen College, Oxford he plunged into the pleasures of sex, drink, partygoing, and the purchase of books beyond his means, while his study of architecture was facilitated by rich and aristocratic friends through whom he gained entry into English and Irish country houses. Failure in Divinity Moderations entailed his being sent down: he nurtured a lifelong hatred for his tutor, C. S. Lewis, who at this crisis displayed a total lack of sympathy. After Betjeman had caused his father acute distress by refusing to enter the family firm, Oxford connections secured him a post in 1931 on the *Architectural Review*, which he left in 1933 to become a freelance journalist. During the war he worked for various government departments, and after 1945 lived by journalism and by engagements on radio and television.

His first book of poems, *Mount Zion* (1931), was published by his rich friend Edward James, a patron of surrealism and husband of Tilly Losch, a beautiful, rapacious Viennese dancer. *Ghastly Good Taste*, a study in architectural fashion, appeared in 1933, the year of Betjeman's marriage to Penelope, the daughter of Field-Marshal Sir Philip (later Lord) Chetwode. Three volumes of verse, *Continual Dew* (1937), *Old Lights for New Chancels* (1940), and *New Bats in Old Belfries* (1945), increased Betjeman's reputation in the small, sophisticated coteries of his admirers, and W. H. *Auden's introduction to his choice of Betjeman's verse and prose, *Slick but not Streamlined* (1947), advanced Betjeman's claims to be regarded as a serious poet, a judgement echoed by John Sparrow in his preface to Betjeman's *Selected Poems* (1948). *A Few Late Chrysanthemums* (1954), his finest collection, foreshadowed the enormous success of *Collected Poems* (1958). His verse-autobiography, *Summoned by Bells* (1960), was more interesting for its revelations about the poet than for the quality of its poetry, nor did *High and Low* (1966) and *A Nip in the Air* (1974) compare with his earlier work.

In his Preface to *Old Lights for New Chancels* Betjeman spoke of his 'topographical predilection': throughout his career he was a masterly painter of landscapes and townscapes with figures, whom he portrayed with love, affection, or satire, or with a mixture of all three. Some of his best-known characters, such as Pam, that 'great big mountainous sports girl', Miss J. Hunter Dunn, silken Myfanwy, and the girl in the liquorice fields at Pontefract, are young and amorous. But his sympathies encompass older women who are not particularly likeable: the elderly nun in 'Felixstowe, or The Last of her Order', the dying nightclub hostess in 'Sun and Fun'. For Betjeman the topographical and the emotional are inextricably conjoined. In 'Middlesex' the sight of 'Fair Elaine the bobby-soxer' evokes the countryside of his childhood and the more distant vision of Victorian England, as enshrined in *The Diary of a Nobody*, and of those who lie 'Long in Kensal Green and Highgate silent under soot and stone'. That note of mortality sounds more often and more deeply in Betjeman's later verse.

His mastery of metre, rhyming, and stanzaic patterns offers continual delight, and he showed considerable skill in the handling of blank verse. He was often content to employ traditional forms or to compose variations on other men's themes; but his original tunes are among the most dazzling examples of his metrical resourcefulness and delicacy. 'Wantage Bells', 'Ireland with Emily', 'A Shropshire Lad', and the intricate 'I. M. Walter Ramsden' display his art at its most assured.

His poetry enjoyed immense popularity; his knighthood in 1969 and his appointment as Poet Laureate in 1972 were almost universally welcomed; he accumulated honours and public appointments; he achieved fame as an eccentric, and as a virtuoso performer on television. Some of his poetry, including what he came to regard as 'merely comic verse', is forced and feeble, but his lyrical cunning, his

gusto, the originality of his topographical and amatory verse, his resonant melancholy, and his power to evoke an idiosyncratic world have secured him a place among the most gifted poets of his generation.

See *Collected Poems* (Murray, 4th edn., 1979) and Bevis Hillier's three-volume authorized biography, published as one volume in 2006. Betjeman's journalism and radio talks have been collected in a series of paperback volumes from John Murray, edited by Stephen Games. Hugo *Williams made a selection of the poetry for Faber in 2006.   JP

Beveridge, Judith (1956–) Born in London, Beveridge came to Australia as a child. She has worked as creative writing teacher, a library assistant, and a bush regenerator. Since 2002, she has been a lecturer at Sydney University, and since 2005 poetry editor of the journal *Meanjin*.

Beveridge began to write poetry in 1974. Her first collection, *The Domesticity of Giraffes* (Black Lightning, 1987) won multiple awards and was reprinted three times. Clive *James has praised her work for its microscopic examination of 'the order of natural events'—famously, in the title poem of her debut, the interaction in captivity between a giraffe and her mate. It was almost a decade until Beveridge's second collection, *Accidental Grace* (University of Queensland Press, 1996). The precision of her free-verse observations (a spider 'pegging out her web | thin as a pressed flower in the bleaching light') is achieved by extensive redrafting, resulting in poems of polished imagery reminiscent of Elizabeth *Bishop.

The meditative quality of Beveridge's poetic stance between the worlds of man and animal is dramatized in a sequence from her third collection, *Wolf Notes* (Giramondo, 2003), 'Between the Palace and the Bodhi Tree', concerning the Buddha's journey to enlightenment. She continued to explore this boundary with a 30-poem portrait of a trawler crew, 'Driftgrounds: Three Fishermen', in her fourth collection, *Storm and Honey* (Giramondo,

2009—the title is a quotation from Kenneth *Slessor).   JNT

Bhatt, Sujata (1956–) Born in Ahmedabad, but grew up in America where her scientist father had settled. Part of her university education was at Iowa University's creative writing department. She lives in Germany, is married to a German, and is a freelance writer.

Bhatt's early work employs her native Gujarati for onomatopoeic effect, and because for her certain subjects cannot be described in English. In 'Search for my Tongue' she writes of the anguish of immigrants when they start to lose their first language and interweaves Gujarati and English into a successful bilingual poem. Bhatt travels through many cultures, using myth and symbol from Greek mythology, Hinduism, Buddhist history, Nordic lore, and science. She connects across the cultures—the Kama Sutra connects with Leda and the swan in an erotic love poem; Parvati, the goddess, connects with Twinings, the tea merchants, in a sardonic commentary on colonialism.

Her collections include *Brunizem* (1988; repr. 2008), *Monkey Shadows* (1991), *The Stinking Rose* (1995), *A Colour for Solitude* (on the painter Paula Modersohn-Becker and her friendship with Rainer Maria Rilke, 2002) and *Pure Lizard* (2008), which includes an exchange with Gillian *Clarke. *Point No Point* (1997—all Carcanet) was a selection from her first three books. She has also translated German and Gujarati poetry.   RA

Bidart, Frank (1939–) Grew up in Bakersfield, California, and was, he claims, infected from earliest youth onward with the dream of making great movies. While the choice of expressive medium has changed over the years, the impulse toward a dramatic staging of material has not. The work gathered in *In the Western Night: Poems 1965–90* (Farrar, Straus, 1990), shows the poet moving the locus of dramatic tension steadily inward.

After a childhood riven by family conflicts, Bidart moved east to attend Harvard. As he wrote in the early poem, 'California

Plush', 'I made myself an Easterner'. At Harvard, Bidart formed important friendships with Elizabeth *Bishop and Robert *Lowell, whose collected poems he later edited. *Golden State* (Braziller, 1973), Bidart's first collection, reflects the Lowell influence—the terse lines recount the particulars of family history and have a harsh, fluorescent glare: 'You punished Ruth | when she went to Los Angeles for a weekend, by | beginning to drink.'

The fascination with exacerbated states grew stronger, but by *The Book of the Body* (Farrar, Straus, 1977), Bidart had freed himself from any traces of the Lowell stance. In his well-known poem 'Ellen West', the poet uses the mask of an anorexic woman to explore the soul's conflicting impulses towards salvation (bodilessness) and the necessary penance of physicality. Bidart appears drawn to existential and religious themes, even as he refuses the consolation of any doctrine.

In his third book, *The Sacrifice* (Random House, 1983), Bidart continued to utilize the dramatic confrontations made possible by the adoption of a persona. 'The War of Vaslav Nijinsky', the *tour-de-force* of the book, projects the torments of madness and spiritual obsession upon a larger screen—that of a world on the verge of war. The lines effectively transmit the deranged fury of an innocent-become-martyr flaying himself: 'I said to myself: | *I must join MY GUILT | to the WORLD'S GUILT.*' The poem makes full use of Bidart's staggered lineation and emphatic capitalizations.

Desire (1997) was nominated for several major awards. It opens with elegiac lyrics from the poet's life as a gay man during the early AIDS era, followed by a continuation of his long narrative poem, 'The Second Hour of the Night'. *Star Dust* (2005—both Farrar, Straus) contains the third part of this work, as well as the chapbook *Music Like Dirt* (Sarabande, 2002), which was nominated for a Pulitzer Prize. In 2007, Bidart was awarded the Bollingen Prize for Poetry. *Watching the Spring Festival* (Farrar, Straus), a book of shorter poems, appeared in 2008.

Bidart lives in Cambridge, Massachusetts, and teaches at Wellesley College.

See *On Frank Bidart*, ed. Liam Rector and Tree Swenson (University of Michigan Press, 2007).   SPB*

Bila, Vonani (1972–   ) Born near Elim, Limpopo, Bila grew up in a large, impoverished family, and studied at Tivumbeni College of Education. He is the founder and editor of *Timbila*, a poetry journal, and director of the Timbila Poetry Project in Limpopo, which has published two of his collections: *In the Name of Amandla* (2004) and *Magicstan Fires* (2006). His staccato, storytelling verse honours those poets who protested against apartheid by continuing their critical perspective on contemporary injustice (see 'on the march', a tribute to Dennis *Brutus). His first book, *No Free Sleeping* (Botsotso, 1998), was a joint publication with two other members of the Botsotso poetry collective, Donald Parenzee and Alan Finlay. See *Handsome Jita: Selected Poems* (University of KwaZulu-Natal Press, 2007). He has performed his work around the world, and also released a musical recording of his poem 'Dahl Street, Pietersburg'.   JNT

Binyon, (Robert) Laurence (1869–1943) Born in Lancaster, the son of a clergyman, and educated at St Paul's and Trinity College, Oxford. He worked in the British Museum in the Department of Prints and Drawings, where he became an authority on Oriental Art; his *Painting in the Far East* (1908) was the first book on the subject in any European language.

His first volume of verse, *Lyric Poems*, was published in 1894; early poems show him experimenting (after *Bridges and Hopkins) with the natural stress-accent of English (see, for example, the anthologized lyric 'The Little Dancers'). During the First World War he wrote a number of poems collected as *The Four Years*, one of which, 'For the Fallen', is among the best-known of all war poems; the fourth stanza provided the inscription for thousands of memorials. Other poems from that collection have been undeservedly neglected: 'The Zeppelin', 'The Witnesses', and 'The Bereaved' are good examples of a discredited genre, the war poem from the Home Front;

'Guns at the Front', 'Dark Wind', and 'The Arras Road', while still celebrating 'the beauty of the dead', are physically closer to the reality of battle. After these, two long traditional odes written in the 1920s, 'The Sirens' (1924) and 'The Idols' (1928), read somewhat remotely. Aside from his lyric poetry, Binyon wrote nine verse plays, including *Arthur* (1923)—one of several treatments of Arthurian legends—which was staged at the Old Vic with music by Elgar.

After the publication of the *Collected Poems* in two volumes in 1931 (Macmillan), Binyon embarked on a fine translation of the whole of Dante's *Divine Comedy* in terza rima—completed in 1943, and rougher in texture than most of his original verse—in which some commentators have found the best use of his craft. Elsewhere his grave, academic style has been judged too monotonously refined. Poems in the posthumous *The Burning of the Leaves* (Macmillan, 1944) show that half-a-century made little impact on his stubbornly pure technique; on the other hand, the timely title sequence (formerly published as 'The Ruins') and the beautiful fragment 'Winter Sunrise' are some of the best (if also the last) of all 'Edwardian' poetry.   MI

Birney, (Alfred) Earle (1904–95) Born in Calgary, Alberta. Birney grew up in Calgary and on a farm in Erickson, British Columbia. His 1981 memoir, 'Child Addict in Alberta', tells of the influence of Calvinism and of his early infatuation with words. An honours student at the University of British Columbia, he went on to doctoral study in Old and Middle English at the University of Toronto, after which he taught at the University of Utah. His involvement in Trotskyite causes during the 1930s, however, led to his leaving the USA. After severing his leftwing political connections, he served actively with the Canadian Army to 1945. From 1946 to 1965 he taught at the University of British Columbia, in later years setting up Canada's first creative writing programme. In 1965 he moved east, took up various writer-in-residence positions, and performed with the sound poetry and jazz group Nexus. Until disabled by a severe heart attack in the mid-1980s, he published regularly. *David and Other Poems* (Ryerson, 1942) exemplifies Birney's early verse, though many lyrics from these years were substantially rephrased when gathered in the two-volume *Collected Poems* (McClelland & Stewart, 1975). 'David', Birney's most popular narrative poem, recounts a mountain-climbing accident which leads the young narrator to an acute ethical choice. 'Anglosaxon Street', combining Old English metrics with modern political slogans, exposes the wartime attitudes of urban Toronto. *The Strait of Anian* (Ryerson, 1948), the first of several volumes of selected verse, illustrates the poet's continuing fascination with the fact of war and the idea of wilderness.

With *Ice Cod Bell or Stone* (1962) and *Near False Creek Mouth* (1964), Birney turned in different formal directions, using non-linear meditation and colloquial idiom to confront the disparity between his community's post-war values and the continuing value of community. His travels abroad led to some of his most evocative lyrics, including 'The Bear on the Delhi Road', and some of his most barbed social critiques, including 'Billboards Build Freedom of Choice'. Satirist as well as metaphysical lyricist, Birney twice updated his mordant national analysis, 'Canada: Case History', and he experimented increasingly with visual design and verbal play. Along with other late volumes, *Rag & Bone Shop* (1971—all McClelland & Stewart) wittily condemns inequities but equably muses on the passing of time.

Altogether, Birney published thirty-six books of poetry, fiction, radio plays, and commentary. Several literary essays appear in *Spreading Time* (1980). *The Creative Writer* (1966) and *The Cow Jumped Over the Moon* (1972) comment on the reading and writing of poetry. Two novels—the picaresque *Turvey* (1949; unexpurgated edn., 1976) and the realist *Down the Long Table* (1955)—respectively satirize military bureaucracy and condemn McCarthyism. See *One Muddy Hand: Selected Poems*, ed. Sam Solecki (Harbour, 2006).   WHN

Bishop, Elizabeth (1911–79) Born in Worcester, Massachusetts, the only child of an American father with Canadian antecedents, and a Canadian mother. Her father died when she was 8 months old; her mother then suffered a series of mental breakdowns which led to her being permanently confined. From the age of 5 Bishop was looked after by relatives, first her maternal grandparents in Nova Scotia, then members of her father's family in Worcester and South Boston, and she never saw her mother again. After boarding at Walnut Hill School near Boston, she entered Vassar, intending to study music (composition and piano), but she soon switched to English and graduated in 1934. The rest of her life was characterized largely by a sense of uprootedness and—in spite of a number of close friendships with other writers, a poetry consultantship at the Library of Congress in Washington in 1949/50, and a post at Harvard in her last years—detachment from literary and academic centres of power. She travelled widely and had homes, successively, in New York, Florida, Brazil, and Boston.

The loss of Bishop's parents and abrupt changes of home in childhood seem to have been decisive in the formation of her later habits of mind and poetic practice. As a young girl she made her own discovery of the poems of George Herbert, and his influence may be traced through both her juvenilia and her mature work. It is most clearly evident in her first published collection, *North & South* (Houghton Mifflin, 1946), whether in her witty transplanting of Herbert's own words ('Wading at Wellfleet'), or in a more thorough adaptation of his poetic procedures to her special requirements ('The Weed'); and this lends the book some of its distinctiveness. *North & South* already shows a voice unlike that of any other American poet, and it lays claim to themes that its author was to explore more fully in subsequent volumes.

Much has been made of Bishop's indebtedness to Marianne *Moore, and the value of the older poet's friendship and encouragement is fondly acknowledged by Bishop herself in a prose piece, 'Efforts of Affection: A Memoir of Marianne Moore'. But apart from a shared enthusiasm for accurate observation, the two poets have little in common, either formally or materially, beyond what might have been expected from the accidental overlapping of their lives. Moreover, it appears that it was Bishop's need to find in poetry a means of addressing her unique experience of alienation that drove her to Herbert and other English writers of the seventeenth century, rather than to any closer example, specifically because they stood at such a fixed distance from the culture of her own time. Another identifiable strain in *North & South*, also markedly un-American, but serving to counterbalance any tendency to mere antiquatedness, was that of surrealism—used, too, for the purpose of distancing.

Visual representations and artefacts, whether real or imaginary, play a significant part in many of these early poems. In 'The Map' and 'Large Bad Picture', the inadequacy or misleading suggestiveness of certain images stands figuratively for the broader perils of intercourse with the perceived world. The 'Monument' supplies scrupulously detailed information about a strange wooden structure of unyielding incomprehensibility. The toy horse and its acrobat rider, which are described in 'Cirque d'Hiver', allow, surprisingly, for a meditation on the soul, while elsewhere ('The Weed', 'Sleeping Standing Up') the attempt to objectify inner states has inevitably bizarre or disconcerting results. Even those poems in *North & South* which purport to deal directly with the real world are prone to hints of bafflement and futility, as expressed by the oddly assorted inventory of domestic trappings in 'Jerónimo's House', or the unedifying riot of nature in 'Florida'.

In exploring and signposting her poetic domain, Bishop's first book is like that of many another writer. What distinguishes it is the assurance with which she sets about the task—an assurance sometimes ironically at odds with a quiet and professedly tentative manner—and the richness of the material she finds there. Significantly, the book won her the admiration of, among others, two fellow poets: Randall *Jarrell, who discussed it perceptively in *Partisan Review*, and Robert *Lowell, who became a lifelong friend and literary confidant. Lowell's later debt to Bishop's example is a matter of record; whether she learned as much from him is more doubtful.

North & South was followed by three further collections of new work within Bishop's lifetime: an incorporation of *North & South* with *A Cold Spring* under the title *Poems* (Houghton Mifflin, 1955; Chatto & Windus, 1956), *Questions of Travel* (Farrar, Straus, 1965), and *Geography III* (Farrar, Straus/Chatto & Windus, 1976). As at least three of the titles indicate, the problem of establishing one's place in the world continued to be of central interest to her. The practice of taking extraneously given images and artefacts as pretexts for meditations on the subject was gradually dropped, although it still supplies the focus of the argument in an important poem, 'Over 2,000 Illustrations and a Complete Concordance'. Bishop came to depend less, too, on overtly surrealistic devices. Instead, her travels and foreign domicile afforded her the opportunity to look at landscapes whose strangeness was simply a fact, and to use her powers of vivid description and animistic metaphor as a means of co-ordinating and fixing the abundance of sensations to which she was exposed.

The tension generated by the clash between extravagantly proliferating imagery and the modesty of the mind set on putting it in order is what lends point to the most successful of the poems in this category— 'The Bight', 'At the Fishhouses', and 'Questions of Travel' among them. Traditional metres, which Bishop handled skilfully elsewhere, would have been inappropriate here. So she evolved her own, idiosyncratic system of lines governed less by considerations of prosody than by an ear finely attuned to the music of assonance, colloquial pacing, and aptly judged pauses and breaks. The mimetic purpose is to show the poet's mind as it improvises its way towards a resolution, in so far as that may be said to occur. The method is one of unflappable diffidence. It appears that Hopkins's metrical experiments gave Bishop the incentive to pursue her own, but she took a far different course from his in her cultivation of looseness and avoidance of insistent stress. Only occasionally does her voice modulate to something like declamation, as in the visionary last lines of 'At the Fishhouses'.

A notable feature of Bishop's later poems is their more frequent use of biographical material. In the section of *Questions of Travel* headed 'Elsewhere', she includes a number of poems about childhood experiences that seem taken from life. 'Sestina' and 'First Death in Nova Scotia' relate troubling incidents in the lives of children, while 'In the Waiting Room', from *Geography III*, offers a startling account of a moment of traumatic self-awareness in Bishop's own seventh year. But while such poems are a long way in spirit from the studied obliqueness of *North & South*, it would be a mistake to think of Bishop's development as a straightforward homing-in on early experiences. Besides the autobiographical poem cited here, *Geography III* contains exercises in dramatic monologue ('Crusoe in England'), rueful comment, and metaphorical fantasy, as well as her characteristic anecdotal and descriptive modes ('The Moose', 'Poem'). The scope is as wide as ever; nuance and intimation are still the preferred means. When Bishop wished to reflect on her misfortunes as a child she was more likely—whatever the reasons may have been—to choose prose, whether in the form of a short story (e.g. 'In the Village'), or of a memoir ('The Country Mouse').

Bishop's output of poems was a small one, by the standards of her time. Apart from her translations (from the Portuguese, Spanish, and French), *The Complete Poems 1927–1979* contains just over one hundred titles, and this is counting juvenilia and occasional light verse. The quality, however, is formidably high. It is perhaps for this reason that Bishop was so admired by her peers and came to have the reputation of being something of a 'poet's poet'. The impression is of a creative intelligence bent solely on satisfying the strictest inner demands, writing only what was necessary, and undeflected by fashion. The assiduously cultivated uniqueness of Bishop's style set her apart from her contemporaries and has made her a dangerous poet to imitate, but her example will no doubt continue to be an inspiration, and her poems read. Although she was recognized in her own day and her books won her such signs of esteem as the Pulitzer Prize and the National Book Award, her standing has, if anything, risen since her death, and it is not uncommon to hear her placed among the greatest of American poets.

A *Complete Poems* was published in 1969, but *The Complete Poems 1927–1979* (Farrar, Straus/Chatto & Windus, 1983) now gives the standard text of Bishop's poetical works. *The Collected Prose* (Farrar, Straus, 1984) contains short stories and writings under the heading, 'Memory: Persons & Places'. *The Diary of 'Helena Morley'* (1957) was translated from the Portuguese by Bishop, and has an introduction by her. She also collaborated with Emanuel Brasil in editing *An Anthology of Twentieth-Century Brazilian Poetry* in her own translations. A biography, *Elizabeth Bishop: Life and the Memory of It* (University of California Press) by Brett Miller, appeared in 1993.

See also *Conversations with Elizabeth Bishop* (University Press of Mississippi, 1996), ed. George Monteiro; *One Art*, a selection of her letters (Farrar, Straus, 1994; Pimlico, 1996); and *Words in Air*, her correspondence with Lowell (Farrar, Straus/Faber, 2008). Anne *Stevenson, who wrote the first study of Bishop in 1966, returned to her subject in 1998 with *Five Looks at Elizabeth Bishop* (Bloodaxe; repr. 2006), a critical introduction which draws on the author's correspondence with the poet. *Elizabeth Bishop: Poet of the Periphery* (Bloodaxe, 2002), ed. Linda Anderson and Jo *Shapcott, is a collection of essays by critics and British poets, including Vicki *Feaver and Deryn *Rees-Jones. *Edgar Allen Poe & The Juke-Box*, ed. Alice Quinn (Farrar, Straus/Carcanet, 2006), an annotated volume of uncollected poems and fragments, reproduces the drafts of her celebrated villanelle, 'One Art', as an appendix. A one-volume Library of America edition of Bishop's *Poems, Prose and Letters* appeared in 2008.   CJR*

bissett, bill (William Frederick Bissett) (1939–   ) Born in Halifax, Nova Scotia, but since the late Fifties he has lived in Vancouver, British Columbia, where in the Sixties he became a leader among counter-culture writers, founding the radical magazine *Blew Ointment* (1963) and beginning his prolific career as a poet. His work was once attacked by politicians as pornographic and sensational. By 1990 he had published over fifty volumes of poetry, much of it in small presses like his own blewointmentpress, which he founded in 1967.

bissett's refusal to capitalize his name is consistent with his attacks on conventional spelling, punctuation, and typography. His radical poetics celebrate the shamanic potential of language, always emphasizing the visual, oral, and aural elements of words so that their significance does not emerge univocally from their conventional meanings, but strikes the senses more immediately through their sight and sound. bissett is one of Canada's best-known sound poets, frequently performing and chanting his verse, which often depends on repetition and incantation for its power.

On the page, bissett's language forces readers to look at familiar words with new eyes: 'the' becomes 'th', 'and' becomes 'nd', 'some' becomes 'sum', 'station' becomes 'stashun'. Often words are run together and lines repeated until a visual pattern is established, only to be disrupted by a deft typographical variation. bissett often illustrates his poems with his own drawings.

A latter-day romantic visionary, bissett wishes to recover essential ecstasy and purity through rapt invocations of the body and spirit. His poems deplore the mundane, attack sophistry, and exalt revolutionary simplicity.

Beyond Even Faithful Legends: Selected Poems 1962–1976 (Talonbooks, 1980) offers a generous collection of bissett's early work. Since then, he has continued to publish prolifically, mainly through Talonbooks in Vancouver. The characteristically titled *inkorrect thots* (1993) and the dystopian *peter among th towring boxes/text bites* (2003) both won the B. C. Books Dorothy Livesay Prize. *radiant danse uv being,*

a blewointment book (2006, Nightwood) contains tributes to bissett from a wide range of other poets, including Margaret *Atwood, P. K. *Page, and Steve *McCaffery. In 2007 he received the George Woodcock Lifetime Achievement Award. His latest book of poems is *time* (2010). *novel* (2011— all Talonbooks) he describes as 'a novel with connekting pomes n essays'.   NB*

Blackburn, Paul (1926–71) Son of the poet Frances Frost, was born and raised in St Albans, Vermont. He remained there until he was 14, when his mother brought him to New York. Though he spent some years at the University of Wisconsin (where he began corresponding with Ezra *Pound), and travelled extensively in Europe, Blackburn remains largely associated with New York City and the alternative poetry scene that flourished there throughout the 1960s.

The publication of *The Collected Poems of Paul Blackburn* (Persea, 1985) did much to bring this poet into larger public awareness. For Blackburn had been, hitherto, a poet of fugitive small-press appearances, largely neglected by the critical establishment. But he is increasingly seen, along with his friend Robert *Creeley, as an important link between the modernist innovations of Pound, the experimentalism of the *Black Mountain poets, and the peculiarly American celebrations of the *Beats.

Blackburn's oeuvre can be seen to fall into at least three distinct phases. The earliest work, much of it written while he travelled in Europe in the early 1950s, reflects the influence of Creeley (with whom he had an extensive correspondence) and of Pound's troubadour renderings. The poems from this period are lyrical and subdued, extremely effective in playing off sound patterns and pauses—already Blackburn is using white space to maximal expressive advantage.

The 1960s find the poet living in New York, working to open his prosody to the energies and collisions of an urban subject-matter. The early calm has yielded to the clamour of streets, voices; the surface is increasingly making room for diary-like notations. The poet himself, however, elects to remain largely absent—certainly we hear next to nothing from the inner man. Blackburn has become an extraordinarily effective medium for the transmission of daily moments excerpted from time: 'The loudest sound in this public room | is the exhaust fan in the east window | or the cat at my back | asleep there in the sun | bleached tabletop, golden | shimmer of ale' (from 'The Island'). Blackburn's collection *The Cities* (Grove, 1967) is the apotheosis of this phase of his development.

In early 1970 Blackburn was diagnosed as having cancer of the throat. In the time before his death the following year his poetry becomes more and more like an extended personal journal. The poems—entries—are likely to baffle the first-time reader, but those familiar with the earlier work will find the ease and immediacy thrilling.

Some of Blackburn's small-press publications are: *Early Selected Y Mas* (Black Sparrow, 1972); *In. On. Or About the Premises* (Cape Goliard, 1968); *The Journals* (Black Sparrow, 1975).   SPB

Blackmur, R. P. (Richard Palmer) (1904–65) Born in Springfield, Massachusetts. After high school, instead of going to university he worked in the Dunster House bookshop in Boston and, in 1929, edited *Hound & Horn* with Lincoln Kirstein before the magazine moved from Harvard to New York. In 1930 he married Helen Dickson, an artist from Harrington, Maine, where they lived on and off until 1951 when they divorced. From 1928 to 1940 Blackmur was a freelance critic and poet; then Allen *Tate, who liked his 'vigorous, tough-minded' criticism, appointed him to assist in the newly established course in creative English at Princeton. He remained at Princeton—first as resident fellow (1940–8), then as professor (1948–65)—for the rest of his life.

Two Guggenheim Foundation grants, in 1936 and 1937, had enabled Blackmur to research a large-scale work on the historian Henry Adams, but the book was never completed (although various studies have been gathered posthumously in *Henry Adams*, 1980); the medium best suited to his deliberately provisional insights was always the essay, not the monograph, and modern poetry and criticism the subjects on which he wrote most persuasively. In his first two books of essays, *The Double Agent: Essays in Craft and Elucidation* (1935) and *The Expense of Greatness* (1940), he advocates the 'technical approach' to poetry, which is 'concerned, first and last—whatever comes between—with the poem as it is read and as what it represents is felt'. Typically, his own readings (of *Stevens, *Moore, and *Yeats, among others) are brilliant analyses of the techniques good poems use to exceed discursive statement and create, rather than merely reflect, sensibility. Later books of criticism include *Language as Gesture* (1952), which prints both new and previously published essays, *The Lion and the Honeycomb* (1955), and *Form and Value in Modern Poetry* (1957). Blackmur's prose is fluent and entertaining, and it is generally agreed that of all the New Criticism his essays will have the most lasting influence.

His poetry, first published in *From Jordan's Delight* (1937), *The Second World* (1942), and *The Good European and Other Poems* (1947), consists mainly of lyric sequences on personal and intellectual themes. 'Dedications' is about the end of a relationship and 'A Labyrinth of Being' about marriage and fatherhood, while 'Judas Priest', a sequence of four sonnets, celebrates 'all those who shun the dogma's dreadful weight', and 'The Cough' considers the respective claims of non-verbal and verbal expression, the cough and the word. Blackmur's poetry, unlike his prose, has never been widely enjoyed, a fact which he attributed to his 'own defects—of style and sensibility and scope'. His sequences weave subtle and paradoxical arguments; but their considerable moral intelligence is often obscured by archaic syntactical inversions, formal diction, and wooden obedience to traditional (usually iambic) metres.

Blackmur's poetry has been collected in *Poems of R. P. Blackmur* (Princeton University Press, 1977); the best selections of his prose are *Language as Gesture* (Harcourt,

Brace, 1952; repr. 1981) and *Selected Essays of R. P. Blackmur* (Ecco, 1986). See Russell Fraser, *A Mingled Yarn: The Life of R. P. Blackmur* (Harcourt, Brace, 1979; new edn. Transaction, 2010).   NE*

Bland, Peter (1934–   ) Born in Scarborough, Yorkshire, and went to school in the Midlands; he emigrated to New Zealand in 1954 after the deaths of his parents and lived in Wellington, where he worked as a clerk, social worker, journalist, and broadcaster, and read English at Victoria University. He became friendly with the poets James K. *Baxter and Louis *Johnson, and with them edited the literary journal *Numbers* in the early 1960s. Johnson was a particularly significant influence; Bland shared his views on the importance of social realism in poetry, using imagery from suburban life and popular culture. With these *Wellington poets he argued against the loftier, chthonic vision of New Zealand poetry advocated by the Auckland group.

In 1964 Bland became one of the co-founders of the Downstage Theatre Company and worked as a writer, director, and actor; in 1968 he returned with his family to England, and for many years earned his living as an actor, mostly in Britain but with further interludes in New Zealand. His poems feed on exile and displacement. The eponymous persona of *Mr Maui* (1976) is described in a prefatory note as 'a young tribal outcast' who later returns 'to the country of his birth as head of his own tribe; cultural dislocation and the struggle for survival are recurring themes. Subsequent titles such as *The Crusoe Factor* (1985—both London Magazine) and *Ports of Call* (Steele Roberts, 2003) hint at his migratory way of life, as does his complicated publishing history, with collections sometimes overlapping and appearing in both countries.

One of Bland's strategies is humour; he has remarked that he does not write about acting and the theatre, but the techniques of comedy and timing learnt from his stage and film work find a place in his poetry, together with a relaxed colloquial tone which does not preclude literary and historical allusions. His *Selected Poems* were published by Car-canet in 1998 and a memoir, *Sorry I'm a Stranger Here Myself* (Vintage), in 2004. In 2011 he returned to live in New Zealand, where in that year he was given the Prime Minister's Award for Poetry and his most recent collection, *Coming Ashore*, appeared from Steele Roberts.   FKA

Blaser, Robin (1925–2009) Born in Denver, Colorado, and educated at the University of California, Berkeley. He worked as a librarian at Harvard University from 1955, moving to San Francisco State University in 1959. In 1966 he emigrated to Vancouver, and taught English at Simon Fraser University. He received the Order of Canada in 2005, and a Griffin Trust Lifetime Recognition Award for Excellence in Poetry in 2006.

In 1946, Blaser met Robert *Duncan and Jack *Spicer (both later featured in his 'Great Companions' sequence). As a group they were influential in the *San Francisco Renaissance, working out their ideas about the 'serial poem' as an aleatory method of composition. Blaser began to write the poems of *Cups* (Four Seasons, 1968) during his first year in San Francisco, and in 1964 published *The Moth Poem* (Open Press), a set of free-verse poems haunted by the creature of the title. Another sequence accumulated throughout his life was *Image-Nations*. Blaser had a significant influence on both the West Coast and Canadian poetry scenes as a teacher, poet, and editor. *The Collected Books of Jack Spicer* (1975) contains his essay on the serial poem, 'The Practice of Outside', which emphasizes his belief in the importance of a poetics that 'reopens the real' in opposition to 'the presuming discourse'. He also edited the selected poems of George *Bowering and Louis *Dudek.

A second edition of Blaser's collected poems, *The Holy Forest*, appeared in 2007. See also *The Fire: Collected Essays of Robin Blaser* (2006—both University of California Press), ed. Miriam Nichol.   JNT

Blessing, Richard (1939–83) Born in Bradford, Pennsylvania. His first two books were studies of Wallace *Stevens and Theodore *Roethke. He also published a novel, *The Passing Season* (Little, Brown, 1982). At the time of his death, from a brain tumour, he was chairman of the graduate programme in English at the University of Washington.

There are fine poems in his first two collections—some of them tart ('Teaching You to Think'), some lyrical ('The Eagle'), and some ('Elegy for Elvis') both at once. And there are effective touches in the numerous poems about his father. Frequently, however, the poems seem willed rather than achieved, marked by easy surrealism, evasive use of the second person, and piled details that do not always cohere. But the fifteen poems in his last book, *Poems and Stories*, published almost simultaneously with his death, are easily his best. In 'State of Women', 'Late News' (about a mass murderer), and especially the ten-poem sequence on his illness and attempts at recovery, he writes with a sureness and power not previously seen in his work. The poems of this sequence are reflective, resonant, and rich with word-play and allusions that reinforce, rather than disrupt, the seriousness of theme. Stoic in the assimilation of the worst that life can offer, and cheerful in the resolve to go on as best one can, they are a well-wrought and moving testament to the human spirit.

Blessing's three collections are *Winter Constellations* (Ahsahta, 1977), *A Closed Book* (University of Washington Press, 1981), and *Poems and Stories* (Dragon Gate, 1983).   MP

Bletsoe, Elizabeth (1960–) Born and raised in Dorset, Bletsoe returned there in 1997 after teaching at Cardiff University for some years. She has trained as a homeopath and works at Sherborne Museum. The Welsh landscape was the subject of her first publication, *The Regardians* (Odyssey Poets, 1993). Her native English county is the *Landscape from a Dream* of a later volume (2008), which concludes with a series of poems re-voicing West Country women from the novels of Thomas *Hardy. Her fascination with deep histories and sacred knowledge of the natural world is expressed in highly visual, consciously archaic verse and prose that breaks and compounds words to reveal their essences, suggesting a tradition of radically eccentric British

modernism running from David *Jones to Maggie *O'Sullivan and Brian *Catling. See *Pharmacopœia and Early Selected Works* (2010—both Shearsman).   JNT

Blight, John (1913–95) Born in South Australia but lived most of his life in Southern Queensland, whose coast of sunken river valleys, mangrove swamps, coral reefs, and sand dunes provided him with much of his poetic inspiration. For many years he ran a sawmill near Maryborough. He lived in Brisbane.

Blight was a sort of mystic biologist of poetry. He recorded the natural world with materialist concentration which amounts to ecstasy. His 'Sea Sonnets' in *A Beachcomber's Diary* (1963) and *My Beachcombing Days* (1968—both Angus & Robertson) re-create the ever-changing turbulence of the Queensland coast just before the beginnings of the Great Barrier Reef. He was entirely at home with such subjects as a beached whale, a bee's sting, or the shadowy world of mangroves.

Blight's early books, *The Old Pianist* (Dymock's Book Arcade, 1945) and *The Two Suns Met* (Lyre-Bird Writers/Commonwealth Literary Fund, 1954), his two *Beachcombing* volumes, and *Hart* (1975) make up the bulk of his poetry, which was brought together in *Selected Poems 1939–1975* (1976—both Thomas Nelson). See also *Selected Poems 1939–1990* (University of Queensland Press, 1992).   PNFP

Blumenthal, Michael (1949–) Grew up in a German-speaking household in Washington Heights, New York City. After graduating with a degree in economics from the State University of New York in Binghamton (1969), he took a law degree at Cornell (1974) and practised for a year as an attorney for the Federal Trade Commission. His interest in writing led him successively to an arts administration position with the National Endowment for the Arts, writing positions at Time-Life Books and the National Endowment for the Humanities, and a television production post with West German Television, before he went to Harvard as a teacher of creative writing

(1983–92). He has had Fulbright Fellowships to Israel (1987) and Hungary (1992), and a Guggenheim Fellowship (1988), and has held visiting professorships at universities in Europe and the United States.

Blumenthal's first five books of poetry were *Sympathetic Magic* (Water Mark, 1980), *Days We Would Rather Know* (Viking, 1984), *Laps* (University of Massachusetts Press, 1984), *Against Romance* (Viking, 1987), and *The Wages of Goodness* (University of Missouri Press, 1992); he has also edited an anthology of marriage poems, *To Wed and to Woo* (Poseidon, 1992). Though Blumenthal is a poet of deft social commentary (see 'Jungians and Freudians at the Joseph Campbell Lecture') and of social protest ('The Heart of Quang Duc'), he writes most often of the conflict between idealization ('romance') and disillusion. A marriage followed by a divorce, and a subsequent marriage followed by the birth of a son, have given Blumenthal material for a series of poems for and against romance, while his own uncertain status as a bilingual child in a family of German-Jewish refugees has given him an abiding interest in foreignness, family dynamics, marginalization, and solitude.

His poems often display a poignant mixture of melancholy and comedy, bewilderment and resolve. He casts himself frequently as a *naif* enduring painful enlightenment; or an erring 'Puer Aeternus' (as one poem has it) resolving to do better; or an analysand coming, perhaps too late, to a revealing truth. Blumenthal's affinities for the moralist literature of aphorisms and *pensées* can sometimes tinge his poems with the homiletic or the sentimental. In *Laps*, he writes a prologue putting himself under the patronage of Aristippus of Cyrene, who believed in 'the primacy of pleasure as a source of moral good'. The conflict between law and pleasure is one of Blumenthal's chief themes, down to his most recent meditations on 'the wages of goodness'.

His later collections are *Dusty Angel* (1999) and *And* (2009—both BOA). He has also published a novel satirizing academic life at Harvard, *Weinstock Among the Dying* (Zoland, 1993). See *All My Mothers and Fathers: A Memoir* (Harper, 2002), which includes a selection of poems.   HV

Blunden, Edmund (Charles) (1896–1974) Educated at Christ's Hospital and Queen's College, Oxford, served in the First World War from 1916 to 1918, and was awarded the Military Cross. *The Waggoner* (1920) and *The Shepherd* (1922), for which he won the Hawthornden Prize, included poems from five slender volumes published in 1914 and 1916. *Undertones of War* (1928), a chronicle of the war in verse and prose, gained him a wider reputation that was enhanced by *The Poems of Edmund Blunden 1914–1930* (1930).

Blunden is underestimated today as a war poet, largely because the work of *Owen, *Rosenberg, and *Sassoon has overshadowed his achievement. Ironically enough, it was Blunden's edition of Owen's poems in 1931 that inaugurated the revival of interest in his work. Blunden's war poems are more restrained than those of the other three men, but his hatred of the war and his grief for the dead, whom he commemorated in an elegy of passionate lyricism, 'Their Very Memory', were as intense as theirs. Moreover, he expressed a horror at the devastation of the French countryside that is almost absent from their poetry: 'I have seen a green country, useful to the race, | Knocked silly with guns and mines, its villages vanished.' He was unique also among his fellow poets in acknowledging that there were moments of happiness amid the insensate slaughter. 'At Senlis Once' celebrates a brief interval of rest and refreshment, just as 'Concert Party: Busseboom' recalls an hour of innocent entertainment 'While men in the trenches below Larch Wood | Were kicking men to death'.

Blunden's poems about the English countryside are among his finest. They combine a formal, at times almost archaic, utterance with an exact portrayal of the scene, a delicacy of perception, and an air of unease and foreboding. His sympathies embrace alms-women, lovers young and old, village forefathers, midnight skaters, even the cornered weasel in 'Winter: East Anglia' that 'stands his ground | And hard as winter dies'.

Between the wars Blunden lived by literary journalism, as professor of English literature at Tokyo University from 1924 to 1927, and as a fellow and tutor in English at Merton College, Oxford, from 1931 to 1943.

During the ten years after the outbreak of war in 1939 Blunden published three volumes. *Poems 1930–1940* (1940) bore traces of his preoccupation with the earlier conflict. In the Preface he denied 'morbidly wishing to go back that road', yet 'that tremendous time does not easily give up its hold'. *Shells by a Stream* (1944) and *After the Bombing* (1949) reflected his sombre meditation on the darkness of the times, lightened by his belief in traditional values and the hope of renewal.

After leaving Merton, Blunden worked for the *Times Literary Supplement* until he joined the UK Liaison Mission in Tokyo in 1948. In 1950 he began a second spell with the *TLS*; and was appointed emeritus professor of English literature at Hong Kong University in 1953, returning to England in the early 1960s. When living in Hong Kong he was permitted by the Chinese authorities to visit the Great Wall of China. His terse, poignant sonnet about the Wall describes how it stretches for thousands of miles, defending the frontier with 'stairway, sally-port, loop, parapet'. The parallels between the Wall and the trenches of the 1914–18 war, though never spelled out, pervade the sonnet. And 'This new-set sentry of a long dead year', whom the poet half-knows, is the brother of the sentries on the Western Front.

A *Hong Kong House: Poems 1951–1962* (1962) and *Eleven Poems* (1965) were Blunden's last two volumes. He was elected Professor of Poetry at Oxford in 1966, but ill health forced him to resign in 1968. He spent his final years with his third wife, Claire, and their four daughters in the Suffolk village of Long Melford, writing a guide in 1966 to its magnificent parish church.

Blunden devoted much time to editing, biography, and criticism. His editions of John Clare in 1920 (with Alan Porter) and of Ivor *Gurney in 1954 performed for them the service he had rendered Owen in 1931. His most important studies were of writers major and minor who flourished between the later seventeenth and mid-nineteenth centuries. He had a particular affection for Shelley, Keats, Lamb, Leigh Hunt, their friends and, among later authors, Thomas *Hardy.

Yet it is by his poetry that he will be longest remembered. In his preface to his 1930 collection he spoke of the Great War as an experience so early 'as to mould and colour the poetry throughout this book'. It continued to do so throughout all his poetry. His other major theme was the English countryside in which he was born and to which he returned after his wanderings. See *Poems of Many Years*, ed. Rupert Hart-Davis (Collins, 1957); *The Poetry of Edmund Blunden*, by Michael Thorpe (Bridge, 1971); *Selected Poems*, ed. Robyn Marsack (Carcanet, 1982).   JPr

Bly, Robert (1926–) An important figure in contemporary American poetry—because of his own writings, because of his influence on such poets as James *Wright, and because of his prominence as a public figure. Bly was born on a farm in western Minnesota and, though he graduated from Harvard University and has given poetry readings and attended conferences all over the United States and in Scandinavia, has lived all his life in Minnesota. He is the author of many volumes of poetry—ranging from *Silence in the Snowy Fields* (Wesleyan University Press, 1962; Cape, 1967) to *Eating the Honey of Words: New and Selected Poems* (Harper, 1999)—and was the founding editor of a magazine called, depending upon the decade, *The Fifties*, *The Sixties*, and *The Seventies*. The magazine was the chief vehicle for the expression of his ideas about poetry during the time of its existence. Bly presented his ideas in essays (at least one per issue) written by himself. Perhaps most important among these are those on such younger American poets as Louis *Simpson, Donald *Hall, W. S. *Merwin, John *Logan, Gary *Snyder, James *Dickey, and James *Wright, that Bly printed under the pseudonym 'Crunk'.

At times the figure of Bly as teacher, preacher, and reformer has seemed to dominate that of Bly the poet. The public donation of his National Book Award money (received in honour of *The Light Around the Body* (Harper) in 1968) to the anti-war group Resistance was an entirely typical gesture for Bly; much of his poetry is outwardly political, a result largely of his concern over the war in Vietnam.

Bly has always tended to view the world in terms of dualities, polarities. Throughout his career he has argued, with an almost Messianic fervour, that there exists an opposition between the poetry of the Cartesian mind—logical, empirical, straightforward, businesslike—and the poetry of the subconscious mind. He strongly feels that the former type is characteristic of the American literary tradition, just as Cartesian thought is typical of the American mind; thus his programme of searching out and translating the work of exemplars of the latter type—Neruda, Tranströmer, Jiménez, Vallejo, Trakl, and others.

It is largely because of Bly's efforts in this direction that America has recently had a poetry of the '*deep image'—an image that comes from the unconscious mind and that communicates a meaning that is not logical. Such images create bridges between the two layers of the mind, making them one: 'We are approaching sleep:...|... a tunnel softly hurtling into darkness.' In the outer world, too, Bly sees dualities; just as man's mind has both its conscious and unconscious aspects, so the natural world has both its physical and its spiritual aspects: in the poem 'Driving Toward the Lac Qui Parle River' are soybeans 'breathing on all sides', water 'kneeling in the moonlight', and lamplight falling 'on all fours on the grass'. The desire to unite all these elements is the major impetus behind both Bly's poetry and his public career. Though predominantly good-natured, even humorous, in his writings, Bly has his more sombre side, as can be seen in his volume *The Man in the Black Coat Turns* (Doubleday, 1981; Penguin, 1983).

With his best-selling Jungian study *Iron John* (Addison-Wesley, 1990) Bly has more recently become known as a leading figure in the American 'men's movement', advocating a mythopoetic reassertion of male identity after feminism. His influential prose poems were partly collected in 1992 as *What Have I Ever Lost By Dying?* and a selection of his many translations as *The Winged Energy of Delight* in 2004. *Morning Poems* (1997), which saw Bly follow William *Stafford in writing a poem every day, is widely considered to be one of his best later books. Since *The Night Abraham Called to the Stars* (2001) Bly has composed extensively in an adapted 'American' form of the Middle Eastern ghazal, including a number of poems in protest at the Iraq war. See also *My Sentence Was a Thousand Years of Joy* (2006—all Harper) and *Talking into the Ear of a Donkey* (Norton, 2011).

For criticism see Howard Nelson, *Robert Bly: An Introduction to the Poetry* (Columbia University Press, 1984), Richard Jones and Kate Daniels (eds.), *Of Solitude and Silence: Writings on Robert Bly* (Beacon Press, 1981), and Joyce Peseroff (ed.), *Robert Bly: When Sleepers Awake* (University of Michigan Press, 1984).   PS*

Boey, Kim Cheng (1965–) Born in Singapore, Boey studied English Literature at the National University of Singapore, German Studies at Murnau, and attended the International Writing Program at the University of Iowa. He has indicated the importance to his work of a broad international tradition of poetry-as-wisdom, rooted in personal encounter with the world, from Seamus *Heaney to Rilke, Cavafy, and Du Fu. Boey's early collections *Somewhere Bound* (1989), which won the National Book Development Councils Book Award for Poetry, *Another Place* (1992—both Time), and *Days of No Name* (EPB, 1996) were all well-received. But they also charted his growing disillusionment with modern Singaporean society. In 1997 he emigrated to Australia, where he teaches at the University of Newcastle. It was a decade until his fourth collection, *After the Fire: New and Selected Poems* (firstfruits, 2006). See also *Between Stations* (Giramondo, 2009), a collection of travel essays.   JNT

Bogan, Louise (1897–1970) One of three children, Bogan was born in Maine to parents of Irish descent and spent her early life in a series of New England mill towns, victimized by parental battles. She would lose one brother to the First World War, and the other to alcoholism at the age of 33. She began writing poetry as a 'life-saving process' at the Girls' Latin School in Boston, and went on to Boston University. She won a scholarship to Radcliffe but married Curt Alexander instead, accompanying him as an army wife to Panama in 1917, where her daughter Mathilde was born. In 1919 she left Alexander, who died a year later, and moved to Manhattan to pursue a literary career. She married Raymond Holden, an affluent poet and novelist, in 1925, but they were separated by 1934 and divorced in 1937.

Bogan's first three collections of verse, *Body of This Death* (1923), *Dark Summer* (1929), and *The Sleeping Fury* (1937), presented the melancholy insights of a strict formalist much influenced by W. B. *Yeats but lacking his genius. Even her most successful lyrics, such as 'Medusa', 'Knowledge', and 'Women', suffer from a remote fastidiousness and relentless intellectuality, though these same qualities helped make her an acute and important poetry critic. Starting in the 1930s and continuing until her death, she wrote most of *The New Yorker*'s poetry reviews. A number of these appeared in *Selected Criticism: Poetry and Prose* (1955) and doubtless underlay *Achievement in American Poetry, 1900–1950* (1951), her incisive critique of modernism's variegated impact on the poets of her era.

Bogan's *Poems and New Poems* (1941) and *Collected Poems 1923–1953* (1954) failed to generate the sort of broad acclaim she thought they deserved, although she did share the 1954 Bollingen Prize with Léonie *Adams. Her last years were harrowed by several bouts of clinical depression, and she died alone in her apartment from a coronary occlusion early in the morning of 4 February 1970.

Her poetry is available in *The Blue Estuaries: Poems, 1923–1968* (Farrar, Straus, 1968; repr. Octagon, 1975), and much of her criticism in *A Poet's Alphabet: Reflections on the Literary Art and Vocation*, ed. Robert Phelps and Ruth Limmer (McGraw-Hill, 1970).

See also *What the Woman Lived: Selected Letters of Louise Bogan 1920–1970*, ed. Ruth Limmer (Harcourt Brace Jovanovich, 1973) and *Louise Bogan: A Portrait* (Knopf, 1985), by Elizabeth Frank.   EB

Bök, Christian (1966–) Born in Toronto, Bök claims to have been christened Christian Book, but changed the spelling to 'avoid unseemly confusion with the Bible'. He studied at York University, Toronto, and teaches on the Creative Writing faculty at the University of Calgary.

Bök's first book, *Crystallography* (1994; revd. edn., 2003), announced his interest in the poetics of science—the title literally means 'lucid writing'. Concrete poems and quasi-encyclopaedic apparatus present the language of geology itself as the subject of ludic investigation ('a fractal is a fatal arc'). The years until *Eunoia* (2001; upgraded edn., 2009—both Coach House) were spent reading the dictionary repeatedly in order to compose five chapters of poetic prose, each obeying the *Oulipian imperative of a single vowel. The book won the Griffin Poetry Prize and became a bestseller in Canada and Britain.

Bök is a fascinated advocate of the history of *conceptual processes in avant-garde poetry. 'A', the first chapter of *Eunoia*, is dedicated to 'Dada bard' Hans Arp. He has also given performances of Dada poems, such as Kurt Schwitters' *Ursonate. Pataphysics: The Poetics of an Imaginary Science* (Northwestern University Press, 2001) is his study of the pseudoscience invented by Alfred Jarry. Since 2003, he has been working on *The Xenotext*, a pair of mirrored sonnets to be encoded as DNA in a bacterium: see 'The Xenotext Experiment' (2008) in volume 5, issue 2 of the journal *SCRIPTed*.   JNT

Boland, Eavan (Aisling) (1944–) The youngest daughter of the painter Frances Kelly and the Irish diplomat F. H. Boland. Though born in Dublin, her school-days were in the main passed outside Ireland—in London, where her father was Irish Ambassador, and in New York, where he was Representative at the United Nations. In 1966 she graduated in English from Trinity College Dublin, and lectured there until 1968. She has taught creative writing in Ireland and in America, and collaborated with the actor Micheál MacLiammóir on a study of W. B. *Yeats. A noted reviewer and award-winning broadcaster, she is a member of the Irish Academy of Letters, and lives in Dublin and the United States, where she is a Professor of English at Stanford University.

New Territory (Allen Figgis, 1967) dealt largely with what it might mean to be a poet, and was remarkable for suppleness and ingenuity of rhythm. It included translations from the Irish; she has since made distinguished verse translations after Horace, Mayakovsky, and Nelly Sachs. During the 1970s she took on themes of Irish identity, engaging with history and with the marginalization of women, enlarging and complicating lyric forms to accommodate voices of oppression and insult alongside protest against indignity. In the 1980s her poetry began a disengagement from these wider social concerns, focusing instead on details of home-making and domesticity, politics giving way to issues of aesthetics and philosophy. Selected Poems (Carcanet, 1989) provides an overview of her early work, but is meagre in its representation of the translations which appeared in The War Horse (Gollancz, 1975).

Boland's revised Collected Poems in 1995 (Carcanet), published in the States as An Origin Like Water (Norton, 1996), was accompanied by a critical memoir, Object Lessons: The Life of the Woman and the Poet in Our Time (Carcanet/Norton). In 2001, with Mark *Strand, she edited The Making of a Poem (Norton), a handbook of poetic forms. She has also translated an anthology of German-speaking women poets from the twentieth century, After Every War (Princeton University Press, 2004), and made a selection of Charlotte *Mew's poetry (Carcanet, 2008). See New Collected Poems (Carcanet, 2005; Norton, 2008), which restores first printings without revision, and

Eavan Boland: A Sourcebook, ed. Jody Allen Randolph (Carcanet, 2007), which includes a number of her uncollected essays. A Journey with Two Maps: Becoming a Woman Poet (Carcanet/Norton, 2011), a sequel to Object Lessons, features her 'Letter to a Young Woman Poet'.   PL*

Bonney, Sean (1969–) Born in Brighton and raised in Hull. He then settled in London, where he was for many years a regular attendee of Bob *Cobbing's Writers Forum workshops.

Much of Bonney's work has a visual element to it, and is influenced by Cobbing in its treatment of the page as a score for performance. Baudelaire in English (Veer, 2008) is notably produced on a typewriter, with nonstandard lineation, palimpsestic layering of words and lines, and esoteric use of punctuation. Bonney is also known for his energetic, breathless live performances, reflecting his interest in punk music.

Bonney's work engages with political issues, in particular those pertaining to class struggle, and his poetry can be described as socialist in its representation of contemporary British society. It is also concerned with the history of visionary, revolutionary poets such as William Blake and the French Symbolists: Baudelaire in English consists of a series of homophonic and pseudo-translations, while Happiness (Unkant, 2011) responds to the poems and politics of Arthur Rimbaud. Bonney's publications include Blade Pitch Control Unit (Salt, 2005), Document (Barque, 2008), and The Commons (Openned, 2011). See also Don't Start Me Talking: Conversations With Contemporary Poets (Salt, 2006), ed. Tim Allen and Andrew Duncan.   SRO

Booth, Philip (1925–2007) Born in Hanover, New Hampshire. His father was a professor at Dartmouth College, and Booth grew up in an environment both bookish and athletic. He was a varsity skier at Dartmouth until the Second World War interrupted his undergraduate education. He served in the US Army Air Force, 1944–5, then returned to Dartmouth, where he was taught by Robert *Frost, and took his AB in 1948. The following year he received his Master's degree from Columbia University. He taught at Bowdoin, Dartmouth, Wellesley, and finally Syracuse University, where he remained from 1961 until his retirement twenty-five years later as senior poet in the creative writing programme. He lived for many years in Castine, Maine, in the house that belonged to his family for five generations.

Booth's first collection, *Letter from a Distant Land*, appeared in 1957, when the poet was 32. It won the Lamont Poetry Prize. It was characteristic of the seven collections which were to follow. Written in a spare and colloquial style, the poems fell into short lines as laconic as New England conversation. The Maine Coast was a metaphor for man living on the edge. In Booth's later books the ebb and flow of tides become associated with the give and take of time. *Lifelines: Selected Poems, 1950-1999* (1999), which won the Poet's Prize, contained selections from nine previous volumes, including *Selves* (1990) and *Pairs* (1994—all Viking). See also *Trying to Say It: Outlooks and Insights on How Poems Happen* (University of Michigan Press, 1996).   RSP

Bornholdt, Jenny (1960–) Born in Lower Hutt, Wellington and studied at the University of Wellington with Bill *Manhire. In 2005 she was named the fifth New Zealand Poet Laureate.

Bornholdt's first book was *This Big Face* (Victorian University Press, 1988). Her characteristically dry, conversational treatment of the pleasures and pains of everyday life has been widely admired for the way its homely imagery suddenly reveals wider vistas (an egg in a frying pan 'sounds like distant hooves | crossing a dusty plain'). Such casual freshness, which can take the form of verse or prose, has American examples in view. The long poem 'Confessional' owes more to the *New York School than Robert *Lowell, although it positions its speaker playfully between the two ('I was also thinking about || personal poetry and how it's not given much | time of day any more').

Summer (2003), in which this poem appears, describes her family's stay in France during a Katherine Mansfield fellowship. Bornholdt's other books include *Waiting Shelter* (1991), *These Days* (2000), *The Rocky Shore*, (2008), and *The Hill of Wool* (2011). *Miss New Zealand: Selected Poems* appeared in 1997, and *Mrs Winter's Jump* (2007—all Victoria University Press) collects the poems from her laureate tenure. She was a co-editor, with Mark Williams and her husband, Gregory *O'Brien, of *An Anthology of New Zealand Poetry* (Oxford University Press, 1997).   JNT

Borson, Roo (1952–) Born in Berkeley, California, Borson studied at the University of California, Santa Barbara, Goddard College, Vermont, and the University of British Columbia, where she received an MFA in Creative Writing. She has taught, held writing residencies, and travelled frequently in Australia. With her partner, the poet Kim Maltman, she performs in the collaborative poetry group Pain Not Bread. See *Introduction to the Introduction to Wang Wei* (Brick, 2000).

The haiku-like imagery of Borson's landscapes can evoke 'Abundance' as 'A field without a man in it. | A rusted plow filling with snow'. Her first book, *Landfall* (Fiddlehead Poetry, 1977) was followed in 1980 by two collections, *Rain* (Penumbra) and *In the Smoky Light of the Fields* (Three Trees). *The Whole Night, Coming Home* (McClelland & Stewart, 1984) and *Night Walk: Selected Poems* (Oxford University Press, 1994) were both nominated for the Governor General's Award, which Borson won with *Short Journey Upriver Towards Oishida* (2004), also awarded the 2005 Griffin Poetry Prize. Her latest volume is *Rain; Road; An Open Boat* (2012—both McClelland & Stewart), published in Australia by Random House.   JNT

Boruch, Marianne (1950–) Grew up in Chicago and studied at the University of Massachusetts with James *Tate. She teaches writing at Purdue University and Warren Wilson College, and has held several prestigious residencies and fellowships. Her collections include *View from*

the Gazebo (1985), *Descendant* (1989—both Wesleyan University Press), *Poems: New and Selected* (Oberlin, 2004), and *Grace, Fallen from* (Wesleyan University Press, 2008). In 2011 she published a memoir, *The Glimpse Traveler* (Indiana University Press) and her seventh book of poems, *The Book of Hours* (Copper Canyon), a sequence of sixteen-line poems arranged in eight groups of eight, which bring a meditative order to the haphazard perceptions of modern life: 'the computer screen, day or night, | illuminated as a manuscript'. See also her two books of critical essays, *Poetry's Old Air* (University of Michigan Press, 1995) and *In the Blue Pharmacy* (Trinity University Press, 2005).   JNT

Bottoms, David (1949–) Born in Canton, Georgia, the only child of a funeral director and a registered nurse. Educated at Mercer University, West Georgia College, and Florida State University, Bottoms became an associate professor of English in 1987 at Georgia State University, where he teaches creative writing.

Bottoms gained critical recognition with his first book of poetry, *Shooting Rats at the Bibb County Dump* (1980), which was chosen by Robert Penn *Warren as winner of the 1979 Walt Whitman Award of the Academy of American Poets. In this work Bottoms draws from his strong Southern background—his childhood in a small town, his life on the road as a bluegrass and country-and-western musician, and his knowledge of the outdoors—to create characters and situations which capture the eccentricity and isolation of many contemporary Southern lives. The voices in his poems are those of the people of his region; images of Southern swamps, creatures, and cultural oddities predominate. His other collections are *In a U-Haul North of Damascus* (1983) and *Under the Vulture-Tree* (1987—all Morrow). He is also the author of two well-received novels, *Any Cold Jordan* (1988) and *Easter Weekend* (1990).

Since *Armored Hearts: Selected and New Poems* (Copper Canyon, 1995) he has published three further collections, all with Copper Canyon Press: *Vagrant Grace*

(1999), *Waltzing Through the Endtime* (2004), and *We Almost Disappear* (2011). Since 2000, he has been Poet Laureate of Georgia.   LRi

Bottrall, Ronald (Francis James) (1906–89) Born in Cornwall. He won a scholarship to Cambridge, and spent his working life abroad. His few successful poems occur amongst a mass of intelligent work which seldom comes into focus. He wrote too rapidly and too much under the influence of *Pound. He was insecure, and tended to rely on the goodwill of other poets to advertise his talents. But these (e.g. *Eliot and *Graves) were only ever half convinced, although there was justice in G. S. *Fraser's remark that they could not all be 'entirely wrong'. He was not 'rediscovered', along with Graves, *Empson, and *Cameron, in the post-war period. *Collected Poems* (Sidgwick & Jackson, 1961) made little impact. His best work is to be found in later volumes, in particular *Poems 1955–1973* (Anvil, 1974), which contains a vivid narrative, 'Talking to the Ceiling', and a number of almost surrealistic short poems. See also *Against a Setting Sun* (Allison & Busby, 1984).   MS-S

Bowering, George (Henry) (1935–) Born in Penticton, British Columbia, and educated in schools in the Okanagan Valley. After high school he served in the RCAF as an aerial photographer (1954–7), then enrolled in the University of British Columbia, where he received a BA in history in 1960 and an MA in English in 1963. While at university Bowering discovered the work of William Carlos *Williams, and readily fell under the influence of the creative theories and compositional practices of the American poets Charles *Olson, Robert *Creeley, and Robert *Duncan. The latter two were visitors to his university in the early 1960s, and Creeley was an adviser on Bowering's creative writing thesis, *Points on the Grid*, which was published in 1964.

Bowering was a founding co-editor of an important avant-garde magazine of poetry *Tish* (1961–3), and from 1964 to 1974 published his own occasional journal, *Imago*. He has also published widely in little magazines and has since 1965 been a contributor to the postmodernist journal, *Open Letter*.

Bowering's creativity has been closely associated with the little-press movement in Canada, while his career as a writer has been nurtured by academic life, with teaching appointments at several universities. He is now professor emeritus at Simon Fraser University in Burnaby, British Columbia.

Since the appearance of his first book of poems, *Sticks and Stones* (Tishbooks, 1963), with a preface by Creeley, Bowering has produced a prolific stream of poetry, prose fiction, and criticism. He won the Governor General's Award for poetry in 1969 for two collections, *Rocky Mountain Foot* (M&S) and *The Gangs of Kosmos* (Anansi). His long poems were collected in *West Window* (General, 1982). A *George Bowering Selected* (McClelland & Stewart) was published in 1993.

The autobiographical *His Life: a Poem* appeared from ECW Press in 2000—see also the later verse diary of a year, *My Darling Nellie Grey* (2010). In 2002, Bowering became an Officer of the Order of Canada, and was named Canada's first Parliamentary Poet Laureate. Work from his tenure is included in *Vermeer's Light, Poems 1996–2005* (2006), as well as an essay on one of his best-known poems, 'Grandfather'. *Changing on the Fly: The Best Lyric Poems of George Bowering* (Raincoast, 2004) was shortlisted for the Griffin Poetry Prize. A second edition of *Kerrisdale Elegies*, his contemporary rewriting of Rilke from 1984, appeared in 2008 (all Talonbooks).

An opinionated yet skilful critic, Bowering has published a small book on the Canadian poet Al *Purdy (1970), and several collections of essays, including *Left Hook* (Raincoast, 2005), and *Horizontal Surfaces* (BookThug, 2010). For more information, including a selected bibliography, see the feature on Bowering in the online magazine *Jacket*, 28 (October 2005).   MG*

Bowering, Marilyn (1949–) Born in Winnipeg, and raised in Victoria, British Columbia. She took her BA and MA degrees at the University of Victoria, where she taught in the creative writing department. She is now a professor at Vancouver Island University.

Bowering's first collection, *The Liberation of Newfoundland* (Fiddlehead, 1973), employs graphic images of whaling to depict the violence implicit in male-female relations. Her next several books continue to break down the boundaries of form through a surreal use of imagery. *The Sunday Before Winter* (General, 1984) offers a good selection from this first phase of her development. After the mid-1980s she turned to poetry of a quasi-historical bent. *Grandfather was a Soldier* (1987) tells of her own journey to the battlefields of the First World War where her grandfather fought. *Calling All the World* (1989—both Porcepic) recounts the story of the dog Laika sent into space by the Soviets in 1957. *Anyone Can See I Love You* (Porcupine's Quill, 1987) offers a first-person portrait of Marilyn Monroe. Her later books of poetry since *Human Bodies: New and Selected Poems* (1999) include *The Alchemy of Happiness* (2003—both Beach Holme), *Green* (2007), and *Soul Mouth* (2012—both Exile). In 1977 Bowering co-edited with David Day the collection *Many Voices: An Anthology of Contemporary Canadian Indian Poetry*. She has also published several well-received novels.   RH

Bowers, Edgar (1924–2000) Born in Georgia, served with the US Army in Europe during the Second World War. He took his BA in 1947 from the University of North Carolina and his PhD in 1953 from Stanford University, where he studied with Yvor *Winters. From 1958 to 1991 he was a professor of English at the University of California, Santa Barbara. His main collections were *The Form of Loss* (1956), *The Astronomers* (1965—both Swallow), *Living Together* (Godine, 1973; Carcanet, 1977), and *For Louis Pasteur* (Princeton University Press, 1989). In 1989 Bowers was awarded the Bollingen Prize.

A poet of great intellectual sophistication and historical awareness, Bowers was perhaps chiefly concerned with the human spirit as it relates to nature and as it expresses itself in different times, places, and cultures. Such earlier poems as 'Aix-la-Chappelle' and 'The Stoic' deal with the Second World War and with the vulnerability of culture in the face of ignorance and violence; such later poems as 'Thirteen Views of Santa Barbara' evoke the beauties of the natural world and speak of the threats posed to them by human indifference and greed. Other poems examine interconnections between durable forms of existence and their transient manifestations in individual lives and events. Certain of these poems (e.g. the 'Autumn Shade' sequence) explore the relationship between the real self, which is necessarily involved in the corruptions and disappointments of life, and an ideal self, which serves as an exemplar to which the real aspires but which it can never fully attain.

Bowers wrote in traditional forms, which he employed with unmannered dexterity. The earlier work generally features rhymed stanzas, whereas the later work is principally in blank verse. If the earlier poems, such as the eerily beautiful 'Astronomers of Mont Blanc', are striking in their concentration, the later work shows a greater range of circumstantial detail.

See *Collected Poems* (Knopf, 1997). Among critical studies are those in Yvor Winters's *Forms of Discovery* (Swallow, 1967) and Richard Howard's *Alone with America* (Atheneum, 1969).   TS

Boyle, Charles (1951–) Born in Leeds and educated at Loretto School and St John's College, Cambridge, where he graduated in English in 1972. He taught English first in a Sheffield comprehensive school and then in North Africa, in Cairo and Rabat (1976–9). North African subjects appeared in his first collection, *Affinities* (1977), and Boyle returned to them in *House of Cards* (1982) and in *Sleeping Rough* (1987). Previously he had appeared in the anthology *Ten English Poets*, edited in 1976 by Michael Schmidt; although his empiricism is characteristically English, Boyle's ironic, urbane poetry of instability and alienation has more in common with the work of Michael *Hofmann and Stephen *Romer than with that of the writers he originally appeared with. He also has affinities with the American poet Louis *Simpson and the short-story writer Frederick Barthelme. Since 1980 he has been married to the painter Madeleine Strindberg and living in London, where he has worked as an editor with Time-Life Books and Faber and Faber. After *The Very Man* (1993—all Carcanet) he had two further collections with Faber: *Paleface* (1996) and *The Age of Cardboard and String* (2001) which was nominated for the T.S. Eliot and Whitbread prizes. He now runs the small press CB Editions, through which he has published prose under the *noms de plume* 'Jack Robinson' and 'Jennie Walker' (2011).   MHu

Brackenbury, Alison (1953–) Born in Lincolnshire and educated at Brigg High School and St Hugh's College, Oxford, where she read English. Since 1976 she has lived on the outskirts of Cheltenham, with her husband and daughter, and now works in the family electroplating business.

Alison Brackenbury won a Gregory Award in 1981. She is a prolific poet whose first Carcanet collections, *Dreams of Power* (1981), *Breaking Ground* (1984), and *Christmas Roses* (1988), were all twice as long as the average collection. The volumes have a diffuse feel, but she has written a clutch of poems which place her firmly in the tradition of Edward *Thomas, Ivor *Gurney, and more recently P. J. *Kavanagh and E. J. *Scovell. Unfashionably for a poet who emerged in the urban Eighties, she is a countrywoman, apparently uninterested in the urban *Zeitgeist*. Like *Larkin, she writes of provincial lives—people who work in shops, watch a once-desired house grow derelict, drive home on wet Friday nights and find a frog in the road, balance the books at home—and these neglected byways become luminous in her poetry.

Stylistically, Brackenbury's poems have a strong rhythmic momentum, and a reek of the pathos of things: the hot dust of electric fires, forlorn assemblages of junk, an industrial piggery, are as familiar presences in her work as fields and horses. But her imagination is also stirred by travel, reading, and music, and she regularly writes documentary poems for national radio. Since *Selected*

Poems (1991) Brackenbury has published *1829* (1995), *After Beethoven* (2000), *Bricks and Ballads* (2004), and *Singing in the Dark* (2008—all Carcanet).   PF*

Brady, Andrea (1974–   ) Born in Philadelphia, Brady studied at Columbia University and the University of Cambridge, and has lived in Britain since 1997. She counts among her influences Renaissance and early modern poetry, which she teaches at Queen Mary, University of London, as well as the *New York and *Cambridge avant-gardes. She herself has been influential not only through her poetry but also through her establishment of Archive of the Now, a print and audio archive of innovative poetry, and as co-founder and editor, with Keston *Sutherland, of Barque Press. As an early modern scholar, she has also published two critical works, *English Funerary Elegy in the Seventeenth Century: Laws in Mourning* (Palgrave, 2006), and, co-edited with Emily Butterworth, *The Uses of the Future in Early Modern Europe* (Routledge, 2009).

Her first collection, *Vacation of a Lifetime* (Salt, 2001), interrogates Western representations and considers contrary truths through a dense, constantly shifting lyricism whose momentum conveys urgency. This concern takes another tack in *Embrace* (Object Permanence, 2005), where beauty and violence appear inseparable. Her more recent work manifests new directions, as their full titles suggest: *Wildfire: A Verse Essay on Obscurity and Illumination* (Krupskaya, 2010) and *Mutability: Scripts for Infancy* (Seagull, 2012)—namely the infancy of her daughter, Ayla. In *Mutability*, Brady alternates between taut lyric poems and exquisite prose accounts, dated like journal entries, that consider both mother's and child's experiences, physically and metaphysically. As Brady remarks, 'Ayla is the beginning of that thought which starts from her'.   CE

Brand, Dionne (1953–   ) Born in Trinidad and moved to Canada in 1970, where she studied at the University of Toronto. She is a poet, novelist, film-maker and essayist, Professor of English at the University

of Guelph and third Poet Laureate of Toronto (2009–12). Brand's first collections were '*Fore Day Morning* (Khoisan Artists, 1978) and, for children, *Earth Magic* (Kids Can, 1979). Political activism informs her 1980s work, including *Chronicles of the Hostile Sun* (Williams-Wallace, 1984), on the invasion of Grenada while she was working for the revolutionary government. In Canada, she was a founding editor of the black women's newspaper, *Our Lives*. The essays in *Bread Out of Stone* (Coach House, 1994) reflect on her life as a black lesbian writer and community organizer in Toronto. *No Language Is Neutral* (Coach House, 1990; revd. edn., McClelland & Stewart, 1998) returned to Trinidad—the title quotes Derek *Walcott's *Midsummer*—and announced a new, urgently wide-reaching style. As she writes of Canada in *Land to Light On* (McClelland & Stewart, 1997): 'It | always takes long to come to what you have to say, you have to | sweep this stretch of land up around your feet and point to the | signs'.

Brand's 1996 documentary, *Listening for Something*, records a conversation with Adrienne *Rich. *Fierce Departures* is a selection of her poetry since the 1990s (Wilfrid Laurier University Press, 2009). Her first novel was *In Another Place, Not Here* (Knopf, 1996) and in 2010 she published *Ossuaries*, a novel in verse (McClelland & Stewart).   JNT

Brandt, Di (1952–   ) Born and raised in Manitoba, Brandt grew up in a Mennonite farming village. She studied at the universities of Manitoba and Toronto, and has taught English at the University of Winnipeg. She published her PhD thesis as *Wild Mother Dancing: Maternal Narrative in Canadian Literature* (University of Manitoba Press, 1993) and is now a professor of creative writing at Brandon University.

A feminist poet who has often written about family relationships, Brandt's first collection was *questions i asked my mother* (1987). It was followed by *Agnes in the sky* (1990—both Turnstone), *mother, not mother* (Mercury, 1992), and *Jerusalem, beloved* (Turnstone, 1995). *Now You Care* (Coach House, 2003), which develops her work in the direction of ecopoetics, was shortlisted for several major Canadian poetry prizes. *Speaking of Power* (Wilfrid Laurier University Press, 2006) is a selection edited with an introduction by Tanis MacDonald and an afterword by Brandt. See also *Dancing Naked: Narrative Strategies for Writing Across Centuries* (Mercury, 1996).   JNT

Brasch, Charles (1909–73) Born into an established mercantile family in Dunedin, and educated at Waitaki Boys' High School and St John's College, Oxford. He lived and worked overseas from 1931 to 1946, when he returned to permanent residence in New Zealand.

His first three books of poetry—*The Land and the People* (1939), *Disputed Ground, Poems*, 1939–45 (1948), and *The Estate and other poems* (1957) associate him with that group of poets who were exploring issues of national identity and treating the concerns of the settler-migrant establishing a European society in New Zealand. Brasch's own verse style had a conservative reticence that distinguished it from some of the more exuberant and experimental work of his contemporaries. His last three books spanning the 1960s—*Ambulando* (1964), *Not Far Off* (1969), and the posthumously published *Home Ground* (1974)—show an innovative change of poetic style and direction, and a new voice, less discursive, speaking of personal themes with a distinctly modernist tone.

As important as his verse was Brasch's editorship of the quarterly *Landfall*, which he established in 1947 and edited for its first eighty issues. The periodical would be 'distinctly of New Zealand without being parochial', and literary, but not solely literary. It would be like *Horizon*, which Brasch read and admired, but guided, as the *Criterion* was and, Brasch felt, *Horizon* was not, by 'general ideas' about 'imaginative truth ... truth in history, philosophy, religion'.

The seriousness, and at the same time an element of the grandiose and the vague in Brasch's commitment, helps to explain both *Landfall*'s importance and its limits under his guidance. It became without a doubt the best literary periodical New Zealand has ever had. It was the focus for liter-

ary performance and debate, a platform and a means by which writers scattered down the length of the two islands could get to know one another's work. The standard was always high, without ever being adventurous. Anything of importance published in or by New Zealand writers was at least intelligently reviewed, and sometimes discussed at length. Almost every New Zealand writer of consequence during the Fifties and Sixties appeared there. But many young writers chafed against the authority of *Landfall*, resenting what they saw as Brasch's prissiness, his solemnity, his inflexibility.

A man of wide cultural interests, he was a generous benefactor of the arts, particularly in his home city Dunedin. See *Collected Poems*, ed. Alan Roddick, (Oxford University Press, 1984), and Brasch's autobiography to 1947, *Indirections* (Oxford University Press, 1980). See also James Bertram, *Charles Brasch* (Oxford University Press, 1976).   WSB/CKS*

Brathwaite, E. K. (Edward Kamau) (1930–) Born Lawson Edward Brathwaite in Bridgetown, Barbados. He was educated at Harrison College, and at Pembroke College, Cambridge (on an island scholarship), where he read history. His doctoral dissertation at Sussex University was on *The Development of Creole Society in Jamaica, 1770–1820* (Oxford University Press, 1971). From 1955 to 1962 he taught in Ghana, which was a great formative experience for a poet who identifies so strongly with his African roots. He was subsequently professor of Social and Cultural History at the University of the West Indies and latterly Professor of Comparative Literature at New York University. In 1994 he was awarded the Neustadt International Prize for Literature, and in 2006 a Gold Musgrave Medal from the Institute of Jamaica.

His poetic techniques include allusiveness, loosely linked imagery, and multiple voices. In this, he resembles early modernists like *Eliot and *Pound, but where they detected disintegration and decay in Western civilization, Brathwaite seeks to revive, and synthesize with other strands, African traditions and culture. Sections in dialect and rhythms derived from jazz further enrich his poetry. *The Arrivants* (Oxford University Press, 1973) is generally considered to be his finest work. Subtitled 'A New World Trilogy', it combines three earlier volumes, *Rights of Passage* (1967), *Masks* (1968), and *Islands* (1969). Expansive in its range, both historical and stylistic, the trilogy can be described as an open-ended epic of the black diaspora; hence, of the African contribution to the varied cultures and societies of the Americas.

Mother Poem (1977), and *Sun Poem* (1982) and *X-Self* (1987) comprise a second trilogy, recast into Brathwaite's later 'Sycorax Video Style', with its word-processed 'calibanisms', and collected as *Ancestors* in 2001 (New Directions). *Third World Poems* (Longman, 1983) is mainly a selection from previous volumes. A revised edition of *Black + Blues* (Casa de las Américas, 1979) appeared in the USA in 1995 (New Directions). Since *Middle Passages* (Bloodaxe, 1991; New Directions, 1993), his books include *Words Need Love Too* (House of Nehesi, 2000; Salt, 2004), *Born to Slow Horses* (2005), which won the Griffin International Poetry Prize, and *Elegguas* (2010—both Wesleyan University Press). *The Zea Mexican Diary* (1993), Brathwaite's response to the death of his wife in 1986, was republished by University of Wisconsin Press in 2003.

Brathwaite's views on dialect are expounded in *History of the Voice: The Development of Nation Language in Anglophone Caribbean Poetry* (New Beacon, 1984). The later two-volume *Magical Realism* is an experimental study of the literary genre as 'a black caribbean blues perspective on post-cosmological disruption' (Savacou North, 2002). See Stewart Brown, *The Art of Kamau Brathwaite* (Seren, 1995) and also the expanded transcript of Brathwaite's *Conversations with Nathaniel Mackey* (We Press, 1999). Charles W. Pollard, *New World Modernisms* (University of Virginia Press, 2004) discusses Brathwaite's achievement in relation to Derek *Walcott and T. S. *Eliot.   MR*

Braun, Richard Emil (1934–   ) A native of Detroit, took a master's degree in Latin from the University of Michigan and a doctorate from the University of Texas. He taught classics for many years at the University of Alberta in Canada, and is thus neither fish nor fowl in either country. He is, in addition, a difficult poet in offbeat, even macabre ways.

Braun is often a narrative poet, but the stories he tells are enigmatic. The interests of his lyrics are similarly unconventional. Things on their surfaces appear to be normal; details are crystalline, hard-edged— yet at the peripheries of vision existential terrors loom.

These are features of Braun's first three collections, *Companions to Your Doom* (n.p. 1961), *Children Passing* (University of Texas, 1962), and *Bad Land* (Jargon Society, 1971). In his fourth volume, *The Foreclosure* (University of Illinois Press, 1972), he began to modify the nightmare, modulating to a point where it was not so overtly surreal, and the effects became more subtle. He has also published translations of Euripides, Persius, and Sophocles. His later collections are *Last Man In* (Jargon Society, 1990) and *The Snow Man is No One* (Corriedale, 2001).   LT

Breeze, Jean 'Binta' (1957–   ) Born in Jamaica, Breeze was a contemporary of Michael *Smith at the Jamaican School of Drama, and is acknowledged as the first female *dub poet of that generation. She has worked as an actress, scriptwriter, director, and lecturer in Theatre Studies, and has also released several recordings of her work. In 1986 she moved to London. She now lives in Leicester and is a contributing editor of *Critical Quarterly* magazine.

Breeze has spoken publicly about her experience of schizophrenia, and mental illness is also treated dramatically in her poetry. The title poem of her debut collection, *Riddym Ravings* (Race Today, 1998), is a lament subtitled 'The Mad Woman's Poem' which describes the repeated harassment of the speaker by 'de dactar and de lanlord'. Breeze's use of the dramatic monologue as a form for social comment and broad humour has been influential on later performance poets such as Patience *Agbabi: see 'The Wife of Bath Speaks in

Brixton Market'. Her later collections include *Spring Cleaning* (Virago, 1992), *On the Edge of an Island* (1997), *The Arrival of Brighteye* (2000), *The Fifth Figure: A Poet's Tale* (2006—all Bloodaxe), a personal history of five generations of Jamaican women told in poetry and prose. In 2011, Bloodaxe published *Third World Girl*, a selected poems accompanied by a DVD of Breeze's live performances and an interview. She received an MBE in 2012.   JNT

Brennan, Christopher (1870–1932) Born in Sydney, the son of an Irish brewery worker, was educated by Jesuits as a scholarship boy and at the University of Sydney. He won a fellowship to the University of Berlin, became engaged to his landlady's daughter while there, and discovered the poetry of Mallarmé, which was the most important influence on his work. Returning to Sydney, he worked for a decade in the public library, passed over for appointment to the university even though his scholarship was such that he could have 'graced', a colleague later said, the chairs of philosophy, classics, modern languages, or literature in any institution. His drunkenness, 'immoral' poems, and unconventional behaviour were already held against him. When he was eventually appointed professor of German and comparative literature, Brennan's lectures were hugely popular, but before long had to be scheduled for early in the day, because of his drinking.

Three years after his return, Brennan's fiancée came to Australia. They were married and had four children, but eventually Brennan left home to live in sailors' hotels. With his family he was something of a tyrant, but in Sydney's bohemia he was sought after for his wit, erudition, and ebullience. A massive figure, with a great hooked nose and vast meerschaum pipe, he became the legend of a thousand brilliant and drunken nights; conversing in, quoting from, construing six languages. When the university heard that he had deserted his family and was living with a much younger woman he was dismissed, but the blow came some months after his companion had been killed, run down by a tram, and when Brennan was still in the depths of grief. From then on he degenerated rapidly, becoming filthy and gross, and living without any support except charitable contributions. Certain Catholic clergy helped, giving him occasional teaching work, and old friends bought him drinks and food so as to hear his often still-marvellous talk. He lived amongst the *demi-monde* of Kings Cross, moving between the prostitutes and the nuns, and finally returned to the Church, which he had dismissed since schooldays, as he was dying.

The main body of Brennan's work is in *Poems 1913*, a sometimes contrived *livre composé*, which records his Symbolist quest for an absolute reality, an intimation of which will transform this world for the initiate. Such an experience is called, after Mallarmé, 'Eden'. Mallarmé wrote admiringly to him ('Poet, wonderful Poet') in response to the gift of Brennan's first book, and chose to defend him against a hostile Parisian reviewer. Brennan's poems often have fresh, Whitmanesque flourishes as their opening lines—'Once, when the sunburst flew'; 'My heart was wandering in the sands'; 'The banners of the king unfold'; 'I saw my life as whitest flame'; 'O life, O radiance'; 'Fire in the heavens, and fire along the hills'—but the promise, again and again, fails, lost in tangled syntax, portentousness, archaism, generalizations, and ponderous, sub-Miltonic rhetoric.

His best poem, by far, is 'The Wanderer', in which the quest for an Absolute is abandoned, and the material world and its sufferings accepted with a calm resignation. The language in the sequence is generally less pretentious and the rhythm more supple than in anything else that Brennan wrote. There are perhaps four or five other poems, lyrics, in which something of his potential was realized.

Frank Kermode has written appreciatively of 'The Wanderer'; Clive James, in his book of essays, *Snakecharmers in Texas* (1989) is interested by Brennan but disappointed by the poetry; Axel Clark's *Christopher Brennan* (1980) is the definitive biography; and G. A. Wilkes's *New Perspectives on Brennan's Poetry* (1953) is an outstanding study. *Selected Poems* (Angus &

Robertson, 1992) includes *Poems 1913* together with letters between Brennan and Mallarmé. The anthology *Christopher Brennan* (University of Queensland Press, 1984), edited by Terry Sturm, contains, as well as the poetry, selections of Brennan's still-excellent literary criticism on the Symbolist movement. RGr

Brew, (O. H.) Kwesi (1928–2007) Born in Cape Coast, of an old Gold Coast family whose connections with the Fante-speaking area of what is now central Ghana go back as far as 1745. Educated locally, he embarked on a career as diplomat, serving in his country's foreign service in Britain, France, India, and Germany. The title of his volume of 1968, *Shadows of Laughter* (Longmans), suggests the ambience of his verse, which is of a pictorialism etched by menace. The poetry is multivalent, subtly ambiguous. In 'The Executions Dream' he employs the almost Daliesque image of a disembodied eye sticky in the palm of a hand, 'Glittering, wet and sickening | Like a dull onyx of thorns'. The poem is a supplication, but whether from the victim to his executioner or the executioner to his victim we are not sure. In 'Plea for Mercy' a group of wanderers return to an ancestral shrine, but their faith is unrewarded, their requests unheard. In 'Locusts' the brilliant pink of an approaching swarm presages ruin, while in 'Questions of Our Time' the inquiries of the title are addressed, not as custom would demand to an elder, but to a child playing in the dust, who answers gnomically 'perhaps'. Most famously, in 'The Sea Eats our Lands', Brew evokes the continual erosion of the sea coast around Keta in Eweland in the country's eastern region. A frequent theme is that of return, but it is to a domain blasted by poverty and decimated by ruin. A reductionist account of his verse would interpret it as an expression of the destruction of Ghana's national aspirations at the hands of her immediately postcolonial governments, but the delicacy and remoteness with which these anxieties are expressed carry his work well beyond the preoccupations of any one period or stage of political growth. Brew was a traveller who wrote about home, a pessimist

whose sadness is redeemed by beauty, and a religious poet whose appeals are addressed to shrines which lie empty. His later publications, in Ghana, were *Return of No Return* (Afram, 1995), on the history of slavery, and *The Clan of the Leopard* (Anansesem, 1996). RF

Brewster, Elizabeth (1922–) Born in the small lumber town of Chimpman, New Brunswick. With Alfred *Bailey, she was involved in founding *The Fiddlehead* magazine. She received her first degree at the University of New Brunswick and her PhD at the University of Indiana in 1962. For many years she worked as a librarian. In 1972 she joined the English department at the University of Saskatchewan, where she taught until 1990. From the time she began publishing in the 1940s, Brewster has taken for her subject-matter the small events of everyday life. In her first poems she employed rhymed quatrains, but soon forsook rhyme for free verse and the verse tale. Frequently her short stories in verse portray people isolated within their communities by their inability to express themselves. Her earlier poetry resembles that of the eighteenth-century English poet George Crabbe, on whom she wrote her doctoral dissertation. During the 1960s she increasingly turned to events in her own life as her main subject. Her usual procedure is to voice a personal anxiety and then undermine its importance by placing it in the wider human context.

A good selection of her work can be found in the two-volume *Selected Poems* (*1944–1977* and *1977–1984*: Oberon, 1985). Brewster has also written two novels, *The Sisters* (1974) and *Junction* (1983), as well as three short-story collections, *It's Easy to Fall on the Ice* (1977), *A House Full of Women* (1983), and *Visitations* (1987). Paul Denham's 'Speeding Towards Strange Destinations: A Conversation with Elizabeth Brewster', in *Essays on Canadian Writing*, 18/19 (Summer/Fall 1980) offers a good introduction to Brewster's poetry. In the 1990s, she published two autobiographical volumes: *The Invention of Truth* (1991) and *Away from Home* (1995). In 2001, Brewster was made a Member of the

Order of Canada, and won the Saskatchewan Book Award for Poetry in 2003 with *Jacob's Dream* (2002). See *Collected Poems of Elizabeth Brewster*, in two volumes (2003–4—all Oberon).   RBH

Bridges, Robert (1844–1930) Son of a landowner, was born in Walmer, Kent, and educated at Eton and Corpus Christi College, Oxford, where he first met Gerard Manley Hopkins. Bridges trained to be a medical doctor at St Bartholomew's Hospital, London, and after working as a physician at other London hospitals he retired to Yattenden, Berkshire, in 1881. From 1907 until his death he lived at Boar's Hill, Oxfordshire. In 1913 he succeeded Alfred Austin as Poet Laureate.

Though at Yattenden he wrote long poems (*Prometheus the Firegiver*, 1883, and *Eros and Psyche*, 1885) and eight plays (1885–94), his early reputation was built on his short poems. These, almost devoid of memorable meaning or strong feeling, are beautifully crafted and display a rare gift for verbal melody; as *Yeats wrote of one of them: 'Every metaphor, every thought a commonplace, emptiness everywhere, the whole magnificent.' Determinedly un-Victorian, Bridges harks back instead to the chaste lyrics of Campion and the young Milton. (He had a lifelong interest in words for music, and provided lyrics for four works by Parry.) The second book of short poems was dedicated to Hopkins, whose influence can occasionally be felt in much-anthologized pieces like 'London Snow' and 'On a Dead Child'; and Bridges was himself an innovator of an academic sort, ambitious to loosen the traditional metres of English verse and write 'by the rules of a new prosody'.

In the late part of his career he wrote largely in a flexible twelve-syllable line with variation in the placing of the accents, what he called a 'loose alexandrine'. *The Testament of Beauty*, his last work, is a long philosophical poem in four books ('Introduction', 'Selfhood', 'Breed', and 'Ethick'); but the central myth of 'the Chariot of the Soul' is not interesting, and the frigidity of thought and style obscures the work's technical virtues. The twentieth century has expressed more gratitude for his edition of Hopkins's poems (1918) than for his own writings.

The Testament of Beauty was added to the *Poetical Works* (Oxford University Press) in 1953. See also *A Choice of Bridges' Verse* (Faber, 1987). Bridges did not want a biography, and destroyed his documents; Catherine Phillips's scholarly life (Oxford University Press, 1992) defies him respectfully. (*See also* DARYUSH, ELIZABETH.)   MI

Bringhurst, Robert (1946–) Born in Los Angeles of Canadian parents and has lived variously in Alberta, Beirut, London, Montana, Utah, and (since 1973) on the British Columbia coast. Two suites of multiple lyric meditations on thinking, one about the Pre-Socratics ('The Old in Their Knowing', 1973–82), and the other using ancient Taoist and Buddhist writers ('The Book of Silences', 1986), are among his finest representative poems. He has also worked with the elders of native North American thought in poems ('Tzuhalem's Mountain', 1982) and in his prose versions of Haida mythology, *The Raven Steals the Light* (with Bill Reid, 1984). Poetry with complex musical and prosodic structures which attends centrally to the human intelligence is his particular contribution to Canadian poetry. He is married to the poet Jan *Zwicky.

Bringhurst's selected poems, *The Beauty of the Weapons* (McClelland & Stewart, 1982; Copper Canyon, 1985), has the major poems to 1982; *Pieces of Map, Pieces of Music* (McClelland & Stewart, 1986; Copper Canyon, 1987) has the subsequent poems with two important autobiographical essays. *Selected Poems* has been published in Canada, Britain, and the States (Gaspereau, 2009; Cape, 2010; Copper Canyon, 2011).

Bringhurst, who composes with a sensuous precision reminiscent of *Pound, is also an expert typographer. His textbook on the subject, *The Elements of Typographic Style*, has been through several editions since its appearance in 1992. See also *A Story as Sharp as a Knife* (Douglas & McIntyre, 1999), a study of the classical Haida myth-tellers, and *The Tree of Meaning*:

Language, Mind and Ecology (Counterpoint, 2006). His translation of *Nine Visits to the Mythworld* (Douglas & McIntyre, 2001) was shortlisted for the Griffin Poetry Prize.   RB*

Brissenden, R. F. (Robert Francis) (1928–91) Born in Wentworthville, Sydney, the son of a schoolteacher. Educated at the universities of Sydney and Leeds, he taught principally in Canberra from 1953 until his retirement, in 1984, as reader in English at the Australian National University. As a writer, editor, critic, teacher, and arts administrator he played a significant role in the development of contemporary Australian literature.

A lyric poet, he had a gift also for comic and satiric verse. Although his subjects range from major issues of the 1970s and 1980s (the Vietnam War, the conservation movement) to the classical world and more personal preoccupations (literature, jazz), he returns most repeatedly and effectively to the shorescapes and fauna of the south coast of New South Wales.

His principal collections are *Winter Matins* (Angus & Robertson, 1971), *Building a Terrace* (Australian National University Press, 1975), *The Whale in Darkness* (Australian National University Press, 1980), *Sacred Sites* (The Phoenix Review, 1990), and a posthumous selected poems, *Suddenly Evening* (McPhee Gribble, 1993). Other significant publications are *Virtue in Distress* (on Samuel Richardson; Macmillan, 1974), and two thrillers, *Poor Boy* (Allen & Unwin/St Martin's, 1987) and *Wildcat* (Allen & Unwin, 1991). He co-edited *The Oxford Book of Australian Light Verse* (1991).   DRB

Brock, Edwin (1927–97) Born in London and is one of the few poets to have served as a policeman (1951–9). He also worked in advertising, and was poetry editor of *Ambit* magazine. His poetry, mainly autobiographical (or, as he put it, 'self-defining') offers an interesting and revealing British contrast to the American *confessional genre; it has more affinities with prose than has most of the latter. Where many poets omit what they feel to be the too-mundane, Brock supplies

it in detail. Rough-hewn, dogged, deliberately unsubtle, and full of incongruous echoes from other poets, his work is also disarmingly genuine.

See *Penguin Modern Poets 8* (with Geoffrey Hill and Stevie Smith, Penguin, 1966), *Invisibility is the Heart of Survival: Selected Poems* (New Directions, 1972)—with its introduction by Alan Pryce-Jones—and *Five Ways to Kill a Man: New and Selected Poems* (Enitharmon, 1990); also his autobiography *Here, Now, Always* (Secker & Warburg/New Directions, 1977). *And Another Thing* is a selection from his later poems (Enitharmon, 1999).   MS-S

Brock-Broido, Lucie (1956–) Grew up in Pittsburgh; her hyphenated name combines her mother's maiden name and her father's name. She received her BA and MA from the writing seminars at Johns Hopkins, and took an MFA in writing at the School of the Arts of Columbia University. She has subsequently taught writing at Wheaton College, Tufts, and Harvard, and now directs the Poetry programme at Columbia University School of the Arts. Knopf published her first volume of poetry, *A Hunger*, in 1988 (2nd edn. 1992).

Brock-Broido's poems often show a ventriloquist's talent exerted through arresting personae (a survivor of the police bombing of the MOVE group—a black clan—in Philadelphia; two mad female twins, 'elective mutes', who share a private language and commit murder; a child who has fallen down a well). Brock-Broido's 'domestic mysticism' declares that her work is 'peopled by Wizards, the Forlorn, | The Awkward, the Blinkers, the Spoon-Fingered Agnostic Lispers . . . | The Charlatans. I am one of those.' The stagey and the coy are weapons in her arsenal, which also uses irony and the theatrical to stage dramas of a life where 'a hunger' is obsessive but strange rewards attend its vigils. *The Master Letters* (1995) is a series of poems inspired by Emily Dickinson's letters to an unknown man whom she addressed only as 'Master'. In Brock-Broido's hands the Master can be God, a lover, or an interior exaction; and the language of the letter-writer can range from Amherst archaic to postmodern eclectic. She has published one further volume in the States, *Trouble in Mind* (2004—both Knopf), and a selected poems in Britain: *Soul Keeping Company* (Carcanet, 2010). She has also edited a new edition of Thomas James's *Letter to a Stranger* (1973) for Graywolf Press.   HV

Brodsky, Joseph (1940–96) Born in Leningrad to Russian-Jewish parents. The family shared a communal apartment while Brodsky attended public schools, which he quit at 15. In the decade that followed he changed jobs many times, along the way working as a milling-machine operator at a factory which produced cannons and at a hospital morgue where he cut and sewed up bodies. For a time, like his mother, he was able to support himself as a translator. This hand-to-mouth existence was not satisfactory in the view of Soviet authorities, who arrested him in 1964 on the charge of social parasitism. In 1960 he met Anna Akhmatova (1889–1966), who, when Brodsky was sentenced to five years' forced labour on a state farm in Siberia, championed his cause. This, along with transcripts of his trial smuggled to the West, helped to make Brodsky's plight internationally known. He was released in 1965 after serving eighteen months of his sentence. In 1972 he was expelled from the Soviet Union. That same year he was hired as poet-in-residence at the University of Michigan. In 1980 he moved to New York City's Greenwich Village. In 1987 he received the Nobel Prize for literature. Almost a decade later, he died of a heart attack at age 55. He was buried on the cemetery island in Venice, Italy, a short distance from Ezra *Pound.

In his introduction to Brodsky's *Selected Poems* (Harper & Row, 1973), translated by George L. Kline, W. H. *Auden identified Brodsky as 'a traditionalist . . . interested in what lyric poets of all ages have been interested in . . . encounters with nature . . . reflections upon the human condition, death, and the meaning of existence'. Certainly Brodsky has benefited from his gifted poet-translators, most conspicuously in

A Part of Speech (Farrar, Straus, 1980), his second major collection in English, which includes translations by Anthony *Hecht, Howard *Moss, and Richard *Wilbur. His own translations into English have been criticized for lacking a native speaker's musicality. Brodsky's third collection in English was *To Urania* (1988), and his last book, published posthumously, was *So Forth* (1996). He also published two highly readable essay collections: *Less than One* (1986) and *On Grief and Reason* (1995—all Farrar, Straus). Appointed Poet Laureate of the United States in 1991, he wrote: 'Books find their readers. And if they will not sell, well, let them lie around, absorb dust, rot, and disintegrate. There is always going to be a child who will fish a book out of the garbage heap. I was such a child, for what it's worth.' A literary biography, by the poet Lev Loseff, appeared in English translation in 2010 (Yale University Press).   HC

Bronk, William (1918–99) Born in the small upstate town of Hudson Falls, New York, into an old Dutch patrician family whose name goes back to the early Dutch settlement that later became the borough of New York City called the Bronx. Except for occasional travel, in particular his important visits to the pre-Columbian ruins of Tikal and Machu Picchu, he lived in Hudson Falls, running a family-owned lumber business.

Bronk's poetry, austere and consummately metaphysical in tone, is a sustained, brooding body of work which seeks to articulate the most fundamental questions, the nature of human consciousness, of desire, time, and location. Though often linked by critics to the work of *Stevens, Bronk's poems proceed by more naked, stripped-down means: a preference for direct statement over metaphor, and a fierce, almost syllogistic logic. Bronk's remarkable imagery, subdued and bleak, often drawing on the winter-struck landscapes of the American north-east, is suggestive of the fragile nature of perception and thought. As in his essays, partly collected in *The New World* (Elizabeth Press, 1974), where he ponders the meaning of archaic culture and our encounters with its otherness, Bronk's aim in his poems is to investigate the paradoxical nature of existence, our need to construct mental or physical worlds by which we confirm who we are and that we do exist. Ambitious in theme, Bronk's poetry is simultaneously a contemplation of, and eloquent quarrel with, the human condition.

The most complete collection of Bronk's early poetry is *Life Supports: New and Collected Poems* (North Point, 1981) which won the American Book Award. It was reprinted by Talisman House in 1997, along with the essays of *Vectors and Smoothable Curves* (North Point, 1983). After *Selected Poems* (New Directions, 1995) he published several further volumes, collected as *Bursts of Light* (Talisman House, 2012).   MH

Brooke, Rupert (Chawner) (1887–1915) Born in Rugby, where his father was a housemaster at Rugby School, and grew up in the comfortable security of a home dedicated to ideals of 'godliness and good learning'. Having discovered the power of poetry—from a chance reading of Browning—at the age of 9, Brooke entered his father's school in 1901. From the start, he did well both in the class-room and on the playing-field; for although early on he adopted the pose of the decadent aesthete, winning the school poetry prize in 1905, he found time to play in the cricket XI and the rugger XV. He was strikingly handsome, and his physical presence was matched by a sharpness of intellect, a charm and vitality of manner that affected everyone with whom he came into contact. Popular and successful at Rugby, he was even more so at King's College, Cambridge, where he went as a scholar in 1906. He read voraciously, and threw himself into acting and the activities of the University Fabian Society, of which he became president.

Having gained a second class in the Cambridge Classical Tripos, Brooke established himself in the house afterwards made famous by his poem 'The Old Vicarage, Grantchester', and began to work at a dissertation on Webster and the Elizabethan dramatists. His pastoral existence, however, was interrupted by an unhappy love affair, and in 1912 he travelled through France and Germany in search of peace of mind. Partially recovered, he returned to England and was elected to a Fellowship at King's. He divided his time between Cambridge and London literary and political circles.

Falling in love again, Brooke decided that he needed a change of scene while considering what to do with his life, and in May 1913 he sailed for America. He had been commissioned by the *Westminster Gazette* to write a series of articles on his impressions of the United States and Canada, and over the coming months sent back a dozen vivid dispatches. After an idyllic interlude in the South Seas (that resulted in some of his best poems), he returned to England and enlisted within weeks of the outbreak of the First World War. He served with the Royal Naval Division in the retreat from Antwerp, and was on his way to Gallipoli when he contracted blood-poisoning, from which he died on 23 April 1915.

England at this time needed a focal point for its griefs, ideals, and aspirations, and Brooke was promptly iconized by Church and State: his sonnet 'The Soldier' read aloud in St Paul's Cathedral, his *Times* obituary appearing over the initials of Winston Churchill. His *1914 and Other Poems* and subsequent *Collected Poems* sold 300,000 copies over the next decade. This elevation into a tragic figure of almost mythical stature is highly ironic, since his friends—who included Violet Asquith, Frances *Cornford, Henry James, Geoffrey and Maynard Keynes, and Virginia Woolf—would remember him above all for his laughter and the laughter he induced in them. Brooke once quoted the remark of Hugo to Baudelaire, 'You have created a new shudder', and went on to suggest that one might say of Ernest Dowson: 'He has created a new sigh.' Similarly, we might say of Brooke that he created a new laugh. Laughter is audible in no less than a third of the poems and fragments in Keynes's edition of the *Poetical Works*, a statistic doubly surprising given the nature of his central subject: the place of love and life and laughter after death. This is the theme of the best of his early poems, such as 'Oh! Death will find me' and 'The Hill', and the elegant satires 'The Fish' and 'Tiare Tahiti', in which he engages Christianity and Platonism with 'the sword of laughter'.

Brooke's 1914 sonnets celebrate the discovery of a cause, a vision—found also in the contemporary poems of *Owen, *Rosenberg, and others—of an exhausted civilization rejuvenated by conflict. The start of the war prompted what he had earlier, ironically, described as 'Nineteenth Century grandiose thoughts, about the Destiny of Man, the Irresistibility of Fate, the Doom of Nations, the fact that Death awaits us All'. Forsaking Marvellian tetrameters for Tennysonian pentameters, he yielded to the temptations of a high style that in his better poems he had resisted. He should not, however, be seen as a 'war poet'. He is a poet of peace, a celebrant of friendship, love, and laughter.

The standard edition of the poems is *Rupert Brooke: The Poetical Works*, ed. Geoffrey Keynes (Faber; 2nd edn., 1970). Keynes also edited *The Letters of Rupert Brooke* (Faber, 1968). The standard biography is *Rupert Brooke*, by Christopher Hassall (Faber, 1964).

See, too, *Rupert Brooke: A Reappraisal and Selection from his Writings, Some Hitherto Unpublished*, ed. Timothy Rogers (Routledge & Kegan Paul, 1971) and *The Neo-Pagans: Friendship and Love in the Rupert Brooke Circle*, by Paul Delany (Macmillan, 1987).   JHS

Brooks, Gwendolyn (1917–2000) Born in Topeka, Kansas, and graduated from Chicago's Wilson Junior College in 1936. She married Henry Blakely in 1939, and had two children. In 1971 she was made Distinguished Professor of the Arts at New York's City College. Her first three books of poetry, *A Street in Bronzeville* (1945), *Annie Allen* (1949), winner of a Pulitzer Prize, and *Bronzeville Boys and Girls* (1956—all Harper), treated urban black life with satiric rage and erudite objectivity, utilizing ballads, dramatic monologues, and lyric forms to simulate novelistic sweep.

Her basic approach, except perhaps for a sharper protest note, changed little in later volumes such as *In the Mecca: Poems* (Harper, 1968) and *Aloneness* (Broadside,

1971). Although 'The Womanhood' and similar poems are usually praised for their ambitious reach, Brooks does best in terser, simpler efforts—in 'The Empty Woman', for instance, a few Bronzeville portraits, and salutes to *Frost and Langston *Hughes. Her *Selected Poems* (Harper, 1963) contains important early work. In 1985 she served as Consultant in Poetry to the Library of Congress, the year before the post was renamed Poet Laureate.

See also *Gwendolyn Brooks: Poetry and the Heroic Voice* (University Press of Kentucky, 1989), by D. H. Melhem, and *A Life Distilled: Gwendolyn Brooks, Her Poetry and Fiction*, ed. Maria K. Mootry and Gary Smith (University of Illinois Press, 1987). Elizabeth *Alexander edited *The Essential Gwendolyn Brooks* for the Library of America American Poets series (2005).   EB

Brown, George Mackay (1921–96) A native of the Orkney Islands, from which he was absent only to attend Newbattle Abbey College (where Edwin *Muir was Warden) and the University of Edinburgh (1956–60; 1962–4) as a mature student. His subjects almost invariably pertain to his remote northern homeland. Not only in his prose account *An Orkney Tapestry* (Gollancz, 1969) is he a scholar and historian of his place, but also in his poetry (and novels, short stories, and plays). Norse sagas, the Catholic liturgy, Hopkins, Dylan *Thomas, and the ballads are among the sources of a poetry which at its best assumes pellucid imagery and narrative as its ideals.

Real and imagined histories overlap in Brown's lyrical evocation of his islands and the traditions from which their sense of community stems. A narrowness of range might seem to follow from a position so firmly located to the point of a determined rootedness. However, the timescale of Brown's poetry stretches from pre-history to the present day. There is a good deal in his work about the Vikings and the pre-Reformation past of the Orkneys, of voyages and the sea. As a historical vision, Brown's is omnibus and kaleidoscopic, as well as densely populated with characters and incidents. It might only be by sleight-of-hand that Brown can be claimed as a Scottish poet: like Edwin Muir, he admitted to feeling more Norse than Scottish, and, therefore, untroubled by the usual questions of nationality which tend to beset many Scottish writers.

Loaves and Fishes (Hogarth, 1959) introduced the town of Hamnavoe (his name for Stromness, where he lived), and it reappeared consistently thereafter. *The Year of the Whale* (Chatto & Windus, 1965) saw him perfect the kind of poem with which he came to be associated—a narrative lyric, often focusing on one or more characters, as in 'The Funeral of Ally Flett', 'Farm Labourer', 'Old Fisherman with Guitar', 'Trout Fisher', and 'Hamnavoe Market'. The first and last of these risk an obvious listing of events, or, in the case of 'Hamnavoe Market', seven kinds of consequence of heavy drinking. Runes, bestiaries, calendars, seasonal lists, and so on occur frequently enough to become repetitive. Taken in quantity, Brown's poems can at times feel as if they depend on too much of the same thing. Duplicated sensations, however, are by and large redeemed by scrupulous writing, clarity, certainty of diction, and an engaging honesty.

Fishermen with Ploughs (Hogarth, 1971) is an ambitious cycle, convincing in its individual parts, but doctrinally insecure. By the end of the book a 'Black Pentecost', or apocalypse, is imagined as having obliterated most of the world. An Orcadian rescue of humanity is witnessed through the agency of women and a return to the old ways of farming and fishing.

Poems New and Selected (Hogarth/Harcourt, 1973) was followed by *Winterfold* (Chatto & Windus, 1976), *Selected Poems* (Hogarth, 1977), *Voyages* (Chatto & Windus, 1983), *The Wreck of the Archangel* (1989), and a new *Selected Poems* (1991—both John Murray). Brown also wrote lyrics and opera libretti for the composer Sir Peter Maxwell Davies, and edited *Selected Prose of Edwin Muir* (1987). His novels include *Greenvoe* (1972), *Magnus* (1973), and *Time in a Red Coat* (1984). There is a study by Alan Bold (Oliver & Boyd, 1978). His last volume of poems, *Following a Lark* (1996), was followed posthumously by an autobiography, *For the Islands I Sing* (1997). See *The Collected Poems of George Mackay Brown* (2005), ed. Archie Bevan and Brian Murray, and Maggie Fergusson, *George Mackay Brown: The Life* (2006—all John Murray).   DED

Brown, James (1966–) Grew up in Palmerston North, a 'bustling, go-ahead city | at the heart of the Manawatu Plains', as he reports in the deadpan autobiographical poem 'I Come from Palmerston North'. Brown studied with Bill *Manhire at Victoria University, where he now teaches, and worked as an editor on the journal *Sport*, who published his booklet *Instructions for Poetry Readings* (2001) under the *nom de plume* 'Dr. Ernest M. Bluespire'.

Brown has written of the importance of Jenny *Bornholdt's work to his own use of 'relatively plain language'. His verse has been called a kind of 'anti-poetry', but its manner remains user-friendly, and might be described as faux-naïve with an adult undertow: *Favourite Monsters* (2002), has a child's painting of 'a person drowning' for its cover. His other collections are: *Go Round Power Please* (1995), which won the Jessie Mackay Best First Book of Poetry Award, *Lemon* (1999), *The Year of the Bicycle* (2006), and *Warm Auditorium* (2012—all Victoria University Press). He has also published short fiction, and an anthology of New Zealand landscape poems, *The Nature of Things* (Craig Potton, 2005).   JNT

Brown, Pam(ela) (1948–) Born in Seymour, Victoria, grew up on military bases in Queensland, and has lived in Sydney since 1968. She has worked as a librarian, silkscreen printer, and lecturer in film, and has published poetry, prose, and plays. She was the poetry editor of the journal *overland* and associate editor of the online magazine *Jacket*.

Like her contemporary John *Forbes, Brown's quick-witted, lower-case lyricism brings postmodern techniques to contemporary Australian experience. Her early books of poetry include *Sureblock* (Woolley, 1972) and *Cocabola's Funny Picture Book* (Tomato, 1973). They comment obliquely on life after the liberations of the

Sixties and in particular the ongoing questions of feminist politics. *Correspondences* (Red Press, 1979) was a collaboration with joanne *burns. Brown's early style tends towards brevity, and is often satirical about a chauvinist 'album cover' Australian landscape. John *Tranter described it as having 'the flavour of Gertrude *Stein sung to a blues guitar' (see 'Honky tonk sunset': 'the chickens || the guitar || the chickenshit'). There are also strongly colloquial and observational notes too, though, indicating her attraction to the particulars of place. Her later verse is more discursive and given to travel—see *This World/This Place* (University of Queensland Press, 1994). *Dear Deliria: New and Selected Poems* (Salt, 2003) won the Kenneth Slessor Prize for Poetry in 2004. Recent books include *True Thoughts* (Salt, 2008) and *Authentic Local* (Papertiger, 2010).   JNT

Brown, Sterling A. (1901–89) Born in Washington DC, the son of a professor of religion. He was educated at Harvard and in 1926 began a lifelong career in teaching, most of it spent at Howard University. Brown began publishing during the 1920s, the era of the *Harlem Renaissance, but he always resisted being labelled a Renaissance poet. In his first volume, *Southern Road* (Harcourt, 1932), he exhibited the range of his poetic voice. The book includes some pastoral lyrics written in a plain English with archaic echoes ('Grief has been hers, before this wintry time. | Death has paid calls, unmannered, uninvited'), but has many more of the dialect poems for which Brown is better known. These draw on mainly musical sources, the ballad, the work-song, and the blues. Certain stanzas from poems such as 'Odyssey of Big Boy', 'Long Gone', and 'Southern Road' could fit easily into the blues lyrics sung by Brown's contemporaries, such as Blind Lemon Jefferson. In a cycle of poems chronicling the adventures of a character called Slim Greer, Brown incorporates elements of fable as he sets his ironic hero loose among the black world, the white world, and the afterworld.

After *Southern Road* Brown published only sporadically, though he continued to write verse. His *Collected Poems*, ed. Michael S. Harper, was published in 1980 (Harper & Row; repr. Northwestern University Press, 1996). Mark A. Sanders has edited a selection of Brown's essays, *A Son's Return* (Northeastern University Press, 1996) and written a critical study, *Afro-Modernist Aesthetics and the Poetry of Sterling A. Brown* (University of Georgia Press, 1999).   JC

Brown, Wayne (Vincent) (1944–2009) Born in Trinidad. He was educated at St Mary's College, Port of Spain, the University of the West Indies, and the University of Toronto. His father was a distinguished judge but, as his mother died giving birth, he was brought up mainly by relatives. As an only child he spent many holidays alone exploring shorelines, and indeed seascapes are prominent in his poems. He held the Gregory Fellowship in Poetry (1975–6) at the University of Leeds, wrote a long-running column for the *Trinidad Guardian*, and taught at the University of the West Indies.

Derek *Walcott was one of his mentors when he first started writing poetry, and a poem like 'Ballad of the Electric Eel', though distinctively elegant and supple, could not have been written without the example of Ted *Hughes. One of his best poems, 'Noah', wears its archetypal symbolism lightly, and reveals the poetic imagination in blinding flashes of imagery. *On the Coast* (Andre Deutsch, 1973) won the Commonwealth Prize for Poetry. It was reprinted by Peepal Tree Press in 2010, with poems from his second collection, *Voyages* (1989). Brown also wrote a biography of *Edna Manley* (Andre Deutsch, 1975), a prominent Jamaican literary figure. A collection of stories from his newspaper column, *The Scent of the Past*, appeared posthumously (Peepal Tree, 2011).   MR

Browne, Michael Dennis (1940–   ) A native of Walton-on-Thames, England, he became a naturalized American in 1978, more than a decade after enrolling at the University of Iowa. Before taking an

MA there in 1967 he was educated at Hull University and Oxford. From 1971 he taught at the University of Minnesota.

Browne's first volumes contain poems of spare narrative context, fractured syntax, and startlingly juxtaposed metaphors. 'The King in May', for instance, creates a surrealistic effect by combining a mythic, unnamed speaker and setting with a series of vivid, unpredictable figures of speech, while 'The Delta' (set in Vietnam) conveys the nightmarish unreality of war by means of archetypal imagery and unpunctuated syntactic repetitions. Browne's later work also reveals his interest in dreams, but his style has become more direct, more personal, and more accessible, without sacrificing psychological depth, as a poem like 'Her Garden' demonstrates.

Browne's publications include *The Wife of Winter* (1970), *The Sun Fetcher* (1978), and *Smoke From the Fires* (1984). See *Selected Poems 1965–1995* (1995) and *Things I Can't Tell You* (2005—both Carnegie Mellon University Press).   MCB

Brownjohn, Alan (1931–) Born in London, which has been his home for most of his life. He was educated there and at Oxford; he has been a lecturer in English at colleges of further education, poetry critic on the *New Statesman* and *The Sunday Times*, a member of the Arts Council Literature Panel, a Labour borough councillor and parliamentary candidate, chairman of the Greater London Arts Association Literature Panel, and chairman of the Poetry Society. He has been a freelance writer and broadcaster since 1978. He has a son by his first wife, Shirley Toulson, whom he married in 1960 (the marriage ended in divorce in 1969). In 1972 he was married again, to Sandra Willingham; this marriage too was dissolved.

Brownjohn's political sympathies and domestic concerns inform a poetry that aims for, and achieves, stylistic correctness, emotional reticence, modest understatement: qualities frequently associated with English poetry of the 1950s and (though Brownjohn was a member of the *Group) particularly with the *Movement. Brownjohn's early work did not appear in either of Robert *Conquest's *New Lines* anthologies, though it would have looked, with its touches of *Auden, *Graves, and *Empson, perfectly at home there. His *Collected Poems* is arranged chronologically by decades, beginning with the 1950s, and there are no radical departures in the 1960s, 1970s, 1980s or 1990s. There is, though, a steady deepening and darkening of the poems' 'virulent proprieties', 'moments of disquiet', and 'meticulous disenchantment' (all phrases from the poems themselves); and a growing confidence and conviction in the approach to social, personal, and philosophical themes—the failures and follies of 'progress' in postwar England, the various pressures on love and marriage, and an acutely self-questioning sense of moral and epistemological doubt. Trim and orderly stanzas, a facility with moralized anecdote and metaphorical exempla, have never been abandoned; nor, more damagingly, has the tendency to baldly abstract diction and philosophizing-in-verse.

The most rewarding developments have been in Brownjohn's gift for elliptical narrative (as in his longer sequences) and in his mastery of tonal nuance, his trust in the ability of a deliberate plainness to suggest much that the poem leaves unsaid. An ear for the accents of social tact and the discreetly avoided 'painful subject' is pertinent here, as is his own comment on his 'styles of reticence': 'I don't feel like making apology for this because I greatly admire certain English puritan values and feel that English rationalism, democracy and humanity would be our best post-imperial contribution to the world at large.' The 'puritan values' have always been evident in the ordinariness of Brownjohn's subjects, his acknowledgement of unexceptional happiness, his sober facing-down of futility and fear; while 'post-imperial' overtones in his later work have been accompanied by a plangent sense of the inexpressible, often associated with the sea or seaside settings.

The even later invention of Ludbrooke—a fiction who shares his age, vocation, and urban environment with his author—has enabled Brownjohn to explore, with detachment but without mockery, the amorous disappointments, vanities and self-deceptions of an ageing white male artist of left-liberal views and educated sensibility in a world that poses ever more exasperating challenges to his 'aplomb'. Ludbrooke's gallantry and resilience are the keynotes in a quietly comic portrait of cultivated disaffection; the sixty thirteen-line blank-verse poems devoted to him that open *Ludbrooke & Others* (Enitharmon, 2010) represent a remarkable late flowering of Brownjohn's uniquely quizzical, truthful, and exacting voice.

The most recent *Collected Poems* (Enitharmon, 2006; there were two earlier editions) gathers work from all the eleven volumes that preceded *Ludbrooke & Others*; while that volume is represented in *The Saner Places: Selected Poems* (Enitharmon, 2011). Brownjohn has also published four novels, including *The Way You Tell Them* (Deutsch, 1990) and *Windows on the Moon* (Black Spring, 2009); a novel for children (as John Berrington), *To Clear the River* (Heinemann, 1964); a critical study, *Philip Larkin* (Longman, 1975); and a translation (with Sandy Brownjohn) of Goethe's *Torquato Tasso* (Angel, 1985).   AJ

Brutus, Dennis (1924–2009) Born in Salisbury (Harare), Zimbabwe, of South African parents, and in early life moved with them back to South Africa. He studied at Fort Hare and the University of Witwatersrand, and taught for fourteen years in South African high schools. Classified as Coloured, he campaigned and protested against the Apartheid regime, and this led to his arrest in 1963. He escaped whilst on bail but was re-arrested and shot in the back during a further escape attempt. He was sentenced to eighteen months hard labour and served his sentence at the penal colony of Robben Island. He emigrated to England in 1966 and then to the USA, where he was a professor of literature at Northwestern University and later Pittsburgh University. He was president of SANROC (South African Non-Racial Olympic Committee), acting chairman of the International Campaign Against Racism

in Sport, and United Nations Representative for International Defence and Aid. He was 'unbanned' in South Africa in 1990 and returned in the Nineties, based at the University of KwaZulu-Natal.

Brutus's volumes of poetry, *Sirens Knuckles Boots* (1963), *Letters to Martha* (1968), *Poems from Algiers* (1970), and *Thoughts Abroad* by 'John Bruin' (1970) were republished with additional poems in *A Simple Lust* (Heinemann/Hill & Wang, 1973). His other published works are *Stubborn Hope* (Heinemann/Three Continents, 1978) and *Airs and Tributes* (Whirlwind, 1989). In *Letters to Martha* Brutus excelled: gracefully poised lines, unextravagant emotions, perceptive observations of prison life defined this volume. See *Poetry & Protest: A Dennis Brutus Reader* (Haymarket, 2006) and *The Dennis Brutus Tapes: Essays at Autobiography* (Boydell & Brewer, 2011).   FO

Bryce, Colette (1970–   ) Born in Derry, Bryce moved to England to study at eighteen. She has held writing fellowships at the universities of Dundee, Newcastle, and Durham, and is an editor of *Poetry London*.

The Heel of Bernadette (2000) won the Aldeburgh Best First Collection Prize. Typically drawn to self-contained, enigmatic poems in the first person, Bryce's verse often plays with threads of rhyme, obliquely catching itself in the act of composition as it addresses other subjects: a poem on her Northern Irish background is titled 'Line'; a monologue spoken by an anorexic, 'Form'. The prize-winning title poem of her second collection, *The Full Indian Rope Trick* (2004), transmutes her experience of leaving Ireland (via 'a braid | eighteen summers long') into a metaphor for personal growth and poetic creation, mingling Sylvia *Plath with magical realism. Her third collection is *Self-Portrait in the Dark* (2008—all Picador).   JNT

Buckley, Vincent (1925–88) Born at Romsey, Victoria (Australia), and educated at the universities of Melbourne and Cambridge. The first of his eight volumes of verse, *The World's Flesh*, appeared in

Melbourne in 1954, while *Last Poems* was published posthumously in 1991, also in Melbourne. In this long career Buckley maintained grave central concerns: with provenance—his roots in rural Victoria and in Ireland—asking: 'How can I find my fathers in this darkness?'; with the Roman Catholic faith; with wives and families; with politics, especially its formal hypocrisies and the tactics of totalitarian regimes. In *Masters in Israel* (Angus & Robertson, 1961), Buckley described his father and himself as: 'Two small, self-wounding, fearful men.' Their relationship is treated at more length in the sequence 'Stroke', influenced by Robert *Lowell, in *Arcady & Other Places* (Melbourne University Press/Cambridge University Press, 1966). In that volume a group of political poems anticipated his autobiographical work *Cutting Green Hay* (1983), which dealt with sectarian and party politics in the 1950s, and *Memory, Ireland* (1985), an account of time spent in that country.

Buckley held a personal chair in English at Melbourne University for more than two decades and was an influential teacher. His literary criticism, including *Essays in Poetry, Mainly Australian* (Melbourne University Press, 1957), *Poetry and Morality* (Chatto & Windus, 1959), *Poetry and the Sacred* (Chatto & Windus/Barnes & Noble, 1968), belongs to his younger days. From 1958 to 1964 he edited the pluralistic Catholic quarterly *Prospect*, and was also poetry editor of the *Bulletin* in this period. His volume of verse, *Golden Builders* (Angus & Robertson, 1976) showed Buckley in experimental vein, echoing Blake's prophetic poetry in his exploration of urban fragmentation. Later books dealt with Ireland—*The Pattern* (1979)—and with the birth of a daughter—*Late-Winter Child* (1979—both Dolmen). His *Collected Poems* (Leonard, 2009) have been edited by Chris *Wallace-Crabbe.   PP

Buckmaster, Charles (1950–72) Born in the country town of Gruyere, Victoria (Australia), and left school shortly before matriculating. He worked briefly at various manual jobs and at the Source Bookshop in Melbourne. He became one of the leaders of the youthful poetry 'explosion' in the Vietnam War years, and edited the short-lived mini-mag *The Great Auk*. Although he travelled widely through Australia he is associated with the Melbourne avant-garde of the late 1960s. He committed suicide in 1972.

Because of his early death Buckmaster was seen as a tragic and representative figure of the confrontationalist period when a whole generation of Australian 19-year-olds were conscripted for active service in a war to which they had no commitment. Established values were challenged and alternatives explored. Buckmaster's life and his literary activities illustrate both romantic defiance and tragic self-doubt.

It was not until the publication of his *Collected Poems* (University of Queensland Press, 1989), edited by Simon MacDonald, that a proper survey of Buckmaster's poetic output became possible. Not surprisingly for someone who died at 22, there is much ephemera, but his poems about his home area (most notably the long poem 'A history of the father') have gained a secure place in the poetry of his epoch. For further reference, see *Parnassus Mad Ward: Michael Dransfield and the New Australian Poetry*, by Livio Dobrez (University of Queensland Press, 1990).   TWS

Bukowski, Charles (1920–94) Born in Germany, he moved to America at the age of two. For most of his life he lived in and around Los Angeles, where he worked at a variety of menial jobs before gaining recognition as a writer in the Sixties. He stands at the centre of a group of Los Angeles-based writers who glorify a gritty street life that encompasses bars, racetracks, and other seedy urban haunts. Bukowski thus represents the antithesis of the academic poet. Instead he hints at the possibility of a genuinely popular poetry; in the US he has a wide following among readers who do not generally keep up with contemporary poetry, and he is also much admired in Europe. This is undoubtedly to do with the candour and ease of his style, coupled with the raunchiness of his subject-matter; in many ways his work has more in common with rock music than with literature.

Yet Bukowski cannot be dismissed as a poet simply because he is popular, or because his poems are easy to read and full of racy or seamy items from his private life. In a sense his work is a natural culmination of the ongoing revolt against formalism, the academic, and the intellectual that has periodically energized American poetry since its inception. For Bukowski the poem is manifestly not sacred; its purpose is simply to record events and emotions with a compression and directness not available in prose (though he also wrote novels and stories). While it is possible to detect in his work vestiges of modernist poetics, these elements are integrated within a seemingly artless, improvised utterance that exhibits no discernible formal structure. Bukowski makes fairly obvious use of free-verse devices like enjambment and indentation, but for the most part he shows little interest in technique. His effects are primarily narrative, and involve the collision of his own gruff, funny, idiomatic voice with the random incidents of his daily life.

His many books of poems were published by small presses like Black Sparrow in Santa Barbara, who continued to issue volumes of unpublished work after his death, as well as editions of his correspondence. John Martin, his publisher, has also edited a selected volume, *The Pleasures of the Damned: 1951–1993* (Ecco, 2007).   RG

Bunting, Basil (1900–85) Born into a Quaker family in Northumberland, where he grew up and spent the latter part of his life. In between, however, he lived an adventurous, cosmopolitan existence. Educated at a Quaker boarding school in Yorkshire, he served six months in prison as a conscientious objector in 1918. The following year he went to London, where he did odd jobs and spent a year at the London School of Economics. In 1923 he went to Paris, met Ezra *Pound and worked for Ford Madox *Ford on the *Transatlantic Review*, and then followed Pound to Rapallo in 1924. He worked for a time as a sailor,

and subsequently spent a nomadic life in London, Germany, Italy, the United States, and the Canary Islands. During this period, with Pound's encouragement, he began publishing poetry and brought out his first book, *Redimiculum Matellarum*, in Milan in 1930. Pound's Faber *Activist Anthology* (1933) contained fifty pages of Bunting, and he became closely acquainted with another Poundian protégé, Louis *Zukofsky.

Bunting joined the RAF on the outbreak of war and was posted to Persia, partly on the strength of his having taught himself classical Persian in Rapallo. He fell deeply in love with the country and became Vice-Consul in Isfahan in 1945, marrying a Persian woman in 1948. His *Poems 1950* was published in Texas in 1950. After another stint in Italy, this time as a journalist, he returned to Persia as a correspondent for *The Times*, but was eventually expelled by Mosaddeq. He spent the rest of his life in Northumberland, doing odd jobs and working as a journalist on the local paper. With the encouragement of Tom *Pickard in 1963 he began to write again after a period of dryness, publishing in England for the first time in the 1960s: his name was made with the long poem *Briggflatts* in 1966. His *Collected Poems* was published in 1968. In the latter part of his life he was much in demand as a visiting poet at various American universities, and also had close ties with the University of Newcastle upon Tyne, which awarded him a D. Litt in 1971. There is a Bunting archive at the University of Durham.

Bunting's many short 'odes' make frequent reference to the scenes and episodes of his nomadic and bohemian life in France, Italy, and Persia, one of the finest (no. 36) being a meditation on the forms of Persian poetry compared to mosque architecture; and his many translations and versions, which he calls 'Overdrafts', testify to an exceptional inwardness with a number of different languages and cultures. His long poem *The Spoils* (1951) is a vivid evocation of historic and contemporary Persia, containing a powerful critique of the results of British imperialism in that country. The longer poem held a continual fascination for Bunting, from *Villon* (1925) to

Briggflatts (1966), presumably partly as homage to Pound, whose *Cantos* he celebrated in 'On the Fly-Leaf of Pound's Cantos', referring to them as 'the Alps'. In the *Collected Poems* all his long poems are grouped under the general title 'Sonatas'; and, although he talks rather speciously in interviews about musical form in relation to poetic composition, the analogy does have force. Repeated images, reiterated motifs, the sense of variations being performed on central themes, all help to give his work an integrity of organization rare in the modernist long poem, and certainly not apparent in Pound's *Cantos*.

One of Basil Bunting's major themes is the necessity for leaving home and the constant desire to return there. *Briggflatts* employs a number of Northumbrian dialect words; in several sections it takes elements of the Dark Age history of the north of England as its theme; it uses, in places, a heavy alliteration and abrupt syntax which strongly recall Anglo-Saxon poetic forms. These obeisances to Bunting's origins are combined, however, with elaborate notations of his travels and reading: the poem's imagery of voyaging takes in references to his life in London, Italy, and Persia which justify its subtitle, 'An Autobiography'. If there is an element of Poundian inclusiveness in this, the poem is also indebted to one of Bunting's other poetic heroes, Wordsworth, for its return, across the years, to a 'spot of time' from Bunting's childhood. Having lived most of his life well outside the usual framework of literary production and reception, Bunting had to wait until late in life for any acclaim in his own country; but his has since come to seem a significant modern reputation.

Complete Poems (Bloodaxe, 2000), edited with an introduction by Richard Caddel, includes the posthumous *Uncollected Poems*. Bloodaxe have also issued an edition of *Briggflatts* with additional material, including a recording of Bunting reading his poem and a documentary (2009). *Basil Bunting on Poetry*, ed. Peter Makin, collects a number of illuminating lectures (Johns Hopkins University Press, 2003). See also Carroll F. Terrell (ed.), *Basil Bunting: Man and Poet* (1981), Peter Makin, *Bun-*

ting: The Shaping of his Verse (Oxford University Press, 1992), and Keith Aldritt, *The Poet as Spy: The Life and Wild Times of Basil Bunting* (Aurum, 1999). *The Star You Steer By: Basil Bunting and British Modernism* (Rodopi, 2000), edited by James McGonigal and Richard Price, is a collection of essays and tributes from other poets. Don Share has edited *Bunting's Persia* (Flood, 2012), a volume of translations, and is working on a fully annotated *Complete Poems*. NC*

Burke, Kenneth (1897–1993) Born in Pittsburgh, Pennsylvania, and educated at Ohio State and Columbia universities. His wide intellectual interests and talents were evident from the start: he studied Marx and Freud; did research for the Laura Spellman Rockefeller Foundation (1926–7) and editorial work for the Bureau of Social Hygiene (1928); was music critic for the *Dial* (1927–9) and the *Nation* (1934–6); and translated several German books (including Mann's *Death in Venice*, 1925; revd. edn., 1970). His first book of critical essays, *Counter-Statement* (1931), was shortly followed by his only novel, *Towards a Better Life* (1932). From 1938 he taught and lectured at several universities and published many critical books. *Permanence and Change: An Anatomy of Purpose* (1935) was an attempt to reconcile his growing Marxist sympathies with his earlier aestheticism. His search for an all-inclusive intellectual framework, however, culminated in 'dramatism', the purposive theory of language described in *A Grammar of Motives* (1945) and *A Rhetoric of Motives* (1950), which sees—and analyses—all forms of language as revelations of motive.

Burke began writing as a poet but was much more prolific, and widely read, as a literary and philosophical critic. His poems are all lyrics, as he defines the term: terse summaries of momentary moods and motives. They are accessible, light, playful, and witty, despite their frequently abstract and metaphysical themes; 'ideally', he says, 'the complete lyrist would love ideas at least as strongly as sensations, and preferably more'. His criticism has often been attacked for its proliferation of abstract terms, abstruse arguments, and frivolous associative leaps; but his analysis of rhetoric is now seen to have anticipated the cross-disciplinary and highly theoretical work of Michel Foucault and other post-structuralists.

See *Collected Poems, 1915–67* (University of California Press, 1968); *The Complete White Oxen: Collected Shorter Fiction* (University of California Press, 1968); *The Philosophy of Literary Form: Studies in Symbolic Action* (Louisiana State University Press, 1941; revd. edn., Vintage, 1957); and for assessments of all his writing, *Critical Responses to Kenneth Burke, 1924–1966*, ed. William Rueckert (University of Minnesota Press, 1969). *Late Poems, 1968–1993*, ed. Julie Whitaker and David Blakesley, was published in 2005 by the University of South Carolina Press.   NE

burns, joanne (1945–   ) Born in Sydney and studied at the university there. She has worked as a teacher of English and creative writing, and is a well-known performer of her work. In 1970 Burns came to London, where she was involved in the poetry-reading scene and published her first book, *Snatch* (Strange Faeces, 1972). She has since published over a dozen more. *Correspondences* (Red Press, 1979) was a collaboration with Pam *Brown, with whom she shares a satirical wit and a preference for lower-case typography. burns' vernacular poetic moves readily from verse to prose. *on a clear day* (University of Queensland Press, 1992; repr. 1997) presents short, fantastic anecdotes with unexpected punchlines. The title poem, for example, describes the 'utopian waves' concealed in a woman's 'inner ear', only to end with her apprehension of 'loads of tourists comfortably draped around the edges of glassbottomed speedboats'.

Her exploration of heightened states of mind also often takes the form of the monologue (see *ventriloquy: monologues 1977–1980* (Sea Cruise, 1981)). Later books include *aerial photography* (1999), *footnotes of a hammock* (2004—both Five Islands Press), *an illustrated history of dair-*

ies (2007) and *amphora* (2011—both Giramondo). *kept busy*, a CD of burns reading her work, was issued by River Road Press in 2007.   JNT

Burnshaw, Stanley (1906–2005) Born in New York City. He attended Columbia University, the University of Poitiers, and the University of Paris, and received a BA from the University of Pittsburgh in 1925 and an MA from Cornell in 1933. From 1933 to 1936 he was an editor of *New Masses*; from 1939 to 1958 founder, president, and editor-in-chief of the Dryden Press; and from 1958 to 1967 vice-president at the publisher Holt, Rinehart, and Winston. He received the National Institute of Arts and Letters award for literature in 1971.

Burnshaw's varied literary output includes verse (*In the Terrified Radiance*, Braziller, 1972), criticism (*The Seamless Web*, Braziller/Allen Lane, 1970, 1991), fiction (*The Refusers*, Horizon, 1981), translation (*The Poem Itself*, Horizon, 1960, 1989; Penguin, 1964; *The Modern Hebrew Poem Itself*, Holt, Rinehart, 1965; Harvard University Press, 1989), and biography (*Robert Frost Himself*, Braziller, 1986). Central to his work is an insistence on the indissoluble unity of mind and body in all human experience, including the production of art; this forms the theme of *The Seamless Web* and, together with the evocation and acceptance of mortality, the preoccupation of much of his poetry. See *The Collected Poems and Selected Prose* (University of Texas Press, 2002).   RZ

Burnside, John (1955–   ) Born in Dunfermline, Fife, and read English and European studies at Cambridge College of Arts and Technology. He has worked as a risk analyst in computers and is now Professor of Creative Writing at the University of St Andrews. He received a Scottish Arts Council Literary Award for his first collection *The Hoop* (Carcanet, 1989), which combines autobiographical elements with history and natural observation. These staple ingredients are refreshed by quiet intensity and meticulous detail. Burnside offers a highly personal account of parts of

England and Scotland, rarely touching on public themes. He dramatizes the pleasures and anxieties of ordinariness and privacy: a lamplit study and its hoarded objects ('The hoop') are in one way a defence against the terrors of the past and the uncertainties of identity; in another they are the imagined threshold of a quite different place: 'everybody, knows | magic is somewhere else, where no one goes' ('Inside'). His romanticism is intensified in *Common Knowledge* (1991), where a religious dimension clearly emerges (for example, in the prose poems 'Annunciations'). *Feast Days* (1992—both Secker & Warburg) continues this development, negotiating between the loss of religious assurance ('a life recalled, that could not happen now') and the persistence of the uncanny. Stylistically, Burnside is walking the line between scruple and hyperaesthetic affectation.

As the *Times Literary Supplement* commented on his eleventh collection, *The Hunt in the Forest* (2009), 'his attraction to indefinable and indefinite experiences, and his delight in poetic irresolution, have frustrated some readers, as well as enticing others'. Since *The Asylum Dance* (2000), however, his fluently dream-like free verse, with its mingling of philosophy, theology, and ecology, has been highly acclaimed, and can be seen as a British outcrop of a contemporary North American tradition of meditative landscape writing, which would include Jorie *Graham, Tim *Lilburn, and Charles *Wright. *Selected Poems* (2006) was followed by *Gift Songs* (2007), which engages with *Eliot's *Four Quartets* in a North European coastal sequence of the same name. *Black Cat Bone* (2011) won both the Forward and the T. S. Eliot prizes in Britain. Burnside has also written several novels on contemporary gothic themes, and two memoirs of his early life: *A Lie About My Father* (2006) and *Waking Up in Toytown* (2010—all Cape).   SO'B*

Butler, Guy (1918–2001) Born at Cradock, Cape Province, and educated at Rhodes University, Grahamstown. During the war he served with the South African forces in the Middle East and Italy, after which he took up a scholarship at Oxford. From 1948 to 1950 he lectured at the University of Witwatersrand, and from 1952 until 1983 he was professor of English at Rhodes University. He served as English editor of the Afrikaans journal *Standpunte*, and helped found the poetry journal *New Coin*. Several of his plays were performed by the South African National Theatre.

Butler's pioneering poems reflect the tension between what he saw as his two 'homes' of Europe and Africa. He considered 'old-fashioned techniques' most suitable for Africa's cultural soil; and his forms are regular, his imagery often literary in origin. In 'Myths' the alien veld is suddenly familiarized by the pastoral vision of a guitar-strumming black Orpheus with his Eurydice. His *Essays and Lectures: 1949–1991* (1994) were edited by Stephen *Watson. A *Collected Poems* appeared in 1999 (both David Philip).

See also *African English Poetry: A Modern Perspective*, by Michael Chapman (Donker, 1984).   JB*

Butlin, Ron (1949–) Lives in Edinburgh where he was born. Brought up in Hightae, a small village near Dumfries, he was educated at Edinburgh University and has held a number of writer-in-residence posts in Scotland. In 2008 he was appointed as the third Edinburgh Makar, a laureate post.

Butlin's poems often view things from unusual angles, and have accordingly been variously tagged surrealist, imagist, and erotic, but he is essentially a lyric poet. Music is a recurrent theme, as in the longish title-poem of *Ragtime in Unfamiliar Bars* (Secker & Warburg, 1985), and Butlin employs a range of subtle free-verse rhythms. The bleak side to his work is evident in the stories in *The Tilting Room* (1983) and his first novel, *The Sound of My Voice* (1987—both Canongate), the latter on the nervous breakdown of an alcoholic businessman 'thirty-four years old and already two-thirds destroyed'.

Butlin's first two booklets, *Stretto* (1976) and *Creatures Tamed by Cruelty* (1979), contained some poems in *Scots, but he now writes exclusively in English. He has translated poems from a number of other languages, including Chinese in *The Exquisite Instrument: Imitations from the Chinese* (Salamander, 1982). For his later poetry see *Histories of Desire* (Bloodaxe, 1995) and *Without a Backward Glance: New and Selected Poems* (Barzan, 2005).   JDB

Bynner, Witter (1881–1968) Most commonly remembered as one of the perpetrators of 'Spectrism', perhaps the century's major literary hoax. Writing as Emanuel Morgan, Bynner published with Arthur Davison Ficke (as Anne Knish) the poems collected in *Spectra: A Book of Poetic Experiments* (Kennerley, 1916), which found enthusiastic support among poets as radically different as Edgar Lee *Masters, John Gould *Fletcher, and William Carlos *Williams. William Jay *Smith's *The Spectra Hoax* (Wesleyan University Press, 1961) contains the complete text of *Spectra* as well as other 'Spectric' poems by Bynner, Ficke, and their subsequent collaborator 'Elijah Hay' (Marjorie Allen Seiffert).

Although Spectrism was initially intended as a spoof of literary movements like *Imagism, Bynner found that writing under the mask of Emanuel Morgan freed him from the restraints he had felt in his early poems and so continued using it in such works as those collected in *Pins for Wings* (Sunwise Turn, 1920).

Shortly after the Spectra episode, Bynner, in collaboration with the Chinese scholar Kiang Kang-hu, began translating poems from the Chinese anthology *Three Hundred Pearls of the T'ang Dynasty*. These translations, collected in *The Jade Mountain* (Knopf, 1929), may be Bynner's major achievement. Few have translated Chinese poetry as well. One who did was Kenneth *Rexroth, whose translations of Tu Fu were undertaken largely at Bynner's instigation.

Bynner was capable of a great range of poetry, from witty social verse to deeply expressive lyrical works dealing with his homosexuality and, as he said in 'No Anodyne', 'perfect loneliness'.

The Works of Witter Bynner (Farrar, Straus, 1978–9) include *Selected Poems, Light Verse and Satires, Prose Pieces*, and *The Chinese Translations*. The first of these volumes offers an extensive biographical introduction by James Kraft and a judicious critical introduction by Richard *Wilbur. See James Kraft, ed., *The Selected Witter Bynner* and (as author) *Who is Witter Bynner?: A Biography* (both University of New Mexico Press, 1995).   EHF

Caddy, Caroline (1944–) Born in Western Australia, Caddy spent her early childhood in America. She worked on Road Dental Units across Western Australia, and later lived on a farm there. Her early poetry reflects her fascination with the state. *Singing at Night* (1980) was followed by *Letters from the North* (1985—both Fremantle Arts Centre), which was divided into several sections and sequences concerned with questions of landscape, travel, and history that move between the mining towns of the north and the coastline of south. Contemplating 'King George Sound', the poet reflects: 'Hit with a mallet it would ring with its own name'. Later books, which draw on her travels in China and elsewhere, include *Conquistadors* (Penguin, 1991), *Antarctica* (1996)—an account of a voyage on an icebreaker—*Editing the Moon* (1999), and *Burning Bright* (2010). *Esperance: New and Selected Poems* (2007—all Fremantle Arts Centre) won the Wesley Michel Wright Prize for Poetry.   JNT

Cage, John (1912–92) Born in Los Angeles and spent most of his life in New York. He studied music with Arnold Schoenberg at the University of California in the 1930s, and went on to be one of the most original artists of the twentieth century, introducing aleatory principles into composition and performance that have been widely influential in postmodernist poetry.

In 1952, Cage staged his first 'happening' at *Black Mountain College, with poetry read by Charles *Olson. He also gave lectures composed in verse-like patterns. His emphasis on the phatic nature of poetic language—famously, 'I have nothing to say ‖ and I am saying it ‖ and that is poetry ‖ as I need it' ('Lecture on Nothing')—was influenced by Gertrude *Stein, as he acknowledged in the introduction to *Silence: Lectures and Writings* (Wesleyan University Press, 1961). In the 1960s, impressed by the experiments of Jackson *Mac Low, Cage began to employ chance procedures in his writing. He invented the mesostic, a form of acrostic in which a central word is traced across others sharing its component letters. Using this technique, Cage 'wrote through' *Joyce's *Finnegans Wake* and *Pound's *Cantos*, finding the author's name in fragments of already fragmented writing (e.g 'and thEn with bronZe lance heads beaRing yet Arms | sheeP slain Of plUto stroNg praiseD').

See *M* (1973), *Empty Words* (1979), *X* (1983), *Anarchy* (2001), and *Musicage: Cage Muses on Words Art Music,* with Joan *Retallack (1996—all Wesleyan University Press).   JNT

Cameron, (John) Norman (1905–53) The son of a Scottish cleric who was senior presidency chaplain in Bombay (now Mumbai), went to school at Fettes, and then to Oriel College, Oxford. He published poems in *The Fettesian* and *Oxford Poetry*, and later became one of the most frequent contributors to *New Verse*. In person he was tall, thin, and fair, a bohemian but slightly intimidating character, contemptuous (Geoffrey *Grigson said in a brief memoir) of most kinds of literary ambition, 'a literate original, not a literary man'. He spent the years from 1930 to 1932 as an education officer in Southern Nigeria, and later became an advertising copy-writer, work which he enjoyed. He is said to have been the inventor of the expression 'Night Starvation', a condition curable by taking Horlicks, and he wrote for the *Graves-*Riding magazine *Epilogue* an article on 'The Fairy-Tale Element in Advertising'.

In the Second World War he worked with a small group that included the film director Alexander Mackendrick and the literary editor T. R. Fyvel, producing political propaganda. He married three times, was a hard drinker, and became a Roman Catholic convert two years before his death. *The Winter House* (1935) was the only original collection published during his lifetime. *Collected Poems* (Hogarth), with an introduction by his close friend Robert Graves, appeared in 1957, and the *Complete Poems*, which contains a dozen more poems, in 1985 (Barth). He was also a notable translator, of Rimbaud and Villon and much French prose, including *Candide, Cousin Pons*, and Stendhal's letters.

Cameron's total poetic output, including his juvenilia, amounted to no more than seventy-odd short pieces, several ironic or deliberately comic, yet the slightest of them makes an impact, and the earliest are marked by the Manichaean struggle between puritanism and paganism that ordered his life. An early poem, 'Nunc Scio Quid Sit Amor' expresses his longing for and terror of the 'fierce outlander' who visits him from the land 'where the wild rainbow like a great giraffe | Curves down its neck to drink upon the sea...I fear you and I fear you, barbarous Love. | You are no citizen of my country.'

But Cameron's poetic country was just this divided land. The outrageous images, like that of the 'wild rainbow', are always under the strict control of what Graves called the Presbyterian moralist; the metres are definite, the rhymes exact, the insoluble problem stated over and over in various forms but always sharply and with a sense of style. 'The Dirty Little Accuser' is condemnatory about an unnamed Dylan *Thomas, but the poet reflects that when the 'crapulous lout' has been ejected his accusation can never be answered. 'The Invader' contemptuously dismisses Nazism in terms of its greed, not for conquest but for love. In technical terms Cameron owed a debt to Graves, perhaps something to Laura Riding, yet he hardly wrote a derivative or conventional phrase. There is something merciless about the way in which he turned his deepest feelings into demeaning comedy: 'When you confess your sins before a parson, | You find it no great effort to disclose | Your crimes of murder, bigamy and arson, | But can you tell him that you pick your nose?' Below the surface this is no more light-hearted than *Larkin, and behind the metronomic exactness, the contempt for casualness and concern for style, was a passionate seriousness that gives his few poems their strange authority.

Collected Poems and Selected Translations, ed. Warren Hope and Jonathan Barker, came out in 1990 (Anvil; new edn., 2011).   JGS

Campbell, Alistair (Te Ariki) (1925–2009) Born in Rarotonga, Cook Islands, of a Polynesian mother from Tongareva (Penrhyn Island) and a New Zealand father. Orphaned in 1933, he and his siblings were shipped to Dunedin and grew up in an orphanage. The landscape of Central Otago furnished images for his *Yeats-influenced first book, *Mine Eyes Dazzle* (Pegasus Press, 1950). After moving to Wellington in 1944 he trained as a teacher and then worked for the School Publications branch of the Department of Education until his retirement in 1972. His first wife was the poet Fleur *Adcock; in 1958 he married Meg Andersen, also a poet.

His traumatic childhood caused him for many years to live in denial of his Polynesian heritage, but a breakdown in 1960 put him in touch with it, and much of his later work celebrated Polynesian themes. With maturity the romantic, lyrical impulse of his youth broadened out to embrace narrative forms; he wrote of the Gallipoli campaign in which his father had served, and *Maori Battalion* (Wai-te-ata Press, 2001) was inspired by the experiences of his brother, killed in action in 1945. He also published fiction and an autobiography, *Island to Island* (Whitcoulls, 1984). *The Dark Lord of Savaiki: Collected Poems* (Hazard Press, 2005) includes his most important poetry.   FKA

Campbell, David (1915–79) Born near Adelong in the Monaro district of New South Wales, and educated in Australia and at Cambridge. He served with distinction in the Second World War in the RAAF, and after the war lived on various properties in the Canberra area, dividing his life between farming and writing. In 1964 he became poetry editor of the *Australian*, and edited *Australian Poetry* 1966 and *Modern Australian Poetry* (1970).

Like other emerging poets of the 1940s, Campbell used traditional forms in his attempt to link popular Australian subject-matter to the European tradition of pastoral and the metaphysical lyric. He focused on characteristic Australian subjects ('Harry Pearce', 'The Stockman') in an attempt to capture a vanishing world. He also experimented with the ballad, the tall story, and the pastoral sequence in 'Cocky's Calendar' and 'Works and Days'. The lyricism of early poems like 'Night Sowing' and 'Who Points the Swallow' gives way in his post-1970 volumes to restless experiment. *The Branch of Dodona* (1970) reinterprets classical myth to comment on the modern world; sequences like 'Starting from Central Station' and 'Deaths and Pretty Cousins' are autobiographical variations on life-studies themes, influenced by *Roethke and *Lowell, while series like 'Ku-Ring-Gai Rock Carvings' and 'Letters to a Friend' experiment with haiku-like arrangements. Campbell's later volumes free themselves from the formal polish of his early work and have the qualities of notebook entries and sketches. Part of his work consisted of translations and imitations from the Russian (published in collaboration with Rosemary *Dobson). He also wrote two volumes of short stories, *Evening Under Lamplight* (1959) and *Flame and Shadow* (1976). See *Collected Poems*, (Angus & Robertson, 1989) and *Hardening of the Light: Selected Poems* (Indigo, 2006), edited with an introduction by Philip Mead.   vs

Campbell, George (1916–2002) Born in Panama of Jamaican parents, and educated in Kingston and New York, where he lived from 1994. In the 1940s he was one of the poets associated with Edna Manley's *Focus* group.

Often biblically allusive, his poems tend to have a liturgical flavour, but at the service of a secular, and politically radical outlook. 'Holy', which opens with the lines, 'Holy be the white head of a Negro | Sacred

be the black flax of a black child', was quoted by Derek *Walcott in *Another Life*, very much as a tribute. 'In the Slums', on the other hand, ends with great simplicity of imagery: 'Here | Here is | The world we accept | From our glass houses.' Another poem, 'History Makers', graphically describes women stone-breakers, and focuses on them as symbolic of women's endurance in general.

Collections include *First Poems* (1945), published by Manley, which was reprinted in vol. 10 of the Yale series, *Critical Studies on Black Life and Culture* (1981), and *Earth Testament* (George Campbell Associates, 1983), with illustrations by Manley and an introduction by Edward *Baugh.

See also *From Our Yard: Jamaican Poetry Since Independence*, ed. Pamela Mordecai (Institute of Jamaica, 1987). *First Poems* was reprinted in 2011 by Peepal Tree Press.   MR

Campbell, (Ignatius) Roy(ston) (Dunnachie) (1902–57) Born in Natal, came to England in 1918 and published in 1924 *The Flaming Terrapin*, an allegory in which the terrapin stands for the renewal of life. After returning to South Africa he joined forces in 1926 with William *Plomer and, later, Laurens van der Post to produce *Voorslag* (Whiplash), a literary magazine that satirized everything held sacred by the Afrikaners. He compounded the offence with *The Wayzgoose* (1928), a satirical poem about South African life.

Adamastor (1930) a volume of exuberant lyrical power, written after his move to Provence, was followed by *The Georgiad* (1931), a long, virulent attack on the Bloomsbury Group in which his contempt for their work was sharpened by his fury at his wife's involvement with Vita *Sackville-West and her associates. *Flowering Reeds* (1933) marked a return to a gentler lyricism, and a further collection of poems, *Mithraic Emblems*, was published in 1936.

In *Broken Record* (1934), a prose autobiography, Campbell paraded his sympathies with Fascism and in 1935 he became a Roman Catholic. *Flowering Rifle* (1939), a strident eulogy of Franco as the upholder of Christian values, is one of the nastiest and worst poems ever written by a man of Campbell's gifts. His claim, made in this mixture of rodomontade and religiosity, to have fought for General Franco is false; but, greatly to his credit, he volunteered in 1942 for the British army in the Second World War and spent most of his military service in East Africa as a coast-watcher, after training briefly with Wingate's commando force.

Sons of the Mistral (1941) is a selection of his poems. *Talking Bronco* (1946), a disappointing volume, contains a number of accomplished but lightweight poems about East Africa, of which the liveliest are 'Heartbreak Camp' and 'Dreaming Spires', Campbell's playful name for giraffes.

There are, however, two poems in the collection that rank among the finest verse he ever wrote. One is the sonnet, 'Luis de Camões', in which he claims an affinity with the sixteenth-century Portuguese poet, the author of *The Lusiads*, who had, like himself, been a Catholic and a servant of Spain, and had sailed past Fort Jesus to endure the life of a common soldier in Mombasa: 'He shouldered high his voluntary Cross, | Wrestled his hardship into forms of beauty, | And taught his gorgon destinies to sing.'

The second poem of outstanding merit in *Talking Bronco*, a version of *En Una Noche Oscura* by St John of the Cross, foreshadows Campbell's major post-war undertakings. He translated a dozen Spanish and Portuguese works of fiction, among them *Cousin Basilio*, the nineteenth-century masterpiece of Eca de Quieroz. Campbell's verse translations are the crown of his poetic achievement. *The Poems of St John of the Cross* (1951) and his version of Baudelaire's *Les Fleurs du Mal* (1952) are worthy of the originals. His translations and appraisal of Lorca in 1952 may seem an unlikely tribute from an aggressively heterosexual Roman Catholic apologist for General Franco to a Communist homosexual murdered by the General's supporters. But apart from the aberrations of *Flowering Rifle* and of the autobiographies—the second, *Light on a Dark Horse* (1951), reiterated the old beliefs—all Campbell's work was inspired by a generous love of poetry and a pursuit of imaginative truth.

Some readers find certain of Campbell's most celebrated poems, such as 'Tristan da Cunha' and 'Choosing a Mast', too self-consciously heroic and elaborately rhetorical. Yet their exuberance and élan carry them irresistibly to their triumphant conclusions, and his shorter lyrics, such as 'The Serf', 'The Zulu Girl', and 'The Sisters', burn with a controlled sensuousness.

Campbell was a quarrelsome and, at times, a truculent figure. He fell out with his co-editors of *Voorslag*; he pursued a variety of literary vendettas; and his married life was stormy. Although some of his accusations against Bloomsbury may have been justified, his diatribes against Communists, homosexuals, and wowsers (a favourite term of abuse) were often ludicrous and wearisome. Yet all these flaws were powerless to spoil the vein of pure lyricism and the nobility of mind that inform the finest of his poems.

Campbell died in a car crash in Portugal. His *Collected Poems* were published in three volumes in 1949, 1957, and 1960 (Bodley Head), the third volume being devoted to his translations.

See also *Selected Poems* (1982), ed. Peter F. Alexander, author of *Roy Campbell* (1982—both Oxford University Press) and Joseph Pearce, *Bloomsbury and Beyond: The Friends and Enemies of Roy Campbell* (Harper, 2002).   JPr*

Capildeo, Vahni (1973–) Born in Port of Spain, Capildeo grew up in Trinidad before moving to Britain in 1991, where she read English at Oxford University, and wrote a doctoral thesis on Old Norse literature. She has worked for the *Oxford English Dictionary*, been a Research Fellow at Girton College, Cambridge, and taught creative writing at the universities of Kingston and Leeds.

Capildeo's first collection, *No Traveller Returns* (Salt, 2003) introduced a sophisticated writer, drawn to working in sequences and multiple voices. Her cosmopolitan imagination is capable of exuberantly satirical humour on questions of identity, as in the 'Person Animal Figure' monologues from her second collection *Undraining Sea* (2009). *Dark and Unaccustomed Words*

(2011—both Eggbox), was shortlisted for the Guyana Prize for Literature. Taking its title from George Puttenham's *The Arte of Poesie* (1589), and an epigraph from Martin *Carter, it offers formally inventive lyrics to friends and fellow poets, as well as the meditative prose poetry that has become one of her most distinctive modes.   JNT

Carruth, Hayden (1921–2008) Born in Connecticut and educated at the universities of North Carolina and Chicago, he spent most of his life in New England and upper New York state. He began publishing collections of his work in 1959. Several well-regarded books followed, particularly *The Bloomingdale Papers* (University of Georgia Press), published in 1975 but written twenty-two years earlier when he was a patient in an asylum.

With the publication of *Brothers, I Have Loved You All* (Sheep Meadow, 1978), Carruth found his own voice. Utilizing New England character and diction with a facility equal to Robert *Frost's, many of his strongest poems in this and subsequent volumes involve stoic resolve in the face of hardship and defeat.

In his introduction to *Effluences from the Sacred Caves* (University of Michigan Press, 1983), a collection of essays and reviews, he said that he defined himself 'only *against* the Platonic and Romantic aspirations', which, none the less, held for him 'a powerful, though I think false, allure'. In this he turned against the transcendental ambitions characteristic of many of his New England predecessors. Carruth's New England is a land of pragmatists and sceptics. Given his very hard-edged sensibility, it is not surprising that he also included William Carlos *Williams and Ezra *Pound among his masters.

The Sleeping Beauty (Harper, 1982), a long meditative poem written in his own 15-line 'paragraph' stanza, was reprinted in a revised edition by Copper Canyon Press in 1990. *Collected Shorter Poems* (1992) and *Collected Longer Poems* (1993) were followed by *Scrambled Eggs and Whiskey* (1996), which won the National Book Award, and *Doctor Jazz* (2001). *Last Poems* appeared posthumously in 2012. See also *Selected Essays and Reviews* (1995) and *Reluctantly: Autobiographical Essays* (1998— all Copper Canyon).   EHF

Carson, Anne (1950–) Born in Toronto and studied Classics at the university there and at St Andrews, Scotland. As a professor she has taught in Canada and the States, and has also held writing residencies and fellowships.

Carson's doctoral thesis on Sappho and the 'hole' at the heart of love poetry later became her first book of criticism, *Eros the Bittersweet* (Princeton University Press, 1986). Her first small-press volume of poetry was *Short Talks* (Brick, 1992). The appearance of *Glass, Irony and God* (New Directions) and *Plainwater: Essays and Poetry* (Knopf) in 1995 brought her to critical recognition, a major publisher, and a wider readership. Her writing effaces the line between verse and prose, lyricism and scholarship, with arresting if variable effect. The secret of its popularity lies in its conversational voice, which roams freely from *Confessional subject matter ('Father's Old Blue Cardigan') to the wisdom of Greek fragments, guided by a respect for the ineffable. She has also published translations of *Electra* (Oxford University Press, 2001), Sappho (*If, Winter* (Knopf, 2002)), and *An Oresteia* (Faber, 2009).

Autobiography of Red: A Novel in Verse (1998) was an acclaimed contemporary retelling of the tenth labour of Hercules. *Men in the Off Hours* (2000) and *The Beauty of the Husband: A Fictional Essay in 29 Tangos* (2001) won the Griffin and the T. S. Eliot prizes respectively. *Decreation* (2005—all Knopf) collected verse, essays, an unfilmed screenplay, and a libretto about female mystics. Her poetry is published in the UK by Picador. *Nox* (New Directions, 2010), an illustrated, fold-out elegy in a box, continued her exploration of hybrid forms.   JNT

Carson, Ciaran (1948–) Born in Belfast into an Irish-speaking family, and educated at Queen's University Belfast. He worked in the Civil Service, as a teacher, and as a musician, before becoming Traditional

Arts Officer for the Northern Ireland Arts Council. He is now Professor of Poetry at Queen's, where he directs The Seamus Heaney Centre.

The New Estate (Blackstaff Press, 1976), Carson's first collection, though promising, consisted largely of a poetry of domesticity. His distinctive voice appeared in his second collection, *The Irish for No* (1987). There he began to use with assurance the long line which is a hallmark of his writing and which allows him the room to develop his free-wheeling narratives. This trend was continued in his third volume, *Belfast Confetti* (1989), in which his concern with Belfast was also intensified. Through an attentiveness to representation Carson avoids sensationalism and sentimentality. He considers that maps and language can never capture the shifting urban landscape: language is always turned aside into digression; maps show roads which no longer exist. The only mode of narrative is digressive, the only map of the city is the city itself. The metaphor 'Belfast confetti'— the name given to the bricolage of nuts, bolts, and half-bricks used by rioters— balances the elements of danger and celebration which Carson successfully combines in poetry which is exhilarating, funny, and exact.

The New Estate and Other Poems (1988) reprinted his first collection with additional poems. *First Language* (1993), which included translations of Baudelaire and Rimbaud into his characteristically expansive verse line and colloquial manner, won the inaugural T. S. Eliot Prize. Carson's prosody has been attributed in part to the American example of C. K. *Williams, but also to Irish ballad metre, which he foregrounded in the sequences of his next collection, *Opera Et Cetera* (1996). His nonfiction book on Irish traditional music, *Last Night's Fun*, appeared the same year from Cape. *The Alexandrine Plan* (1998— all Gallery Press), a collection of sonnets translated from the French Symbolists, was followed by *The Twelfth of Never*, which employed the same form in a utopian fantasia, and *The Ballad of HMS Belfast*, a collection of his poems about the city (1999—both Picador). See also his autobiographical history of Belfast, *The Star Factory* (Granta, 1997). *Breaking News* (2003), whose starker realism and shorter line looked to William Carlos *Williams, won the Forward Poetry Prize. It was followed by *For All We Know* (2005), a novelistic sonnet sequence. Since *Collected Poems* (2008) Carson has published *On the Night Watch* (2009) and *Until Before After* (2010—all Gallery Press).

Carson has also written prose fiction, including *Shamrock Tea* (2001), and made a translation of Dante's *Inferno* (2002— both Granta). He is published in the States by Wake Forest University Press: see *Selected Poems* (2001). For criticism see Neal Alexander, *Ciaran Carson: Space, Place, Writing* (Liverpool University Press, 2011).   EH*

Carter, Martin (Wylde)

Carter, Martin (Wylde) (1927–97) Born in Georgetown, British Guiana (now Guyana), and educated there, at Queen's College. He was actively involved in the nationalist movement, and a spell of three months in detention for his political activities led to *Poems of Resistance* (Lawrence & Wishart, 1954), the collection which established his reputation. This volume reflects Carter's commitment to the People's Progressive Party of Dr Cheddi Jagan, and its Marxist orientation. The stark, militant rhetoric of a poem like 'I Clench My Fist', however, is counterbalanced by the compassion and startling imagery of one like 'Cartman of Dayclean'. Carter at his best also fuses the confessional and the political, as in 'I Come from the Nigger Yard'.

After independence, Carter joined the cabinet of Prime Minister Forbes Burnham as Minister of Public Information and Broadcasting, and represented Guyana at the United Nations. His later poetry loses some of its political urgency, but it gains in sibylline irony.

Poems of Succession (New Beacon, 1977) also contained poetry from his earlier books. His last collection was *Poems of Affinity: 1978–1980* (Release, 1980). *Hinterland: Caribbean Poetry from the West Indies and Britain*, ed. E. A. Markham (Bloodaxe, 1989), contains a substantial selection of his poems, and also a probing interview with Peter Trevis. In 1989, Carter's *Selected*

Poems (Demerera) won the Guyana Prize for Literature. See *University of Hunger: Collected Poems and Selected Prose*, ed. Gemma Robinson (Bloodaxe, 2006).   MR

Carver, Raymond (1939–88) Best known as a short-story writer, but his interest as a poet is oddly independent of his prose, though perhaps a growth from it, at least in terms of a certain spare and tight-lipped style. The stories of Carver operate often in a low-keyed, blue-collar world, where a stark ashcan brilliance illuminates a sort of bleak heroism. These stories take place in the darkness at the edge of town.

The best of Carver's stories are likely to last, but his poems remain more controversial. Most of them strike the ear with a deliberate flatness of diction, an absence of metaphor, and an air of being arranged in roughly chopped lengths, as if a backwoodsman has been at a copse of prose with an axe. But his plain look is part of a sound American tradition, rooted in *Frost and *Jeffers, flowering in Robert Penn *Warren. Indeed, the very extremity of Carver's drive towards casualness—his conscious willingness to leave his finished text with the freshness of a first draft or note for a poem—is what gives his work its genuine originality and importance. We are being invited to accept in verse what was once very difficult to accept even in prose when we had it offered first by Hemingway: the gas turned down towards its lowest level without the flame going out.

The justification for this bare style can perhaps be found most easily in the poignant and bitter experiences from which Carver has taken his material. We form a relationship with a persona—close to Carver but not quite him—who has endured alcoholism, loves hunting and the American wilderness, and is dying of cancer. This last element dangerously qualifies our responses, but inevitably so. We watch a brave man counting out his time, seeing this happen through a verse medium as clear as glass, the perfect, neutral focus for our emotions.

Carver's collections include: *Near Klamath* (English Club of Sacramento State College, 1968), *Winter Insomnia* (Kayak, 1970),

At Night the Salmon Move (Capra, 1976), *In a Marine Light: Selected Poems* (Harvill, 1987), and *A New Path to the Waterfall* (Atlantic Monthly Press/Harvill, 1989); see also *Fires: Essays, Poems, Stories* (Harvill, 1985) and the posthumous *No Heroics, Please* (Random House, 1992). *All of Us: The Collected Poems* (Knopf), with an introduction by his second wife, Tess *Gallagher, appeared in 1998.   GMacB

Cassity, Turner (1929–2009) Born in Jackson, Mississippi, where he grew up, and was educated at Millsaps College, BA 1951; Stanford University, MA, 1952; and—after two years in the US Army—at Columbia University, MS, 1955. At Stanford University he became associated with Yvor *Winters' *Stanford School.

Cassity's extensive travels included South and Central America, Russia, Hong Kong, Europe, the West Indies, Australia, and West Africa. He lived for three years in Johannesburg and Pretoria. In 1991 he retired as catalogue librarian in the library of Emory University after twenty-nine years of service.

The locales of his poems are as geographically far-flung and exotic as his travels, but the extreme variety of place and subject is given unity by several dominant themes—social injustice, greed, vanity, hypocrisy, lust, and vulgarity of taste. He is primarily a satirist. In his poetic procedure he employs logical structure and conventional prosody, but in the confines of his strict forms there is a variety of rhythm and an impressive display of exotic and unconventional imagery and diction. Occasionally there are poems of serious metaphysical substance, such as his meditations on chance and determinism in 'Calvin at the Casino'; on time versus beauty, in the ingenious 'A Clock with a Mirror Face, Presented to a Lady'; and on death in 'Allerseen', all from his first book, *Watchboy, What of the Night?* (Wesleyan University Press, 1966). Caustic comment on contemporary culture continues in *Steeplejacks in Babel* (Godine, 1973), notably in 'Off the Freeway', and 'The Shropshire Lad in Limehouse'. There is a heartless dissection of the heritage of imperialism in the South African poems and in the play on Cecil Rhodes in *Yellow for Peril, Black for Beauty* (Braziller, 1975). *The Defense of the Sugar Islands* (Symposium, 1979) is a psychological study of an American soldier who, during the Korean War, is stationed in Puerto Rico, far from the military action.

The Destructive Element: New and Selected Poems (1998, Ohio University Press) drew on the later collections *Hurricane Lamp* (1986) and *Between the Chains* (1991—both University of Chicago Press). Cassity's last books were *No Second Eden* (2002) and *Devils and Islands* (2007—both Ohio University Press), which won the Georgia Author of the Year Award in Poetry.   DS

Catalano, Gary (1947–2002) Born in Brisbane but soon moved to Kellyville, on the outskirts of Sydney, where his Italian father was a market gardener. He attended Trinity Grammar School in Sydney, but left at the age of 16 to begin an intensive course of self-education. Without any formal training he managed to become one of Australia's leading art critics, an achievement recognized in 1986 when he was appointed by the Melbourne *Age* as its art correspondent. He published several volumes of art criticism and a collection of short stories, in addition to his poetry.

Catalano's early poems, in *Remembering the Rural Life* (University of Queensland Press, 1978), are touchingly detailed childhood recollections, but this first book already bore indications of the minimalist direction his poetry was later to take, concluding with a group of tersely introspective meditations. In *Heaven of Rags* (Hale & Iremonger, 1982) and *Slow Tennis* (1986) his verse became increasingly abstract, cryptic, and refined, its form attenuated in ultra-short lines and repetitive two- or three-line stanzas. *Fresh Linen* (1988—both University of Queensland Press) was a volume of prose poems, which would become one of his most characteristic modes: see *Light and Water: Forty Prose Poems 1980–1999* (Finlay Press, 2002). *Selected Poems* (1993) drew on *The Empire of Grass* (1991—both University of Queensland Press), whose title poem refers to the 'real empire' of the non-human

world—says the poet—'of which I dream'. See *New and Selected Poems* (Indigo, 2007).   JG*

Catling, Brian (1948–) Born in London and studied at North East London Polytechnic and the Royal College of Art. He is an internationally recognized sculptor, performance artist, and poet—activities, as he has said, 'that sometimes fuse together into a hybrid event'. He taught for many years at art schools in Brighton and London, and is now Professor of Fine Art at the Ruskin School, Oxford.

Catling has cited the poetry of Samuel *Beckett as an important early influence. The shadow of William Blake also falls across his neo-Gothic visions of London (see 'The Pittancer' and 'The Flea'). His first books, beginning with *Necropathia*, were published by Iain Sinclair's Albion Village Press in the early 1970s. *The Stumbling Block its Index* (Bookworks, 1990) is Catling's best-known work. A series of densely wrought prose poems, it describes a non-existent sculptural object using elusively *surrealist metaphors ('a graphite font', 'a spirit bench', 'an atlas swallowing its tongue').

Catling's wide-ranging, often ritualistic interests suggest a shamanistic conception of the artist's role. In 2006, he was commissioned to produce a monument for the site of execution at the Tower of London, which features a circular text and a glass pillow as 'a gesture of repentance'. His collected poems, *A Court of Miracles*, were published by Etruscan Books in 2009. See *Tending the Vortex: the Works of Brian Catling*, ed. Simon Perril (CCCP, 2001).   JNT

Causley, Charles (1917–2003) Born in Launceston, Cornwall, and lived there for most of his life. He attended the local grammar school, and later worked in an office before serving in the Royal Navy, 1940–6. On demobilization Causley trained as a teacher and subsequently worked in schools ('thirty years in chalk Siberias') before resigning in his fifties to become a full-time author. He remained based in Cornwall but increasingly ventured across the world to take up literary appointments in Australia, Canada, and the USA. He received the Queen's Gold Medal for poetry in 1967.

Causley published plays in the Thirties—*Runaway* (1936), *The Conquering Hero* (1937)—but had to wait until 1951 before his first collection of poems was printed—*Farewell, Aggie Weston*. After that he produced an abundance of verse for adults and for children; his principal publisher in London (Macmillan) brought out a *Collected Poems* in 1975, which went into several expanded editions.

Experiences gained in the navy offered Causley a meaty subject-matter, as did the Cornish landscape and its people. He stood quietly apart from the machinations and in-fighting of the poetry world, and consistently eschewed trends and fashions, preferring instead to use traditional forms to create a readable poetry which appeals to a wide audience. Causley's strengths are his clarity, sensitive use of rhyme, freshness of language and imagery, and an ability to combine recognizable poetic forms with contemporary reference-points. The collections of poems for children include a generous slice of humour.

Later work, such as the collection *A Field of Vision* (Macmillan, 1988), offers great diversity of material as Causley records his childhood, and includes observational poems gathered from his literary travels around the globe. *Causley at 70* (Peterloo, 1987) is a compilation of appreciative poems and prose contributed by leading literary figures, while *The Young Man of Cury* (Macmillan, 1991) is a rich and rewarding collection for young people. See *Collected Poems 1951–2000* (Picador, 2000), which ends with the late lyric 'Eden Rock', and *I Had a Little Cat: Collected Poems for Children* (Macmillan, 2009).   WM

Ceravalo, Joseph (1934–88) Born in New York City to Italian parents. He began writing poetry in 1957 while on Army service in the German Alps. On returning to New York, he studied for a degree in civil engineering and joined Kenneth *Koch's poetry workshop.

Ceravalo's association with Koch and contemporaries such as Ted *Berrigan places him among the *New York School. There is a purity and minimalism to his verse, though, which contrasts with the expansive, pop-culture irony that often characterizes New York poetry. The title poem of *Spring in this World of Poor Mutts* (Columbia University Press, 1968)—a volume which won the inaugural Frank O'Hara Award—admittedly features 'a robot... looking at a bird | his penis... hanging down'. But it also expresses fragmentary pain in elemental imagery more reminiscent of a European poet such as Paul Celan ('I kiss your lips | on a grain: the forest').

Ceravalo's fractured syntax was most pronounced in *Fits of Dawn* ('C' Press, 1965). By his final volume, *Millennium Dust* (Kulchur Foundation, 1982), the writing is more directly mystical. As in William Carlos *Williams, whom Ceravolo admired, the pastoral world of the seasons reveals the essential poetry of urban American life (another title was *Wild Flowers Out of Gas*). Like Williams, he spent his adult life in New Jersey, working and raising a family. He died suddenly of bile duct cancer. *The Green Lake Is Awake* (Coffee House, 1994) is a selection edited by friends and introduced by Koch. Ceravalo's *Collected Poems* appeared from Wesleyan University Press in 2013.   JNT

Cervantes, Lorna Dee (1954–   ) Called by *Alurista 'probably the best Chicana poet active today'. Both *Emplumada* (University of Pittsburgh Press, 1981) and *From the Cables of Genocide: Poems on Love and Hunger* (Arte Publico, 1992), and the work published in magazines like *Mango*, the *Revista Chicano-Riqueña*, and *Red Dirt*, exhibit considerable skill and variety. She can be toughly unsentimental yet lyric, as in 'Beneath the Shadow of the Freeway', a recollection of her cross-blood Chicano and Native American welfare-family upbringing in California. She can speak forcefully, as in 'Barco de Refugios/Refugee Ship', about America's non-recognition of her *mestiza* heritage, causing her to feel 'orphaned from my Spanish name'. She can assume an intimate, teasing tone as in her love poem 'The Body As Braille'. In 'Cannery Town in August' she invokes nameless women 'who smell of whiskey and tomatoes, | peach fuzz reddening their lips and eyes', working through the night to can California fruit and vegetables. And though 'political' only in the most oblique fashion, she can write with well-placed irony of cultural outsiderness, as in 'Poem for the Young White Man Who Asked Me How I, an Intelligent, Well-Read Person Could Believe in the War between Races'. Few contemporaries, chicano or otherwise, match her powers of articulating *barrio* and blue-collar family life and labour—or the intimacies of a hard-won, anti-patriarchal femininity. Cervantes' later poems have been collected in five books as *Drive: The First Quartet* (2006), which won a Latino Book Award. See also *Ciento: 100 100-Word Love Poems* (2011—both Wings).   ARL

Challis, Gordon (1932–) Born in Wales and emigrated to New Zealand in 1953. He studied at Victoria University College in Wellington in the later 1950s, completing a degree in psychology in 1960. He published extensively in the small periodicals associated with Wellington's literary activities in those years, and was recognized as one of the emerging poets of his generation.

His poetry was often metaphysical, developing conceits that explore the metaphorical attributes of a persona created out of what Kendrick *Smithyman called 'nominal unreality'. The figures of his poems are often grotesque and allegorical, but they always suggest insightful awareness of human behaviour and temperament.

The editor of *Landfall*, Charles *Brasch, presented him as one of four new 'poets of the sixties' in the first issue of the decade (issue 53, Mar. 1960), and Challis' first book, *Building* (Caxton, 1962), was well-reviewed. Smithyman wrote on him in his study of New Zealand poetry, *A Way of Saying* (Collins, 1965), but Challis himself did not publish again until he retired from a career in mental health in 1989. *The Other Side of the Brain* (2003) has been followed

by the lighter-hearted *Luck of the Bounce* (2009—both Steele Roberts).   WSB*

Chappell, Fred (1936–) Born in Canton, a mill town in the mountains of western North Carolina, and raised on the family's farm. Educated at Duke University, he taught creative writing at the University of North Carolina at Greensboro for over twenty-five years.

Chappell's early reputation was based on the four novels he published between 1963 and 1973, one of which, *Dagon* (New York, 1968), received France's Prix de Meilleur des Livres Étrangers. His first volume of poems, *The World Between the Eyes* (1971), earned little recognition. Not until the publication of the tetralogy *Midquest* (1981), which reprinted four previously published books (*River, Bloodfire, Wind Mountain*, and *Earthsleep*), did Chappell's poetry attract significant critical attention. In 1985, largely on the strength of *Midquest*'s achievement, Chappell was named, along with John *Ashbery, co-recipient of the Bollingen Prize. His other publications in the 1980s included a collection of short stories, two novels, and three additional books of poems.

Chappell's art derives from two major sources: his childhood and youth in the Appalachian mountains and his wide reading in the books, philosophical as well as literary, that have shaped Western culture. Among the most notable qualities of his poetry are its carefully crafted variety of forms, its fine story-telling and creation of character, its humour, and its serious moral intent. Chappell's poems reveal both enormous erudition and a profound commitment to what he has called 'folk art'. In addition to the mountain community whose life *Midquest* records, the book also creates a striking sense of literary community and of a vital literary tradition through its varied poetic forms, its verse epistles to contemporary author-friends, and its countless references to other writers, especially Dante, whose spiritual quest Chappell's persona emulates. *Castle Tzingal* (1984), a moral allegory presented through a series of voices, *Source* (1985), and *First and Last Words* (1989), a volume largely composed of prefaces and afterwords to Chappell's reading, confirm his poetic range and power.

The Fred Chappell Reader (New York, 1987) reprinted thirty-four of the author's poems, including over a third of *Midquest*, together with a generous selection from his fiction. Since *Spring Garden: New and Selected Poems* (1995), he has published three further collections: *Family Gathering* (2000), *Backsass* (2004), and *Shadow Box* (2009—all Louisiana State University Press). Between 1997 and 2002 he was Poet Laureate of North Carolina.

A Way of Happening: Observations of Contemporary Poetry (Picador, 1998), includes Chappell's essays on A. R. *Ammons, Alfred *Corn, and others. His short stories have been selected in *Ancestors and Others* (St Martin's Press, 2009). See Patrick Bizarro (ed.), *Dream Garden: The Poetic Vision of Fred Chappell* (Louisiana State University Press, 1997), and John Lang, *Understanding Fred Chappell* (University of South Carolina Press, 2000). JLa*

Charles, Faustin (1944–) Born in Trinidad, and educated at the universities of Kent and London. He has lived in England since 1962, has been a visiting lecturer for the Commonwealth Institute, a part-time teacher in London, and a Community Literacy Officer. Richly imagistic, his poems tend to be lush and fertile with implication, but also elegant in execution. He excels in phantasmagoric effects, most strikingly in 'Nude Black Nymph Riding a Black Stallion at Midnight'. His aims as a poet are strongly suggested in 'Calypso Cricketer' and 'Cricket's in my Blood'.

His collections include *The Expatriate* (1969), *Crab Track* (1973—both Brookside), and *Days and Nights in the Magic Forest* (Bogle-l'Ouverture, 1986). He has also novels, short stories, and several works for children, including the best-selling *The Selfish Crocodile* (Bloomsbury, 1998). See *Children of the Morning: Selected Poems* (Peepal Tree, 2008). MR

Charman, Janet (1956–) Born in Auckland, Charman trained to be a nurse, and has worked as a secondary-school teacher of English. Her poems have been called 'understated' in their elliptical, playful notations of everyday life. Their feminist ambition, however, is openly declared in her first full volume, *2 Deaths in 1 Night* (New Women's Press, 1987), which presents a series of narrative 'lectures' on poets such as Maya *Angelou, Sylvia *Plath, and Adrienne *Rich. In 1997 Charman was Literary Fellow at the University of Auckland. During this time she wrote on Ursula *Bethell, arguing that her neglect in New Zealand literary history 'is due to critical ambivalence regarding her lesbian identity'. Her subsequent collection, *Rapunzel Rapunzel* (Auckland University Press, 1999), includes poems about Bethell's partner, Effie Pollen. Her other collections, all from Auckland University Press, are *red letter* (1992); *end of the dry* (1995); *snowing down south* (2002); and *Cold Snack* (2007), which won the Montana Poetry Prize. JNT

cheek, cris (1955–) Born in London, cheek co-founded Chisenhale Dance Space in Mile End, London in 1981. In the early 1990s he began attending Bob *Cobbing's Writers Forum workshops. Along with Caroline *Bergvall, he taught on the Performance Writing course at Dartington College of Arts, and later received a PhD from the University of Leicester. Subsequently, he moved to the United States, where he is a professor at Miami University in Oxford, Ohio.

cheek's poetry is characterized by his interests in interdisciplinarity and performance. Much of his work is produced in collaboration with other artists. He also frequently employs other media in his compositions, such as computer programs, found texts, and sound and video recordings. With Kirsten Lavers, he worked for many years on an interdisciplinary writing project, *Things Not Worth Keeping*.

cheek's publications include *a present* (Bluff, 1980), *mud* (Spanner/Open Field, 1984), *Cloud Eyes* (Microbrigade, 1991), *Stranger* (Sound & Language, 1996), *Songs from Navigation* (Reality Street, 1998), and *the church, the school, the beer* (Critical

Documents, 2007). Iterations of his work can often be found in more ephemeral settings such as art galleries, improvised performance evenings, and websites.   SRO

Cheney-Coker, Syl (1945–) Born in Freetown, Sierra Leone. He studied at the universities of Oregon and Wisconsin before returning to Africa, where, after working as a journalist in Sierra Leone, he taught for many years at the University of Maiduguri in Nigeria. He also taught for two years at the University of the Philippines, but eventually returned to live in Freetown, where he edited and published the radical newspaper *The Vanguard*. He has published one novel, *The Last Harmattan of Alusine Dunbar* (1990), which won the Commonwealth Writers Prize, and three collections of poetry: *Concerto for an Exile* (1973) which was reissued as a part of his second collection, *The Graveyard Also Has Teeth* (1980), and *The Blood in the Desert's Eyes* (1990—all Heinemann).

Syl Cheney-Coker's poetry has always seemed an adjunct to his calling as a radical, campaigning journalist. His are poems of causes, essentially intended as interventions into the various debates that his life's wanderings and his intellectual enquiries have touched on—so he has written about South Africa, black America, the Arab-Israeli conflict, the duties and fates of poets everywhere, as well as the struggles in Sierra Leone, about which he has always been outspoken. Cheney-Coker is unashamedly opinionated, rhetorical, and verbose. His work is characterized by a surging, discursive, long-lined verse that at times teeters on the verge of the prosaic. His best poems, however, assume the force of poetic manifestos on behalf of the world's 'sufferers'.

After the military coup d'état in 1997, Cheney-Coker went into exile from Sierra Leone until 2003. In 2000 he was the first writer-in-residence under the City of Asylum programme in the United States. See *Stone Child and Other Poems* (HEBN, 2008).   SB

Chesterton, G. K. (Gilbert Keith) (1874–1936) Born in London. He made his first reputation with his comic drawings,

but had become a well-established journalist by the turn of the century. He was associated in the public mind with his Roman Catholic friend Hilaire *Belloc ('The Chesterbelloc'); but he was not actually received into the Roman Catholic Church until 1922. Chesterton is most famous as the creator of the priest-detective Father Brown, and as a capable, witty, paradoxical essayist. His profundity has been questioned, but never in regard to his poetry, which is unashamedly lightweight. He wrote in the tradition of Browning, and never made the slightest effort to accommodate himself to modernism, which he regularly mocked (his last radio broadcast, 'We Will End With a Bang', pokes fun at *Eliot). The chief influences upon him were Walt Whitman and Belloc, the nonchalance of whose light verse he at first tried to emulate. At its worst Chesterton's poetry declines into trite doggerel. At its best ('The Donkey' has been much anthologized, but 'The Rolling English Road' is more characteristic) it has a pleasant charm and sincerity, although—perhaps surprisingly—Chesterton could never express paradox in poetry as successfully as he could in prose. *Collected Poems* (Methuen, 1933) is the most complete edition.   MS-S

Chiasson, Dan (1971–) Born in Burlington, Vermont, Chiasson read English at Harvard University. He is a poetry editor at the *Paris Review* and teaches at Wellesley College, Massachusetts. His criticism has been widely published.

The Afterlife of Objects (University of Chicago Press, 2002) knowingly plays with *Lowellian tropes in its dream-like treatment of grief for family, friends, and the 'souvenirs of youth'. In his second collection, *Natural History* (2007), with its deployment of Horace and Pliny, Chiasson takes a deliberately literary step away from this autobiographical debut. As he reflects on himself through the voice of another poet-critic, Randall *Jarrell, 'He tried on the *confessional style for a while.' *Where's the Moon, There's the Moon* (2010—both Random House) moves further towards the spacious American lyric 'I' this writing evidently aspires to inhabit, though youthful fancy remains a touchstone of its charm ('Stadium' imagines the poet's childhood 'bobbing like a raisin' in a 'vast cereal bowl'). Both have been published in the UK by Bloodaxe. Chiasson's first critical book, *One Kind of Everything: Poem and Person in Contemporary American Poetry* (University of Chicago Press, 2007), contains essays on Lowell, Elizabeth *Bishop, Frank *Bidart, Frank *O'Hara, and Louise *Glück.   JNT

Chimombo, Steve (1945–) Born at Zomba, Malawi, and studied at the universities of Malawi, Wales, Leeds, and Columbia. He joined the staff of Chancellor College, University of Malawi, in 1972, where he became professor of English. He has published a play, *The Rainmaker* (1978), a novel, *The Basket Girl* (1990), and a critical study of Malawian oral literature. He also edits a literary journal, *Wasi Writer*. *Napolo Poems* (Manchichi, 1987), his first collection, received honourable mention in the prestigious 1988 Noma Award for publishing in Africa. A selection of the poems from this volume, as well as a previously unpublished poem, 'A Death Song', appeared in the *Heinemann Book of African Poetry in English* (1990).

According to the poet himself, the Napolo of the title is 'the mythical subterranean serpent residing under mountains and associated with landslides, earthquakes and floods in Malawi'. The last serious manifestation of this mythical serpent was in 1946, when Zomba mountain erupted and thousands of people were killed. The local population thought it was a sign of the end of the world, and still talk of it to this day. At an immediate level, the poems in the collection draw on the newspaper reports, folk-songs, and stories associated with the event; at a deeper level, however, they form an oblique commentary on one of the most ruthless dictatorships anywhere in the world. A selected poems, *Napolo and the Python*, appeared in 1994 (Heinemann). He continues to publish through his own WASI imprint: see *The Wrath of Napolo* (2000), a novel.   AM-P

Chin, Marilyn (**Mei Ling**) (1955–) Born in Hong Kong, Chin's family emigrated to the United States in her childhood. She studied Chinese Literature at the University of Massachussets, an MFA in Creative Writing (University of Iowa), and undertook postgraduate work at Stanford University. Chin currently teaches in the department of English and Comparative Literature at San Diego State University.

Poet and anthologist, translator, teacher, and activist, Chin has won numerous awards and fellowships, and has published three volumes of poetry to date, a surrealist novel/manifesto, *Revenge of the Mooncake Vixen* (Norton, 2009), and a play *The Love Palace* (2002). She has edited collections of Asian-American and world poetry, and translated the work of the modern Chinese dissident poet Ai Qing, and the Japanese poet Gozo Yoshimasu.

Self-described as a 'hyphenated American poet', Chin's poetry explores marginalization, exile, cultural inheritance, and sexual politics, and demonstrates an overtly political feminism. She draws on sources ranging from contemporary popular American culture and the poetry of Adrienne *Rich and June George, to Cantonese opera and Persian ghazals. *Dwarf Bamboo* (Greenfield Review, 1987) was dedicated to *Ai. *The Phoenix Gone, The Terrace Empty* (Milkweed, 1994) saw Chin win her first Pushcart prize, and included a section, 'Beijing Spring', addressing the Tiananmen Square atrocities. *Rhapsody in Plain Yellow* (Norton, 2002) shows the influence of music on Chin's poetry (from classical Chinese folk music to blues and ancient Persian forms), and contains elegies for her mother and maternal grandmother.   HY

Chingono, Julius Sekai (1946–2011) Born on a commercial farm near Harare, Chingono worked for most of his life as a rock blaster in mines. He wrote in Shona and English. His English poetry is included in *Not Another Day* (Weaver, 2006), *State of the Nation: Contemporary Zimbabwean Poetry* (The Conversation Paperpress, 2009), and *Together*, with John *Eppel ('amaBooks, 2011). He also wrote a novel (*Chipo Changu*, 1978), a play (*Ruvimbo*,

1980), and a collection of short stories (*Not Another Day*, 2006).

Chingono's writing is direct and transparent. He is preoccupied with everyday, seemingly mundane matters. But he brings his humour, his sense of irony, and a thoroughgoing interest and empathy for his subjects to bear on the ordinary. In 'Recipe' he wrote 'Take a sizable number | of township residents | adults of varying ages | cram them into a combi | until full | allow time to heat | . . . let mixture simmer | and then allow to cool | in bed at night. | May be served as bad temper.' This is Chingono at his most ferocious: the poem is well paced, the images exact, the narrative is taut, and the impact devastatingly humorous.   FO

Chipasula, Frank Mkalawile

(1949–) Born in Malawi and studied at Chancellor College, University of Malawi, until he was forced into exile in 1973. He lived for one year in Tanzania, then moved to Zambia. He obtained a BA from the University of Zambia in 1976, and for the next two years worked as an English editor for NECZAM, the national publishing house. He moved to the United States in 1978. He studied first at Yale University, where he obtained an MA in 1982, and then at Brown University, where he obtained a PhD in 1987. He was an associate professor in the Black Studies Department at the University of Nebraska at Omaha, and is now a professor at Southern Illinois University. He has edited an anthology of poetry from Central and Southern Africa, *When My Brothers Come Home* (Wesleyan University Press, 1985), and published four volumes of poetry: *Visions and Reflections* (NECZAM, 1972); *O Earth, Wait for Me* (Ravan, 1984); *NIGHTWATCHER, Nightsong* (Green, 1986); and *Whispers in the Wings* (Heinemann, 1991). His prize-winning poem, 'Manifesto on Ars Poetica', was published in *The Fate of Vultures* (Heinemann, 1989), an anthology of new African poetry from the 1988 BBC Arts and Africa Poetry Award. Chipasula's work was banned in his own country.

Living in exile enabled Chipasula to write openly against the dictatorship of Life-President Dr H. Kamuzu Banda, who ruled Malawi from independence in 1964 to his death in 1997. In the 'First Word' to his three-part poem, *NIGHTWATCHER, Nightsong*, he speaks of the need to 'break out of [the] vicious shell of silence' that is 'familiar to our people'. In 'Manifesto on Ars Poetica', he promises to 'undress our raped land and expose her wounds'. He has edited, with Stella B. Chipasula, *The Heinemann Book of African Women's Poetry* (1995), and an anthology of African love poetry, *Bending the Bow* (Southern Illinois University Press, 2009).   AM-P*

Chitre, Dilip Purushottam (1938–

2009) Born in Baroda, where he had his early education. His family moved to Bombay (now Mumbai) when he was thirteen. After taking a degree in English from Bombay University in 1959, he went to Ethiopia for three years to teach in schools, and in the late Sixties and Seventies he was associated with the magazine *Quest* (later *New Quest*), for which he wrote essays, reviews, and a regular column of comment. He edited *An Anthology of Marathi Poetry: 1945–65* (Nirmala-Sadanand, 1967), doing most of the translations himself, and his translations of Tukaram (seventeenth century) are collected in *Says Tuka* (Penguin, 1991). He also directed a feature film, many documentaries, and held exhibitions of his paintings.

A prolific writer in two languages, Marathi and English, Chitre created a large body of work, much of it uncollected. *Travelling in a Cage* (Clearing House, 1980), his first book in English, contains merely a fraction of his English poems. The title poem was written between 1975 and 1977, when he lived in the United States. Its epigraph, 'The heart is placed obliquely in the chest' is from Gray's *Anatomy*, and a sexual encounter, not always obliquely dealt with, appears to be at the heart of the sequence. Chitre sees language, sex, even death, as a prison or cage, with self-murder, 'the greatest of all forms', holding the key to freedom. The book's shorter poems play down his *De Profundis* side, and employ a plainer, less inward-turning voice and a raconteur's tone.

See *As Is, Where Is* (2007), a new and selected volume which draws on several later publications, and also *Shesha*, a translated selection of his Marathi poems, which were collected in three volumes between 1992 and 1999 (2008—both Poetrywala). AKM

Christopher, Nicholas (1951–) Born in New York; his life and work have centred on that city, where he is now a professor at Columbia University. He attended the Horace Mann School and Harvard, where he studied with Robert *Lowell and Anthony *Hecht. Two strains are discernible in his work: a tough, urban temperament, alert to the bizarre juxtapositions and speed of modern life; and a lyrical, sensuous strain, traceable perhaps to Christopher's Greek ancestry. His first book of poems, *On Tour with Rita* (Knopf, 1982), was remarkable for its striking imagery and cosmopolitan geography; Christopher is fascinated by the romantic figure of the wanderer, the traveller, the artist perpetually 'on tour'.

The related theme of the essential solitude of the artist is at the core of his vision; two sections of *On Tour with Rita* are titled 'Solos', and the book opens with a poem called 'Double Solitaire' and has, as its penultimate poem, 'The Soloist'—the title, as well, of Christopher's novel (1986) about a concert pianist. A second book, *A Short History of the Island of Butterflies* (1986), develops further the twin themes of wandering and solitude. A more unusual, original, and challenging work, is the long poem, *Desperate Characters*, subtitled 'A Novella in Verse' (1988—both Viking). Christopher has always had a rich sense of popular culture—comic strips, films, rock music. His long poem, set mainly in Hollywood, is nourished by his interest in film culture, especially *film noir*. Written in a taut free verse, it is a vivid, fast-moving narrative of shady characters living on the edge.

See also his critical book *Somewhere in the Night: Film Noir and the American City* (Free Press, 1997). His later volumes of poetry include *In the Year of the Comet* (1992), *Five Degrees and Other Poems* (1995—both Viking), *Atomic Field: Two Poems* (2000), and *Crossing the Equator: New and Selected Poems* (2007—both Harcourt). CB

Chuilleanáin, Eiléan Ní (1942–) Born in Cork, the daughter of the writer Eilis Dillon and Cormac Ó Chuilleanáin, professor of Irish at University College, Cork. She was educated at UCC, and is Professor in Medieval and Renaissance English at Trinity College Dublin. Her first volume of poems was *Acts and Monuments*, published by Gallery Press (1973), and she has published several further volumes with Gallery, including *The Magdalene Sermon* (1989), *The Brazen Serpent* (1994), *The Girl Who Married the Reindeer* (2001). *Selected Poems* (co-published in the UK with Faber) appeared in 2008, and was followed by *The Sun-Fish* (2009), which won the Griffin International Poetry Prize. She is published in the States by Wake Forest University Press.

Ní Chuilleanáin's early poems were written in a free form, and their virtues (which made her a prize-winner from the first) were evocativeness and imaginative imagery. These gifts were well exemplified, for example, in her volume *Cork* (1977), which was accompanied by Fintan Lalor's drawings. Her later poetry is more ambitious and has more direction to it. Like other Irish women poets of her era, such as Eavan *Boland, this work is an absorbing mix of mythology, mostly Irish and centring on female archetypes, and contemporary domestic experience. As the objective has become more focused, the style has become more precise. Edna Longley in *The Irish Review*, 8 (Spring 1990) characterized Ní Chuilleanáin's poetry as 'even-paced and temperate . . . inclined to repeat structural patterns', but saw it moving beyond her usual concerns (national identity and femininity) in a metaphysical direction in the strange, imaginative 'Observations from Galileo'. Ní Chuilleanáin has edited several volumes of Irish writing and critical essays, including *Irish Women: Image and Achievement—Women in Irish Culture from Earliest Times* (Arlen, 1985), and with Mebh *McGuckian has been a significant translator of the Gaelic poems of Nuala Ni Dhomhaill (see *The Water Horse* (Gallery, 1999). She has also translated poetry from Italian and Romanian. A founding editor of the journal *Cyphers*—with Leland Bardwell,

Pearse *Hutchinson, and Macdara Woods—she has latterly edited several issues of *Poetry Ireland Review*. *Irish University Review* vol. 37, no. 1 (2007) was a special issue devoted to her work. She is a member of Aosdána.   BO'D*

Clampitt, Amy (1920–94) Born in New Providence, Iowa, and pursued a career in publishing and librarianship, mainly in New York, before her richly intelligent poems began to attract attention in the 1970s. Her debut with *The Kingfisher* (Knopf) came as late as 1983, when she was 63. This long incubation period suggests two things: an intelligence that ripened into a learned and mature sensibility, and a stubbornly maintained fastidiousness during the 'confessionalist' 1960s.

Amy Clampitt's elegantly crafted meditations, more cultured and less eccentric than Marianne *Moore's, manifest a profound feeling for nature. A biographer's gift for re-creating character and situation informs long poems on Keats, George Eliot, and other writers with whom she identifies. Chiefly, however, Clampitt is a moralist. Her openly baroque, complex stanzas are usually sustained by the working out of a gradually revealed idea. In more personal poems, like 'The Cove' in *The Kingfisher*, the fine stitching of the verse creates distinctive, womanly interiors: 'cross-stitch | domesticates the guest room', while outside, warblers 'flirt' through foliage which is 'all ombre | and fine stitchery'. In 'Gradual Clearing' the sea, which had been a 'wavering | fishnet plisse', takes on the 'smoothness | of peau-de-soie or just-ironed | percale, with a tatting | of foam out where the rocks are'. In the best of her long poems, such as her meditation on life and death in 'A Procession at Candlemas', the accumulated effect of forty-eight three-line stanzas is grand and unfussy.

Clampitt's second major collection, *What the Light Was Like* (Knopf, 1985; Faber, 1987) consisted chiefly of elegies dedicated to the memory of her brother. A subsequent collection, *Archaic Figure* (Knopf, 1987; Faber, 1989) dwells on European travel, with the usual accompaniment of sympathetic reflection on art, artists,

migraine, and time. Her last collection was *A Silence Opens* (Knopf, 1994). *The Collected Poems of Amy Clampitt* appeared in the States in 1997 (Knopf) and in the UK in 1998 (Faber). See also *Predecessors, Et Cetera: Essays* (University of Michigan Press, 1991), which discusses Wordsworth, Moore, and T. S. *Eliot, among others, and *Love, Amy: The Selected Letters of Amy Clampitt* (Columbia University Press, 2005).   AS

Clanchy, Kate (1965–   ) Born in Glasgow and studied in Edinburgh and Oxford. She has worked as a school teacher and a journalist.

Clanchy attributes the clarity of her writing to reading Sylvia *Plath with her pupils and becoming 'fed up' with trying to elucidate obscurities. The loose, colloquial formalism of her image-led monologues shows the early influence of Carol Ann *Duffy and Simon *Armitage, combined with an intimate physicality and frankness that reflects her admiration for Sharon *Olds. Her first, widely praised volume, *Slattern* (Chatto & Windus, 1995), informs a 'Man with No Sense of Smell' that 'beneath the spray of my expensive scent | my armpits sound a bass note strong | as the boom of a palm on a kettle drum'. *Samarkand* (1999) similarly explored female desire with humour and exuberance, and concluded in the domestic sequence 'The Newhome Cabaret'.

Newborn (2004) focused on the experience of being a mother in 'naked, unembarrassed' language, continuing Clanchy's dialogue with Plath and Olds. In 2006 she adapted Dorothy *Porter's verse novel, *The Monkey's Mask*, for radio. *What Is She Doing Here? A Refugee's Story* (2008—all Picador) is a non-fiction account of her friendship with a woman from Kosovo.   JNT

Clark, Thomas A. (1944–   ) Born in Greenock, Scotland. In 1973, whilst living in Gloucestershire, he started Moschatel Press with his wife, the artist Laurie Clark, which published small verse booklets and postcards. In 1986, they founded the Cairn Gallery, for minimalist and conceptual art, moving to Scotland in 2002.

Clark's crisply visual verse, with its concern for the presentation of the printed word, has been compared to that of Ian Hamilton *Finlay, whom he published. *Some Particulars* (Jargon Society, 1971) included concrete, collaged, and found texts. Clark is less a concrete poet than a pastoral minimalist, though, in the *Objectivist tradition of Lorine *Niedecker. His lower-case lettering, short lines, and compact stanzas showcase simple but precisely related phrases: 'the flute of the ring-ouzel | lingering melts | like a snow crystal'. Clark's poetry returns repeatedly to the experience of walking isolated Scottish landscapes. His characteristic mode has been called 'a litany of Highland images'—for a book-length series, see *The Hundred Thousand Places* (Carcanet, 2009).

The ambition of his work to re-see the human situation is indicated by the short manifesto statement 'On Imaginative Space': 'Whole spaces, precincts and localities should be subject to the imperative "as if . . ."' More recently, he has worked on site-specific installations, such as the texts provided for New Stobhill Hospital, Glasgow. See also *Madder Lake* (Coach House, 1981) and *The Path to the Sea* (Arc, 2005).   JNT

Clark, Tom (Thomas Willard Clark) (1941–   ) Born in Chicago, Clark served as poetry editor for the *Paris Review* from 1963 until 1973. Much of his verse (he had published thirty-six collections by 1990) has been issued by small presses in small editions. His main inspiration comes from European *surrealism and the laid-back, conversational procedures of Ted *Berrigan, with whom Clark, together with Ron *Padgett, shared an early collection, *Back in Boston Again* (Telegraph, 1972). In the spirit of the *New York School, Clark's poems embrace a wide range of subject matter, from *Baseball* (The Figures, 1976) to the lives of the poets. But he can also be a pure lyricist, as in the early 'Like musical instruments . . .', and, latterly, an epic poet: see *Empire of Skin* (Black Sparrow, 1997). Clark spent two years in Cambridge, England as a Fulbright Scholar, where he studied the work of Ezra *Pound. He is also a prolific, anti-academic biographer of *Olson, *Kerouac and others. See *Light and Shade: New and Selected Poems* (Coffee House, 2006).   MS-S*

Clark Bekederemo, J. P. (John Pepper) (1935–   ) Born of Ijo and Urhobo parents in Kiagbodo, mid-western Nigeria. He studied at Government College, Ughelli, and later obtained a BA in English at University College, Ibadan. He has held fellowships at Princeton University and at the University of Ibadan. Formerly professor of English at the University of Lagos, he was also artistic director of PEC repertory theatre in Lagos.

Clark's early work was published in *Black Orpheus*, the pioneering African arts and literature journal from Nigeria. It was founded in 1957 by Ulli Beier, and under the expatriate European regime of Beier, Jahnheinz Jahn, and Gerald Moore its editorial stance was 'inspirational' rather than critical. After Beier left for Papua New Guinea in 1966, the editorship fell to the Nigerians, Abiola Irele and Clark, who adopted a new approach: 'There was no point any more in presenting African literature as new literature that had to be defended and all that' (Irele). In 'The Legacy of Caliban' (Issue 2:1), Clark attacked European distortion of Africa. Issues 2:2 and 2:3 focused on traditional African literature and on politics. But Longmans had withdrawn, and it emerged that the Fairfield Foundation, one of the journal's backers, was funded by the CIA. Amid multiplying organizational problems, Irele left in 1974 (to found the *Benin Review*, which died after one issue), and Clark left in 1975.

A selection of his earlier works, *Poems* (Mbari, 1962), *A Reed in the Tide* (1965), and *Casualties* (1970), have been collected together in *A Decade of Tongues* (1981). Other volumes of poetry are *State of the Union* (1985) and *Mandela and other poems* (1988—all Longman). He has also written plays, critical works, and a travelogue. His translation of an Ijo oral epic poem, *The Ozidi Saga*, is highly regarded, and two of his poems, 'Ibadan' and 'Abiku', have already become classics of modern African poetry and are widely known by schoolchildren in Nigeria. He is at his best when capturing the essence of a place or phenomenon in a few descriptive lines. For critical reviews, see *Understanding African Poetry* (Heinemann, 1982), by Ken Goodwin and 'J. P. Clark's Poetry', in *Perspectives on Nigerian Literature* (Guardian, 1988), ed. Yemi Ogunbiyi. See *Collected Plays and Poems* (Howard University Press, 1991). Several later volumes of poetry have appeared in Nigeria.   FO/JB*

Clarke, Austin (1896–1974) Born in Dublin and lived there throughout his life, except for a period in London from 1921 to 1937. Although he wrote nearly twenty verse plays, three novels, two literary autobiographies, and a substantial body of criticism and journalism, his principal significance is as a poet. He disputes with *MacNeice and Patrick *Kavanagh the title of the leading Irish poet in the generation after *Yeats. He was born to a relatively well-off family in Dublin, although six of his nine siblings died in infancy. He was given a first in his English MA at University College, Dublin, in 1917, and succeeded to the lectureship made vacant there by the execution of Thomas *MacDonagh for his part in the 1916 Easter Rising. In 1919 he had a mental breakdown (on which he drew for what is perhaps his greatest poem, 'Mnemosyne lay in dust' in 1966). After a brief first marriage in 1920, he lost his UCD lectureship in 1921 and subsequently lived mostly by his writing.

In 1917 his first collection of poems, *The Vengeance of Fionn*, was warmly received. It is an eloquent, epic-styled evocation of Irish legend in the manner of early Yeats, whom Clarke then revered. His fifth volume of poems, *Pilgrimage* (1929), mixes with this earlier legendary style a new spare realism and eroticism, representing a departure from the prevailing modes in Irish poetry of the time. Its principal stylistic innovation is to attempt (with varying success) to incorporate into poetry in English the assonantal patterns of Gaelic poetry, as prescribed by Larminie and MacDonagh. After his first *Collected Poems* in 1936, the short confessional volume *Night and Morning* (1938) introduced

what were later to be his principal themes: sexual freedom and conscience, and the constricting effects of the Church, which he saw in operation in his medieval 'Celto-Romanesque' world as well as in contemporary Ireland. But *Night and Morning* was followed by a seventeen-year poetic silence, which is not fully explained by Clarke's statement that he was working on plays in that period. He returned to poetry with the angrily topical and public *Ancient Lights*, published in 1955 when he was nearly 60. The best of these forceful pieces are much admired as a flourish of 'lust and rage' in old age, as prescribed by Yeats, though they often seem too willed.

Clearly an important figure, with gifts of style and imagination that few can match, Clarke remains often uncompelling. It has been suggested that politically inclined Irish writers were disablingly marginalized by Irish neutrality in the Second World War. In any case, Clarke's unvaryingly Irish perspective, combined with his anti-clericalism and distaste for the politics of the new state (which Clarke saw as a disastrous failure of republican idealism), meant that he had no obviously sympathetic catchment area. But, pending a full-scale biography and a detailed critical account that is more than introductory, his reputation remains to be established conclusively.

See: *Collected Poems* (Dolmen/Oxford University Press, 1974; new edn., Carcanet, 2008); *Selected Poems*, ed. Hugh Maxton (Dolmen, 1991); and *Twice Round the Black Church: Early Memories of Ireland and England* (Routledge & Kegan Paul, 1962); also Susan Halpern, *Austin Clarke: His Life and Works* (Dolmen, 1974); G. Craig Topping, *Austin Clarke: A Study of His Writings* (Academy Press, 1981—this has a useful appendix listing Clarke's journalism); M. Harmon (ed.), *Irish University Review: Austin Clarke Special Issue*, 4:1 (Spring 1974). See also *Reviews and Essays of Austin Clarke* (1995), published in the Irish Literary Studies series and edited by Gregory A. Schirmer.   BO'D

Clarke, George Elliott (1960–) Born in Nova Scotia to Canadian parents of African-American ancestry, Clarke studied at the universities of Waterloo, Dalhousie and Queen's, and is E. J. Pratt Professor of Canadian Literature at the University of Toronto. He has worked as a parliamentary aide, editor, social worker, and journalist. In 2008, he was made an Officer of the Order of Canada.

Clarke's first book was *Saltwater Spirituals and Deeper Blues* (Pottersfield, 1983). He has described the black Nova Scotian heritage that he 'sings' in his work as 'Africadian', a word which combines Africa with Acadia, the old name for the maritime provinces of Canada. *Whylah Falls* (Polestar, 1990; 10th and revd. edn., 2000) describes the inhabitants in an earthy, rhapsodic style which mingles the poet's learning with the impoverished realities of small-town Africadian life. Ezra *Pound's 'The River Merchant's Wife: A Letter', for example, is readdressed to a girl called 'Shelley' on the banks of the fictional Sixhiboux.

Execution Poems (Gaspereau, 2001) tells the story of two black brothers who 'smacked a white taxi driver, Silver, with a hammer, to sack his silver', later reworked in Clarke's novel *George & Rue* (Harper, 2004). He has also written a play about Trudeau, the Liberal politician, and a libretto, *Beatrice Chancy* (Polestar, 1999). Clarke's major critical work is *Odysseys Home: Mapping African-Canadian Literature* (University of Toronto Press, 2002). For a selection of his verse with an afterword, see *Blues and Bliss* (Wilfrid Laurier University Press, 2008).   JNT

Clarke, Gillian (1937–   ) Born and educated in Cardiff, where she took a degree in English. After two years in London as a news researcher for the BBC, she returned to Wales in 1960. She has since lectured in art history, from 1976 to 1984 edited the *Anglo-Welsh Review*, and taught Creative Writing at the University of Glamorgan.

The Sundial, Clarke's first collection, was published by Gwasg Gomer, a small Welsh press in 1978, and immediately established the territory of her work as both isolated and luminous. Bleak meditations on the passing of time, of journeys made by car through a landscape of slate and coal-

mines, modulated into a lyricism associated with the experience of giving birth, and the 'tugging pleasure' of its 'bruised reordering'. In the long title-poem of *Letter From a Far Country* (1982; repr. 2006) there was still a promise of lyricism, yet the bruises suffered in comparative silence by generations of Welsh women proved the more emphatic preoccupation. Writing home in English from her ancestors' future, she commemorated but also identified herself with their confinement: her letter of release remained 'unfinished, unposted'. *Letting in the Rumour* (1989) struck a more positive note. Still, 'At One Thousand Feet' on her hillside, Clarke now mined her family's history to celebrate its affinity with a contemporary world of 'glasnost, | golau glas, | a first break of blue'.

Since *Selected Poems* in 1996 and *Collected Poems* in 1997, Clarke has increasingly been a poet of public themes and subjects. The urban writing of *Five Fields* (1998) reflects her time as a writer-in-residence at the Bridgewater Hall in Manchester; *Making the Beds for the Dead* (2004) records the effect on rural life of the 2001 UK foot-and-mouth outbreak; and *A Recipe for Water* (2009) explores the source of life. See also *At the Source* (2008), a writer's journal which meditates on the river landscape where she lives. In 2008 Clarke became the National Poet of Wales and in 2010 she received the Queen's Gold Medal for Poetry. *Ice* (2012—all Carcanet) includes poems written to commission, as well as her response to recent hard winters in Wales.   MRW*

Clarke, John Cooper (1949–   ) Born in Salford, Lancashire, Clarke left school at fifteen and worked in various part-time jobs. In the late 1970s, he became known as the 'Punk Poet', performing his verse in Manchester clubs, and touring with bands such as the Sex Pistols and The Fall, in the cross-over tradition of the Mersey poets (*see* ROGER MCGOUGH).

Clarke released four albums, and two books: *The John Cooper Clarke Directory* (Omnibus, 1979) and *Ten Years in an Open-Necked Shirt* (Arena, 1981). He spent much of the 1980s suffering from a heroin addiction, and has not published another book, but his work has been anthologized and set for school examinations. It is admired for qualities that also characterize British songwriting of the era: wry social observation, rapid play with cliché, and inventive rhyme. Poems such as 'beezly street' conjure a cartoon-like vision of late-twentieth-century hard times: 'light bulbs pop like blisters | the only form of heat | where a fellow sells his sister | down the river on beezly street'. *Word of Mouth* (Sony, 2002) is a 'Best Of' album.   JNT

Clemo, Jack (Reginald John Clemo)

(1916–94) Born the son of a Cornish clay-worker in a granite cottage near St Austell which, in the first of two autobiographies (*Confessions of a Rebel*, 1949), he describes as 'a fitting birthplace for me, being dwarfed under Bloomdale clay-dump, solitary, grim-looking, with no drainage, no water or electricity supply, and no back door'. With little formal education, and for most of his writing career, both deaf and blind, Clemo lived there all his life, though the conditions improved.

Clemo first came to attention with his novel *Wilding Graft* (1948) which was admired by T. F. Powys, and writing of Powys in his second volume of autobiography (*Marriage of a Rebel*, 1980) Clemo stressed an affinity in that both men had 'chosen the unworldly borderline, the terrible wrestle with God'. Like Powys, too, Clemo had become preoccupied by 'the struggle between the ascetic and the sensualist'.

Dominated by the stark landscape of the claypits, Clemo's best-known poems explore the forces of nature and the workings of a hard-won grace. His earliest work, of which the characteristically titled 'Christ in the Clay-Pit' is a good example, is marked by the self-wounding, exclusively tortured spirit of Calvinism, and his development as a poet was informed by a search for reconciliation which he described as 'mystical-erotic' in poems full of a charged, evangelical language. Powerful, intense, and often chillingly austere, his poetry nevertheless became mellower in later years and more reconciled to the human condition.

In a telling portrait by Charles *Causley which introduces Clemo's 1961 collection *The Map of Clay*, the poet's cottage is seen to contain a portrait of Billy Graham on the mantelpiece and volumes of D. H. *Lawrence and Karl Barth in the bookcase, suggesting vividly the components of his vision. Clemo's *Selected Poems* was published by Bloodaxe Books (1988), as was *Approach to Murano* (1992) and, posthumously, *The Cured Arno* (1995), which continued his imaginative exploration of Italy. See also *The Awakening: Poems Newly Found* (Francis Boutle, 2003).   JM

Clifton, Lucille (1936–2010) Born in

Depew, New York, to a working-class family. Educated at the State University of New York at Fredonia and Howard University, she married Fred James Clifton, an educator, in 1958, and raised six children. She was distinguished professor of humanities at St Mary's College, Maryland.

Clifton gained national attention in 1969 with her first volume, praised for its craft and its evocation of urban black life. Thus her early work is significant to the *Black Arts Movement; however, subsequent volumes demonstrate that hers is a poetry not of race but of revelation, in the manner of Denise *Levertov. Characterized by brevity, simplicity of language, and polyrhythmical phrasing, her work celebrates the spiritual revealed in the ordinary. Many poems (e.g. the 'two-headed woman' and 'Lucifer' sequences) depend on voice for their dramatic situation, yet they are not dramatic monologues, like those of Gwendolyn *Brooks, but rather voiced meditations. Clifton wrote that she heard characters speak, including family members and mythic figures.

Good Woman (1987), which collects the memoir (*Generations*, 1976) and poems from 1969 to 1980, and *Next* (1987) were both nominated for a Pulitzer Prize. *Quilting* (1991), contains her funny and poignant menopausal poems 'to my uterus' and 'to my last period'. *Blessing the Boats: New and Selected Poems, 1988–2000*, which won a National Book Award, draws on both books as well as *The Book of Light* (Copper Canyon, 1993) and *The Terrible Stories*

(1998). Her last volumes were *Mercy* (2004) and *Voices* (2008). In 2007, she was awarded the Ruth Lilly Poetry Prize and in 2010 the Poetry Society of America's Robert Frost Medal. See *The Collected Poems of Lucille Clifton* (2012—all BOA), with a foreword by Toni Morrison and an afterword by Kevin *Young. She also wrote many books for children.   JTC*

Clouts, Sydney David (1926–82) Born in Cape Town, and educated there at the South African College School and the University of Cape Town, where he studied law and philosophy. He married Marjorie Leftwich in 1952. His poetry first appeared in South African magazines during the 1950s, and in 1961 he departed for the UK to become a literary agent. Some poems were broadcast by the BBC in 1965, and in 1966 his volume *One Life* was published in South Africa. On completion of an MA at Rhodes University in Grahamstown in 1969, he returned to the UK, where he worked as a librarian until his death in 1982.

Clouts' prominence in South African poetry is assured but controversial. Criticism has ranged from descriptions of him as South Africa's 'purest poetic talent', to readings of the poetry as 'blinkered' because it tends to ignore social issues or deals with them from a position of naïve romanticism. These ideological difficulties are compounded by what for many is an unnecessary impenetrability, often the result of the poet's attempt to reduce language to the barest minimum, although he exhibits a *Stevensian relish for the words he chooses, and also shares Stevens' philosophical concern with the place of the imagination (see 'Poetry Is Death Cast Out').

See his *Collected Poems* (David Philip, 1984), ed. Marjorie and Cyril Clouts, and *English in Africa*, 11:2 (1984), dedicated to him. See also Kevin Goddard, 'Sydney Clouts' Poetry', *English in Africa*, 19:2 (1992).   KG*

Cobbing, Bob (1920–2002) Born in Enfield, Middlesex, Cobbing trained as an accountant and teacher. He was the most influential British sound and visual poet of the twentieth century. In the late 1950s, he began the long-running Writers Forum workshop, which also became a prolific small press, publishing Allen *Ginsberg, John *Cage, and Lee *Harwood among others, and reaching its thousandth publication in 2001. Around the same time, he left teaching to run a bookshop. In the 1970s, he was involved in temporarily modernizing the Poetry Society in London.

Cobbing was raised by Plymouth Brethren parents. He was a lay preacher in his youth and a conscientious objector during the Second World War. But he rejected religion (and politics) for the 'more honest' communication of art, saying 'gone is the word as the word'. His seminal first book, *ABC in Sound* (Writers Forum, 1965, and several later editions), presented alliterative and asyntactic combinations of words and syllables ('Tan tandinan tandinane | Tanan tandina tandinane'). It was broadcast by BBC radio in 1966. Experiments with office printing processes also produced poems primarily visual in effect, such as the early 'Worm'.

Cobbing published many works in many forms, and collaborated with experimental poets around the world. A short pocket primer is *kob bok: selected texts 1948–1999* (Etruscan, 1999). Selected recordings of Cobbing's performances can be heard on *The Spoken Word: Bob Cobbing* (British Library, 2009). See also Doreen King, *Poetology of Bob Cobbing* (Feather, 2003), a brief biography with interviews.   JNT

Cochrane, Geoff (1951–) Born in Wellington, where he attended St Patrick's College and still lives. He is also a fiction writer.

Like his first novel, *Tin Nimbus* (1995), Cochrane's prolific later verse often reflects his experience as a recovering alcoholic, as well as his life as a long-time observer of the city of Wellington. His poetic style brings the precision of realist prose to the momentary insight: as he says in *Acetylene* (2001), 'I write in order to have | degrees of clarity– | if not solutions, legible diagrams.' *Aztec Noon* (1992—both Victoria

University Press) selects from earlier work published through small presses, beginning with *Images of Midnight City* (Hauraki, 1976). Other volumes include *Vanilla Wine* (2003), *Hypnic Jerks* (2005), *84-484* (2007), and *The Worm in the Tequila* (2010—all Victoria University Press). In 2009 Cochrane received the Janet Frame Award for Poetry.   JNT

Coffey, Brian (1905–95) Born near Dublin and read arts and sciences at the University College there. In the 1930s, he studied physical chemistry and then philosophy (with Jacques Maritain) in Paris. In 1947, Coffey moved to St Louis, Missouri, where he taught philosophy. Returning to England in 1952, he worked as a school teacher.

Coffey's first book, *Poems*, was a privately printed collaboration with Denis *Devlin (1930). In 1934, Samuel *Beckett called them 'without question the most interesting of the youngest generation of Irish poets'. Coffey met Beckett through Thomas *MacGreevy, and they remained close friends. In 1938, the year of his marriage, he published *Third Person* (Europa). The discursively personal 'Missouri Sequence' did not appear until 1962, having been begun during an unhappy post-war period in the States ('bitter necessity no monopoly | of Irish soil'). It describes family life with tenderness. In 1964, Coffey edited Devlin's *Collected Poems*, and in 1965 published a translation of Mallarmé (*Dice Thrown Will Never Annul Chance*—both Dolmen). In 1966, he began his own press, Advent Books, with *Monster*, a concrete poem.

Coffey was absorbed by the example of Mallarmé, alluding to the French Symbolist at the start of his long poem 'Advent' (1975), and publishing a longer volume of translations in 1991. The late modernism of his verse evinces his Catholicism, the densely sounded and argued 'making' of its English recalling Hopkins and David *Jones. See Dónal Moriarty, *The Art of Brian Coffey* (University College Dublin Press, 2000).   JNT

Cohen, Leonard (1934–) Born in Montreal, Cohen attended McGill Univer-

sity, and began graduate work at Columbia University, but left to pursue his career as a writer and singer. He is now better known internationally as the latter, and many readers of *Poems and Songs* (Knopf, 2011) will have difficulty seeing the words of 'Suzanne' or 'Bird on a Wire' without hearing Cohen's distinctive intonation and accompanying guitar. As Paul *Muldoon has written, 'his songs have meant more to me | than most of the so-called "poems" I've read'. Nevertheless, *Stranger Music: Selected Poems and Songs* (Cape, 1993) lists an equal number of books and albums, beginning with *Let Us Compare Mythologies* (1956), and Cohen's poetry was important in Canadian literature as a *Beats-era reinvention of traditional lyricism, bringing the *Yeatsian pursuit of wisdom to a world of popular culture and casual sex. Michael *Ondaatje wrote an early study. See also *Intricate Preparations: Writing Leonard Cohen* (ECW, 2000), ed. Stephen Scobie.   JNT

Cole, Henri (1956–) Born in Fukuoka, Japan, to American and French-Armenian poets, Cole grew up in Virginia, and studied for an MFA at Columbia University. In the 1980s, he was executive director of The Academy of American Poets. He has taught at Harvard University and Yale, and received many fellowships and awards. He is currently a professor of Creative Writing at Ohio State University.

Cole's post-*confessional verse is distinguished by its fascination with the relationship between sexual and religious experience, and the contradictions of identity—in particular, between his Catholic upbringing and homosexuality, as recalled in the early poem 'White Spine'. See also 'Anagram', which plays with the poet's own name ('HERON LICE . . . LION CHEER') in modern metaphysical fashion.

His collections are *The Marble Queen* (Atheneum, 1986), *The Zoo Wheel of Knowledge* (1989), *The Look of Things* (1995—both Knopf), *The Visible Man* (1998), *Middle Earth* (2003), nominated for the Pulitzer Prize, *Blackbird and Wolf* (2007), and *Touch* (2011). See *Pierce the Skin: Selected Poems* (2010—all Farrar,

Straus). For a discussion of Cole's early work, see Helen Vendler, *Soul Says: On Recent American Poetry* (Harvard University Press, 1995). JNT

Colebatch, Hal Gibson Pateshall (1945–) The son of Sir Hal Colebatch, a former premier of Western Australia, whose biography he has written (*Steadfast Knight* (Fremantle Arts Centre Press, 2004)). After completing a degree in politics at the University of Western Australia he enrolled in a law course, graduating to become a solicitor. In his student days, he worked as a journalist and radio scriptwriter, and even offered himself as a political candidate for a state election in the 1970s: at his electoral rallies he read his poetry to captive audiences. He has also been the Australian manager for Debrett's Peerage.

Two early books, *Spectators on the Shore* (1975) and *In Breaking Waves* (1979), are incorporated in Colebatch's third published book *Outer Charting* (1985). It is not to Colebatch's discredit that there is no sign of development from his first book to his fourth, *The Earthquake Lands* (1990—both Angus & Robertson): he established a distinctive and successful style from the outset and has persisted with it ever since. His poems are all in rhyming forms, most commonly quatrains and sonnets, though the rhythm is that of the plainest discursive prose. A number of his poems are dispassionate descriptions of seascapes, but more deal with political matters as Colebatch rails against the left-wing orthodoxies of present-day Australia.

His seventh collection, *The Light River* (Connor Court, 2007), came with a foreword by Les *Murray, and won the Western Australian Premier's Prize for Poetry. In his critical study, *Return of the Heroes* (Australian Institute for Public Policy, 1990), Colebatch argues in favour of the values embodied by such modern-day mythologies as *The Lord of the Rings* and *Star Wars*. He has also written science fiction and political commentary: see *Blair's Britain* (Claridge, 1999). JG*

Coles, Don (1928–) Born in Woodstock, Ontario and educated at the University of Toronto and at Cambridge, from which he received an MA in 1954. He spent the next ten years in various European centres before returning to Canada. He taught creative writing at York University, Toronto, and was poetry editor at the Banff Centre for the Fine Arts until 1994.

Coles' poetry is notable for its elegance, sophistication, and urbane intelligence. These qualities are as evident in his first book, *Sometimes All Over* (Macmillan, 1975) as in the later, *K. in Love* (Véhicule, 1987), a series of concentrated 'notes' inspired by a reading of Kafka's letters and journals. Coles is equally at home in the Europe of Munch and Mann and in the Canada of his Bergmanesque childhood; combining lofty eloquence with wry off-handedness, he can produce a *tour de force* on subjects as disparate as Pushkin's fiancée and Major Hoople. *Landslides: Selected Poems 1975–1985* (McClelland & Stewart, 1986) shows an impressive range of subject-matter and technique. See also *Someone Has Stayed in Stockholm* (1994), a new and selected volume published in the UK by Arc, and *The Essential Don Coles* (Porcupine's Quill, 2009), chosen by Robyn *Sarah.

Coles' other books of poetry are *Anniversaries* (1979), *The Prinzhorn Collection* (1982—both Macmillan), *Little Bird* (Véhicule, 1991), *Forests of the Medieval World* (1993), which won the Governor General's Award for Poetry, *Kurgan* (2000—both Porcupine's Quill), and *Where We Might Have Been* (Véhicule, 2010). He has also written a novel (*Doctor Bloom's Story*, 2004), a memoir (*A Dropped Glove in Regent's Street*, 2007), and translated the Swedish poet Tomas Tranströmer. *How We All Swiftly* (Véhicule, 2005) collects his first six books of poetry. JKK

Collins, Billy (William) (1941–) Born in New York City in 1941, Collins has been a professor of English at Lehman College, City University of New York since 1971. Between 2001 and 2003 he was Poet Laureate of the United States, and has been called 'the most popular poet in America' by *The New York Times*.

Collins wrote his PhD on 'Wordsworth and the Romantic Search for an Audience'.

He has found his own audience by employing what he misses in Romanticism: humour. Collins' poems are conversational musings that wear their Wordsworthian ambition to be 'a man speaking to men' modestly (as in 'Lines Composed Over Three Thousand Miles from Tintern Abbey'). His first significant collection was *The Apple That Astonished Paris* (University of Arkansas Press, 1988). Further collections appeared in the 1990s—including *Picnic, Lighting* (University of Pittsburgh Press, 1998)—to growing acclaim. At the end of the decade Collins signed an unprecedented (for a poet) six-figure deal with the publisher Random House. *Sailing Alone Around the Room: New and Selected Poems* appeared in 2001. He has continued to publish a new volume every three years or so.

Collins is an accomplished performer of his own work and a public advocate for the reading of poetry. He has called his use of humour 'a door into the serious', although critics have heard a tendency to hover on the threshold of whimsy. His belief in the free verse of the 'ordinary' American voice, though, continues the tradition of Edgar Lee *Masters with an easy wit.   JNT

Collis, Stephen (1965–) Born in Victoria, British Columbia, Collis worked in the fishing and service industries for many years before moving to Vancouver, where he became associated with the *Kootenay School of Writing and studied at Simon Fraser University. He is now Associate Professor of English at SFU, where he teaches contemporary poetry and poetics.

'The Barricades Project' collects three of Collis' most recent books: *Anarchive* (New Star, 2005), *The Commons* (2008), and *To the Barricades* (2013). Taking the work of John Clare, Henry Thoreau, and Robert *Frost as his springboard, Collis explores the commons in their present state as a gap, or lesion, in capital's ever-expanding body, and hence one of the last remaining social spaces to represent an alternative to neoliberal capitalism's imperative of privatization. Both in this project and a separate collection, *On the Material* (2010—all Talonbooks), grammatical ambiguity and an expansive range of reference situate Collis' work within a North American (post)modernist tradition: 'Were the bees . . . | . . . or where the hive? | the drive home | to the honey of place | no trace | to return to die singly'. Collis' poetics incorporate a Marxist materialism and are closely aligned with his activist work and recent critical writings on social movements and political change. As such, his poetry has been compared to the direct language and simplicity of Pablo Neruda and Nicanor Parra. *On the Material* was awarded the British Columbia Book Prize for Poetry.   ADA

Coloquhon, Glenn (1964–) Born in South Auckland, Coloquhon trained as a doctor and works as a general practitioner. Coloquhon's poetry has won wide popularity for its tender observation of everyday life (see 'The morning after a night spent taking blood') and its humorous reflections from the perspective of an 'indigenous Pakeha' (the Maori term for those of European descent). *The Art of Walking Upright* (1999) won the Jessie Mackay Award for Best First Book of Poetry and was followed by *An Explanation of Poetry to My Father* (2001). *Playing God* (2002), his third collection, was a best-selling book in New Zealand, and has been published in the UK by Hammersmith Press. In 2004 coloquhon won the prestigious Prize in Modern Letters. See also *How We Fell* (2006) and *North South* (2009—all Steele Roberts).   JNT

Colum, Padraic (1881–1972) Born at Longford in Ireland, the son of the master of the workhouse there. As a young man he associated with *Yeats, *Joyce, James *Stephens, Lady Gregory, and a host of others. Later he worked for the state of Hawaii on a folklore programme for schoolchildren, and he and his wife, the writer Mary Colum (née Maguire), whom he had married in 1912, became American citizens. But he journeyed regularly to Ireland for the remainder of his life.

Colum's poetry is almost all in traditional forms, and based in Irish lore; but it was never in the artificial, later Celtic Twilight style of the minor poets of the first decades of the twentieth century who were content to imitate the early Yeats. Colum achieved such genuine simplicity that he was universally respected; but his work seldom drew the attention it deserved. On the other hand, such poems as 'She Moved Through the Fair' became so well known that they went back into the tradition. Others, such as 'Ploughing', are starkly contemplative. *Carricknabauna*, a musical based on his poems, was produced in New York in 1967.

See his *Collected Poems* (Devin-Adair, 1953) and *Life and the Dream* (Doubleday, 1947) by Mary Colum. Also *The Dublin Magazine*, 6 (Spring, 1967).   MS-S

Conn, Stewart (1936–) Born in Glasgow, and his first book, *Stoats in the Sunlight* (1968), identified him as a fastidious recorder of the landmarks, relatives, and farms of his boyhood. His reunions with the past elicited measurements of personal and agricultural change. What emerged was the image of a dwindling rural Lowland Scotland worked out in crafted lines and stanzas.

An Ear to the Ground (1972) and *Under the Ice* (1978—all Hutchinson) saw him extend his range, but with a similar appreciation of form applied to different subjects. 'Family Visit' and 'To My Father' drew from the family concerns of some of the earlier work. Much in these two volumes was domestic and marital, with an unnerving sense of the fragility of life as well as an unmodish awareness of its decencies and delights. By and large, these have been Conn's chief poetic interests since; see, for example, the third part of *In the Kibble Palace: New and Selected Poems* (1987). Subdued rhythms, half-rhymes, and a plain vocabulary are characteristic of his unassertive but attractively honest voice. *The Luncheon of the Boating Party* (1992—both Bloodaxe) was a long ekphrastic sequence in response to Renoir, and *At the Aviary* (Snail Press, 1995) a South African sequence. Bloodaxe published a second selected volume, *Stolen Light*, in 1999, and two subsequent collections: *Ghosts at Cockcrow* (2005) and *The Breakfast Room* (2010).

Conn is also the author of many plays for stage and television. He worked as a drama producer for BBC Radio from 1962 to 1992 and was head of BBC Radio Scotland's drama department. In that capacity, his contribution to Scottish poetry, and Scottish writing in general, has been significant. From 2002 to 2005 he served as the first Makar (Poet Laureate) of Edinburgh and has edited *100 Favourite Scottish Poems* (Luath, 2006). See also his memoir, *Distances* (Scottish Cultural Press, 2001).   DED

Connolly, Kevin (1962–) Born in Mississippi, Connolly grew up in Ontario, and studied at York University in Toronto, where he lives. A poet, editor, and journalist, with Jason Sherman he co-founded the influential literary magazine *What!* As an editor he has worked for several major Canadian poetry publishers, including Coach House Press, who published his first collection *Asphalt Cigar* (1995), and ECW Press, who published his second, *Happy/and* (2002). Connolly's drily humorous imagination, like that of David *McGimpsey, is attracted to the surreal simulacra of contemporary life, and what he calls 'the familiar joust | of the real and the seen | that means everything | and settles nothing at all' ('Porcelain Jesus'). His third book, *Drift* (2005) won the Trillium Book Award for Poetry. *Revolver* (2008—both Anansi) presents a series of individual poems each intentionally unlike the others. It was shortlisted for the Griffin Poetry Prize.   JNT

Connor, Tony (John Anthony Augustus) (1930–) Born in Manchester and left school at the age of 14. He worked as a textile designer until 1960, and the following year joined Bolton Technical College as a liberal studies assistant. His first collection of poems, *With Love Somehow*, appeared in 1962 (Oxford University Press). He spent the academic year 1967/8 as visiting poet at Amherst College, Massachusetts, and subsequently became visiting poet, lecturer, and between 1971 and 1999 professor of English at Wesleyan University, Middletown, Connecticut.

Connor's early books established him as an acute and wide-ranging social poet, with an engagingly bluff sense of wit. A change of tone was signalled by his *Twelve Secret Poems* (published as a pamphlet, 1965, and incorporated in *Kon in Springtime*, 1968) with their journeys into the 'suburbs of Hell', which preceded his permanent move to the USA. *In the Happy Valley* (1971—all Oxford University Press) presents his adopted country with sometimes baffled admiration as a brilliantly fragmented, almost surreal mosaic. His later collections include *Spirits of the Place* (1986) and *Metamorphic Adventures* (1996). See *Things Unsaid: New and Selected Poems 1960-2005* (2006—all Anvil). NP

Conquest, (George) Robert (Ackworth) (1917–) Educated at Winchester and Magdalen College, Oxford, served in the army from 1939 to 1946, and then spent ten years in the foreign service. Subsequently he has been a freelance writer and reviewer, literary editor of the *Spectator*, and more recently has become famous as an expert on Russian affairs. He has held various posts at American universities, and since 1981 has been based at the Hoover Institution, Stanford University. *The Great Terror* (1968) and *The Harvest of Sorrow* (1986), the first dealing with Stalin's organized terror and persecution in the late Thirties, the second with the death by starvation of millions in the Ukraine, have made him internationally known.

Conquest's poetry has been little touched by his other interests. Indeed, the work of his that is most nearly political comes in his first collection and, as in poems like 'A Minor Front' and 'On The Danube', is perhaps implicitly left-wing, and so at odds with his later prose writings. In general, he is a personal rather than a social poet, his characteristic tone lyrically enthusiastic, the verse vigorous and varied, the appreciation of the visible world powerful. A lesser strain in his poetry is ironic or satiric, and he is capable also of fanciful, near-metaphysical speculation, as in 'On an X-Ray Photograph of the Poet's Skull' or 'The Phases of Venus'. His early master was *Auden, and there are residual traces in his later work of *Graves' offhand and quirky humour. At times his rhetoric is too high-flown for his subject, occasionally he ties himself up in verbal or metaphysical knots, but his best work celebrates the acts and emotions of love in a manner clear, elegant, and easy.

Poems (Macmillan/St Martin's, 1955) was succeeded by *Between Mars and Venus* (Hutchinson/St Martin's, 1962), *Arias from a Love Opera* (Macmillan, 1968), and *Forays* (Chatto, 1979). *New and Collected Poems* appeared in London in 1988. Conquest also championed the *Movement poets in the Fifties, when he edited the anthology *New Lines*, and he has produced a vigorous translation of Solzhenitsyn's *Prussian Nights* (Fontana, 1977; Farrar, Straus, 1978). His latest collections, in his ninth decade, are *Penultimata* (2009) and *Blokelore & Blokesongs* (2012—both Waywiser), which reflect on the world from the *Amis-esque perspective of 'Old Fred'. JGS

Constantine, David (1944–) Born in Salford; he lectured in German at the University of Durham from 1969 to 1981, and is now a fellow in German at the Queen's College, Oxford. He has translated Hölderlin and written a book about him, and the German poet's 'Half of Life', with its balance between celebration and anxiety, classical restraint and romantic longing, might be a manifesto for Constantine's own work. *A Brightness to Cast Shadows* (1980) uses an impassioned, skilful lyricism to clarify a vision of experience that is both light and dark: love is affirmed, yet social wretchedness—the subject of a novel by Constantine, *Davies* (1985)—is treated with straightforward tenderness and Brechtian irony. *Watching for Dolphins* (1983) demonstrates a poignant obsession with loss and longing, often revivifying traditional myth. *Madder* (1987)—one of Constantine's best collections—is written in a leaner, seriously playful style that is responsive both to the sombre 'noise | And shadow' of history and to the 'manifest beauty of breathing'.

Since *Selected Poems* (1991) he has published four further collections: *Caspar Hauser* (1994), a long Browningesque poem on the mysterious nineteenth-century

German, *The Pelt of Wasps* (1998), *Something for the Ghosts* (2002), and *Nine Fathom Deep* (2009). *Collected Poems* appeared alongside a book of lectures on poetry, *The Living Language*, in 2004 (all Bloodaxe). In 1996 Constantine won the European Poetry Translation Prize for his *Selected Poems* of Hölderlin. He has also translated contemporary French and German poetry, and written two volumes of short stories.   MO'N*

Coolidge, Clark (1939–   ) Born in Providence, Rhode Island, and studied at Brown University, where his father was a professor of music. He has lived in New York, San Francisco, Italy, and California, and is an accomplished jazz drummer.

Coolidge majored in geology, but left university without finishing his degree after reading *On the Road* by *Kerouac, whose improvisatory poetics he has cited as an inspiration. The paratactic early work collected in *Space* (Harper & Row, 1970) was famously dismissed as 'psychedelic word salad' ('what buck last cattle lap form pits'). But he has proved a substantial and ambitious writer, embracing a wide range of modes and subjects. *Quartz Hearts* (This Press, 1978) lists sources from Watergate to Beethoven; 'Subject to a Film' recounts watching the shoot for *Jaws* in clipped prose; *The ROVA Improvisations* (Sun & Moon, 1994) are jazz poems; *Far Out West* (The Figures, 2001) is a cowboy sequence; *The Act of Providence* (Qua Press, 2010) returns to his home town.

Coolidge has been associated with—and admired by—the *Language poets, but the spirit of his writing remains closer to the freehand verve of the *New York School and the *Beats. The occluded yet discursive quality of his later work ('whatever you can't know you do write', *The Crystal Text* (The Figures, 1986)) has been compared to that of John *Ashbery. Coolidge's critical prose can be found in *Now That's Jazz* (Living Batch, 1999). He has also edited the writings of his collaborator, the painter Philip Guston.   JNT

Cooper, Jane (1924–2007) Born in Atlantic City, New Jersey, and educated at Vassar College, the University of Wisconsin, and the University of Iowa. From 1950 to 1987 she taught at Sarah Lawrence College. She lived in New York City and was New York State Poet from 1995 to 1997.

The relative sparseness of Cooper's poetic oeuvre is matched by the economy of individual poems: her work has a sinewy, thought-through quality. In cool language, careful syntax, and controlled structures, she looks steadily at family, love, work, cities and loneliness.

A journal passage from the early 1950s which Cooper retrieved for her 1974 essay, 'Nothing Has Been Used in the Manufacture of This Poetry That Could Have Been Used in the Manufacture of Bread', captures the integrity with which she has approached her art: 'I have a very old-fashioned idea of what poetry should do. It is the soul's history and whatever troubles the soul is fit material for poetry.'

Like her friends and contemporaries, Adrienne *Rich, Jean *Valentine, Grace Paley, and other New York women writers, Cooper was intensely concerned from the late 1960s with the problems, themes, and achievements of women's writing, which is the subject of her 'Poetry . . . Bread' essay. Cooper's books of poetry were *The Weather of Six Mornings* (1968), *Maps and Windows* (1974—both Macmillan), *Scaffolding: New and Selected Poems* (Anvil, 1984)—also published in the States by Tilbury House in 1993—*Green Notebook, Winter Road* (Tilbury, 1994), and *The Flashboat: Poems Collected and Reclaimed* (Norton, 1999).   RHa

Cope, Wendy (1945–   ) Born in Erith, Kent, Cope took a history degree at St Hilda's College, Oxford, and was a primary-school teacher for some years, specializing in music. Her first collection of poetry, *Making Cocoa for Kingsley Amis* (1986) was followed by *Serious Concerns* (1991—both Faber). Both quickly reached the best-seller lists, and established her as the most popular English poet of the Eighties and Nineties.

Cope writes skilfully in the traditional compact verse-forms and, in *The River Girl* (1988), a children's poem which originated as a puppet-play, demonstrates ease with the longer narrative. She is a gifted parodist—of T. S. *Eliot, Seamus *Heaney and Geoffrey *Hill among others—and has invented a memorable comic character in the shape of the pretentious suburban poet, Jason Strugnell. Her satire, however, like the melancholy of her more serious poems, is gentle and often appealingly self-mocking.

In the later collections, *If I Don't Know* (2001), shortlisted for the Whitbread Award, and *Family Values* (2011), her own voice has come to the fore, demonstrating fewer pressures to distrust and ironize the language of emotion. Her selected poems, *Two Cures for Love: Poems 1979-2006,* is a teacher-friendly edition, containing notes and descriptions of the verse-forms (all Faber). Cope has also written a number of collections for children, and has edited a variety of anthologies, including *Is That the New Moon? Poems by Women Poets* (HarperCollins, 1989). She selected and introduced *George Herbert's Verse and Prose* (SPCK, 2003).   CAR

Corless-Smith, Martin (1965–) Born in Worcestershire, England, Corless-Smith studied painting before moving to the States where he attended the University of Iowa Writer's Workshop and gained a PhD at the University of Utah. He teaches on the MFA programme at Boise State University and edits the 'Free Poetry' imprint.

Sometimes described as neo-Romantic, Corless-Smith brings postmodernist instability to bear on an antiquarian English imagination. Like Susan *Howe, he presents precisely fragmented, palimpsestic texts, in which literary tradition and historical record are quoted, broken, and overlaid with unruly, anonymous voices: see 'Worcestershire Mass' in *Complete Travels* (West House, 2000). His other collections are: *Of Piscator* (University of Georgia Press, 1997) *Nota* (2003), *Swallows* (2006), and *English Fragments: A Brief History of the Soul* (2010—all Fence), wherein he adopts the personae of two historical poets, 'Thomas Swan' and 'William Williamson'.   JNT

Corman, Cid (Sidney Corman) (1924–2004) Born in Boston. After university, in

1948, he began America's first poetry radio show. He became associated with Charles *Olson, Robert *Creeley, and Louis *Zukofsky, whose poetry he published in the first series (1951-7) of his magazine *Origin*. Paul *Blackburn and Denise *Levertov were among the early guest editors; and work by Robert *Creeley, Robert *Duncan, and Larry *Eigner also featured prominently. In 1958 he went to Japan and set up his publishing activities there (including Origin Press), returning to America between 1970 and 1982. Corman extended editorial policy in subsequent series (1961-4; 1966-71; 1977-80; 1983-6) to include any work he felt deserved a wider audience, whenever it had been written. Thereafter the magazine became more diverse, though it continued to favour poems in free and experimental forms. Its translations—from a wide range of languages— helped establish or extend the American reputations of a number of European and Far Eastern poets, most of them modern (Antonin Artaud, Gottfried Benn, René Char, Paul Celan), but a few (like Basho) whose work is centuries old.

By 1987 Corman had published over seventy volumes of his own verse, most of them being short collections from small or private presses. He is still better known for his early and influential advocacy of William Carlos *Williams, Creeley, and other poets who were not accepted in America in the 1950s and 1960s than for his own poetry, for which he made few claims, asking only that it 'sing into you a little moment'. In 1990, he began to collect it in a series of volumes under the general title *Of*. It resembles the work of the *Black Mountain school, being in very short lines, and consisting mainly of momentary impressions, most of these personal and frequently verbless. The latter feature became increasingly pronounced, doubtless owing to his long residence in Japan and the effect of its poetry on him. He translated much French and Japanese poetry, and made the first English translations of Celan. *The Gist of Origin, 1951–1971* (Grossman, 1973), is an anthology of poems, short stories, and essays from the magazine's first three series. Corman's poetry is selected in *The Next One Thousand Years*, edited by Bob Arnold and Ce Rosenbow (Long-house, 2008). NE/MS-S*

Corn, Alfred (1943–) Born in Georgia, where he graduated from Emory University. Following doctoral studies in French literature at Columbia, Corn began writing poetry and literary criticism for numerous magazines and quarterlies. He has since taught at Yale, Columbia, and UCLA (among others), and has edited a book of essays by contemporary writers on The New Testament, *Incarnation* (Viking, 1990). A collection of critical essays on fiction and poetry, *The Metamorphoses of Metaphor* (Viking, 1987), includes pieces on many of the poets who influence his work most consistently: *Stevens, *Ashbery, Robert *Lowell, *Bishop, and Hart *Crane.

Corn's first book, *All Roads at Once* (1976), ranges formally from imagistic short lyrics to an ambitious narrative poem ('Pages from a Voyage'), and reflects his interest in the relation of art to experience. His subsequent four volumes similarly balance autobiographical episode and anecdote with his wide knowledge of art and literature. If his first book emphasizes natural observation, his second, *A Call in the Midst of the Crowd* (1978), celebrates the urban landscape of New York City in its long title sequence. With *The Various Light* (1980), Corn achieves a smoother syntax and greater clarity in lyric poems about loss and impermanence. His fourth book, *Notes from a Child of Paradise* (1984), is a full-length narrative poem, partly written in *terza rima*, which chronicles Corn's courtship, marriage, and divorce, and, less successfully, aspires to a grand vision of America in the Sixties. A prolific poet, Corn departs somewhat from his previous mandarin work in the long poem 'An Xmas Murder' (in *The West Door*, 1988—all Viking), a chilling and plain-spoken tale diminished only by its weak narrative frame.

Stake: Selected Poems, 1972–1992 (Counterpoint, 1999) was followed by *Contradictions* (Copper Canyon, 2002). Corn has also written a novel, *Part of His Story* (Mid-Line, 1997). For his later writing on poetry as a practitioner and critic, see *The Poem's Heartbeat: A Manual of Prosody* (Story

Line, 1997; repr. Copper Canyon, 2008) and *Atlas: Selected Essays 1989–2007* (University of Michigan Press, 2008). TDeP

Cornford, Frances (née Darwin) (1886–1960) Born in Cambridge, and privately educated. She was a granddaughter of Charles Darwin, the wife of the classical scholar, F. M. Cornford, and the mother of the poet, John *Cornford, who was killed in the Spanish Civil War.

She was comparable at her best with Walter *de la Mare and W. H. *Davies. But neither the advocacy of Rupert *Brooke nor that of J. C. *Squire could persuade Edward Marsh to put her work into his *Georgian anthologies.

Her poems rejoice at the tranquillity of life in Cambridge where she lived almost all her life. But, at the same time, she shows a quirky apprehension of decay and death. Best of all, perhaps, is 'Childhood', with its perception of the mutual incompetence of a small child and a senile great-aunt. Her poignant epitaph for Charlotte Brontë sits alongside her mock-epitaph for a reviewer, the latter chirping 'I hope to meet my Maker brow to brow | And find my brow the higher'.

Frances Cornford's first book was *Poems* (Priory, 1910), and this was followed by five others, consolidated into a *Collected Poems* (Cresset, 1954). She also published a morality play, *Death and the Princess* (Bowes & Bowes, 1912). PDH

Cornford, (Rupert) John (1915–36) Born in Cambridge, the son of the classicist Francis Cornford and the poet Frances *Cornford, and studied at the London School of Economics and Trinity College, Cambridge. He joined the Young Communist League in 1933, and the Communist Party in 1935. He graduated in June 1936, a month before the Spanish Civil War began, and in August left for Spain, where he was one of the first Englishmen to join the Anarchist POUM. He was in the battles for Madrid and Boadilla, and was killed in December on the Cordoba front on his twenty-first birthday or the day after.

Cornford's precocious achievements and his early death in Spain have made him a literary legend, though he in fact left about two-dozen poems, only half of which were written after he was 18. His writings, which consisted largely of political essays and letters, were brought together as *John Cornford: A Memoir* (Cape, 1938: enlarged as *Understand the Weapon, Understand the Wound*, 1976) and *Collected Writings*, ed. J. Galassi (1986—both Carcanet).

Cornford saw his poems as instrumental to his political views; yet 'Full Moon at Tierz' remains a work of remarkable power, largely because of its directness and the intensity of its conviction. The firmness and simplicity of its diction is also a feature of 'To Margot Heinemann', one of the most touching personal poems of the period.

See also *Journey to the Frontier* (Constable, 1966), by P. Stansky and W. Abrahams, an authoritative study.   ATT

Corso, (Nunzio) Gregory (1930–2001)

Born in New York City to a poor family. He was one of the original *Beats, along with *Ginsberg and *Kerouac. It has been said that 'if Kerouac was the father-figure and Ginsberg the rabbi-figure, Corso was the child-figure and the clown'. As a young man he got into trouble with the police and served three years in prison for an attempted robbery. He read much there, and on his release was supported by a number of Harvard students, who helped him to publish his first book, *The Vestal Lady on Brattle and Other Poems* (1955). Then Ginsberg discovered him. The best poems of *The Happy Birthday of Death* (City Lights, 1960)—such as 'Marriage' and 'Bomb'—were outrageous, often funny, very much that of an autodidact (full of 'hard' words), and sometimes touching. Later, under the influence of Kerouac, with his philosophy of spontaneity, his poems became more grandiose; it also became clear that he had been reading Hart *Crane, and wished to emulate his singing line. 'Elegiac Feelings American', in memory of Kerouac, was the title poem of his 1970 New Directions volume. One of his most prominent personae began to resemble that of Charles *Bukowski, but was more self-consciously literary. But he remained, as he said, 'un-Faustian . . . naive . . . strange—sweet—smart—why not'. Unlike his old associates, he refused to succumb to the White House or literary agents and, for many, his was the only surviving authentic Beat voice—beat up, certainly, and faded, but still full of good-hearted hatred for the establishment. On his death, Robert *Creeley wrote: 'Lots of us propose to be poets but who finally stakes all, or just takes all, as being that way?'

See *Mindfield: New and Selected Poems* (2nd edn., Thunder's Mouth, 1998) and *An Accidental Autobiography: The Selected Letters of Gregory Corso* (New Directions, 2003). Also Gregory Stephenson, *Exiled Angel: A Study of the Work of Gregory Corso* (Hearing Eye, 1989).   MS-S*

Coulette, Henri (Anthony) (1927–88)

Born in Los Angeles, where he lived almost all of his life, except for a short stint in the army (1945-6) and the time he spent in graduate school at the University of Iowa. On his graduation from Iowa he returned to his alma mater, California State University, Los Angeles, and taught there until his death from an apparent heart attack at his home in South Pasadena.

Coulette's best-known book, *The War of the Secret Agents and Other Poems* (1965), received the Lamont Poetry Award of the Academy of American Poets. The book's title poem is about a ring of spies operating in occupied France during the Second World War. The poem depicts the sadly comic delusions of the spies and reveals the larger web of interlocking duplicities that destroys them. At the end of the poem the author addresses the reader, saying 'there is no meaning | or purpose; only the codes'. Coulette's second book, *The Family Goldschmidt* (1971), was accidentally shredded by the publisher before it was widely distributed.

Usually written in traditional verse forms but sometimes in carefully wrought free verse, Coulette's poetry often looks to popular culture for its subject-matter—spy novels, Hollywood movies, computer poets, life in the 1960s—but considers it with classical wit and contemporary ambivalence.

His tone might best be characterized as serio-comic.

Posthumously published by the University of Arkansas Press, *The Collected Poems of Henri Coulette* (1990) contains the two published books, along with a new book that Coulette had readied for publication and a small selection of uncollected poems.   AH

Cowley, Malcolm (1898–1989) Born in western Pennsylvania and raised in Pittsburgh, where he became a lifelong friend of Kenneth *Burke. At Harvard, Cowley met Conrad *Aiken and E. E. *Cummings, and attended the literary salons of Amy *Lowell, who gave him much practical advice on his early poetry. Although he is best known as an editor, a literary critic, and a cultural historian, Cowley began his illustrious career in letters as a poet, and was influenced early on by the French Dadaist and *Surrealist poets, many of whom he met in Paris, where he translated their poetry into English. *Blue Juniata: A Life* (Penguin, 1985) incorporates his three earlier volumes of poetry (*Blue Juniata*, 1929; *The Dry Season*, 1941; and *Blue Juniata: Collected Poems*, 1968) into an autobiographical sequence modelled on Whitman's *Leaves of Grass*, which Cowley celebrated as a critic.

Following the 'shapes of his childhood, patterns of his growth', Cowley recalls, in many poems, his idyllic boyhoood, a simpler time marred only by the death of his adoptive sister ('The Pyre' and 'The Red Wagon'). 'Tomorrow Morning' captures the revolutionary fervour of literary radicalism in the Thirties, when Cowley uncritically supported the Soviet Union. His best poems, like his best prose writings, are generational portraits. 'The Flower and the Leaf' and 'Ezra Pound at the Hôtel Jacob' profile his renowned friends with the same verve as his unforgettable prose memoir of Hart *Crane in *Exile's Return* (1951), his definitive chronicle of the so-called lost generation of expatriate American writers.

A selection of Cowley's poems and his prose about poets can be found in *The Portable Malcolm Cowley*, ed. Donald Faulkner (Viking, 1990).   TDeP

Crane, (Harold) Hart (1899–1932) Born in Garrettsville, Ohio, of continually quarrelling parents and committed himself to a poetic career after having had one of his poems accepted by a New York magazine when he was 16. He was encouraged in his ambition by the widow of William Vaughn Moody, and when his parents separated in 1916 he moved to New York, abandoned his intentions of preparing for college, and plunged into the Greenwich Village world of poetry, painting, avant-gardisme, and moral and ideological unorthodoxy.

After making many literary contacts, Crane returned to Ohio in late 1919 to try to support himself by menial work in his father's chocolate business while reading and writing in the little spare time that was left to him. During this time he acquainted himself with a wide range of writers who had come to his notice through the criticism of T. S. *Eliot and Ezra *Pound. In 1922 he obtained work as an advertising copy-writer, which he believed would free him from his enslavement to the business world and be congenial to his poetic abilities. He was drawn back to New York in 1923, and from this time onwards made a precarious living, mostly from copy-writing, and came to feel increasingly isolated from the values of 1920s America, both because of his homosexual life-style and deepening alcoholism, and also because of his unproductive and socially non-respectable vocation as a poet.

Crane's reaction against the poetic pessimism of Eliot's *The Waste Land* was partly responsible for his determination to 'launch into praise' in an affirmative and visionary poem about America which eventually became *The Bridge*. A personal grant from the banker Otto Kahn allowed him time to work on this project; meanwhile his first collection of lyrics, *White Buildings*, was published in 1926. The disorder of his personal life continued to intensify, while his private faith in the meaning and value of his optimistic poem steadily declined. On a short trip to Europe in 1928 he spent most of his time in Paris among American expatriate writers and artists. Awarded a

Guggenheim Fellowship after the publication of *The Bridge* in 1930, he embarked for Mexico in 1931 with the intention of writing an epic poem about the Spanish conquest of that country. This last phase of his career included an attempt to establish a heterosexual identity for himself in an affair with the estranged wife of Malcolm *Cowley, Peggy Baird. On a return trip to the United States in April 1932 he committed suicide by leaping overboard from the stern of his ship.

Like much of the poetry of the period, Crane's very earliest lyrics exhibit many 1890s-ish qualities, and they have usually been dismissed rather patronizingly by critics. These poems nevertheless possess a lyrical delicacy and fragility which may define the true nature of Crane's talent better than most of his later, more willed and declamatory work. Poems like 'My Grandmother's Love Letters', 'Pastorale', or 'Voyages I'; the more obviously derivative and literary 'Legende' or 'Forgetfulness'; or the piece of seasonal imagery 'October-November', written when he was 17, show a sensitivity in the handling of free verse which is unsurpassed by any other English-language poet. If he had been more sure of the real nature of his poetic powers, and if he had been able to assimilate more of his twentieth-century subject-matter within his lyric capacities (as he occasionally did in *The Bridge*) without doing violence to them, it seems possible that Hart Crane might have marked out a more Romantic and intuitive path for American poetry than the one which it in fact took.

Crane's sensitivity to the connotative or associational dimension of words is a noticeable characteristic of his earlier poems, but it also helped to open the way to his later poetic undoing. Partly under the influence of the Elizabethan poets and dramatists, but also that of the French Symbolists, and particularly of Rimbaud, he gave himself over in many poems to the creation of complex knots of meaning which were not easily intelligible without some kind of accompanying interpretation from the poet himself. Some of the later lyrics of *White Buildings* such as 'Possessions', 'Lachrymae Christi', or 'Recitative',

embody a great sense of visionary aspiration and occasional lines of intense beauty, but without yielding any clearly grasp-able overall significance. Crane also abandoned his earlier delicate free verse for blank verse, and thereby laid the basis for the rather oratorical idiom which became the anchoring mode of his major poem, *The Bridge*. This 'turn' in Crane's work took place around 1922, principally in his three-part poem 'For the Marriage of Faustus and Helen', which was an attempt to relate these archetypal or mythic figures to the actual circumstances of modern city life.

Crane's ambition in *The Bridge* was to write a visionary poem about America in which America's past history since the Spanish conquest and its present-day realities of business, engineering, and democratic optimism would be held together by one over-arching and exaltational symbol—the Brooklyn Bridge—in an almost Dantesque manner. Other emblems which serve to integrate the poem on a symbolic level include Columbus, Pocahontas, Rip Van Winkle, Walt Whitman, the clipper ship Cutty Sark, the Mississippi river, and the New York subway. From the start, the success of such an enterprise seemed doubtful, even to Crane himself, but the large-scale and loose framework of the long poem nevertheless allowed him room to explore many different poetic styles and materials, and between its opening 'Proem' and its closing 'Atlantis'—both of them written in high-toned and annunciatory blank verse—*The Bridge* contains extended passages and many individual lyrics which are both easily readable and poetically successful. 'The Harbor Dawn' is one of Crane's most subtle and authentically modern lyrics. 'The Rivers', set firmly in the twentieth-century world of railroads and railroad hobos, perhaps comes closest to Crane's aim of tracing living links between America's past and its present, and does so by making historical and psychological, rather than merely symbolic connections. 'Cutty Sark' contains some interesting formal experiment, 'National Winter Garden' has some sharp contemporary observation, 'Virginia' is a playful and innocent love lyric. 'The Tunnel', set in the New York subway—cast in the role of a Dantean hell or purgatory—is persuasively infernal, but at the same time reveals the main flaws of Crane's method in so far as this subterranean symbol of desolation is of course realistically a product of the very same forces which produced its would-be uplifting counterpart, the Brooklyn Bridge. Crane's last collection, assembled shortly before his death, shows a successful return to simplicity in such lyrics as 'Island Quarry', or even the Hopkinsesque 'The Hurricane', but by this time his life was in chaos and his talent largely destroyed.

The key to Crane's 'failure' to do all that he might have done is almost certainly to be found in his continuing, if largely unconscious, acceptance of the American bourgeois values which surrounded and beset him. By these criteria he could only see himself as a non-achiever, and his attempts by way of compensation to achieve a public affirmation in his poetry (rather than authentically and more personally to register despair or defeat, as he had done in a poem like his homage to Chaplin, 'Chaplinesque') led to a distortion of his talent and a loss of poetic direction; meanwhile his life, and his talent, were being undermined by real-life forces which he tried to ignore as he toiled away at his mystical bridge-building. The many mid-century poets (for example, Robert *Lowell) who have been fascinated by Crane have perhaps seen him as anticipating some of their own conflicts with twentieth-century American society.

Crane's *Complete Poems and Selected Letters* were edited by Langdon Hammer for the Library of America in 2006. See also Hammer's study of Crane and Allen *Tate, *Janus-Faced Modernism* (Princeton University Press, 1993). The biographies by Philip Horton (*Hart Crane*, Norton, 1937), Brom Weber (*Hart Crane*, Bodley, 1948), and John Unterecker (*Voyager*, Farrar, Straus, 1969) have been followed by Clive Fisher, *Hart Crane: A Life* (Yale University Press, 2002). The most penetrating comments on Crane's work are perhaps still to be found in the essays of such poet-critics of his own generation as

Allen Tate, Yvor *Winters, and R. P. *Blackmur. See also John T. Irwin, *Hart Crane's Poetry* (Johns Hopkins University Press, 2011), an eclectically scholarly study of *The Bridge* as an epic of Western culture.   CF

Crapsey, Adelaide (1878–1914) Born in Brooklyn Heights and named for her mother, she was the third child of the Revd Algernon Crapsey, a free-thinking Episcopal minister, who moved his family to Rochester, New York, soon after her birth. Crapsey grew up in a hectic but intellectual household as her father's favourite. She graduated in 1901 from Vassar College and taught prep school for two years before attending Rome's School of Archaeology, returning in 1905 for her father's widely reported heresy trial. She also accompanied him to the 1907 Hague Peace Conference, but bouts of fatigue forced her to resign another teaching post. She spent two more years abroad, researching a study of English metrics.

Her own poetry was conventionally Romantic, often Keatsian, but exposure to recently translated Japanese *tanka* and haiku, as well as to Emily Dickinson and Landor, encouraged a new tautness. Early in 1911, while teaching at Smith College, she invented the cinquain: an unrhymed, five-line poem with a 1,2,3,4,1 accentual scheme. She also learned that tuberculin meningitis was ravaging her brain, and passed her last year in a sanatorium.

Though a minor poet, anticipating the *Imagists, Crapsey was a pioneer in the shift away from Victorian rhetoric and sentimentality, as the sardonic 'To the Dead in the Grave-Yard under my Window' confirms. Pressured by death, her modest gift forged a group of cinquains—'November Night', 'Trapped', 'The Guarded Wound', 'Amaze', 'The Warning', 'Night Winds', 'Triad'—that have entered the canon. Her unfinished thesis was published as *A Study in English Metrics* (Knopf, 1918), and Susan Sutton Smith has edited *The Complete Poems and Collected Letters of Adelaide Crapsey* (State University of New York Press, 1976). See also *Adelaide Crapsey* (Twayne, 1979), by Edward Butscher and *Alone in the Dawn*

(University of Georgia Press, 1988; repr. 2008) by Karen Alkalay-Gut.   EB

Crase, Douglas (1944–   ) Born in Battle Creek, Michigan, and received a BA from Princeton University. He dropped out of law school at the University of Michigan in order to write campaign speeches for the Democratic candidate for governor of the state. He then moved to Rochester, New York, where he spent three years working as a speech-writer for Eastman Kodak. He now lives and works in New York City as a freelance writer.

To date Crase has published only one volume, *The Revisionist* (Little, Brown, 1981), yet that was enough to establish him as one of the most important poets of his generation, displaying a rare ambition and an explicitly Whitmanian concern with American landscape and history. As Crase himself acknowledges, his major influence among living poets has been *Ashbery; unlike other second-generation *New York School poets, however, Crase picks up not Ashbery's playfully surrealist mannerisms but the deeply American strain in his work that reaches back through Hart *Crane, *Stevens, and Whitman to its ultimate origins in Emerson (whose essays Crase has recently edited). Where older poets like *Ginsberg, *Simpson, and James *Wright have bemoaned what they regard as modern America's betrayal of Whitman's vision, Crase steadfastly continues to affirm the sense of infinite possibility, in however attenuated a form, that has been at the centre of American mythology since Emerson. As the title of his book suggests, the renewal of American possibility depends for Crase on revision in all its senses, political as well as literary; in his poems he explores these modes of revision as they connect with specific landscapes. Crase is a topographical poet in an almost eighteenth-century sense; he writes lovingly and meticulously about places as such, rather than incidents or epiphanies for which they provide convenient backdrops. His style is discursive, argumentative, at times verging on the prosaic in its abstract diction and pursuit of intricate logical structures; but these qualities (which may reflect and to some extent parody his work as a corporate speech-writer) are balanced by an intense lyricism that breaks out unexpectedly in the midst of dry patches, much like the beauty Crase continues to find cropping up in the barren landscapes of *fin-de-siècle* America.

See also *AMERIFIL.TXT: A Commonplace Book* (University of Michigan Press, 1997) and *Both: A Portrait in Two Parts* (Pantheon, 2004), a biography of the bohemian botanists, Rupert Barneby and Dwight Ripley.   RG

Crawford, Robert (1959–   ) Educated at the universities of Glasgow and Oxford, and now Professor of English at St Andrews. This academic background sets up expectations which are agreeably confounded by Crawford's poetry. His work is lively, sentient, and eclectic—Scottish qualities, perhaps, but rarely found controlled by such a wide-ranging and astute critical intelligence. *A Scottish Assembly* (1990) was followed by *Talkies* (1992—both Chatto & Windus), which shows a similar scope as well as a Scottish particularity but with an enhanced confidence. His growth as a poet can be sensed in the bravura inventiveness of two longer poems, 'Z' and 'Customs'. His work is also topical within the context of the recent regeneration of the Scottish cultural and political scene, especially in his critical but positive engagement with Scottish subjects and personalities.

Crawford has also written in a densely textured *Scots, as in *Sharawaggi* (Polygon, 1990) which he shared with W. N. *Herbert. *Selected Poems* (2005) also draws on *Masculinity* (1996), *Spirit Machines* (1999), which continued his *Informationist interest in imagining the technologized Scottish landscape, and *The Tip of My Tongue* (2003). He has since published *Full Volume* (2008—all Cape), which includes occasional poems as well as versions of Gaelic lyrics from his literary history, *Scotland's Books* (Penguin, 2007).

As a critic, Crawford has published *The Savage and the City in the Work of T. S. Eliot* (Clarendon, 1987) and *Devolving English Literature* (1992), and has co-edited collections of essays, *About Edwin Morgan* (1990), *The Arts of Alasdair Gray* (1991), *Reading Douglas Dunn* (1992), and *Liz Lochhead's Voices* (1994—all Edinburgh University Press). He was also a founder and co-editor of the poetry magazine *Verse*, and, with Mick *Imlah, edited *The New Penguin Book of Scottish Verse* (2000). Among his other books are *The Modern Poet* (Oxford University Press, 2001)—a study of poetry and academia—and a biography of Robert Burns.   DED*

Creeley, Robert (White) (1926–2005) Born in Arlington, Massachusetts. He lost his father, and the use of his left eye, before he was 5, and was subsequently brought up on a farm in West Acton. A year with the American Field Service in India and Burma (1944/5) interrupted his time at Harvard; on his return he married, left Harvard without graduating, and, in 1948, went to New Hampshire to try subsistence farming. His attempt two years later to launch his own magazine failed, but prompted a long correspondence with Charles *Olson and provided material for Cid *Corman's journal, *Origin*. In search of a cheaper way of life, the Creeleys moved in 1951 to France and the following year to Mallorca (the setting for Creeley's only novel, *The Island*, 1963), where they stayed until their divorce in 1955. There they set up the Divers Press and printed books by Creeley himself (including *The Gold Diggers*, 1954; eleven stories), Robert *Duncan, Olson, and others. At Olson's invitation Creeley taught at Black Mountain College (spring 1954 and autumn 1955) and founded and edited the *Black Mountain Review* (1954–7: *see* BLACK MOUNTAIN POETS).

His first three books of poetry, *Le Fou* (1952), *The Kind of Act of* (1953), and *The Immoral Proposition* (1953), appeared in quick succession while he was in Europe, and his next two, *All That Is Lovely in Men* (1955) and *If You* (1956), shortly after his return to America. In 1956 Creeley settled in Albuquerque, New Mexico, where he remarried, taught at a boy's school until 1959, and took an MA from the University of New Mexico in 1960. Having worked as a tutor on a Guatemalan plantation, in the early 1960s he began a new academic career—which led in later years to the State University of New York, Buffalo—and became nationally known with *For Love: Poems 1950–1960* (1962). He divorced again, and married for the third time in 1977.

Creeley's poetry is predominantly concerned with love and the emotions attending intimate relationships. Among his strongest influences he listed not only poets, like Olson, William Carlos, *Williams, and *Ginsberg, who reassured him that 'you can write directly from that which you feel', but also jazz musicians, who demonstrated that feelings could be expressed no less powerfully for eschewing prescribed forms. Creeley's early poems, collected in *Poems 1950–1965* (1966), are minutely detailed—often obscure—analyses of feelings, their verse invariably free, their lines and stanzas short, and their sentences terse. A new disillusionment with analytical thinking is evident in *Words* (1967), *Pieces* (1969), and *A Day Book* (1972), and a less exalted view of love in *Later* (1978) and *Echoes* (1982). More notable for its continuities than for its changes, however, his poetry sustained its unique brand of vigilant minimalism.

Creeley continued to publish prolifically through a variety of presses. *Just in Time* (2001) collected poems written between 1984 and 1994. Following *Life & Death* (1998) he was awarded the Bollingen Prize for Poetry. The last collection he published was *If I Were Writing This* (2003—all New Directions). See the posthumous *On Earth: Last Poems and an Essay* (2006) and *The Collected Poems of Robert Creeley* in two volumes (2006–8). Benjamin Friedlander has edited a *Selected Poems* from all six decades of verse (2008—all University of California Press).

See also *The Collected Essays of Robert Creeley* (University of California Press, 1989), *Charles Olson and Robert Creeley: The Complete Correspondence*, ed. George F. Butterick and Richard Blevins, 9 vols. (Black Sparrow, 1980–90), *Robert Creeley's Poetry: A Critical Introduction*, by Cynthia Dubin Edelberg (University of New Mexico Press, 1978), *Robert Creeley and the Genius of the American Common Place*, by Tom

*Clark (New Directions, 1993)—an extended interview which includes the poet's own 'Autobiography' (1990)—and *Robert Creeley: A Biography*, by Ekbert Faas with Maria Trombaco (University Press of New England, 2001).   NE*

Croggon, Alison (1962–) Born in South Africa to English parents, and lived in England before coming to Australia in 1969. She was educated in Ballarat and began her career as a journalist. Since the mid-80s, she has worked as a theatre critic in Melbourne. Her own writing includes plays and libretti.

Croggon's first collection, *This Is the Stone* (1991), appeared in Penguin's *Australian Poetry Series* alongside poems by Fiona Perry. She then published a novella, *Navigatio* (1995) and a second collection, *The Blue Gate* (1997—both Black Pepper). Her work is often concerned with forms of desire, from the sexual to the political and metaphysical. She has written that 'carnality, combined with poetry's encounter with otherness, is the source of the eroticism of the poetic'.

In 2000, Croggon was Australian Council writer-in-residence at Cambridge University, and her work has been published around the world. Recent small-press chapbooks include *Mnemosyne* (Wild Honey, 2003), *November Burning* (Vagabond, 2004) and *Ash* (Cusp, 2007). Her third collection, *Attempts at Being* (2002), was nominated for the Kenneth Slessor and Pushcart Prizes. *Theatre* (2009—both Salt) essays a variety of 'lyrical effusions', with the wars of the decade flickering in the wings.

The Common Flesh: New and Selected Poems (Arc) appeared in 2003. Croggon has been poetry editor for several magazines and is founding editor of the online literary journal *Masthead*. She has also published an acclaimed quartet of fantasy novels, *The Books of Pellinor*, with Candlewick Press.   JNT

Cronin, Jeremy (1949–) Grew up in Simonstown, South Africa, where his father was a naval officer. He became a Marxist during his student years at the University of Cape Town and the Sorbonne, where he gained his MA in philosophy. In 1976 he was arrested for distributing pamphlets for the banned African National Congress. His seven years in gaol as a political prisoner gave rise to the poems of his first volume, *Inside* (Ravan, 1983), which won the Ingrid Jonker Prize in 1984. He spent three years in exile in London and Lusaka before returning home in 1990. He is Deputy General-Secretary of the South African Communist Party and a member of the National Executive of the African National Congress. In 2012 he became Deputy Minister of Public Works.

Prison freed Cronin from the fear that lyricism is self-indulgent in a context of oppression: his personal suffering became part of the collective suffering and resistance of his comrades. This African humanism is enhanced in many of his poems by indigenous diction and oral repetition, and his work is perhaps best encountered in performance. Cronin has been called the precursor of the 'low mimetic' style of South African poetry in the 1990s.

In 1987 *Inside* was published in London by Cape. His later books are *Even the Dead: Poems, Parables and a Jeremiad* (Mayibuye, 1997)—selected along with poems from his debut in *Inside & Out* (David Philip, 1999)—and *More than a Casual Contact* (Umuzi, 2006).   CWO*

Cronin, M. T. C. (Margie) (1963–) Born in New South Wales, and studied at the University of Queensland, where she majored in political science. During the 1990s she worked in law, and later wrote a doctoral thesis exploring the relationships between law and literature (see *Squeezing Desire Through a Sieve: Micro Essays on Judgement and Justice* (Puncher & Wattmann, 2009)). She has taught creative writing in schools and universities, and lives on an organic farm in Queensland.

Cronin is among the most prolific of the generation of Australian poets who emerged in the 1990s, and has published over a dozen volumes around the world. Her first collection was *Zoetrope: We See Us Moving* (Five Islands, 1995), which established the philosophical interest of her work in the flow of human history. Her long poem *More or Less Than 1–100* (Shearsman, 2004), which won the C. J. Dennis Prize for Poetry, begins 'not simply the stream but they who thought of following', and comprises one hundred sections which increase and then decrease by a line each time.

Like her contemporary John *Kinsella, Cronin ranges readily from short anecdotal lyrics to longer discursive forms. Her surreal humour and curiosity is open to an international range of influences, as in her 2001 book, *Talking to Neruda's Questions* (Vagabond). *How Does a Man Who Is Dead Reinvent His Body? The Belated Love Poems of Thean Morris Caelli* (Shearsman, 2009) is a collaboration with Peter Boyle on an imaginary, amorphous poet.   JNT

Crozier, Andrew (1943–2008) Born in Hertfordshire to a family evacuated from London during the Blitz. He studied at Dulwich College and the University of Cambridge. From 1973 he lived in Sussex, where he was a professor in English and American Studies.

An important figure in the trans-Atlantic networks of the 'British Poetry Revival', in 1964 Crozier began the Ferry Press, and went to America on a Fulbright Scholarship, where he studied with Charles *Olson. In 1965, he corresponded with the poet Carl *Rakosi, who resumed writing as a result. Returning to England, Crozier started the mimeographed 'worksheet' *The English Intelligencer*, a key document in the emergence of the *Cambridge School. He began lecturing at Essex on the invitation of Donald *Davie, and went on to work at Keele alongside Roy *Fisher. In 1983, he co-edited the influential anthology *A Various Art*, and published 'Thrills and Frills: Poetry as Figures of Empirical Lyricism', a critique of British poetry's dominant naturalism. He also edited the poems of John Rodker.

Crozier's own poetry, partially collected in *All Where Each Is* (Allardyce, Barnett, 1985), celebrates the lived environment of post-war England with an *Objectivist frugality. Diary-like sequences such as *The Veil Poem* (Burning Deck, 1974), *Pleats* (Great Works, 1975), *High Zero* (Street Editions, 1978), and 'Free Running Bitch' (1997) are open in form but reserved in their respect for the 'hemmed round' condition of an individual life. *An Andrew Crozier Reader* (Carcanet, 2012), ed. Ian Brinton, reprints the major poems with contextual material.   JNT

Crozier, Lorna (1948–) Born and raised in Swift Current, Saskatchewan, where she worked as a teacher (1972–7) after graduating from the University of Saskatchewan, Saskatoon. Crozier has taught creative writing, held a number of writer-in-residence positions, worked as a radio correspondent with the Canadian Broadcasting Corporation, and in 1986 was appointed a Special Lecturer at the University of Saskatchewan. She is now Chair of the Writing Department at the University of Victoria.

Crozier's early verse, *Inside Is the Sky* (Thistledown, 1976), *Crow's Black Joy* (NeWest, 1978), and *Humans and Other Beasts* (Turnstone, 1980), explores the landscape of poetry and celebrates the simple virtues and vices of prairie people. Her later poetry, in *The Weather* (Coteau, 1983), *The Garden Going on Without Us* (1987), *Angels of Flesh, Angels of Silence* (1988), and *Inventing the Hawk* (1992) analyses gender and sexual politics, anatomizes the lifeline from foetus to angel to death, and questions the seeming invulnerability of nature. *Inventing the Hawk* won the Governor General's Award. Her later collections include *Everything Arrives at the Light* (1995), *A Saving Grace* (1996)—which imagines the poems of 'Mrs. Bentley', the narrator of Sinclair Ross' prairie novel, *As For Me and My House* (1941)—*What the Living Won't Let Go* (1999), and *Whetstone* (2005—all McClelland & Stewart).

Before the First Word (Wilfrid Laurier University Press, 2005) is an introductory selection of poems from 1985 to 2002 with an afterword by Crozier. For a fuller volume, see *The Blue Hour of the Day: Selected Poems* (McClelland & Stewart, 2007). She has also written a memoir of prairie life, *Small Beneath the Sky* (2009) and edited, with her husband Patrick *Lane, two collections of new Canadian poetry: *Breathing Fire* (1994) and *Breathing Fire 2* (2004).   PMStP*

Cruz, Victor Hernandez (1949–) Born in Aguas Buenas, Puerto Rico (where he now lives), grew up in Spanish Harlem. Early *Beat- and *Black Arts-influenced collections like *Papo Got His Gun!* (Calle Once, 1966) and *Snaps* (Random House, 1969) established him as a leading *nuyoriqueño* (or New York-Puerto Rican) poet. His adeptness in Spanish and English, and in using a blend of both, has served a now considerable body of poetry whose key theme has been the contrasting worlds of Manhattan and Puerto Rico, an American metropolis of the *barrio* and the tenement as against a Caribbean homeland as luxuriant in its people as its topography. Thus an early poem like 'urban dream', in *Snaps*, can speak of New York apocalypse ('things blowing up. | times square | electrified'), while a later poem, like 'Areyto', in *Red Beans* (1991), can invoke a Puerto Rico at once Arawak-Indian, Afro-Caribbean, and eclectically 'Spanish'. A similar multicultural vibrancy and reference marks out all his stronger poetry, as, for instance, in his New York-inspired 'Mountain Building', or his lyric, Puerto Rico-inspired 'Geography of the Trinity Corona', both in *By Lingual Wholes* (Momo's Press, 1982). From the 1960s on, Cruz has been a major energy in America's Latino renaissance, able to shift from an oral street voice to an almost Wallace *Stevensish versatility. The principal collections include *Mainland* (1973), *Tropicalization* (1976—both Random House), *Rhythm, Content & Flavor* (Arte Publico, 1989), *Red Beans* (1991), *Panoramas* (1997), *The Mountain in the Sea* (2006), and *In the Shadow of Al-Andara* (2011), which continues his vision of how 'national languages melt, sail into each other' by exploring the artistic influence of Islam in Europe, Africa, and the Caribbean. See also *Maraca: New and Selected Poems* (2001—all Coffee House), which was shortlisted for the International Griffin Poetry Prize.   ARL*

Cullen, Countee (1903–46) Probably born in Louisville, Kentucky. He was adopted by a Harlem preacher and his wife at the age of 15, and later attended both New York University and Harvard. With the publication of his first volume of poems in 1925, *Color*, Cullen assumed the place of a central figure in the *Harlem Renaissance. The book stated the themes—the injustice of colour-prejudice, the black man's African legacy, religious doubt and belief—that were to dominate his work over the twenty years until his death. A frequently anthologized poem is 'Incident', in which an 8-year-old boy has his visit to a strange city spoiled when he is called 'nigger'.

Cullen had other interests besides race, however, and a wider formal range than most of his Renaissance contemporaries. His verse is often crisp, subtle, and intelligent at once, taking special pleasure in manipulating the paradoxes thrown up by the modern treatment of the black man brought forcibly to the Land of the Free.

A selected poems was published as *On These I Stand* (Harper, 1947). See also *A Many-Colored Coat of Dreams: The Poetry of Countee Cullen* (Broadside, 1974). *My Soul's High Song: The Collected Writings of Countee Cullen*, ed. Gerald Early, appeared in 1991 (Doubleday).   JC

Cullinan, Patrick (1932–2011) Born in Pretoria and educated at Charterhouse and Oxford. He worked as a saw-miller in the Eastern Transvaal and, latterly, as a lecturer in English at the University of the Western Cape.

First coming to prominence in the 1960s, Cullinan rapidly established himself as one of South Africa's leading poets. He also distinguished himself as an editor of the influential journal, *The Bloody Horse*, as a translator of Montale, and an historian of early European explorers in South Africa.

In his first collection, *The Horizon Forty Miles Away* (Polygraph, 1973), many of the distinctive concerns of the white South African poet find expression. But Cullinan gives new resonance to these through a verse that is so unadorned as to be almost a form of anti-poetry. He also reveals a gift, rare in South Africa, for the use of myth and parable.

Throughout this first volume there is a note of controlled anguish which is all the more powerful in his second collection, *Today Is Not Different* (1978). Although Cullinan was never a 'protest' poet, here he uses past South African history to reflect, albeit indirectly, upon present troubles. Moreover, in such poems as 'The Billiard Room', he shows himself also to be a striking historian of family relations.

As a poet, Cullinan early showed the type of concern with language which marked him as something other than a realist. This is all the more conspicuous in *The White Hail in the Orchard* (1984—both David Philip). In this volume his themes become ever more metaphysical. At the same time, his skilful focusing on questions of language and reality, particularly in a poem like 'Mimesis', served to underline his position as one of the few genuine modernists in English South African poetry.

See *Selected Poems 1961-1994* (1994), *Transformations* (1999—both Snailpress), and *Escarpments*, a later selection (Umuzi, 2008). Cullinan also wrote a novel, *Matrix* (Snailpress, 2002), and edited a selection of the work of Lionel *Abrahams. See also *Imaginative Trespasser: Letters between Bessie Head and Patrick and Wendy Cullinan, 1963-1977* (Wits University Press, 2005).   sw

Cummings, E. E. **(Edward Estlin)** (1894-1962) Born in Cambridge, Massachusetts, to liberal, indulgent parents who from early on encouraged him to develop his creative gifts. While at Harvard, where his father had taught before becoming a Unitarian minister, he delivered a daring commencement address on modernist artistic innovations, thus announcing the direction his own work would take. In 1917, after working briefly for a mail-order publishing company, the only regular employment in his career, Cummings volunteered to serve in the Norton-Harjes Ambulance group in France. Here he and a friend were imprisoned (on false grounds) for three months in a French detention camp. *The Enormous Room* (1922), his witty and absorbing account of the experience, was also the first of his literary attacks on authoritarianism. *Eimi* (1933), a later travel journal, focused with much less successful results on the collectivized Soviet Union.

At the end of the First World War Cummings went to Paris to study art. On his return to New York in 1924 he found himself a celebrity, both for *The Enormous Room* and for *Tulips and Chimneys* (1923), his first collection of poetry (for which his old classmate John Dos Passos had finally found a publisher). Clearly influenced by Gertrude *Stein's syntactical and Amy Lowell's *imagistic experiments, Cummings' early poems had nevertheless discovered an original way of describing the chaotic immediacy of sensuous experience. The games they play with language (adverbs functioning as nouns, for instance) and lyric form combine with their deliberately simplistic view of the world (the individual and spontaneity versus collectivism and rational thought) to give them the gleeful and precocious tone which became a hallmark of his work. Love poems, satirical squibs, and descriptive nature poems would always be his favoured forms.

A roving assignment from *Vanity Fair* in 1926 allowed Cummings to travel again and to establish his lifelong routine: painting in the afternoons and writing at night. In 1931 he published a collection of drawings and paintings, *CIOPW* (its title an acronym for the materials used: charcoal, ink, oil, pencil, watercolour), and over the next three decades had many individual shows in New York. He enjoyed a long and happy third marriage to the photographer Marion Morehouse, with whom he collaborated on *Adventures in Value* (1962), and in later life divided his time between their apartment in New York and his family's farm in New Hampshire. His many later books of poetry, from *VV* (1931) and *No Thanks* (1935) to *Xaipe* (1950) and *95 Poems* (1958), took his formal experiments and his war on the scientific attitude to new extremes, but showed little substantial development.

Cummings' critical reputation has never matched his popularity. The left-wing critics of the 1930s were only the first to dismiss his work as sentimental and politically naïve. His supporters, however, find value not only in its verbal and visual inventiveness but also in its mystical and anarchistic beliefs. The two-volume *Complete Poems*, ed. George James Firmage (Granada, 1981; revd. edn., 1994) is the standard edition of his poetry. *Selected Poems* (1994) was edited by Richard S. Kennedy, who also wrote *Dreams in the Mirror*, the standard biography (1980—both Liveright). See also Christopher Sawyer–Lançanno, *E. E. Cummings* (Sourcebooks, 2004). *e. e. cummings: The Art of His Poetry*, by Norman Friedman (Johns Hopkins University Press/Oxford University Press, 1960) is still among the best critical studies of his poetic techniques. Cummings' long correspondence with Ezra *Pound was published by University of Michigan Press in 1996. *AnOther E. E. Cummings* (Liveright, 1999), ed. Richard Kostelanetz, is a selection of his more avant-garde writings, and *Erotic Poems* (Norton, 2010) collects his erotic poems and drawings. Liveright have also issued a series of edited reprints of Cummings' individual volumes.   NE*

Cunningham, J. V. (James Vincent) (1911–85) Born in Cumberland, Maryland, to Irish Catholic parents. The family moved to Montana, then to Colorado, where at 16 Cunningham graduated from a Jesuit high school. His father having died the year before in an industrial accident, Cunningham drifted from job to job, making several abortive attempts at college. He settled at Stanford University, studying with Yvor *Winters and W. D. Briggs, and publishing poems as an undergraduate in prominent magazines. Cunningham received an AB in classics in 1934, a PhD in English eleven years later. *The Helmsman*, his first of six poetry collections, appeared in 1942. In a long career Cunningham taught at numerous universities, including Harvard and Brandeis, where he remained from 1953 until retirement in 1980. He was married three times and had one child, a daughter.

Perhaps because his work is severe and his oeuvre small, Cunningham has not been as widely read as he deserves to be. When he is praised it is usually as a great epigramma-

tist, but Cunningham was a poet (he preferred to be called a verse-maker) of complex vision, confronting the incongruities of modern life with directness and purifying anger. His quest for virtue in 'sinuous exacting speech' suggests that he found little virtue elsewhere. If his poems display the plain style associated with Winters and the *Stanford School, they are also the best and most searching poems that school has produced. Cunningham was unafraid of the pithy abstraction, yet his sequences, 'Doctor Drink' and 'To What Strangers, What Welcome', as well as short poems like 'Montana Pastoral', are full of incisive images.

Cunningham's critical and scholarly essays discuss Shakespearean tragedy, Dickinson, *Stevens, and poetic form. In 'The Quest of the Opal' and 'The Journal of John Cardan' he poses questions of technique in relation to the uncertainty and dividedness of human nature.

The Collected Poems and Epigrams (Swallow/Faber, 1971) lacks several good poems found in *The Exclusions of a Rhyme* (1964). *The Collected Essays* (1976—both Swallow) includes both scholarly and critical work.

See also *The Poetry of J. V. Cunningham*, by Yvor Winters (Swallow, 1961), and 'An Interview with J. V. Cunningham' by Timothy *Steele, in *The Iowa Review* (Fall 1985). Steele also edited Cunningham's collected poems for Swallow Press/Ohio University Press in 1997.   DM

Curnow, (Thomas) Allen (Munro) (1911–2001) Born in Timaru, New Zealand, of Scottish and English stock. He did not move directly to a university education but first became a journalist and then studied for the Anglican ministry, returning before ordination to newspaper work. More significant than his early career moves were the friendships he made with New Zealand writers, including Denis *Glover, R. A. K. *Mason and A. R. D. *Fairburn. From the outset Curnow was perceived to be a key figure in the emergence of an authentic New Zealand literature. Later involvements with James K. *Baxter and C. K. *Stead helped confirm Curnow's importance as a catalyst to newer generations of poets, and by the end of his life, he was the unquestioned doyen of his country's writing. He edited two of the landmark anthologies of New Zealand poetry, *A Book of New Zealand Verse* (Caxton, 1945 and 1951) and the *Penguin Book of New Zealand Verse* (1960). Soon after the Second World War he came to England and worked on Fleet Street, after which he was invited to join the English department of Auckland University. Curnow's life since the Fifties was devoted to university teaching, with extended periods travelling in the United States and Europe. He also worked on compiling a definitive canon of his poetry.

Curnow's first major book, *Not in Narrow Seas* (Caxton, 1939), with its determination to add to 'the antimyth about New Zealand', was, significantly, reprinted entire in his Penguin *Selected Poems* of 1982. Poets' first published collections often distil an essence they later deplore but recognize as important. This Penguin culls Curnow's prodigious forty-year output severely and may be seen to mark the two-thirds point of his career. The later volumes drawn upon by the selection show the remarkable development of Curnow as a quirky, experimental, perhaps even 'postmodernist' poet. This phase is summed-up in his second collection, *Continuum* (Auckland University Press, 1988), sub-titled *New and Later Poems, 1972–1988*, to which must also be added a further book of *Selected Poems 1940–1988* (Penguin, 1990). The title of one of his late poems serves as a clue to those qualities in his poetry which tend to elude criticism—'An Incorrigible Music'. In his hands, the English language makes music continually, and yet he is faithful to that journalistic particularity which resists any too-ready recourse to the sublime.

In all his verse Curnow reveals himself as a quiet virtuoso with a complete command of poetic resource. He combines a vernacular diction with a high baroque tone, and never wrenches the tessitura of his language even over an extended range. His collected work has a consistent feeling of maturity, a philosophical calm which also manages to include the scabrous, the vulgar, and the sheerly ordi-

nary. His poetry got more, not less, audacious with age, so that *Continuum* and its successors constantly surprise the reader, being skittish and profound by turns.

Early Days Yet: New and Collected Poems 1941–1997 was published by Auckland University Press and was followed by *The Bells of Saint Babel's* (2001). Curnow won the New Zealand Book Award six times, and received a CBE, the Queen's Gold Medal for Poetry, and the Order of New Zealand. *Look Back Harder* (Auckland University Press, 1987) contains his critical writings, and *Whim Wham's New Zealand*, edited by Terry Sturm (Vintage, 2005), reprints the best of the satirical verse column that he wrote between 1937 and 1988.   PNFP

Curtis, Tony (1946–   ) Born in Carmarthen and educated at University College, Swansea, and Goddard College, Vermont. He is now Emeritus Professor of Poetry at the University of Glamorgan. His first four collections of verse were *Album* (1974), *Preparations* (1980), *Letting Go* (1983), and *The Last Candles* (1989). Many of his poems are concerned with his family (especially his dead father) and friends, but they are more celebratory than elegiac, and tender-hearted rather than sentimental. A wide range of historical and contemporary perspectives is brought to play in some of his longer narrative poems, such as 'The Death of Richard Beattie—Seaman' and 'Soup'.

A *Selected Poems 1970–85* (Poetry Wales), together with an American edition, *Poems: Selected and New* (Storyline) appeared in 1986; see also the interview the poet gave to Robert Minhinnick in *The New Welsh Review*, 2:4 (Spring 1990), and the article by Tony Brown on the poetry of Tony Curtis in the same number of that magazine. Curtis has also been a prolific editor and critic: see *How Poets Work* (1996) and *Wales at War: Critical Essays on Literature and Art* (2007). His later volumes of poetry are *Taken for Pearls* (1993), *War Voices* (1995), *Heaven's Gate* (2001), and *Crossing Over* (2007—all Seren), which includes a number of poems in response to visual art.   MS

Dabydeen, Cyril (1945–) Born in British Guiana (now Guyana), and educated at Queen's College in Georgetown, and the University of the West Indies. His cousin is David *Dabydeen. He moved to Canada in 1970, eventually becoming a Canadian citizen. In keeping with the Canadian cultural ethos, his poetry has gradually mellowed and become more relaxed in tone, the concluding lines of 'As An Immigrant' being characteristic: 'And let the beaver draw me closer | As I quarry silence and talk | In riddles so that the maple leaf | Itself will understand.' He could not have chosen two more familiar symbols of Canada than the beaver and the maple leaf, but by doing so he paradoxically secures his own distinctive vision as a Guyanese who grew up on the periphery of a wilderness. Dabydeen's poetry in general explores borderlines of all kinds, keeping at bay inscrutable tropical and arctic landscapes.

He was Poet Laureate of Ottawa from 1984 to 1987 and is now a professor in the English department at the university there. Since *Coastland: New and Selected Poems* (Mosaic, 1989) he has been a prolific author both of poetry and prose fiction, publishing in the UK and Canada. See *Imaginary Origins: New and Selected Poems* (Peepal Tree, 2004) and *Play a Song Somebody: New and Selected Stories* (Mosaic, 2005). In 2010 he received a Lifetime Achievement Award for Excellence from the Guyana Council of Canadians.   MR*

Dabydeen, David (1955–) Born in British Guiana (now Guyana), and educated at the universities of Cambridge and London, completing his doctorate in 1982. Academic appointments have included a research fellowship at Wolfson College, Oxford, and at the directorship of the Centre for Caribbean Studies, University of Warwick, where he is a professor.

The poems in *Slave Song* (Dangaroo, 1984), are distinguished by innovative use of Guyanese Creole dialect. Primarily dramatic monologues, the poems deal with the harsh lives and frustrated sexual fantasies of sugarcane cutters. The cumulative effect is that of an anti-pastoral inferno, the protagonists trapped in physical and spiritual pain, though still capable of being gripped by tender emotion. It won the Commonwealth Poetry Prize and was reprinted with an afterword by Peepal Tree Press in 2005. More wide-ranging and autobiographical, the poems in *Coolie Odyssey* (Hansib, 1988) explore the experience of East Indians, both in Britain and in the Caribbean. Dabydeen's views on forms of English, and their often hidden political and cultural implications, are expounded in 'On Not Being Milton: Nigger Talk in England Today', his contribution to *The State of the Language*, eds. Christopher Ricks and Leonard Michaels (Faber/University of California Press, 1990).

Other books include the studies *Hogarth's Blacks* (Manchester University Press, 1987), *The Intended* (Secker, 1991; repr. Peepal Tree, 2005), his first novel, and *Turner: New and Selected Poems* (Cape, 1994; repr. Peepal Tree, 2002), whose long title poem responds to a submerged figure in the foreground of J. M. W. Turner's 1840 painting 'Slavers Throwing Overboard the Dead and Dying—Typhoon Coming On' (also known as 'The Slave Ship'). He has published four further novels, and co-edited *The Oxford Companion to Black British History* (2007). See Kevin Grant, ed., *The Art of David Dabydeen* (Peepal Tree, 1997).   MR*

D'Aguiar, Fred(erick) (1960–) Born in London of Guyanese parents. He grew up in Guyana, and returned to London in 1972. He later trained and worked as a psychiatric nurse before reading English and Caribbean studies at the University of Kent. He is now Professor of English and Africana Studies at Virginia Tech State University.

D'Aguiar's poems are deeply rooted in Caribbean folk-wisdom, reinterpreting its homilies in terms of the contemporary world. They are also informed by a humane humour quite different from any kind of steely wit, but not at all sentimental. In his first collection, *Mama Dot* (1985), the title refers—as E. A. *Markham put it—to the 'archetypal grandmother, an elemental force'. The ostensibly anecdotal poems about her, some in the vernacular, are in fact subtly rhetorical in structure. The poems in *Airy Hall* (1989—both Chatto) survey his early years in Guyana, often capturing the vivid sensuousness of childhood vision.

The 'Black British Poetry' section of *The New British Poetry* (Paladin, 1988) was edited by him. A selection of his early poems, and a short essay on his childhood, 'Zigzag Paths', are available in *Hinterland: Caribbean Poetry from the West Indies and Britain*, ed. E. A. Markham (Bloodaxe, 1989).

British Subjects (Bloodaxe, 1993) considers the nation of D'Aguiar's passport and the colonial history of his identity—see also his 1991 play *A Jamaican Airman Foresees His Death*, published in *Black Plays: Three* (Methuen, 1995). He has since written several novels, including *Feeding the Ghosts* (Chatto, 1997), which imagines the survival of a woman on the slave ship that was also the subject of David *Dabydeen's long poem *Turner* (1994). Two book-length narrative poems—*Bill of Rights* (1998) and *Bloodlines* (2000)—were followed by a new and selected volume, *An English Sampler* (2001—all Chatto). *Continental Shelf* (Carcanet, 2009) includes a long sequence, 'Elegies', on the victims of the 2006 shootings at Virginia Tech, as well as a group of new Guyanese poems, 'Local Colour'.   MR*

Dale, Peter (John) (1938–) Studied at Oxford, where he met Ian *Hamilton and Kevin Crossley-Holland. With William Cookson, he was co-editor of the magazine *Agenda* until 1996. His main achievement has undoubtedly been as translator of François Villon (*The Legacy, The Testament and Other Poems*, revd. edn., Anvil, 2001), in which he attempts to reproduce the metres of the originals. He has also written imitations of Tamil poetry in *The Seasons of Cankam* (Agenda, 1975), in the tradition of *Pound's adaptations from the Chinese, versions of Laforgue, and a translation of Dante's *Divine Comedy*. As an original poet Dale is quiet and, essentially, neo-*Georgian. He writes, usually, in a controlled free verse, and often in sequences, as in the sonnets of *One Another* (Carcanet/Agenda, 1978; revd. edn., Waywiser, 2002) and *Local Habitation* (Anvil, 2009). *Diffractions: New and Selected Poems* was published by Anvil Press in 2011. See also his *Introduction to Rhyme* (Agenda/Bellew, 1998).   MS-S*

Dallas, Ruth (1919–2008) Born in New Zealand's southernmost city, Invercargill, Dallas lived most of her life in Dunedin. She began publishing in local papers as a child, and was the most frequent woman contributor to the literary quarterly *Landfall* during the period of Charles *Brasch's editorship (1947-67). Six volumes of her verse were published by the Caxton Press, Christchurch, between 1953 and 1979, and *Song for a Guitar and Other Songs* by Otago University Press, Dunedin, in 1976. She also wrote stories and several children's books. In 1968 she held the Robert Burns Fellowship at the University of Otago, which in 1978 awarded her an honorary D.Litt. *Walking on the Snow* (1976) won the 1977 New Zealand Book Award for Poetry.

Dallas' poems characteristically focus on natural phenomena—whether within the Southland countryside or Dunedin's gardens and parks—to meditate on the cycle of the seasons and on human transience. She peopled her landscapes with figures who are apt to be representative rather than individual. Receptive to oriental influences, she will address a Chinese poet, emulate a Japanese potter or printmaker, or respond to the spirit of Buddhist sculpture. In some of her later volumes she cultivated a vein of dream imagery.

Her development may be traced in the second edition of her *Collected Poems* (2000). See also *The Joy of a Ming Vase* (2006—both Otago University Press). An autobiographical account of her 'Beginnings' as a writer was published in *Landfall, 76* (1965), and reprinted in *Beginnings*, ed. Robin Dudding (Oxford University Press, 1980).   MacDJ

Dangor, Achmat (1948–) Born and educated in Johannesburg. In 1973, following years of anti-apartheid campaigning, Dangor was declared a banned person by the South African Government. After the ban was rescinded in 1978, he worked as a manager for a multinational company in Johannesburg. He has also been director of the Kagiso Trust, an agency providing humanitarian and educational aid to the victims of apartheid, and is now Chief Executive of the Nelson Mandela Foundation.

Dangor's first volume of verse, *Bulldozer* (Ravan, 1983), bears the stamp of his political commitment. The poetry moves from the lyricism of 'The Colour of Love' and 'My Africa' to the more explicitly political 'Die Patriot' and 'Leila', where the voice is thunderously public, merging Afrikaans street-talk with standard English. His second collection was *Private Voices* (Congress of South African Writers, 1992). Dangor has published a short-story collection, *Waiting for Leila* (1981), a novella, *The Z Town Trilogy* (1990—both Ravan), and two acclaimed novels, *Kafka's Curse* (Kwela, 1997), which won the Herman Charles Bosman Prize, and *Bitter Fruit* (Atlantic, 2003), which was shortlisted for the Man Booker Prize. He has also written for the stage, and his play *Majiet* won him critical acclaim.   M-HM

Daruwalla,   Keki   Nasserwanji (1937–) Born in Lahore into a Parsee family, completed his Masters degree in English literature at Punjab University, and has since worked as assistant to the inspector-general of police in Uttar Pradesh and, latterly, as a career diplomat, whose career included a posting to the Indian

High Commission in London and an appointment in India as Special Assistant to the Prime Minister on International Affairs. He is now retired and lives in Delhi.

Since his first collection of poems, *Under Orion* (Harper, 1970; repr. Rupa, 2000), he has published over a dozen books. He won the prestigious Sahitya Akademi Award for *The Keeper of the Dead* (1982) and the Commonwealth Poetry Prize (Asia Region) for *Landscapes* (1987—both Oxford University Press). He is a discriminating anthologist himself, and the introduction to his selection *Two Decades of Indian Poetry* (Vikas, 1980) provides a concise and stimulating overview of developments since the 1960s.

Daruwalla's poetry evinces an intensity of vision, an ability to evoke landscape and environment that won the praise of Robert *Graves. *Crossing of Rivers* (Oxford University Press, 1976) is a sequence of linked poems recording a personal pilgrimage along the River Ganges. Written in a taut style, it weaves a web of allusion, drawing upon Hindu, Zoroastrian, and personal myth, but there is also a satirical edge.

Unlike many of his contemporaries who write in English, Daruwalla is untroubled by notions of 'Indian authenticity', perhaps because of his own minority status as a Parsee and his peripatetic life-style. His attitude towards the language he writes in is summarized in a witty and elliptical poem, 'My Mistress'.

His later volumes include *A Summer of Tigers* (Indus, 1995), *Night River* (2000), *The Scarecrow and the Ghost* (2004—both Rupa), and *Collected Poems* (2006), published in India by Penguin. He has also written a historical novel, *For Pepper and Christ* (Penguin, 2009). See Asha Viswaw, *Keki N. Daruwalla: The Poet and Novelist* (Bahri, 2011).   RW

Daryush, Elizabeth (1887–1977) Born in London, the daughter of Robert *Bridges, the future Poet Laureate, and Monica Waterhouse, whose father Alfred was the famous architect. She was brought up in the family manor house, Yattendon, and at Boar's Hill, Oxford, where under the guidance of her father she developed an early interest in the flowers of rural England. She refers to her father's teaching in her moving memorial verses 'Bye Flowers'. In 1923 she married Ali Akbar Daryush whom she met while he was engaged in Persian studies at Oxford. They lived in Persia until 1926, when they moved to their permanent home, Stockwell, on Boar's Hill, close to the home of her parents.

In her first book, *Charitesse* (1911) and throughout the many volumes published by the Oxford University Press and later by the Carcanet Press, she established herself as a traditionalist poet writing in conventional prosody but (like her father) willing to experiment in non-traditional forms. One of her best-known poems, 'Still-Life', an ironic critique of the false security of the idle rich, is written in syllabic verse. The subject-matter of her best poems is moral without being didactic—a stoic acceptance of impermanence, the need for discipline, self restraint, and dignity in the face of tragic loss. Among her finest poems are 'Autumn, dark wanderer' (on the feeling of loss brought about by seasonal change), 'Faithless familiars', 'Fresh spring', and 'Eyes that queenly sit'.

Perceptive critical and technical comments on her poetry are to be found in Yvor Winters, 'Robert Bridges and Elizabeth Daryush', *American Review, 8* (1936–7); in Winters' foreword to her *Selected Poems* (Swallow, 1948); and in Donald Davie's introduction to her *Collected Poems* (Carcanet, 1976).   DS

Das, Kamala (1934–2009) Born in Punnayurkulum, Kerala, into an aristocratic Nair family. Married off while still an undergraduate, she did not publish any poetry until the Sixties. She received the PEN Asia prize in 1963. Her poetry collections include *Summer in Calcutta* (Rajinder Paul, 1965; repr. DC, 2004), *The Descendants* (Writers Workshop, 1967), *The Old Playhouse* (Orient Longman, 1973; repr. 2004), *Only the Soul Knows How to Sing*, a selected volume published by DC Books in 1996. Hers is a personalized poetry of marital unhappiness, the quest for love outside of marriage, the terrors of mental illness, and

the joys of childhood memories. Much of her verse is written with a sense of urgency in a language she described as half-English, half-Indian, its distortions and queernesses hers alone. Some of her strongest poems, like 'The Old Playhouse' and 'Sunshine Cat', describe the husband persona as a jailer. In others, like 'The Freaks', she discovers love to be 'grand, flamboyant lust'. When she turns despairingly to her matriarchal roots—as in her most anthologized work, 'My Grandmother's House'—she finds it lying in silence with snakes moving about the books.

Das' poetry is available in her *Collected Poems* (Kamala Das, 1984). Her autobiography, *My Story* (Sterling, 1976; repr. Harper, 2010), translated by her from the Malayalam, provides the context for her verse. In 1999 she converted to Islam, changing her name to Kamala Surayya. See also her memoir *A Childhood in Malabar* (Penguin, 2003).   RA

Das, Mahadai (1954–2003) Born in Eccles, British Guiana, Das studied first at the University of Guyana and later at Columbia University in New York, graduating with a BA in philosophy.

Das is best remembered for 'They Came in Ships', her early and often-anthologized recounting of Indo-Guyanese history. The strident nationalism of her youth is captured in the title of her first book, *I Want to Be a Poetess of My People* (Guyana National Service Publishing Centre, 1977). But a sense of disillusion with the dark turns in Guyanese politics pervades *My Finer Steel Will Grow* (1982), published as a volume of the Vermont-based journal *Samisdat*. Das cultivated a more wary voice and inward vision in her later work. By this time she was based in the United States, where her PhD research at the University of Chicago was ultimately cut short by declining health. *Bones* (1988) meditates on both geographical displacement and mortality, often corporealized in the female body.

At her early death, Das left dozens of poems uncollected, which were finally published in *A Leaf in His Ear* (2010—both Peepal Tree). The title poem suggests a new path cut off. Concise, elusive, in

quick flashes of imagery it describes a dia-
mond prospector whose solitary labour is a
deliberate withdrawal from the human
world. 'A Leaf in His Ear' offers both an
allegory of submission to a higher power
and an elegy to the poet's brother, who
disappeared 'into Guiana forests' in 1973
and never returned.   NL

Davey, Frank(land Wilmot) (1940–)
Born in Vancouver and brought up in
the nearby Fraser Valley. He was educated
at the University of British Columbia and
University of Southern California, where he
wrote a dissertation on Charles *Olson's
poetics. For two decades he taught English
and writing at Toronto's York University,
before going to University of Western On-
tario (London) in 1990.

Like his modernist predecessor, Louis
*Dudek, Davey favours the long poem or
sequence, is wary of metaphor and lyric,
and has always published his books with
selected literary presses. But Davey sees
himself as a post-modernist. He has said
that the serious poem cannot be finished
but must be abandoned.

His subject in books such as *Popular
Narratives* (1991) is often childhood, ado-
lescence, and young manhood, but his re-
creating of those personal years is always
related ironically to issues in history, poli-
tics, industry, and education. He fashions
links between individual pathology and
public crises. See *The Arches: Selected
Poems* (1980—both Talonbooks).

Davey has devoted a large part of his
time to criticism and editing. He was the
central force in the successful 1980s attack
on the thematic criticism of Northrop Frye,
whose influence dominated the Canadian
critical and academic worlds in the 1970s.
His several critical books and collections
consider literature as ideological and dis-
cursive. Works such as *Reading Canadian
Reading* (Turnstone, 1988) and *Canadian
Literary Power: Essays on Anglophone-Ca-
nadian Literary Conflict* (NeWest, 1994),
expound on the relationships between
writing and the economics of publishing.

Davey was managing editor of the poetry-
poetics newsletter *Tish* (1961–3), and since
1965 has been editor of *Open Letter*, a jour-

nal of postmodern theory and criticism. A
key guide to his ideas at mid-career can be
found in a long interview, 'Starting at Our
Skins', in a 1979 issue of *Open Letter*.

In 1984, with Fred *Wah, he founded
SwiftCurrent, the world's first online liter-
ary magazine. His later books of poetry
include *Cultural Mischief* (1996), *Back to
the War* (2005), and *Bardy Google*, written
using Internet searches (2010—all Talon-
books). See also his little-magazine
memoir, *When TISH Happens* (ECW,
2011).   GHB*

Davidson, Donald (Grady) (1893–1968)
Born in Tennessee and taught at Vanderbilt
University from 1920. He was one of the
founders and editors of the *Fugitive* maga-
zine, and one of the foremost Southern
*Agrarians, contributing to the manifesto
I'll Take My Stand. He was also the close
friend and confidant of such poets as Allen
*Tate and John Crowe *Ransom. He wrote
the libretto to the opera *Singin' Billy* (pro-
duced 1952), to music by Charles Faulkner
Bryan. As a poet in his own right, Davidson
has not been reckoned one of the outstand-
ing Fugitives. He was more important to
the movement as an austere influence and
setter of guide-lines, especially in the early
and more conservative years.

His poetry, like his prose, is noted for its
lucidity and its chiselled correctness. After
a collection of shorter poems, *An Outland
Piper* (1924), he published *The Tall Men*
(1927), a blank-verse narrative. *Lee in the
Mountains* (1938—all Houghton) con-
tained short poems about Southern figures.
Of all his group Davidson remained the
most steadfastly committed to Agrarian
principles (*Still Rebels, Still Yankees* (1957)
consists of essays which some thought were
reactionary). Some of the poems in *The
Long Street* (Oxford University Press,
1961), however, intelligently view the con-
flict in Davidson between nostalgia for an
old order and awareness of the contempo-
rary situation, and this is his best collection.
See *Poems 1922–1961* (University of Min-
nesota Press, 1966).   MS-S

Davie, Donald (1922–95) Born in Barns-
ley, Yorkshire, spent his childhood in the

industrialized West Riding, and received his earliest education at Barnsley Holgate Grammar School. In 1941 his studies at St Catharine's College, Cambridge (which he had entered in 1940), were interrupted by service in the Royal Navy, which posted him to Murmansk and Archangel until 1943. He married Doreen John in 1945, returned to Cambridge University to receive his BA in 1947, his MA in 1949, and his PhD in 1951. His career as a university teacher began in Trinity College, Dublin, in 1950, and he became a fellow in 1954. He resigned his fellowship in 1957, and subsequently taught as a visiting professor at the University of California, Santa Barbara, and at Gonville and Caius College, Cambridge. In 1964 he was a co-founder of the University of Essex and a professor of English there. In 1968 he accepted a professorship at Stanford University, where he remained until 1978 when he removed to Nashville, Tennessee, as Andrew W. Mellon Professor in Humanities at Vanderbilt University. He retired from Vanderbilt in 1987 and lived in Devonshire.

Davie was born of Baptist parentage and for a number of years considered himself to be a conservative member of the English dissenting tradition, with an admiration for the hymns of Isaac Watts and Charles Wesley and a dislike for bohemianism, Bloomsbury, and 'sentimental leftists'. There is, therefore, a strong ethical element in much of his verse, expressed in its plain style. At Cambridge he considered himself to be a disciple of F. R. Leavis, and his native tendencies towards moralism and plain writing and speaking were reinforced by contacts with Yvor *Winters' Stanford School—he read Winters very early in his career, and established personal contacts with the Winters group when teaching in the States. In England Davie was a leading member of the *Movement, of which he considered his critical book, *Purity of Diction in English Verse* (Chatto, 1952), to be a manifesto. Of his numerous volumes of verse, perhaps the best-known are *Essex Poems* (1969) and *The Shires* (1974), where as a traditionalist he develops one of his most cherished themes—the importance of a sense of place in life and in poetry. Among his best-known poems are 'Woodpigeons at Raheny', 'The Fountain', 'Remembering the Thirties', 'A Winter Landscape near Ely', 'Iona', 'Lowlands', and 'In the Stopping Train'.

Davie held several lectureships in Europe which enabled him to pursue his interest in Polish, Hungarian, and Russian literature, and which resulted in his verse translations and adaptations. *The Forests of Lithuania* (Marvell, 1959) is an adaptation of the Polish poet Adam Mickiewicz's romantic epic *Pan Tadeusz*. *The Poems of Dr Zhivago* (Manchester University Press, 1985) and *Pasternak: Modern Judgements* (Macmillan, 1969; Aurora, 1970), edited by Davie and Angela Livingstone, contain his verse translations of poems by Boris Pasternak, whom Davie considered to be among the greatest poets of our time. Among Davie's most important books of criticism are *Articulate Energy: An Inquiry into the Syntax of English Poetry* (Routledge, 1955; Harcourt, Brace, 1958); *Ezra Pound: Poet as Sculptor* (Penguin, 1964; Fontana, 1965); *Thomas Hardy and British Poetry* (Oxford University Press, 1972; Routledge, 1973); and *Under Briggflatts: A History of Poetry in Great Britain, 1960–1988* (Carcanet, 1989). Among his critical books on European literatures are *Czeslaw Milosz and the Insufficiency of the Lyric* (University of Tennessee Press, 1986) and *Slavic Excursions: Essays on Russian and Polish Literature* (Carcanet, 1990). Among volumes he edited are Elizabeth Daryush's *Collected Poems* (Carcanet, 1976); *Collected Poems of Yvor Winters* (Carcanet, 1978; Swallow, 1980); and the *New Oxford Book of Christian Verse* (Oxford University Press, 1981). Biographical information is in Davie's *These the Companions: Recollections* (Cambridge University Press, 1982).

See *Selected Poems* (1997) and *Collected Poems* (2002), ed. Neil Powell, which includes the posthumous volume *Poems and Melodramas* (1996). *With the Grain* (1998) is a selection of Davie's essays on modern British poetry, ed. Clive *Wilmer, which includes *Thomas Hardy and British Poetry*. Wilmer also edited a volume of Davie's *Modernist Essays* (2004). See also *Two Ways Out of Whitman: American*

Essays (2000) and *A Travelling Man: Eighteenth-Century Bearings* (2003), both edited by Doreen Davie. *Purity of Diction in English Verse* and *Articulate Energy* were reprinted as one volume in 2006 (all Carcanet).   DS

Davies, Idris (1905–53) Born at Rhymney, in Monmouthshire. He left school at the age of 14 to work in a coal-mine, but after the General Strike of 1926 he studied at the University of Nottingham and became a teacher in London and Wales.

His first volume of verse, *Gwalia Deserta* (1938), is concerned with the aereliction of industrial south Wales during the years of the Depression. All the poems in it are either short lyrics in the style of A. E. *Housman or in the accumulative, long-line form which was to become characteristic of his later work. They include the poem which, set to music by Pete Seeger, became famous as the song 'The Bells of Rhymney'.

The long poem entitled 'The Angry Summer' (1943) consists of fifty short, untitled sections, and is a loosely chronological record of the General Strike, from the high spirits of its beginning to the miners' ignominious return to work. A further volume appeared during the poet's lifetime under the title *Tonypandy and Other Poems* (1945).

Early judgements of Idris Davies tended to emphasize his integrity as man and poet while criticizing the somewhat narrow range of his work, but the wry humour and passionate indignation which inform the best of his poems are now recognized as self-imposed limitations which help to throw his main themes into relief.

The fullest edition of Idris Davies' poems is to be found in the volume of his *Collected Poems* compiled by Islwyn Jenkins (Gomer, 1972; repr. 2003). Islwyn Jenkins has also written a monograph on the poet in the Writers of Wales series (University of Wales Press, 1972) and a book-length study, *Idris Davies of Rhymney* (Gomer, 1986). See Glyn Jones, *The Dragon has Two Tongues* (Dent, 1968); Anthony Conran, *The Cost of Strangeness* (Gomer, 1982); and the special number of *Poetry Wales*, *16:4* (Spring 1981), which is devoted to his work. See also *A Carol for the Coalfield and Other Poems* (Carreg Gwalch, 2002).   MS

Davies, Kevin (1958–   ) Born in Nanaimo, British Columbia, Davies was peripherally involved in the *Kootenay School of Writing during the 1980s, before moving to New York, where he has worked as a writing instructor and financial proofreader. He studied at the Empire State College of the State University of New York and obtained a Master's degree in English from the University of Maine. He lives in Brooklyn.

Davies' three collections of poetry, *Pause Button* (Tsunami, 1992), *Comp.* (Edge, 2000), and *The Golden Age of Paraphernalia* (Edge, 2008), have in recent years begun to receive much critical attention, and can be characterized as an ongoing work of social critique. Davies' method across these collections—dubbed his 'trilogy of error'—re-appropriates and subverts language drawn from a variety of textual and discursive frames and, by way of their disjunctive relations and subsequent gaps, enacts a dialogue that foregrounds their ideological character. From 'Lateral Argument': 'The papier-mâché Potemkin | village we've spread, spreadable | cheese over the surface of ‖ what we call Earth.' Davies' wry humour, often conspiratorial in tone, contributes to what Brian Kim *Stefans has called 'a positive, communal sense of disgust with the social world'.   ADA

Davies, W. H. (William Henry) (1871–1940) Born in Newport, Monmouthshire, and brought up by his grandparents in the Church House Inn there. He left school at 14, was apprenticed to a picture-framer, read avidly, and attended classes in the evening. At the age of 22 he received a small weekly legacy from the estate of his grandmother, and sailed for America, where he spent six years tramping back and forth. In 1899, he injured his right foot when jumping a moving train in Canada and had to have his leg amputated above the knee. From then on he wore an artificial limb. These years are re-created in Davies' *The Autobiography of a Super-*

Tramp (Cape, 1908), a modern classic of autobiography. Davies returned to Newport, then settled in London where he lived in cheap lodging-houses and concentrated on writing full time. In 1905 he published *The Soul's Destroyer and Other Poems* at his own expense under the imprint: 'Of the Author, Farmhouse, Marshalsea Road, S. E.' The book was favourably reviewed by Edward *Thomas, who encouraged Davies to write *Super-Tramp*. In 1923 Davies married Helen Matilda Payne, a young countrywoman in her early twenties whom he had picked up in a London street. The story is vividly told in *Young Emma* (1980), a book written in 1924 but impossible to publish at the time due to its candour. The couple settled in the Cotswold town of Nailsworth where they lived until Davies' death in 1940.

In his lifetime Davies wrote just under 800 poems published in twenty individual volumes, which generally sold well. He was quick to find his own style: his first book, *The Soul's Destroyer*, contained 'The Lodging House Fire', a portrait of a poor lodging-house. Other realist urban poems include the violent picture of urban degradation in 'Saturday Night in the Slums', the down-and-out of 'The Heap of Rags', and 'The Bird of Paradise', on the delusions of a dying prostitute. These poems can be set against work such as his best-known poem 'Leisure' ('What is this life if, full of care, | We have no time to stand and stare'), or 'In the Country', which counterbalances urban squalor with an idealized rural world of lost innocence: 'This life is sweetest; in this wood | I hear no children cry for food.'

See: Richard J. Stonesifer, *W. H. Davies: A Critical Biography* (Cape, 1963); *Complete Poems*, intro. Osbert Sitwell, foreword Daniel George (Cape, 1963); *Selected Poems*, ed. Jonathan Barker (Cape, 1985); *The Autobiography of a Super-Tramp*, preface George Bernard Shaw (Cape, 1908; repr. Oxford University Press, 1980); *Later Days* (Cape, 1925; repr. Oxford University Press, 1985); *The Essential W. H. Davies*, ed. Brian Waters (Cape, 1951); *Young Emma*, foreword by C. V. Wedgwood (Cape, 1980). See also Lawrence Normand, *W. H. Davies* (Seren, 2003). There is a chapter on Davies' poetry

in Peter Howarth, *British Poetry in the Age of Modernism* (Cambridge University Press, 2005).   JDB

Davis, Dick (1945–) Born in Portsmouth. After graduating from King's College, Cambridge, he worked as a teacher in, among other places, Iran, and gained a doctorate in Persian from Manchester University in 1989. He teaches Persian at Ohio State University, Columbus.

An early passion—and one that has not been lost—was for Edward Fitzgerald's *Rubáiyát of Omar Khayyám*, a new edition of which Davis edited in 1989; this passion may explain the most obvious characteristic of his own poetry: its dependence on traditional metrical skills. But it was evident from his first collection, *In the Distance* (Anvil, 1975), that Davis uses metre and rhyme in no outdated manner. He creates with them intricately wrought poems that move in a quiet and measured way. There is a notable exactness of thought and perception.

Davis has translated works by Natalia Ginzburg, Attar's *The Conference of the Birds* (with Afkham Darbandi), and *The Legend of Seyavash* (a translation of part of Ferdowsi's *Shahnamah*). His second collection of poems was *Seeing the World* (Anvil, 1980). There are both British and American selections of his early work: *Devices and Desires: New and Selected Poems 1967–1987* (Anvil, 1989) and *Selected and New Poems* (University of Arkansas Press, 1991).

Touchwood (Anvil, 1996) includes the comic sequence 'A Translator's Nightmare', and has been followed by *Belonging* (Ohio University Press/Anvil, 2002) and *A Trick of Sunlight* (Ohio University Press, 2006; Anvil, 2007). See also his *Medieval Persian Epigrams* (Anvil, 1996; expanded edn. published as *Borrowed Ware* (Mage, 1997)).   TJGH

Davis, Jack (1917–2000) Born in Perth, Western Australia and spent his early childhood in the small country town of Yarloop, one of a family of eleven Aboriginal children in a white community. Neither of his grandfathers was Aboriginal—one was a

Sikh, the other a Scotsman. His parents were taken from their Aboriginal mothers as children. Davis himself was sent to the Moore River Nature Settlement for education and training. His experience there is recalled in his poems and plays, and in Keith Chesson's *Jack Davis: A Life-Story* (Melbourne, 1988). See also his own memoir, *A Boy's Life* (Magabala, 1991).

Davis' first three books of poems were *The First-Born and Other Poems* (Angus & Robertson, 1970); *Jagardoo: Poems from Aboriginal Australia* (Methuen, 1978); and *John Pat and Other Poems* (Dent, 1988). In each of these books an Aboriginal persona speaks for his people, lamenting their tragic defeat by the white invaders, reflecting on a loss of identity and purpose among contemporary Aborigines, especially in the cities. His last volume of poetry was *Black Life* (University of Queensland Press, 1992).   BB

Davison, Peter (1928–2004) Born in New York, grew up in Colorado, and was educated at Harvard College and Cambridge University. From 1956 until 1985 he was a book editor at the Atlantic Monthly Press; he then became a senior editor at Houghton Mifflin; he was also poetry editor of *The Atlantic* for many years. His first wife, writer Jane Davison, died in 1981; he married Joan Edelman Goody, an architect, in 1984. His first book of poems was *The Breaking of the Day*, which won the Yale Series of Younger Poets Award in 1963. It was characterized by a sharp wit and strongly physical sense of language. Davison's work was also drawn to traditional forms.

Much influenced by Robert *Frost, Davison was increasingly attracted to rural images and has relied heavily on iambic patterns broken up by the patterns of ordinary speech. His quietly sophisticated, contemplative voice recalls the English *Georgians, a school of poets with whom his father, Edward Davison, was often associated. Though essentially a nature poet, Davison also wrote poems about his family and personal life; this '*confessional' vein was mined most fully in his autobiography, *Half Remembered: A Personal History* (Harper, 1973; revd. edn., Story Line,

1991). He published several further volumes, including *Walking the Boundaries: Poems 1957–1974* (1974); *Praying Wrong: New and Selected Poems, 1957–1984* (1985—both Atheneum); *The Great Ledge* (1989), *Collected Poems* (1994), and *Breathing Room* (2000—all Knopf). See also *One of the Dangerous Trades: Essays on the Work and Workings of Poetry* (University of Michigan Press, 1991) and *The Fading Smile* (Knopf, 1994), a memoir of literary Boston in the late 1950s, which includes reminiscences of Frost, *Lowell, and *Plath. He also wrote a life of George Orwell.

For criticism, see Guy Rotella, *Three Contemporary Poets of New England* (1983).   JP

Dawe, (Donald) Bruce (1930–   ) Born in Geelong, Victoria, Australia, to working-class parents. He left school at 16 to begin a series of short-lived, mostly unskilled jobs. After a year at Melbourne University, Dawe returned to unskilled jobs until 1959, when he began a nine-year period of service with the Royal Australian Air Force, working in the education section in Australia and Malaysia, and rising to the rank of sergeant. In 1964 he married Gloria Blain; their four children are the subject of poems. After his Air Force service, Dawe worked as a teacher. He completed his Arts degree, and subsequently, through part-time study, gained other degrees, including a PhD.

From his very first volume, *No Fixed Address* (1962), Dawe's work has been popular with critics and the public. He is probably Australia's best-selling poet and has won many awards. His collected poems, *Sometimes Gladness*, was the only volume of poetry included in a list of the ten best Australian books of the decade in 1984.

Dawe has always acknowledged his indebtedness to the small-town ordinariness of Edgar Lee *Masters and Edwin Arlington *Robinson, an influence evident not only in his poems but also in his stories. His sympathies are with the 'bottom-dog', the 'battler', the person puzzled and overwhelmed by life. He writes about cities, suburbs, and—perhaps most tellingly—about the places on the outskirts where city and country meet.

World events, especially those involving war or injustice, figure in some poems, notably the Vietnam War poem, 'Homecoming'. He has written many satirical poems about Australian politics, especially concerning Queensland's long-serving populist premier, Sir Joh Bjelke-Petersen. Other poems have concerned the ill-treatment of Australian Aborigines. His commonest form is the dramatic monologue, of which 'A Victorian Hangman Tells His Love' (a black-humour protest against capital punishment spoken by the hangman) is typical.

His current collected volume is *Sometimes Gladness: Collected Poems*, now in its sixth expanded edition (Pearson, 2006). *Bruce Dawe: Essays and Opinions*, ed. Ken Goodwin (Longman Cheshire, 1990), contains a set of prose statements and a bibliography. *Over Here, Harv! and Other Stories* (Penguin, 1983) contains short stories. For critical studies, see Ken Goodwin, *Adjacent Worlds: A Literary Life of Bruce Dawe* (Longman Cheshire, 1988), Peter Kuch, *Bruce Dawe* (Oxford University Press, 1995), and Dennis Haskell, *Attuned to Alien Moonlight: The Poetry of Bruce Dawe* (University of Queensland Press, 2002). In 1992 Dawe was made an Officer of the Order of Australia.　KGO

Dawes, Kwame (1962–) Born in Ghana, Dawes grew up in Jamaica and studied at the University of the West Indies at Mona, and the University of New Brunswick in Canada. The son of novelist, poet, and Marxist critic Neville Dawes, he has been an actor, playwright, broadcaster, and singer in a reggae band. From 1992 he taught at the University of South Carolina, and is now a Chancellor's Professor of English at the University of Nebraska. Since winning the Forward Prize for Best First Collection in the UK for *Progeny of Air* (Peepal Tree, 1994), which tells stories of his Jamaican youth, Dawes has been an extraordinarily prolific figure in the world of Anglophone Caribbean poetry. See the collection of interviews, *Talk Yuh Talk* (University of Virginia Press, 1999). His other books include *Prophets* (1995), *Jacko Jacobus* (1996), two contemporary Biblical epics, *Shook Foil: A Collection of Reggae*

Poems (1997—all Peepal Tree), *Wisteria: Twilight Poems from the Swamp Country* (Red Hen, 2006)—on Sumpter, the small town where he lived in South Carolina—and *Wheels* (2011), a large book in prophetic mood which addresses contemporary events such as the election of Barack Obama and the Haitian earthquake. Among his other publications are a study of Bob Marley, a prose memoir, a book of stories, and an anthology of contemporary black poetry in Britain (*Red* (2010)). See *New and Selected Poems* (2003—all Peepal Tree).　JNT

Day, Jean (1954–) Born in Syracuse, New York, Day studied at Antioch College before moving to the San Francisco Bay Area. She has lived and worked here, in literary publishing, ever since, in close contact with many other Bay Area writers and publishers, especially those associated with the *Language movement.

Day's six books of poetry reveal a style characteristic of this movement's experimentalism, though with an emphasis on its *Objectivist heritage; her work is more visual than most other Language poetry, yet full of movement and surprise. 'Exact and muscular' is how Ron *Silliman described Day's most recent book *Enthusiasm: Odes & Otium* (Adventures in Poetry, 2006). 'Enthusiasm' and 'otium' are words that also fit the moods of her earlier books: *Linear C* (Tuumba, 1983), *Flat Birds* (Gaz, 1985), *A Young Recruit* (Roof, 1988), *The I and the You* (Potes & Poets, 1992), and *The Literal World* (Atelos, 1998), though a darker 'undersong'—the name of a recent poem—runs through her oeuvre too.

Day's poetry has been widely anthologized—in, for instance, *In the American Tree* (1986), *Moving Borders: Three Decades of Innovative Writing by Women* (1998), and *The Best American Poetry 2004*—as have her translations of Russian poetry.　ECr

Day, Sarah (1958–) Born in Lancashire,England and migrated with her family to Tasmania in 1964. She studied at the University of Tasmania, and has taught English and creative writing in schools and universities. She is the former poetry editor of the Tasmanian literary magazine *Island* and lives in Hobart.

The title poem of Day's debut collection, *A Hunger to Be Less Serious* (Angus & Robertson, 1987) replies to *Larkin's 'Church Going' (which speaks of 'a hunger to be more serious') with a vision of cars waiting at a canal bridge as a carnival occasion of 'strayed dreams and wish-fulfilments'. Like her contemporary Judith *Beveridge, Day's precise, conversational poems often describe an urban pastoral with an eye for the jarring encounter between man and nature (roadkilled wombats are 'meaty silhouettes receding | into ignominious shadows'). As Chris *Wallace-Crabbe has said, 'her pinpoint diction and elastic syntax stretch our assumptions by way of aesthetic play'.

From the intimate and local, Day's imagination radiates out into national and global histories. Thus, the submerged emotions of her canal poem return magnified to a 'dangerous lust' at the end of her debut in 'TITANIC DISCOVERED'. Her second volume was *A Madder Dance* (1991), followed by *Quickening* (1997—both Penguin). *New and Selected Poems* was published in the UK by Arc in 2002. *The Ship* (2004) won three major awards. See also *Grass Notes* (2009—both Brandl & Schlesinger).   JNT

Day Lewis, C. (Cecil) (1904–72) Born in

Ireland. Proud of his Anglo-Irish connections, he moved with his family to England in 1905. He was educated at Sherborne and at Wadham College, Oxford, where he read classics. His first two volumes of verse, *Beechen Vigil* (1925) and *Country Comets* (1928), were slight. *Transitional Poem* (1929), *From Feathers to Iron* (1931), *A Time to Dance* (1935), and *Noah and the Waters* (1936) deployed images of comrades, frontiers, blood, red dawns, and saviours. Day Lewis excluded a number of these poems from his *Collected Poems* (1954).

He turned to prose in *A Hope for Poetry* (1934) and edited a left-wing symposium, *The Mind in Chains*, in 1937, the year in which he joined the Communist Party. Although the imminence of war did not alter Day Lewis' beliefs, it awakened certain ideas and emotions not hitherto expressed in his poems. The title of his volume *Overtures to Death* (1938) indicates his prevailing mood. In 1940 he joined the Home Guard, and from 1941 to 1946 worked for the Ministry of Information. Many of the poems in *Word Over All* (1943) and *Poems 1943–47* (1948) concerned his childhood and the turbulence of his emotional life; they show also the influence of *Hardy and, to a lesser extent, of Edward *Thomas that marked his later verse.

After the war Day Lewis became influential in academic and orthodox literary circles. His 1946 Clark Lectures at Cambridge were published as *The Poetic Image* (1947); he was the elected Professor of Poetry at Oxford from 1951 to 1956; and *The Poetic Impulse* (1965) was based on his 1964 Charles Eliot Norton Lectures at Harvard. After the ending of his first marriage and of his long association with Rosamond Lehmann, he married the actress Jill Balcon in 1951. They gave many readings together, often under the auspices of the Apollo Society. Their son is the actor Daniel Day Lewis.

Collections of verse appeared regularly. *An Italian Visit*, a lyrical narrative poem (1953), was succeeded by *Pegasus* (1957), *The Gate* (1962), *The Room* (1965), and *The Whispering Roots* (1970). The craftsmanship of these poems was not disputed, but some critics believed that he had ensconced himself in a bland conservatism, sadly at variance with his youthful ardour.

He lavished skill and metrical ingenuity on his translations of Virgil's *Georgics* (1940), *Aeneid* (1952), and *Eclogues* (1963), and published in 1946 a version of Valéry's *Le Cimetière Marin*. He wrote three mainly autobiographical novels and, from 1935 onwards, a score of detective tales under the pseudonym of Nicholas Blake. Appointed Poet Laureate in 1968, he brought to his office a fine presence, courtesy, eloquence and administrative ability. Like most of his predecessors though, he was unfitted to write poems on major public themes.

The Complete Poems (Sinclair-Stevenson, 1992) and the centenary *Selected Poems* (Enitharmon, 2004), were both edited by

d

Jill Balcon (Entharmon, 2004). For Day Lewis' life, see his autobiography, *The Buried Day* (Chatto/Harper, 1960); *C. Day-Lewis* (Weidenfeld, 1980), by Sean Day-Lewis, the elder son of his first marriage, and Peter Stanford, *C. Day Lewis: A Life* (Continuum, 2007). For criticism, see Albert Gelpi, *Living in Time: The Poetry of C. Day Lewis* (Oxford University Press, 1998). JPr

Deane, John F. (1943–) Born on Achill Island, Co. Mayo, Deane has been an influential figure in Irish poetry since the 1970s, when he founded Poetry Ireland, the national poetry society, and its magazine *The Poetry Ireland Review*, becoming editor in 2011. In 1985, he also founded The Dedalus Press, which has published a number of important Irish poets, including Thomas *Kinsella, and poets in translation, including Deane's own versions of the Swedish poet Tomas Tranströmer. He has been Secretary-General of the European Academy of Poetry and is a member of Aosdána.

Deane is also a novelist, published by Blackstaff Press. *Snow Falling on Chestnut Hill* (Carcanet, 2012) selects from the five poetry collections he has published with Carcanet: *Toccata and Fugue* (2000), *Manhandling the Deity* (2003), *The Instruments of Art* (2005), *A Little Book of Hours* (2008), and *Eye of the Hare* (2011). Notable among contemporary poets for his Christian philosophy, Deane's ecumenical theology is more gregarious than the 'distant, difficult' God of Geoffrey *Hill or R. S. *Thomas, his moments of vision in rural Ireland, or during the encounter with art, closer in spirit to the quotidian mysticism of Seamus *Heaney. As he has said, 'I write to set the Christ-life echoing', a knowing echo of Heaney's 'Personal Helicon' ('I rhyme | . . . to set the darkness echoing'), and Christ is repeatedly invoked in the daily life of Deane's poems as 'the urgency, the exemplar and the ground'. JNT

de Hoyos, Angela (1940–2009) Mexican-born but raised in San Antonio, Texas, announced her poetic debut with *Arise, Chicano! and Other Poems* (1975), strong Chicano-nationalist 'protest' verse written

from the late 1960s onwards. Its title-poem speaks from the vantage-point of the migrant worker trapped doubly by 'the shrewd heel of exploit' and by an English language in which 'not even your burning words are yours'. That compares with 'The Final Laugh', a bold, keenly satirical and anti-racist soliloquy, in which she treats the key Chicano issues of assimilation and loss of cultural pride. With *Chicano Poems for the Barrio* (1975—both Backstage) her range increases—especially in bilingual poems like 'Hermano', an extolling of Chicano heritage which takes the Alamo and the white American triumphalism which surrounds it as its presiding metaphor, and in 'Small Comfort', which treats the issue of language and custom, the 'burial', as she says, of *chicanismo* beneath an overlay of 'Anglo' Americanism. De Hoyos, too, has shown considerable skill in developing the use of personae, not least in 'One Ordinary Morning' from *Selecciones* (Xalapa, 1976), metaphysical verse both in form and theme, or 'Ex Marks The Spot' from *Woman, Woman* (Arte Publico, 1985), a careful (and bilingual) lament at the loss of a close feminine friendship.

Criticism includes *The Multi-Faceted Poetic World of Angela de Hoyos*, by Marcela Aguilar-Henson (Relámpogo, 1985) and *Angela de Hoyos, A Critical Look*, by Luis Arturo Ramos (Pajarito, 1979). ARL

de Kok, Ingrid (1951–) Born in Johannesburg and grew up in Stilfontein, a mining town in the Western Transvaal. She studied at the universities of Witwatersrand, Cape Town, and (after emigrating to Canada in 1977) Queen's, Kingston. In 1984, she returned to South Africa and became active in adult education and extramural studies at the University of Cape Town, where she is a fellow.

De Kok's intimately observed poems bring the pre- and post-apartheid South African landscape close, scaling its histories down to personal scenes. The well-known 'Our Sharpeville' describes the prejudice instilled through childish fear. Like Seamus *Heaney in Northern Ireland, de Kok employs an innocent's perspective to discover a deeper resonance in the seemingly mundane. Her first collection was *Familiar Ground* (Ravan, 1988). *Terrestrial Things* (Kwela/Snailpress, 2002), her third, alludes to a phrase from *Hardy's 'The Darkling Thrush', suggesting the search for hope against despair. Half of the book describes the proceedings of the Truth and Reconciliation Commission and the suffering of the AIDS epidemic. The other half is given to poems of love and family life, continuing the pattern of her second collection, *Transfer* (Snailpress, 1997). *Seasonal Fires: New and Selected Poems* (Random House, 2006), also appeared in the States. De Kok's fifth volume, *Other Signs* (Kwela/Snailpress) was published in 2011. With Karen *Press she edited *Spring Is Rebellious*, a book of responses to ANC leader Albie Sachs' essay 'Preparing Ourselves for Freedom' (Buchu, 1990).   JNT

de la Mare, Walter (1873–1956) Born at Charlton, Kent, and educated at St Paul's Cathedral Choir School in London. In 1890, aged 16, he began work in the statistics department of the London office of Anglo-American Oil. He married Constance Elfrida Ingpen in 1899; they had four children. His first book of poems, *Songs of Childhood* (Longmans, 1902), was published under the pseudonym Walter Ramal. He was author of nineteen books of poems published between 1902 and 1953, two of the best-known of which are *The Listeners* (1912) and *Peacock Pie* (1913—both Constable), the latter for children. De la Mare's poems were included in each of Edward Marsh's *Georgian Poetry* anthologies between 1912 and 1922. He was made Companion of Honour in 1948 and awarded the Order of Merit in 1953.

De la Mare is essentially an inward-looking poet of escape, skilled at depicting atmosphere and mood as in his elliptical narratives such as 'The Railway Junction', 'The Listeners', or the remarkable 'The Feckless Dinner Party', a poem written almost entirely in dramatic voices. The best poems are shot through with a disturbing sense of mystery and unease in which dream can shift into nightmare. He writes

chillingly on supernatural and unearthly themes.

De la Mare's writing is technically assured. It is conservative in form yet capable of a wide range of subtle and virtuoso effects. His variations on established verse forms helped direct modern British poetry away from the experiments of early modernism, and back to the traditional methods into which W. H. *Auden was to breathe new life in the 1930s.

De la Mare's poems for children are models of their kind and include numerous small masterpieces, such as 'The Song of the Mad Prince', 'Old Shellover', 'Hi!', and 'Tit For Tat', collected in *Collected Rhymes and Verses* (Faber, 1944). What starts out as a children's poem can, in a few lines, turn unexpectedly into an exercise in controlled terror, as in 'John Mouldy', 'smiling there alone' in his rat-infested cellar.

Graham Greene praised the best of de la Mare's short stories for 'a prose unequalled in its richness since the death of James, or dare one, at this date, say Robert Louis Stevenson', and it may indeed be argued that de la Mare is overall even more interesting as a prose writer than a poet. The language of the stories is generally sharper and avoids the archaic diction of the poems, and his novels are overdue for rediscovery—in particular *Henry Brocken* (1904) and *The Return* (1910). *Memoirs of a Midget* (1921) was reprinted in 1982, with a preface by Angela Carter.

De la Mare was also a compendious, original, and influential poetry anthologist, keen to include the out-of-the-way along with the well known. *Come Hither; A Collection of Rhymes and Poems for the Young of All Ages* (Constable, 1923) contains everything from mainstream poems to anonymous border ballads, folk songs, children's chants, and nursery rhymes. In 1939, Auden commented that it, 'more than any book I have read before or since, taught me what poetry is'. Other brilliant, labyrinthine anthologies are *Desert Islands* (1930), *Behold This Dreamer* (1939), and *Love* (1943). De la Mare's two books of literary criticism, *Pleasures and Speculations* (1940) and *Private View* (1953—all Faber), are full of unexpected insights, as in the lecture

'Rupert Brooke and the Intellectual Imagination'.

See also: Forrest Reid, *Walter de la Mare: A Critical Study* (Faber, 1929); *Tribute to Walter de la Mare on his Seventy-Fifth Birthday* (Faber, 1948); Walter de la Mare, *Collected Poems* (Holt, 1941; Faber, 1942); *Collected Rhymes and Verses* (Faber, 1944, 1989); *Walter de la Mare: A Selection from his Writings*, ed. Kenneth Hopkins (Faber, 1956); *The Complete Poems of Walter de la Mare* (Faber, 1969); *Selected Poems*, ed. R. N. Green-Armytage (1st edn., 1954; repr. Faber, 1973); *A Choice of de la Mare's Verse*, ed. W. H. Auden (Faber, 1963); Theresa Whistler, *Imagination of the Heart: The Life of Walter de la Mare* (Duckworth, 1993). A later selection of de la Mare's verse has been made by Matthew *Sweeney (Faber, 2006). JDB

(⊕) SEE WEB LINKS

• More information may be found on the website of the Walter de la Mare Society.

Delanty, Greg (1958–) Born in Cork, Delanty attended University College Cork, where he edited the literary magazine *Quarryman*. At UCC he studied under John *Montague and became associated with a circle of young writers that included Maurice *Riordan. In 1983, Delanty received the distinguished Patrick Kavanagh Poetry Award (given to an Irish poet who has not previously published a book), and in 1986 his first full-length work, *Cast in the Fire* (Dolmen) appeared. That same year he received a fellowship enabling him to travel to the United States, where he has remained, becoming an American citizen in 1994.

Since 1987, Delanty has been associated with Saint Michael College, Vermont, initially as a teacher and currently as artist-in-residence. It is here that his poems began to explore the themes of exile and family which would dominate his later work. His collection *American Wake* (Blackstaff, 1995), which envisions a fifth Irish province 'where all exiles naturally land', was followed by *The Hellbox* (Oxford University Press, 1998), whose title alludes to the printing trade to which his father had de-

voted his life. *The Blind Stitch* (Carcanet, 2001), extends the geography of Delanty's poems to include India, and was followed by *The Ship of Birth* (Carcanet, 2007), a collection inspired by fatherhood and committed to 'affirming the sustaining continuity of life'. *Collected Poems* was published by Carcanet/Oxford Poets in 1996.

In addition to his own poems, Delanty has published translations of the Gaelic poet Seán O Ríordáin and is co-editor of *The Word Exchange: Anglo-Saxon Poems in Translation* (Norton, 2010). KGr

Denby, Edwin (1903–83) Born in Tientsin, China, where his father was the American Consul. After attending the Hotchkiss School in Connecticut he entered Harvard, but although he appears to have been academically brilliant he dropped out of college and travelled to Europe with a friend. He spent the Twenties and early Thirties as a dancer, choreographer, and librettist in Austria, Germany, and France. After returning to New York in 1935, he concentrated on writing poems, opera and ballet libretti, and dance criticism. He is now known as one of the most influential dance critics of this century. Denby's literary significance lies chiefly in his having provided a link between Hart *Crane and Frank *O'Hara, the two major twentieth-century poets of Manhattan. While Denby's own poetic output was sporadic and uneven, it displays striking originality and inventiveness. In it we can see him gradually pushing Crane's high rhetoric, clotted diction, and pseudo-rational syntax toward the looser, more vernacular idiom of O'Hara's 'lunch poems'. The result is a poetry that retains traditional formal values (most of Denby's poems are sonnets or rhymed stanzas) while opening itself to the contingencies and dislocations of city life. At its best his work offers an effortless blending of intelligence and immersion; at its weakest these two elements fail to cohere, and the poems become knotted and opaque.

His first book of poems, *In Public, In Private*, appeared in 1948, and was followed by only two more small-press collections. Horrified at the prospect of senility,

Denby committed suicide on 12 July 1983. *The Complete Poems*, ed. Ron Padgett (Random House, 1986) is out of print, but see *Dance Writings and Poetry*, ed. Robert Cornfield (Yale University Press, 1998). There are also selections in *The New York Poets II*, eds. Mark Ford and Trevor Winkfield (Carcanet, 2006) and *The Reality Street Book of Sonnets* (2008), ed. Jeff Hilson. A special feature on Denby appeared in issue 21 of the online magazine *Jacket* (February 2003).   RG

Dennis, C. J. (Clarence James) (1876–1936) Born in South Australia. After a varied career as clerk, barman, and journalist, he moved to Toolangi near Melbourne in 1908, where he remained to the end of his life. He is especially popular for his dramatic monologues in verse: *The Songs of the Sentimental Bloke* (1915; new edn. Angus & Robertson, 1992), *The Moods of Ginger Mick* (1916), and *Digger Smith* (1918). He married Olive Herron in 1917.

Dennis is most noted for his mastery of the larrikin slang that defines the voices of his main characters. Sentimental and nationalistic, his vernacular captures the aspirations of a mythical Australian lower class, contemptuous of the 'self-made slaves' of the middle and ruling classes, while aspiring to their values.

The best available collection of Dennis' verse is *The Sentimental Bloke and Other Selected Verse* (Angus & Robertson, 1973). A. H. Chisholm's *The Making of the Sentimental Bloke* (Georgian, 1946) is a helpful biography, while G. W. Hutton's *C. J. Dennis, The Sentimental Bloke* (Premier's Dept., 1976) provides a useful modern appraisal.   AU

Dennis, Carl (1939–) Born in St Louis, Missouri, Dennis attended the universities of Chicago, Minnesota, and Berkeley. From late 1960s until his retirement in 2001 he taught English at the University of Buffalo.

Dennis' understated, ruminative poems on the lives of small-town, middle-class America are typically between one and two pages in length and written in a leisurely pentameter line, evincing his sympathy for a world where literature has a small but

traditional place. As 'A Colleague Confesses' in a dramatic monologue on the academic life which is also a gently ironic *ars poetica*, 'the poems and stories we're teaching | are less important to me than they are to you': 'I try to content myself | with working in harmony with the world'. He has gradually found a wider readership since his first volume, *A House Of My Own* (Braziller, 1974). Dennis began to publish with Penguin in the 1990s, and in 2001 won the Pulitzer Prize for *Practical Gods*. See *New and Selected Poems 1974–2004* (2004—all Penguin) and also an 'essay for writers', *Poetry as Persuasion* (University of Georgia Press, 2001).   JNT

Derksen, Jeff (1958–) Born in New Westminster, British Columbia, Derksen completed his PhD at the University of Calgary under Fred *Wah, and was a Research Fellow at the Center for Place, Culture, and Politics at the City University of New York. He is Associate Professor of English at Simon Fraser University in Vancouver.

Derksen's books include *Down Time* (1990), winner of the British Columbia Book Prize for Poetry, *Dwell* (1993), and *Transnational Muscle Cars* (2003), all from Talonbooks. Former editor of *Writing* magazine and a founding member of Vancouver's writer-run centre, the *Kootenay School of Writing, Derksen has had a formative influence on contemporary Canadian poetry. Like that of Charles *Bernstein, much of his poetry works at the level of the sentence and draws language from contrasting registers, foregrounding its politics in what Derksen himself has called 'the socialist one-liner'. To quote 'But Could I Make a Living From It': 'I'll stand in for form, for me. | It's the "political economy of genitals" that puts us inside production.' Derksen's poetic practice, always a dimension of wider theoretical projects, is articulated in the recent collection of essays, *Annihilated Time: Poetry and Other Politics* (2009), and informed by his work with the visual research collective Urban Subjects, based in Vancouver and Vienna. *The Vestiges* (2012—both Talonbooks) explores the relation between the social subject and urban spaces, and the possibility of a 'social sincerity' to be found in art, poetry, and new social movements.   ADA

Derricotte, Toi (1941–) Born and raised in Detroit, Derricotte studied at Wayne State University, and is Professor of English at the University of Pittsburgh. With Cornelius *Eady, she was a founder member of the *Cave Canem group: see *Gathering Ground* (University of Michigan Press, 2006).

Derricotte has characterized the black middle-class area in which she grew up by its 'pervasive sense of vulnerability', and the poems of her first collection, *The Empress of the Death House* (Lotus, 1978), are fired with anger at the legacy of racial segregation and female subjection. Her next book, *Natural Birth* (The Crossing Press, 1983), narrates in diary-like detail her violently obstetric experience of becoming a mother at the age of eighteen. A new edition, with an introduction by the author, appeared in 2000 from Firebrand Books. *Captivity* (1989) returns to childhood to address her physical abuse by her father. The poems of *Tender* (1997—both University of Pittsburgh Press) also identify violence as 'central in our lives', while holding out the possibility of understanding through a poetry intimate with the body. See also her memoir, *The Black Notebooks* (Norton, 1997), and most recently, *The Undertaker's Daughter* (University of Pittsburgh Press, 2011).   JNT

de Silva, Alfreda (1920–2001) Born in Sri Lanka, and worked as a freelance journalist, broadcaster, and television scriptwriter. Her poems were published in *Out of the Dark the Sun* (Sarvodaya, 1977) and *The Unpredictable Blood* (Alfreda de Silva, 1988). She also wrote books of verse for children. Her most notable pieces are 'Collages', a frightening sketch of personal relationships; 'First-Born', which involves the reader in the violence of birth; and 'Crows and Children', in which the creatures of the title compete for food at a garbage can: 'Someone has willed them the dark | The Sun goes on without them.'   LdeS

de Souza, Eunice (1940–) Born into a Goan Catholic family in Bombay (now Mumbai) and is a graduate of both the University of Bombay and Marquette University, Wisconsin. She was a lecturer in English literature at St Xavier's College, Bombay until her retirement. Her journalism is widely appreciated in India for its impatient and acerbic tone, and her poetry criticism is seen as a healthy reaction against a tradition of derivative, lifeless, 'Indo-Anglian' verse.

Although she is not a prolific poet, de Souza's voice is individual and challenging. The poems in her first collection, *Fix* (Newground, 1979), are firmly located in the Goan Catholic community of her childhood. They are direct, often witty, always iconoclastic. Her targets, as identified by a range of contrasting personae, are the casual tolerance of social injustice, the sexual mores inculcated by Jansenism, and the omnipresent oppression of women. Many of her funniest pieces reproduce the dated argot of the period and ambience in which they are set.

De Souza's second collection, *Women in Dutch Painting* (Praxis, 1988), is more personal, betraying a wider range of sympathies and interests. Both collections were published in a third volume, *Ways of Belonging* (Polygon, 1990), together with some new material. See *A Necklace of Skulls: Collected Poems* (Penguin, 2009) and *Talking Poems* (Oxford University Press, 1999), a book of interviews with other Anglo-Indian poets. De Souza has also edited several anthologies of Indian poetry and published two novels.   RW

Devlin, Denis (1908–59) Born in Greenock, Scotland, to an Irish family which returned to Ireland in 1918. He was educated at Belvedere College, University College, Dublin, Munich University, and the Sorbonne. Between Belvedere and UCD he spent a year at All Hallows College, a seminary, but decided against the priesthood. As a student, he was one of an academically brilliant and artistically outward-looking generation of the Thirties in Ireland, which also included Brian O'Nolan (Flann O'Brien), Mervyn Wall, Brian *Coffey (with whom Devlin published *Poems*, Dublin, 1930), and somewhat more marginally, Samuel *Beckett, who considered Devlin one of the most interesting poets of his generation. He took a degree in languages, but despite a period of research and a spell as an assistant lecturer in English at UCD, he joined the Irish Foreign Service in 1935. Thereafter his life was that of a successful career diplomat. He became Irish ambassador to Italy in 1958.

Devlin's early work was highly cerebral— not to say precious and obscure. Later on his poems, although still densely packed, became more accessible and better controlled, and they adopted a distinct but surprisingly rare Irish Catholic perspective. His central themes are exile and love. In each case Devlin identifies both a secular and a divine aspect without merely reiterating that time-worn opposition. Thus, exile is both the life of the diplomat and the condition of humanity, expelled to the vale of tears that is the fallen world. Human and divine love, similarly, have secular and divine aspects: the love of God, given and received by humanity, is subject to secular transformations, while mortal love can achieve timelessness, as in 'The Colours of Love'. In Devlin's thought, metaphysical and physical passion are not just reflections of each other—they are mutually dependent components, brought together only rarely, as in the figure of Christ in the sequence 'The Passion of Christ'. Throughout his life Devlin translated widely from the French, notably from St John Perse (also a diplomat). His translations are not a separate part of his work but an extension of it, for they deepen his concern with language as negotiation: between cultures, between lovers, between consciousness and silence, and between God and humanity.

Because of Devlin's erratic publication history and constant revisions, both of his own poetry and of his translations, Brian Coffey's editions of the *Collected Poems* (1964) and *The Heavenly Foreigner* (1967—both Dolmen) need to be supplemented by the *Selected Poems*, eds. Robert Penn Warren and Allen Tate (Holt, 1963). J. C. C. Mays' edition of the *Collected Poems of Denis Devlin* (Dedalus, 1989) was followed by *Translations into English*, ed. Roger Little (Dedalus, 1992). See Alex Davis, *A Broken Line: Denis Devlin and Irish Poetic Modernism* (University College Dublin Press, 2000).   EH

Dewdney, Christopher (1951–)
Born in London, Ontario, his father was Selwyn Dewdney, the archaeologist, artist, and writer. He has spoken of the importance of an education in both science and the arts to his own writing, saying 'all poetry deals with information'. He lives in Toronto, where he teaches at York University.

Predators of the Adoration (McClelland & Stewart, 1983) was a selection of Dewdney's early, geologically inspired work published through Coach House Press, where was also poetry editor. In 1982 he appeared in Ron Mann's documentary on experimental poets in North America, *Poetry in Motion*. His later collections, which increasingly explore the interconnection of mind and environment, include *The Radiant Inventory* (1988) and *Demon Pond* (1994). *Signal Fires* (2000—all McClelland & Stewart) contains the later parts of his sequence 'A Natural History of Southwestern Ontario', begun in *Spring Trances in the Control Emerald Night* (The Figures, 1978), and collected in *The Natural History* (ECW, 2002). Dewdney has been nominated four times for the Governor General's Award. See *Children of the Outer Dark* (Wilfrid Laurier University Press, 2007), a selection edited by Karl E. Jirgens, with an afterword by the author. He has also written several popular works of non-fiction on the secular revelation of science, including *The Secular Grail* (Somerville House, 1993) and *Soul of the World: Unlocking the Secrets of Time* (HarperCollins, 2008).   JNT

Dharker (or Dharkar), Imtiaz (1954–)
Born in Lahore to Pakistani parents, Dharker was brought up in Glasgow, studying Literature and Philosophy at the University of Glasgow. Poet, artist, and documentary film-maker, Dharker, a self-described 'Scottish Muslim Calvinist', lives between London, Wales, and Mumbai.

Dharker's mixed cultural heritage informs her self-illustrated volumes of poetry. Like

Sujata *Bhatt and Kamala *Das, Dharker's poetry gives a new, and multiculturally feminist, voice to contemporary Anglo-Indian poetry. Early volumes equate displacement negatively with exile, an itinerant life-style, and the idea of a self and home 'between borders' (*Purdah* (Oxford University Press, 1988)), but later volumes have moved to revel in this displacement. *Postcards from God* (1997) and *I Speak for the Devil* (2001) expand, in Dharker's characteristically direct address, the personal visions of earlier volumes to encompass the socio-political world, writing in protest against violence and power-play. *The Terrorist at my Table* (2006) and *Leaving Fingerprints* (2009—all Bloodaxe) continue her preoccupation with identity and gender politics, effecting a stripping down of both images and verse-forms in order to reach a common ground unconstrained by borders or cultural mores.   HY

Dickey, James (1923–97) Born in Atlanta, Georgia. After serving as a pilot in the Second World War, he attended Vanderbilt University. Having earned an MA in 1950, Dickey returned to military duty in the Korean War, serving with the US Air Force. Upon return to civilian life Dickey taught at Rice University in Texas and then at the University of Florida. From 1955 to 1961, he worked for advertising agencies in New York and Atlanta. After the publication of his first book, *Into the Stone* (Wesleyan University Press, 1962), he left advertising and began teaching at various colleges and universities. He was poet-in-residence and Carolina Professor of English at the University of South Carolina.

Dickey's third volume, *Buckdancer's Choice* (Wesleyan University Press, 1965), won the prestigious National Book Award in Poetry. From 1966 to 1968 he served as poetry consultant to the Library of Congress. In 1977 Dickey read his poem 'The Strength of Fields' at President Carter's inauguration. The Hollywood film of his novel *Deliverance* (Houghton, 1970) brought Dickey fame not normally enjoyed by poets.

Dickey's poems are a mixture of lyricism and narrative. In some volumes the lyricism dominates, while in others the narrative is the focus. The early books, influenced obviously though not slavishly by Theodore *Roethke and perhaps Hopkins, are infused with a sense of private anxiety and guilt. Both emotions are called forth most deeply by the memories of a brother who died before Dickey was born ('In the Tree House at Night') and his war experiences ('Drinking From a Helmet'). These early poems generally employ rhyme and metre.

With *Buckdancer's Choice*, Dickey left traditional formalism behind, developing what he called a 'split-line' technique to vary the rhythm and look of the poem. Some critics argue that by doing so Dickey freed his true poetic voice. Others lament that the lack of formal device led to rhetorical, emotional, and intellectual excess. The truth probably lies somewhere between these two assessments, and it will be left to the reader to decide which phase of Dickey's career is most attractive.

Dickey's most comprehensive volume is *The Whole Motion: Collected Poems 1945–1992* (1992). His early poems are collected in *The Early Motion* (1981). Later individual volumes include *The Eagle's Mile* (1990) and *Falling, May Day Sermon, and Other Poems* (1982—all Wesleyan University Press). Dickey also published collections of autobiographical essays, *Self Interviews* (Doubleday, 1970; repr. Louisiana State University Press, 1984) and *Sorties* (Doubleday, 1971; repr. Louisiana State University Press, 1984).

See *James Dickey: The Selected Poems*, ed. Robert Kirschten (University Press of New England, 1998) and *The James Dickey Reader*, ed. Henry Hart (Simon & Schuster, 1999). *Crux: The Letters of James Dickey* (Knopf), eds. Matthew J. Bruccoli and Judith S. Baughman, appeared in 1999. *Classes on Modern Poets and the Art of Poetry* (University of South Carolina Press, 2004), ed. Donald J. Greiner, gathers transcriptions of his lectures. For the biography see Henry Hart, *The World as a Lie* (Picador, 2000) and *The One Voice of James Dickey: His Letters and His Life, 1942–1969*

(University of Missouri Press, 2003), ed. Gordon van Ness. For criticism see *The Way We Read James Dickey: Critical Approaches for the Twenty-First Century* (University of South Carolina Press, 2009), eds. William B. Thesing and Theda Wrede.   RS

Dickey, William (Hobart) (1928–94) Born in Bellingham, Washington state, and attended Harvard, the University of Iowa, and Oxford. He taught at Cornell and Denison University in Ohio, and from 1962 until his retirement in 1991 at San Francisco State University. From formal beginnings, markedly influenced by *Auden—who chose his first book, *Of the Festivity* (Yale University Press, 1959), for the Yale Series of Younger Poets—and Richard *Wilbur, Dickey moved to an 'open' style, including 'multimedia poems combining text, graphics, sound recordings and animation on computers', and taught a course on this subject. The transition was not abrupt: poems of the late 1960s and early 1970s, such as those collected in *More under Saturn* (Wesleyan University Press, 1971), owe an obvious debt—perhaps too obvious—to *Imagism and to *Pound. *Rainbow Grocery* (University of Massachusetts Press, 1978), Dickey's most widely read collection, displays a shift towards 'local' (*San Francisco) poetry and the subject of his own homosexuality.

See *In the Dreaming: Selected Poems* (University of Arkansas Press, 1994). *The Education of Desire* (Wesleyan University Press, 1996), his last collection, appeared posthumously, with an introduction by W. D. *Snodgrass.   MS-S

Dickinson, Patric Thomas (1913–94) Born at Nasirabad in India. His father was killed early in the First World War, and he was educated at St Catherine's College, Cambridge, where he won a blue for golf. After teaching at a preparatory school he served in the Artists' Rifles from 1939 to 1940, but was invalided out. He joined the BBC in 1942, working in the Feature and Drama Department until he resigned in 1948 to become a freelance writer.

Beginning in 1946, Dickinson published more than twenty volumes of poems and verse translations. All his poetry is lyrical but the early romanticism and *Yeatsian symbolism have given way to a tauter, darker, more concentrated utterance. *This Cold Universe* (Chatto & Windus, 1964) presents, as the title suggests, a characteristically sombre view of lonely man in an impersonal world, lost and despairing unless redeemed by love.

Dickinson published translations of Aristophanes in 1959 and 1970, and of *The Aeneid of Vergil* (Penguin, 1960). He wrote and produced many radio poetry programmes, including the series 'Time for Verse', and a number of feature programmes, of which those on Keats and on Wilfred *Owen were particularly memorable.   JPr

Didsbury, Peter (1946–) Born in Fleetwood, Lancashire, but moved to Hull at the age of 6 and has been closely associated with that city ever since. He read English and Hebrew at Oxford, taught English for eight years, and worked at Hull museums for two. In 1987 he became a research assistant with Humberside County Council's Archaeological Unit, writing reports on Roman and medieval pottery. The 'historical imagination', historical erudition, a thorough immersion in the urban-domestic life of Hull and in its estuarial hinterland of rain-drenched farms, drains, ditches, and dykes: all these are powerfully present in Didsbury's poems. But his most characteristic genre is playful invention, and his fictions often depend on little more than a 'necessary premiss' (though this may be arbitrary or fanciful) and authorial whim to sustain them. Intimations of dread or compassion, wonder and disenchantment; nods to *Surrealism and Sterne, John *Ashbery and John Keats; visionary disjunctions and flurries of archaic or pedantically formal diction; inconclusive revelations or portentously offhand gestures: these have secured Didsbury, like the comparably mercurial Roy *Fisher, widespread admiration among his peers. Fellow Hull poet Sean *O'Brien has praised his 'large and peculiar imagination' and 'sense of adventure', even if it is only (as in 'An Expedition') to the end of the garden with milk, a cigarette, and 'light from the new kitchen window'.

Didsbury's collections, all published by Bloodaxe, are *The Butchers of Hull* (1982), *The Classical Farm* (1987), *That Old-Time Religion* (1994), and *Scenes from a Long Sleep: New and Collected Poems*, which includes his fourth volume, *A Natural History* (2003). See Sean O'Brien, 'Peter Didsbury: Getting Some Things Down', in *The Deregulated Muse* (Bloodaxe, 1998). Didsbury's literary opinions are given in interview with David *Wheatley in *Metre*, 16 (Autumn 2004).   AJ*

di Michele, Mary (1949–) Born in Lanciano, Italy, and has lived in Canada since 1955. Educated at the universities of Toronto and Windsor, Ontario, she teaches creative writing at Concordia University in Montreal. A strong feminist, she edited an anthology of Canadian women poets, *Anything Is Possible* (Mosaic, 1984); a visit to Pinochet's Chile inspired a strong group of poems examining the interconnections between sexual and power politics. They have been published in *Luminous Emergencies* (McClelland & Stewart, 1990).

Lyrical, metaphorical, yet also interrogative and unsettling, Di Michele's poetry explores the transformative powers of language, memory, and love. Influenced by artists as diverse as Rilke, Frieda Kahlo, and Leonard *Cohen, her writing also acknowledges the work of other women poets, notably Bronwen *Wallace, with whom she co-published *Bread and Chocolate/Marrying into the Family* (Oberon, 1980).

Di Michele's publications include *Mimosa and Other Poems* (Mosaic, 1981), *Necessary Sugar* (Oberon, 1983), *Immune to Gravity* (McClelland & Stewart, 1986), and *Debriefing the Rose* (Anansi, 1998). See *Stranger in You: Poems Selected and New* (Oxford University Press, 1995). She has also published two novels, *Under My Skin* (Quarry, 1994), and *Tenor of Love* (Simon & Schuster, 2005).   JKK

Dinh, Linh (1963–) Born in Saigon, Dinh came to the United States in 1975. He attended art school, and worked as a house painter in Philadelphia. He writes in English and Vietnamese, and has held residencies in Italy and England. He has also published fiction, autobiography, political commentary, and documentary photography of America's urban underclass.

Dinh's first small-press chapbook, *Drunkard Boxing* (Singing Horse, 1996) was collected, with two others, in *All Around What Empties Out* (subpress/Tinfish, 2003). His poetry evinces a strong appreciation of diverse avant-garde traditions, channelled with a directness that Ron *Silliman has praised as 'a walking example of the role of the real at the heart of the surreal'. It takes both incantatory and narrative forms, recounting the strange and abject with *Beat-like humour ('Toothless man sucking | a pureed porterhouse steak | with straw'). The use of online material in his second collection, *American Tatts* (2005), suggested Flarf sympathies (*see* CONCEPTUALISM). But Dinh's designedly crude diction remains focused on the distortions of the speaking subject. Later books include *Jam Alerts* (2007) and *Some Kind of Cheese Orgy* (2009—all Chax Press). He has edited anthologies of contemporary Vietnamese fiction and poetry, and translated the poems of Phan Nhiên Hao (*Night, Fish and Charlie Parker* (Tupelo, 2006)). See also two collections of stories, *Fake House* (2000) and *Blood and Soap* (2004), and a novel, *Love Like Hate* (2010—all Seven Stories).   JNT

Di Piero, W. S. (1945–) Born in South Philadelphia, where he grew up in an Italian neighbourhood. He lives in San Francisco where he is art critic for the *San Diego Reader* and teaches at Stanford University. A poet of the modern American city, Di Piero's relaxed, particular voice is attracted to the vernacular music of jazz and slang, the seasonal recurrences of life, and the power of the directly-seen image. As he writes 'On a Picture by Cézanne': 'There's no description in the braided stone'. His own characteristic scenes are bars, tenements, street-corners, churches, and subways, with occasional pastoral excursions. *Chinese Apples* (Knopf, 2007) draws on eight previous collections: *The Only*

Dangerous Thing (Elpenor, 1984), *Early Light* (University of Utah Press, 1985), *The Dog Star* (University of Massachusetts Press, 1990), *The Restorers* (University of Chicago Press, 1992), *Shadows Burning* (TriQuarterly/Northwestern University Press, 1995), *Skirts and Slacks* (2001), *Brother Fire* (2004—both Knopf). He has also published several volumes of essays and Italian poetry in translation: see *When I Can See Again: New Art Writings* (Pressed Wafer, 2010) and *Night of Shooting Stars: The Selected Poems of Leonardo Sinisgalli* (Tavern, 2011). His latest collection is *Nitro Nights* (Copper Canyon, 2011).   JNT

Dipoko, Mbella Sonne (1936–2009) Born in Douala, Cameroon and grew up in Western Cameroon and Nigeria. He joined the Nigerian Broadcasting Corporation in 1958 as a news reporter but lived in France from 1960. He studied law for a time at Paris University, and later devoted himself to poetry and painting.

Dipoko's articles, short stories, and poems were published widely; his first poems were broadcast by the BBC African Service. His only volume of poetry, *Black and White in Love* (Heinemann, 1972), was published following his trip from England through France and Spain to Morocco. He also published two novels and a play. His most accomplished work is the title-poem, 'Black and White in Love'. The structure is free verse; the language is evocative and accessible; the concerns are urbane and liberal. There is tenderness and sensitivity in his poetry, but his political ideas are unrefined and fragmentary.   FO

di Prima, Diane (1934–   ) Born in New York City and educated at Swarthmore College, Pennsylvania. Married with three children, she has acted as contributing editor to *Kulchur* magazine, editor of *Signal* magazine, and editor, with LeRoi Jones (Amiri *Baraka), of *Floating Bear* magazine. With her husband, Alan Marlowe, she has also been editor and publisher of Poets Press, based in New York. Her first collection of poetry, *This Kind of Bird Flies Backward*, was published in 1958 (Totem); and since then she has produced many volumes, the

more significant or representative of which include *The New Handbook of Heaven* (Auerhahn, 1963), *Revolutionary Letters* (City Lights, 1971; expanded edn., 1979), and *Kerhonkson Journal, 1966* (Oyez, 1971). Her prolific output of over forty books also includes several novels and plays.

Associated with the *Beat poets, di Prima was prominent as a counter-cultural voice in the 1960s. Her work has been particularly concerned with American life outside the middle-class mainstream: with the culture of travellers and hobos, ethnic minorities, outsiders. However, even the political polemics of *Revolutionary Letters* are punctuated by more intimate moments concerned with friends and family, while *New Handbook of Heaven* is full of magic and incantation, and the poems in *Kerhonkson Journal* are notable for their tenderness and lyricism. Her long poem *Loba* was published by Penguin in 1998.

See *Pieces of a Song: Selected Poems* (City Lights, 2001), and the memoir *Recollections of My Life as a Woman: The New York Years* (Viking, 2001). In 2009 di Prima became Poet Laureate of San Francisco.   RJG*

Disch, Tom (Thomas Michael Disch) (1940–2008) Born in Iowa, grew up in Minnesota, moved to New York City after graduating from high school in 1958, and became a full-time writer after dropping out of New York University four years later. Versatile and prolific, Disch long enjoyed a commanding international reputation for his science-fiction novels, such as *Camp Concentration* (1968), *334* (1972), and *On Wings of Song* (1979). Recognition for his poetry came first in England: three of his collections, including *Burn This* (1982), were published in London. *Yes, Let's*, a volume of new and selected poems (Johns Hopkins University Press, 1989), confirmed his growing stature in America.

The virtues of Disch's prose—wit, invention, boyish wonder, and intellectual sophistication—are to be found in his verse too. He wrote in a wide range of forms: sestinas and villanelles, songs and sonnets, the abecedarius and its opposite, the zewhyexary (a Disch coinage). His approach to form is jubilant in the *New York School manner; he had a flair for clever internal rhymes and an ability to stretch out a conceit to the furthest limit of ingenuity. Disch wrote inspired parodies as well as chatty and urbane verse essays (such as 'On the Use of the Masculine-Preferred') that recall *Auden's efforts in this vein. The novels and poems written jointly with other writers may help persuade sceptics of the value of literary collaboration.

Disch was the author of *Amnesia*, an 'interactive' computer fiction, in addition to children's books, collections of short stories, historical fiction, and verse plays. He served as fiction critic for *Playboy*, and was the theatre critic for *The Nation*. In September 1990 Disch found himself at the centre of a controversy when a New York City production of his short play, *The Cardinal Detoxes*, caused the Roman Catholic Archdiocese of New York to lodge strong protests.

Disch also published two notably critical studies of science fiction literature, *The Dreams Our Stuff Is Made Of* (Simon & Schuster, 1998) and *On SF* (University of Michigan Press, 2005), as well as *The Castle of Perseverance: Job Opportunities in Contemporary Poetry*, a mixture of critical prose and poems (University of Michigan Press, 2002). He committed suicide in 2008, having written, often in verse, about his increasingly unhappy personal circumstances in an online journal.   DL*

Dixon, Isobel (1969–) Born in Umtata, Isobel Dixon grew up in the semi-desert Karoo region of South Africa before studying English Literature at the University of Stellenbosch. With Masters degrees in English Literature and Applied Linguistics from the University of Edinburgh, Dixon currently works as a literary agent in London, representing a number of prominent South African authors. She has published three collections of poetry as well as three joint pamphlets with a group of UK poets.

Dixon's debut poetry collection, *Weather Eye* (Carapace, 2001), won the Sanlam Prize and Olive Schreiner Prize in South Africa. The collection is a reminiscence of family life and childhood but is also very much about South Africa, whose sensuality is cast into relief by life in an often damp and restrained Britain. Dixon's second collection, published in the UK and South Africa, *A Fold in the Map* (Salt/Jacana, 2007), is split into two distinct halves. The first half, 'Plenty', contains many of the warm and nostalgic poems from *Weather Eye* (which was published only in South Africa), and emphasizes the sadness of the second half, 'Meet My Father', which is about her father's illness and death. Dixon's latest collection, *The Tempest Prognosticator* (Salt/Umuzi, 2011), contains the same warm, lyrical, and gently humorous poetry as her earlier books, but is less personal. Many of these poems, like the leech-contraption used to predict a coming storm in the title poem, enlist animals to illuminate what people can't or won't see.   KK

Dobson, Rosemary (de Brissac) (1920–2012) Born in Sydney. Her paternal grandfather was the English poet Austin Dobson (1840–1921). After studying design, which she regarded as a valuable discipline, and attending university, she became a publisher's editor in Sydney. Later she lived abroad with her husband before settling in Canberra. Douglas *Stewart encouraged publication of *In a Convex Mirror* (Dymocks, 1944).

Dobson shared the classicist and formalist orientation of such contemporaries as James *McAuley and A. D. *Hope. Its simplicity, clarity, detachment, and precision give her work a contemplative stillness—what Hope called 'passionate serenity'—which reflects her love of early Renaissance painting. Her effects derive from quiet irony, wit, and formal finesse rather than visual imagery; her sensibility is spare and austere.

Although her career spanned six decades, Dobson was neither prolific nor broad in scope. Her chief preoccupation was always time and its implications for individual experience (notably parenthood) or, more often, art. *Child With a Cockatoo* (Angus & Robertson, 1955) contains her best-known poems, mostly dramatic monologues pertaining to Renaissance paintings. Some poems are informed by a sense of loss

('Cock Crow', 'Jack'), or by a sense of the mystery beyond that which can be apprehended and expressed. But Dobson is resolutely anti-transcendental, as 'Over the Frontier' demonstrates.

With her friend David *Campbell she translated Mandelstam and other Russian poets. *Selected Poems* (Angus & Robertson, revd. edn., 1980) reprinted much of five earlier volumes. *The Three Fates* (Hale & Iremonger, 1984), influenced by Chinese poetry, contained impressive work in the free verse she later favoured. *Collected Poems* (Angus & Robertson, 1991) was followed by two later books, *Untold Lives* (Brandl & Schlesinger, 2000) and *Folding the Sheets* (Picaro, 2004).   AW

Dobyns, Stephen J. (1941–   ) Born in Orange, New Jersey, and teaches at Warren Wilson College. Though primarily a poet, he is also the author of many novels, including ten chronicling the adventures of Saratoga detective Charlie Bradshaw, and the best-selling *The Church of Dead Girls* (Viking, 1997). Whatever medium he happens to write in, Dobyns is always a storyteller, for all his work is based upon narrative. Even in the volume that ought to be his most static, *The Balthus Poems* (Atheneum, 1982), where each poem is based upon a single one of the French artist's paintings, Dobyns brings the characters to life by creating dynamic stories for them.

Perhaps because he was a newspaper reporter early in his life, Dobyns does not look inside his own psyche for the subject-matter of his poems; he writes primarily in the third person. Many of his poems contain traditional stories that bite their own tails, resolving at the end conflicts established at the beginning. Others—for example, 'The Invitation', from *Cemetery Nights* (Viking, 1986; Bloodaxe, 1992)—move in a linear fashion, leaving behind the characters and situations with which they begin. Still others are created like spider-webs; their stories are sticky, confusing, in danger of being broken and flung, at any moment, 'into heaven's blue and innocent immensity'.

Dobyns' first volume, *Concurring Beasts* (Atheneum), was the Lamont Poetry Selection for 1971; his fifth, *Black Dog, Red Dog* (Holt), was chosen for the National Poetry Series in 1984.

Since *Velocities: New and Selected Poems* (Penguin, 1994; Bloodaxe, 1996) his books include *Pallbearers Envying the One Who Rides* (Penguin, 1999; Bloodaxe, 2000), *The Porcupine's Kisses* (Penguin, 2002; Bloodaxe, 2003)—an illustrated collection of prose poems, maxims, and one-line definitions—and *Winter's Journey* (Copper Canyon, 2010). See *Best Words, Best Order: Essays on Poetry* (St Martin's, 1996; second edn., Palgrave, 2003).   PS

Donaghy, Michael (1954–2004) Born in New York, and educated at Fordham University and the University of Chicago. He was poetry editor for the *Chicago Review* before moving to London. His first collection, *Shibboleth* (1988), earned him the year's Whitbread Poetry Prize, and also the Geoffrey Faber Memorial Award of 1989. *Errata* (both Oxford University Press) followed in 1993. They were reprinted in one volume, *Dances Learned Last Night* (Picador, 2000).

Shibboleth records an intelligent literary apprenticeship: Donaghy recalls his precocious childhood with affectionate irony, parades a wide range of learning lightly, and views the oddities of real life—a man carrying a man-length mirror along a girder, or an especially fruitful *Guardian* misprint—with wry amusement. He is fond of unsettling juxtapositions (*Yeats and an angel, Purcell and a twelve-speed bike), and perhaps over-fond of poetic riddles which implicate the reader without troubling to teach him the rules of the game. His allusiveness, too, can become overburdened, as when his precise reference to a cadenza in Mozart (K.285*a*) is called upon to support an entire poem. In love poems, such as 'The Present', there is a more subtly rewarding blend of intimacy and intellect.

A poet who tries on so many suits of clothes is always in danger of looking like a coat-hanger: in his second collection, *Errata*, Donaghy began to settle for longer, more fluent-looking forms (as in the substantial narrative spoken by Benvenuto Cellini), although his imagination remains dartingly anecdotal and often bewilderingly frenetic.

Donaghy consolidated his reputation as a metaphysical formalist with *Conjure* (2000), which contains several original takes on the poetic summoning of a dead parent (see 'Caliban's Books'). It won the Forward Poetry Prize. His sudden death in 2004 brought elegies from a number of British contemporaries, including Simon *Armitage, Paul *Farley, and Don *Paterson. *Collected Poems* (2009) includes a posthumous volume, *Safest* (2005). The introduction by Sean *O'Brien discusses some of the allusive background to the poems, and reads the dramatic monologue 'Black Ice and Rain' as a 'critique of postmodernity'. See also *The Shape of the Dance: Essays, Interviews and Digressions* (2009— all Picador).   NP*

Doolittle, Hilda (H. D.) (1886–1961) Born in Bethlehem, Pennsylvania. Her mother was a Moravian artist, her father a professor of astronomy. The posthumous memoir, *End to Torment*, describes how, as a student at Bryn Mawr College, she fell in love with Ezra *Pound, who was then a postgraduate student at the University of Pennsylvania, and who gave her a hand-bound sheaf of poems entitled *Hilda's Book*. She left college in her sophomore year with poor grades. In 1911 she travelled to London, where Pound was established, intending to stay for the summer; but she never returned, and lived in England and Switzerland for the rest of her life. Instead of Pound she married her fellow-Imagist Richard *Aldington in 1913; they separated in 1919, though they were not divorced until 1938. After Aldington left her she lived with Bryher (Winifred Ellerman) from 1919 to 1946.

It was Pound who labelled her 'H. D. Imagiste' when, in 1912, he sent her poems (and Aldington's) to Harriet Monroe for publication in *Poetry*. She continued to subscribe to *Imagism when the movement was taken over by Amy *Lowell; and her spare, clear, sculptural early poems, like 'Pear Tree' and the famous 'Oread' ('Whirl up, sea—| Whirl your pointed pines . . .'), are among the most successful embodiments of Imagist principles.

After the breakdown of her marriage her poetry began to serve a more complex personal purpose, and the purely Imagist phase of her career can be considered closed by the publication in 1925 of the (first) *Collected Poems*. *Red Roses for Bronze* (1931) shows her moving towards a more discursive treatment of psychic and religious archetypes, a tendency accelerated by her visits to Vienna, in 1933 and 1934, to be analysed by Freud— see the memoir, *Tribute to Freud* (1956; repr. New Directions, 2012), and the poem 'The Master', which transplants their relationship typically to ancient Greece and describes how the Freud-figure sets her free to 'prophesy', to voice her proto-feminist repudiation of 'man-strength'. Subsequent volumes of note include the wartime *Trilogy* (composed 1942–4 and published 1944–6) and the 300-page poem *Helen in Egypt* (1961), her re-creation, composed in the guise of the ancient Sicilian poet Stesichorus, of the Helen-Achilles myth.

H. D. has been variously dismissed as a poet of minor gifts, narrow range, and esoteric concerns, and promoted (especially in America) as the great female modernist in verse. Several poets have expressed their debt: see Robert *Duncan's *H. D. Book*, published by the University of California Press in 2012, and Denise *Levertov's elegy in her volume *O Taste and See*. See also the study by Barbara *Guest, *Herself Defined: the Poet H. D. and Her World* (Doubleday, 1984).

A *Collected Poems* was published in New York by New Directions in 1983 (and in the UK by Carcanet in 1984), and *Selected Poems*, ed. Louis L. Martz, in 1989 (Carcanet). *Trilogy* was republished by New Directions in 1973 and by Carcanet in 1997. *Bid Me to Live* (Virago/Grove, 1960) is an autobiographical novel with lively portraits of Aldington and D. H. *Lawrence. See also *Between History and Poetry: The Letters of H. D. and Norman Holmes Pearson*, ed. Donna Krolik Hollenberg (University of Iowa Press, 1997), and *Analyzing Freud: Letters of H. D., Bryher and Their Circle*, ed. Susan Stanford Friedman (New Directions, 2005).   MI

Dorn, Ed(ward) (1929–99) Born and grew up in eastern Illinois, on the banks of the River Embarrass (a tributary of the Wabash). He never knew his father. His mother was of French ancestry, his grandfather a railroad man. He attended a one-room school, while in high school played billiards with the local undertaker for a dime a point, and after two years at the University of Illinois and two stops at *Black Mountain College, travelled through the transmountain West following the winds of writing and employment. From 1965 to 1970 he lived in England, where he lectured at the University of Essex. He later taught in Kansas, Chicago, and San Francisco; throughout the 1980s he taught in the Creative Writing Program of the University of Colorado, Boulder, and with his wife Jennifer edited the newspaper *Rolling Stock*. He died in 1999 at his home in Boulder.

Dorn's early work is notable for lyrical, gestural style, his later for a humorous and increasingly abrasive moral satire. The American West has been his special subject; the various phases of his writing have in common a strict and angular attention to the particularities of its landscapes and culture. The anti-post-industrial-capitalist mock-epic *Gunslinger* (Duke University Press, 1989) is for Dorn a sort of transitional marker, demonstrating the best qualities of both his early and late modes. Eight years in the making (1967–75), this ambitious, inventive, multi-voiced allegorical narrative plays off pop song and cowboy ballad in assembling an outrageous outlaw metaphysics, extravagantly updating pre-Socratic philosophies and the myths of comic-book gunman and Hollywood/TV frontier hero to fit the subjectivist ethics of the Vietnam War-era drug culture.

Among Dorn's works are *The Collected Poems, 1956–1974* (Four Seasons, 1975; enlarged edn. 1983); *Hello, La Jolla* (Wingbow, 1978); *Yellow Lola* (Cadmus, 1980); and *Abhorrences* (Black Sparrow, 1990). His prose writings include *The Rites of Passage* (Frontier, 1965; revd. edn. issued as *By the Sound*, 1971; new edn., Black Sparrow, 1991); *The Shoshoneans* (Morrow, 1966); and *Views* (Four Seasons, 1980). See also *Ed Dorn Live: Lectures, Interviews, and Outtakes* (University of Michigan Press, 2007), ed. Joseph Richey, and *Way More West: New and Selected Poems* (Penguin, 2007), ed. Michael Rothenberg, with an introduction by Dale Smith. *Collected Poems*, ed. Jennifer Dunbar Dorn et al., with tributes from J. H. *Prynne and Amiri *Baraka, was published by Carcanet in 2012.   TC

Doty, Mark (1953–) Born in Tennessee, Doty studied at Drake University and later took an MFA at Goddard College, Vermont. He lives in New York and teaches at Rutgers University in New Jersey.

Acclaimed as both a poet and memoirist, Doty came to prominence with his third collection *My Alexandria* (University of Illinois Press, 1993). Chosen for the National Poetry Series by Philip *Levine, it went on to win the National Book Critics Circle Award in the USA and the T. S. Eliot Prize in the UK, after being published by Cape in 1995. In poems that responded to the diagnosis of his lover, Wally Roberts, with AIDS, Doty remade the *confessional mode of Robert *Lowell for a new era of openness about gay relationships. *Atlantis* (Harper, 1995; Cape, 1998) dealt with Roberts' death, as did his first memoir in prose, *Heaven's Coast* (Harper, 1996). *Sweet Machine* (Harper/Cape, 1998) saw Doty developing the sensuous and celebratory qualities of his verse ('Glisten fretting the indigo of a plum, | silvered chalk of moth-wing dust') in self-consciously painterly poems: landscapes, portraits, still lives. See also his extended essay *Still Life With Oysters and Lemon* (Beacon, 2001). His later collections are *Source* (Harper/Cape, 2001), *School of the Arts* (Harper/Cape, 2005), *Fire to Fire: New and Selected Poems* (Harper, 2008), and *Theories and Apparitions* (Cape, 2008). He has written two further memoirs, *Firebird* (1999), on his childhood, and *Dog Years* (2007—both Harper), and also *The Art of Description*, on poetry (Graywolf, 2010).   JNT

Douglas, Keith (1920–44) Born in Kent, and brought up near Cranleigh, where his father drifted in and out of work (settling for a while as a chicken-farmer) and his mother succumbed to *encephalitus lethargia*, or 'sleepy sickness'. As soon as he was eligible, Douglas was bundled off to boarding school—in Guildford, first, then in 1931 to Christ's Hospital.

By the time he went up to Merton College, Oxford, in 1938—where his tutor was Edmund *Blunden—the disruptions of home had forced him to evolve a style of living which would remain constant for the rest of his life: rational and pragmatic in thought, hard-hitting and hard riding in deed, brisk and vigorous in his pursuit of affection. The stories and poems he wrote as an undergraduate (for a while he edited *The Cherwell*) show similar qualities: taking their lead from *Auden, they relate private feelings to public issues in a way which allows the poet's sensitivity to be mined but at the same time defended and deflected.

When war broke out Douglas relished the chance it gave him to dramatize these tensions. After training at Sandhurst and Wickwar (the time was heavily punctuated by games-playing and girl-chasing) he was posted in 1941 to Palestine with the Nottinghamshire (Sherwood) Rangers. The history of his time in North Africa is dashingly told in his memoir *Alamein to Zem Zem* (1946), where he is at pains to appear casual and raffish—deserting in order to see action, living it up in Alexandria and Cairo, chasing the enemy across the desert as though they were competitors in a gymkhana. When he returned to England in late 1943 his brave face was still intact. In June the following year he was sent to France, and four days after landing he was killed. He was 24.

As a soldier, Douglas managed to conceal his finer feelings until the very end of his life. His poems—to their credit—are not so sanguine. In an early letter he anticipated that 'one day cynic and lyric will meet and make a balanced style', and from 'Simplify me when I'm dead' (1941) to his last poem, 'On a return from Egypt' (1944), he gives many examples of their conjunction. 'These grasses, ancient enemies' is characteristic: 'devil and angel do not fight, | they are the classic Gemini | for whom it's vital to agree | whose interdependent state | this

two-faced country reflects.' Douglas knew that it was his own mind which contained the 'arguments of hell with heaven', but realized that their terms and resolution were reflected in the actual circumstances of battle. 'Cairo Jag' is typical of several poems in juxtaposing the seedy world of the base town with the battlefields a mere 'day's travelling' away, and explores the truce they are forced to make between their apparent similarities. 'The streets dedicated to sleep | stenches and sour smells' are parodied by the 'new world', where 'the vegetation is of iron | dead tanks, gun barrels split like celery'.

This animation of war by its opposite (the same process occurs in 'Dead Men', 'Landscape with Figures', and 'Vergissmeinicht') produces another of Douglas' major themes. As an undergraduate he wrote that poetry 'is like a man, whom thinking you know all his movements and appearance you will presently come upon in such a posture that for a moment you can hardly believe it is a position of the limbs you know', and as a soldier he regularly finds himself testing the unreality of his impressions. In *Alamein to Zem Zem* he draws images from the 'normal', civilian world to perform this function, admitting that he went to fight 'a little like a visitor from the country going to a great show'. The explosions of gunfire which give the impression of 'watching a magician's trick'; the wounded men 'in an attitude like the humble and resigned attitude of people in long queues'; and the dead Italian soldiers who look 'like trippers taken ill' all bear the same sinister resemblance to scenes of peace as the corpse in 'Vergissmeinicht', who is 'sprawling in the sun' like a sunbather.

In their oblique way these comparisons provide the 'pity' which admirers of First World War poetry find lacking in Douglas. His repeated transformation of people into things (a casualty into a 'cleverly posed waxwork') testifies to war's dehumanizing effect, and redirects the compassion of his predecessors rather than merely re-creating it—which he realized 'a modern poet on active service' would be tempted to do. His heroes are not tortured, sensitive souls, advertising their distress, but the 'obsolescent breed' of his poem 'Sportsmen', who 'under these stones and earth lounge still | in famous attitudes of unconcern'. At the same time that Douglas realizes their stupidity, he admires their nonchalance—the very quality on which so many of his own best poetic strategies depend. The more marked his detachment, the more it suggests his involvement. It is a tone of considerable subtlety, a fine balance of disinterest and commitment, which ably carries out his own commands: 'To be sentimental or emotional now', he stated in a letter, 'is dangerous to oneself and to others. To trust anyone or admit to any hope of a better world is criminally foolish, as foolish as it is to stop working for it.'

Complete Poems, ed. Desmond Graham (Oxford University Press, 1978) was reissued in a new edition with an introduction by Ted *Hughes in 1998. It has since been reprinted by Faber and Faber. See *Keith Douglas 1920–1944*, by Desmond Graham (Oxford University Press, 1974), who also edited *Keith Douglas: A Prose Miscellany* (1985) and *Keith Douglas: The Letters* (2000—both Carcanet).   AM

Dove, Rita (1952–) Born in Akron, Ohio, and educated in Ohio and at the universities of Tübingen and Iowa. She ends her first book, *The Yellow House on the Corner* (1980), by pointing out, in the poem 'Ö', how the finding of a perfect word can allow a writer to 'start out with one thing, end | up with another, and nothing's | like it used to be, not even the future'. The poems in that book begin in the author's childhood neighbourhood in the industrial city of Akron, but reach to worlds as far away as Sweden, Germany, Tunisia, literature, music, geometry, and the American South where Dove encounters her enslaved ancestors—a meeting that helps to shape her identity but does not limit the vision of her work. Her second book, *Museum* (1983), was more cosmopolitan, containing poems that range in reference from 'Shakespeare Say', which tells the story of a black American blues-singer in Paris, to 'The Copper Beech', which describes the signif-

icance of the most rococo tree 'in the park of the castle | at Erpenberg'.

Dove's third collection, *Thomas and Beulah* (1986—all Carnegie-Mellon University Press), for which she was awarded the Pulitzer Prize in Poetry in 1987, uses the lives of the poet's maternal grandparents in order to explore the experiences of those mid-twentieth-century American blacks who journeyed from the South to search for jobs in the industrial North. In addition to containing the most personal poems Dove had yet published, *Grace Notes* (Norton, 1989) also deals with the black experience in America and includes a remarkable section on words ('grace notes') and the possibilities of language.

Her first *Selected Poems* (Pantheon) was published in 1993. In the same year Dove became Commonwealth Professor of English at the University of Virginia in Charlottesville, and was appointed Poet Laureate of the United States. She was the youngest poet, and the first African-American, to hold this post, and used it to promote public interest in literature. *Mother Love* (1995) was followed by *On the Bus with Rosa Parks* (1999), the title sequence of which intertwines the poet's present with a historic moment in the campaign for civil rights. Her later collections are *American Smooth* (2004) and *Sonata Mulattica* (2009—all Norton).

Dove has received many awards and honours for her work, and in 2004 was appointed Poet Laureate of Virginia. She has also written short stories, a novel, a verse drama, a song cycle, and a collection of essays, *The Poet's World* (Library of Congress, 1995). In 2011, she edited *The Penguin Anthology of Twentieth Century American Poetry* and was awarded the National Medal of Arts by President Barack Obama. See Helen Vendler, *Soul Says: On Recent Poetry* (Harvard University Press, 1995) and *Conversations with Rita Dove*, ed. Earl G. Ingersoll (University Press of Mississippi, 2003).   PS*

Dowling, Finuala (1962–) Born in Cape Town to parents who worked as radio presenters, Dowling studied English at the university there, and wrote a doctoral dissertation that was later published as *Fay Weldon's Fiction* (Fairleigh Dickinson University Press, 1998). She has been a lecturer at the University of South Africa in Pretoria, and is now a freelance writer. *I Flying* (2002), the first collection of her poignant, humorous, personal poems—which she describes as having a 'favoured tragic-comic pitch'—was published by Gus *Ferguson's Carapace imprint and won the Ingrid Jonker Prize. *Doo-Wop Girls of the Universe* (Penguin, 2006) won the Sanlam Award for Poetry, and *Notes from the Dementia Ward* (Kwela/Snailpress, 2008) won the Olive Schreiner Prize. She has also published three novels, beginning with *What Poets Need* (2005).   JNT

Downie, Freda (1929–93) Born in London and educated in Northampton, Australia, and Kent. Her first pamphlet collection, *Night Music*, appeared in 1974, and she subsequently published several small-scale editions of her poetry—including *Even the Flowers* (1989)—as well as two full collections: *A Stranger Here* (1977) and *Plainsong* (1981—both Secker).

Freda Downie's poems—elegant, full of gently spiked irony, and oblique, wistful glances at everyday events and familiar landscapes—relish oddity, sometimes skirmishing with the whimsical, but their hallmark is a sharp, controlling intelligence which seldom permits mere eccentricity. Her poem 'Pastime' carries an epigraph from Montaigne—'When I play with my cat, who knows if I am not a pastime to her more than she is to me?'—and this kind of unsettling, contemplative wisdom gives her writing its distinctive edge. As she observes in the title-poem of *A Stranger Here*: 'I wait, every detail waits | For something—for someone recognizable | Approaching with special lotions and explanations.' In her best poems the lotions and explanations she provides herself are refreshingly unexpected. Her *Collected Poems* (1995) were edited George *Szirtes. See also *There'll Always Be an England*, a memoir of her childhood written during the last year of her life (2003—both Bloodaxe).   JM

Dransfield, Michael (1948–73) Divided his life between 'bohemian' areas of his native Sydney and restless motor-bike wanderings round rural east-coast Australia. His poetry reflects the division. Hailed as a harbinger of a Sixties poetic—urban-based; aesthetically, socially, and politically radical—he became a major figure in the 'new' poetry promoted by the University of Queensland Press Paperback Poets and the anthologies of Thomas *Shapcott, *Australian Poetry Now* (Sun, 1969) and John *Tranter, *The New Australian Poetry* (Makar, 1979). However, his city poems speak tellingly of personal and social anomy, of angry despair at environmental degradation and the Vietnam War, and of the ecstasies and desolations of drug-taking. From the beginning he turned to the city's antonym for contrast; not, however, to the bush of social realism, but to idealized lost worlds, those of the cultured graziers of 'Courland Penders' and the spiritually rich aboriginal inhabitants ('On the Land').

In 1973 Dransfield died of a drug-related tetanus infection, leaving the largely prepared *Memoirs of a Velvet Urinal* and some 600 poems. Rodney *Hall's literary executorship culminated in *Collected Poems of Michael Dransfield* (University of Queensland Press, 1990). For a retrospective view of this 'Rimbaud of the suburbs', see 'Remembering Michael Dransfield', in *Literary Memoirs: Biting the Bullet*, by Thomas Shapcott (Simon & Schuster, 1990). *Michael Dransfield: A Retrospective* (University of Queensland Press, 2002) is a selection of the poems made by John *Kinsella.   JS

Draycott, Jane (1954–   ) Born in London, Draycott studied at Kings College, London, and Bristol University. She has frequently worked collaboratively with visual and sound artists, and currently teaches on the creative writing programme at Oxford University. Draycott's pamphlet, *No Theatre* (Smith/Doorstop, 1996), was shortlisted for the Forward Prize for Best First Collection in 1997: an unusual accolade for a pamphlet. Her first full-length collection appeared two years later: *Prince Rupert's Drop* (Oxford University Press, 1999) established Draycott as a poet of tact, concision and careful craft, especially evident in 'Braving the Dark', an elegy for her brother. In 2000, as poet in residence at the River and Rowing Museum, Draycott worked with the Thames watermen, and the resulting poems were collected in a beautifully produced pamphlet, *Tideway* (Two Rivers, 2002). Some of this work reappeared in her second full-length book, *The Night Tree* (2004). By turns sensuous and austere, the poems in *Over* (2009) drew comparisons with the artistry of Vermeer and Hammershøi, and the collection was shortlisted for the T. S. Eliot Prize. Draycott's translation of the anonymous fourteenth-century poem *Pearl* appeared in 2011 (all Oxford Poets/Carcanet).   PBa

Drinkwater, John (1882–1937) Born in Leytonstone, London. He was one of those poets who may safely be described as quintessentially *Georgian, and he is well represented in all five volumes of *Georgian Poetry*. But his work, unlike that of *Graves, *de la Mare, and even (very occasionally) J. C. *Squire, has failed to last. He had a more distinguished theatrical career. At 25 he met Barry Jackson, and with him formed the Pilgrim Players, which led to the founding of the Birmingham Repertory Theatre, of which Drinkwater became manager in 1913. The Pilgrims gave his first verseplay, *Cophetua* (1913); and this was followed in 1918 by the highly successful *Abraham Lincoln*, given by the Repertory. Although the verse of this, and others resembling it, was flat and undistinguished, it had competence, and played well enough in its time. Drinkwater produced a stream of popular biographies and autobiographies. His greatest interest in later life was philately, and he owned a notable collection. See *Collected Poems* (1923); *Collected Plays* (1925—both Sidgwick).   MS-S

Driver, C. J. (Charles Jonathan) (1939–) Born in Cape Town, the son of a clergyman-schoolmaster. He was educated at St Andrews College, Grahamstown, the University of Cape Town, and Trinity College, Oxford.

As an active participant in student politics, and president of the National Union of South African Students, Driver was detained in 1964 under a ninety-day detention law. While at Oxford (1965–7) his South African passport was withdrawn, effectively forcing him into exile. He has been a teacher in Kent and Humberside, a headmaster in Hong Kong, at Berkhamstead School, Hertfordshire, and at Wellington College, Berkshire. He is now a full-time writer.

Driver's poems are characterized by a search for a home, both actual and artistic, as a way of finding meaning, defeating time, and overcoming a lurking sense of absurdity in ordinary life. They sometimes seem occasional, and at times self-conscious, but this is offset by a rigorous honesty and a careful craftsmanship that is nevertheless always aware of aspects of human experience the craft cannot fully tap.

He is better-known as a novelist than a poet, having published four novels, the best-known of which are *Elegy for a Revolutionary* (1969) and *Send War in Our Time, O Lord* (1971), both of which were banned by the South African authorities. His volumes of poetry include *Occasional Light*, published in a Mantis edition with Jack Cope (David Philip, 1979), *I Live Here Now* (Lincoln and Humberside Arts, 1979), and *In the Water-Margins* (1994). See *Selected Poems, 1960–2004* (2005—both Snailpress).   KG

Dubie, Norman (1945–) Raised in isolated communities in New England with books for entertainment. A graduate of Goddard College and the University of Iowa, he has come to write some of the most learned and allusive poetry of his generation. His poems are most often based on stories and characters drawn from history, literature, and art. In technique he is a postmodernist and feels free to alter and combine his materials according to the demands of the imagination; at the beginning of his *Selected and New Poems* (Norton, 1983) he quotes Randall *Jarrell approvingly: 'What the wish wants to see, it sees.' In choosing his materials,

Dubie favours the nineteenth century and often turns to Russia. His first book, *Alehouse Sonnets* (University of Pittsburgh Press, 1971), which he has repudiated, engages the poet in a dense, amusing, and learned dialogue with William Hazlitt; characters from twentieth-century Vermont intermingle with others from nineteenth-century England.

A listing of subjects from another of Dubie's books, *The City of the Olesha Fruit* (Doubleday, 1979), indicates the range of his interests: in 'The Infant', the dead Kafka is berated by his father; in 'The Seagull', Chekhov meditates in his garden at Yalta; in 'The Old Asylum of the Narragansetts' we see the everyday life of an early American Puritan settlement; 'The Ambassador Diaries of Jean de Bosschere and Edgar Poe' is addressed to Conrad *Aiken and draws parallels between his life and theirs.

Dubie became a practising Tibetan Buddhist in the 1990s. After *Radio Sky* (Norton, 1991) he did not publish a new volume until *The Mercy Seat: Collected and New Poems* (2001). Collections since include: *Ordinary Mornings of a Coliseum* (2004), *The Insomniac Liar of Topo* (2007), and *The Volcano* (2010—all Copper Canyon). He is Regents Professor of English at Arizona State University, where he has taught since 1975.   PS

Dudek, Louis (1918–2001) Born and educated in Montreal, receiving his BA from McGill University in 1939. Upon graduating, Dudek looked for work as a journalist and tried his hand at freelance writing before settling into a job in advertising. His early poems began to appear in 1941–2 in the *McGill Daily*, and at about the same time he became involved with the group editing the avant-garde magazine *First Statement*, which marked the beginning of a long history of active participation in the little-press and little-magazine movement in Montreal. In 1944 he married Stephanie Zuperko and moved to New York City, where he studied history and comparative literature at Columbia University. In 1951 Dudek returned to Montreal and took up an appointment in the English department at McGill University where he spent the rest

of his academic career. In the following year, Dudek, together with Raymond *Souster and Irving *Layton, launched Contact Press—destined to become one of the most important little presses in Canada—with the publication of a joint collection of their poetry, *Cerberus*. At the same time, Dudek became involved with a series of avant-garde literary magazines: *Contact* in 1952; *CIV/n* in 1954; and finally his own poetry magazine, *Delta* (1957–66). He was also a co-founder of the little press Delta Canada (1963–71).

Dudek's own poetry, which was characterized initially by colloquial lyricism and strong social concerns, as evidenced in *East of the City* (Ryerson, 1946), developed into the long, meditative statement that began with *Europe* (Porcupine's Quill, 1954), and went on to *The Transparent Sea* (1956) and *En Mexico* (1958—both Contact). He had become (much like his friend and correspondent, Ezra *Pound) a writer concerned with preserving civilization and the values of serious art. Repelled by the literary histrionics and cultural excesses of the 1960s, Dudek retreated into his own work, publishing a long and ruminative poem, *Atlantis*, in 1967 and a *Collected Poetry* (both Delta) in 1971. Between 1965 and 1969 he wrote reviews and a column on the arts for the two English-language dailies in Montreal. In 1967 he co-edited (with Michael Gnarowski) *The Making of Modern Poetry in Canada*. This was followed by several volumes of essays and criticism.

The later Dudek, as exemplified in *Continuation!* (1981) and *Continuation!!* (1990—both Véhicule), is someone engaged in writing 'the poem without end', which takes the form of recording the fragmentary, poetic instant, and suggests a natural creative process rather than the willed structures of conventional poetics. *Infinite Worlds* (Véhicule, 1988), the definitive selected poetry, was edited by Robin *Blaser, while his cultural journalism was collected as *In Defence of Art* (Quarry, 1988).

Dudek's *Notebooks 1940–1994* (1994) and 1998 'definitive edition' of his own poems were published by Golden Dog Press. His later volumes of poetry include

The Caged Tiger (1997) and *The Surface of Time* (2000—both Empyreal). *All These Roads: The Poetry of Louis Dudek* (Wilfrid Laurier University Press, 2008) is a short selection edited by Karis Shearer. For criticism, and an interview with the poet, see *Louis Dudek: Essays on His Works* (Guernica, 2001), ed. George Hildebrand.   MG

Duffy, Carol Ann (1955–) Born in Glasgow, she spent her childhood in Staffordshire, graduating in philosophy from the University of Liverpool in 1977. She first attracted attention with the lively, well-crafted dramatic monologues of *Standing Female Nude* (1985). A number of successful collections followed, culminating in *The World's Wife* (1999—both Anvil), a work which attractively developed a device popular with earlier feminist writers, that of giving a voice to the forgotten women in the lives of male mythological figures. The social criticism of her poetry is never mere polemic, but is channelled through the sensibilities—and sometimes the rich fantasy-lives—of various characters: the artist's model of 'Standing Female Nude', frazzled housewives, lager-sodden husbands, nervy young delinquents, gifted but unrecognized schoolteachers. Some of her finest work is in the genre which eschews direct social commentary—the personal elegy.

A gifted dramatist as well as poet, Duffy combines lyric intensity with vernacular-rich plain-speaking. Her further publications include *Feminine Gospels* (2002), *New Selected Poems* (2004—both Picador), *New and Collected Poems for Children* (Faber, 2009), and *The Bees* (Picador, 2011). A rather florid collection of love-poems, *Rapture* (Picador), received the T. S. Eliot Prize in 2005. Appointed UK Poet Laureate in 2009, Carol Ann Duffy has demonstrated in subsequent occasional and commissioned poems that she is genuinely a people's poet, and not to any degree a courtier. She has developed into an innovative performer, whose collaborations with the musician and composer John Sampson are highly popular with both adult and younger audiences. She has also edited several anthologies and made a

selection of Sylvia *Plath's poetry. For criticism, see Deryn Rees-Jones, *Carol Ann Duffy* (Northcote House, 1999).   CAR

Dugan, Alan (1923–2003) Born in New York and worked as a staff member at the Fine Arts Work Centre at Provincetown, Massachusetts. His first book, *General Prothalamion in Populous Times* (1961), was privately printed, but his second, *Poems* (Yale University Press, 1961) won both the Yale Younger Poets Award and the Pulitzer Prize, and was greeted with unusually wide praise. The stark, usually unrhymed poems in this and succeeding volumes have been aptly described as 'directly stated, dry, bleak'. They were fluent, but the gloomy poet distrusted his own fluency, and questioned himself in every way: 'I guess there is a garden named | "Garden of Love". If so, I'm in it | I am the guesser in the garden.'

Apart from faintly echoing (or resembling) Robert *Creeley's laconic manner, Dugan's work offered a sharp contrast to contemporary American poetry at the time, being on the one hand formal and over-academic, and on the other loose to the point of spilling into undisciplined, impressionistic prose. Dugan was disciplined, but eschewed both extremes, and tended only to write when he was moved to do so. Greatly respected for his honesty and restraint, he disappointed only inasmuch as he did not develop (or try to develop)— almost as if he regarded the notion of development as a kind of artificiality. What has been called the 'stinging note of self-contempt' remained apparent, and so did an extreme pessimism: we are offered the conscientious and intelligent reportage of a spirit which sees itself as dead, or about to die: 'Oh it is here | that I propose to build | it, the Cathedral "Abattoir" ...' See *Poems 7: New and Complete Poetry* (Seven Stories, 2001), which won the National Book Award.   MS-S

Duggan, Eileen (1894–1972) The fourth daughter of Irish immigrant parents from County Kerry, was born in the small settlement of Tua Marina in the South Island province of Marlborough, New Zealand. She attended Wellington Teachers' College and Victoria University College in Wellington, and taught for a brief period before becoming a freelance journalist. For forty-five years she edited 'Pippa's Page' for women in the *New Zealand Tablet*.

Duggan's first two small volumes of poetry, *Poems* (1922) and *New Zealand Bird Songs* (1929), were published in New Zealand, while the subsequent three, *Poems* (1937), *New Zealand Poems* (1940), and *More Poems* (1951), were published in England and America. For some time she was New Zealand's best-known poet, and certainly the first to be internationally recognized. Yet there has never been a collected edition of her poetry. Complicated circumstances also resulted in her omission from the two important New Zealand anthologies edited by Allen *Curnow.

Duggan's profound religious faith is central to her poetry. Many of her early poems were concerned with Ireland and its dispossessed people. There is, however, no sense of exile from 'Home'. She was firmly committed to New Zealand; many of her poems focus on her feelings for its people, both Maori and Pakeha, its emerging nationalism, and the landscape which provided her with appropriate symbols and imagery. A number of her ballads celebrate the strength and courage of pioneer women, while she was also one of the first New Zealand writers to incorporate Maori myth and language into her poetry. Her work is uneven, at times marred by an old-fashioned literariness and an excessive romanticism. At its best, for example in her best-known lyric, 'The tides run up the Wairau', it achieves an impressive economy of thought and image. See *Selected Poems* (Victoria University Press, 1994).   GB

Duggan, Laurie (1949–) Born in Melbourne and studied at Monash University (with a brief sojourn at the University of Sydney). He has had various occupations: lecturing in media studies at Swinburne College, the Canberra College of Advanced Education, and Griffith University, Brisbane (where he was also writer-in-residence), freelancing as a script-writer (1977–82), and writing art criticism for *The Times on Sunday*. From 1994 to 1997 he was poetry editor of *Meanjin*. Like many Australian poets of his generation, Duggan was drawn to modernism in its American embodiment: *Pound is an obvious forebear, but Duggan's commitment to open forms, his play with fragmentation, and his fascination with popular culture show an affinity with William Carlos *Williams and the *New York School. Lyricism and satire have been Duggan's touchstones from his first collections, *East* (Kenny, 1976) and *Under the Weather* (Wild and Woolley, 1978). *Adventures in Paradise* (1982) shows him trying a relaxed, amusing autobiographical poem; it marks the culmination of *The Great Divide* (Hale, 1985).

With *The Ash Range* (Picador, 1987; repr. Shearsman, 2005), Duggan ventured into a longer, more complex work, what he calls an epic in Pound's sense, a 'poem including history'. The work is a collage in verse and prose of journal entries, newspaper clippings, local histories, and other documents relating to Gippsland culture and history: while its content is solidly Australian, its technique has been learned from the *Black Mountain school.

In *The Epigrams of Martial* (Scripsi, 1989), Duggan proved himself to be an incisive translator; many of the poems allude to contemporary writers and literary politics, and are wickedly funny. *Blue Notes* (Picador, 1990) also contains translations from the Italian, chiefly of Ardengo Soffici, and revisits the epigram and the lyric.

Mangroves (2003) won the Australian Literature Society Gold Medal, and *The Passenger* (2006) won the Judith Wright Calanthe Award. See *New and Selected Poems* (1996—all University of Queensland Press) and *Compared to What: Selected Poems* (2005), published in the UK by Shearsman. The quick, diaristic lyrics of *Crab & Winkle* (2009) and *The Pursuit of Happiness* (2012—both Shearsman) reflect Duggan's recent move to south-east England. See also his study *Ghost Nation: Imagined Space and Australian Visual Culture, 1901–1939* (University of Queensland Press, 2001).   KH*

Duhig, Ian (1954–) Born in London to Irish parents and studied at Leeds University.

For fifteen years he worked with homeless people. He has held writing fellowships at universities in the North of England and at Trinity College, Dublin, and was a *New Generation poet.

In 1987, Duhig won the National Poetry Competition with 'Nineteen Hundred and Nineteen', which later appeared in his debut, *The Bradford Count* (Bloodaxe, 1991). The poem ventriloquizes 'Manuel Palafox', a Mexican revolutionary who writes disrespectfully to various famous figures, and turns out to be the unlikely model for W. B. *Yeats' 'Crazy Jane' poems. The twist is typical of Duhig's postmodernist wit, which he mixes with broad humour. As in the work of Paul *Muldoon and Paul *Durcan, the solemn invocation of Irish literature and mythology by Yeats—and, latterly, Seamus *Heaney—is burlesqued. Duhig's writing nevertheless values the poetry of arcane knowledge, as in 'From the Irish', which translates Petrarchan similes into the earthy etymologies of Gaelic ('your hair is the colour of a lake's bottom'), or the more sinister lyricism of 'The Lammas Hireling', which draws its dramatic allegory of guilt from agricultural folklore.

Duhig's second-generation perspective on his Catholic immigrant ancestry has sympathies with that of his late friend, the Irish-American Michael *Donaghy, whom he elegizes as 'one of we hyphenated people' in *The Speed of Dark* (Picador, 2007). His other collections are *The Mersey Goldfish* (1994), *Nominies* (1998—both Bloodaxe), *The Lammas Hireling* (2003), and *Pandorama* (2010—both Picador).   JNT

Duncan, Robert (1919–88) Born in Oakland, California. After his mother died he was adopted by a couple who practised orthodox theosophy. He attended the University of California at Berkeley, then spent several years in New York City as part of Anais Nin's circle. After a brief marriage, he returned to Berkeley for graduate work. In 1951 he met the artist Jess Collins, with whom he lived until his death. During the Sixties Duncan was among the most vocal of the poets writing against the Vietnam War. He also wrote a pioneering gay rights essay, 'The Homosexual in Society' (1944).

Duncan's oeuvre constitutes a sustained and powerful exploration of visionary possibilities. Resolutely clinging to a high, at times archaic style, tempered only by the quirks of spelling associated with the *Beats, he produced a large body of poetry charged with mystical energies, celebrating modes of transcendence ranging from the erotic and the aesthetic to the religious. His inspiration derives from poets like Pindar, Dante, and Blake, and from more recent experimental writers like *Stein, *Pound, and especially H. D. (Hilda *Doolittle), about whom he wrote a critical book. But he is most immediately associated with the group of poets gathered under Charles *Olson's tutelage at *Black Mountain College in North Carolina, where Duncan briefly taught, and his friends in the *San Francisco Renaissance group. Through Olson's theories of projective verse Duncan came to his own understanding of poetic form as process rather than shape or structure; this, together with his Neo-Platonic concern with higher vision, accounts for the general murkiness of his work, its way of moving from topic to topic without providing clear narrative or logical links. At times this penchant for flowing leads to long, amorphous dithyrambs that offer no clear subject beyond a vague mysticism.

His books include *The Opening of the Field* (Grove, 1960; Cape, 1969), and *Ground Work II: In the Dark* (1987), which was reprinted with *Ground Work: Before the War* in a single volume introduced by Michael *Palmer (2006). Robert J. Bertholf has edited a *Selected Poems* (1993) and *A Selected Prose* (1995—all New Directions). Duncan's correspondence with Denise *Levertov was published by Stanford University Press in 2003, and the complete text of *The H. D. Book* by University of California Press in 2012. For a study of Duncan's work, see Mark Andrew Johnson, *Robert Duncan* (Twayne, 1988) and also the biography by Lisa *Jarnot, *Robert Duncan: The Ambassador from Venus* (University of California Press, 2012). A *Collected Writings* is forthcoming from University of California Press.   RG*

Dunmore, Helen (1952–) Born in Yorkshire. After graduating from the

University of York in 1973, she spent some time teaching in Finland, and now lives in Bristol. As demonstrated by her first collection, *The Apple Fall* (Bloodaxe, 1983), Dunmore's ear for phrasing and cadence gives cohesion to her informally structured poems, and is combined with a strong visual, even cinematic, sense. Her poems often give the effect of a panning movement between distance and close detail. Although at times a sharp miniaturist, she is usually at her best in more expansive, medium-length forms. Despite her preoccupation with the organic and domestic worlds and with maternity, political concerns are registered as they impinge on private space, both in the poems and novels. While continuing to write poetry, Dunmore has produced a significant body of fictional writing for both adults and children. Her first adult novel, *Zennor in Darkness* (Viking, 1993), won the McKitterick Prize in 1994, and *A Spell of Winter* won the Orange Prize for Fiction in 1995. Her collections of poetry, all from Bloodaxe, include *The Sea Skater* (1986); *The Raw Garden* (1988); *Short Days, Long Nights* (1991), and *Out of the Blue: Poems 1975–2001* (2001).   CAR

Dunn, Douglas (Eaglesham) (1942–) Born and brought up in Renfrewshire and educated at the Scottish School of Librarianship and the University of Hull, for long worked as a librarian at the University of Hull, where he met Philip *Larkin. In 1991, he became Professor of English at St Andrew's University, Fife. His widely noticed first book, *Terry Street* (1969), was regarded as coming from 'Larkin territory'—fresh and original for all that. Many lines, quoted and praised by critics for their graphic qualities, described such things as 'Old men's long underwear | (Dripping)' and (most notably) frozen dogshit, as well as other appurtenances of working-class Hull.

The bright, sour early poems were indignant, deeply felt, and full of effective description; but *Terry Street* was both poster-colour-promising and immature. Dunn's next two collections, *The Happier Life* (1972) and *Love or Nothing* (1974), disappointed most critics: it was felt that he had

failed to develop his own voice, had included too much frivolous light verse, and was too often wilfully obscure. *Barbarians* (1979) however, confirmed his reputation: he developed his technique and powers of concentration, and was more self-critical. The descriptions of physical and mental squalor had become more sharply focused and suggestive.

St Kilda's Parliament (1981) marked a further advance in its treatment of Scottish history and politics. *Elegies* (1985), a series of poems in memory of his wife, reminiscent of *Hardy's *Poems 1912–13*, was praised by Larkin for its 'subdued tender glowing lyricism', and won several prizes. The more occasional poetry of later collections (including *Northlight*, 1988) has been valued for its honest eschewal of rhetorical embellishment, as well as its colloquial formalism. *Dante's Drum-Kit* (1993) took its title from Dunn's nickname for *terza rima*, imagined as a jazz rhythm. *The Donkey's Ears*, a verse novel, and *The Year's Afternoon*, were both published in 2000. *New and Selected Poems 1964–2000* and a volume of *Essays* appeared in 2003, the year that he was awarded an OBE. Dunn has also written short fiction, translated Racine's *Andromache* (1990), and edited an anthology of *Twentieth Century Scottish Poetry* (2006—all Faber).   MS-S*

Dunn, Stephen (1939–) Born in New York City and educated at Hofstra University, the New School for Social Research, and Syracuse University. He served in the army, played professional basketball for a year, and worked as an advertising copywriter before starting a teaching career. He is a professor at Stockton State College in New Jersey.

Dunn is one of America's foremost poets of middleness, in all its aspects: social, cultural, psychological, stylistic. His poetry is consistently intelligent and even-tempered, rejecting equally the blandishments of illusion and disillusionment. He does not write with the descriptive or sensual fullness common to his generation, instead choosing to pursue a discursive style in which metaphor functions as a kind of logic. Dunn is primarily concerned with the ways we find to live in a world of other people, and hence his imagination is more moral than aesthetic, though he would no doubt find the distinction a false one. He features in his own poems as an almost comic protagonist, stumbling towards a self-conscious wisdom through a series of parabolic encounters with strangeness. Dunn's choice of reason, responsiveness, and responsibility over extravagance makes him one of the less conspicuous but more appealing poets of his generation.

Since *New and Selected Poems 1974–1994* (1994) his collections include *Loosestrife* (1996), *Different Hours* (2000), which won the Pulitzer Prize, *Local Visitations* (2003), *Everything Else in the World* (2006), and *Here and Now* (2011), as well as *What Goes On: Selected and New Poems, 1995–2009* (all Norton). See also *Walking Light: Essays and Memoirs* (Norton, 1993; revd. edn., BOA, 2001), which includes his discussion of 'the good poem'.   RG

DuPlessis, Rachel Blau (1941–) Born in Brooklyn, New York, DuPlessis earned a PhD in modernist poetry from Columbia University in 1970 and went on to lecture in English and Creative Writing at Temple University from 1975 until 2011. Alongside her poetry, DuPlessis is known for her writing on feminism, modernism, and contemporary literature. Her critical publications include *Writing Beyond the Ending: Narrative Strategies of Twentieth-Century Women Writers* (Indiana University Press, 1985); *The Pink Guitar: Writing as Feminist Practice* (Routledge, 1990); *Genders, Races, and Religious Cultures in Modern American Poetry, 1908–1934* (Cambridge University Press, 2001); and *Blue Studios: Poetry and Its Cultural Work* (University of Alabama Press, 2006). In 2002 DuPlessis received the Roy Harvey Pearce/Archive for New Poetry Prize for her lifetime contribution to American poetry and literary scholarship.

Gender is also a primary but not exclusive focus of DuPlessis' 'poetry of critique', which espouses a literary feminism concerned with politics, the social world, and questions of historical location, including 'centers of...otherness' or marginalization. There are parallels between her writing and *écriture féminine*, though DuPlessis has also criticized the restricted focus of this movement. Hers is a positive, playful poetry that seeks deliberately to undercut finality. It is constituted of as many different forms (from a *Poundian 'counter-Cantos'* to 'puppet opera') as subjects. DuPlessis has been composing her 'poem of a life', *Drafts*, since 1986, now collected in several book-length instalments from Wesleyan University Press and Salt.   ECr

Durcan, Paul (1944–) Born in Dublin and studied archaeology and medieval history at University College, Cork. In his first book, *O Westport in the Light of Asia Minor*, published in 1975, he already displayed in his zany verse-narratives the dislocated, conversational vernacular which is his hallmark. Everyday language is made disconcerting by defeating idiomatic expectation, and by whimsical titles such as 'Archbishop of Kerry to have Abortion'. Beginning with the Patrick Kavanagh Award in 1974, Durcan has enjoyed considerable and increasing recognition, culminating in the prestigious Whitbread Poetry Prize for *Daddy, Daddy* (1990). His work has been variously characterized as mystical, surrealist, or facetious. Despite his violent yoking together of heterogeneous ideas and registers (biblical repetition in colloquial contexts, for example), his vivid narratives are more atmospheric than metaphysical. The principal difficulty is deciding how seriously to take the poetry's politics, and how far the narrator of these extravagant stories is to be identified with the poet. There is no doubting Durcan's genuine compassion, for example in the impressive poems about his broken marriage in *The Berlin Wall Café* (1985). He has plausibly been called feminist, and his opposition to the violence of contemporary Northern Ireland is unwavering. Despite the success of some earlier volumes, including two selections—*The Selected Paul Durcan* (1982) and *Jesus and Angela* (1988)—*Daddy, Daddy* was greeted as a major advance in range and seriousness. It was followed in 1991 by *Crazy About Women* (The National Gallery of Ireland). From 1982 his primary publisher was The Blackstaff Press in

Belfast, and, since *A Snail in My Prime* (1993), Harvill in London.

Durcan's prolific later work includes *Christmas Day* (1996), a long poem plus a tribute to Seamus *Heaney, 'A Goose in the Frost'; *Greetings to Our Friends in Brazil* (1999), which includes his response to the 1998 bombing in Omagh; *Cries of an Irish Caveman* (2001); *The Art of Life* (2004); and *The Laughter of Mothers* (2009), on his own mother, who was the niece of John Mac-Bride, executed after the Easter Rising of 1916. *Life is a Dream: Forty Years of Reading Poems* (Random House, 2009) is a selected volume whose title reflects Durcan's popularity as a performer. Between 2004 and 2007 he was the Ireland Professor of Poetry. His latest volume is *Praise in Which I Live and Move and Have My Being* (Harvill, 2012).   BO'D*

Durrell, Lawrence (1912–90) Born in India to an English-Irish family. Although sent back to England for a conventional education, Durrell turned naturally to bohemianism. The eccentric life he lived in childhood and manhood is best known through his zoologist brother Gerald's autobiographical books, and via his own celebrations of places and people, including travel books on Corfu and Rhodes, letters and memoirs of Henry Miller, and that *tour-de-force* of diablerie, *The Black Book* (1938). In many ways, Durrell resembles the British poets of the last century who lived expatriate lives but directed their works back to their homeland—Browning, Landor, Eugene Lee-Hamilton—with the necessary rider that Durrell has always seen Americans and English-speaking Continentals as part of his audience. His tangential relationship with England (he never lived there for any length of time) did not prevent his being employed in various official British capacities, both in wartime and after, chiefly in the Eastern Mediterranean. Durrell's novels, travel books, and comic forays into diplomatic life are better known than his verse. Indeed, the author of *The Alexandria Quartet* is probably not known to many of his readers as a poet.

And yet few poets of any generation have started as brilliantly as Lawrence Durrell.

His precocious early verse culminated in his first book from a major publisher, *A Private Country*, in 1943. This may claim to share with Wallace *Stevens' *Harmonium* and W. H. *Auden's *Poems* (1930) the title of most accomplished debut of the century. But Durrell was to prove more a Mendelssohn than a Mozart: his poetry did not mature and produce the masterpieces his readers had every reason to expect from such youthful achievement. Even so, his next two books, *Cities, Plains and Peoples* (1946) and *On Seeming to Presume* (1948), make the decade of the Forties a time of rich harvest for Durrell. This was the period when his celebration of Mediterranean life was coupled with a fine satirical vision of his English inheritance, and before the sway of the exotic overwhelmed his lyrical impulse.

The beauty of his early poetry, written in and about Greece and Egypt, has not staled. 'Nemea', 'At Epidaurus', and 'On Ithaca Standing' breathe the sharp-edged reality of timeless Greece, its lives and options as hard as the light of the country. The exotic had not turned into the picturesque at this juncture. Early Durrell celebrates more than the genius of place. His sequence 'The Death of General Uncebunke' is the most (perhaps the only) successful example of surrealism in British poetry, David *Gascoyne notwithstanding. His scabrous and satirical poems are brilliant, as 'The Ballad of the Good Lord Nelson' and 'Pressmarked Urgent' show. Perhaps Durrell's greatest gift is his celebration of the antinomy of past and present, of classical persistence and contemporary emotion. For this reason, 'On First Looking into Loeb's Horace' may be considered his most characteristic poem. He finds a copy of the Loeb crib of Horace's poetry annotated by a former lover's hand, and the poem is both a sympathetic analysis of the Roman poet's life, and a lament for vanished love and the Mediterranean civilization that nurtured it.

A revised edition of the *Collected Poems* was published in London in 1980, and a posthumous selection of his poems was made by Peter *Porter in 2006 (both Faber).   PNFP

Dutton, Geoffrey (Piers Henry) (1922–98) Raised on a South Australian sheep station founded by pioneer ancestors. He was a wartime pilot and English lecturer before becoming a publisher. While his social privilege, education (Magdalen College, Oxford), and extensive travels oriented him towards the culture of England and Europe, he came to realize the depth of his attachment to Australia, a subject addressed in such poems as 'A Finished Gentleman' and 'An Australian Childhood'. Retaining an antipathy for Australia's philistine timidity, he became a republican and campaigner against censorship. Only the first of seven volumes reflects his association with the self-consciously modernist *Angry Penguins* movement. Thereafter his poetry is not only accessible but unashamedly conventional. He handles rhyme with facility; the verse is assured, fluent, and usually good-humoured. His many love poems often show a metaphysical or cavalier influence. In some respects the poetry is that of a patrician gentleman, a view belied by his other writings and literary activities. His settings range from Russia to the South Pacific; a talent for description of nature is particularly evident in *Selective Affinities* (Angus, 1985). *Findings and Keepings: Selected Poems 1939–1969* (Australian Letters, 1970) collects the best of the earlier work. For the later work, see *New and Selected Poems* (Angus, 1993). He also wrote a biography of Kenneth *Slessor, whose poems he edited.   AW

Dyment, Clifford (1914–71) Born of Welsh parents in Alfreton, Derbyshire. His home town was Carleon upon Usk until, on the death of his conscripted father in 1918, his mother moved to West Bridgford, near Nottingham. Educated at Loughborough Grammar School, he then ran a cycle-shop, tried commercial travelling, and ended writing film-scripts. During the Second World War he wrote and directed military-training films; afterwards, films on civics and agriculture for the Ministry of Information. Later he worked in BBC radio and television.

Dyment's topics are nature, childhood, personal experience. Religion is also a preoccupation—mostly in the sense of questioning man's role and purpose on earth, though many samples seem purely doctrinal and devotional. His theme is the loneliness of the individual in society and in nature. He writes free and formal verse, uses traditional and modern rhyming, claiming an organic rightness of rhythm where metre deviates from expected norms. The two extremes of Dyment's work are best shown in 'The Axe in the Wood', an unrhymed sonnet, not harmfully reminiscent of Edward *Thomas, and 'The Hedgehog', in free verse. His more direct religious verse is well represented by 'Pietà'. In his last phase, he ventured into poems derived from dream experience: these were appended to his *Collected Poems* (Dent, 1970). An autobiography, *The Railway Game*, appeared in 1971.   PD

Eady, Cornelius (1954–) Born and raised in Rochester, New York, Eady studied at Empire State and Warren Wilson colleges. He now teaches at the University of Missouri, and with Toi Derricotte was a founder of *Cave Canem.

An active popularizer, Eady once edited a series of poetry T-shirts called 'The Shirt Off Your Back'. As a poet he is drawn to the aesthetics and histories of African-American musical culture. *Hardheaded Weather: New and Selected Poems* (Putnam, 2008) juxtaposes two epigraphs: 'Make it new' (Ezra *Pound) and 'Make it funky' (James Brown). His first collection was *Kartunes* (Warthog, 1980). *Victims of the Latest Dance Craze* (Ommation, 1985), a series of poems about the relationship between poetry and dance, was chosen for the Lamont Poetry Award. *You Don't Miss Your Water* (Holt, 1995) was an elegiac volume for the poet's father. *Brutal Imagination* (Putnam, 2001) included a sequence on a fictitious black man accused of a real-life crime, and a libretto, 'Running Man', which was a Pulitzer Prize for Drama finalist in 1999. See also *The Gathering of My Name* (1991) and *The Autobiography of a Jukebox* (1997—both Carnegie Mellon University Press).   JNT

Eberhart, Richard (1904–2005) Born in Austin, Minnesota, the son of a well-off mid-western businessman who worked for a meat-packing company. Eberhart graduated from high school in 1921 and briefly attended the University of Minnesota, before making his way east to Dartmouth College, where he graduated with a BA in 1926. After graduation, Eberhart had a succession of temporary jobs until he signed on to a tramp steamer to sail around the world. He eventually jumped ship and made his way to England, where he enrolled in St John's College, Cambridge, taking another BA in 1929. At Cambridge, he studied with I. A. *Richards and befriended William *Empson. Returning to the States, Eberhart studied in the graduate school at Harvard (1932–3), then took a position as an English instructor at St Mark's School, near Boston, where he taught for seven years; during this time, one of his pupils was Robert *Lowell. During the war, Eberhart served as an aerial-gunnery instructor for the US Navy. This experience led to the writing of his most famous poem, 'The Fury of Aerial Bombardment'. Eberhart married Elizabeth Butcher, the daughter of a wealthy manufacturer, just before the war; after the war he served for several years as an executive of his father-in-law's floor-wax company. Leaving the business world for academe in the early 1950s, Eberhart taught English literature at Princeton, then at Dartmouth, where he was poet-in-residence. Recognition came slowly to Eberhart, though he had an early champion in F. R. Leavis, who was reminded of Blake when he read Eberhart's compact early lyrics, such as 'For a Lamb' and 'The Groundhog'. Leavis also noted a mystical strain in Eberhart which continued.

Eberhart's collections of poetry were usually greeted with mixed reviews; critics have most often complained of unevenness in the volumes, which contain too many ill-formed, awkward poems. But he was widely praised for his best work, which is marked by a peculiar fierceness, a willingness to grapple with issues of human mortality and sin. Eberhart's poems are often set in highly symbolic, northern landscapes. In later years the coast of Maine was often the setting for his work, as in *The Long Reach* (New Directions, 1984). In all, Eberhart published nearly thirty books after *A Bravery of Earth*, his first volume, appeared in 1930. His *Collected Poems, 1930–1986* (Oxford University Press, 1986), is the most comprehensive collection of his work. Among his numerous awards and prizes were the Bollingen Award (1962), the Pulitzer Prize for Poetry (1966), and the National Book Award (1977). In addition to the poetry, Eberhart also wrote verse dramas and criticism. For criticism of his work, see Joel Roache, *Richard Eberhart* (Oxford University Press, 1971) and Bernard F. Engel, *Richard Eberhart* (Twayne, 1971).   JP

Echeruo, Michael (1937–) Born in Okigwi in the Owerri Province of the former East Central State of Nigeria. After studying at Stella Maris College, Port Harcourt, and at the newly established University College of Ibadan, he embarked on a career as a university teacher, firstly at the University of Nigeria at Nsukka, then back at Ibadan, where he held the chair of English. He is now a professor in the English department at Syracuse University, New York. He took further degrees at Cornell University, and has some distinction as a critic, especially of English fiction in its relation to Africa, his 1973 study *Joyce Cary and the Novel of Africa* being probably his *chef-d'oeuvre*. But in the early Sixties he slowly established a reputation as a poet in a quiet, if erudite, mould, contributing to one of the early issues of the journal *Black Orpheus*, and publishing the collection *Mortality* with Longman in 1968. He has been compared to his fellow countryman Christopher *Okigbo, but where Okigbo is a poet of cycles, Echeruo is a poet of moods: declining seasons, the crisis and promise of death. Throughout *Mortality* the controlling images are of autumn and harvest, the melancholy and fruitfulness of which are explored in their private, mythic, and political dimensions.

Mortality was reprinted in Nigeria alongside other poems in 1995 (I. K. Imprints). In 1998, Echeruo published the first comprehensive Igbo-English dictionary, and in 2008 a concordance to Okigbo's poetry.   RF

Edgar, Stephen (1951–) Born in Sydney. From 1971 to 1974 he lived in London, working as a library assistant. After returning to Australia, he worked in libraries in Sydney and Hobart. He read classics at the University of Tasmania, graduating BA in 1978 and Dip. Lib. in 1985.

To date, Edgar has published seven collections of poetry, beginning with *Queuing for the Mudd Club* (Twelvetrees, 1985). Amongst his generation of Australian poets, he is distinctive for a firm commitment to closed forms and for showing considerable panache in handling them. Although he draws strength, in this regard, from writers as various as *Frost, Gwen *Harwood, A. D. *Hope, and *Stevens, his voice is in no way muted by theirs. His writing is by turns lyrical and meditative, guided by music as an exemplary discipline, yet drawn towards exuberance and phantasmagoria. Three main themes recur in his work: rereadings of folk-tales (Sleeping Beauty, the Pied Piper, and Bluebeard); the dislocations and fitful illuminations offered by travel; and the pathos arising from family relations. Throughout his work mordant (and sometimes hilarious) observations of contemporary culture cut figures against a background of classical myth. In 2006, he was awarded the Phillip *Hodgins Memorial Medal. See *History of the Day* (Black Pepper, 2009). *The Red Sea* (Baskerville, 2012), published in the States, is a new and selected volume.   KH

Edmond, Lauris (1924–2000) Born in Hawkes Bay, New Zealand, and educated at Victoria University. She said she always wrote poems and kept them in the cupboard, but her first published book came out only in 1975. After that she was very prolific, and *Summer Near the Arctic Circle* (1988) was her ninth collection.

Edmond is a personal poet; her most memorable successes—such as 'Epitaph' from *Salt from the North* (1980—both Oxford University Press) and 'Hymns Ancient and Modern' from *Seasons and Creatures* (Bloodaxe, 1986)—are about family tragedy or happiness. The poetry's prevailing tone is one of humane observation, expressed in quiet, direct language. Later volumes were divided into three sections, dealing with travel, ageing, and family. But her best poems (such as 'The Outward and Visible Signs' from *Summer Near the Arctic Circle*) cross over all such categoric boundaries as they become a remarkable kind of wisdom poetry.

Edmond was awarded an OBE in 1986, and in 1999 she received the A. W. Reed Award for Contribution to New Zealand Literature. Her anthology of *New Zealand Love Poems* (Oxford University Press, 2000) and her final volume, *Late Song* (Auckland University Press, 2001), both appeared posthumously. See *Selected Poems* (2001), ed. K. O. Arvison and *Lauris Edmond: An Autobiography* (2nd edn., 2001—both Bridget Williams). BO'D

Edmond, Murray (1949–) Born in Hamilton, New Zealand. He took a degree at Auckland University in 1971, and since then has worked in theatre, publishing poetry at regular intervals. In the late Sixties and early Seventies he published in, and edited, two issues of the short-lived magazine *The Word Is Freed*, whose title displays its generation's messianic hopes. In 1974–6 Edmond lived in England and toured Europe, then returned to New Zealand, where he continued to work in experimental and educational theatre. He was writer-in-residence at Canterbury University, Christchurch, in 1983. Since 1985 he has taught at Auckland University, where he wrote a doctoral thesis on experimental theatre in New Zealand. Edmond has written several plays and a full-length musical, *A New South Pacific*.

Edmond's own writing is rhapsodic and linguistically dense, with dramatic and narrative qualities which owe much to his life in the theatre. His books of poetry include *Entering the Eye* (Caveman, 1973); *Patchwork* (Hawk, 1978); *End Wall* (Oxford University Press, 1981); and *Letters and Paragraphs* (Caxton, 1987). With his wife, Mary Paul, he edited *The New Poets: An Anthology of Initiatives in Recent New Zealand Poetry* (1987), and, with Alan Brunton and Michele *Leggott, *Big Smoke: New Zealand Poems 1960–1975* (2000), which includes his essay on the history of innovative poetry in New Zealand, 'Poetics of the Impossible'. Edmond's latest collections are *Fool Moon* (2004) and *Walls to Kick and Hills to Sing From: A Comedy with Interruptions* (2010—all Auckland University Press). IW

Edson, Russell (1935–) Born in New York City, son of Gus Edson, a cartoonist who drew Andy Gump. An accomplished print-maker himself, Edson showed his talent early, winning at 16 the Kimon Nicolaides Scholarship at the Art Students League in New York, an event which triggered his leaving school in the tenth grade. He studied writing briefly at Black Mountain College before settling in Connecticut with his wife Frances. His 21 books include a collection of plays and a novel, though he is most celebrated for his prose poems for which he has received a Guggenheim and three National Endowment for the Arts Fellowships. Edson's poems are brief, strange narratives of an inverse world. Although deeply surreal and never confessional, they have a lifelike clarity even as they record the odd and the monstrous—a man grown so fat he spills completely out of his shoes; another who tells his father he's about to marry his car. Edson's fables are grim, hopelessly comic, rich with non-sequiturs and transforming, mysterious connections. The work is an original lyric mix of Dante and Warner Brothers. *The Tunnel* (Oberlin, 1994) is representative, including new and earlier work. *See Jack* (University of Pittsburgh Press, 2009) is the most recent collection. MB

Ee, Tiang Hong (1933–90) Born in Malacca, the ancestral home-state of the Babas, or Straits-born Chinese. His birthplace figures prominently in his verse, serving as a metaphor for the early splendour and eventual decline of the Baba epoch. Ee received his education at the Universities of Malaya and Reading. He was a lifelong educationist.

Ee's early poetry was written during his undergraduate days in the 1950s. His first small collection of verse, *I of the Many Faces* (Wah Seong, 1960), pays heed to the individual's place in Malaya's plural society. In his second volume, *Lines Written in Hawaii* (East-West Culture Learning Institute, 1973), Ee's 'Malaysianness' gives way to his musings on life in general and the nature of human relationships.

Ee's Baba ancestry shaped his view of himself as a poet. The Babas, although they had assimilated the Malay tongue and culture over generations, were still identified with the more-recent immigrant Chinese. This lack of acceptance gave rise to the note of protest and the theme of dislocation which characterized Ee's best poetry, found in his third publication, *Myths for a Wilderness* (Heinemann, 1976). His disenchantment and growing feelings of helplessness at the gradual erosion of his community's roots finally caused Ee to emigrate to Perth, Australia, with his wife and four children in late 1975.

In *Tranquerah* (National University of Singapore, 1985), Ee's last book of verse, the poet, still speaking in strong Malaysian accents, re-examines his past in order to come to terms with his present status as an 'exile'. *The Second Tongue: An Anthology of Poetry from Malaysia and Singapore* (Heinemann, 1976) contains poems from Ee's third volume.   SPG

Eggleton, David (1952–) Born in Auckland and part Polynesian, Eggleton grew up in New Zealand and Fiji, and now lives in Dunedin. An internationally recognized performance poet, in 1985 he was named London 'Street Entertainer of the Year' in *Time Out* magazine. He has also won the Montana Book Reviewer of the Year award six times, and edits *Landfall* magazine.

Crowd-pleasing, wry, and energetically inventive, Eggleton's vernacular style has been credited with refreshing poetry about the New Zealand landscape ever since his debut *South Pacific Sunrise* (Penguin, 1987). 'God Defend New Zealand', for example, is a rhyming incantation against a time 'When young men no longer pick the peaches at the beaches' and 'the cow-

nipple of green Taranaki ceases to spout'. He has released several recordings of his readings. For recent work, see *Rhyming Planet* (Steele Roberts, 2001), *Fast Talker* (Auckland University Press, 2006), and *Time of the Icebergs* (Otago University Press, 2010). He has also edited an anthology of landscape writing, *Here on Earth* (1999), and written histories of rock music and modern art in New Zealand.   JNT

Eigner, Larry (1927–96) Critically palsied as a result of forceps delivery at birth, Eigner spent most of his life in bed or in a wheelchair. Until 1978 he lived with his family in Massachusetts, but then moved to Berkeley, California, where he was cared for by the poet Robert *Grenier. The example of William Carlos *Williams can be felt in Eigner's attention to detail and precision of observation. His work characteristically derives from sights and sounds in the vicinity of his home—clouds, birds, crickets, cars, rain—but words in the poems are arranged in visual patterns of great elegance and complexity, much as in the work of one of his principal masters, Charles *Olson. Eigner does not merely duplicate Olson's projectivist manner, however. In Ron Silliman's introduction to his anthology of *Language Poetry, *In the American Tree* (National Poetry Foundation, University of Maine, 1986)—dedicated to Eigner— he identifies this poet as one who has 'transcended the problematic constraints' of Olson's speech-based projectivist poetics. Eigner himself pointed out that his poetry originates in 'thinking' rather than speech.

Eigner's *Selected Poems* (Oyez) was published in 1972. Among many subsequent collections are *Things Stirring Together or Far Away* (1974) and *Waters, Places, a Time* (1983—both Black Sparrow). His critical writings were edited by Benjamin Friedlander in *Areas Lights Heights* (Roof, 1989). An earlier selection is *Quiet Harbor Quiet Act Around* (THIS Press, 1978). Some of his letters were gathered by Robert Kocik and Joseph Simas in *Larry Eigner Letters* (Moving Letters, 1987).

See Irving P. Leif, *Larry Eigner: A Bibliography of His Work* (Scarecrow, 1989). *The*

Collected Poems of Larry Eigner (Stanford University Press, 2010), in four volumes, contains over 3,000 poems, edited by Grenier and Curtis Faville to preserve the *mise-en-page* of Eigner's manual typewriter.   EHF

Elder, Anne (1918–76) Born at Auckland and moved to Australia at the age of three. In 1938 she joined the Borovansky Ballet, eventually becoming a soloist. After her marriage in 1945 she settled at Eaglemont, Melbourne. Her first poems were published in newspapers and periodicals from 1956, but near the end of the decade diffidence led her to stop writing, and she did not resume until the late 1960s. Of her three volumes of verse—*For the Record* (Hawthorn, 1972), *Crazy Woman* (Angus & Robertson, 1976), and *Small Clay Birds* (Monash University, 1988)—two were published posthumously. The last drew on the first two and on unpublished poems. Its title comes from the poem 'Apologia', where Elder spoke of the pains of translating into words 'my hard brown-shrouded seed of thoughts'. With a whimsy that she usually kept at bay, Elder called those words 'small clay birds'. More often her verse was elliptical, its tone detached but grieving as she addressed an extensive range of subjects—the death of her father and her own illness, small creatures, the ambience of Spain. The dichotomy between the 'pitiful' and the 'terrible' exercised her, as did obscure menaces to the self and unrealizable desires. Elder's small corpus is technically skilled and temperamentally melancholy; no myth has yet been made of her.   PP

Eliot, T. S. (Thomas Stearns) (1888–1965) Born in St Louis, Missouri, the youngest child of Charlotte Champe Stearns Eliot and Henry Ware Eliot, a southern businessman from a distinguished Bostonian family, then president of the Hydraulic Brick Company. Eliot's grandfather, Walter Greenleaf Eliot, was a prominent Unitarian minister who had moved from Boston to St Louis with a strong sense of educational mission, and his example cast a long shadow over Eliot's childhood and career. Eliot's schooldays were largely spent in and around St Louis, punctuated by long annual holidays on the Massachusetts coast. In 1906 he entered Harvard University and completed his BA in 1909 and MA in 1911, beginning work on a doctoral thesis on the philosophy of F. H. Bradley in 1912 (eventually published as *Knowledge and Experience in the Philosophy of F. H. Bradley*, 1964). Seemingly set on an academic career, in 1912 he was appointed an assistant in philosophy at Harvard. While a student, however, he encountered Symons' *The Symbolist Movement in Literature*, which he later described as a 'revelation', and during these years he began writing his own ironic and Bostonian versions of symbolist poems, such as 'Spleen' and 'Humoresque' after the manner of Jules Laforgue, and then his Jamesian 'Portrait of a Lady', a super-subtle adaptation of the Browning poetic monologue to the climate of the new century.

Eliot's Harvard career was interrupted by a 'romantic year' in Paris (1910–11), in which he attended Bergson's lectures on personality at the Sorbonne, took part in the demonstrations of the *camelots du roi*, a right-wing, anti-Dreyfusard organization, and became friends with Jean Verdenal, to whom he later dedicated his first book of poems. He returned to Europe again in 1914, as a travelling fellow in philosophy at Merton College, Oxford, and though neither Oxford nor academic philosophy was to prove satisfactory, England was henceforward to become Eliot's permanent home. Though he returned to the United States for brief visits in later life, this Bostonian Southerner was to spend the rest of his career in England, and it was with what he called 'the mind of Europe' rather than the literature of his native land that he chose to align himself.

It was in London in 1914 that Eliot met another émigré American poet, Ezra *Pound, the most conspicuous and successful entrepreneur of the literary and artistic experimentalism which flourished in the British capital during the period of the aggressively avant-gardiste journal *Blast* (1914) and the poetic anthology *Des *Imagistes* (1914), and associated with such figures as the writer and painter Wyndham

*Lewis, the brilliant reactionary critic T. E. *Hulme, and the iconoclastic sculptor Henri Gaudier-Brzeska. Pound, on reading Eliot's 'The Love-Song of J. Alfred Prufrock', the culminatory poem of his discreet American poetic apprenticeship, proclaimed that Eliot had 'modernized himself on *his own*' and promoted him to a starring role in the modern movement in literature. He arranged for the publication of 'Prufrock' in *Poetry* (1915), and acted as agent and editor for Eliot's work, a role that culminated in his decisive editorial contribution to *The Waste Land* (1922). Despite subsequent periods of estrangement and disagreement, Eliot was later to act as an advocate and publisher of Pound's work too, publishing his *Selected Poems* and *Cantos* with Faber, and lobbying for his release from St Elizabeth's in the late 1950s. The literary careers of the two expatriate Americans came to be profoundly intertwined.

In 1915, after a two-month courtship, Eliot married Vivien Haigh-Wood, an English girl from a conventional upper-middle-class family. The marriage, though it was to prove extremely unhappy, contributed to Eliot's commitment to living in England as well as to his unnerving vision of marital unhappiness in poems and plays. During this difficult time Eliot earned a living, first as a schoolteacher in High Wycombe and Highgate, then, after 1917, in the colonial and foreign department of Lloyd's Bank in London. In his spare time he continued to oscillate between literature and philosophy. Through his friendship with Bertrand Russell he did some reviewing for philosophical journals, while in the evenings he gave lectures on literature, including a course on modern French literature in 1916. After several unsuccessful attempts to be inducted into the US Navy in 1918, Eliot found himself representing Lloyd's Bank in the complex financial negotiations involved in the Treaty of Versailles at the close of the war. At the same time, with the publication by *The Egoist* of *Prufrock and Other Observations* (1917), the harvest of his first and primarily American poetic phase, Eliot's literary career finally began to take shape. It was followed by the publication of *Poems* (1919) and *Ara Vos Prec* (1920), which included 'Sweeney among the Nightingales' and 'Burbank with a Baedeker: Bleistein with a Cigar', as well as the cunningly contrived historical allegory of 'Gerontion'. They mark a new stage of Eliot's poetic development, predominantly in the form of suavely grotesque exercises in lyric satire of English and European post-war culture, in the severely regular rhymed stanzas prescribed by Pound as a 'remedy' for the 'dilutation of vers libre'. As assistant editor of *The Egoist* (1917–19), Eliot was beginning to play an increasingly influential role as critic as well as poet. He published his first book of criticism, *The Sacred Wood* (1920), which through such important early essays as 'Tradition and the Individual Talent', with its notorious claim that poetry is not 'the expression of personality, but an escape from personality', and 'Hamlet', with its idea of an 'objective correlative', proved to be not only a touchstone for Eliot's poetic thinking but a milestone in the establishing of a peculiarly twentieth-century 'historical sense' of literature.

The strains of professional, literary, and personal responsibilities took a severe toll on Eliot and in 1921 he applied for leave from the bank, then suffered a physical and mental breakdown, going first to Margate and then to Lausanne to recuperate. It was in these months that he wrote the bulk of what was to become *The Waste Land* (1922). A vocal collage of 'fragments shored' against his and his culture's 'ruin', written in a musically unerring and psychologically unnerving idiom, the poem is the culmination of his early work, and its publication, in the year of the appearance of *Joyce's Ulysses*, marks the key moment in the cultural legitimation of Eliot and 'modernism'. With its hallucinatory iconography of post-war London and stammering vision of psychic disintegration, it is one of the inescapable landmarks of twentieth-century poetry. Much of Eliot's later career can be understood as an attempt to escape its consequences.

The Waste Land was published in the first issue of *The Criterion*, a cultural quarterly sponsored by Lady Rothermere, which

Eliot founded and edited until 1939. Through his commentaries in *The Criterion*, his decisive editorial role in the publishing firm of Faber and Faber, which he joined in 1925, and his contributions to other literary periodicals, Eliot soon became an established spokesman for the avant-garde, and probably the most influential literary critic of the twentieth century. In 1924 he published *Homage to John Dryden*, studies of Dryden and the metaphysical poets, which outlined the myth of a 'dissociation of sensibility' occurring in the late seventeenth century, and declared that 'poets in our civilization ... must be difficult'—views which shed as much light on Eliot's need to justify his own poetry as on earlier literary history. This was followed by *For Lancelot Andrewes: Essays on Style and Order* (1928), in which he announced himself to be 'classical in literature, royalist in politics, and Anglo-Catholic in religion'. Thereafter Eliot's criticism and poetry sought to establish an authoritative alignment with 'tradition' and 'orthodoxy of sensibility'. His *Selected Essays* (1932) confirmed his status as conservative controversialist and arbiter of his generation's taste, while with *The Use of Poetry and the Use of Criticism* (1933), a survey of poetry criticism from the Renaissance to the modern period, and the subsequently unreprinted *After Strange Gods: A Primer of Modern Heresy* (1934), a diagnosis of what he found disturbing in contemporary culture, Eliot mapped out his fatefully persuasive sense of the use of poetry and criticism in and for his time.

For Lancelot Andrewes proclaimed Eliot's unrepentantly traditionalist solutions to his problems of cultural identity. He had in fact become a member of the Anglican Church and a British citizen in 1927. In 1932/3 he partially resolved the difficulties of his troubled marriage when he formally separated from his wife Vivien, who later died in a private mental hospital in 1947. In the years following his 'conversion' he published a series of lyrical meditations on religious themes ('Journey of the Magi', 'A Song for Simeon', and 'Marina'), and with his essay on Dante (1929) and *Ash Wednesday* (1930)—a purgatorial Dantesque sequence which impersonally dramatized, in almost liturgical form, the poet's conversion crisis—Eliot's poetry entered a new phase. *The Idea of a Christian Society* (1939) articulated its theology, and 'The Music of Poetry' (1942) its poetics. With *Burnt Norton* (1936) Eliot began a series of quasi-musical and Christian meditations built around and named after places of symbolic importance to the poet, continued during the early years of the war with *East Coker* (1940), *The Dry Salvages* (1941), and *Little Gidding* (1942). They were published together as *Four Quartets* (1943), the culminating work of Eliot's later career, constructed within a rhetoric of traditional mystical paradox and permeated by a profoundly nostalgic and Anglican vision of history, culminating in a vision of seventeenth-century Little Gidding framed by the broken London of the Blitz. For some readers this represents the climax of Eliot's poetic oeuvre; for others, its anti-climactic betrayal.

Eliot's early poetry, as evinced in poems such as 'The Love Song of J. Alfred Prufrock' and *The Waste Land*, was dramatic, lyrical, ironic, and brilliantly discontinuous. His later poetry is marked by a dissociation of that precariously unified sensibility: the 'metaphysical' intelligence issued in the solemn discursiveness of *Four Quartets*, while the poetic playfulness was siphoned off into the virtuoso light verse of *Old Possum's Book of Practical Cats* (1939), and the dramatic imagination into a series of experiments in verse drama. Much of Eliot's criticism was devoted to verse theatre, and his later career was largely taken up by attempts to resurrect poetic drama in the wake of *Yeats. These began with the satirical and jazzily demotic fragment *Sweeney Agonistes* (1932), and two church plays—a laboured ecclesiastical pageant, *The Rock* (1934), and *Murder in the Cathedral* (1935), a ritual drama based on the murder of Thomas à Becket which was to prove Eliot's most theatrically effective work. There followed a set of cleverly contrived but rarely convincing attempts to reconcile Christianity and classical drama, modern poetry, and the well-made play—*The Family Reunion* (1939), *The Cocktail Party* (1950), *The Confidential Clerk* (1954), and

The Elder Statesman (1959). Though these plays earn Eliot a place in the problematic history of modern verse drama, relatively few readers have found them to succeed either as verse or drama. After *Four Quartets*, Eliot published little of poetic significance. Despite the award of the Nobel Prize for Literature and the Order of Merit in 1948, and his belated personal happiness after his marriage to Valerie Fletcher in 1957, Eliot's post-war role was very much that of an elder statesman and successful man of letters. His later prose, from 'What is a Classic' (1945) and *Notes towards the Definition of Culture* (1948) to *On Poetry and Poets* (1957), a collection of later lectures and essays, reflects his own status as a 'modern classic' and confident definer of 'culture', but has little of the polemical energy or provocative clarity of the pre-war criticism. He died on 4 January 1965, and his remains were buried at East Coker. A finally Europeanized American—and Eliot was nowhere more American than in his Europeanism—he was buried in the English village from where his family had emigrated to America in the seventeenth century.

At the end of his life Eliot noted, with characteristically sly modesty, that he would 'perhaps have a certain historical place in the literary history of our period'. It would be more truthful to say that, for better and worse, the canonical literary history of the first half of the twentieth century has been largely shaped by and around T. S. Eliot—with his contemporaries, Pound and Joyce. As poet first and foremost, but also as literary and cultural critic, playwright, and publisher, Eliot's influence on modern literature has been profound, controversial, and irreparable. Eliot's poetic output, including the belatedly published *Poems Written in Early Youth* (1950, 1967), remains relatively meagre, but his *Collected Poems 1909–62* embodies one of the most complete and cunningly contrived oeuvres in twentieth-century literature. John *Berryman named 'Prufrock' the first 'modern' poem, and *The Waste Land* quickly became established as the archetypal monument of poetic modernity in English. During his later career Eliot became a thoroughly establishment figure, an embodiment of cultural conservatism and the doyen of academic criticism. Perhaps as a result, much of the most interesting subsequent poetry and criticism in the USA and Britain appeals to other values and directions than those he came to represent, especially in these later years. Eliot's reactionary politics, religious orthodoxy, cultural élitism, and mandarin temperament have done much to render his work suspect to later readers on both sides of the Atlantic. Eliot, the Wordsworth or Tennyson of our era, has become a modern 'classic' and must suffer the fate of the classic—to be demolished and avoided for a while, in order to be resurrected in another guise.

The standard edition of Eliot's poetry comprises *Collected Poems, 1909–1962* (1963) and *Collected Plays* (1962). For his correspondence, see *The Letters of T. S. Eliot*, vol. 1, *1898–1922*, ed. Valerie Eliot (1988—all Faber). This volume was re-edited and expanded by Hugh Haughton in 2009, with a second volume for the years 1922–25, reflecting the growing scale of Eliot's professional correspondence as an editor. Further volumes seem likely to proceed at the same rate.

See also *The Waste Land* facsimile, with biographical introduction by Valerie Eliot (1971) and Helen Gardner, *The Composition of 'Four Quartets'* (1978—both Faber). There is still no satisfactory biography, but the most useful biographical introduction is *T. S. Eliot* (Hamilton, 1984), by Peter Ackroyd. See also Lyndall Gordon's two volumes, *Eliot's Early Years* (1978) and *Eliot's New Life* (1988—both Oxford University Press), published in one volume as *T. S. Eliot: An Imperfect Life* (Vintage/Norton, 1998). The best selection of his prose remains the one made by Frank Kermode (Faber, 1975). Christopher Ricks published an annotated edition of Eliot's pre-*Prufrock* manuscript, *Inventions of the March Hare: Poems 1909–1917* (Faber, 1996) and is preparing a *Complete Poems*. *The Annotated Waste Land* (Yale University Press, 2006), ed. Lawrence Rainey, adds to Eliot's own notes and reprints his contemporary prose. Since Anthony Julius' *T. S. Eliot, Anti-Semitism and Literary Form* in 1995

(Cambridge University Press; new edn., 2003, Thames & Hudson), the charge of anti-semitism in Eliot's work has been polemically levelled and denied; a balanced overview may be found in the second edition of Louis Menand's *Discovering Modernism* (Oxford University Press, 2007). Eliot's compelling development as a poet continues to attract life-and-works studies: see Denis Donoghue, *Words Alone: The Poet T. S. Eliot* (Yale University Press, 2000), Craig Raine, *T. S. Eliot* (Oxford University Press, 2006), and Colin McCabe, *T. S. Eliot* (Northcote House, 2010).   HH*

Elliot, Alistair (1932–) Born in Liverpool. Between the ages of 8 and 13 he lived, with his two sisters, in America. Subsequently he was educated at Edinburgh and Oxford, where he studied classics. From 1965 to 1967 he lived in Iran. He retired from his position at the Newcastle University Library in 1982, and immediately afterwards went back to America for a visit, writing a number of poems about the experience.

Elliot's forms are traditional, his subjects various, though travel and meditations in connection with writers of the past are favourite themes. These themes are brought together in the entertaining long poem *On the Appian Way* (1984), an account of a journey from Rome to Brindisi in the footsteps of Horace, who made the same journey in 37 BC and wrote about it in his Fifth Satire. Elliot's writing is consistently lively and unlaboured, and rhythmically subtle; the perceptions are quick, sociable, and exact. There is throughout his work a strong feeling for the continuities of European culture.

Elliot's most celebrated book is his translation of Verlaine's two clandestine volumes of erotic poetry, *Femmes/Hombres, Women/Men* (Sheep Meadow Press, 1979). Other translations are *The Lazarus Poems*, by Heinrich Heine (Carcanet, 1979) and *French Love Poems* (Bloodaxe, 1991). *My Country: Collected Poems* (1989) includes work from Elliot's first five collections and a number of previously uncollected poems. His later books include *Facing Things* (1997—both Carcanet) and *The Real Poems* (Shoestring, 2008).   TJGH

Elmslie, Kenward (1929–) Born in New York City, and grew up in Colorado Springs. His father was British and his American mother was the daughter of Joseph Pulitzer. He studied English at Harvard, and became a writer for musical theatre. He published many of the *New York School poets through his Z Press and *Z Magazine*, and has collaborated with painters and performers.

Elmslie's first collection was *Pavilions* (Tibor de Nagy, 1961). Although almost contemporary with *Koch, *O'Hara, and *Ashbery at Harvard, he only became associated with them in the 1960s, when he also met his long-term partner, the artist Joe Brainard (see *Bare Bones* (Bamberger, 1995)). *Motor Disturbance* (Columbia University Press, 1971) won the Frank O'Hara Award. *The Orchid Story* (Doubleday, 1973) is a novel.

Elmslie's verse has taken many forms in over forty publications. Camp social observation is a constant, and his background as a lyricist shows in comic rhymes, as well as the Busby Berkeley chorus rhythms of a performance piece like 'Girl Machine' ('show gets on and is a smasheroo'). His collaborations with Brainard began with *The Baby Book* (Boke) in 1965, the same year that he wrote libretti for two operas: *Lizzie Borden* and *Miss Julie*.

Routine Disruption (Coffee House, 1998) is a selection of both poems and lyrics. In 2004, Elmslie wrote and performed his own off-Broadway retrospective, *Lingo Land*. His online musical animations, including 'Girl Machine', can be viewed at kenwardelmslie.com.   JNT

Empson, William (1906–84) Born at Yokefleet Hall near Howden in Yorkshire. In 1920 he won a scholarship to Winchester College, and five years later a Milner Scholarship to Magdalene College, Cambridge, where he took mathematics. He gained a first in Part 1, but his enthusiasm had waned by the time he took Part II, when he was placed only Senior Optime. But he was unusually allowed a fourth year to read English, under the direction of I. A. *Richards; and in 1929 he gained a 'starred' first in Part I of the English Tripos.

His prospects changed forever in 1929, however, when the Master of Magdalene chose to make a scandal out of an inadvertence: contraceptives were discovered in Empson's possession, and he was debarred from taking up a Bye-Fellowship. But he promptly won himself world-wide fame by publishing his first book at the age of 24. *Seven Types of Ambiguity* (1930), 'a grammatico-critical essay' which grew out of a paper written for Richards, changed the course of literary criticism by elucidating in creative detail the effects, the meanings, and implications, achieved in English poetry. From 1931 to 1934 he taught English literature at Tokyo University of Literature and Science, in an ethos of perniciously developing nationalism. Then in July 1937 he went off to teach at the National University in Peking, where the Japanese invasion obliged him to spend two years as a refugee with the Southwest Associated Universities, ending up in the province of Yunnan. From 1940 he was with the BBC, first in the Monitoring Department and then as Chinese Editor in London (where he befriended Orwell and *MacNeice), organizing short-wave broadcasts to China and writing features for the Home Service; the effectiveness of his work stung the Nazi propagandist Hans Fritzsche into dubbing him a 'curly-headed Jew'. In 1941 he married Hetta Crouse, who bore him two sons. From 1947 to 1952 he taught at Peking University, where he was caught up in the civil war; he was trapped during the siege of Peking, and witnessed the Liberation of 1949 and the advent of Communist China. From 1953 until his retirement in 1971 he held the Chair of English Literature at Sheffield University. He was knighted in 1979.

It was the success of *Seven Types of Ambiguity* that prompted Chatto & Windus to issue *Poems* (1935), though Empson had already gained a high reputation with a selection in *Cambridge Poetry* 1929 which was singled out for praise by Leavis. Other critics were impressed by the poet's intellectual precision and the dense wit of his work. The early poetry is difficult because

Empson's apprehension of the place of science in the modern world charged his work (according to his contemporary Kathleen *Raine) with radical questions about the way in which man tries 'to impose order on fields of knowledge and experience so contradictory as to threaten the mind that contains them with disintegration—the compulsion, as Empson writes, to "learn a style from a despair"'. So far from being the product of sterile over-intellectualization, the poems strive painfully to cope with the contradictions that arise from what Empson called 'the strangeness of the world, in which we are often tripped up and made helpless'. This poetry tended to be undervalued in the 1930s because it seemed not to be engaged with the political divisions embodied in the work of *Auden and others, but later critics came to see that Empson's small body of verses concerned a subject perhaps less topical but no less profound and urgent, the need for a new imaginative synthesis in a non-traditional society. Certainly the poems of his second volume, *The Gathering Storm* (1940), are infused with a baleful sense of cultural crisis and a mood of courageous renunciation.

'I imitated Donne only, which made me appear pointlessly gawky or half undressed', he declared; arguments were what his poetry was made out of. Indeed, so many of his early poems deal with what he called the 'neurotic (uncaused) fear' of individual isolation, the wish to escape that fear through love, and the wish also to transcend the oppressive facts of the known physical world, that the challenge of new knowledge about the universe puts him in a position of remarkable affinity with Donne. He is a 'metaphysical in the root sense', as Richards insisted; not just in the sense of being witty and erudite but also in the sense of passionately enquiring into and arguing about the nature of existence and experience. Adverse critics stress his putatively impersonal concern with ideas; favourable critics, by contrast, have shown that he commands a large, humane, and stoical view of life.

*Eliot, Allen *Tate, *Betjeman, and *Larkin enormously admired his poetry; and several poets of the 1950s, notably those associated with the *Movement, took his work as a model. Robert *Lowell called him the most intelligent poet writing in the English language. But Empson ended his career as a poet when he brought out *Collected Poems* (Harcourt, Brace, 1948; Chatto & Windus, 1955).

A posthumous collection of poems is included in *The Royal Beasts and other works* (Chatto & Windus, 1986; University of Iowa Press, 1987). Empson's critical works include *Some Versions of Pastoral* (Chatto & Windus, 1935—published as *English Pastoral Poetry* in the USA), *The Structure of Complex Words* (1951), *Milton's God* (1961), *Using Biography* (1984—all Chatto & Windus), *Argufying* (Chatto & Windus/ University of Iowa Press, 1987).

See also *William Empson: The Man and His Work*, ed. Roma Gill (Routledge & Kegan Paul, 1974) and *The God Approached: A Commentary on the Poems of William Empson*, by Philip and Averil Gardner (Chatto & Windus, 1978). John Haffenden has edited *The Complete Poems of William Empson* (University Press of Florida, 2000; Penguin, 2001), as well as two collections of Empson's essays on Renaissance literature, and a selected letters. He has also written a two-volume biography: *Among the Mandarins* (2005) and *Against the Christians* (2006—all Oxford University Press).   JH

Engle, Paul (1908–91) Born in Cedar Rapids, Iowa. He attended Coe College there, graduating in 1931. He had studied for the Methodist ministry and preached at Stumptown church at the edge of town, but he heard no call and took an MA from the University of Iowa in 1932 instead. In the same year he published what may have been the first creative thesis ever submitted anywhere for a graduate degree, *Worn Earth* (AMS, 1932), in the Yale Series of Contemporary Poets. Subsequently he studied at Columbia and then travelled to Oxford on a Rhodes Scholarship, taking another set of degrees there.

In 1937 he returned to the University of Iowa as a faculty member and eventually became director of the Iowa Writers' Workshop, the oldest programme of its kind in the world. Under his aegis the Workshop became world-famous as a training ground for young writers. Towards the end of his career Engle founded Iowa's Translation Workshop which draws young poets and novelists from around the globe.

Always a traditionally formal poet, Engle's books include: *American Song* (Doubleday, 1934; Cape, 1935); *Break the Heart's Anger* (Doubleday/Cape, 1936); *New Englanders* (Engle, 1940); *West of Midnight* (1941); *American Child* (1945); *The World of Love* (1951—all Random House); *Book and Child* (Cummington, 1956); *Poems in Praise* (1959); *A Woman Unashamed and Other Poems* (1965); and *Embrace: Selected Love Poems* (1969—all Random House). Notwithstanding these and many other publications including plays and two novels, Engle has never been a celebrated poet, perhaps because he attempted generally to be popular rather than literary, as many of his titles attest. Nevertheless, he played a major role in post-Modernist poetry, for it was his workshop that provided the model for nearly every creative-writing programme in the United States.   LT

Enright, D. J. (Dennis Joseph) (1920– 2002) Born in Leamington, Warwickshire, and educated at Leamington College and Downing College, Cambridge, where he studied English under F. R. Leavis. After taking his doctorate at the University of Alexandria (1949), Enright spent many years teaching abroad in Egypt, Japan, West Berlin, Bangkok and Singapore, experiences recorded in his *Memoirs of a Mendicant Professor* (Chatto & Windus, 1969). Enright's anthology *Poets of the 1950s*, published in Japan in 1955, was a significant first gathering of *Movement poets such as *Larkin and *Amis. From 1975 to 1980 he was honorary professor of English at the University of Warwick. He was co-editor of *Encounter* from 1970 to 1972, and editorial adviser and director of Chatto & Windus from 1971 to 1982; he won the Queen's Gold Medal for Poetry in 1981.

Enrights' early poems bring a cool, undeceived voice to bear on exotic locations and subject-matter. *The Laughing Hyena and Other Poems* (Routledge & Kegan Paul,

1953), *Bread Rather Than Blossoms* (Secker & Warburg, 1956), and *Some Men Are Brothers* (Chatto & Windus, 1960) contain quizzical explorations of oddity yet are warmly humanist in tone, satirizing human pretension, endorsing the unsung kindness of those 'Rooted in precious little, without benefit of philosophy, | Who grew the rice, who deliver the goods, who | Sometimes bear the unbearable' ('Tea Ceremony'). Prolific but uneven, he published five more books in the next thirteen years, including *Unlawful Assembly* (1968) and *The Terrible Shears* (1973—both Chatto & Windus), about his working-class childhood in the Twenties, which is so prosaic as almost to constitute a kind of anti-poetry. Increasingly throwaway and ironic in manner, *Paradise Illustrated* (Chatto & Windus, 1978) and *A Faust Book* (Oxford University Press, 1979) are dry, postmodernist annotations of two cultural monuments. Enright's determination to avoid rhetoric and position-taking means that the poetry tends to court bathos and the exact opposite of the singing line. *Collected Poems* (Oxford University Press, 1998) exhibits his variousness, from early achievements like 'How right they were, the Chinese poets' ('Suffering exists, and most of it is not yours') to the gentle humour of 'Agape', which ruminates slyly on the lightning that struck York Minster in 1985.

He also published novels, children's books, and many volumes of criticism and reviews, and edited *The Oxford Book of Contemporary Verse* (1980) and *The Oxford Book of Death* (1983). *Signs and Wonders: Selected Essays* appeared from Carcanet in 2001, and a posthumous memoir, *Injury Time*, in 2003 (Pimlico).   WS

Enslin, Theodore (1925–2011) Enslin may have been Thoreau's truest descendant among contemporary American poets. A resident of New England from the 1940s and a resident of Maine from 1960, Enslin wrote a poetry attentive to setting and the seasons and the ways in which they transform and define the self. Enslin studied musical composition with Nadia Boulanger when she was living in the United States during the Second World War,

and his work is profoundly musical, one of the finest instances in American poetry of what *Pound called *melopoeia*.

In 1975, Enslin characterized the poem as 'a life process'. Thoreau would have understood that definition, but whereas Thoreau wrote chiefly as an observer, Enslin found ways to transform observation, or the experience of observation, into the experience of poems.

Enslin was one of the more prolific poets of his generation. For the early work, see *The Median Flow: Poems 1943–1973* (Black Sparrow, 1975). Among other works, the five volumes of *Forms* (Elizabeth Press, 1970–4) and two volumes of *Ranger* (North Atlantic, 1978, 1980) deserve particular notice. A collection of essays on Enslin was edited by John Taggart and published in *Truck*, 20 (1978). The National Poetry Foundation published a large selected poems, *Then and Now*, in 1999.

See also *Re-Sounding: Selected Later Poems* (Talisman House, 1999). His last book, *I, Benjamin*, was a 'quasi-autobiographical' novella on the life of the artist (McPherson, 2010).   EHF

Eppel, John (1947–) Born in Lydenburg, South Africa and grew up at Colleen Bawn, Zimbabwe. He was educated at the University of Natal and currently teaches English at Christian Brothers College, Bulawayo. Eppel is a novelist, short-story writer, and an important and influential poet in Southern Africa. His novel *DGG Berry's The Great North Road* (Carrefour/Hippogriff, 1992) won the MNet Prize. Volumes of poetry include *Spoils of War* (Carrefour, 1989) which won the Ingrid Jonker Prize, *Selected Poems 1965–1995* (Childline, 2001), and *Songs My Country Taught Me: Collected Poems 1965–2005* (Weaver Press, 2005). His poems are included in *State of the Nation: Contemporary Zimbabwean Poetry* (The Conversation Paperpress, 2009), and jointly with Julius *Chinongo in *Together* ('amaBooks, 2011).

Eppel is a master of form and structure. He writes sonnets, sestinas, and haikus, and there is an elegance and lyricism to his writing that often belies the intensity and depth of the material with which he is working. His emotional register ranges between sorrow, guilt, regret, anger, and sometimes resignation. Eppel is preoccupied with the flora and fauna of Southern Africa, not merely as a nature writer but as a means of grounding the poetry in a specific place and time. Mimosa, frangipane, geraniums, petunias, and the smells of, for example, woodsmoke, jasmine, and dust, create and sustain the imagined space, as do the sounds of this world. As he writes in 'November': 'Frogs practising scales against the drone | of a filter plant were off-keyed by the | massed choir of mosquitoes, the telephone | ringing. A cadenza of crickets ended the movement...'   FO

Eshleman, Clayton (1935–) Born in Indianapolis and educated at Indiana University. He writes an intensely autobiographical poetry shaped in large part by Reichian theory and attention to myth. He was influenced at the outset of his career by Rilke's assertion in *Letters to a Young Poet* that poetry arises from the self. Eshleman's midwestern values and background were stripped away as he went deeper into a poetic exploration of the fundamental self, which he understood as specifically sexual—a view intensified through his encounter with Reichian therapy in the 1960s. He read James Hillman's *The Dream and the Underworld* in the late 1970s, and this, combined with his investigations of Palaeolithic art, led to an increased understanding of archetypes and to the poems collected in *Hades in Manganese* (1981), *Fracture* (1983), and *Hotel Cro-Magnon* (1989—all Black Sparrow). He is an emeritus professor at Eastern Michigan University.

Eshleman's principal achievements are as a poet, but he has also edited two of the most respected journals of postmodern poetry, *Caterpillar* (1967–73) and *Sulfur* (1981–2000). He is an admired translator of, among others, Pablo Neruda, Aime Cesaire, Antonin Artaud, and César Vallejo. Eshleman has been an enormously productive poet, but *The Name Encanyoned River: Selected Poems, 1960–1985* (Black Sparrow, 1986) provides a good introduction. His selected prose is available in *Antiphonal Swing: Selected Prose, 1962–1987*

(McPherson, 1989). For a study of his work and its place in the development of postmodern American poetry, see Paul Christenson's *Minding the Underworld* (Black Sparrow, 1991).

See also Martha J. Sattler, *Clayton Eshleman: A Descriptive Bibliography* (McFarland, 1988) and *Grindstone of Rapport: A Clayton Eshleman Reader* (Black Widow, 2008). *Companion Spider* (2001), a later collection of his essays, has a foreword by Adrienne *Rich. *Juniper Fuse: Upper Paleolithic Imagination and the Construction of the Underworld* (2003—both Wesleyan University Press) is a study in verse and prose of the cave painting of south-western France.   EHF

Espada, Martín (1957–) Born in Brooklyn of Puerto Rican parents and formerly a tenant lawyer in Boston, writes a socially aware poetry which from the outset has marked his identification with the Spanish-speaking migrant in America. Pablo Neruda has been a key influence. *The Immigrant Iceboy's Bolero* (Ghost Pony Press, 1982) set the note—typically, 'Mrs. Baez Serves Coffee on The Third Floor', about a deranged arsonist setting fire to a Latino tenement building; 'Waiting For the Cops', a portrait of drugs and street violence which 'waits' for its larger solution; or 'Red Buzzard of Light Circling in the 25th Precinct', an East Harlem story of false arrest and Puerto Rican victimization. In *Trumpets from the Islands of their Eviction* (Bilingual, 1987), a more personal note enters, as in 'We live by what we see by night' or 'From An Island You Cannot Name', tributes to his father's life as an early immigrant *puertorriqueño*. Even so, he remains essentially a city poet, not least in his wry, vivid account of everyday Puerto Rican life in 'Tony Went to the Bodega but He Didn't Buy Anything'. Espada's third collection, *Rebellion is the Circle of a Lover's Hands* (Curbstone, 1990) favoured an increasing economy of form, notably in 'Clemente's Bullets', his memoir of the struggle for Puerto Rican independence, and 'Latin Night at the Pawnshop', a terse comment on Puerto Rican poverty amid the affluence of Boston.

Espada now teaches poetry at the University of Massachusetts, Amherst. *Alabanza: New and Selected Poems* (2003) includes three later volumes: *City of Coughing and Dead Radiators* (1993), *Imagine the Angels of Bread* (1996), *A Mayan Astronomer in Hell's Kitchen* (2000). *The Republic of Poetry* (2006—all Norton) won the Paterson Award for Sustained Literary Achievement. Its enquiry into the relationship between poetry and social justice includes poems for Robert *Creeley and Dennis *Brutus. See also the prose collected in *The Lover of a Subversive Is Also a Subversive* (University of Michigan Press, 2010) and *Poetry like Bread: Poets of the Political Imagination* (Curbstone, 1994; new edn., 2000). His latest collection is *The Trouble Ball* (Norton, 2011).   ARL*

Evaristo, Bernadine (1959–) Born in London to Anglo-Nigerian parents, Evaristo trained as an actor and has worked in the theatre and written plays. A popular reader of her work, who has held residencies in America and Britain, she is an active editor and reviewer, and Reader in Creative Writing at Brunel University. *Blonde Roots* (Penguin, 2008), her first prose novel, continues the imaginative exploration of European and African history that informs all her work. Her first book was a collection of poems, *Island of Abraham* (Peepal Tree, 1994): the central sequence concerns a journey to Madagascar. In between these two modes come her verse-novels, from the lyrical, semi-autobiographical *Lara* (Angela Royal, 1997; revd. edn., Bloodaxe, 2009), to the fast-paced satirical narratives of *The Emperor's Babe* (2001) and *Soul Tourists* (2005—both Penguin), a novel in prose 'with' verse. Like her Australian contemporary Dorothy *Porter, Evaristo has employed the hybrid form to find a popular audience for stories that subvert their inherited genres. With Daljit Nagra, she co-edited an anthology of black and Asian British poets, *Ten* (Bloodaxe, 2010). In 2009 Evaristo received an MBE.   JNT

Everson, R. G. (Ronald Gilmour) (1903–92) Born in Oshawa, Ontario, of United Empire Loyalist stock, and educated at the University of Toronto and Osgoode Hall Law School. He chose not to practise law at the beginning of his career, preferring instead to try his hand at professional writing. This led him into thrillers and western fiction, a good deal of which he published pseudonymously in the pulp market. Everson then moved into public relations, becoming a partner in a prominent Montreal firm which specialized in advertising and business communications; he worked there until his retirement.

Everson began to write verse seriously in the 1920s, and in spite of their occasional nature, his poems continued to appear steadily in American and Canadian magazines, eventually leading to the appearance of his first, privately published collection, *Three Dozen Poems* (Cambridge Press, 1957) which was closely followed by *A Lattice for Momos* (Contact, 1958). These were poems of a mature sensibility reflecting Everson's thoughtful but cryptically matter-of-fact manner, a quality which became the hallmark of his writing. Variously described as possessing an 'innocent vision' and being 'almost greatly gifted', Everson showed adroitness in reconciling his innate philosophic conservatism with an entirely modern spirit. In 1963 he published *Blind Man's Holiday* (Ryerson), and later that year, he helped found in Montreal, with Louis *Dudek, Glen Siebrasse, and Michael Gnarowski, a small literary press called Delta Canada (1963–71), the first publication of which was his collection of poems, *Wrestle with an Angel* (1965). His *Selected Poems 1920/1970* appeared in 1970 (Delta Canada) and was followed by *Indian Summer* (1976), *Carnival* (1978) and *Everson at Eighty* (1983—all Oberon). The later collections, heavily dependent upon reminiscence, a strong sense of history, and the impressions garnered during extensive travel, became more elaborate in their delivery and more sombre in their mood. Everson's last collection, *Poems About Me*, came out in 1990 (Oberon).   MG

Everson, William (1912–94) Born in Sacramento, California, to Francelia and Louis Everson, a Norwegian composer. He dropped out of Fresno State College, where he had ingested Robinson *Jeffers' 'mystical pantheism', to marry a high-school sweetheart. Drafted as a conscientious objector, he spent the war years in Oregon work camps, then gravitated to the San Francisco *Beat circle orbiting Kenneth *Rexroth. A Catholic convert in 1949, he became a Dominican monk two years later, teaching and writing under the name Brother Antoninus.

His first volume, *The Residual Years: Poems 1934–1948* (1948, revd. edn. 1968), established his bold poetic signature: Jeffers' muscular metaphysical quest entwined with the Beats' hatred of both formalism and American materialism. A potent sensuality also marked that signature, as evident, for instance, in *The Hazards of Holiness: Poems 1957–1960* (1962) and *The Rose of Solitude* (1967). He left the Dominicans late in 1969, an event treated in *Man-Fate: The Swan Song of Brother Antoninus* (1974). Everson published several later poetry collections, including *The Veritable Years: 1946–1966* (Black Sparrow, 1978; expanded edn., 1998), *The Blood of the Poet: Selected Poems* (Broken Moon, 1994), and *The Integral Years: Poems, 1966–1994* (Black Sparrow, 2000). See also *Dark God of Eros: A William Everson Reader*, ed. Albert Gelpi (Heyday, 2003).   EB

Ewart, Gavin (Buchanan) (1916–95) Ewart had poems published in *New Verse* while still a schoolboy at Wellington and was later an exhibitioner at Christ's College, Cambridge. He served in the Royal Artillery from 1940 to 1946, and later worked for the British Council and in advertising. After the publication of *Poems and Songs* in 1938 his next volume did not appear until the Sixties, when *Pleasures of the Flesh* (1966) disgusted or angered some readers by its explicit and sly sexual references. Among the 'Eight Awful Animals' described in this collection were the Dildo, the Masturbon, and the Panteebra ('The Panteebra rhymes with zebra and is a very slinky cockteaser'). A joke about Virginia Woolf's last period (the name changed later to Emily Brontë) gave much offence.

'Its bad taste jokes are myriad', Ewart said of 'The Dildo', and a deliberate outrageousness remained a conspicuous element in the several collections he published after breaking public silence. *The Collected Ewart 1933–1980* appeared in 1980, a completely new collection called *The New Ewart* only two years later, a volume of clerihews, another of very short poems, and *Penultimate Poems* in 1989. Two selections appeared in the USA: *The Gavin Ewart Show* (Bits, 1986), and *Selected Poems 1933–1988* (New Directions, 1988).

Ewart's fecundity was extraordinary, and so was his technical skill. He was ready, and indeed eager, to experiment with any verse-form, rhyme-scheme, or metre. When a reviewer suggested that he wrote two or three poems a week, Ewart responded that he produced far more than that. He refused to be selective about his work, believing that time would do the necessary editorial weeding. He expressed a preference for light over heavy poetry, saying that 'Good light verse is better than bad heavy verse | any day of the week', but his refusal to contemplate any grandeur of style or manner inevitably limited his achievement. Many of the comic poems are delightful, the high spirits with which they are written persuasive, and it is easy to accept that 'by writing the one-line sagas | and fooling about with the norm | the Poet Ewart may have answered | the vexing Question of Form'.

But there remains the question of content, and here Ewart's self-imposed restrictions are regrettable. His best poems are those in which the tone remains light but the material is seriously treated, like the sonnets about his parents and his children, or 'Lovers in Pairs', which tells of old lovers keeping each other warm in 'the penultimate bed | before the one with the gravestone'. But it would be wrong to be stuffy about a poet who on his chosen level offers such a varied and emotionally generous comic view of twentieth-century English manners, beliefs, and behaviour. See *Collected Poems* (Hutchinson, 1991) and *Civil Humor: the Poetry of Gavin Ewart* by Stephen W. Delchamps (Fairleigh Dickinson University Press, 2002).   JGS

Ezekiel, Nissim (1924–2004) Born into a Jewish (Bene-Israel) family in Bombay (now Mumbai). He studied philosophy at Birkbeck College, London and had a distinguished academic career teaching English literature at Bombay University. As an undergraduate he was a member of the Radical Democratic Party and an intense concern for social justice is seldom far from the surface of his writing. He also worked as an advertising copy-writer and was the first editor of the celebrated intellectual bimonthly, *Quest* (now *New Quest*). He served as a member of the council of Indian PEN and of the Lalit Kala Akademi and the Sahitya Akademi, India's national academies of art and literature. He was for a time the editor of *Poetry India*, which was generally regarded as the most important Indian poetry journal. He published widely on Indian art and literature. In 1983 he was presented with the much-coveted Sahitya Akademi Award and in 1988 with the Padma Shri for his contribution to Indian literature in English.

Despite his achievements in so many different fields, it is almost certainly for his poetry that Ezekiel will be remembered. Many critics regard him as the first major Indian poet to write in English. After the publication of his first collection, *A Time to Change* (Fortune, 1952) there were seven further volumes. These were gathered into one volume as *Collected Poems* (Oxford University Press, 1989), which includes a preface by the poet Gieve *Patel, who provides a perceptive introduction to Ezekiel's work. The second edition in 2005 replaced this with a preface by Leela Gandhi and an introduction by John Thieme.

Ezekiel's poems exhibit a varied range of tone and concerns. His personal use of religious metaphor in *Hymns in Darkness* (1976) and *Latter-day Psalms* (1982—both Oxford University Press) suggests a return to earlier questionings of the problematics of identity, but now being reworked within the imagery of a distinct Indo-Judaic tradition. Other motifs are supplied by the teeming cosmopolitan life of Bombay and the ambiguities of personal and sexual relationships. The fastidious craftsmanship, urbanity of tone, and habitual understatement make many of the poems appear simple, but often the full implications of the myth and metaphor woven into the narration are reserved for the final verse or line.

Another aspect of Ezekiel is revealed in the broad humour of his 'Very Indian Poems in Indian English' and 'Goodby Party for Miss Pushpa T.S.'. In these he exploits the comic incongruities that arise from an imperfectly acquired veneer of western culture at work upon a type of Indian sensibility.

The most extended studies of Ezekiel as a poet are Chetan Karnani, *Nissim Ezekiel* (Heinemann, 1974), and a special issue of *Journal of South Asian Literature*, 11:3–4, guest-edited by Inder Nath Kher. See also the *festschrift* published on his seventieth birthday, *Mapping Cultural Spaces: Post-Colonial Indian Literature in English* (Vision, 1998), and the authorized biography by R. Raj Rao (Viking, 2000).   RW*

Ezenwa-Ohaeto (1958–2005) Studied English at the University of Nigeria, Nsukka and the University of Benin. He taught at Ahmadu Bello University, Zaria, at Anambra College of Education, Awka, at Albert Ikoku College of Education, Owerri, and was Professor of English at Nnamdi Azikiwe University in Nigeria. He was at various times a visiting fellow at universities at Bayreuth, Mainz, Humboldt, Berlin, Harvard, and Austin, Texas.

Ezenwa-Ohaeto won the Association of Nigerian Authors prize for his first volume of poetry, *The Voice of the Night Masquerade* (1996), and the prestigious Association of Nigerian Authors/NDDC poetry prize for his second volume, *Chants of a Minstrel* (2004—both Kraft). He was also the author of a highly praised and authorized biography of Chinua *Achebe. Ezenwa-Ohaeto's poetry is deeply rooted in Igbo culture. In *The Voice of the Night Masquerade*, he assumed an oracular, mystical voice that took in the idiom of proverbs, affirmations, praise songs and wedded these to the rhythm of everyday speech and of incantations. The effect was hypnotic. His untimely death foreclosed the possibilities of further invention in this direction.   FO

Fahey, Diane (1945–) Born in Melbourne, where she was educated. After spending some years abroad she has returned to live in South Australia. Her first collection, *Voices from the Honeycomb* (Jacaranda, 1986), established her as a new poet of considerable strength and flexibility, writing through a range of subjects drawn from art, cinema, personal observation, and with an eye for the quirky newspaper report. Her second collection, *Metamorphoses* (Dangaroo, 1988) draws on Greek myths to 'tell the story of contemporary woman journeying from patriarchy to reclaim her own space and authenticity'. The book includes an extended section of 'Notes and Illustrations'. Diane Fahey expanded on her preoccupations as developed in this book in a prose essay published in *Poetry and Gender: Statements and Essays in Australian Women's Poetry and Poetics*, ed. Brooks and Walker (1989). Her third collection was *Mayflies in Amber* (Angus & Robertson, 1993).

Although the reinterpretation of classical myths has been at the heart of much twentieth-century invention and pastiche, Fahey's work in Australia has gained from recent feminist theory and from the poet's own belief in poetry as 'an integrating process'. She has published four further collections—*Listening to a Far Sea* (Hale & Iremonger, 1998), *The Sixth Swan* (2001), *Sea Wall and River Light* (2006—both Five Islands), and *Winter Solstice and Other Poems* (Picaro, 2008)—and a poetic crime novella, *The Mystery of Rosa Morland* (Clouds of Magellan, 2008).   TWS

Fainlight, Harry (1935–82) Born in New York of Jewish parents, his father being English and his mother American. He grew up in England but was evacuated to the United States during the Second World War. After reading English at Cambridge, he moved to New York to join the *Beat poets.

He returned with a celebrated long poem, 'The Spider', an account of an LSD trip. He performed it at the Albert Hall reading in London in 1965 which was filmed as *Wholly Communion*. In a state of drug-induced paranoia, he later suppressed the poem.

The one pamphlet he allowed to be published in his lifetime, *Sussicran* (Turret, 1965), reflects another suppression that must also have left its mark: the English law's suppression of male homosexuality. Poems like 'Meeting', a bleak variation on *Owen's 'Strange Meeting', evoke the homosexual underworld as it was before the law changed in 1963.

His reworking of Owen, as of Shelley, shows the poetic ambition that underlay his suppressions and his recurrent breakdowns. He ended in a remote cottage in Wales where he was found dead of pneumonia. He had lived out the role of the poet as Saul Bellow imagines it in *Humboldt's Gift*: incompetent in the world's terms, but keeping imagination's gate.

His *Selected Poems* (1986) were edited by his sister, Ruth *Fainlight. They were followed by a cache of newly discovered poems, *Journeys* (1992—both Turret).   RGa

Fainlight, Ruth (1931–) Born in New York, Fainlight was educated at schools in the USA and England, and at art colleges in Birmingham and Brighton. In 1985 she was poet-in-residence at Vanderbilt University, Tennessee. She married the novelist Alan Sillitoe in 1959.

Ruth Fainlight's poetry combines fidelity to the complicated realities of life with an intense, almost mystical apprehension of the woman poet's role as seer: 'Sibyls' is an extended sequence about just such women. Yet, perhaps because she has also published short stories, her most assured pieces seem often to be vignettes of people observed, with thoughtful candour, in their characteristic contexts. Undeterred by apparently intractable subject-matter, she has even recycled a poem from 'The New Science of Strong Materials'.

Her first full-length collection, *Cages* (Macmillan) appeared in 1967. Since then she has published over a dozen books of poetry, several pamphlets, and two *Selected Poems*, in 1987 and 1995; *Daylife and Nightlife* (1971) and *Doctor Clock's Last Case* (1994) are volumes of her short stories, and she edited the *Selected Poems* of her brother, Harry *Fainlight. She has also written libretti and translated Sophocles' Theban plays. Her later collections have been published by Bloodaxe, who issued a *New and Collected Poems* in 2010.   NP

Fairburn, Arthur Rex Dugard (A. R. D. **Fairburn** or **Rex Fairburn**) (1904–57) Fairburn was among the most vigorous and forceful personalities to emerge in New Zealand poetry in the years between 1930 and 1950. He was always associated with Auckland, where he lived all his life except for two years in England, and where he worked at a variety of jobs from journalism to university tutoring. An essayist and polemicist as well as a poet, he contributed prolifically to local journals on matters relating to art, politics, and society.

The youthful effusion of his first volume, *He Shall Not Rise* (1930), gave way to a more mature poetry in the years of the Depression. Those years produced the long poem 'Dominion', published first in 1938, and many of his best shorter poems. Though much of his satire and comic work retains its force, his most enduring verse is lyrical, expressing a Romantic belief in human experience being at its most vital when it is in harmony with nature. Fairburn's concerns seem to owe much to Blake and *Lawrence, but also much to his eclectic enthusiasm for the art, literature,

and popular philosophical writings of his own time.

His best poems are found in *Poems 1929–1941* (1943) and *Strange Rendezvous* (1952—both Caxton). *Three Poems* (New Zealand University Press, 1952) contains his longer works, 'Dominion' and the post-war poems 'The Voyage' and 'To a Friend in the Wilderness'.

See also *Collected Poems* (Pegasus, 1966); *The Woman Problem and other prose*, selected essays, (Blackwood & Janet Paul, 1967); *The Letters of A. R. D. Fairburn*, ed. Lauris Edmond (Oxford University Press, 1981); and Denys Trussell, *Fairburn* (Auckland University Press, 1984).   WSB

Fallon, Padraic (1905–74) Born in Athenry, Co. Galway. He was educated at St Joseph's School, Roscrea. At eighteen he moved to Dublin and became a customs official, working until 1939 in Dublin and subsequently in Wexford. In Dublin, the poet AE encouraged him and helped him get his first poems published. His work appeared regularly in the *Dublin Magazine* until it folded in 1958. He died during a visit to England at Aylesford, Kent. His body was taken back for burial in Kinsale, Co. Cork, where he had settled after retirement. In the same year the first extensive collection of his work, *Poems*, was published.

With Austin *Clarke's and *Kavanagh's, Fallon's work marks the emergence of a specifically Irish, as opposed to Anglo-Irish, sensibility in poetry written in English, an emergence that involved standing against the tremendous example of *Yeats, though Fallon was in some ways less successful in this than the former two poets. He was helped in his struggle to achieve stylistic independence by the example of *Pound, though he never became a modernist in the Poundian mould. There is often a stylistic faltering even in Fallon's best work, but throughout his oeuvre can be found fine, coherent poems that display a subtle ear for cadences and a freshness of thought and perception.

The fullest edition of the poems, including a number of poems from the plays he wrote for Radio Eireann as well as translations, is *Collected Poems* (1990), which has an introduction by Seamus *Heaney and an afterword by the poet's son, Brian Fallon. A new selection, *A Look in the Mirror and Other Poems*, appeared in 2003, with an introduction by Eavan *Boland, and a volume of radio plays, including *The Vision of MacConglinne*, in 2005 (all Carcanet).   TJGK

Fanthorpe, U. A. (Ursula Askham)

(1929–2009) Born in London and studied at St Anne's College, Oxford (1949–53) and the University of London Institute of Education (1953–4). She became an assistant English teacher, and later head of English, at Cheltenham Ladies' College, Gloucestershire, and from 1972 to 1983 did hospital clerical work in Bristol. In 1983–5 she was Arts Council Writing Fellow at St Martin's College, Lancaster, and in 1987–8 she was Northern Arts Literary Fellow at the universities of Newcastle and Durham.

U. A. Fanthorpe is a notable exponent of a tendency in English poetry which Harry Chambers' Peterloo Poets press did much to encourage—wry, observant, humane, inclined to the proverbial, faithful to place and experience, sharing some of *Larkin's attitudes, if not his habitual formality. Fanthorpe's poems often begin in the everyday, working to disclose the common experience—frequently the expectation of death. Her hospital work enabled her to observe the stripping of identity and the importance of ritual in the face of mortality ('Lament for the Patients').

Attachment to 'ordinary' people is matched by love of 'this narrow island charged with echoes | and whispers' ('Earthed'), her account of which is anecdotal rather than political. Place also provides access to myth: her account of London's lost rivers, 'Rising Damp', ends by naming the rivers of Hell. The more directly mythological poems seem less successful, working towards a point rather than a discovery, but her best work (for example, 'Seminar: Felicity and Mr Frost') succeeds by noticing, overhearing, and divining.

Fanthorpe's collections include: *Side Effects* (1978); *Standing To* (1982); *Voices Off* (1984); *A Watching Brief* (1987); and *Neck-Verse* (1992—all Peterloo). *Selected Poems* (Penguin) appeared in 1986; and a *Collected Poems*, incorporating several more Peterloo volumes, in 2004 (Peterloo). *Christmas Poems* (2002) collects seasonal verses that she circulated among friends. Fanthorpe became a CBE in 2001, and was awarded the Queen's Gold Medal for Poetry in 2003. *New and Collected Poems* (2010—both Enitharmon) appeared posthumously, with a preface by Carol Ann *Duffy.   SO'B

Farley, Paul (1965–   ) Born in Liverpool,

Farley studied at the Chelsea School of Art and is Professor of Poetry at Lancaster University. His first collection, *The Boy from the Chemist Is Here to See You* (1998), won a Forward Prize, and in 1999 he was named the *Sunday Times* Young Writer of the Year. His second book, *The Ice Age* (2002), won the Whitbread Prize, and his third, *Tramp in Flames* (2006—all Picador), was shortlisted for several awards.

Farley's appeal for a British audience lies in his combination of the demotic range of Simon *Armitage—both write out of working-class upbringings in the age of pop culture—with the elegiac formality of Philip *Larkin. Many poems are occasioned by memory, and invoke a collective feeling about the post-war quotidian somewhere between nostalgia and irony ('When I see some kids springing the gallery doors | I lament the great revolvers' (Automatic Doors)). The subjects of his curatorial realism are to be found in every home: tins of treacle, diary moons. There is anger, too, on behalf of neglected lives.

Field Recordings, the text of a decade of radio-poems for the BBC, appeared from Donut Press in 2009. A selected poems, *The Atlantic Tunnel*, has been published in the States (Faber, 2010). Farley has also written a study of Terence Davies' 1988 film *Distant Voices, Still Lives* (BFI, 2006). A book of prose on semi-urban landscapes, *Edgelands: Journeys into England's True Wilderness* (Cape, 2011), with Michael *Symmons Roberts, appeared in 2011, and a fourth collection, *The Dark Film* (Picador), in 2012.   JNT

Fearing, Kenneth (Flexner) (1902–61)

Born in Oak Park, Illinois, the son of a

Chicago attorney. After leaving the University of Wisconsin he did a variety of jobs, including millhand, salesman, and sports reporter, and later worked as a journalist on *Time*, the magazine serving as background for his crime story *The Big Clock*, the best of his several novels. His first collection of poems *Angel Arms* (1929) was followed by four others, and *New and Selected Poems* (Indiana University Press) appeared in 1956. He was twice married, and had one son.

'For practical purposes I should say I was in the Whitman tradition,' Fearing said, but this obvious derivation took a personal colouring from a simplistic but strongly held radicalism and the use of current slang, advertising slogans and copy, phrases on posters, and neon signs. There are a few poems justifying the comment that Fearing converted the bromides of tabloid journalism into art, but sentimentality is never far away. Radical Fearing can sometimes carry a reader along on his Whitmanesque wave, lyrical Fearing is to be avoided. Yet although the form of the verse was derivative, from Carl *Sandburg as well as Whitman, the result was sometimes original. Nobody else wrote like Fearing in the Thirties and Forties. In manner he was a forerunner of the *Beats, although he would have found their nihilism deeply uncongenial. See *Selected Poems* (Library of America, 2004), ed. Robert Polito.   JGS

Feaver, Vicki (1943–) After a childhood in Nottingham, Feaver studied music at Durham University. She later read English at University College, London, and went on to be a lecturer in English and Creative Writing at University College, Chichester, where she is now emeritus professor. She lives in Scotland.

Feaver's three collections of poetry, published over three decades, have been widely admired for the intensity of their execution. The imagistic depiction of domestic life in *Close Relatives* (Secker & Warburg, 1981) recalls the example of Douglas *Dunn's *Terry Street*, but from darker, female perspectives. Shortly after the appearance of *The Handless Maiden* (1994), Feaver featured in the *Penguin*

Modern Poets series alongside Carol Ann *Duffy and Eavan *Boland. 'Judith', a monologue of murderous tenderness ('it's easy | like slicing through fish'), won a Forward Prize in 1993. *The Book of Blood* (2006—both Cape) continues Feaver's unflinching exploration of a gothic lyricism after *Plath.   JNT

Feinstein, Elaine (1930–) Born in Bootle, Lancashire, and took her degree at Newnham College, Cambridge. Feinstein began writing under the influence of various American poets, notably William Carlos *Williams, Wallace *Stevens, and Emily Dickinson, and her first poems were published in *Poetry Introduction, 1* (Faber, 1969). Through translating the poems of Marina Tsvetaeva she discovered a more open, fluid syntax, immediately responsive to shifts of narrative and mood. Tsvetaeva's influence is visible in her first novel, *The Circle* (Hutchinson,1970; Penguin, 1973; Faber, 2008), and throughout her subsequent early fiction. The directness and freshness of tone in her poems link them to the same source. Her life's work on Tsvetaeva culminated in the biography, *A Captive Lion* (Hutchinson, 1987*)* and *Bride of Ice: New Selected Poems of Marina Tsvetaeva* (Carcanet, 2009).

Feinstein has contributed to all the major literary genres. She is a prolific novelist as well as biographer, playwright, poet, and translator. Her primary vocations as poet and novelist are interestingly fused with memoir in *The Russian Jerusalem* (Carcanet, 2010). Her most recent poetry collections, all from Carcanet, are *Gold* (2000), *Collected Poems and Translations* (2002), *Talking to the Dead* (2007), and *Cities* (2010). Her biography of Ted *Hughes was published by Weidenfeld & Nicolson in 2001.   CAR

Feldman, Irving (1928–) Born in Coney Island, New York, and educated at City College and Columbia University. He has lived in Puerto Rico, France, and Spain, and the echo of European literary styles, especially *Surrealism, is evident in his work. He was awarded a MacArthur Fellowship in 1992, and retired from the State

University of New York at Buffalo, where he was Distinguished Professor of English, in 2002. The profoundest influence on his poetry is not, however, a fashion but an event, the Jewish Holocaust. A teenager in New York during the early 1940s, Feldman suffered the destruction of European Jewry at a distance that was nonetheless close to home, as the title-poem of his book *The Pripet Marshes* (1964) makes clear. And in the middle of the poem which follows it, 'To the Six Million', he writes: 'There is someone missing. | Is it I who am missing?'

His *New and Selected Poems* (Viking, 1979) shows a mastery of tone and style and a broadening circle of concerns, always, however, fretted by a pessimistic wisdom. Lyrics, aphorisms, tales, psalms, prose poems, jokes, and disquisitions range over the whole sad, funny backlot of modern life, from 'The Handball Players at Brighton Beach', to poetry readings in the Hamptons, to Bette Davis, 'fantastic and compelled', slamming the door behind her. His *Collected Poems, 1954–2004* were published by Knopf in 2004. Feldman never ceases to wonder over the way we freely invent our lives and yet are driven by powers looming behind or within us.   EG

Fenton, James (1949–) Born in Lincoln and educated at Repton and Magdalen College, Oxford, where he followed a degree course in psychology and philosophy and won the Newdigate Prize with 'Our Western Furniture', a sonnet-sequence about European influences on Japan. *Terminal Moraine* (Secker & Warburg, 1972), a first volume of high promise, displayed a variety of forms and unconventional subject-matter, ranging from topical satire (his 'Open Letter to Richard Crossman') to startling assemblages of recondite and alarming detail from anthropology ('The Pitt-Rivers Museum, Oxford'), biology ('A Frog'), or horticulture ('The Fruit-Grower in Wartime').

The title-poem of this first book touches on an important element in Fenton's writing: a restless yearning for changing scenes and experiences. This is treated entertainingly in 'The Skip', in his second volume, *The Memory of War* (Salamander, 1982;

reprinting several poems from *Terminal Moraine* and including everything in his 1978 pamphlet, *A Vacant Possession*). Here, as before, he can be abundantly mysterious and sinister, with the same strong hint of intellectual games-playing (in 'Nest of Vampires' or 'A Staffordshire Murderer'). But between books he had worked in Germany and south-east Asia, and he was now writing from personal experience with a new authority and emotional strength. 'A German Requiem' is a laconic and formal exploration of collective memory and collective forgetfulness in post-1945 Germany. 'In a Notebook', like the later 'Children in Exile', draws movingly on his Cambodian journeys and their aftermath.

Manila Envelope (1989), privately published from the Philippines where he was a correspondent, comprised a book of thirteen substantial poems, a poster of one of them, and a broadsheet poetic manifesto, advocating different, even reckless directions in poetry and attacking prescriptive critics. His abandoned, surreal word-play threw off constraints of prosody and even meaning (in 'Here Come the Drum Majorettes' and 'The Ballad of the Shrieking Man'), though both the topical, and the personal and reflective poet are still present, in 'Jerusalem' and 'The Mistake'. His last new collection was *Out of Danger* (Penguin, 1993; Farrar, Straus, 1994), which showed him also to be a skilfully simple love poet.

Fenton has also published collections of his theatre criticism and reportage, travel writing (with Redmond O'Hanlon), and a collaboration with John *Fuller in a collection of satirical poems, *Partingtime Hall* (Viking/Salamander, 1987). His lectures as Oxford Professor of Poetry between 1994 and 1999, *The Strength of Poetry* (Oxford University Press), appeared in 2001, and were followed by his lucid and concise *An Introduction to English Poetry* (Penguin, 2003; Farrar, Straus, 2004). In 2007 Fenton was awarded the Queen's Gold Medal for Poetry. His latest selected poems is *Yellow Tulips* (Faber, 2012).   AB*

Ferguson, Gus (1940–) Born in Scotland and raised in South Africa, Gus

Ferguson is a poet, publisher and illustrator. He has published nine collections of poetry as well as several books of cartoons. As well as working as a pharmacist, Ferguson has run the small poetry imprints, Snailpress, Firfield Press, Carapace Poets, and the Unpublished Manuscript Press, and edited the poetry journal, *Carapace*. He lives in Cape Town.

Ferguson is arguably the best-known humorous poet in South Africa, with many of his poems providing bathetic philosophy, making fun of poets, or documenting his love of snails and cycling. His books include *Snail Morning* (1979), *Doggerel Day* (1982—both Donker), *Carpe Diem* (Carrefour, 1992), *The Herding of the Snail* (Firfield, 1995), *Icarus Rising* (Dye Hard, 1995), *Light Verse at the End of the Tunnel* (1996), *Stressed-Unstressed* (2000—both David Philip), *Arse Poetica* (Kwela, 2003), and *Holding Pattern* (Quartz, 2009). Ferguson has received a Molteno Silver Medal and the South African English Academy Gold Medal for poetry. His illustrations have been widely exhibited.   KK

Ferlinghetti, Lawrence (Mendes-Monstanto) (1919–) Born in Yonkers, New York. The publisher of Allen *Ginsberg's *Howl* (City Lights Books), Ferlinghetti is indelibly identified with the San Francisco *Beat movement. He was a co-founder of the movement, and remains its chief apostle. Like Ginsberg, he has a shrewd business sense, and his poetry has immense popular appeal: *A Coney Island of the Mind* (New Directions, 1958) was one of the big poetry best-sellers of the century. The poems in *A Coney Island of the Mind* owe considerable debts to Carl *Sandburg and Vachel *Lindsay, as well as the less likely E. E. *Cummings, but were original in their time for use of explicit language and direct, no-holds-barred attacks on the 'Terrible People' (i.e. politicians and bankers). Ferlinghetti does write with the 'immediacy, power and passion' that have been claimed for him; but as society has changed so his message has come to look less startling. Abrasiveness and bad language have begun to look ordinary, too. Thus, *To Fuck Is to Love Again*, published

by Fuck You Press in New York (1985), has quite lost its revolutionary impact. But Ferlinghetti's persistence impresses, and his earlier poems were often, above all, funny.

See *These Are My Rivers: New and Selected Poems, 1955–1993* (1993) and *How to Paint Sunlight: Lyric Poems and Others, 1997–2000* (2001—both New Directions). B. Silesky, *Ferlinghetti: The Artist in his Time* (Warner, 1990) is a biography. In 1998 Ferlinghetti became Poet Laureate of San Francisco, and in 2008 a fiftieth-anniversary edition of *A Coney Island of the Mind* was issued, with a recording of the poet reading his million-selling volume.   MS-S*

Fernando, Patrick (1931–83) Combined a career in Sri Lanka's Department of Inland Revenue with the writing of a meticulous, mannered poetry shaped by his classical education and Roman Catholic upbringing. Often ironic in its perceptions, as in 'The Late Sir Henry' and 'Obsequies of the Late Antonio Pompirelli, Bishop', it evinces a concern for discipline and precision in matters of technique.

Although his inspiration was rooted in Western classical literature, Fernando strove during the 1950s to find common ground with Sri Lanka's Sinhala-speaking majority culture. He worked on doggedly during a period of chauvinistic cultural resurgence that was openly hostile to Western arts and letters, describing his situation in those years as one of 'unhelpful isolation'.

During his lifetime Fernando published one collection, *The Return of Ulysses: Poems* (Hand & Flower, 1955). *Selected Poems* was published posthumously by OUP (India) in 1984.

See also: Y. Gooneratne (ed.), *Poems From India, Sri Lanka, Malaysia and Singapore* (Heinemann, 1979); Y. Gooneratne (ed.), 'The Poetry of Sri Lanka', *Journal of South Asian Literature* special issue, 12:1/2 (Fall–Winter 1976), Asian Studies Center, Michigan State University.   YG

Ferry, David (1924–) Born in Orange, New Jersey. He is professor emeritus of English at Wellesley College in Massachusetts, where he began teaching in 1952. His wife Anne, whom he married in 1958, was a well-known critic of English poetry of the sixteenth and seventeenth centuries.

Ferry's first two collections are brief (together they comprise only seventy-three pages), and unified in tone, style, and theme. *On the Way to the Island* (Wesleyan University Press, 1960) employs a style of conscious artifice, with occasional echoes of *Yeats, *Stevens, and *Ransom. In *Strangers* (1983), the writing is quieter and the imagery more wide-ranging. The best poems—'out at Lanesville', 'After Spotsylvania Court House', and others—impress with the richness of their human concerns, but impress also, as the title suggests, with the knowledge that our deepest longings for connection and fulfilment cannot, in the nature of things, be satisfied. A third volume, *Dwelling* Places, appeared in 1993 (both University of Chicago Press). He has also published a verse translation of *Gilgamesh* (Farrar, Straus, 1992), and, latterly, acclaimed versions of Virgil and Horace. *Of No Country I Know* (1999) was a new and selected volume of poems and translations. In 2011, Ferry was awarded the Ruth Lilly Poetry Prize for Lifetime Achievement by the Poetry Foundation. See also *Bewilderment* (2012—both University of Chicago Press).   MP

Field, Edward (1924–) Born in Brooklyn, New York. He attended New York University and served in the US Army Air Force during the Second World War. He won the Lamont Poetry Award for his first book, *Stand Up Friend, With Me* (Grove, 1963).

Writing a conversational, unadorned poetry, Field takes on a variety of unlikely subjects, including aliens from outer space, faith-healers, spiritual gurus, and televised football games, creating entertaining exposés of contemporary life in America. He also explores more traditional subjects, such as his own Jewish heritage and troubled love affairs. His sensitive examination of his family and their effects on one another and him is given its fullest treatment in 'Visiting Home', a long poem in his volume *A Full Heart* (Sheep Meadow, 1977).

Field combines a self-deprecating, painful, even at times maudlin voice with the keen ability to look at extremely personal material with an objective eye. He is, furthermore, a poet unbound by intellectual systems, either philosophical or psychological, and in fact examines such thought patterns with a deft scepticism in a number of poems. See *After The Fall: Poems Old and New* (University of Pittsburgh Press, 2007). His memoirs of life as a gay man in post-war New York have been published as *The Man Who Would Marry Susan Sontag, and Other Intimate Literary Portraits of the Bohemian Era* (University of Wisconsin Press, 2005).   RS

Figueroa, John Joseph Maria (1920–99) Born in Kingston, Jamaica. He was educated at St George's College, Jamaica, a Jesuit institution. He went on to study at Holy Cross College, Worcester, Massachusetts, and do postgraduate work at the University of London. He had many academic appointments as a Professor of Education. He contributed to the BBC's 'Caribbean Voices' programme, also the title of an important two-volume West Indian poetry anthology that he edited, and was general editor of the Heinemann Caribbean Writers Series.

At their best, Figueroa's poems tend to be sensuous, yet formally stringent, and expansive in their breadth of reference. He can be precise about 'Chartres Window', for instance, or subtly ironic in 'Christmas Breeze', which counterpoints religious observances in England and Jamaica. As Spanish was his second language he also wrote adaptations of Lorca and St John of the Cross. Sensitivity to cultural crosscurrents leavens his most effective imagery. In this respect, Derek *Walcott's poems may owe something to Figueroa's practice. *The Chase* (Peepal Tree, 1991) collects poems from five decades.   MR

Finch, Annie (1956–) Studied at the universities of Yale and Stanford and now teaches at the University of Southern Maine. She has co-edited a collection of essays on Caroline *Kizer, and translated the poems of Louise Labé.

Finch's first books were a critical study, *The Ghost of Meter: Culture and Prosody in*

American Free Verse (University of Michigan Press, 1993), and an anthology, *A Formal Feeling Comes: Poems in Form by Contemporary Women* (1994). Her first full collection, *Eve* (1997—both Story Line), saw her associated with the *New Formalism, but an earlier work, *The Encyclopaedia of Scotland*, written for performance in 1982 and published in the UK by Salt in 2004, reveals the experimentalism underlying her writing and thinking. *The Body of Poetry: Essays on Women, Form, and the Poetic Self* (University of Michigan Press, 2005) collects Finch's essays on women's poetics after modernism, advocating her idea of a 'radical formalism' or 'omniformalism', dedicated to poems that 'pound the blood' and 'move freely between schools'. Her own work insists on the fundamental nature of metric experience, and the way its 'pulse' links language to other rhythms and cycles, as in the neopagan chant poems of *Calendars* (Tupelo, 2003).   JNT

Finch, Peter (1947–   ) Born in Cardiff, Finch has been an influential figure in Welsh poetry for decades, working as a poet, publisher, editor, critic, and self-described 'literary entrepreneur', as concerned with encouraging others as with promoting his own writing. With handbooks such as *How To Publish Your Poetry* (Allison & Busby, 1985; 4th revd. edn., 1999) and *The Poetry Business* (Seren, 1994), he seeks to demystify, to 'open the gates'. He has also written a popular series of guides to *Real Cardiff*. Chief Executive of Literature Wales from 1998 until 2011, and treasurer of the Association of Little Presses for more than twenty years, Finch also edited *Second Aeon*, a journal of poetry, graphics, fiction, and reviews, from late 1966 to early 1975, and ran weekly poetry readings in Cardiff through the 1970s and 1980s.

He is known as a lively reader of his work, performing with Bob *Cobbing and others, and a poet of technical range, working in traditional forms as well as visual and collaborative practices. He has published over twenty-five books of poetry, many through Cobbing's Writers Forum and Seren in Wales. See *The Welsh Poems* (Shearsman, 2006), which includes his Internet-generated collage of 'information' about the Anglo-Welsh poet R. S. *Thomas, and *Selected Later Poems* (Seren, 2007). The invertor of many kinds of poem, his use of found language now seems a British anticipation of *Conceptualism. In 2011, he was given the Ted Slade Award for Service to Poetry.   NH

Finkel, Donald (1929–2008) Husband of the poet and novelist Constance *Urdang, Finkel was a native of New York City. He left New York early in his career, however, and accepted a series of university teaching positions, culminating with his appointment to the faculty of Washington University in 1960–91, where he was poet in residence from 1965 until his death. He also taught at Bennington College and Princeton University.

In spite of his Eastern background, Finkel seems pre-eminently a Midwestern poet, and it is in this landscape and diction that much of his work occurs. His poems may borrow from classical myth or a very extensive and profound knowledge of Western culture, but they repeatedly return to the concerns of the emotionally parched world associated with the Midwest. His stronger poems include 'The Detachable Man', a sequence collected in a volume of that name (1984), in which the title figure identifies himself as one who does '*without*'. *Adequate Earth* (1972) is a long poem which draws on a visit which Finkel made to Antarctica in 1969. He returned to Antarctica for subject-matter in another long poem, *Endurance: An Antarctic Idyll* (1978—all Atheneum). Richard *Howard, in an essay on Finkel in *Alone with America* (Atheneum, 1969, 1980), argues that the poetry's 'prime compulsion' is 'the escape from myth into individuality, history and death'.

See *Not So the Chairs: Selected and New Poems* (Mid-List Press, 2003).   EHF

Finlay, Ian Hamilton (1925–2006) Born in Nassau, Bahamas. Lived in various parts of Scotland until settling, in 1966, at Stonypath, near Dunsyre, where, with Sue Finlay, he created the garden 'Little Sparta'. In 1961, with Jessie McGuffie, Finlay co-founded the magazine *Poor.Old.Tired. Horse* and Wild Hawthorn Press.

Finlay's earliest work from the 1950s—collected in *The Dancers Inherit the Party: Early Stories, Plays and Poems* (Polygon, 1996)—comprises short stories and plays set in the rural landscapes where he lived. The early poems, *The Dancers Inherit the Party* (Migrant, 1960) show his move 'towards formalism, concision and transformation', as well as tones of humour and melancholy, which characterize Finlay's later work. A major innovator in concrete poetry, Finlay claimed it was 'concerned with intelligence & order, not the self, "thought" & fuss'. Wild Hawthorn published much of the work as cards, prints, and booklets. Books include *The Blue and the Brown Poems* (Jargon, 1968) and *Poems to See and Hear* (Macmillan, 1972). Subjects include fishing cultures; pastoral; the French Revolution; and Neo-Classicism. Finlay's martial allusions include, contentiously, Nazi imagery.

Finlay saw his interest in 'architecture & avant-gardening' as 'the logical development of earlier concrete poetry—from the poem as an object on the page to the poem as an object'. This led to collaborations with numerous artists and artisans and commissions for public gardens and installations. Comprehensive introductions to Finlay are Yves Abrioux's *Ian Hamilton Finlay: A Visual Primer* (Reaktion, 1994) and Alec Finlay's *Selections* (University of California Press, 2012).   ROH

Fisher, Allen (1944–) Born in South London, Fisher worked in the lead and plastic industries before studying art at Goldsmiths College and then Essex University in the 1980s. He was a member of the English Fluxus group, and taught at Hereford College of Art. He is now Emeritus Professor of Poetry and Art at Manchester Metropolitan University. Fisher began to write poetry in the 1960s, and was an active figure in what has been called the British Poetry Revival. In 1974 he began the journal *Spanner*, and has published his own writing in over a hundred pamphlets and books. He is also a painter and performer.

An early instance of Fisher's process-ravaged Romanticism was *Thomas Net's TREE-BIRST* (Edible Magazine, 1970), an 'auto-destructive' version of *The Prelude*, Book First. His output has often been gathered under larger projects. Between 1971 and 1979, he wrote the five books collected as *PLACE* (Reality Street, 2005), developing the 'open field poetics' of Charles *Olson in relation to his own territory of South London. Another sequence, *Gravity as a Consequence of Shape* (a 'history of ideas for a future culture'), began in 1982, and has been collected in three books: *Gravity* (Salt, 2004), *Entanglement* (The Gig, 2004), and *Leans* (Salt, 2007).

The fascination with a multiplicity of 'spacetimes' in Fisher's work makes it impossible to summarize in a sentence. A succinct expression of his aesthetics of consciousness can be found in 'The Poetics of the Complexity Manifold' (*Boundary 2, vol. 26, no. 1* (1999), pp. 115–8).   JNT

Fisher, Roy (1930–) Born at Handsworth, Birmingham, and educated at Handsworth Grammar School and Birmingham University. He taught at Midlands schools and colleges from 1953 to 1971, and as senior lecturer in American Studies at the University of Keele, 1972–82. Since then he has worked as a freelance writer and musician.

Fisher is an elusive, skilful poet who has absorbed an unusual number of influences. 'I get used as a between-worlds counter in reviewers' debates', he has said, the worlds in question being those of the 'underground' and the 'establishment'. This is borne out by his publishing history: his early *Collected Poems 1968: The Ghost of a Paper Bag* (1969) was published by Fulcrum Press, noted for its championship of neglected figures; his later *Poems 1955–1980* (1980) and *Poems 1955–1987* (1988) by Oxford University Press.

The Fulcrum *Collected* demonstrates his variousness. Fisher can write traditional, well-made poems such as 'The Hospital in Winter', wittily metaphysical poems such as 'The Billiard Table' and 'Starting to Make a Tree', and ambitious modernist poems like 'City', an extended meditation in prose and verse on his native Birmingham. This has been likened to William Carlos *Williams' *Paterson*. It began as a series of discrete short poems and prose observations, and was only later fused or agglomerated into one. 'The openness of my preferred forms', he has remarked, 'is . . . imaginative self-preservation as well as . . . a political attitude'—i.e. a rejection of metrical closure and consensus politics. One of his constant themes is the nature of perception itself, and the role of an imperious imagination. 'The human mind makes the world. The examination of this organism that makes the world is of paramount interest.' In lesser poems, for example in much of *The Thing About Joe Sullivan* (Carcanet, 1978), this reflexivity seems rather cloudy and whimsical, a means of evading the emotions that lie beneath the quiet surface of his best work.

Jazz, 'violent and ordinary', is clearly one influence on his method of composition, West Coast and *Black Mountain poetry another. Fisher himself insists that he is a 'realist'; the element of surreal caprice in his poems simply mirrors that of our perceptual apparatus and the world at large. 'On the Neglect of Figure Composition', a witty poem containing proposals for 'a fresh Matter of Britain', is both playful and serious, and far from indifferent to conceptual thought.

Fisher's formal variety and sustained achievement has made him one of Britain's most widely admired contemporary poets. In 2005 he was elected as a Fellow of the Royal Society of Literature. *The Long and the Short of It: Poems* (2005; expanded edn., Bloodaxe, 2012) covers the range of half a century, from the experimental prose of *The Cut Pages* (Fulcrum, 1971) to the long poem *A Furnace* (1986), and later collections *Birmingham River* (1994—both Oxford University Press) and *Standard Midland* (Bloodaxe, 2010). Published to mark his eightieth birthday, *An Unofficial Roy Fisher* (Shearsman, 2010), edited by Peter *Robinson, includes uncollected writing, poems in homage, critical essays and a bibliography. See also *The Thing About Roy Fisher* (Liverpool University Press, 2000), a collection of critical essays, edited by John Kerrigan and Peter Robinson.   ws*

FitzGerald, R. D. (Robert David) (1902–86) Born in Sydney into two distinguished families. His father's family were colonial civil servants, and his mother's, the le Gay Breretons, included his uncle John, professor of English at Sydney University and a poet himself. FitzGerald qualified as a land surveyor in 1925 and followed that profession in Fiji and Australia for the rest of his life.

He published poetry consistently from the early 1920s to the 1980s, acquiring a reputation by the time he was in his late twenties. His standing was at its highest in the 1950s, but his classical forms and uncompromising metrics were not popular in the last few decades of his life.

FitzGerald attempted most of the traditional forms of poetry—the lyric, the long narrative, the meditation, and the ballad. He was least successful with the lyric, but his long meditative poems were some of the finest written in Australia. His subjects were often domestic and personal, but his major contribution was in uniting speculation in aesthetics with the new theories of physics. FitzGerald's ideas grew out of late nineteenth-century vitalism and twentieth-century notions of time. In combining them, he added to what has been called the 'metaphysical' tradition in Australian poetry. These ideas are best seen in such poems as 'The Hidden Bole' (1938), 'Essay on Memory' (1938), and 'The Face of the Waters' (1944). He was also one of the initiators of what became known as 'Voyager Poems'—poems about Australia's history which stress heroism and national creative energy—for example, 'Heemskerk Shoals' (1944) and his most anthologized poem, the convict portrait, 'The Wind at Your Door' (1958). His views on politics and history were illustrated in 'Between Two Tides' (1952), an epic-length poem about Tonga in the early nineteenth century. His spare, elliptical style and jagged rhythms have alienated some readers, but they have the attraction of individuality and the immediacy of the struggle to articulate complex thought.

The most recent edition of FitzGerald's poetry, together with a selection of his prose, may be found in *Portable Australian Authors: Robert D. FitzGerald*, ed. Julian Croft (University of Queensland Press, 1987).   JCr

Fitzgerald, Robert (Stuart) (1910–85) Born in Geneva, New York, but grew up in Springfield, Illinois. His Irish-American parents were actors who had met in a road company. Fitzgerald's early life was marked by tragedy. His mother died when he was 3; his only sibling five years later. When he was 17 his long-invalided father also died. Despite these losses, Fitzgerald became a model scholar-athlete whose literary ambitions received early encouragement from his fellow townsman Vachel *Lindsay. Before attending college, Fitzgerald spent an extra year of preparation at The Choate School where he met the Latin master, Dudley Fitts, with whom he would eventually collaborate on their widely performed translations of Euripides' *Alcestis* (1935) and Sophocles' *Antigone* (1938) and *Oedipus Rex* (1948). At Harvard Fitzgerald took honours in English and Greek. Graduating in 1933, he worked first as a reporter for the *New York Herald Tribune*. In 1936 he joined the staff of *Time*. In the Second World War he served in the US Navy at Guam and Pearl Harbor. In 1945 he returned to the Catholic Church, an experience which suffuses his subsequent poetry. Quitting *Time* in 1949, Fitzgerald divided his time between teaching in the USA and writing in Italy, where he eventually settled his large family. In 1965 he was appointed the Boylston Professor of Rhetoric and Oratory at Harvard, where his charismatic teaching proved influential to the younger poets who would later become known as the *New Formalists. He won many honours, including the first Bollingen Prize in translation. He died in Hamden, Connecticut.

Fitzgerald is generally acknowledged as his generation's pre-eminent translator of classical poetry. His reputation rests primarily on his celebrated versions of Homer's and Virgil's epic poems, *The Odyssey* (1961), *The Iliad* (1974), and *The Aeneid* (1983), but is equally supported by his commanding translations of Sophocles and Euripides. Fitzgerald's *Odyssey* demonstrates the combination of virtues which made his translations invaluable: he created a compelling narrative line, which makes every character and incident memorable, without ever sacrificing the poetry. Cast in flexible but resonant blank verse, Fitzgerald's language mixes archaic and contemporary diction to achieve a lucid but dignified tone capable of both narrative speed and lyric expansion. Showing how the classical epic could be re-created as living contemporary poems, Fitzgerald's translations have not only become the standard against which later versions have been measured; in their form, tone, and texture they have also provided an influential example of how contemporary narrative poems might be written.

Fitzgerald's achievements as a translator have tended to overshadow his genuine talent as a lyric poet. His most powerful early poems are elegiac meditations on particular landscapes. In 'Midsummer' he considers the small-town neighbourhoods of his lost youth. In 'Souls Lake' and 'Colorado' the natural scene becomes a mirror for philosophical speculation. If Fitzgerald's early work reflects spiritual longing, his deeply Catholic later poetry—like 'Solstitium Saeculare'—displays a radiant religious peace.

Spring Shade: Poems 1931–1970 (New Directions, 1971) remains the definitive collection of Fitzgerald's verse. His translations of *The Odyssey* (Doubleday, 1961; Heinemann, 1962), *The Iliad* (Doubleday/Collins, 1974), and *The Aeneid* (Random House/Harvill, 1983) have stayed continuously in print since publication. Fitzgerald's interview in *The Paris Review* (Winter, 1984) is a rich source of biographical and critical information.   DG

Flecker, James Elroy (originally Herman Elroy Flecker) (1884–1915) Born at Lewisham, South London. He went up to Trinity College, Oxford, in 1902, on a classical scholarship. While there he became well known for his agnosticism, his *fin de siècle* style, and for the promising precociousness of his poetry. He later studied modern languages, became friendly with Rupert *Brooke, and worked in the consular service (Constantinople, Beirut). Flecker was one of the more gifted poets of the Edwardian era; there is reason to suppose that he might have developed had he not fallen victim to tuberculosis. He had fruitfully studied French poets, Heredia in particular, and the colourful style he evolved, while over-lush and devoted to verbal effect at the expense of content, was more than competent. He had a reliable ear, and certain phrases in his work (there are twenty in the *Oxford Dictionary of Quotations*) are memorable and shot through with genuinely fervent, if diffused and sometimes commonplace, feeling. 'The Dying Patriot' offers a good example of his strengths and weaknesses. Flecker was best known for his play *Hassan* (Heinemann, 1922), which had a vogue some years after his death; but, although agreeably luxuriant in its faintly decadent manner, it has dated and is now read less than individual poems such as 'The Old Ships' and 'To a Poet a Thousand Years Hence'. He served as a role-model for the *Georgians.

See *Collected Poems* (Secker & Warburg, 1946), and *James Elroy Flecker: From School to Samarkand* (Merle, 1952), by T. S. Mercer.   MS-S

Fletcher, John Gould (1886–1950) Born in Little Rock, Arkansas, the son of a banker and Confederate Civil War veteran, and educated at Harvard. Like several contemporaries, he abandoned America for the richer culture of Europe, living in London, 1909–14 and 1918–33. Finding no takers for his copious early poems, he published five volumes simultaneously at his own expense in 1913 (he later pulped all the unsold copies). In the same year he met *Pound in Paris, but found him too stern a critic, and it was not until Amy *Lowell took over the *Imagist movement that he was ushered into that fold, appearing in each of her three anthologies (1915–17). His five-movement 'Blue Symphony' in the first of these is typical of his early work, whose formal innovations have artistic or musical models (or both). In fact Fletcher was too

individual a spirit to embrace the Imagist programme: in 1916 he wrote to Lowell: 'I do not believe that a poem should present an "image". I do not believe in cadence but in rhythm.' In America during the war years, he wrote a series of pieces on American subjects in what he called 'Polyphonic Prose' (see, for example, 'Clipper Ships'), as well as a number of poems influenced by Oriental art, later collected in *Japanese Prints* (1918). He was still incorrigibly over-productive, and his fortunes took a down-turn when three separate volumes were rejected by publishers in 1917. The next distinct phase of his career, beginning in the mid-Twenties, was religious, its most significant product the Blakean long poem *Branches of Adam* (1926). After a nervous breakdown in 1932 he returned for good to Arkansas, where he followed the *Fugitives in affirming a Southern agrarian culture against Yankee materialism; his last books, *South Star* (1941) and *The Burning Mountain* (1946) have strong regional associations. In 1950 a recurrence of mental illness caused him to drown himself.

Fletcher's *Selected Poems* (Farrar & Rinehart, 1938) won him the Pulitzer Prize; but even within this volume, as a contemporary reviewer remarked, '[his] best and most concentrated work is often lost in the wide reaches of a diffuse whole'. Prose works include *Paul Gauguin* (1921), the first biography of the painter in English, and the autobiography *Life Is My Song* (1937).   MI

Flint, F. S. (Frank Stuart) (1885–1960) Born in Islington, north London, the son of a commercial traveller, and was brought up in what he later described as 'fleabitten' poverty. He left school at 13 and, after a succession of odd jobs, joined the civil service as a typist at 19; he studied French and Latin at night school, and eventually became proficient in ten languages. At 24 he married, and, already a contributor—chiefly of articles on contemporary French literature—to journals such as the *New Age* and the *English Review*—published his first book of poems, *In the Net of the Stars*. This records, for the most part in conventional late-Romantic terms, with occasional flashes of French Symbolism and *Georgian rural nostalgia, the yearnings and disenchantments of a sensitive soul dismayed by urban squalor and redeemed by passionate love; the rhyming stanzas may be unadventurous, the inversions and poeticisms those of an exhausted idiom, but the poems have an affecting awkwardness and sincerity.

It was in this year too—1909—that Flint first came into contact with T. E. *Hulme; out of their close friendship and shared stylistic preoccupations grew an informal group of poets whose attachment to *vers libre* and 'the Image' made them precursors of the movement that Ezra *Pound (who was introduced to Hulme and Flint at about the same time) later christened *Imagisme. Flint, in fact, collaborated in the first printed statement of Imagist precepts, in *Poetry* for March 1913 ('Pound's direct treatment of the "Thing", whether subjective or objective', and so on); his poems appeared in the Imagist anthologies and he remained—despite a bitter falling-out with Pound—a loyal supporter of the movement's aims and principles.

Many of the poems in his collection *Cadences* (Poetry Bookshop, 1915) seem merely pared-down versions of the themes—and sometimes even the subject-matter, as in 'The Swan'—of *In the Net of the Stars*: clearer, plainer, and undoubtedly more 'modern', but thinner in texture and less spontaneous in feeling. When he came to publish *Otherworld: Cadences* (Poetry Bookshop, 1920), Flint was as stalwart as ever in his defence of the free verse he now called 'unrimed cadence', and just as dismissive of rhyme and metre, which he called 'dead or dying devices' that 'strangle and stifle the natural cadence of our emotion'. Almost all trace of the other Imagist virtues has, however, disappeared from the prolix, ruminative title-poem of this book, which provides Flint's fullest exploration of his distinctive theme—defeated aspiration, the contrast between drab reality and a lushly idealized 'otherworld' based on domestic affections; though some of the shorter pieces find more concrete correlatives for Flint's characteristic mood of wistful (self-) disappointment. He published no more collections, and seems to have stopped writing poetry, after *Otherworld* (though his miniature verse-drama, 'The Making of Lilith', was included in *Imagist Anthology*, Chatto & Windus, 1930); instead, he rose to a senior position in the statistics division of the Ministry of Labour and steadily contributed articles and reviews to periodicals such as the *Chapbook*, *Poetry Review*, and the *Times Literary Supplement*. He also published two volumes of translations from the French of Jean de Bosschère (John Lane, 1917) and Émile Verhaeren (Constable, 1916). See *The Fourth Imagist: Selected Poems of F. S. Flint*, ed. Michael Copp (Fairleigh Dickinson University Press, 2007).   AJ

Flynn, Leontia (1974–) Born in County Down, and studied English at Edinburgh and Belfast, where she wrote a doctoral thesis on the poetry of Medbh *McGuckian. In 2005, she became a Research Fellow at the Seamus Heaney Centre for Poetry, Queen's University, Belfast.

These Days (2004) won the Forward Prize for Best First Collection. Its insouciant wit was widely admired, not least for the way it ironizes the world of Northern Irish poetry (one poem is entitled 'When I Was Sixteen I Met Seamus Heaney'). For this and other qualities, including her combination of 'ordinary-sounding anecdotal language' with inventive formal facility, Flynn has been compared to Paul *Muldoon. But Philip *Larkin and Denise *Riley indicate the range of her acknowledged influences.

Drives (2008), which won the Rooney Prize for Irish Literature, features a series of biographical sonnets on other writers. Flynn has referred to these as 'Wikipedia poems'—an updating, perhaps, of W. H. *Auden's 'shilling life'. *Profit and Loss* (2011—all Cape), her third collection, includes a long poem modelled on Auden's 'Letter to Lord Byron', which surveys a life arrived at motherhood and middle-age, with all the 'old junk' of youth still to sift ('Letter to Friends').   JNT

Fogarty, Lionel G. (Lionel George) (1958–) Born in Barambah, Queensland, now Cherbourg Aboriginal Reserve. Leaving high school, he became involved in Aboriginal activism in Brisbane, protesting about Land Rights and custody deaths. He was one of the 'Brisbane Three', arrested but acquitted on conspiracy charges. In 1993 his brother was murdered in a police van.

Fogarty's 'guerrilla poetry' brings the standard English of an unfinished formal education into his own Murri creole, with a passionate insistence on the language of a people as a form of political and spiritual life. The results are disjunctive and incantatory arguments for a poetics of community: 'These words, not vocation | Born, inbred by Aboriginal people | I'm blood. Sheer and delightful.' He prefers to call himself a 'speaker' rather than a 'writer', and has said 'poetry is only relevant when it changes the bloody law'. John *Kinsella has called Fogarty the greatest living 'Australian' poet.

Fogarty cites Kevin *Gilbert and Oodgeroo *Noonuccal as early influences. His first book was Kargun (Cheryl Buchanan, 1980), followed in 1982 by Yoogum Yoogum (Penguin), the name of his grandfather's tribe. Later collections include Minyung Woolah Binnung: What Saying Says (Keeaira, 2004) and Connections Requital (Vagabond, 2010). Booyooburra tells a story of the Wakka Murri for children (Hyland House, 1993). A new and selected poems was published by Hyland House in 1995.   JNT

Forbes, John (1950–98) Born in Melbourne but endured a peripatetic childhood in New Guinea and Malaya before undergoing a Catholic education at De La Salle College in Sydney. He was briefly at Monash University in Melbourne, where he associated with Alan *Wearne, Laurie *Duggan, and John A. *Scott, before graduating from Sydney University with a degree in fine arts.

A long poem by Forbes, 'Four Heads & How To Do Them', was the most frequently anthologized piece in Australia for the 1970s, but his first full-length book, Stalin's Holidays (Transit, 1980), did not appear until the end of that decade, and eight more years elapsed before his second

collection, The Stunned Mullet (Hale & Iremonger, 1988). A New and Selected Poems, which in fact included nearly all the poetry he had written, was published (Angus & Robertson) in 1991.

Despite his small output, Forbes was an influential and imposing figure after the Monash Readings of 1968, his annus mirabilis. His achievement consists of the introduction of a style, since widely imitated by lesser writers, to Australian poetry. It is a style which invites postmodernist exegesis, a hectic mixture of deliberate non-sequiturs, mixed metaphors, meaningless similes, and private jokes. It moves with a dream-like inevitability, combining sophistication and boyishness, all in a depersonalized tone. The effect can be amusing, exhilarating, and involving. The style is remarkably similar to that of the New York poet Frank *O'Hara, whose work was the subject of a thesis Forbes wrote as a student; but its content is Australian.

Forbes' last collection was Damaged Glamour (1998). He died of a heart attack the same year. Collected Poems: 1970–1998 appeared in 2001. See also Homage to John Forbes, ed. Ken Bolton (2002—all Brandl & Schlesinger).   JG

Forché, Carolyn (1950–) Born Carolyn Sidlosky in Detroit, Michigan, and grew up in its suburbs. She attended Michigan State University and Bowling Green University. Forché's first book of poems, Gathering the Tribes (Yale University Press, 1976), was chosen for the Yale Series of Younger Poets by Stanley *Kunitz, who admired the unabashed eroticism in poems such as 'Taking Off My Clothes' and the Sapphic narrative, 'Kalaloch'. In many of these free-verse poems she meditates on the kinship bonds of Native Americans, and links their tribal rites and rituals to her own ethnic roots in Eastern Europe.

A few weeks spent in civil-war-torn El Salvador inspired a group of sombre poems in Forché's second book, The Country Between Us (Harper & Row, 1981), which includes the often-reprinted prose piece, 'The Colonel', a journalistic account of a dinner with a Salvadoran military man who collects the ears of his victims. Poems about oppression in Czechoslovakia ('Letter From Prague, 1968–78'), a scarred Vietnam veteran ('Joseph'), and an American expatriate in Paris ('Expatriate') all blend the personal and the political. Without irony or humour, many poems in the volume emphasize the naïvety of the poet in the face of world events she cannot fully understand. Forché has also published translations of Claribel Alegría and Robert Desnos.

In 1993, she edited an anthology of twentieth-century poetry of 'witness', *Against Forgetting* (Norton). Her later books, appearing after a long silence—*The Angel of History* (1994) and *Blue Hour* (2003—both HarperCollins)—offer fragmented responses to this material, and to her ongoing work as a translator and human-rights activist. She is Director of the Lannan Center for Poetry and Poetics in Washington D.C.   TDeP

Ford, Ford Madox (1873–1939) Born Ford Madox Hueffer (all his books are thus signed until 1923) in Merton, Surrey, the son of a German music-critic and his English wife. His poetry has not been widely read or noticed, although it was often published in his lifetime. Ford put much less effort into it than into his prose; but it is not negligible, either as an indispensable guide to a complex man or for its intrinsic qualities. It is free and flowing, usually careless, almost wilful in its lack of concentration; he showed little grasp of the technical side of verse-making; but it is also genuinely modest, charming, and (like most things he did) unusual. He had a good enough natural ear to preserve him from rhythmical barbarities. He wrote poetry throughout his life, from *Poems for Pictures and for Notes of Music* (John MacQueen, 1900) to *Collected Poems* (Oxford University Press, 1936), which is incomplete. His best work is in *Antwerp* (Poetry Bookshop, 1914), which *Hardy found 'delightful in its spontaneity', and in the sequence of nine poems called 'Buckshee', occasioned by his pleasure and gratitude

at being loved by a young woman when he was a sick old man.

See *Selected Poems* (Pym-Randall, 1971), ed. Basil Bunting (an excellent selection), and *English Poetry 1900–1950* (Carcanet, 1981) by C. H. Sisson.   MS-S

Ford, Mark (1962–   ) Born in Nairobi, Kenya. He was educated at St Paul's School, Lincoln College, Oxford, and Harvard. He is Professor of English at University College, London, and has been visiting lecturer at Kyoto University (Japan).

Ford's vivacious poems range between the oblique social commentary of 'Passion Play', in which football provides a morose refrain, and the surrealistic exuberance of 'A Swimming-pool Full of Peanuts'. The highly intelligent evasiveness of the verse is influenced by *Ashbery, whose collected poems he has edited. Metaphors which seem entirely private, as in 'Winter Underwear', use objects of public discourse as hollow symbols, ones beyond decoding, in a way which insists on the primacy of the poet's imagination. Ford brings to British poetry a *New York School style of take-it-or-leave-it breeziness which reflects his academic experience yet shows a sharp ear for contemporary idiom. It was this ear in particular which brought Ford early acclaim.

Ford's first collection was *Landlocked* (Chatto & Windus, 1992). *Soft Sift* (2001), a decade later, saw him taken on by Faber and, in the States, Harcourt (2003). His third collection, *Six Children* (2011), continues his exploration of the border between British realism and 'the republic of dreams', employing the sestina and the pantoum to reimagine the Kenya of his childhood, and offering an elegy for Mick *Imlah. Ford has written a biography of Raymond Roussel, the influential French proto-Surrealist (2000—both Faber), whose *New Impressions of Africa* (Princeton University Press, 2011) he later translated. He has also edited selections of Frank *O'Hara, Allen *Ginsberg, and the *New York School poets. His essays and reviews have appeared in two volumes: *A Driftwood Altar* (Waywiser, 2005) and *Mr and Mrs Stevens and Other Essays* (Lang, 2011).   LMacK*

Ford, R. A. D. (Robert Arthur Douglass) (1915–98) Born in Ottawa, and educated at the University of Western Ontario and Cornell. Determined to live a normal life despite a debilitating muscular disease, he joined the Department of External Affairs in 1940. In 1946 he married Maria Thereza Gomez, a Brazilian delegate to the United Nations, and was appointed Secretary to the Canadian Embassy in Moscow. He eventually became Canada's Ambassador to the USSR, a post he occupied from 1964 to 1980. A lifelong interest in Russian history and culture made him one of his country's most thoughtful commentators on East-West affairs.

His first book of poems, *A Window on the North* (1956), won the Governor General's Award for poetry. Critics noted the influence of Bliss Carman and D. C. Scott, particularly in the lovingly described emptiness of the northern landscapes and the fascination with the consolations of bleakness. Translations and adaptations of Russian and Portuguese poetry helped Ford extend the somewhat limited range of this early volume. He published six further books of poetry, in which he essentially explored the same territory: the dark and silent spaces whose oppressiveness can be held at bay by signs of human order—love, memory, cultural artefacts, patterns of meticulously noted details. Ford's laconic suggestiveness often creates a kind of lyric minimalism, a quiet self-assertion in the presence of the century's large and potentially soul-destroying movements and concerns. The vision in the later volumes became, if anything, darker and more personal. Ford's technical and political conservatism makes him something of an anomaly in Canadian poetry of this period, and helps explain the relative neglect in which his verse has languished. He added Serbo-Croatian, Spanish, French, and German poems to his published work as a translator. In retirement, he lived in a chateau near Vichy, France.

The most recent, and fullest, edition of Ford's poetry is *Coming From Afar: Selected Poems 1940–1989* (McClelland & Stewart, 1990).

See also *Our Man in Moscow: A Diplomat's Reflections on the Soviet Union* (University of Toronto Press, 1990), an autobiographical account of Ford's years as Canadian Ambassador in Moscow.   DR

Forrest-Thomson, Veronica (1947–75) Grew up in Glasgow and was educated at the universities of Liverpool and Cambridge. Her poetry has particularly attracted interest since the posthumous publication of her critical work, *Poetic Artifice* (St Martin's, 1978), which is influenced by formalism, structuralism, the criticism of William *Empson, and the philosophy of Wittgenstein, but which is always trenchant and original. Her earlier poems in *twelve academic questions* (1970) and *Language-Games* (1971) were concerned to explore the conventions which decree that a poem is a poem. But under the influence of Empson her work reverted to more traditional models, and the poems became dense with ambiguity, irony, and allusion: so dense with allusion in fact, that some read like a self-conscious inventory of quotations. They are sometimes flippant in tone, and maladroit in their handling of form, especially when emotional suffering is the source of inspiration. Nevertheless, there are some poems where all these factors work successfully together: 'Pastoral' is one such. Her poems were first collected in *On the Periphery* (Street Editions, 1976) with a memoir by J. H. *Prynne. The latest edition is *Collected Poems*, ed. Anthony Barnett (Shearsman/Allardyce Book, 2008). See also Alison Mark, *Veronica Forrest-Thomson and Language Poetry* (Northcote House, 2001).   ETL*

Foulcher, John (1952–) Born in Sydney and educated at Macquarie University. He has worked mainly as a schoolteacher, latterly in Canberra, and has been poetry editor of the *Canberra Times*.

The first of his three volumes of verse, *Light Pressure*, appeared in 1983. The poetry was technically skilled and careful, in the service of precise notations of scenes from the poet's emotional life. The range of Foulcher's work widened in *Pictures from the*

War (1987), winner of the National Library Poetry Award, in which human conflict, 'cruelty, and poverty, and war', was the broad ground of his concern. The death of his father, marriage, and the advent of his own children are conventional subjects that Foulcher treats detachedly. Passive, acted upon, 'kidnapped from school | in the alien craft of university', he writes at length of the self observed, though this egoistic concentration features more strongly in *Paperweight* (1991). Perceived from outside ('I sit', 'I lean', 'I recall'), as an actor in his difficult marriage, Foulcher parries the impulse to *confessional poetry by restricting himself to description of the incidentals and externals of his life. All that he needs for a supple and intelligent, not quite self-indulgent poetry, is there, and larger gestures—for instance towards his religious beliefs—are not so successfully handled.

See also *New and Selected Poems* (1993). His later volumes include *The Honeymoon Snaps* (1996—all Angus & Robertson), *The Learning Curve* (Brandl & Schlesinger, 2002), and *The Sunset Assumption* (Pitt Street Poetry, 2012).   PP*

Frame, Janet (1924–2004) Born in Oamaru, New Zealand, the daughter of a railway worker. Frame's childhood was marked by tragedy: her two sisters were drowned and her younger brother was epileptic. As a young woman Frame suffered a breakdown and was admitted to Seacliff Hospital outside Christchurch. She spent eight years in psychiatric hospitals and narrowly escaped a leucotomy.

Frame's writing carries the marks of this background, but we should be wary of projecting on to the poetry the images of distress and loneliness associated with her life. In the poems light and dark are always in balance, shifting continually from comic to tragic modes and from the sublime to the ridiculous, often within a single sentence. Popular speech-forms, the language of advertising, and suburban clichés are set alongside echoes of Shakespeare or *Masefield's 'Sea-Fever'. Pastiche abounds, along with a Joycean predilection for puns and

double entendre. Above all, there are continual deflations of the 'poetic' by the mundane. There are also images of death, loss, and terror, but these are controlled by a richly comic delight in language-play.

Frame published only one book of poems in her lifetime, *The Pocket Mirror* (Braziller, 1967). But to focus on the work published under the category 'poetry' while ignoring the wealth of poetry worked into her novels is to misrepresent her; she is not one of those novelists who happen to have written poems which are mere footnotes to the major work. All her writing challenges the distinction between poetry and prose. Her novels include *The Lagoon* (1951), *Owls Do Cry* (1961), and *The Carpathians* (1988); her three volumes of autobiography were made into a film by Jane Campion under the title of the second volume, *An Angel at my Table*. A posthumous volume, *The Goose Bath* (Random House/Vintage, 2006), is a selection from hundreds of unpublished poems that she kept in the homely container of the same name, with an introduction by Bill *Manhire. *Storms Will Tell* (Bloodaxe, 2008) contains poems from both volumes.   MW

Francis, Matthew (1955–) Born in Hampshire, and currently lives in West Wales, where he is Reader in Creative Writing at the University of Aberystwyth. Originally a writer of fiction, he has published a novel, *WHOM* (Bloomsbury, 1989) and a collection of short stories, *Singing a Man to Death* (Cinnamon, 2012). He has edited the *New Collected Poems* of W. S. *Graham and published a critical study, *Where the People Are: Language and Community in the Poetry of W. S. Graham* (Salt, 2004).

His collections of poetry are *Blizzard* (1996), *Dragon* (2001—both Faber), *Whereabouts* (Rufus, 2005) and *Mandeville* (Faber, 2007). *Dragon* was shortlisted in 2001 for both the Forward Prize and the Welsh Book of the Year. Applying metafictional techniques to verse, *Mandeville* is Francis' most ambitious collection. In a richly imaginative series of forty linked poems, all in tercets, the speaker reports on strange, evocative places ('Of the

Gravelly Sea') and species ('Of Ants that Dig for Gold'), as he pursues the itinerary of the fourteenth-century explorer, John Mandeville, in his perhaps apocryphal account, *The Travels of Sir John Mandeville*. As poetic magic realism, these studies are far from mere whimsicality. They engage more profoundly with the experience of the journey, literal and metaphorical, than much factual travel-writing, and at times draw close in spirit to Dante's epic poem of pilgrimage, *La Divina Commedia* (1300). CAR

Francis, Robert (Churchill) (1901–87) Born in Upland, Pennsylvania, and attended Harvard. From 1926 until his death he lived in Amherst, Massachusetts. His home since 1940, a small, tree-shaded house he called 'Fort Juniper', inspired the name of the Juniper Prize for Poetry, which the University of Massachusetts Press established in his honour.

Although he enjoyed his seclusion in Amherst, he often travelled to Europe and taught variously at home and abroad. He served as Phi Beta Kappa poet at Tufts and at Harvard, and he taught at the American University in Beirut, Lebanon. He spent a year in Rome, having won the Rome Prize of the American Academy of Arts and Letters, 1957–8.

From his first collection, *Stand with Me Here* (Macmillan, 1936), the poems of Robert Francis are marked by an excited curiosity about ordinary things. In them, passion is restrained by a clipped, conversational tone and an original use of form. 'Altitude', in *The Face Against the Glass* (published by the author, 1950), begins with a startled perception of a hawk circling around shrieking crows, and gains momentum as the birds rise and disappear. Much of his later work deals with the drama of human perception as related to art: remarkable poems in this genre are 'Part for the Whole' (1950), 'Exclusive Blue' and 'Three Darks Come Down Together' (1960).

His ten volumes of poetry are represented in *Collected Poems, 1936–1976* (University of Massachusetts Press, 1976). Among his seven prose works are a novel,

We Fly Away (Swallow, 1948), a book of essays, *The Satirical Rogue on Poetry* (1968), and an autobiography, *The Trouble with Francis* (1971—both University of Massachusetts Press). GS

Fraser, Kathleen (1937–) Grew up in Oklahoma, Colorado, and California, where she read English Literature at Occidental College. Moving to New York, she worked as a journalist, and studied poetry with Stanley *Kunitz and Kenneth *Koch. She began to teach in universities from the late 1960s, and was Professor of Writing at San Francisco State University until 1992. During the 1980s, she edited *HOW(ever)*, a journal dedicated to innovative practice in women's writing. She lives in America and Italy.

Fraser's first book was *Change of Address* (Kayak, 1966). Her early work was imagistic, and visual art is an important subject (see *Magritte Series* (Tuumba, 1977)). Her later books developed a more self-consciously textual style: see *Notes preceding trust* (Lapis, 1987), *when new time folds up* (Chax, 1993), and *Discrete Categories Forced into Coupling* (Apogee, 2004). The feminism of Fraser's work often focuses on the literary 'overwriting' of women, with a playfulness that foregrounds 'this | language we come up against' on the printed page. As 're:searches (fragments, after Anakreon, for Emily Dickinson)' has it: 'pink pearl eraser | erasing her face her | ee face meant | her face meant'. *Translating the Unspeakable: Poetry and the Innovative Necessity* (University of Alabama Press, 2000) collects some of Fraser's writings on poets who have been important to her, such as Barbara *Guest and Hannah *Weiner. She has also translated several Italian poets. *il cuore: the heart*, a new and selected volume, was published by Wesleyan University Press in 1997. JNT

French, Anne (1956–) Born in Wellington. She graduated from Victoria University of Wellington in 1980 and moved to Auckland as managing editor of Oxford University Press in New Zealand. In 1993 she became Massey University's inaugural Writer's Fellow. Her first collection of poems, *All Cretans are Liars* (1987), won the 1988 New Zealand Book Award for Poetry. Its title, which alludes to the famous paradox of Epimenides, acknowledges the tricksiness of language and the tendency of truth to recede even as one attempts to formulate it. And it points to the poet's concern with the evasions and subterfuges of verbal communication, and to the witty, paradoxical, game-playing qualities of her poems. French is candid, sophisticated, literate, and sharp. She is an effective commentator on sexual politics. Her second book, *The Male as Evader* (1988), recognizes that women collude in the drama of deception. Her third collection, *Cabin Fever* (1990), while still concerned with 'knowledge and belief', ventures into the outdoors, to range widely around northern New Zealand and its coastal waters.

Her later collections are *Seven Days on Mykonos* (1993), *Boys' Night Out* (1998), and *Wild* (2004—all Auckland University Press). There is a long interview with her in *Landfall, 171* (1989).   MacDJ

Frost, Robert (1874–1963) Born in San Francisco, where he spent his first eleven years. After the death of his father, a journalist, he moved with his mother and sister to eastern Massachusetts near his paternal grandparents. He wrote his first poems while a student at Lawrence High School, from which he graduated as co-valedictorian with the woman he was to marry, Elinor Miriam White. He entered Dartmouth College in the fall of 1892 but stayed for less than a term, returning home to teach school and to work at various jobs, including factory-hand and newspaperman. In 1894 he sold his first poem, 'My Butterfly: An Elegy', to a New York magazine, *The Independent*. That same year, unable to persuade Elinor to marry him (she wanted to finish college first), he headed south on a reckless journey into Virginia's Dismal Swamp. After emerging unscathed he came home to Lawrence where he and Elinor were married in December 1895.

Both husband and wife taught school for a time, then in 1897 Frost entered Harvard College as a special student, remaining there just short of two years. He performed well at Harvard, but his health was uncertain and he rejoined his wife in Lawrence, where she was about to bear a second child. In October of 1900 he settled with his family on a farm just over the Massachusetts line in New Hampshire, purchased for him by his grandfather. There, over the next nine years, he wrote many of the poems that would make up his first published volumes. But his attempt at poultry farming was none too successful, and by 1906 he had begun teaching English at Pinkerton Academy, a secondary school in New Hampshire. That same year two of his most accomplished early poems, 'The Tuft of Flowers' and 'The Trial by Existence', were published. Meanwhile he and Elinor produced six children, two of whom died in infancy. After a year spent teaching at the State Normal School in Plymouth, New Hampshire, he sold the Derry farm and in the fall of 1912 sailed with his family from Boston to Glasgow, then settled outside London in Beaconsfield.

Within two months of his arrival in England, Frost placed his first book of poems, *A Boy's Will* (1913) with a small London publisher, David Nutt. He also made acquaintances in the literary world, such as the poet F. S. *Flint, who introduced him to Ezra *Pound, who in turn reviewed both *A Boy's Will* and *North of Boston*, which followed it the next year. He became friends with members of the *Georgian school of poets—particularly with Wilfred Gibson and Lascelles *Abercrombie—and in 1914, on their urgings, he moved to Gloucestershire to be nearer them and to experience English country living. The most important friend he made in England was Edward *Thomas, whom Frost encouraged to write poetry and who wrote sharply intelligent reviews of Frost's first two books. While many reviewers were content to speak of the American poet's 'simplicity' and artlessness, Thomas recognized the originality and success of Frost's experiments with the cadences of vernacular speech—with what Frost called 'the sound of sense'. His best early poems, such as 'Mowing', 'Mending Wall', and 'Home Burial', were composed under the assumption that, in Frost's formulation from one of his letters, 'the ear does it. The ear is the only true writer and the only true reader.' The best part of a poet's work, he insisted, was to be found in the sentence-sounds poems made, as of people talking. Like Wordsworth (as Edward Thomas pointed out in one of his reviews of *North of Boston*), Frost boldly employed 'ordinary' words and cadences ('I have sunk to a diction even Wordsworth kept above', he said in another letter) yet contrived to throw over them—in Wordsworth's formulation from his preface to the *Lyrical Ballads*—'a certain colouring of imagination'.

England's entry into the First World War hastened Frost's return to America early in 1915. By the time he landed in New York City, his American publisher, Henry Holt, had brought out *North of Boston* (Holt would continue to publish Frost throughout his life). He was fêted by editors and critics in the literary worlds of both New York and Boston, and he continued shrewdly to publicize himself, providing anthologists and interviewers with a vocabulary to describe his poetic aims. A third volume of verse, *Mountain Interval*, published in 1916 but still drawing on poems he had written in England and before, showed no falling off from his previous standard. In fact such poems as 'The Road Not Taken,' 'An Old Man's Winter Night,' 'The Oven Bird,' 'Birches,' 'Putting in the Seed,' and 'Out, Out—' were among the best he had written or was to write. Like the somewhat latecoming and even drab oven bird of his poem, Frost knew in 'singing not to sing', and a century after the ecstatic flights of romantic poets like Keats and Shelley, Frost's bird remained earthbound (the oven bird, in fact, builds its nests on the ground) and, like the poet who created him, sang about the things of this world.

Soon after he re-established himself in America, Frost purchased a farm in Franconia, New Hampshire (he would purchase a number of farms over the course of his life) and then, at the behest of President Alexander Meiklejohn, joined the faculty of Amherst College in Massachusetts. Frost was later to teach at the University of Michigan and at Dartmouth College, but his relationship to Amherst (sometimes a troubled one) was the most significant educational alliance he formed. Meanwhile he had begun the practice of reading his poems aloud—or rather, 'saying' them, as he liked to put it—at public gatherings. These occasions, which continued throughout his life, were often intensive ones in which he would read, comment on, and reflect largely about his poems and about the world in general. Particularly at colleges and universities he commanded the ears and often hearts of generations of students, and he received so many honorary degrees from the academy that he eventually had the hoods made into a quilt.

Frost won the first of four Pulitzer Prizes in 1924 for his fourth book, *New Hampshire*, and followed it with *West-Running Brook* (1928) and *A Further Range* (1936), which also won a Pulitzer. Yet the latter volume occasioned, from critics on the left, the first really harsh criticism Frost's poetry had received. One of those critics, Rolfe *Humphries, complained in *New Masses* (his review was titled 'A Further Shrinking') that Frost no longer showed either a dramatic or a sympathetic attitude toward his New England characters; that in setting himself against systematic political and social reforms (especially Franklin Roosevelt's New Deal), he had become querulous and sarcastic, all too personally present in his quarrel with the way things were going. It is true that, for one reason or another, Frost no longer wrote poems like the dramatic monologues and dialogues in *North of Boston*, and that poems from *A Further Range*, such as 'Two Tramps in Mud Time' or 'Provide, Provide', were argumentative and at times didactic in their thrust. But he had become expert at composing poems that had affinities with light verse and that consisted of a pointed, witty treatment of issues and ideas. Such a treatment purchased its surface brilliance at the cost of deeper sympathies and explorations.

Those deeper concerns were to make themselves felt once again, however, in what was to be Frost's last truly significant book of verse, *A Witness Tree* (1942). During the 1930s, as he became ever more honoured and revered, Frost endured a terrible series of family disasters. In 1934 his youngest and best-loved child, Marjorie, died a slow death from the puerperal fever contracted after giving birth to her first child; in 1938 his wife Elinor died suddenly of a heart attack; then, when he seemed to be pulling things together once more, his son Carol committed suicide in 1940. Another daughter, Irma, suffered—as did Frost's sister Jeannie—from mental disorders and was finally institutionalized. A number of poems in *A Witness Tree* undoubtedly derived their dark tone from the family tragedies suffered over the decade; but at any rate lyrics such as 'The Silken Tent', 'I Could Give All to Time', 'Never Again Would Birds Song Be the Same', and 'The Most of It' stand in the top rank of Frost's work (he himself thought that some of his best poetry was contained in this book). In words from his prose essay 'The Figure a Poem Makes', they exhibit both 'how a poem can have wildness and at the same time a subject that shall be fulfilled'.

Except for the publishing of a major poem, 'Directive', in his 1947 volume, *Steeple Bush*, Frost's poetry after the Second World War was mainly occasional, a relaxation from earlier intensities. He made a triumphant return to England in 1957 to receive honorary degrees from Oxford and Cambridge; he expended his efforts to have Pound released from St Elizabeth's Hospital; and under the Kennedy administration he made a somewhat less-than-satisfactory visit to Russia, in which he attempted, in conversation with Premier Khrushchev, to mediate between the superpowers. His last reading was given to a large audience in Boston in December 1962; the following day he went into hospital for a prostate operation and suffered a severe heart attack while convalescing, then a series of embolisms, one of which killed him in January of 1963.

Frost once wrote about Edwin Arlington *Robinson that 'his life was a revel in the felicities of language', and surely the claim could be made, even more appropriately, of Frost himself. While standing apart from the modernist work of his famous contemporaries—*Eliot, Pound, *Stevens—his own poetry, in its complication of tone and its delicate balancing of gravity and wit ('I am never more serious than when joking', he said more than once), asks for constant vigilance on the reader's part: a listening ear for the special postures of speech and the dramatic effects of silences. Like the works of his great predecessor, Emerson, Frost's poetry has never been sufficiently appreciated in England, the country which gave him his start. This neglect may be in part a reaction to the rather promiscuous admiration he inspired from so many different sorts of American readers (and non-readers), many of whom would have no time for Eliot or Stevens. But if, for some Americans, the homely nature of Frost's materials—cows, apples, and snow-covered woods—predisposes them to like his poetry, such readers are no more narrow than the 'cosmopolitan' ones who accept mythical allusions in Eliot or Pound but disdain stone walls as a fit vehicle for serious poetry. Frost's own formulation to an American friend in 1914 is helpful in thinking about his achievement: he told the friend, Sidney Cox, that the true poet's pleasure lay in making 'his own words as he goes' rather than depending upon words whose meanings were fixed: 'We write of things we see and we write in accents we hear. Thus we gather both our material and our technique with the imagination from life; and our technique becomes as much material as material itself.' It was this principle that Pound saluted in Frost when, in his review of *North of Boston*, he remarked conclusively: 'I know more of farm life than I did before I had read his poems. That means I know more of "Life".'

Robert Frost: Collected Poems, Prose, and Plays, ed. Richard Poirier and Mark Richardson (Library of America, 1995), also contains a selection of Frost's letters. *Robert Frost: A Biography*, by Lawrence Thompson and R. H. Winnick (Holt, 1981), is a one-volume edition of Thompson's three-volume biography. *The Notebooks of Robert Frost*, ed. Robert Faggen (2006), and *The Collected Prose of Robert Frost*, ed. Mark Richardson (2007), have been published by Belknap Press of

Harvard University. See also *Robert Frost: The Work of Knowing* by Richard Poirier (Oxford University Press, 1977); *Frost: A Literary Life Reconsidered* by William H. Pritchard (University of Massachusetts Press, 1993, 2nd edn.); and *Robert Frost: A Life* by Jay Parini (Holt, 1999).   WHP

Fuller, John (1937–) Born in Ashford, Kent, the son of the poet Roy *Fuller and Kathleen Fuller (née Smith). He was educated at St Paul's School and New College, Oxford and in 1966 became a fellow of Magdalen College, Oxford.

In his first book, *Fairground Music* (1961), he showed a remarkable facility for composing poetry in a variety of conventional verse-forms, a talent for vivid descriptive writing, and a sophisticated wit and verbal virtuosity, as in the outlandish rhymes of 'Snapshot'. Of the expertly written sonnets, 'A Kiss in Galloway' is the most moving. Wit and verbal pyrotechnics are prevalent in Fuller's next volume, *The Tree that Walked* (1967—both Chatto & Windus), as in 'De Sade', a sequence of eight limericks. *Epistles to Several Persons* (London, 1973), written in Burns stanzas, are random satirical comments on the fads and pretensions of contemporary culture. They were published simultaneously with annotation in *Poems and Epistles* (Godine, 1973), together with a group of poems including 'The Two Sisters', a sombre character-portrayal reminiscent of *Masefield, and 'The Art of Love', a devastating comment on a world dominated by feminism and sexual permissiveness. *Lies and Secrets* (Secker & Warburg, 1979) is notable for 'The Most Difficult Position', a study of the complex psychological rivalry between two nineteenth-century chess masters— Howard Staunton, British chess expert for the *Illustrated London News*, and the American master from New Orleans, Paul Morphy. The quarrel is famous in chess history. Staunton's part is spoken in blank verse, first in a monologue to his wife, later in soliloquy as epilogue. The style is Browning pastiche, but it is first-rate pastiche. Morphy's part is in hexameters, an epistle written in the summer and fall of 1858, to his mother. The best introduction to Fuller's

early poetry is *Selected Poems 1954 to 1982* (Secker & Warburg, 1985), which reveals a modern sensibility expressing extremely eclectic subject-matter in a variety of traditional verse-forms. It is now complemented by *New Selected Poems: 1983–2008* (2012).

Fuller's *Collected Poems* (2002—both Chatto & Windus) includes *Partingtime Hall* (with James *Fenton) (Salamander Press, 1987), *The Grey among the Green* (1988), *The Mechanical Body* (1991), and *Stones and Fires* (1996—all Chatto & Windus), which won the Forward Prize. In 1998, Faber published his magisterial commentary on W. H. *Auden's poetry. *Ghosts* (2004), his fifteenth collection, is a meditative, elegiac volume, while *Song & Dance* (2008) displays his light verse, including 'The Spellchecker's Guide to Poetry'. *Who is Ozymandias?* offers 'poetry puzzles' in prose (2011—all Chatto & Windus).   DS*

Fuller, Roy (Broadbent) (1912–91) Born in Failsworth, Lancashire, and grew up in Blackpool, where he attended Blackpool High School and later qualified as a solicitor. After a spell in private practice he joined the Woolwich Equitable Building Society in 1938, becoming a director in 1969. He was legal adviser to the Building Societies Association, of which he was a vice-president, and at one time a governor of the BBC. His lectures as Oxford Professor of Poetry (1968–73) are published under the titles *Owls and Artificers* (1971) and *Professors and Gods* (1974). He received many prizes and awards, including a CBE and the Queen's Gold Medal for Poetry, both in 1970; he was also chairman of the Literature Panel of the Arts Council and of the Poetry Book Society.

During the war Fuller served as a radar mechanic in East Africa and then as a radio and radar officer at the Admiralty in London, experiences commemorated in his first books: *Poems* (Fortune, 1939), *The Middle of a War* (1942), and *A Lost Season* (1944—both Hogarth). *Auden's powerful influence is visible throughout, but is gradually subsumed into Fuller's own flexible voice. 'The Middle of a War' and 'During a Bombardment by V-Weapons' are minor classics, expertly condensing all the mixed, unheroic emotions induced by war, and distinguishing between 'ridiculous detonations' and 'the permanent and real | Furies . . . settling in upstairs'. Less death-haunted and less lyrical than his fellow war poets Alun *Lewis and Keith *Douglas, his poetry coolly but honestly records the boredoms and deprivations suffered by most civilians during the aftermath of the Blitz, anticipating *Larkin sometimes in its wry colloquialism ('The 'Nineties would have seen me thrive, | Dyspeptic, bookish, half-alive') and refusal to make large gestures. With *Epitaphs and Occasions* (Lehmann, 1949), *Counterparts* (Verschoyle, 1954), and *Brutus' Orchard* (Deutsch, 1957), he settled into the middle style that continued to serve him throughout a prolific and distinguished career.

Politically, he moved from Thirties neo-Marxism to an undogmatic, left-of-centre Welfare Statism. His poetry characteristically pits reason and a well-stocked mind against lust and terror, a wry stoicism against 'amatory botherations', concluding that 'the world belongs to the obtuse and passionate, and that the bosom's small | But noticeable curve subtends its tall | Explosions and orations of mad abuse' ('The Perturbations of Uranus'). Linguistically too the dialectic is always between the decorous and the rude, 'ruminant . . . art' attempting to digest a world 'weltering in blood'.

'Poetry is something between the dream | And its interpretation', he has said. Fuller cherished art for its coherence and lucidity, but persistently worried about its ability to deal with the quotidian: 'Girl with fat legs, reading Georgette Heyer, | Shall I arrange you in my pantheon?' ('Romance'). Another girl spotted at the baker's eyeing 'a bogus | Farm-house cob' has 'gathered herself together from | The chaos of parturition and | Appears now with a lacquered bouffant | Top-knot and her old wiles unimpaired' ('Metamorphosis'). Fuller rejoiced in the mixture of savagery and civilization that characterizes urban life. He also seized on the posthumous tense, as it were, with Hardyesque relish: 'My photograph already looks historic'; 'Already one's actions

smack of the legendary, | If only to oneself'. Like Auden and *Hardy too he was a dedicated experimenter, using a wide variety of poetic forms, including syllabics, though the pentameter remained his norm.

There are perhaps rather too many quirky meditations and journeyman pieces on favourite topics—gardening, music, poetry, birds, cooking, dreams, insomnia, bits and pieces of science—in the 550 pages of *New and Collected Poems 1934–84* (Secker & Warburg, 1985), but this is merely to say that Fuller benefits from selection. His last substantial collection, *Available for Dreams* (Collins Harvill, 1989), recording the 'unegotistical sublime' of illness and old age and the pleasures of the daily round, showed little diminution of his remarkable powers.

See *Selected Poems*, ed. John Fuller (Carcanet, 2012). Fuller also published eight novels, eight children's books, and three volumes of memoirs. *Roy Fuller: Writer and Society*, by Neil Powell, is a literary biography (Carcanet, 1995).   WS

Fuller, William (1953–) Born in Illinois, Fuller attended Lawrence University in Wisconsin and wrote a PhD at the University of Virginia on the seventeenth-century neo-Platonism of Sir Thomas Browne and Thomas Traherne. He has since lived in Chicago where he is Chief Fiduciary Officer at the Northern Trust Corporation.

Fuller's first book, *byt* (1989), was published by Leslie *Scalapino's press, O Books. His grammatically restless writing is both impassioned and deadpan in its rediscovery of poetic mystery for the post-*Language era ('the flowering crab, the diving bird, the flaming heart | all stand accused of delusion'). *Hallucination* (Flood, 2011), his sixth collection, was described as 'a masterpiece' by Cal Bedient in the *Boston Review*, who singled out Fuller's development of an 'incessantly *thinking*' prose poetry. See also *The Sugar Borders* (O Books, 1992), *Sadly* (2003), and *Watchword* (2006—all Flood), and the British chapbooks *Three Poems* (2006), *Three Replies* (2009—both Barque), and *Dry Land* (Equipage, 2007).   JNT

Fulton, Alice (1952–   ) Born and raised in Troy, New York, where she lived until the age of 25. The industrial, northern city of Troy and its mythic homonym loom large in her second book of poems, *Palladium* (University of Illinois Press, 1986), as well as her recent collection of short stories *The Nightingales of Troy* (2009). She transforms her Catholic, working-class background into the stuff of myth through her inventive and evocative language. *Cascade Experiment: Selected Poems* (Norton, 2005) reveals as well her fascination with modern science and by extension modernity itself. Fulton loves words, and her poems are full of triple-*entendre* and coinages. She re-creates speech at all levels of diction: the scientist, nun, pimp, and child sing equally in her poems. Her book *Powers of Congress* (Godine, 1990) makes the least aspect of modern life seem poetic: computers, hotel decor, junk bonds, and this tendency continues in her most recent work, where she reveals the cruelty of everyday life, of childbirth and war, with an uncommon fierceness. She is Ann S. Bowers Distinguished Professor of English at Cornell University, and received a MacArthur Fellowship in 1991.   EG

Gallagher, Tess (1932–) Born in Port Angeles, Washington. She was taught creative writing by Theodore *Roethke at the University of Washington, and the poems of *Stepping Outside* (Penumbra, 1974) and *Instructions to the Double* (1976) combine Roethke's verbal exuberance with his metaphysical inclinations, but without at all trying to imitate his style or manner. Her third husband, Raymond *Carver, died in 1988. *Willingly* (1992) consists of poems about and to Carver, and lovingly mirror his style and approach to life. *Moon Crossing Bridge* (1992—all Graywolf) was a sequence for Carver. Gallagher's elegiac writing has continued in the later volume *Dear Ghosts* (Graywolf, 2006; Bloodaxe, 2007). See *A Concert of Tenses: Essays on Poetry* (University of Michigan Press, 1986), *Midnight Lantern: New and Selected Poems* (Graywolf, 2011; Bloodaxe, 2012), and *The Man from Kinvara*, a volume of her selected stories (Graywolf, 2009).   MS-S*

Gander, Forrest (1956–) Born in California's Mojave Desert and raised in Virginia, Gander holds a BA in geology from the College of William and Mary and an MA in literature from San Francisco State University. He presently serves as Adele Kellenberg Seaver Professor of Literature at Brown University in Providence, Rhode Island.

Highly acclaimed as both a poet and a translator, Gander has published eight full collections of poetry, ten works of translation, a novel (*As a Friend*, New Directions, 2008), and a book of essays (*A Faithful Existence: Reading, Memory and Transcendence*, Counterpoint, 2005). Additionally he has edited two anthologies, *Mouth to Mouth: Poems by Twelve Contemporary Mexican Women* (Milkweed, 1993) and *Connecting Lines: New Poetry from Mexico* (Sarabande, 2006).

His most recent collection of poems, *Core Samples from the World* (New Directions, 2011), was a finalist for the 2012 Pulitzer Prize and the 2011 National Book Critics Circle Award in Poetry. He has also been awarded fellowships from the Library of Congress, United States Artists, the Guggenheim Foundation, and (twice) the National Endowment for the Arts.

Robert *Hass has described Gander as 'a restlessly experimental writer', a quality evinced in the innovative range of form and style employed across his work. Widely regarded as a leader in ecopoetics in both his poetry and criticism, Gander's latest book is *Redstart: An Ecological Poetics*, co-written with John *Kinsella in poetry and prose (University of Iowa Press, 2012).   CE

Gardner, Isabella (Stewart) (1915–81) Born in Newton, Massachusetts, daughter of an investment banker. After attending private schools, she studied drama, first in East Hampton, New York, and then in London. She was a professional actress from 1939 to 1942. Her first poetry collection did not appear until 1955, when she was 40.

From 1950 to 1956 she was associate editor of *Poetry* magazine in Chicago. The last of four marriages was to poet-critic Allen *Tate, who was in residence at the University of Minnesota. After divorcing Tate, Gardner made her home in Ojai, California, and later in New York City, where she died. A slow, often blocked writer, Gardner produced four collections in her lifetime. Her lyrics are admired for their spontaneity of voice, playfulness and economy of language, and formal accomplishment. Her best poems, like 'The Widow's Yard', deal with personal relationships and the failure of love.

The fullest edition of Gardner's poetry is *Isabella Gardner: The Collected Poems* (BOA, 1990). It includes all previously collected poems as well as thirty unpublished or uncollected. See Marian Janssen, *Not at All What One Is Used To: The Life and Times of Isabella Gardner* (University of Missouri Press, 2010).   RSP

Garfitt, Roger (1944–) Born in Melksham, Wiltshire, and educated at Merton College, Oxford. He edited *Poetry Review*, 1978–81 and was poetry reviewer for the *London Magazine*, 1973–6.

Landscape is the centre of Garfitt's work. He is both a meticulous re-creator of, for example, the effects of light, and a sociable poet who sees place as expressive of its inhabitants. His collection *Given Ground* (Carcanet, 1989), concentrates on the unsung lives of the many whom official history excludes ('Hares Boxing', 'Lover Lumb Mill') and extends into the mythological ('The Hooded Gods' are three unnamed household deities). The minuteness of his attention is often rewarding. Clearly socialist in outlook, and combining formality with freer verse, Garfitt is an intriguing counterpart to the more public work of Douglas *Dunn and Tony *Harrison.

His earlier collections were: *Caught on Blue* (1970); *West of Elm* (1974—both Carcanet); *The Broken Road* (Northern House, 1982). See also *Selected Poems* (Carcanet, 2000). Garfitt edited the *Collected Poems* of his wife, Frances *Horovitz. *The Horseman's Word* (Cape, 2011) is a memoir of his youth.   SO'B

Garioch, Robert (Sutherland) (1909– 87) Born in Edinburgh and educated at that city's Royal High School and University. He began publishing in newspapers in the 1930s. *Seventeen Poems for Sixpence* (1940) was a slender collection shared with Sorley MacLean. Conscripted in 1941, Garioch spent the rest of the war as a POW. The experience is recorded in 'The Wire', a harrowing poem virtually medieval in atmosphere and amounting to a chilling vision of captivity. *Two Men and a Blanket* (written 1946, published 1975)—he referred to it as 'that *Kriegsgefangenschaft* book'—is a prose evocation of his years as a prisoner.

Writing of Garioch's 1940 pamphlet in 1955, George Kitchin referred to Garioch's 'rough-tongued satire, and his language reeking of the closes of Edinburgh'. He went on to state that they 'should not blind us to his real talent'. Kitchin meant the poems in English in *Chuckies on the Cairn* (1949). Garioch's English poems are far from negligible ('Chalk Farm 1945', 'Property', 'Now I Remember You, McAlister') but his 'real talent' turned out to be for poetry in *Scots. His literary affections owed much to Robert Fergusson (1750– 74), the precursor of Burns; he is addressed in 'To Robert Fergusson' and commemorated in the sonnet 'At Robert Fergusson's Grave'. The first of these poems employs the 'Standard Habbie' or Burns Stanza, first used by Robert Sempill of Beltrees in the seventeenth century. Hugh *MacDiarmid's revival of poetry in Scots in the 1920s deliberately avoided Burnsian and other older verse-forms as part of his strategy of dissociating new Scottish poetry from the taint of Burns' trivializing imitators and the thoughtless populism which had grown around Scotland's national poet. Reintroducing these stanzas with contemporary verve rather than archaeological piety constitutes a large part of Garioch's achievement. 'Embro to the Ploy', for example, a high-spirited dig at the pretensions of the Edinburgh Festival, makes use of the bob-and-wheel stanza of the fifteenth-century poems 'Peblis to the Play' and 'Christis Kirk on the Grene'. Stanzas like these support the classically indigenous force of Garioch's work; they are perfect foils for a craftsmanship that is at times stunning in its vernacular confidence, and rarely if ever inadequate. They also assisted him to tap the directness and fast tempos of Scottish verse, in keeping with his persona as Edinburgh's Everyman, a wry, observant,

g

satirical, witty, and elusive figure, whose puzzled smile disguised a wealth of erudition.

Much of Garioch's poetry is humorous; he had a sharp eye for modernist affectation, fakery, hypocrisy, and unearned magnitude of self. Poems like 'The Wire' and 'The Muir', however, could have been undervalued as a consequence. The outcome of his attempt to understand the 1953 Reith Lectures by J. Robert Oppenheimer, 'The Muir' is especially interesting as a meditation on science written in Scots.

Garioch taught in England from 1946 to 1959, which might help to explain the relative slowness with which he came to an established reputation, although he was well known in Scottish literary circles since the newspaper publication of *The Masque of Edinburgh* as early as 1933. A new and expanded version of that work appeared in 1954. Subsequent volumes, as well as cherished public readings, extended his work to a wider readership and considerable popularity. *Collected Poems* (Carcanet, 1977) was replaced by *Complete Poetical Works*, ed. R. Fulton (1983). *A Garioch Miscellany* (1986—both Macdonald) contains brief memoirs, letters, reviews, and the text of *The Masque of Edinburgh*. His translations, of which there are many, especially his versions of Belli's sonnets, are included in *Complete Poetical Works*.   DED

Garlick, Raymond (1926–2011) Born in London and educated at the University College of North Wales, Bangor. He later taught English at Pembroke Dock and at Blaenau Ffestiniog. He was the founder of *Dock Leaves* and edited the magazine (later *The Anglo-Welsh Review*) from 1949 to 1961, when he left Wales to teach at an international school in the Netherlands. Six years later he returned to Wales to take up a post as senior lecturer in the English department at Trinity College, Carmarthen, and he remained there until his retirement.

As editor and critic he made a significant contribution to the study of Anglo-Welsh literature, arguing in numerous essays, and in his *An Introduction to Anglo-Welsh Literature* (1970), that from the late fifteenth century there has been a tradition of writing by Welshmen in the English language which deserves wider recognition, particularly in the schools of Wales. He also edited, with Roland Mathias, an influential anthology, *Anglo-Welsh Poetry 1480–1980* (1984; revd. edn., Seren, 1993).

Before his departure for the Netherlands, Garlick published two volumes of his verse, *Poems from the Mountain-House* (1950) and *The Welsh-speaking Sea* (1954), as well as a long poem for radio, *Blaenau Observed* (1957). On his return he published a trilogy of verse collections: *A Sense of Europe* (1968), *A Sense of Time* (1972), and *Incense* (1976). The unity of these three volumes is in their verse-forms, often intricately structured, and in their common themes, which include a nationalist view of Wales, the poet's adopted country, as an integral part of European civilization, a passionate concern for justice and an admiration for the non-violent campaigns of *Cymdeithas yr Iaith Gymraeg* (The Welsh Language Society), and a preoccupation with language, especially English as one of the languages of a fully bilingual Wales.

A number of new poems, written after he left the Roman Catholic Church, appeared in Raymond Garlick's *Collected Poems 1946–86* (Gomer, 1987). It was followed by *Travel Notes* (Gomer, 1992) and *The Delphic Voyage* (Carreg Gwalch, 2003). See Don Dale-Jones, *Raymond Garlick* (University of Wales Press, 1996). R. S. *Thomas' correspondence with Garlick was published in 2009.   MS

Garrett, George (1929–2008) Born in Orlando, Florida, and educated at Columbia and Princeton. From the mid-1950s he held a number of academic appointments, most prominently at Hollins College, the University of South Carolina, and the University of Virginia, where he was appointed Henry Hoyns Professor of Creative Writing in 1984. Garrett was a complete man of letters who published in all genres, including short stories, screenplays, and literary criticism, and who edited anthologies and literary reviews. His first collection of poems, *The Reverend Ghost*, appeared in

1957 in Scribner's Poets of Today series. He subsequently published six collections, including *For a Bitter Season: New and Selected Poems* (University of Missouri Press, 1967) and *The Collected Poems of George Garrett* (University of Arkansas Press, 1984), as well as numerous chapbooks and broadsides.

Garrett's wit, literary sophistication, and deft handling of traditional forms linked him to the academic poets of the 1950s, like *Nemerov and *Wilbur, but he also wrote a substantial number of free-verse lyrics. He is at his best as a writer of intelligent light verse, satirical epigrams and invectives, and topical poems, all genres that have become rare in contemporary American poetry. A lifelong Episcopalian, Garrett drew on religious subjects for poems like 'Revival', which describes ironically the fervour of Southern fundamentalists. 'Buzzard', a frequently anthologized poem, depicts a predatory bird as the appropriate emblem of both religious and poetic inspiration. He was also the author of a number of sensitive love poems. In later years Garrett concentrated on writing fiction, including *An Evening Performance: New and Selected Short Stories* (1985); *Poison Pen* (1986), an entertaining work of social and literary satire; and a trilogy of novels about Elizabethan England. See also *Days of Our Lives Lie in Fragments: New and Old Poems, 1957–1997* (Louisiana State University Press, 1998).   RSG

Garrigue, Jean (1912–72) Born in Evansville, Indiana. Her pre-Revolution ancestry was of mixed French, English, and Scottish origin. She received her BA degree at the University of Chicago, and in 1943 an MFA at the University of Iowa. She settled in New York's Greenwich Village and taught occasionally at various colleges, and from 1968 to 1970 she was appointed scholar, Radcliffe Institute for Independent Study. She died of Hodgkins disease in December 1972.

The individuality evident from her first publication in the Fall 1941 issue of the *Kenyon Review* accounted for her swift emergence as one of her generation's leading poets. In addition to the seven volumes

of poems that followed, she also published a novella, *The Animal Hotel* (1966), and the collection *Chartres and Prose Poems* (1971—both Eakins). Among American poets her strongest affinities were with Hart *Crane, and among English poets with Keats. She also admired greatly *Stevens and Marianne *Moore on whose poetry she published a highly regarded monograph (University of Minnesota Press, 1965; Oxford University Press, 1966).

In her poetry Garrigue relates to all things ephemeral with an intensity so charged that only language which aims to exceed itself is adequate. That she managed to combine excess with the strictness of art remains her triumph. She detects the unseen not as absence but as felt reality. This vision, running through much of her work, is suggested by the title of what was perhaps her best book, *Country Without Maps* (Macmillan, 1964). By the time of her death, attention to her work had somewhat declined—she had little appeal for a criticism concerned solely with feminist causes—but a revival of interest followed. Her papers have been acquired by the prestigious Berg Collection (New York) and articles on her have appeared in scholarly journals, including a symposium in *Twentieth Century Literature* (1983).

Her most representative collection remains *New and Selected Poems* (Macmillan, 1967). For critical studies see the chapter on Garrigue in *Unassigned Frequencies*, by Laurence Lieberman (University of Illinois Press, 1977), and *Jean Garrigue, A Poetics of Plenitude*, by Lee Upton (Fairleigh Dickinson University Press, 1991).   AG

Gascoyne, David (Emery) (1916–2001) Born at Harrow and educated at Salisbury Cathedral Choir School and Regent Street Polytechnic in London. In 1932, while still at school, he published his first book of poems, *Roman Balcony*. In 1933 his poems appeared in *New Verse*, and his semi-autobiographical novel, *Opening Day*, was published. On the advance of royalties he visited Paris, home of the *Surrealist movement that he already admired. In *A Short Survey of Surrealism* (1935) he gave one of the first accounts of the movement published in England. He was then 19. He was one of the few British poets to be strongly influenced by the movement, as is evident from his second book of poems, *Man's Life Is This Meat*, published in 1936, the year of the Surrealist Exhibition in London. In September he joined the Communist Party, and the following month went briefly to Spain.

In the autumn of 1937 he came upon Pierre Jean Jouve's *Poèmes de la Folie de Hölderlin* (1930), which had a profound effect on him, as described in *Paris Journal* (1978); and in 1937 he published a volume of original poems and translations, *Hölderlin's Madness*. The influence of Jouve was an abiding one and is felt in Gascoyne's most important book, *Poems 1937–42*, where there is a new, religious quality.

During the latter years of the Second World War Gascoyne worked as an actor and wrote little poetry. In 1947 he returned to Paris, out of which came the title-poem of his next book, *A Vagrant* (1950). It contained some powerful poems, but was marred by what the author called 'makeweight verse'. By this time he was much engaged by Existentialism, particularly the work of the Russian philosopher Leon Chestov.

In the early Fifties he was commissioned to write a long poem for radio, which was finally broadcast in 1955 and published the following year as *Night Thoughts*. During the Fifties he lived in France and suffered medical and psychological problems due to the use of amphetamines, to which he alludes in *The Sun at Midnight* (1970). He wrote hardly any poetry after *Night Thoughts*.

Gascoyne is an uneven writer, but his work includes visionary poems of an often harrowing religious and philosophic intensity, unusual in poets of his generation. His work is marked by a depth of response, seldom encountered in British writing, to modern European poetry, his translations from which appeared as *Collected Verse Translations* (1970). His *Collected Poems* (1988) contains a valuable memoir that serves as an introduction to the poems. See Robert Fraser, *Night Thoughts: The Surreal*

Life of the Poet David Gascoyne (2012—all Oxford University Press). ATT

Geddes, Gary (1940–) Born in Vancouver and grew up in British Columbia and Saskatchewan. Educated at the University of British Columbia and the University of Toronto, he was once writer-in-residence at the University of Alberta. He taught at Concordia University in Montréal and later at Western Washington University. The settings of his poems reflect his wide travel—notably in the Far East.

Political, but not in any partisan way, Geddes is deeply concerned with 'what we can't afford to forget about our private and collective pasts'. Like Al *Purdy, he often finds himself among graves, archaeological relics, and 'lost manuscripts | charting connections'. There is a strong narrative element in his poetry: see, in particular, 'Sandra Lee Scheuer' and longer, fragmented poems such as *War & other measures* (1976) and *The Terracotta Army* (1984). 'Sandra Lee Scheuer' is about a student killed at Kent State University on 4 May 1970 by the Ohio National Guard. *War & other measures* is a collection of related lyrics and narrative fragments imaginatively reconstructing the life of Paul Joseph Chartier, who died in the men's washroom of the Canadian House of Commons on 18 May 1966, when the bomb he was carrying accidentally exploded. *The Terracotta Army* is a series of dramatic monologues in which the imagined speakers are clay soldiers from China of the third century BC. It was reprinted in Britain by Peterloo Poets in 2007, and in an illustrated edition by Goose Lane in 2011.

Since *Active Trading: Selected Poems 1970–1995* (1996), Geddes has published a series of documentary volumes: *Flying Blind* (1998), on travelling through Israel with a blind poet and scholar; *Skaldance* (2004), on the history of the Orkney Islands; *Falsework* (2007), on the collapse of the Vancouver Second Narrows Bridge in 1958; and *Swimming Ginger*, a poetic commentary on the twelfth-century Chinese Qingming Shanghe Tu scroll (2010—all Goose Lane).

His prose memoir about returning to live in British Columbia, *Sailing Home: A Journey Through Time, Place and Memory* (HarperCollins, 2001), was a bestseller, and his influential anthologies of Canadian poetry and modern poetics have been frequently reprinted. In 2008, Geddes received the British Columbia Lieutenant Governor's Award for Literary Excellence.   DRB*

Ghiselin, Brewster (1903–2001) Born in Webster Groves, Missouri, and for most of his life worked as a teacher of English at the University of Utah, Salt Lake City, where from 1971 he was emeritus professor. Although admired during the 1950s by such poets as W. S. *Merwin and, later, James *Dickey and Kathleen *Raine, his poetry, the bulk of which may be read in *Windrose: Poems 1929–1979* (University of Utah Press, 1980), has not reached an international audience. He wrote that his 'central subject' is 'man's struggle for breath, for being and light', and his poetry is concomitantly fervid—although always in a disciplined manner—owing much to *Eliot, Hopkins and, perhaps above all, to St-John Perse. It is never less than carefully and conscientiously written. Ghiselin's earlier verse, as in his first collection, *Against the Circle* (Dutton, 1946), was polished and elegant, reflecting the then prevailing New Criticism; this later gave way to a broader and more (as it has been described) 'tidal' style ('Behind you the toppling bells and foam-like waving farewell'). His last collection was *Flame* (University of Utah Press, 1991). There is a chapter on Ghiselin's poetry in Henry Taylor, *Compulsory Figures: Essays on Recent American Poets* (Louisiana State University Press, 1992).   MS-S*

Ghose, Zulfikar (1935–) Born in Sialkot, Pakistan. He took a degree in English and philosophy at Keele University, and, before becoming a teacher in London, was cricket correspondent of the Observer. He was a professor of English at the University of Austin, Texas until his retirement. He has written over a dozen novels—including one, *The Texas Inheritance* (1980), under the name of William Strang—as well as books of criticism and five collections of

poetry. At first associated with the novelist B. S. Johnson, with whom he co-authored a book of stories (*Statement Against Corpses*, 1964), and with Johnson's somewhat misconceived poetic experimentation, he has latterly—especially in his fiction—gravitated to more sophisticated genres, demonstrating the influence of his philosophical studies. Philip *Hobsbaum said that Ghose's 'precision of detail is a pattern about a void'. But students of 1960s so-called 'syllabics' and of predominantly intellectual poetry, such as was most notably and polemically practised by the Romanian mathematician Ion Barbu (called by him 'passion on ice'), would find his work rewarding.

See his autobiography, *Confessions of a Native Alien* (Routledge & Kegan Paul, 1965), *In the Ring of Pure Light: Lectures on Language and Literature* (2011), and *50 Poems: 30 Selected 20 New* (2010), both published in Pakistan by Oxford University Press.   MS-S

Gilbert, Jack (1925–2012) Born in Pittsburgh, Pennsylvania, and educated at the University of Pittsburgh and at San Francisco State College. Recipient of the Yale Younger Poets Award for *Views of Jeopardy* (Yale University Press, 1962), he served as chief lecturer on American Literature for the US State Department in the 1970s. His second collection, *Monolithos: Poems, 1962–1982* (New York, 1982), chronicles his later migratory and reclusive life in Italy, Japan, and Greece, where he lived with the poet Linda *Gregg.

His preference for writing brief, elliptical, understated poems is best understood as a corrective to the discursive excesses of *Beat and conversational poetry. Despite his distrust of artfulness, many of his most memorable poems, like 'The Abnormal Is Not Courage', 'Don Giovanni on His Way to Hell', and 'In Dispraise of Poetry', focus on literary and historical subjects. Narrating the frustrations of a self seeking to build a redeeming spirituality through Eros, asceticism, and travel, his best poems gain depth and resonance from their allusive Aegean settings. His work is unified in theme and tone; but, out of print for many years, it seemed fragmentary, mysteriously incomplete, like the statuary of the Mediterranean vistas he often described.

The second half of Gilbert's career began at the end of his sixties with his third book, *The Great Fires: Poems 1982-1992* (1994). *Refusing Heaven* (2005), his fourth, won the National Book Critics Circle Award. In the same year, he was interviewed for the *Paris Review*'s 'Art of Poetry' series. Reflecting on his long life and costive oeuvre, he observed that Ezra *Pound's motto 'make it new' was missing a word: 'it should be make it importantly new'. *The Dance Most of All* (2010) was followed by *Collected Poems* (2012—all Knopf). *Transgressions*, a selected poems, was published in the UK by Bloodaxe in 2006.   DWF*

Gilbert, Kevin J. (1933–93) Born in Condobolin, New South Wales, the son of an English-Irish father and Aboriginal-Irish mother. His mother's Wiradjuri people fiercely resisted the white invasion. Orphaned at seven, Gilbert remembered seven Wiradjuri elders 'who knew of the old things'—namely the language, customs, sacred spots, and massacre sites. In 1957 he was charged with the murder of his white wife; no defence witnesses were called, he was given life, and spent the next fourteen-and-a-half years in some of the state's worst gaols. His first play (and the first by an Aboriginal), *The Cherry Pickers* (written 1970; pub. 1988) and many poems were written while he was incarcerated.

His release, after a public campaign, coincided with the publication of his first volume of poems, *End of Dream-Time* (1971), and a new wave of Aboriginal militancy. Gilbert played a pivotal role: in 1972 he helped organize the Black Moratorium and the famous Aboriginal Embassy on the lawns of Parliament House; he was charged (and exonerated) with threatening to kill the queen; and he published *Because a White Man'll Never Do It* (1973), his first attempt to contribute to 'the regeneration of the Aborigine'. In the next twenty years, through his passionate espousal of Aboriginal rights and the publication of *Living*

Black—Blacks Talk To Kevin Gilbert (1977; repr. Allen Lane, 1978), *Inside Black Australia—an Anthology of Aboriginal Poetry* (1988), and *Aboriginal Sovereignty Justice the Law and Land* (1988), Gilbert emerged as the most political and iconoclastic of all Aboriginal writers. He ran the Treaty '88 Campaign, and in 1990 began Australian Aboriginal Community Aid Incorporated.

Like virtually all Aboriginal creative writers of his generation, Gilbert was an activist first and a writer second. His poetry in the 1970s falls broadly into four categories—Aboriginal character studies, strident social protests, indictments of 'Jackies' (career Aboriginals, 'lickin' smilin' lyin''), and calls to action, such as 'Mister Man', 'The Flowering . . .', 'Look Koori', and 'Me and Jackamari Talkin' About Land Rights'. His later poems maintain the rage but he is now more positive, at times even cautiously optimistic.

The Blackside—People Are Legends and other poems (1990) was followed by *Black from the Edge* (1994—both Hyland House). They are complemented by Gilbert's essays (and new poems) in *Imagining the Real: Australian Writing in the Nuclear Age* (1987) and *Looking Beyond Yesterday: The Australian Artist and New Paths to Our Future* (1990).   DH

Gillies, Valerie (1948–   ) Born in Canada, but was brought up and educated in Edinburgh, where she attended the University. A year at the University of Mysore in southern India provided the subjects of the best poems in her first collection *Each Bright Eye* (1977).

Whether about people, places, children, animals, or objects, Gillies' poetry hinges on uncluttered observations and insights, often delivered in moods of puzzled affection. Disclosures of a more unnerving kind run through her work too; however, its general effect is gentle, settled, and benign, although without an excess of understatement or soft-hearted benevolence. The unshowy lyricism of her first two collections stems from a technique that is essentially one of free verse leaving room for the possibilities of a near-musical tonality. Some poems in *Bed of Stone* (1984) attempt more organized rhythm and rhyme ('The Pause', 'Eagle', 'The Drill'). Her relaxed, scrupulous formality is extended in *The Chanter's Tune* (1990—all Canongate).

She has translated Gaelic poetry, taught writing in hospitals, and participated in public art collaborations around Scotland: see *Men and Beasts* (Luath, 2000), with the photographer Rebecca Marr. In 2005 she became the first female Makar (Poet Laureate) of Edinburgh. Her later books include *The Lightning Tree* (Polygon, 2002) and *The Spring Teller* (Luath, 2008).   DED*

Gilmore, Mary (Mary Jean Cameron) (1865–1962) Born into a family of pioneer settlers in southern New South Wales, Mary Gilmore was the first woman member of the Australian Workers Union and the first woman on its executive. In 1893 she helped to found the socialist New Australia settlement in Paraguay; marrying there, she returned to Australia with her husband and son in 1902. Editor for many years of the women's page of the *Worker* newspaper, she became famous for her essays and articles, which often rise to the quality of prose poetry, especially in the reminiscences she collected in the volume *Old Days: Old Ways* in 1933. Through her own and other newspapers Mary Gilmore championed many causes over the years, from invalid pensions to a proper status for illegitimates.

Her reputation as a poet began to grow with the publication of her first collection, *Marri'd*, in 1910, and was consummated by the rapturous reception of her second volume, *The Passionate Heart*, in 1918. Of a reformist rather than a revolutionary temper, fiercely patriotic, with a real love for the downtrodden of all periods of Australian history, she could extol the convicts and pioneers and yet write with clearer eyes than any of her contemporaries about the great glossed-over crime of settlement days, the wholesale slaughter of the Aborigines. In the latter half of her long life she became the legendary elder and remembrancer of the Labor movement, then of the nation, and even thirty

years after her death her legend continues, to a degree, to inhibit a clear assessment of her published work. The beloved figure of Dame Mary may be hiding a better poet than recent criticism has allowed. Since the 1960s, she has tended to be represented fairly sparsely in anthologies, and very often by the same few short, concentrated lyrics: 'Nationality', 'Old Botany Bay', sometimes 'Never Admit the Pain'. All of these do represent one side of her verse, a side equally well illustrated by the less familiar but deeply moving elegy 'The Little Shoes That Died'.

Perhaps surprisingly for a cradle Presbyterian and lifelong socialist, Mary Gilmore at times evinced a mystical and rather Catholic spirituality, which not only allowed her to contribute simultaneously, in the 1950s, to the Communist paper *Tribune* and the *Catholic Weekly*, but evoked several fine religious poems, notably the title-poem of her 1931 collection *The Rue Tree*. Living across a great span of literary epochs, and tugged this way and that by the impulses of Victorian romanticism, bush balladry, and the pre-modernist modernity of contemporary newspaper verse, she seems at times uncertain in her diction, veering between the colloquial, the poeticizing, and many usually unfortunate strains of dialect. On the other hand, there is a lesser-known side of her verse which connects with the manner and sensuous particularity of her best essays, and achieves the supple density of poems such as 'The Harvesters'.

See *The Collected Verse of Mary Gilmore*, edited in two volumes by Jennifer Strauss (University of Queensland Press, 2006–2007).   LM

Ginsberg, Allen (1926–97) Born in Newark, New Jersey and grew up in Paterson where his father, Louis, a published poet, was a high school teacher. Ginsberg attended Columbia University in New York, where he met Jack *Kerouac and William Burroughs, friendships that would be central to the *Beat group of writers. With Neal Cassady and Carl Solomon, they were the dedicatees of *Howl and Other Poems* (1956), the sequence in which he found his voice as the Whitmanic poet-prophet of a 'generation destroyed by madness'. Ginsberg's poems prior to 'Howl', such as 'In the back of the real' (1954), show the influence of Paterson's most famous poet, William Carlos *Williams, as well as the mysticism of William Blake. (Ginsberg heard Blake reciting his poems during an 'illumination of eternal consciousness' in Harlem in 1948.) The wilder language and long verse line of 'Howl', written when Ginsberg was living among the *San Francisco Renaissance poets, reflected Kerouac's Buddhist-influenced notion of writing the moment of consciousness through a 'spontaneous bop prosody', analogous to improvisation in jazz.

James *Joyce once observed that T. S. *Eliot's *The Waste Land* (1922) ended the idea of 'poetry for ladies'. *Howl and Other Poems* had the same effect in post-war America. As Williams wrote in an introductory note to the volume, 'Hold back the edges of your gowns, Ladies, we are going through hell.' The 'other poems' included classics of Ginsberg's gregarious humour such as 'America', which ends 'I'm putting my queer shoulder to the wheel', one of several references to his homosexuality. An attempt to prosecute the volume for obscenity failed.

Ginsberg's next major poem was the title sequence of *Kaddish and Other Poems* (1961), an autobiographical lament for his mother, Naomi, a Communist party member who suffered from schizophrenia and died in 1956. Breaking up 'Howl''s sweeping line with agitated dashes as memories flash in upon each other, the ritual form of 'Kaddish' saw Ginsberg deepening his poetic engagement with his Jewish background. (The Kaddish is a prayer in praise of God, recited by mourners.) In the late 1950s Ginsberg began to travel with his long-term partner Peter Orlovsky, living in Paris with other Beats, and going to India in the early 1960s. His fame as a spokesperson for libertarian political and religious beliefs began to spread.

The poems of Ginsberg's later volumes such as *Reality Sandwiches* (1963) can be occasional and diaristic, but *Planet News* (1968) in particular contains some of his most original post-*Howl* writing, such as the anti-Vietnam sequence 'Wichita Vortex Sutra', improvised onto tape during a long bus journey through the Midwest, and 'Studying the Signs', a London aubade. Significant later collections include *The Fall of America: Poems of These States* (1973) and *Plutonium Ode* (1981), which won the National Book Award. All were first published in 'pocket' format by Lawrence *Ferlinghetti's City Lights Books in San Francisco, and remain in print, having sold hundreds of thousands of copies.

Writing openly about spiritual and sexual experience, Ginsberg's activism and charismatic readings—including one at the Royal Albert Hall in London, recorded in Peter Whitehead's documentary *Wholly Communion* (1965)—made him a counterculture hero in the 1960s. From 1974 until his death he directed and taught at the Jack Kerouac School of Disembodied Poetics, Naropa, a writing programme that he co-founded with Anne *Waldman. His example as a popular experimental poet, whose expansive, omnivorous voice is by turns comic and prophetic, continues to resonate in contemporary American verse, from Clark *Coolidge and Ron *Silliman to C. K. *Williams and D. A. *Powell.

Selected Poems 1947–1995 (1997) and *Collected Poems 1947–1997* (2006) were published in the US by Harper and in the UK by Penguin, as was *Deliberate Prose* (2000), a substantial gathering of his non-fiction and criticism. Ginsberg's readings and performances can be heard on the CD box set *Holy Soul Jelly Roll* (Rhino, 1994). A selection of his letters to poets and friends such as Kerouac, Gregory *Corso, Philip *Whalen, and Gary *Snyder, was edited by Bill Morgan for Da Capo Press in 2008. For criticism, see *On the Poetry of Allen Ginsberg*, ed. Lewis Hyde (University of Michigan Press, 1984), and for biography, *Ginsberg* (Simon & Schuster, 1989; revd. edn., 2001), by Barry Miles, who also edited an annotated edition of *Howl*, with notes by the poet (Harper, 1986; repr. 2006). Ed Sanders' *The Poetry and Life of Allen Ginsberg* (Overlook, 2000) is a personal portrait in verse. See also Jonah Raskin, *American Scream: Allen Ginsberg's* Howl *and the Making of the Beat Generation* (University of California Press, 2004). JNT

SEE WEB LINKS

- A range of further reading is available at the website of the Allen Ginsberg Project.

Gioia, Dana (1950–) Born in Los Angeles of Italian and Mexican descent and raised in the blue-collar suburb of Hawthorne. He attended Catholic schools before moving on to Stanford University, where he edited its literary magazine *Sequoia*. He spent two years doing graduate work in comparative literature at Harvard where he studied with Robert *Fitzgerald and Elizabeth *Bishop and received his MA in 1975, before returning to Stanford for his MBA. From 1977 to 1992 he worked as a business executive in New York while contributing poetry and critical essays to such journals as *The New Yorker* and *The Hudson Review*. In addition, he has edited the stories of Weldon *Kees, co-edited two anthologies of Italian poetry, and translated Montale's *Mottetti: Poems of Love* (1990).

Gioia's poems range in subject-matter from meditations on the landscape of California ('California Hills in August') and his youth spent there ('Cruising with the Beach Boys') to ones on his life as a business man in suburban Westchester County ('Eastern Standard Time' and 'In Cheever Country'); from poems that examine the 'Lives of the Great Composers' to such brief lyrics on the evanescence of love and the nature of mortality as 'Parts of Summer Weather' and 'The Gods of Winter'. 'The Room Upstairs' and 'Counting the Children' are psychologically astute dramatic monologues whose isolated speakers contemplate the complexities and varieties of love. His sequence, 'Daily Horoscope', is a philosophical musing on how to accept the limitations of everyday existence in the context of brief epiphanic glimpses into a world of ideal

beauty. A man adeptly juggling, like *Stevens, business and poetic careers, Gioia makes this his animating theme. His poetry is grounded in traditional metrics and characterized by distinct musical cadences and technical virtuosity, gifts which, in conjunction with his essays, especially the much-reprinted 'Notes on the *New Formalism', place him at the front of that movement.

His collections, all published by Graywolf Press, are *Daily Horoscope* (1986), *The Gods of Winter* (1991), *Interrogations at Noon* (2001), which won the American Book Award, and *Pity the Beautiful* (2012).

Can Poetry Matter? Essays on Poetry and American Culture (1992) includes his much-discussed 1991 critical essay of the same name. *Barrier of a Common Language: An American Looks at Contemporary British Poetry* (University of Michigan Press, 2003) includes appreciations of James *Fenton, Charles *Causley, Philip *Larkin, and Wendy *Cope. See also *Disappearing Ink: Poetry at the End of Print Culture* (Graywolf, 2004). From 2003 to 2009, Gioia was chairman of the National Endowment for the Arts, promoting Shakespeare, poetry recitation, creative writing for US troops ('Operation Homecoming'), and jazz. In 2011, he became Judge Widney Professor of Poetry and Public Culture at the University of Southern California. RMCP*

Giovanni, Nikki (1943–) Born Yolande Cornelia Giovanni, Jr., in Knoxville, Tennessee. Entering Fisk University in 1960, she edited the university literary magazine and founded a chapter of SNCC (Student Non-Violent Coordinating Committee) on campus. Previously a right-wing Republican, she became involved in the *Black Arts Movement and, after studying further at the universities of Pennsylvania and Columbia, she immersed herself in black community and cultural projects. Her first two books, *Black Feeling, Black Talk* (1967) and *Black Judgement* (1969) grew out of this activity and reflect her commitment at the time to the development of a separate African-American identity.

Her third collection *Re: Creation* (1970—all Broadside) was not notably different from her first two. In 1969, however,

Giovanni gave birth to a son to whom she dedicated her first book of poems for children, *Spin a Soft Black Song* (Hill & Wang, 1971); and in 1971, after travelling to the Caribbean, she published *Gemini: An Extended Autobiographical Statement on my First Twenty-Five Years of Being a Black Poet* (Bobbs-Merrill, 1976). These two books reveal a more introspective style and approach. 'I'm into a very personal thing now... and I'm more settled', she said at the time of the publication of her next collection *My House* (Morrow, 1972). She was also achieving wider fame thanks to the popularity of her album, *Truth Is On Its Way* (1971), on which she reads some of her poetry against the background of gospel music. Work published since has continued to tap a more personal vein while also promoting ideals of universal human relatedness. Notable later collections include *Cotton Candy on a Rainy Day* (1978) and *Those Who Read the Night Winds* (1983).

Since 1987 Giovanni has taught at Virginia Tech, where she is now University Distinguished Professor. *The Selected Poems of Nikki Giovanni* (1996) was followed by *Blues: For All the Changes* in 1999 and *Quilting the Black-Eyed Pea* in 2002. *The Collected Poetry of Nikki Giovanni* (2003) was accompanied by a Grammy-nominated spoken-word retrospective, *The Nikki Giovanni Poetry Collection*, and a collection of her non-fiction (including *Gemini* and *Racism 101*), *The Prosaic Soul of Nikki Giovanni*. Her most recent volumes are *Acolytes* (2007) and *Bicycles: Love Poems* (2009—all Morrow).   RJG

Giscombe, C. S. (Cecil S.) (1950–) Born in Dayton, Ohio. He studied at SUNY at Albany and Cornell University. From 1983 to 1989, Giscombe edited the Cornell-based literary magazine *Epoch*. He has worked as a taxi driver, a hospital orderly, and a railroad brakeman, and taught at various universities. He is currently Professor of Creative Writing at the University of California, Berkeley.

Giscombe has described the poems of his first book, *Postcards* (Ithaca House, 1977) as 'kind of closed cages': 'I wanted poetry to do more'. He did not publish another book until *At Large* (St Lazaire, 1989), followed in 1994 by *Here* (Dalkey Archive, 2004). As these titles suggest, Giscombe's later work is concerned with the North American landscape, in which he traces histories of his own Afro-Caribbean ancestry. The long, *Olsonian mapping of *Giscome Road* (Dalkey Archive Press, 1998, repr. 2000 and 2004) arose from his research into 'the constellation of places in northern British Columbia that were named, directly or indirectly, for John Robert Giscome', a nineteenth-century Jamaican miner and explorer.

Into And Out of Dislocation (North Point/ Farrar, Straus, 2000) is an experimental prose memoir that reflects Giscombe's fascination with travel and journal writing. The prose poems of *Prairie Style* (Dalkey Archive, 2008) continue to explore the poetic challenge of American space: 'Everybody wants to be the singer but here's the continent' ('Afro-Prairie').   JNT

Gizzi, Peter (1959–) Born in Pittsfield, Massachusetts, and studied at New York and Brown universities. He teaches at the University of Massachusetts. Between 1987 and 1993 he co-edited *o•blék: a journal of language arts*, and later published an annotated edition of the lectures of Jack *Spicer (*The House that Jack Built* (Wesleyan University Press, 1998)). His brother was the poet Michael Gizzi.

In 1994, Gizzi was selected by John *Ashbery for a Lavan Younger Poet award. *Artificial Heart*, his first full collection, was published in 1998 (Burning Deck). The critic Marjorie Perloff saw Gizzi as part of a generation of avant-garde American poets returning to the tradition of lyric voice after the *Language poets. 'Song' is a resonant word in Gizzi's work. He has described his fascination with lyricism as a way of telling 'the story of where we go' in moments of emotional intensity. These range from the limpid observations of *Some Values of Landscape and Weather* (2003) to the vast palindromic address of 'Vincent, Homesick for the Land of Pictures' in *The Outernationale* (2007). The life of the poet as political citizen is also an important theme. In 'A Panic That Can Still Come Upon Me', urgent anaphora and flashed imagery combine in prophetic panorama. *Threshold Songs* (2011—all Wesleyan University Press), a more introspective and elegiac volume, deepens Gizzi's vision of the continuities between American and European poetry after *Eliot (see 'Tradition & the Indivisible Talent'). JNT

Glassco, John (Stinson) (1909–81) Born in Montreal of a prominent family, was educated in private schools and briefly attended McGill University before going to Paris in 1928, an experience fictively retold in his *Memoirs of Montparnasse* (1970).

He published his first collection of verse, *The Deficit Made Flesh*, in 1958 (McClelland & Stewart), and this was followed by *A Point of Sky* (1964), *Selected Poems* (1971—both Oxford University Press), and *Montreal* (DC Books, 1973), a long satire/parody. As a writer of prose, Glassco, who had a highly adaptable style, tried his hand at completing Aubrey Beardsley's (1872–98) *Under the Hill* (1959), and went on to more titillating work in *The English Governess* (1960), *The Temple of Pederasty* (1970), *Fetish Girl* (1972), and *The Fatal Woman* (1974). In addition, Glassco had a distinguished career as a sensitive and skilful translator of French-Canadian writing, beginning with an early interest in Saint-Denys Garneau (1912–43), whose *Journal* he translated in 1962 and *Complete Poems* in 1975. He also edited (translating many of the selections himself) a landmark anthology, *The Poetry of French Canada* (Oxford University Press, 1970).

In his poetry Glassco has shown himself to be a traditional stylist concerned with the decaying landscape of a particularly stony but picturesque part of rural south-eastern Quebec. Widely read, occasionally decadent in spirit and given to the fine phrasings of a genuinely elegant sensibility, Glassco fashioned a strong if elegiac statement out of the tension between a remembered, relic-strewn past and the acquisitive stresses of contemporary life. See *Selected Poems with Three Notes on the Poetic Process* (Golden Dog, 1997), ed. Michael Gnarowski. MG

Glover, Denis (1912–80) Born in Dunedin, New Zealand, was both poet and printer, and he began both careers at Canterbury University College. The Caxton Press, which he established first as a university club press in 1933 and then as a commercial venture in Christchurch, gave to a generation of New Zealand writers the chance of publication with a quality of typography that commanded international respect. In the Second World War he served with the Royal Navy, and helped interest John *Lehmann, the editor of *Penguin New Writing*, in New Zealand authors of the time.

Glover's poetry celebrates the vitality of individual toil and delights in the sea and his country's landscape. It also reflects his pleasure in sport and his wide knowledge of classical and renaissance literature. But, like many of his generation, Glover reveals a melancholy in his treatment of mortality and human insignificance in the presence of the landscape. Though parts of his prolific output are ephemeral, the best of his work—the 'Sings Harry' cycle and the 'Arawata Bill' poems—remain valued, while his ironic ballad 'The Magpies' may now be the single most-recognized poem in his own country.

Selections of Glover's poems were published in his lifetime in *Enter Without Knocking* (Pegasus, 1964 and 1971) and posthumously in *Selected Poems*, introduced by Allen Curnow (Penguin, 1981).

See also his autobiography *Hot Water Sailor* (Reed, 1962), and J. E. P. Thomson, *Denis Glover* (Oxford University Press, 1977). WSB

Glück, Louise (1943–) Born in New York and raised on Long Island. Glück, who was married to John Dranow, a writer, made her home in Plainfield, Vermont, for many years. From this base she taught at various American colleges and universities, including Columbia, the University of Iowa, and Williams College. She currently teaches at the universities of Yale and Boston. Her first book of poems, *Firstborn*, appeared in 1968. That volume, deeply influenced by the poetry of Sylvia *Plath, dealt in images of contemporary wastelands and focused on lost lives, figures moving through a postmodern suburban landscape with severe physical or emotional damage. 'The poison | that replaces air took over', she writes in 'The Chicago Train', which opens this collection of harsh, elliptical poems. Though many of the poems centre on domestic scenes, they consistently reach for a larger, symbolic meaning, as in the title-poem, 'Firstborn', where even a 'lone onion' in a bowl of soup is seen to be 'floating like Ophelia, caked with grease'.

Glück's breakthrough came with *The House on Marshland* (1975), which began the work of turning the family circle into a kind of symbolic galaxy, with biblical and other mythical allusions underpinning the literal level of the poems. Glück's characteristic style: terse, hard, deeply imagistic and lyrical, emerges here in full force. One of the best poems of this volume, 'The Pond', opens with a haunting image typical of Glück: 'Night covers the pond with its wing.' The pond becomes emblematic—of memory, the reservoir of all myths, hopes, and dreams. Having by now moved to Vermont, Glück begins to rely heavily on natural imagery, as in 'Flowering Plum', where she says in a typical line: 'In spring from the black branches of the flowering plum tree | the woodthrush issues its routine | message of survival.'

This 'message of survival' is consistently mixed with a harsher message of despair in Glück's work. *Descending Figure* appeared in 1980, taking up again the themes of family life and human loss, and featuring a memorable sequence, 'The Garden', a subtle meditation on the theme of human solitude and death in the context of the poet's origins and love relations. Glück's fourth collection was *The Triumph of Achilles* (1985), a volume dedicated to issues of 'knowing' and 'clarifying' the poet's sense of the world, whose title-poem ends with Achilles grieving for Patroclus in his tent, 'a victim of the part that loved, | the part that was mortal'. It was followed by *Ararat* (1990), and *The Wild Iris* (1992), which won the Pulitzer Prize.

Glück's first four books were reprinted in one volume in 1995. *Meadowlands* (1996) contains lyrics of married life loosely based on *The Odyssey*. It was followed by *Vita Nova* (1999), which won the Bollingen Prize, and *The Seven Ages* (2001—all Ecco). In 2003, she became the twelfth US Poet Laureate. Her most recent books are *Averno* (2006), which takes up the psychodynamics of the Persephone myth, and *A Village Life* (2009—both Farrar, Straus), a narrative departure for Glück's work. See also *Proofs and Theories: Essays on Poetry* (Ecco, 1994). Since *The Wild Iris*, she has been published in the UK by Carcanet. For criticism, see Helen Vendler, *Part of Nature, Part of Us* (1980) and *The Music of What Happens* (1988—both Harvard University Press).   JP*

Gogarty, Oliver St John (1878–1957) Born in Dublin. After a leisurely education, which included a term at Oxford as well as medical school in Dublin, he qualified as an ear-and-throat surgeon. For a time, owing to the demands of medical etiquette, he was obliged to keep his literary persona, such as that of playwright for the Abbey, under wraps. He was most famous for his bawdiness and wit, and for being the model for Buck Mulligan in *Joyce's Ulysses*. In verse he was a gifted epigrammatist, but *Yeats was scarcely justified in describing him as 'one of the great lyric poets of our age'. Now his graceful, if old-fashioned verse is a little neglected. His much-anthologized 'Leda and the Swan' is often quoted as evidence of his mastery of form, as are 'Ringsend' and 'The Crab Tree'. Insistently anti-modernist, he could be ponderous and, for an esteemed wit, portentous and 'poetical'; but at his best he is sonorous, if never wholly original. He lived in America from 1939 till his death.

See *Collected Poems* (Constable, 1951) and *Unselected Poems* (Contemporary Poetry, 1954). See also, J. B. Lyons, *Oliver St John Gogarty* (Bucknell University Press, 1976) and U. O'Connor, *Oliver St John Gogarty: A Poet and his Times* (Cape, 1964).   MS-S

Goldbarth, Albert (1948–) Raised in Chicago and studied at the universities of Illinois, Iowa, and Utah. He has taught at Cornell and the University of Texas: he is currently Distinguished Professor of Humanities at Wichita State University.

Albert Goldbarth is one of the most prolific poets of his generation, having published numerous volumes and chapbooks since 1973, sometimes as many as two a year. This fact is not merely incidental to his poetry, but has everything to do with its identifying traits, above all its almost manic prolixity. Goldbarth was one of the first poets to revolt against the minimalist poetics established in the 1960s by poets like James *Wright, *Bly, *Merwin, and *Strand. Rather than offering quiet, bare epiphanies insulated from the chaos and vulgarity of contemporary America, Goldbarth wades into his cultural surroundings with equal measures of glee and disgust. In his poetry the 'discursive' style called for by the slightly older poet Robert *Pinsky takes on a nearly pathological quality; Goldbarth's many essay-poems seem less interested in their ostensible subjects (the history of glass, novelty stores, etc.) than in their own compulsion to generate language as profusely as possible. In a wry self-critique appended to his long poem *Opticks* (Seven Woods, 1974), Goldbarth writes that his 'radical style consists of never using one word when three can be substituted', a principle that seems expressly designed to flout writing-workshop conventions. What makes Goldbarth's poetry engaging is its dense and intricate texture, which is achieved in part through his ear for bizarre words from diverse vocabularies, some technical ('*syzygial*', 'defalcation'), some colloquial ('rinkydink'), and in part through his eye for eccentric particulars of all kinds: kitsch objects, outlandish news items, odd scientific or historical facts. These strands are skilfully woven together, always with some central thread of earnest meditation serving to unify, however tenuously, the motley fabric. Reading Goldbarth can be both exhilarating and fatiguing; few poets offer a greater sense of profusion, yet ultimately his poems are more concerned with the enervating effects of culture than with its capacity to nourish. *Heaven and Earth: A Cosmology* (University of Georgia Press, 1991) and *Saving Lives* (Ohio State University Press, 2001) both won the National

Book Critics Circle Award. See also *The Kitchen Sink: New and Selected Poems* (2007), a suitably generous volume. *To Be Read in 500 Years: All New Poems* followed in 2009. Goldbarth has also published several collections of essays, and a novel, *Pieces of Payne* (all Graywolf).   RG

Goldsmith, Kenneth (1961–) Poet, artist, and critic, Kenneth Goldsmith was born and lives in New York. He is senior editor of the Pennsound website, a founding editor of UBUweb, and teaches poetics at the University of Pennsylvania.

Marjorie Perloff situates Goldsmith's work 'on the border between "poetry" and "prose" . . . poetry and "not poetry" . . . "literature" and "art"'. Like Christian *Bök, Caroline *Bergvall, and Craig Dworkin, Goldsmith has been a pioneer of *Conceptual poetics. Employing a technique of 'uncreative' recycling, Goldsmith's poetry explores the intersections of the aural and oral, and the narrative potential of accreted repetition and rhyme. *Nos. 105* (Artists Museum, 1993) and *111* (The Figures, 1997) collect phrases ending with 'ee' and 'ah', arranged alphabetically by syllable count. *Fidget* (Coach House, 2000) is a 'Bloomsday' dictation of Goldsmith's body movements; expanding on Andy Warhol's *A: A Novel* (1968), *Soliloquy* records every word spoken for a week; inspired by John *Cage's *One Minute Stories* (1959), *The Weather* (Make Now, 2005) transcribes New York's WINS Radio daily one-minute weather reports.

Goldsmith has created an edition of Gertrude *Stein's *On Punctuation* (Abaton, 2000), and has edited an anthology of conceptual poetry with Craig Dworkin (*Against Expression*, Northwestern University Press, 2011). *I'll Be Your Mirror: The Selected Andy Warhol Interviews* (Carrol & Graf, 2004) has been adapted as an opera, *TRANS-WARHOL* (2006). *Sucking on Words* (dir. Simon Morris, 2007) is a documentary film of Goldsmith's life and practice, and *Letter to Bettina Funke* (Documenta, 2011) narrates his career to date.   HY

Goldsworthy, Peter (1951–) Born in Winlaton, South Australia, and educated in medicine at the University of Adelaide. He has sought since then to combine medical practice with writing, in more or less equal measures. In 1982 he published both his first book of verse, *Readings from Ecclesiastes*, and his first collection of short stories, *Archipelagoes*. His first novel *Maestro* (1989) approaches the racing wit of his best poetry. He has since published several more, as well as collections of short stories.

The small, skinny poems in Goldsworthy's earlier volume give little hint of the intellectual sharpness which distinguishes the prize-winning *This Goes with That* (ABC Books, 1988). These stylishly chiselled poems offer rueful ironies at the expense of the universe. Reaching into parody, domestic lyricism and an inventive use of kennings, they spell out an acute, if modest, epistemology. In every line the poet strives to make language elegant enough to do justice to the world as comedy. In the process he is frequently self-dismantling. See *New Selected Poems* (Duffy & Snellgrove, 2001) and also *Navel Gazing: Essays, Half-Truths and Mystery Flights* (Penguin, 1998).   CW-C

Gonzales, Rodolfo 'Corky' (1928–2005) Literally fought his way out of the *barrio* in Denver, Colorado, by becoming a one-time Golden Gloves boxing champion and national prize-fighter. In the early 1950s, however, he turned to politics, founding, in 1966, the influential Denver Crusade for Justice. In 1967 he published *I Am Joaquín/Yo Soy Joaquín*, a bilingual, free-verse history-in-small of *chicanismo* in which 'Joaquín' serves as the everyman voice of *la raza*, the people. Beginning from the defeat and Hispanicization of the Mayan and Aztec civilizations, Joaquín delineates each stage in the Amerindian-Spanish history of *los chicanos*—through, in turn, Mexican Independence (1821), the ceding of much of northern Mexico to the United States (1848), the Mexican revolution (1910–20), and, finally, the modern 'border' Mexico-America of the American south-west. As the persona for his community, Joaquín ends with a near Whitman-esque flourish against poverty and exploitation: 'La Raza! | Mejicano! | Español! | Latino! | Hispano! | Chicano! | or whatever I call myself, | look the same | I cry | and | sing the same.'

The complete text is to be found in *I am Joaquín/Yo Soy Joaquín* (self published, 1967; 2nd edn., Bantam, 1972). See also *Message to Aztlán: Selected Writings of Rodolfo 'Corky' Gonzales*, ed. Antonio Esquibel (Arte Publico, 2001).   ARL

Goodby, John (1958–) Born in Birmingham, Goodby has combined a career as a translator, lecturer, and critic with his work as a poet. Having taught at Leeds and Cork, he is currently Senior Lecturer at the University of Swansea. His first collection, *A Birmingham Yank* (Arc, 1998), was praised by Sean *O'Brien as 'at once lush and abrasive...Goodby's music can at moments be as orotund as *Stevens and as abrupt as Les *Murray'. He is a member of the Welsh multimedia ensemble Boiled String, which was founded to perform his most experimental book, *uncaged sea* (Waterloo, 2008). This is a John *Cage-inspired reworking of Dylan *Thomas' *Collected Poems 1934–1952* which transforms its text into a sequence of open-field 'mesostic' games through full-page re-patternings of Thomas' name. Goodby's *Illenium* (Shearsman, 2011) is darker and more personal, a sequence of seventy-two sonnets—all broken or partial—recounting the particularities of life, love, and language in a corner of 'South Wets Wales', the swirled name of his personal locale. Oscillating between *mise-en-page* lacunae and lines lost sagging or folding into blankness, it is also traumatized in content, trying to retell or reframe memories of desire and of loss. As well as writing on Thomas, he has published a critical study, *Irish Poetry Since 1950: From Stillness into History* (Manchester University Press, 2000).   LMe

Goodison, Lorna (1947–) Born in Kingston, Jamaica. She studied at the Jamaica School of Art and at the School of the Art Students' League in New York. She has previously worked as an artist, designer, painter, and illustrator, and now teaches at the University of Michigan. Many of her poems allude to modern art and mythological subjects. 'The Mulatta and the Minotaur', for instance, is an exploration of the nature of poetry, in which feminine and masculine principles interlock. It ends by mocking Picasso's patriarchal pretensions. Her elegy, 'For Don Drummond', a musician who committed suicide after killing his girl-friend, confronts Jamaican social tensions. Her poems have become increasingly more mystical and religious, but she is a seeker rather than a dogmatist.

Goodison's books are frequently graced by covers illustrating her paintings; her first three collections were *Tamarind Season* (Institute of Jamaica, 1980), *I Am Becoming My Mother* (1986), and *Heartease* (1989—both New Beacon).

Goodison's later poetry has been highly praised by Derek *Walcott, and Edward *Baugh has admired the way in which 'English is flavoured and extended' by its Jamaican sensibility. Since *Selected Poems* (University of Michigan Press, 1992) she has published *To Us, All Flowers Are Roses* (1995), *Turn Thanks* (1999), and *Controlling the Silver* (2005—all University of Illinois Press) in the States, *Travelling Mercies* in Canada (McClelland & Stewart, 2001), and two selected poems in the UK: *Guinea Woman* (2000) and *Goldengrove* (2006—both Carcanet). *From Harvey River* (McClelland & Stewart, 2008) is a prose memoir of Goodison's family, and in particular her mother, an important figure in her poetry. She has also published two collections of short stories.   MR*

Goodland, Giles (1964–) Born in Taunton, Somerset, Goodland studied at the universities of Wales, California, and Oxford. He works for the *Oxford English Dictionary*. Like Tony *Lopez, his formal shaping of found text has affinities with the procedures of *Oulipo and *Conceptual poetry, in ways that implicitly reflect on the history of English as a poetic language. The 'systematic collage' of *A Spy in the House of Years* (Leviathan, 2001) combined his interest in 1940s documentary montage with his training as a lexicographer, mining the printed century for a hundred synchronic sonnets. *Capital* (Salt, 2006) continued this

method in response to a series of contemporary compounds ('Burnt Capital', 'Seed Capital', 'Symbolic Capital'). *What the Things Sang* (Shearsman, 2009) employs alphabetical patterns and proverbial idioms to generate a playfully philosophical lyric sequence. In 2010 Goodland's poem 'The Bees' won the Cardiff International Poetry Competition. See also *Gloss* (Knives Forks and Spoons, 2011).   JNT

Gooneratne, Yasmine (1935–) Educated at the universities of Ceylon and Cambridge and is the foundation director of the Post-Colonial Literatures and Language Research Centre of Macquarie University, Sydney. She has published critical books on Jane Austen, Pope, and on the novelist Ruth Prawer Jhabvala. In her first book of verse, *Word, Bird, Motif* (1971), she captures tones varying from the trenchant to the tender, the poignant, or the suavely savage. *The Lizard's Cry* (1972) employs the Sanskrit and Sinhala message-poem convention and reveals a keen, if anguished, perception of the socio-economic factors behind the 1971 insurgency. *6000 ft Death Dive* (1981), published after nine years' domicile in Australia, exploits a lucent sensuousness without sacrificing wit or pith. See *Celebrations and Departures*, a selected poems (self published, 1991). She has since published prose fiction: *The Sweet and Simple Kind* is a family narrative of Sri Lankan history (Perera Hussein, 2006; repr. Little, Brown, 2009).   Ldes

Gould, Alan (1949–) Born of British-Icelandic parents; he graduated from the Australian National University in 1971. He has travelled widely and worked as a teacher, a nuclear-physics technician, and an agricultural labourer.

Gould's poetry revolves around themes of necessity and will; memory and observation; space, time, and the sea; myth-making and history. His accounts of journeys by sea and air stress a sense of continuity between the individual self and other life-forms, and the universe.

Icelandic Solitaries (1978) and *Astral Sea* (1981) both contain poetic sequences featuring Icelandic myth. Further volumes of poetry (all Angus & Robertson) include *The Pausing of the Hours* (1984), *The Twofold Place* (1986), *Years Found in Likeness* (1988)—part of which is a libretto, 'The Great Circle', written for a choral symphony by Graham Hair—and *Formerlight* (1992), a selected poems. He has also published seven books of fiction. *The Past Completes Me* (2005), a later selected poems from University of Queensland Press, won the Grace Leven Prize. His appointment as poet-in-residence at the National Folk Festival in Canberra resulted in *Folk Tunes* (Salt, 2009).   PK

Graham, Jorie (1950–) Daughter of sculptress Beverly Pepper, grew up in Italy and was educated at the Sorbonne, Columbia University, and the University of Iowa, where she also taught. She is now Boylston Professor at Harvard University. Graham's first collection, *Hybrids of Plants and of Ghosts* (1980) suffered from intellectual vagueness. But *Erosion* (1983—both Princeton University Press) conveyed a sense of liberated coherence. The poems chronicled a longing for spiritual attainment in the clamorous here and now, often making use of an ingenious inventory of Donne-like conceits: 'we | stitch the earth, | it seems to me, each time | we die, going | back under, coming back up . . . ' (from 'I Watched a Snake').

The End of Beauty (1987) departs radically from her previous volumes. The poems reflect the influence of Michael *Palmer and Susan *Howe. Connections are attenuated, leaps between fragmented sections often require reserves of faith in the leaper. *The Dream of a Unified Field* (1995) contained selections from her six volumes up to *Materialism* (1993). It won the Pulitzer Prize, and confirmed her standing as one of the most admired and ambitious American poets of her generation. Graham's later books are restless, sequential works, their poems responding equally to *en plein air* experience and the poet's reading with an increasingly extended and indented verse line. Always an apocalyptic writer, attracted to mythological and mystical tropes, since *Never* (2002) she has been preoccupied by

an ecopoetics of temporal presence: see *Overlord* (2005), which meditates on the beaches of Northern France, *Sea Change* (2008), and *P L A C E* (2012—all Ecco), which won the Forward Prize. Since 1996, her books have been published in the UK by Carcanet. Helen Vendler, one of Graham's most consistent champions, has discussed the evolution of her work in *The Breaking of Style: Hopkins, Heaney, Graham* (Harvard University Press, 1995). See also Thomas Gardner, ed., *Jorie Graham: Essays on the Poetry* (University of Wisconsin Press, 2005).   SPB*

Graham, W. S. (William Sydney) (1918–86) Born in Greenock, on the Clyde. He worked for a while as a structural engineer. His first book of verse, *Cage Without Grievance*, came out in 1942. This was followed by *The Seven Journeys* (1944) and *2ND Poems* (1945). But it was *The White Threshold* (1949) and *The Nightfishing* (1955) that secured his reputation, and these were followed by *Malcolm Mooney's Land* (1970) and *Implements in their Places* (1977). His *Collected Poems 1942–1975* came out in 1979, and, posthumously in 1993, *Aimed at Nobody*, forty-four poems in notebook and worksheet form, ed. Margaret Blackwood and Robin Skelton. From 1949 his poetry was published by Faber and Faber.

Graham is often described, aptly enough, as a Romantic, for his celebration of moments of intense significance, especially those of love, in a lyrical, and sometimes bardic manner. The manner is especially at issue. For since the Forties, when Graham's work first appeared, the term 'Romantic' in discussion of contemporary poetry has come to encompass a technique associated particularly with the work of Dylan *Thomas: a high density of metaphor, especially metaphor created through the surprising use of misapplied parts of speech. Graham's early verse is very much of its time in this respect, as in 'Explanation of a Map': 'Near farms and property of bright night-time | By mileaway dogbark how there is means to say | What unseen bargain makes heavier where I walk | The meanwhile word . . . '.

The purified style of *The Nightfishing* dramatizes the uncertainty of individual identity in the context of a night fishing for herring. 'To work at waking. Yet who wakes?' The sea becomes a metaphor for the protean nature of the 'I', a flux against which credible identity can occasionally be defined in successful action. This concern becomes linked to an anxiety about the difficulties of communicating from such uncertainty. In 'Malcolm Mooney's Land' the difficulty is symbolized by the narrator's isolation in an arctic landscape where the snow and ice are 'the obstacle | Of language'. In true Romantic fashion, Graham sees the self as subject to unconscious drives. This belief, together with his interest in words, produces the memorable poem, 'What is the Language Using Us For?' The answer, it seems, is hard to find. As for the question, it only matters when we want to tell 'Each other alive about each other | Alive', as we want to do in love. Love is one of Graham's chief subjects, and he conveys a considerate tenderness in his elusive rhythms.

From the mid-Forties Graham lived mainly near St Ives in Cornwall. Among his finest late poems are elegies for the painters he knew there, such as Peter Lanyon and Bryan Wynter. Impoverished for much of this time, he received a Civil List pension in 1974. He is now one of the most widely admired of the mid-century British poets mentored by T. S. *Eliot at Faber and Faber, praised by writers as diverse as Denise *Riley and Harold *Pinter. The first full-length study of his work was *The Poetry of W. S. Graham* (Edinburgh University Press, 1989), by Tony *Lopez. The expanded *New Collected Poems* (Faber, 2005) was edited by Matthew *Francis, who has also written a study, *Where the People Are: Language and Community in W. S. Graham* (Salt, 2004). A selection of Graham's letters, *The Night Fisherman*, ed. Michael and Margaret Snow, appeared in 1999 (Carcanet). See also *Selected Poems* (Faber, 1996).   ETL*

Grant, Jamie (1949–) Born in Melbourne, Australia, and has worked in publishing and book-selling. He has done occasional editing and book reviews and has toured England with a national cricket team (and has written on that subject).

Grant has become associated with a small group of poets who have claimed allegiance to Les *Murray, whose concept of a 'vernacular republic' has stressed the endurance of rural and family values as against the eclecticism of city modishness. Grant's own verse is wry, sharply observed, and with a quasi-ruminative discursiveness that is perhaps closer in spirit to the work of Geoffrey *Lehmann, a friend and contemporary of Murray. In the feuds and factions of contemporary Australian poetry, Grant's work represents an essentially conservative urban vision—nervous about expressing emotional commitment, taut, habitually ironic, but its strengths are in its uncluttered imagist decorum and selection of detail, and in a sometimes rueful self-recognition in poems that are ostensibly maps of social behaviour.

Selected Poems (Duffy & Snellgrove/Carcanet, 2001) selects from his five major collections: *The Refinery* (1985), *Skywriting* (1989—both Angus & Robertson), *Mysteries* (1993), *The Valley Murders* (1995—both Heinemann), and *Relativity* (Duffy & Snellgrove, 1998). He has also edited *100 Australian Poems You Need to Know* (Hardie Grant, 2008).   TWS

Graves, Robert (von Ranke) (1895–1985) Born in Wimbledon, the son of the Irish poet and folklorist Alfred Perceval Graves and his second wife. He began to write poetry while still at Charterhouse School, being encouraged by one of his schoolmasters there, the mountaineer George Mallory, as well as by Edward Marsh. When war broke out, he joined the Royal Welch Fusiliers. He came to know Siegfried *Sassoon while serving in France, where he was wounded and supposed dead. He became known as one of the war poets with his first collection, *Over the Brazier* (1916). His war poetry was not, however, of the calibre of Sassoon's or *Owen's, and later he suppressed it. During the war Graves married Nancy Nicolson, daughter of William Nicolson and sister of the painter Ben Nicolson. He went up to St John's College, Oxford, where one of his tutors was Percy Simpson, whose

Shakespearean Punctuation influenced his and Laura *Riding's analysis of Shakespeare's Sonnet 129 in their *A Survey of Modernist Poetry* (1927), which in turn influenced the critical methods of the young William *Empson, and thus the course of English criticism.

Graves' poetry appeared regularly in Marsh's *Georgian Poetry* anthologies, but by 1922 it had become apparent, in volumes such as *The Pier Glass* (1921), that, although traditional in form—as it always remained—it was by no means typically Georgian. The early Graves wrote in complex experimental schemes often derived from Welsh prosody, depended heavily on nursery rhyme and ballad, and explored his feelings of guilt on lines (as his critical study *Poetic Unreason* (1925) made clear) heavily influenced by Freud. In 1925 he met the American poet Laura Riding, and from that time his attitude and style changed. He was affected not by her poetic procedures, which he never sought to imitate, but by her unique and antinomian personality, by the fact that he was in love with her, and by her major role in relieving him from the post-war trauma, or 'neurasthenia' as it was then called, from which he suffered. He began to distrust everything that had been imposed upon him by convention, and to defend some aspects of modernism (for example, the poetry of E. E. *Cummings and Gerard Manley Hopkins, then regarded as modernistic). His poetry became a means of self-critical exploration of his own psyche. Riding became the muse to whom he submitted all his work for judgement, and his belief in her powers was, for many years, absolute. After a scandal involving her attempted suicide, Graves and Riding went to the island of Majorca (1929–36), where they carried on with publishing activities on their Seizin Press (mostly their own work, but also that of Gertrude *Stein, James *Reeves, and one or two others), and issued three volumes of the miscellany *Epilogue*. They returned to England at the outset of the Spanish Civil War, and then went to America (1939), where they parted company.

The experience of Riding soon became the basis for Graves' 'historical grammar of poetic myth', *The White Goddess* 1948; revd. and enlarged, 1952, 1961), a highly individualistic and influential variation on themes explored in Mario Praz's *The Romantic Agony*, and for his theory—to which he more or less adhered throughout his life—that every poet must have a muse actively destructive of all but his capacity to love. The rationale behind this is not masochistic, but rather an almost mystical desire to be purified of the kind of 'grossness' described in such poems as 'The Succubus': a reappearance, albeit in a more sophisticated form, of Graves' pre-Riding dedication, first to the Christian faith he lost in the war, and then to conventional morality. No poet, he had solemnly told Peter Quennell at Oxford, could possibly be successful if he did not observe strict conventional morality. Many of the poems of his first phase, together with a few of his second, are collected in *Poems 1914–27* (1927). In *Poems* (1929) the new, harder manner, purged of whimsicality and sentimentality, is fully in evidence. From this time onwards Graves subjected his poems to continual revision in a series of *Collected Poems* published some in London, some in New York, some in both (1938, 1948, 1955, 1959, 1961, 1965, 1966, 1975). They first appeared in separate small collections. The poems' uniquely pungent quality comes less, perhaps, from their preoccupation with romantic love than from the poet's resistance, often ironically, sceptically, or even cynically expressed, to its demands and existential inconveniences. Thus, in Graves' best poetry, mostly written between 1930 and 1950, a naturally lyrical voice is undercut and challenged by a down-to-earth, gritty, paradoxical enlightenment on the subject of the poet's own motives and desires. Graves' more obvious exemplars include Skelton, the Metaphysicals, and, in particular, Rochester. *Hardy was the chief contemporary influence. But the flavour is Graves' own. In the last twenty-five years of his poetic activity his work became more lapidary, a textbook demonstration of poetic devotion to the muse. But it retained its epigrammatic force and its technical mastery.

Graves was a gifted translator from the classics (Apuleius' *The Golden Ass* (1950), and others), a powerful historical novelist (*I, Claudius* (1934), and many others), and a stimulating but unreliable critic. Much of the best of his criticism was done in collaboration with Riding; the rest is collected in *The Common Asphodel* (1949). His Clark Lectures, *The Crowning Privilege* (1959), and his lectures as Oxford Professor of Poetry, *Oxford Addresses on Poetry* (1962), are best approached as guides to his own idiosyncratic approach, although they contain indispensable insights. He himself privately acknowledged that the stresses of the muse, in her various appearances to him, had taken their toll of his later criticism so far as thoroughness and accuracy were concerned. His *Greek Myths* (1955) has delighted general readers and enraged scholars. The anthropological assumptions of the unscholarly *The White Goddess* are dubious, but the book remains a classic statement of an unusual and drastic romantic thesis. *Goodbye To All That* (1929, revd. edn. 1957), the least self-consciously literary of all the British First World War memoirs, also has classic status. Martin Seymour-Smith's full biography, *Robert Graves: His Life and Work* (Holt, Rinehart, 1982; revd. edn. Bloomsbury, 1995) is based on extensive personal knowledge; Richard Perceval Graves' *The Assault Heroic* and *The Years with Laura* (Weidenfeld & Nicolson, 1986–90), which cover the years 1895–1939, add family lore and some other detail. In 1995, the centenary of the poet's birth, Carcanet initiated a reissue of all Graves' major works with a new *Selected Poems*, edited by Patrick Quinn, followed by a three-volume *Complete Poems* (1995–1999).   MS-S

(⊕) SEE WEB LINKS

• For further information see the website of the Robert Graves Trust.

Gray, Sir Alexander (1882–1968) Born in Dundee, economist, poet, and translator Alexander Gray studied mathematics and economics at Edinburgh University, Göttingen University, and the Sorbonne. In 1920 he was appointed Professor of Political Economy at Aberdeen University, and in 1934 into the same post at Edinburgh University; his academic career was punctuated by work in the civil service during both world wars. He is best known for his poem 'Scotland', a part of which features on the Canongate wall at the New Scottish Parliament building. In 1939 he was awarded the CBE, which was followed by election as Fellow of the Royal Society of Edinburgh in 1942, and the KBE in 1947.

Gray's poetry is written in English and *Scots, and selections of his early work were published by Hugh *MacDiarmid in *Northern Numbers* (1922). It is characterized by clarity, directness, good humour, and a concern for the common man. A *Selected Poems* (MacLellan, 1948) was edited by Maurice Lindsay. Influenced by the Scottish ballad tradition as well as his own translations of Danish, German, and other European balladry into Scots, Gray's verse is highly formal, and often takes on a ballad form. His translations into English of the Heine poems which make up Schumann's *Dichterliebe* are still widely performed.   HY

Gray, John (1866–1934) Born in London. Taken out of school in 1879, he was successively a metal-turner, civil servant, aesthete, Catholic convert, and, from 1901, priest. His *Silverpoints* (subsidized by Oscar Wilde, designed by Charles Ricketts, published by the Bodley Head, 1893) contained sixteen poems and thirteen translations from the French Symbolists; as both text and object, it was the quintessential Nineties volume. After two decades of silence following his ordination, he resumed writing and publishing in his last years. His novella *Park: A Fantastic Story* (1932) was reissued in 1966 and again in 1984. Gray died four months after the death of his lifelong friend and benefactor André Raffalovich.

'The Barber' and 'Mishka' stand out from the merely decorative effects of his earliest verse, as does 'The Tree of Knowledge' from the mass of devotional poetry written between his conversion and ordination; 'The Flying Fish' (1896) is also notable. His late work is compressed, precise, and individual (at times eccentric); 'Quatrains' and 'Ode' show to especially good effect his reading of modernist poetry.

The Poems of John Gray have been edited by Ian Fletcher (ELT, 1988). Fr. Brocard Sewell has compiled *Two Friends* (1963; essays on Gray and Raffalovich) and written *Footnote to the Nineties* (1968) and *In the Dorian Mode: A Life of John Gray* (1983). Jerusha Hull McCormack's *John Gray: Poet, Dandy, and Priest* (1991) is a critical biography.   MP

Gray, Robert (1945–) Grew up in a rural environment on the north coast of New South Wales, which provides most of his settings, and left school without matriculating. Gray's poetry is notable for its clarity and objectivity; it evokes mood (often melancholy) through carefully selected sensory details and often manifests the static, epiphanic quality of *haiku*. Indeed this is a favourite form, though Gray is also given to leisurely, loosely structured meditations or narratives in free verse. While drawn to nature, he also addresses the morose patterns of lower-class life (urban and rural), family relationships, and the corruptions of civilization.

For Gray the world apprehended by the senses is real, sufficient, and autonomous. He is attracted to those principles of Buddhism consistent with materialism and positivism; these are adduced in several poems which extol non-attachment, the mind 'light-footed upon all things'. Contemplation of the world involves both escape from self and a salutary empathy, hence Gray's ideal of 'disinterested care', which has social and aesthetic dimensions, justifying both his socialism and his meticulous craftsmanship, which Jamie *Grant has praised for its 'claritas'.

New Selected Poems (Duffy & Snellgrove, 1998) drew on two decades of work, from *Creekwater Journal* (University of Queensland Press, 1974) to *Lineations* (Duffy & Snellgrove, 1996). Gray has twice won the Victorian Premier's Literary Award, for *Certain Things* (Heinemann, 1994) and *Afterimages* (Duffy & Snellgrove, 2002). See also *Grass Script: Selected Earlier Poems* (2001) and *Nameless Earth* (2006—both Carcanet)

and *The Land I Came Through Last* (Giramondo, 2008), a memoir. He has also edited several influential anthologies; most recently, with Geoffrey *Lehmann, *Australian Poetry Since 1788* (University of New South Wales Press, 2011).   AW*

Gray, Stephen (1941–) Born in Cape Town. After studying at the University of Cape Town, he proceeded to Queens' College, Cambridge, where he edited *Granta* and produced Shakespeare. He took an MA at the Iowa Writers' Workshop, then travelled briefly in Chile before settling back in South Africa where he taught at the Rand Afrikaans University in Johannesburg until his retirement in 1991.

Gray is highly conscious of belonging to the South African tradition of Roy *Campbell and William *Plomer; indeed his verse, which is always versatile and idiomatic, can be seen as an attempt to extend that tradition by applying it to the developing South African scene and thus to produce 'a history of local endeavour'. His first collection, *It's About Time* (David Philip, 1974), inclined towards the derivative, but in *The Hottentot Venus* (1979), and above all in *Love Poems, Hate Poems* (1982—both David Philip/Collings), he evolved a style which is fluent, racy, aurally astute but innocent of commas. He is at his best when wedded to tighter forms, as in *Love Poems, Hate Poems*, where a protracted variety of sonnet allows him just the right vehicle for meditations on love, violence, and betrayal. He is above all a poet of process, of becoming, an interpreter of *actualités*. While others fled the country, or indulged in furious sniping from within, Gray preferred to stay and observe. *Apollo Café* (1989), confirmed him as a bitter eulogist of his own torn land, 'my nourishment and obsession'.

Selected Poems (1994—both David Philip) also drew on *Season of Violence* (Dangaroo Press, 1992). In an introductory note, Gray describes his two preoccupations as 'love and apartheid' and his two modes as 'lyric and satire'. His later books include *Gabriel's Exhibition* (MayibuyeBooks-UWC, 1998) and *Shelley Cinema* (Protea, 2006). *Accident of Birth* (COSAW, 1993), his autobiography, broke new ground in the South African memoir with its discussion of his bisexuality. Gray has been an influential editor, biographer, and critic, and in 2007 received the South African Literary Award for Lifetime Achievement.   RHF*

Greacen, Robert (1920–2008) Born in Londonderry, Northern Ireland, and educated at the Methodist College, Belfast, and Trinity College, Dublin. Having once worked for the UN, Greacen went on to teach and work as a freelance writer. His early work was overwhelmed by the influence of *Auden, *Thomas, and *Yeats, and he did not discover his own voice until quite late, in the sequence of poems that make up *A Garland for Captain Fox* (Gallery, 1975). In the inscrutable figure of the fictional Captain Fox, Greacen found a focus for his energies and attentions, and he produced a mischievous and captivating portrait. Significantly, Greacen's work as an anthologist of Northern Irish poetry and prose helped to establish the distinctive voice of the province.

Greacen's other collections of verse include *The Bird* (Gayfield, 1941), *One Recent Evening* (Favil, 1944), *The Undying Day* (Falcon, 1948), *Young Mr. Gibbon* (Profile Poetry, 1979), *A Bright Mask* (Dedalus, 1985), *Protestant Without a Horse* (1997) and *Lunch at the Ivy* (2002—both Lagan). He also published an autobiography, *Even Without Irene* (Dolmen, 1969; repr. Lagan, 1995), and edited a number of anthologies of work from Northern Ireland, including *Northern Harvest* (MacCord, 1944) and, with Valentin Iremonger, the Faber *Contemporary Irish Poetry* (1949). His *Collected Poems* (1995) won the Irish Times Literature Prize for Poetry. See also *Rooted in Ulster: Nine Ulster Lives* (2001—both Lagan), a study of his generation, and *Selected & New Poems* (Salmon, 2006).   IES

Greenberg, Samuel (1893–1917) Born in Vienna. His father, a Jewish worker of gold and silver brocade, emigrated to America with his wife and children when the poet was 7, and the family settled in New York City's lower East Side, where Greenberg attended public schools until his parents' distressed circumstances made it necessary for him to begin working in a sweatshop at the age of 12. Poverty and long hours of tedious labour notwithstanding, he read voraciously, graduating from dime novels to Keats, Shelley, and Emerson, and on weekends he went to concerts, took sketching lessons, and studied paintings in museums. As his intellectual world expanded, the landscape of his life contracted: his mother died in 1908 and his father in 1913, a year after Greenberg himself was diagnosed tubercular. His last four years were spent largely in charity hospitals, and in these bleak surroundings he wrote most of his exuberantly mystical poetry. After his death, his brothers and a friend, the art critic William Murrell Fisher, managed to preserve several hundred poems and prose fragments, and in 1923 Fisher showed some of the manuscripts to Hart *Crane, who recognized the originality underlying the awkwardness and incoherences that were the result of poor schooling and worse health. Especially impressed by the dead poet's highly charged vocabulary, replete with curious archaisms and idiosyncratic coinages, and by his densely impacted musical sentence structure, Crane composed and published a collage of lines taken almost verbatim from several of Greenberg's 'Sonnets of Apology', and it was the story of this appropriation that led to the publication of *Poems from the Greenberg Manuscripts*, ed. James Laughlin (New Directions, 1939), which led in turn to a much larger collection, *Poems by Samuel Greenberg*, ed. Harold Holden and Jack McManis (Holt, 1947).

See also Marc Simon, *Samuel Greenberg, Hart Crane and the Lost Manuscripts* (Humanities Press, 1978).   RH

Greenlaw, Lavinia (1962–) Born in London and grew up in Essex. She studied for an MA in Art History at the Courtauld Institute, and is Professor of Creative Writing at the University of East Anglia.

Greenlaw comes from a family of scientists, and her work is often interested in the poetics of other arts and disciplines. Following her first collection, *Night*

Photograph (1993), she was poet-in-residence at the Science Museum in London, which inspired several poems in *A World Where News Travelled Slowly* (1997). The title poem of Greenlaw's second collection describes the history of communication systems in typically cool yet particular images, from ink and paper to the Internet. It ends on an ambivalent vision of the speed and scales of modernity.

Minsk (2003) drew Greenlaw's self-contained lyricism into the autobiographical territory of adolescence, which was also the subject of her first novel, *Mary George of Allnorthover* (2001) and a memoir, *The Importance of Music to Girls* (2007—all Faber). The collection ended with travel poems, an interest continued in *Questions of Travel*, a reworking of William Morris' Icelandic journal (Notting Hill) and *Audio Obscura*, the text of a railway station soundwork (Full Circle—both 2011). Her fourth volume, *The Casual Perfect* (Faber, 2011) takes its title from Robert *Lowell's praise of Elizabeth *Bishop, an abiding influence, though its pared-down, dream-like imagery is more European in its inwardness with things ('The intimacy of the telescope. | The becoming of quartz or iron.')   JNT

Greger, Debora (1949–) Born in Walsenburg, Colorado, and raised in Richland, Washington, the eldest of seven children. Since 1974 she has lived with William *Logan, to whom she was married in 2010. She attended the University of Washington and the University of Iowa, and taught at the University of Florida for twenty-five years. With the assistance of the Amy Lowell Poetry Travelling Scholarship and awards from the Guggenheim Foundation, the National Endowment for the Arts, and the Ingram Merrill Foundation, she has travelled extensively, and she lives part of each year in Cambridge, England.

Greger's poems are reticent autobiographically, employing a fanciful, cerebral mode, while making use of fairy-tale, description, and both memory and myth, but not in a traditional narrative manner. Rather, the poems seem cleverly conjured, and sometimes are as hermetic as symbols on a cave wall.

Greger has published nine collections of poetry: *Movable Islands* (1980), *And* (1986), *The 1002nd Night* (1990—all Princeton University Press), *Off-Season at the Edge of the World* (University of Illinois Press, 1990), *Desert Fathers, Uranium Daughters* (1996), *God* (2001), *Western Art* (2004), *Men, Women, and Ghosts* (2008), and *By Herself* (2012—all Penguin). She is also an accomplished visual artist.   HC

Gregg, Linda (1942–) Born in Suffern, New York, and soon moved in 1943 to Marin County in California. Her parents were both active educators, and her father was also an architect and an author.

Gregg has travelled widely, living for times in Greece, Sweden, Nicaragua, and elsewhere, and has kept up an intermittent life as a teacher, taking up residencies at the universities of Syracuse, Iowa, and Houston, and other literary centres throughout America. Even more than most of her peripatetic generation, Gregg has been one to 'burn with the speed | of endless departures', as the poet W. S. *Merwin, an aesthetic compatriot of Gregg's, has put it. She received a BA (1967) and MA (1972) from San Francisco State University, where she studied with the poet Jack *Gilbert, an important influence on her life and work. But her poetry also has about it a pared-down and elliptical motion reminiscent of George *Oppen.

Czesław Miłosz called Gregg 'one of the best American poets'. *All of It Singing* (2008) selects from six previous collections, all published by Graywolf Press: *Too Bright to See* (1981), *Alma* (1985), *The Sacraments of Desire* (1991), *Chosen by the Lion* (1994), *Things and Flesh* (1999), *In the Middle Distance* (2006). It won the William Carlos Williams Award and the Lenore Marshall Poetry Prize.   LR*

Gregor, Arthur (1923–) Emigrated to the United States from Vienna in September 1939, two weeks after the Second World War had broken out in Europe, a refugee from Nazism. His first book of poems, *Octavian Shooting Targets*, appeared in New York in 1954. After a trip to India he discovered the theme of self-realization that was to unfold in his eight subsequent volumes, from *Declensions of a Refrain* (1957) to *Secret Citizen* (1989).

From 1974 to 1988 Gregor directed the creative writing programme at Hofstra University; from 1989 he was poet-in-residence there for one semester each year, while spending the remaining months in France. *Embodiment and Other Poems* is a selected volume (Sheep Meadow Press, 1982). Gregor's own description of his life and work, 'Basic Motivations', appears in *Contemporary Authors Autobiography Series, 10*. Later collections include *The River Serpent* (1994), *That Other Side of Things* (2001) and *The Hand Upon His Head* (2004—all Sheep Meadow).　　GS

Gregory, Horace (Victor) (1898–1982) Born in Milwaukee and studied Lucretius and Catullus at the University of Wisconsin. From the first his work seemed modern— spare in form, urbane in tone, urban in imagery—yet deeply rooted in classical influences. As Winfield Townley *Scott wrote, Gregory 'employed his spirit not to avoid the confusing modern world but to clarify and enrich it'. Gregory was a true man of letters: he published ten collections of poetry, three books of translations (Catullus and Ovid), eight books of literary criticism, an autobiography, edited or co-edited ten anthologies, and co-wrote with his wife, the poet Marya *Zaturenska, the controversial *History of American Poetry, 1900–40*. His *Collected Poems* received the Bollingen Award. Gregory was also a distinguished teacher. From 1934 to 1960 he lectured on classical literature in translation and modern poetry at Sarah Lawrence College.

All this he accomplished while in frail or precarious health. He was born with tuberculosis of the bone that left him partially paralysed, as well as causing a tremor in the right hand. When he walked he was unstable, and later in life he was confined to a wheelchair. Due to illness, he was first educated at home by a tutor. Later he went to a private school, the German-English Academy. For three summers he attended the Milwaukee School of Fine Arts, and thought he would become a painter. ('I decided to switch when I found myself writing poems on canvas', he said. Later he wrote a book-length study of James McNeill Whistler.) When he attended the University of Wisconsin (1919–23), he met his future wife.

After graduation, in what was to be the most important influence on his work, Gregory turned his back on Milwaukee and his affluent family. He moved to New York City, where he lived in the Chelsea district among the artistic and the poor. What he saw there motivated him to destroy the manuscript of his first book of poems, composed of highly conventional lyrics. In its place he wrote *Chelsea Rooming House* (Covici, Friede, 1930; published in London in 1932 as *Rooming House*), one of the strongest and most individual first books by a modern poet. Its free-verse dramatic monologues of the underdog set the tone for the entire body of his poetry.

The most complete edition is *Collected Poems* (1964), though it omits certain admired early works and all of *Another Look* (1976). See also *The House on Jefferson Street, A Cycle of Memories* (1967—all Holt, Rinehart) and *Spirit of Time and Place: Collected Essays* (Norton, 1972).　　RSP

Greig, Andrew (1951–　) Born in Bannockburn, raised in Fife, and attended the University of Edinburgh.

Surviving Passages (1982), his second collection after *Men on Ice* (1977—both Canongate), demonstrates an essential liveliness, at its best in a firm free verse (see 'In the Tool-Shed') which allows his imagination to work. *A Flame in Your Heart* (1986), written with Kathleen *Jamie, is an interesting poetic fiction about the love affair between a Second World War fighter pilot and his girl-friend. Greig's work, however, began to find its achievement in *The Order of the Day* (1990—both Bloodaxe). American (such as John *Berryman) and other influences on his work have become truly digested and fructifying. They help to provide Greig with a poetic manner which diverges from Scottish averages without ignoring the insistent priorities of recent Scottish culture. What makes his work distinctive is a hard and vivid contemporary diction.

An experienced mountaineer and inveterate traveller, Greig has also published prose works which reflect his love of the high places, *Summit Fever* (1985) and *Kingdoms of Experience* (1986—both Hutchinson), and several novels. *This Life, This Life* (2006), a selected poems, was followed by *As Though We Were Flying* (2011—both Bloodaxe). *Getting Higher: The Complete Mountain Poems* were published by Polygon in 2011. *At the Loch of the Green Corrie* (Quercus, 2011) is a memoir that recalls the formative influence of Norman *MacCaig. DED

Grenier, Robert (1941–   ) Born in Minneapolis. He studied at Harvard, where he was taught by Robert *Lowell, and took an MFA at the University of Iowa. He lives in California, where he has taught literature and writing, and acted as an assistant to the poet Larry *Eigner, whose *Collected Poems* he edited.

Grenier's importance to the *Language poets is attested by his leading place in Ron *Silliman's anthology, *In the American Tree* (1986). Silliman also reprints the 1971 essay, 'On Speech', first published in the magazine Grenier edited with Barrett *Watten, *This*. Its declaration, 'I HATE SPEECH', symbolized Language poetry's turn from the oral poetics of *Williams, *Olson, and *Creeley towards self-consciously textual methods. Grenier's work nevertheless shows strong affinities with these poets. He wrote a thesis on Williams' 'organic' prosody, edited Creeley's *Selected Poems*, and has used the typed page in a way that recalls Olson's theory of projective verse: see *Phantom Anthems* (O Books/Trike, 1986). The speech that his writing actually rejects is the first-person naturalism of a poet such as Lowell. Instead, the American urban pastoral of *OAKLAND* (Tuumba, 1980) looks back to the *Objectivists for its quotidian imagery and *Stein for its playful abstractions ('A ROUND | the block').

Sentences (Whale Cloth, 1978), comprising 500 short poems on index cards, has now been published digitally and can be found at the Whale Cloth Press website. JNT

Grennan, Eamon (1941–   ) Born in Dublin and studied English and Italian at the city's University College. He has lived in the United States since the 1960s, travelling frequently to the West of Ireland. Grennan obtained a PhD from Harvard University in 1972, and taught English at Vassar College, Poughkeepsie, New York for many years until his retirement in 2004.

Grennan published his first volume in his forties. *Wildly for Days* (1983), begun in 1977, came with a foreword by his friend Derek *Mahon, who points to Wallace *Stevens, Patrick *Kavanagh, Elizabeth *Bishop, and James *Wright as guiding lights to its poetry of epiphany. *What Light There Is* followed in 1987 (both Gallery), with an expanded American edition from North Point Press in 1989. Like Seamus *Heaney, to whom he dedicates the poem 'Men Roofing', Grennan's poetry seeks a post-*Yeatsian vision of the everyday world redeemed through art. There is something of Mahon's irony too in Grennan's acknowledgement of the aestheticized quality of his quotidian, and its implicit political tensions.

Later books include *As If It Matters* (1992), *So It Goes* (1995), *Selected and New Poems* (2000), *The Quick of It* (2004—all Gallery), a book-length sequence of untitled observations, and *Matter of Fact* (Graywolf Press, 2008). Grennan's prize-winning translations of Leopardi were published in 1997 by Princeton University Press. *Facing the Music: Irish Poetry in the Twentieth Century* is a collection of critical essays (Creighton University Press, 1999). JNT

Griffiths, Bill (1948–2007) Born in Middlesex, Brian Bransom Griffiths, known as 'Bill', received early encouragement from Eric Mottram and Bob *Cobbing. Cobbing's enthusiasm for the small-press scene led Griffiths to set up the Pirate Press, through which he published his own work as well as that of other young poets.

After living in Germany for two years, Griffiths returned to England to study Old English at King's College, London, receiving a PhD in 1987. His studies informed his subsequent work for the Centre for

Northern Studies at Northumbria University, where he compiled several books on dialect, including *A Dictionary of North East Dialect* (Northumbria Press, 2004).

Griffiths' work is structured not by imagery or linear argument, but by lexical associations and rhythmic patterns, in particular the rhythms of spoken, non-standard forms of English, whether that means Romany dialect, prison slang, or the patois of biker gangs (as a young man, Griffiths was part of such a gang). His poetry can be challenging in its compression and its frequent switches of register, but it is also playful and musical, and Griffiths is equally at home translating pre-modern poetry or writing poems about cartoons or sport. A selection of Griffiths' work from 1969 to 1989 appears in *Future Exiles* (Paladin, 1992) alongside work by Allen *Fisher and Brian *Catling. *The Mud Fort* (Salt, 2004) selects from work 1984–2004. *The Salt Companion to Bill Griffiths*, edited by William Rowe, appeared in 2007. In 2011, Reality Street published Griffiths' *Collected Earlier Poems (1966–1980)*.   PBa

Griffiths, Jane (1970–) Born in Exeter and raised in the Netherlands, Griffiths read English at Oxford University, where she won the Newdigate Prize for her poem 'The House'. After working as a bookbinder, she returned to Oxford to complete her doctorate on John Skelton, the basis for her monograph *John Skelton and Poetic Authority: Defining the Liberty to Speak* (Oxford University Press, 2006). She has taught in Oxford, Edinburgh, and Bristol, and is now Lecturer in English and Fellow of Wadham College, Oxford. She received an Eric Gregory Award in 1996, and subsequently published four books with Bloodaxe: *A Grip on Thin Air* (2000), *Icarus on Earth* (2005), *Another Country: New and Selected Poems* (2008), and *Terrestrial Variations* (2012). 'Crystal Palaces' won the *TLS*/Blackwells Poetry competition in 2002. Her work relishes journeys, boundaries, and exile; she has a painterly eye, and poems are often 'views' or 'portraits'; rarely using rhyme, rhythms arise through syntactical repetition; well-known scenes (Icarus, the Annunciation, Orpheus Ascending), or proverbs (Heraclitus on rivers) are given a modern spin, as in much contemporary poetry: the challenge for Griffiths is to stand out from the crowd. Her most successful poems might be her least self-conscious: see 'Floating Poem' or 'Clairvoyance'.   GR

Grigson, Geoffrey (1905–85) Born the seventh son of a Cornish vicar in the parish of Pelynt and educated in Devon, Surrey, and at St Edmund Hall, Oxford. In his autobiography *The Crest on the Silver* (1950), with a characteristic blend of acerbity and affection, he describes his elderly father as 'a sample of the negative, passive culture which passed for scholarship', and from an early age Grigson took up the contrary position, regarding himself as 'a childish and hungry sensualist, finding and finding and, as I still am, unsatisfied'. His passion for discovering, for noticing the overlooked, and—as an anthologist—rescuing the single good poem by an otherwise indifferent author is matched by a savagely critical desire to scorn the mediocre and pillory the inadequate.

Between 1933 and 1939, while literary editor of the *Morning Post*, he held to the view expressed by Coleridge—that praise of the unworthy is robbery of the deserving, and during the same period, as editor of the magazine *New Verse*, he put this maxim ever more forcefully into practice. Although he claimed to have come to recognize that 'the tactic was too uncharitable, and dust lies down sooner or later of its own accord', age can hardly be said to have mellowed Grigson the journalist and critic. There was something increasingly predictable about his cantankerous spleen and paying-off of old scores, and his last collection of essays, *Blessings, Kicks and Curses* (1982), though thoroughly readable, relishes the benediction rather less than putting the boot in.

It is, however, in his poetry—the first volume of which appeared in 1939—that Grigson's keen-eyed, unsentimental appreciation of nature, his eclectic curiosity, his reverence for hallowed objects, and what he describes in the autobiography as 'a localized sense of life and a sense of history'

g

come to the fore. Many of the poems are occasional, quirkily conversational jottings, their syntax strained by inversion and multiple parentheses, but they sound the authentic note of instant speech—vivid, declaratory, much more carefully shaped than might at first appear. Their visual accuracy has much in common with the poems and notebooks of Clare and Hopkins, about both of whom Grigson wrote with insight, and it should be remembered that as well as championing *Auden and *MacNeice, Grigson did much to draw attention to the work of Ben Nicholson and Henry Moore, and to the paintings of Samuel Palmer.

Grigson's poems, too, are of a piece with his own notebooks. Although he maintained that *Notes from an Odd Country* (1970) should be seen as the best gloss on his poems, *A Private Art* (1982) is equally illuminating. Both books are full, like the poems, of precise observation, idiosyncratic opinion, high relish, and quick temper. His *Collected Poems 1963–1980* (Allison & Busby, 1982) was followed by several individual volumes, the last of which—*Persephone's Flowers* (Secker & Warburg, 1986)—contains five poems written during the last few weeks of his life and found among his papers. One of these poems recalls his awkward relationship with his father. Grigson was prolific and argumentative to the very end.   JM

Groarke, Vona (1964–) Born in Edgeworthstown in the Irish Midlands, and studied at Trinity College, Dublin and University College, Cork. She has been a writer-in-residence at Galway and Maynooth, and taught at universities in the UK and the States. Since 2007, she has been a faculty member of the University of Manchester's Centre for New Writing.

Groarke's first volume was *Shale* (1994). Poems such as 'Patronage' established her ambition to address historical questions from a personal perspective. 'I was born in the ballroom of Maria Edgeworth's house,' she writes, reflecting on the overlap of the work of the nineteenth-century novelist with 'my mother's screams' in the family's converted property. *Other People's Houses* (1999) continued to explore the theme of domestic politics with short imagistic poems such as 'The Big House' and longer, colloquially assured pieces such as 'Open House', which holds forth satirically on social and sexual relationships. *Flight* (2002) contained prize-winning poems on the Irish Famine and the Easter Rising, and was followed by *Juniper Street* (2006), the title poem of which describes family life in North America.

All Groarke's books are published in Ireland by The Gallery Press. Since *Flight and Earlier Poems* (2004), she has also been published in the States by Wake Forest University Press. In 2008, she produced *Lament for Art O'Leary*, a version of Eibhlín Dubh Ní Chonaill's eighteenth-century Irish poem which imagines a pregnant widow's grief for her husband. Her fifth collection, *Spindrift*, appeared in 2010.   JNT

Grosholz, Emily (1950–) Born in Bryn Mawr, Pennsylvania. She was educated at the universities of Chicago and Yale. She is a member of the philosophy department at Pennsylvania State University and serves as an advisory editor for the *Hudson Review*.

Grosholz's poetry ranges from relatively short meditative pieces to narrative (see her 'Cypress and Bitter Laurel'). Much of her work is about absence of one kind or another, and a significant number of her poems deal with paintings. Another preoccupation is travel. Travel is a figure for process and pausing to visit a place often means taking stock of the self. Often this process is broadened as the speaker addresses someone not present. Many of Grosholz's poems are epistolary and are the occasions for meditations about the way relationships evolve, especially within the changing circumstances of travel. She has moved from the singular meditative stance of her earlier poems to a perspective that entails the presence of others, and this increased objectivity has produced some deft love poems.

Grosholz's collections of poetry to date are *The River Painter* (University of Illinois Press, 1984); *Shores and Headlands* (Princeton University Press, 1988); *Eden* (Johns Hopkins University Press, 1992); and *The Abacus of Years* (Godine, 2002). Her

Cartesian Method and the Problem of Reduction was published by Oxford University Press in 1991. She has also edited a collection of poems and essays on the work of Maxine *Kumin, *Telling the Barn Swallow* (University Press of New England, 1997). WP

Gross, Philip (1952–) Born at Delabole, Devon, 'beside the slate mine'. His father was an Estonian refugee and Gross has written memorably of the Holocaust and the world of the wartime refugees. His mother was the village schoolmaster's daughter. He read English at the University of Sussex and worked as a librarian before moving to Bristol in 1984. He is now Professor of Creative Writing at Glamorgan University.

There is a touch of the chameleon about Philip Gross, which is not to say that he is derivative; rather, that he has an extraordinarily plastic imagination, and his technique is tuned to the occasion of each poem. He is an animist, apparently able to get under the skin of any being or phenomenon. In this he resembles Ted *Hughes, but Gross' muse is less muscle-bound. If influences are sought, Craig *Raine was a presence in his first full collection, *The Ice Factory* (1984). (There was an earlier short volume from Peterloo, *Familiars* (1983), which contains a few poems not in *The Ice Factory*.) This *Martian influence is largely absent, though, from his second book, *Cat's Whisker* (1987—both Faber), which the publisher advertised as a miscellany, there being no recurrent themes. Further evidence of his versatility can be found in *The Air Mines of Mistila* (Bloodaxe, 1988), written in collaboration with Sylvia *Kantaris.

A selected poems from Bloodaxe, *Changes of Address* (2001), drew on *I. D.* (Faber, 1994) and *The Wasting Game* (1998), which addressed his daughter's anorexia. It has been followed by *Mappa Mundi* (2003), *The Egg of Zero* (2006), *The Water Table* (2009), an ecological meditation which won the T. S. Eliot Prize, and *Deep Field* (2011—all Bloodaxe). He has also written poetry and fiction for young people. PF

Grossman, Allen (1932–) Born in Minneapolis and studied at Harvard and Brandeis universities. He was the Paul E. Prosswimmer Professor of Poetry and Education at Brandeis and Andrew W. Mellon Professor of Humanities at Johns Hopkins University from 1991 until his retirement in 2006.

Though he has never received the kind of attention given to many other poets of his generation, Grossman has over the years become something of a legend in certain circles, particularly in the Boston area. This cult status doubtless reflects his power and eloquence as a teacher passionately committed to the redemptive functions of poetry; his book *The Sighted Singer* (Johns Hopkins University Press, 1992) comprises a series of fascinating conversations with the poet Mark Halliday and a remarkable work of 'speculative poetics', 'Summa Lyrica', which outlines a conception of poetry at once fiercely Romantic and profoundly humane. His own poetry is uncompromising in its engagement of the high style, as derived chiefly from such modernist giants as *Yeats, *Stevens, and Hart *Crane. His insistence on the visionary, prophetic dimension of poetic speech, and the intense rhetoric that accompanies it, may have led some readers and critics to dismiss him as an anachronism. But Grossman does not simply repeat Romantic modernism; he also corrects it, particularly in the sphere of morality. Rejecting the notion that vision and prophecy entail a solipsistic withdrawal from other selves, Grossman has evolved a subtle and moving ethic based on the idea of care—an ethic that may owe something to his Judaism, which he frequently invokes. Poetry, in his view, is one of the primary ways in which human beings 'affirm one another', preserving their voices and images 'against our vanishing'. Thus Grossman's most striking departure from his high modern forebears lies in his frequent reference to other people, who are always granted full humanity—his childhood nurse; a woman seen on the street;

most especially his parents, Louis and Beatrice, who figure in many of his poems. Stylistically Grossman's poetry has moved from an austere, stark mode to a more baroque and playful manner that verges on pastiche yet never relinquishes its fundamental seriousness. His poetry may be read in *The Ether Dome and Other Poems: New and Selected 1979-1991* (1992). His later volumes are *The Philosopher's Widow* (1995), *How to Do Things with Tears* (2001), and *Sweet Youth* (2002), a later selected poems. In 2009 Grossman was awarded the Bollingen Prize for *Descartes' Loneliness* (2007—all New Directions).   RG*

Guest, Barbara (1923–2006) Born Barbara Ann Pinson in Wilmington, North Carolina, Guest studied at the University of North Carolina and also the University of California at Los Angeles and Berkeley. In the 1950s she was an editorial associate of *Art News*. She also made collages and later published several collaborative books with artists.

Although Guest is known as the only first-generation female member of the *New York School, the perceptions of a lyric 'I' are much less important to her work than, say, that of her friend Frank *O'Hara. Instead, she proceeds by sensory associations and verbal substitutions, placing an emphasis on the composed quality of images and scenes in a way that evinces her interest in visual art and, in particular, Abstract Expressionism (see the refracted still life of 'Red Lilies'). Guest's early publications include *The Locations of Things* (Tibor de Nagy, 1962), *The Blue Stairs* (Corinth, 1968), and *Moscow Mansions* (Viking, 1973). During the 1960s she also wrote several plays. *Seeking Air* (Black Sparrow, 1978; repr. Sun & Moon, 1997) was a stream-of-consciousness novel. In 1984 Guest published a biography of Hilda *Doolittle, *Herself Defined: The Poet H. D. and Her World* (Doubleday). The later collections *Fair Realism* (1989) and *Defensive Rapture* (1993—both Sun & Moon) reflected an engagement with *Language poetry, refining her style through intense parataxis and abstraction ('stilled grain of equinox').

Selected Poems was published in the USA by Sun & Moon Press in 1995, and in the UK by Carcanet in 1996. In 1999 Guest was awarded the Robert Frost Medal for Distinguished Lifetime Achievement. Her last volume was *The Red Gaze* (Wesleyan University Press, 2005). *The Collected Poems of Barbara Guest*, ed. Hadley Haden Guest, appeared from Wesleyan University Press in 2008, with an introduction by Peter *Gizzi.

Guest's example as a female avant-garde poet whose work opened up an imaginative space that, in her own words, 'overruns the boundaries', has been acknowledged as an influence by many others, including Kathleen *Fraser, Marjorie *Welish, and Wendy *Mulford. For her criticism, see *Dürer in the Window: Reflexions on Art* (Roof, 2003) and *Forces of Imagination: Writing on Writing* (Kelsey Street, 2003). *Chicago Review* 53:4–54:1/2 (Summer 2008) was a Barbara Guest special issue.   JNT

Gunn, Thom(son William) (1929–2004) Born in Gravesend and raised principally in Hampstead. His father was a journalist, as his mother had been before her marriage. In 'My Life Up to Now', an autobiographical essay written in 1977, Gunn warmly recalls growing up in a household full of books and playing with friends on the Heath. However, his parents divorced, and his mother, with whom he lived after the divorce and who encouraged his interest in reading and writing, took her life when he was 15. It is possible that the emphasis, in certain of his poems, on self-definition and self-reliance reflects not only such literary influences as the French existentialists, but also personal circumstances that required independence and resilience of him while he was still relatively young.

After two years of national service in the army, Gunn went in 1950 to Cambridge. Here he attended lectures by F. R. Leavis, who impressed him with his passion for literature, his belief in the value of realized imagery, and his insistence on the expressive significance of verse rhythm. Gunn also discovered Donne and read all of Shakespeare, both authors contributing to the formation of his early style, which is exemplified in 'Tamer and Hawk' and

'The Beach Head', and which is characterized by a masterful control of the metaphysical conceit, the extended metaphor or analogy. In 1954 he travelled to California, where he held a fellowship at Stanford University and studied for a year with Yvor *Winters, about whom he wrote a fine reminiscence, 'On a Drying Hill'. After living and teaching briefly in Texas, Gunn returned to the San Francisco Bay area, settling in San Francisco itself in 1961. From 1958 to 1966 he taught at the University of California at Berkeley, but resigned his professorship to devote more time to writing. He subsequently held occasional visiting appointments at different schools; from the late 1970s he taught at Berkeley for one term a year.

While at Cambridge, Gunn wrote most of the poems that appeared in his first collection, *Fighting Terms* (Fantasy Press, 1954; revd. edns. 1958, 1962). Impressive for their concentration, their vigour, and their effective fusion of traditional metre with contemporary idiom, these poems established him as one of the most arresting voices of his generation. Though critics associated him with the *Movement, his predilections were never as sharply anti-modernist as those of such Movement poets as *Larkin and *Amis. Indeed, Gunn soon began to investigate different tonalities, a development encouraged by his move to the United States and by his reading of Williams Carlos *Williams, *Stevens, and other American experimentalists. Gunn's second book, *The Sense of Movement* (1957), and more especially his third, *My Sad Captains* (1961), feature poems in syllabic measures, poems which, like 'Vox Humana' and 'Considering the Snail', show the poet speaking in a quieter, more tentative manner. Gunn remarked that syllabics provided him with a transitional form to work his way into free verse, and *Touch* (1967) contains his earliest free-verse poems.

Unlike many of his contemporaries, however, who began with conventional forms and switched exclusively to free verse, Gunn continued to work in metre too; and *Moly* (1971), with such memorable poems as 'At the Centre' and 'Sunlight', employs strict forms to render illumina-

tions related to experiences with hallucinogenic drugs. *Jack Straw's Castle* (1976) in part explores darker aspects of these experiences. The title piece, a sequence of poems examining consciousness nightmarishly isolated from its customary contexts, recalls Gunn's earlier 'Misanthropos' sequence, which appears in *Touch* and which has as its protagonist a man who has survived a terrible world war and who believes himself to be the only survivor, 'the last man' on earth. *The Passages of Joy* (1982) shows a growing concern with friendship and its social virtues. Gunn was gay, and in the mid and late 1980s he wrote a number of powerful poems about the AIDS epidemic, collected in *The Man with Night Sweats* (1992).

Overall, Gunn's poetry evolved towards a more directly humane treatment of its subjects. This evolution may be seen in the changing aspects of two abiding qualities in his work: his sympathy with the outsider-rebel and his interest in the nature of courage. Whereas the outsider-rebels of earlier poems tend to exhibit, as do the motorcyclists in 'On the Move', romantic self-sufficiency, those in later work are more likely to be injured or lost, as with 'Sparrow' or 'Slow Walker'. And if the characteristic gesture of courage in early poems like 'Lerici' and 'In Santa Maria del Popolo' is that of opening the arms wide to the existential void, in the later work courage is perhaps best expressed by the comforting embrace that the man dying of AIDS in 'Memory Unsettled' confers on a friend more sick than he.

From 1957 Gunn's major collections were published in England by Faber and Faber, and in the States by University of Chicago Press and later by Farrar, Straus and Giroux. *Collected Poems* appeared in 1994. *Boss Cupid* (2000), his final collection, included a sequence of dark love lyrics ('Troubador') imagined for the serial killer and cannibal, Jeffrey Dahmer. August *Kleinzahler has edited a posthumous *Selected Poems* (Faber, 2007; Farrar, Straus, 2009).

Gunn also collaborated with his brother, the photographer Ander Gunn, on *Positives* (1966), supplying verse to accompany his brother's photographs. *The Occasions of Poetry, Essays in Criticism and Autobiography*, ed. Clive Wilmer (Faber, 1982; enlarged edn., 1985) displays the wide range of Gunn's reading and literary sympathies. A second collection of his prose, *Shelf Life*, appeared in 1993 (Faber/University of Michigan Press).

Jack W. C. Hagstrom and George Bixby's *Thom Gunn, A Bibliography 1940–1978* (1979) offers, as well as data on the poems, a list of interviews with Gunn and entries for his uncollected book-reviews. *Three Contemporary Poets: Thom Gunn, Ted Hughes and R. S. Thomas*, ed. A. E. Dyson (Macmillan, 1990) reprints George Fraser's fine 1961 essay, 'The Poetry of Thom Gunn', and Wilmer's illuminating 'Definition and Flow: Thom Gunn in the 1970s'. Gregory Woods' *Articulate Flesh* (Yale University Press, 1987) has a chapter on Gunn as a gay poet. In addition, *PN Review*, 70 (1989), devoted chiefly to Gunn, contains useful discussions of his work. See also Joshua Weiner, ed., *At the Barriers: On the Poetry of Thom Gunn* (University of Chicago Press, 2009).   TS*

Gurney, Ivor (1890–1937) Born in Gloucester, the son of a tailor. His musical abilities were recognized early and in 1906 he enrolled as an articled pupil to the cathedral organist. Even at this early age the stabilizing influence of musical colleagues (one of them was Herbert Howells), his intoxication with what his friend Will Harvey called 'the very fact of being Gloucester bred', and his deep love of the local countryside were disturbed by poor health, reckless solitariness, and a confused egoism which made him passionately independent in his impulses but vulnerably derivative in his utterance.

In 1911 he won a scholarship to the Royal College of Music in London to study composition under Stanford, and here he achieved his first real success: a setting of five Elizabethan lyrics. Here too his sense of Englishness was sharpened—in music by his increased exposure to the work of Elgar and Vaughan Williams, and in poetry by the opportunity to meet and hear the *Georgian poets whom Edward Marsh was promoting. 'Our young men must write on a diet largely composed of Folk Song and

Shakespeare', he told his friend Marion Scott.

When war broke out his career as a composer was stunted. After he had reached France (in 1916, as a private in the 2nd/5th Gloucesters) he found time to compose no more than five songs. Instead, he intensified his interest in writing poems, and his two collections (*Severn and Somme*, 1917, and *War's Embers*, 1919), contain several of the lyrics on which his reputation still rests—notably 'To His Love' and 'Song' ('Only the wanderer . . . '). In 1917 he was gassed at Ypres and posted back to England, where he suffered a breakdown in the late spring of the following year. In 1922 he was incarcerated in the City of London Mental Hospital at Dartford, suffering from schizophrenia. He died fifteen years later.

Gurney wrote a great deal of poetry during his asylum years, and it was only when the poems were collected and edited by P. J. *Kavanagh (1982), and later, the best selected (1990—both Oxford University Press) that Gurney's status as a major war poet became apparent. His preoccupations were those of the Georgians—the sanctity of place, the threat of change, the delights of seclusion, the barbarism of conflict—but his treatment is recognizably modern: broken rhythms, buckled diction (he had read Hopkins in Robert *Bridges' anthology *The Spirit of Man*), idiosyncratic syntax, breathless celebration (in 'Cotswold Ways', for instance), undermined by despairing regret. Like Edward *Thomas, whom he greatly admired, his work forms a link between Victorian and contemporary sensibilities, and the pressures and problems of occupying such a position give his work its power as well as being the means by which it was overwhelmed. See Michael Hurd, *The Ordeal of Ivor Gurney* (Oxford University Press, 1978).

In the late 1990s, Carcanet published Gurney's poems in a series of individual volumes, reconstructing his original intentions. *Selected Poems*, ed. Kavanagh, followed in 2001, and a revised and expanded edition of the *Collected Poems* in 2004. See Donald Davie, 'Ivor Gurney Recovered', in *Under Briggflatts* (University of Chicago Press/Carcanet, 1989).   AM

Gustafson, Ralph (1909–95) Born of Anglo-Swedish stock in Lime Ridge, Quebec. He studied at Bishop's University, then at Oxford. After a brief stint at teaching in Canada he returned to England, where he published his first two collections of poetry and remained from 1933 to 1939. During the war he worked for the British Information Services in New York, summarizing attitudes to Britain in the American press. From 1963 he lived in North Hatley, Quebec, where he worked as writer-in-residence at Bishop's, as a music critic for radio, and as a freelance writer and anthologist, editing various editions of the *Penguin Book of Canadian Verse*.

Gustafson's critical writings in *Plummets and Other Partialities* (1987) provide clues to some of his poetic concerns. His early work is notable for its craftiness, particularly its compression, verbal wit, and musicality, although feeling and idea are at times overwhelmed by form in these somewhat overwrought poems. In mid-career Gustafson explored longer forms, experimenting with sequences, or what he called 'the poem by sections'. His later work was characterized by a mix of what he called witness poems, on significant public events, and quiet, meditative pieces about the life and landscape of the Eastern Townships of Quebec where he lived.

Gustafson also wrote two books of stories, *The Brazen Tower* (1974) and *The Vivid Air* (1980). *The Collected Poems of Ralph Gustafson* were published by Sono Nis Press in three volumes between 1987 and 1994. His last book, published posthumously, was *Visions Fugitive* (Véhicule, 1996). See Dermot McCarthy, *A Poetics of Place: the Poetry of Ralph Gustafson* (McGill-Queens, 1991) and *Selected Poems* (Véhicule, 2001).   GG

Guthrie, Ramon (1896–1973) Born in New York City and served in the American Field Service and US Army Air Corps from 1916 to 1919. He married Margarite Maurey in 1922 and pursued an expatriate life in Paris through most of the 1920s. Beginning in 1930, he taught French and comparative literature at Dartmouth College. He also wrote two novels and, with George E.

Diller, edited *French Literary Thought since the Revolution* (1941) and *Prose and Poetry of Modern France* (1964).

Guthrie's first books of verse, Graffiti (1959) and *Asbestos Phoenix* (1968), seem to have been preparations for his minor masterpiece in satiric melancholia, *Maximum Security Ward: 1964–1970* (Farrar, Straus, 1970). Influenced by Laforgue, *Pound, and young *Eliot—the main voice in the 'poem' echoes Prufrock's self-conscious estrangement—this work builds a dramatic collage of affects, tropes, and literary references around the interior monologue of a doomed but erudite member of Gertrude *Stein's 'lost generation', which helps explain its archaic aura of Baudelairean posturing.

For a sympathetic explication of Guthrie's poetic sequence, see *Ramon Guthrie's Maximum Security Ward: An American Classic* (University of Missouri Press, 1984), by Sally M. Gall.   EB

Gwala, Mafika Pascal (1946–) Born in Verulam, near Durban, in South Africa's Natal province and educated at Vryheid where he matriculated. He has worked as a legal clerk, secondary-school teacher, factory worker, and publications researcher, notably as the editor of *Black Review* in 1973, in which he appeared as a leading exponent of the Black Consciousness philosophy in South Africa. In the black township of Hammarsdale in 1982 he was a founder member of the Mpumalanga Arts Ensemble which has contributed substantially to the ensuing working-class poetry and arts movement. In the early 1990s he was a student at the University of Manchester. He is married and has several children.

He is often grouped by critics with the Johannesburg-based poets, Oswald *Mtshali, Mongane *Serote, and Sipho *Sepamla, as a leader of the 'Soweto poets' group which came to prominence after the Soweto uprising of 16 June 1976, but, although his work deals in protest terms with the Soweto condition, it is not literally Soweto-based. His poems began to appear in journals like *Ophir* (Pretoria) from 1970 and his first collection was published in 1977—*Jol'iinkomo* (Donker). This was followed by his only other collection to date, the substantial *No More Lullabies* (Ravan, 1982), No. 15 in the Staffrider series. His work is characterized by a bluesy-jive idiom that stresses black African creative usages of English, and is often strongly satirical of the pretensions of bourgeois urbanites.

His later work is well represented in *Exiles Within*, an anthology produced in 1986 by the Writers Forum in Johannesburg. A fair summary of his career is John Povey, 'The Poetry of Mafika Gwala', *Commonwealth, 8: 2* (Spring 1986). Gwala also co-edited and translated, with Liz Gunner, an anthology of Zulu poetry, *Musho! Zulu Popular Praises* (Michigan State University, 1991). SG

Gwynn, R. S. (Robert Samuel) (1948–) Born in Eden, North Carolina, of a middle-class family which had been in the South for generations. A high-school athlete, Gwynn attended Davidson College on a partial football scholarship until a sports injury forced him to abandon the game. He completed his education at the University of Arkansas. Since 1976 he has taught at Lamar University in Beaumont, Texas.

Gwynn's early collections, *Bearing and Distance* (1977) and *The Narcissiad* (1981—both Cedar Rock), revealed a poet almost entirely at odds with the literary temper of his times. Formal and satiric, his poems pilloried the excesses of contemporary American culture. *The Narcissiad*, a mock epic, recounts the adventures and apotheosis of Narcissus, an ambitious but talentless poet. In *The Narcissiad* American poets simultaneously realize that to achieve artistic pre-eminence in the overcrowded field of verse they must kill all competitors. After a series of outrageous battles, fought by caricatures of fashionable American poets, Narcissus ineptly triumphs.

The Drive-In (University of Missouri Press, 1986) stands as one of the representative volumes of the *New Formalist movement. Gwynn's metres are traditional but his language is aggressively contemporary and colloquial. The volume is a small encyclopaedia of historical genres—elegy, satire, anacreontic, epistle, dialogue, ode, sonnet-sequence—but Gwynn usually employs the forms in deliberately irreverent, even obscene ways. The early cynicism remains but now is balanced by a lyrical impulse. *The Drive-In*'s signature piece, 'Among Philistines', retells Samson's downfall in a lurid American setting of shopping malls and tabloid journalism. This dark, comic poem unexpectedly rises to a lyric epiphany as the captive hero finds redemption in his mutilation. *Body Bags* (1990) further explores the lyric potential of the ludicrously doomed, especially in the title sequence of three vernacular sonnets about the pointless deaths of high-school acquaintances.

Gwynn has also been an active critic. His monograph-length summaries of 'The Year in Poetry', appeared in the *Dictionary of Literary Biography Yearbook* from 1987 to 1992. He has edited *American Poets Since World War II: Dictionary of Literary Biography, vol. 105* (1992); a reader of modernist-era American poet-critics, *The Advocates of Poetry* (University of Arkansas Press, 1996); and an anthology of writing on the 'New Expansive Poetry' of *New Narrative and New Formalism (revd. edn., 1999). See *No Word of Farewell: Selected Poems 1970–2000* (2001—both Story Line), with an introduction by Dana *Gioia. DG

Hacker, Marilyn (1942–   ) Born in New York City and educated at the Bronx High School of Science, Washington Square College of New York University, and the Art Students League. The author of five books of poems and winner of the National Book Award (1974), Hacker has taught at several universities, including the City College of New York. She divides her time between New York City and Paris.

Hacker's fluent command of technique, fully evident in her first book, *Presentation Piece* (Viking, 1974), has been maintained in subsequent collections. Her sonnet-sequences, villanelles, and various stanzaic poems share a restless, dynamic quality and a conversational tone: this is a poetry largely addressed to friends and lovers which usually transcends the merely intimate exchange. Meditations on love and grief arise from sketched city-scapes, notes on meals, weather, travels, furnished interiors.

Hacker's lesbianism became increasingly explicit in her verse novel, *Love, Death, and the Changing of the Season* (Arbor House, 1986) and *Going Back to the River* (Random House, 1989). These alert and sensuous accounts of urban love affairs have an urgent yet casual rapidity and wit. Yet the later books are perhaps less ambitious than Hacker's earlier work, notably *Separations* (1976) and *Taking Notice* (1980—both Knopf). See *Selected Poems 1965–1990* and *First Cities: Collected Early Poems 1960–1979* (2003). *Winter Numbers* (1994) reflects on the AIDS epidemic and the poet's own experience of cancer, while *Desperanto: Poems 1999–2002* (2003—all Norton) articulates political anger in such pieces as 'Elegy for a Soldier'. *Essays on Departure* (2006) was a new and selected volume published in the UK by Carcanet.   RHa*

Hadas, Rachel (1948–   ) Hadas spent her childhood in New York City. She was educated at Radcliffe College, Johns Hopkins University, and Princeton, and is now Board of Governors Professor of English at Rutgers University. She has published many books of essays, most recently a memoir *Strange Relation* that considers the dementia of her husband, the composer George Edwards, who died less than a year after the book's publication in 2010. They were married in 1978, and have one son.

During the early Seventies Hadas spent four years in Greece, and was trained as a classicist, so the real and imagined landscape of Greece looms large in her early books of poetry, especially *Slow Transparency* (1983). These earlier poems bear traces of Seferis' metaphysical re-imagining of sea and island, the accidents of history, and the essence of time; and James *Merrill's word-play, textual abridgements, borrowings, and bridgings.

Her later poetry, however, has become all her own. The suite of her dozen books of poetry is marked by *Halfway Down the Hall: New and Selected Poems* (1998—all Wesleyan University Press), which was a finalist for the Lenore Marshall Poetry Prize. Playful diction is controlled by a sober consciousness of limits, the scope of the Aegean spiralled back into glints on a Manhattan window-pane. In *Pass It On* (Princeton University Press, 1989), her themes are friendship, marriage, and (most centrally) the connections that persist between parent and child. Her poems on bearing and nursing a child, reading to him, and watching him begin to speak, are touching but unsentimental, inventive and yet steeped in literary and family tradition.

To pass on what we know and love, she says, we have 'no way but words'. See also *The Golden Road* (Northwestern University Press, 2012).   EG

Haines, John (Meade) (1924–2011) Born in Norfolk, Virginia. He served in the US Navy, 1943–6, and homesteaded in Alaska, supporting himself by hunting and trapping, 1946–69. From 1972 he held positions as poet-in-residence at several universities.

Well known for his deft renderings of Alaskan frontier life, his range of subjects broadened steadily after the publication of his first book, *Winter News* (1966). His poetry indicts post-industrial culture for making the non-essential seem essential, for its despoiling of nature, and for its wilful delusions and selfish offices. Despite the heftiness of such themes, Haines' poems seldom lose their winsome lyricism, wit, or concision. His poetry is celebratory as well. In each of his books Haines evokes the Alaskan wilderness—beautiful, generous, and unspoiled—and can thus afford understatement; post-industrial life appears, in comparison, hideous and aberrant. Where other American poets adopt an elemental vocabulary and archetypal imagery merely as components of a fashionable style, Haines speaks of wind, stone, ice, leaf, and branch as a true initiate. His is the hard-earned language of an original and self-reliant naturalist.

His other books of poetry include *The Stone Harp* (1971); *Cicada* (1977); *News from the Glacier: Selected Poems 1980* (1980—all Wesleyan University Press). His collected poems appeared from Graywolf Press as *The Owl in the Mask of the Dreamer* in 1993, and a volume of early poems, *At the End of This Summer*, from Copper Canyon Press in 1997. Later poems are collected in *For the Century's End* (University of Washington Press, 2001). See also his own essays and autobiographical stories, *The Stars, the Snow, the Fire* (1989) and *Fables and Distances: New and Selected Essays* (1996—both Graywolf).   DWF

Hall, Bernadette (1945–) Born in Alexandra, Central Otago, of Irish ancestry, Hall studied Latin at the University of Otago, and lived for many years in Christchurch, where she was a classics teacher. She has been poetry editor of *Takahe* magazine, and has also written plays. Among her native inspirations in the 'high and low of language' she cites James K. *Baxter, Hone *Tuwhare, and Janet *Frame. There is often a sense of discovery in her poems, as they break moments of love and reflection into verse depicting daily life in New Zealand while touching lightly on the spiritual language of her Catholic upbringing. *Heartwood* (Caxton, 1989), her first collection, was followed by *Of Elephants etc* (Untold, 1990). Since *The Persistent Levitator* (1994) she has been published by Victoria University Press, for whom she also edited the poems of the artist Joanna Margaret Paul. See *The Merino Princess: Selected Poems* (2004) and also *The Ponies* (2006), written after a travelling fellowship to Antarctica, and *The Lustre Jug* (2009), which reflects on six months spent in Ireland.   JNT

Hall, Donald (1928–) Born in New Haven, Connecticut, and educated at Phillips Exeter Academy, New Hampshire, Harvard, and Oxford, where his poem 'Exiles' won the Newdigate Prize (1952). In 1952 he married Kirby Thompson, by whom he has two children, and was made creative-writing fellow at Stanford University the following year. He spent another three years at Harvard, this time as a junior fellow, and from 1957 was a professor of English at the University of Michigan.

Hall's first two books of poetry—*Exiles and Marriages* (1955) and *The Dark Houses* (1958)—harness moral arguments and social observations to traditional forms. Ideas, ironies, and metres give way to images, emotions, and free rhythms in *A Roof of Tiger Lilies* (1964) and *The Alligator Bride* (1969); the latter's fragmented syntax and surrealist juxtapositions make it Hall's most experimental work. *The Yellow Room: Love Poems* (1971) and *Kicking the Leaves* (1978; 1979), elegies and memories, reflect Hall's growing conviction that 'the poem is a vehicle for self-discovery'. Later collections include *The Twelve*

Seasons (1983), *Great Days in the Cow's House* (1984), and *The One Day and Poems 1947–1990* (1991).

In 1975 Hall retired from Michigan and, with his second wife, the poet Jane *Kenyon, returned to his ancestral farmhouse in Danbury, New Hampshire, to live by his writing alone. He was made Poet Laureate of New Hampshire in 1984. He has published books on baseball, a critical biography of the sculptor Henry Moore (1966), a critical study of Marianne *Moore (1970), personal and literary reminiscences, and books for children. His strongest influence, however, has been as an editor: of poetry for the *Paris Review* (1953–62); and of numerous widely read selections and anthologies, most notably *Contemporary American Poetry* (Penguin, 1962; revd. edn., 1971), the *Oxford Book of American Literary Anecdotes* (1981), and the *Oxford Book of Children's Verse in America* (1985).

See *Breakfast Served Any Time All Day: Essays on Poetry New and Selected* (University of Michigan Press, 2003), *Willow Temple: New and Selected Stories* (2003), and *White Apples and the Taste of Stone: Poems 1946–2006* (2006—both Houghton).   NE

Hall, J. C. (John Clive) (1920–2011) Born in London and educated at Leighton Park School, Reading, and Oxford. While at Oxford, Hall was an editor of *Fords and Bridges* and contributed to its successor, *Kingdom Come.* He was a friend of Keith *Douglas; and, while Douglas was in Egypt, arranged the publication of *Selected Poems* (1943) by K. C. Douglas, J. C. Hall, and Norman *Nicholson. Of strong Quaker sympathies, Hall was exempted from military duties and did farm-work during the Second World War. After the war he made his career in publishing and was for some years on the staff of *Encounter.*

From 1943 to 1947 he seems to have written little or no poetry; and he was a very sparse poet throughout his career. In 1952 he edited Edwin *Muir's *Collected Poems;* and Muir's influence is particularly felt in his third book, *The Burning Hare* (1966). Keith Douglas said that Hall's early poetry could do with a little more cynicism;

and thirty years later, in *A House of Voices* (1973), Hall seemed to find himself in a style more direct and less involved with conventional rhetoric than was his earlier poetry. *Long Shadows* (Shoestring, 2003; repr. Faber, 2010) selects from seven decades of verse.   ATT

Hall, Rodney (1935–) Born in Solihull in England of Australian parents. His father died when he was six months old, and the family returned to Australia after the Second World War. Hall went to Queensland, where he left school at 16, later taking a degree from the University of Queensland in 1971. He has worked as a script-writer, actor, film critic, youth officer for the Australian Council for the Arts, and as teacher of music and creative writing. From 1967 to 1978 he was poetry editor of the *Australian*, and from 1972 to 1975 adviser to Angus and Robertson, both influential positions. Since 1981 he has concentrated on prose: among his novels, *Just Relations* (1982) won the Miles Franklin Award; he has also written studies of artist Andrew Sibley (1968), writer John Manifold (1978), a number of accounts of Australia, libretti, and has edited numerous anthologies, most notably, with Tom *Shapcott, *New Impulses in Australian Poetry* (1968), as well as three volumes of Michael *Dransfield's poetry.

His poetry is witty, detached, and wears considerable learning with an easeful grace. Often ironic, it is technically flexible and well crafted. His first publication, which appeared in England, was *Penniless till Doomsday* (Outpost, 1961), followed in Australia with a small selection in *Four Poets* (Cheshire, 1962). Eight volumes followed in the next thirteen years. His *Selected Poems* (University of Queensland Press, 1975), extracts the best of his first eight books, excepting *The Law of Karma* (Australian National University, 1968), a 'progression of poems' in which discrete lyrics accumulate in an interrelated whole. In 1990, Hall was made a Member of the Order of Australia, and chaired the Literature Board of the Australia Council until 1994. See *The Owner of My Face: New and Selected Poems* (Paper Bark, 2002) and *Popeye Never Told You* (Pier 9, 2010), an experimental memoir.   JD

Halpern, Daniel (1945-) Born in Syracuse, New York, and grew up in Los Angeles and Seattle, the eldest of four children. His father was a scrap-metal dealer. He was educated at San Francisco State College, California State University at Northridge, and Columbia University. For two years, from 1968 to 1970, he lived in Tangier, where he met the composer and writer Paul Bowles. With financing from Bowles, together they founded the international literary magazine *Antaeus* in 1970, which Halpern continued to edit until 1994. He is also president and publisher of Ecco, an imprint of HarperCollins publishers in New York City (where his authors include Nobel Laureates Czesław Miłosz and Tomas Tranströmer). As Halpern's artistic mentor and friend in those early years, Bowles introduced him to the avant-garde in contemporary literature and music. For many years, he taught at Columbia University.

Like the work of his teachers Stanley *Kunitz and Mark *Strand, Halpern's poetry is spare in its diction. Often his poems are studies in *film noir* surfaces. But there are also poems of Maine light and New York urbanity, where the senses are continually stimulated by landscape, mood, and gastronomic delights.

Halpern has published nine volumes of poetry, of which the most recent are *Something Shining* (1999) and *Selected Poems* (1994—both Knopf). He also translated *Songs of Mririda*, by Mririda n'Ait Attik, from a French translation of the original Berber, and (co-translated) *Orchard Lamps*, by Ivan Drach, from the Ukrainian. He has edited *The American Poetry Anthology* (Avon, 1975), *The Antaeus Anthology* (Bantam, 1986), and *The Art of the Tale: an International Anthology of Short Stories* (Penguin, 1986), among other anthologies.   HC

Hamburger, Michael (1924–2007) Born in Berlin and emigrated to England in 1933. He was educated at schools in Edinburgh and London, and studied modern languages at Christ Church, Oxford. During the war he served as an infantryman, non-commissioned officer, and lieutenant in the Royal Army Educational Corps, 1943–7. After the war he held posts at University College, London and the University of Reading. In the 1960s and 1970s he was a guest lecturer and visiting professor at various American universities. Later, he settled in rural Suffolk, and mostly devoted himself to freelance writing and translation. His translations won many distinguished prizes and awards.

Hamburger's memoirs, *A Mug's Game* (Carcanet, 1973 and—retitled *Spring of Beginnings*—1991) tell his life story up to the early 1950s. His contemporaries at Oxford included *Larkin and the wartime generation of Sidney *Keyes, Drummond *Allison, David *Wright, and John *Heath-Stubbs. Later he became an admirer of Herbert *Read. Much of his poetry shows the pervasive influence of T. S. *Eliot. He has explored social dilemmas, personal loneliness, and the impersonal sanities of nature: 'Come late into the freedom his from birth, | To breathe the air, and walk the ownerless earth' ('Confirmist'). His major critical book was *The Truth of Poetry* (Weidenfeld & Nicolson, 1969).

As a translator of classic and modern German poetry Hamburger made a significant contribution to Anglo-American understanding of the German poetic canon. His career as a translator began in 1942 with a volume of Hölderlin from The Harvill Press, and he produced important early versions of Paul Celan, with Christopher *Middleton (Penguin, 1972). He later translated the poetry of W. G. Sebald. Hamburger was awarded an OBE in 1992. *Collected Poems 1941-1994* (1995) was followed by five further collections, the last of which was *Circling the Square* (2007—all Anvil).   WS*

Hamilton, George Rostrevor (1888–1967) The only son of a clergyman, Hamilton was born in London and educated at Exeter College, Oxford. In 1912 he joined the Inland Revenue and there pursued a distinguished career, for which he was knighted in 1951. He settled in London, living first by the Thames at Chiswick then moving to Blackheath, where he was a friend of Roy *Fuller, another poet and man of letters committed to the professional world.

The first of eighteen volumes of verse, *Escape and Fantasy*, appeared in 1918, the year of Hamilton's marriage to Marion Hermine; *The Making*, a selection of his poetry to 1925, was significantly dedicated to Henri Bergson, a study of whose philosophy Hamilton published in 1921. He claimed that Bergson taught him 'immediacy of sight', and to 'immerse [his] life's movement . . . in a living, streaming universe'; but Hamilton's verse rarely repaid the debt. In later life Plato replaced Bergson as a presiding influence in his somewhat mannered meditations on nature, in which the Thames continued to figure, uneasily, as a unifying presence. His taste for formality was perhaps best suited to the polished epigrams he produced in great numbers. His study of *The English Verse Epigram* appeared in 1965; but his most impressive criticism is in *The Tell-Tale Article* (1949), an acute, admirably focused discussion of language in T. S. *Eliot and W. H. *Auden.

Selected Poems and Epigrams (Heinemann, 1945) represents Hamilton's poetic career. For a brief memoir, see Roy Fuller, *Spanner and Pen* (Sinclair-Stevenson, 1991).   MRW

Hamilton, Ian (1938–2001) Born in King's Lynn, Norfolk, and educated at Darlington Grammar School and Keble College, Oxford. He edited *The Review*, 1962–72, and *The New Review*, 1974–9, and was the first editor of this *Companion*.

Despite the parish-magazine-like appearance of its early issues in 1962, *The Review* rapidly established itself as the most influential and stylish of post-war British poetry magazines. The poems of its regular contributors—among them Douglas *Dunn, Colin Falck, John *Fuller, David *Harsent, Hamilton himself, and Hugo *Williams—tended to be sparse, intense, and intelligent; but the magazine will be more widely recalled as a forum for rigorous and sometimes ferocious critical writing. Over ten years, in thirty numbers, *The Review* covered most important English

and American poets of the time, giving particularly sympathetic, sustained attention to Robert *Lowell, who was in some respects its literary mentor; the final double number included a substantial and entertaining symposium on 'The State of Poetry' in 1972. Less serious but equally entertaining were the regular satirical columns of 'Edward Pygge'. A selection of essays from the first fifteen issues, compiled by Hamilton, was published as *The Modern Poet* (1968). The magazine was succeeded in 1974 by *The New Review*, an ambitious literary monthly.

Hamilton himself was a famously glacial poet, publishing three volumes with Faber in as many decades, which were in fact cumulative editions of his complete output. *The Visit* (1970) was reprinted with revisions in *Fifty Poems* (1988), to which *Sixty Poems* added ten more. *Collected Poems* (Faber, 2009), edited with an introduction by Alan *Jenkins, expands the work of fifty years with two poems published in 2001, and a handful of unpublished or uncollected pieces. An appendix illustrates the intensive editorial process to which Hamilton subjected his writing.

In the preface to *Fifty Poems*, he commented on his decision 'to stop thinking like a poetry pro' and only to write when 'prompted by circumstance'. The result is a spare oeuvre of measured reflections—often arriving at last lines resonant with unspoken pain—that exemplifies the understated craft he admired in others. Hamilton's phrasing and attitudes sometimes echo the plain-speaking of Philip *Larkin, but his recurrent concern with the question of poetic speech, its simultaneous power and impotence, also suggests an affinity with the hesitant postmodernism of, say, W. S. *Graham: see 'Poem' ('Sleep on | And listen to these words . . . Refuse to waken you'). He was less impressed by the kind of American free versifier whom he caricatured as writing 'Two words a line, at most'.

Hamilton's critical style was famously judicious and unflinching: 'supple, pointed, acidly laconic', said Clive *James. See *Walking Possession: Essays and Reviews 1968–1993* (Bloomsbury, 1994). He also wrote a biography of Lowell. In *Little Magazines:*

A Study of Six Editors (Weidenfeld & Nicolson, 1976) and *Keepers of the Flame* (Hutchinson, 1992), a study of literary estates, he surveyed the sociology of the literary world. His attempt to write a critical biography of the reclusive American novelist J. D. Salinger ended at the US Supreme Court and a change in American copyright law: see *In Search of J. D. Salinger* (Heinemann/Random House, 1988; repr. Faber, 2010).

It is characteristic of the range of Hamilton's interests that, in 1998, he published a biography of the poet-critic Matthew Arnold and a study of the English footballer Paul Gascoigne, both figures whose difficult relationship to youthful talent he brought sympathetically to life. *Against Oblivion*, a twentieth-century *Lives of the Poets*, appeared posthumously (Viking, 2002). See *Another Round at the Pillars* (Cargo, 1999), a festschrift edited by David Harsent, and *Ian Hamilton in Conversation with Dan Jacobson* (Between the Lines, 2002), an extended interview from the last year of his life.   JNT/NP/POM

(⊕) SEE WEB LINKS

• More information including a full bibliography of Hamilton's work is available at the Ian Hamilton website.

Hampton, Susan (1949–) Born in Inverell, New South Wales. Her published poetry includes *Costumes* (Transit, 1981) and *White Dog Sonnets: A Novel* (Fab Press, 1987), and a collection of monologues, prose poems, stories, and performance pieces, *Surly Girls* (Collins, 1989). With Kate *Llewellyn, she edited the *Penguin Book of Australian Women Poets* (1986) and worked with the Aboriginal writer, Ruby Langford, on Langford's autobiography *Don't Take Your Love to Town* (1989). Hampton has also written, with Sue Woolfe, a teaching textbook *About Literature* (1984). She taught writing in universities for many years, and has latterly worked as an editor.

Hampton's early poems 'The Crafty Butcher' and 'Yugoslav Story' were her most often anthologized, possibly because they do not call attention to her commitment to a lesbian feminist aesthetic. Hampton has assembled an eloquent statement of her feminism in David Brooks and Brenda Walker's *Poetry and Gender* (1990). Though she is committed to challenging representations of women, and to creating a poetry which breaks down genre barriers, Hampton consistently writes about relationships and examines the failure of romantic, monogamous love. At the same time, she attends to the social and political implications of personal life, and her writing about lesbian women, particularly in *Surly Girls*, has a polemical intent. She has published three later collections: *A Latin Primer* (Cerberus, 1998), a sonnet sequence; *The Kindly Ones* (2005), a travel poem which brings the Greek Furies to modern Australia; and *News of the Insect World* (2009—both Five Islands Press).   SMCK

Hannah, Sophie (1971–) Born in Manchester and read English and Spanish at the university there. She has taught at Manchester Metropolitan University and held writing residencies, including one at Trinity College in Cambridge, where she now lives.

Hannah began publishing her poetry while still a student. Her first pamphlets, *Early Bird Blues* (Smith/Doorstep, 1993) and *Second Helping of Your Heart* (Frogmore, 1994), were collected in her 1995 debut, *The Hero and the Girl Next Door*, which won an Eric Gregory award. *Hotels like Houses* followed the next year. Her facility as a writer of witty verse in regular rhyming form was immediately popular, and her wry, often satirical attitude to love poetry drew comparisons with Wendy *Cope. Hannah is not a parodist, though, and beyond relationships tends to social observation (including, latterly, reflections on the life of a professional poet) and the pleasure and pathos of familiar things. 'The Norbert Dentressangle Van', which concludes *Leaving and Leaving You* (1999), her third collection, exemplifies the more ludic tendencies of her formalism.

First of the Last Chances appeared in 2003, and *Pessimism for Beginners* in 2007 (all Carcanet). Since *Selected Poems* (Penguin, 2006), she has published several crime novels and a book of short stories, *The Fantastic Book of Everybody's Secrets* (Sort Of, 2008).   JNT

Haq, Kaiser (1950–) Born in Dhaka and educated at St Gregory's School, Dhaka College, and Dhaka University. In 1971 he joined the Bangladesh Liberation Army when the war of liberation broke out. After liberation he resigned his commission to resume his studies at Dhaka University, and in 1975 joined the English department as a lecturer. Between 2002 and 2003 he was a Fellow at the School of Oriental and African Studies in London.

Haq writes about the contemporary Bangladeshi scene, exposing life's little incongruities and ironies, exploiting a form of colonial English which, even so many years after the departure of the British, still seems to dominate academic and media discourse. His poetry relies heavily on irony and understatement. It combines flashes of insight with a journalistic detailing of objects; it is moving and insightful but smart and refreshingly witty at the same time. Haq likes to see himself as belonging to an Indo-Anglian tradition which has attained a distinct identity and idiom of its own, and one of his favourite themes is the alienation and rootlessness of the educated middle class.

Haq has appeared widely in poetry reviews and journals at home and abroad, and has published five volumes of poems: *A Little Ado*, *Starting Lines* (both Granthabithi, 1978), *A Happy Farewell* (University Press, Dhaka, 1994), *Black Orchid* (Aark Arts, 1996), and *The Logopathic Reviewer's Song* (University Press, Dhaka/Aark Arts, 2002). See *Published in the Streets of Dhaka: Collected Poems 1966–2006* (Writers.ink, 2007). He has also edited an anthology, *Contemporary Indian Poetry in English* (Ohio State University Press, 1990), and translated many Bengali poems into English.   SMI

Hardy, Thomas (1840–1928) Born in Higher Bockhampton, Dorset, a hamlet three miles from the county town of Dorchester. His father, also named Thomas, was an independent builder; his mother, Jemima, was in domestic service at the time of her marriage. Both were members of families with extensive connections throughout southern and western Dorset. Thomas Hardy senior was a gifted amateur musician; Jemima, who was far more energetic and ambitious than her husband, encouraged all her children—her bookish and delicate older son in particular—to seek the best education available to them, within the family's limited means.

Hardy left school at 16 and was apprenticed to a local architect. In 1861 he moved to London, where he was to live for the next five years, and took a job as an architect's assistant. A notebook he kept shows that it was during this period that he began to write verse. His first novel, *Desperate Remedies*, was published in 1871. By then he was once again in Dorset (he made his home there for the rest of his life), and was engaged to be married to Emma Gifford, whom he had met during a visit to Cornwall. Over the next twenty-six years he published a large number of novels, of which the most famous are probably *Far From the Madding Crowd, Tess of the D'Urbervilles*, and *Jude the Obscure*.

Throughout these years he continued to write poems, or to jot down lines and ideas for poems. However, he published nothing of what he had written in this form until the last of his novels, *The Well-Beloved*, had appeared in 1897. *Wessex Poems and Other Verses* came out the year after; it was followed by a further eight volumes of verse, the last of which, *Winter Words*, was published posthumously. He also wrote a verse drama on the Napoleonic Wars, *The Dynasts*, which appeared in three parts between 1904 and 1908. Hardy's decision to give up fiction and confine himself to verse owed something to the hostile reception given to *Jude the Obscure*, on the grounds of the novel's supposed obscenity; but the biographical and literary evidence shows that poetry was anything but a *pis aller* for him. Rather, it could be called his earliest as well as his last calling.

Anyone looking into the *Complete Poems* for the first time might well be struck by two apparently contradictory features of the massive volume in their hands. The first is of the uniformity of Hardy's poetry; the second is of its variety. What is meant by 'uniformity' here is that it is impossible to trace any kind of development, any growth or decline in power, any change in subject-matter, technique, or even emotional tone, from the beginning to the end of Hardy's poetic career. No doubt this is in part due to the fact that he had been accumulating poems or drafts of poems for so long before appearing in public as a poet; these were then drawn in irregular fashion into his successive collections. The felicities of his verse are manifest as frequently in the first volume as in the last; so are the lapses into awkwardness and bathos to which he was always prone; so are those turns of phrase and rhyme which somehow combine the felicitous and the awkward in a manner which is quite unlike anything to be found elsewhere in English poetry.

There are, of course, sequences of poems which plainly belong to one or another specific period of Hardy's life—those he wrote during the Anglo-Boer War, for example; or even more notably, those written after Emma Hardy's death, which celebrate and mourn the brief period of happiness he and she had known together, as well as the decades of conjugal misery that had followed. However, groups of poems like these do not differ in style or vocabulary from the rest of his output; even the themes, moods, and preoccupations which they explore with their own special intensity are familiar from other contexts and in other guises.

As for the 'variety' of his verse: he wrote hundreds of lyrics and love-songs, ballads, sonnets, dramatic, descriptive, and meditative poems of all kinds, drinking songs, character sketches, poems on public issues and events (the sinking of the *Titanic*, the outbreak or the ending of wars, an eclipse of the moon), tributes to other poets (Shakespeare, Shelley, Keats, Swinburne)—as well as poems which combine these genres, or elements of them, in often unexpected ways. In addition, the verse-forms, rhythms, and rhyme-schemes used by the poet vary from poem to poem in what seems to be a positively compulsive manner. No particular form is matched consistently to any particular genre or type of subject-matter. (Blank verse, however, is found only in *The Dynasts;* all Hardy's other poetry is rhymed.) To complicate matters yet further, he will frequent-ly begin a poem in one elaborate stanzaic form, very possibly a form newly invented for the occasion, only to switch to another half-way through; sometimes he will then return to the original form before the end of the poem, sometimes not.

The effect of all this on the reader is bound to be, intermittently at least, one of bewilderment. The formal restlessness of the poet, and the strained ingenuities and improbabilities of rhyme and vocabulary into which it occasionally drives him, can make an almost childlike impression at times. Nor does it seem unfair to call child-like some of the delight which Hardy takes, in his dramatic and narrative verse especially, in malign, melodramatic coincidences, or in a generalized, sepulchral spookiness, or in moments of heavily contrived self-disclosure on the part of his protagonists. These faults will, of course, be familiar to readers of his novels and short stories too. When Hardy gives the name *Satires of Circumstance* (1914) to one collection, the reader is entitled to fear that all too many of its poems will mechanically fulfil the ominous promise of the title; and this indeed turns out to be the case. Yet that particular volume also contains the sequence of poems about the death of Emma Hardy, which (under the sub-heading 'Poems of 1912–13') includes many examples of his finest and most heartfelt work. One cannot help feeling that there is something typically perverse and Hardyesque in his choosing to link together in so uncritical a manner some of the best and the worst of which he was capable.

However, all criticisms made, Hardy remains for his admirers an indispensable poet: one of that smallish group of whom one might say that his absence would be felt not just as a depletion of the canon of English poetry but as a personal loss. That his work was to affect so deeply successors as different as W. H. *Auden and Philip *Larkin is perhaps just one illustration of this point. The sources of his appeal may be identified, crudely enough, in threefold fashion: first, in the delicacy of his observations of the natural world; secondly, in his capacity to stare straight into the duplicities of human passion; and thirdly, in the philosophical scope of his mind. But one must at once add that his greatest strength as a poet ultimately shows itself not by way of a movement in his verse from one to another of these elements, but in the unique and indissoluble fusion of them which it again and again offers.

For Hardy, nature is never inert—neither in itself as a theatre of continual change; nor as the terrain, begrudging and generous in turn, from which we and all other animals have to glean a living; nor in the ever-renewed power it has to evoke a response in those who regard it. In fact, a paradox that the verse presses upon us—and here we come on one of its philosophic dimensions—is that even when it is at its harshest, bleakest, its apparently most remote and indifferent, nature is to be understood as having these aspects only because we ourselves are compelled to see it as such. Thus, almost in spite of ourselves, we remain a part of it, and it remains a part of us. ('We' in this context refers not only to the human race, incidentally: Hardy is always sensitive to the possibility that the humblest animals are conscious of more than we dare to credit them with. See, for instance, the little poem 'An August Midnight'.)

If Hardy looks on both nature and our relations to it as continually undergoing a process of change, he is positively obsessed with the instability and transience of all human emotions—and hence of all human life. Here again, however, the essentially philosophic nature of his verse makes itself apparent. To say that he is preoccupied with transience is also to say that he is constantly engaged in a search for permanence; or for such permanence as we are capable of experiencing. Recurrence across the generations is one form of it; memory is another; both are at once beyond all value and yet inherently and ironically subversive of value. We possess our memories only at the cost of knowing that we can never recover or go back to that which we are remembering; the individuality we treasure, and all the passions which sustain it, turn out to be nothing but an ineluctable miming of the lives of the dead and the yet-to-be born.

In the light of all this, and given also Hardy's unflinching (if often aggrieved) refusal of the comforts offered by religious belief, it is hardly surprising that the emotions and states of mind most eloquently expressed in his verse are those of bewilderment, dismay, regret, remorse, loss, failure, and misunderstanding; a longing for times past together with an exacerbated sense of opportunities not taken or simply not noticed when that same past was actually present, available, malleable; a consciousness of motives wholly or partly hidden at times of action, and revealed or understood too late to be of any use; above all, a never-to-be-evaded awareness of mortality. Feelings like these are inevitably taken both to reflect and to account for Hardy's famous 'pessimism'; and that pessimism is in turn commonly identified with his 'philosophy' (Hardy himself does it from time to time). Enough has been said here, however, to suggest that the latter word should be used both more widely and more carefully in thinking about his work.

In the end, what makes Hardy a philosophic poet is something more than his bleak view of human possibilities, however deeply he held that view and however central it was to his overall achievement. He is a philosophic poet because he struggles so hard to extend the range of the sayable, and hence of the thinkable, whether it be by the poet himself or by anyone who reads his work. What is the true nature of the relation between animate creatures and an apparently inanimate world, and in what terms can it best be described? Is it possible for conscious beings to imagine an absence of consciousness—and if so, how? What is it of the dead that lives in us and in what forms does it manifest itself? How are we able to apprehend the limits of our own knowledge and experience; and what kind of knowledge, what kind of experience, is it to feel that very apprehension within us? These are the questions which his verse asks of itself and of its readers, even as it talks (or sings) of hedgehogs and thrushes, raindrops, birch trees, fresh love, embittered love, and a long-dead sister 'laughing, her young brown hand awave'.

See the *Complete Poetical Works*, ed. Samuel Hynes, in three volumes (Clarendon, 1982–5), and *Thomas Hardy: A Selection*, also ed. Samuel Hynes (Oxford University Press, 1994).

See also Robert Gittings' *The Young Thomas Hardy* (1975) and *The Older Hardy* (1978—both Heinemann); and Michael Millgate's *Thomas Hardy: A Biography* (Oxford University Press, 1982). Hardy's novels are readily available in various editions; his deeply uninteresting *Collected Letters*, ed. R. L. Purdy and Michael Millgate, were published in seven volumes between 1978 and 1988. Of more interest is *Thomas Hardy's 'Poetical Matter' Notebook* (Oxford University Press, 2009), ed. Pamela Dalziel and Michael Millgate, a fragmentary record of his imaginative life. Donald *Davie's *Thomas Hardy and British Poetry* (Routledge & Kegan Paul, 1973) is a study of Hardy's twentieth-century legacy. See also Barbara Hardy, *Thomas Hardy: Imagining Imagination* (Athlone, 2000).   DJ*

Harford, Lesbia (1891–1927) Born Lesbia Keogh in Melbourne, where she studied philosophy and law, being one of the first women graduates in law at Melbourne University. Both her life and her art were shaped to conform to her commitment to the socialism of the radical labour movement. Despite congenital heart disease, she spent years in manual work in clothing factories; despite seriousness about writing, she published few of her often untitled poems, and remained remote from Sydney's literary world, although maintaining Melbourne contacts with Frank *Wilmot and Nettie Palmer; aware of contemporary movements in poetry, she chose to write 'little fresh songs', accessible to the fellow-workers she frequently made her subject-matter.

Palmer edited a selection in 1941, and national anthologies like Serle's *An Australasian Anthology* (Collins, 1927) kept some poems in circulation, but major attention came with feminist criticism, attracted by her expression of the tensions and contradictions experienced by women seeking independence in work, politics, and love. *The Invaluable Mystery*, her novel on these themes, was finally published (McPhee Gribble, 1987) following *The Poems of Lesbia Harford* (Melbourne University Press, 1985), a complete edition with a comprehensive introduction by Drusilla Modjeska.   JS

Harjo, Joy (1951–) Born in Tulsa, Oklahoma, to Muskogee Creek and Canadian parents, Harjo studied at the universities of New Mexico and Iowa, where she attended the Writers' Workshop. Also a painter and musician, she has taught at various universities in the United States, and plays saxophone in the band Poetic Justice.

An important feminist voice in Native American writing, like her contemporary Leslie Marmon *Silko, Harjo began to publish in the 1970s. Her early collections include *What Moon Drove Me to This?* (Reed, 1980) and *She Had Some Horses* (Thunder's Mouth, 1983; repr. Norton, 2008), the title poem of which is a surreal incantation of contradictions. *In Mad Love and War* (Wesleyan University Press, 1990) won the National Book Award, the Delmore Schwartz Memorial Award, and the William Carlos Williams Award. Its prose poems, such as 'Deer Dancer', blend colloquial realism with mythological symbolism ('The woman inside the woman who was to dance naked in the bar of misfits blew deer magic'). See also *The Woman Who Fell from Sky* (1994), *A Map to the Next World: Poetry and Tales* (2000), and *How We Became Human: New and Selected Poems* (2002—all Norton). In 1995 Harjo received the Lifetime Achievement Award from the Native Writers' Circle of the Americas. See also, with Gloria Bird, *Reinventing the Enemy's Language: Contemporary Native Women's Writing of North America* (Norton, 1997); *Soul Talk, Song Language: Conversations with Joy Harjo* (Wesleyan University Press, 2011); and *Crazy Brave* (Norton, 2012), a memoir.   JNT

Harper, Michael S. (Michael Steven) (1938–) Born in Brooklyn, but received his high-school education in Los Angeles. He took degrees from the City College and California State College there, and from the

Iowa Writers' Workshop. He taught in several colleges and universities on the West Coast, but since 1973 has taught at Brown University in Providence, Rhode Island, with honorary stints at many schools.

His first book of poems was *Dear John, Dear Coltrane* (1970), and he has published several collections since, including *Song: I Want a Witness* (1972—both University of Pittsburgh Press), *Nightmare Begins Responsibility* (1974), *Images of Kin: New and Selected Poems* (1977), *Honorable Amendments* (1995), and *Use Trouble* (2009). Harper writes out of his black heritage, using the referents and rhythms of jazz and blues. *Songlines in Michaeltree: New and Collected Poems* appeared in the USA in 2000 (all University of Illinois Press). A *Selected Poems* has been published in the UK by Arc. *To Cut Is to Heal: A Critical Companion to Michael S. Harper's* Debridement (2000) contains essays and an extended interview with Ben *Lerner on his Vietnam-era sequence, previously published in separate parts (see *Debridement* (2001—both Paradigm)). He has also edited several anthologies, including *The Vintage Book of African American Poetry* (2000).   LT*

Harris, Max (1921–95) Born in Adelaide but grew up in Mount Gambier, a large country-town near the border between South Australia and Victoria. A nearby town appears in the name of perhaps his best-known poem, 'The Tantanoola Tiger'. Harris worked briefly as a journalist, then completed a degree in economics at Adelaide University.

In 1944, when still a student, he gained inadvertent celebrity as the victim of Australia's most spectacular literary hoax. *Angry Penguins*, the literary magazine he had founded two years earlier, invited some such treatment: its content, much of it written by Harris himself, consisted mainly of clumsy imitations of Dylan *Thomas and T. S. *Eliot, while its editorial stance was precociously pompous. James *McAuley and Harold Stewart, young poets only a few years older than Harris, resolved to deflate his pomposity by invent-

ing a non-existent poet whose verse was even worse than Harris' own; they named their creation 'Ern Malley' and submitted his work to *Angry Penguins*, where Harris swallowed the bait. In the subsequent fracas Harris was prosecuted for publishing 'indecent advertisements', and his career as an avant-gardist ended in humiliation. It was not, however, the end of his literary career. Ten years later he completed *The Coorong and Other Poems* (Mary Martin, 1955) in which he revealed himself as an impressively mature and accomplished, if somewhat conservative, poet. *A Window at Night* (ABR, 1967) overlaps the previous book but adds new poems as well. The quality of Harris' best poetry tends to be overlooked in the face of his other pursuits, from his youthful misadventures, through his appearances as a television personality in the 1960s, to his latter-day manifestation as a crusty newspaper columnist.   JG

Harrison, Jim (James Thomas Harrison) (1937–) Born in Grayling, a small county seat in northern Michigan, the state in which he has spent most of his life. After attending Michigan State University, where he studied comparative literature, he taught for two years at the State University of New York, Stony Brook, before returning to live on a farm in the region of his birthplace. He has been poetry editor of the *Nation* and co-editor of *Sumac*. His local rootedness and rural loyalties are disclosed in several titles of his volumes of poetry, which, in addition to *Selected and New Poems, 1961–1981* (1982), include *Locations* (1968), *Returning to Earth* (1977), and *The Theory and Practice of Rivers* (1986). He is also the widely acclaimed author of nine volumes of prose fiction, from which may be singled out *Legends of the Fall* (1979), three novellas exploring the ways of violent revenge.

Characteristically a free verse of short, imagistic lines, Harrison's is a poetry both of natural particulars and the universals of human experience. Though most happily grounded close to home, he is a poet of large sympathy and concern, who names amongst the primary influences upon him

Whitman, *Yeats, Rilke, Lorca, Neruda, and *Pound, and whose *Letters to Yesenin* (1973) enact a passionate correspondence between the contrasting kinds of Russian and American anguish.

See *The Shape of the Journey: New and Collected Poems* (1998) and three subsequent volumes, all with Copper Canyon Press. *Braided Creek: A Conversation in Poetry* (2003) collects an exchange of short poems with Ted *Kooser. RWB

Harrison, Tony (1937–) Born in Leeds and educated at Leeds Grammar School (1948–55) and Leeds University (1955–60), where he read classics and took a diploma in linguistics. He lectured in English at Ahmadu Bello University, Nigeria, 1962–6 and at Charles University, Prague, 1966–7. In 1968–9 he co-edited *Stand*. In 1977/8 he was resident dramatist at the National Theatre.

Tony Harrison's achievement springs from apparent contradiction: he is a classicist from the working class; a writer of considerable scholarship seeking a mass audience in the theatre and on television; a poet of great technical accomplishment whose work insists that it is speech rather than page-bound silence; a pessimist with a relish for life; above all, perhaps, a poet repeatedly troubled by the knowledge that the very gift which enables him to speak for his class is what separates him from it. These shaping tensions have bred Harrison's conviction that poetry 'is not something I can take for granted': hence, perhaps, the scale and ambition of his work.

Harrison's first full collection, *The Loiners* (London Magazine, 1970) showed a ready transition between the personal and the larger stage of power in history—from sex on a Leeds tombstone to the burning victims at Philip of Spain's wedding in 'The Nuptial Torches'. It is in the ongoing series *The School of Eloquence* that he begins to make a history for himself, turning to address language as a form of power and exclusion (for example, 'Them & [uz]'). To 'occupy' the 'lousy leasehold poetry' involves not only the inclusion of supposedly unpoetic materials, but also mastery of the

forms tradition has proposed as the possession of the élite—notably the sonnet. A struggle is waged both by and in the poems, and Harrison's emotional frankness, while sometimes risking sentimentality, has an undeniable force. At the same time, his travels, notably to the USA, have provided him with a less class-burdened context from which a more ample and sensual poetry has emerged (for example, 'A Kumquat for John Keats').

The 1987 television broadcast of the controversial *V*. (new edn., Bloodaxe, 1989) a meditation on death and division in a vandalized Leeds graveyard, written during the 1984–5 miners' strike, brought Harrison wide attention. He has continued to use television as a medium for poetry in *Loving Memory* (1987) and *The Blasphemers' Banquet* (1989). His conviction that poetry is a public art is further demonstrated by the publication of his Gulf War poems, 'Initial Illumination' and 'A Cold Coming' in the *Guardian* on 5 and 18 March 1991, during the conflict.

Harrison has also worked extensively as a theatre poet and as a librettist, writing acclaimed versions of Racine, Molière, and Aeschylus, as well as *The Mysteries* (1985) and *The Trackers of Oxyrhynchus* (1990). His plays have been collected in five volumes by Faber. *A Cold Coming: Gulf War Poems*, and *The Gaze of the Gorgon*, which won the Whitbread Award, both came from Bloodaxe in 1992.

Tony Harrison: Bloodaxe Critical Anthologies 1 (1991), ed. Neil Astley, is a comprehensive critical introduction to his work up to 1990. In 1995, his film-poem *The Shadow of Hiroshima* was shown on the fiftieth anniversary of the dropping of the first nuclear bomb: see *Collected Film Poetry* (Faber, 2007). *Permanently Bard*, a selected poems, appeared in the same year from Bloodaxe. *Laureate's Block and Other Occasional Poems* (2000) collected Harrison's topical poems from across the decade. It included writing on the war in Bosnia commissioned by the *Guardian* newspaper, but was criticized in the same paper by Robert Potts as a 'falling off' in technique from his earlier work. *Under the Clock*

(2005—both Penguin) was a pocket volume of new poems. Harrison's *Collected Poems* appeared from Viking in 2007.   SO'B*

Harry, J. S. (Jan S.) (1939–) Born in Adelaide, South Australia. A reclusive and unpredictable poet, J. S. Harry has been praised for her 'wit and lyrical argumentation', and for her stylistic versatility. Each new volume has seemed like a leap into the dark, or a demonstration of her ability to range from experimental modishness to formal tautness, from scintillation to savagery. There is sometimes an unevenness of pace, but Harry is perhaps best read in volume form, rather than for individual poems. Because of this, perhaps, her work has been difficult to anthologize adequately.

Her early collections were *The Deer under the Skin* (University of Queensland Press, 1971); *Hold for a Little While, and Turn Gently* (1979); and *A Dandelion for Van Gogh* (1985—both Island). Peter *Porter called Harry 'the most arresting poet working in Australia today'. Her *Selected Poems*, which won the Kenneth Slessor Award, was published by Penguin in 1995. In the same year, *The Life on the Water and the Life Beneath* (Angus & Robertson) introduced her inquisitive rabbit-hero, Peter Henry Lupus. *Not Finding Wittgenstein*, a volume devoted to Lupus' search for philosophical conversation, was published in Australia by Giramondo Press in 2007, and in the UK by Bloodaxe in 2012.   TWS*

Harryman, Carla (1952–) Born in Orange, California and studied at the University of California at Santa Barbara and San Francisco State University. She teaches creative writing at Eastern Michigan University and is married to Barrett *Watten. She is also a playwright and was co-founder of the Poet's Theater in San Francisco.

Harryman's first book was *Percentage* (Tuumba, 1979). The prose poem 'For She', from her second, *Under the Bridge* (This Press, 1980), was cited by Ron *Silliman in his essay 'The New Sentence' as an instance of the *Steinian disjunction that characterizes much *Language writing: 'I came from an odd bed, a vermilion riot attracted to loud dogs.' Harryman has de-

scribed her prose-based practice as an attempt 'to distribute narrative', leading to reflections on the fictions of writing and the self: 'If I were a realist would I say something else instead?' ('Realism'). *Memory Play* (O Books, 1994) explores recollection as a theatrical experience. *There Never Was a Rose Without a Thorn* (City Lights, 1995) is a selection of her prose. She describes several of her works, which include experimental novels, as 'new genre': see *Adorno's Noise* (Essay Press, 2008). Harryman has co-edited a collection of essays on the writing of Kathy Acker. *The Wide Road* (Belladonna, 2011) is a collaboration with Lyn *Hejinian.   JNT

Harsent, David (1942–) Born in Devon. From his first collection, *A Violent Country* (1969), his central subject has been the relationship, or non-relationship, between men and women. This he treats with a deftly tuned bleakness; his lines are often short, his words and syllables always weighed. Typically, 'Home Movies' sketches an emotional drama by focusing on the act of seeing, yet leaves its implications suggestively unstated; less typically, observation points the way towards release from unhappiness for both watcher and watched at the end of the poem. An intent record of moods close to desperation, 'The Woman's Soliloquies' moves skilfully between speech and silence, 'she' and 'I'. Here as elsewhere in Harsent's work, the human and the natural interact, sharing a need for endurance.

After Dark (1973) includes more ventilated lines and poems about parents and childhood, of which 'Two Postscripts to my Father' and 'Encounter' are impressive examples, the first unsentimentally direct, the second haunting. The slow-motion, cinematic clarity of Harsent's images marks his third collection, *Dreams of the Dead* (1977). By now he had mastered the art of making larger wholes out of short pieces. Two sequences of brief poems, 'Dreams of the Dead' and 'Moments in the Lifetime of Milady', reach inner states by way of an inventive documentation of externals: weather, a Berlin bar, spiders, deathbed silks. Narcissism is a risk the volume faces and surmounts.

Harsent's next volume, *Mister Punch* (1984—all Oxford University Press), extends the poet's fascination with dream, nightmare, lust, and loss in a sequence of grimly humorous poems featuring Punch, a trickster-like persona who challenges comparison with *Berryman's 'abominable' Henry. But Harsent's dream songs eschew the fractured idiom patented by Berryman in favour of a polished, bitter control (evident in the virtuoso rhyming of 'Rouault: A Portrait').

Fiona *Sampson has praised Harsent's later work for 'a clarity that takes no hostages and is unmatched in contemporary British verse'. Since *A Bird's Idea of Flight* (1998), his major volumes have all been published by Faber and Faber and shortlisted for most British prizes. The title sequence of *Marriage* (2002) explores the relationship between Pierre Bonnard and his model. *Legion* (2005) begins with a series of 'despatches' from an unnamed war zone, obliquely reflecting Harsent's work in the 1990s as a translator of the Serbian poet, Goran Simic. *Night* (2011) narrates dark episodes from an England where chthonic forces lurk in run-down suburbs, ending in the long poem, 'Elsewhere'. It won the International Griffin Poetry Prize. Harsent has also written mythological opera libretti for Harrison Birtwhistle, and crime fiction and television drama under a pseudonym. He is a Distinguished Writing Fellow at Sheffield Hallam University. See *Selected Poems* (2007).   MO'N*

Hart, Kevin (1954–) Born in London, grew up in Brisbane, and was educated in Canberra. He has taught both philosophy and English at universities in Victoria. Apart from his distinction as a poet, he is the foremost literary theorist of his generation in Australia. He was Associate Professor of Comparative Literature and Theory at Monash University and is now Professor of Christian Studies at the University of Virginia. He has examined the relations between deconstruction and mysticism in his challenging book, *The Trespass of the Sign: Deconstruction, Theology and Philosophy* (Cambridge University Press, 1989; repr.

Fordham University Press, 2000). He has also published extensively on the work of Maurice Blanchot.

Hart's own poetry started out quietly enough among the Canberra formalists. However, in *The Lines of the Hand* (Angus & Robertson, 1981) and *Your Shadow*, three years later, his mature characteristics emerged: passionate declaration, purity of diction, and a hunger for ontology. Hart's fondness for tercets can suggest a Wallace *Stevens turned Christian, but he is more physical than Stevens. Often he bypasses modernist irony altogether at the behest of Eros or Agape. *Peniel* (Golvan Arts, 1990) is a formally triune work of which the tercet is the essential unit. In 1994 he edited *The Oxford Book of Religious Verse*.

The best essay on Hart's early work is Peter Steele's 'Kevin Hart', *Overland, 122* (1991), which links the poetry with the criticism and with the translations from Ungaretti. *Flame Tree*, published in Australia by Paper Bark Press (2001) and in the UK by Bloodaxe (2002), is the latest selection of his poems. See also *Young Rain* (Giramondo, 2008; Bloodaxe, 2009) and *Morning Knowledge* (University of Notre Dame Press, 2011), his thirteenth collection, which deals with the death of his father. The title poem is a simple but affecting expression of his view of God as the 'Dark One'.   CW-C*

Hartigan, P. J. ('John O'Brien') (1878–1952) Born in Yass, a New South Wales country town, of Irish immigrants. He was ordained a Roman Catholic priest in 1903 and worked as a pastor in rural areas of New South Wales until retirement in 1944. Hartigan's verse provides a humorous yet sympathetic record of the lives of his congregations, mainly Irish settlers, and their responses to Australian outback life. His collection *Around the Boree Log* (1921), published under the pseudonym 'John O'Brien', was immensely popular and reprinted five times in as many years. Hartigan's unpublished verse appeared posthumously in *The Parish of St Mels* (1954).

The subjects and form of Hartigan's verse locate it in the popular tradition of the Australian rural ballad, epitomized by A. B. (Banjo) *Paterson. His most enduring piece, 'Says Hanrahan', satirizes the pessimism of the farmer whose refrain: 'We'll all be rooned', echoes throughout the poem, regardless of dramatic, positive changes in fortune.

For a detailed discussion of Hartigan's life and work see *'John O'Brien' and the Boree Log*, by James Mecham (Angus & Robertson, 1981). A brief assessment is given in *The Oxford Companion to Australian Literature*, ed. William Wilde, Joy Hooton, and Barry Andrews (Oxford University Press, 1985). 'Says Hanrahan' is printed in the *Penguin Book of Australian Ballads*, ed. Russel Ward (Penguin, 1964).   EMCM

Hartnett, David (1952–   ) Read English at Oxford and went on to write a D Phil on James *Merrill. He shares with Merrill a formal resourcefulness exemplified by 'Prehistories', four villanelles included in his second collection, *House of Moon* (Secker & Warburg, 1988). Their skills communicate an emotional depth typical of this poet; exact and daring metaphors explore rather than decorate. Hartnett's work combines delicacy and force, figurative brilliance and trust in feeling, acute self-consciousness and openness to experience. His first collection, *A Signalled Love* (Anvil, 1985), unsentimentally affirms, even as it investigates, the significance of the personal. Especially affecting is the title-poem, a sequence concerned with the birth of the poet's son. *House of Moon* builds on and extends the thematic and stylistic range of *A Signalled Love*. Rooted in the actual yet suffused with symbolic nuance, 'The Other Side of the Mountain', the second collection's final poem, moves hauntingly between a childhood self and 'Europe—| Her wars, this last exhausted peace'. His later collections are *Dark Ages* (Secker & Warburg, 1992) and *At the Wood's Edge* (Cape, 1997). He has also written two novels.   MO'N

Hartnett, Michael (1941–99) Born on a farm in Newcastle West, Co. Limerick, and died in Dublin. He is recognized as one of the principal Irish poets of his era, but he has suffered critical neglect. The reasons for this are evident: Hartnett does not fit very neatly into the various schools of Irish-English poetry—post-Yeatsian or Ulster—and his principal influences are not from English or Anglo-Irish literature at all but from classical Irish-language poets, like Daibhi Ó Bruadair (from Hartnett's locality and translated by him in 1985), and from Lorca (also translated by Hartnett, who lived for a time in Spain). Also, his poetry varies greatly, from the loose, adolescent extravagance of his first volume, *Anatomy of a Cliché* (1968), to the exact spareness of the translations from his own Irish lyrics in *A Necklace of Wrens*.

In 1975 Hartnett declared his intention to write only in Irish in the title-poem of what remains his most substantial volume, *A Farewell to English*, and he kept primarily true to that principle. His powerful manifesto-poem, 'A Small Farm' (1970), takes an un-nostalgic, anti-pastoral view of rural life.

See *A Necklace of Wrens* (Gallery Press, 1987), *Selected and New Poems* (Wake Forest University Press/Gallery, 1994), and *Collected Poems* (Gallery, 2001). *Remembering Michael Hartnett*, eds. Stephen Newman and John McDonagh, is a collection of essays and tributes (Four Courts, 2006).   BO'D

Hart-Smith, William (1911–90) Born in Tunbridge Wells, England, emigrated to New Zealand in 1924, and moved to Australia in 1936. He earned his living as a radio mechanic in Sydney before enlisting in the Australian army in 1940. After the war he went back to New Zealand as an adult-education tutor and returned to Australia again in the early 1960s as a radio technician.

Hart-Smith was associated with the *Jindyworobak Movement in the 1940s which aimed at linking white and aboriginal Australia. He was drawn to its use of anthropology and myth in the depiction and interpretation of landscape and the spirit of place, but his abiding affinities were with the *Imagists and the early poetry of Ezra *Pound, D. H. *Lawrence, William Carlos *Williams, and Marianne *Moore. Immensely productive, Hart-Smith was one of the most experimental, eclectic, and individual poets in the Australia of his time. He wanted his poems to be 'poems of discovery, recording brief moments of insight and understanding' in language spare and unadorned. His best lyrics, like 'Boomerang', 'Kangaroos', 'Gulls at Pareora', 'Native Violets', and 'Bathymeter' are usually short, astringent, and imagistic. A verse-sequence *Christopher Columbus* (1943) was an important contribution to the historical narrative (the voyager poem) in Australia and New Zealand. He was the author of ten collections, and three selections have appeared: *Poems of Discovery* (1959), *Selected Poems* (1985—both Angus & Robertson), and *Hand to Hand: Selected Poems 1935–90* (Butterfly, 1991).   vs

Harwood, Gwen (1920–95) Born in Brisbane but lived in Tasmania from 1945. Her education prepared her for a career in music, and she subsequently combined the careers of music teacher and poet. The ongoing sequence of poems about the drunken, disreputable, self-pitying but ultimately sympathetic musician, Professor Kröte, gives a painfully comic insight into the predicaments of all those forced to earn a living from receiving 'an earful | of Gounod' with their pupils' scales. Throughout a long writing life Harwood repeatedly turned to music as the subject-matter for her elegant, invariably closely rhymed, lyrical poems, but she is by no means confined to the one subject; her fascination with the philosophy of Wittgenstein is another recurrent inspiration (see '1945'). She also created a more scabrous academic character, Professor Eisenbart, and published some of her early work under (mostly male) pseudonyms, such as 'Walter Lehmann' and 'Timothy Kline', partly to counter editorial prejudice against female poets.

Apart from a number of fine occasional poems, of which the one to A. D. *Hope is outstanding, she is capable of lively social satire, as in 'Cocktails at Seven'; of acute and almost *Larkin-like observation and commentary, as in 'Home of Mercy', and 'In the Park', and—perhaps most remarkably—of deeply felt and powerfully executed love poetry. This ranges from the teasing out of dark ambiguities in 'Triste, Triste', to the unabashed eroticism of 'Carnal Knowledge I and II' and the second 'Meditation on Wyatt'. *Bone Scan* (Angus & Robertson) won the 1989 Victorian Premier's Literary Award. She also composed several libretti, working with various composers.

Stephanie Twigg's study of Harwood's work appeared from Oxford University Press in 1994. *The Present Tense* (Imprint, 1995), ed. Alison Hoddinott, is a posthumous miscellany. See *Collected Poems* (University of Queensland Press, 2003) and *Mappings of the Plane: New Selected Poems*, eds. Gregory Kratzmann and Chris Wallace-Crabbe (Carcanet, 2009).   JL*

Harwood, Lee (1939–) Born in Leicester and attended London University. He has published over twenty books of poetry, given readings and lectures in Europe and North America, and edited various little magazines. He has lived in Brighton since the late 1960s, where he has worked as a bus conductor and Post Office clerk and run a bookshop. His work has an accessible, un-literary manner, and a concern with the present moment. Like his friend the American poet John *Ashbery—to whom the love poems of his second book, *The Man With Blue Eyes* (Angel Hair, 1966), are addressed—he cultivates a loose, flowing, sometimes flippant, and often lyrical style in which to depict the movement of the mind on the spot. There are surprises and surreal moments, but these tend to be folded into the smooth flow of the poem. Much of his work seems 'painterly' in the sense that it displays a keen sensitivity to colour and a careful attention to landscape—his work has a pastoral bias—enacted through a broad and detailed survey of a scene. These qualities are well displayed in *Landscapes* (Fulcrum, 1969). But in the end Harwood's concern is to let his consciousness take him where it will. His selected poems, *Crossing the Frozen River* (Paladin), were published in 1988, with a foreword by Ashbery, who praised them as 'carelessly wise'. His *Collected Poems* (2004) have been followed by a later *Selected* (2008—both Shearsman). He has also published translations of Tristan Tzara: see *Chanson Dada* (Coach House, 1987; revd. edn., Black Widow, 2005). *Not the Full Story* (Shearsman, 2008) is a series of interviews with Harwood about his life and work by the poet Kelvin Corcoran.   ETL*

Hashmi, Alamgir (1951–) Born in Lahore, educated in Pakistan and the United States, and has worked as a professor of English, editor, and broadcaster. His early work, which includes a collection of love poems, *Oath and Amen* (1976), and a long poem recording his travels across America, *America is a Punjabi Word* (1979), is characterized by a terse, witty, imagistic style, and reveals a recurring preoccupation with language, time, and place. The poet's peripatetic career in America, Europe, and Pakistan is reflected in the concerns of his subsequent collections, *My Second in Kentucky* (1981), *This Time in Lahore* (1983), *Neither This Time/Nor That Place* (1984), *Inland and Other Poems* (1988), and *Sun and Moon and Other Poems* (1992). As Hashmi has developed, there has been a broadening of human sympathies and an emerging political awareness which have modified the virtuosity and self-absorption of some of his earliest writing. His most recent publications are *The Poems of Alamgir Hashmi* (National Book Foundation, 1992), *A Choice of Hashmi's Verse* (Oxford University Press, 1997), and *The Ramazan Liberation* (Arc, 2003), with an introduction by John *Kinsella, which selects from his seven volumes.   SS

Haskell, Dennis (1948–) Born and raised in the working-class western suburbs of Sydney. After completing a commerce degree in 1968, he worked as an accountant over the next few years in Sydney and London, travelled in America and Europe, married, and developed an interest in philosophy and literature. He completed an arts degree in 1976, received his doctorate in 1982, and presently lectures in English at the University of Western Australia.

His first book of poems, *Listening at Night* (Angus & Robertson, 1984), exhibits a religious sensibility in an essentially god-less world, celebrated as the search for the extraordinary in a mundane urban environment. While many of Haskell's earlier poems are imagist in technique, he also writes more abstract pieces that explore his philosophic concerns, especially in his second book, *Abracadabra* (Fremantle Arts Centre, 1993). His academic writing includes many articles on modern poetry, and studies of Keats and Bruce *Dawe. He has co-edited (with Hilary Fraser) an anthology of contemporary Western Australian verse, *Wordhord* (1989), and (with Geoffrey Dutton) the complete poems of Kenneth *Slessor (1994). *A Touch of Ginger* (Folio, 1992) was a pamphlet with Fay *Zwicky. *Samuel Johnson in Marrickville*, a selection from his work up to *The Ghost Names Sing* (Fremantle Arts Centre, 1997), appeared in the UK from Arc in 2000. See also *All the Time in the World* (2006) and *Acts of Defiance: New and Selected Poems* (2010—both Salt).   AU

Haslam, Michael (1947–) Born in Bolton, Lancashire and studied at Cambridge University, where he was taught by J. H. *Prynne. In 1970, he moved to a cottage near Hebden Bridge, West Yorkshire, and worked for many years as a semi-skilled labourer.

Haslam's oeuvre comprises an ongoing, tragicomic celebration of his life in this South Pennines landscape (the same area is rather differently depicted by Ted *Hughes in *Remains of Elmet*). His verse is animated by a strong iambic pulse, much internal rhyme, broad wordplay, and esoteric symbolism, which sees the worlds of man and nature as vividly interwoven. Haslam's early poems were encouraged by Peter *Riley, and published in *various ragged fringes* (Turpin, 1975). His major work began with the long poem, *Continual Song*, published by his own press, Open Township, in 1986. This sequence of 'improvisations upon double-sonnets' is arranged so as to be read forwards, backwards, or outwards from the middle.

A trilogy of book-length works, *Music*, has appeared in the last decade: *The Music Laid Her Songs in Language* (2001), *A Sinnner Saved by Grace* (2005), and

A Cure for Woodness (2010—all Arc). Haslam is a frequent reviser of his work, and different versions of earlier poems can be found in two collected volumes: *A Whole Bauble* (Carcanet, 1995) and *Mid Life* (Shearsman, 2007). See Andrew Duncan, 'Froths and Delphs of the Atlantic Fringe', in *Centre and Periphery in Modern British Poetry* (Liverpool University Press, 2005).   JNT

Hasluck, Nicholas (1942–) Born in Canberra, Australia, son of Dame Alexandra and the late Sir Paul Hasluck, both of them authors. He graduated from the University of Western Australia in 1963 and Oxford in 1966, and practised law in Perth. From 2000 to 2010 he served as a judge on the Supreme Court of Western Australia. Hasluck has become recognized as one of the notable fiction stylists in Australia, but his poetry, too, is important, particularly in its relation to an energetic regional 'explosion' of creativity in Western Australia from the end of the 1970s and into the 1980s.

Anchor and Other Poems (1976) initiated the West Coast Writing series from Fremantle Arts Centre Press and was to establish that press as one of Australia's leaders in small-press activity, an exemplar of its kind. Hasluck's poetry set a standard of urbanity and specific vividness of observation. The title-poem, 'Anchor' is a sequence in thirteen sections exploring an essential Australian theme of shoreline and littoral; in this it presages the two major sequences in his second book of poems, *On The Edge* (Claremont, 1980; poems by William Grono and Nicholas Hasluck). The most substantial of these, 'Rottnest Island', balances precision of image with an edgy, open-ended reflectiveness. See *A Dream Divided* (Access, 2005).   TWS

Hass, Robert (1941–) Born in San Francisco and studied under Yvor *Winters at Stanford University in the 1960s. The recipient of the Yale Series of Younger Poets Award in 1972, Hass has taught at various American universities, including the State University of New York at Buffalo and the University of Virginia. He is now a professor of English at the University of Berkeley, and is married to the poet Brenda *Hillman. His first book, *Field Guide*, was published in 1973 (Yale University Press) and was followed by *Praise* (Ecco, 1981). In addition to his volumes of original poetry, he is also well-known as a critic and essayist (his collection *Twentieth Century Pleasures* won the National Book Critics Circle award in 1984) and as co-translator of the work of the Nobel-Prize-winning Polish poet Czesław Miłosz.

It is easy to see why Hass would respond to the intense lyrical fantasia of Miłosz, in which a history of suffering and oppression is carried with great tact and grace along the fine lines of a sensibility which, for all its privacy, stays engaged, alert, and lucid. Hass' own best poems strive for a comparable lucidity. Their evocations of place, particularly California, are always suffused with a vividly responsive human consciousness, making it apparent why one of his favourite forms is the haiku. Yet his intensely rendered states of nature and consciousness are rarely entirely innocent of history: the fate of the American Indian, the lot of working-class Polish-Americans, the Vietnam war, and the squalor of contemporary urbanization all provide a context of anxiety and unease; it is unsurprising to find Hass writing passionately about Robert *Lowell. His tone, however, is usually meditative, ruminative, occasionally almost entranced, one of its major signatures being a bitter-sweet, Chekhovian sadness (Chekhov is himself the hero of more than one of the poems). It is hard to manage this at length without affectation or complacency, and Hass is certainly a poet of variable quality; but the distilled eroticism, all yearning and nostalgia, of a poem such as 'Meditation at Lagunitas', goes well beyond any mere absorption of earlier Romantic models.

Between 1995 and 1997 he served as US Poet Laureate, committing the role to public engagement and education. Among his causes was the promotion of 'ecoliteracy': see the sequence 'State of the Planet' in *Time and Materials: Poems 1997–2005* (Ecco, 2007), which won the National

Book Award and the Pulitzer Prize. In 2011, Hass was hit with a police baton during a student protest at Berkeley, an experience that he wrote about in the *New York Times*. See *The Apple Trees at Olema: New and Selected Poems* (Ecco, 2010; Bloodaxe, 2011) and *What Light Can Do: Essays on Art, Imagination, and the Natural World* (Ecco, 2012).   NC*

Hawken, Dinah (1943–) Born in Hawera, Hawken trained in physiotherapy, psychotherapy, and social work, and teaches creative writing at the International Institute of Modern Letters in Wellington. She studied for an MFA in poetry with John *Ashbery at Brooklyn College in New York, and mentions American poets such as Adrienne *Rich among her early inspirations, as well as the New Zealander, James K. *Baxter. *It Has No Sound and Is Blue* (1987), won the Commonwealth Poetry Prize for Best First-Time Published Poet in 1987, establishing Hawken's place among an innovative generation of women poets in New Zealand. It was followed by *Small Stories of Devotion* (1991), published in the UK by Arc in 1994, and *Water, Leaves, Stones* (1995). *Oh There You Are Tui!* (2000) is a new and selected volume. Critics have noted the Ashberian, dream-like drift of Hawken's work between verse and prose. *One Shapely Thing* (2006— all Victoria University Press) presents both poems and journals. In 2007 she received the Lauris Edmond Award for Distinguished Contribution to Poetry.   JNT

Hay, George Campbell (1915–84) Brought up in Tarbert Loch Fyne by his mother and her aunts. Here he learned Gaelic and developed a lifelong love of the landscape and seascapes of Kintyre, admiration for the Tarbert fishermen, and a fascination for their boats. Hay's linguistic talents were nurtured through a classical education at Fettes and Oxford. By then, however, his interests embraced many other languages and literatures, including Irish Gaelic and Welsh. He translated poetry into and out of all of these, and composed in many. War service widened the scope of his linguistic explorations, and he became especially interested in Arabic language and culture. Surviving the war, he was seriously injured by a bomb-blast in Greece in 1946. His health never really recovered, and he was hospitalized several times during his later years, which were spent in Edinburgh.

Hay's most productive period began when he joined the circle of Oxford Scots led by Douglas *Young, and continued until his injury. His poetry shows both an ardent nationalism and a wider concern for the common man. He is a connoisseur of languages, enthralled by the challenge of creating and of translating the creations of others. His Gaelic and *Scots poems are distinguished by a consistent and occasionally overwhelming musicality.

Hay's poetry is best known through the collections *Fuaran Sléibh* ('Upland Spring', MacLellan, 1948), *Wind on Loch Fyne* (1948), and *O na Ceithir Airdean* ('From the Four Airts', 1952—both Oliver & Boyd). A selection with introduction appeared in the bilingual anthology *Nua-bhàrdachd Ghàidhlig/Modern Scottish Gaelic Poetry*, ed. D. MacAulay (Southside, 1976), and Hay's complete works are in M. Byrne (ed.), *Collected Poems and Songs of George Campbell Hay* (2 vols., Edinburgh University Press for the Lorimer Trust).   WG

Hayden, Robert (1913–80) Born in Detroit and educated at Wayne State University and at the University of Michigan, where he took his MA in 1944. He began teaching at Fisk University, a predominantly black college, in 1946, and he ended his career back at Michigan.

Hayden was always a formal poet, but his formalism was not—except in his earliest work—of a traditional nature, for he experimented with language approaches; however, unlike some of his ethnic contemporaries, he was not radically politicized by the Civil Rights Movement of the 1960s. Hayden did not want to be judged by specialized, 'Negro-only' criteria. On the other hand, he did not shrink from utilizing his heritage and his family background.

Heart-Shape in the Dust (Falcon, 1940) was his first book, and *The Lion and the Archer*, with Myron O'Higgins (n.p., 1948), his second. Only one collection appeared during the next decade, however: *Figures of Time* (Hemphill, 1955). Two collections were issued during the 1960s—*A Ballad of Remembrance* (Breman, 1962) and *Selected Poems* (1966). In the next decade there were *Words in the Mourning Time: Poems* (1970—both October House) and *The Night-Blooming Cereus* (Breman, 1972). *American Journal: Poems* (Liveright, 1982) appeared posthumously. There is a study by Robert Fetrow, *Robert Hayden* (Twayne, 1984). LT

Haynes, John (1936–) Born in Cornwall to parents who worked as seaside entertainers, Haynes attended boarding school in England, and later trained as a teacher. From 1970 he lectured at Ahmadu Bello University in Zaria, Nigeria, before returning to England at the end of the 1980s. His time in Africa is reflected in all his work.

Haynes' early poetry appeared in *Sabon Gari*, published in 1974 by London Magazine Editions, and *First the Desert Came and Then the Torturer* (RAG, 1986), printed in Zaria under the pseudonym of 'Idi Bukar', an imagined Nigerian poet. During this time he also wrote books on teaching English and African poetry, as well as a PhD thesis on versification. He only became known as a poet, however, with *Letter to Patience* (2006), an autobiographical verse-letter addressed from England in the early 1990s to the female owner of a bar in Nigeria. A remarkable work of postcolonial imaginative travel written in *terza rima*, it won the Costa Prize for Poetry. Critics have admired Haynes' formalism, which enjambs his relaxed speaking manner within strict limits, and draws knowingly but lightly on a lifetime's reading. *You* (2010—both Seren) is a sequel to *Patience*, addressed to the poet's Nigerian wife in rhyme royal stanzas. JNT

H. D. *See* DOOLITTLE, HILDA.

Healy, Randolph (1956–) Born in Scotland but moved to Ireland in early childhood. After stints as a telex-typist and security guard, he studied at Trinity College, Dublin, and now works as a mathematics teacher. Logic and information technology have proved subjects of abiding interest: 'writing is mind made visible', as he insists in 'Vertices'. Healy is usually grouped with Trevor *Joyce, Michael Smith, Catherine *Walsh, Geoffrey Squires, and Billy Mills as belonging on the neo-modernist wing of Irish poetry, though his fondness for onomastic and other wordplay suggests *Oulipian tendencies too. A veteran of the small press scene, he collected his work in *Green 532: Selected Poems 1983–2000* (Salt, 2002). Healy's major work is *Arbor Vitae* (Wild Honey, 1997), which mixes poetry and prose and extrapolates from the theme of deafness to wider considerations of semiotics. Describing the disastrous effects of 'oralist' approaches to teaching deaf students, Healy lodges an implicit plea for a bold and pluralist understanding of language. Exploiting other recondite subject matter from early Christian saints to the habits of frogs, Healy's work is adept at providing what the sequence 'Flame' calls 'Access to ground denied' by more conventional writing. Subsequent publications include *Rattling the Bars* (Oystercatcher, 2009) and *Hex* (2012), from his own Wild Honey Press. DW

Heaney, Seamus (1939–) Born in Mossbawn, Co. Derry, Northern Ireland, the eldest of nine children and the son of a Catholic farmer and cattle-dealer. In 1951 he won a scholarship to St Columb's College, where he was a boarder, and then in 1957 to Queen's University, Belfast, where he returned as a lecturer, after some years schoolteaching, in 1965. That same year he married Marie Devlin, and in 1966 published his first book of poems in the UK and the USA, *Death of a Naturalist*. After two more collections, and a year in California, he became a full-time writer and moved to Co. Wicklow in 1972, returning from the countryside to live in Dublin in 1976. In 1984 he was appointed Boylston Professor of Rhetoric and Oratory at Harvard, and in 1989 he became Professor of Poetry at Oxford, two prestigious lecturing posts that took him away from Dublin for extensive periods but also allowed him time to pursue his own work. He was awarded the Nobel Prize for Literature in 1995.

Richly physical in its descriptions of rural life (digging, blackberry-picking, churning, thatching, etc.), Heaney's early work in *Death of a Naturalist* and *Door into the Dark* (both Faber/Oxford University Press, 1969) shows the influence of both Ted *Hughes and Patrick *Kavanagh. At its freshest, it conveys a country-boy's first troubled encounters with sexuality, responsibility, and death; at its most pious, a merely sentimental affection for a disappearing, peasant-simple world. Beyond the rustic homage can be glimpsed Heaney's anxiety about how he can best keep faith with the values of his tribe and ancestors while not lapsing into their grunting curtness and silence.

Similar concerns were brought to a head by political events in Northern Ireland in the early 1970s, as Heaney, in solidarity with his fellow Catholics during the civil-rights marches, bombings, and terrorism of the Troubles, found himself searching 'for images and symbols adequate to our predicament' while not wishing to become a mere propagandist. *Wintering Out* (Faber, 1972; Oxford University Press, 1973) lovingly rolling its tongue round childhood words and place-names, finds a deeper structure for the present hostilities by uncovering a history of linguistic and territorial dispossession. The verse-form—narrow, two-stress, unrhymed quatrains which owe something to William Carlos *Williams and which run like mine-shafts down the page—becomes a means of drilling into the past. A recurrent image is that of the peat-bog which, with its unique preservative properties, Heaney sees as a kind of 'memory bank', spectacularly so in the case of the 'bog people' of northern Europe, about whose remarkably intact Iron Age corpses Heaney composes a number of his finest poems both in this collection and its successor, *North* (Faber, 1975; Oxford University Press, 1976).

Divided into two parts, the first (historical and highly wrought) tracing the invasions of Ireland from the Vikings to the Elizabethans, the second (contemporary and journalistic) attempting a colloquial, head-on reportage of the Troubles, *North* is Heaney's most politically overt book, a

myth by which to understand the history of Ireland. It is hardly surprising that his next, *Field Work* (Faber/Farrar, Straus, 1979), should have been a self-conscious retreat or 'escape from the massacre', its core a group of sonnets about living in the Wicklow countryside, the 'hedge-school' of Glanmore, though in fact his finest political poem, 'Casualty', is to be found here, and it is—despite the quieter, more celebratory domestic note sounded in the two fine love poems, 'The Skunk' and 'The Otter'—his most troubled, elegiac, questioning book.

Heaney's work in the Eighties moves into a more allegorical and spirit-haunted terrain, with the influence of Homer and Dante, and Miłosz and *Brodsky, more telling than that of Hughes and Kavanagh. But even his most grandiose or elliptical work none the less retains its roots in his childhood. The central sequence of *Station Island* (Faber, 1984; Farrar, Straus, 1985) is about Lough Derg, an ancient place of pilgrimage, and includes a series of ghostly encounters, one of them with *Joyce, who urges Heaney to strike out on his own. *Sweeney Astray* (1984) is his version of the medieval Irish *Buile Suibhne*. *The Haw Lantern* (1987) contains a moving sonnet-sequence about his mother's death, and *Seeing Things* (1991—all Faber/Farrar, Straus) a number of poems about his dead father. This last collection saw Heaney at his most buoyant, discovering miracles at 50 and regaining some of the palpability and physicality of his first book—another twist in the development of a poet whose constant struggle is to honour his origins without surrendering to the restraints he fears they place on him.

Seeing Things ushered in a distinctive late period for Heaney's poetry, which has seen him playing variations on familiar themes while remaining open to new experience. 'Tollund', for example, from his next book, *The Spirit Level* (1996), contemplates 'a new beginning' at the site of the bog-people discoveries. The poem is dated 'September 1994', the year of the IRA ceasefire. *Electric Light* followed in 2001 and *District and Circle* in 2006. These volumes are more occasional in their tributes, translations, and reminiscences, and Heaney's ripest late style arguably dallies with self-parody ('the slush and rush and hiss'). Each nevertheless contains sequences which develop the intertwined narrative of the poet's life and work, such as 'Route 110' from *Human Chain* (2010), his twelfth collection, which maps his early manhood onto *Aeneid VI*.

All Heaney's later volumes are published by Faber and Faber in Britain and Farrar, Straus, and Giroux in the United States. *Opened Ground* (1998) is a substantial selected poems from three decades which also includes his Nobel lecture, 'Crediting Poetry'. In 1999, he made a widely praised verse translation of the Anglo-Saxon heroic epic, *Beowulf* (Faber, 1999; Farrar, Straus, 2000; Norton critical edn., 2001). His three books of essays, *Preoccupations: Selected Prose 1968-1978* (1980), *The Government of the Tongue* (1988), and his Oxford lectures, *The Redress of Poetry* (1995), are useful companions to the work and fascinating in their own right. They have been selected in *Finders Keepers* (2002). Critical studies include Blake Morrison's *Seamus Heaney* (Methuen, 1982), *The Art of Seamus Heaney*, ed. Tony Curtis (1982; fourth revd. edn., Seren, 2001), Neil Corcoran, *The Poetry of Seamus Heaney* (Faber, 1998), and Helen Vendler, *Seamus Heaney* (Harvard University Press, 2000). *Stepping Stones* (Farrar, Straus, 2008; Faber, 2009) is a collection of interviews with Dennis *O'Driscoll.   PBM*

Heath-Stubbs, John (1918–2006) Born in London and educated at Worcester College for the Blind and Queen's College, Oxford. He has often been described as a Romantic, perhaps because any serious interest in Romanticism seemed highly unusual in the early 1940s, when he began to be published (*Eight Oxford Poets*, 1941, *Wounded Thammuz*, 1942). In fact, he might just as well be called a Classicist if one were to be guided by his call in 1941 for 'the return to the classical tradition of English poetry'. During this period, when he was an undergraduate, he published an article on the poetry of John Gay. His early work is indebted to the Augustans, to the minor Romantics, and to Milton's shorter poems. His originality was to weave a distinctive modern, pastoral style out of these unexpected strands. His admiration for Le-

opardi (a selection of translations from whom he published in 1946) is in part owing to the fact that the Italian poet is 'at once a Romantic and a Classicist', but also to his sense that Leopardi was one who had to construct a system of his own from past mythologies, from 'erotic passion', and from 'natural beauty'. For the same reason he admired the French Symbolists and Hart *Crane. This view of poetry might seem to align him with *Yeats more than with any other modern poet, and he can strike a note redolent of Yeats' power, and of his confidence with symbolism, as in 'Titus and Berenice'. But the characteristic tone of Heath-Stubbs, from the mid-Fifties, is dry and ironic, as in the 'Epitaph' in A *Charm Against the Toothache* (Methuen, 1954). Increasingly he comes to seem like a neoclassicist, albeit one who often chooses to write in free verse. He is sometimes reminiscent of Cavafy, whose work he admired. But he remained a master of traditional forms: 'Sestina', from *The Watchman's Flute* (Carcanet, 1978) offers only one among many examples of his versatility. A more ambitious and less ironic side of his work is displayed in the long Arthurian poem *Artorius* (Enitharmon, 1973).

See *Collected Poems 1943–1987* (1988) and *Selected Poems* (1990). His last collection was *Pigs Might Fly* (2005—all Carcanet). Heath-Stubbs' criticism includes *The Darkling Plain* (Eyre & Spottiswoode, 1950), a study of Victorian Romantic poetry, and *The Literary Essays*, ed. Trevor Tolley (Carcanet, 2008).   ETL

Hecht, Anthony (1923–2004) Born in New York City. He graduated from Bard College in 1944 and served in the army in Europe and Japan. After the war he studied at Kenyon College, where he began a long and distinguished career as a professor, lastly at Georgetown University, Washington. His second collection, *The Hard Hours*, won the Pulitzer Prize for poetry in 1968; his many other awards include the Bollingen Prize and the Librex-Guggenheim Eugenio Montale Award. Apart from poetry collections, he published critical essays (*Obbligati*, 1986), light verse (*Jiggery-Pokery*, 1967, with John *Hollander), and translation, most notably of Aeschylus (*Seven Against Thebes*, 1973, with Helen Bacon) and Joseph *Brodsky.

Some editions of his work (*Collected Earlier Poems* and *The Transparent Man*—both Knopf/Oxford University Press, 1990) employ on their covers a photograph of the poet's face reflected in a mirror—on the latter book a photographic negative—most appropriate images for his substantial and remarkable oeuvre, which holds the glass up to the worst of centuries and looks it squarely in the eye, neither glossing its beauty nor flinching from its horror. The work of Anthony Hecht shatters the cosy notion that a fragmented, fractured age should be reflected in the forms of its art, that ugliness and shapelessness demand payment in kind. Like *Auden, he absorbed the evils and grotesqueries of his unhappy century into a verse both highly formal and all-encompassing, stitching wounds with iambs, sculpting pentameters of sustained, Latinate beauty, sounding a healing music.

Thirteen years after his first book (*A Summoning of Stones*, 1954) in which, as he rightly admits, 'advanced apprenticework', craft, and polish have priority, Hecht published *The Hard Hours*, where pity and terror rise to the placid surface of his tones, sometimes an even simplicity (as in the famous '"It Out-Herods Herod. Pray you, avoid it"', where he counterpoints the innocence of his children in front of the television with the observation that he 'could not, at one time, | Have saved them from the gas'); sometimes a numbed lyricism: 'Father, among these many souls | Is there not one | Whom thou shalt pluck for love out of the coals? | Look, look, they have begun | To douse the rags' ('Rites and Ceremonies'). In the latter poem Hecht goes further towards confronting the Holocaust than perhaps any other English-language poet. Elsewhere, he weaves together biblical and classical history, modern America, myth, and fine art with a painter's detailed observation and transformation of the physical.

Millions of Strange Shadows (1977) continues and expands the work, notably into love poems which are all the more intense and conquering for being part of the same dread world as the cruelty, tyranny, and spiritual inertia by which such love is encircled and threatened. The Horatian range and dexterity of Hecht's lines also allow some happy ventures into comedy ('The Ghost in the Martini') and current affairs ('Black Boy in the Dark'), always anchored on the twin foundations of the poet's historical awareness and his generous, embracing intelligence.

These strands continue through *The Venetian Vespers* (1980) and *The Transparent Man* (1990). See in particular 'The Short End' and the title-poem in the former, one a tragicomedy of an American woman, the other an exile's monologue of childhood memory, aspiration, and decay; and in *The Transparent Man*, the enchanting 'Love for Four Voices', a masque of the lovers from *A Midsummer Night's Dream*. *Collected Later Poems* (2003) includes his last, elegiac books *Flight Among the Tombs* (1998) and *The Darkness and the Light* (2001). A *Selected Poems* (2011—all Knopf) has been edited by J. D. *McClatchy. In 1993 Hecht published a long study of Auden, *The Hidden Law* (Harvard University Press). See also the wide-ranging reflections gathered in *On the Laws of the Poetic Art* (Princeton University Press, 1995) and *Melodies Unheard: Essays on the Mysteries of Poetry* (Johns Hopkins University Press, 2003).   GM*

Hegley, John (1953–) Born in London, Hegley grew up in Luton, read Literature and Sociology at Bradford University, and has worked as a bus conductor. He is well-known for his comic performances of his poems, which can be heard, along with his songs, on the album *Family Favourites* (2006). Beginning with *Glad to Wear Glasses* (Deutsch, 1990) and *Can I Come Down Now, Dad?* (Methuen, 1991) he has published a number of popular books of verse, illustrated—after the example of the comedian Spike Milligan—with his own cartoons. Cultivating the naïve voice of an underdog, Hegley's is nevertheless a verbally ingenious poetry able to make sharp observations about social history and family life, and conscious of its place in a popular English tradition that includes Stevie *Smith and Adrian *Mitchell. With

Sophie *Hannah, he has edited an anthology of poetry for young readers, *The Rope: Poems To Hold On To* (Diamond Twig, 2008). JNT

Heighton, Steven (1961–) Born in Toronto and grew up in Red Lake, Northern Ontario. He studied at Queen's University, Kingston, where he took creative writing classes with Victor Coleman. After graduation, Heighton edited *Quarry* magazine, and has worked as a translator and teacher. He also writes prose fiction.

Heighton's prize-winning work has been hailed by Todd *Swift and Evan Jones in their anthology *Modern Canadian Poets* (Carcanet, 2010) as 'the beginning of a new consciousness in Canadian poetry' which connects with 'a more anglophile appreciation of form and style'. Heighton's own advice to writers ('stand on the side of artifice') is of a piece with his imperative to 'avoid earnestness and solemnity—those Upper Canadian birthrights—by cultivating a grown-up, crap-detecting irony'. The resulting poetry has a fascination with unsentimental poses and personae. *Stalin's Carnival* (Quarry, 1989) presented the poems of the dictator. 'The Machine Gunner', from Heighton's second collection, *The Ecstasy of Sceptics* (1994) twists the pathos of the Wilfred *Owen-esque war poem with a merciless formalism: '[I] laid them three deep in the wire' ends the final tercet. The title poem of *Address Book* (2004) is a dramatized, satirical self-examination of the writer.

His fourth collection is *Patient Frame* (2010—all Anansi). He has also published two collections of short stories, three novels, and three works of non-fiction, including *Foreign Ghosts* (Oberon, 1990), a Basho-esque travelogue from Japan, and *Workbook: Memos & Dispatches on Writing* (ECW, 2011). JNT

Hejinian Lyn (1941–) Born in the San Francisco Bay Area and teaches at the University of California, Berkeley. Hejinian is a poet, translator, editor, and publisher. She has published and collaborated with many of the poets associated with *Language writing, and co-edited *Poetics Journal* with Barrett *Watten until 1999. In 2006, she was elected as a Chancellor of the American Academy of Poets.

In 1976, Hejinian began Tuumba Press with her second collection, *A Thought Is the Bride of What Thinking* (1976—her first, *a gRReat adventure*, was also self-published, in 1972). Its opening essay, 'Variations: A Return of Words', exemplifies the post-*Stein style of prose poetry that she would also use for her best-known work, *My Life* (Burning Deck, 1980). Composed in 37 sections of 37 sentences, *My Life* embodies the poet's age at the time of writing. A second edition in 1987 was revised and expanded accordingly to 45. Like Ron *Silliman's similarly structured *Tjanting* (1981), its lucid yet discontinuous memories ('a pause, a rose, something on paper') foreground sentence rhythm over narrative momentum. *My Life in the Nineties* is a sequel volume (Shark, 2003).

Oxota (The Figures, 1991), a 'short novel' of free sonnets after Pushkin, reflects Hejinian's interest in Russian literature as a critic and translator. *The Language of Inquiry* (University of California Press, 2001) collects her critical essays, including 'The Rejection of Closure'. Many more volumes have followed, including the serial poem, *A Border Comedy* (Granary, 2001), *The Beginner* (Tuumba, 2002), and *Saga/Circus* (Omnidawn, 2008). JNT

Hendriks, A. L. (Michael Arthur Lemière) (1922–92) Born in Kingston, Jamaica, of West Indian and French parentage, and educated at Jamaica College, Jamaica, and Ottershaw College, England. Dividing his time mainly between Britain and America in later life, he travelled widely in Europe and the Americas. Executive posts included: general manager of the Jamaican Broadcasting Corporation; international director of Thomson Television International; chairman of the Arts Council of Jamaica; and president of the Jamaican Centre of International PEN.

His poetry has much in common with that of John *Figueroa in its cosmopolitan outlook, sensuousness, and sacramental imagery. He is particularly effective when he writes about the sea, even finding epic similes for it, like 'pathways of the fish' and 'Sandless highways'. His attachment to the ocean, and fascination with how it has shaped the lives of West Indian islanders, he shares with Derek *Walcott.

Two long sequences, 'The Islanders' and 'D'où Venons Nous? Que Sommes Nous? Où Allons Nous?' (after the Gauguin painting) are particularly distinctive. The former quietly imposes its dream-like logic on the reader, as the poet carves out a landscape of meditation on Caribbean realities; the latter achieves a prophetic intensity of vision. His later poems are more spare, almost bitter in tone, but also lucidly detached. 'Ennui' and 'Where It's At' are especially powerful in this bleak vein.

Collections include *On This Mountain* (Deutsch, 1965); *These Green Islands* (Bolivar, 1971); *Muet* (Outposts, 1971); *Madonna of the Unknown Nation* (Workshop, 1974); and *To Speak Simply: Selected Poems 1961–1986* (Hippopotamus, 1988).   MR

Hendry, J. F. (James Findlay) (1912–86)

Born in Balgrayhill near Glasgow and educated at Whitehill School, Dennistoun, and Glasgow University, which he left without taking a degree. During the Second World War he was with Army Intelligence. After the war he was a translator and founded the School of Translating and Interpreting at Laurentian University in Canada. He died in Toronto in 1986.

Hendry is best known as the principal founder of the *New Apocalypse movement, and his essays 'Myth and Social Integration' and 'The Art of History' remain insightful and stimulating. Herbert *Read thought well of him and published his first two books of poems, *The Bombed Happiness* (1942) and *The Orchestral Mountain* (1943), which elegizes the poet's wife, killed in an air raid.

The reception of Hendry's first two volumes of poetry did not measure up to the ambitions for literature expressed in his essays, and he did not publish any more until the long poems *Marimarusa* (Caithness, 1979) and *World Alien* (Borderline, 1980) at the end of his life. A selection of the war poems was made by Andrew *Crozier in *Conductors of Chaos*, ed. Iain Sinclair (Picador, 1996).   ATT*

Henry, Paul (1959–)

Born in Aberystwyth, Henry began his career as a songwriter, and won an Eric Gregory Award for his poetry in 1989. He works as a creative writing tutor and arts presenter on radio and television.

Henry's musical background is often present in his lyrical work, which has been admired by Carol *Rumens for its 'beautiful economy'. He has spoken of the importance of mid-century poets such as Louis *MacNeice and W. S. *Graham to his sense of a line balanced between speech and song. Irregular but recurrent rhyme is an important device in his dream-like evocations. *The Brittle Sea: New and Selected Poems* (2010) draws on six previous collections, all from Seren: *Time Pieces* (1991); *Captive Audience* (1996); *The Milk Thief* (1998); *The Slipped Leash* (2002); *The Breath of Sleeping Boys* (2004); and *Ingrid's Husband* (2007).   JNT

Herbert, W. N. (William N.) (1961–)

Born in Dundee and studied at Oxford University, where he wrote a doctoral thesis on Hugh *MacDiarmid: see *To Circumjack MacDiarmid* (Oxford University Press, 1992). He is Professor of Poetry and Creative Writing at the University of Newcastle.

Herbert's first volume of poetry was in *Scots: *Sterts and Stobies* (Obog, 1985). In 1989 he began the *Informationist poetry magazine, *Gairfish*, with Richard *Price, and the following year published *Sharawaggi* (Polygon) with Robert *Crawford. Later collections mix poems in English and Scots with dialectic wit—see 'Mappamundi', on the Anglocentric poetic map of the world ('Ireland's | bin shuftit tae London'). With *Forked Tongue* (1994), he began to publish regularly with Bloodaxe Books.

Since *Dundee Doldrums* (Galliard, 1991), Herbert has been attracted to extended narrative fantasias. These are typically inspired by the postmodern encounter of quasi-heroic figures and popular culture, as in *The Testament of Reverend Thomas Dick*, a nineteenth-century Dundee astronomer (Arc, 1994) and *The Laurelude* (1998), a reimagining of Wordsworth's *The Prelude* for comic actor Stan Laurel, born in the Lake District. *Cabaret McGonagall* (1996), *The Big Bumper*

Book of Troy (2002), and *Bad Shaman Blues* (2006) demonstrate Herbert's formal variety as a versifier, for whom the vernacular ballad remains a vigorous form. He continues to publish criticism, often on Scottish poetry, and with Matthew Hollis edited *Strong Words: Modern Poets on Modern Poetry* (2000—all Bloodaxe), an anthology of statements about writing.   JNT

Herrera, Juan Felipe (1948–   ) Born in Fowler, California, to Mexican migrant farmer parents, Juan Felipe Herrera studied Social Anthropology at UCLA and Stanford University, and holds an MFA (Creative Writing) from the University of Iowa. Writer, activist, community worker, actor, and performance artist, Herrera lives in California with his partner, poet and performance artist Margarita Robles, and has published over twenty-five books of poetry and prose for adults and children. He is Tomás Rivera Chair in Creative Writing at University of California, Riverside. In 2011 he was elected a Chancellor of the Academy of American Poets, and in 2012 he became the first Hispanic writer to hold California's Poet Laureateship.

Influenced by Allen *Ginsberg, and the Chicano movement of the 1960s and 1970s, which included writers such as Alberto Delgado, Trinidad Sanchez, and Rodolfo *Gonzales, Herrera's politically fuelled, self-consciously hybrid poetics blends languages (English, Spanish, Chicano), and articulates the possibilities of a life without borders. *CrashBoomLove* (University of Mexico Press, 1999), a novel in verse for young adults, won the America's Award, and a collection of poetry, *187 Reasons Mexicanos Can't Cross the Border: Undocuments 1971–2007* (City Lights, 2007) won the PEN (West) Poetry Award. A subsequent selection, drawing on his poetry for adults only, *Half the World in Light* (University of Arizona Press, 2008), was awarded the National Book Critics Circle Prize, the PEN Beyond Margins Award, and the Latino International Award in Poetry.   HY

Hewett, Dorothy (1923–2002) Born in Perth, Western Australia, was brought up on a wheat and sheep farm at Malyalling via Wickepin in the Great Southern Region of Western Australia. Hewett discovered in these childhood years a basis for her pastoral vision of 'the Garden', a place of dangerous innocence against which she counterpoints, in her poetry and plays, 'the City' of Sydney, where she lived for a time in the late 1940s, and returned to live in 1974. In 1991, she moved to the Blue Mountains.

Hewett's poetry of the 1960s was strongly influenced by the ideology of the Communist Party, which she joined at 19 and left in 1968. Theatrical and romantic by temperament, she wrote poetry and plays which incline towards the personal and *confessional, though the early populist ballads and socially critical verse also reflect a desire to upset conservative social attitudes and practices. Poems such as 'Legend of the Green Country' and 'The Puritans' in *Windmill Country* (1968) recall Robert *Lowell's *Life Studies*, but dramatize an undeniably Australian ruralism. Hewett's poetry of the 1970s is more urban, influenced by Sydney 'new romantics' Robert *Adamson, John *Tranter, and others and the American *Black Mountain poets Charles *Olson, *Creeley, and *Duncan. A third phase, in the 1980s, is notable for this poet's experiments with myth and legend.

Hewett's volumes of verse included: *What About the People!* (with Merv Lilley, 1963); *Windmill Country* (1968); *Rapunzel in Suburbia* (1975); *Greenhouse* (1979); *Alice in Wormland* (1987); and *Peninsula* (1994). She also wrote plays and three novels: *Bobbin Up* (1959), *The Toucher* (1994), and *Neap Tide* (1996). The selection of her poetry in *A Tremendous World in her Head* (Dangaroo Press, 1990) was followed by a further *Selected Poems* (1991) and *Collected Poems* (1995), which won the Western Australian Premier's Poetry Award. Her last books were *Wheatlands*, with John *Kinsella (2000) and *Halfway Up the Mountain* (2001—all Fremantle Arts Centre). A *Selected Poems* appeared in 2010, edited by her daughter, Kate Lilley. *Wild Card: An Autobiography, 1923–1958* (Virago, 1990; repr. Penguin, 2001) describes her early marriages, family life, and factory job.   BB*

Hewitt, John (1907–87) Born and grew up in Belfast where his parents were teachers of nonconformist Protestant background. From 1930 to 1957 he worked in the Belfast Museum and Art Gallery, and from 1957 to 1972 he was director of the Herbert Museum, Coventry. His last fifteen years were spent back in Belfast. Hewitt always avowed socialist principles and a lack of religious affiliation, although his sense of community identification was unwavering ('my own' is a recurrent construction in his writing). In the *Irish Times* in 1974, he declared himself to be 'an Ulsterman of planter stock...born in the island of Ireland, so secondarily...an Irishman. I was born in the British archipelago and English is my native tongue, so I am British...I'm European. This is my hierarchy of values.'

This hierarchical order of identifications explains much about Hewitt's poetry and its reception. Though of *Auden's era, his poetry was largely ignored for most of his career. (Geoffrey *Grigson included him in his 1949 anthology, *Poetry of the Present*.) But the Ulster poets since the 1960s have all claimed Hewitt as a standard-bearer of non-sectarian, northern regionalism, with the result that in the last decade of his life he was regarded as a major figure, recognized by the founding of a summer school in his name in 1988.

The adjective used by Hewitt of himself, picked up by most commentators, is 'mannerly', which suggests well the low-key Augustanism of his poetry, in form and tone. His poetry also manifests a marked sense of place, as physical location and native region; the place is always Ulster, and the identity always the Protestant settler. This is first strikingly stated in one of Hewitt's best-known poems 'The Colony' (1950), in which the Ulster planters are represented as Roman legionaries, garrisoned on the native 'barbarians', 'squatting at our gates'. As well as political allegories, Hewitt wrote fine personal and nature lyrics like 'The swathe uncut' and 'The little lough'. His edition of the Rhyming Weavers, *The Rhyming Weavers, and Other Country Poets of Antrim and Down* (1974), has been an important influence in Ulster writing, broadening the literary community.

Hewitt's *Collected Poems* appeared in 1992, ed. Frank Ormsby. A good introductory essay is '"The Dissidence of Dissent": John Hewitt and W. R. Rodgers', by John Wilson Foster, in *Across a Roaring Hill: The Protestant Imagination in Modern Ireland: Essays in Honour of John Hewitt*, ed. Gerald Dawe and Edna Longley (1985). See too T. Clyde (ed.), *Ancestral Voices: The Selected Prose of John Hewitt* (1987—all Blackstaff).   BO'D

Higgins, Bertram (1901–74) Born in Melbourne, son of a hotelier. After a year at Newman College, Melbourne, in 1918, he read languages at Oxford. From 1922 to 1930 he worked in London as a book reviewer and was closely associated with the *Calendar of Modern Letters*, which published a number of his poems and articles. From 1930 to 1933 he lived in Australia, publishing there his most important poem *Mordecaius' Overture* (1933). He then returned to Europe and served in the RAF during the Second World War. After the war he and his family settled permanently in Australia. Higgins was greatly influenced by the French Symbolists and the literary milieu of London in the 1920s. It has been claimed that he wrote the first and finest modernist poem in Australia—'Mordecaius'. His style was richly allusive in the manner of *Pound and *Eliot, but utilized a late-nineteenth-century diction. He had little influence in Australia and his poetry was generally ignored until 1981, when the first collection of his poems, *The Haunted Rendezvous* (Alella) appeared. The volume also contains criticism and a memoir.   JCr

Higgins, F. R. (Frederick Robert) (1896–1941) Born in Foxford, Co. Mayo, son of a Protestant engineer. He founded the Irish Clerical Workers' Union, and was the editor of trade-union journals, and of Ireland's first magazine for women. His first significant collection was *The Dark Breed* (Macmillan, 1927); this was followed by *Arable Holdings* (Cuala, 1933) and *The Gap of Brightness* (Macmillan, 1940). Higgins believed that poetry should resemble music, and so, although never incoherent or even very mannered, he tended to allow the sense of his poems to look after itself. His verse achieved a considerable degree of musicality. His poems are usually wistfully erotic or celebratory of the Irish folk. After 1933 Higgins tried to abandon lyricism, and, under the influence of his by-then close friend *Yeats, attempted a more symbolic style (e.g. 'Auction!' from the final volume), but this won him little subsequent admiration. His best poems, such as 'The Grief' (from *The Dark Breed*) and 'The Wife of the Red-Haired Man' (from *Arable Holdings*), with their evocative, song-like diction, are now neglected.   MS-S

Hill, Sir Geoffrey (1932–) Born in Bromsgrove, Worcestershire. Educated at Oxford, he subsequently taught in the University of Leeds, where he was elected to a professorship in English literature in 1976. He has since been a fellow of Emmanuel College, Cambridge, and in 1988 moved to the United States, where he taught at Boston University until his retirement. In 2010, he was elected Professor of Poetry at Oxford. He was knighted in 2012 for services to literature.

Hill won an Eric Gregory Award for his poetry, the first of many plaudits, in 1961; in the glare of the esteem now surrounding him, it is worth recalling that his early work, *For the Unfallen: Poems 1952–1958* (1959), defeated as many readers as it fascinated. Hill began his book with a sternly formal treatment of the Genesis creation myth; neither the subjects of his poems nor the voices he chose to approach them had much in common with the work of his contemporaries. While other university poets of the 1950s reacted against modernist difficulty by standing under the banner of accessibility, Hill had other, older objects in mind. 'Against the burly air I strode, | Crying the miracles of God': the combination this work presented of a personal investment in explicitly religious struggle, a daunting breadth of scholarly allusion, and the clear suggestion that such expression cost him genuine pain, seemed to forbid its assimilation by a reading public. Even his 'Two Formal Elegies', the first of many poems on Nazi atrocities and the persecution of the Jews in Europe, deterred the easy response. They contained instead dark ironies directed, by a motivation that was as yet obscure, at 'the pushing midlanders' who survive in wilful, complicit ignorance of the horrors Hill memorialized.

Not until the publication of *King Log* (1968) did Hill's reputation begin to spread. He continued to address the tensions between history, myth, legend, and the more personal imperatives of memory, giving agonized voice—in sequences such as 'Funeral Music'—to victims of a violence that the compelling density of his work refused to consign to its ostensibly remote historical context, and developing a cold, impassioned, Yeatsian rhetoric to address the horrors which Hill believes, after *Pound, it is the poet's duty to address. He continued to insist that contemporary Europe is irredeemably burdened with its past, and that lyric poetry must confront the uncomfortable fact of such territory's status as both 'nest and holocaust'. But his insistence carries another weight, that of personal conviction. Hill's disgusted fascination for the inevitable horrors of the individual human body, alive as well as dead, makes an enemy of himself, and, indeed, of his own corpus. His celebration, in *The Mystery of the Charity of Charles Péguy* (1983), of the French Catholic intellectual who intervened disastrously in the Dreyfus affair before dying heroically in the first days of the First World War, makes Hill's distrust of poetry's commemorative and potentially political rhetoric more explicit, as it does his own attitude to the relationship of poetry to action.

Neither that poem, nor the collection *Tenebrae* (1978), constitutes his early masterpiece. *Mercian Hymns* (1971), a series of thirty formally innovative prose poems reanimating and reinhabiting the life of the eighth-century King Offa, comes closer than any of Hill's other work to achieving the atonement he has continually sought of the currency of historical chronicle, devotional religious lyric, and twentieth-century poetic idiom. Allusive, inventive, but also surprisingly exuberant, the collection represents a remarkable late addition to the two traditions—of doubting Romanticism and of modernism—to which Hill has such close affinities.

Hill's early volumes, all published by André Deutsch, were gathered in a *Collected Poems* that appeared in the UK and USA (Penguin, 1985; Oxford University Press, 1986).

Canaan (Penguin, 1996; Houghton, 1997), with its terse address to contemporary England, can now be seen as a transitional work, prefiguring a remarkably prolific and avowedly 'prophetic' late period. A trilogy of autobiographical book-length sequences followed. *The Triumph of Love* (Houghton, 1998; Penguin, 1999), which first appeared in the States, saw Hill breaking open his early style and subjects with a discursive free verse, American in manner, though still determinedly English in its lexical quibbles. *Speech! Speech!* (Counterpoint, 2000; Penguin, 2001) is a more cryptic satire on public language, which also obliquely elegizes Diana, Princess of Wales. *The Orchards of Syon* (Penguin/Counterpoint, 2002) combines stylistic innovations from both books in a mystical and pastoral celebration of the 'harvests' of a long life.

Scenes from Comus (2005), a trans-Atlantic sequence concerned (through its sustained allusion to Milton) with the morality of poetry-as-music, reads in some ways as a postscript to this trilogy, though it also contains the most virtuoso lyric writing of the group. Two later volumes, *Without Title* (2005) and *A Treatise of Civil Power* (2007—all Penguin) collect shorter sequences and occasional poems. *Oraclau/Oracles* (Clutag Press, 2010), a meditation on Wales, and *Clavics* (Enitharmon, 2011) are the first parts of a new six-part sequence in rhyming verse, to be published as *The Daybooks* in *Collected Poems 1952–2012* (Oxford University Press, 2013).

Hill's *Collected Critical Writings*, including episodes from his long quarrel with T. S. *Eliot, appeared in 2008 (Oxford University Press). Praised by some as England's 'greatest living poet', Hill's obscurities can still be called 'sheerest twaddle' by newspaper reviewers, although he remains a strongly ratiocinative writer. His *Paris Review* interview in 2000 with Carl *Phillips is revealing about the autobiographical origins of the recent work.

For critical studies, see Christopher Ricks, *The Force of Poetry* (Oxford University Press, 1984); Vincent Sherry, *The Uncommon Tongue: The Poetry and Criticism of Geoffrey Hill* (University of Michigan Press, 1987); Jeffrey Wainwright, *Acceptable Words: Essays on the Poetry of Geoffrey Hill* (Manchester University Press, 2005); and *Geoffrey Hill: Essays on his Later Work*, ed. John Lyon and Peter McDonald (Oxford University Press, 2012).   MRW*

Hill, Selima (1945–) Educated at the University of Cambridge. She lived in London for some years before settling on the Dorset coast. Her first collection, *Saying Hello at the Station* (1984) was followed by *My Darling Camel* (1988). In the same year she consolidated her growing reputation when she won first prize in the 1988 Arvon International Poetry Competition for a poem-journal charting the life of a young woman schizophrenic, *The Accumulation of Small Acts of Kindness* (1989—all Chatto & Windus). A fascination with remote geographical and archaeological space gives innovative breadth to her earlier work. Her later poetic world may seem hermetic, but this is offset by earthiness and quirky humour. Her poems are frequently short, concentrating imagery and narrative into a suggestive microcosm. While, like Medbh *McGuckian, she aims to subvert the rational, and foreground free-spirited eccentricity linked to gender politics, her style is less dream-like and divagatory. Both 'on the page' and in performance, Selima Hill is one of the few poets who can achieve comedy without the aid of rhyme. Her recent collections, published by Bloodaxe Books, include *Red Roses* (2006), *Gloria: Selected Poems* (2008), and *Fruitcake* (2009).   CAR

Hillmann, Brenda (1951–) Born in Tucson, Arizona, Hillmann studied at Pomona College and the Iowa Writers' Workshop, and worked for a decade at University Press Books in Berkeley. She is Professor of Poetry at St Mary's College in Moraga, California, and is married to Robert *Hass.

Hillmann's eight collections of poetry have all been published by Wesleyan

University Press: *White Dress* (1985); *Fortress* (1989); *Death Tractates* (1992); *Bright Existence* (1993—shortlisted for the Pulitzer Prize); *Loose Sugar* (1997); *Cascadia* (2001); *Pieces of Air in the Epic* (2005); and *Practical Water* (2009). The last three form part of a projected tetralogy, alchemically themed around the four elements: earth, air, water, and fire. Hillman's interest in a 'poetics of alchemy' combines an early enthusiasm for the chance associations and subconscious processes of *Surrealism with later reading in occult mysticism and feminist literary theory. Robert *Duncan is also, as Marjorie *Welish has said, 'a tutelary spirit'. She has related the 'decentred subject' of her increasingly ambitious poetic structures to the experience of living on the faultlines of the Californian landscape, one of the 'earth' subjects of *Cascadia* (see 'A Geology').

A committed non-violent activist, Hillman explicitly addresses political and ecological issues in her work. She has edited a collection of Emily Dickinson's poems (Shambhala, 1995), co-edited, with Patricia Dienstfrey, *The Grand Permission: New Writings on Poetics and Motherhood* (Wesleyan University Press, 2003), and co-translated Korean poet Jeongrye Choi's selected poems. JNT

Hillyer, Robert (1895–1961) Born in New Jersey but belonged to an old Connecticut family. He graduated from Harvard in 1917, the same year his first volume appeared, *Sonnets and Other Lyrics*. After serving as an ambulance driver in the First World War, he returned to teach at Harvard. In 1926 he married Dorothy Hancock Tilton, and they had one son. Though friends with John Dos Passos and Conrad *Aiken, Hillyer was an adamant foe of modernism in any form, describing himself as 'a conservative and religious poet in a radical and blasphemous age.' He did attempt to inject some measure of the harsher realism gleaned from E. A. *Robinson and *Frost into his technically deft traditional verses. Satire was more suitable to his minor talent and aristocratic temperament, however, as in the mildly witty use of Pope's heroic couplets in a series of poetic 'letters'. His *Collected Verse* (1933) won a Pulitzer Prize.

Divorced in 1943, he resigned from Harvard the next year and served as president of the conservative Poetry Society of America, leading the fight against the 'new estheticism' represented by *Pound, *Eliot, and other 'expatriate' intellectuals—he protested against awarding the first Bollingen Prize to Pound in two vituperative articles for the *Saturday Review of Literature*. Hillyer's *Collected Poems* (Knopf, 1961) contains the bulk of his verses. EB

Hilson, Jeff (1966–) Born in Singapore, Hilson grew up in Bedford, and read English Literature at Cambridge University. He lives in London, where he teaches creative writing at Roehampton University and founded the Crossing the Line reading series with Sean *Bonney and David Miller. Like his contemporaries Tim *Atkins and Simon *Smith, Hilson is an English poet who takes his experimental bearings from American reference points, including Gertrude *Stein, Louis *Zukofsky, and Jack *Spicer. Early publications such as *A Grasses Primer* (Form, 2000) and *The As* (2000), from his own Canary Woof Press, were followed by *Stretchers* (Reality Street, 2006), a sequence of column-like poems written while living on the Isle of Dogs. In an afterword Hilson speaks of his love of 'naïve language', 'verbal detritus', and 'spelling mistakes'. All are evident in the sequences *Bird Bird* (Landfill, 2008) and *In the Assarts* (Veer, 2010), which punningly drags the Renaissance sonneteering of Sir Thomas Wyatt into modern Britain ('The van travel hath wearied me so sore'). Hilson also edited *The Reality Street Book of Sonnets* (2008). See Stephen Thompson, 'The Forlorn Ear of Jeff Hilson', *Complicities: British Poetry 1945–2007* ed. Robin Purves and Sam Ladkin (Litteraria Pragensia, 2007). JNT

Hine, Daryl (1936–2012) Born in Burnaby, British Columbia. He was educated at McGill University in Montreal and, after several years in France on a fellowship, at the University of Chicago where he taught until 1968, when he assumed the editorship of *Poetry* magazine. After leaving that post in 1978 he continued to teach in the Chicago area.

Hine is one of those North American poets who, along with others like Anthony *Hecht and John *Hollander, is sometimes classed as a 'university wit'. While the label accurately suggests the enormous erudition his work displays, it fails to do justice to both its formal brilliance and its emotional and meditative depth. Hine's poetry can be forbidding in its technical polish, its allusiveness, and frequent lack of clear narrative occasion; above all in its abstract diction and difficult syntax. He quite consciously refused the various counter-traditional modes and idioms of modernism in favour of a verse modelled in form on the seventeenth century, and in elegance and urbanity on the Alexandrian school of Theocritus (whom Hine has translated). Yet for all his emphasis on craft and finish, Hine's poetry often has a muted but eloquent pathos, particularly when it takes up erotic themes, that keeps it from becoming too dry or brittle. Though he never abandoned his devotion to strict verse-forms, his poetry gradually moved closer to his own experience, culminating in his long autobiographical poem *Academic Festival Overtures* (Atheneum, 1985), which centres on the poet's adolescent confrontation with his own homosexuality.

See also *In & Out: A Confessional Poem* (1975; repr. Knopf, 1989). *Recollected Poems: 1951–2004* arranges a selection of Hine's verse under four themes: Art, Love, Place, and Time. *&: A Serial Poem* (2010—both Fitzhenry & Whiteside) is a work of similar abstraction, cast in complexly rhymed ten-line stanzas. He also published an award-winning verse translation of Hesiod and the Homeric Hymns (University of Chicago Press, 2005).   RG*

Hippolyte, Kendel (1952–) Born in St Lucia and educated in Jamaica. He is a poet and dramatist. In 1984, he co-founded the Lighthouse Theatre Company, and has directed productions and taught poetry workshops around the world. He is married to the poet Jane King.

Birthright (Peepal Tree, 1997) introduced a poet with a wide range of voices and forms, from rhyming sonnets to reggae-influenced incantations, standing, like his contemporary Kwame *Dawes, in a broad Caribbean

tradition that encompasses both Derek *Walcott and Kamau *Brathwaite. Hippolyte's denunciation of the colonial legacy in St. Lucia can be satirical, as in 'City Grafitti', from *Night Vision* (Northwestern University Press, 2006): 'so my city | in your half-assed state, | what should you do? | perhaps emigrate?'. In 2000 he was awarded the St Lucia Medal of Merit. His latest collection is *Fault Lines* (Peepal Tree, 2012).   JNT

Hirsch, Edward (1950–) Educated at Grinnell College in Iowa and at the University of Pennsylvania, where he studied with the poet Daniel *Hoffman. Formerly a professor at the University of Houston, Hirsch became president of the Guggenheim Foundation in 2002. He has won a number of awards, including the Delmore Schwartz Award for his first book, *For the Sleepwalkers* (1981), and the National Book Critics Circle Award in Poetry for his second collection, *Wild Gratitude* (1986). In Hirsch's first volume the world is seen through the eyes of a magic realist and rendered by a skilful rhetorician. The book has a playful beginning, dominated by verbal experimentation and insincerity ('The guardian | Angel of poetry sits in a wicker chair . . . | Ceaselessly trying to astonish us: | To astonish, yes, and to offend'), and progresses to an elegiac ending. The two impulses are intimately related through Hirsch's view of poetry, as expressed in one of his elegies: 'These imaginings make it possible | To survive, to endure the hard light, | Though darkness is floating in.' Feeling seems mostly to replace playfulness in Hirsch's second and third books (*The Night Parade* was published in 1989), even—in the eyes of some critics—to the point of sentimentality. *Wild Gratitude* in particular was criticized for its reliance on modifiers to convey nuance. In addition, each volume showed an increasingly autobiographical subject-matter, which seemed to leave behind Hirsch's early regard for pure imagination. His later volumes are *Earthly Measures* (1994), *On Love* (1998), *Lay Back the Darkness* (2003), *Special Orders* (2008), and *The Living Fire: New and Selected Poems* (2010—all Knopf). Hirsch is

also a popular writer about poetry: see the best-selling *How to Read a Poem: and Fall in Love with Poetry* (1999), and his collection of weekly columns for the *Washington Times*, *Poet's Choice* (2006—both Harcourt). PS

Hirshfield, Jane (1953–) Born in New York City, Hirshfield graduated from Princeton University in 1973, and spent eight years studying at the San Francisco Zen Center and Tassajara Zen Mountain Center, receiving lay ordination in Soto Zen in 1979. Writer, editor, translator, and teacher, Hirshfield lives in California and has published nine volumes of poetry to date. In 2004 she was awarded a fellowship for distinguished poetic achievement by the Academy of American Poets, and was appointed a Chancellor in the same year (2012) as Arthur *Sze and Toi *Derricotte.

Hirshfield sees the act of writing poetry as way to gain a renewed understanding and awareness of the world. Her poetry articulates the fleetingness of life, and the importance of experience, judgement, ethical awareness, and transformation. The tight forms of Hirshfield's early poetry have gradually opened up, and Czesław Miłosz noted its sensuality, seeing in it 'empathy for the suffering of all living beings'. *After* (2006) contains elegies for both Miłosz and his wife, and was shortlisted for the T. S. Eliot Prize.

Nine Gates: Entering the Mind of Poetry (1997—both HarperCollins) collects many of her essays on poetry. Hirshfield, who was in part responsible for bringing the tanka form to an American audience, has translated the poetry of Ono no Komachi and Izumi Shikibu (Vintage, 1990), and edited *Women in Praise of the Sacred* (HarperCollins, 1994) which collects spiritual poetry by women between 2300 BC and the early 1900s. HY

Hoagland, Tony (1953–) Born in North Carolina, Tony Hoagland grew up on Army bases in the USA (his father was a military doctor). He studied at Williams College and the universities of Iowa and Arizona, and now teaches writing at the University of Houston. In 2005 he received both the O. B. Hardison Jr. Prize for poetry

and teaching, and the Mark Twain Award for humour in American poetry.

The everyday, anecdotal quality of Hoagland's poems from mall-culture America, which spin flat reflection into wry fantasy, invites comparison with Billy *Collins. His humour, however, is more willing to wander into taboo subjects, including race, than many American poets 'from the galaxy of Caucasia' (see 'The Story of White People'). In interview, Hoagland has positioned himself between Frank *O'Hara and Sharon *Olds, but his frankness takes its licence as much from stand-up comedy as *New York or *Confessional poetry. He is also well aware of the relationship of his unwelcome 'truth-telling' to Romantic irony: see 'Negative Capability: How to Talk Mean and Influence People' in *Real Sofistikashun: Essays on Poetry and Craft* (Graywolf, 2006). *What Narcissism Means to Me* (Graywolf, 2003), his third collection in the USA, was also the title of a selected poems in the UK (Bloodaxe, 2005). His other volumes are *Sweet Ruin* (University of Wisconsin Press, 1992), *Donkey Gospel* (Graywolf, 1998), and *Unincorporated Persons in the Late Honda Dynasty* (Graywolf/Bloodaxe, 2010). JNT

Hobsbaum, Philip (1932–2005) Born in London and educated at Bellevue Grammar School, Bradford. He read English at Downing College, Cambridge, under F. R. Leavis, and took his doctorate at the University of Sheffield, under William *Empson. He later taught at Queen's University, Belfast and at the University of Glasgow, where he was reader in English.

Hobsbaum founded the *Group (with Edward *Lucie-Smith, George *MacBeth, Martin *Bell, Peter *Porter, and others) in London in 1955, and took its principles with him to form other groups in Belfast and Glasgow. In Belfast Hobsbaum's arrival coincided with, and may have helped the emergence of, young Northern Irish poets such as Seamus *Heaney, Michael *Longley, and Derek *Mahon (he was the dedicatee of Heaney's early poem 'Blackberry-Picking').

Hobsbaum's first book of poems, *The Place's Fault* (1964), takes its title from a *Larkin poem, and that indicates its general tenor and indebtedness. *In Retreat* (1966) varies the ordinary-life poems with a number of dramatic monologues. *Coming Out Fighting* (1969) tells the story of a failed love affair with a younger woman. *Women and Animals* (1972—all Macmillan) is about the poet's subsequent divorce.

Hobsbaum also published critical works on Dickens, *Lawrence, *Lowell, and *Essentials of Literary Criticism* (Thames & Hudson 1983). See also his *Metre, Rhythm and Verse Form* (Routledge, 1996).   ws*

Hodgins, Philip (1959–95) Born in Shepparton, a country town in Victoria, and grew up on a dairy farm at Katandra West, a place-name which figures in several of his poems. He was educated at Geelong College, and then worked in publishing for seven years. At the age of 24 he was diagnosed as having leukaemia, and was told that he could expect to live for as few as three more years. He survived for twelve.

Though he had already begun to publish poetry of promise, Hodgins was galvanized as a writer by this news. He rapidly completed his first book, *Blood and Bone* (Angus & Robertson, 1986), in which many of the poems deal with the prospect of an early death; the calm, reasoned tone of these poems, and the impressive command of technique in them, makes them all the more wrenching to read. Hodgins' second book has a humorous title, *Down the Lake With Half a Chook* (ABC, 1988), and expands his range from the hospital ward to memories of his country childhood and boarding-school life. Hodgins' third book, *Animal Warmth* appeared in 1990. Three further books were published: *Up on All Fours* (1993), *Dispossessed* (1994), and a posthumous work, *Things Happen* (1995—all Angus & Robertson). See *New Selected Poems* (Duffy & Snellgrove, 2000).   JG*

Hodgson, Ralph Edwin (1871–1962) Born in Darlington, Co. Durham, the son of a coal merchant. He was a recluse with a strong sense of privacy, and little is known about his early life: adept at boxing and billiards, he worked in the theatre in New York and as a draughtsman on a London evening paper. In 1913 he founded (with Lovat Fraser) the publishing house The Sign of the Flying Fame; his own *Eve and Other Poems*, with coloured cuts, was one of its first productions. His appearance in the second volume of *Georgian Poetry* won him admirers, and he enjoyed the friendship of *de la Mare, *Sassoon, and *Eliot, whose affectionate 'Lines to Ralph Hodgson Esqre.' refers to his love of dogs (he bred bull-terriers, and judged them at Crufts).

Hodgson was editor of *Fry's Magazine* for a while, but he mistrusted literary cliques and left England in 1924 to take up the post of lecturer in English Studies at Tohoku University at Sendai in Japan. Edmund *Blunden records an eccentric, inveterate talker, quick to take offence, who referred to himself as 'The Last of the Fancy'. From his retirement in 1938 he lived in Minerva, Ohio.

Hodgson's reputation, once considerable, was based on a relatively small body of work: *The Last Blackbird* (1907) and *Poems* (1917). The latter furnished the anthologists of two decades with standards like 'Time, you old Gipsy Man', 'Stupidity Street', and 'The Bells of Heaven', with their simple rhythms and clear sentiments, though 'The Bull' (especially), 'The Moor', and others are subtler and more substantial. After the First World War, however, Hodgson stopped writing poetry until he was in his seventies, when he began to send out broadsheets or 'Flying Scrolls' to his friends. Colin Fenton collected these in *The Skylark and Other Poems* (Macmillan, 1958).

Hodgson's main inspiration was always the enchantment of nature, and man's idiotic abuse of it. His most-praised poem, 'The Song of Honour' (modelled on Smart's 'Song to David') is a rapturous recital of the world's harmonious hymn of being; his longest finished poem, 'To Deck a Woman', is an angry attack on trade in furs and feathers, originally published (in 1910) as propaganda in favour of prohibitive legislation. In style, however, his late poems differ markedly from those of his '*Georgian' period; they are humorous and cryptic, and make much use of direct speech (see 'Tobit', 'Hever Picnic', and all the miniatures collected in *The Skylark*). His last long poem, 'The Muse and the Mastiff', is a curiosity. Ten years in the writing and not finished, it takes off from a single line of Coleridge's 'Christabel' and is as vigorous and strangely charming as it is cranky and incoherent.

Hodgson's *Collected Poems* was published in London in 1961. See John Harding, *The Life and Times of Ralph Hodgson* (Greenwich Exchange, 2008). MI

Hoffman, Daniel (1923–) Born and grew up in Larchmont, New York. He attended Columbia University, with three years (1943–6) out for active service in the US Army Air Force. After receiving his doctorate he taught at Columbia and at Swarthmore and was poet-in-residence at the University of Pennsylvania.

In his eleven books of poems Hoffman has explored the fragile bond between man and nature in language which veers sharply from the vernacular to the heroic. He writes of the contemporary scene with a spiritual integrity that is akin to that of the Transcendentalists. Hope, for Hoffman, is a live issue: he 'defies desolation'. These concerns are mirrored in the title of his *New and Selected Poems: Hang-Gliding from Helicon* (Louisiana State University Press, 1988). Equally at home in formal and free verse, Hoffman is never afraid to go to an extreme, to risk the outrageous. He knows how to spin believable tales. He is an expert mimic and a parodist of the obvious. Nowhere is history or nature taken straight: it is always sifted through myth and folklore. Hoffman is responsive to 'things | whose archetypes | have not yet been dreamed' ('On the Industrial Highway').

In *Brotherly Love* (Random House, 1981; repr. University of Pennsylvania Press, 2000), he gives his interest in folklore and myth an historical setting. The poem's hero is William Penn, founder of the city of 'brotherly love', and Hoffman's task is to construct a poem in the same spirit as Penn. 'Penn, in the Quaker tradition, was trying to found a commonwealth in which everyone could live by the light of Divine grace. That's why his treaty with the Indians, whom he approached as his spiritual equals, became the governing image of my whole shebang' (from 'Daniel Hoffman:

Education of the Poet', in *Envoy*, 53). In an age of deconstruction Hoffman is reconstructing, like Penn, what the 'age' has torn apart. He sees his task as picking up the pieces in search of a new country.

See *Beyond Silence: Selected Shorter Poems 1948–2003* (2003) and *The Whole Nine Yards: Longer Poems* (2009—both Louisiana State University Press). For his criticism, see *Words to Create a World: Interviews, Essays, and Reviews of Contemporary Poetry* (University of Michigan Press, 1993). *Zone of the Interior* (Louisiana State University Press, 2000) is a memoir of his non-combatant war years. MRU

Hofmann, Michael (1957–) Born in Freiburg, Germany. He is the son of the novelist Gert Hofmann, some of whose works he has translated. He came to Britain at the age of 7 and was educated at schools in Edinburgh and Bristol, and then at Winchester College. He took an English degree at Magdalene College, Cambridge, and pursued graduate studies at the University of Regensburg and Trinity College, Cambridge. Since 1983 he has worked as a freelance writer.

Hofmann's first book, *Nights in the Iron Hotel* (1983), announced an unusual talent, one given to wringing poetry out of flat, prosaic rhythms and containing many elisions and ironies, somewhat in the manner of Robert *Lowell's later poems. The title-poem is a sad and witty reflection on a stalled love affair in which sex is characterized as 'a luxury, | an export of healthy physical economies'. His second book, *Acrimony* (1986), confirmed the promise of the first. The first half is devoted to modern urban life. Even the titles of poems—'Between Bed and Wastepaper Basket', 'From Kensal Rise to Heaven'—suggest a slightly off-beat, surreal approach to experience. The second half of the book, however, entitled 'My Father's House', explores the uneasy son-father relationship—complicated in Hofmann's case by literal divisions of language and culture, and by the fact that both are writers—with memorable honesty and precision.

Gert Hofmann died in 1993, the same year that *Corona, Corona* appeared. His absence haunts Hofmann's fourth collection, *Approximately Nowhere* (1999)

('My father | for once not at his post'). *Selected Poems* (2008—all Faber) includes seven new pieces. He is a prolific translator, and has edited *The Faber Book of Twentieth Century German Poems* (2005).   ws*

Holden, Molly (1927–81) Born in Peckham, South London, the granddaughter of Henry Gilbert, a novelist and children's author. When she was thirteen her family moved to Swindon, and the broad spaces and historical resonance of the Wiltshire landscape proved to have a lasting influence on her work. She was educated at King's College, London, taking her MA in 1951.

In the 1960s, when her two children were still young, she was stricken by multiple sclerosis. She had always written poetry, but it was during the years of illness that she became most consistently productive. Some early pamphlets were followed by three full collections, published by Chatto & Windus/The Hogarth Press in the Phoenix Living Poets series: *To Make Me Grieve* (1968), *Air and Chill Earth* (1971), and *The Country Over* (1975). She also published four novels for children.

She was first influenced by Thomas *Hardy, though *Housman seems a presence behind the bitter-sweet simplicity of the shorter lyrics. Some of her most moving poems are those in which she confronts with candour the sadness and frustration of her disablement. (She acknowledges too, though, the value of the watchful stillness it encouraged.)

New and Selected Poems, ed. Simon Curtis (Carcanet, 1987) includes work from her uncollected manuscripts and a memoir by her husband, Alan Holden. Commentary on her work may be found in Colin Falck, *American and British Verse in the Twentieth Century: the Poetry that Matters* (Ashgate, 2003) and *A History of Twentieth-Century British Women's Poetry* by Jane Dowson and Alice Entwhistle (Cambridge University Press, 2005).   CAR

Hollander, John (1929–   ) Born in New York, and took two degrees at Columbia before moving on to further graduate study at the University of Indiana. He was elected a junior fellow of the Society of Fellows at Harvard University and later taught at Hunter College of the City University of New York, before taking up his position as A. Bartlett Giamatti Professor of English at Yale University, where he is now emeritus professor.

Hollander's career as a poet began when W. H. *Auden chose his first volume, *A Crackling of Thorns*, for the Yale Series of Younger Poets Award in 1958. Auden's poetic kinship is evident throughout Hollander's poems; one finds in them a deep commitment to traditional forms joining an effort to bring contemporary issues, private and public, to bear in original ways. Since publishing that first volume Hollander has written more than fourteen collections. In some of these, Hollander—like the seventeenth-century poets he admires—writes poems in concrete figures, using, for instance, the shapes of a key, a crescent moon, an umbrella, or a swan while writing poems focused on those images. He often begins a poem with an ordinary image and proceeds, through a sequence of elaborate metaphysical turns, to widen the scope of the poem. His best-known early poem, for instance, is 'The Great Bear', in which the poet contemplates the sky at night, searching for patterns in a patternless splay of light.

The best of Hollander's early work is collected in *Spectral Emanations: New and Selected Poems* (1978). Later volumes include *Powers of Thirteen* (1983), *In Time and Place* (Johns Hopkins University Press, 1986), and *Harp Lake* (1988—all Atheneum). The final poem in this highly accomplished volume is 'The Mad Potter', a Yeatsian meditation that becomes, in the end, an elegy for the poet himself and an exploration of the relation of art and language to human mutability. Since *Selected Poetry* in 1993, he has published four further volumes, all with Knopf, and continues to be active as an editor and anthologist. Hollander's books of criticism—all philosophically concerned with the relationship between form, language, and meaning—include *The Untuning of the Sky* (1961), *Vision and Resonance* (1975), *The Figure of Echo* (1981), *Melodious Guile* (1988), and *Poetry and Music* (2003). *Rhyme's Reason* (Yale University Press, 1981) is a popular guide to versification wittily written in the forms it describes.   JP*

Hollo, Anselm (1934–2013) Born in Helsinki, Finland, and attended the universities of Helsinki and Tübingen, Germany, before moving first to England, where he worked for the BBC, and then to the United States, where he was visiting professor at numerous universities and latterly, from 1989, lecturer at the Naropa Institute, Boulder, Colorado. He published more than forty volumes of poetry. He also published many volumes of translated poetry, from Finnish, Russian, Swedish, German, and French. In 2001, the influential SUNY Buffalo Poetics email list nominated Hollo as US 'anti-laureate' in response to the appointment of Billy *Collins.

Energy, versatility, and continuous movement are the hallmarks of Hollo's poetry and character of mind. Expatriated, he made his home in 'the new American poetry . . . a very real place to be . . . It moved me here, & it's still moving, faster and more variously than ever.' Light-hearted, agile-witted, open-spirited, essentially joyful and benign, Hollo is tolerant of and receptive to all kinds of experience. 'Phew! wow! pow! *zat* voss somsink', exclaims his 'professor albert hofman', as he 'inadvertently inhaled' and thus discovered LSD. Yet he is also a poet who can convey poignantly the haphazard forlornness of transient American lives, where 'in the neverness motels of the bitter country | lovers lie sleeping & loving in fits & starts'. See, in the US, *Notes on the Possibilities and Attractions of Existence: Selected Poems, 1965–2000* (Coffee House, 2000) and, in the UK, *Braided River: New and Selected Poems 1965–2005* (Salt, 2005).   RWB*

Hongo, Garrett (Kaoru) (1951–) Born in Volcano, Hawaii, grew up there and in Southern California, and spent one year studying in Japan. He attended Pomona College, studying with the late Bert Meyers, and the University of Michigan, and received an MFA in writing from the University of California at Irvine. Since graduating, he has taught poetry at UC Irvine, the University of Southern California, the University of Missouri at Columbia (where he also served as a poetry editor for *The Missouri Review*), and the University of Oregon, where until 1993 he directed the creative-writing programme.

His first book of poetry, *Yellow Light* (Wesleyan University Press, 1982), presents ruminative lyric portraits of family and childhood set against the suburban Los Angeles of the Fifties and early Sixties. Often nostalgic and melancholy, the poems strive both to celebrate and preserve a coherent record of the poet's own bi-cultural history and the older Japanese heritage preceding it. The poems of his second book, *The River of Heaven* (Knopf, 1988), focus this dual effort on the Hawaiian branch of the poet's family and display a greater willingness to call on narrative techniques to tell their stories. He has also edited *The Open Boat: Poems from Asian America* (Doubleday, 1993) and written a memoir of Hawaii, *Volcano* (Knopf, 1995).   RMCD

Honnalgere, Gopal (1942–2003) Born in Karnataka, India, and raised in Mysore and Bangalore, Honnalgere studied science and then painting at the university founded by Rabindranath Tagore in Santiniketan, and eventually settled into the life of a schoolteacher at small private schools across India. Unjustly forgotten, his work has seen a new surge of interest after Jeet *Thayil's anthology *Sixty Indian Poets* (Penguin, 2008) brought some of his poems back into print. The author of six books—currently out of print—and quite likely many unpublished poems, he certainly ranks among the most original and important Indian writers in English. Honnalgere's first two books, *A Wad of Poems* (1971) and *A Gesture of Fleshless Sound* (1972—both Writers Workshop), are apprentice works, flailing, like much Indian writing of the time, between 'Marx, Mao [and] American democracy' ('War'). Yet they also introduce the surprising leaps of thought that would mark his later verse. In *Zen Tree and the Wild Innocents* (Gray Book, 1973), as well as in *The Nudist Camp* (Release, 1978), he achieves a new lightness of form and diction. *The Fifth* (Broomstick, 1980) and *Internodes* (Samkaleen, 1986) fine-tune his ability to intertwine fable and realism, memory, and found speech. 'Internodes' is a term taken from plant biology, and Honnalgere's consistently recurring themes might be understood as ecological, concerned with the complexity of relations between species and, equally, among humans themselves. These are never presented sentimentally, but with an emphasis on paradoxes, inversions, and a playful linguistic irony.   VN

Hooker, (Peter) Jeremy (1941–) Born in Warsash near Southampton. A career lecturing in English and creative writing has taken him to Wales, the Netherlands, and Somerset, as well as his native Hampshire. Since his first book, *Soliloquies of a Chalk Giant* (1974), he has published fifteen books of verse, culminating in *The Cut of Light: Poems 1965–2005* (2006—both Enitharmon). His extensive criticism includes essays on David *Jones and John Cowper Powys, both writers central to his outlook.

Though Hooker's poetry touches on his travels, it is dominated by his feeling for his home territory: the chalk downs, forest paths, and muddy estuaries of the region he celebrates in *Solent Shore* (Carcanet, 1978), which is, like nearly all his poetry, an integrated sequence of short lyrics. He has called his work a 'poetry of place', which partly means a poetry of fact, shaped from and by the substance of the world. But his facts grow from invisible roots—in a shared human history and the mysterious otherness of non-human creation. Much of Hooker's originality as a poet derives from his very English use of historically resonant language in the spacious forms of American modernism.   CW

Hope, A. D. (Alec Derwent) (1907–2000) Born in Cooma, New South Wales, the son of a Presbyterian minister. He spent most of his childhood in rural Tasmania, where his parents fostered his interest in the classics and in English poetry. Despite an early interest in science, he graduated in 1928 with an arts degree and took up a scholarship at Oxford, returning to Australia in 1931. After training as a teacher, and marrying, he followed an academic career in Sydney and Melbourne, eventually holding the chair of English at the Australian National University, Canberra, from which he retired in 1968. As emeritus professor he remained closely associated with the ANU.

Hope wrote his first poem at the age of eight, and continued to write thereafter, though almost all his early work was lost in a fire a few years before his first collection of verse, *The Wandering Islands*, appeared in 1955. This collection, however, made a great impact in a country to some extent still parochial in outlook. Though Hope's poetry is largely traditional in form, and reminiscent in this respect of *Yeats, *Frost, and *Graves, his voice is more powerfully satiric than any of these poets, and his sexual explicitness, combined with his erudition, has often been analysed unsympathetically when it has been analysed at all. His poetry is much concerned with man's ambiguous and adversarial relationship with nature, which is seen either to succumb to, or to ignore, his urge to master her through ingenuity, blind destructiveness, or both. This opposition is frequently translated into terms of sexual struggle and conflict, themselves illustrated by mythological and biblical material. Similarly, the seriousness with which Hope regarded the role of poetry in the world manifested itself in a reverence for, and a familiarity with, poets of the past which some readers will not share. This seriousness is by no means incompatible with an unforgiving, sardonic brand of humour, somewhat un-Australian in nature. A combination of these factors led to Hope's having an uneasy relationship with his native literary culture. In a country with its own particular idea of the democratic vistas writers should address, he was accused, wrongly, of being élitist, misogynist, and anti-Australian in attitude. This last accusation was particularly unjust: as an academic Hope consistently supported the teaching of Australian literature at Australian universities.

Hope's love for traditional verse-forms can occasionally seem self-indulgent; his vision of man's struggle with nature portentous, and his view of sex both old-fashioned and wilfully 'poetic'. His scepticism and the ferocity of his wit, however, are provocative in the fullest sense. They transcend the purely satirical, and betray a compassionate impatience with human folly which is both traditional and timely.

Hope's *Collected Poems 1930–1970* (1972) was followed by *A Late Picking: Poems 1965–1974* (1975), *A Book of Answers* (1978), *Antechnicus: Poems 1975–1980* (1981—all Angus & Robertson), *The Age of Reason* (Melbourne University Press, 1985), and *Orpheus* (Angus & Robertson, 1991). See also *Selected Poems*, ed. Ruth Morse (Carcanet, 1986), and *Selected Poetry and Prose*, ed. David Brooks (Halstead, 2000). His essays on poetry were collected in *The Cave and the Spring* (Rigby, 1965), on Australian literature in *Native Companions* (Angus & Robertson, 1974); and on books in general in *The Pack of Autolycus* (1978). *The New Cratylus* (1979—both Australian National University Press) is a study of the craft of poetry. See also *A. D. Hope*, by Leonie Kramer (1979), and *A. D. Hope*, by Kevin Hart (1992—both Oxford University Press). RL

Horovitz, Frances (1938–83) Born in London in 1938 and educated at Bristol University and the Royal Academy of Dramatic Art. She became a distinguished reader and presenter of poetry, and made a number of recordings for BBC Radio 3 and the Open University. The first of several pamphlets, *Poems*, appeared in 1967. Her first full-length collection, *Water Over Stone* (Enitharmon, 1980) was followed by *Rowlstone Haiku* (Five Seasons, 1982) written in collaboration with Roger *Garfitt, and *Snow Light, Water Light* (Bloodaxe, 1983). In 1982 she moved to Herefordshire, where after a long illness she died from cancer in 1983. *Collected Poems*, ed. Roger Garfitt, was published by Bloodaxe in 1985.

Perhaps not surprising in a poet drawn to the haiku form, a spare, *Imagist quality informs her best work. It conveys spontaneity and a feeling of organic process, as if shaped by the landscapes and natural objects that are so often its subject matter. CAR

Horovitz, Michael (1935–) Born in Frankfurt, Horovitz emigrated as a child to the UK from Nazi Germany and still lives in London. While studying at Oxford (1954–60) Horovitz founded (with Pete Brown) the eclectic *New Departures*, a publication committed to popularizing experimental writing. Among those published were Samuel *Beckett, Stevie *Smith, and William Burroughs. He edited it for fifty years and in that time oversaw numerous spin-off initiatives, such as the Poetry Olympics reading series. Eccentric, erudite, and anti-establishment, he was a participant in the International Poetry Incarnation at the Royal Albert Hall, London in June 1965. The event included Allen *Ginsberg, on his first visit to the UK, who later described Horovitz as a 'popular, experienced, experimental, New Jerusalem, Jazz Generation, Sensitive Bard'. In the *Beat tradition, Horovitz's work has been artistically collaborative and stylistically wide-ranging. He has published twelve collections, most recently *A New Waste Land: Timeship Earth at Nillennium* (New Departures, 2007). He edited the well-known anthology *Children of Albion* (Penguin, 1969), and a sequel, *Grandchildren of Albion* (New Departures, 1992), each paying homage to the 'liberating spirit' of William Blake and the British tradition of literary dissent. Horovitz stood for election as the Oxford University Professor of Poetry in 2010, coming second to Geoffrey *Hill. See *Wordsounds & Sightlines: New & Selected Poems* (Sinclair-Stevenson, 1994). NH

Hoskote, Ranjit (1969–) Based in the suburbs of Mumbai his entire life, Hoskote began his career as a writer on art and religion for the *Times of India* and later became an influential curator of Indian art. The influence of painting manifests itself very directly in Hoskote's poetry as a repeated concern with perspective, light and colour; to this he also adds a sustained interest in history (especially the medieval and post-medieval history of India and the

Near East) and contemporary politics. These elements are all present in his precocious first collection, *Zones of Assault* (Rupa, 1991), which was both celebrated and notorious for its supposed 'complexity' and 'difficulty'—that is, for its range of references, its obliquity, its vocabulary, and its density of expression. *The Cartographer's Apprentice* (Pundole Art Gallery, 2000), a shorter, chapbook-length work in collaboration with the artist Laxman Shrestha, and a full-length collection, *The Sleepwalker's Archive* (Single File, 2001), attempt to leaven this density with more direct, plain-spoken diction and forays into contemporary slang and usage. *Vanishing Acts* (Penguin, 2006) is a new and selected volume that excerpts from the first three collections and adds fifty new poems. Hoskote's significant books also include a co-translation of the Marathi poet Vasant Abaji Dahake and a translation of the fourteenth-century Kashmiri poet Lal Ded. He has edited an anthology of contemporary Indian poetry, *Reasons for Belonging* (Penguin, 2002) and, most recently, the *Selected Poems* of Dom *Moraes (Penguin, 2012).   VN

Houédard, Dom Sylvester ('dsh') (1924–92) Born in Guernsey, Houédard served in British Army Intelligence and studied at Jesus College, Cambridge and St Anselmo, Rome. In 1949 he joined the Benedictine Abbey at Prinknash, Gloucestershire, and was ordained as a priest in 1959. A respected theologian, Houédard was active in the ecumenical movement and a founder member of the Eckhart Society. He was closely involved with the Ibn 'Arabī Society and, in 1961, became the literary editor of the New Testament Jerusalem Bible. A key innovator in British concrete poetry, in the 1960s Houédard pioneered the 'typestract' poem, which uses combinations of words, letters, and symbols to 'think in images alone'. Examples are included in *like contemplation* (Writers Forum, 1972).

The earlier poetry of the 1940s and 1950s, written primarily in French, betrays the influence of Guillaume Apollinaire, John-Paul Sartre, and André Breton. The

work of the 1960s reveals Houédard's interest in Eastern philosophies and Beat writing. His translation of Bashō—'frog | pond | plop'—and reversible poems such as 'deus|snap' display the impersonal formal spareness that also characterizes subsequent work. All of Houédard's poetry expresses what has been called his 'convincing, but ironic, restatement of the Idealist position' which reflects his belief in an interfaith ecumenism and a longstanding interest in mystical traditions.

In 1963, with John Furnival and Edward Wright, Houédard launched Openings Press, publishing Louis *Zukofsky, Ian Hamilton *Finlay, and bp *Nichol, among others. See *Notes from the Cosmic Typewriter: The Life and Work of Dom Sylvester Houédard* (Occasional Papers, 2012), ed. Nicola Simpson.   ROH

Housman, A. E. (Alfred Edward) (1859–1936) Born in Fockbury, Worcestershire, and educated at Bromsgrove School and St John's College, Oxford. After taking first-class honours in classical moderations, he disastrously failed his final examinations and took a clerical job in the Patent Office, London, for the next ten years. However, he kept up his own rigorous classical studies, was awarded his MA, published in specialist journals, and took up the chair of Latin at University College, London, in 1892. In 1911 he was elected a fellow of Trinity College, Cambridge, and Kennedy Professor of Latin in the university, posts he held until his death.

Housman's gifts as a poet have sometimes been seen as being much like his gifts as a classical scholar: narrow, profound, isolated, brooding, and on occasion ferocious. He brought his highly trained and subtle powers as a textual critic to bear on one of the least-considered (some would say least-rewarding) Roman writers, Manilius, and guarded him as a dragon would its cave. In the same way, he guarded his poems and the emotional wounds from which they welled: wounds he suffered in his youth, and which he could hardly bring himself to mention except through the obliquities of his apparently stark and simple verse.

His first book, *A Shropshire Lad* (1896), was originally published at his own expense, before being taken up by Grant Richards, who continued to be his publisher. Its poems soon began to become popular, the South African war helping to draw attention to Housman's memorable mixture of patriotic pride and stoical gloom, pessimism, and nostalgia. The 'Shropshire' of the book's title and its poems, though often apparently reinforced with place-names (Clun, Ludlow, Wenlock Edge), is a region of evocative emotions rather than an actual locality. This is a 'land of lost content'. Housman was not a rural writer; instead, he based a personal mythology (of country lads betrayed in love, drinking themselves into oblivion, committing suicide, being hanged for nameless crimes) on a pastoral tradition which he helped to rediscover.

In his lifetime, Housman published only one other book of poems, the decisively titled *Last Poems* (1922). This is a gathering of pieces from the 1890s until the end of the First World War. It shows no real development from *A Shropshire Lad*: its strengths, and its few weaknesses (an occasional mawkishness, and what might be called a hopeless emotional vulgarity—'Little is the luck I've had | And oh, 'tis comfort small | To think that many another lad | Has had no luck at all'), are the same, virtually interchangeable. The almost marmoreal words are matched with an extraordinarily seductive, though simple, rhythmical inspiration: 'In gross marl, in blowing dust, | In the drowned ooze of the sea, | Where you would not, lie you must, | Lie you must, and not with me.'

After Housman's death, his brother Laurence, as his literary executor, gathered together *More Poems* (1936). There then appeared a *Collected Poems* (1939, paperback, 1967—both Cape), edited by John Carter, which included a few 'Additional Poems'. In 1988 Christopher Ricks edited a *Collected Poems and Selected Prose* (Allen Lane). Another important text is Housman's Leslie Stephen Lecture at Cambridge, *The Name and Nature of Poetry* (1933), in which he spoke about his basic attitude to poetry—chiefly, that it strikes to the pit of the emotions and bypasses 'thought'. This simple intuitiveness is not as simple as it looks. Nor, indeed, is Housman's poetry, which has been sporadically carped at by critics who find it 'adolescent'; but the popularity of the poetry cuts across many boundaries and barriers, of age and taste.

See also John Bayley, *Housman's Poems* (Clarendon, 1992); Norman Page, *A. E. Housman: A Critical Biography* (Macmillan, 1983); and Richard Perceval Graves, *A. E. Housman: The Scholar Poet* (Oxford University Press, 1979). Archie Burnett has edited the complete edition of *The Poems of A. E. Housman* (1997), with a commentary, and a two-volume edition of the correspondence (2007), both for Oxford University Press. Tom Stoppard's play *The Invention of Love* (Faber, 1997) is a dramatization of Housman's life.   AST

Houston, Douglas (1947–) Born in Cardiff and read English at Hull University. He now lives near Aberystwyth.

Houston's work is striking in its combination of large and local themes in language both literary and vernacular, and for a vein of fantasy by turns amusing and disquieting. Apocalyptic pieces like 'Sic Transit' are juxtaposed with comic monologue ('To the Management'), bizarre ritual ('Devotions') with imaginative additions to history ('Horst Wessel on Alcatraz'). An atmosphere of nightmare pervades a number of poems dramatizing dreams or madness ('From the Corner', 'After the Anaesthetic').

An admirer of both W. H. *Auden and Derek *Mahon, Houston also looks back to Baudelaire and Keats: an aspiration to Romantic grandeur is habitually checked by irony and humour. At his best, when philosophical leanings are bedded in the particular, Houston is a poet of strangeness and charm.

Houston's first collection of poems *With the Offal Eaters* (1986) was followed by *The Hunters in the Snow* (1994—both Bloodaxe). *The Welsh Book of the Dead* (Seren, 2000) treats the subject of divorce using traditional forms such as the sonnet and villanelle. See *Beyond the Playing Field: New and Selected Poems* (Shoestring Press, 2010).   SO'B*

Houston, Libby (1941–97) Born in London, brought up in the West Country, and educated at Lady Margaret Hall, Oxford. In 1966 she married the artist Malcolm Dean, who illustrated her early books. She was widowed in 1974 and returned to Bristol, where she researched local-history projects and contributed regularly to BBC Radio schools programmes.

Especially in her first two books, *A Stained Glass Raree Show* (1967) and *Plain Clothes* (1971), her poetry typifies the spirit of the 1960s, and shows the influence of the American *Beat poets. At the same time her use of vernacular forms such as the ballad and limerick, the debunking humour, flights of pastiche, and the comic-sympathetic approach to the animal world, connect her to English traditions. In the later volumes, *At the Mercy* (1981—all Allison & Busby) and *Necessity* (Slow Dancer, 1988), her mood is darker and more meditative, and she is drawn to the longer, mythological narrative poem. Her refusal to find the easy answer or the pleasant cadence often brings unexpected rewards. *Cover of Darkness: Selected Poems, 1961–1998* was published by Slow Dancer Press in 1999.   CAR

Hove, Chenjerai (1956–   ) Born in Mazvihwa, Zimbabwe (then Rhodesia), and educated at the University of Rhodesia. A former teacher, he worked as a cultural journalist in Harare until his two-year appointment as writer-in-residence at the University of Zimbabwe in 1990. His novel, *Bones* (Harare, 1988), won the 1988 Zimbabwean Publishers/Writers Literary Award, as well as the 1989 Noma Award for publishing in Africa. He has published four volumes of poetry: *Up In Arms* (Zimbabwe Publishing House, 1982), *Red Hills of Home* (Mambo, 1985), *Rainbows in the Dust* (Baobab, 1997), and *Blind Moon* (Weaver, 2004). While his early poems reflect the violence he witnessed during the civil war, his later work laments the political history of Zimbabwe post-independence. Since 2001, he has lived in exile at Brown University in the United States.

Much of Hove's poetry is informed by the natural world to an extent that is unusual in modern African poetry. Only the Nigerian Niyi *Osundare communicates the same depth of feeling for the landscape of his birth, as is evident in the opening stanza of the title-poem from his second collection: 'Father grew up here | tuning his heart | to the sound of the owl from the moist green hills, | beyond, the eagle swam in the air | while mother-ant dragged | an unknown victim to a known hole | printed on the familiar unreceding earth…'

Hove also contributed to *And Now the Poets Speak: Poems Inspired by the Struggle for Zimbabwe* (1981). Some of his poems can be found in the *Mambo Book of Zimbabwean Verse in English*, ed. Colin and O-lan Style (Gweru, 1986) and in the principal anthologies of African poetry. He has also published novels and non-fiction essays.   AM-P

Howard, Richard (1929–   ) Born in Cleveland, Ohio, and educated at Columbia University and the Sorbonne. A prolific translator from French, Howard was made a Chevalier de l'Ordre National du Gouvernement Français (1980) for his many translations from authors including Gide, Barthes, Baudelaire, and Proust. Honoured by the Pulitzer Prize in poetry (1970), Howard has taught at many universities, including Johns Hopkins and the universities of Houston, Cincinnati, and Columbia. He lives in New York City and, from 1993 to 1995, was State Poet Laureate.

The formal versatility and fluent ease with abstractions of Howard's early poetry recall *Auden, but as early as *The Damages* (Wesleyan University Press, 1967) many poems begin to locate either historical or imagined characters in vividly evoked settings. Howard's voice has moved steadily away from the directly personal; rather, a poem may feature Goliath addressing Donatello's David, or the aged Browning holding forth in Florence, or a figure in a Caspar David Friedrich canvas musing, or a pair of fictional Americans in Paris describing the (apocryphal) visit to that city of the old Wallace *Stevens.

In such dramatic guises, and in suave, sinuous, and often witty language, Howard offers meditations on art and society, mortality and love. The poems are rich in aphorisms and cultural history alike, but transcend such ingredients; most tend toward a melancholic abstractness very different from the verve and bustle of a dramatic monologue by Browning. The urbane voice is recognizably Howard's.

Howard's translations from French are too numerous to list. Notable volumes of poetry are *Two-Part Inventions* (1974) and *Misgivings* (1979—both Atheneum). Howard is also the author of a capacious study of American poetry in the mid-twentieth century, *Alone with America* (Atheneum, 1969, expanded edn. 1980). His later poems have addressed the subject of homosexuality directly: see *Like Most Revelations* (Pantheon, 1994), which reflects on the AIDS epidemic, and 'My Last Hustler', another nod to Browning. *Inner Voices* (2003) is a selection from four decades of verse. See also *Paper Trail: Selected Prose 1965–2003* (2004—both Farrar, Straus). RHa*

Howe, Fanny (1940–) Born in Buffalo, New York, and grew up in Cambridge, Massachusetts, where her father was a law professor at Harvard. Her sister is the poet Susan *Howe. She attended Stanford University and taught for two decades in Boston, before becoming Professor of English at the University of California, San Diego.

Howe's *Selected Poems* from the University of California Press in 2000 included work from the three decades since *Eggs* (Houghton, 1970). It is notable for its theological passion and egalitarian vision (in her youth, she was a civil rights activist). As she writes in the prose poem, 'Catholic', 'I only stop for eucharist in a church where there are sick, vomiting, maimed, screaming, destroyed, violent, useless, happy, pious, fraudulent, hypocritical, lying, thieving, hating, drunk, rich, poverty-stricken people'.

O'Clock (Reality Street, 1995), Howe's first publication in Britain, is a spiritual journal set in the Ireland of her mother, who was a friend of Samuel *Beckett. Later collections include *On the Ground* (2004), *The Lyrics* (2007), and *Come and See* (2011—all Graywolf). *Emergence* (Reality Street, 2010) is a selection of earlier poems. Howe has also written novels and

fiction for young adults. See *Radical Love: Five Novels* (Nightboat, 2006). Her autobiographical critical essays are collected in *The Wedding Dress: Meditations on Word and Life* (University of California Press, 2003) and *The Winter Sun: Notes on a Vocation* (Graywolf, 2009). See Clair Wills, 'Marking Time: Fanny Howe's Poetics of Transcendence', in *Contemporary Women's Poetry* (Macmillan, 2000), ed. Alison Marks and Deryn Rees-Jones.   JNT

Howe, Susan (1937–) Born in Boston, Massachusetts, where she trained as a painter at the Museum School of Fine Arts. She also studied acting in Dublin (her mother, Mary Manning, worked with *Yeats at the Abbey Theatre). From 1989 to 2006 she was a professor of English at SUNY-Buffalo. Her sister is the poet Fanny *Howe.

Howe's early publications through small presses are collected in *Frame Structures: Early Poems 1974–1979* (New Directions, 1996). She has been associated with the *Language movement, but her approach to English as 'a wood for thought' is a singular project, scattering lines of verse on the page in a visual dramatization of textual instability, as in the 'turning' sequences of *The Nonconformist's Memorial* (New Directions, 1993).

Like Charles *Olson, Howe practises an eclectic scholarship, seeking to recover the 'stutter' of marginal voices from American and European history. The poet has attributed this fascination to her wartime childhood. In works such as *The Liberties* (Loon, 1980) and *The Midnight* (New Directions, 2003), it is also an exploration of her Irish ancestry, and in *Singularities* (Wesleyan University Press, 1990), *Pierce-Arrow* (1999), and *Souls of the Labadie Tract* (2007), of her New England and Puritan intellectual background. *That This* (2010—all New Directions) won the Bollingen Prize.

Howe's *My Emily Dickinson* (North Atlantic, 1985) is a classic of creative literary criticism. Later essays are collected *The Birth-Mark: Unsettling the Wilderness in American Literary History* (Wesleyan

University Press, 1993). See Will Montgomery, *The Poetry of Susan Howe* (Palgrave, 2010).   JNT

Howes, Barbara (1914–96) Born and raised in Boston, and attended Bennington College. In the mid-Forties she edited the literary journal *Chimera* in New York, but for many years she lived in North Pownal, Vermont. She married William Jay Smith in 1947; they had two sons and were later divorced. Her first book of poems, *The Undersea Farmer*, was published by Banyan in 1948, and was followed by a suite of critically acclaimed volumes. Her fifth book *The Blue Garden* (1972) reveals in smaller compass what *A Private Signal: New and Selected Poems* (1977—both Wesleyan University Press) shows in full, a poetic world located between the geographical poles of New England and the island of Tobago in the Caribbean. That world is rich in the lore of nature, and of neighbours described with a naturalist's precision and sympathy. *The Collected Poems of Barbara Howes 1945–1990* (University of Arkansas Press, 1995) was nominated for the 1995 National Book Award.

Howes was a formalist of sorts, though inventive and self-determined. Her formalism is not so much a refusal of free verse as the expression of a taste for symmetry and complication; she usually chooses forms that work against the grain of any easy, unimpeded flow of thought or speech. The more she hems and dams her poems, the more interesting they become, and the more insistent their music.

Her Vermont poems are naturally more inward and personal, reflecting the farmers and animals she lived among, her children and memories. Her pastoral poems are not sentimental, but candidly reveal the violence and physical hardship of winter and mud-season in the green mountains: the dog shot by hunters, the old cow and her untimely calf dead together in the field, the 'windmares' brought on by blizzard, the abused child who shot his father four times. All these sombre themes, together with life's ordinary celebrations, she finds worthy of poetry.   EG

Hudgins, Andrew (1951–) Born in Kileen, Texas, and holds degrees from Huntington College and the University of Alabama. In 1985 he joined the faculty at the University of Cincinnati, and is now Distinguished Professor of English at Ohio State University.

Hudgins' first volume, *Saints and Strangers* (1985), is divided into four unequal parts containing a total of thirty-three poems. Characters of familiar name appear throughout, including St Francis, Audubon, Zelda Fitzgerald, as well as biblical figures. The fourth section comprises an eight-part poem from which the volume takes its title. The poems deal with death and images of horror, and most of his narrators are ironic angels at best: the best tend to be pathetically mad or significantly depressed. His collection of personae—drunk drivers, female convicts, murdered girls—suggest a sense of the grotesque that is in good company with the Southern Gothic poets he says he admires.

In his second book, *After the Lost War: A Narrative* (1988), Hudgins focuses on a single figure, a poet, Sidney Lanier, and follows Lanier's sensibility through the American Civil War and the knowledge of his own, impending death. *The Never-Ending* (1991) was nominated for a National Book Award. His verse autobiography, *The Glass Hammer: A Southern Childhood* (1994 —all Houghton), has a prose companion in the personal and critical essays of *The Glass Anvil* (University of Michigan Press, 1997). Hudgins' dark sense of humour is given full rein in *Shut Up You're Fine: Instructive Poetry for Very, Very Bad Children* (Overlook Press, 2009). For his later poetry, see *American Rendering: New and Selected Poems* (Houghton, 2010).   CR

Hueffer, Ford Madox See FORD, FORD MADOX.

Hughes, Glyn (1935–2011) Born in Middlewich, Cheshire, and educated at Altrincham Grammar School and the Regional College of Art, Manchester. He taught art and liberal studies at schools and colleges in Lancashire and Yorkshire until 1972, and then became a freelance writer.

His poems are largely set in 'that block of the Pennines made of millstone grit, and ringed with the Yorkshire wool towns to the east and the Lancashire cotton towns to the west' vividly described in his prose book *Millstone Grit* (1975). In his first collection, *Neighbours* (Macmillan, 1970), he explores both the landscape and its people, dour, uningratiating, taciturn, more concerned with survival than with the niceties of friendship or love. Occasionally northern stereotypes intrude, and the tone of voice probably owes something to his namesake Ted *Hughes, but the chaos and poetry of the high moors is subtly realized, mirroring personal and national (post-industrial) hardship.

Rest the Poor Struggler (Macmillan, 1972) circles round similar places and themes, showing some American influence in its free-verse rhythms, and a greater interest in narrative. *Best of Neighbours: New and Selected Poems* (Ceolfrith, 1979) reprints the best of the earlier work and begins to explore the Nonconformist, evangelical world—'mills for souls called "chapels"'— he went on to write about at greater length in his novels and plays.

His prize-winning novels include *Where I Used To Play On The Green* (Gollancz, 1982), *The Hawthorn Goddess* (1984), and *The Rape of the Rose* (1987—both Chatto & Windus). He also wrote stage plays and verse plays for radio. Hughes returned to poetry at the end of his life with *Dancing Out of the Dark Side* (2005) and two autobiographical sequences: *Two Marriages* (2007) and *Life Class* (2009—all Shoestring). *A Year in the Bull-Box* describes the time he spent in an isolated stone hut after his diagnosis with cancer (Arc, 2011).   ws

Hughes, Langston (1902–67) A native of Joplin, Missouri, but grew up in various places in the American Midwest and in Mexico, where he taught and was a ranch-hand for his father. He moved on to manual labour in New York City, France, and Washington, DC; however, Hughes was also the first black American to make a living as a writer. Although he began as a poet, his literary output was enormous, covering drama, fiction, autobiography, li-

bretti for musicals, opera, and a cantata. Furthermore, Hughes wrote in a variety of styles and techniques: he was as capable of penning a traditionally formal poem as a prose poem in the style of Whitman.

Although Hughes is associated with the '*Harlem Renaissance' of the 1920s and 1930s, he lived into the Decade of Protest and served as a model for postmodernist black poets such as Robert *Hayden, Gwendolyn *Brooks, Amiri *Baraka, and Don L. Lee. Hughes was accused by some critics, both black and white, of not writing enough consciousness-raising material, but he was in fact the first black American to write civil-rights protest poetry that was identifiable as such, and he did it when it was quite dangerous to do so.

Hughes tried hard to bring into American literature not only the black experience, but Afro-American musical traditions as well, for many of the poems he wrote were conceived of as 'jazz' poems, as Steven C. Tracy discussed in *Langston Hughes and the Blues* (University of Illinois Press, 1988). Hughes is given credit for making the 'blues' as much a part of American literature as it had become of American music. Blues first appeared as a consciously literary form in Hughes' poem, 'The Weary Blues', which won *Opportunity magazine*'s poetry prize in 1925 and, in the following year, was the title-poem of his first book (Knopf, 1926). The synthesis of these efforts was *Montage of a Dream Deferred* (Holt, 1951) which is a 'street epic' full of all sorts of jazz effects, as is *Ask Your Mama: 12 Moods for Jazz* (Knopf, 1961). His autobiographies are *The Big Sea* (Knopf, 1940) and *I Wonder As I Wander* (Rinehart, 1956). Jemie Onwuchekwa's book *Langston Hughes: An Introduction to the Poetry* (Columbia University Press, 1976) provides a good overall view of the poet's work, as does Arnold Rampersad's *The Life of Langston Hughes* (Oxford University Press, 1986–8; new edn., 2002) of his career. See *The Collected Poems of Langston Hughes* (Knopf, 1994) and also the first three volumes of *The Collected Works of Langston Hughes*, ed. Arnold Rampersad (University of Missouri Press, 2001).   LT

Hughes, Ted (Edward James Hughes) (1930–98) Born in Mytholmroyd in Yorkshire. His father, William Hughes, was a carpenter who fought in the First World War (he was one of only seventeen survivors of an entire regiment which perished at Gallipoli). The family moved to Mexborough, a coal-mining town in South Yorkshire, when Hughes was 7, and his parents took a newsagent's and tobacconist's shop. In 1948 he won an Open Exhibition to Pembroke College, Cambridge. Before attending university he did two years' National Service in the RAF. After leaving Cambridge, he worked as a rose-gardener, night-watchman, and a script-reader for Rank at Pinewood, before becoming a teacher.

He married the American poet Sylvia *Plath in 1956 and the couple went to the USA in the following year. Hughes taught English and creative writing at Amherst College, and Plath taught literature at Smith College. After spending several months in the writers' colony of Yaddo in Saratoga Springs, the couple returned to England in December 1959. Plath committed suicide in 1963, an event that would overshadow the rest of his life.

Hughes' first collection of poems, *The Hawk in the Rain*, was published in 1957, and its vigorous vernacular won immediate acclaim. Its terse celebration of raw natural energies contrasted with the rational ironies of *Movement verse and since the late 1950s Hughes has been viewed as a nature poet. His appointment as Poet Laureate in 1984 sealed his essentially shaman-like conception of his poetic mission and enabled him to speak out on environmental issues while celebrating royal weddings and babies.

During a prolific writing career, Hughes was regarded as a poet who wrote about the natural world rather than society, but the feral forces he celebrates are disguised metaphors for a series of historical struggles—Reformation, Industrial Revolution, First World War—which echo and combine in his radically unsettled imagination. Rooted like D. H. *Lawrence in dissenting culture, Hughes follows Lawrence both as a literary model and as a writer who attempts to abolish society by locating the self-justifying act of individual witness in a primordial wilderness. Hughes' primitivism embodies this wounded search for an original wholeness and forms the basis of his writing for children (a gifted children's writer, his story, *The Iron Man*, is widely popular).

In his early poems, Hughes sometimes uses rhyme, but he does so uneasily. Drawing on Walt Whitman and Robinson *Jeffers, his verse-line is most confident when unconstrained by the demands of formal rhyme or metre. His imagination is drawn to horizons, open space, the impacted bunching of strong monosyllables ('short fierce fuse' in 'The Jaguar', 'sudden sharp hot stink of fox' in 'The Thought-Fox'). Locating North American wilderness poetry in England, he expresses a type of puritan, entrepreneurial striving, a visceral populism which scorns what Hughes termed the 'crippled court-artifice' of polite speech. His second volume, *Lupercal* (1960), aims to challenge the cultural dominance of southern English culture by designing heroically English figures on recognizably Yeatsian principles. Like *Yeats, Hughes likes to set up imaginative polarities—salt-bleached Viking warriors against the 'elaborate, patient gold of the Gaels'.

In his verse, Hughes constructed a myth in which the Germanic/puritan/masculine is eternally at war with the Celtic/catholic/feminine. The driven, gruelling texture of his poems is intensely puritan—they are written to the moment in a type of absolute present tense. Hughes' poems do not develop; instead, he appears to have been endlessly re-drafting the same poem. Hughes' visionary spontaneity is a form of born-again evangelical earnestness which is integral to Yorkshire dissent. In their fascination with an elemental energy, his poems may also be read as protests against the post-war consensus which was challenged by the election of a radical conservative government in 1979. By coincidence, Hughes' most assured volume, *Moortown*, was published that year. The poems in the opening sequence are elegies for an island economy which is self-reliant and not 'at the mercy of foreign politicians' (this remark is taken from Hughes' introduction to *Moortown Diary*, the reprint of the volume's opening sequence which was published in 1989). Insistently, these poems enact the means by which individual enterprise reclaims a natural wilderness. Paradoxically, they also express the desire to occupy a primal natural world before 'industrial servitude'. Such a wish is an expression of Hughes' primitivist imagination, his celebration of what Nietzsche terms 'the free powers without ethics'. The volume is dedicated to the memory of Jack Orchard, the Devonshire farmer whose daughter, Carol, Hughes married in 1970.

Hughes won many literary awards and in 1968 he set up the Arvon Foundation to encourage new writing. His most important volumes, published from the first in the UK and the USA, include *The Hawk in the Rain* (1957); *Lupercal* (1960); *Wodwo* (1967); *Gaudete* (1977); *Remains of Elmet* (1979—all Faber/Harper); *Moortown* (Faber, 1979, Harper, 1980; title-sequence reprinted separately as *Moortown Diary*, 1989); *Wolfwatching* (Faber, 1989). He is perhaps best known for *Crow* (Faber, 1970, revd. edn. 1972; Harper, 1971), whose subtitle 'from the Life and Songs of the Crow' points to its status as a fragmentary epic. These 'super-crude' episodes of mythological violence are modelled on Native American 'Trickster' cycles, as well as modern American cartoons. Begun in the mid-1960s, Hughes abandoned work on the *Crow* poems after the suicide of his second partner, Assia Wevill, in 1969.

In 1992 he published *Rain-Charm for the Duchy and Other Laureate Poems* and a prose work, *Shakespeare and the Goddess of Being. Winter Pollen*, a selection of his critical prose edited by William *Scammell, appeared in 1994. In 1997, Hughes' free translations of the *Metamorphoses, Tales from Ovid* (all Faber), won the Whitbread Book of the Year. His last original volume after *New Selected Poems 1957–1994* (Faber, 1995; Farrar, Straus, 2002) was *Birthday Letters* (1998), a raw account in verse of life with and after Plath. It was published shortly before his death and won the 1999 Whitbread Poetry Prize.

Collected Poems (2003—both Faber/Farrar, Straus, 2003), ed. Paul Keegan, includes many uncollected pieces, although it omits the prose episodes of *Gaudete*. *Collected Poems for Children* (2005) contains the fine *Season Songs* (1975), a volume that 'grew up'. Elaine *Feinstein published a short biography in 2001 (*The Life of a Poet*, Weidenfeld & Nicolson). See also the selected *Letters of Ted Hughes*, ed. Christopher Reid (Faber, 2007; Farrar, Straus, 2008) and *Selected Translations*, ed. Daniel Weissbort (Faber, 2006; Farrar, Straus, 2008). There is a shorter *Selected Poems* (Faber, 2000), chosen by Simon *Armitage. In 2011, a memorial to Hughes in Poets' Corner at Westminster Abbey was unveiled by Seamus *Heaney. Keith Sagar, *The Laughter of Foxes* (Liverpool University Press, 2000) is the first survey of the complete oeuvre. For more information see the online journal of The Ted Hughes Society: www.thetedhughessociety.org. TP*

(⊕) SEE WEB LINKS

Hugo, Richard (1923–82) Born in Seattle and educated at the University of Washington. He is sometimes said to have taken a radical turn in his poetry with the volume *31 Letters and 13 Dreams* (1977), from a distanced formality to something like *confessionalism. The change is more apparent than real, however; Hugo is both more personal in his early work and more formal in his later work than is generally perceived. What he did in 1977 was not so much change his style as expand the range of his subject-matter, making it franker and more inclusive. He was always an unusually self-analytical poet; but before *31 Letters and 13 Dreams* he presented his feelings largely through persons and objects separate from himself. With that volume he began to speak much more directly of his own life. The story that gives psychological energy to Hugo's poems is by turns painful, tragic, and triumphant. His father, a man named Hogan, abandoned Hugo's mother shortly after the poet was born. She then married a man named Hugo and left the baby with her parents, who raised him within a strict and emotionally impoverished environment. Out of this childhood, not surprisingly, came feelings of worthlessness, guilt, and shame, all of which were, for years, projected outward on to the surrounding landscape. This is why Richard Hugo is so famous for the many early poems—like 'Degrees of Gray in Philipsburg'—that he wrote on the abandoned, failed small towns of the Pacific Northwest; they are a mirror to his soul. And yet Hugo is no literalist; as explained in his collection of essays, *The Triggering Town* (Norton, 1979), he followed a principle of composition that resembles the process of psychoanalysis: 'when you are writing you must assume that the next thing you put down belongs not for reasons of logic, good sense, or narrative development, but because you put it there. You, the same person who said that, also said this.' In *31 Letters and 13 Poems* Hugo relaxed his forms in order to say things he could not say otherwise. A kind of balance is achieved in *White Center* (1980), which revisits territory covered earlier but from a happier perspective.

All of Hugo's individual books are republished in *Making Certain It Goes On: The Collected Poems* (Norton, 1984). See also Michael S. Allen, *We Are Called Human: The Poetry of Richard Hugo* (1982), Jack Myers (ed.), *A Trout in the Milk: A Composite Portrait of Richard Hugo* (1982), and Donna Gerstenberger, *Richard Hugo* (1983). PS

Hulme, T. E. (Thomas Ernest) (1883–1917) Born in Endon, Staffordshire, and educated at the High School, Newcastle under Lyme, and St John's College, Cambridge. He was sent down in his second year, for—in one account—'indulging in a brawl'. Pugnacity in one form or another seems to have characterized many of Hulme's public dealings—he is said to have carried a brass knuckleduster made for him, at his request, by Gaudier-Brzeska. Hulme was killed in action with the Royal Marine Artillery; though fascinated by military strategy, he appears not to have approached warfare with the same truculent relish he showed for argument. Before this he worked in Canada and Brussels;

while living in London he joined the 'experimental' Poets' Club (in 1908) and published (in the *New Age* for January 1912) 'The Complete Poetical Works of T. E. Hulme', five poems, the longest of which is nine lines. He published only six poems during his lifetime. Some two dozen other poems and fragments survive, but like his prose writings these remain uncollected, and Hulme might seem a very marginal figure were it not for the considerable impact he had made on twentieth-century taste. In his own words a 'philosophic amateur', influenced both by Bergson and *L'Action française*, Hulme developed the 'classical, reactionary and revolutionary' outlook later embraced by T. S. *Eliot; he championed the semi-abstract, geometrical art of Wyndham *Lewis, Henri Gaudier-Brzeska, and Jacob Epstein; and his propaganda on behalf of *vers libre* and the primacy of the image in poetry was effectively taken up (along with Hulme's combative stance) by Ezra *Pound. Hulme was not among the contributors to Pound's or Amy *Lowell's 'official' *Imagist anthologies, but Pound signalled an affinity (or acknowledged a debt) by reprinting the 'Complete Poetical Works' as an addendum to his own 1912 volume, *Ripostes*.

In his attack on Romanticism, on conventionally poetical subject-matter, and outworn expression, in his repeated demands for a 'visual, concrete language' to convey 'vividly felt actual sensation', Hulme provided polemical buttressing for the kind of poetry that he and others such as F. S. *Flint and Pound had begun to write. His own poems, which predate his most 'classical' phase, are graceful mood pieces, focusing a 'state of soul' through striking but homely images, reaching towards the rhythms of conversational speech while retaining the inversions of a more antiquated style. Yet their very modesty and charm could now be seen— along with his insistence on freshness, novelty, 'an accidentally seen analogy or unlooked-for resemblance', and on keeping to 'the exact curve of the thing' or feeling—to anticipate the tendencies of much

British post-war poetry. T. S. Eliot considered them 'some of the finest short poems in the English language'.

Speculations: Essays on Humanism, and the Philosophy of Art, ed. Herbert Read (Kegan Paul, 1924; last repr. 1987) contains a selection from Hulme's prose and the five poems that comprise 'The Complete Poetical Works'; more poems and fragments, with textual details, are published in *The Life and Opinions of T. E. Hulme*, by Alun R. Jones (Gollancz, 1960); see also *T. E. Hulme*, by Michael Roberts (Faber, 1938, repr. Carcanet, 1982), *Selected Writings*, ed. Patrick McGuinness (Carcanet, 1998), and *The Short Sharp Life of T. E. Hulme* by Robert Ferguson (Penguin, 2002, repr. Faber, 2012).   AJ

Hummer, T. R. (1950–) Born and raised in Macon, Mississippi. He received a BA and MA in English literature from the University of Southern Mississippi in Hattiesburg, and later a PhD in English and creative writing from the University of Utah. He has served as editor of several literary periodicals, including *Quarterly West, the Cimmarron Review*, and the *New England Review*. He has taught creative writing at several US universities, most recently Arizona State.

From the publication of his first book, *The Angelic Orders* (1982), T. R. Hummer's poetry has been characterized by moral seriousness. He has written personal narratives and dramatic monologues exploring the complexities of politics, labour, racism, and other themes. But he has proved most successful in the substantial number of poems in each of his collections that deal with the meaning and mystery that love and sexuality have for human beings at the end of the twentieth century. In these, Hummer has sought to combine both passion and philosophy: see his sonnet sequence, 'Axis', on Martin Heidegger, from *Useless Virtues* (2001—both Louisiana State University Press). His books include *The Passion of the Right-Angled Man* (1984), *Lower-Class Heresy* (1987—both University of Illinois Press), *The 18,000-Ton Olympic Dream* (Morrow, 1990), *Walt Whitman in Hell* (1996), and *The Infinity Sessions*, a cycle of jazz poems (2005—both Louisiana

State University Press). See also *The Muse in the Machine: Essays on Poetry and the Anatomy of the Body Politic* (University of Georgia Press, 2006) and, in the UK, *Bluegrass Wasteland: Selected Poems* (Arc, 2005).   LS*

Humphreys, Emyr (1919–) Best-known for his television plays and for the many novels he has written since the 1950s, when he won the Somerset Maugham Award for *Hear and Forgive* (1952) and the Hawthornden Prize for *A Toy Epic* (1958). His prose-works are his major achievement, but he also has a reputation as a poet, having published four volumes of verse: *Ancestor Worship* (1970); *Landscapes* (1979); *The Kingdom of Brân* (1979); and *Pwyll a Riannon* (1980). His verse is more direct than his prose (which is subtle and finely wrought) and more personal. It nevertheless shares with the novels a concern with 'the Welsh condition', often from a nationalist and Protestant point of view, and it makes little concession to readers who are not familiar with the history, literature, and legends of Wales.

A selection of Emyr Humphreys' verse (with that of John *Ormond and John *Tripp) appeared in *Penguin Modern Poets* (1978). A study of his work has been contributed to the Writers of Wales series (1980) by Ioan Williams. Since *Collected Poems of Emyr Humphreys* (University of Wales Press, 1999) he has published several works of fiction and a study of Welsh literary history, *The Taliesin Tradition* (Seren, 2000).   MS

Humphries, Rolfe (1894–1969) Born in Pennsylvania; the family moved to California in 1912, but he graduated from Amherst in 1915. Influenced by his schoolteacher mother, he was attracted to strong women, and both Genevieve *Taggard and Louise *Bogan became close friends after he moved to New York City in 1923. He began teaching Latin at the Woodmere Academy on Long Island in 1925, the same year he married Dr Helen Spencer. Over his career he produced six volumes of poetry—controlled, well-executed lyrics more intelligent than intense—but he is better known for his vigorous translations, especially Lorca's *The Poet in New York* (1940), Virgil's *The Aeneid* (1951), and Ovid's *Metamorphoses* (1955).

A liberal, concerned with the dangerous world situation in the 1930s, and not above writing political verses, Humphries joined the Communist Party but left in 1940. His reputation for integrity was confirmed in 1948 when he refused to remove a reference to *Pound's anti-Semitism from his introduction to that poet's *Selected Poems* (1949), which was then published without the introduction. He returned to Amherst as a lecturer in English in 1957, though he also gave a seminar in translation at Yale.

All of Humphries' poetry is in his *Collected Poems* (1965) and *Coat on a Stick* (1969—both Indiana University Press). See also *Poets, Poetics, and Politics: America's Literary Community Viewed From the Letters of Rolfe Humphries, 1910–1969*, ed. Richard Gillman and Michael Paul Novak (University Press of Kansas, 1992).   EB

Hunt, Sam (1946–) Born in Auckland, New Zealand. After being expelled from school he worked at various jobs around the country, mainly truck-driving and labouring, before settling at Bottle Creek, an estuary north of Wellington. He has made his living ever since almost entirely from writing, publishing, and performing. A troubadour poet with a gravelly voice, Hunt travels New Zealand reading his poems and singing his songs in schools, theatres, and taverns, where he reaches a wide popular audience. With his sheepdog Minstrel (d.1988) he rapidly became a national figure. He has also toured Australia and the United States.

His poetry is simple, personal, and strongly autobiographical. It is performance material, Romantic in nature, with a strong sense of place. His first small hand-bound collection of poems, *Between Islands* (1964) was followed in quick succession by thirteen further volumes which sold very well. His *Collected Poems* (1980) saw him dismissed as 'the Pam Ayres of New Zealand poetry' by one critic, but (like Ayres) he continues to outsell his more literary contemporaries. Hunt stopped publishing for a decade after 1997, returning with *Doubtless: New and Selected Poems* (2008). *Backroads: Charting a Poet's Life* is a memoir (2009—both Potton). Hunt has also edited a selection of the work of James K. *Baxter, a friend and mentor whose poems he often recites (Auckland University Press, 2009). In 2010 he was made a Companion of the New Zealand Order of Merit.   HMCQ*

Hutchinson, Pearse (1927–2012) Born in Glasgow to Irish Catholic parents. Later, the family moved to Dublin, where he was educated. In the 1950s and 1960s he lived in Switzerland, the Netherlands, and Spain, and worked as a translator. In the 1970s he returned to Dublin, where he gave radio broadcasts on Irish culture. Hutchinson's first English poems appeared in *The Bell* in 1945. His first book was a translation of the Catalan poet Joseph Carner, published by Dolphin Books in 1962. *Tongue Without Hands*, his debut, appeared from The Dolmen Press in 1963, followed by *Expansions* in 1969. He published five volumes with The Gallery Press, as well as a *Collected Poems* (2002).

Hugh *MacDiarmid was an important exemplar for Hutchinson's writing, which brings socialist and nationalist politics to a concern with language as the site of beauty and violence. 'The Frost is All Over', his 1973 poem dedicated to Michael *Hartnett, expatiates, with a *Yeatsian sweep, on the idea that 'To kill a language is to kill a people'. Hutchinson began to publish poems in Irish in the 1950s. *The Soul that Kissed the Body* (1990) is a selection with his own translations. *Done into English* (2003—both Gallery Press) selects his translations of other poets in over a dozen languages or dialects. *Reading Pearse Hutchinson: From Findrum to Fisterra*, ed. Philip Coleman and Maria Johnston (Irish Academic Press, 2011) is a book of tributes and essays.   JNT

Hyde, Robin (1906–39) Pseudonym of Iris Guiver Wilkinson, born in South Africa of an English father and Australian mother who shortly took her to Wellington, New Zealand, where she grew up and began work as a journalist. She suffered from recurrent ill health, including mental break-downs, depression, and a painful physical illness which left her permanently lame and caused her to become intermittently addicted to morphine. She had two children, one of whom died in infancy. Until her health made it impossible she worked for newspapers in several parts of the country; she then struggled to earn her living by writing (five novels, two other prose books, and much journalism). All the time she was writing poetry, which she regarded as her true work. In 1938 she set out for England but stopped on the way to visit China and report on the Sino-Japanese war; after gruelling experiences there she travelled to London, where some months later, suffering from depression, poverty, and a tropical disease caught in China, she committed suicide.

The collections of poems published in her lifetime—*The Desolate Star* (1929), *The Conquerors* (1935), and *Persephone in Winter* (1937)—tended to be over-pretty and marred by 'poetic' language; they were based on faded literary models and contained little reference to her New Zealand surroundings. Often they resorted to historical, biblical, or literary subject-matter. However, she left a great deal of unpublished work, much of which showed more vigour and flexibility; in this she brought her novelist's skills to bear on subject-matter which was familiar to her or genuinely experienced; her verse-forms became less rigid and her language more straightforward. A substantial selection from this later work was published as *Houses by the Sea & The Later Poems* (1953), ed. Gloria Rawlinson. It includes the title sequence, a vivid evocation of her childhood, and poems written in New Zealand, China, and England. See *Young Knowledge: The Poems of Robin Hyde*, ed. Michele *Leggott (Auckland University Press, 2003).   FKA

(⊕) SEE WEB LINKS

- To access Leggott's notes to the Poems visit the New Zealand Electronic Poetry Centre website.

Ignatow, David (1914–97) Born in Brooklyn, the only son of Jewish-Russian immigrants. The onset of the Depression forced him to leave college in his freshman year and take a series of low-paying jobs. He married artist Rose Graubart in 1938, and they had two children. Showing the clear influence of William Carlos *Williams, his first book, *Poems* (Decker, 1948), was as simple and direct as its title, mostly urban, spare free verse in service of a 'hard core realism literally presented'.

The main literary current, still under the spell of *Eliot and *Pound's neoclassic modernism, ran against him, but a second volume, *The Gentle Weight Lifter* (Morris Gallery, 1955) had the help of a positive review by Williams himself. The next few decades, which included publication of his strongest work, *Figures of the Human: Poems* (1964) and *Rescue the Dead* (1968—both Wesleyan University Press), involved editing and teaching, while recognition grew as Ignatow deepened his naturalistic mode with surreal invention, narrative functioning as metaphor to limn an unjust world. His verse became a species of social protest but also explored domestic, even *confessional themes, particularly fierce father-son conflicts.

Ignatow won the Bollingen Prize in 1977. Robert *Bly edited a *Selected Poems* (Wesleyan University Press, 1975), and parts of his candid journals were published as *The Notebooks of David Ignatow*, ed. Ralph J. Mills, Jr. (Swallow, 1973). *Against the Evidence: Selected Poems, 1934–1994* appeared in 1993, followed by *I Have a Name* (1996—all Wesleyan University Press). *Living is What I Wanted: Last Poems* was published posthumously by BOA Editions in 1999. For appreciations by poets and critics, see *Meaningful Differences: the Poetry and Prose of David Ignatow*, ed. Virginia R. Terris (University of Alabama Press, 1993).   EB

Imlah, Mick (1956–2009) Brought up in Milngavie and London, Imlah read English at Magdalen College, Oxford, where he did research on Victorian poetry and was junior lecturer in English. He was founding editor of *Oxford Poetry* (1983) and editor of *Poetry Review* 1983–6. From 1989 to 1993 he was poetry editor for Chatto & Windus.

Imlah's first full collection, *Birthmarks* (Chatto & Windus, 1988), is the work of an accomplished technician with an appetite for eccentric and at times baroque narrative ('Goldilocks', 'The Zoologist's Bath'), blackly and at times cruelly humorous. An overt literariness and pleasure in the play element of poetry, along with his formal skill, suggest the influence of his former college tutor, John *Fuller, who published a pamphlet collection, *The Zoologist's Bath and Other Adventures*, through his Sycamore Press in 1982. Imlah shared the widespread interest in monologue while making his interest in Browning more apparent than most of his contemporaries. The subjects of his work might seem academic but the effect is quite otherwise: at once fastidious and extravagant.

Imlah made selections of Tennyson and Edwin *Muir and, with Robert *Crawford, co-edited *The New Penguin Book of Scottish Verse* (2000). His second and final collection, *The Lost Leader* (2008), dwelt from many angles on the history of Scotland, with a virtuosic formal variety that reflected two decades of patient accumulation. It was awarded the Forward Prize in 2009, shortly after his death from motor neurone disease. A *Selected Poems* (both Faber) appeared in

2011, edited by Mark *Ford, with an intro-
duction by Alan Hollinghurst. The *Times
Literary Supplement*, where Imlah was poet-
ry editor for sixteen years, praised its 'weird-
ly wonderful inventiveness'.   SO'B*

Inada, Lawson (Fusao) (1938–) Born
in Fresno, California, Inada attended the
University of California at Berkeley and
Fresno State College, where he took his
BA in 1959. Subsequently he attended the
Iowa Writers' Workshop and the University
of Oregon, where he received an MFA in
1966. He began his teaching career at the
University of New Hampshire, and went to
Southern Oregon State College (now South-
ern Oregon University) in 1966, where he is
emeritus professor of English.

His first substantial publication was a
group of poems in *Three Northwest Poets*,
with Albert Drake and Doug Lawder (Qui-
xote, 1970). His three solo books are *Before
the War* (Morrow, 1971), *Legends from Camp*
(1992), and *Drawing the Line* (1997—both
Coffee House). Inada co-edited *Aiiieeeee!:
An Anthology of Asian-American Writers*
(Howard, 1974) and *The Big Aiiieeeee!* (Pen-
guin, 1990). He shared another book, *The
Buddha Bandits Down Highway 99* (Buddha-
head, 1977) with Garrett *Hongo and Alan
Lau. Despite Inada's intense involvement
with Asian-American poetry, his own work
owes more to American sources than to
Asian; the five-poem sequence 'Since When
As Ever More', for instance, is an even stricter
catalogue of parallel structures than most
Walt Whitman pieces—as strict, in fact, as
Allen *Ginsberg's *Howl* or Christopher
Smart's *Jubilate Agno*, but the catalogues
are fragmentary in nature and they rely
heavily on repetitions. His anthology of the
Japanese-American internment experience,
Only What We Could Carry (Heyday)
appeared in 2000. In 2006, he was appointed
as the fifth Oregon Poet Laureate.   LT

Ingamells, Rex (1913–55) Born in
Orraroo, South Australia, and read history
at the University of Adelaide. He worked in
turn as an adult-education tutor, a high-
school teacher, and a publisher's agent.
Ingamells was the driving spirit of the Jin-
dyworobak Club which he founded in 1938

and which developed into the influential
and controversial *Jindyworobak move-
ment. *Jindyworobak*, an Aboriginal word
which Ingamells paraphrased as 'to annex,
to join', encapsulated for him the means of
developing a uniquely Australian poetry: he
advocated rejecting the forms and direc-
tions of other world literature, focusing on
the Australian environment and distinc-
tively Australian experience which he di-
vided into three eras: 'primaeval, colonial
and modern'.

Ingamells' poetry, conventionally lyric in
form and tone, attempts to apprehend the
Aboriginal experience, but he was also in-
spired by records of the early European
explorers and their quest for the mythical
terra australis, which he describes in
poems such as 'Luis De Torres' and 'The
Great South Land'.

Ingamells published eight collections of
poetry, one novel, and critical works. *The
Jindyworobaks*, ed. Brian Elliott (University
of Queensland Press, 1979) gives a selec-
tion of Jindyworobak poetry, including that
of Ingamells, and discusses its impact on
later poets.   EMCM

Ireland, Kevin (1933–) Born in Auck-
land, New Zealand, of pioneer Irish and
English stock, Ireland was educated at
Auckland University College, leaving in
1952 in protest at the position the Students'
Association took during the Waterfront
Strike. In 1959 he travelled to Australia
and on to England and Eastern Europe. In
London he took a job at *The Times*, where
he found a literary bolthole as a printer's
reviser for almost twenty years. During that
time he published eight books of poetry,
all with New Zealand publishers, although
he rarely visited New Zealand during his
self-imposed 'exile'. His sixth book, *Literary
Cartoons*, won the New Zealand Book
Award for Poetry in 1978. Ireland returned
to New Zealand in 1985, where he has held
several writing fellowships.

The strongest influence on Ireland's
early poetry was the New Zealand poet,
R. A. K. *Mason, whose short, spare,
unpunctuated lines and gruff unsentimen-
tality he admired. By his second book
Ireland had found his subject and his own

distinctive voice: this book and the next half-dozen conduct a wry, urbane, self-deprecating examination of love and lovers' folly. The elegant wit of *Literary Cartoons* (Islands/Hurricane, 1977) was repeated in *Tiberius at the Beehive* (Auckland University Press, 1990), where the satirist's attention turned from literature to politics. Ireland's earlier poetry was largely unpunctuated, and was just as often in regular stanzas, using varieties of half-rhyme, as it was *vers libre*. In his later work he has attempted longer poems, much longer punctuated lines, and he now writes with greater detachment, often on historic subjects. *Anzac Day: Selected Poems* appeared in 1997. Ireland has also published prose fiction and two memoirs. His books of poetry since 2000 include *Fourteen Reasons for Writing* (2001), *Walking the Land* (2003—all Hazard Press), and *Table Talk* (Cape Cantley, 2009).   AF

Jackson, Michael (1940–) By education and experience, Jackson is a social anthropologist. Born in New Zealand at Inglewood, Taranaki, and educated at Auckland and Cambridge universities, he taught anthropology at Massey University before moving to Australia in 1982 to teach and write. In 1989 he was given an endowed research professorship at Indiana University, where he was able to combine scholarly research with his creative work. Since 2005, he has been Distinguished Visiting Professor of World Religions at Harvard Divinity School.

His first collection, *Latitudes of Exile*, won the 1976 Commonwealth Poetry prize. While conservatively following in the tradition of *Yeats and *Eliot, and unaffected by the debate about form in New Zealand poetry, the poems typically show the intersection of an educated Western mind with the facts of strange cultures, or with remembrances of family things past. In *Wall* (1980), the poems open up more, are less constricted by tradition. *Going On* (1985) is a logbook of the illness and death of his wife.; the poems are hard-edged, yet do not always escape sentimentality or preciousness.

Duty Free: Selected Poems 1965–88 (1989—all McIndoe) covers the three volumes, adding a dozen new poems. *Pieces of Music* (Random House, 1994) is a prose work of linked 'autobiographical fictions' set around the world, as are the poems of *Antipodes* (1996). Jackson has been academically prolific in the last decade, but has published only one further volume of poetry, *Dead Reckoning* (2006—both Auckland University Press).   RB*

James, Clive (1939–) Born in Sydney and educated at Sydney and Cambridge universities. He has achieved fame as a television personality, but it was as a writer of verse that he first attracted literary attention: his four mock-epics *The Fate of Felicity Fark* (1975), *Peregrine Prykke's Pilgrimage* (1976), *Britannia Bright's Bewilderment* (1976), and *Charles Charming's Challenges* (1981—all Cape), appeared before his fictionalized autobiography began to be published in best-selling instalments. While extravagant claims cannot be made for these epics—their author, with his habitual self-deprecation, said of the last of them that 'the West End critics demanded that its perpetrator be transported to Botany Bay, and were not to be mollified by the information that he was born there'—they established James as the most adept practitioner of light verse in his generation of Australians.

Had he not left Australia for England as soon as he graduated from Sydney University his epics might not have been published, even if they had been written. In the years of James' absence from Australia, light verse has fallen there into intellectual disrepute. Few of his other accomplishments would have been possible, either, if he had stayed at home. Liberated by success, he published *Other Passports* (Picador, 1986), an interim 'collected poems'. To those readers who did not feel obliged to sneer at his public persona, a customary treatment for Australia's successful expatriates, it was apparent that his poetic skill extended beyond light verse. He is a considerable poet with a voice all his own, versatile, witty, and technically rigorous.

James' second collected poems, *The Book of My Enemy* (Picador, 2003), announced a late renaissance. An American selected poems covering fifty years of writing, *Opal Sunset* (Norton), appeared in 2008. In the same year, James published a new British volume, *Angels Over Elsinore*, which includes his witty piece of pedantry for the word-processing age, 'Windows is Shutting Down' ('and grammar are | On their last leg'). See also *Nefertiti in the Flak Tower: Poems 2008–2011* (2012—both Picador).   JG*

James, John (1939–) Born in Cardiff and educated there at Saint Illtyd's College. He studied literature and philosophy at the universities of Bristol and Keele, where he met Roy *Fisher. Andrew Duncan has called him 'the most gifted poet using the English language ... to come out of Wales since the Second World War'. In the 1960s he published *Resuscitator*, an important *Cambridge School magazine. For many years he was Head of Communication Studies at Anglia Ruskin University, Cambridge.

Over the course of an oeuvre, James has emerged as one of the most demotic practitioners of the lyric dailiness that characterizes the poetry of his peers (including that of his first wife, Wendy *Mulford). His conversational style has often been compared to that of Frank *O'Hara, with whom he shares a flaneurial wit. But James' humour is more politically sardonic than O'Hara's ('If there is always memory in working-class life | it is because things are always being taken away'), and the poet's loves, drinks, and landscapes are lonelier pleasures.

James' early lyrics evince his friendship and exchange with J. H. *Prynne. *mmm ... ah yes* (Ferry) and *The Welsh Poems* (Grosseteste) both appeared in 1967. *A Theory of Poetry* (Street Editions, 1977) expounds mock-solemnly on a textuality of 'openings windows apertures leaks' and 'delicate smears & caresses'. *Toasting* (Garden Centre Gallery, 1979) is one instance of his punk-era interest in art and performance. *Collected Poems* appeared in 2002, and *The Salt Companion to John James*, ed. Simon Perril, in 2010 (both Salt).   JNT

Jamie, Kathleen (1962–) Born in Renfrewshire, Jamie grew up on the outskirts of Edinburgh, studying philosophy at the university there. She is Professor of Creative Writing at Stirling University and a Fellow of the Royal Society of Literature.

Her early work was encouraged by Douglas *Dunn. A pamphlet, *Black Spiders* (Salamander, 1982), established her as a crisply observant poet. *The Way We Live* followed in 1987, and *A Flame in Your Heart*—a wartime romance in verse with Andrew *Greig—in 1988. In 1994, she was announced as one of the *New Generation poets, and published *The Queen of Sheba* (all Bloodaxe).

Jamie's diction in this book dramatizes the class tensions between *Scots and standard English. Her concern with the construction of female identity in this culture can be heard in satirical fantasies such as 'Wee Wifey' and 'Mr and Mrs Scotland are Dead' (also the title of a selected volume from Bloodaxe in 2002). Since *Jizzen* (1999—the word is Scots for childbed), her prize-winning work has increasingly inclined to a lyrically direct ecopoetics: see *The Tree House* (2004) and *The Overhaul* (2012—all Picador). *Waterlight: New and Selected Poems* (Greywolf, 2007) appeared in America. In 1981, Jamie used an Eric Gregory award to travel to the Himalayas. She has also written nonfiction prose and made radio programmes about travel and landscape: see *The Golden Peak: Travels in North Pakistan* (Virago, 1992), which was revised and reprinted as *Among Muslims* (2002), and *Findings* (2005—both Sort Of Books).   JNT

Jarman, Mark (1952–) Born in Kentucky, the son of a minister, Jarman grew up in California and Scotland. He studied at the University of Santa Cruz, California, and received an MFA from the Writers' Workshop at the University of Iowa. He has taught at Vanderbilt University in Tennessee since 1983, where he is now Centennial Professor of English.

A leading figure in the *New Narrative movement of the 1980s, Jarman edited *The Reaper* magazine with Robert McDowell: see *The Reaper Essays* (1996). The pair subsequently founded Story Line Press. Robinson *Jeffers is an important influence on Jarman's work, notably in the long poem *Iris* (1992). Often autobiographical, it has latterly rediscovered the Christian faith of his childhood: see *Questions for Ecclesiastes* (1997), which won the Lenore Marshall Poetry Prize, *Unholy Sonnets* (2000—all Story Line), and the prose poems of *Epistles* (2007). *Bones of Fire: New and Selected Poems* (2011—both Sarabande) draws on eight collections, beginning with *North Sea* (Cleveland State University Poetry Center, 1978). Jarman has published two collections of essays: *The Secret of Poetry* (Story Line, 2001) and *Body and Soul* (University of Michigan Press, 2002).   JNT

Jarnot, Lisa (1967–) Born in Buffalo, New York, Jarnot attended the university there, where she was taught by Robert *Creeley. She also has an MFA from Brown University. In the 1990s, she edited the *Saint Mark's Poetry Project newsletter, and co-edited *An Anthology of New (American) Poetry* (Talisman, 1997). In 2004, she played the main character in Jennifer Todd Reeve's film, *The Time We Killed*. She now works as a horticulturalist.

After several chapbooks, beginning with *Phonetic Introductions* (Northern Lights, 1988), Jarnot came to prominence with her first full-length book, *Some Other Kind of Mission* (Burning Deck, 1996; repr. 2008). This 'mock-epic', influenced by the serial poetics of Robert *Duncan and Jack *Spicer, collages prose and verse with graphic work.

Jarnot's distinctively incantatory lyricism emerged in her next book, *Ring of Fire* (Zoland, 2001; Salt, 2003), where a high Romantic register meets *Steinian iteration: as Tom *Raworth has put it, 'Gertrude Blake pirouettes in a fun house of auditory mirrors'. 'Ye White Antarctic Birds', for example, refracts New York's art galleries, birdlife, and bank machines through a chant of 'antarctic longings'.

Black Dog Songs (2003) and *Night Scenes* (2008—both Flood) develop a post-*Language pastoralism with an implicitly political thrust (the terse poems of 'My Terrorist Notebook' are dedicated to members of the Bush administration, then at war in Iraq and Afghanistan). Her biography of Duncan, *The Ambassador from Venus*, appeared in 2012 from University of California Press.   JNT

Jarrell, Randall (1914–65) Born in Nashville, Tennessee, moved with his parents to Los Angeles soon after, then returned to Nashville with his mother after his parents divorced. In 1926-7 a visit to his paternal grandparents in Los Angeles would provide him, decades later, with the remembered sensations and experiences that inform 'The Lost World' the three-part title-poem of his last and best book of verse. Jarrell graduated from Vanderbilt University in Nashville, where he studied with Robert Penn *Warren and John Crowe *Ransom. (Later his mentor would be, for a short time, another Vanderbilt graduate, Allen *Tate.) These poet-critics were associated with the *Fugitive group of writers that had come together in Nashville in the 1920s; but Jarrell showed little interest in Fugitive or 'Southern' political and cultural ideas. His early poetry, some of it published while he was still an undergraduate, is apocalyptic, surreal, and humourless— much indebted to *Auden's example, though lacking Auden's wit and formal brilliance.

When Ransom accepted a job at Kenyon College in Ohio, Jarrell followed him as an assistant, taught courses in the English department, and wrote his Master's thesis on A. E. *Housman's poetry. At Kenyon he roomed first with Robert *Lowell, then with a group of talented literary people which included Lowell and the fiction writer Peter Taylor, who later became Jarrell's closest friend. After two years at Kenyon he took a job at the University of Texas, married Mackie Langham in 1940, and brought out his first book of poems *Blood for a Stranger*, in 1942. Meanwhile, encouraged by Edmund Wilson, who published him in *The New Republic*, he made a reputation for himself as a fierce and fiercely humorous critic of other poets. His penchant for the devastating one-line dismissal (e.g. Oscar Williams' poems give the impression of 'having been written on a typewriter by a typewriter') caused recipients acute pain, but established Jarrell, in his twenties, as a highly readable force to be reckoned with.

In 1942 he entered the Army Air Force, but failed to qualify as a flyer and became a celestial training navigator in Tucson, Arizona. During his nearly four years of service he wrote many poems about the army and the war, accumulating the bulk of his next two books, *Little Friend, Little Friend* (1945) and *Losses* (1948). In these poems his earlier, Audenesque style modulated into a flatter, greyer, more homely idiom, appropriate for re-creating the dailyness of barracks life as well as the disasters of combat. During the latter part of his service, in 1945, he wrote a number of letters to Lowell about the manuscript of Lowell's soon-to-be-published book of poems, *Lord Weary's Castle*—letters filled with valuable suggestions for improving what Jarrell thought would be the most important poetry collection since Auden's *Poems* (1930). After the war Jarrell spent a year as literary editor of the *Nation*, whose back pages he filled with poems and reviews from many of the best writers in America and England. He also taught at Sarah Lawrence College, which he would later make use of as a model for the mythical Benton College in his satiric novel, *Pictures from an Institution* (1954).

Jarrell's post-war appreciations of Lowell, Elizabeth *Bishop, and William Carlos *Williams helped to establish their reputations as significant American poets; they also marked a change of emphasis in his criticism, in that he now mainly celebrated poets rather than awarded them demerits. His essays on *Frost (whose influence on his own poems was significant), Whitman, Marianne *Moore, *Stevens, Williams, Ransom, and others (mainly collected in *Poetry and the Age*, 1953) remain classics of clear-eyed, informed, and loving description, written in a wholly accessible and always humorous prose. His poetic reputation however did not keep pace with his critical one, and it was not until *The Woman at the Washington Zoo* (1960), which won the National Book Award, and *The Lost World* (1965) that he showed how original and attractive a poet he could be. The best

of his later poems—like 'The Woman at the Washington Zoo', 'Next Day', 'The Lost Children', 'The Lost World', and 'Thinking of the Lost World', are narratives, frequently spoken by women, which have some of the strength and human compassion of Frost's dramatic monologues (much admired by Jarrell). They also express, in a distinctive way, what Karl *Shapiro called 'the common dialogue of Americans'.

Jarrell married his second wife, Mary von Schrader, in 1952, and for most of his remaining years taught, with notable success and pleasure, at the University of North Carolina at Greensboro. He was an active poetry consultant at the Library of Congress in Washington for two years, and—during periods in the late 1950s and early 1960s when his rate of poetry production was low—he translated *Faust, Part I*, a Chekhov play, and several of Grimm's tales. Near the end of his life he wrote some remarkable children's stories, of which *The Bat Poet* (1964) and *The Animal Family* (1965) are pre-eminent. Soon after completing *The Lost World* he became mentally ill, first elated and later depressed, and eventually attempted suicide by slashing his wrist. Recovering, he went back to teaching in the fall of 1965, then entered a hospital in Chapel Hill for therapy on his wrist. While there, and while walking at dusk on a nearby highway, he was struck by a car and killed immediately. The coroner's verdict was accidental death, although the circumstances will never be entirely clear.

Jarrell will be remembered for his poems which, as Lowell claimed, rank with 'the best lyric poets of the past'; for his brilliantly engaging and dazzling criticism; and for his passionate defence, in what he termed 'the age of criticism', of writing and reading poems and fiction. *The Complete Poems* (1969) includes hitherto uncollected and unpublished work; while *Selected Poems*, ed. William H. Pritchard (1990—both Farrar, Straus), contains fifty of his best. *Randall Jarrell's Letters*, ed. Mary Jarrell (University of Virginia, 2002), has much valuable commentary. *No Other Book*, ed. Brad Leithauser (HarperCollins, 1999) is a generous selection of Jarrell's essays and reviews. See also *Randall Jarrell: A Literary Life*, by William H. Pritchard (Farrar, Straus, 1990) and *Randall Jarrell and His Age*, by Stephen Burt (Columbia University Press, 2002).   WHP

Jeffers, Robinson (1887–1962) Jeffers is one of the few American poets of the twentieth century who can be approached in terms of ideas rather than technique. As a classical scholar, Jeffers was able to absorb the principles of repetition and antithesis without feeling a need to retain the division into feet of the traditional British metric line. The result is a long-winded, clamorous free verse which manages a rare dignity and ease in the handling of large themes. For Jeffers, these large themes were summed up in his philosophy of Inhumanism, with its symbols of the falcon and the rock: violent energy and stoic endurance, 'bright power, dark peace'. In the course of the 1920s, while other American writers were travelling to Paris and London, or seeking a home base in the great cities of the east, Jeffers retired into the wild ocean landscape of north California, where he built himself a stone tower with his own hands. There, living in comparative isolation with his wife Una, Jeffers began work on a dual series of poems: long verse narratives basing their emotions—and occasionally their plots—on the dramas of the Greek tragedians, and short meditative poems arising out of personal experience in the wilderness.

These two extremes might be illustrated by the book-length poem *The Women At Point Sur*, and the brief lyric 'Hurt Hawks', with its liberal-challenging line: 'I'd sooner, except the penalties, kill a man than a hawk'. Inevitably, this kind of statement made Jeffers enemies. His best book, *The Double Axe*, appearing in 1948 just after the Second World War (revd. edn., Liveright, 1977), carried a disclaimer from the publishers, who wanted to disassociate themselves from the views expressed in some of the (apparently) pro-Nazi poems. In fact, Jeffers was years ahead of his time in noting the bitter ferocity of the Allied Powers in victory. Poems like 'The Bloody Sire' were perhaps provoking, and remain so, but there is an almost sublime detachment from worldly affairs in a lyric like 'The Eye', about the Pacific Ocean: 'what it watches is not our wars.' What can surprise and may survive best of Jeffers' copious output are the moments where satire and tenderness meet, as in poems like 'Original Sin', where early men are seen slaughtering a mammoth.

The Collected Poetry of Robinson Jeffers has now been published in five volumes by Stanford University Press, as well as a substantial new *Selected Poetry* (2001), ed. Tim Hunt. A three-volume *Collected Letters* is in progress. For criticism, see Robert Zaller, *Robinson Jeffers and the American Sublime* (Stanford University Press, 2012).   GMacB

⊕ SEE WEB LINKS

• For more information see the website of the Robinson Jeffers Association.

Jenkins, Alan (1955–) Born in London and read English and French at Sussex University. Since 1981 he has worked for the *Times Literary Supplement* and is presently deputy editor.

Love, sex, violence, and relations between the personal and political are central themes in Jenkins' poetry. His first collection, *In The Hothouse* (1988) ranges from oblique erotic reminiscence to the ambitious narrative centrepiece, 'Or Would You Rather Not Be Saved'. The latter's elliptical structure and multiple allusiveness show the influence of Paul *Muldoon, as do Jenkins' rhythmic flexibility and ingenuity of rhyme.

Unabashed by the uncertainties of tone allegedly discovered by some reviewers of his debut, in the title poem of *Greenheart* (1990) Jenkins produced a *tour de force* of exotic horror in which elements of postmodernist play coexist with an attempt to uncover the roots of violence by recasting *Heart of Darkness* in the drug economy of South America. Alongside this, a series of poems about the author's father indicate growing confidence in the more direct expression of feeling.

A stylish, inventive, highly literary poet with an appetite for risk, Jenkins won the Forward Prize for his next collection, *Harm* (1994). An 'intensely personal' fourth collection, *The Drift* (2000—all Chatto & Windus) was followed by an American volume of new and collected poems, *A Short History of Snakes* (Grove), in 2001. *A Shorter Life* (Chatto & Windus, 2005), continues his post-*Larkinian exploration of *confessionalism, English understatement, and a long-standing fascination with the French Symbolists (he translated Rimbaud in *Drunken Boats* (Sylph, 2007)). Jenkins edited Ian *Hamilton's *Collected Poems* (Faber, 2009).   SO'B*

Jennings, Elizabeth (1926–2001) Born in Boston, Lincolnshire, and educated at St Anne's College, Oxford. She worked first in advertising, then in Oxford City Library, and briefly in publishing before becoming a full-time writer. Her early work in volumes like *Poems* (1953), *A Way of Looking* (1955), and *Song for a Birth or a Death* (1961) won praise for its clarity and orderliness. It avoided the incoherence and formlessness of much contemporary neo-Romantic poetry, and revealed (in poems like 'The Climbers', 'Kings', and 'The Storm') a preference for regular verse-forms and an allegorical approach deriving from *Muir, *Graves, and occasionally *Auden. But although she was included in Robert *Conquest's *Movement anthology, *New Lines* (1956), her verse did not share the academic wit of some poets in that book, or the ironic, down-to-earth tone of others. Jennings' individual, highly sensitive treatment of love, childhood, or religious experience (as in her sequence 'Notes for a Book of Hours') does, however, show the quality of mature restraint often advocated by Movement poets and critics. The address of this quietly rhymed, finely crafted work is intimate, but real persons are not named and actual situations not developed. Jennings' poems about illness and hospital scenes, in *Recoveries* (1964) or *The Mind Has Mountains* (1966), sometimes register acute personal suffering but never go beyond a proper reticence. Conscious, perhaps, that her technical skill and imaginative resource might be further stretched, she made some successful attempts in later books, like *Growing Points* (1975) and *Extending the Territory* (1985),

to vary the shape and diversify the subject-matter of her poems (examples are 'Thunder and a Boy' and 'A Time Ago').

In 1992, Jennings was awarded a CBE. Her last collection was *Timely Issues* (2001). She died in Oxford, where a road is named after her. *Every Changing Shape* (1961), a collection of critical essays, was reprinted in 1996, and there was a new edition of her translation of *The Sonnets of Michelangelo* (1961) in 2003. *The Collected Poems* (2012—all Carcanet), ed. Emma Mason, puts Jennings' oeuvre in the context of her faith, drawing on unpublished verse and theological writings.   AB*

(⊕) SEE WEB LINKS

- For more information, visit the website of the Elizabeth Jennings Project.

Jensen, Laura (1948–) Born in Tacoma, Washington. Her grandparents emigrated from Scandinavia in the 1880s. The first literary influence on Jensen was Laura Ingalls Wilder's *Little House* series read aloud to her in childhood, stark accounts of American frontier life. Other influences were David *Wagoner and Mark *Strand at the University of Washington (BA 1972), before she entered the Iowa Writers' Workshop (MFA, 1974). Jensen has published three poetry collections and many chapbooks, and has taught for extended periods at Tacoma Community College and in residencies at the University of Minnesota and elsewhere. A 1989 Guggenheim Fellowship enabled her to travel to Scandinavia.

Although drawing from the *imagist and *surrealist traditions of the last half-century, Jensen remains a poet of high originality, from her first book *Bad Boats* (Ecco, 1977) through to her third, *Shelter* (1985). Her work is characterized by an intensely private yet impersonal vision. Never sensational in her subject-matter, Jensen none the less transforms the most ordinary situation into mystery, finding occasion there for wonder. Her dramatic design is elliptic rather than rational, austere rather than wily or lush. Gradually her work has opened toward more public concerns, such as war and poverty. Her second collection, *Memory* (1982—both Dragon Gate), was republished in 2006 in the Carnegie-Mellon University Press Classic Contemporaries Series. MB

Jensma, Wopko (1939–?) Born in Middelburg, Cape Town. Jensma began at the University of Potchefstroom, but withdrew after a motorcycle accident. He later studied fine art at the University of Pretoria. In the 1960s, he lived and worked in Mozambique and Botswana, returning to South Africa at the end of the decade, where he began to publish and exhibit visual art. The white Jensma had married a black woman and requested (like Tatamkhulu *Afrika) to be reclassified as black under the apartheid system. In 1993, he left the Salvation Army hostel where he was living in Johannesburg. His whereabouts are currently unknown.

Jensma's three large format volumes, which he designed himself, were among the first books published by the anti-apartheid Ravan Press: *Sing for Our Execution* (1973), *where white is the colour, where black is the number* (1974), and *i must show you my clippings* (1977). All include verse written in English, Afrikaans, and phrases from other African languages, alongside found text, photos, and creature-like woodcuts. Some critics admired the 'jazz' freedom of the writing and its *Joycean ambition to collage the languages of a divided society. Others disdained it.

Jensma's own divided mind appears eventually to have overwhelmed him. As he put it in his 1975 poem 'Spanner in the What? Works': 'i suffer from schizophrenia | (they tell me)'. Interviewed in 1991 he said, 'Don't speak to me about poetry.' His work has been selected by Adam *Schwartzmann in *Ten South African Poets* (Carcanet, 1999). JNT

Jiles, Paulette (1943–) Born in Salem, Missouri. She grew up in Blackwater and other towns, and received a BA in Spanish Literature from the University of Missouri (1968). Emigrating to Canada in 1969, Jiles worked briefly as a freelance journalist with the Canadian Broadcasting Corporation. Her first poems appeared in the anthology *Mindscapes* (1971), edited by Ann Wall. After travelling in Europe and Africa (1970–2), and publishing *Waterloo Express* (Anansi, 1973), she spent the years 1973–83 in the Canadian Arctic, working in aboriginal communications. Here she explored the themes of silence-utterance, wilderness-community, and dream-nature that distinguish her verse, notably *Celestial Navigation* (McClelland & Stewart, 1984), which won a Governor General's Award (1985). *Blackwater* (Knopf, 1988), *The Jesse James Poems* (1988), and *Song to the Rising Sun* (1989—both Polestar) followed. She has been a lecturer at David Thompson University Centre in British Columbia, and writer-in-residence at Phillips Academy in Massachusetts. A selected poems, *Flying Lessons*, appeared in 1995 (Oxford University Press). Jiles has since been better known for her historical fiction. PMStP

Johnson, Amryl (*c.*1960–2001) Born in Tunapuna, Trinidad. She came to England when she was 11, and later lived in Coventry and taught at the University of Warwick. Her degree from the University of Kent was in African and Caribbean studies, and she gave many poetry readings and writing workshops in schools. What she said in *Sequins for a Ragged Hem* (Virago, 1988), her memoir of a return visit to Trinidad, is applicable to her poetry: 'My emotions would knot and turn, twist and fragment in the whirlpool of existence. At times, I felt like a ghost who was haunting herself.' Many of her poems endow the Trinidad Carnival with archetypal significance, and one of her finest, 'The Wheel', displays Yeatsian authority in its sense of history as recurring agony: 'It stood silhouetted against the sky | drawing in the pain and suffering.' A note explains: 'In Tobago a gigantic iron wheel, now reclaimed by nature, is almost all that remains of what was once a sugar mill.' Amryl Johnson's first book of poems was *Long Road to Nowhere* (Sable, 1982), but a second volume of the same title, published by Virago in 1985, contained work that was entirely new. Her later volumes, *Gorgons* (Cofa, 1992) and *Calling* (Sable, 2000), developed an interest in myth as a way of voicing female experience, and have been called 'allegories about poetry': see Bruce King,

The Internationalization of English Literature (Oxford University Press, 2004).   MR*

Johnson, Colin (Mudrooroo Narogin)
(1938–) Born in East Cuballing near Narrogin, in the south-west of Western Australia. He was one of the leading figures in the second generation of Australian Aboriginal writers in English. Since 2001 he has lived in Nepal.

Johnson's first works were the novels *Wild Cat Falling* (1975), *Long Live Sandawara* (1979), and *Doctor Wooreddy's Prescription for Enduring the Ending of the World* (1983). His first two volumes of poetry were *The Song Circle of Jacky and Selected Poems* (Hyland House, 1986) and *Dalwurra, the Black Bittern* (Centre for Studies in Australian Literature, 1988). Both volumes adapt aspects of traditional Aboriginal song-cycles to the author's understanding of contemporary realities. One of these realities is that the fourteen tribes of south-west Australia have now gone and only one tongue remains: that of the Nyoongah or Bibbulman people, a distinctive version of Australian English, on which Johnson draws.

Like Jack *Davis, Johnson recognizes the facts of change but introduces a more defiant voice. His poems in *The Song Circle of Jacky* recall traditional tribal perceptions and customs from the perspective of a fringe-dweller of both Aboriginal and European Australia. *Dalwurra, the Black Bittern* uses the symbolic figure of this now-displaced bird to trace the author's travels through Asia, Europe, and back to Australia. Significant in these travels is India, where the author himself lived for some years as a Buddhist monk.

The Garden of Gethsemane: Poems From the Lost Decade (Hyland House, 1992) reflected the influence on Mudrooroo's writing of Lionel G. *Fogarty, and was a double winner in the W A Premier's Book Awards in 1992. *Pacific Highway Boo-Blooz: Country Poems* (University of Queensland Press, 1996) is a blues poetry travelogue. In 1997, he published a revised edition of his study of modern Aboriginal literature, *Writing from the Fringe* (1990), under the title *The Indigenous Literature of Australia: Milli Wangka*, in response to controversy over his own non-Aboriginal ancestry. See *Mongrel Signatures: Reflections on the Work of Mudrooroo*, ed. Annalisa Oboe (Rodopi, 2003).   BB*

Johnson, Denis
(1949–) Born in Munich, and works as a freelance writer. His first two collections, *The Man Among the Seals* (Stone Wall, 1969) and *Inner Weather* (Graywolf, 1976), demonstrated that he was an obliquely satirical poet with a preference for odd subjects seen from weird perspectives.

Where *Ginsberg's *Howl* speaks for a generation invigorated by rebellion and self-expression, Johnson's *Incognito Lounge* (Random House, 1982) speaks for a generation dissipated by its own self-gratification; it is a raw and original examination of contemporary suburban and urban life, of secular humanism becoming mere consumerism. Intimate and surreal, the poems are confessions of an Everyman turned Anycustomer, who tries to dissipate his failures through cinematic fantasies, shopping, drinking, and changing sexual accomplices. Johnson's subsequent book of poetry, *The Veil* (Knopf, 1987), is neither as concentrated nor as unified a book, although it contains a few splendid dramatic monologues, such as 'The Monk's Insomnia' and 'Talking Richard Wilson Blues'.

In 1995, he published a new and collected volume under the title *The Throne of the Third Heaven of the Nations Millennium General Assembly* (HarperCollins). Since then, Johnson has concentrated on his career as a writer of fiction—notably, with a semi-autobiographical collection of stories about addiction, *Jesus' Son* (Farrar, Straus, 1992)—and latterly as a playwright.   DWF

Johnson, James Weldon
(1871–1938) Born in Jacksonville, Florida, studied law, and became the principal of the grammar school he had attended. He moved to New York City and in 1900 collaborated with his brother, J. Rosamond Johnson, on 'Lift Every Voice and Sing', extremely popular among black Americans, as well as on a number of other songs and musicals.

The multi-talented Johnson served the US consular service in Venezuela and Nicaragua between 1906 and 1913, and his novel about 'passing', *The Autobiography of an Ex-Colored Man* (1912), published anonymously, caused a stir, although *God's Trombones* (1927), sermons by a black preacher in free-verse paragraphs that simulated impelling oratory rhythms, had a greater critical impact. He rejected the minstrel dialect employed in early poems, and among his later successes are 'O Black and Unknown Bards', a tribute to the creation of the spiritual, and 'Brothers', a graphic account of a black man burned to death by a white mob that echoes Edwin Markham and foreshadows William Faulkner.

Ever conscious of his historic racial mission, Johnson compiled *The Book of American Negro Poetry* (1922), a pioneering anthology, and with his brother edited *The Book of American Negro Spirituals* (1925). He also served as field secretary for the NAACP (National Association for the Advancement of Colored People) then became its general secretary. In 1930, however, he resigned to assume the post of professor of creative literature at Fisk University. He was killed in a car accident.

Johnson's verses can be found in *The Poetry of the Negro 1746–1970*, ed. Langston Hughes and Arna Bontemps (Doubleday, 1970) and *The Black Poets*, ed. Dudley Randall (Bantam, 1971).   EB

Johnson, Kent (1955–) Born in Springfield, Massachusetts, Johnson grew up in Latin America, and studied at the University of Wisconsin-Milwaukee. He taught literacy in Nicaragua for the Sandinistas in the 1980s, and now teaches at Highland Community College, Illinois. An engaged satirist of domestic avant-garde movements such as *Language and *Conceptual poetry, Johnson is a literary internationalist, who has edited anthologies of poetry from Russia and Uruguay, and, with Forrest *Gander, translated the Bolivian poet Jáime Saenz. Often mixing fact and fiction in his writing, Johnson was involved in bringing the invented Japanese poet 'Araki Yarasuda' to an American reader-

ship: see *Doubled Flowering: From the Notebooks of Araki Yarasuda* (Roof, 1998).

Collections of his own verse include *Epigramititis: 118 Living American Poets* (BlazeVox, 2006), which summarizes the contemporary scene in sardonic, imagistic snapshots, and *Homage to the Last Avant-Garde* (Shearsman, 2008), a British volume that includes his parodies of the *New York School. In 2010, *A Question Mark Above the Sun*, Johnson's critical 'thought experiment' proposing that Kenneth *Koch wrote one of Frank *O'Hara's best-known poems, was published by Punch Press. Despite legal threats, an expanded edition appeared from Starcherone Books in 2012.   JNT

Johnson, Linton Kwesi (1952–) Born in Chapleton, Jamaica, and educated at Tulse Hill Comprehensive School (Brixton) and Goldsmiths' College of the University of London, where he took a BA in sociology. As a political activist with the Black Panther Movement, he organized a poetry workshop which was expanded to include musicians, the group calling itself Rasta Love. The poetry he performed with this band was influenced by reggae rhythms, but the poems stand on their own, though performed with musical accompaniment. These poems of articulate, if highly demotic, protest came to be called '*dub poetry' by Johnson. The style of dub poetry has been described by James *Berry as 'over-compensation for deprivation'. Rage and belligerent overstatement are its keynotes, but also optimistic vitality, energy, and exuberance. Other prominent practitioners in Britain include John *Agard and Benjamin *Zephaniah.

Johnson's work includes *Voices of the Living and the Dead* (Race Today, 1974), *Dread Beat An' Blood* (Bogle L'Ouverture, 1975), *Inglan is a Bitch* (Race Today, 1980), and *Tings an Times: Selected Poems* (Bloodaxe, 1991). His recordings include, on the Virgin label, *Dread Beat An' Blood* (1978) and, on the Island label, *Forces of Victory* (1979), *Bass Culture* (1980), and *Making History* (1984). A CD, *LKJ A CAPELLA LIVE*, was issued on his own label, LKJ Records, in 1996. In 2002 *Mi Revalueshanary Fren*, a selected poems introduced by Fred *D'Aguiar, was published by Penguin Classics (new edn., 2006). In 2005, Johnson was awarded a Silver Musgrave Medal for poetry by the Institute of Jamaica.   MR

Johnson, Louis (1924–88) Born in Feilding, New Zealand, son of a policeman. In the late 1940s he entered Wellington Teachers' College and quickly became the angry young man of the capital's literary life during a drab period of post-war austerity and repression. He was a leading member of the socially conscious *Wellington Group of poets, and in 1951 he published a collection of poems, *Roughshod Among the Lilies*, with the Pegasus Press. He was editor of two important literary magazines of the period, *Arachne* and *Numbers*, established the *New Zealand Poetry Yearbook* (1951–64), and founded the Capricorn Press.

In 1968, feeling that New Zealand had become 'an unacceptably suppressive society', Johnson moved to Papua New Guinea. This was followed by a long period as a lecturer in creative writing at the Mitchell College of Advanced Education in New South Wales. He published two collections in Australia, the second of which, *Fires and Patterns* (Jacaranda), was awarded the New Zealand Book Award in 1975. He returned to Wellington in 1980 to take up the annual literary fellowship at Victoria University, serving on the New Zealand Literary Fund Advisory Committee from 1982 until his death in England in November 1988. He was awarded the OBE in 1987.

As a poet Louis Johnson looked beyond the historical and landscape-painting poetry of the Thirties and Forties and opened up a new urban subject-matter. Probably his best collection is *Bread and a Pension* (Pegasus, 1964) in which the influence of *Auden is augmented by a growing feeling for the vernacular. He was a passionate, sometimes clumsy, and often witty poet, dedicated to his own creative sources, with a recognizable voice and 'a concern with the *what* of a poem rather than the How'.   PB

Johnson, Ronald (1935–98) Born Ashland, Kansas and studied at the University of Kansas and Columbia. Johnson wrote several successful cookbooks including *The American Table* (Morrow, 1983).

Johnson's poetry expresses what has been described by Eric Selinger as an Orphic drive to explore the interactions 'between the world and the mind that has evolved to behold and re-create it'. Eye and ear are pivotal. Emphasis is on vision and an innovative use of 'different musics': modernist collage poetics; outsider art; cosmology and physics; Charles Ives; William Blake; and Henry David Thoreau. *The Book of the Green Man* (Norton, 1967), Johnson's 'attempt, as a brash American, to make new the traditional British long seasonal poem' stems from his travels in the UK. *Songs of the Earth* (Grabhorn-Hoyem, 1970) is the lyrical culmination of Johnson's involvement with concrete poetry via his friendship with Ian Hamilton *Finlay.

The major books are *Radi os* (Sand Dollar, 1977)—a rewriting-by-excision of the first four books of Milton's *Paradise Lost*—and *ARK* (Living Batch Press, 1996). Written over twenty years, and comprising ninety-nine poems in three parts—*The Foundations* (North Point Press, 1980), *ARK 50: Spires 34-40* (E. P. Dutton, 1984), and 'The Ramparts'—*ARK* counters the 'risks and shipwrecks' of the American modernist epic (i.e. *Pound's *Cantos*) by being 'a poem without history'. *ARK*'s democratic scope, its embrace of 'kosmos', and its celebration of the American grain (particularly Kansas), also invites comparison with *Leaves of Grass*. See Ross Hair, *Ronald Johnson's Modernist Collage Poetry* (Palgrave, 2011).   ROH

Johnston, Andrew (1963–   ) Grew up in the Hutt Valley, and studied at the universities of Otago and Auckland. He was literary editor of the *Wellington Evening Post* before moving to Europe, where he lived in France and worked for the *Observer* in London, and later the *International Herald Tribune* in Paris. Johnston has been called 'the most important new poet to come out of New Zealand in the Nineties'. His first collection, *How to Talk* (1993), which won the New Zealand Book Award for Poetry, established his interest in the poetry of casual speech, something he shares with his compatriot Jenny *Bornholdt. The title poem of his second book, *The Sounds* (1996), is a sestina which revolves the words 'plain', 'small', 'the', 'listening', 'water', and 'touch'. His third book, *The Open Window* (1999), a new and selected volume, published in the UK by Arc, was followed by *The Birds of Europe* (2000). All his books have been published in New Zealand by Victoria University Press. *Sol* (Victoria University Press, 2007; Arc, 2008) features an elegy for the poet's father, 'The Sunflower', in double-sestina form. He founded the online poetry digest, *The Page*, and edited, with Robyn Marsack, *Twenty Contemporary New Zealand Poets* (Carcanet, 2009).   JNT

Johnston, George (Benson) (1913– 2004) Born in Hamilton, Ontario, and educated at the University of Toronto. From 1950 to 1979 he taught English at Carleton University in Ottawa, specializing in Old English and Old Norse. In 1971 he was awarded an honorary degree by Queen's University, and in 1979 by Carleton University.

Johnston started as a writer of fiction, and began to write poetry regularly only after the Second World War, publishing in journals. By the time he was almost 60 he had published only two small volumes of original poetry. *The Cruising Auk* (1959) revealed his talent for serious light verse as it wittily, and with a kind of melancholy comedy, depicted an almost surreal landscape, a small city and its characters through childhood, innocence, domesticity, happiness, adult disappointments, and doom. The same qualities are displayed in *Home Free* (1966), which includes two long poems, 'Under the Tree', about capital punishment, and a narrative poem, 'Love in High Places'. These two collections, along with new poems—lyrics and brief narratives—made up *Happy Enough: Poems 1935–1972* (1972—all Oxford University Press), in which Johnston's true

nature as a serious poet of personal and domestic themes became clear. His later volumes were *Taking a Grip* (Golden Dog, 1978), perhaps his best book; *Ask Again* (Penumbra, 1984); and his collected poems, *Endeared by Dark* (Porcupine's Quill, 1990).

In Johnston's later volumes many poems are of a valedictory nature, and in their lack of formal ostentation and their relaxed, unpretentious diction, they seem to come as close to the commonplace and the prosaic as they can. In the introduction to *Endeared by Dark* he emphasizes the importance of knowing the medium intimately in terms of its history, diction, syntax, and rhythms. The naturalness of his art hides such a sophisticated awareness, and a density of suggestion is attained in his seemingly uncontrived presentation of experience.

Johnston translated from the Old Norse *The Saga of Gisli* (1963), *The Faroe Islanders' Saga* (1974), and *The Greenlanders' Saga* (1976). He also translated works by modern Norwegian, Icelandic, and Faroese writers, including an anthology of Faroese poetry, *Rocky Shores* (1981). He emphasized the importance of translation, both as a cultural act and as a creative discipline.   ATT

Johnston, Martin (Clift) (1947–90) The son of the writers George Johnston and Charmian Clift. He was born in Sydney but grew up and went to schools on the Greek islands of Kalymnos and Hydra where the Johnston family lived and worked between 1954 and 1964. Johnston's adult life was divided between Sydney and Greece, before his untimely death in Sydney in 1990, and his writing often reflects these cross-cultural experiences. While a student at Sydney University in the late 1960s Johnston was heavily involved in anti-Vietnam protests; he became an important figure in the young generation of Australian intellectuals and writers who began to publish in the early 1970s.

Johnston's earliest poetry is surreal in its imagery and dazzlingly erudite, qualities which his writing displays throughout. The elegance of his lyricism is never compromised by his eye for exotic detail or the swiftness and complexities of his thought. (The analogy between Johnston's poetry and his expert interest in chess is one that reviewers have noticed.) As well as intellectuality and allusiveness, there is an underlying elegiac mood, present from early poems such as the one in memory of his father, 'The Sea-Cucumber', which breaks through at moments with great power, as in these lines from the posthumously published 'Grief': 'Love is the subject and love's loss the text. | Grief breaks the heart and yet the grief comes next.'

Johnston's poems are represented in most anthologies of contemporary Australian poetry. He published three collections during his lifetime, *Shadowmass* (Arts Society Publications, 1971), *The Sea-Cucumber* (University of Queensland Press, 1978), and *The Typewriter Considered as a Bee-Trap* (Hale & Iremonger, 1984), and a series of translations *Ithaka: Modern Greek Poetry in Translation* (Island, 1973). He also published an experimental novel *Cicada Gambit* (Hale & Iremonger, 1983). *Selected Poems and Prose*, ed. John Tranter, came out in 1993 (University of Queensland Press).

See also *George Johnston: A Biography*, by Garry Kinnane (Nelson, 1986).   PM

Jones, Brian (1938–2009) Born in London, and was a schoolmaster by profession. He later lived in France. His first two collections, *Poems* (1966) and *A Family Album* (1968), attracted a good deal of attention and had unusually high sales for poetry. Here, it seemed to many readers and reviewers, was an energetic, blunt poet using conventional procedures without recourse to clichés, archaisms, or poeticisms. Critics discerned the intelligently exploited influence of Edward *Thomas, as well as potentialities for narrative. The contents of *A Family Album*, especially the 'Aunt Emily' poems, demonstrated an ability for lucid characterization not often seen in English poets at the time. Expectations were maintained with *Interior* (1969) and *For Mad Mary* (1974—all London Magazine), whose title-poem evoked wide praise. His two succeeding collections, *The Island Normal* (1980) and *The Children of Separation*

(1985—both Carcanet), contained both lyrics in the old manner, and more experimental narratives. *The Spitfire on the Northern Line* (Chatto & Windus, 1975) was a collection for children. His last book of verse was *Freeborn John* (Carcanet, 1990). Interviewed in 2001, Jones acknowledged that publication had become less important to him that 'the absolutely vital' process of writing.   MS-S*

Jones, David (Michael) (1895–1974) Born in Brockley, Kent, to an English mother and Welsh father. He attended Camberwell School of Art and joined the Royal Welch Fusiliers as a private in 1914, serving until 1918. His experiences in the earlier phase of the war became the basis for his long poem, *In Parenthesis*, eventually published in 1937 (Faber; Chilmark, 1961). In 1921, he became a Roman Catholic, and the following year joined Eric Gill's community of artists and craftsmen at Ditchling, Sussex, remaining there, at Capel-y-ffin in Wales, and at Pigotts in Buckinghamshire for a number of years, and being briefly engaged to Gill's daughter, Petra. In 1928 he visited Lourdes and Salies-de-Bearn, country which figures prominently in his paintings, and in 1934 he went to Cairo and Jerusalem with Gill, a trip influential on both the conception and imagery of his later writings, *The Anathemata* (Faber, 1952; Chilmark, 1963) and *The Sleeping Lord and Other Fragments* (Faber, 1974). He subsequently lived a fairly solitary life in Sidmouth, Devon, and, after 1939, in London, occasionally suffering depression and breakdown and becoming increasingly withdrawn, but maintaining his output as poet, painter, engraver, and calligrapher; he was supported partly by various kinds of patronage. From 1940 he also wrote an increasing number of reviews, radio talks, and essays, primarily on the arts, mythology, and aesthetic theory: they are collected in *Epoch and Artist* (Faber/Chilmark, 1959) and *The Dying Gaul* (Faber, 1978). Praised by T. S. *Eliot (who wrote an introduction for the paperback edition of *In Parenthesis* in 1963, calling it 'a work of genius') and W. H. *Auden, he was awarded the CH in 1974.

All of Jones' work is essentially interdependent, drawing on a central fund of preoccupations and motifs, deriving partly from heterogeneous and arcane sources: Welsh mythology, particularly *The Mabinogion;* Malory; the liturgy and forms of his heterodox Catholicism; certain key texts of archaeology and anthropology. Motifs from sources such as these are woven into *In Parenthesis*, where they create a rich verbal texture and place the First World War in a large historical and mythological perspective. *In Parenthesis* is his only narrative poem: both *The Anathemata* and *The Sleeping Lord* are more fragmentary and episodic. *The Anathemata* comes with a lengthy introduction, dense annotation, and Jones' own illustrations. It is an attempt to define his own complex cultural identity as an Anglo-Welshman; to articulate a view of the history of Britain and a Christian understanding of the relationship between history and the Incarnation; and to celebrate various manifestations of man as artist. The individual poems of the *Sleeping Lord* sequence are more straightforwardly approachable, being dramatizations of historical moments, particularly that of the Crucifixion, and monologues spoken in the characters of, for instance, Roman centurions. Both these works, however, depend on an even larger conception which Jones never brought to realization: its remaining fragments were edited by Harman Grisewood and Renè Hague and published in 1981 as *The Roman Quarry and Other Sequences*. *Wedding Poems* (Enitharmon, 2002), ed. Thomas Dilworth, prints two private celebrations written during the Blitz. A late British modernist, indebted to Eliot and *Joyce (though not to *Pound, with whom he has more frequently been compared), Jones has never been fully assimilated by English literary criticism, though his strength and significance have been attested by such later poets as Seamus *Heaney, Geoffrey *Hill, and John *Montague. His letters are available in *Dai Greatcoat: A Self-Portrait of David Jones in His Letters* (Faber, 1980).

See also John Matthias (ed.), *David Jones: Man and Poet* (National Poetry Foundation, 1989), Keith Aldritt, *David Jones: Writer and Artist* (Constable & Robinson, 2003), and Thomas Dilworth, *Reading David Jones* (University of Wales Press, 2008).   NC

Jones, D. G. (Douglas Gordon) (1929–)
Born in Bancroft, Ontario, and educated at McGill University and Queens University, Kingston, bastions of Anglo-Canadian tradition. He taught English in Quebec, at Sherbrooke, a French-language university. He was one of the founding editors of *Ellipse*, a magazine in which Canada's English and French poetries are translated.

Jones has published nine books of poetry since the mid-Fifties. He also translated a volume of selected poems by the Quebec poet Paul-Marie Lapointe, for publication in the United States. The Quebec journal *Urgences* published a Jones poem, 'Rock Garden: October', along with forty translations of it by Quebec's prominent poets. In 1993, his translation of Normand de Bellefeuille's *Categorics One, Two and Three* (1992) won the Governor General's Award for Translation.

Jones' poetry is lyrical and imagist, marked by economy and precision. Typically he attends to the details of seasonal change, especially around his home in Quebec's Eastern Townships. But as did one of his literary sources, William Carlos *Williams, he has also found fellowship and energy in the works of painters, such as the Canadian painter David Milne in *Under the Thunder the Flowers Light Up the Earth* (1977), and Balthus, in *Balthazar and Other Poems* (1988), which received the A. M. Klein Prize for Poetry, as did his 1995 volume, *The Floating Garden* (1995—all Coach House). Jones might best be described as a meditative poet, but one who resembles a painter or a composer more than a philosopher. His longer poems are suites rather than excursions.

In 1970 Jones published *Butterfly on Rock* (University of Toronto Press), a thematic study of Canadian literature which has become a standard work of criticism. It explores biblical echoes in Canadian writing, especially images of the expulsion of Adam and Eve. Jones honours Northrop Frye and prizes human courage that will face down the human fear of the other: 'The only effective defence for a garrison culture is to abandon defence, to let down the walls and let the wilderness in, even to the wolves.' His later collections include *Wild Asterisks in Cloud* (1997) and *Grounding Sight* (1999—both Empyreal). In 2007 Jones became an Officer of the Order of Canada. *The Stream Exposed with All its Stones: Collected Poems* (Véhicule/Signal) appeared in 2010.   GHB

Jones, Evan (1931–   ) Born and brought up in Melbourne, Jones is a product of Melbourne University and taught there, in the English department, for many years. His first book, *Inside the Whale* (Cheshire, 1960) and its successor *Understandings* (Melbourne University Press, 1967) are filled with skilfully wrought lyrics, songs, extended odes, and a variety of forms such as villanelles and nursery rhymes. In these poems Jones moulds the vernacular with great verve and displays an eye for exact observation, together with a wide knowledge of western European myth. His early 'Address to the Pure Scholars' and his late 'Insomnia' are those rare things, sestinas which are not otiose.

Jones held a Stanford Writing Fellowship in the period 1958 to 1960 and the influence of Yvor *Winters, succeeding that of *Auden, confirmed him in his didactic and heuristic approach to poetry. Thus his work was at variance with the tone which prevailed in Australian poetry during the Sixties and Seventies, a time when his technical skill and pre-eminence as a formal master should have afforded him wide recognition and influence. There is an irony inherent in Evan Jones' position as a formalist among a people which distrusts tradition and virtuosity. He, more than any of his colleagues, celebrates ordinary human emotions in the vernacular mode.

See also: *Recognitions* (Australian National University, 1978) and *Left at the Post* (University of Queensland Press, 1984). In 2010, Picaro Press printed a second edition of *Understandings* and a volume of new work, *Alone at Last*.   PNFP

Jones, Glyn (1905–95) Born in Merthyr Tydfil, Glamorgan, and worked for most of his life as a teacher at schools in Cardiff.

His early work, published as *Poems* (1939), shows in its alliteration the author's lifelong fascination with poetic disciplines in Welsh and attempts to reproduce in English the effects of Welsh prosody and the Welsh praise-tradition. The long poem *The Dream of Jake Hopkins* (1944), originally written for broadcasting, deals with his often unhappy experience as a teacher, while 'Merthyr' takes as its subject (as does the work of Leslie *Norris) the town in which he grew up. The short stories and novels of Glyn Jones reveal the same qualities as his poetry: full of pathos and humour, they are essential for an understanding of the themes and special effects of his verse. Among his other works are the translations *The Saga of Llywarch the Old* (1955) and two collections of Welsh harpstanzas.

Although his output as a poet was comparatively small, Glyn Jones continued to write well into old age. His *Selected Poems* (Gomer, 1975) reprints his early work; a second edition, subtitled *Fragments and Fictions* (Seren, 1988), presents a further eighteen poems.

There is an essay on Glyn Jones in the Writers of Wales series (1973); see also the author's memoir of literary life in Wales, *Setting Out* (1982). Most important of all is his autobiography, *The Dragon Has Two Tongues* (1968). *The Collected Poems of Glyn Jones*, ed. Meic Stephens, was published by University of Wales Press in 1996. On National Poetry Day 2005, the Glyn Jones Centre opened in Cardiff as a resource for Welsh writers.   MS

Jones, Jill (1951–   ) Born in Sydney in 1951, she has worked in a variety of fields, including legal publishing, journalism, public policy, arts administration, and as a freelance writer and editor. She was a co-founder of the gay and lesbian imprint Black Wattle Press in the late 1980s, and a member of the collective producing Refractory Girl, then Australia's longest-running feminist magazine. With Judith Beveridge and Louise Wakeling, she edited the poetry anthology *A Parachute of Blue* (1995), and with Michael Farrell, she co-edited *Out of the Box: Contemporary Australian Gay and Lesbian Poets* (2009). She is currently a senior lecturer in creative writing at the University of Adelaide.

Her first book, *The Mask and the Jagged Star*, appeared from the New Zealand publisher Hazard Press in 1992 and won the Dame Mary Gilmore Award in 1993. She has since published eight poetry collections, including *Screens Jets Heaven: New and Selected Poems* (Salt), winner of the Kenneth Slessor Prize in 2003. Her poetry brings a Romantic sensibility to urban contexts, explicitly arguing against a nationalistic 'bush tradition' that ignores the largely urban experience of Australians.   ACr

Jones, LeRoi See BARAKA, AMIRI.

Jones, Rae Desmond (1941–) Born in the mining town of Broken Hill in western New South Wales, a city memorably depicted in his first novel, *The Lemon Tree* (Angus & Robertson, 1990). He graduated at 35 from the University of Sydney, by which time he was well established as one of a new, urban generation of Australian writers loosely centred on himself and John *Tranter, and now generally tagged as the *Generation of '68.

Jones helped project the image of the 'new poetry' through personal performances of his work in a wide range of settings, especially in venues not normally associated with literature. In his private life he took a number of casual jobs before joining the Commonwealth Employment Service and, later, becoming an English and history teacher at Granville Boys' High School in Sydney's western suburbs. He has released an LP, *Two Voluminous Gentlemen* (1977) with Norman Talbot, and a video, *Rae Jones: Poet With A Tuba* (1985). He was founding editor of the journal *Your Friendly Fascist*, which appeared for several years.

In his early poetry Jones projected a violent and anarchic persona with strong self-destructive attitudes but also an underlying sensitivity of response, echoing a back-

ground later developed with clarity in his first novel. *The Mad Vibe* (Fragment, 1975), his second collection, tellingly enunciates this stage of his creative development. It was succeeded by *Shakti* (Makar, 1977), which retains the tone of personal assertiveness but focuses more on the external world. *Walking the Line* (1979), a collection of short stories, may be seen as an exploration of more extended forms and of prose as a device for 'poetic' expression.

Jones' work is discussed in two books that explore the poetry of this period: *A Possible Contemporary Poetry: Interviews with Thirteen Poets from The New Australian Poetry*, ed. M. Duwell (1982), and *Parnassus Mad Ward: Michael Dransfield and the New Australian Poetry*, ed. L. Dobrez (1990). After *The Palace of Art* (Makar, 1981) Jones did not publish another collection until *Blow Out* (Island, 2009), which followed a period during which he served as Mayor of Ashfield Council in Sydney.   TWS

Jones, Rodney (1950–) Born in Falkville, Alabama, and reared in rural northern Alabama. He attended the University of Alabama where he met the poet Everette *Maddox, an early formative influence on his poetry. Jones graduated from the University of Alabama in 1971 with a degree in English literature. He then attended the University of North Carolina at Greensboro, receiving an MFA in creative writing in 1973. Since that time he has taught English and creative writing in public schools and universities. He has been on the faculty of the department of English at Southern Illinois University since 1984.

Like many poets of the southern United States, Jones writes often about the power of the past. A theme that runs through his work is the ability of the imagination to give meaning to personal memory and thus define the present in terms of the past. This theme is central to his first book, *The Story They Told Us of Light* (University of Alabama Press, 1980), although most poems in the book seem to be well-made apprentice works. It was not until the publication of *The Unborn* (Atlantic Monthly, 1985), that Jones found his own voice, using a longer line combined with devices of conversational poetry as diverse as those employed by Robert *Frost and C. K. *Williams. After the publication of his second book he received a number of grants and awards. Most significant of these was the 1990 National Book Critics Circle Award given to his third book, *Transparent Gestures* (1989). He has published a number of volumes since then, including *Apocalyptic Narrative and Other Poems* (1993), *Elegy for the Southern Drawl* (1999), and *Salvation Blues: One Hundred Poems 1985-2005* (2006), which won the Kingsley Tufts Poetry Award. His ninth collection is *Imaginary Logic* (2011—all Houghton).   LS

Jones, Sally Roberts (1935–   ) Born in London but brought up in north Wales and educated at the University College of North Wales, Bangor. Formerly a reference librarian, she lives in Port Talbot, West Glamorgan, where she and her husband own the Barn Owl Press, a children's books imprint. Many of her precise, ironical poems deal with the darker side of everyday life, often in an urban setting, but she is also concerned with aspects of local history and with her family over several generations. Her volumes of verse include *Turning Away* (1969), *The Forgotten Country* (1977 —both Gomer), and *Relative Values* (Poetry Wales, 1985). She has also published a monograph on the novelist Allen Raine in the Writers of Wales series (University of Wales Press, 1979). *Notes for a Life*, a new and selected volume, appeared in 2010 from Headland.   MS

Jones, T. Harri (Thomas Henry) (1921– 65) Born on a hill-farm near Llanafan Fawr, Builth, Breconshire. He was educated at the University College of Wales, Aberystwyth, where he read English, and his first teaching post was at the Naval Dockyard Apprentices' School in Portsmouth. In 1959 he emigrated to Australia where he became a lecturer at the University of New South Wales in Newcastle.

His first volume, *The Enemy in the Heart* (1957), showed promise in its exploration of the tension between a young man's sexual passion and the curbing influence of a narrowly religious upbringing. In Australia he was active in literary and academic circles but suffered from depression and the problems associated with heavy drinking. He nevertheless began to free himself in his next volume, *Songs of a Mad Prince* (1960), from the influence of Dylan *Thomas and R. S. *Thomas and from the metaphysical conceits on which he had relied too much in his early work. In *The Beast at the Door* (1963) there are a number of memorable love-portraits and some moving evocations of the Wales from which he had escaped but which he could not put out of mind. In the complexity of its emotions and its mastery of colloquial language this volume was his best achievement. Among his other themes were the sea, war, and the loss of religious belief. The *confessional mode of his later writing, collected in the posthumous volume, *The Colour of Cockcrowing* (1966), pointed towards the possibility of further development which was not to be. The poet was found drowned in a disused bathing-pool near his home on 29 January 1965.

The *Collected Poems* of T. Harri Jones was edited by Don Dale-Jones and Julian Croft (Gomer, 1977); the latter also contributed an essay on the poet in the Writers of Wales series (Cardiff, 1976).   MS

Jordan, June (1936–2002) Born in Harlem to Jamaican immigrant parents, Jordan grew up in New York, where she studied at Barnard College and Columbia University. She held many academic positions, culminating in a professorship of Afro-American studies and women's studies at the University of California, Berkeley, where she founded the Poetry for the People teacher-training programme. She was also a playwright, essayist, and leading voice in African-American activism and progressive politics, who early in her career worked with Buckminster Fuller on an architectural project for the redesign of Harlem.

Directed by Desire: The Complete Poems of June Jordan (Copper Canyon, 2005) collects ten books of poetry, with a foreword by Adrienne *Rich, who describes how Jordan 'believed in and lived the urgency of the word—along with action'. Her poetry begins with the ekphrastic *Who Look At Me* (Crowell, 1969), a series of portraits of black America for young adults written in a corresponding idiom, looking back to the example of Langston *Hughes. Emphatic orality is an important quality of her free verse, which ranges from poems of social protest to love lyrics.

She also edited *Soulscript: Afro-American Poetry* (Doubleday, 1970), an influential anthology for young people. Jordan's memoir *Soldier: A Poet's Childhood* (2000) reflects on her difficult relationship with her father. Her last book was *Some of Us Did Not Die: New and Selected Essays of June Jordan* (2002—both Basic/Civitas). See Valerie Kinloch, *June Jordan: Her Life and Letters* (Greenwood, 2006).   JNT

Joseph, Anthony (1966–) Born in Trinidad, Joseph studied creative writing at Goldsmiths College, University of London, where he also teaches. He was the first poet-in-residence for the British Council at California State University, Los Angeles, and performs and tours with The Spasm Band. He has said, 'For me, poetry is music.' His first collections, *Desafinado* (1994) and *Teragaton* (1998), were published by Poison Engine Press, which also issued a spoken-word CD, *Liquid Textology* (2005). The autobiographical *Bird Head Son* (2009) brought his combination of syncopated prosody, surreal imagery, and Trinidadian speech patterns to a wider audience. Its title poem, dedicated to Kamau *Brathwaite, ends: 'Ai, you is bird head son? | You mus be bird head son f'true | cause your father head | did small too.' Joseph has also published a novel, *The African Origins of UFOs* (2006). His latest collection is *Rubber Orchestras* (2011—all Salt).   JNT

Joseph, Jenny (1932–) Born in Birmingham, and educated at St Hilda's College, Oxford. She has worked as a newspaper reporter, an adult-education lecturer, and a pub landlady, and has lived in South Africa. Her first collection of poems, *The Unlooked-for Season* (Scorpion Press, 1960), won an Eric Gregory award. *Selected Poems* (Bloodaxe, 1992) draws on her first four collections, among them *Rose in the Afternoon and Other Poems* (Secker, 1974). It was a poem from the latter collection, 'When I am Old, I Shall Wear Purple' which won a BBC poll for Britain's Favourite Modern Poem in 2006. Jenny Joseph has published experimental fiction, children's books, a gardening memoir, and further collections of poetry, including a new and later selected poems, *Extreme of Things* (Bloodaxe, 2006), and a selection of her love poems, *Nothing Like Love* (Enitharmon, 2010).

Intellectually astringent, philosophical, intense, occasionally prolix, Jenny Joseph has always been drawn to the longer poem, an interest that culminates in the engrossing counterpoint of her prize-winning poem-novel, *Persephone* (Bloodaxe, 1985).   CAR

Joseph, M. K. (Michael Kennedy) (1914–81) Born in Chingford, Essex, but spent much of his post-war childhood in Belgium and France, gaining the international range of sympathy and polyglot cultivation which enrich his work. His parents settled in 1924 in New Zealand, where he became a professor of English at Auckland University. He died there shortly after retirement.

The only interruption was artillery service in the Second World War, an experience which dominated his literary and moral thought. Usually regarded as a poet of scholarly elegance, and indeed skilled in word-play, satire, and learned meditation, Joseph also brought an intense visual memory to his treatment of war and other contemporary subjects. He borrowed forms from film and a sense of cosmic scale from science-fiction (in which he was a superior novelist), notably the awesome Wellsian montage of past and future in 'Epilogue to a Poetry Reading'. In novels like *A Soldier's Tale* (1976) and in varied poems, including the Owen-like 'Elegy on the Unburied Dead', Joseph is a truthful and powerful writer on war.

Eschewing *confessional intimacies, his work more obliquely frames personal feeling, as in pastiches such as 'Meditation on a Time-Piece'. Most distinctive, however, is his habitual confrontation of the moral complexities of cruelty and mercy, apocalypse and hope, based in, but not constrained by, his Catholic faith.

Inscription on a Paper Dart (Oxford University Press, 1974) is his selected poems.   RR

Joyce, James (Augustine Aloysius) (1882–1941) Born in Dublin and educated in Jesuit schools there. He studied English, French, and Italian at University College, and took Gaelic League Irish classes under Padraig Pearse. In 1904 he and Nora Barnacle (they married in 1930) left Ireland for Trieste, where he wrote *Dubliners* (1914) and *A Portrait of the Artist as a Young Man* (1916). He lived in Zurich from 1915 to 1919, and in 1920 moved to Paris where he spent most of the rest of his life. At the outbreak of the Second World War he left Paris for Zurich, where he died. His major works are the novels *Ulysses* (1922) and *Finnegans Wake* (1939); he published a play, *Exiles*, in 1918.

Joyce's first literary ambitions were in poetry but his gift for detailed circumstantiality was more suited to the extensive novel form. Attempts have been made to describe *Finnegans Wake* as poetry because of its highlighting of language rather than narrative (and *Giacomo Joyce* can be seen as a linked series of elegant prose poems, describing a love-affair). Joyce published two slight volumes of lyric poems: *Chamber Music* (1907: his first published work), and *Poems Penyeach* (1927). These are formally tight and conventional in diction, remote from the experimental language of *Finnegans Wake*. The persona in the thirty-six poems of *Chamber Music* (single-voiced like a Schubert song-cycle: Joyce called the collection 'a suite of songs' and set one of the poems to music himself) is the young lover, alternately lovelorn and sensual, as he serenades his beloved. The cycle has been variously interpreted as codedly suggestive (chamber-pots) or symbolic (the chamber-size constrictions of the lover's mind).

Apart from several Swiftean broadsides on the Irish literary revivalists, most notably 'The Holy Office' (1904) and 'Gas from a Burner' (1912), and the exquisite 'Eccepuer' marking the birth of his grandson (1932), *Poems Penyeach* (1927) collects the rest of Joyce's poetic output. These thirteen poems illustrate Joyce's enduring taste for the nostalgic (*Pound told him they were not worth publishing), and 'Tilly' is the only one which is much anthologized.

The best guide to Joyce's poems is Richard Ellmann, *James Joyce* (revd. edn., Oxford University Press, 1982). They are included in R. Ellmann, A. Walton Litz, and John Whittier-Ferguson (eds.), *James Joyce: Poems and Shorter Writings* (Faber, 1991).   BO'D

Joyce, Trevor (1947–) Born and grew up in Dublin, reading English and philosophy at the University College. He later read mathematical sciences at University College, Cork, and worked as a business systems analyst for Apple. In 1997, he founded the SoundEye Cork International Poetry Festival, and has been a full-time writer since 2000. As a student in Dublin in the late 1960s, Joyce co-founded New Writers' Press with the poet Michael Smith. Their aim was to promote a more eclectic poetry in Ireland, publishing volumes by Paul *Durcan, Jack *Spicer, César Vallejo, and Brian *Coffey, as well as a magazine of international modernist poetics, *The Lace Curtain*.

Joyce's debut was *Sole Glum Trek* (1967). A cover note warned readers that the reality described by poetry 'is not yet accessible to scientific methods'. *Watches* (1969) and *Pentahedron* (1972—all New Writers' Press) followed. In 1976, Joyce published *The Poems of Sweeny Peregrine*, his 'working' of the Middle Irish *Buile Suibhne,* later rendered by Seamus *Heaney as *Sweeney Astray*. In the 1980s, Joyce studied and taught Chinese and Japanese poetry. The lyricism of *stone floods*, his next volume (New Writers' Press, 1995), evinces this influence; *Syzygy* (Wild Honey, 1997), that of John *Cage and Tom *Raworth. *with the first dream of fire they hunt the cold* (New Writers' Press/Shearsman, 2001) is a collected volume. See also *What's in Store* (The Gig, 2007) and *Courts of Air and Earth* (Shearsman, 2008), a book of translations.   JNT

Jussawalla, Adil (Jehangir) (1940–) Born in Bombay (now Mumbai) and educated at the Cathedral School there. He read English at University College, Oxford, and returned to India in 1970. Between 1972 and 1975 he was lecturer in English at St Xavier's College, Bombay. He has edited the seminal *New Writing in India* (Penguin, 1974) and worked for various Bombay newspapers and magazines. He has also been associated with two small presses, Clearing House and Praxis.

Though he tends to be dismissive about his first book, *Land's End* (Writers Workshop, 1962) is a remarkably confident volume. Its anxieties and attitudes may belong to a young man, but a much older person seems to have handled the verse. Jussawalla wrote these poems in England or some part of Europe, and has said they are 'about a resentment' at being abroad. This is not entirely true, for many of them are strongly affected by the sense of place. His longest and most ambitious work so far, however, is the title sequence of *Missing Person* (Clearing House, 1976). 'Missing Person' is a metaphor for the Indian bourgeois intellectual, 'our two-bit hero', for whom English, the language learnt in school, becomes, for the rest of his life, 'a piece of tin' aimed at his throat. The sequence maps an area of historical rifts few Indian poets have looked at.

Jussawalla's collections are now out of print, but poems from them are included in two recent anthologies, *The Oxford India Anthology of Twelve Modern Indian Poets*, ed. Arvind Krishna Mehrotra (Oxford University Press, 1992) and *The Bloodaxe Book of Contemporary Indian Poetry*, ed. Jeet Thayil (2009). For a discussion of his work, see *Modern Indian Poetry in English*, by Bruce King (Oxford University Press, 1987; revd. edn., 2001). Jussawalla's long-awaited third volume, *Trying to Say Goodbye* (Almost Island, 2011), surveys the whole of his life, including his time as an architecture student in London in the late 1950s.   AKM*

Justice, Donald (1925–2004) Born and raised in Miami where he attended the public schools and studied piano, eventu-ally with the composer Carl Ruggles at the University of Miami from which he graduated in 1945. After receiving his MA from North Carolina, he studied for a year at Stanford with *Winters, from whom he learned much about poetic metre, before going on to receive his PhD from Iowa in 1954. He taught at the Iowa Writers' Workshop from 1957 to 1982, remaining firmly committed, as the interviews and essays in *Platonic Scripts* (University of Michigan Press, 1984) attest, to the idea of the poem as a crafted work of art. In 1982 he returned to Florida, and taught at the University of Florida in Gainesville until his retirement.

Having spent many of his childhood summers on his grandparents' farm in Georgia during the Depression, his view of the South differed from that of the *Fugitives and *Agrarians, despite early admiration for the work of *Ransom. He did not share their idealization of the area as a lost paradise, knowing primarily its poverty, and eventually ceased to consider himself a Southern writer. Nevertheless, it is to the Florida and Georgia of his childhood that he returns again and again with a Wordsworthian ambition to poetically memorialize this landscape. If his first book, *The Summer Anniversaries* (Wesleyan University Press, 1960), is notable for its mastery of such forms as the sonnet and the sestina, it also begins to sketch in the Southern landscape from which he emerged in such poems as 'Landscape with Little Figures', 'Sonnet: The Poet at Seven', and 'Tales from a Family Album'. The volume's strongest poems are 'Sestina: Here in Katmandu', an experimental piece contrasting the poet's successful quest for sublime transcendence with the subsequent necessity of living in the flat, real world, and the brief, resonant elegy, 'On the Death of Friends in Childhood'. His next two books, *Night Light* (1967—both Wesleyan University Press) and *Departures* (Atheneum, 1973), extend his vision to encompass his adult experiences in places as various as Kansas, Syracuse, San Francisco, and Iowa City in such poems as 'American Sketches', 'Bus Stop', and 'Men at Forty'. *Departures* is his most experimental book, though his forays into free verse are always kept in check by his formal decorum. Here he also began to imitate musical forms in poetry, as in 'Sonatina in Green' and 'Sonatina in Yellow'.

The publication of his *Selected Poems* (Atheneum, 1979), which won the Pulitzer Prize, and *The Sunset Maker* (Atheneum/ Anvil, 1987) confirmed his reputation as one of the pre-eminent American lyric poets of his generation. The previously uncollected poems in the former book return to traditional form while extending his evocation of his childhood in such poems as 'First Death', 'Memories of the Depression Years', and his most luminous evocation of Miami in the Thirties, the prose-annotated 'Childhood'. The new poems in the latter collection combine with two stories and an essay to give a portrait of the artist as both a young and an older man, highlighted by elegies to old music teachers and fellow poets, the most moving being his villanelle, 'In Memory of the Unknown Poet, Robert Boardman Vaughn'. His own selection from his poems, *Orpheus Hesitated Beside the Black River*, appeared in the UK in 1998 (Anvil). From 1997 to 2003, Justice was a Chancellor of the Academy of American Poets. *Collected Poems* appeared in America shortly before his death in 2004 (Knopf; Anvil, 2006).   RMCP

Kamal, Daud (1935–87) Born in Abbottabad, Pakistan, received his early education at a public school, and later attended the universities of Peshawar and Cambridge. He was professor of English in the University of Peshawar. During an academic tour in December 1987 he died of heart failure in New York.

Kamal published two volumes of translations of Urdu poetry before his own first collection, *Recognitions*, appeared in England (1979) with an introduction by Anthony *Thwaite, who wrote of Kamal's unsentimental wistfulness and of his concern for 'the fragments of the past, summoned up in brilliant but reticent images'. In his second book, *A Remote Beginning* (1985—both Interim Press), Kamal continued to join imagist practice to the poetics of the Urdu *ghazal* and the haiku. Sadness alternates with outrage, and two styles are discernible throughout: lyric-narrative, as in 'The Street of Nightingales' and 'Water Carrier', and the staccato-telegraphese of 'River Mist'. His poems were collected in *Before the Carnations Wither* (Daud Kamal Trust, 1995). See also *A Selection of Verse* (Oxford University Press, 1997).   AHa

Kantaris, Sylvia (1936–) Born in the Derbyshire Peak District, and now lives in Cornwall, where she was elected the first Writer in the Community. She studied at Bristol University and at the University of Queensland, Australia, and wrote her MA and PhD theses on the French Surrealists. Her translations of twentieth-century French poetry are too little-known. Her first two collections *Time and Motion* (Prism/Poetry Society of Australia, 1975) and *The Tenth Muse* (Peterloo, 1983) were reissued by Menhir Press in 1986. *Dirty Washing: New and Selected Poems* (1989) draws on three earlier collections and was followed by *Lad's Love* (1992). A narrative fantasy, *The Air Mines of Mistila* (1988—all Bloodaxe), co-written with Philip *Gross, reveals the playful aspects of her imagination.

Generally, Kantaris deals with unpretentious, everyday subjects in fluent, loosely structured verse. Her strengths are her emotional directness and ready humour. She can be a moving love poet, notwithstanding a lively streak of feminist rebellion (see *News from the Front* (Arc, 1983), written in collaboration with D. M. *Thomas, and her two autobiographical essays in *Delighting the Heart: Notebook by Women Writers*, ed. Susan Sellers (The Women's Press, 1989)).   CAR

Kasischke, Laura (1961–) Born in Grand Rapids, Michigan, Kasischke obtained her BA in writing and literature and Masters of Fine Arts in creative writing at University of Michigan, where she is now a professor. She has published eight collections of poetry, from *Wild Brides* (New York University Press, 1992) to *Space, in Chains* (Copper Canyon, 2011), which won the National Book Critics Circle Award in Poetry. Often following the speaker's consciousness and using both conversational and heightened language, the poems deftly move between narrative and lyric, the physical and metaphysical. While technically free verse, her poems employ partial and full, internal and end rhyme without pattern, and vary line length (and sometimes employ prose) to alter the pace. As 'Wasps' from *Space, in Chains* concludes, 'In our fading animal memories: | The humming gold of being, and ceasing to be. The exposed motor of eternity.'

She has also published six novels for adults, two for young adults, a novella, and a collection of short stories. Translations of her adult novels appear in Dutch, French, German, Hebrew, Italian, Japanese, Romanian, Russian, and Spanish. Her awards include the Alice Fay DiCastagnola Award from the Poetry Foundation of America and fellowships from the Guggenheim Foundation and the National Endowment for the Arts. CE

Kavanagh, P. J. (Patrick Joseph Gregory) (1931–) Born in Sussex; his father was Ted Kavanagh, noted for his ITMA sketches on radio. Kavanagh read English at Merton College, Oxford, after National Service in Korea. He has worked as an actor, in publishing, and in television. He now works as a freelance writer.

Although Kavanagh's influences (Edward *Thomas, *Auden, *MacNeice) place him squarely in the English mainstream, he is a maverick poet, an outsider, affiliated to no group. He has spoken admiringly of MacNeice's 'wristy manner' and this is present in the best of his own poetry and prose. He has written pastoral, eclogues, and satires, but the shorter lyrics are his finest achievement. See, in particular: 'Perfection Isn't Like a Perfect Story', 'The Temperance Billiards' Room', and 'On the Way to the Depot'.

Kavanagh's crucial subject was his first wife Sally (daughter of Rosamond Lehmann), who died two and a half years after their marriage. Kavanagh's prose account of his life up to her death, *The Perfect Stranger* (1972; repr. Carcanet, 1995), is a classic. It is the story of an insouciant misfit (in Korea he had deliberately courted death), redeemed by a rare woman.

Kavanagh's early collections of poetry, from *One and One* (Heinemann, 1959) to *Life Before Death* (Chatto & Windus/Hogarth, 1979) are out of print. His *Collected Poems* was published by Carcanet in 1992. *Something About* (2004) contains later observations of the rural and the numinous. Kavanagh has also edited the *Collect-*

ed Poems of Ivor *Gurney (1982; revd. edn., 2004—both Carcanet). PF

Kavanagh, Patrick (1904–67) Born in the parish of Inniskeen, Co. Monaghan, and succeeded his father as a cobbler and small farmer. He is the most popular and influential Irish poet of the generation after *Yeats, but the controversy that he fomented and suffered throughout his life survived him. He is the century's most prominent representative of the 'rural' as against the 'urban' side of an established Irish literary dichotomy—at least before Seamus *Heaney, whose consistent championing of Kavanagh has helped to stabilize his high standing.

Kavanagh finished his Irish national primary schooling at the age of 12, coming from an entirely unbookish background, but he says he was already writing verses at that stage. His first book, *Ploughman and other Poems* (1936), was uneven, not surprisingly, but it contained some of his now most admired lyrics, especially 'Inniskeen Road: July Evening', which has his hallmark: a rough immediacy combined with a feeling for the transcendent power of the imagination. In 1938 he published *The Green Fool*, a loosely autobiographical novel which he later deplored as 'stage-Irish', but which some readers still regard as the most successful of his three versions of that material—the other two being *Tarry Flynn* (1948), which Kavanagh called 'the only authentic account of life as it is lived in Ireland this century', and *By Night Unstarred* (published by his brother Peter in 1978).

In 1939 he moved to Dublin, a step he later called 'the worst mistake of my life'. There he published his most famous poem, *The Great Hunger* (1942), a powerful, if over-long, account of the spiritual and social privation of the Irish small farmer. Kavanagh later criticized it for its too-explicit concern 'with the woes of the poor'.

The poems of Kavanagh's middle period often lack objectivity, being too concerned with the role and reception of the poet. In 1952 he and Peter used the latter's American savings to launch *Kavanagh's Weekly*, which ran for thirteen issues between April and July, extending into polemic Kavanagh's resentments at the Dublin literary establishment and the pettinesses of Irish politics. There followed a disastrous period in his life: he sued the insignificant weekly the *Leader* for libel and was treated with contemptuous hostility in the courts, and in 1953 he developed lung cancer. But then, miraculously, followed his happiest years, referred to as his 'Canal Bank' period from a 'rebirth' he says he underwent one summer's day in 1955 on the banks of the Grand Canal in Dublin, when he learnt the virtues of 'simplicity' and 'not to care'. The poems of his last decade were again uneven, often prosodically unconvincing or tending towards reductiveness after the magnificent sonnets of the 'Canal Bank'. In April 1967 he married Katharine Moloney.

Paradoxically, Kavanagh has been underrated because of the immediate appeal of his most popular poems ('Kerr's Ass', 'On Raglan Road', 'Shancoduff'), which has tended to establish them as the measure of his achievement. Recently the corpus has been read as a whole, balancing sentimentality, touchiness, and pomposity about 'art', against philosophical insight and social generosity. He gave Irish poetry a salutary shift towards reality, away from its Celtic high ground.

See: *Collected Poems* (Penguin, 2004) and *A Poet's Country: Selected Prose* (Lilliput, 2003), both edited by Antoinette Quinn; *The Green Fool* (1938; Penguin, 2001); *Tarry Flynn* (1948; Penguin, 2000); *By Night Unstarred*, ed. Peter Kavanagh (Hand Press, 1978); *Kavanagh's Weekly* (complete in one volume, Goldsmith, 1981). Also, Antoinette Quinn's life, *Patrick Kavanagh* (Gill & Macmillan, revd. edn. 2003), and, for background, Anthony Cronin, *Dead as Doornails: A Chronicle of Life* (1976; Lilliput, 1999).   BO'D

Kay, Jackie (1961–) Born in Edinburgh to a Scottish mother and Nigerian father, Kay grew up in Glasgow with adoptive parents. She is Professor of Creative Writing at Newcastle University and in 2006 was awarded an MBE. Her first poetry collec-

tion, *The Adoption Papers* (1991), dramatized the history of her identity through the voices of birth mother, adoptive mother, and daughter. This has remained a central theme of her work, which has successfully sought a wide readership through formal simplicity, emotional clarity, and wry humour about familial and romantic love.

'In My Country', from *Other Lovers* (2003), describes being challenged about her mixed origins by a stranger ('Where do you come from?'), and answering with a quietly meaningful colloquialism: '"Here," I said. "Here. These parts."' The book also features a sequence about the blues singer, Bessie Smith. *Life Mask* (2005—all Bloodaxe) included vignettes from the experience of tracing her birth father, which was the subject of her prose memoir, *Red Dust Road* (2010). Kay's latest collection, *Fiere* (2011), continued her interest in *Scots diction and ballad form (the title is a word found in Robert Burns' 'Auld Lang Syne', meaning 'companion' or 'equal'). She has also written a novel (*Trumpet* (1998)), short stories (*Why Don't You Stop Talking?* (2002—all Picador)), drama (*The Lamplighter* (Bloodaxe, 2008)), and poetry and fiction for children. *Darling: New and Selected Poems* was published by Bloodaxe in 2008.   JNT

Keene, Dennis (1934–2007) Born in London and educated at Sheen Grammar School and St John's College, Oxford. He spent most of his adult life abroad, teaching in Malaysia, Ethiopia, and Japan, where he was professor of English literature at Japan Women's University, Tokyo (1976–81; 1984–9). In 1993 he returned to Oxford.

Keene first made a name as a poet while an undergraduate at Oxford. In his mid-twenties he stopped writing poetry, beginning again in his fortieth year. His first book, *Surviving*, appeared in 1980. His poetic practice is linked intimately with his apprehension of temporal experience, which accounts for the circling, repetitive mode he often employs. There is also, throughout his work, an argument with Romantic and symbolist modes of comprehending and representing experience.

Keene's major achievement is the long poem 'Universe', which combines deliberately prosaic blank verse, prose passages, and traditional verse-forms, and deals with astronomy, atomic physics, history, and personal experience, not drawing them into any factitious and comforting relationship, but holding them in their incomprehensibility and irreducibility.

See *Universe and Other Poems* (Carcanet, 1984). Keene's many translations of twentieth-century Japanese work include *The Modern Japanese Prose Poem* (Princeton University Press, 1980). He also edited a selection of the verse of Henry Howard, Earl of Surrey (Carcanet, 1985; repr. 2003). TJGH

Kees, Weldon (1914–55) Born in Nebraska and, growing up in the Depression, his obsessions were the Communist Party (he was a Trotskyite) and the stupidities of middle-class America.

Kees published his first story when he was 16. A novel, *Slow Parade*, went the rounds in 1937 and another, *Fall Quarter*, met a similar fate (since rectified by Story Line Press). His first poem, 'Subtitle', was published in the same year. His first book of poems, *The Last Man*, was published in San Francisco in 1943, though the poems have less to do with the horrors of war than those of a man 'alone in a worn out town in wartime'. Less obviously indebted to *Auden, his second book, *The Fall of the Magicians*, was published in New York in 1947. By this time he had quit his job as a librarian and taken up painting. Kees was also a competent jazz pianist and composer, and in later years made films and put on revues. He earned his living writing for *Time*, *The New Yorker*, and the *Nation*.

Kees' last book, *Poems 1947–1954*, was published just before his death and contains an epigraph from Hawthorne: 'those dark caverns into which all men must descend, if they would know anything beneath the surface and illusive pleasures of existence.' On 18 July 1955 his car was found near the entrance to the Golden Gate Bridge. The body was never found.

Today Kees is known for a smaller body of work, about 150 poems, than any other poet of comparable standing in America. Indeed, he is best known for just four poems, the strange 'Robinson' poems, which pre-date and prefigure John *Berryman's 'Henry' dream songs. Where Berryman's poems are perversely modernistic, Kees' are urbane and accessible: 'Through sounds of ice cubes dropped in a glass, an osteopath, | Dressed for the links, describes an old Intourist tour |—Here's where old Gibbons jumped from, Robinson.'

This is the period of *ciné noir*: betrayal, corruption, and murder in the public sector, the lone gumshoe, possibly called Robinson, going about his hopeless but poetic calling, alone, terminally depressed, and inevitably drunk.

Weldon Kees was largely ignored by anthologists during his life and even now is usually represented by one or two poems. A notable exception was Conrad *Aiken's *Twentieth Century American Poetry*, which printed nine poems, more than by any other poet after *Eliot and *Pound. Kees' *Collected Poems*, ed. Donald Justice, were published by the University of Nebraska Press (1962; 3rd edn., Bison, 2003, with a new introduction by David *Wojahn).

Kees' work has become better known in Britain through Simon *Armitage's second volume, *Kid* (Faber, 1992), which contains its own 'Robinson' sequence, as well as the poem 'Looking for Weldon Kees', which begins 'I'd heard it said by Michael *Hofmann | that *Collected Poems* would blow my head off'. They were reprinted by Faber in 1993. See James Reidel, *Vanished Act: The Life and Art of Weldon Kees* (University of Nebraska Press, 2003). HW*

Keesing, Nancy (Hertzberg) (1923–93) Born in Sydney, Australia, and graduated from the university there. She was most widely known as a freelance writer and active executive member of numerous literary organizations. She was a founding member of the Literature Board and chairman from 1944 to 1947. She was made a Member of the Order of Australia in 1979.

Keesing's poetry remains the key to her literary activity. She was one of a generation of poets who emerged in the 1940s under the shadow of the Second World War and who revitalized the craft, combining lyrical exactitude with a quality of wit and playfulness notably absent in the work of many writers in that period. Her later poetry is suffused by her warm concern for people and by the telling, idiosyncratic detail.

As a poet, she published *Imminent Summer* (Lyre Bird Writers, 1951), *Three Men and Sydney* (1955), *Showground Sketchbook* (1968—both Angus & Robertson), and *Hails and Farewells* (Edwards & Shaw, 1977). She edited, with Douglas Stewart, the important anthologies *Australian Bush Ballads* (1955) and *Old Bush Songs* (1957—both Angus & Robertson). There are also books of criticism and social commentary, historical monographs, and children's fiction. Her book of memoirs, *Riding the Elephant* (Allen & Unwin, 1988) is a colourful personal document. *The Woman I Am*, a collection of unpublished poems, edited by Meg Stewart, appeared posthumously from the State Library of New South Wales Press in 1995. TWS

Kefala, Antigone (1935–) Born in Romania of Greek parents and has lived in Romania, Greece, New Zealand, and Australia. She graduated from Victoria University in 1960 and has worked as a librarian, English teacher, and arts administrator.

Although she has published several works of fiction, it is as a poet that Kefala has established a reputation. She is one of the increasingly influential writers in Australia who uses the English language to reveal a poetic sensibility profoundly influenced by non-English origins. Her subject-matter is often the characteristic theme of displacement, alienation, and rootlessness found in much writing of the diaspora, but Kefala refines this with a lyrical delicacy and she has a subtle understanding of antipodean nuances.

Her three verse collections are *The Alien* (Makar, 1973), *Thirsty Weather* (Outback, 1978), and *European Notebook* (1988). See *Absence: New and Selected Poems* (1992; 2nd edn., 1998—both Hale & Iremonger),

and *Sydney Journals: Reflections 1970–2000* (Giramondo, 2008). TWS

Kell, Richard (Alexander) (1927–) Born in Youghal, Co. Cork, and educated at Trinity College, Dublin. He lectured in English at Isleworth Polytechnic 1960-70, and was senior lecturer at Newcastle Polytechnic 1970-83. From 1960 to 1973 he reviewed poetry for the *Guardian*.

Linked at times both with the *Movement and the *Group, Richard Kell shares a background in the Irish Protestant clergy with Louis *MacNeice and is similarly drawn to dualisms. A strong sensuous appetite ('River') is matched by a sense of order enlivened by paradox and wit, as in the sequence *Humours* (Ceolfrith, 1978). *Heartwood* (Northern House, 1978) is an extended examination of bereavement following the death of the poet's wife by drowning. Kell's humanistic attempt to reconcile reason and emotion is nowadays unusual, and is matched by his formal accomplishment and the elegance of his improvisations.

Kell's other main collections are *Control Tower* (1962); *Differences* (1969—both Chatto & Windus); *The Broken Circle* (Ceolfrith, 1981); and *In Praise of Warmth: New and Selected Poems* (Dedalus, 1987). Volumes published since his *Collected Poems* (2001) include *Under the Rainbow* (2003—both Lagan), *Letters to Enid* (2004), and a collection of limericks, *Taking a Break* (2008—both Shoestring). SO'B

Kelly, Brigit Pegeen (1951–) Born in Palo Alto, California, Kelly has held fellowships from the Guggenheim Foundation and the Academy of American Poets. She teaches English and creative writing at the University of Illinois in Urbana-Champaign.

Although not a prolific writer, Kelly's evocations of a mystical, pastoral America have been widely admired for their painterly colour and musical patterning. *To the Place of Trumpets* (1987) was awarded the Yale Younger Poets Prize by James *Merrill. It was followed in 1994 by *Song*, which won the Lamont Poetry Prize, and, a decade later, *The Orchard* (2004—both BOA), which was shortlisted for the National Book Critics Circle Award and the Pulitzer Prize. The latter two volumes were published together in the UK by Carcanet in 2008.   JNT

Kelly, Robert (1935–   ) Born in Brooklyn, New York, and educated at the City College of New York and Columbia University. After a brief career as a translator he took a series of posts as lecturer or writer-in-residence at various institutions, including Tufts University, the California Institute of Technology, and Bard College. The editor of *Chelsea Review* from 1958 to 1960, he also helped to launch *Trobar*, an influential poetry magazine, and Trobar books; and with seven other poets he formed The Blue Yak, a poet's co-operative, in New York. He has also been editor of *Matter* magazine and Matter publishing company. In 1961, he coined the term '*Deep Image'.

The first of his many collections, *Armed Descent*, appeared in 1961. During the 1960s he published no fewer than twenty-five volumes, with some of his best work to be found in *Finding the Measure* (Black Sparrow, 1968) and *A California Journal* (Big Venus, 1969). Kelly has described his poetry as 'news from nowhere', adding 'my work is not *my* work . . . my personality is its enemy'. Experimenting with a variety of forms, and using language that always pivots on an image, he tries to dramatize life as process, impersonal energy. Deploying a technique that offers a haunting mixture of dream, chant, and ritual, he attempts to translate the interpenetration of things into intelligible, although not necessarily paraphraseable, sounds. He has continued to be a prolific writer of plays, novels, and essays as well as poems. His many volumes of poetry since the 1960s include *Flesh: Dream: Book* (1971); *The Convections* (1978); *Spiritual Exercises* (1981); and *Not This Island Music* (1987—all Black Sparrow). *Mont Blanc* (Otherwind, 1994) is a 'writing into' Shelley's poem of the same name. Since *Red Actions: Selected Poems 1960–1993* (1995) he has also published *The Time of Voice: Poems 1994–1996* and *Lapis* (2005—all Black Sparrow).   RJG

Kennard, Luke (1982–   ) Born in Kingston-upon-Thames, Kennard grew up in Luton and took his BA, MA, and PhD at Exeter University. He received an Eric Gregory award in 2005, and, at 26, became the youngest ever nominee for the Forward Poetry Prize with his second collection, *The Harbour Beyond the Movie*. His work is already widely influential on a younger generation of British poets. He currently teaches at the University of Birmingham.

Kennard has stated in interview that he writes out of 'anger. And wanting to make that anger into something funny.' He describes his own work as cultivating 'a fairytale-like [quality] to comment on society'. Critics frequently highlight his poetry's *surrealism; commonly overlooked is its political thrust. The ironic lyricism and prose poetry of his first three collections, *The Solex Brothers* (Stride, 2005; Salt, 2007), *The Harbour Beyond the Movie* (2007), and *The Migraine Hotel* (2009), modulates between manic despair and farce in response to a universe of maddening, tyrannical forces. Kennard constructs and populates an absurdist *mise-en-scène* as a reflexive reassertion of personal agency in a relativist world. His fourth collection is *A Lost Expression* (2012—all Salt).   NH

Kennedy, X. J. (1929–   ) Born Joseph Charles Kennedy in Dover, New Jersey ('X. J.' is a pseudonym). Raised as a Roman Catholic, he attended Seton Hall, Columbia, and the University of Michigan, where he completed all work for a doctorate except the dissertation. In 1977 he gave up his tenured professorship at Tufts in order to devote himself full time to writing and editing. His college textbooks, a few of which are co-written with his wife, Dorothy, are best-selling introductions to literature and composition, and include *Literature* (10th edn., Longman, 2007) and *An Introduction to Poetry* (13th edn., Longman, 2010).

Kennedy likes to refer to himself as 'one of an endangered species: people who still write in meter and rime'. Though formal verse was unpopular in the early Seventies, he and his wife published the little magazine, *Counter/Measures*, a short-lived but influential refuge for traditional poets. Kennedy's first volume, *Nude Descending a Staircase* (Doubleday, 1961), which won that year's Lamont Award, established him as a technical virtuoso who combines metaphysical wit with idiomatic diction. *Cross Ties* (University of Georgia Press, 1985) selects the best from this and subsequent volumes, and includes everything from limericks to sonnets, as well as epigrams, elegies, heroic couplets, and villanelles. Many of his finest poems express an irreverent, sometimes profane, view of religion ('First Confession', 'Nothing in Heaven Functions As It Ought', 'The Atheist's Stigmata', and 'Hangover Mass'). His frank sexual humour surfaces in poems about flagellation, masturbation, and his own buttocks.

An expert at parody and satire ('Among Stool Pigeons' and 'Emily Dickinson in Southern California'), Kennedy excels at verse set to popular music, such as his often-anthologized lamentation on fading beauty, 'In a Prominent Bar in Secaucus One Day'. Mocking much about the poetry trade, Kennedy bemoans the bleak state of American culture. Not strictly a nay-sayer, he also celebrates the richness of everyday life with its simple epiphanies. He elevates the vulgar with his effortless technique and deflates pretence with his sardonic wit. Since the mid-Seventies Kennedy has written mostly children's verse, work full of sophisticated nonsense and much inspired silliness, including *Brats* (Atheneum, 1986) and *Ghastlies, Goops, and Pincushions* (McElderry, 1989). See *The Lords of Misrule: Poems, 1992–2001* (Johns Hopkins University Press, 2002).   TDeP

Kennelly, Brendan (1936–) Born in Ballylongford, Co. Kerry, and educated at Trinity College, Dublin, where he became professor of modern English literature, and at Leeds University. His first four books of poetry were published jointly with Rudi Holzapfel; his reputation was established by his impressive second solo volume, *My Dark Fathers* (1964). After four further volumes in fairly rapid succession and the AE Memorial Prize for Poetry (1967), his *Selected Poems* were published in 1969. He pub-

lished two early novels and edited his acclaimed *Penguin Book of Irish Verse* in 1970. The volumes of the next twelve years demonstrate the same characteristics as this earlier poetry: a free-form, individualistic, romantic expressionism which is forceful but can seem flat and unrelieved. *Cromwell* (1983) changed Kennelly's status dramatically: this series of 160 poems on the themes and obsessions of Irish history confronts that history's bogeyman, Cromwell, with Buffán, its hapless consumer. Kennelly's graphic force was ideally suited to this clamorous sequence, of which there is a stage version, and which is now regarded as one of the principal poetic commentaries on the recent vestigial turbulence of the Irish past. A new selected, *A Time For Voices* was published by Bloodaxe in 1990, as was *Cromwell* in 1987, and a 400-page epic poem *The Book of Judas* in 1991 (a shorter version appeared as *The Little Book of Judas* (2002)). A good short introduction to this period is Gerard Quinn's 'Brendan Kennelly: Victors and Victims', *The Irish Review*, 9 (Autumn 1990).

In 1992 Bloodaxe published *Breathing Spaces: Early Poems*, followed by a volume of selected prose in 1994 (*Journey into Joy*) and 350-page new volume, *Poetry My Arse*, in 1995. *Familiar Strangers* (2004) selects from all Kennelly's work up to *Martial Art*, his engagement with the 'punchy' Roman satirist (2003—all Bloodaxe). For a full critical study, see John McDonagh, *A Host of Ghosts* (Liffey, 2004). See also *The Essential Brendan Kennelly*, ed. Terence Brown and Michael Longley (Bloodaxe, 2011), which includes a recording of the poet reading his work.   BO'D*

Kenney, Richard (1948–) Born in Glen Falls, New York and graduated from Dartmouth College in 1970. After graduation Kenney studied Celtic lore in Ireland and Scotland, then worked for several years as a school-bus driver and house painter in Winooski, Vermont. Married to botanist Mary Hedberg, he is currently teaching at the University of Washington, in Seattle.

Kenney's first book of poems was *The Evolution of the Flightless Bird* (1984), selected by James *Merrill for the Yale

Series of Younger Poets; Merrill writes in his introduction to that volume that Kenney 'is not out to disguise the liveliness of his mind or the breadth of his learning. He has read science and history and philosophy as well as Hopkins and Browning, Crane and Frost.' Kenney's deeply allusive, elliptical but firmly drawn work is marked by a recondite, often inward, diction and an interest in myth and language. 'The Hours of the Day', a sonnet-sequence that opened his first volume, is a meditation on the echoes between self and world that haunt the poet's 'hero' through twenty-four hours and sonnets in a complex, interrupted narrative of loss and recovery. Kenney's preference for the long poem is seen in 'Notes from Greece', the elaborate final poem of that first volume centred on a visit to the Byzantine monastic communities at Mount Athos. *Orrery* (Atheneum, 1985), Kenney's second collection, opens with a narrative 'crown' of sonnets; 'Apples' is an extended sequence of lyrics that moves through a single year on a cider-milling farm in Vermont. It was followed by *The Invention of Zero* (Knopf, 1993), six long poems on the history of the universe, and *The One-Strand River: Poems 1994–2007* (Random House, 2008). JP

Kenyon, Jane (1947–95) Born in Ann Arbor, Michigan, and educated at the university there. In 1972 she married the poet Donald *Hall, and by 1975 they had left Ann Arbor to take up residence in Hall's ancestral farmhouse in Danbury, New Hampshire, where she was later the state poet laureate. Kenyon's first book of poems, *From Room to Room* (Alice James, 1978), was marked by meditations on the subject of *residing*—both in terms of locale and of character—in the life of the country. Her translation of *Twenty Poems*, by Anna Akhmatova (Eighties, 1985) further framed the progress of her work, which then went on to find a more solid voice in *The Book of Quiet Hours* (1986).

Kenyon made something of an aesthetic of quiet, and her poems have a brooding introversion. Rare among American poets, she is also able to infuse her poetry with a lightly worn sense of Christian humility,

and an active—if worried—sense of mercy. These are among the qualities which give her verse both the tones and the turns of serious prayer. Within the subtle, yet dramatic, use of rhyme and sound in *Let Evening Come* (1990), she evokes not only the drama of her need to speak, but also the deep communion and solace within any reader's need to listen.

The new-and-selected volume *Otherwise* (1996), published following her death from leukaemia, includes poems from Kenyon's final collection, *Constance* (1993), which explores grief and depression. See also *A Hundred White Daffodils*, a miscellany of writings (1999—all Graywolf), and *The Best Day the Worst Day: Life with Jane Kenyon*, a memoir by Hall (Houghton Mifflin, 2005). Her *Collected Poems* came out in the USA in 2005 (Graywolf), the same year that *Let Evening Come: Selected Poems* appeared in the UK as part of the Bloodaxe World Poets series. LR*

Kerouac, Jack (Jean-Louis) (1922–69) Born in Massachusetts and studied at Columbia. His first language, until school, was the Joual dialect of his French-Canadian parents. He joined the Navy during the War, but was discharged on psychiatric grounds. He lived in New York, California, and Florida.

Kerouac is credited with coining the term '*Beat Generation' and is best known for the autobiographical novels which describe the life of that group, such as *On the Road* (1957) and *The Dharma Bums* (1958). He theorized his style as a 'prosody', however, and its example has influenced a number of American poets, including his friend, Allen *Ginsberg, who wrote that the incantatory free verse of *Howl* took off from Kerouac's 'inspired prose line'.

'Spontaneous bop prosody' was an ideal that Kerouac derived from jazz improvisation, although it stands in a history of speech-based poetics from Wordsworth to Charles *Olson. Like those poets, Kerouac emphasizes the primacy of voice in composition, with a *Surrealist insistence on 'free deviation (association) of mind into limitless blow-on-subject seas of thoughts'. Kerouac's most sustained experiment with this idea in verse is *Mexico City Blues* (Grove, 1959), a series of numbered 'choruses' in short page-long bursts. He also wrote 'American haiku', freed of the discipline of seventeen syllables. *Scattered Poems* (City Lights, 1971) appeared posthumously. In 1974, the Jack Kerouac School of Disembodied Poetics at Naropa was named in honour of his Buddhist principles (see *The Scripture of the Golden Eternity* (Totem, 1960)).   JNT

Keyes, Sidney (Arthur Kilworth) (1922–43) Educated at Tonbridge School and Queen's College, Oxford. An elegy on his grandfather, written when Keyes was 16, is an example of his precocious talent, which he extended and deepened at Oxford, where he became the centre of a group of poets and edited with Michael Meyer *Eight Oxford Poets* (1941). He wrote with astonishing fluency: for example, he composed the first of his Oxford poems, 'Remember Your Lovers', in an examination room, having finished his papers early. He came to dislike the poem for its 'lush sensuality'.

Keyes, an omnivorous reader and lover of paintings, found inspiration in such visionaries as El Greco, Blake, Hölderlin, and Schiller and in masters of the macabre, notably Webster, Goya, Beddoes, Picasso, and Rouault. He loved also Wordsworth, Clare, *Hardy, *Housman, and Edward *Thomas, regretting that he had not been born in nineteenth-century Oxfordshire or Wiltshire, 'because then I might have been a good pastoral poet, instead of an uncomfortable metaphysical poet without roots'. His early poems were influenced by *Yeats (overwhelmingly) and Rilke, especially an ambitious poem of over 400 lines, 'The Foreign Gate', written in February and March 1942.

Even more potent than his intellectual allegiances was his intense but unreciprocated passion for Milein Cosman, a refugee from Düsseldorf who had come to Oxford when the Slade School had moved there from London. The epitaph on his love for Milein is 'North Sea', written in October 1942.

In April 1942 Keyes joined the army and one month later was posted to the Officer Cadet Training Unit at Dunbar. Between then and the end of the year he wrote some of his finest verse, including two linked poems, 'Dido's Lament for Aeneas' and 'Rome Remember', which celebrates 'the singers | That cry with dead voices along the African shore'. He wrote a long poem in December 1942 and January 1943, 'The Wilderness' which, like 'The Foreign Gate' is immensely ambitious but a partial failure. He thought both his 'nearest misses'.

Keyes was killed in action in Tunisia towards the end of April, fighting with great gallantry. A posthumous collection of poems, *The Cruel Solstice*, was published in 1943.

See *Collected Poems*, ed. Michael Meyer (Routledge, 1945; repr. Carcanet, 2002). J. Guenther's *Sidney Keyes* (London Magazine, 1967) is a biographical study. Tim Kendall, in *Modern English War Poetry* (Oxford University Press, 2006), compares Keyes and Keith *Douglas as poets of 'self-elegy'.   JPr

Kgositsile, Keorapetse (William) (1938–) Born in Johannesburg, Kgositsile was a member of the African National Congress who went into exile from South Africa in 1961, spending the next decade in the United States, becoming an important figure in the *Black Arts Movement. He studied for an MFA at Columbia University in New York and began to perform and publish his poetry, which was influenced by his interest in jazz as a black art form. *My Name is Afrika* (1971) was published with an introduction by Gwendolyn *Brooks. He also edited an anthology, *The Word is Here: Poetry from Modern Africa* (1973—both Doubleday).

A founding member of the ANC Departments of Education and Arts and Culture while in exile, he returned to Africa in 1975, where he taught in various countries. He did not go back to South Africa until 1990, which saw the publication of *When the Clouds Clear* by the Congress of South African Writers. See the selected volumes *If I Could Sing* (2002) and *This Way I Salute You* (2004—both Kwela/Snailpress), and also his *Approaches to Poetry Writing* (Third World, 1994).

Popularly known as 'Bra Willie', in 2006 Kgositsile became National Poet Laureate of South Africa. JNT

Khalvati, Mimi (1944–) Born in Tehran, and went to school on the Isle of Wight, England. She studied at the University of Neuchâtel, Switzerland, and at the Drama Centre and School of African and Oriental Studies in London. She settled in Britain in her twenties, and worked for many years as a theatre actor and director.

Khalvati's poetry first appeared in a pamphlet with David *Morley in 1990 (*Persian Miniatures/A Belfast Kiss*, Smith/Doorstop). Her full-length debut, *In White Ink*, was published in 1991, followed by *Mirrorwork* (1995) and *Entries on Light* (1997). During this period, she became active as a creative-writing tutor, and in 1997 was a founder of the Poetry School in London.

As poet-in-residence at the Royal Mail in 2000, Khalvati compared postage stamps to lyric poems as two kinds of 'miniature art' that contain 'huge worlds'. Her own writing is noted for its inventive formalism, from the title sequence of her fourth collection, *The Meanest Flower* (Carcanet, 2007)—a dozen unrhymed sonnets, all ending 'open'—to her use of the Persian ghazal as a mode of contemporary love lyric. Khalvati's subject matter is often autobiographical, reflecting her formative experience of two cultures, as well as her early reading of Wordsworth: *The Chine* (2002) is named after a ravine on the Isle of Wight ('every childhood has its chine, upper world | and lower'). *Child: New and Selected Poems* appeared in 2011 (all Carcanet). JNT

Kilmer, Joyce (1886–1918) The son of a chemist, he was born in New Brunswick, New Jersey, and attended Rutgers between 1901 and 1906, but earned his AB from Columbia in 1908, the same year he married Alice Murray. After teaching Latin for a year, Kilmer worked on the *Standard Dictionary* and served as literary editor with the *Churchman*, an Episcopal outlet, before joining the staff on the Sunday Magazine and Book Review sections of the *New York Times*. His first book of poems, *Summer of Love* (1911), showed the strong influence of early *Yeats and the Celtic poets. He converted to Roman Catholicism after his daughter contracted infantile paralysis, which in turn inspired 'Trees', the only poem of his still remembered. *Trees and Other Poems* appeared in 1914 (it was reissued in London in 1941), followed by a book of prose, *The Circus and Other Essays* (1916), *Main Street and Other Poems* (1917), and, posthumously, *Joyce Kilmer: Poems, Essays and Letters* (Doran, 1918). Kilmer enlisted as a private when the United States entered the First World War and was killed at the second Battle of the Marne. EB

King, Amy (1971–) After a childhood and early education in the American South, King completed her MA in Poetics at SUNY Buffalo, where she studied with Charles *Bernstein and Susan *Howe, and her MFA in Poetry at Brooklyn College, where she worked with Ron *Padgett. Subsequently she moved to New York, where she founded and curated the Stain of Poetry Reading Series. She teaches literature and writing at SUNY Nassau Community College.

King is the author of four books of poetry: *Antidotes for an Alibi* (2006), *I'm the Man Who Loves You* (2007), *Slaves to Do These Things* (2009), all from Blazevox Books, and *I Want to Make You Safe* (2012), from Litmus Press. King has written of her queer poetics as a means of imagining alternative modes of being that are never grounded, but always 'beyond the determinable'. Her gender politics emerge within a single poem's constantly mutable subject matter and shifting subjectivities, as in 'Failed to Include': 'ushered | chameleon people of the female | to cradles, through kitchens | and the iris, backwashing the tomb'. King's poetry has been described by John *Ashbery as bringing 'abstractions to brilliant, jagged life, emerging into rather than out of the busyness of living'. Her work also reflects her pedagogical and activist work with several organizations including VIDA: Women in Literary Arts, for which she was honoured by The Feminist Press as one of the '40 Under 40: The Future of Feminism' awardees.   ADA

Kinloch, David (1959–) Born in Glasgow and educated at the universities of Glasgow and Oxford, Kinloch was a founder editor of the magazine *Verse*, and a founder of the Scottish Writers' Centre. He was also associated with the *Informationists group. Having taught French language and literature for many years, Kinloch is currently Reader in Poetry at the University of Strathclyde.

Kinloch's poetry ranges from traditional lyric poems to experimental prose poems, and he has translated into both English and *Scots. Edwin *Morgan and Hugh *MacDiarmid are significant antecedents, but Kinloch also draws on North American and modern European traditions. His first pamphlet, *Dustie-Fute* (Vennel, 1992), is an elegiac sequence for a gay man who died of AIDS. It is included in his first full-length collection, *Paris-Forfar* (Polygon, 1994). In *Un Tour d'Ecosse* (2001), Kinloch explores Scottish identity, sometimes playfully, as in the title sequence, which imagines Whitman and Lorca on a cycling tour of Scotland. *In My Father's House* (2005) concludes with a powerful long poem, 'Baines His Dissection', in which a seventeenth-century medic embalms his deceased lover. *Finger of a Frenchman* (2011—all Carcanet) considers the influence of French culture on five centuries of Scottish art. In 2004 Kinloch received the Robert Louis Stevenson Memorial Award.

Kinnell, Galway (1927–) Born in Providence, Rhode Island, and studied at Princeton and the University of Rochester. He served in the United States Navy and then visited Paris on a Fulbright Fellowship. Returning to the United States, he worked for the Congress on Racial Equality and then travelled widely in the Middle East and Europe. He has taught at several colleges and universities, including California, Pittsburgh, and New York. The poems of his first volume, *What a Kingdom It Was* (1960), were informed by a traditional Christian sensibility. However, while retaining a sacramental dimension, his later work burrows fiercely into the self away from traditional sources of religious authority or even conventional notions of personality. 'If you could keep going deeper and deeper', he has said, 'you'd finally not be a person . . . you'd be a blade of grass or ultimately perhaps a stone. And if a stone could read poetry would speak for it.'

The poems issuing from this conviction may be found in such collections as *Flower Herding on Mount Monadnock* (1964), *Body Rags* (1968), *The Book of Nightmares* (1971), and *Mortal Acts, Mortal Words* (1980). Short, chanting lines, a simple, declarative syntax, emphatic rhythms, bleak imagery, and insistent repetition: all are used here to generate the sense of the poet as shaman who throws off the 'sticky infusions' of speech and becomes one with the natural world, sharing in the primal experiences of birth and death. *Walking Down the Stairs* (1978) is a useful selection of interviews with Kinnell; he has also published a number of translations. His *Selected Poems* (1982) won a Pulitzer Prize. A *New Selected Poems* appeared in 2000 (revd. edn., 2001).

Kinnell's first collection since *Imperfect Thirst* (1994), *Strong is Your Hold* (2006—all Houghton), includes his long poem on the 2001 World Trade Center attack, 'When the Towers Fell'. It was published in the UK by Bloodaxe. In 2010 Kinnell received the Wallace Stevens Award from the Academy of American Poets.   RJG

Kinsella, John (1963–) Born in Perth and studied at the University of Western Australia. He is a Fellow of Churchill College, Cambridge, and has taught at universities in Australia and the United States.

Kinsella's prolific career as a published poet began at seventeen, shortly after his discovery of the work of Judith *Wright. He has written over thirty books of verse, fiction, autobiography, and criticism since *Night Parrots* (1989). Harold Bloom, who edited *Peripheral Light: New and Selected Poems* (2003—both Fremantle Arts Centre), has called Kinsella an 'Orphic fountain', and the flow can inevitably dilute the potency. But Kinsella has achieved a wide readership by writing poems that span the spectrum of contemporary styles, in a diction that is diverse, empirical, challenging, and tactile. *Doppler Effect* (Salt, 2004), introduced by Marjorie Perloff, collects his more formally innovative work since the sequence *Syzygy* (Fremantle Arts Centre, 1993), which reflected the influence of both *Cambridge poetry in England and *Language poetry in the States.

In *Disclosed Poetics* (Manchester University Press, 2008), Kinsella describes himself as 'a vegan anarchist pacifist'. His poetry is often concerned with the ecological degradation of the Western Australian landscape where his family farmed: see *Shades of the Sublime and Beautiful* (Fremantle/Picador, 2008). As well as founding the publishing house Salt, and the journal of the same name, Kinsella has been an active anthology editor: see *Vanishing Points: New Modernist Poems* (with Rod Mengham, Salt, 2003) and *The New Penguin Anthology of Australian Poetry* (2008). *The Jaguar's Dream* (Herla, 2012) gathers his free translations.   JNT

Kinsella, Thomas (1928–) Born in Dublin and abandoned a science degree at University College, Dublin, to work in the Irish Civil Service until 1965 when he retired from the Department of Finance. Since then he has taught at various universities in the United States. He has been a director of the Dolmen and Cuala presses in Dublin; in 1972 he started his own Peppercanister Press which has published most of his work before publication in larger volumes by Dolmen and by Oxford University Press in Oxford and New York. His first volume *The Starlit Eye* (1952) is lyrical but already somewhat cryptic because of its breadth of mythological and literary allusion, from *Eliot to medieval Irish legend. *Another September* (1958) was enthusiastically received in Ireland, England, and America (his poetry has always shown American influence), and his standing as a principal figure in contemporary poetry was confirmed by the reception of *Nightwalker and other poems* in all three centres in 1968. The tendency towards greater

crypticism and more subdued imagery of that intellectual volume has continued, through *Notes from the Land of the Dead and other poems* (1972) to the various numbered brief Peppercanister volumes.

Kinsella's writing has become increasingly allusive and the symbolic coding has become even more internalized, with his eye on Jung, Irish myths, and his own Joycean Dublin topography. The principal interest lies in watching Kinsella building towards a definitive structure as he attempts (like *Yeats) to make of his work a myth of modern Irish life. This is not a self-indulgence but a painstaking record of the accumulation of experience and sensation from an internal vantage-point.

Kinsella's second major significance in Irish literary history is his translating of earlier Irish poetry, both of the medieval period (*The Táin*) and the classical period (*An Duanaire*), in a campaigning attempt to give a clear vernacular hearing to poets who have lacked it. He has famously (and controversially) defined the Irish tradition as 'gapped': that is, as a single national culture which is fragmented by a change of vernacular—an idea that nowadays seems recognizably modernist, in Eliot's tradition. He has also occasionally turned aside from his psychic odyssey towards public events, most famously in *Butcher's Dozen* (1972: Peppercanister only), an impassioned broadside against the Widgery Tribunal's anodyne judgement on the events of 'Bloody Sunday' in Derry. Less sensationally, he has sustained Austin *Clarke's hostilities against Dublin's architectural planners.

Kinsella's crypticism means that he benefits from being read with an informed guide, such as Maurice Harmon's *Thomas Kinsella: Designing for Exact Needs* (Irish Academic Press, 2008). He edited The *New Oxford Book of Irish Verse* (Oxford University Press, 1986), and his principal translations are *The Táin*, with illustrations by Louis le Brocquy (Dolmen, 1969; Oxford University Press, 1970) and, with Seán Ó Tuama, *An Duanaire, 1600–1900: Poems of the Dispossessed* (Dolmen, 1981).

His own historical study of Irish poetry is *The Dual Tradition* (Carcanet, 1995).

Readings in Poetry (Carcanet, 2006) contains essays on Yeats and Eliot. See *Collected Poems* (Carcanet, 2001; Wake Forest University Press, 2006) and *Selected Poems* (Carcanet, 2007; Wake Forest University Press, 2010), which extends to Peppercanister 24, *Marginal Economy* (2006). The Peppercanister pamphlets continue to appear, and are distributed in Ireland by The Dedalus Press, in the UK by Carcanet, and in the United States by Dufour Editions.   BO'D*

Kinzie, Mary (1944–) Born in Montgomery, Alabama, and raised in the South. She was divorced in 1992 and has one child, Phoebe, born in 1985. Kinzie attended Northwestern University and Johns Hopkins University, and is a professor of English at Northwestern.

Kinzie's poems surprise the reader as much with their verbal complexity as with the human story they disclose. They are often lyrics in the purest sense, for their revelation of a tragic element, and can seem both 'masculine' and 'feminine' in their thematic domains: war, passion, history, maternal love, and the landscapes of the earth. She writes both taut, spare lyrics and longer free-verse meditations.

Kinzie has published seven volumes of poetry, most recently: *The Ghost Ship* (1996), *Drift* (2005), and *California Sorrow* (2007—all Knopf). For many years she was a staff reviewer for the *American Poetry Review*, and she has published a book of critical prose entitled *The Cure of Poetry in an Age of Prose* (1993), in addition to *A Poet's Guide to Poetry* (1999—both Chicago University Press), a resource for beginners and experts alike.   HC

Kipling, Rudyard (1865–1936) Born in Bombay (now Mumbai), sent (at the age of six) with his sister to horrible foster-parents in Southsea, and then to an equally horrible public school. He returned to India to work as a journalist, and, by way of short prose pieces and poems, embarked on a literary career.

Somebody once said of Kipling: 'Even if he's not a great poet, he's certainly a great

something!' His best novel, *Kim*, could be called great, and the same contentious epithet could be applied to the best short stories. The poetry is a different matter. *Eliot regarded it as 'verse', though he did admit that Kipling could write 'poetry' accidentally. Kipling, from the first, wrote in strict forms, the forms of ballads and music-hall songs: light verse at first, then with moral and political purpose—like Brecht. However, by these simple means, he could achieve remarkable effects. Eliot has shown how the variations of pace in 'Danny Deever' (probably his best poem) enhance the total effect. Orwell contended that Kipling's Cockney verse would have sounded better in standard English, more dignified and more stately. Lines like 'When 'Omer smote 'is bloomin' lyre' don't inspire confidence, because they suggest that Kipling's soldiers are only puppets expressing Kipling's opinions.

Kipling's poetry was always overwhelmingly popular with the English middle classes. 'If' has been elevated almost to the height and dignity of an alternative Creed. But most of his poems—including 'If'—are 'political' in some sense, and unless you agree with Kipling's line, you may not like the poem. He once gave a talk on literature to senior boys at Wellington College, in which he recommended them, when they met people who advocated the reading of *lurid* literature, to think to themselves whether 'they strike you as the kind of men you'd like to be with in a tight place'. In other words (this was in 1912) the virtues of junior officers are the key virtues: courage, awareness of danger, improvisation.

Kipling's Indian knowledge and experience was not beneficial only for the writing of *Kim* and the Indian stories. 'Arithmetic on the Frontier', an early poem, compares the Afghan tribesman with his inaccurate rifle ('a ten-rupee *jezail*') to the Sandhurst-trained infantry subaltern, trained for seven years ('Two thousand pounds of education'), and concludes: 'The odds are on the cheaper man.' Nor does the soldier-talk always seem theatrical. See 'Mandalay'. Kipling also wrote overt political satires. 'Gehazi' (on the Marconi scandals) now depends too much on knowledge of the case, and of the Old Testament. He also wrote one fine 'prophetic' poem, warning of the troubles to come—'The Storm Cone', written in 1932, four years before his death.

The best introduction to the poems, with a long essay, is T. S. Eliot's *A Choice of Kipling's Verse* (Faber, 1941; many later impressions). Craig Raine edited an alternative selection for Penguin in 1992. In 1995, 'If' was voted Britain's favourite poem in a BBC poll. GE

Kirkup, James (Falconer) (1923–2009) Born in South Shields, Co. Durham. From 1977 he lived mostly in Japan and Andorra. Highly respected in Japan for his work as a translator, Kirkup had technical ability, and his earlier poetry abounded in difficult verse-forms. His first collection was *The Drowned Sailor* (Grey Walls, 1947), and his early reputation was at its apogee when he published the less rhetorical *A Correct Compassion* (1952), the long, documentary title-poem of which describes a heart-operation. See also *The Prodigal Son: Poems 1956–1959* (1959), *The Refusal to Conform* (1963—all Oxford University Press), and *The Body Servant: Poems of Exile* (Dent, 1971). In 1976, a poem about Christ published in *Gay News* achieved a brief notoriety when it was prosecuted for alleged blasphemy.

Kirkup published several volumes of autobiography including, latterly, *I, of All People* (1988, Weidenfeld & Nicolson,); *A Poet Could Not But Be Gay* (1991); and *Me All Over* (1993—both Peter Owen). He remained prolific to the end of his life, and wrote increasingly about the North-East of England where he grew up. His final collection was *Marsden Bay* (Red Squirrel, 2008). MS-S*

Kizer, Carolyn (1925–) Born in Spokane, Washington, and educated at Sarah Lawrence College. She has held a number of positions both in and out of the academy, including teaching appointments in the Iowa Writers' Workshop. Her first book was *The Ungrateful Garden* (1961). The long poem, 'Pro Femina', from *Knock Upon Silence* (Doubleday, 1965), was an early feminist work, reprinted by BkMk Press in 2000.

Kizer's poems are formal and lyrical, but a particular element of her success is her sense of narrative, as in *Yin: New Poems* (BOA, 1984). She gets and keeps the reader's attention without resorting to the sensational or the hortatory. In 'Semele Recycled', for instance, the poet tells a tale out of Greek myth, but makes it familiar and compelling: a narrative embodiment of the war between the sexes and the truce that is eternally struck. In 1998, Kizer and Maxine *Kumin resigned as Chancellors of the Academy of American Poets in protest at the under-representation of women and ethnic minorities on the board. See *Cool, Calm, and Collected: Poems 1960–2000* (2001) and *Proses: Essays on Poems and Poets* (1993—both Copper Canyon). LT*

Klappert, Peter (1942–) Born in Rockville Center, New York, and grew up in Connecticut. He was educated at Cornell University and the University of Iowa and taught at George Mason University until his retirement in 2006. His first collection, *Lugging Vegetables to Nantucket* (Yale University Press, 1971), won the Yale Series of Younger Poets competition. 'The Babysitters', the book's central poem, displays his characteristic qualities and concerns: satire, wordplay, structural experimentation, and a sense of alienation. In *Circular Stairs, Distress in the Mirrors* (Griffin, 1975), a shorter collection, he explored the theme of the double.

With *The Idiot Princess of the Last Dynasty* (Knopf, 1984), Klappert produced a work of epic proportions. The book is a long series of poems in the form of monologues by 'Doc' Dan Mahoney, a character based on Dr Matthew O'Connor from Djuna Barnes' 1936 novel *Nightwood*. In its setting (1939–40), structure, allusiveness, and metaphysical perspectives, *Idiot Princess* is a product of late modernism, recalling *Eliot, *Pound, and other influences. Mahoney is the archetypal outsider—abortionist, homosexual, alcoholic—whose complex, multivalenced voice allows Klappert to make full use of his own heterogeneous talents. The large ambition, moral intensity, omnivorous learning, and technical accomplishment that mark *Idiot Princess* have attracted widespread praise. See *Chokecherries: New and Selected Poems* (Orchises, 2000).   TWi

Klein, A. M. (Abraham Moses) (1909–72) Born in Ratno, Ukraine, to Jewish parents who moved to Montreal in 1910. While studying at McGill (1926–30), he published poems and essays in Canadian and American periodicals. He graduated from the Université de Montréal law-school in 1933, and practised law until his retirement in 1956. During the 1920s and 1930s he was actively involved in the Zionist youth group Young Judaea. From 1938 to 1955 he edited the *Canadian Jewish Chronicle*. During this time he was also employed by the Jewish philanthropist, Samuel Bronfman, as a speech-writer and public-relations consultant. Teaching as a visiting lecturer in poetry at McGill (1945–8) and running unsuccessfully for the Federal Socialist Party (1949) added pressures to a busy life. In 1955 Klein suffered a mental breakdown from which he never fully recovered.

As a Jew living in a French-Canadian province, which in turn was surrounded by an English-speaking majority, Klein was acutely conscious of his vulnerable minority status. His first verse collection, *Hath Not a Jew . . .* (1940), gathered over a decade of poems on Jewish themes. Enthusiastic reception led to a second collection, *Poems* (1944) and *The Hitleriad* (1944), a mock-epic indictment of Nazi Germany. *The Rocking Chair and Other Poems* (1948) conveyed the tensions of life in Quebec with characteristic wit and affection. The highly wrought novella, *The Second Scroll* (1951), an expression of his Zionism, reflected his deep knowledge of *Joyce's Ulysses*. There were also numerous essays, reviews, editorials, stories, and translations from Hebrew and Yiddish.

The most recent and authoritative edition of Klein's poetry is *A. M. Klein: The Complete Poems*, ed. Zailig Pollock (University of Toronto Press, 1990). See also: *A. M. Klein: Literary Essays and Reviews*, ed. Usher Caplan and M. W. Steinberg (University of Toronto Press, 1987); *A. M. Klein: Short Stories*, ed. M. W. Steinberg (University of Toronto Press, 1983); *A. M. Klein, Beyond Sambation: Selected Essays and Editorials 1928–1955*, ed. M. W. Steinberg and Usher Caplan (University of Toronto Press, 1982); *Like One That Dreamed: A Portrait of A. M. Klein*, by Usher Caplan (McGraw-Hill, 1982); and *A. M. Klein and His Works*, by Noreen Golfman (ECW, 1990).   NG

Kleinzahler, August (1949–) Born and grew up in New Jersey. After high school in New York, he began studying at the University of Wisconsin, before dropping out under the influence of the *Beats. He later majored in English at the University of Victoria, Canada, where he was taught by Basil *Bunting. He has worked as a locksmith, cab driver, lumberjack, and music critic for the *San Diego Reader*, as well as latterly teaching writing at various institutions.

Kleinzahler has criticized *Language poetry's self-conscious theorizing, and attributes the development of his own verse to his lack of an academic career. His poems evince an eclectic range of enthusiasms, from *New York poets such as *O'Hara and *Schuyler, to blues, jazz, and the Elizabethan lyrics he encountered through Bunting. William Carlos *Williams' love of American urban life and vernacular is also an important influence.

Kleinzahler's early poems were published in Canada in the late 1970s. His breakthrough fourth book, *Red Sauce, Whiskey and Snow* (1995), was published in America by Farrar, Straus, and in England by Faber. *Green Sees Things in Waves*—the title poem describes the LSD-altered visions of a homeless veteran—followed in 1998. *The Strange Hours Travelers Keep* (2004) won the Griffin International Prize. *Sleeping it Off in Rapid City* (2008—all Farrar, Straus/Faber) is a volume of new and selected poems. The prose essays of *Cutty, One Rock* (Farrar, Straus, 2004) describe his early life among New Jersey mafia families.   JNT

Knight, Etheridge (1931–91) Born in Corinth, Mississippi. Self-educated, he served in the US Army (1947–51), and while recuperating from shrapnel wounds, he began a life-long cycle of drug-addiction and recovery. Three marriages (to poet Sonia *Sanchez, Mary Ann McAnally, and Charlene Blackburn) ended in divorce. During Knight's incarceration for robbery at Indiana State Prison (1960–8), Dudley Randall, founder of Broadside Press in Detroit became his mentor.

Knight's aesthetic emphasizes the relationship between the poet, the poem, and the people: the poet witnesses through his own experience the truth of the collective vision of the people and returns it to them as the poem. Like Whitman, as well as many poets of the African-American oral tradition, he views the poet as one with the people, rather than a 'poet-preacher', such as *Baraka. Knight's commitment to the spoken poem is notable, although he published widely. Technically, he combines traditional metrical devices with accentual rhythms of black street-talk, blues, and toasts (rhyming, humorous, often vulgar narratives extolling the subculture's power).

A dominant motif in Knight's poems is the tension between love, freedom, and various forms of imprisonment, especially in the earlier collections *Poems from Prison* (1968) and *Belly Song and Other Poems* (1973—both Broadside). In later collections an expanded thematic and technical range does not diminish his life-affirming tone. *Born of a Woman: New and Selected Poems* (Houghton, 1980) received a Pulitzer Prize nomination and won the National Book Award; the most comprehensive collection, *The Essential Etheridge Knight* (University of Pittsburgh Press, 1986), won the American Book Award.   JTC

Knister, (John) Raymond (1899–1932)

Born in the village of Ruscomb, Ontario. He attended, briefly, the University of Toronto and Iowa State University. His peripatetic life took him to Iowa City where he became involved as associate editor with the Midwestern avant-garde literary magazine, *The Midland*. Knister's stories, sketches, and poems appeared in the popular press as well as in avant-garde publications such as *This Quarter* in Paris. A rural background

which included work on the family farm was balanced by the experience of big-city life in Chicago, Toronto, and Montreal. Knister's tragically shortened life as a professional writer was one of struggle burdened by the responsibilities of a young family.

Knister was not only a practitioner of new literary modes in the modified imagism of his poetry and the psycho-realism of his fiction, but he was also actively engaged in furthering modernism in Canada. He edited a landmark anthology, *Canadian Short Stories* (1928), and engaged in thoughtful critical journalism. He died in a tragic drowning accident while vacationing with his family. In 1949 the Canadian poet Dorothy *Livesay published his *Collected Poems* (Ryerson). Six of his best stories were collected by Michael Gnarowski and published as *Selected Stories of Raymond Knister* (1972), and David Arnason edited *Raymond Knister: Poems, Stories, and Essays* (1975). Anne Burke assembled *Raymond Knister: An Annotated Bibliography* (1981).   MG

Knott, Bill (William Kilborn) (1940–)

Born in Michigan, and spent some of his childhood on a Michigan farm. His mother died when he was 6, his father when he was 11, and he spent the years between 8 and 16 in an orphanage. After serving in the US Army as a medic, he made his way to Chicago where he studied with poets Gwendolyn *Brooks and John *Logan. Knott went on to take an MFA from Vermont College, and has held appointments at a number of colleges, including Emerson College in Boston.

Knott published his first book of poems, *The Naomi Poems: Book One: Corpse and Beans* (Follett, 1968) under the pseudonym of St Geraud (who, according to Knott, was the hero of a French pornographic novel, the head of an orphanage who debauched his charges). After this auspicious beginning Knott went on to publish *Aurealism: A Study; Autonecrophilia; The—Poems: Book 2; Love Poems to Myself;* and, with the poet James *Tate, a collaborative prose-work titled *Lucky Darryl*.

Knott's self-referential world of words is in the tradition of the *Surrealists, *Stein, *Joyce, and others. His influences are decidedly European: Desnos, Eluard, and Michaux. But as Knott published *Becos* (Random House, 1983), *Outremer* (University of Iowa Press, 1989), and *Poems 1963–1988* (University of Pittsburgh Press, 1989), it became apparent that he had long ago outlived any label that might have been conferred upon him. His work is individual, not to say eccentric, and has about it an inner logic which is now self-generative. In the volume of selected poems he pared down some poems to as little as one line or one phrase from their former, published incarnations, and this kind of ongoing revision and reassemblage—reinvention, as from his beginning—remains a signature of Knott's aesthetic. See *Laugh at the End of the World: Collected Comic Poems 1969–1999* (BOA, 2000) and *The Unsubscriber* (Farrar, Straus, 2006).　LR

Kocan, Peter (1947–　) Born in Newcastle, New South Wales, and in 1966 sentenced to life imprisonment for the attempted assassination of Arthur Caldwell, leader of the Australian Labor Party. *The Other Side of the Fence* (1975), a gallery of institutional portraits, was completed before his release, after nearly ten years in Morriset Mental Hospital. He has lived in Tuggerah, Newcastle, Sydney, and Brisbane.

In *Armistice* (1980) Kocan juxtaposes institutional themes with the horrors confronting the trench poets, and in *Freedom to Breathe* (1985) makes apparent his sympathy for those like the Jacobites, who espouse lost causes. In *Standing with Friends* (1992) his historical pessimism extends from the battle of Cannae to the Tienanmen Square massacre. *Primary Loyalties* (1999), a volume shared with Hal *Colebatch and Andrew *Lansdown, satirizes contemporary vanities, while *Fighting in the Shade* (2000) balances exposure of hypocrisy with tributes to composers and writers who help hold the line of traditional values.

The Other Side of the Fence (University of Queensland Press, 1975) and *Fighting in the Shade* (Hale & Iremonger, 2000) are Kocan's main collections of poems, and *Fresh Fields* (Fourth Estate, 2004) his most engaging novel.　CP

Koch, Kenneth (1925–2002) Born in Cincinnati, Ohio, and served as a rifleman in the Pacific theatre during the Second World War. After graduating from Harvard in 1948 he moved to New York City, where his close circle of friends included the poets John *Ashbery and Frank *O'Hara and the painters Jane Freilicher and Larry Rivers. In France and Italy, where Koch spent three fellowship years, he found inspiration in the ambience of foreign languages imperfectly understood, and he set out to communicate the same 'incomprehensible excitement' in his poetry.

Thank You (Grove, 1962) remains Koch's most influential collection. Radiating comic energy, the book illustrates *par excellence* certain seminal strategies associated with the *New York School, such as the 'list' poem, where the inventory as a structural device serves an ideal of inclusiveness and a delight in humorous incongruity. Koch's tone, often imitated, is one of exclamatory exuberance and hyperbolic wit, as in his invention of a conceptual artist who plans to paint the Pacific Ocean and has, to this end, ordered 16 million tons of blue paint.

If the spirit of pastiche is definitive of postmodernism, Koch must be considered one of that movement's pioneers. A gifted and versatile parodist, he built his comic epic *Ko, or a Season on Earth* (Penguin, 1959) on *ottava rima*, the stanza of Byron's *Don Juan*. *The Art of Love* (Random House, 1975), a spoof on pedagogy, offers unconventional instruction on matters of aesthetics and love. *One Thousand Avant-Garde Plays* (Knopf, 1988)—actually consisting of 112 miniature verse plays—takes on the concept of avant-garde art, mindful that it may be beautiful and ridiculous at once.

At Columbia University, where he taught for many years, Koch developed innovative techniques for teaching the writing of poetry. He attained a degree of celebrity when he applied these methods to schoolchildren and elderly nursing-home residents. The best-known of his books on education are *Wishes, Lies, and Dreams* (Chelsea House, 1970) and *Rose, Where Did You Get That Red?* (Random House, 1973). Koch's *Selected Poems* appeared from Random House in the USA in 1985 and from Carcanet in the UK in 1991.

A later selected poems, *On the Great Atlantic Rainway*, followed in 1994. *Sun Out: Selected Poems 1952–1954* (2002) reprints some of his most challengingly disjunctive early writing, in which Koch said he tried 'to keep my subject up in the air as long as possible'. His last volume was *A Possible World* (2002). See *The Collected Poems of Kenneth Koch* (2005) and *On the Edge: Collected Long Poems* (2009—all Knopf); *Collected Fiction* (2005) and *Collected Plays* (2012—both Coffee House); and *Selected Poems*, ed. Ron *Padgett (Library of America, 2005).   DL*

Koethe, John (1945–) Born in San Diego, California. He attended Princeton University as an undergraduate, and took a PhD in philosophy at Harvard. Until 2010 he was a member of the philosophy department at the University of Wisconsin in Milwaukee. In 2000 he became the state's first poet laureate.

In his later poetry Koethe has perfected and purified the autobiographical lyric mode developed by John *Ashbery. The subtle relations between time and desire form Koethe's primary theme; for this reason his poetry offers few tangible objects or landscapes, instead evoking the abstract yet intimate space of life itself, as experienced by an intensely introspective mind. Yet in Koethe's hands the medium of language itself takes on a silken sensuality. The influence of his work as a professional philosopher is clear in his poetry, but it does not lead to sterility; for Koethe, ideas themselves are infused with pathos.

Since *North Point North: New and Selected Poems* in 2002 he has published *Sally's Hair* (2006) and *Ninety-fifth Street* (2009—all HarperCollins). See also *The Continuity*

of Wittgenstein's Thought (Cornell University Press, 1996) and a collection of essays, *Poetry at One Remove* (University of Michigan Press, 2000).   RG*

Kolatkar, Arun Balkrishna (1932–2004) Born in Kolhapur and worked as a graphic artist in a Bombay advertising agency. He was one of the few genuinely bilingual poets of contemporary India, writing in both English and Marathi. Although his poems appeared in a number of anthologies and journals in India, Britain, and the United States, his only two published collections for many years were *Arun Kolatkarchya Kavita* (a selection of his Marathi verse) and a collection of thirty-one linked poems in English, *Jejuri* (1976), both from Ashok Shahane's small press, Pras Prakashan. For this volume he was awarded the Commonwealth Poetry Prize. Notable among his verse is the long poem 'The Boatride', which was originally published in Arvind *Mehrotra's short-lived little magazine, *Damn You*. It was subsequently published in R. *Parthasarathy's *Ten Twentieth Century Indian Poets* (Oxford University Press, 1976).

Kolatkar's most sustained achievement, *Jejuri*, ostensibly records a pilgrimage to the temple of Khandobi at Jejuri, a small town in Western Maharashtra. The poet views Hindu tradition sceptically. His laconic verse borrows something from the medieval *bhakti* poets of Maharashtra, especially Tukaram (who Kolatkar has translated into English), and juxtaposes this with the relaxed diction of the American *Beat poets. An idiosyncratic humour pervades much of Kolatkar's writing; it derives some of its force from viewing commonplace detail at an unaccustomed angle. In the short poems this can produce original, surreal effects. Longer poems display a skilfully sustained handling of narrative and irony.

Shortly before his death from cancer, Kolatkar published three further collections in Marathi, and two in English: *Kala Ghoda Poems* (on the neighbourhood in South Mumbai where he socialized) and *Sarpa Satra*, a contemporary verse fable. Arvind Mehrotra edited a selection of uncollected work in 2008, *The Boatride and Other Poems* (all Pras Prakashan), which also includes translations from Marathi. *Jejuri* was reprinted in the New York Review of Books Classics series in 2006, with an introduction by Amit Chaudhuri. Kolatkar's *Collected Poems in English*, edited with an introduction by Mehrotra, was published in the UK by Bloodaxe in 2010, and recognized as the work of a major poet.   RW*

Komunyakaa, Yusef (1947–) Born James William Brown Jr. in Bogalusa, Louisiana, Komunyakaa changed his name to reflect his Caribbean ancestry. He served in Vietnam as correspondent and editor of the *Southern Cross*, and received the Bronze Star. He has taught at the universities of Indiana, Princeton, and New York.

Highly compressed, Komunyakaa's poetry has the virtues of both lyrical and narrative poetries: lush cadences, dense imagery, and dramatic conflicts. Discordant then melodic, riffing across a range of dialects, gritty then opulent in its imagery, his work is inspired by blues, jazz, and the historic suffering of black Americans. In his first major collection, *Copacetic* (1984), the conflicts are usually those of racism, but despair and rage are abated by a will to persevere and to sing. Where *Copacetic* often deals with the rural South during the first half of this century, *I Apologize for the Eyes in My Head* (1986) relates episodes of class-strife in present day urban America, dramatizing the enduring aftermath of slavery: poverty and the psychic violence of more repressed—but still insidious—forms of racism. Some of Komunyakaa's most memorable poems appear in *Dien Cai Dau* (1988—all Wesleyan University Press): 'Re-Creating the Scene', 'To Do Street', and 'Facing It' are among the most moving poems written about the Vietnam war.

Neon Vernacular: New and Selected Poems (1993) won both the Pulitzer Prize and the Kingsley Tufts Poetry Award. Since *Pleasure Dome: New and Collected Poems* (2001—both Wesleyan University Press) he has published a dramatic adaption of the Gilgamesh epic and several new volumes, including *Taboo* (2004) and *The Chameleon*

Couch (2011—both Farrar, Straus). He has also edited a two-volume anthology of jazz poetry. See *Blue Notes: Essays, Interviews & Commentaries* (University of Michigan Press, 2000). In 2001 Komunyakaa received the Ruth Lilly Poetry Prize, and in 2011 the Wallace Stevens Award.   DWF

Kooser, Ted (1939–) Born in Ames, Iowa, and studied at the universities of Iowa State and Nebraska. For much of his life, he worked as a life-insurance executive. Between 2004 and 2006 he was US Poet Laureate, and is now Professor of English at the University of Nebraska at Lincoln.

Sure Signs (University of Pittsburgh Press, 1980) was a selection from a decade of work that established Kooser's characteristic mode as conversational observation of rural Midwest life, in image-led verse recalling the shorter poems of William Carlos *Williams. *The Blizzard Voices* (Bieler, 1986; repr. Bison, 2006) was a series of monologues based on reminiscences of the 1888 Great Plains 'Schoolhouse Blizzard'. After *Weather Central* (University of Pittsburgh Press, 1994), Kooser stopped publishing until *Winter Morning Walks* (Carnegie-Mellon University Press, 2001), a hundred 'postcard' poems sent to his friend Jim *Harrison following a cancer diagnosis (see also *Braided Creek: A Conversation in Poetry* (Copper Canyon, 2003)). *Delights and Shadows* (Copper Canyon, 2004) won the Pulitzer Prize.

As Laureate, Kooser was a prominent and eloquent advocate of poetry for the 'ordinary' reader, and began a free syndicated newspaper column, 'American Life in Poetry'. He has said that his own ideal reader would rather get her raincoat cleaned than buy a book of poems. He has also written nonfiction prose—see *Local Wonders* (2002) and *Lights on a Ground of Darkness* (2009—both University of Nebraska Press)—and two books about the writing of poetry.   JNT

Kreymborg, Alfred (1883–1966) A native of New York City who, during the earliest period of modernism, became an editor and literary entrepreneur on a par with Ezra *Pound, whom he met in Paris in 1921 after a correspondence of eight years. Originally an experimental poet and the editor of *Broom*, which was published in Rome, Berlin, and New York between 1921 and 1924, and other pioneering modernist magazines including *The Glebe* (1913) and the *Others* anthologies (1916–19), Kreymborg was once described as the 'patron saint of the modern "little magazine" movement'. *Broom* gave equal space to European and to American writers such as Pound and British ones such as *Aldington. Kreymborg also wrote the first comprehensive history of American poetry, *Our Singing Strength* (Coward-McCann, 1929). Those sections concerning the modernist poets were full of insights into the work of his contemporaries; they often read like insiders' gossip which, indeed, they were. In his later life he suffered from Parkinson's disease and wrote little.

Kreymborg is neglected, perhaps because, though he began as an offbeat writer of *imagist and impressionist poems, he turned away from avant-garde work quite early and became a strict formalist. His *Love and Life* (1908) and *Apostrophes* (1910—both Grafton), which he straightforwardly called 'prose poems', were among the century's earliest examples of *vers libre*. *Mushrooms* (Marshall, 1916) and *Blood of Things* (Coward-McCann, 1920) were typified by aphoristic, often imagistic work, such as 'Vista' or 'Theology'. 'Overheard in an Asylum' is a remarkable anti-war poem; other work was epigrammatic and whimsical, as for instance 'Race Prejudice'.

Traditionally formal work began to make inroads into *Less Lonely* (Harcourt, 1923), and by the time of *Scarlet and Mellow* (Boni & Liveright, 1926) Kreymborg's transformation was virtually complete. Other books of his poetry were *The Lost Sail* (1928); *Manhattan Men* (1929); *The Little World* (1932); and *The Selected Poems 1912-1944* (1945—all Coward-McCann). *Man and Shadow, an Allegory* (Dutton) appeared in 1946. A lifelong pacifist, Kreymborg's last book was, appropriately, *No More War and Other Poems* (Bookman, 1950). Kreymborg also scripted and produced many plays and puppet plays,

from *Lima Beans* in 1918 to *The Four Apes* of 1939. He wrote a novel, two novelettes, and an autobiography, *Troubadour* (Boni & Liveright, 1925). MS-S/LT*

Kroetsch, Robert (1927–2011) Born in Heisler, Alberta. After graduation, he worked for the US Army as a civilian education and information specialist in Labrador. He held graduate degrees from Middlebury College and the University of Iowa. After teaching for several years at the State University of New York at Binghampton and editing *boundary 2*, a journal of postmodern literature, he returned to Canada, where he taught mainly at the University of Manitoba. Kroetsch's critical writings are to be found in *The Lovely Treachery of Words: Essays Selected and New* (Oxford University Press, 1989).

In his poetry, Kroetsch moves from fairly traditional beginnings in *The Stone Hammer Poems* (Oolichan, 1975) to vigorous experimentation in *Seed Catalogue* (Turnstone, 1977), which explores history and place in comic-opera or mock-epic fashion. Using the flat and, at times, commercial diction of seed catalogues and their testimonials as a counterpoint to his lyrical and anecdotal meditations on place, growing up, family, and the advent of sexual awareness, Kroetsch is able to construct a touching, evocative, and at times hilarious patchwork quilt of life in the vanished prairie that is at once both a portrait of the artist as farm-boy and a testament to the perennially transforming power of art. It was reprinted with woodgravings by Jim Westergard in 2005 (Fitzhenry & Whiteside).

Kroetsch published nine novels. The final text of a long-running *Olson-esque sequence appeared as *Completed Field Notes* in 1989 (McClelland & Stewart), and was reprinted by the University of Alberta Press in 2000 with an introduction by Fred *Wah. Kroetsch's later books include *The Hornbooks of Rita K.* (2001) and *Too Bad: Sketches Towards a Self-Portrait* (2010—both University of Alberta Press). GG*

Kumar, Shiv K. (1921–) Born three years before Nissim *Ezekiel, Kumar is technically the most senior statesman of the new post-independence Indian English poetry; however, he began writing and publishing only in his late forties, after his mother's death. Since then, he has become one of the most productive writers of his generation, eventually publishing ten books of poetry in English—the last three of those in his still-lucid eighties—and one in Urdu, as well as five novels, two short story collections, a play, and a translation of Faiz Ahmed Faiz's selected poems (Viking, 1995). He has also published a retelling of the Mahabharata (HarperCollins, 2011). Kumar is the author of a significant critical study relating Bergson to the modernist stream-of-consciousness novel (New York University Press, 1963); however, his own poems appear to owe a greater debt to Sigmund Freud and Robert *Lowell.

An interest in spirituality, the perishability of the body and the Hindu/Buddhist concept of karma runs as a constant from Kumar's first poems to his last. These themes are always refracted through the lens of modernist irony, but in the later collections they also acquire more texture when sieved through social observation and a gently deployed classical symbolism. *Subterfuges* (Oxford University Press, 1976) focused on travel and cultural alienation in America, remains Kumar's best-known collection, but it is not necessarily his best or most representative. *Cobwebs in the Sun* (Tata McGraw Hill, 1974), *Subterfuges*, and *Woodpeckers* (Sidgwick & Jackson, 1979) together initiated the new frankness of sexual confession for which Kumar would come to be known. The principal section of *Trapfalls in the Sky* (Macmillan, 1986), which won the Sahitya Akademi award, dwells more closely on Delhi and the Indian urban experience. Kumar's later collections do not diminish in their intensity and energy; if anything, he becomes more oblique and takes greater risks. *Which of My Selves Do You Wish to Speak To? Selected Poems* (Penguin, 2011) excerpts from all of his published work.   VN

Kumin, Maxine (1925–) Born and raised in Philadelphia, the daughter of prosperous Jewish parents, and educated at Radcliffe College. Kumin's friends in Boston included Sylvia *Plath and Anne *Sexton. The versatile author of novels, short stories, essays, and children's books as well as poetry, Kumin won the Pulitzer Prize in 1973. She has taught at Columbia, Brandeis, and Princeton, has served as poetry consultant to the Library of Congress, and now lives in New Hampshire, where she has been state poet laureate.

Increasingly since her move to the country, Kumin's poetry has concerned itself with the natural world. In matter-of-fact tones sometimes darkened by elegy, her work chronicles the lives and deaths of animals and the cycle of the seasons. The fragile state of the environment is another compelling theme. Except as an occasion for mourning illnesses and deaths (the later poems abound in dark dreams), the human world seems marginal in Kumin's imagination, in contrast to the rural poems' rootedness in daily experience.

Kumin's work is less daring and stylistically distinctive than that of such contemporaries as Plath and Sexton (Kumin has a poem about surviving her friend Sexton). The tone is steady, grounded, almost stoical in comparison; the language less likely to transcend its occasion and engage in lyric flights. Kumin's early work is more concerned with formal structures than her later work, but always her language is subordinated to observation and thought.

Notable collections are *Up Country: Poems of New England* (Harper, 1973) and *The Retrieval System* (Viking, 1978). *Bringing Together* contains uncollected poems from 1958 to 1988 (Norton, 2003). Kumin's thoughts on poetry are collected in *To Make a Prairie* (University of Michigan Press, 1979) and *Always Beginning* (Copper Canyon, 2000). Her *Selected Poems 1960–1990* (1997) draws on nine volumes, and has been followed by *The Long Marriage* (2002), *Jack and Other New Poems* (2005), and *Still to Mow* (2007). See *Where I Live: New and Selected Poems 1990–2010* (2010). *Inside the Halo and Beyond* is a memoir of recovery after a serious accident (2000—all Norton).   RHa

Kunene, Mazisi (1930–2006) Born in Durban, South Africa, and took his MA at the University of Natal. In 1956 he won the Bantu Literary Competition and in 1959 went to the School of Oriental and African Studies, University of London, where he wrote a dissertation on Zulu Poetry. While there, he helped found the Anti-Apartheid Movement in Britain. Upon his return to Southern Africa he became the head of the Department of African Studies at the University of Lesotho. He later taught African studies at the University of California and represented the African National Congress both in Europe and the United States. In 1993, after taking up a post at the University of Natal, he was named Africa's Poet Laureate by UNESCO, and Poet Laureate of South Africa in 2005.

Kunene was an indigenous poet who saw himself as part of a specific African tradition of written and oral culture. Most of his poetry in English was in fact first written in Zulu. Kunene employs such traditional genres as the funeral dirge, the war song, the praise-song, and the elegy. He also includes elements of traditional religion and cosmology, such as ancestor-worship.

Above all, Kunene's poetry is political; it describes the inhumanity of the Apartheid regime in South Africa and looks back to the values of pre-colonial Africa. He published the following collections: *Zulu Poems* (Deutsch, 1970); *Emperor Shaka the Great* (1979); *Anthem of the Decades* (1981); and *Ancestors and the Sacred Mountain* (1982—all Heinemann). See the posthumous volume *Echoes from the Mountain: New and Selected Poems* (Malthouse, 2007). M-HM

Kunitz, Stanley (1905–2006) Born in Worcester, Massachusetts, where he grew up; he studied at Harvard College, receiving a BA in 1926 and an MA in 1927. He then moved to New York, taking a job with the H. W. Wilson company as an editor of the *Wilson Library Bulletin*; he also began at this time the work of collaboration with Howard Haycraft on four important biographical dictionaries of English and American authors. His first book of poems, *Intellectual Things* (1930) was barely recognized, and Kunitz did not publish his second book, *Passport to War*, for another fourteen years. The Second World War interrupted his career as editor, and when he was released from the army he joined the faculty of Bennington College, the first of several academic jobs. Real recognition came slowly to Kunitz, culminating in his receiving the Pulitzer Prize for Poetry in 1958 for his first *Selected Poems*. In 2000, at the age of ninety five, he became the tenth Poet Laureate of the United States.

The witty, even defiantly intellectual first poems of Kunitz gave way, gradually, to a more autobiographical verse (as in *The Testing Tree*, 1971), which reminded some critics of Randall *Jarrell and Robert *Lowell in their *confessional phases. The poems of later years have been restrained but quietly passionate, as in 'The Layers', where Kunitz writes: 'I have walked through many lives, | some of them my own, | and I am not who I was, | though some principle of being | abides, from which I struggle | not to stray.' Always, Kunitz writes with an almost passionate clarity and with attention to formal details.

Kunitz also worked as a translator, creating deft English versions of Russian poems by Mandelstam, Yevtushenko, Stolzenberg, Akhmatova, and Akhmadulina. His critical essays are collected in *A Kind of Order, A Kind of Folly* (Little, Brown, 1975). *Passing Through: Later Poems, New and Selected* (1995) won a National Book Award. *The Collected Poems* appeared in 2000. Kunitz's last book, written with Genine Lentine, was *The Wild Braid: A Poet Reflects on a Century in the Garden* (2005—all Norton).

For criticism and context, see Marie Henault, *Stanley Kunitz* (Twayne, 1980), Gregory Orr, *Stanley Kunitz* (Columbia University Press, 1985), and *Interviews and Encounters with Stanley Kunitz*, ed. Stanley Moss (Sheep Meadow, 1993). JP

Kuppner, Frank (1951–) Born in Glasgow and studied English and German at Glasgow University, later training as an electronics engineer. From his debut collection, *A Bad Day for the Sung Dynasty* (1984), he has specialized in book-length sequences marked by pugnacious scepticism, a ribald and zany wit, an interest in Chinese poetry, and a principled aversion to the diminished horizons and expectations of the conventional short lyric. His second collection, *The Intelligent Observation of Naked Women* (1987), underlines his concern to combine eroticism with the life of the mind, a desire persistently sabotaged by the poet's instinctive scatology.

Kuppner's confession of 'nursing the impossible dream of emigrating to Edinburgh' situates him in a recognizably Scottish tradition of 'Cosmopolibackofbeyondism', in Robert *Crawford's term, flaunting an impossible urbanity in the face of less than inspiring local prospects. His wish 'to develop the ability to write literature, and then to write something else' captures the restlessness of his gift, if not the underlying near-mania with which he has pursued his dominant themes of human insignificance and the chaotic infinities of the imagination.

Later books include *Ridiculous! Absurd! Disgusting!* (1989), *Everything Is Strange* (1994), *Second Best Moments in Chinese History* (1997), *A God's Breakfast* (2004), *Arioflotga* (2008)—an 'index of first lines' from a fictional anthology—and *The Same Life Twice* (2012—all Carcanet). He has also written a novel 'of sorts', *A Very Quiet Street* (Polygon, 1989).   DW

k

Laing, Kojo (1946–) Born in Kumasi, Ghana. After taking an MA at Glasgow University in 1968 he spent nine years in administrative positions in provincial Ghana, followed by a year in Accra. From 1980 to 1985 he was secretary to the Institute of African Studies at the University of Ghana, and has been chief executive of a private school in Accra founded by his mother.

Laing describes his poetic medium as 'verbal fireworks'. One poem has a different poem inserted into it in single capitalized words every other line; another places the same five lines in a different order in each of its first three stanzas. His themes are unusually varied. 'The same corpse' is a robust satire on the corruption of Ghanaian society. 'Africa sky' is a lyrical mood piece. 'I am the freshly dead husband' is the quirky monologue of a dead man in his coffin, observing the false grief of his fashionable widow. In 'Funeral in Accra' clocks become 'anachronistic' and the deceased is sung 'slowly to death'. The relentless flow of witticism may irritate, but it can also seem imaginatively liberating.

Laing's poetry is collected in *Godhorse* (Oxford University Press, 1989). He has since become better known as a novelist: see *Search Sweet Country* (1986; repr. McSweeney's, 2011). M. E. Kropp-Dakubu discusses Laing's early trilogy of long poems—one unpublished ('Christcrowd')—in 'Kojo Laing's Poetry and The Struggle for God', *Contemporary Ghanaian Literature, Theatre and Film*, eds. Kofi Anyidoho and James Gibbs (Rodopi, 2000). JB

Lamantia, Philip (1927–2005) Born in San Francisco and educated at public schools there. At the age of 15 he saw his work published by Henri Ford and Parker Tyler in their magazine *View*. André Breton described him at the time as 'a voice that rises once in a hundred years'. His first collection was published in 1946. Lamantia then travelled extensively and, of the younger *San Francisco group poets, became one of the first to experiment with altered states of consciousness. He was initiated into the Washo Indian peyote rites in Nevada in 1953 and afterwards spent three years in Mexico, living for a while with the Cora Indians of Nayarit. At the end of his wanderings he tried to destroy all his earlier work: this was, however, eventually published in 1962. Beginning to write again in the late 1950s, Lamantia claimed that 'he broke with surrealism in 1946'. Nevertheless, the volumes that followed, among them *Ekstasis* (1959), *Destroyed Works: Hypodermic Light, Manic Notebook, Still Poems, Spansule* (1962), and *Touch of the Marvelous* (1966), all have the essential surrealistic quality of revealing the inner life via explosive patterns of imagery. A useful selection of the work from these years is to be found in *Selected Poems 1943-1966* (City Lights, 1967). In the 1960s Lamantia travelled in Europe and continued to publish: the work sustaining a development noticeable in his 1966 collection away from an almost obsessive consciousness of cruelty and towards a poetry of affirmation.

His later volumes were *The Blood of the Air* (1970), *Becoming Visible* (1981), *Meadowlark West* (1986), and *Bed of Sphinxes: New and Selected Poems, 1943–1993* (1997—all City Lights). See Steven Frattali, *Hypodermic Light: The Poetry of Philip Lamantia and the Question of Surrealism* (Lang, 2005). RJG

Lane, Patrick (1939–) Born in Nelson, British Columbia, into a working-class family and educated at the University of British Columbia. After working at a variety of jobs, including carpet-salesman and medic in a lumber camp, Lane took up poetry as a serious vocation following the death in 1964 of his elder brother, Richard Stanley 'Red' Lane, a pop poet of the early Sixties who has assumed a slightly mythic standing in Canadian poetry, and who Patrick Lane memorialized in an early chapbook, *Carnival Man* (1966).

From his early collections—*The Sun Has Begun to Eat the Mountains* (Ingluvin, 1972), *Passing into Storm* (Traumerei, 1973), and *Beware the Months of Fire* (Anansi, 1973)—to his later works—*The Measure* (Black Moss, 1980), *Old Mother* (Oxford University Press, 1982), *A Linen Crow, A Caftan Magpie* (Thistledown, 1984), *Selected Poems* (Oxford University Press, 1987—an update of his *Selected Poems*, 1978), and the sequence *Winter* (Coteau, 1990)—Lane has stressed that, although he is not a political writer in an overt sense, he is a writer of the working class, a witness and chronicler, not only of the political world, but of the private domestic tensions shared by two people.

Throughout his poetry Lane has professed a voice in search of a home, whether that home is found in the remains of his parents' house in the interior of British Columbia, or in the prairie, or in distant lands and times. His travels to South America in the early 1970s led to *Unborn Things: Poems of South America* (Harbour, 1975), which chronicles the blurred distinction between barbarity and culture. Anarchy and violence are at the heart of Lane's early poetry. For him, history is something which dies in the vastness, the obliqueness of working-class Canada; the memory of the poet is its only, somewhat ambivalent, repository. In an early essay, 'To the Outlaw', Lane writes that the poet is both trapped and defined by history, and the voices which survive it are essentially pathetic.

In *No Longer Two People* (Turnstone, 1981), which Lane co-wrote with the poet Lorna *Crozier, what begins as a male-female argument is synthesized, humanized, and ultimately unified, and in his

more recent works, such as the poems at the conclusion of *Selected Poems* and those in *Winter*, a more pensive, less vernacular voice has emerged.

Too Spare, Too Fierce (Harbour, 1995) won the Dorothy Livesay Poetry Prize, and was followed by a further *Selected Poems* (Graphic Arts, 1997); the latest is *Witness* (2010). Later collections include *The Bare Plum of Winter Rain* (2000) and *Last Water Song* (2007). See *The Collected Poems of Patrick Lane* (2011—all Harbour) and, in the UK, *Syllable of Stone: Selected Poems* (Arc, 2005), with an introduction by John *Kinsella. Lane has also edited, with Crozier, two influential anthologies of new Canadian poetry under the title *Breathing Fire* (1995 and 2004).   BM

Langley, R. F. (Roger Francis) (1938–2011) Born in the West Midlands, Langley spent his working life as a secondary schoolteacher there. He studied English at Jesus College, Cambridge, where he met J. H. *Prynne, and was taught by Donald *Davie. In 1999, he retired to Suffolk, a county that inspired much of his writing.

Langley's *Collected Poems* (2000) numbered seventeen, from two decades of small-press publication. All are densely-layered compositions in which (as he wrote in a note on his methods) 'every brush stroke changes the picture'. 'Matthew Glover', the first poem he preserved, brings *Olson's 'open field' poetics to the enclosure of the English countryside. Another early poem, 'The Ecstasy Inventories', includes found text, a characteristic technique of this work. Later poems develop a more centripetal prosody, shaped by syllabic lines, irregular rhyme, and a meditative observational voice: see, in particular, the group clustered around the Puckish figure of *Jack* (Equipage, 1998). The poems of *The Face of It* (2007—both Carcanet) attend to art history, insects, and birdlife, as well as philosophy and psychology. The original occasions of several are recorded in the remarkable prose of his *Journals* (Shearsman, 2007).

Emerging from a personal canon that included W. S. *Graham, William Carlos

*Williams, and Wallace *Stevens—as well as a lifetime's teaching of Shakespeare—Langley's work was admired for many years by his *Cambridge School contemporaries: see *Sneak's Noise*, a sixtieth-birthday tribute (infernal methods, 1998). The uncollected 'To a Nightingale' was posthumously awarded the 2011 Forward Prize for Best Single Poem.   JNT

Lansdown, Andrew (1954–) Born in Pingelly, a small town south-east of Perth in Western Australia. He gained arts degrees from both the Western Australian Institute of Technology and the Murdoch University before becoming for a time a tutor in creative writing at the former institution, which later was renamed the Curtin University. Since then he has worked as an education officer in various prisons in Western Australia, a grim occupation which has done surprisingly little to affect his work.

Few Australian poets have been so prolific and consistent. By 37 he had already published six collections of verse, with a seventh ready for publication. From his first book, *Homecoming* (Fremantle Arts Centre, 1979), he has adopted a Christian stance and, perhaps as a result, his work has been neglected and undervalued. A collection of poems for children, *A Ball of Gold*, was followed by *Counterpoise* (Angus & Robertson, 1982), *Windfalls* (Fremantle Arts Centre, 1984), *Waking and Always* (Angus & Robertson, 1987; repr. Picaro, 2007), and *The Grasshopper Heart* (Collins/Angus & Robertson, 1991), *Between Glances* (Heinemann, 1993), and *Fontanelle* (Five Islands, 2004). Lansdown is a miniaturist, a poet attentive to the smallest details of nature, and to subtle domestic emotions. The effect of his work is cumulative, so that his poems can seem slight when considered separately; their style is precise and direct, and never ostentatious. Unusually for a poet of the late twentieth century, the mood in his poems is generally one of contentment or joy, causing fashion conscious readers to overlook his consistent technical excellence.

Birds in Mind (2009) collects his poems on the natural world of Australia. Lansdown's formalism, as discussed in *Allsorts: Poetry Tricks and Treats* (2010—both Wom-

bat), has increasingly employed syllabic Japanese forms. See the collection *The Colour of Life* in *Two Poets*, with Kevin Gillam (Fremantle Arts Centre, 2011).   JG

Larkin, Peter (1946–) Born in the New Forest, and for many years Philosophy and Literature Librarian at Warwick University, Larkin's interests include ecocriticism, postmodern theology, and Romantic poetry. An avant-garde figure whose work combines the pastoralism of the *Cambridge School with the textuality of the *Language poets, Larkin published much of his early work in fine, large-format pamphlets through his own Prest Roots Press: see *Additional Trees* (1992), *Three Forest Conformities* (1997), *Parallels Plantations Apart* (1998). All these and other works were collected in *Terrain Seed Scarcity* (Salt, 2001). Titles such as *Prose Woods* (1985) give notice of his concentrated concern with the nature of language and being in sequences meditating on arboreal landscapes. The result is an intellectually demanding, exhilaratingly defamiliarized writing of ecological apprehension ('Go steep, trees, where roots are soaked by sideways blocked creep.') See *Leaves of Field* (2006) and *Lessways Least Scarce Among* (2012—both Shearsman).   JNT

Larkin, Philip (1922–85) Grew up in Coventry (where his father served as City Treasurer), attended King Henry VIII School, and went up to read English at St John's College, Oxford, in 1940—the austere, war-disrupted atmosphere of his undergraduate years in Oxford, during which he formed a lasting friendship with Kingsley *Amis, is evoked in his novel *Jill* (1946). After graduating, Larkin went to the small town of Wellington, where he ran the local library, 'single-handed and untrained', and still found time to write both *Jill* and his second novel, set in a small-town library, *A Girl in Winter* (1947); a third novel was begun and worked at for five years, but never completed. Temperamentally, Larkin seems to have needed a full-time job, and without realizing it he had already embarked on the career which was to last to the end of his life, and which took him subsequently to the university libraries of Leicester (1946–50), Belfast (1950–5), and Hull (1955–85). Hull was where he spent the second half of his life, and he wrote vividly about the place in his poem 'Here', but even after thirty years would have hesitated to call it home. He never married, and liked to portray himself as a hermit-like bachelor, despite several long and intense relationships with women, one of whom, Monica Jones, was his companion and lover for three decades. As a reviewer he wrote perceptively about both poetry and jazz, often taking the side of the 'pleasure-seeking audience' against the alleged drabness and difficulty of modernism, though his own work's relationship with modernism was a good deal more complex than he liked to pretend. In the autumn of 1984, a year before his death, he was offered the Poet Laureateship but turned it down.

Regarded for much of his career as a minor poet with a narrow range of subject-matter, Larkin now seems to dominate the history of English poetry in the second half of the twentieth century much as *Eliot dominated it in the first. Though detractors speak of his gloom, insularity, and anti-modernism, the authority and grandiloquence of his long poems, and the grace, sharpness and humour of his shorter ones, continue to attract new generations of admirers, and the eloquence of his engagement with major themes—love, marriage, freedom, destiny, ageing, and death—has become clearer with the passage of time. The appearance of his *Collected Poems* in 1988, while turning up no new masterpieces, added over eighty poems to the Larkin canon, considerably enlarging our sense of a poet who had published only four slim volumes in his lifetime. And there has been a further sense of enlargement since, not least with the publication in 2012 of *The Complete Poems*, which runs to over 700 pages.

For all the seriousness of his early ambitions as a novelist, Larkin's achievement and reputation were made as a poet: he liked to say, not that he chose poetry, but that it chose him. Yet there was little maturity in his first volume, *The North Ship* (1945), which if anything seems to go back-

wards from the tough, witty Audenesque verse he wrote as a schoolboy. Its frail, inward, *Yeatsian rhetoric of hearts and silences and stony places has a consistency of tone he might have been pleased with for a time, but which he soon tried to toughen and correct, in part through the flatter, less deceived manner of Thomas *Hardy. He was blocked and seemingly depressed through the late 1940s (when his father died), but in 1950, in the autumn of which he moved to Belfast, he wrote 'At Grass', 'Deceptions', 'Spring', 'Wants', 'No Road', and a number of other poems that were to appear in *The Less Deceived* (1955). It was in this collection that Larkin constructed the poetic persona—plain-speaking, sceptical, modest, unshowy, awkward, commonsensical, even rather dry and dull—that was to be associated not only with him but with the *Movement, the post-war generation of poets anthologized in Robert *Conquest's *New Lines* (1956). It is a persona that owes something to modernist forebears like Laforgue and Eliot, but also to the Englishness of *Betjeman and Orwell. There can be something faintly comic in the Larkin narrator's miserable exclusion from the joys of sex, or the consolations of religion, or the excitements of social rebellion, his life compromised or squatted on by 'the toad work'. But at best Larkin makes matters of obsessive concern to him—whether to marry, how to face the idea of death, what we owe to others (especially our parents) and ourselves, to what extent we control our lives—into rich dramatic monologues, inviting the reader to listen in as he thinks aloud, venturing one tentative explanation then overturning it with another, filling his speech with the hesitations and self-corrections ('Yes, true; but . . . ', 'No, that's not the difference: rather, how . . . ') that seem to guarantee the speaker's honesty. The Larkin persona is a subtle and elaborate construct, even a mask, though he was perhaps right to feel that his work was far more direct, emotional, and even naïve than critics acknowledged.

The effect of a man speaking to other men (rather less, perhaps, to women) is even more pronounced in Larkin's two other mature collections, *The Whitsun*

Weddings (1965) and *High Windows* (1974), which in nearly all respects are a refinement of the manner and widening of the scope of *The Less Deceived*, not a departure (Larkin remained as contemptuous of the idea of 'development' as he did of free verse or poetry in translation). In these volumes, the close pact with the reader is enhanced by Larkin's use of the vernacular, the slangy familiarities and obscenities not only counterpointing and holding down more elevated diction but also delivering some of his most famous lines ('Books are a load of crap', 'They fuck you up, your mum and dad'). The epigrammatic quality of Larkin's verse would be hard to overemphasize: many of his best lines seem to float magnificently free of their immediate context—'Life is first boredom, then fear', from 'Dockery and Son', for example; or 'Nothing, like something, happens anywhere', from 'I Remember, I Remember'; or 'What will survive of us is love', from 'An Arundel Tomb'—but he would rarely allow himself to fire his big guns without first patiently winning the reader's trust: the verse-form which dominates the poems on which his reputation seems likely to rest—'Church Going', 'The Whitsun Weddings', 'Dockery and Son', 'The Old Fools', 'Aubade'—is spacious (eight-to-twelve lines), complex-rhyming, and can run to as many as eight stanzas. The pattern is nearly always the same: the siting of the speaker in a particular place, then the slow opening out of one man's tentative musings into a large, confident, universal statement.

The mood of Larkin's poems is often sombre, glimpsing the loneliness, emptiness, and mortality that lie underneath social rituals. The ideas in his poems, baldly stated, can sound chilling and depressing, nearer to *Beckett than Betjeman: that we always make the wrong choice, supposing we have any choice at all; that the sense we have of a 'life lived according to love' makes the compromised, loveless reality almost unendurable; that human existence is only bearable because the prospect of death is worse. But his gloom is often overstated by critics. He rather relished the role of misanthrope, and there is something energetic and life-enhancing about his determina-tion to find phrase-making, disabused summations of everything from childhood ('A forgotten boredom') to marriage ('two can live as stupidly as one'). Even his darkest poems have their element of black comedy, and there are, besides, a number of exercises in light verse, whether satirical about social mores ('Sexual intercourse began | In nineteen sixty-three'), sardonic about human relationships ('He married a woman to stop her getting away | now she's there all day'), or gently mocking of academic life ('Jake Balokowsky, my biographer | Has this page microfilmed'). The tone here is affectionate rather than scabrous, and though Larkin has been accused of loftiness and condescension—as in his image of the 'cut-price crowd, urban yet simple'—this is to ignore his imaginative engagement with ordinary lives: the empathy he shows towards the young mothers in 'Afternoons', pushed to the side of their own lives, or towards the patients and stretcher-cases in 'Ambulances' and 'The Building'. Larkinesque affirmation of another kind comes from the metaphors of air and light, the transcendent Utopian gleams which appear throughout his work, highlighting the limitations of the real world, yet offering a vision of hope and integrity which is more than merely cruel.

Despite the emergence since his death of a substantial body of unpublished work, Larkin was not a prolific writer. After *High Windows*, he came to feel that poetry had given him up, turning increasingly to drink, becoming partially deaf (and so losing the consolations of jazz), and deriving professional comfort only from the acclaim for his collected prose, *Required Writing*. Apart from 'Aubade' (the definitive statement of his fear of death), 'Love Again' (a haunting poem of sexual jealousy), and 'The Mower' (prompted by the accidental killing of a hedgehog), he wrote few poems worth preserving in his last ten years. Though his work repeatedly denies the possibility of life after death, Larkin survives through his art as an original, deep-feeling poet who courageously refused the consolations of conventional belief. Larkin's *Collected Poems*, ed. Anthony Thwaite (Marvell/Faber

1988; Farrar, Straus, 1989), was the first attempt to bring together his published and unpublished poetry, and remains the most attractive and accessible volume in print. *The Complete Poems*, edited by Archie Burnett (2012), adds further unpublished poems from workbooks and letters, with extensive and often illuminating annotations. *The Early Poems and Juvenilia*, ed. A. T. Tolley (2005), consists of apprentice work which Larkin himself would not have wanted to see published. *Trouble at Willow Gables*, ed. James Booth, (2002—all Faber) gathers his unpublished fiction, including the pastiches of schoolgirl romances he wrote under the pseudonym Brunette Coleman. *Required Writing* (Faber, 1983; Farrar, Straus, 1984) is Larkin's own selection of his miscellaneous prose and critical pieces, which *Further Requirements*, ed. Anthony Thwaite (2001), supplements by including interviews, broadcasts and statements about writing. *All What Jazz* (1970—both Faber), Larkin's collection of jazz reviews, is similarly supplemented by *Reference Back*, ed. Richard Palmer and John White (University of Hull Press, 1999; repr. as *Jazz Writings*, Continuum, 2001), forty years of his uncollected jazz writings. *Selected Letters of Philip Larkin*, ed. Anthony Thwaite, came out from Faber in 1992 (Farrar, Straus, 1993), and *Letters to Monica*—the same editor's selection of letters exchanged between Larkin and Monica Jones—in 2010 (Faber).

Andrew Motion's *Philip Larkin: A Writer's Life* (Faber, 1993) remains the definitive biography. Other useful biographical information is contained in *Larkin at Sixty*, ed. Anthony Thwaite (Faber, 1982) and *Philip Larkin, 1922–1985: A Tribute*, ed. George Hartley (Marvell, 1988), as well as in two memoirs written by women close to Larkin: Jean Hartley's *Philip Larkin, The Marvell Press and Me* (Carcanet, 1989) and Maeve Brennan's *The Philip Larkin I Knew* (Manchester University Press, 2002). Among critical books, Andrew Motion's short study, *Philip Larkin* (Methuen, 1983), Janice Rossen's *Philip Larkin: His Life's Work* (Harvester Wheatsheaf, 1989) and Stephen Regan's *Philip Larkin* (St Martin's Press, 1992) provide useful introductions. Recent criticism has emphasized

Larkin's literary sophistication as a poet: see *New Larkins for Old* (Palgrave, 1999), ed. James Booth, and M. W. Rowe, *Philip Larkin: Art and Self* (Palgrave, 2011). PBM

Lasdun, James (1958–) Born in London and read English at Bristol University. He now lives in New York and has taught at New York University. He has won an Eric Gregory Award for his poetry and the Dylan Thomas Award (in 1986) for the stories in *The Silver Age* (Cape, 1985).

Lasdun's early poetry combined brilliant, dense-packed imagery reminiscent of Anthony *Hecht with deft rhythmic control. In style and mood he was a poet of the Eighties: not the Eighties of urban dereliction, graffiti, and cardboard cities, but its brittle antipode of decadent wealth.

His first collection, *A Jump Start* (Secker & Warburg, 1987) displayed his neo-Jacobean sensibility, as did *The Silver Age* in rather cruel stories of spoilt people, told in a conventional style but with considerable panache. In his poems, similar people and places are rendered in a style that is particularly good at fleshing out indeterminate states: the feathery evocation of 'On the Road to Chenonceaux', the bravura metaphysics of 'Vanishing Points'.

A Jump Start was very much a young man's book. Like the youths in his poem 'Vindice at the Oyster Bar' he is 'turned to the brine of sex', a theme pursued in his novels, *The Horned Man* (2002) and *Seven Lies* (2006), and his third collection of stories, *It's Beginning to Hurt* (2009). His later collections of poetry are *The Revenant* (1995; published in the USA as *Woman Police Officer in Elevator*), *Landscape with Chainsaw* (2001), an evocation of life in rural America which was nominated for the T. S. Eliot Prize, and *Water Sessions* (2012—all Cape). With Michael *Hofmann, he edited *After Ovid: New Metamorphoses* (Faber, 1994). PF*

Laughlin, James (1914–97) Born in Pittsburgh and attended Harvard University, at the end of his freshman year there visiting Ezra *Pound in Rapallo. Pound advised the wealthy young Laughlin that he could make his best contribution to literature as a publisher of new writing, rather than as a poet. Subsequently in 1936 Laughlin established New Directions, publishing first Pound and William Carlos *Williams and thereafter a wide range of American and international work, until New Directions became, as it has remained, the foremost disseminator of modernist and related writing in the English-speaking world.

However, he continued throughout his life to write and publish his own poetry, some twenty volumes in all, including *Selected Poems, 1935–1985* (1986). His poems, sometimes in what he himself called 'long and languid' lines, but more usually in shorter, regularly defined, but freely measured couplets or triplets, employ a language that is cool, clear, unstrained, and unaffected. They call to mind most often, amongst his immediate seniors, Williams and *Cummings. Laughlin was modest about his own poetic achievement. Yet he is a poet capable of considerable beauty of image and movement, of good-humoured irony and bitter-sweet reminiscence, of compassion for 'the succession of the generations'.

Hayden *Carruth edited *The Collected Poems of James Laughlin* in 1994 (Moyer Bell), and wrote a memoir of his friend, *Beside the Shadblow Tree* (Copper Canyon, 1999). See also *Poems, New and Selected* (New Directions, 1998). Selections of Laughlin's letters to poets such as Pound, Delmore *Schwartz, and Kenneth *Rexroth have also been published. His long, unfinished verse-autobiography, *Byways*, was published by New Directions in 2005, ed. Peter Glassgold, with a preface by Guy *Davenport.   RWB

Lauterbach, Ann (1942–) Born in New York City, she took a BA in English at the University of Wisconsin-Madison, and worked at Central St Martin's School of Art and the ICA in London before returning to New York. Lauterbach balances the world of art with the world of poetry and poetics; she has authored thirteen volumes of poetry, many collaborations, and a volume of prose writings, and is Schwab Professor of Language and Literature at Bard College, and Visiting Core Critic at Yale School of Art.

Influenced by poets as diverse as Wallace *Stevens and George *Oppen, Lauterbach finds experience and poetic experiment inextricable. Her poetry pays attention to the changeability and infinite possibilities of experience, and the disjunctions between subject and object, cause and effect, leading John *Ashbery to write that it 'goes straight to the elastic, infinite core of time'. The title poem of *Hum* (2005) addresses the poet's experience of the World Trade Center attacks of 2001 in restrained elegiac couplets. For Lauterbach, poetry after 9/11 'continues to elucidate the vital topography between individual and historical accounting' (*The Night Sky: Writings on the Poetics of Experience* (2005)). *Or to Begin Again* (2009—all Penguin) is an exploration of narrative and rupture, which was nominated for a National Book Award. Its central sequence, 'Alice in the Wasteland', meditates on the differences between spoken and written language, reading, and consciousness.   HY

Lawrence, Anthony (1957–) Though known as the author of the novel *In the Half Light* (Picador, 2000), Anthony Lawrence has made his reputation as a poet of pastoral and interior landscapes. Born in Tamworth in rural New South Wales, Lawrence left school at sixteen and worked around Australia as a jackeroo, fisherman, gardener, and teacher. His first collection, *Dreaming in Stone* (Angus & Robertson, 1989), won the Harri Jones Memorial Prize with its lyrical coagulation of harshness and epiphany influenced as much by Les *Murray and Judith *Beveridge as John *Berryman, Wallace *Stevens, Bob Dylan, and Ted *Hughes. After *Three Days Out of Tidal Town* (Hale & Iremonger 1992) and *The Darkwood Aquarium* (Penguin, 1993), Lawrence's *New and Selected Poems* (University of Queensland Press, 1998) and *Skinned by Light: Poems 1989–2002* secured his reputation, the former winning the inaugural Judith Wright Calanthe Award in 1999.

His other prestigious prizes include the Peter Porter Poetry Prize (2010), Josephine Ulrick National Poetry Prize (2001), the Kenneth Newcastle Poetry Prize (1997), the Kenneth Slessor Poetry Prize (1997), and the Gwen Harwood Memorial Poetry Prize (1996). His latest publications are *Bark* (University of Queensland Press, 2008) and the verse novella *The Welfare of My Enemy* (Puncher & Wattman, 2011).   TD

Lawrence, D. H. (David Herbert) (1885–1930) Born in Eastwood, Nottinghamshire, the fourth son of a coal-miner. His mother, whose influence dominated the first half of his life, belonged to the middle class and had been a teacher. In 1898 he won a scholarship to Nottingham High School, and in 1906 went to University College, Nottingham.

Lawrence, according to his own note in the *Collected Poems* (1928), wrote his first two poems, 'if poems they were, when I was nineteen'; he identifies them as 'To Guelder-Roses' and 'To Campions'. Though these pieces suffer from *Georgian and Romantic diction, and a rather clumsy handling of traditional form (a limitation we find in much of Lawrence's poetry), they nevertheless have certain unmistakable features—for instance, a choice of adjectives and nouns evoking colours, textures, and sensations—which foreshadow the later verse; here we find Lawrence on his way to creating his personal poetic language without yet having anything to say in it. An account of his reading in his youth can be found in *A Personal Record* (1935), by Jessie Chambers (whom he portrayed as Miriam in *Sons and Lovers*). He apparently knew most of the poems in Palgrave's *Golden Treasury of Songs and Lyrics*, but what she remembers most vividly are his recitations of Shelley, Wordsworth, and Keats. A crucially important influence on his poetry was that of Walt Whitman. According to Chambers, 'Whitman's *Leaves of Grass* was one of his great books. He would sometimes write, "I'm sending you a Whitman-esque poem," when he was enclosing one of his own.' Lawrence later used Whitman's free, brimming long line and his extrovert poetic voice for his own purposes in his verse; his vision—mythopoeic and sceptical at once—was, however, very different from the American poet's. An acute and characteristically idiosyncratic essay by him on Whitman can be found in *Studies In Classic American Literature* (1923).

In 1909 Lawrence's poetry was published in the *English Review*, after Jessie Chambers sent three poems—'Discipline', 'Dreams Old and Nascent', and 'Baby Movements'—to the journal's editor, Ford Madox Hueffer (later *Ford). Hueffer was deeply impressed, and wished to meet Lawrence personally; thus was formed the latter's first literary friendship, and through Hueffer came his initial contact with London's literary world. *The White Peacock*, his first novel, was published in 1911, and a book of verse, *Love Poems and Others*, in 1913. Among the successful pieces here are the ones based on his experiences as a schoolteacher at Croydon, and poems that explore themes of love and sexuality while subtly attending to the details of the Midlands landscape. Also in this volume is 'End of Another Home-Holiday', in which a smoky, understated mood of parting (in this case, from his mother) lies beneath the scrupulously observed and casually animated particulars of a small town; moreover, that important Lawrentian symbol the moon is suggestively present. All this is developed through finely judged rhythmic and prosodic variations which both preserve and liberate the ambiguity of the moment; there is a balance of subject-matter and a form not quite traditional and not quite *vers libre* which Lawrence seldom achieves again until the poems in *Birds, Beasts and Flowers* and his last poems about death. For an interesting reading of this poem, see A. *Alvarez's essay on Lawrence in *The Shaping Spirit* (1958). We also find in *Love Poems and Others* the dialect poems, which reveal insights into the small-scale tragedies and the unexpected humorousness of working-class life reminiscent of *Hardy's novels; these poems were much admired by Ezra *Pound. The book was critically well-received, Pound calling it 'the most important book of poems of the season', and Edward *Thomas welcoming it as 'the book of the moment in verse'.

Amores (1916), his next collection of poetry, once more has some powerful pieces about family life ('Discord In Childhood'; 'Sorrow', a slight and touching elegy on his mother); some of the events recorded here are to be found in a more realized form in the novel *Sons and Lovers* (1913). In 1912 Lawrence eloped with Frieda Weekley (the aristocratic German wife of his former modern-languages tutor) to Germany; they were married after returning to England, in July 1914. *Look! We Have Come Through* (1917) is a sequence of poems mostly about married love and happiness: two themes relatively rare in modern poetry. 'Gloire De Dijon', 'Song Of A Man Who Is Loved', and 'Song Of A Man Who Has Come Through' represent, after his mother's death, a phase of renewal and creativity, and suggest a profound, albeit slightly threatened, conjugal calm; what is most wonderfully expressed, perhaps, is the sense of *gratitude* to the woman in the poems. By now Lawrence had also discovered his aims and desires as a poet. In his nervously sensitive but forcefully conversational manner, he articulates his ideas (which owe something to his reading of F. T. Marinetti and the Italian Futurists) in his remarkable essay, 'Poetry of the Present', in *New Poems* (1918). His intention, he says, is to write a 'poetry of that which is at hand: the immediate present', of the 'moment' in which there is nothing 'fixed, set, static', and to employ a Whitmanesque free verse that would do away with 'clichés of rhythm as well as phrase'.

Meanwhile, Lawrence's novel *The Rainbow* was completed in 1915; it was banned on publication. After the war he travelled extensively with Frieda in search of societies that could offer him an alternative to the modern Western civilization he had come to hate. Most of the poems in *Birds, Beasts and Flowers* (1923), which he (and many others) considered his 'best book of poems', are set in places as diverse as Italy, Sicily, Australia, New Mexico, and Ceylon. Some of his most impressive poetry— 'Almond Trees', 'Bat', the tortoise-sequence,

and the much-anthologized 'Snake', among others—is to be found here, written in an unprecedented, flickering free verse, in a style at once celebratory and wittily hectoring. They convey, through their peculiar language, an almost occult empathy with the landscape; 'empathy', however, is an inadequate word for the complex Lawrentian relationship with natural phenomena. The energy of many of these poems also derives from a concealed misanthropy, an intense and irrational longing for a 'world empty of people', converted here, through the healing power of the imagination, into a positive feeling of reverence for non-human life.

In 1925, the Lawrences returned to Europe, and in 1928 *Lady Chatterley's Lover* was banned. *Pansies* (1929)—from the French *pensées*, thoughts—contains poems that show a deepening disgust with English society; in some, however, the disgust provides the impulse for genuinely funny satire. After Lawrence's death of tuberculosis in Venice, Richard *Aldington published *More Pansies* and *Last Poems* in 1932 from manuscripts found among his last writings. Besides some memorable pieces about the sea, God (a distinctively Lawrentian, excitable, and amoral God), and the Etruscans, are, in *Last Poems*, the great sonorous poems on death, including 'The Ship of Death' and 'Bavarian Gentians'. These poems, which divulge his personal myth of death and the afterlife, interweaving images from Etruscan culture and the Etruscan tombs, are perhaps the most serene and affirmative he ever wrote, and are full of a haunting and even tragic optimism about a 'new life'—an idea always precious to Lawrence. They remind us that his poetry (even on the eve of death) is essentially a poetry of wonder, of possibilities, and of departures.

See *Complete Poems*, ed. V. de S. Pinto and W. Roberts (Heinemann/Viking, 1964; paperback, 1967), and also two full-length studies of Lawrence's verse: *Acts Of Attention* (Cornell University Press, 1972; 2nd edn., 1990), by Sandra M. Gilbert, and *Thinking In Poetry* (Macmillan, 1987), by M. J. Lockwood. See also Amit Chaudhuri, *D. H. Lawrence and 'Difference':*

Postcoloniality and The Poetry of the Present (Oxford University Press, 2003) and Bethan Jones, *The Last Poems of D. H. Lawrence: Shaping a Late Style* (Ashgate, 2010). Tom *Paulin has made a recent selection of Lawrence's verse (Faber, 2007). AC

Lawson, Henry (1867–1922) Born on the Grenfell (New South Wales) gold-fields. Educated in country schools, he worked as a coach-and house-painter. By 1883 he had joined his mother Louisa (later editor of the feminist journal *Dawn*) in Sydney. His first published poem, 'A Song of the Republic', appeared in the *Bulletin* in 1887. The early bent of his verse was radical (as spokesman for 'the Army of the Rear') and nationalist (warning against the danger of 'old-world errors and wrongs and lies | Making a hell in a Paradise'). Lawson's poems of outback life mingled celebration of bush characters with a realistic appraisal of hardship. In his 1892 verse debate with A. B. 'Banjo' *Paterson in the *Bulletin* he took the pessimistic side. A note of threnody informs Lawson's outback poems, for instance in the lament of how 'The mighty Bush with iron rails | Is tethered to the world'.

Lawson published many, sometimes best-selling, volumes of verse. These have been valued less highly than his short fiction. A. A. Phillips referred to the 'ventriloquial folk-voice' that spoke through Lawson's poetry. Like his contemporary Rudyard *Kipling, Lawson's ballads were a rich fount of aphorism, apparent crystallizations of popular feeling, even if a racist and militarist strain was pronounced in his later years.

See *Poetical Works of Henry Lawson* (Angus & Robertson, 1918, new edn. 1979). Phillips' *The Australian Tradition* (1958) and Brian Matthews' *The Receding Wave* (1972) contain important criticism. George Mackaness' *An Annotated Bibliography of Henry Lawson* (1951) and Colin Roderick's *Henry Lawson Criticism 1874–1971* (1972) are significant, if not recent, reference works. Roderick also wrote *Henry Lawson: A Life* (Angus & Robertson, 1992). PP

Layton, Irving (Peter) (1912–2006) Born Israel Pincu Lazarovitch in Romania, he was brought to Montreal by his immigrating parents who settled in the working-class ghetto of that city. Educated at local schools, Layton received a BSc from Macdonald College and an MA in political science from McGill University. He taught school at various levels, and evening classes at Sir George Williams College. His success as a poet led to a professorship of English at York University, Toronto, from which he retired in 1978. He died in Montreal.

Layton harboured strong left-wing ideals from his college days which found an outlet in the 1940s in his association with a modernist little magazine called *First Statement*. This was the beginning of a series of involvements with the little-press movement, most important of which was Layton's connection with Contact Press in the early 1950s which, in turn, led to a friendship with the Americans Robert *Creeley and Jonathan *Williams, the latter publishing Layton's breakthrough collection, *The Improved Binoculars* (1956; repr. Porcupine's Quill, 1991) with an enthusiastic foreword by William Carlos *Williams. In 1959 Layton won the Governor General's Award for *A Red Carpet for the Sun*, a collection which established his reputation and standing in the literary community. The frank and passionate rhetoric of his poems disturbed the critics of the day, and led Layton into a war of words with reviewers and anthologists, whom he accused of smothering the creative process. His poetry shows great swings between a Dionysian celebration of life on the one hand and much tenderness and sorrowing about the dark side of existence. Given to the self-conscious verbal strut, the occasional vulgarism, the declamatory posture of poet and prophet, Layton won a large audience both for himself and for contemporary poetry in Canada. Well read in Marx, D. H. *Lawrence, and Nietzsche, Layton took upon himself the various roles of social rebel, raunchy poet, and poetic will personified. A slow publishing start in the Forties with two slim collections led to a productive decade in the Fifties, and ultimately would see Layton as the author of some fifty volumes of verse and a memoir,

Waiting for the Messiah (McClelland & Stewart, 1985; repr. 2012). His first *Collected Poems* came out in 1965. With the advent of the Seventies, Layton began to exhibit a growing social conservatism coupled with a self-conscious Jewishness, tendencies characterized by support for American politics and anti-Christian rhetoric. A major volume, *The Collected Poems of Irving Layton* (both McClelland & Stewart) appeared in 1971, while his *Uncollected Poems 1935–1959* was published by Mosaic Press in 1976. *Engagements: The Prose of Irving Layton* (McClelland & Stewart, 1972) was followed by *Taking Sides: The Collected Social and Political Writings* (Mosaic/Valley) in 1977. There are three collections of letters: *An Unlikely Affair* (Mosaic, 1980), *Wild Gooseberries: The Selected Letters of Irving Layton* (Macmillan, 1989), and *Irving Layton and Robert Creeley, The Complete Correspondence 1953–1978* (McGill-Queen's University Press, 1990). Layton was inducted into the Order of Canada in 1976. See *A Wild Peculiar Joy: The Selected Poems* (McClelland & Stewart, 1982; repr. 2012).   MG

Lea, Sydney (1942–) Grew up in the affluent suburbs of Philadelphia, and graduated from Yale University with a BA and PhD before taking up teaching positions at Dartmouth College, Yale, and Middlebury College. In 1976, Lea co-founded, with Jay Parini, *New England Review*, a literary journal, which he edited until 1989.

Lea's poetry is densely concrete, often formal in structure and style. His affection for the woodland areas of New England, especially New Hampshire and Maine, and his interest in hunting and fishing, provide a regional aspect to his poems, which frequently move in autobiographical directions, as in 'The Tracks on Kenyon Hill' or 'For My Son Creston at the Solstice', both of which affect an outdoor, woodsy setting that becomes increasingly symbolic. In Lea's best work outer landscape merges with inner to create a sense of the physical presence of the spiritual world—much in the American tradition of Emerson and Thoreau.

Lea's second book, *The Floating Candles* (University of Illinois Press, 1982) contains a memorable long narrative, 'The Feud', which depends on a strongly colloquial voice and finely tuned dramatic sense for its effects. The narrative impulse continues through Lea's more recent volumes, including *No Sign* (University of Georgia Press, 1987) and *Prayer for the Little City* (Scribner's, 1989), which take his poetry in an explicitly Christian direction. Lea's first novel was *A Place in Mind* (Scribner's, 1988; repr. Story Line, 1997). He has also edited a volume of essays on Anthony *Hecht's poetry.

To the Bone: New and Selected Poems (1996) was followed by *Pursuit of a Wound* (2000—both University of Illinois Press), a finalist for the Pulitzer Prize. His later books include *Ghost Pain* (Sarabande, 2005) and *Young of the Year* (Four Way, 2011). In 2011 Lea became Poet Laureate of Vermont. See also *Hunting the Whole Way Home: Essays and Poems* (Lyons, 2002) and *A Little Wildness: Some Notes on Rambling* (Story Line, 2006).   JP

Ledwidge, Francis (1887–1917) Born in Slane, Co. Meath, where for a time he worked as a labourer and clerk. From boyhood Ledwidge wrote poetical, untutored verses. Lord Dunsany, local landlord and an aspiring writer of the Celtic revival, introduced him to *Yeats' poetry and to Katherine Tynan with whom he corresponded. Ledwidge was an organizer of the Irish Volunteers; like many of the Volunteers, he enlisted in the British Army in 1914, in Dunsany's regiment. His years in the war were marked by homesickness, highlighted by news of the 1916 Rising (his best-known poems are 'Thomas McDonagh' and 'The Blackbirds', elegies for the executed poet-leaders of the Rising, *MacDonagh and Plunkett). He was killed near Ypres in 1917.

Ledwidge is like a lesser Keats: his stylized diction and syntax are vivified by colloquial idiom ('The Singer's Muse' 'made a poet of her servant boy'), in a mixture that anticipates Patrick *Kavanagh or early *Heaney. The poeticisms too are often vivid: the 'spider-peopled wells'; 'this poor bird-hearted singer of a day'. His mixed language is perhaps learned from Yeats; its archaizing recalls Mangan. Neither his poeticality nor his national sentiments have current appeal; but it is sad that his nature poetry has not been discovered by Clare's readership. Ledwidge's *Complete Poems* were edited by Alice Curtayne (1974); she also wrote *Francis Ledwidge: A Life of the Poet* (1972—both Brian & O'Keeffe), which was reprinted by New Island Books in 1998.   BO'D

Lee, Don L. *See* MADHUBUTI, HAKI R.

Lee, Laurie (1914–97) Born, the eleventh of twelve children, in Stroud in Gloucestershire, where he went to school. He described those among whom he grew up as the country's first literate peasantry, the inheritors of an oral tradition of language. He left home at 19 and walked to London, where he worked as a labourer. In 1935 he went to Spain, supporting himself by playing his violin in the streets or cafés. In the Second World War he worked as a scriptwriter and in the Ministry of Information. His first volume of autobiography, *Cider With Rosie* (1959) brought him fame and independence.

Although a number of his poems were written in the 1930s, he had almost no contact with the literary world during those years. His poems were included in the third volume of John *Lehmann's *Poets of Tomorrow* in 1944; and his first book, *The Sun My Monument*, appeared that year (Hogarth/Doubleday, 1947). Lee's second book, *A Bloom of Candles*, twelve 'verses from a poet's year' (Lehmann), came out in 1947. His last book of new poems, *My Many-Coated Man*, appeared in 1955 (Deutsch; Coward-McCann, 1957). He wrote two verse dramas, *Peasants' Priest* (1947) and *The Voyage of Magellan* (1948).

Although Lee had little education and wrote about the life from which he came, the imagery of his early poems shows the influence of the sophisticated poetry of *Auden and *Spender and possibly of the Spanish poet, Federico Garcia Lorca. His best work has a sharpness and brightness of imagery and a lightness of movement

that are unmistakable; but these effects are also a measure of his limited range. He is none the less a poet of enduring charm. His work can be explored in *Selected Poems* (Deutsch, 1983; repr. Penguin, 1985). See Valerie Grove, *Laurie Lee: The Well-Loved Stranger* (Viking, 1999).   ATT

Lee, Li-Young (1957–) Born in Jakarta, Indonesia, of Chinese parents. His maternal grandfather was Yuan Shikai, the first president of the Republic of China, who attempted to make himself into Emperor. In 1959 Lee's father, who had been a personal physician to Mao Zedong in China, fled to Indonesia with his family and after spending a year as a political prisoner in President Sukarno's jails, the family travelled throughout Hong Kong, Macau, and Japan, before arriving in America in 1964. Lee studied at the University of Pittsburgh, the University of Arizona, and the State University of New York, Brockport. Lee has written, 'I think immigrants have beautiful stories to tell. But the problem is to make art out of it.' His critics fault his poetry for its slackness, both emotional and linguistic; but his admirers speak of his modesty and of the unsentimental intimacy with which he handles his often sensational subject matter.

Li-Young Lee is the author of four collections of poetry: *Rose* (1986), which received the Delmore Schwartz Memorial Poetry Award, *The City in Which I Love You* (1990), which was the Lamont Poetry Selection of the Academy of American Poets, *Book of My Nights* (2001—all BOA), and *Behind My Eyes* (Norton, 2008). He has also published a lyrical memoir, *The Wingéd Seed: a Remembrance* (Simon & Schuster, 1995). Lee lives in Chicago with his wife Donna and their two children.   HC

Lee, Tzu Pheng (1946–) Lee began writing poetry while still at school. During her undergraduate years at the University of Singapore her poems came to the attention of Edwin *Thumboo, among others, and she was encouraged to publish. Essentially a private poet, she made a public impact with the appearance in 1966 of her

'My Country and My People'. Many Singaporean readers saw this piece as encapsulating the peculiar history of the nation in its convoluted progress from British colony to independent republic. Lee's later work is more personal. Both *Against the Next Wave* (1988) and *The Brink of an Amen* (1991—both Times) register emotional anguish, but they also celebrate the embracing of a religious faith which has intensified over the years, and now provides the secure emotional basis of her work.

See also *Prospect of a Drowning* (Heinemann, 1980) and *Lambada by Galilee and Other Surprises* (Times, 1997). For criticism, see Felicia Chan, *Silences May Speak: the Poetry of Lee Tzu Pheng* (Times, 1999). KS

Leggott, Michele (1956–) Born in Stratford, New Zealand, Leggott read English at the University of Canterbury before moving to Canada in 1980 to pursue doctoral studies at the University of British Columbia. She is an Associate Professor of English at Auckland University.

Leggott's doctoral thesis on Louis *Zukofsky was published as *Reading Zukofsky's '80 Flowers'* (Johns Hopkins University Press, 1989). Her work as a poet, critic, and editor testifies to an interweaving interest in the history of poetic innovation in North America and New Zealand. She has co-edited a collection of essays, *Opening the Book: Essays on New Zealand Writing* (1995), and an influential anthology, *Big Smoke: New Zealand Poems 1960–1975* (2000—both Auckland University Press). She also edited the poems of Robin *Hyde.

Leggott's first poems were published in Vancouver. *Like This?* (Caxton, 1988), her debut volume, collected the writing of a decade. The unrhymed, rhapsodic sonnet has become a recurrent form in Leggott's work. *Dia* (1994) featured a sequence of thirty, 'Blue Irises', which incorporated lines from the love poetry of earlier New Zealand female poets. *As Far as I Can See* (1999) addressed the poet's failing sight in sonnets and prose poems. Since 2001, Leggott has led the development of the New Zealand Electronic Poetry Centre (nzepc), an online resource. From 2007 to 2009 she was New Zealand Poet Laureate, which resulted in the poems of *Mirabile Dictu* (2009—all Auckland University Press). JNT

Lehman, David (1948–) Born in New York City and educated at Columbia University and Cambridge, writing a dissertation at Columbia on the prose poem. He has taught at Brooklyn College and Hamilton College. He currently lives with his wife and son in Ithaca, New York, where he works as a freelance writer, editor, and book-reviewer, and teaches at the New School. In 1988 Lehman instigated the annual series of anthologies titled *Best American Poetry*. He remains series editor.

Lehman's own poetry began in the mode of the *New York School, with obvious debts to Frank *O'Hara, Kenneth *Koch, and John *Ashbery. But in his second book, *Operation Memory* (1990), his imagination was drawn to the nightmares of twentieth-century history. Lehman eschews a literal accounting of horrors, opting instead for a mythopoeic mode that converts the traumas of war and genocide into slippery dream narratives. His poems draw freely on popular culture, especially movies, and the result is an uneasy mixture of the conventional and the unspeakable, as though the truth of history could only be glimpsed through the protective gauze of cliché. His first book was *An Alternative to Speech* (1986—both Princeton University Press).

Later volumes include two 'poetry journals', *The Daily Mirror* (1998) and *The Evening Sun* (2002), from a period when he wrote a poem a day, *When a Woman Loves a Man* (2005), and *Yeshiva Boys* (2009—all Simon & Schuster). Lehman has written non-fiction on deconstructionism, detective novels, Jewish American songwriters, and a history of the New York School, *The Last Avant-Garde* (Doubleday, 1998). He is also the editor of *The Oxford Book of American Poetry* (2006). RG

Lehmann, Geoffrey (1940–) Grew up at McMahon's Point on Sydney Harbour, his father the owner and pilot of a small ferry. He attended Shore (Sydney Church of England Boys' School) and graduated in arts-law from the University of Sydney. At university he met Les *Murray and co-edited a literary magazine with him. They published a joint first volume of their own poetry, *The Ilex Tree* (1965). Lehmann practised as a solicitor until 1976, then taught law in the faculty of commerce at the University of New South Wales. He was a partner in an international accounting firm, working in Sydney. As well as poetry, he has published a novel, a book on Australian naïve painters, has edited or co-edited anthologies of poetry, and is co-author of the major treatise on Australian tax law. Married twice, he has five children.

Lehmann has a predilection for exploring a subject in a series of poems, and has written in this way on his family background, Roman history (including a book in the persona of the Emperor Nero, who is depicted sympathetically), and the daily life of his then father-in-law, Ross McInerny, a farmer in inland New South Wales, whose anecdotes become a vehicle for the author's own liberal-humanist attitudes (*Ross' Poems*, 1978). The earlier poetry is mostly in a supple, plain-spoken blank verse, with a somewhat formal tone; the later eases its limbs in free verse and relaxes its diction. Lehmann can be seen as continuing the ethos of the Sydney 'vitalist' school, of which the artist Norman Lindsay was the theorist and Kenneth *Slessor the leading exponent: his work, like theirs, celebrates 'pagan' values—sensuousness, aestheticism sexuality, vitality, and considerations of quality above those of equality. He combines successfully the influence of Slessor and of C. P. Cavafy. *Children's Games* (1990), appearing after a ten-year silence, contains some of his best work, particularly the title-poem. *Spring Forest* (1992—all Angus & Robertson), published in the UK by Faber and Faber in 1994, was an expanded and revised version of *Ross' Poems*. See also *Collected Poems* (Heinemann, 1997). With Robert *Gray, Lehmann was co-editor of the anthology *Australian Poetry Since 1788* (University of New South Wales Press, 2011).   RGr

Lehmann, John (Frederick) (1907–87) Born in Buckinghamshire and educated at Eton and Trinity College, Cambridge, where he was a contemporary of William *Empson, Kathleen *Raine, and Julian *Bell. His early admirations were the *Georgian poets and T. S. *Eliot; and the economy of style of the best Georgian poetry was reflected in his first book, *A Garden Revisited*, in 1931. Left-wing political leanings emerge in *The Noise of History* (1934), whose Rilkean prose poems communicate the feeling of menace underlying middle-European life in the 1930s. In 1936 Lehmann started the periodical *New Writing*, and during the late Thirties wrote little poetry. He began writing again during the Second World War, producing *Forty Poems* (1942) and *The Sphere of Glass* (1944), his best single volume.

He established *The London Magazine* in 1954, three years after the collapse of *New Writing*. It took its name from the periodical which, between 1820 and 1829, published some of the most celebrated work of Hazlitt, Keats, De Quincey, and Leigh Hunt, and was backed by the newspaper magnate Cecil King of the *Daily Mirror*. The intention was that it should discover and encourage new writers as well as publishing established names, and that it should carry the work of American and Commonwealth writers along with English ones, and also Europeans in translation. Its editorial board included John Hayward, Elizabeth Bowen, William *Plomer, Rex Warner, C. V. Wedgwood, and Thom *Gunn. New stories and poems were to be the principal offerings each month, together with reminiscences and confessions by contemporary authors. There would be a substantial reviews section, where 'lucidity, seriousness and freshness of approach' were required of the contributors. Lehmann was determined not to let his magazine become a vehicle either for academic theory or for political ideology. 'There are no Keep Out notices', he wrote in his first issue, 'except for those who *in their writings* put political propaganda—or any kind of propaganda—before art, and those who should never have strayed into the field of literature at all.' Lehmann edited the magazine for seven years, after which it was taken over by Alan *Ross.

During the rest of his career, he ran his own publishing house and wrote his autobiography and many works of criticism, biography, and history, but produced little poetry. However, his last book of new poetry, *The Reader at Night* (1974), contains one or two of his best poems.

Despite a certain conventionality of diction, his poems have an unostentatious directness and economy. He was one of the few British poets to attempt the prose poem—at length in *Christ the Hunter* (1965), but most successfully in *The Noise of History*.

He may be sampled in *New and Selected Poems* (Enitharmon, 1985). See also *John Lehmann: A Tribute*, ed. A. T. Tolley (Carleton University Press, 1987).   ATT/CKS*

Leithauser, Brad (1953–) Born in Michigan where he also grew up. After graduating from Harvard College and Harvard Law School, he married the poet Mary Jo *Salter and spent several years in Japan as a research fellow at the Kyoto Comparative Law Centre. Since then Leithauser has travelled widely in Europe and has lived for short periods in Rome, London, Reykjavik, and Paris. He is now a Professor of Writing at Johns Hopkins University.

Leithauser is a formalist. He specializes in urbane, detailed descriptions of the minutiae and exotica of life. His poems frequently record strange incidents or artefacts he comes across on his travels. Like Marianne *Moore, whom he deeply admires, Leithauser delights in the oddness of unfamiliar things; a stuffed tortoise, a Japanese moss garden, a Bonsai nursery. He excels also in capturing the peculiarities of animals, reptiles, and fish. One of his best poems is a fanatically precise evocation of sea-horses, while others describe rabbits, snakes, an ostrich, fireflies, and a toad and a damselfly who momentarily confront one another on an empty road.

Leithauser has also applied his deft poetic craftsmanship to longer narrative poems. 'A Ghost of a Ghost' is a dramatic monologue delivered by a ghost condemned to haunt the house of his bereaved family. In 'Two Incidents On and Off Guam' the protago-

nist watches with a crowd on the beach the rescue by helicopter of two drowning swimmers. Later in the poem he goes snorkelling, and the bubbles emitted by some scuba divers below suddenly overwhelm him with a sense of the miraculousness of everything: 'a breath- | taking incandescence so intense the | body is as nothing in the path | of its streaming . . . '.

Leithauser's first collections were *Hundreds of Fireflies* (1982) and *Cats of the Temple* (1986—both Knopf). A selection from both books, *Between Leaps*, was published by Oxford University Press in 1987. His later volumes include *The Mail from Anywhere* (1990), *The Odd Last Thing She Did* (1998), and *Curves and Angles* (2006).

He has also written six novels, the most recent of which is *The Art Student's War* (2009), and an acclaimed verse-novel, *Dartington's Fall* (2002). See also *Penchants & Places*, a collection of his widely published non-fiction and criticism (1995—all Knopf).   MF

Leonard, Tom (1944–) Born and educated in Glasgow and took an MA at Glasgow University, where he is now an Honorary Senior Research Fellow. *Six Glasgow Poems* (The Other People, 1969) and *A Priest Came on at Merkland Street* (Midnight, 1970) established Tom Leonard as an uninhibited and original writer whose innovation was the serious use of working-class Glasgow speech. It was apparent from the beginning that the language he used amounted to more than a comically notated dialect based on near-phonetic misspelling. Glasgow's unique accent, its phrasings and cadences, were accurately reproduced.

Leonard uses humour to serve his critical indignation. 'The Voyeur', 'Pffff', 'No Light', 'Unrelated Incidents', and parts of 'Ghostie Men', for example, seem calculated to leave the reader (or listener) in a state where amusement rubs against worried shock. Leonard's work in this vein has a linguistic unexpectedness from start to finish.

In *Intimate Voices: Selected Work 1965– 1983* (Galloping Dog, 1984) Leonard's approach to language is illuminated by an essay on William Carlos *Williams—'What I like about Williams is his presentation of voice as a fact, as a fact in itself and as a factor in his relationship with the world as he heard it, listened to it, spoke it...'. Leonard seems to have found much of his own release in that recognition. In its turn, his urban *Scots has helped to instil confidence in younger writers as far as 'voice' is concerned, and its helpful, and unhelpful, links with English-English. Peter *Manson has written of *Intimate Voices* that 'no book of poetry has done more to articulate the experience of working, thinking, simply being in the languages of working-class Scotland in the last fifty years'.

Situations Theoretical and Contemporary (1986) and *Nora's Place* (1990—both Galloping Dog) were in 'ordinary' English. His anthology *Radical Renfrew* (Polygon, 1989) unearths a neglected, virtually suppressed tradition of working-class poetry in the west of Scotland from around 1790 to the early twentieth century. He has also written a biography of the nineteenth-century Scottish poet James 'B. V.' Thomson. Leonard has cited the radical spoken and visual poems of Bob *Cobbing and Ian Hamilton *Finlay as early influences. His own poster poems have continued his campaign—made famous by the frequently anthologized poem 'The Six O'Clock News'—against the hegemony of standardized usage (e.g. 'AN | OXFORD | DICTIONARY | OF | AN | ENGLISH | LANGUAGE'). See *access to the silence: poems and posters 1984-2004* (Etruscan, 2004) and *outside the narrative: poems 1965-2009* (Etruscan/Word Power, 2009).   DED*

LePan, Douglas (1914-98) Born in Toronto and educated at the universities of Toronto and Oxford. After serving with the Canadian Army during the Second World War he joined the Canadian Department of External Affairs, and later he served as principal of University College at the University of Toronto. In addition to his poetry he wrote fiction (see *The Deserter* (1964) and *Macalister* (1995)), and a collection of memoirs, *Bright Glass of Memory* (1979).

Characterized by elaborate language and a highly figurative style, LePan's poetry meditates on the longing of the human

spirit for freedom and dignity in a hostile world. Essentially traditional in form and formal in diction, several poems in his first book, *The Wounded Prince and Other Poems* (1948), published in London by Chatto & Windus, examine a quest through the Canadian landscape for both a personal and a national identity. In contrast, the poems of *The Net and the Sword* (1953), which won the Governor General's Award, are set in wartime Italy where LePan's heroes struggle to maintain their ideals in a bleak world of entrapment, violence, and death. Although the self-conscious ornateness of these earlier volumes is less apparent in two later collections, *Something Still to Find* (1982) and *Far Voyages* (1990), these poems reveal a similar search for love, peace, and justice amidst moral confusion and brutality. (The elegiac *Far Voyages* was the first volume to be open about his homosexuality.)

LePan's achievement is well represented in *Weathering It: Complete Poems* (McClelland & Stewart, 1987). See also 'The Wounded Eye: The Poetry of Douglas LePan' by J. M. Kertzer, *Studies in Canadian Literature*, 6 (1981), and S. C. Hamilton, 'European Emblem and Canadian Image: A Study of Douglas LePan's Poetry', *Mosaic* (Winter, 1970).   DD*

Lerner, Ben (1979–) Born and raised in Topeka, Kansas, Lerner has fast become an influential figure in contemporary American poetry. His first book, *The Lichtenberg Figures* (2004), a cycle of fifty-two unrhymed, untitled sonnets, won the Hayden Carruth Prize. *Angle of Yaw* (2006—both Copper Canyon), written on a Fulbright scholarship to Madrid, was a finalist for the National Book Award. His acclaimed first novel, *Leaving the Atocha Station* (Coffee House, 2011) takes its title from John *Ashbery (in *The Tennis Court Oath*) and is concerned with the relationship of art to life: the book's protagonist is a young poet on a scholarship in Madrid, and his views on the role of poetry are discussed at length. Lerner studied at Brown University, where he gained a BA in political theory and an MFA in poetry. Critics have drawn attention to the pronounced differences in style between Lerner's collections, moving from formal verse, to prose poem, to the fragmented, spacious use of line in *Mean Free Path* (Copper Canyon, 2010). In a 2004 interview, Lerner described himself as interested in 'the commercialization of public space and speech...the ways that technologies of viewing...feed our spectacular culture an image of itself.' In 2008 Lerner became poetry editor of *Critical Quarterly*, a British academic journal. He has taught at California College of the Arts, the University of Pittsburgh, and since 2010 in the English department at Brooklyn College.　SR

Levertov, Denise (1923–97) Born in Ilford, Essex, her mother being 'descended from the Welsh tailor and mystic Angel Jones of Mold' and her father 'from the noted Hasid, Schneour Zaiman, "the Rav of Northern White Russia"', although he himself had converted to Christianity and become an Anglican priest. Levertov's own heterogeneous spirituality is, therefore, in the first instance very much an ancestral inheritance. She was educated privately in a bookish home enlivened by many and diverse visitors, and learned to dance at Sadler's Wells. A nurse in wartime London, in 1946 she published her first volume of poems in thoroughly English, neo-romantic vein. In 1948 she emigrated to the United States, where by her husband, Mitchell Goodman, she was introduced to Robert *Creeley, Cid *Corman, who published her poems in *Origin*, the organicist and objectivist poetics of William Carlos *Williams and Charles *Olson, and to Robert *Duncan, to whom, because of his mystical and mythic way of perceiving, she felt an especial affinity. By 1955, when she became an American citizen, she was already a distinctly American poet, on her way to becoming one of the significant voices of the age. Levertov published over twenty volumes of poetry and taught at numerous universities. From 1982 to 1993 she was professor of English at Stanford University.

Levertov wrote as both a maker and a seer, as a proponent of both scrupulous craftsmanship and organic form, whereby 'the poet can discover and reveal' the form that is in all things. Her poem 'September 1961' celebrates 'the old great ones', specifically *Pound, Williams, and H. D. (Hilda *Doolittle), whilst elsewhere she names Duncan and Creeley 'as the chief poets among my contemporaries'; and, very roughly to locate her, it might be said that, just as she is more etherially inclined than Williams or Creeley, so she is more materially grounded than H. D. or Duncan. 'The world is | not with us enough. | O taste and see', she writes in the title-poem of one of her volumes: 'bite, | savor, chew, swallow, transform...'. But though a poet possessed continually of spiritual curiosity, she was also a poet of personal experience and relationships, who strenuously explored the conflicting claims of the domestic and the artistic; a poet of memory and commemoration, who, expatriated in the United States, recalled her Essex childhood in radiant detail, and who, many years later, celebrated her mother enduring, then dying, at great old age in Mexico; and a poet of public statement and witness, who was outraged by all forms of destruction but who came less precociously and self-tormentingly to political consciousness than her elder sister, Olga, whose premature death is hauntingly mourned in the 'Olga Poems' of 1967. However, Levertov's radical politics are always to be seen within the larger context of her fundamentally religious, sacramental sense of the holiness of all things: 'Blessed | be the dust. From dust the world | utters itself. We have no other | hope, no knowledge.' Her final volumes were *Sands of the Well* (1998) and, posthumously, *The Great Unknowing: Last Poems* (1999—both New Directions). See *Selected Poems*, with a preface by Creeley (New Directions, 2002), published in the UK as *New Selected Poems* (Bloodaxe, 2003). A selection of Levertov's essays was published by New Directions in 1992, and an autobiographical volume, *Tesserae*, in 1995. Editions of her correspondence with Williams and Duncan have also been published.

Levertov's most industrious critical reader has been Linda Wagner, who published her study, *Denise Levertov* (Twayne), in

1967, edited *Denise Levertov: In Her Own Province* (New Directions, 1979), and, as Linda Wagner-Martin, edited *Critical Essays on Denise Levertov* (Hall, 1990). Bibliographies include Robert A. Wilson, *A Bibliography of Denise Levertov* (Phoenix, 1972) and Liana Sakelliou-Schulz, *Denise Levertov: An Annotated Primary and Secondary Bibliography* (Garland, 1989). See also *Denise Levertov: Selected Criticism*, ed. Albert Gelpi (University of Michigan Press, 1993) and *Conversations with Denise Levertov*, ed. Jewel Spears Brooker (University Press of Mississippi, 1998).   RWB*

Levi, Peter (Chad Tigar) (1931–2000) Born in Middlesex, he was a Jesuit priest until he resigned orders in 1977. He was elected Professor of Poetry at Oxford (1984–9). His abundant verse has not yet been widely studied. Most attention was paid to his early poems, particularly those in *The Gravel Ponds* (1960) and *Water, Rock and Sand* (1962—both Deutsch). These, although they displayed the debt to Wallace *Stevens apparent throughout his work, were more conventional in form than those written later, and sounded a more personal note, sometimes reminiscent of *Graves, at others of *Auden. Succeeding collections saw the growing influence of Greek surrealism (Levi translated modern Greeks such as Elytis), and of a multitude of European poets. Levi's later verse is open to the strictures that have been levelled at his prose: over-enthusiastic and hasty. That he had much of interest to say is undoubted; the general effect is blurred. *The Noise Made by Poems* (1977) is a critical commentary.

See: *Collected Poems 1955–1975* (1976) and *Goodbye to the Art of Poetry* (1989). His last collections were *Reed Music* (1997) and *Viriditas* (2001—all Anvil).   MS-S

Levine, Philip (1928–) Born in Detroit, Michigan, and educated in local schools and at Wayne State University. He was Professor of English at California State University in Fresno. Levine has periodically lived in Spain, a country whose people, landscape, and history remain a strong presence in his poems. From 2011 to 2012 he was Poet Laureate of the United States.

A prolific poet, Levine has published collections at regular intervals since *On the Edge* appeared in 1963. His earliest poems were relatively formal in character, but *Not This Pig* (1968), his second book, marks the emergence of Levine's mature style, characterized by a haunting lyricism, an inward sense of the natural world (frequently invoked for symbolic purposes), and a strong identification with ethnic and working-class issues. There is an undertone of rage and defiance throughout this, and other, volumes. (In 'Animals Are Passing from Our Lives', for instance, a pig refuses to be butchered, crying in the last line: 'No. Not this pig.')

Levine is particularly well known for his poems set in Detroit, a blighted urban landscape about which he has written with visionary intensity. *1933* (1974) was his most explicitly autobiographical work, in which family members and the physical geography of Detroit were uniquely invoked. 'Letters for the Dead', 'Uncle', and '1933' are among the finest poems of his maturity, followed in *The Names of the Lost* (1976) by more poems set in Detroit, such as 'Belle Isle, 1949', which describes a young couple who 'baptize' themselves in the polluted Detroit River with its 'brine | of cars parts, dead fish, stolen bicycles, | melted snow'.

Levine's strong identification with the antifascist side of the Spanish Civil War has given his poetry a decidedly left-populist political slant, as in his elegy for a Republican soldier, 'To P. L., 1916–1937', which appeared in *They Feed They Lion* (1972), one of Levine's strongest collections. Another strong poem focused on this period is 'On the Murder of Lieutenant Jose Del Castillo by the Falangist Bravo Martinez, July 12, 1936'—a vivid historical piece, published in *The Names of the Lost*. Here, as in Levine's best work generally, he re-creates a particular milieu with freshness and originality.

Though he has written well about Spain and Detroit, Levine has lived much of his adult life in northern California, and a number of his poems reflect the dry dust and hot climate of the Fresno Valley, as in 'A Sleepless Night', which begins: 'April, and the last of the plum blossoms | scatters on the black grass | before dawn'. Levine is, ultimately, a religious poet, and he invests whatever landscape he chooses to write about—geographical or mental—with a fervent spirituality. A volume called *Ashes* (1979) contains many of his most explicitly religious poems, many of which explore his Jewish roots, as in 'On a Drawing by Flavio', which summons the image of the Rabbi of Auschwitz, who 'bows his head and prays | for us all'.

Levine's *Selected Poems* (Atheneum, 1984) was a major collection of the poet's work. Later books include *A Walk with Tom Jefferson* (1988), *New Selected Poems* (1991), *What Work Is* (1991), which won the National Book Award, *The Simple Truth* (1994), which won the Pulitzer Prize, *The Mercy* (1999), *Breath* (2004), and *News of the World* (2009). *The Bread of Time* (2004—all Knopf) is a memoir. *Stranger to Nothing: Selected Poems* was published in the UK by Bloodaxe in 2006.

For criticism, see *Cry of the Human*, by Ralph J. Mills, Jr. (University of Illinois Press, 1975). For interviews, see *Don't Ask* (1981) and *So Ask* (2002—both University of Michigan Press). JP

Levis, Larry (Patrick) (1946–96) Born, raised, and educated in Fresno, California. He received an MA from Syracuse University and a PhD from the University of Iowa. After many years at the University of Missouri, he later taught at the University of Utah and Virginia Commonwealth University.

Levis may fairly be described as a typical exponent of the mainstream Iowa Writers' Workshop/*American Poetry Review* style that dominated late-twentieth-century American poetry. In so far as that style changed, Levis' poetry changed with it, though not in far-reaching ways: his lines grew longer and correspondingly more discursive, his rhetoric a touch more flamboyant, his subjects more narrative, but essentially he continued to write a hybrid of *confessional and *Deep Image poetry—labels one might ordinarily prefer to avoid,

but which seem quite appropriate for a poet as generic as Levis. Bits of anecdotal reminiscence centred on family or lovers, an indiscriminately reverent tone, a programmatic emphasis on loss and equally programmatic turns toward reconciliation, gratuitous phrases that create little dramatic frames ('I think', 'You can almost believe', 'Look'): these are the ingredients of the period style as Levis and many other workshop-based poets practise it. Levis' success, measured in the many prizes and fellowships he received, reflects the skill with which he deployed this shared style. See *The Selected Levis* (University of Pittsburgh Press, 2000). RG

Lewis, Alun (1915–44) Born and grew up in Cwmaman, a small mining village near Aberdare in Mid-Glamorgan, the eldest son of two Welsh schoolteachers. He was educated at Cowbridge Grammar School as a boarder, and Aberystwyth College, where he took a first in history and contributed poems and stories to the college magazine. This was followed by a miserable period in Manchester, where he lived in a slum and did postgraduate research on thirteenth-century religious and economic history.

From an early age he was torn by conflicting private and public impulses, which occasionally led to severe depression. Social injustice was all around him, exacerbated by the Depression. Lewis' strong sense of duty, socialist and nonconformist, urged him to put his talents to public use as a journalist, teacher, or academic. His private emotional life, however, rich and confused, pulled him in the opposite direction, towards literature and the contemplative life, 'alone in a People's Age'. The declaration of war solved, or rather postponed, his dilemma, and in 1940 he enlisted in the Royal Engineers. But 'the perversions of Hitler . . .', he wrote, 'affected me less profoundly than my own destructive impulses'.

He married Gweno Ellis in July, 1941 and transferred to the 6th Battalion, South Wales Borderers, eventually rising (after a characteristic struggle as to whether he should become an officer or stay in the ranks) to the rank of captain. The army kept training and retraining him in various skills, and he spent most of his time moving around England, far from action, writing stories and poems, which began to attract the attention of Robert *Graves and other writers. Eventually the battalion was sent to India, on a long sea voyage via South Africa, and finally on to Burma to engage with the Japanese. While in India he fell in love with a married woman, Freda Akroyd, and also came increasingly under the spell of eastern religious attitudes, especially Buddhist renunciation of material reality. 'Acceptance seems so spiritless, protest so vain. In between the two I live', he wrote to Gweno. And, in a late poem, 'I am seeking less and less of world'. He died in mysterious circumstances, possibly by his own hand, in March 1944, near Goppe Bazar, Burma.

Two of the strongest influences on his poetry are Keats and Edward *Thomas, to the latter of whom he addressed such fine early poems as 'All Day It has Rained . . .' and 'To Edward Thomas'. Both mentors were death-haunted, in their different ways, and both clearly spoke to Lewis' own troubled nature. His early work is marred by over-reliance on capitalized abstractions such as Death, Love, Time, Beauty, and by sub-Yeatsian plangency, but shows also a remarkable lyric strain which deepened throughout his short life. *Raiders' Dawn* (1942), his first book of poems, captured many of the experiences of enlisted men and went through several editions, as did his collection of stories *The Last Inspection* (1943). *Ha! Ha! Among the Trumpets* (1945—all Allen & Unwin), published posthumously, shows him absorbing India, turning inwards more and more, working towards a sort of testament in his late poem 'The Jungle', whose 'green indifference' and 'jungle pool | That drowns its image in a mort of leaves' mirror his own predicament as soldier-predator and dreamer-prey: 'The killing arm uncurls, strokes the soft moss'. It ends in large rhetorical questions about death, which recall both Rilke and the *Yeats of 'Among School Children'. Together with the very different Keith *Douglas—Douglas asserts, Lewis

questions—he is probably the finest of the poets who fought in the Second World War.

Lewis' publishing history has been unfortunately scrappy. *Letters from India*, ed. Gweno Lewis and Gwyn Jones (Penmark, 1946), and *Letters to Gweno*, ed. Gweno Lewis (Seren, 1989) contain much of his voluminous correspondence. *In the Green Tree* (Allen & Unwin, 1948) contains poems and extracts from Lewis' excellent journals. The best critical introduction to his work is *Alun Lewis: Selected Poetry and Prose*, ed. Ian *Hamilton (Allen & Unwin, 1966). *Selected Poems of Alun Lewis*, ed. Jeremy Hooker and Gweno Lewis (Allen & Unwin, 1981) is a useful sampler, and much interesting uncollected work is available in *Alun Lewis: A Miscellany of his Writings*, ed. John Pikoulis (Poetry Wales, 1982). *Alun Lewis: A Life*, by John Pikoulis (Seren, 1984) was the first full biography. Cary Archard edited the *Collected Stories* and *Collected Poems* for Seren in 1995. ws

Lewis, C. Day. *See* DAY LEWIS, C.

Lewis, Gwyneth (1959–) Born in Cardiff to a Welsh-speaking family. She read English at Cambridge, and went on to study at Harvard, Columbia, and Oxford. She has worked as a freelance journalist and documentary maker for the BBC. In 2005 she became the first National Poet of Wales.

Lewis writes in both Welsh and English. She composed the bilingual motto that can be seen in six-foot letters across the front of the Wales Millennium Centre in Cardiff: 'Creu Gwir fel Gwydr o Ffwrnais Awen [Creating truth like glass from inspiration's furnace] | In These Stones Horizons Sing'. Her first collection was *Llwybrau bywyd* (Urdd Gobaith Cymru, 1977). Her debut in English was *Parables & Faxes* (1995). *Keeping Mum* (2003—both Bloodaxe) began as a translation of *Y Llofrudd Iaith* (Barddas, 2000), but became an original collection. The opening section, 'The Language Murderer', makes a crime drama of the relationship between Lewis' two tongues. Her shorter poems are often homely in their starting points, from which they pursue more abstract trains of thought ('How to

Knit a Poem'). See *Sparrow Tree* (2011), which won the Roland Mathias Poetry Award.

Lewis' first three books in English are collected in *Chaotic Angels* (2005). *A Hospital Odyssey* (2010—all Bloodaxe) concerns a wife's quest through the National Health Service to save her husband from cancer. She has written two memoirs, *Sunbathing in the Rain: A Cheerful Book on Depression* (Flamingo, 2002) and *Two in a Boat: A Marital Voyage* (Fourth Estate, 2005).   JNT

Lewis, Janet (1899–1998) Born near Chicago. Her father, Edwin Herbert Lewis, professor of English at the Lewis Institute, Chicago, encouraged her early interest in writing. Growing up in the Chicago suburb of Oak Park, she spent her summers with her family in northern Michigan and Canada where, from childhood on, she became well acquainted with the Indians and their culture, drawing on these experiences for her first book of poems *The Indians in the Woods* (Monroe Wheeler, 1922; repr. Matrix, 1980) and her first novel, *The Invasion* (Harcourt, 1932). She married the poet and critic Yvor *Winters in Santa Fe in 1926 and settled in semi-rural surroundings in Los Altos, California, near Stanford University where her husband taught until his death in 1968.

Although she experimented with free verse early and late in her career, most of her luminous and resonant lyrics are written in conventional prosody. Her subjects are love, protracted illness (she was at a Santa Fe sanatorium for tuberculosis for several years), death of friends, friendship, domestic duties, and other themes of universal scope. Among her best-known poems are 'Earth-Bound', 'During illness', 'In an Egyptian Museum', 'Love Poem', and 'To Helen'. She began a series of libretti in verse with *The Wife of Martin Guerre: An Opera* (1958), drawn from her second novel published in 1941. Her volume of poems *The Ancient Ones* (No Dead Lines, 1979) reflected a lifelong interest in the native cultures of New Mexico.

Her poems were collected in *Poems Old and New, 1918–1978* (1981). See *The Select-*ed *Poems of Janet Lewis* (2000—both Ohio University Press), ed. Robert L. Barth.

See also Mitzi Berger Hamovitch, 'My Life I Will Not Let Thee Go Except Thou Bless Me: an Interview with Janet Lewis', *Southern Review*, 18 (Apr. 1982).   DS

Lewis, (Percy) Wyndham (1882–1957) Lewis made many enemies during a career as visual artist, social philosopher, polemical critic, and novelist. He is little regarded as a poet, but the 2,000-line *One-Way Song* (1933) is an accomplished and wholly individual work. As a statement of Lewis' socio-political stance and an argument about the reactionary nature of those who clung to what Lewis regarded as the mock-revolutionary idea of 'Progress', the poem is often unclear, but the parts are much more eloquent and effective than the whole.

The opening section, 'Engine Fight-Talk', is genially critical of the Audenic poetic concern with machinery; 'Song of the Militant Romance' looks at the extravagant verbalism of Joyceans; 'If So The Man You Are' is a statement of Lewis' own position. The verse-forms used are the old-fashioned fourteener and the heroic couplet, both handled with freshness, humour, and an at times overwhelming vigour.

See *Collected Poems and Plays*, ed. Alan Munton (Carcanet, 1979). Jeffrey Meyers' *The Enemy* (Routledge & Kegan Paul, 1980) is a comprehensive biography, and *The Essential Wyndham Lewis* (Deutsch, 1989) a useful introduction to the various aspects of the work.   JGS

Liardet, Tim (1959–) Born in London, Liardet read history at the University of York, obtaining BA and MA degrees. He worked in cabinet-making, information technology, and marketing for many years before he began teaching creative writing at Bath Spa University in 2001, where he is now Professor of Poetry.

His first collection, *Clay Hill* (Poetry Wales, 1988), displays the dense linguistic precision that continues to characterize his style. Though they bear a certain formal gravity, Liardet's poems, besides a regularity of line and stanza, do not strictly adhere to traditional constraints. *Fellini*

Beach (1994), *Competing with the Piano Tuner* (1998), and *To the God of Rain* (2003) continue in this vein. Based upon his work in a juvenile prison, *The Blood Choir* (2006—all Seren), marks an important departure in its tighter thematic focus on the sustained, nuanced exploration of imprisonment. It received wide critical acclaim and was shortlisted for the T. S. Eliot Prize. His sixth collection, *The Storm House* (Carcanet, 2011), focuses on his younger brother's mysterious death and richly explores the psychodrama of family. In 'Goose Flesh' for example, mother and brother struggle to inhabit the same physical and psychological skin, such that it is unclear 'which body musk seeped out | from which armpit, which thought originated first || in his head or her encompassing head behind, | so little the lapse, the spaces between them.'   CE

Lieberman, Laurence (1935–) Born in Detroit, Michigan, and educated at the University of Michigan, Ann Arbor, and the University of California, Berkeley. His teaching career has included a post at the College of the Virgin Islands, St Thomas (1964–8), where he developed the interest in life in the Caribbean and the underwater world of the coral reefs which has remained a persistent theme in his poetry. Since 1970 he has been a professor of English at the University of Illinois, Urbana, where he served as poetry editor for its press.

Drawing on Whitman, Lieberman has developed a long cadenced verse line and an emphasis on narrative uncommon in twentieth-century poetry. An inveterate traveller, he views the customs and scenery of the Caribbean—and, in *God's Measurements*, Japan—with the eye of a tourist/poet.

His collections include *The Osprey Suicides* (1973); *God's Measurements* (1980); *Eros at the World Kite Pageant: Poems 1979–1982* (1983); and *The Mural of Wakeful Sleep* (1985—all Macmillan). His criticism can be found in *Unassigned Frequencies: American Poetry in Review* 1964–77 (University of Illinois Press, 1977) and *Beyond the Muse of Memory: Essays on Contemporary American Poets* (University of Missouri

Press, 1995). See *New and Selected Poems, 1962–1992* (University of Illinois Press, 1993), *The Regatta in the Skies: Selected Long Poems* (University of Georgia Press, 1999), and *Carib's Leap: Selected and New Poems of the Caribbean* (Peepal Tree, 2005).   LD

Lilburn, Tim(othy) (1950–) Born in Regina, Saskatchewan, Lilburn has lived in Africa, trained as a Jesuit priest, and worked as a farmer. In 2004, he joined the Creative Writing department of the University of Victoria, having previously taught philosophy and English literature at St Peter's College, University of Saskatchewan.

His debut, *The Names of God* (Oolichan, 1986), introduced an ecstatically descriptive nature poetry, which was compared to that of Gerard Manley Hopkins. Lilburn's interest in mysticism and ecology is expounded by the essays collected in *Living in the World as if It Were Home* (Cormorant, 1999) and *Going Home* (Anansi, 2008). His second collection, *Tourist to Ecstasy* (Exile, 1989), was a finalist for the Governor General's Award, which he later won with his sixth volume of poetry, *Kill-site* (2003). Lilburn repeatedly philosophizes on the non-human fact of the prairies where he was born. His third collection, *Moosewood Sandhills* (1994), turned towards this locality in a simpler style of meditative free verse, more akin to Charles *Wright than Hopkins. *To the River* (1999—all McClelland & Stewart) continued the attempt to inhabit the South Saskatchewan landscape.

Desire Never Leaves (Wilfrid Laurier University Press, 2008) is a selected poems, edited by Alison Calder, with an afterword by the author. Lilburn has also edited *Thinking and Singing: Poetry and the Practice of Philosophy* (Cormorant, 2002). *Contemplation and Resistance: an Exchange* (2003), published by his own JackPine Press, is a dialogue between Lilburn and Jan *Zwicky.   JNT

Lim, Shirley Geok-lin (1944–) Born and raised in Malacca, Malaysia, the only daughter in a family of five sons. She was educated in the University of Malaya, and remained in Malaysia until the late 1960s, when she left to study in America. Although she has since settled there, her poetry has maintained strong links with her Malaysian past. Lim's first collection of poems, *Crossing the Peninsula and Other Poems* (Heinemann), won the 1980 Commonwealth Poetry Prize. This was the first time the prize had been won by an Asian and a woman. Her subsequent publications include *Another Country and Other Stories* (Times, 1982), *No Man's Grove and Other Poems* (National University of Singapore English Department, 1985), *Modern Secrets: New and Selected Poems* (Dangaroo, 1989), *Monsoon History: Selected Poems* (Skoob Pacifica, 1994), and *What the Fortune Teller Didn't Say* (West End, 1998).

Of Chinese origins in a non-Chinese cultural landscape, Lim writes best about the culturally colonized and marginalized individual. Her poetry is dominated by sharp delineations of fragmented identities, and sustained by a strong, penetrating style and an ironic, unsentimental delivery. She has furthered this theme significantly by addressing the question of her female identity within the context of her received patriarchal culture.

See also *The Writer's Sense of the Contemporary*, ed. Bruce Bennett *et al.* (Perth, 1982), for Anne Brewster's essay on Lim. Her memoir, *Among the White Moon Faces* (1996), and her novel, *Joss and Gold* (2001), were published in the USA by Feminist Press and in Singapore by Times Books. She is a professor of English at the University of California, Santa Barbara.   WMY

Lindop, Grevel (1948–) Born in Liverpool, he studied English at Oxford, and taught at Manchester University. After a romantic and bookish pamphlet, *Against the Sea* (1969), he published his first full-size volume, *Fools' Paradise*, in 1977, demonstrating a harder and more achieved technique, especially in two poems about manual work, 'The Spot-Welder's Song' and 'The Barrel-Dance'. His second full volume, *Tourists* (1987), was more wide-ranging and ambitious. This has more public concern than its predecessors, but its principal merit is its power of precise observation and description, as in the long title-poem, set on a South-East Asian island, and in a series of poems illustrating twenty-one wood engravings by Bewick. Lindop's easy and exact vernacular is the vehicle for a perceptiveness and intelligence which, perhaps because of his slow rate of production, have still to be accorded proper recognition.

Lindop's collections have all been published by Carcanet. *Selected Poems* (2000) was followed by *Playing with Fire* (2006). He is also the author of a literary guide to the Lake District, a travel book about salsa dancing, and *The Opium-Eater: a Life of Thomas de Quincey* (Oxford University Press, 1981).   BO'D

Lindsay, Graham (1952–) Born in Wellington, Lindsay studied at the University of Canterbury, and has lived in Dunedin and Christchurch, working as a teacher, librarian, and taxi-driver. He began to publish poetry in the late 1970s, when he also edited the journal *Morepork* for three influential issues. *Thousand-Eyed Eel* (1976), published by Hawk Press, recalled the American *Objectivists in its scrupulously pared lyricism of the immediate present, observing a world named in both Maori and English ('Nga tamariki sit between the iron wheels | Of a rust-chipped seed machine—'). Later books include *Big Boy* (1986), which essays a more garrulous vernacular ('Oh ah yeah there's this little boy'), and *The Subject* (1994), which reflects variously on the 'telling pictures' of poetry. His seventh collection was *Lazy Wind Poems* (2003—all Auckland University Press).   JNT

Lindsay, Vachel (1879–1931) Born in Springfield, Illinois, to religious-fundamentalist parents. He entered Hiram College in 1897 but left after three years to study art in Chicago and New York until 1905. Fired by a desire both to preach temperance and bring verse to the masses, he tramped around the country begging, and bartering broadsides of his poems. He was part of the literary revival hailed as America's 'poetry renaissance' and anchored in the Midwest by Harriet Monroe's 1912 founding of *Poetry* magazine.

Lindsay's first book, *General Booth Enters Heaven and Other Poems* (1913) was a popular success, aided by its author's dramatic readings of the title-poem and of the naïvely racist title poem of his second collection, *The Congo and Other Poems* (1914). Like his lectures on 'The Gospel of Beauty', the public readings were sincere, evangelical attempts to elevate national taste. If his jingle-rhymed and syncopated poems were not profound, they were genuinely modern in their reformist (populist) stance, conversational ease, and readiness to experiment, scoring the Booth poem, for instance, with a revival hymn, or apeing popular music in *The Daniel Jazz* (1920).

Lindsay, however, was victimized by success, forced to perform the same poems repeatedly even as he lost faith in their worth. Always prey to self-doubts, he was hurt by criticisms of his third volume, *The Chinese Nightingale and Other Poems* (1917), and the flop of *The Golden Book of Springfield* (1920), prose revelations. The 1922 death of his mother led to a total, if temporary, collapse, and in 1924 he learned he was epileptic. Marriage a year later only deepened his depression. He swallowed a bottle of Lysol in a hotel room during yet another reluctant reading tour.

See Lindsay's *Collected Poems* (1923, revd. edn. 1925) and *Johnny Appleseed and Other Poems* (1981—both Macmillan). See also *Letters of Vachel Lindsay*, ed. Marc Chenetier (Franklin, 1979) and *City of Discontent: An Interpretive Biography of Vachel Lindsay* (Bobbs-Merrill, 1952; repr. Octagon, 1975) by Mark Harris.   EB

Liu, Timothy (Ti Mo) (1965–) Born in San Jose, California to Chinese immigrant parents, Timothy Liu spent two years in Hong Kong as a missionary, and then studied at the universities of Brigham Young, Houston, and Massachusetts (Amherst) universities. No longer a practising Mormon, he is the author of eight volumes of poetry and two chapbooks, and edited *Word of Mouth* (Talisman, 2000), an anthology of gay American poetry. Early poetic mentors include Leslie *Norris and Richard *Howard. He is currently Professor of English at William Paterson University, and lives in Manhattan.

Liu's poetry addresses themes of travel, identity politics, sexuality, and violence. In spite of its sometimes explicit nature, his subject matter is never sensationalized or romanticized. *Vox Angelica* (Alice James, 1992) reworked Liu's MA thesis and won the PEN Norma Farber First Book Award, establishing a poetics characterized by a free yet economical line, and a pervasive sense of immanence in a similar vein to John *Ashbery.

The central sequence of *For Dust Thou Art* (Southern Illinois University Press, 2005) is a meditation on the events of 9/11; as with many of Liu's volumes, the poems here indulge in a wide range of formal experimentation, using both traditional and innovative verse forms. His poetry eschews narrative and obvious correlations, seeking to complicate rather than to explain. This has led Charles Altieri to note the 'enthymematic' nature of Liu's work in his introduction to *Polytheogamy* (Saturnalia, 2009), a collaboration with painter Greg Drauler.   HY

Livesay, Dorothy (1909–96) Born in Winnipeg, Manitoba, of a family with strong interests in writing and journalism. She was educated at Glen Mawr private school for girls and, with interruptions, at the University of Toronto and the Sorbonne. Strongly influenced by a free-thinking father and left-wing ideas and personalities—Engels, Marx, Emma Goldman, and Shaw—Livesay embarked on a career in social work and joined the Communist Party. Her first book of poems, *Green Pitcher* (1928) was a precocious effort showing considerable craft and a developing social conscience. In 1932 she published *Signpost*, in which a demonstrated technical skill is matched by a growing sense of her own persona. The 1930s saw Livesay working actively for leftist causes as a social worker, organizer, and contributor to left-wing periodicals. Committed to the ideal of the working class and its contribution to the war effort, Livesay published

Day and Night (1944) and the appropriately named, *Poems for People* (1947). Much of her literary effort of the Thirties and Forties is marred by the stereotypical language of leftist rhetoric.

After the death of Livesay's husband in 1959 she went to teach in Zambia, and returned in the early 1960s to enter her most impressive phase as poet, teacher, and pioneer feminist. Two collections, *The Unquiet Bed* (1967) and *Plainsongs* (1969) reveal a mature, sensual, and outspoken writer. There is also the beginning of an unabashed self-awareness which, appropriately enough, serves as a rehearsal for the strong autobiographical elements that colour her later work. In 1968 she published *The Documentaries*, which stands as an important contribution to the long poem in Canada. Her major collection, *Collected Poems: The Two Seasons* (McGraw-Hill) appeared in 1972. Intense and confessional in her old age, Livesay's output and energy were truly remarkable. She remembered herself and her times in a series of reminiscences: *Beginnings: A Winnipeg Childhood* (1973); *The Raw Edges: Voices from our Time* (1983); and, latterly, *Journey with my Selves* (1991). Livesay edited the anthology *Forty Women Poets of Canada* (Ingluvin, 1971), and helped to found *CV/II*, a magazine of poetry and criticism. She was an Officer of the Order of Canada. See also *Archive for Our Times: Previously Uncollected and Unpublished Poems of Dorothy Livesay*, ed. Dean Irvine (Arsenal Pulp, 1998).   MG

Livingstone, Douglas (1932–96) Born in Kuala Lumpur, and went to Africa at the age of ten. He lived for a time in the old Federation of Rhodesia and his poems reflect something of the energy, if not the optimism, of that short-lived experiment. Marine biologist, diver, sometime pugilist, jazz *aficionado*, Livingstone in his verse was a scrupulous craftsman. There is broad humanity, though his interest in microscopic organisms suggests that he saw them as more successful than anything to be found in the human species.

His early poems, which appeared in the pamphlet *The Skull in the Mud* (1960), set out what were to become continuing themes of blood and bone, the destructive energies of African wildlife, human and animal, set against the indifference of the continent and the violent shifts in its history. This last is evident in his verse play *The Sea My Winding Sheet* (1978), which looks at the myth of Adamastor.

Sjambok, and Other Poems from Africa (1964), established his reputation as one of the leading English poets in South Africa after Roy *Campbell. The curious, distinctive combination of large, sometimes violent, themes with a meticulous eye for the telling detail is evident in his *Poems* (1968) and dramatically reinforced in *Eyes Closed Against the Sun* (1970—all Oxford University Press).

Menacing gallantry and steely lyricism are Livingstone's trademarks. The poems in *A Rosary of Bone* (David Philip, 1975; revd. edn., 1983) seemed pallid after the intensity of his earlier work, and Livingstone omitted many of them from his *Selected Poems* (1984). *The Anvil's Undertone* (1978—both Donker) was a welcome return to form. His strengths as a satirist are to be seen in the Giovanni Jacopo meditations, a series of mordant reflections on his life and times since the 1970s. His scientific interests were summarized in his *Microbial Studies in the Sea off Durban, 1964–88* (1988). See *A Ruthless Fidelity: Collected Poems of Douglas Livingstone*, ed. Malcolm Hacksley and Don Maclennan (Donker, 2004).

For a critical study of Livingstone's work, see Michael Chapman, *Douglas Livingstone* (Donker, 1981).   CH*

Llewellyn, Kate (1940–) Born in Tumby Bay, South Australia. She gained early qualifications as a registered nurse and later a BA in history and classics from the University of Adelaide (1978). From 1965 to 1972 she was an owner/director of various Adelaide art galleries. She began writing poetry in the mid 1970s. *Her Trader Kate and the Elephants* (Friendly Street, 1979) won the Anne Elder Award for a first book of poetry. She published three subsequent collections (*Luxury*, Women's Redress, 1985; *Honey*, 1988; and *Figs*,

1990), before a *Selected Poems* (1992—all Hudson). She is the author of a prose trilogy (*The Waterlily*, 1986; *Dear You*, 1988; and *The Mountain*, 1989) based on diaries of her life in the Blue Mountains of New South Wales, where she now lives, and in 1991 published *Angels and Dark Madonnas*, an account of travels in India and Italy. With Susan *Hampton, she edited the influential *Penguin Book of Australian Women Poets* (1985). Her poetry, 'with all its precise moments of bitterness and ecstasy, lust and folly, irony and grief' (Marie Tulip), reflects the *Confessional and *Deep Image poetries of North America, and is known for its candour, sensuality, and what some construe as a stubborn disregard for a prevailing, predominantly patriarchal, Australian poetic.

Her later collections include *Crosshatched* (Angus & Robertson, 1994) and *Sofala* (Hudson, 1999). A new selection appeared in 2010 from Wollongong University Press. See also *The Dressmaker's Daughter* (Fourth Estate, 2008), a memoir.   DBr

Lochhead, Douglas Grant (1922–2011) Born in Guelph, Ontario, and educated at the universities of McGill and Toronto. His father was a distinguished bacteriologist. Through his mother's family, the Van-Warts, Lochhead experienced life in rural New Brunswick. Childhood summers were spent in Fredericton and on the shore of the Bay of Fundy. After academic retirement in 1987 Lochhead continued to live in Sackville, New Brunswick, a small university town surrounded by the Tantramar Marshes which provided one of the landscapes in much of his later work.

Lochhead's early poetry was influenced by Dylan *Thomas, *Auden, *Yeats, and *Roethke. His mature work starts with *Millwood Road Poems* (1970). This collection's seemingly improvisational airs about domestic, small city, and small wildlife matters are partly indebted to *Souster and W. C. *Williams, but Lochhead's free verse here, as elsewhere, is distinguished not only by convincing line-breaks, accurate stresses, and cogent forms but also by an unpretentious yet insistent attempt to balance nature and humanity, love and

the poetic imagination. Lochhead's work is often spry, elegant, and comic. At other times, and increasingly so in later collections such as the prose-poem sequences of *High Marsh Road* (1980) and *The Panic Field* (1984), his work is abrupt and sardonic. It deals with personal loss, guilt, blocked metaphysical ambition, self-betrayal, and with the survival of a beleaguered poetics still based upon generosity and trust.

After *Tiger in the Skull: New and Selected Poems, 1959–1985* (Goose Lane, 1986) he published many more books: see *Weathers: Poems New and Selected* (Goose Lane, 2002). His last, meditative works were *Love on the Marsh* (2008) and *Looking into Trees* (2009—both Sybertooth) with illustrations by his brother, the painter Kenneth Lochhead.

See also *The Red Jeep and Other Landscapes: A Collection in Honour of* Douglas Lochhead (Goose Lane, 1987), ed. Peter Thomas, and *As the Eyes of Lyncaeus: A Celebration for Douglas Lochhead* (Anchorage, 1990) by Peter Sanger.   PMS*

Lochhead, Liz (1947–) Born and brought up in industrial Lanarkshire. She attended the Glasgow School of Art and taught for several years. *Memo for Spring* (Reprographia, 1972) introduced her up-tempo, bitter-sweet, feminine self-awareness to the male-centred Scottish poetry world.

Dreaming Frankenstein and Collected Poems (Polygon, 1984; repr. 2003) draws from *Memo for Spring*, with more recent work added. 'What the Pool Said, On Midsummer's Day', 'The Grim Sisters', 'My Mother's Suitors', and a number of other poems demonstrate that the range of Lochhead's talent can work at levels deeper than those of audience-nudging entertainment. Couplets in 'Fourth of July Fireworks', for example, have a *Lowellian hardness. At times, too, she writes a singing line which seems as much haunted by the lyrics of popular songs as by more formal poetry. Expert timing and a natural narrative-dramatic gift have contributed to her success as a public performer of her work.

True Confessions and New Clichés (Polygon, 1985; repr. 2003) is a selection of monologues, songs, and other pieces for revue performance. It is poetry in cabaret mood and often extremely funny. *Bagpipe Muzak* (Penguin, 1991) contains a section of similar 'recitations' (as she calls them), which, if anything, are satirically sharper and more achieved. The theatre seems a natural home for such work and Lochhead, unsurprisingly, is the author of several plays, notably *Mary Queen of Scots Got Her Head Chopped Off* (1989). However, *Bagpipe Muzak* also contains a section of poems. Here too there is an increased assurance, a seriousness which can handle the paraphernalia of contemporary life with jaunty affection as well as a critical, measuring eye for its darker side.

In 2011, Lochhead was named the second Scots Makar, succeeding Edwin *Morgan. See *A Choosing: The Selected Poetry of Liz Lochhead* (Polygon, 2011). For criticism, see *Liz Lochhead's Voices*, ed. Robert Crawford and Anne Varty (Edinburgh University Press, 1993).   DED

Loewinsohn, Ron(ald William)
(1937–   ) Born in the Philippines. He first went to the United States in 1945, living in Los Angeles and the Bronx before settling with his parents in San Francisco. After graduating from high school in 1955 he spent two years travelling around America. Returning to San Francisco, he then married in 1957. Work as a lithographer was followed by undergraduate and graduate study at San Francisco State College, the University of California, Berkeley, and Harvard. Having taught writing in California and at Harvard, he became a member of the Department of English at Berkeley in 1970. He has also edited a number of little magazines, including *change, Sum*, and *R. C. Lion*.

His first volume of poetry, *Watermelons*, was published by Totem Press in 1959, with a prefatory commendation from William Carlos *Williams and an introduction by Allen *Ginsberg that described Loewinsohn as part of the 'great wave of Poetry . . . breaking over America now'. Deeply indebted to Williams, Loewinsohn dwells on the local, the minute particulars of the ordinary world, meditating on the beauty, violence, and the surprises of everyday life in poems that are notable for their tender feelings and colloquial vigour. Some of his work is particularly memorable for its sexual frankness (one of his poems bears the title, 'The Romaunt of the Rose Fuck'); but a more frequent mode is a pellucid, unforced lyricism, the desire, as Loewinsohn has put it, 'to fill our days with beauty | from whatever faucet's available'. Other volumes include *The World of the Lie* (1963); *The Sea, Around Us* (1968); *The Step* (1968); and *The Leaves* (1973). A useful selection is to be found in *Meat Air: Poems 1957–1969* (Harcourt, 1970). His ludic novel, *Magnetic Field(s)* (Knopf, 1983) was reprinted by Dalkey Archive Press in 2002.   RJG

Logan, John
(1923–87) Born in Red Oak, Iowa. He earned a BS in zoology at Coe College in Cedar Rapids and an MA in English at the University of Iowa. The father of nine children, he taught at St John's College in Maryland and the University of Notre Dame (Indiana) before becoming a professor of English at the State University of New York in Buffalo. His first book, *Cycle for Mother Cabrini* (1955), was metrically and religiously conventional, influenced as much by Rilke as by the Old Testament. His second and third collections, *Ghosts of the Heart; New Poems* (1960) and *Spring of the Thief: Poems 1960–1962* (1963), evinced a technical loosening into syllabics and slant rhymes, though still concentrated on a metaphysical vision. The latter collection also introduced a bolder note of sensuality as it explored the lives of poets and religious figures.

This sexual motif intensified in both *The Zig-Zag Walk: Poems 1963–1968* and *The Anonymous Lover: New Poems* (1973), often amplified or mocked by witty rhymes and absurd puns, as Logan's orthodox Catholicism acquired a Zen openness. His prose has been collected in *A Bullet for the Ear: Interviews, Essays, and Reviews*, ed. A. Poulin, Jr. (University of Michigan Press, 1983) and his verse in *The Collected Poems* (BOA, 1989).

See also *Dissolve to Island: On the Poetry of John Logan*, ed. Michael Walters (Ford-Brown, 1984).   EB

Logan, William (1950–) Born in Boston, and grew up in the north-eastern United States. He attended Yale and the University of Iowa, where he studied with Donald *Justice, later a colleague at the University of Florida. Logan divides his times between his academic job in Gainesville and a home in Cambridge, England.

Logan distinguishes himself from his American contemporaries by his unfailing commitment to a poetry of impersonality and statement. In vigorous, simple diction, his first book, *Sad-Faced Men* (Godine, 1982) reflects a classical sensibility in poems about fate, abandoned gods, and the dullness of the material world. Nature, as manifest in imagery of water throughout the volume, is a source of awe, discomfort, and cruelty ('Ice' and 'Maelstrom'). *Difficulty* (Salamander, 1984; Godine, 1985) declares its denser textures in its title, and supports Logan's complex philosophical intentions with its linguistically demanding verse. As sombre as his previous volume, Logan's more mature work displays a hard-earned wit in cynical poems about loneliness, betrayal, and decay ('Hard Waters', 'Cartography', and 'Dream Contract'). Many of these poems resume the poet's ongoing struggle against his true 'enemy', silence. In Logan's third volume, *Sullen Weedy Lakes* (Godine, 1988), he turns to politics, but only in the abstract. His poems on affairs of state explore corruption, conspiracy, and tyranny, and he peoples these narratives with unnamed mercenaries, generals, emperors, assassins, and exiles ('The Ancient Economy', 'Methods of Empire', 'Banana Republics').

Vain Empires (1994) was published by Penguin in New York and Peterloo Poets in the UK. Although it has been compared to the early work of Geoffrey *Hill, Logan's poetry has yet to find a significant British readership. His later collections are *Night Battle* (2003), *Macbeth in Venice* (2003), *The Whispering Gallery* (2005), and *Strange Flesh* (2008—all Penguin). Since 1998, he has also published four volumes of his poetry criticism, which appears regularly in *The New York Times. The Undiscovered Country: Poetry in the Age of Tin* (Columbia University Press, 2005) won a National Book Critics Circle Award. He also co-edited, with Dana *Gioia, a book of essays on Donald Justice. Logan's biannual 'Verse Chronicle' in the *New Criterion* offers a rare instance of a contemporary poetry reviewer licensed to express scepticism, which he does even-handedly and with epigrammatic gusto.   TDeP*

Logue, Christopher (1926–2011) Born and educated in Portsmouth, and served in the British Army 1944–8. In 1951 he moved to Paris, where his first book of poems, *Wand and Quadrant*, was published in 1953 (Collection Merlin); from 1956 he lived in London. He worked as a playwright, screen-writer, anthologist, actor, and contributor to the British satirical magazine, *Private Eye*. A memoir, *Prince Charming* (Faber, 1999), describes his early life and post-war literary milieu.

Logue's interest in verse had cosmopolitan beginnings; he was among the first English writers to appreciate Pablo Neruda, whom he translated and adapted in the late Fifties. He was equally responsive to world events and to trends in youth culture, so that his poems, both in their straightforwardly political content and in their slangy, jazzy address, are strongly affixed to their particular time. Typical of his career in the Sixties were a series of poster poems, distributed by Turret Books, London, including *I Shall Vote Labour* (1966), and the readings he gave, with Adrian *Mitchell and others, in protest against the Vietnam War. He had more than thirty verse publications, in various forms, to his credit; the more durable of these are preserved in *Selected Poems* (Faber, 1996). He is best known, however, not for his 'popular' contemporary work but for his racy, clangorous adaptations (including extraneous elements from later history) of some books of the *Iliad*, after the example of Ezra *Pound. This critically acclaimed project began with *War Music* (Cape, 1981). The first three volumes, revised and collected as *Logue's Homer: War Music* in 2001, was a finalist for the Griffin International Poetry Prize. Two more instalments followed: *All Day Permanent Red* (2003) and *Cold Calls* (2005—all Faber/Farrar, Straus), which won the Whitbread Poetry Award. In 2007 he received a CBE. There is an extended interview with Logue in *Areté*, 13 (2003).   MI*

Lo Liyong, Taban (1938–) Born of Southern Sudanese and Ugandan parents and grew up in Uganda. He studied at Howard University and at Iowa, where he was the first African to receive an MFA from the Iowa Writers' Workshop. He has taught at the universities of Nairobi, Kenya, Papua New Guinea, Venda, South Africa and is currently Acting Vice Chancellor of Juba University, South Sudan.

Lo Liyong has published a number of volumes of poetry including: *Frantz Fanon's Uneven Ribs: Poems, More and More* (1971), *Another Nigger Dead* (1972—both Heinemann), *Ballads of Underdevelopment* (East African Literature, 1978), *Words that Melt a Mountain* (East African Educational, 1996), *Carrying Knowledge up a Palm Tree* (Africa World Press, 1997), and *Corpse Lovers and Corpse Haters* (Tambila Poetry Project, 2005). He is an authority on the oral literature of the Lwo and Masai and has published his own transmutation of Lwo oral poetry, *Eating Chiefs* (Heinemann, 1970), and collections of short stories from the oral tradition. He is also an essayist and has translated Okot *p'Bitek's *The Defence of Lawino* (Fountain, 2001).

Lo Liyong's approach to poetry is highly individualistic. The poems take the form of unedited stream-of-consciousness material. The literary allusions are endless and the content often clever and infuriating. However, it is arguable whether his ideas work as poetry. Lo Liyong is aware of this, and in response to the charge that 'all this is prose' he argues that 'prose is poetry now'.

See *Understanding African Poetry* (Heinemann, 1982), by Ken Goodwin, for a sympathetic critical review of Lo Liyong's work.   FO

Lomas, Herbert (1924–2011) Grew up in Southport, Lancashire. He served in the army in India (1943–6) and read English at Liverpool University (MA, 1952), before lecturing at the University of Helsinki (1952–65) and Borough Road College, London (1966–82). He lived in Aldeburgh, Suffolk.

Lomas is an idiosyncratic poet. His language is both meticulous and conversational, blending sometimes surreal imagery with anecdote and meditation. He is an adept improviser in received forms. His interests extend beyond poetry—*Who Needs Money?* (1972), is a work on economic reform—and his attitude is characteristically enquiring, as he ranges over love, sex ('The Groves of Academe'), music, family history (the sequence 'Todmorden'), and religious belief—the subject of *Letters in the Dark* (1986)—via vampires, photography, and translations from Valéry, Horace, and Finnish poets. At once urbane and astonished, lyrical and down-to-earth, Lomas' is an attractive voice.

Lomas' other collections include *Chimpanzees Are Blameless Creatures* (Mandarin, 1969); *Private and Confidential* (London Magazine, 1974); *Public Footpath* (Anvil, 1981); *Fire in the Garden* (Oxford University Press, 1984), *Trouble* (Trafalgar Square, 1992), and *A Useless Passion* (London Magazine, 1998). A prolific translator of Finnish, he edited *Contemporary Finnish Poetry* (Bloodaxe, 1991). See *Selected Poems* (Sinclair-Stevenson, 1995) and *A Knack of Casual Living: Collected Poems* (2009). His last volume was the autobiographical *The Vale of Todmorden* (2003—both Arc).   SO'B

Longley, Michael (1939–) Born in Belfast and educated at Trinity College, Dublin, where he read Classics. He worked as a school-teacher in Dublin, London, and Belfast until, in 1970, he joined the Arts Council of Northern Ireland, eventually becoming director of literature and the traditional arts. He published his first volume, *No Continuing City* (Dufour), in 1969. He is married to the critic Edna Longley, who has written widely on the contemporary poetry of Northern Ireland. He shares with her a devotion to the work of Louis *MacNeice, and his advocacy resulted in his revisionist edition of MacNeice's *Selected Poems* in 1988.

Michael Longley is a poet of the personal life, a quiet, punctilious observer of love and landscape (particularly that of Co. Mayo). His exact and elegant notations, often minimalist in their brevity, are nevertheless enlivened by a certain disconcerting strangeness in which realism may bewilderingly swerve into fantasy or even the surreal, natural description into emblem, the quotidian into parable, topographical into imaginary location. In *An Exploded View* (Gollancz, 1973), his verse letters to Seamus *Heaney, Derek *Mahon, and James *Simmons (with whom he was associated in the Belfast 'Group') suggest that the discursive is not his most successful mode. Reticent, tentative, and unpresuming, he is more memorable as an elegist, where his capacity to disconcert produces a number of exceptional poems. In 'Wounds', from *An Exploded View*, he links his father's experience in the Ulster Division at the Somme with contemporary terrorist atrocities to produce a deeply poignant sense of hapless involvement in political process; and in probably the best known of his poems, 'The Linen Workers', from *The Echo Gate* (Secker & Warburg, 1979), he complicates a relationship between his father, the eponymous victims of sectarian assassination, and a chillingly surreal Christ, 'fastened forever | By his exposed canines to a wintry sky'. Refusing to settle for any appropriate *gravitas*, the poem achieves a far more appropriate terror, disgust, and helplessness.

Longley did not publish a new collection in the 1980s. His prize-winning later work has been characterized by an increasing lightness of touch and brevity of form, though his classical themes remain the memory of war and the transience of the natural world. *Gorse Fires* (1991) won the Whitbread Poetry Prize, and *The Weather in Japan* (2000) won the T. S. Eliot Prize. His other collections are *The Ghost Orchid* (1995), *Snow Water* (2004), and *A Hundred Doors* (2011—all Cape/Wake Forest University Press). In 2001, Longley was awarded the Queen's Gold Medal for Poetry, and received a CBE in 2010. Between 2007 and 2010 he served as Ireland's Professor of Poetry. See *Selected Poems* (Cape, 1998; Wake Forest University Press, 1999) and *Collected Poems* (Cape, 2006; Wake Forest University Press, 2007). Longley has also edited the poems of W. R. *Rodgers. For criticism, see Fran Brearton, *Reading Michael Longley* (Bloodaxe, 2006).   NC*

Lopez, Tony (1950–   ) Raised in Brixton, South London, Lopez began work as a freelance writer in the early 1970s, publishing five crime and science-fiction novels. He then studied for a BA at the University of Essex, and a PhD at Cambridge University on the poetry of W. S. *Graham, which became the first full-length published study (Edinburgh University Press, 1989). He taught poetry for many years at the University of Plymouth.

Lopez published his early poetry through small presses: see *Snapshots* (Oasis, 1976), *Change* (New London Pride), and *The English Disease* (Skyline—both 1978). After *A Handbook of British Birds* (Pig Press) and *Abstract & Delicious* (Secret Books) in 1982, Lopez stopped publishing until *A Theory of Surplus Labour* (Curiously Strong) in 1990. Throughout the next decade, he worked on the widely acclaimed *False Memory* (The Figures, 1996; revd. edn., Salt, 2003), a sequence of fourteen-line poems composed of found text which 'samples and blends the white noise of 1990s Britain' (Robert Potts). Its juxtapositions are surprisingly poignant, its irony clinical.

Lopez's criticism on a range of poets associated with *Language and *Cambridge poetry is collected in *Meaning Performance: Essays on Poetry* (Salt, 2006). He has continued to develop his use of cut-up techniques in *Covers* (Salt, 2007)—which includes reworkings of Ezra *Pound and Ted *Berrigan—and *Only More So* (University of New Orleans Press, 2011; Shearsman, 2012).   JNT

Lorde, Audre Geraldin (1934–92) Born in New York City and educated there at Hunter College and Columbia University, where she took a master's degree in library science which she practised until 1968 when she began a career as an academic at Tougaloo College. She later held various academic posts, including that of Thomas Hunter Professor at Hunter College. She was a member of the editorial staffs of various periodicals and received sundry awards.

Audre Lorde's first book was *The First Cities* (Poets Press, 1968); this was followed by nine others including *Coal* (1976; repr. 1996), *The Black Unicorn* (1978; repr. 1995), and *Undersong: Chosen Poems— Old and New* (1992). Lorde's range of personal experience was central to her poetry: as Marilyn *Hacker wrote, 'Black, lesbian, mother, cancer survivor, urban woman: none of Lorde's selves has ever silenced the others.' Lorde died of cancer in 1992; her last volumes were *Our Dead Behind Us* (1986) and *The Marvelous Arithmetics of Distance* (1993—all Norton). *Collected Poems* was published by Norton in 1997. See Alexis de Veaux, *Warrior Poet: A Biography of Audre Lorde* (Norton, 2006). The title is a phrase Lorde applied to herself in *The Cancer Journals* (Aunt Lute, 1980; new edn. 2006).   LT*

Lowbury, Edward (Joseph) (1913–2007) Son of a Hampstead doctor, was educated at St Paul's School and University College, Oxford, where he won the Newdigate Prize and the Matthew Arnold Memorial Prize. He did his clinical studies at the London Hospital and took a medical degree at Oxford before specializing in pathology. After spending three years of the Second World War in the RAMC in East Africa, Lowbury began his long career in Birmingham working under the auspices of the Medical Research Council. For his distinction as a pathologist he was awarded the OBE and received honorary doctorates from the universities of Aston and of Birmingham.

Edward Lowbury's poetry reflects his scientific knowledge, his love of music, and his wide reading in literature and philosophy. His shorter poems combine lyrical purity, meditative subtlety, and technical assurance; while the epistolary poems exhibit narrative strength, the power to portray complex characters, and a sense of history.

His first book, *Port Meadow* (1936), was followed in 1947 by *Crossing the Line*, which had won a competition organized by Hutchinson and judged by Edmund *Blunden and Louis *MacNeice. *Time for Sale* (Chatto & Windus, 1961) assembled his best work of the previous decade and a half. His *Selected and New Poems 1935–89* (1990) superseded an earlier selection published in 1978, and was followed by *Mystic Bridge* (1997— both Hippopotamus). See also *Hallmarks of Poetry: Reflections on a Theme* (University of Salzburg, 1994).   JPr

Lowell, Amy (Lawrence) (1874–1925) Poet and foster-parent of the *Imagist movement. Born in Brookline, Massachusetts, of an aristocratic family and educated privately, she came late to poetry after years of travel, voluntary work, and society life. Her first volume, *A Dome of Many-Coloured Glass* (1912), is derivative late Romanticism, thought 'fluid, fruity, facile stuff' by Richard *Aldington. In January 1913, however, she took as a 'revelation' the signature 'H.D. Imagiste' which she came upon in *Poetry* magazine; and in the following year she arrived in England to link up with Aldington, H. D. (Hilda *Doolittle), and *Pound (who published one of her poems in his 1914 anthology *Des Imagistes*) in promoting and directing the new movement. As Pound grew fed up with her headstrong 'democratizing' methods, she assumed leadership and edited three volumes of the anthology *Some Imagist Poets* (1915–17).

Pound derided what he called 'Amygism', and the movement certainly changed under her influence. In the first place, her own verse, while it has its (somewhat long-winded) versions of Imagist formulae ('Do you think you see a young man in a swallow-tailed coat leading an orchestra? | I tell you it is a white, pointed flame in a silver dish'), is better described as a mystical sort of impressionism. Secondly, though her 1915 'Preface' restates Pound's principles of exactness, clarity, and concentration, she was principally concerned, as he foresaw, to promote *vers libre* of all sorts. The Preface to her own *Sword Blades and Poppy Seeds* (1914) expresses a debt to the French Parnassians for their example (borrowing F. S. Flint's phrase) of 'unrhymed cadence'; in 1915, J. Gould *Fletcher credited her with the innovation of 'Polyphonic Prose', restoring to the Imagist 'skeleton' the panoply of 'assonance, alliteration, rhyme and return'. Lowell herself ascribed this form to Paul Fort; in her own work, it has been applied both to her lush prose poems and to the method of alternating prose and verse used in 'Guns as Keys: and the Great Gate Swings' in *Can Grande's Castle* (1920).

Lowell's flamboyant wealth, large figure, and eccentric behaviour (she smoked cigars and slept on sixteen pillows) set her up for ridicule. D. H. *Lawrence's estimate of her as 'a good amateur' embodies a general suspicion of one who seemed to play at poetry. Yet she maintained a prolific output after the dispersal of Imagism, producing twelve volumes (three published posthumously) in her thirteen active years; one of these, *Men, Women and Ghosts*, runs to 360 pages, even while excluding the 'purely lyrical' part of her recent writing. *The Complete Poetical Works* was published in 1955 by Houghton Mifflin, and while it confirms the durability (for example) of her oriental fixation, it also records aspirations to a broader formal and thematic range—see the colloquial dramatic poems of *East Wind* (1926)—than she is normally allowed. The major task of her later years was her two-volume *Life of Keats* (1925), largely based on MS materials. Lives of Lowell include those by S. Foster Damon (1935), Horace Gregory (1958), and Jean Gould (1975). See *Selected Poems* (Library of America, 2004), ed. Honor Moore.   MI

Lowell, Robert (Traill Spence) (1917–77)

Born in Boston, descended on his mother's side from the Winslows who arrived on the *Mayflower*, and related through his father to the poets James Russell Lowell (his great-great-uncle) and Amy *Lowell (his cousin). Educated first at St Mark's School, where his English teacher was the poet Richard *Eberhart (Eberhart would recall being shown a manuscript of some sixty poems, full of 'raw power'), he entered Harvard College in 1935. This Lowell, however, was not set to follow the family tradition of smooth academic passage and comfortable installation within the cultural and civic life of Boston. After an unsatisfactory freshman year, he got himself engaged to a woman five years his senior, and at Christmas 1936 found himself in a quarrel with his father, during which he famously knocked the parent to the floor. The episode was probably brought on by one of those bouts of mania which would recur with cruel regularity until his death, so Lowell was lucky to have been attended at the time by his mother's psychiatrist, the poet Merrill *Moore. Moore directed his patient away from Harvard towards a more intensely literary milieu, one which included the distinguished poet-professors Allen *Tate and John Crowe *Ransom. Under Ransom's supervision, Lowell studied classics at Kenyon College in Ohio, and there met two of his lifelong friends and mentors, the short-story writer Peter Taylor and the poet-critic Randall *Jarrell. During this time he also met and married the novelist Jean Stafford, who remained a vital energy in his writing life until the couple separated in 1946.

After graduating in 1940, Lowell went south to Louisiana State University, worked with the famous New Critics, Cleanth Brooks and Robert Penn *Warren, developed a Southern accent, and, more drastically, converted to Catholicism. Further deliberate swerves from the paths of convention ensued: in 1943 he declared himself a conscientious objector to the United States' participation in the Second World War, and was duly incarcerated. The overall result was that when *The Land of Unlikeness* appeared in 1944, its tone of rancorous disaffection and its symbolist habits of baroque Catholic allusion and elaboration had been thoroughly underwritten by this rite of passage from blue-eyed boy to blue-blooded *enfant terrible*. Already Lowell was marked by his aura of great distinction, and from then until his death his name would remain synonymous with the effort by a contemporary poet to attain classic status, to pitch the force of his pugnacious intellect and his traditional 'European' sensibility against the grain of media-dominated, consumerist-oriented, imperially inclined late-twentieth-century America. (*Imitations*, his book of translations from great poets in different European languages, appeared in 1961, and constituted an oblique assertion that he placed his own career under the aegis of such masters.)

Lowell's second volume, *Lord Weary's Castle* (1946), won great critical esteem and many literary honours: its author seemed to have secured a history for American poetry after the achievements of the modernists. Poems like 'The Quaker Graveyard in Nantucket' served notice that this voice was equal to the burden of the past. Along with Elizabeth *Bishop, John *Berryman, Sylvia *Plath, and, to a lesser extent, Theodore *Roethke, Lowell would create the fashion and generate the force of American poetry for the next three decades. Only Allen *Ginsberg and the *Beats would possess anything like the same impact and glamour, and it was partly in response to the head-on simplicity of the Beats that Lowell's style changed in the 1950s, and he produced his greatest single volume, the epoch-making *Life Studies*, in 1959. This collection initiated an autobiographical project which would henceforth dominate his oeuvre, and resembled both a cubist self-portrait and a gallery of ancestral busts. It is the book of 'a man who has come through', a firmly braced utterance combining the strict feel of traditional form with the free-hanging voice of *vers libre*, and its subjects include the whole private matter of mental collapse and recovery. It felt intimate, new and powerful, and it created the need for a new critical term, '*confessional poetry', which nominated the genre *Life Studies* had established.

With poems like 'Man and Wife', 'Skunk Hour', 'Waking in the Blue', and 'Memories of West Street and Lepke', Lowell had invented a way of getting at life, of making poetry kick and freak at the edge of contemporary reality, and his next two books of original poems, *For the Union Dead* (1964) and *Near the Ocean* (1967), extended the effort to arrive at an inclusive, rhetorically heightened contemporary art, one that pushed beyond the domestic and the psychic into the realm of the political. The

crises of the Civil Rights movement and the Vietnam War, arising to trouble the aftermath of the Kennedy years, provide the background for poems like 'Fall 1961' and 'Waking Early Sunday Morning', but they also provide a kind of enhanced acoustic which sustains the poetry's aspiration towards a nobler, unconstrained state of being.

During these years Lowell was very much a public figure. His Catholicism behind him, remarried since 1949 to the writer Elizabeth Hardwick, he now lived in New York and enjoyed the status of unofficial poet laureate. He spent his summers writing in Maine and, in the early Sixties, began to teach poetry courses at Harvard every spring; yet he also continued to undergo regular periods of hospitalization, to the great distress of his friends and his deeply afflicted self.

It has been suggested that the drug prescribed for his illness contributed to the change of style which became evident in Lowell's 1969 volume, the aptly entitled *Notebook* 1967–68. This is a massive accumulation of unrhymed sonnets, poems of immediate, unprepossessing, blunt-edged force, which record not so much the public events of those days as the reactions which the events provoked in Lowell's consciousness. Certainly, the writing is different from the more pointed articulation of the earlier books; his poetic intelligence is on the rampage, swooping into all kinds of biblical, classical, and historical sources for analogies and omens, and deliberately shunning the old, orchestral melodiousness.

Notebook 1967–68 was subsequently revised, reorganized, and vastly extended into three more thematically coherent volumes, *History, For Lizzie and Harriet*, and *The Dolphin*, all published in 1973. The content and focus of the second and third of these books reflect yet another upheaval in Lowell's affairs. This occurred when he left New York and Elizabeth Hardwick to become resident in England with the novelist and essayist Lady Caroline Blackwood, whom he married in 1972. These books represent the extreme of Lowell's push to get at life and 'say what happened', making use of letters from Elizabeth ('Lizzie')

Hardwick, and generally opening to the scrutiny of readers an intimate world of pain which he had both endured and inflicted. 'Is art worth this?' Elizabeth Bishop asked, and many others contended that it was not. *For Lizzie and Harriet* and *The Dolphin* showed Lowell at the height of his wilfulness and daring. Secular, knowing, incriminatory, unconcerned to cajole the ear or to win sympathy, the best poems in them, such as 'Fishnet' and 'Dolphin', manage to acknowledge all the self-awareness and belatedness of the postmodern consciousness, yet they reconfirm poetry as a value-challenging and value-producing activity.

Even so, his next book made it look as if he had been preparing for diminuendo. The mood of *Day by Day* (1977) is autumnal, ruminant, uninsistent, indulgent. 'We are poor passing facts', he says in 'Epilogue', one of the several self-epitaphs which this last collection contains. There is a mood of general absolution, of simultaneous comprehension and renewal. From the opulent, resurgent *poème-à-clef* which opens the collection ('Ulysses and Circe', a mythological treatment of the Lowell/Blackwood/Hardwick triangle), to the elegiac valediction of 'Marriage', the poetry is steadily a-tremble between stylistic self-denial and debilitated impulse—a poetry which only Robert Lowell could write, and only at this stage of his life, a life with which (as he acknowledged in 'Dolphin') he 'plotted perhaps too freely'.

Lowell's oeuvre also contains critical essays, tough-minded, knottily composed autobiographical prose, and brilliant memoirs of his personal friends and literary mentors. He also made adaptations for the stage of a trilogy of stories by Melville and Hawthorne, published as *The Old Glory* in 1964. He did a translation of Racine (*Phaedra*, 1961) and versions of Aeschylus (*Prometheus Bound*, 1969, and *The Oresteia*, 1978). Even so, it is as a poet that he has established his sure place in literary history: his achievement is major, original, and undislodgeable. Beginning with aspirations that were Marlovian and impatient of limit, he ended by coming to accommodations that were virtually Chekhovian. All through

his career he believed in the mystery of the resonant line, and achieved many that had the formal conclusiveness and proverbial density of major poetry from the past. The strain of the ambition often shows, however, and the price he paid for such magnificence appears in a certain rhetorical assertiveness, an overweening triumphalism of tone which can provoke resistance by its very assuredness. Towards the end of his life and after his death his reputation suffered because of a reaction in critical and academic circles against those New Critical qualities which had originally made him preeminent. In a period when the poetics of indeterminacy were in the ascendant, and critics were intent upon exposing the discriminations entailed by a writer's gender or minority status, Lowell's 'canonical' steadfastness and cultural certitudes did not win many advocates. Indeed, the new climate favoured the more tentative art of his great friend and influence Elizabeth Bishop, a poet whom he unfailingly honoured and inevitably overshadowed when he was alive. But there is a linguistic foundedness and perfected form about Lowell's always-intelligent art which secures its inherent poetic value and guarantees its survival.

See *Collected Poems* (2003), ed. Frank Bidart and David Gewanter, *Selected Poems* (2006), ed. Frank Bidart, and *Collected Prose*, ed. Robert Giroux (1987—all Farrar, Straus/Faber). See also *Robert Lowell: A Biography*, by Ian Hamilton (Random House, 1982; Faber, 1983), *Robert Lowell, Interviews and Memoirs*, ed. Jeffrey Meyers (University of Michigan Press, 1988), and Paul Mariani, *Lost Puritan: A Life of Robert Lowell* (Norton, 1996). Saskia Hamilton has edited *The Letters of Robert Lowell* (2005) and, with Thomas Travisiano, *Words in the Air* (2008—both Farrar, Straus/Faber), his correspondence with Bishop.   SH

Lowther, Pat(ricia Louise) (1935–75)

Born in Vancouver and raised there in a working-class suburb. After leaving school at 16, she worked in the office of a shipbuilding company for two years, then married and had two children. In 1968, having divorced the husband of her first marriage, she married Roy Lowther, an elementary-school teacher and poet with strongly left-wing political views. Deeply committed to socialism herself, Pat Lowther actively supported the New Democratic Party. She also taught creative writing at the University of British Columbia and, just before her death, was elected co-chair of the League of Canadian Poets. Lowther was murdered by her second husband in 1975.

Most of Lowther's verse is written from a feminist perspective. Its expressive power is partly a product of strong contrasts (as in 'Remembering How'), suggestive metaphors (as in 'Seven Purgative Poems'), delicate analogies (as in 'Amphibia'), and variety of descriptive detail (as in 'Two Babies in Two Years'). Several of her poems are concerned with the politics of exploitation from an historically materialist perspective (e.g. 'Regard to Neruda', 'The Dig', 'Chacabuco, The Pit'); one of them ('Coast Range') suggests that simple natural things are the basis of all truth about life.

Lowther's best work may be found in *This Difficult Flowering* (Very Stone House, 1968) and in the posthumously published volume, *A Stone Diary* (Oxford University Press, 1977). Her other publications include *Milk Stone* (Borealis, 1974) and a short—and rather cryptic—broadside, *The Age of the Bird* (Blackfish, 1972). Her juvenilia was published in *Final Instructions: Early and Uncollected Poems*, ed. Dona Sturmanis and Fred Candelaria (Orca Sound, 1980). See *Time Capsule: New and Selected Poems* (Polestar, 1996; repr. Raincoast, 2004) and *The Collected Works of Pat Lowther* (NeWest, 2010), edited by Christine Wiesenthal, who has also written a critical biography, *The Half-Lives of Pat Lowther* (University of Toronto Press, 2006).   JST

Loy, Mina (1882–1966) Born Mina Gertrude Lowy in London into a well-to-do middle-class English family descended from Hungarian Jews and English Protestants, a lineage she made the subject of her long poem, 'Anglo-Mongrels and the Rose'. She studied art in Europe and England and developed a style of painting resembling that of the Decadents.

She lived in Florence from 1907 to 1916. After divorcing her first husband, in 1918 she married Arthur Cravan, a poet and boxer who disappeared the following year in Mexico. Loy lived in New York for a few years and then settled in Paris. She numbered among her friends avant-garde painters and writers including Carl Van Vechten, Guillaume Apollinaire, Mabel Dodge, Djuna Barnes, and William Carlos *Williams.

Her highly experimental free-verse poems began appearing from 1914 on in *Others*, the *Dial*, and *The Little Review*. Her most important book of poems, *Lunar Baedeker*, was first published in 1923. Biting satire and caustic cynicism expressed in savage, violent imagery are characteristic of her verse, as in 'Apology for Genius' and 'Der Blinde Junge'. Visual art was also an important interest. Loy wrote a poem on the sculpture of Brancusi, and was later friends with the collagist Joseph Cornell (her own last artworks were 'constructions' of found material from the Bowery). In 1936 she moved to New York City, which is the scene of much of her later poetry, and in 1954 to Aspen, Colorado, to be with her daughters. She died in Aspen.

The definitive edition of her work is *The Lost Lunar Baedeker*, edited with an introduction by Roger L. Conover, first published by the Jargon Society (1982). Virginia M. Kouidis, *Mina Loy: American Modernist Poet* (Louisiana State University Press, 1980) is a critical biography. See also Caroline Burke, *Becoming Modern: The Life of Mina Loy* (Farrar, Straus, 1996).

Since *Mina Loy: Woman and Poet*, ed. Maeera Shreiber and Keith Tuma (National Poetry Foundation, 1998), critical appreciation of Loy's wittily feminist modernism has steadily spread. The 1917 sequence 'Songs to Joannes', with its opening image of 'Pig Cupid', describes sex with a physicality remarkable for the time ('wild oats sown in mucus membrane'). All her work is characterized by an ability to respond to and rework the aesthetics of the various movements with which she was associated, as well as by an inventive approach to prosody and diction. A new edition of *The Lost Lunar Baedeker* appeared in the USA from Farrar, Straus and Giroux

(1996), and in the UK from Carcanet (1997). Her novel, *Insel*, a critique of *Surrealism, was published by Black Sparrow Press in 1991. *Stories and Essays of Mina Loy* (Dalkey Archive, 2011), ed. Sara Crangle, includes an early essay on the poetry of her friend, Gertrude *Stein, as well as a satire on the misogyny of her former lover, the Italian Futurist F. T. Marinetti ('The Sacred Prostitute'). See *The Salt Companion to Mina Loy*, ed. Rachel Potter and Suzanne Hobson (2010).   DS*

Lucie-Smith, (John) Edward (McKenzie)

(1933–) Born in Kingston, Jamaica. His earliest verse, as exemplified in *A Tropical Childhood* (1961), was largely *Georgian in inspiration. Later he was a leading figure in the *Group, experimenting with dramatic monologues in the manner of Browning; some of these appeared in *Confessions and Histories* (Oxford University Press, 1964). In the early 1970s, after the appearance of his collection *Towards Silence* (Turret, 1968), he announced that he was tired of 'conventional verse forms' and 'their lack of real flexibility', and that he 'hated the term "poet"'; he began to experiment with poster and concrete verse, and poems written to be recited, by his friends, to the accompaniment of musical instruments. His themes, he has said, are 'erotic…historical and aesthetic…and occasionally religious'. Most of his later collections, with the exception of *The Well Wishers* (Oxford University Press, 1974), have been limited editions containing only a few poems. Lucie-Smith's anthology, *British Poetry Since 1945* (Penguin, 1970) was reprinted in 1985, with a new preface lamenting the waning of modernism's influence. *Changing Shape* (Carcanet), a selection of his verse, appeared in 2002.   MS-S*

Ludvigson, Susan

(1942–) Born in Rice Lake, Wisconsin. In her twenties she moved to North Carolina and has lived in either North or South Carolina since that time. She is currently professor emeritus of English at Winthrop University in South Carolina, and spends half of each year in southern France.

Ludvigson's early poetry, collected in her first two full collections, *Northern Lights* (1981) and *The Swimmer* (1984), was written in short, carefully crafted lines. The subjects were various, ranging from the concerns of women in both the modern world and throughout history to comic views of life and love in the late twentieth century. Occasionally the poems would take on a satirical or even grotesque quality, as in the often-anthologized 'Man Arrested in Hacking Death Tells Police He Mistook Mother-in-Law for Raccoon'. In her later work Ludvigson abandons the devices of satire and comedy in an attempt to come to serious conclusions about the meanings of life and death in what she perceives to be a faithless world. In her later poems she focuses on both art and love as the sources from which the meaning that she seeks can be discovered.

Ludvigson's later volumes of poetry include *The Beautiful Noon of No Shadow* (1986), *To Find the Gold* (1990), *Everything Winged Must Be Dreaming* (1993), *Trinity* (1996), and *Escaping the House of Certainty* (2006). See *Sweet Confluence: New and Selected Poems* (2000—all Louisiana State University Press).   LS

Lumsden, Roddy

(1966–) Born in St Andrews and now lives in London, where he teaches at the Poetry School. He received an Eric Gregory Award in 1991 and since published five collections of poetry with Bloodaxe, beginning with *Yeah Yeah Yeah* (1997). His work shares characteristics with the '*New Generation' poets who came to prominence in 1990s Britain such as Glyn *Maxwell and Don *Paterson. It is often surreal or darkly romantic in its treatment of urban life, generally formalist and colloquial in tone, with elements of song-like wordplay and self-referential irony (e.g. *Roddy Lumsden is Dead* (Wrecking Ball, 2001)). Despite this commitment to formalism, of his own work he has said, 'I try to retain a certain air of spontaneity…I can hone and craft too, but I like the poem to have a certain rawness.' He has remarked regularly on his lack of fondness for poems relating to family, describing them as often 'artless', and locates himself on 'the ludic wing of the mainstream'.

Lumsden has brought these tastes to bear as an influential editor and anthologist. He presided over Tall Lighthouse's Pilot series of pamphlets for poets under 30 and edited *Identity Parade* (Bloodaxe, 2010), an anthology of younger British and Irish poets which proposed a 'pluralist' UK scene. He has also been a quizmaster and compiler of trivia books, and now works as poetry editor for Salt. See *Mischief Night: New and Selected Poems* (2004), *Third Wish Wasted* (2009), and *Terrific Melancholy* (2011—all Bloodaxe).   NH

Lux, Thomas (1946–) Born in Massachusetts and educated at Emerson College. He taught creative writing at Sarah Lawrence College in New York for two decades, and is now a professor at the Georgia Institute of Technology.

Lux casts a scathing eye on the human experience, especially the chaotic version manifest in the United States during the decades following the Second World War. Cruelties inflicted, both consciously and unconsciously, degradations and sorrows borne, misguided aspirations, and above all confusion about how to live—these are the subjects of his poems, but Lux neither judges nor condemns.

His early books include *The Drowned River* (Houghton, 1990), *Half Promised Land* (Houghton, 1986; repr, Carnegie Mellon University Press, 1994), *Sunday* (Houghton, 1979), *The Glassblower's Breath* (Cleveland State University Poetry Center, 1976), and *Memory's Handgrenade* (Pym-Randall, 1972). A self-described 'recovering *surrealist' since the late 1980s, his *Split Horizon* (1994) won the Kingsley Tufts Poetry Award. Since *New and Selected Poems* (1997), he has published *Street of Clocks* (2001), *The Cradle Place* (2004), and *God Particles* (2008—all Houghton), which includes an elegy for his editor, Peter *Davison ('The Gentleman Who Spoke Like Music').   RS*

Lynch, Thomas (1948–) Born in Michigan, and raised in a large Irish Catholic family, his father was an undertaker. He attended Oakland University, where he met the poet Michael Heffernan. In 1974, alongside two of his brothers, he entered the family business, running a funeral home in the small town of Milford, on the Huron River. He has a daughter and three sons, two of whom now also work for Lynch and Sons. He has combined writing with full-time work as an undertaker, and spends part of each year in Ireland.

Lynch has described his life and work in two books of essays: *The Undertaking: Life Studies from the Dismal Trade* (1997) and *Bodies in Motion and at Rest* (2000). These collections were followed by *Booking Passage: We Irish and Americans* (2006) and a collection of short stories: *Apparitions and Late Fictions* (2010—all Norton). Cape has published three poetry collections in the UK: *Grimalkin* (1994), *Still Life in Milford* (1999), and *Walking Papers* (2010). *Skating with Heather Grace* (1986), his debut collection, was published in the USA by Knopf. Death is generally Lynch's subject. His knowledge of its details and rituals, social and commercial, make him unusual among contemporary writers; and he can be read for curiosity-value alone. At its best, his amiable voice can be honest and darkly funny (e.g. 'Inviolata', on his Catholic schooling). He has sometimes bemoaned his typecasting as 'mortician/poet'; but it has spared him the restless eclecticism of his contemporaries and made him readable.   GR

McAuley, James (1917–76) Born at Lakemba, New South Wales. He wrote his first poems as a teenager at Fort Street High School and his first journalism for student publications while at the University of Sydney (1935–40). In 'Self-Portrait, Newcastle 1942' he described himself at a frustrated time in his life, teaching dull classes in his first job, talking anarchism with friends, and reading Rilke. That year he married.

In 1943 McAuley was transferred to the Directorate of Research and Civil Affairs, and a first visit to New Guinea the following year began a long-standing concern with the affairs of that country. The next year saw his first fame, or notoriety, when (with Harold Stewart, later noted for his translations of Japanese poetry) he perpetrated the Ern Malley hoax, in the magazine *Angry Penguins*, publishing the 'posthumous' quasi-apocalyptic poems (titled *The Darkening Ecliptic*) of an imaginary Australian modern bearing a resemblance to George *Barker and Henry *Treece. A special issue of poems, critical essays, and an imaginary portrait by Sidney Nolan was devoted to Malley in Autumn 1944, but the hoax soon came out. Mockery followed in the press, and one of the editors of the magazine, Max Harris, was fined for obscenity.

McAuley's traditionalist antipathy to modernism was to be thoroughly documented in subsequent critical writing, particularly *The End of Modernity* (1959). A Roman Catholic convert (in 1952), McAuley held many hieratic, anti-egalitarian views; but his more personal writings also revealed a man of considerable compassion and affection. These qualities mark the best of his poetry in *Under Aldebaran* (1946), *A Vision of Ceremony* (1956), *Captain Quiros* (1964), *Surprises of the Sun* (1969), and *Time Given* (1976). The widely anthologized 'Because' (remembering his parents), 'Pietà' (remembering the death of a day-old son), and 'Terra Australis' are written in the rhyme and iambic metre McAuley preferred. His symbolism is most effective when at its lightest.

A prolific critic (*The Grammar of the Real*, 1975) and editor (*A Map of Australian Verse*, 1975), James McAuley founded the Sydney magazine *Quadrant* in 1956 (remaining its sole editor till 1963) and from 1961 was Reader in Poetry at the University of Tasmania. *Collected Poems* (Angus & Robertson, 1993) is introduced by Leonie Kramer, who edited *James McAuley: Poetry, Essays and Personal Commentary* (University of Queensland Press, 1988); this has a valuable introduction and notes. There are useful books on McAuley by Vivian Smith (Oxford University Press, 2nd edn., 1970) and Peter Coleman (Wildcat, 1980), and helpful essays by David Bradley in Geoffrey Dutton (ed.), *The Literature of Australia* (Penguin, 2nd edn., 1976), and by Judith Wright in *Preoccupations in Australian Poetry* (Oxford University Press, 1965). See also *Collected Poems of Ern Malley*, introduced by Albert Tucker and Max Harris (Angus & Robertson, 1993); Michael Heyward, *The Ern Malley Affair* (University of Queensland Press/Faber, 1993); and Michael Ackland, *Damaged Men: The Precarious Lives of James McAuley and Harold Stewart* (Allen & Unwin, 2001). In 2002, the online magazine *Jacket* ran a special issue devoted to Ern Malley.   MHu

(⊕) SEE WEB LINKS

• Visit the website of Ern Malley for more information.

MacBeth, George (Mann) (1932–92) Born in Shotts, Lanarkshire, the son of a miner and an antique-dealer's daughter. When MacBeth was three the family moved to Sheffield, where he was educated at the King Edward VII School, later going to New College, Oxford. From 1957 he lived in London as a producer of talks and poetry programmes for BBC radio, and was an influential member of the *Group; from 1976 he earned his living as a freelance writer. MacBeth's first two marriages, to Elizabeth Robson and Lisa St Aubin de Téran were both dissolved; in 1989 he married Penelope Ronchetti-Church and settled in Ireland, where he died of motor neurone disease three years later.

MacBeth's admirers have seen a boldly experimental and playful poetic intelligence behind his copious output in a wide variety of styles and forms, while others have found in it a succession of self-dramatizing poses and evidence of 'extraordinary gifts extravagantly wasted'. Some of the lighter 'performance' pieces are ingenious, accurate and amusing, but the relish for pain and violence, the addiction to sick jokes and unconvincing slang, the modish properties and themes, all of which marked much of MacBeth's work in the Sixties and Seventies, have worn less well. MacBeth's most interesting writing is obsessively autobiographical. The early experiences that shaped his adult life and work (the death of his father in an air-raid in 1941, and of his mother ten years later; his own bout of rheumatic fever at the age of 12, which left him an invalid for much of his adolescence) are described in a memoir, *A Child of the War* (Cape, 1987). His long poem, *A War Quartet* (Macmillan, 1969), evokes the experience of combatants in the Second World War. Again and again, in shorter poems, MacBeth returns to the war, his parents' deaths, or the pre-war years of their prime in the attempt to untangle the 'war-tied knot' of 'illness or guilt' that presses through his marital crises or sexual unhappiness. Later poems attempt—and sometimes achieve—a spacious pastoral elegance (though often seeming tricked out in traditional dress) and a more scrupulous, tentative approach, celebrating 'the luck of settlement, of finding a piece of land to feel secure on' and

'someone to live there with'; later still, MacBeth evoked the bitter break-up of this idyll (always troubled by undercurrents of sado-masochistic fantasy), resettlement in Ireland, and a new relationship.

Collected Poems 1958–1982 (Hutchinson, 1989) superseded *Collected Poems 1958–1970*, and was a fairly rigorous selection from fourteen books of verse, four others—*A War Quartet; Lusus: A Verse Lecture* (Fuller d'Arch Smith, 1972); *The Cleaver Gardens* (Secker & Warburg, 1986); and *Anatomy of a Divorce* (1988)—being unrepresented. *Trespassing: Poems from Ireland* (1991) and *The Patient* (1992—all Hutchinson) appeared subsequently. MacBeth also published *My Scotland: Fragments of a State of Mind* (Macmillan, 1973), several novels, and books for children; and edited a number of anthologies. A posthumous *Selected Poems* was edited for Enitharmon Press by Anthony *Thwaite, with an introduction by Carol Ann *Duffy.   AJ

Steve McCaffery (1947–) Born in Sheffield, England, and moved to Toronto in 1968. He is currently David Gray Chair of Poetry and Letters, University at Buffalo, State University of New York. He is married to the poet Karen Mac Cormack.

Along with Rafael Barreto-Rivera, Paul Dutton, and bp *Nichol, McCaffery was a member of The Four Horsemen, a collaborative group of sound poets. In 1967, he began *Carnival*, one of his best-known publications to date. The work consists of a complex, large-scale visual poem, produced on the typewriter, broken into pages and designed to be re-assembled into large panels by the reader. McCaffery's work with the aural and visual elements of poetry are explicit examples of the way in which he pushes the boundaries of syntax and meaning, and challenges habitual patterns of reading and listening.

McCaffery's publications include *Carnival* (1967–1975), *Evoba* (1987—both Coach House), *The Black Debt* (Nightwood, 1989), *Theory of Sediment* (Talonbooks, 1991), *The Cheat of Words* (ECW, 1996), *Seven Pages Missing: Selected Texts 1969–2000* (Coach House, 2000), and *The Basho Variations* (BookThug, 2007). For a discussion of some of the ideas that inform his work, see *Prior to Meaning: The Protosemantic and Poetics* (Northwestern University Press, 2001). For criticism and context, see Clint Burnham, *Steve McCaffery and His Work* (ECW, 1996) and Peter Jaeger, *ABC of Reading TRG: Steve McCaffery, bp Nichol, and the Toronto Research Group* (Talonbooks, 1999).   SRO

MacCaig, Norman (orig. McCaig)

(1910–96) Born in Edinburgh. After graduating in classics from the University of Edinburgh in 1932, MacCaig entered on a career as a primary-school teacher. It was interrupted by the Second World War, during which he was a conscientious objector and suffered the usual penalties. He continued to teach until 1970 when he became Lecturer, and then Reader in Poetry, at the University of Stirling.

MacCaig's first collections were *Far Cry* (1943) and *The Inward Eye* (1946). Both were heavily influenced by the *New Apocalypse school. MacCaig described his disenchantment with encrusted obscurity in an anecdote. A friend, having read both books, asked: 'When are you publishing the answers?' There then followed what MacCaig has called 'the long haul back to lucidity'. He did not reprint the poems in his lifetime.

Riding Lights (1956) established the mature style which he developed and modified in subsequent phases of his work. His poems are usually short, and, in the four books preceding *Surroundings* (1966) neat metricality, rhyme, and stanza were matched with habits of mind and figuration which soon attracted the label 'metaphysical'. As well as Elizabethan and Jacobean conceited poetry, Wallace *Stevens has been cited as an influence. More enabling affections could be poetry by Andrew *Young, John Crowe *Ransom, W. H. *Auden, and Louis *MacNeice.

MacCaig's poems are informed by agnostic common sense, sensuous wonder, and a generous, welcoming sanity. His freer style, its looseness markedly different from that of earlier poems like 'Byre', 'Summer Farm', or 'Fetching Cows', did not prevent his ingenious similes. Free verse,

though, from *Surroundings* on, has been accompanied by a tendency to question the metaphor-making once typical of his work. But it is the instinctive if also reasonable free play of the 'five senses' (see 'Centre of Centres') which is close to the animating force of his poetry, and to its figurative techniques. For example, a trout jumping is seen as having 'hung high its drizzling bow | For a count of three—| Heraldic figure on a shield of spray.' A scene is observed, then transformed; an accurate perception is noted and then ornamented. Examples of his ingenious precision are plentiful. Unusually for a Scottish poet, he was a disinterested pictorializer as well as a writer whose imagination was profoundly ethical. Many of his poems celebrate Assynt in north-west Scotland—to some extent his background is that of a Gael disinherited of the Gaelic language. However, many poems also describe Edinburgh; his imagery is more than adaptable to the urban scene.

MacCaig once called history 'filthy', and a strong anti-political thread runs through his work from the mid-1960s ('Old Edinburgh' and 'No Interims in History' are two examples). Along with a number of satirical pieces (chastising pedants, dullards, the sanctimonious, etc.), these bring about a complicating contrast with his many poems about creatures, places, lochs, rivers, mountains, weather, country people, love, and friendships. Intellectually nimble lyricism is, however, the strongest feature of his poetry. Over the range of his work his dextrous imagery, intelligence, compassion, unpredictable similes, metrical skill, and unflagging lyrical energy cumulate into a substantial body of work which has yet to receive the critical attention it deserves.

In the Scottish, and every other, context MacCaig maintained a characterful, garrulous independence. 'Patriot', for example, declares: 'My only country | is six feet high | and whether I love it or not | I'll die | for its independence.' Although little more than a squib, 'Patriot' suggests that personal autonomy is not always an easy stance for a Scottish poet to take. It could be the more remarkable in MacCaig's case when it is kept in mind that he was a close friend of Hugh *MacDiarmid, whose poetry MacCaig admired without sharing its underlying beliefs and designs. His work has been influential on younger Scottish writers. Douglas *Dunn made a posthumous selection of the poems for Chatto & Windus in 1997.

See *The Poems of Norman MacCaig*, ed. Ewen McCaig (2005), and *The Many Days: Selected Poems of Norman MacCaig*, ed. Roderick Watson (2010—both Polygon).

Criticism of MacCaig's poetry includes: Erik Frykman, *Unemphatic Marvels* (Gothenburg University Press, 1977), J. Hendry and R. Ross (eds.), *Norman MacCaig: Critical Essays* (Edinburgh University Press, 1990), and Alasdair Macrae, *Norman MacCaig* (Northcote, 2011).   DED

McClatchy, J. D. (Joseph Donald) (1945–) Born in Bryn Mawr, Pennsylvania and educated at Georgetown University and Yale. He has written six collections of poetry, *Scenes from Another Life* (Braziller, 1983), *Stars Principal* (Macmillan, 1986), whose title derives from Gerard Manley Hopkins' 'Spelt from Sybil's Leaves', *The Rest of the Way* (1990), *Ten Commandments* (1998), *Hamat* (2002), and *Mercury Dressing* (2009—all Knopf). McClatchy's verse is intricately wrought in a variety of complex rhyme-schemes. His best poems combine a rich bravura surface with a sophisticated dialectic or narrative. In the ambitious 'Ovid's Farewell', for instance, he develops a complex parable about the poet's ambivalent relations with art and life in flowing verse. In the poem Ovid relates how, knowing his younger brother was about to be bitten by a poisonous snake, he spell-bound the boy with verse, allowing the snake to strike. Occasionally McClatchy's poems can seem too fastidious in their perceptions, and rather complacent about their own powers of formal ingenuity, but often he is a delicate and intriguing poet. He edited *The Vintage Book of Contemporary American Poetry* (1990; revd. edn., 2003); he is also an influential poetry critic, and has written interestingly on Robert *Lowell, Elizabeth *Bishop, and James *Merrill, whose collected works he edited. A collection of his essays,

White Paper, was published in 1989; another, *Twenty Questions*, in 1998 (both Columbia University Press). McClatchy has taught creative writing at a number of American universities, including Princeton and Yale, where he is a professor of English and edits *The Yale Review*. Since the 1990s he has also been a prolific librettist. His verse translation of seven Mozart operas was published by Norton in 2010.   MF

McClure, Michael (Thomas) (1932–) Born in Kansas, and formerly professor at the California College of Arts and Crafts, Oakland. A prolific writer and reader of his work, McClure believes that poetry 'is a muscular principle—an athletic song or whisper of fleshly thought'. He began as an associate of the *Beat poets, and writes in a style sometimes reminiscent of *Creeley and Charles *Olson, but he never gives an impression of being quite as serious or earnest as these two exemplars. Kenneth *Rexroth in his political mood is another influence. His interest in the animal consciousness of man is elaborated in *Meat Science Essays* (City Lights, 1963). He has published many broadsides, including *GRAHHR GROOOOOOOOOOOOOO NYARR GARHOOOOOOOOSH ROSE* (1963), a line from his ululating *Ghost Tantras* (privately printed, 1964). McClure is also a playwright, whose 1965 play *The Beard* was unsuccessfully prosecuted for indecency. He has recorded his poetry in collaboration with Ray Manzarek, keyboardist in 1960s rock band, The Doors. *Of Indigo and Saffron: New and Selected Poems* (University of California, 2011) has an introduction by Leslie *Scalapino.   MS-S*

McCuaig, Ronald (1908–93) Born in Newcastle, New South Wales, Ronald McCuaig resembled his friend and admired contemporary Kenneth *Slessor in two respects: he spent his working life in journalism, and he ceased writing poetry in middle life. His conceits and madrigals in the manner of the seventeenth century have not worn well; where he shines is in colloquial realistic monologues and satires, usually of urban life and clearly influenced by the strongly proletarian tradition of his native city. A fear of censorship on the part of publishers caused him to publish his first collection, *Vaudeville*, privately in 1938, though its sexually explicit passages, as usual in his work, were fairly mild and the attitude to sex hardly joyous.

In all, McCuaig published four collections of verse and one of essays and short stories (*Tales out of Bed*, 1944). All are long out of print. They relate strongly to the half-innocent, half-deeply sophisticated world of urban low-life in Australia before the present era of multiculturalism, and are thus out of fashion now, but a *Selected Poems* was published by Angus & Robertson in 1992.   LM

MacDiarmid, Hugh, pseudonym of Christopher Murray Grieve (1892–1978). Born, a postman's son, in Langholm, Dumfriesshire. MacDiarmid's formal education ended with his father's death in 1911 when the poet was training to be a schoolteacher in Edinburgh. Between 1912 and enlistment in the Royal Army Medical Corps in 1915 he worked on local newspapers in Scotland and South Wales. War service followed, including periods in the Balkans and France where he seems to have enjoyed sufficient leisure to form energetic literary and cultural plans. *Northern Numbers* (1920–2) was followed by his periodical *Scottish Chapbook*. Editorials under the name C. M. Grieve promulgated justifications for writing in the *Scots language (see especially, 'A Theory of Scots Letters'), while he published lyrics in Scots under his pseudonym. In Grieve's case a pseudonym was a liberating device more than a sly disguise. Self-publication indicates something of the provincial climate which the dichotomous poet-critic was determined to sweep away. The Scots language was expounded for its modernist opportunities. He described it as 'an inchoate Marcel Proust—a Dostoevskian debris of ideas—an inexhaustible quarry of subtle and significant sound'.

Annals of the Five Senses, six prose pieces and six poems in English, appeared in 1923 but was written earlier; 1925 saw the publication of his Scots lyrics, *Sangschaw*, followed in 1926 by *Penny Wheep* and his long, audacious, and compelling masterpiece *A Drunk Man Looks at the Thistle*. Using J. Jamieson's *Etymological Dictionary of the Scottish Language* (1808; new edn. in four vols., 1879–82) and Warrack's *Chambers' Scottish Dictionary* (1911) as well as memory, MacDiarmid 'synthesized' his diction by taking words and expressions from the dialects of different districts of Lowland Scotland. The practice has now become established, but MacDiarmid's poetry of the 1920s has not been surpassed.

Outspoken fervour and incautious ambition typified MacDiarmid's career from beginning to end, and was matched by prodigious productivity. Norman *MacCaig suggested that MacDiarmid's motto might have been 'excess is not enough'. Inconsistency, recklessness, and passionate intellectualism were among the risks MacDiarmid took. 'I'll hae nae hauf-way hoose, but aye be whaur | Extremes meet' expresses perfectly his aesthetic, and perhaps also his temperamental delight in turbulence. In politics, a thoroughly foregrounded concern, his extremism is more controversial. His use of Scots was perhaps inseparable from nationalist passion, although not its primary motive. In the early 1920s he advocated Italian fascism; he was a founder member of the National Party of Scotland (1928), from which he was expelled in 1933 on grounds of communism. He joined the Communist Party soon after and was expelled in 1938 on grounds of nationalism. He rejoined in 1956 as a gesture of support for the Soviet invasion of Hungary.

His personal circumstances in the 1930s reflected the poetic, philosophical, and political turmoil into which his work led him and to which his mind always seemed predisposed. The ruthless 'First Hymn to Lenin' and adamant but sweeping 'On a Raised Beach' express his political and private determination. He was divorced in 1931, married Valda Trevlyn soon after, and in 1933 moved to the remote Shetland island of Whalsay. He suffered a nervous breakdown in 1935. Not far off 50, in 1942, he was conscripted for war work in Clydeside industry.

MacDiarmid ceased writing in Scots around 1934 and the collection of that year, *Stony Limits*, marks the extent to which he chose to engage with philosophy, science, linguistics, communism, and facts as poetic material. 'A poetry full of erudition, expertise, and ecstasy', was how he stated his ambition for an intellectual epic in which Mind would be the hero and which was to be called *Mature Art*. Parts of this largely unrealized *magnum opus*— the work of a poet who believed in 'giganticism'—came out separately as *In Memoriam James Joyce* (1955), 'The Kind of Poetry I Want', 'Cornish Heroic Song for Valda Trevlyn', and others.

Although acknowledged in Scotland as crucial to Scottish poetry, culture, and politics, MacDiarmid's significance as a major figure of modernism has been harder to establish. In England particularly he is little more than a reputation assembled from misleading reports and unsympathetic assessments.

There is an annotated edition of *A Drunk Man Looks at the Thistle*, ed. K. Buthlay (Scottish Academic Press, 1987). Alan Bold edited *The Letters* (Hamilton, 1984; see also C. Kerrigan (ed.), *The Hugh MacDiarmid—George Ogilvie Letters*, 1988). There is a biography by Alan Bold (Murray, 1988). In 1992, Carcanet began a programme to put all of MacDiarmid's major works back into print, under the general editorship of Alan Riach. This has included a corrected edition of the two-volume *Complete Poems*, a *Selected Poems* (1992; new edn., 2004), a *Selected Prose*, and a *New Selected Letters* (2001). *The Revolutionary Art of the Future* (2003) is a selection from three hundred unpublished poems discovered in the National Library of Scotland archives. See also *The Edinburgh Companion to Hugh MacDiarmid*, ed. Scott Lyall and Margery Palmer McCulloch (Edinburgh University Press, 2011).   DED

MacDonagh, Thomas (1878–1916) Born in Cloughjordan, Co. Tipperary. After various periods of teaching, he took his BA (1910) and wrote an MA on Thomas Campion for University College, Dublin, where he was a lecturer from 1912. He joined the Gaelic League in 1901 and in 1908 began teaching with Pádraig Pearse at St Enda's School. A leader of the Easter Rising and one of the seven signatories of the proclamation of a provisional Irish Republic, he was executed in May 1916.

MacDonagh had plays performed at the Abbey and in Edward Martyn's Irish Theatre. He published several volumes of poems from 1903 onwards—collected by James *Stephens as *The Poetical Works of Thomas MacDonagh* (Fisher Unwin, 1916). His earlier poetry is slight and conventional, but from *Songs of Myself* (1910) onwards his manner becomes less artificial. His best collection was *Lyrical Poems* (1913), and the best of those are translations from the Irish where (most famously in 'The Yellow Bittern') he reproduces Irish metrical forms in English. Of related importance are the chapters in *Literature in Ireland: Studies Irish and Anglo-Irish* (Talbot, 1916) where he acutely identifies 'the Irish mode'—the prosody of Irish English induced by the Irish language. His theory and practice here influenced later writers such as Austin *Clarke (who succeeded to his lectureship at UCD).   BO'D

MacDonald, Cynthia (1928–) Born in New York City. After graduating from Bennington College, she pursued a career as an opera and concert singer. In 1970 she earned an MA from Sarah Lawrence College and began a new career as poet and teacher. She taught at Johns Hopkins University before settling at the University of Houston, Texas, where she was a professor; she has also been a research fellow at the Houston/Galveston Psychoanalytic Institute.

Macdonald's extra-literary vocations as opera singer and psychoanalyst together hint at the distinctive flavour of her poetry, which features a gaudy theatricality placed in the service of a thorough anatomy of human compulsions. She writes with great wit and a refreshing freedom of invention; for Macdonald poetry is not confession or documentary but a peculiarly fabulous species of fiction. Her poems are populated by a variety of grotesque and comic types, from circus freaks to cheerleaders, each one becoming an allegorical caricature of some essential human trait. In form her poetry is generous, making full and expressive use of the page-as-stage; and while precision is not one of her most notable qualities, the energy of her imagination, by turns boisterous and ominous, gives her language its own baroque contours. See *Living Wills: New and Selected Poems* (1991) and a later volume, *I Can't Remember* (1997—both Knopf).   RG

McDonald, Ian (1933–) Born in St Augustine,Trinidad, McDonald read history at Clare College, Cambridge, then joined the Booker Group of Companies in British Guiana in 1955. He had a long career in the sugar industry, retiring in 2007, and was also a tennis champion for many years.

His very early poems were published in West Indian journals like *BIM* and *Kyk-Over-Al* in the 1950s, but his first book, *The Humming-Bird Tree* (Heinemann, 1969) was a novel based on his childhood in Trinidad. Although he was active in literary circles in now-independent Guyana, befriending Martin *Carter and A. J. *Seymour, among others, McDonald's career allowed little time for writing, until a new creative period in the 1980s, triggered by his second marriage. A pamphlet *Selected Poems* published by the Guyana *Labour Advocate* in 1983 was followed by *Mercy Ward* (1988), offering bittersweet portraits of the elderly indigent in a Georgetown hospital. *Essequibo* (1992—both Peterloo) won the Guyana Prize for poetry, and *Jaffo the Calypsonian* (1994) collected many of McDonald's very early poems.

The meditative and hymn-like *Between-Silence and Silence* (2003—both Peepal Tree) marked the beginning of a late-career preoccupation with time, age, death, and the meaning of a 'good' life. McDonald's 2008 *Selected Poems* (Macmillan) was shortlisted for the Ondaatje Prize. *The Comfort of All Things* (Moray House, 2012) includes a sequence of haiku-like 'Garden Poems', joyful observations of the natural world.   NL

McDonald, Nan (1921–74) Born at Eastwood in Sydney, graduated from the University of Sydney in arts, and worked for the publishers Angus and Robertson as an editor. McDonald published three volumes of poetry and a *Selected Poems* (Angus & Robertson, 1969). She was unmarried, lived always with members of her family, and died of cancer when she was 52.

McDonald's poetry is mostly sombre and deathward-drawn. Its style is muted and austere, refined and unpretentious, and it exults in cold, inhuman places (like the smoky blue vistas of the coast south from Sydney, the alpine country of New South Wales, and the steep Hawkesbury River area). Her relatively early death was evidently long anticipated and accepted. A stoic, Protestant religion underlies much of her work.   RGr

McDonald, Peter (1962–) Born in Belfast and educated at Oxford, where he won the Newdigate Prize. His 1989 debut *Biting the Wax* (Bloodaxe) is marked by a classical temperament and a skilful handling of narrative verse. McDonald's is a deeply moral imagination. Eschewing the tricksy postmodernism of his immediate Northern Irish predecessors, he practises a taut and understated style, and in 'Sunday at Great Tew' offers a powerful response to the IRA bombing of a Remembrance Day parade in Enniskillen in 1987.

McDonald has written extensively on Northern Irish poetry, with a particular interest in Louis *MacNeice: he has edited MacNeice's plays and poems and is the author of *Louis MacNeice: The Poet in his Contexts* (Clarendon, 1991). Like MacNeice, McDonald is drawn to parables, and in *Adam's Dream* (Bloodaxe, 1996) turns to the Lisbon Earthquake as a defining encounter of civilization and disaster, and the 'geography of ruin' that results.

His other collections are *Pastorals* (2004), *The House of Clay* (2007), and *Torchlight* (2011), with a *Collected Poems* in 2012 (all Carcanet). He has experimented with prose poems ('Academic Sentences') and quasi-imagist minimalism ('The pieces'), and is also a skilled classicist, translating from Latin and Greek. A trenchant observer of the contemporary scene (see *Serious Poetry* (Clarendon, 2002)), he has taught at the universities of

Bristol and Oxford, where he directs Tower Poetry, a poetry education organization, from Christ Church College, and edits its online magazine, *Poetry Matters*.   DW

McDowell, Robert (1953–) Born in Los Angeles and went to local public schools. He attended the University of California, Santa Cruz, received an MFA in writing from Columbia University in 1976, and taught at Indiana State University, Evansville from 1978 to 1984. He was the most outspoken proponent of the *New Narrative movement. From 1981 through 1990 he and Mark *Jarman edited *The Reaper*, which was devoted to narrative poems and became a sounding board for its editors' hyperbolic manifestos on the vitality of contemporary narrative poems in comparison to the lyric, which they once proclaimed dead. Since 1985 he has been publisher and editor of Story Line Press, a small press publishing poetry, fiction, and criticism. His first book of poems, *Quiet Money* (Holt, 1987), consists of eighteen narratives focusing on the lives of ordinary men and women—businessmen, librarians, bowlers—often down on their luck, though never less than spirited. At their weakest, the poems are sentimental and melodramatic. At their strongest, they are acute renderings of character brought sharply into focus within the flux of everyday life. This is true of 'In the Photograph You See', a chilling psychological portrait of the imaginary life of a small-town tailor. The title-poem is about a bootlegger who made transatlantic flights for liquor during the depression before Lindbergh's historic trip and, in the aftermath of Lindbergh's public tragedy, learns to appreciate the compensatory pleasures of an unheroic domestic life. His narrative poem, *The Diviners* (Peterloo, 1995), was published in Britain with an introduction by Dana *Gioia, who praised it as 'one of the most absorbing and original long poems of recent years'. More recently he has been a professional speaker on the subject of *Poetry as Spiritual Practice* (Free Press, 2008).   RMCP

MacEwen, Gwendolyn (1941–87) Born in Toronto and raised there and in Winni-

peg. She dropped out of school at 18 to pursue a career in poetry. Following a short marriage to poet Milton *Acorn, she published the chapbooks *Selah* (1961), *The Drunken Clock* (1961), and *The Rising Fire* (1963, with Raymond *Souster's influential Contact Press), before she established her reputation with *A Breakfast for Barbarians* (Ryerson, 1966).

Both *A Breakfast for Barbarians* and *The Shadow Maker* (Macmillan, 1969) contain poems where the musicality of the language and vividness of image are elucidated with a surging, almost anarchic energy. An eye for the absurd in the commonplace and for emotional power in the serene are hallmarks of MacEwen's work.

Her collections *The Armies of the Moon* (1972), *Magic Animals* (1975—both Macmillan), and *The Fire Eaters* (Oberon, 1976), as well as the volume of travel writings about Greece, *Mermaids and Ikons* (1978), owe a debt to mythology. MacEwen's second husband, Greek singer Nikos Tsingos, introduced her to the Mediterranean mentality, and the voice she developed during this period is haunted by doubts about the border between dream and reality, a theme which underlies her novel about the Egyptian Pharoah Akhenaton, *King of Egypt, King of Dreams* (1971).

A fascination with the Arab world drew her to the subject of Lawrence of Arabia in *The T. E. Lawrence Poems* (Mosaic/Valley, 1982)—her most completely integrated work. In it, the poet questions the line between psychotic delusion and rational disintegration.

MacEwen's interest in narrative was first manifested in *Terror and Erebus: A Verse Play for Radio*, written in 1965. Her treatment of the fateful Franklin Expedition of 1848 (which Northrop Frye had dubbed the 'unwritten Canadian epic') perceives the Canadian Arctic as an interior landscape rather than an exterior realm, a place inhabited by disembodied voices which exist only through the power of description, memory, and chronicle. MacEwen included the play in the 'Apocalypse' section of her final volume, *Afterworlds* (McClelland & Stewart, 1987), a hauntingly poignant book; many of the poems foreshadow her death in the November of its year of publication. Throughout *Afterworlds* the poems flirt with the abstract, the inconceivable, and the ethereal, as if the voice of the poet were looking back from some point beyond life, still chronicling, still witnessing, transcribing, and describing. Her collected poems in two volumes were edited for Exile Editions in 1993 by Margaret *Atwood and Barry Callaghan. See also Rosemary Sullivan, *Shadow Maker: the Life of Geraldine MacEwen* (Harper, 1995; repr. 2012) and *The Selected Gwendolyn MacEwen*, ed. Meaghan Strimas (Exile, 2008).   BM

McFadden, David W. (1940–) McFadden lived all of his first thirty-eight years in the small city of Hamilton, Ontario. He has been a proof-reader, newspaper reporter, journal editor, novelist, and a prolific poet. His early *Letters from the Earth to the Earth* (Coach House, 1968) presented observations of domestic and local life, its blissful strange ordinariness, but in the 1970s his poems took on a darker tone, as in the well-known 'A Typical Canadian Family Visits Disney World'.

In 1978 McFadden's great change of life led him away from the family to British Columbia, and into a series of long poems whose subjects are darkness, chance, and the emotional and mystical elements of the everyday. The 1980s poetry is personal, but more fictive; the poet's progress is through the darker corners of life and imagination, but he still looks quirkily beyond appearances for the real forms of human life. Four novels (three in the 'Great Lakes' series) parallel this progress, which culminates in the hundred Baudelairean prose sonnets of *Gypsy Guitar* (Talonbooks, 1987). In all of this work McFadden remains the comic metaphysician reporting on the experimental nature of daily life.

In 2001, his 1974 illustrated novel, *The Great Canadian Sonnet*, was reissued by Coach House Press. His later selected poems, *Why Are You So Sad?* (2007), drew on over twenty volumes, and was nominated for the Griffin Poetry Prize. A collected volume of McFadden's long poems, *Why Are You So Long and Sweet?*, followed in 2009. Both books were edited by Stuart

Ross for Insomniac Press. See also the later sonnet sequence, *Be Calm, Honey* (Mansfield, 2008).   RB

McFadden, Roy (1921–99) Born in Belfast, read law at Queen's University in that city, and lived there his entire life with his wife and a large family, practising as a solicitor. Encouraged especially by Herbert *Read, McFadden published a promising first collection during the Second World War, but it seems to have been lost among more metropolitan voices. What may have gone against McFadden is that the vision of war he presented was largely Yeatsian. After his third book he published no major collection for twenty-four years, but the bitter circumstances of Ulster enabled a distinct narrative voice to emerge. Of the law-courts revisited McFadden says: 'Keep handy in your briefcase | A summons and a shout: | Not everyone who comes here | Is certain to get out.' By purging his voice of oratory he gained eloquence, and by remaining in Northern Ireland he came to stand at stage centre.

There is a *Selected Roy McFadden*, ed. John Boyd (Blackstaff, 1943), but it is slight in relation to the total oeuvre. This includes *Swords and Ploughshares* (1943); *Flowers for a Lady* (1945); *The Heart's Townland* (1947—all Routledge); *The Garryowen* (Chatto & Windus, 1971); *Verifications* (1977); *A Watching Brief* (1979—both Blackstaff); *Letters to the Hinterland* (Dedalus, 1986); and *After Seymour's Funeral* (Blackstaff, 1990). *Collected Poems*, published by Lagan Press in 1996, contains some later work.   PDH

McGimpsey, David (1962–) Born in Montreal, and studied there at Concordia University, where he now teaches, after obtaining a PhD from Dalhousie. He also plays in the rock band, Puggy Hammer, and is a travel writer and newspaper columnist.

McGimpsey's critical study, *Imagining Baseball: America's Pastime and Popular Culture* (Indiana University Press, 2000), examines the relationship between popular and literary culture by which his poetry is also fascinated ('in the future . . . | to get younger people more interested | in poems, Browning's "Pippa Passes" | will be retitled "Whatevs"'). His comically voracious poems, beginning with *Lardcake* (ECW, 1996), frequently present mythopoetic continuations of television programmes and celebrity lives. *Li'l Bastard* (Coach House, 2011), a cartooning tribute in 'chubby sonnets' to the *confessional sequences of John *Berryman and Robert *Lowell, was nominated for the Governor General's Award for Poetry.

McGimpsey's other collections are *Dogboy* (1998), *Hamburger Valley, California* (2001—both ECW), and *Sitcom* (Coach House, 2007). He is a popular performer of his own work, and his ironic take on Americana has been influential in Canadian poetry. See *Population Me*, a collection of critical essays edited by Alessandra Porco (Palimpsest, 2010). *Certifiable*, a book of short stories, appeared in 2004 from Insomniac Press.   JNT

McGinley, Phyllis (1908–78) Born in Oregon and educated at the universities of Utah and California. She won the Pulitzer Prize for Poetry in 1960, and, with Dorothy *Parker as her only equal, she is the best woman writer of light verse that America has produced. Yet to call this poetry 'light' is not altogether accurate, if by this we mean poetry that is jokey or entirely frivolous. W. H. *Auden, introducing the prize-winning selection, claims that her poetry could not have been written by a man because it is not nostalgic, like the verse of *Betjeman. Certainly this is very much the verse of the normal wife-and-mother ('Why, if (according to A. Gesell) | The minds of children ring clear as a bell, | Does every question one asks a tot | Receive the similar answer—"What?"'). Also, in its rhyming ingenuity, it is very close to Praed or Byron ('Let sobs be broken, let tears be saline. | Charles & Company has no male line'); but, as Auden notes, it is never ostentatious in rhyme (Ogden *Nash rhymes such as 'anthropophagi/sarcophagi' don't occur). Another of McGinley's conspicuous talents is to be able to write poems about the minutiae of everyday life that are neither silly nor facetious: for example, 'My Six Toothbrushes'. When she is satirical, the satire is gentle. She can write a *Graves-like 'serious' poetry (see 'The Landscape of Love'). In her 'religious' verse, mainly about saints and theologians, she seems a little embarrassed by the sometimes conflicting demands of piety and common sense. The literary satires, such as 'Publisher's Party', seem more assured; and some of the Second World War poems (like 'Landscape Without Figures') are both moving and difficult to reconcile with Auden's definition. She uses, exclusively, conventional forms and metres. The volume, with Auden's introduction, is *Times Three* (Viking, 1960; Secker & Warburg, 1961).   GE

McGough, Roger (1937–   ) Born in Liverpool and studied at Hull University. A prolific writer, performer, and broadcaster, McGough is one of the most popular post-war English poets for adults and children. He was awarded an OBE in 1997 and a CBE in 2008.

Underdog, his 1965 small-press debut, announced a rebellious yet self-deprecating persona, famously dramatized in the poem 'Let me die a youngman's death'. McGough then appeared alongside Adrian Henri and Brian *Patten in the million-selling *Mersey Sound* (1967) volume, the tenth in the Penguin Modern Poets series. The trio became known as the Liverpool or Mersey Poets, and were marketed as the literary equivalent of The Beatles (McGough was also a member of the pop group, The Scaffold, with Paul McCartney's brother). See Phil Bowen, *A Gallery To Play To: The Story of the Mersey Poets* (Stride, 1999).

His early influences were *Beats such as Gregory *Corso, as well as oral forms such as playground songs and ballads. McGough's populism, like that of his contemporary Adrian *Mitchell, has been criticized as 'an unliterary principle of making poems' (Douglas *Dunn). The simplicity is a skilful one, though, with a familiar conception of modern lyricism at its heart (one of his favourite poets is Norman *MacCaig). McGough has also written plays and made translations of Molière's comedies. See *Collected Poems* (Penguin, 2003) and *Said and Done* (Century, 2005), an autobiography. *As Far as I Know* (Penguin,

2012) includes the new poem, 'Not for Me a Youngman's Death'. JNT

McGrath, Thomas (1916–90) Born the grandson of Irish Catholic homesteaders on a farm near Sheldon, North Dakota. His childhood was punctuated by often-violent labour unrest, which gave him a deep feeling for social justice. McGrath was educated in a grab-bag of places, from a one-room schoolhouse to the University of North Dakota, Louisiana State University, and New College, Oxford, where he was a Rhodes Scholar. His itinerant resumé includes work as a dockyard labour organizer in New York, two years stationed in the Aleutians during the Second World War, and stints of film-writing and college teaching that were interrupted in the 1950s when he was blacklisted as a communist.

McGrath's political views have contributed to his neglect by mainstream literary critics and publishers. His pseudo-autobiographical epic, *Letter to an Imaginary Friend* (Book I, 1970; Book II, 1985) contains vivid images from a turbulent life transmuted into verse that is alternately lyrical, fragmentary, imitative, and unruly, but often subtly controlled and poised. Written over thirty years in at least six countries, the poem builds toward a dream-vision of a better world not unlike the New Jerusalem of Blake and *Auden.

Though he occasionally succumbed to sentimentality, McGrath was a superb craftsman, comfortable with a rich variety of forms and diction. Lyrics like 'The World of the Perfect Tear' and 'The Buffalo Coat' make good use of traditional metres and rhyme. In 'The Bread of this World' one hears the full sounds of Hopkins and Dylan *Thomas. Often compared to Whitman's, McGrath's technique has, except for its occasional invective, as much in common with *Eliot's, Auden's, and *MacNeice's.

Selected Poems, 1938–1988 (1988) contains the best of McGrath's shorter work. Sam Hamill edited his last poems as *Death Song* in 1991. A one-volume edition of *Letter to an Imaginary Friend* appeared in 1997 (all Copper Canyon). See also *Praises and Dispraises*, by Terence Des Pres (Viking, 1988) and *The Revolutionary Poet in the United States*, ed. Frederick C. Stern (University of Missouri Press, 1988). DM

MacGreevy, Thomas (orig. **'McGreevy'**) (1894–1967) Born in Tarbert, Co. Kerry. After active service at Ypres and the Somme he took a degree at Trinity College, Dublin and taught at the École Normale Supérieure in Paris, where he became friendly with James *Joyce and later Samuel *Beckett.

Short monographs on Richard *Aldington and T. S. *Eliot were followed by his only poetry collection, *Poems* (1934), praised by Beckett for its 'endopsychic clarity'. Too modernist for the Irish Free State, but intellectually committed to his homeland in a way that Joyce and Beckett were not, MacGreevy suffered a long creative attrition in later life, serving instead as the Director of the National Gallery and editor of *The Capuchin Annual*. Beckett's advocacy, notably in 'Recent Irish Poetry' (1934), has helped cement MacGreevy's association with the Thirties generation of Irish modernist poets, though the *esprit de corps* of the four writers concerned (MacGreevy, Beckett, Denis *Devlin, and Brian *Coffey) may be largely notional.

'Crón Tráth na nDéithe', his longest poem, meditates on frustrated Republican hopes against the backdrop of squalid civil war. MacGreevy was an important confidant of Beckett's in the 1930s (though his side of their correspondence has not survived), and forged a close friendship in later life with Wallace *Stevens, as reflected in the latter's 'Our Stars Come from Ireland'. A *Collected Poems* appeared in 1991 from Anna Livia Press. Though few in number, MacGreevy's exquisite short lyrics offer us 'alps, ice, stars and white starlight | In a dry, high silence'. DW

McGuckian, Medbh (1950–) Born in Belfast. She studied at Queen's University, taught English at St Patrick's College, Knock, and was the first woman to be writer-in-residence at Queen's.

McGuckian has described her territory as 'the feminine subconscious or semi-consciousness'. Rivers, clouds, clothes, flowers, ferns, and shadows are her favoured archetypes, predictable in themselves but never treated predictably. There are few abstractions in her work: ideas are translated directly into imagery, giving the sense of a keen intellect at play, or opulently dreaming. Quotations from other authors' texts may be interwoven. Consistently inventive and witty, sometimes obscure but syntactically cogent, McGuckian's work often has a strong political subtext. Formally, it seems closer to the poetry of John *Ashbery and some of the American *Language poets than to current British and Irish writing. The significant volumes in her prolific output include: *The Flower Master* (1982); *Venus and the Rain* (1984); *On Ballycastle Beach* (1988—all Oxford University Press); *Marconi's Cottage* (Bloodaxe, 1992); *Selected Poems: 1978–1994* (1997); and *My Love has Fared Inland* (2008—both Gallery Press). A critical study, *The Poetry of Medbh McGuckian: The Interior of Words*, ed. Shane Alcobia Murphy and Richard Kirkland, appeared from Cork University Press in 2010.   CAR

McHugh, Heather (1948–) Born in California. By the time McHugh, as a Radcliffe undergraduate, had been admitted to Robert *Lowell's graduate workshop at Harvard, her first published poem had already appeared in *The New Yorker*. Educated further at Denver University (MA 1972), she taught at SUNY Binghamton and elsewhere, most recently at the University of Washington and Warren Wilson College. She has published eight poetry collections, four books of translations, and a collection of essays, *Broken English: Poetry and Partiality* (Wesleyan, 2007). Her awards include fellowships from the Guggenheim, Rockefeller, and MacArthur Foundations, and from the National Endowment for the Arts.

McHugh's affection for jazz and her early experiments with painting give her poems an uncommon physicality, the immediate heard quality of speech. Characteristic too are her witty turns of phrase, the sense of the mind observing itself. ('That's the trick,' she said in a 1999 interview, 'the sudden unexpectedness inside the overknown.')

Although rich in image, the work is often abstract rather than narrative. Since the late 1980s, however, McHugh's poems have grown darker, and more emotional in impulse. Representative is her fifth collection, *Hinge and Sign: New and Selected Poems* (Wesleyan University Press, 1994). The most recent is *Upgraded to Serious* (Copper Canyon, 2009).   MB

McKay, Claude (1889–1948) Born in Sunny Ville, Jamaica. His father was a prosperous farmer. As a young man, he lived in Kingston, where he met the English folklorist Edward Jekyll, and it was Jekyll who encouraged him to write poems in dialect. His first two books of poems, all in dialect, *Songs from Jamaica* (1912) and *Constab Ballads* (1912), are much concerned with the harsh lives of ordinary people, both in rural, mountainous areas, where he grew up, and in cities. He encountered the worst aspects of city life during a brief stint with the constabulary. Shortly after, McKay left Jamaica for the United States, never to return. He lived mainly in New York, but travelled widely in Europe. He was an early advocate of black liberation, both in America and in colonial Africa, and became an American citizen in 1940. In his last years he converted from communism to Roman Catholicism, and taught at a Catholic school in Chicago.

His first American volume of poems, *Harlem Shadows* (1922) inaugurated the *Harlem Renaissance. It was preceded by *Spring in New Hampshire* (1920). His later poetry tended to treat politically radical themes within traditional verse-forms. Two of his most famous poems, 'If We Must Die' and 'The White House', for instance, are sonnets. The former, which was reputedly quoted by Churchill as wartime prime minister, exhorts victims of racist oppression to fight back, however hopeless the odds. The latter is a bitter indictment of presidential indifference.

Other collections include *Selected Poems* (Bookman, 1953), *Selected Poetry of Claude McKay*, ed. Wayne F. Cooper (Schocken, 1973), and *Selected Poems*, ed. Joan R.

Sherman (Dover, 1999). *Banana Bottom* (Harper, 1933) is his most successful novel. *A Long Way from Home* (Furman, 1937) and *My Green Hills of Jamaica* (Heinemann, 1975) are autobiographical works. McKay's *Complete Poems* (University of Illinois Press, 2003), including many unpublished pieces, were edited by William J. Maxwell. See James R. Giles, *Claude McKay* (Twayne, 1976), Wayne F. Cooper, *Claude McKay: A Biography* (Louisiana State University Press, 1987; repr. 1996), and Tyrone Tillery, *Claude McKay: A Black Poet's Struggle for Identity* (University of Massachusetts Press, 1992).   MR

McKay, Don(ald) (1942–) Born and raised in Ontario, McKay gained a PhD at Swansea University College in Wales, and went on to lecture at the universities of Western Ontario and New Brunswick. Since 1975 he has edited and published Brick Books, and has also been editor of *The Fiddlehead* magazine.

A leading figure to other Canadian ecopoets of his generation, such as Tim *Lilburn and Jan *Zwicky, McKay is concerned with the relationship between civilization and wilderness, as mediated by poetry itself. His ongoing series of 'songs for the song of' acknowledges the vulnerable limits of anthropocentrism in vigorously colloquial verse on the otherness of birds: 'Were the geese to quit their existential yammer, talk | would also cease' ('Song for the Song of the Canada Geese'). See also his collection of essays, *Vis à Vis: Field Notes on Poetry & Wilderness* (Gaspereau, 2001).

His early books include *Birding, or Desire* (1983). *Strike/Slip* (2006), a meditation on geology, won the 2007 Griffin Poetry Prize. *Paradoxides* (2012) continues his exploration of this subject. Two recent selections are available: *Camber: Selected Poems* (2004—all McClelland & Stewart) and *Field Marks: The Poetry of Don McKay* (Wilfrid Laurier University Press, 2006), ed. Méira Cook. In 2008 McKay became a Member of the Order of Canada.   JNT

McKendrick, Jamie (1955–) Born in Liverpool and studied at Nottingham University. He lives in Oxford, where he teaches and works as a reviewer.

McKendrick's first two collections, *The Sirocco Room* (1991) and *The Kiosk on the Brink* (1993), gained him a place among the Poetry Society's *New Generation poets. His visually attentive and historically inquisitive writing is often cast in anecdotal moulds, weighing whole cultures in small details. The title of his third collection, *The Marble Fly* (1997—all Oxford University Press), refers to a Pompeiian wall-relief. It won the Forward Prize for Best Collection. With the closing of the Oxford University Press poetry list, McKendrick moved to Faber and Faber, who published *Sky Nails: Selected Poems 1979–1997* in 2000. Sean *O'Brien hailed his fourth collection, *Ink Stone* (2003), as 'the best of an impressive series of books', and a work of 'significant authority'. The widening political sweep and colloquial vigour of McKendrick's later poems suggest the influence of Tom *Paulin, to whom *Crocodiles & Obelisks* (2007) is dedicated. Dwelling on the ruins of men and empires, it continues the interweaving of McKendrick's own verse with his work as a translator of Italian (a 'crocodile' is an Italian slang term for obituary). He is the editor of *The Faber Book of Twentieth-Century Italian Poems* (2004), and has also published a prize-winning selection of the poetry of Valerio Magrelli. His latest collection is *Out There* (2012).   JNT

Mackenzie, Kenneth Seaforth (1913–55) Born in Perth, Western Australia. He was disowned by his family after he failed to persevere in three attempts at his education: he ran away from high school, agricultural college, and a university law course.

Mackenzie went to Sydney at 21, taking his poems and arriving unannounced on Kenneth *Slessor's doorstep. Work was found for him in journalism, but he proved an unreliable employee and moved about amongst various newspapers. He married at 21 and was to have two children. At 24 he published his first novel and first volume of poetry. The novel, *The Young Desire It* (1937), appeared under the name Seaforth Mackenzie, as did all he wrote in that form, and is usually considered the best of his four works of fiction. He had already become an alcoholic and was sexually promiscuous. Drafted into the army, Mackenzie was a prison guard at Cowra in 1944 when there was a mass, intentionally suicidal breakout of Japanese prisoners of war (although he was not on duty that night). This event became the subject of his novel *Dead Men Rising* (1951). During the war he published one further book of poetry, *The Moonlit Doorway* (1944).

On his discharge from the army, Mackenzie was hospitalized for his drinking, and then separated from his wife and children. He lived in the Blue Mountains, outside Sydney, in a bark-roofed hut without electricity or water, on a block of land his wife owned. In the remaining ten years of his life he produced three novels, receiving three one-year Commonwealth Literary Fund fellowships (awarded by Slessor), and the best of his poetry, which was left unpublished until it appeared in *The Poems of Kenneth Mackenzie* (Angus & Robertson, 1972). He occasionally worked as a labourer in his last years, was hospitalized again, and was reduced at times, his wife said, to drinking methylated spirits. At the age of 42, while he was on a visit to a friend at Goulburn, south of Sydney, he was found lying drowned in a small creek.

Mackenzie's is overwhelmingly the poetry of a painful consciousness. His facile early work is full of an assertive sexuality, but for all its efforts after sensuousness has something irritable, divided, and metallic about it. He was later influenced by Edward *Thomas (too plainly so in pieces like 'By one small stream . . .'), and these poems about suffering and its occasional lapses (written either formally or in free verse) are limpid, cleanly crafted, natural, without self-pity, and full of a helpless compassion. Most notable are the poems set in hospitals, such as 'An Old Inmate'. See *The Model: Selected Writings of Kenneth Seaforth Mackenzie* (University of Western Australia Press, 2000), ed. Richard Rossiter. RGr

Mackey, Nathaniel (1947–) Born in Miami, Florida and grew up in California. He studied English at the universities of Princeton and Stanford. From 1979 to 2010 he taught at the University of California in Santa Cruz, where he also hosted a jazz and world music radio show. He is now Professor of Creative Writing at Duke University. From 2001 to 2007 he was a Chancellor of the Academy of American Poets.

Jazz music has been an inspiration for Mackey's improvisatory, staccato verse ever since his first chapbook, dedicated to John Coltrane, *Four for Trane* (Golemics, 1978). Amiri *Baraka was an important early influence, along with William Carlos *Williams and the *Black Mountain poets.In the ongoing serial poem 'Song of the Adoumboulou', Mackey speaks of his fascination with the 'Supreme Friction' of human creativity and sexuality, a dissonant version of Wallace *Stevens' 'Supreme Fiction'.

His full-length books of poetry are: *Eroding Witness* (University of Illinois Press, 1985), *School of Udhra* (1993), *Whatsaid Serif* (1998—both City Lights), *Splay Anthem* (2006), and *Nod* (2011). *Bass Cathedral* (2008—all New Directions) is the fourth volume of an ongoing prose work called *From a Broken Bottle Traces of Perfume Still Emanate* (the first three volumes were republished by New Directions in 2010). Mackey's critical writing has been collected in *Discrepant Engagement: Dissonance, Cross-Culturality, and Experimental Writing* (Cambridge University Press, 1993) and *Paracritical Hinge: Essays, Talks, Notes, Interviews* (University of Wisconsin Press, 2005). *Chicago Review* 43:1 was a special Mackey issue.   JNT

Mackie, Alastair (1925–94) Born to working-class parents in Aberdeen, where he went to university after war service in the Royal Air Force and Navy, Mackie lived for most of his life on the east coast of Scotland, and worked as an English teacher. He has been called 'the best and most woefully-neglected *Scots-writing poet of his generation'.

Mackie began writing after he met George Mackay *Brown while teaching in Orkney. Brown introduced him to the work of Hugh *MacDiarmid, whom he later addressed in a sonnet, 'To Hugh MacDiarmid Whiles' (1958), which compares the older poet to St

Anthony in the desert. Elsewhere he spoke of the 'enormous shadow' cast by the 'Chinese Wall' of MacDiarmid's revolutionary Scots modernism. Another important discovery was that he could translate the French of Rimbaud more easily into his own dialect than standard English. *Soundings* (1966) contained only two poems in Scots, but *Clytach* (1972—both Akros) was composed exclusively in it. His third collection, *Back-Green Odyssey and Other Poems* (Rainbow, 1980), was followed by a selection for Aberdeen University Press, *Ingaitherins* (1987). *Collected Poems 1954–1994* (Two Ravens, 2012), ed. Christopher Rush, has a foreword by Andrew *Greig, who recalls being taught by Mackie in the Fife town of Anstruther. It contains four hundred pages of poetry, including several longer sequences such as *At the Heich Kirk-Yaird* (Akros, 1974), and translations of Rimbaud, Virgil, and Osip Mandelstam. JNT

Mackinnon, Lachlan (1956–) Born in Aberdeen and educated at Charterhouse and Christ Church College, Oxford. He teaches English at Winchester College and is a regular reviewer of new verse.

Mackinnon's first collection, *Monterey Cypress* (1988), showed a talent for economical, evocative poems deriving from place ('Here'), identity ('Fallodon Wood'), and exile (a sequence of Parisian pieces). His interest in uncertainty provides the book's most direct and successful poem, 'In a French Court', the monologue of an abused child, although other attempts at directness can seem rhetorical and grandiose ('La Cimetière Montparnasse').

The Coast of Bohemia (1991—both Chatto & Windus) was far more powerful, focused on the experience of breakdown and distinguished by honesty and painstaking accuracy ('Nature Poem', 'Mania'). His third collection, *The Jupiter Collisions* (2003), was a volume of occasional lyrics arranged around two longer sequences on memory and perception ('Pips in a Watermelon' and 'A Water Buffalo in Guangdong Province'). At the heart of his fourth, *The Small Hours* (2010—both Faber), is an elegiac prose poem, 'The Book of Emma'.

His critical books are: *Eliot, Auden, Lowell: Aspects of the Baudelairean Inheritance* (1983); *Shakespeare the Aesthete: An Exploration of Literary Theory* (1988—both Macmillan); and *The Lives of Elsa Triolet* (Chatto & Windus, 1992). SO'B*

Maclean, Alasdair (1926–94) Born in Glasgow. Despite some self-regarding views on 'the pain and indignity' of writing poetry, and occasional hectoring, Alasdair Maclean's *From the Wilderness* (1973) announced a late-arriving talent willing to engage with nature in the raw and the hard crofting life of Ardnamurchan in northwest Scotland from the basis of convincingly unsentimental experience. Maclean's best work was harsh and mediated through a voice which he described as that of 'a peasant who writes poetry'. He was ruefully conscious of the distance which had grown between him and his origins, although it could be argued that his vivid disclosures of waning Highland life made that ostensible gap unimportant.

Waking the Dead (1976) closes with a sequence in memory of the poet's mother—'to draw the thin milk from two half-starved cows | she swung her sickle in a field of stones'. There is an anger and virulence in his writing about nature ('Hen Dying', for example, or 'Rams'), and in many poems a relentless, sometimes wooden iambic rhythm lends an appropriate pulse to what in the end seems the limitation of a misanthropic point of view. On the positive side, there is nothing meek, humble, or yielding in Maclean's poetry. An angry assertiveness, however, sometimes leads to a damaging contempt and a punitive relish for the hurts on which much of his vision is founded. *Night Falls on Ardnamurchan* (1984—all Gollancz) is a ruminative, impressive prose account of 'the twilight of a crofting community'. DED

MacLeish, Archibald (1892–1982) Born and brought up in Glencoe, Illinois. He graduated from Yale in 1915 and—having married and served at the front in the First World War—from Harvard Law School in 1919. After three frustrating years as a lawyer in Boston, he went to Paris to live by his poetry alone, returned to America in 1928, and spent most of the 1930s as a journalist on *Fortune* magazine. Appointed Librarian of Congress in 1939, MacLeish quickly won his way into President Roosevelt's circle of confidential advisers, becoming director of the newly created Office of Facts and Figures in 1941 (which placed him in a key position respecting wartime propaganda in America), Assistant Secretary of State in 1944, and chairman of the US delegation at the formation of UNESCO in 1945. After Roosevelt's death MacLeish's days as a government official were numbered, and in the late 1940s he turned from public to academic life, moving back to Boston to become Boylston Professor at Harvard (1949–62).

MacLeish's poetry—like his professional career—reflects the changing intellectual trends of his time. The traditional lyric forms and lilting rhythms of his first two books, *Songs for a Summer's Day (A Sonnet-Cycle)* (1915) and *Tower of Ivory* (1917), as he later commented, 'took off from Swinburne'. In Paris he discovered modernism and French Symbolism: *The Pot of Earth* (1925) and *The Hamlet of A. MacLeish* (1928), long poems on the conflict between personal desire and natural law, take many of their techniques and symbols from *The Waste Land*; and the lyrics in *Streets in the Moon* (1926) are indebted to *Pound, Laforgue, and Mallarmé. Back in America, MacLeish's new patriotic and political concerns joined an equally new declamatory style in *New Found Land: Fourteen Poems* (1930), *Frescoes for Mr. Rockefeller's City* (1933), and *Panic: A Play in Verse* (1935), and soon became vigorously partisan: *Public Speech: Poems* (1936) defines true (liberal-democratic) against specious (communist) brotherhood, while *America Was Promises* (1939) urges Americans to remain loyal to the government's New Deal doctrines. Wanting a more immediately far-reaching vehicle for his topical themes, MacLeish wrote verse plays for radio (*The Fall of the City*, 1937, and *Air Raid*, 1938), and verse illustrations to a sequence of photographs (*Land of the Free—U.S.A.*, 1938). Less choric and more personal, *Actfive and Other Poems* (1948) shows a fresh clarity and formal variety,

thus launching the last phase of MacLeish's poetry. His *Collected Poems 1917–1952* (1952) won a Pulitzer Prize, a National Book Award, and a Bollingen Prize; but the later elegies and reflections on old age in *The Wild Old Wicked Man and Other Poems* (1968) are perhaps his best (if least ambitious) poems, and the Oscar for the documentary screenplay, *The Eleanor Roosevelt Story* (1965), his most notable award. The later verse plays include *J. B.* (1958), a modern version of Job, and *Herakles* (1967), a modern version of the Greek myth. *A Time to Speak: The Selected Prose* (1941) and *A Time to Act: Selected Addresses* (1943) are good companions to his poetry of the 1930s; *Poetry and Experience* (Riverside, 1961), however, contains more sober criticism. See also *New and Collected Poems 1917–1976* (Houghton, 1976), *MacLeish* by Signi Lenea Falk (Twayne, 1965), and *Archibald MacLeish: An American Life* (Houghton, 1992) by Scott Donaldson and R. H. Winnick. NE

Macleod, Joseph (Gordon) (1903–84) A poet and theatre director, Macleod was best known in his lifetime as an announcer on BBC radio. Educated at Rugby School and Oxford University, his friends included Graham Greene and Adrian Stokes. A cameo role in Humphrey Jennings' film *Listen to Britain* (1942) showcases his gravitas at the microphone, but his work from the 1930s—visionary, tightly-wrought modernist fragments—has remained largely hidden since early appreciation by Basil *Bunting and Ezra *Pound. Macleod's major book-length work is *The Ecliptic* (Faber, 1930), divided into the signs of the zodiac, with each offering visual and alliterative associations. The text owes much to the *Eliotic myth-kitty, but it exudes force and brooding power. 'Cancer' begins thus: 'Moonpoison, mullock of sacrifice, | Suffuses the veins of the eyes | Till the retina, mooncoloured, | Sees the sideways motion of the cretin crab | Hued thus like a tortoise askew in the glaucous moonscape'. From the late 1930s onwards Macleod also published under a pseudonym, 'Adam Drinan'; these works attempted to replicate in English the sound patterning of

Gaelic poetry and dealt with Scottish subjects: i.e. *The Ghosts of the Strath* (Fortune, 1943). Macleod is also notable for his work as producer and actor at the Cambridge Festival Theatre with Terrance Gray in 1927–36, and for his sequence of books on Soviet theatre. See *Cyclic Serial Zeniths From the Flux: The Selected Poems of Joseph Macleod*, edited with an introduction by Andrew Duncan (Waterloo, 2008).   LMe

Mac Low, Jackson (1922–2004) Born in Chicago and studied at the university there, and later at Brooklyn College. He worked as a reference-book editor, and taught widely. He was a founding member of the avant-garde group Fluxus, and has been called, by Jerome *Rothenberg, 'the principal experimental poet of his time', influencing *Language and *conceptual writers.

In the early 1950s, Mac Low set W. H. *Auden's alliterative long poem *The Age of Anxiety* to music. Shortly afterwards, he began to 'engage with contingency' in poetry, in response to John *Cage's use of chance methods in music, informed by principles of Zen Buddhism and Jewish mysticism. *22 Light Poems* (Black Sparrow, 1968) includes one dedicated to Cage, which splices different kinds of 'light' with astrology-column cliché ('Orange light yields revenue yielding ideas').

The Pronouns (Mac Low and Judson Dance Workshop, 1964) was a 'collection of 40 dances', written in verse intended as a cue for improvised performance. Their abstract juxtaposition of phrases recalls Gertrude *Stein, whom Mac Low later reworked using a 'diastic' computer program developed to automate his acrostic procedures (cf. Cage's use of the 'mesostic'). Although Mac Low's guiding ideal was one of 'non-ego', his later work moved from using source texts to language he largely originated himself, as in *From Pearl Harbor Day to FDR's Birthday (7 December 1981–30 January 1982)* (Sun & Moon, 1982). For an overview, including some pre-1950s poetry, see *Thing of Beauty: New and Selected Works* (University of California, 2009).   JNT

McMaster, Rhyll (1947–) Born in Brisbane and attended Queensland University. In her early twenties she married the poet and novelist Roger McDonald, and much of her time in the years which followed was taken up with their three children. In the late 1970s she moved from Brisbane to Canberra, where she studied to qualify as a nurse, but before she began work in a hospital she and McDonald bought a farm near Braidwood, outside Canberra, where they have lived ever since. Farming has proved as time-consuming as child-rearing for McMaster, and for this reason her poetic output has been sparing.

She is, nevertheless, one of Australia's most highly regarded woman poets. *The Brineshrimp* (University of Queensland Press, 1972) was notable for its close observation of commonplace things, and for its weight of unstated emotion. *Washing the Money* (Angus & Robertson, 1986; repr. Picaro, 2008) won a major prize, though it contained less than thirty pages of poetry, alongside photographs. Its best poems are detailed and quirky recollections of childhood events. Her third collection was *On My Empty Feet* (1993). *Flying the Coop: New and Selected Poems 1972–1994* (1994—both Heinemann) was joint winner of the Grave Leven Prize, and was followed by *Chemical Bodies: A Diary of Probable Events* (Brandl & Schlesinger, 1997). In 2007 she published her first novel, *Feather Man*.   JG

McMichael, James (1939–) Born in Pasadena, a poet of southern California, a region better represented in American politics—Nixon and Reagan—than in American poetry. McMichael is unusually sensitive to place: what Paterson, New Jersey, was to William Carlos *Williams, Pasadena is to him. His father's profession—he was a real-estate developer—increased that sensitivity. His long poem *Four Good Things* (Houghton, 1980), is a sprawling autobiographical meditation on life, death, and real-estate, set in—of course—southern California. McMichael's poetic line and rhythm verge on prose; the weakly enjambed verse paragraphs allow an essayistic voice to emerge, following its own connections and associations. The poem opens with the poet's mother dying of cancer, his father pushing the development of Pasadena—two kinds of modern blight, cell division out of control. It is loose and capacious enough to hold a capsule history of Pasadena, its architectural growth amid the surrounding desert serving as a figure for the growth of the poet's mind and of the poem. See also *The World at Large: New and Selected Poems* (University of Chicago Press, 1996) and *Capacity* (Farrar, Straus, 2006), a collection of meditations on settlement, which was nominated for a National Book Award. McMichael's earlier books were *Against the Falling Evil* (Swallow, 1971) and *The Lover's Familiar* (Godine, 1978); he has also written a study of James *Joyce, *Ulysses and Justice* (Princeton University Press 1991). A discerning essay on his work is included in Robert *Hass' *Twentieth Century Pleasures* (Ecco, 1984). He teaches at the University of California at Irvine. *Five American Poets* (Carcanet, 2010), ed. Michael Schmidt and Clive Wilmer, has a selection of poems with an autobiographical afterword.　CB

McMillan, Ian (1957–　) Born in Barnsley, Yorkshire, where he still lives, McMillan learnt his stage technique as a stand-up comic in Yorkshire, before forming Versewagon with John Turner and Martyn Wiley, a poetry performance group later renamed the Circus of Poets. He has also written radio comedy, plays, and poetry for children, and is well known as a broadcaster and poet-in-residence at various institutions, including Barnsley Football Club and Humberside Police Force.

McMillan's poems cover a wide range of contemporary subjects, but he does not write down to his audience by offering a loaded 'message'. Although primarily aiming to entertain, his poems work equally well on the printed page as in performance. He has written with verve and invention in a wide variety of verse-forms. He is never dull and can often be extremely funny, as in the satirical 'Poem Badly Translated from the Language', which sends up translatorese, 'The Soft White Pillowcase Boys', on an interview for a writer-in-residenceship, or 'Cracking Icicles in Totley Tunnel', on the

1984–5 mineworkers' strike. *Selected Poems* (1987) was reprinted several times. Since then he has published *Dad, the Donkey's on Fire* (1994), *I Found This Shirt* (1998), a volume of poems and prose, and *Perfect Catch* (2000—all Carcanet), a gathering of his work in various forms. See *Talking Myself Home: My Life in Verses* (Murray, 2008).　JDB

MacNeice, Louis (1907–63) Born in Belfast and educated at Marlborough and Merton College, Oxford, where he took a first-class degree in classics and philosophy. He taught classics for a time in Birmingham and London, but for most of his working life he was a writer and producer for BBC radio, especially in the legendary Features Department.

Though MacNeice's precocious first book, *Blind Fireworks* (1929), attracted little attention, he emerged in the early 1930s as a bright, sharp, intelligent, and sophisticated poet. He was conventionally ranked with his Oxford contemporaries *Auden, *Day Lewis, and *Spender—and indeed often continues to be so ranked—but it should now be possible to see him in better perspective, relating him more interestingly to his Northern Irish background and upbringing, for example. His father was a senior clergyman in the Church of Ireland, a strict and brooding presence over the son, who often seems to have felt more at home in the less puritanical south of the island. Nevertheless, one has to bear in mind MacNeice's inherited, if deflected, notions of account-books and duty. There is also the fact of his conventional English public-school and Oxford education, in which he was both the rebel and the dandy.

Poems (1935), MacNeice's contributions to *Letters from Iceland* (prose and verse, written with Auden, 1937), and *The Earth Compels* (1938) all contain attractive and memorable poems and lines. But it was *Autumn Journal* (1939), written during the Munich crisis, that most brilliantly captures the essence of the best of MacNeice, not in miniature but at length. He had already shown a gift for sensing the temper of the time in such poems as 'An Eclogue for Christmas' ('I meet you in an evil time') and 'Bagpipe Music' ('It's no go the merry-goround, it's no go the rickshaw'). *Autumn Journal* discursively reacts to the events of the moment, to his own public and private responses, and catches them all in a colloquial, flexible, argumentative, and yet relaxed mode which (as John Press has remarked) reminds one of Byron's Don Juan.

The 1940s and 1950s were prolific but difficult years for him. He wrote a great deal to order for the BBC: whatever was ruminative, occasional, and gregarious in him as a poet was perhaps given too easy a ride. Nevertheless, there are poems from these years of a dark energy (particularly those concerned with the bombing of London, such as 'Brother Fire') which are among MacNeice's best.

When he died in the autumn of 1963, MacNeice was going through a rich and extended creative phase. The evidence of this can be seen in his last two books, *Solstices* (1961) and *The Burning Perch*, which he had prepared for press and which appeared only a few days after his death. They are not in any ordinary sense the poems of a dying man, for MacNeice's death was sudden and unexpected (he died of pneumonia, brought on when making radio recordings in a damp cave); yet they are indeed much concerned with slow decline, extinction, and nullity, watched with his usual jaunty and devil-may-care insouciance.

MacNeice's *Collected Poems*, carefully edited by E. R. Dodds, appeared in 1966 and a *Selected Poems* in 1988 (both Faber). There are also several verse plays (including versions of the *Agamemnon* of Aeschylus and Goethe's *Faust*, in collaboration with E. L. Stahl), and an unfinished autobiography, *The Strings Are False* (Faber, 1965; Oxford University Press, 1966), also edited by E. R. Dodds.

MacNeice's importance to contemporary Northern Irish poetry has become increasingly apparent—it is 'Louis', for example, who speaks the last lines of Paul *Muldoon's long poem on Auden's departure for America ('7, Middagh Street') in *Meeting the British* (1987). In 2007, Faber and Faber published a new selection of MacNeice's poems made by Michael *Longley, and a new *Collected Poems*, edited by Peter

*McDonald, which restores the order of MacNeice's individual volumes and adds previously uncollected material. See also *Letters of Louis MacNeice*, ed. Jonathan Allison (Faber, 2010) and *Incorrigibly Plural: Louis MacNeice and His Legacy* (Carcanet, 2012), ed. Edna Longley and Fran Brearton. AST*

McNeill, Anthony (1941–96) Born in Kingston, Jamaica, and educated at Excelsior College and St George's College. He had MA degrees from both Johns Hopkins University and the University of Massachusetts (Amherst). From 1975 to 1981 he was assistant publishing director at the Institute of Jamaica.

In an interview for *Jamaica Journal* (Dec. 1970) McNeill declared: 'For poetry to have any immediate value in the West Indies, it has got to be concerned with the identity crisis which exists here.' But such a stance did not lead to parochialism in his case. 'St. Ras', for instance, scrutinizes Rastafarian behaviour in terms of a general malaise left to the reader to interpret. Indeed, his treatment of Rastafarianism, a 'local' phenomenon but of universal significance, emerges as rather more subtle, complex, and questioning than that by other poets, such as Dennis *Scott and Benjamin *Zephaniah.

His books included *Hello Ungod* (Peaceweed, 1971), *Reel from 'The Life-Movie'* (Savacou, 1975), and *Credences at the Altar of Cloud* (Institute of Jamaica, 1979). His final collection, published posthumously, was the lyrical and valedictory *Chinese Lanterns from the Blue Child* (1998). See Daryl Cumber Dance, *New World Adams: Interviews with West Indian Writers* (1992; 2nd edn., 2002—both Peepal Tree). MR

Macpherson, Jay (1931–2012) Born in England, but she and her brother were taken to Newfoundland when she was nine, and in 1944 to Ottawa. She was educated there, at McGill University, Montreal, and at Victoria College, University of Toronto, where she was influenced by Northrop Frye, and where she later taught. Her first collection, *Nineteen Poems* (1952), was published by Robert *Graves' Seizen Press. Her own small press, Emblem Books, published *O Earth Return* (1954), which was later to become a section of *The Boatman* (1957), the book that established her reputation and won the Governor General's Award. Her next collection, *Welcoming Disaster*, did not appear until 1974. These two collections were reprinted in *Poems Twice Told* (Oxford University Press, 1981), which also contains other poems.

The Boatman is an intricately unified sequence of short poems in six sections. Though simple in diction and in metrical forms, they lightly and wittily—even colloquially—bear the weight of a whole cosmos of the poet's invention and contain biblical and classical allusions along with echoes of ballads, Elizabethan verse, carols, nursery rhymes, hymns—and of William Blake. The titles of two sections, 'O Earth Return' and 'The Plowman in Darkness', are from the 'Introduction' to Blake's *Songs of Experience*; and his idea that the human spirit must pass from innocence, through experience, to a higher innocence informs the entire collection. The boatman of the title is Noah, the 'anagogic man', who carries, 'balancing with care, | A golden bubble round and rare. | Its gently shimmering sides surround | All us and our worlds, and bound | Art and life, wit and sense, | Innocence and experience.' *Welcoming Disaster* is Macpherson's exploration—in similar light, epigrammatic, metrically strict verses—of life's 'dark places', and has as its daring and poignant central symbol Tedward, who is not only a 'guide' and 'finder of lost direction', but also a 'friendly substitute for Him'. Tedward is a teddy-bear. See also her critical study, *The Spirit of Solitude: Conventions and Continuities in Late Romance* (Yale University Press, 1982).   WT

McPherson, Sandra (1943–) Raised in San Jose, California, by foster-parents (her eventual reunion with her birth parents provides the occasion for some of her most moving poems). She went to college in California, then studied with Elizabeth *Bishop at the University of Washington, leaving after one year to have her daughter. McPherson has taught at the Iowa and Oregon writers' workshops; she currently tea-

ches in the creative-writing programme at the University of California, Davis.

McPherson is the poet who has most successfully extended the style and vision of Elizabeth Bishop into the feminist era. She shares Bishop's concern with the look of things, illuminating them through slightly odd or incongruous metaphors, often conjoining the domestic and the natural in ways that make each seem to partake of the other. Like Bishop, she speaks in a somewhat flattened, reticent tone, not given to climaxes or emotional outbursts, but pervaded by sadness and sympathy. But McPherson's subjects are often more directly human and social than Bishop's; she writes of her relationships with husband, daughter, parents, teachers, and friends with a sense of both the possibilities and limits of intimacy.

She also writes about the way gender, particularly the female, is coded and caricatured; her poem 'Streamers' takes a huge jellyfish as a poignant emblem for woman in her double guise of poisonous Medusa and protective mother. Her poems are oblique and often difficult, yet are always firmly anchored in perception and experience; if we sometimes have trouble making out their biographical occasions, it is because McPherson's sensibility insists on transforming life into metaphor in such a way that neither side is subordinated. The most striking characteristic of her language is its precision, which in her case leads not to transparency but to controlled complexity. She writes equally well in free verse and fixed forms, though she tends to prefer loosely shaped stanzas of various kinds. Her recent collections include *The Spaces Between Birds: Mother/Daughter Poems 1967–1995* (1996), *A Visit to Civilization* (2002—both Wesleyan University Press), and *Expectation Days* (University of Illinois Press, 2007).   RG

McQueen, Cilla (1949–) Born in Birmingham, England, McQueen came to New Zealand in the 1950s. She was educated in Dunedin and at the University of Otago, where she became interested in both poetry and theatre. She has worked as a teacher, and is also a performer and multimedia artist. A triple winner of the New Zealand Book Award, from 2009 to 2011 she was New Zealand Poet Laureate.

McQueen has called poetry a practice of 'intuition and concentration', arising from her daily handwritten diary ('The hardest thing is seeing | straight and saying plainly', 'Vegetable Garden Poem I'). *Axis* (University of Otago Press, 2001) is a selection of poems and drawings from her first five volumes, beginning with *Homing In* (1982). Her next collection after *Crĭk'ey: New and Selected Poems* (1994—both McIndoe) was *Markings* (2000), which reflects on colonialization, family history, and her life in Bluff, South Island. Her later volumes include *Soundings* (2002), *Fire-Penny* (2005), and *The Radio Room* (2010). She has also made a musical recording of a selection from her work, *A Wind Harp* (2006—all University of Otago Press). In 2010 McQueen received the Prime Minister's Award for Literary Achievement.   JNT

MacSweeney, Barry (1948–2000) Born in Newcastle upon Tyne, MacSweeney left school at sixteen, and worked all his life as a journalist on local newspapers in Kent, Bradford, and South Shields. He ran The Blacksuede Boot Press, which published work by Eric Mottram and Nicholas *Moore among others.

MacSweeney's first book, *The Boy from the Green Cabaret Tells of his Mother* (Hutchinson, 1968), appeared when he was nineteen years old. The title alludes to Rimbaud, and the book also shows the influence of Frank *O'Hara, Allen *Ginsberg, and Jeremy *Prynne, as well as more popular figures such as the Liverpool poets and Bob Dylan. In the 1970s, MacSweeney's work became increasingly experimental: *Brother Wolf* (Turret, 1972) and *Odes* (Trigram, 1978) are characterized by fragmentation, compression, and collage, while *Jury Vet* (Bath Place Community Arts, 1981) is a long poem that blends consumer-culture satire with an aggressive masculinity.

A change of direction was signalled in 1985 with *Ranter* (Slow Dancer), a long poem that draws on the history of radical religious and political dissent in England.

After a period of writer's block and alcoholism, MacSweeney returned with some of his finest work: *Pearl* (Equipage, 1995) is a collection of contemplative lyrics about his rural Northumbrian youth. In 1997, Bloodaxe published it in *The Book of Demons*, alongside a sequence of that name charting his struggles with alcoholism in 1990s Newcastle. The same year, MacSweeney won a Paul Hamlyn Award. *Wolf Tongue*, a generous selection, appeared from Bloodaxe in 2003.   PBa

Maddox, Everette (1944–89) Born in Montgomery, Alabama, he lived there and later in Mobile until he entered the University of Alabama in Tuscaloosa, where he received both a BA and MA in English literature. In 1975 Maddox moved to New Orleans where he held teaching positions in creative writing and English at Xavier University and the University of New Orleans. He left teaching in 1978 to devote his energies to writing. During the next ten years Maddox wrote a considerable amount of poetry and acquired a local reputation in New Orleans as a writer and reader of his own work. His life became that of a Bohemian, and he played the role of the alcoholic poet with dedication. In the 1980s he became a fixture at *The Maple Leaf Bar* in the Carrollton section of New Orleans, and his poetry began to reach an audience of admirers throughout the southern United States.

Maddox's first full-length collection of poetry was *The Everette Maddox Song Book* (New Orleans Poetry Journal, 1982), and the influences of such poets as Alan *Dugan and Frank *O'Hara are occasionally apparent in the book. But Maddox combined with these influences, and with his own comic vision, the dark surrealism found in the fiction of Donald Barthelme to produce an original voice. In his poetry Maddox is the literary equivalent of Charlie Chaplin's little tramp. His spare poems present a persona aware of and vulnerable to the inhumanities of man but still hoping for the best. His love poems in particular contain an innocent idealism rarely found in the literature of his generation. Maddox published his second book, *Bar Scotch* (Pirogue, 1988), only months before his death from throat cancer, a complication of alcoholism and malnutrition.   LS

Madge, Charles (Henry) (1912–96) Born in Johannesburg, South Africa, and educated at Winchester College and at Magdalene College, Cambridge, where he was a pupil of I. A. *Richards. His first book of poems, *The Disappearing Castle* (Faber, 1937) appeared when he was 24, by which time his work had been anthologized in the *Faber Book of Modern Verse* (1936) and the *Oxford Book of Modern Verse* (1936). Despite this acclaim, his second book of poetry, *The Father Found* (Faber, 1941), was followed by a gap of fifty years. In 1994 came *Of Love, Time and Places* (Anvil), Madge's own selection from his earlier books together with more recent work. In 1936, with Tom Harrisson, he had founded Mass Observation; and from 1950 to 1970 Madge was professor of sociology at Birmingham University.

Madge developed under the influence of slightly older poets, William *Empson and W. H. *Auden, who themselves had been influenced by modernist poetry. Madge's years at Cambridge saw the beginnings of the left-wing literary movement of the Thirties, and in 1932 he joined the Communist Party. However, his orientation to politics and society had more in common with *Surrealism, and his poetry has a visionary quality and is concerned to explore our imaginative apprehension of the world and society. This interest was also the basis of his work with Mass Observation.   ATT

Madhubuti, Haki R. (1942–) Born Don L. Lee in Little Rock, Arkansas, and raised in the 'black bottom' of Detroit, Michigan. His early life was difficult: his father deserted the family when Madhubuti was still very young, and when he was 16 his mother died. After studying in Chicago and at the University of Iowa, he served in the army, 1960–3. Different jobs followed, as a cleaner, apprentice curator, stock clerk, and post-office clerk: but after the publication of *Think Black* (1967) and *Black Pride* (1968), two collections combining autobiographical elements with a strong commitment to *Black Arts activism,

Madhubuti devoted himself full time to teaching, publishing, and writing. A writer-in-residence at several universities, he is also the founder and editor of *Black Books Bulletin* and Third World Press, both based in Chicago and dedicated to publishing new black writers. *Don't Cry, Scream* (1969), his third collection, continued the style of the other two: radically experimental, it used rhythmic violence and verbal play to capture the movements of black speech. However, it reflected Madhubuti's growing conviction that 'most, if not all, black poetry will be *political*' by largely discarding the personal dimension. *Directionscore: New and Selected Poems* (1971) is a useful selection of this earlier work.

Book of Life (1973—all Broadside), the first collection published after he had discarded his 'slave name' in favour of one meaning 'justice' (Haki) and 'precise, accurate, dependable' (Madhubuti) in Swahili, retains the political commitment while moving towards the use of standard English. Political writing and activity preoccupied Madhubuti for the next ten years: but *Earthquakes and Sun Rise Missions: Poetry and Essays of Black Renewal, 1973–1983* (Third World, 1984) continued his development of a more mainstream style, and he has since published a number of bestselling non-fiction books on black American experience. Useful information is to be found in Marlene Mosher, *New Directions from Don L. Lee* (Exposition, 1975). See *Groundwork: Selected Poems of Haki R. Madhubuti/Don L. Lee* (Third World, 1996). Until his early retirement in 2010 he was a Distinguished Professor at Chicago State University, where he founded and directed the Gwendolyn Brooks Center for Black Literature and Creative Writing.   RJG*

Maguire, Sarah (1957–) Born in West London, Maguire left school to train as a gardener, and later studied English Literature at the University of East Anglia. She has worked as a broadcaster and in 2004 founded the Poetry Translation Centre at the School of Oriental and African Studies in London, which she directs.

Her first collection, *Spilt Milk* (Secker & Warburg, 1991) was reprinted by the Poetry

Book Society in 2007, the same year that her fourth volume, *The Pomegranates of Kandahar*, appeared from Chatto & Windus. She has also edited an anthology, *Flora Poetica: The Chatto Book of Botanical Verse* (2001). Her own poetry has unfolded a thoughtful floral feminism, from the *Plathesque 'A Cherry Tree' to 'Cow Parsley, Bluebells', dedicated to Kathleen *Jamie. Her other collections are *The Invisible Mender* (1997) and *The Florist's at Midnight* (2001 —both Cape).

Over two decades, Maguire has emerged as a prominent translator of Arabic verse, travelling widely in the Middle East, and finding stimulation there for her precisely sensuous, international imagination. In 2003, a selection of her poems was translated by the Iraqi poet Saadi Yousef, and published in Syria.   JNT

Mahapatra, Jayanta (1928–) A scientist and academic who turned to writing poetry in English in the late Sixties. Born in Cuttack, Orissa, he became known to western readers through poems in *Critical Quarterly* and *Poetry*, which awarded him the Glatstein Prize in 1975. He joined the Iowa Writers' Workshop's international writing programme (1976) and has been much published in American literary journals. He is a prolific poet with over a dozen collections, beginning with *Close the Sky, Ten by Ten* (1971). He also translates modern Oriya poets and has edited a literary magazine, *Chandrabhaga* (1979–85).

His poetry, often obscure and elliptical, draws on symbols from Orissan landscape and history, Hindu mythology and philosophy. He is preoccupied with Hindu ritual, from which he feels alienated since his grandfather converted to Christianity. In *A Rain of Rites* (University of Georgia Press, 1976) there are several pieces about the great Puri temple and the poverty and squalor outside, as in his best-known poem, 'Hunger'. *Life Signs* (Oxford University Press, 1983) includes some of his best verse, like 'The Lost Children of America', in which vivid images of Cuttack lanes where the unkempt hippies live develop into a complex interweaving of their search and the poet's in 'haunted wood and

hunted myth'. His most ambitious work, *Relationship* (Greenfield Review, 1980) is a near-epic, some 600 lines long, in which Mahapatra delves into the self through history which he traces to mythic time when the great god Siva roamed among the wild beasts in 'the night of the wild elephants'. Guilt and ambivalent feelings towards parents are dissolved in the course of a psychic journey ending with the dance of the temple dancers.

Mahapatra's *Selected Poems* (Oxford University Press, 1987) includes a representative sample of his early work. In 2009 he made a selection of all his poems—including two later volumes from D.C. Books, *Shadow Space* (1997) and *Bare Face* (2000)—in *The Lie of Dawns: Poems 1974–2008* (2009). In the same year he received the Padma Shri award from the Indian government. See also the essays and memoirs collected in *Door of Paper* (2007—both Authors Press).

For critical evaluation, see Bijay Kumar Das, *The Poetry of Jayanta Mahapatra* (Writers Workshop, 1992; 4th edn., 2009) and *The Indian Imagination of Jahanta Mahapatra*, ed. Jaydeep Sarangi and Gauri Shankar Jha (Sarup, 2006).   RA

Mahon, Derek (1941–) Born in Belfast and educated at Trinity College, Dublin, where he took a degree in French. After leaving university, Mahon travelled in France, Canada, and the United States, teaching and doing a variety of odd-jobs, and publishing his first book, *Night-Crossing* (Oxford University Press), in 1968, before settling in London in 1970. He now lives in Kinsale, Co. Cork. He was associated in the mid-1960s with the Belfast '*Group'. Apart from a return to Northern Ireland in 1977–9 as writer-in-residence at the New University of Ulster in Coleraine, he has since earned his living as a freelance writer, reviewing widely and writing screenplays for the BBC from such sources as novels by his fellow Northern Irish writers Jennifer Johnston and Brian Moore. His Francophile enthusiasms, clearly evident in his own poetry, issued in 1984 in *High Time* (Gallery), a Molière translation for the Field Day Theatre Company, and in 1988 in his translations of the *Selected Poems* of Philippe Jaccottet (Penguin).

Mahon is a poet of great stylistic zest whose polish ironizes a scepticism, gloom, and even apocalypticism of temperament. Admiring Louis *MacNeice's outsider attitudes, and drawn to 'Beckett's bleak *reductio*', he often evokes settings, sometimes futuristic, devoid of human beings. In 'One of these Nights' in *The Hunt by Night* (Oxford University Press, 1982; Wake Forest University Press, 1983) he imagines the 'radiant warplanes' of a future war as they approach London. These larger perspectives situate the plight of Northern Ireland in a context of wider contemporary breakdown and entropy. This happens strikingly in what is probably his single most admired poem, 'A Disused Shed in Co. Wexford', in *The Snow Party* (Oxford University Press, 1975). He discovers there an unforgettable emblem for Irish historical suffering in what begins as the almost humorous fantasy of a 'thousand mushrooms' crowding to the keyhole of a shed as the poet-photographer opens its door. A subtle and penetrating meditation on the poet's responsibility and the dangers of his appropriation of human suffering as material, the poem is eloquent testimony to an artful but scrupulously undeceived imagination.

The rhyming meditations and epistles of Mahon's later work, from *The Hudson Letter* (1996) and *The Yellow Book* (1998—both Gallery/Wake Forest University Press) to *An Autumn Wind* (2010), have been compared to MacNeice's *Autumn Journal* (1939) for the way they relate the individual life to the international present. After charting his personal disillusionment against the *fin-de-siècle* backdrop of America in the 1990s, Mahon's pessimism has more recently concerned itself with environmental crisis: see 'Homage to Gaia' in *Life on Earth* (2008) and 'The Seasons' in *An Autumn Wind* (2010), which rewrites the first line of 'A Disused Shed in Co. Wexford' ('there are still corners where a lark can sing'). Yet critics agree that the volumes since *Harbour Lights* (2006) also represent a 'late flowering' in which the poet writes with a playful relish for the worlds revealed

by art. *Adaptations* (2006) and *Raw Material* (2011) are two selections of Mahon's poetic 'versions' from classical Greek and Latin to French, Irish, and Chinese verse. The latter volume also includes the fictitious Hindi poet 'Gopal Singh'. See *New Collected Poems* (2011) and *Selected Prose* (2012—all Gallery). For criticism and context, see Hugh Haughton, *The Poetry of Derek Mahon* (Oxford University Press, 2007).   NC*

Maiden, Jennifer (1949–) Born in Penrith, New South Wales. After casual jobs she completed an arts course at Macquarie University, Sydney (1974). She tutors in creative writing, has received writing fellowships from the Literature Board of the Australia Council, and has worked with the New South Wales Torture and Trauma Rehabilitation Service.

Critical attention has steadily increased since *Tactics* (1974) appeared in the University of Queensland Paperback Poets series. Of her collections from the 1970s and 1980s, *The Problem of Evil* (Prism, 1975) is the most demanding, and *For the Left Hand* (South Head, 1981) the most accessible. Her *Selected Poems* (Penguin, 1989) offered a first overview of a distinctive poetic world that has been called 'Maidenland': a place of fragmented narrative clues, concentrated, idiosyncratic personal feeling, and often acerbic social observation.

Since *The Winter Baby* (Angus & Robertson, 1990), Maiden's poetry has addressed itself more directly to the everyday world of family, fellow poets, and politicians (see 'Madeleine Albright Wears Two Lapel Pins'). In 1999, she received the Christopher Brennan Award for lifetime achievement in poetry. *Intimate Geography* (2012), a later selected volume published in the UK by Bloodaxe, draws on four collections: *Acoustic Shadow* (Penguin, 1993), *Mines* (Paper Bark, 1999), *Friendly Fire* (2005), and *Pirate Rain* (2010—both Giramondo), which saw Maiden win the Kenneth Slessor Prize for the third time, the only writer to have done so. She has also written two novels: *The Terms* (1982) and *Play With Knives* (1990).   JRO*

Major, Clarence (1936–) Born in Atlanta, Major grew up in Chicago, where he attended art school, and then spent two years in the US Air Force. A poet, painter, and fiction writer, he taught at the University of Colorado, Boulder, and is emeritus professor of English at the University of California at Davis.

Major made contact with *Beat generation and *Black Mountain poets through his magazine, *Coercion Review*, in the late 1950s. He moved to New York at the time of the *Black Arts movement and began to exhibit his painting and publish. In 1969 he edited an anthology, *The New Black Poetry*, and in 1970 a dictionary of African-American slang (revd. edn., *Juba to Jive* (1994)). In the same year his first major poetry volume, *Swallow the Lake* (Wesleyan University Press), reflected in a 'middle | passage blues' on the necessity of moving from the Midwest ('I could not whistle and walk in storms | along Lake Michigan's shore. Concrete walks. | I could not swallow the lake'). *Configurations: New and Selected Poems 1958–1998* (Copper Canyon, 1998) draws on several later collections, including *Inside Diameter: The France Poems* (Permanent, 1985), a sequence of improvisatory, meditative verse. It was nominated for the 1999 National Book Award. See also *Waiting for Sweet Betty* (Copper Canyon, 2002) and *Myself Painting* (Louisiana State University Press, 2008). Major has also written nine novels, and edited an anthology of twentieth-century African-American poetry, *The Garden Thrives* (HarperCollins, 1996). JNT

Malley, Ern See MCAULEY, JAMES.

Malouf, David (1934–) Born in Brisbane and educated at the University of Queensland. From 1959 to 1968 he lived in Europe, acquiring that unselfconscious intimacy with its history and urban sites which characterizes his poetry. Returning to Australia, he taught English at the University of Sydney until 1977. In that time three of his six volumes of verse were published. *Bicycle and Other Poems* (1970) began the University of Queensland Press Paperback Poets series. Malouf's deep at-

tachment to his home state (despite subsequent annual sojourns in Tuscany) is indicated in 'The Year of the Foxes', a meditative reminiscence of wartime Brisbane, and for its author 'a touchstone poem'. Here, as in much of his verse and the fictions that it presaged, Malouf showed his intense awareness of life being determined by the particulars of place, as by unsuppressible historical memories.

Neighbours in a Thicket (University of Queensland Press, 1974), took its title from the poem 'An Ordinary Evening at Hamilton', where Malouf's remembrance of his childhood home (whose 'Familiar rooms | glow, rise through the dark—exotic islands') anticipated the memoir *12 Edmonstone Street* (Chatto & Windus, 1985) as well as his first novel, *Johnno* (University of Queensland Press, 1975).

Malouf's fifth book of verse, *First Things Last* (1980), was followed by his *Selected Poems* (Angus & Robertson) the next year. Since then the concerns of his poetry with provenance and Australianness, severance and conjunction, the primitive and the civilized have been translated into prose fiction. *An Imaginary Life* (1978) treated Ovid in exile. The Great War was the subject of *Fly Away Peter* (1981); the Second World War and its Australian aftermaths, of *The Great World* (1990). Malouf has also written the libretto for Richard Meale's opera *Voss* (based on Patrick White's novel), volumes of short stories, and a play. *David Malouf* (1990) by James Tulip contains a useful bibliography. Philip Neilsen and Ivor Indyk have written critical studies: *Imagined Lives* (1990) and *David Malouf* (1993), respectively. *Selected Poems 1959–1989* was published in the UK by Chatto & Windus in 1994. See *Typewriter Music* (2007), a later collection of poems which won the Judith Wright Calanthe Award, and *Revolving Days: Selected Poems* (2008—both University of Queensland Press). PP

Mandel, Eli (as Wolf) (1922–92) Born in Estevan, Saskatchewan, and grew up in the Jewish community of the region. During the Second World War he served with the Canadian Army Medical Corps. He received his PhD from the University of Toronto in 1957 with a dissertation on Christopher Smart. For many years he was professor of English literature at the University of York, Toronto.

Mandel's early poems of the late 1950s portray a speaker who wanders helplessly through a closed and violent landscape. Mythic figures such as the minotaur and Cain appear and seem to offer an explanation of the darkness and horror. In the later poems the atmosphere of terror continues, but it becomes increasingly difficult to distinguish the internal and psychic dimension from the external and public one. The poetry no longer describes an objective world to be explained by mythic patterns, but one in which the speaker's own violent tendencies interweave with public events. The duplicity of language remains a central concern in Mandel's poetry, as is the struggle to create poems which allow us to glimpse a world of being outside language. *Dreaming Backwards* (General, 1981), offers a selection of his poetry, and his essays in literary and social criticism can be found in *Another Time* (Porcépic, 1977) and *The Family Romance* (Turnstone, 1986). There is an interview with Mandel and an article on his poetry, by Peter Stevens, in *Essays on Canadian Writing*, 18/19 (Summer/Fall 1980).

See *The Other Harmony: The Collected Poetry of Eli Mandel* (Canadian Plains Research Center, 2000), published in two volumes, and *From Room to Room* (Wilfrid Laurier University Press, 2010), a selection edited by Peter Webb. For criticism, see Andrew Stubbs, *Myth, Origins, Magic: A Study of Form in Eli Mandel's Writing* (Turnstone, 1993).   RBH

Manhire, Bill (1946–   ) Born in Invercargill, New Zealand, and grew up in various small towns in the far south of the country, where his parents worked as publicans. His poems first appeared in New Zealand journals in the 1960s, while he was an undergraduate at the University of Otago. Set against the protracted, egocentric effusions of his contemporaries, his terse, cryptic imagism was immediately striking. He made his debut in British magazines in the early 1970s, when he was

studying Norse sagas at University College London. He returned to New Zealand in 1973 to teach in the English Department of Victoria University of Wellington, where he now is Director of the International Insitute of Modern Letters. Among his duties there, he runs a highly esteemed creative-writing course: see the anthology *Spectacular Babies* (Flamingo, 2001). He has also edited several popular anthologies of New Zealand literature, including *100 New Zealand Poems* (Godwit, 1993), updated in 2005 as *121 New Zealand Poems*.

Much of the power in Manhire's poetry comes from the tension between the conservative and the avant-garde sides of his personality. He is continually determined to surprise, but he also wants to remain accessible. He places a high value on both imagination and common sense. Most of his poems assume a tidy stanzaic form, but his syntax is often deliberately odd, so that the reader's sense of security is undermined almost as soon as it is established. Manhire's influences are disparate enough to include both Philip *Larkin and John *Ashbery. Although he is an academic he has a dislike of jargon, which he is consequently fond of satirizing. Inimical to preciousness, he purposefully includes comic-book references, racetrack terminology, and other supposedly 'lowbrow' material in his poems. Yet there are also playful allusions to Spenser, Keats, Matthew Arnold, and other figures from the English literary tradition.

Manhire's first book, *Malady* (Amphedesma, 1970), consisted of just four words, 'malady', 'melody', and 'my lady', arranged on the page in sundry patterns, with accompanying drawings by the New Zealand painter Ralph Hotere. Throughout his career, Manhire has never lost his fondness for word-play, experimentation, and disrupting his audience's expectations. He has a sly and unpredictable sense of humour. Nevertheless, his reputation rests on a solid, seriously intentioned body of work, notable for its oblique lyricism and sense of wonder at the strangeness of both life and language. Although he frequently embarks on surreal flights of fancy and has always shied away from the role of either autobiographer or sage, his work, viewed as a whole, can still be said to follow the trajectory of ordinary domestic life, commenting on courtship, marriage, the vicissitudes of adult love, and the anxieties of parenthood, ageing, bereavement, and death.

After the publication of his fifth book of verse, *Good Looks*, in 1982, Manhire directed his attention more towards prose fiction, producing *The Brain of Katherine Mansfield* (1988), a parody of teenagers' choose-your-own-adventure books, and *The New Land* (1990), a largely satirical collection of stories. *Milky Way Bar* (Victoria University Press/Carcanet, 1991), also playfully manipulates narrative structures. *Zoetropes: Poems 1972–1982* (Port Nicholson, 1984; Carcanet, 1985) is the most comprehensive selection of his early work.

In 1997, Manhire was appointed as New Zealand's first Poet Laureate: *What To Call Your Child* (Godwit, 1999) contains poems written during his two-year term. *Collected Poems* (Victoria University Press, 2001) has been followed by *Lifted* (Victorian University Press, 2005; Carcanet, 2007), and *The Victims of Lightning* (2010). See also *Doubtful Sounds: Essays and Interviews* (2000) and *Selected Poems* (2012—all Victoria University Press). Winner of four New Zealand Book Awards, Bill Manhire was made a Companion of the New Zealand Order of Merit in 2005, and in 2007 received the Prime Minister's Award for Literary Achievement in Poetry.   IS

Mann, Chris(topher Zithulele) (1948–) Born in Port Elizabeth, South Africa, and educated at the University of the Witwatersrand, at Oxford as a Rhodes scholar (where he won the Newdigate Prize for Poetry), and at the School of Oriental and African Studies in London where he took a master's degree in African oral poetry. In 1982 he adopted the Zulu name Zithulele as his second name to express his solidarity with black praise-poets whose work he has translated into English. He was the director of the Valley Trust near Durban, a grassroots organization involved in educational projects, and founded Wordfest, the multilingual South African literature festival. He is now Professor of Poetry at Rhodes University, Grahamstown.

His first volume, *First Poems* (Bataleur, 1977), established him as a poet whose unembellished, plain-talking style was designed for oral delivery and performance. A characteristic theme—inspiration and guidance from the shades or ancestors—was further developed in his *New Shades* (1982). The title poem of *Kites*, his third volume (1990—both David Philip), when it first appeared had this note attached: 'These poems are written in a prosody derived from my study and practice of African oral verse.' He has also translated poetry from his own original work in Zulu (see 'Where is the Freedom for Which We Died?'), and written for public performance and multimedia works, often collaborating with his wife, the artist Julia Skeen. His later volumes include *South Africans* (1996) and *Heartlands* (2002—both University of Natal Press). See *Home from Home: New and Selected Poems* (Echoing Green, 2010).   SG

Manson, Peter (1969–   ) Born in Glasgow and studied at the university there. He worked for several years at the Land Register, and was Judith E. Wilson Fellow in Poetry at the University of Cambridge in 2005.

In 1994, Manson began *Object Permanence* magazine, with Robin Purves, in order to put experimental British and American poetry into circulation in Scotland. The first issue featured work by Charles *Bernstein, Bob *Cobbing, and Tom *Raworth. At the same time, Manson began publishing verse and visual poetry through Cobbing's Writer's Forum: see *iter atur e* (1995) and *me generation* (1997).

The pamphlet *Birth Windows* (1999) is collected with other work in the volume *For the Good of Liars* (2006—both Barque). *Between Cup and Lip* (2008) was his first American collection. Both display the variety of Manson's work, from densely compacted lyrics to diaristic prose poems. These poles are separately marked by *Stéphane Mallarmé: The Poems in Verse* (2012—both Miami University Press), which collects his acclaimed translations of the French Symbolist poet, and *Adjunct: an Undigest* (Edinburgh Review, 2005), a randomly ordered, seven-year journal of personal, verbal, and cultural solecisms ('Stéphane Mallarmé spellchecks as Stephanie Mallard'). JNT

Mapanje, Jack (1945–) Born in Kadango, Mangochi District, in southern Malawi. He was educated at Kadango, Chikwawa Mission, and at Zomba Catholic Secondary School. He has a BA degree and Diploma in Education from the University of Malawi, Zomba and a doctorate from the University of London. In 1975 he joined the department of English at Chancellor College, University of Malawi, as a lecturer. He was arrested on 25 September 1987 and detained without charge until he was released in 1991. He is now living in the United Kingdom and has taught at York, Newcastle-upon-Tyne, and latterly York St John University.

Mapanje is acknowledged as an authority on African oral literature and edited *Kalulu*, a Malawi-based journal of oral literature. He also co-edited with Landeg White the anthology *Oral Poetry from Africa* (London, 1983). Mapanje's published volumes of poetry include *Of Chameleons and Gods* (1981), *The Chattering Wagtails of Mikuyu Prison* (1993—both Heinemann), *The Last of the Sweet Bananas: New and Selected Poems* (2004), and *The Beasts of Nalunga* (2007—both Bloodaxe). Mapanje's early poems are mournful in tone, lamenting the loss of the dignity of traditional Africa. The vulgarity and poverty of contemporary urban and rural communities are assiduously described. The poems which he wrote during his earlier stay in London analysed his experience of English manners. His disappointment with English society was apparent; however, he was able to use the experience to reaffirm his own identity. The later poems are more evidently political. In these poems Mapanje's poetic voice is assured, steadfast, and distinctive. His poems are ironic and humorous in tone. Where the true content was once veiled and the messages transmitted through elaborate codes, sometimes derived from the oral tradition, the later poems are now bolder, more direct, but yet evocative of the African environment despite his writing from exile. FO

Marechera, Dambudzo (1952–87) Born in Rusape, Zimbabwe (then Rhodesia). He began his studies at the University of Rhodesia in 1972, but was expelled the following year for protesting against racial discrimination on the campus. He was awarded a scholarship to resume his studies at New College, Oxford, but was sent down two years later for his 'outrageous behaviour'. Apart from a spell as writer-in-residence at the University of Sheffield in the first half of 1979, Marechera found it impossible to settle anywhere for long. He moved from one squat to another, mostly in London, and drank heavily. In December 1977 he was arrested and charged with theft, possession of cannabis, and being an illegal immigrant, and spent three months in jail. None of this, however, stopped him writing. His first book, *The House of Hunger* (Heinemann, 1978), a collection of short stories, was joint winner of the *Guardian* fiction prize for 1979. This was followed by two further volumes in his lifetime, *Black Sunlight* (Heinemann, 1980), a novel, and *Mindblast* (College Press, 1984), a collection of prose and poetry, and a posthumous collected poems, *Cemetery of Mind* (Baobab, 1992).

Marechera returned to Zimbabwe in 1981, where he appears to have continued a 'dissipated way of life' until his death at the age of 35. A second novel, *The Black Insider* (Africa World Press, 1990), was published posthumously, as well as another collection of assorted prose and poetry, *Dambudzo Marechera 1952–1987*, ed. Flora Veit-Wild and Ernst Schade (Baobab, 1988). Marechera was unquestionably one of the most talented writers of his generation. His poems, which are largely autobiographical, explore his abiding sense of alienation within the newly liberated society, and demonstrate the eclectic range of his influences: William Blake, Rainer Maria Rilke, and Allen *Ginsberg. Unlike most of his contemporaries he had little interest in politics, which did not stop him pouring scorn on his many critics who accused him of 'irrelevance'. His collected poems, *Cemetery of Mind* (Baobab, 1992), were edited by Flora Veit-Wild, who also co-edited a collection of essays, *Emerging Perspectives on Dambudzo Marechera* (Africa World Press, 1999). See also *Moving Spirit: The Legacy of Dambudzo Marechera in the 21st Century* (LIT Verlag, 2012), ed. Juli Carnie and Dobrota Pucherova. The novelist Helon Habila has been researching a biography.   AM-P

Markham, E. A. (Edward Archibald) (1939–2008) Born in Montserrat, West Indies. He moved to Britain in 1956 and read English and philosophy at St David's University College (Lampeter). He directed the Caribbean Theatre Workshop in the West Indies (1970–1), and worked as a media co-ordinator in Papua New Guinea (1983–5): see his memoir *A Papua New Guinea Sojourn* (Carcanet, 1998). He also held writing fellowships at Hull College of Higher Education (1978–9) and the University of Ulster (1988–91), and was editor of several publications, including *Artrage* (1985–7).

Markham was one of the most cosmopolitan of the post-war West Indian poets in style and subject-matter. He also showed great partiality for the long poem, usually autobiographical in content. Dry wit pervades much of his work, and free verse is his most frequent poetic medium. In 'Late Return', a long poem which describes a return visit to Montserrat, his wit emerges as a probing, self-critical exercise in cold detachment. 'Grandmother-poem' is more moving, drawn from childhood memories, but stern in spirit: 'I step | on the wrong end of a rake | and crack my skull: the yellow scream of grandmother burns the head.' 'Don't Talk to me about Bread' describes in great detail a woman kneading dough, but it is highly sensuous, and treats work as sublimated frustration. A delightful poem, and one of his best, it suggestively encapsulates Markham's views about the poetic process.

His collections included *Family Matters* (Sow's Ear, 1984), *Towards the End of a Century* (1989), and *Misapprehensions* (1995—both Anvil). Markham also edited an important anthology of Caribbean poetry, *Hinterland* (Bloodaxe, 1989), and wrote fiction: see *Marking Time* (1999), a campus novel featuring his academic alter ego, Pewter Stapleton, and *Taking the Drawing Room Through Customs: Selected Stories 1972–2002* (2003—both Peepal Tree). *A Rough Climate* (2002), his seventh collection, was nominated for the T. S. Eliot Prize.

Lambchops with Sally Goodman (Salt, 2004) was an expanded edition of the poems collected in *Living in Disguise* (Anvil, 1986), originally published under two pseudonyms, one female, one male. The latter, 'Paul St. Vincent', writes in turn about a Caribbean immigrant character called 'Lambchops', the hero of a series of bleakly funny episodes about race relations in Britain. From 1995 to 2005 Markham was Professor of Creative Writing at Sheffield Hallam University. He died in Paris. *Looking Out, Looking In*, a new and selected volume chosen by the poet, appeared posthumously from Anvil Press in 2009.   MR*

Marlatt, Daphne (Buckle) (1942–) Born in Australia, and in 1951 moved to Vancouver, Canada. In the early 1960s she became active with the poets involved in the magazine *Tish* and studied with some of the major *Black Mountain poets. *Rings* (1971), with its extended poetic line to register the nuances of pregnancy and birth in the midst of a failing marriage, became part of her book of poetics and autobiography, *What Matters* (Coach House, 1980). She explores the past and present of a fishing and cannery town in *Steveston* (Talonbooks, 1974/1984; anthologized in Michael Ondaatje's *The Long Poem Anthology*, Coach House, 1979), the geography and history of her city in *Vancouver Poems* (Coach House, 1972), and her mother's inheritance in *How Hug a Stone* (Turnstone, 1983). Her stance is now strongly feminist, stimulated by collaborations with Quebec feminist writer, Nicole Brossard, and her companion, Betsy Warland, to whom *Touch to My Tongue* (Longspoon, 1984), a prose poem conflating the roles of Demeter and Persephone, is dedicated. 'Musing with Mothertongue', its accompanying essay, argues that language is 'a living body we enter at birth'. *Double Negative* (Gynergy, 1988) is a collaboration with Warland; *Salvage* (Red Deer, 1991) is Marlatt's feminist rewriting of her work since 1970.

She has also published two novels that explore the meeting point of history and fiction in the retelling of women's lives: *Ana Historic* (Coach House, 1988) and *Taken* (Anansi, 1996). *This Tremor Love Is* (Talonbooks, 2001) is a collection of her love poems from three decades. Her later long poem *The Given* (McClelland & Stewart, 2008) won the Dorothy Livesay Prize for Poetry. She has also written a Canadian-Japanese Noh play, *The Gull* (Talonbooks, 2008). Daphne Marlatt became a Member of the Order of Canada in 2006 and in 2012 was the recipient of the George Woodcock Lifetime Achievement Award.   DBa

Marquis, Don(ald Robert Perry)

(1878–1937) Born in Walnut, Illinois, he was best known as a newspaper columnist. In his early career, under the encouragement of the journalist and humorist Joel Chandler Harris, he began two columns: 'The Sun Dial' in the New York *Sun* and 'The Lantern' in the New York *Tribune*. He developed his comic and satirical perspective into a series of popular texts. *Hermione and Her Little Group of Serious Thinkers* (1916) was a satire on the social and artistic pretensions of Greenwich Village 'socialites', just as his play, *The Old Soak* (1922) offered a caustic view of American prohibition. During this period he published three books of 'serious' verse, beginning with *Dreams and Dust* (1915). However, he is best remembered for a series of books which, beginning with *archy and mehitabel* (1927), feature the rantings (in comic form) of archy the cockroach, who in a previous life was a free-verse poet. These were written at night in the deserted newspaper office. The upper case was absent because archy could not work the shift key on the typewriter. *the lives and times of archy and mehitabel*, a cat (motto: 'toujours gai'), was published in 1940 (Doubleday), and included the original collections of the 'col-

umn'. Other humorous books of verse include *Sonnets to a Red-Haired Lady (by a Gentleman with a Blue Beard)* and *Famous Love Affairs* (1922) and *Love Sonnets of a Cave Man* (1928). Among Marquis' other writings are a posthumously published and unfinished autobiographical novel, *Sons of the Puritans* (1939), and *The Dark Hours*, a play based on the last period of Christ's life.

See E. O. Anthony, *O Rare Don Marquis: A Biography* (1962). A selection of unpublished 'archy and mehitabel' poems, *archyology*, ed. Jeff Adams, appeared from University Press of New England in 1996.   GC

Marriott, Anne (1913–97) Born in Victoria, British Columbia. One of the early Canadian modernists, she sought to capture in poetry the uniqueness of the Canadian experience and landscape. Along with Dorothy *Livesay, whose social concerns she shared, she co-founded in 1941 *Contemporary Verse*. She assisted with its editing until 1945, when she moved to Ottawa to work for the National Film Board; she was also assistant editor of *Canadian Poetry Magazine* (1946–8). She married Gerald McLellan in 1947, and three years later they moved to Prince George, British Columbia, where she was women's editor of the *Prince George Citizen*. The couple settled in North Vancouver in 1959. She was co-author, with Joyce Moller, of *A Swarming in My Mind* (1977), a poetry-writing workbook for elementary school students.

Her first poetry collection, *The Wind Our Enemy* (1939), is an episodic documentary of a prairie farmer's plight during the Depression; her second, *Calling Adventurers!* (1941) celebrates the romantic Canadian north. She then published little for more than a quarter-century. Her later work, primarily set on the west coast, examines the plight of the elderly and the displaced.

The fullest edition of her poetry is *The Circular Coast: Poems New and Selected* (1981). Her eight short stories are gathered in *A Long Way to Oregon* (1984—both Mosaic).   DS

Marshall, Tom (1938–93) Born in Niagara Falls, Ontario, and lived in the southern

United States as a child. Educated at Queen's University in Kingston, Ontario, and the University of London (1966–8), he taught in the English department at Queen's from 1964.

Marshall's major work as a poet (he also wrote short stories and two novels) comprises a quartet of books—*The Silences of Fire* (Macmillan, 1969), *Magic Water* (Quarry, 1971), *The Earth-Book* (1974), and *The White City* (1976—both Oberon)—in which he creates a four-part vision of the universe based on the four elements.

Marshall sees the poet as a modern shaman, attempting to make beautiful and meaningful order in art. Although his poetry sometimes alludes to Canadian history and literature (as in 'Macdonald Park', his long poem invoking Sir John A. Macdonald, Canada's first prime minister), Marshall more frequently uses natural landscapes as ways into his reflections on more universal themes of alienation and mortality.

In his later book of poetry, *Playing With Fire* (Oberon, 1984), Marshall grapples with his heightened sense of mortality and with his haunting visions of children menaced by an approaching nuclear holocaust.

Marshall edited a collection of essays on the Canadian poet A. M. *Klein (1970) and wrote a book on D. H. *Lawrence's poetry, *The Psychic Mariner* (1970). His most important critical work is *Harsh and Lovely Land: The Major Canadian Poets and the Making of a Canadian Tradition* (University of British Columbia Press, 1979). *The Elements* (Oberon, 1980) contains selections from Marshall's four previous books of poems. His last poems were published posthumously as *Some Impossible Heaven of the Senses* (Oberon, 1994).   NB

Marson, Una (1905–65) Born in Jamaica. During the early 1930s she lived in London, where she became secretary of the League of Coloured People and editor of its journal. She also became secretary to Haile Selassie, the then-exiled emperor of Ethiopia. She returned to Jamaica in 1936, where she founded the Readers and Writers Club and the Jamaica Save the Children Fund, but was back in London in 1938 to work for the BBC World Service, finally returning to Jamaica in 1945.

Much of her poetry is characterized by experimentation with dialect, in a manner anticipating Louise *Bennett. In her 'blues' poems she experimented with jazz-derived rhythms. She could also, however, and in a strikingly witty manner, deploy traditional forms. 'To Wed or not to Wed', for instance, effectively parodies Shakespeare's most famous soliloquy from *Hamlet*, but also poses pertinent conundrums about the institution of marriage.

She published three volumes of poetry in Kingston, Jamaica: *Tropic Reveries* (1930), *Heights and Depths* (1932), and *The Moth and the Star* (1937). *Towards the Stars* (University of London Press, 1945) mostly reprints poems from the earlier volumes. See Delia Jarrett-Macauley, *The Life of Una Marson* (Manchester University Press, 1998) and *Selected Poems* (Peepal Tree, 2011), ed. Alison Donnell.   MR

Martin, Charles (1942–) Born of German and Irish descent in the Bronx, where he attended Catholic schools, including Jesuit-run Fordham Prep and University. It was here that he acquired his training in Latin and the interest in Catullus which would ultimately lead him to write his doctoral dissertation for SUNY-Buffalo on the Latin poet's influence on *Pound, and to translating Catullus' complete works. His *The Poems of Catullus* (Abbatoir, 1979; revd. edn., Johns Hopkins University Press, 1990) is notable both for its skilful rendering of Catullus' Latin hendecasyllabic line into the more natural English blank-verse line, and for its preserving his colloquial vulgarity in a contemporary American idiom. See also his critical study of Catullus, published by Yale University Press in 1992.

Martin's first book, *Room for Error* (University of Georgia Press, 1978), reflects the Catullan influence, particularly in 'Calvus in Ruins', a *tour de force* based upon the few extant fragments by one of Catullus' closest friends. Martin has been identified as one of the *New Formalists, and there is intelligence and wit in his treatment of a wide range of topics, from film to literature to science fiction, and of landscape, from ancient Rome to Buffalo (where he lived in the Sixties), to Brooklyn, where he has lived since 1968, teaching at Queensborough Community College and later at Johns Hopkins University as well. His second collection, *Steal the Bacon* (1987), confirmed his reputation for technical and thematic virtuosity and was a finalist for the Pulitzer Prize. It is highlighted by a narrative poem, 'Passages from Friday', a retelling, in eighteenth-century English, of *Robinson Crusoe* from Friday's perspective. Martin's later collections include *What the Darkness Proposes* (1996) and *Signs & Wonders* (2011—all Johns Hopkins University Press). See also the Pulitzer-nominated *Starting from Sleep: New and Selected Poems* (Overlook, 2002) and his acclaimed translations of Ovid's *Metamorphoses* (Norton, 2003).   RMCP

Martin, William (1925–2010) Born in Silksworth, a pit village in the Durham coalfield, and his childhood memories of its communal life form the matrix of his poetry.

A key image is the Durham Miners' Gala, when the huge silk banners of the miners' lodges are paraded through the city streets. The poems themselves are like banners, woven of many different threads—the Gnostic Gospel of St Thomas, the legend of St Cuthbert, the industrial history of strikes and evictions, children's songs and street-games—to make emblems of community.

Locally based but wide-ranging in reference, Martin represents a development from the work of David *Jones, taking the fragments of past traditions and using them as 'rubble to build with'. He compacts his images, adding layer upon layer over long poems, and they can seem too compressed. When the language clarifies and the rhythms become songlike, he sustains a terse, haunting music. He received a Northern Arts Award in 1984, and a set of children's songs, *Battledore*, was set to music by John Woolrich in 1985.

There are two collections from Taxus, *Cracknrigg* (1983) and *Hinny Beata* (1987), and two from Bloodaxe, *Marra Familia* and *Lammas Alanna* (2000). His long poem 'Arl' has been published online.   RGa

Masefield, John (Edward) (1878–1967) Born in Ledbury, Herefordshire. His mother died when he was 6, and his solicitor father soon after, following a mental breakdown, and he was brought up by an aunt unsympathetic to his juvenile literary ambitions. A career in the merchant navy was prescribed for him, and at thirteen he joined the training ship HMS *Conway* on the Mersey. On his second voyage, however, he left his ship at New York, and worked as a bartender and in a Yonkers carpet factory before returning to London in 1897 determined to be a writer. (These adventures are recounted in the autobiographical volumes *New Chum*, 1944, and *In the Mill*, 1941.) For most of his twenties, a decade fondly remembered in the poem 'Biography' (1912), he struggled to make a living, but enjoyed the friendship of *Yeats, *Binyon, Synge, and others. He began to write poems flavoured by his youthful experiences, pledging himself in 'A Consecration' to sing of the uncelebrated, 'the ranker, the tramp of the road ... The sailor, the stoker of steamers'. His first two volumes, *Salt-Water Ballads* (1902) and *Ballads* (1903), contained the pungent, rhythmical poems of the sea ('Sea-Fever' and 'Cargoes') which are still his best-known works.

Contemporary fame came, however, with the publication in the *English Review* in 1911 of the controversial narrative poem *The Everlasting Mercy*. This tells, in octosyllabic couplets, the story of Saul Kane, a poacher and drunkard converted by the Quaker, Miss Bourne, and juxtaposes scenes of religious fervour with pub brawls and a sort of dialogue ('You closhy put!', 'You bloody liar!') new to poetry. Further narrative poems reviving Chaucerian metres, including *Dauber* (1913), the story of the seaman-painter who proves himself and drowns, and *Reynard the Fox* (1919), an account of the Ledbury Hunt in bristling couplets, earned Masefield a high reputation on both sides of the Atlantic.

In the First World War he worked initially with the Red Cross; instead of war poems there were the prose studies *Gallipoli* (1916), *The Old Front Line* (1917), and the *Battle of the Somme* (1919). After the war he settled at Boar's Hill near Oxford, where he continued his prolific output including plays, and novels, of which *Sard Harker* (1924) and *Odtaa* (1926) are the best; but all the valuable poetry had been written by the time he was appointed Poet Laureate, succeeding *Bridges, in 1930.

Masefield's *Collected Poems*, first published in 1923, sold 200,000 copies. There is a sympathetic biography by Constance Babington Smith (Macmillan, 1978), and several volumes of letters. Phillip W. Errington has edited a new selection of Masefield's poems, *Sea-Fever* (2005), and a critical edition of *Reynard the Fox* (2008—both Carcanet).   MI

Mason, R. A. K. (Ronald Allison Kells) (1905–71) Born and educated in Auckland, eventually taking a classics degree. He began writing while still a schoolboy, and had written most of his major poems by the time he was 25.

Mason's work, along with Ursula *Bethell's, is widely recognized as marking the beginning of a significant New Zealand poetic tradition in the 1920s. His first properly published book, *The Beggar* (1924), was hardly noticed locally but was seen by Harold *Monro, and provided two poems for the *Chapbook Miscellany* in 1924. The earliest poems were often ornate and conventionally *Georgian, though many were revised with a newly austere diction on republication. The poems have a pessimism that stresses a concern with mortality and death; their universe appears to be godless and devoid of charity, yet this harsh vision is presented in verse of considerable compassion and intensity.

At the centre of Mason's finest book, *No New Thing, Poems 1924–1929* (Spearhead, 1934) is a Christ figure, the good man of the heresy of Arius, wearing the 'gallant mask' of a pretension to divinity but finally manifesting only a stoic determination to accept the fatal consequences of a humanistic commitment to goodness.

By the 1930s Mason had turned to political and trade-union activity and largely ceased writing poetry, though an interest in drama continued. A selection of his work was published as *This Dark Will Lighten* in 1941, and his *Collected Poems* (Pegasus) ed. Allen Curnow, appeared in 1962.

See also, Charles Doyle, *R. A. K. Mason* (Twayne, 1970), J. E. Weir, *R. A. K. Mason* (Oxford University Press, 1977), and Rachel Barrowman, *Mason: The Life of R. A. K. Mason* (Victoria University Press, 2003).   WSB

Massingham, Harold (1932–2011) Born and grew up in Mexborough, Yorkshire, the son of a collier. After graduating in English from Manchester in 1954, he spent fifteen years as a schoolteacher, and taught in the extramural department of Manchester University. He also set cryptic crosswords for national newspapers under the pseudonym 'Mass'.

In his first book, *Black Bull Guarding Apples* (Longmans, 1965) a determination to voice violent, animal sensations and impressions was reminiscent of that other son of Mexborough, Ted *Hughes. An early poem defines its locus, a local farm, as 'cold home for honest gutturals'. The landscape of industrial Yorkshire, and Massingham's memories of his childhood, continued to provide the source of many of his striking if also perplexing images and much of his densely, sometimes excessively textured syntax. A tendency to favour compound epithets and rugged alliteration reflects Massingham's other major influence, Anglo-Saxon poetry, and *Frost-Gods* (Macmillan, 1971) contained an impressively energetic version of 'Creation' to add to other translations of Exeter Book riddles and poems.

Massingham then fell largely silent. But *Sonatas and Dreams* (Arc, 1992) contains an admirable Pennine sequence, new work for children in the manner of his earlier 'Magician' poems, and a treatment of Van Gogh, with whom he had long been fascinated.   MRW

Masters, Edgar Lee (1868–1950) Born in Garnett, Kansas, and grew up on his grandfather's farm in Illinois. Largely an autodidact, Masters spent only a single year (1889) at Knox College in Galesburg, Illinois; his mid-life tribute (in *Songs and Satires*, 1916) to William Marion Reedy 'descanting on Yeats, | With a word on Plato's symposium, | And a little glimpse of

Theocritus, | Or something of Bruno's martyrdom, | Or what St Thomas Aquinas meant | By a certain line obscure to us' indicated both his willingness to be impressed by learning and a lurking sense of inferiority.

Masters began his working life as a printer, but entered his father's law office under pressure and was admitted to the Illinois Bar in 1891. He established a practice in Chicago, made a successful career, and in 1898 married Helen M. Jenkins, with whom he had three children. The same year saw publication of his first collection *A Book of Verses*, and by his mid-forties he had followed it with *The Blood of the Prophets* (1905) and the two-volume *Sons and Sonnets* (1910–12), as well as seven plays. This early work was derivative of Whitman, Swinburne, and Keats.

The book which made Masters famous was prompted partly by his mother's lively accounts of people the family had known in Petersburg and Lewistown, Illinois, and partly by J. W. Mackail's *Select Epigrams from the Greek Anthology*, given to him by Reedy (editor of *Reedy's Mirror* in St Louis). The *Spoon River Anthology* (Macmillan, 1915) contained well over two hundred free-verse epitaphs. 'When the book was put together in its definitive order', Masters wrote ten years later in the *American Mercury*, 'the fools, the drunkards, and the failures came first, the people of one-birth minds got second place, and the heroes and the enlightened spirits came last, a sort of *Divine Comedy*'. Psychologically and socially acute, sympathetic in tone, the *Spoon River Anthology* marked out Masters as a leading spirit in the Chicago Renaissance, alongside Carl *Sandburg and Vachel *Lindsay. As a portrait of a community, it has often been compared with Anderson's *Winesburg, Ohio*, Wilder's *Our Town*, and Dylan *Thomas' *Under Milk Wood*. It was made into an opera (*La Collina*) by the Italian composer Mario Pergallo.

Unfortunately Masters proved to be a one-book writer, in spite of his prolific output. His next collection, *The Great Valley* (1916), included accomplished monologues which deserve to be better known ('Emily Brosseau: In Church', 'Hanging the Picture'), arresting portraits ('Theodore Dreiser', 'John Cowper Powys'), and a poem, 'The Bay Window', which strikingly shares the tone of *Eliot's 'Portrait of a Lady'; but most of the book is little more than attitudinizing fustian. *Domesday Book* (1920) and *The Fate of the Jury* (1929) are the only other of Masters' two-dozen volumes of verse that are still read; *The New Spoon River* (1924), like the original volume, was a best-seller, but its assault on modern city life was too crude. Masters wrote several historical plays (largely in verse), seven novels (partly autobiographical), and biographies of Mark Twain, Whitman, Vachel Lindsay, and (a controversial attack) Lincoln; but he remained the Spoon River poet. Interviewed by the *New York Times* in 1942, he described himself as 'a Hellenist', claiming that the marvel of Greek civilization was that 'they thought in universals [whereas] we are provincial in our thoughts'.

In 1920 Masters gave up his Chicago law practice and moved to New York, where in 1925 he divorced his wife, marrying Ellen Coyne the following year. Towards the end of his life he was awarded a fellowship of the Academy of American Poets (1946). Masters died in 1950 and was buried in the cemetery at Petersburg amidst those he had written of in the *Spoon River Anthology*. The most useful study is John T. Flanagan's *Masters: The Spoon River Poet and His Critics* (Scarecrow, 1974). An annotated edition of *Spoon River Anthology* was published by University of Illinois Press in 1992, ed. John E. Hallwas. See also Herbert K. Russell, *Edgar Lee Masters: A Biography* (University of Illinois Press, 2005).   MHu

Mathew, Ray(mond Frank) (1929–2002) Born in Sydney, Australia and worked as a schoolteacher, journalist, and freelance writer. He left Australia in 1961 when his play *The Life of the Party* (1961) was produced at the Royal Court Theatre, London. He lived for many years in New York, but his last published work was his one novel, *The Joys of Possession* (Chapman & Hall, 1967), based extensively on his personal experiences as a teacher in rural New South Wales.

Ray Mathew was the most important new poetic voice in Australia in the 1950s and the first Australian writer to reflect the stimulus of American poetic experimentalism of the period. His work, lyrical, verbally playful, and increasingly concerned with the delicate balance within interpersonal relationships, confirmed the established line of Australian lyrical poetry while at the same time infusing it with a measure of sophistication and political insight that was ahead of its time. A decade later, when the stridencies of protest-poetry in the Vietnam-War years came to dominate much Australian writing, Mathew's earlier experiments in social observation and his concern for humanistic values were largely ignored, and his work continued to languish in comparative obscurity. Yet a rereading of his three volumes of poetry reaffirm a freshness of verbal dexterity and a sharp ear for social inflections, both rural and urban. His three collections are *With Cypress Pine* (1951), *Song and Dance* (1956—both Lyre Bird Writers), and *South of the Equator* (Angus & Robertson, 1961). See also *Tense Little Lives: Uncollected Prose of Ray Mathew* (National Library of Australia, 2007), ed. Tom Shapcott.   TWS

Mathews, Harry (1930–) Mathews has lived primarily in France since graduating from Harvard in 1952. Despite this geographical remoteness, Mathews' American audience has steadily increased in recent years, and it always made up in intensity of admiration whatever it may have lacked in size. Mathews serves an uncompromisingly experimental muse. A good portion of his work eludes classification, blurring genres and amalgamating forms. The centre-piece of *Armenian Papers* (Princeton University Press, 1987), a retrospective selection of his poetry from 1954 to 1984, is 'Trial Impressions', a sequence of thirty versions of the text of an Elizabethan song. The song turns into a multiple-choice narrative here and an equivoque there; Mathews favours homemade forms as well as recondite ones.

Much American poetry is predicated on the repudiation of strict forms. For Mathews the problem with traditional forms is that they are not constrictive enough. In *Selected Declarations of Dependence* (Z Press, 1977; repr. Sun & Moon, 1996), written with Alex Katz, Mathews devises and demonstrates a brilliantly eccentric set of formal procedures based on 'perverbs' (in which the first half of one adage is coupled with the second half of a different one) and 'paraphrases' (in which the perverbs are elaborated, transformed, made into metaphors or allegories). Mathews seems determined to create poetry out of some of the most unpromising materials that language hurls up. In 'Histoire', a madcap and hilarious sestina, the six recurring end-words are 'militarism', 'Marxism-Leninism', 'sexism', 'racism', 'fascism', and 'Maoism'.

Mathews is the only American member of the *Oulipo (Ouvroir de Litterature Potentielle, or Workshop for Potential Literature), a Paris-based association of mathematicians and writers committed to the development of ingenious new forms and methods of composition. See *The Oulipo Compendium* (Atlas, 1998; 2nd edn., 2005). With John *Ashbery, Kenneth *Koch, and James *Schuyler, he founded the literary magazine *Locus Solus* in 1960. *The Conversions* (1962), his first novel, is a picaresque adventure based on a rich man's capricious will. He has published five novels since, including *Cigarettes* (Weidenfeld & Nicolson, 1987; Carcanet, 1988; repr. Dalkey Archive, 1998), a fictional application of the Oulipian method of composition known as 'Mathews' algorithm'.

Since *A Mid-Season Sky: Poems 1954–1991* (Carcanet, 1992), he has published one new volume of poems, *The New Tourism* (Sand Paper, 2010), which the critic Barry Schwabsky described as 'more than ever…imbued with a childlike sense of wonder at both language and the world it can conjure'. His stories have been collected as *The Human Country* (2002) and his essays as *The Case of the Persevering Maltese* (2003). See also the quasi-memoir *My Life in the CIA: A Chronicle of 1973* (2005—all Dalkey Archive).   DL

Mathias, Roland (1915–2000) Born at Talybont-on-Usk, Breconshire, and educated at British military schools in Germany, where his father was an army chaplain, and at Jesus College, Oxford. After teaching history at schools in England, he returned to Wales to become headmaster of Pembroke Dock Grammar School in 1948, but later resumed his career as headmaster of schools at Belper in Derbyshire and in Birmingham.

In 1949 Mathias was one of the founders of *Dock Leaves* (later the *Anglo-Welsh Review*) and edited the magazine between 1961 and 1976, contributing a large number of poems, reviews, and articles, as well as substantial editorials, and in this role he was highly respected and influential.

He published five collections of verse: *Break in Harvest* (1946), *The Roses of Tretower* (1952), *The Flooded Valley* (1960), *Absalom in the Tree* (1971), and *Snipe's Castle* (1979). Many of the poems in these volumes have to do with Wales and its history, with specific places and people, but they are also intensely personal, following no fashion and showing little significant change in theme, style, or vocabulary over the thirty years of their composition. They are sometimes difficult in their allusion and syntax, usually reflecting the poet's erudition, but they are honest and scrupulously crafted.

A selection of Mathias' writings on Anglo-Welsh literature was published under the title *A Ride through the Wood* (1985); this volume contains essays on Henry Vaughan, Vernon *Watkins, Dylan *Thomas, David *Jones, Alun *Lewis, R. S. *Thomas, and Emyr *Humphreys. The volume entitled *Anglo-Welsh Literature, an Illustrated History* (1987) is a broad survey of its subject. He was also the author of a study of the poetry of John Cowper Powys, *The Hollowed-out Elder Stalk* (1979), and a monograph on Vernon Watkins in the Writers of Wales series (1974), and the editor, with Raymond *Garlick, of the anthology *Anglo-Welsh Poetry 1480–1980* (1984).

Roland Mathias' Selected Poems are to be found in *Burning Brambles* (1983). There is an autobiographical essay in *Artists in Wales*, ed. Meic Stephens (1971—both Gomer), a critical essay by Jeremy Hooker in *Poetry Wales*, 7:1, (1971), and an interview with the poet in *Poetry Wales*,

18:4 (1983). Sam Adams, who wrote a study of Mathias in 1995, also edited two posthumous volumes: *Collected Stories* (2001) and *Collected Poems* (2002—both University of Wales Press).   MS

Mattawa, Khaled (1964–) Born in Benghazi, Libya, Mattawa emigrated to the USA in 1979, and went to high school in Louisiana. He studied Political Science and Economics at the University of Tennessee, and English and Creative Writing at Indiana University. The stories of his verse evoke a personal history in which American and Arab culture are simultaneously familiar and strange ('Growing Up With a Sears Catalog in Benghazi, Libya'). In 1995, the year of his first collection from The Sheep Meadow Press, *Ismailia Eclipse*, he was Alfred Hodder Fellow at Princeton University. His other volumes include *Zodiac of Echoes* (2003), *Amorisco* (2008—both Ausable), and *Tocqueville* (New Issues, 2010). He currently teaches at the University of Michigan. Mattawa has translated several volumes of Arabic poetry into English, edited two anthologies of Arab-American literature, and is a contributing editor to *Banipal* magazine. His selection from the work of the Syrian poet Adonis for Yale University Press was shortlisted for the 2011 Griffin International Poetry Prize.   JNT

Matthews, Harley (1889–1968) Born in Sydney and educated at Sydney High School. He was an articled clerk in a solicitor's office until he enlisted in the Australian Infantry Forces in 1914. Matthews was among the Anzacs who landed at Gallipoli beach in a campaign against the Turks which became a legendary disaster. He survived the slaughter there to fight in France. After the war he worked for a Sydney afternoon newspaper, and in 1920 went to the United States, where he was a freelance writer for two years. In 1922 he established a vineyard at Moorebank, outside Sydney, which was to become a weekend meeting place for writers as diverse as Kenneth *Slessor and Roland *Robinson.

In 1942 Matthews was arrested and interned in an army prison camp for six months because of his association with members of the Australia First movement (an isolationist, anti-British, quasi-fascist organization), although he himself was not a member. During this time his elderly mother died and his vineyard was ruined through neglect. After the war a Royal Commission exonerated him of any connection with subversion and he was awarded £600 compensation. He lived the remainder of his life on another small farm on the outskirts of Sydney.

It was not until twenty years after the First World War that Matthews published his poems on Gallipoli. Their tone occasionally suggests Robert *Frost's narrative voice. They are written in lines of various metres and with opportunistically occurring rhymes. The long delay in these poems' appearance, their publication just before the Second World War, and their being too long for most anthologies have caused them to be overlooked. Les *Murray rediscovered 'Women Are Not Gentlemen' for *The New Oxford Book of Australian Verse* (1986). At least one other long poem from *Vintage* (1938), 'Two Brothers', is equally fine, and these are among the outstanding English-language poems of the First World War. Matthews', shorter and less successful work, to be found mainly in *Patriot's Progress* (1965), has typically a note of aggrieved patriotism, along with its praise of the Australian bush. All of his books are long out of print.   RGr

Matthews, William (1942–97) Born in Cincinnati, Ohio, and educated at Yale University. While he was working towards a PhD degree (never completed) at the University of North Carolina, Matthews founded, with Newton Smith and Russell Banks, the magazine *Lillabulero*. A prolific writer, Matthews also served as a member of the literature panel of the National Endowment for the Arts and as president of the Poetry Society of America. Though he writes basically a free-verse line, Matthews is a master of the well-turned phrase; he is known for both the lyric and the aphoristic qualities of his poems. They are peppered with wise sayings, often cast in a metaphorical form.

The richness of Matthews' use of metaphor was already evident by the time of his third volume, *Rising and Falling* (1979), where it can be seen in complete poems, in passages, and in single lines, as when he describes 'abandoned | mines' as 'vaccinations that didn't take'. Such resemblances lie at the heart of his best poems and account in large part for their success. Matthews' most intentionally wise book is his fifth, *A Happy Childhood* (1984—both Little, Brown), which investigates the psychological basis of human life by taking its text from Freud. No simple exercise in nostalgia, the volume makes clear that we as much create our childhoods as we remember them. Matthews' next book, *Foreseeable Futures* (Houghton, 1987), carried this principle even further by pointing out that a creative use of lying, or fiction, is at least as important to wisdom as an understanding of the truth.

Matthews' later books included *Time & Money* (1996), which won the National Book Critics Circle Award, and *After All: Last Poems* (1998). See *Selected Poems and Translations* (1992—all Houghton), *The Poetry Blues: Essays and Interview* (University of Michigan Press, 2001), and *Search Party: Collected Poems* (Houghton, 2004), ed. Sebastian Matthews and Stanley Plumly.   PS

Maurice, Furnley See WILMOT, FRANK.

Maxwell, Glyn (1962–) Born of Welsh parents, but grew up in Welwyn Garden City. He took a first in English at Oxford, but abandoned research to concentrate on his writing. In 1987 he won a scholarship to Boston University, where he worked on a creative-writing programme under Derek *Walcott and George *Starbuck.

Maxwell's first full collection, *Tale of The Mayor's Son* (1990), reflected the sharp restlessness of his talent. Quirky 'tales' oscillate playfully between the realms of the library and of 'the skinhead world', in both of which the narrator emphatically and intrusively tells, and knows he tells, before he shows. Syntax is continually interrupted, broken open as readily as the ideas it governs. It is a constantly invigorating poetry, which exploits Maxwell's ear for conversational rhythms; but such immediate effects risk swamping its subjects—love in an English garden city; the ethics of advertising; small-town and national politics—with a jauntiness and an eagerness to strike a pose. *Auden has been detected as an influence, particularly in the way Maxwell establishes a conspiratorial but also meretricious relationship with his readers, and in the importance of striking rhythms in the work; a barbed Brechtian social impulse may perhaps be detectable too; but the eccentricity of Maxwell's manner is original.

Poems from *Tale of the Mayor's Son* were reprinted with selections from Maxwell's second and third collections, *Out of the Rain* (1992) and *Rest for the Wicked* (1995), in *The Boys at Twilight* (2000—all Bloodaxe). Together they form a witty trilogy of English life in the early 1990s, comparable in its sympathetic presentation of the sensitive 'bloke' to the work of Maxwell's Northern contemporary, Simon *Armitage. Both were chosen as part of the Poetry Society's *New Generation group in 1994, and in 1996 commissioned by Faber and Faber to collaborate on *Moon Country*, a contemporary version of Auden and *MacNeice's *Letters from Iceland* (1937).

In 1996, Maxwell moved to America. He taught at Amherst College in Massachusetts, Columbia University, and The New School in New York, and was also poetry editor of *The New Republic*. In 1997 he received the E. M. Forster Award from the American Academy of Arts and Letters. His next collection, *The Breakage* (Faber, 1998), marked a self-conscious maturation of tone, notably in the central sequence 'Letters to Edward *Thomas'. In 2000 he published his first verse-novel, *Time's Fool*, a narration in *terza rima* of the nightmarish journey of 'Edward Lea' through modern England. His second was *The Sugar Mile* (2005), which moves between New York in September 2001 and London during the Blitz. Two later collections, *The Nerve* (2002) and *Hide Now* (2008—all Picador), reflect on transatlantic life and middle age, the jaunty worldliness inflected now more anxiously by the unmistakable syntax and rhythms of Maxwell's interlocutory voice. As he argues in his critical essay, *On Poetry* (Oberon, 2012), 'A poem coherently expresses the presence of a human creature.' See *One Thousand Nights and Counting: Selected Poems* (Picador, 2011). Since 1999 Maxwell's poetry has also been published in the USA by Houghton Mifflin.

He has also written two novels in prose (*Blue Burneau* (1994) and *The Girl Who Was Going to Die* (2008)) and a number of verse-plays: see *Gnyss the Magnificent* (Chatto & Windus, 1993), *Plays One* (2005), *Plays Two* (2006), and *After Troy* (2011—all Oberon). He currently teaches at the University of Essex in England.   MRW*

Mayer, Bernadette (1945–) Born in Brooklyn, Mayer received her BA from the New School for Social Research in 1967. She has spent the majority of her life in New York City. Mayer often employs experimental techniques in her poetry, such as stream-of-consciousness and time-limited writing. *Midwinter Day* (Turtle Island, 1982), for example, consists of a book-length prose poem composed in a single day. Her poetic prose has often been compared to the work of Gertrude *Stein. Mayer is also known for her engagement with the sonnet form. Her approach to writing is best summarized through her poetic essay 'Experiments', in which she gives many process-based ideas for composition, including the use of journals, erasure, repetition, and collage. It ends: 'Work your ass off to change the language & dont ever get famous.' The essay was reprinted by her former students Bruce *Andrews and Charles *Bernstein in *The L=A=N=G=U=A=G=E Book* (Southern Illinois University Press, 1984).

Mayer taught writing workshops at the *St. Mark's Poetry Project, New York City, for many years. Due to her process-based approach to writing, Mayer's work is often used in pedagogical contexts. Her publications include *Memory* (North Atlantic, 1976), *Studying Hunger* (Big Sky, 1976), *Sonnets* (Tender Buttons, 1989), *The Formal Field of Kissing* (Catchword Papers, 1990), *A Bernadette Mayer Reader* (New Directions, 1992), *The Desires of Mothers* to *Please Others in Letters* (Hard Press, 1994), and *Poetry State Forest* (New Directions, 2008).   SRO

Meehan, Paula (1955–) Born and raised in Dublin, Meehan attended Trinity College there and also Eastern Washington University, where she received an MFA in poetry. A member of Aosdána, she is also a playwright and has run writing workshops in prisons. Two early volumes from The Gallery Press, *The Man Who Was Marked By Winter* (1991) and *Pillow Talk* (1996), were shortlisted for the *Irish Times* Literature Prize for Poetry. A selection of her work appeared as *Mysteries of the Home* (Bloodaxe, 1996). Since then she has published two further collections in the UK and USA: *Dharmakaya* (Carcanet/Wake Forest University Press, 2000) and *Painting Rain* (Carcanet, 2008; Wake Forest University Press, 2009). She was also included in Eavan *Boland's anthology *Three Irish Poets* (Carcanet, 2003). Boland praises the 'zest' and 'daring' of Meehan's treatment of women's lives in Ireland, including her own working-class childhood. *An Sionnach*, 5 (2009) was a special issue of essays on Meehan's work.   JNT

Mehrotra, Arvind Krishna (1947–) Born in Lahore, educated at Allahabad and Bombay (now Mumbai), is an academic in the English studies department of Allahabad University. He began writing early, and in order to promote experimental verse he started the little magazines *damn you* (1965–8) and *ezra: an imagiste magazine* (1967–71). His iconoclastic reputation was strengthened by his long poem, 'Bharatmata: a Prayer' (1966) which turns Mother India into a septic tank filled with World Bank loans. He was invited to the first international exposition of concrete and mechanical poetry (Paris, 1967), and published his collection of concrete poems, *Woodcuts on Paper* (Gallery Number Ten, 1967) in London. His association with fellow experimental poets and painters continued and two early volumes of *surrealist verse— *Pomes/Poems/Poemas* and *Twelve Poems from the Good Surrealist*—were published

by avant-garde publishers in Baroda and Bombay (1971–2). The collection *Nine Enclosures* (1976) contains his best-known poem, 'The Sale', in which a single metaphor, life as a saleroom, is wittily developed.

Mehrotra, like Arun *Kolatkar and Dilip *Chitre, is an accomplished translator of verse, ranging widely from translations of second-century Prākrit love poetry to the contemporary Macedonian poet, Gjuzel. He has been influenced by the cryptic, deceptively simple aphorisms of the medieval weaver-mystic Kabir, in poems like 'After Kabir' in *Distance in Statute Miles* (1982—both Clearing House). See also his translation *Songs of Kabir* (New York Review, 2011).

Mehrotra acknowledges the influence of André Breton's Surrealist manifestos on his own discordant images, sometimes nightmarish, often amusing and clever. His later works, even when fractured and disjointed, retain an inner rationality, as in 'Eleven Cross-sections'.

Middle Earth (Oxford University Press, 1984) is a representative selection. He has published one further volume, *The Transfiguring Place: Poems* (Dayal, 1998), and a translation of Prākrit love poetry, *The Absent Traveller* (Penguin, 2008). In 2009 Mehrotra received a PEN Translation Fund Grant and was nominated for the Oxford Professorship of Poetry. He has edited *The Oxford India Anthology of Twelve Modern Indian Poets* (1992) and *A History of Indian Literature in English* (Hurst, 2003). His own criticism has been published as *Partial Recall: Essays on Literature and Literary History* (Permanent Black, 2012), which includes 'Death of a Poet', a tribute to his friend, Arun Kolatkar.

For criticism of his poetry, see *Modern Indian Poetry in English*, by Bruce King (Oxford University Press, 1987; revd. edn., 2001).   RA

Menashe, Samuel (1925–2011) Born and lived in New York City. Having enlisted in 1943, he served as an infantryman in Europe; following the Second World War he earned a doctorate at the Sorbonne.

Extremely terse poems, often no more than a few lines long, constitute the bulk of Menashe's work. Although often unpunctuated, the poems are usually syntactically complete and are more reminiscent of the Greek Anthology than of haiku. He treats the classic topics of love, loss, and time in tones that can be sombre, wry, or funny. Sometimes the poem functions like a wink, signifying a shared joke; at other times Menashe's use of imagery familiar from the Bible gives his poems a psalm-like cast.

In their cramped physical dimensions, Menashe's poems enact the limitations that form part of his subject-matter—the boundaries of the body, for example. 'The niche narrows | Hones one thin | Until his bones | Disclose him', is a characteristically laconic example. Other well-defined and vivid themes that arise in Menashe's work are tiny landscapes (most often cityscapes), momentary observations, and summaries of the evanescent: a change of weather, or waking from a dream.

His first book, *The Many Named Beloved*, was published in London by Victor Gollancz, with a foreword by Kathleen *Raine. Several later volumes appeared in America, including *Collected Poems* (National Poetry Foundation, 1985). In 2004 he was the first recipient of the Poetry Foundation's Neglected Masters Award, and in 2005 Christopher Ricks edited a *New and Selected Poems* for the American Poets Project. This was republished in an expanded UK edition by Bloodaxe in 2009, featuring tributes from Stephen *Spender and Donald *Davie, and a DVD documentary of the octogenarian poet reciting and discussing his work.   RHa*

Meredith, William (1919–2007) Born in New York City, graduated from Princeton in 1940, and served as a naval aviator in the Second World War. *Love Letter from an Impossible Land*, his first poetry collection, was chosen by Archibald *MacLeish for the Yale Younger Poets Series in 1944. Five volumes followed, including *The Wreck of the Thresher and Other Poems* (1964) and *Earth Walk: New and Selected Poems* (1970—both Knopf). Meredith also translated Apollinaire's *Alcools* (1964). He

taught at Princeton, the University of Hawaii, Middlebury College, Bread Loaf, and for many years at Connecticut College, until a stroke in 1983 led to his retirement.

Throughout his career Meredith's poetic voice was notable for its lyrical reticence. The poems are rarely obscure but almost always noticeably, sometimes insistently, quiet, even when the subject-matter (such as Meredith's wartime experiences) might warrant drama. This characteristic tone accompanies graceful syntax and an often stately pace; the effect can be paradoxically sly or evasive, as the reader struggles to determine the poet's exact stance.

Meredith's many meditations on the New England landscape link him more strongly than most poets of his generation to Robert *Frost, but he has ties with various contemporaries as well. The war poems may recall Randall *Jarrell, the fastidious language and lurking humour James *Merrill or Richard *Wilbur, the minute yet shifting perspectives of observed nature (as in 'Whorls') Elizabeth *Bishop ('Last Things', dedicated to Robert *Lowell, glances at both Lowell's 'Skunk Hour' and Bishop's 'The Armadillo'). Finally, though, Meredith's gift for the odd angle and the wry understatement is, however it limits his poetic range, distinctively his own.

Occasionally Meredith seems to anticipate or echo the effect of defamiliarization achieved by the *Martian poets in Britain in the 1970s. In 'Navy Field' (1944), an airman reads 'The numbered sheets that tell about weather'; in 'Hazard Faces a Sunday in the Decline' (1976), a cat has seen 'the big thrush taken from the cold | box, dressed and put in the hot'—a Thanksgiving turkey transferred from refrigerator to oven. With such eloquently clumsy periphrases Meredith evokes, in a memorably circumlocutory fashion, the things of this world. Hampered by the expressive aphasia which followed his stroke, Meredith did not publish a full new volume after 1980, but *Partial Accounts: New and Selected Poems* (Knopf, 1987) won the Pulitzer Prize and *Effort at Speech: New and Selected Poems,* TriQuarterly/Northwestern University Press, 1997) won the National Book Award.   RHa

Merrill, James (1926–95) Born in New York City, the son of the immensely wealthy financier Charles E. Merrill, the founder of Merrill Lynch, and the second of his three wives, Hellen Ingram. His parents divorced in 1939 when he was thirteen, a traumatic experience to which he often alluded in his poetry. Merrill attended Amherst College; he took a year off to serve in the army and graduated in 1947. Although he occasionally taught semesters at a variety of American universities, Merrill's freedom from financial pressures has meant that he was able to live how and where he pleased, a privilege almost unique among modern poets. In 1954 he moved with his companion David Jackson (DJ of *The Changing Light at Sandover*) to Stonington, Connecticut. Merrill travelled widely, and his poems are often directly concerned with the exotic discoveries and alienating displacements of his journeys abroad. For two decades starting in 1964 he spent a part of each year in Greece, where some of his best-known poems are set.

Merrill's early poems, collected in *Black Swan* (1946) and *First Poems* (1951), are stiff formal exercises in a rather remote high-symbolist rhetoric. Although they exhibit a precocious facility with a wide range of metres and rhyme-schemes, and great skill in their elaborations of stock *fin de siècle* conceits, few of these early pieces add up to more than the sum of their decorative properties. Merrill's breakthrough in the Sixties was to find a way of uniting his formal gifts with a conversational tone capable of including the more mundane aspects of life. As he realizes in 'About the Phoenix': 'But in the end one tires of the high-flown.' 'An Urban Convalescence', the opening poem of his 1962 collection *Water Street* (Atheneum), is obviously pivotal in this transition. Merrill here rejects both the precious decadence of his earlier work and the temptation to windy denunciations of 'the sickness of our time', resolving instead to devote himself to the more practical business of day-to-day living, 'the dull need to make some kind of house | Out of the life lived, out of the love spent'.

This more personal tone allows Merrill to be autobiographical, but he is rarely *con-fessional. His poems are sheathed in manners in a way unusual in American poetry (Proust and *Auden are without doubt the two dominant influences on his overall poetics). Merrill called manners 'an artifice in the very bloodstream'; his own nature poems are instinct with an unfailing courtesy, occasionally patrician, occasionally camp, and this social dimension is reflected also in the multiple frames and stylistic devices through which he habitually angles his material. His work is full of puns, extravagant word-games, mythical allusions, intricate metres, and complex rhyme-schemes. Much of it has an almost operatic lushness and self-delight.

Merrill's *chef d'oeuvre* is undoubtedly his 17,000-line epic trilogy *The Changing Light at Sandover* (Atheneum, 1982). Its three long poems—'The Book of Ephraim' (included in *Divine Comedies*, Atheneum, 1976; Oxford University Press, 1977); *Mirabell: Books of Number* (Atheneum, 1978; Oxford University Press, 1979); and *Scripts for the Pageant* (Atheneum, 1980)—are all based on Merrill's and his friend David Jackson's experiences at the ouija board. The various spirits they contact, who include the poet W. H. Auden along with other recently departed friends, gradually educate them in the ways of the scientific and the spiritual worlds, somewhat in the manner of Virgil's instructions to Dante. The poem is composed in a dazzling array of styles, ranging from blank-verse narrative to *canzone* to the uppercase shorthand of the spirits' communications through the ouija board, the different segments of which govern the poem's structure. Merrill also wrote two novels, *The Seraglio* (1957) and *The (Diblos) Notebook* (1965), and a collection of his occasional prose pieces was published under the title *Recitative* (North Point, 1986).

His last book was *A Scattering of Salts* (1995). Merrill's posthumous *Collected Poems* (2001), *Collected Novels and Plays* (2002), *Collected Prose* (2004), and *Selected Poems* (2008—all Knopf) were edited by Yenser and J. D. McClatchy. See Stephen Yenser, *The Consuming Myth: The Work of James Merrill* (Harvard University Press, 1987). MF

Merton, Thomas (1915–69) Son of an English painter father and an American Quaker, was born in Southern France and brought up amongst artistic people. In the early 1930s he worked with the communists; in 1938 he joined the Roman Catholic Church, but without losing his liberal sympathies. In 1941 he entered the Cistercian Trappist Monastery at Gethsemane, in Kentucky, where he remained for six years. Eventually he was ordained priest, as Father M. Louis. *The Seven Storey Mountain* (Harcourt, 1948), an autobiography dealing with his wild youth, conversion, and experiences as a Trappist became an international bestseller. His verse, beginning with *Thirty Poems* (1944), written 'in the first flush of his conversion', and owing more to William Blake than to Catholic devotional poets in its fervour, is perhaps best regarded as an adjunct to his main achievement as a religious thinker and mystic, or as a part of modern American Roman Catholic poetry (cf. Daniel *Berrigan) than as in the mainstream of American poetry. In the poems of the second collection, *Figures for an Apocalypse* (1947), the original fervour and passion are modified by doctrinal considerations and by a more intellectual note. Subsequent work, reflecting Merton's reading of St John of the Cross and his study of oriental religion and the Christian mysticism of the European Middle Ages, becomes more of a piece with the prose meditations of *Seeds of Contemplation* (1949), a series he continued until his premature death as a result of an accident with an electric fan. It is likely that his best poetic work has a proper place in any anthology of modern Catholic or mystical verse.

See also *Cables to the Ace* (1968—all New Directions). MS-S

Merwin, W. S. (William Stanley) (1927–) Born in New York City and grew up in Union City, New Jersey, and Scranton, Pennsylvania. His father was a Presbyterian minister. 'I started writing hymns for my father as soon as I could write at all', Merwin has said. He attended Princeton University, where he studied writing with John *Berryman and R. P. *Blackmur,

to whom his fifth book, *The Moving Target* (1963), was dedicated. Merwin spent a postgraduate year at Princeton studying Romance languages, an interest that would lead, eventually, to his much-admired work as a translator of Latin, Spanish, and French poetry.

Having left Princeton, Merwin travelled in France, Spain, and England. He settled in Majorca in 1950 as a tutor to Robert *Graves' son. Graves, with his interest in mythology, would become a primary influence on young Merwin. Moving to London in 1951, Merwin made his living as a translator for several years. Meanwhile, back in America, his first book of poems won the Yale Series of Younger Poets Award for 1952, selected by W. H. *Auden, who remarked in his introduction on the young poet's technical virtuosity. That volume, *A Mask for Janus*, is immensely formal, neoclassical in style. For the next decade Merwin would regularly publish collections of intensely wrought, brightly imagistic poems that recalled the poetry of Wallace *Stevens as well as Robert Graves and other influences.

Merwin's early subjects were frequently tied to mythological or legendary themes, while many of the poems featured animals, which were treated as emblems in the manner of Blake. A volume called *The Drunk in the Furnace* (1960) marked a change for Merwin, in that he began to write in a much more autobiographical way. The title-poem is about Orpheus, seen as an old drunk. 'Where he gets his spirits | It's a mystery', Merwin writes; 'But the stuff keeps him musical'. Another powerful poem of this period is 'Odysseus', which reworks the traditional theme in a way that plays off poems by Stevens and Graves on the same topic.

In the 1960s Merwin began to experiment boldly with metrical irregularity. His poems became much less tidy and controlled. He played with the forms of indirect narration typical of this period, a self-conscious experimentation explained in an essay called 'On Open Form' (1969). *The Lice* (1967) and *The Carrier of Ladders* (1970) (which won a Pulitzer Prize) remain his most characteristic and influential volumes. These poems often used legendary subjects (as in 'The Hydra' or 'The Judgment of Paris') to explore highly personal themes.

In Merwin's later volumes, such as *The Compass Flower* (1977), *Opening the Hand* (1983), and *The Rain in the Trees* (1988), one sees him transforming earlier themes in fresh ways, developing an almost Zen-like indirection. His later poems are densely imagistic, dream-like, and full of praise for the natural world. He has lived in Hawaii in recent years, and one sees the influence of this tropical landscape everywhere in the recent poems, though the landscape remains emblematic and personal.

Migration: New & Selected Poems (Copper Canyon, 2005) won the National Book Award, and draws on four volumes since 1990: *Travels* (1993), *The Vixen* (1996), *The River Sound* (1999), and *The Pupil* (2001). An expanded edition, published in the UK by Bloodaxe in 2007, also includes poems from *Present Company* (2005) addressed to a range of people and things, from 'My Teeth' to 'The Gods'. *The Shadow of Sirius* appeared in 2008 (both Copper Canyon). He has also published translations of Dante's *Purgatorio* (Knopf, 2000) and the Middle English poem *Sir Gawain and the Green Knight* (Bloodaxe, 2002), and a 'memorial anthology' for his poetic contemporaries, *Lament for the Makers* (Counterpoint, 1996). Merwin's volumes of autobiography include, *Unframed Originals* (Atheneum, 1982; repr. Counterpoint, 2004), and *Summer Doorways* (2005). His latest collection of essays is *The Ends of the Earth* (2005—both Counterpoint), and his short, poetic prose has been collected in *The Book of Fables* (Copper Canyon, 2007). For criticism, see H. L. Hix, *Understanding W. S. Merwin* (University of South Carolina Press, 1997) and *Until Everything Is Continuous Again: American Poets on the Recent Work of W. S. Merwin*, ed. Jonathan Weinert and Kevin Prufer. From 2010 to 2011 Merwin was Poet Laureate of the United States.   JP*

Metelerkamp, Joan (1956–) Born in Pretoria, Metelerkamp grew up on a farm in KwaZulu-Natal before completing a BA and diploma in acting at the Universities of Natal and Cape Town. She was editor of the South African poetry journal *New Coin* between 2000 and 2003. She lives on a farm in the Southern Cape.

Metelerkamp's first collection of poetry, *Towing the Line* (Carrefour, 1992), which won the SANLAM literary award, initiates the privileging of an individual, and specifically female, experience over political life which distinguishes all of her work within its South African context. In *Stone No More* (1995) and *Into the day breaking* (2000—both Gecko), Metelerkamp writes out of her preoccupation with what it means to be—and how to be—a mother, daughter, and writer. The poems perceive and articulate simultaneously, thinking and rethinking their subjects through a distinctive halting, circling, repeating poetic voice. Metelerkamp's most recent books have all been long poems. *Floating Islands* (Mokoro, 2001), which shares its title with poems by Dorothy Wordsworth and South African poet Ruth *Miller, explores aspects of the female experience in the form of an exchange between a mother and her daughters. *Requiem* (Deep South, 2003) and *Carrying the Fire* (Substance, 2005) are emotionally intimate book-length introspective sequences which deal with her mother's suicide and a romantic relationship. Most recently, *Burnt Offering* (Modjaji, 2009) is a meditation on the transformative effects of writing.   KK

Mew, Charlotte (1869–1928) Born in London into a genteel Victorian middle-class family which was neither literary nor highly educated. Her father's death when she was 29 forced Mew to take employment as a teacher, and she lived with her mother and sister all her life in varying degrees of hardship. A history of mental instability in the family dissuaded her from considering marriage. She wrote a quantity of short stories in the early years of the century and took to writing poetry when she was in her forties. Through her friendship with Alida Monro, Mew's work was published by the Poetry Bookshop in a slim volume, *The Farmer's Bride*, in 1916, and was admired by *Masefield and *Hardy, among others. In 1923 she was awarded a Civil List pension, but did not live long to enjoy it, dying by her own hand in a sanatorium five years later. Her poems are sensual, melancholy, and subjective, reflecting a lonely and eccentric life. Her use of narrative forms and the dramatic monologue is reminiscent of Browning's, which points up an interesting struggle in her poetry between form and content—the first almost wholly Victorian, the latter of the twentieth century. Her themes are death, ephemerality, love (usually lost or hopeless), God (also lost or uncompassionate), and the overriding tone is elegiac. Her work is uneven, but at its best very vivid and eloquent, rooted in the physical world and experienced through a powerful, rather morbid sensuality. The emotional intensity of many of her poems is enhanced by the use of a speaking voice and by highly personal rhythms and syntax, partly the fruit of her confessed ignorance of the rules of punctuation. A second volume, *The Rambling Sailor* was published posthumously in 1929 and *Collected Poems* in 1953. Mew's *Collected Poems and Prose*, ed. Val Warner, was published in 1981 (Carcanet; revd. edn. 1997).

See also Penelope Fitzgerald, *Charlotte Mew and Her Friends* (Collins, 1984). A new selection of Mew's poems was made in 2008 for Carcanet by Eavan *Boland.   CPH

Meynell, Alice (née Thompson)

(1847–1922) Born in Barnes, west London. Her father Thomas Thompson, a friend of Charles Dickens, was a cultured gentleman of independent means who insisted on a solid classical education for his two talented daughters and on frequent travel in Italy to enhance their aesthetic sensibilities.

Alice became a Roman Catholic in 1868. She married Wilfrid Meynell, also a Catholic convert, in 1877. He became a successful editor of the magazine *Merry England* to which the poet Francis Thompson contributed. Thompson subsequently moved in with the Meynell family and accepted their patronage. Alice also developed a friendship with George Meredith and with Coventry Patmore, but this was broken off when Patmore insisted on its being more intimate than she desired.

Alice raised a family of seven children and yet managed to find time to be active in prominent social circles in London and in politics. She marched with the Suffragettes.

Her poems are generally low-keyed, subtle, and non-rhetorical. She employed conventional prosody and defended her use of it in her poem 'The English Metres', first published in 1921 when the *vers libre* movement was at its height. The subjects she treated were usually love, religious belief, response to the beauties of nature, and war. 'Renouncement' is the most famous of her love poems.

For biographical information see Viola Meynell, *Alice Meynell: A Memoir* (Cape/Scribner's Sons, 1929) and June Badeni, *The Slender Tree: A Life of Alice Meynell* (Tabb House, 1981).

Geoffrey Cumberlege, *The Poems of Alice Meynell* (Oxford University Press, 1940), is the standard collected edition of her verse.   DS

Mezey, Robert (1935–) Born in Philadelphia and attended Kenyon College, Ohio, for two years before entering the army in 1953—by his own account, he was discharged as a 'subversive' in 1955. He earned his BA from the University of Iowa by 1960 and spent the next year at Stanford University as a poetry fellow. He married Ollie Simpson in 1963, and they have three children. Besides teaching at Pomona College for many years, he served as poetry editor for *Trans Pacific*.

A gifted metaphysical poet, Mezey's strong first collection, *The Lovemaker: Poems* (1961), won the Lamont Poetry Award. In the volumes to follow, *White Blossoms: Poems* (1965) and *A Book of Dying: Poems* (1970), he abandoned rhyme and metre, attempting to combine his Blakean passion with Philip *Levine's freer naturalism. He also edited, with Stephen *Berg, *Naked Poetry: Recent American Poetry in Open Forms* (1969) and, on his own, edited and translated *Poems from the Hebrew* (1973). With Dick Barnes, he has translated the poems of Jorge Luis Borges.

See *Collected Poems* (University of Arkansas Press, 2000), which won the Poets' Prize.   EB

Middleton, Christopher (1926–   ) Born in Truro, Cornwall. He read German and French at Oxford, and subsequently taught in Zurich and London. In 1965 he emigrated and became professor of Germanic languages and literature at the University of Texas until his retirement in 1998.

As a poet Middleton is compulsively experimental, which explains in part his neglect in England. The first collection he acknowledges, *Torse 3: Poems 1949–61* (1962), was awarded the first Sir Geoffrey Faber Memorial Prize, but it was with his next collection, *Nonsequences/Self-poems* (1965—both Longmans), that the direction he was to take became clear. An early influence was the prose of the Swiss writer Robert Walser, four of whose stories Middleton translated in the Fifties and whom he described in an early essay, included in *Bolshevism in Art and Other Expository Writings* (Carcanet, 1978), as 'a stranger to the realm of ideas'. Throughout his work Middleton resists and subverts the demands of the 'logomorphic' intelligence which tries to explain and interpret experience, seeking instead to disrupt poetic and linguistic modes to create unprecedented structures in which a delicate and often humorous freshness of perception is apparent.

Middleton is an outstanding translator from the German. Among his many translations are *Selected Poems* of Friedrich Hölderlin and Eduard Mörike (1972), *Kafka's Other Trial: The Letters to Felice*, by Elias Canetti (1974), *Selected Stories* of Robert Walser (1982; repr. 2001), and a number of Gert Hofman's novels. A selection of his translations of poets from many languages has been published as *Faint Harps and Silver Voices* (Carcanet, 2000). The best introduction to Middleton's work is *Selected Writings* (1989). See also *Jackdaw Jiving: Selected Essays on Poetry and Translation* (1997), and *Collected Poems* (2008), which includes his most recent volumes in the UK and USA respectively, *The Anti-Basilisk* (2005—all Carcanet) and *The Tenor on Horseback* (Sheep Meadow, 2007). For a judicious ac-count of his early work, see *An Introduction to 50 Modern British Poets*, by Michael Schmidt (Pan/Heinemann, 1979). *Chicago Review* 51:1/2 (Spring 2005) contains tributes, an interview, and a bibliography.   TJGH

Miles, Josephine (1911–85) Born in Chicago and educated at the University of California, Los Angeles. Severely crippled by arthritis, she taught at the University of California, Berkeley, from 1940 until her retirement in 1978. A prolific critic and scholar as well as poet, Miles' works include studies of the characteristic vocabularies of poetry in various eras. In 'Poetry and Tradition,' an essay published in *Pacific Coast Philology* (Nov. 1981), Miles stated that at the beginning of her poetic career, 'one of the assumptions I most resented was that of individual autonomy.'

Miles' early poems do not deserve Kenneth *Rexroth's famous quip ('small, very neat holes cut in the paper'), but their very modesty and attention to formal details set them apart from the broader, romantic work of Rexroth and poets such as William *Everson and Robert *Duncan with whom he was then associated. Her later work is less formal, but extreme attention to detail remains constant. Sometimes seen as one of Rexroth's principal opponents in the mid-century poetry community in the San Francisco Bay Area, she was in fact too independent to ally herself with any poetic faction, and although her work was widely respected among her peers, she had no major disciples.

Miles' *Collected Poems* was published in 1983. *To All Appearances: Poems New and Selected* (1974—both University of Illinois Press) provides a good introduction to the work.   EHF

Millay, Edna St Vincent (1892–1950) Though it seems surprising now, Edna Millay, bohemian rebel and darling of Greenwich Village in the Twenties, was younger by five years than the modernist Marianne *Moore. The most gifted of three talented daughters, Edna (known as 'Sefe' or 'Vincent' to her family) was born in Rockland, Maine on 22 February 1892. Her father was a superintendent of schools, but her parents separated when their daughters were tiny, and it was principally her mother, a musician frustrated into becoming a district nurse, who brought up the family. Although encouraged to develop her gifts, the young Edna Millay had no formal teaching until, in her twenties, she was sent briefly to Barnard College and then to Vassar, from which she graduated in 1917, her reputation already established by the publication of *Renascence and Other Poems*.

Millay soon settled in Greenwich Village where she assimilated the image of the new 'free woman', undertaking to live dangerously in several roles: she acted, wrote plays in verse for the Provincetown Players, and contributed clever, satirical prose to magazines—sometimes under a pseudonym, Nancy Boyd. She also became famous for love affairs (there was an especially turbulent one with the young Edmund *Wilson), while she continued to write popular lyrics. Her second book, *A Few Figs from Thistles* (1920), included her most quoted quatrain: 'My candle burns at both ends; | It will not last the night | But ah, my foes, and oh, my friends—| It gives a lovely light.'

Edna Millay published two more collections of verse (*The Harp-Weaver and Other Poems* won the 1923 Pulitzer Prize) and produced a number of her plays before, at the end of 1923, she married Eugene Boissevain, a businessman who dedicated his life to caring for her. They travelled together and then settled for a while in New York City. After Edna had suffered several nervous breakdowns, they retreated to a farm near Austerlitz, New York State. Here, in desperately bad health, writing steadily despite a waning reputation, Millay, widowed in her later years, lived in painful seclusion until her death in 1950.

In the period between the World Wars Millay's reputation was what Sylvia *Plath's is today. But Millay, though prone to violent mood-swings and recurrent crises of health, was held prisoner, as Plath was not, by the rigidity of lyrical convention. At its most assured, Millay's ear dictated a firm, musical, economical line. Her sonnets, once compared with Shakespeare's and Donne's, to the modern ear often

verge on the bathetic. Her fanciful one-act plays, though (*The Princess Marries the Page*, 1918, and *Aria da Capo*, 1919), are still performed in American schools. And Millay has a faithful following. Many women readily forgive her for sacrificing what John Crowe *Ransom stiffly identified as a woman's typical 'indifference to intellectuality' to uninhibited emotion and a gift for heart-wringing pathos.

Publications include *A Few Figs from Thistles* (1920); *Second April* (1921); *The Harp-Weaver and Other Poems* (1923); *The Buck in the Snow* (1928); *Fatal Interview* (1931); *Wine from These Grapes* (1934); *Conversation at Midnight* (1937); *Huntsman, What Quarry* (1939); *Bright these Arrows* (1940); *Murder of Lidice* (1942). Millay's *Collected Sonnets* were published in 1941 and *Collected Lyrics* in 1943. *Mine the Harvest* posthumously collected sixty-six poems in 1954. Her *Collected Poems* appeared in 1956, *Selected Poems of Edna Millay* (HarperCollins) in 1991, and *Selected Poems*, ed. Colin Falck (Carcanet) in 1992.   AS

Miller, Kei (1978–) Born in Jamaica, Miller studied English at the University of the West Indies, where was mentored by Mervyn *Morris, and Creative Writing at Manchester Metropolitan University. He has been a visiting writer in Canada and America, and currently teaches at the University of Glasgow.

Miller's first book, *Fear of Stones and Other Stories* (Macmillan, 2006), was a collection of stories for teenagers about homophobia in Jamaica. He has also published fiction for adults. His first two novels, *The Same Earth* (2008) and *The Last Warner Woman* (2010—both Weidenfeld & Nicolson), feature Jamaican women who find themselves in England. Miller's poetry exhibits a similar social curiosity, descriptive appetite, and satirical insight: see the sequences 'In Dream Country', from his first collection, *Kingdom of Empty Bellies* (Heaventree, 2006), and 'In This Country', from his second, *There Is an Anger that Moves* (2007). His verse has increasingly celebrated the rhapsodic and visionary power of poetry, as discussed in the autobiographical essay 'The Art of Tongues,

The Craft of Prophecy', published in *PN Review*, 179 (2008). *A Light Song of Light* (2010) goes deeper into the relationship between poetry, music, and history, invoking the figure of the Singerman, who sang to Jamaican gangs breaking stone to make roads. Miller has also edited *New Caribbean Poetry: An Anthology* (2007—all Carcanet).   JNT

Miller, Ruth (née Fridjhon) (1919–69) Born at Uitenhage, Cape Province. Her parents were Jewish but the ethnic influence was offset by circumstances. Deserted by her father, she and her mother lived on a farm with the family of a courtesy aunt who played a formative role in Ruth's early education. Later she attended a convent school.

Once the sole woman in the front rank of South Africa's English-language poets, she is the one whose work most characteristically invokes the note of tragedy. At the same time there is wit, sometimes deployed in satire. One of Miller's emotional motifs is exasperation when weakness of the flesh (such as the fatal cancer in whose grip she probably knew herself to be) or over-domestication of the spirit shrinks her capacity for joyous participation or passionate commitment. In some of her most powerful poems—'Voicebox', 'Come Not Unto Me', 'Submarine', 'Pebble', 'Rat'—the predominant theme is the confrontation of mortality.

Miller's ironical and unexpectant vision implies the possible existence of a deity whose chief attributes, however, are absence and indifference, but this does not preclude an appalled and compassionate identification with all suffering creatures (adventurous men in peril, victims of racist mean-spiritedness, a blind dog, an oil-soaked penguin). Nor does it mean that her poems cannot be celebratory—of love, courage, natural beauty. The sudden death of her 14-year-old son in 1962 brought these feelings more intensely into focus.

After her two collections *Floating Island* (Human & Rousseau, 1965) and *Selected Poems* (Chatto & Windus/Hogarth, 1969) went out of print, certain poems (notably 'The Floating Island', 'Sterkfontein', 'Penguin on the Beach', 'Fruit', 'Aliens at home', 'Plankton', 'The Stranger', 'Spider', 'Mantis') were increasingly in demand for anthologies. Both collections were incorporated, with a choice of uncollected poems and other material, in *Ruth Miller—Poems, Prose, Plays*, ed. Lionel Abrahams (Carrefour, 1990).   LA

Miller, Vassar (1924–98) Born in Houston, Texas, where she lived all her life. Two conditions influenced her poetry: her disease (cerebral palsy), and her religion (Christian mysticism). After 1956, when *Adam's Footprint* appeared, Miller became considered an accomplished lyric poet. Her themes are intensely personal: God ('Nada'); religious faith; acceptance (her need to accept God); silence (the inexpressible); sleep (as seducer); the barren inadequacy of modern technology; the erotic; and death (as reliever of pain). She wrote in both traditional and modernistic forms.

If I Had Wheels or Love: Collected Poems of Vassar Miller (Southern Methodist University Press, 1990) contains all the poems in her earlier eight collections, along with a sampling of new work. The earlier collections are *Adam's Footprint* (1956); *Wage War on Silence* (1960): *My Bones Being Wiser* (1963): *Onions and Roses* (1968); *If I Could Sleep Deeply Enough* (1974); *Small Change* (1976); *Approaching Nada* (1977); and *Struggling to Swim on Concrete* (1984). *Despite This Flesh: The Disabled in Stories and Poems*, which she edited in 1984 (University of Texas Press), is an anthology of poetry and stories. *Heart's Invention: On the Poetry of Vassar Miller*, ed. Steven Ford Brown (Ford-Brown, 1988) contains critical commentary on her work.   JT

Milne, Drew (1964–) Born in Edinburgh, Milne studied English at the University of Cambridge, where he is now Judith E. Wilson Lecturer in Drama and Poetry. He has also taught at the universities of Edinburgh and Sussex, and edited two books of critical theory.

The driving concerns of Milne's poetry are forcefully argued in his prose, which is often concerned with Marxist philosophy and the avant-garde tradition. In particular, he has sought to recover poets such as Mina *Loy and David *Jones for a contemporary canon of 'neo-modernism', and to articulate the political nature of so-called *Cambridge poetry. See in particular the essays and correspondence with Allen *Fisher and J. H. *Prynne from the early 1990s, published in his magazine *Parataxis*.

Two sequences from *Sheet Mettle* (Alfred David, 1994), his first book, exemplify the rhetorical and ludic qualities of Milne's poetry: sonnet-like stanzas bring the language of news, cliché, and lyricism into ironic combination, with a controlling syntactical wit that has been likened to William *Empson ('It's a long way still where love our gulf is war'). The aesthetic is ultimately more imperative than the didactic, however, and Milne's later work has moved away from such monologic forms, splicing voices in constructivist shapes. His books include *Bench Marks* (Alfred David, 1998), *The Damage: New and Selected Poems* (Salt, 2001), *Mars Disarmed* (The Figures, 2002), *Go Figure* (Salt, 2003), and *Blueprints and Ziggurats* (Shearsman, 2012). JNT

Minhinnick, Robert (1952–) Born in Neath and brought up in the village of Pen-y-fai, Mid-Glamorgan. Educated at University College, Cardiff, he has had a variety of jobs, including working for Friends of the Earth in Wales, of which he was a co-founder. He is now an adviser to the charity Sustainable Wales. Between 1997 and 2008 he edited *Poetry Wales* magazine

Minhinnick is concerned with environmental and political questions, but succeeds in avoiding rhetoric and propaganda. Many of the people in his poems live under pressure but they face a hostile world with resilience and humour. He has published eight volumes of poetry, beginning with *A Thread in the Maze* (Davies, 1978), and edited and translated an anthology of contemporary Welsh poets, *The Adulterer's Tongue* (Carcanet, 2003). Minhinnick also writes autobiographical non-fiction, often reporting on his investigative travels. Two collections of essays have won the Wales Book of the Year Award: *Watching the Fire Eater* (1992) and *To Babel and Back*

(2005—both Seren). Drawn to formally diverse lyric sequences, his poetry since the 1990s has transformed these experiences into something more fantastical and image-led: e.g. 'An Opera in Baghdad', from *King Driftwood* (2008). He has twice won the Forward Prize for Best Single Poem, including 'Twenty-Five Laments for Iraq' in 1999. See *New Selected Poems* (2012—both Carcanet). Minhinnick has also published a novel, *Sea Holly* (2007), and a collection of short stories, *The Keys of Babylon* (2011—both Seren). MS*

Minter, Peter (1967–) Born in Newcastle, New South Wales, in 1967, Peter Minter is of English, Scottish, and Aboriginal heritage. He began to publish poetry in his teens. After graduating from the University of Sydney, he moved to the Blue Mountains and co-founded the journal *Cordite Poetry Review*. He taught Indigenous Studies at the University of Western Sydney until 2000 and is Lecturer in Indigenous Studies at the Koori Centre at the University of Sydney. He has edited various anthologies and journals, including *Overland Journal* and *Meanjin*, and is an active critic and advocate for Indigenous writing. With Anita Heiss, he co-edited the *Macquarie PEN Anthology of Aboriginal Literature* (2008).

Minter's first collection of poems, *Rhythm in a Dorsal Fin*, was published by Five Islands Press in 1995. He has since published three further collections, including *Empty Texas: A Selection* (Folio/Salt, 1998), which won the Age Dinny O'Hearn Poetry Prize and the *Age* Poetry Book of the Year in 2000, and *Blue Grass* (Salt, 2006), which was reviewed in the *Times Literary Supplement* as a work of 'conclusive, unillusioned, poetic and visionary possibility'. Minter's modernist lyric is acutely concerned with the politics of colonialization, in relation to the environment as well as Aboriginal people, and is distinctive for its sensual intelligence. ACr

Mishra, Sudesh (1962–) Born in Suva, Fiji, of Indian indentured-worker descent, Mishra is a poet, playwright, and academic. Educated in Fiji and Australia, where he studied for a PhD at Flinders University in

Adelaide, he has taught at Deakin University in Melbourne and is currently a professor of Literature, Language, and Linguistics at the University of the South Pacific.

In 'The Loving Song of R. J. Tangaya', from *Tandava* (Meanjin, 1992), Mishra parodies T. S. *Eliot's 'The Love Song of J. Alfred Prufrock' in Australian and Indian English, satirically confronting the literary canon with the post-colonial question of cultural translation ('Do I dare | Disturb the universe | By serving Les *Murray tandoori chicken?'). These are also themes he has written about in his critical monographs, *Preparing Faces: Modernism and Indian Poetry in English* (Centre for Research in New Literatures in English, 1995) and *Diaspora Criticism* (Edinburgh University Press, 2006). Capable elsewhere of a delicately reflective lyricism with an edge ('Suva; Skye'), his later collections are *Memoirs of a Reluctant Traveller* (CRNLE/Wakefield, 1994) and *Diaspora and the Difficult Art of Dying* (University of Otago Press, 2002).   JNT

Mitchell, Adrian (1932–2008) Born in London, of Scottish descent, and studied at the University of Oxford. His most famous poems are 'performance pieces', rather of the kind known by left-wing students in the Thirties as 'agitprop', verse designed to initiate, or support, political action. Free-wheeling, surrealist, rhyming or unrhyming, there is a lot of vitality in these exuberant declarations ('Snow White was in the News of the World—Virgin Lived With Seven Midgets') though some seem simplistic when written down. Equally, some of the pieces are very funny, as well as subversive ('The Eggs O' God' and 'A Leaflet To Be Dropped On China'). Some even, like 'The Oxford Hysteria Of English Poetry', are funny without any political designs on the reader. A good many, with their repetitions and their banging rhythms, are like sophisticated, politically aware pop songs—'Fifteen Million Plastic Bags', warning of nuclear war, is one of the most famous expressions of his pacifism.

Mitchell famously said in the Preface to his debut volume, *Poems* (Cape, 1964), 'Most people ignore most poetry because most poetry ignores most people.' In the last decades of his life, the range of his work received wider recognition. His early poems were selected as *Greatest Hits* (1991) and collected as *Heart on the Left: Collected Poems 1953–1985* (1997). Later volumes include *Blue Coffee: Poems 1986–1995* (1996—all Bloodaxe). Mitchell also worked as a journalist (the first to interview the Beatles), screenwriter, and children's author. His several theatre adaptations of verse plays include an English version of Peter Weiss' *Marat/Sade*.   GE*

Mlinko, Ange (1969–) Born in Philadelphia, Mlinko studied philosophy and mathematics at St John's College in Annapolis, Maryland, and took an MFA at Brown University, where she later taught. She has lived in Morocco, and currently teaches creative writing at the University of Houston. A former editor of the *St Mark's Poetry Project Newsletter and a regular reviewer of poetry for *The Nation*, in 2009 she received the Randall Jarrell Award in Criticism.

*New York School poetry has often been invoked as the milieu of Mlinko's verse, particularly the baroquely associative phrase-making of John *Ashbery. 'On the strength of this I could prise | piccolo jonquils out of April edemas', she writes in the title poem of her third collection, *Shoulder Season* (Coffee House, 2010). An air of self-examination cools the pleasure taken in such colourful discoveries, however, recalling the wariness of modernists such as Wallace *Stevens or Marianne *Moore towards their own verbal fancies. 'Am I really living more fully, am I making relevant discoveries, by continually delving into these dream-like narratives?' Mlinko has asked in a note on her writing. A recent 'cantata' written in homage to the wartime 'ear raids' of British modernist Lynette *Roberts works through these questions in the form of a verse-essay. Her two other collections are *Matinees* (Zoland, 1999) and *Starred Wire* (Coffee House, 2005).   JNT

Mnthali, Felix (1933–) Born of Malawian parents in Shurugwe, Zimbabwe. After education in Lesotho he obtained a PhD in English in Canada. From 1969 he taught at Chancellor College, University of Malawi. A period in detention was ended with an apology from the authorities, but from 1979 he lived in exile, latterly as professor of English at the University of Botswana, until his retirement in 2010, when he returned to Malawi.

Mnthali's Catholic faith is a strong presence in his work: 'Corpus Christi', for instance, is a characteristically direct and sensuous hymn on his release from jail. Mnthali's free-verse rhythms are controlled towards emphatic rather than delicate effects. He deplores without affectation the negative features of Africa's recent history of colonialism and dictatorship, but is equally fervent in affirmation. His verse declaims well—'Antonina', for instance, is a compact, powerful denunciation of repression in Malawi, while 'Ads and the Man,' despite its seemingly flippant title, celebrates the country's natural grandeur on the way to a simple protestation of human love.

Mnthali's substantial collection is *When Sunset Comes to Sapitwa* (Longman, 1982). Adrian Roscoe discusses his work in 'Proceed with Joy: The poetry of Felix Mnthali', *The Month* (Apr. 1992). He has also written a novel, *Yoranivyoto* (Dudu Nsomba, 1998).   ALRC

Mole, John (1941–) Born in Taunton, Somerset, and has taught English, which he studied at Cambridge. He is married to the artist Mary Norman; with Peter *Scupham he ran the Mandeville Press in Hitchin. His first substantial book was *The Love Horse* (Morten, 1974); since then he has published many more, as well as several highly acclaimed collections of poems for children, to the success of which Mary Norman's delightful drawings have contributed greatly. Mole is also a jazz clarinettist, and has been a poet-in-residence in the City of London and at Magdalene College, Cambridge.

Although Mole's concern is with the unpretentious, intelligent portrayal of everyday experience, his poems vary considerably in their degree of earnestness; what is common to all is skilled craftsmanship. He has said that regularity of form does not squeeze out feeling but squeezes it in—a

claim justified by his successes: 'The Birthday', 'Coming Home', or the poems from the series 'Points of Departure'. His children's poems are metrical *tours de force*; finally, the distinction between serious and juvenile is inessential, because he has the gift of writing in the child's terms at a level that also addresses adult experience. Good examples are 'Wasp Talk', which provides the title for one of Mole's best collections *In and Out of the Apple* (Secker & Warburg, 1984), and the haunting, Blake-like 'The Lost Boy', written for the poet's two sons.

Most of Mole's collections from the last two decades were published by Peterloo Poets, including *Counting the Chimes: New and Selected Poems* (2004). See also *The Point of Loss* (Enitharmon, 2011). Some of his *Encounter* poetry reviews were collected as *Passing Judgements: Poetry in the Eighties* (Bristol Classical Press, 1989).   BO'D

Moll, E. G. (Ernest George) (1900–97) Born in Murtoo, Victoria, Australia, and was educated in Australia and at Harvard University. He was professor of English at the University of Oregon, 1928–66, but retained his Australian citizenship, and published nine collections of poetry in Australia between 1927 and 1971. Of these, *Poems 1940–1955* (Angus & Robertson, 1957) represents a combination of his five previous volumes. His rural background, combined with a breadth of education, and a long period of expatriation which was no doubt intensified by occasional return visits to Australia, all brought the poet's sensibilities to bear on recapturing memorable and minute moments of Australian experience. Although Moll was not a member of the *Jindyworobak movement of the 1930s and 1940s, which sought to redefine a European Australian experience in terms of an Aboriginal understanding of the land, his work was included in some of the Jindyworobak anthologies and, in retrospect, is most securely placed in the context of a lyrical celebration of nature in its harshness and beauty. His later volume, *The Rainbow Serpent* (Angus & Robertson, 1962), included an extended sequence for several voices, 'The Lightless Ferry', based on Aboriginal death ceremonies recounted in Sir Baldwin Spencer's *Wanderings in Wild Australia*. The poem is ambitious in scope, but remains uncomfortable in its linking of Aboriginal with Greek mythologies. See also *The View from a Ninetieth Birthday* (La Jolla Poets, 1992).   TWS

Molloy, Dorothy (1942–2004) Born in Ballina, Co. Mayo. Studied languages at University College Dublin, after which she went to live in France and Spain and worked as researcher, journalist, and arts administrator. She was also a successful painter. After a return to Ireland in 1979, she began writing poetry and became a member of the Thornfield Poets Group, based at UCD. Her first collection, *Hare Soup* (2004), was accepted by Faber and Faber, but she died of cancer ten days before its publication. At her death she left enough unpublished work for two further books, which have been assembled by her husband, Professor Andrew Carpenter, also of UCD: *Gethsemane Day* (Faber, 2007) and *Long-distance Swimmer* (Salmon, 2010).

Often likened to Sylvia *Plath's *Ariel*, *Hare Soup* is marked by arresting imagery and fearless description of bodily ordeals: birth, murder, rape, sexual abuse, and death. Humour and technical skill make this more than an ingenious Grand Guignol; internal rhymes, word-play, and skipping rhythms complicate the horror. Line-breaks are jagged, and add their own jolting shocks. Molloy's posthumous volumes are less theatrical, but look with the same fearlessness at the poet's past and her approaching death. A monograph on her work is forthcoming from Dr Luz Mar González-Arias of the University of Oviedo.   GR

Monk, Geraldine (1952–) Born in Blackburn, Lancashire, Monk has always lived in the north of England. In the 1970s she ran Siren Press, self-publishing her first pamphlet, *Scarlet Opening*, in 1974. She currently runs West House Books with her husband, the poet and artist Alan Halsey.

The complexity and fragmentation of Monk's poetry exist in tension with its intricate sound-patterning. In performance,

these elements combine to great effect: Monk frequently collaborates with musicians and is a compelling reader of her work. She often draws on Yorkshire dialect, folk traditions, and playground chants, but her work is also irreverently literary: a recent sequence, 'A Nocturnall Upon S. Lucies Day Being The Shortest Day' is subtitled 'A Collaboration with John Donne'. Place, landscape, and history are important to her work: the title of *Escafeld Hangings* (West House, 2005) refers to the Anglo-Saxon name for Sheffield, and the sequence concerns Mary, Queen of Scots, who was imprisoned in the city. A good introduction to Monk's work is provided by *Selected Poems* (Salt, 2003). More recent collections include *Ghost & Other Sonnets* (Salt, 2008) and *Lobe Scarps & Finials* (Leafe, 2011). *The Salt Companion to Geraldine Monk*, edited by Scott Thurston, appeared in 2007.   PBa

Monro, Harold (1879–1932) Born in Brussels and read modern and medieval languages at Cambridge. He travelled and lived on the continent and studied for the Bar before taking to poetry. He co-founded the Samurai Press then, eventually, settled in London where he became founder editor of the magazines *Poetry Review* (1912), *Poetry and Drama* (1913–14), and the *Monthly Chapbook* later renamed the *Chapbook* (1919–25). In January 1913 he officially opened the Poetry Bookshop in London, at 35 Devonshire Street, Theobalds Road, London, near the British Museum. He arranged regular readings by poets—including W. B. *Yeats, Walter *de la Mare, W. H. *Davies, T. S. *Eliot, Ezra *Pound, Robert *Graves, and dozens more—from their own work. The poets W. W. Gibson, Robert *Frost, T. E. *Hulme, and Wilfred *Owen at various times stayed in the shop's attic rooms. F. S. *Flint rightly called Monro a 'romantic idealist'. He was certainly hospitable and generous in his encouragement of unpublished poets such as the young Wilfred Owen. In 1926 the shop moved to 38 Great Russell Street. Following Monro's death in 1932 after a long illness, his widow Alida Monro struggled to continue, but the shop had been in financial difficulties for some time and she was forced to close in June 1935.

Monro also founded an influential publishing imprint named The Poetry Bookshop, which published books and pamphlets by many contemporary poets such as Frances *Cornford, Eleanor Farjeon, James Elroy *Flecker, and Edward Shanks. Between the years 1912 and 1922 the imprint published each of the five best-selling *Georgian Poetry* anthologies edited by Edward Marsh. The anthologies launched the *Georgian poets (who included W. H. Davies and Walter de la Mare in their number), and were read by a very wide non-specialist audience. Monro also published the first anthology of *Imagist poetry, *Des Imagistes*, in 1914. Monro's taste as editor and publisher was wide yet conservative and, at times, flawed: astonishingly, he rejected T. S. Eliot's 'The Love Song of J. Alfred Prufrock' and the poems of Edward *Thomas when offered to him for publication. (He was later to acknowledge the importance of both poets.) Yet, these major failures apart, he published poems by many writers, such as Ford Madox *Ford (Hueffer), F. S. Flint, Robert Graves, and Charlotte *Mew, whose work was later to achieve prominence.

Better known in his lifetime as an editor and publisher than as a poet, Monro's own poems have been highly praised by T. S. Eliot, who wrote in the critical note to Monro's 1933 *Collected Poems*, 'I think that his poetry, as a whole, is more nearly the real right thing than any of the poetry of a somewhat older generation than mine except Mr Yeats''. Monro's work is serious and varied, but still rather undervalued. He wrote the unironic 'Week-end', in many ways *the* quintessential Georgian poem, on the weekend flight of a commuter from the city to the 'comfortable joys' of his country retreat. He wrote well, too, on modern urban life in 'The Ocean in London' and 'Suburb'. In his day his best-known poem was the much anthologized 'Milk for the Cat', which manages to be simultaneously domestic and unsettling. But his real achievement is to be found in the longer poem sequences on personal isolation such as 'Strange Meetings', 'The

Silent Pool', and 'Bitter Sanctuary' (this last a bleak portrait of a terminal ward), in which his own grim and authentic voice finally breaks through, expressing what Eliot called Monro's sense of the 'ceaseless question and answer of the tortured mind'. Monro's anthology, *Twentieth Century Poetry* (1929), is a modern classic, drawing attention to the best of widely differing types of poetry by both Georgians and modernists. He wrote one critical book, *Some Contemporary Poets* (1920).

See: *Collected Poems of Harold Monro*, ed. Alida Monro with a biographical sketch by F. S. Flint and a critical note by T. S. Eliot (Cobden-Sanderson, 1933) and Harold Monro *Collected Poems*, ed. Alida Monro with a preface by Ruth Tomalin (Duckworth, 1970); Joy Grant, *Harold Monro and the Poetry Bookshop* (Routledge & Kegan Paul, 1967); and Robert H. Ross, *The Georgian Revolt: Rise and Fall of a Poetic Ideal 1910–22* (Faber, 1967).   JDB*

Montague, John (1929–   ) Born into a Catholic family in New York and grew up in Co. Tyrone, and has been an important influence on the work of several younger Irish poets, including Seamus *Heaney. By them he is regarded as something of a pioneer, especially in his acute sense of the cultural and material spoliation inflicted on the Gael, and in his ambitious determination to explore its history and its effects in the present. Much of Montague's childhood, however, was spent in America, and his poetry has clearly been influenced by the *Pound tradition. He has that fear of rhetoric endemic among post-Yeatsian Irish poets: 'Enlarged profile, gun and phrase', as he nicely puts his association of gesturing politics and language. He praises Tim, the first horse he rode, for 'denying | rhetoric' and forcing him to drink from 'the trough of reality'. This aesthetic is summarized in a poem from *A Chosen Light* (MacGibbon & Kee, 1967), 'A Bright Day', where he speaks of 'The only way of saying something | Luminously as possible', which he equates with 'A slow exactness | which recreates experience | By ritualizing its details'. Montague is well able to achieve this effect, combining it with a tough urbanity of stance and diction. Formally, he has increasingly moved towards the use of fluent, run-on lines.

Perhaps his most important early volume—which has been through five editions—is *The Rough Field* (Dolmen, 1972), an ambitious attempt to link the universal and particular in a view of the Northern Irish Troubles. Thus 'The Cave of the Night' gives a dark view of the violence on both sides, moving from legendary pre-Christian Irish child-sacrifice to the bombing of children in a community centre.

Montague has also translated much poetry from the Irish, as can be seen from the *Faber Book of Irish Verse* (1974), which he edited. These translations are very much in the modern tradition, prizing fidelity to meaning over other values, but they are admirable in this kind.

Montague has taught at universities in Ireland, America, and France. In 1998 he became the first Ireland Professor of Poetry, and in 2010 was made a Chevalier de la Légion d'Honneur. Since his *Collected Poems* in 1995, his volumes include *Smashing the Piano* (1999)—dedicated to 'Fierce lyric truth, | Sought since youth'—*Drunken Sailor* (2004), and *Speech Lessons* (2011— all Gallery), which has a central sequence on the poet's family history, 'In My Grandfather's Mansion'. His poetry is published in the United States by Wake Forest University Press. His fiction, including an erotic novella, *The Lost Notebook* (1987), has been collected in *A Ball of Fire* (Liberties, 2009). He has also published a translation of the contemporary French poet Guillevic (*Carnac* (Bloodaxe, 1999)), two collections of essays—*The Figure in the Cave* (Syracuse University Press, 1989) and *Born in Brooklyn* (White Pines, 1991)—and two volumes of autobiography: *Company* (Duckworth, 2001), and *The Pear is Ripe* (Liberties, 2007). See the John Montague Special Issue of the *Irish University Review* (Spring, 1989) and the festschrift, *Chosen Lights* (2009), ed. Peter Fallon.   ETL

Moolman, Kobus (1964–) Moolman studied English at the University of KwaZulu-Natal in Durban, where he now teaches. Between 1995 and 2007 he edited the journal *Fidelities*. He is also a prize-winning playwright: see *Blind Voices* (Botsotso, 2007).

A spare, elemental poet of the South African landscape, Moolman often strikes a *Beckettian note in his presentation of the lone figure in relation to the world ('Sitting'). His full collections to date are *Time Like Stone* (University of KwaZulu-Natal Press, 2000), *Feet of the Sky* (Brevitas, 2003), which won the Ingrid Jonker Prize, and *Separating the Seas* (University of KwaZulu-Natal Press, 2007). As a member of the Botsotso poetry collective, he was included in the volume *5 Poetry* (Botsotso, 2001) and also the UK anthology *Botsotso* (Reality Street, 2009).   JNT

Moore, Marianne (Craig) (1887–1972) Born in Kirkwood, a suburb of St Louis, Missouri. She was the second child of a father who, failing as an engineer, returned permanently to his parents after a nervous breakdown, and a mother who assumed the burden of bringing up her family. Mrs Moore housekept for her own father, a Scotch-Irish Presbyterian minister, until his death in 1894, after which she moved with her children to Carlisle, Pennsylvania. Marianne attended the Metzger School, where her mother had a teaching job, before entering Bryn Mawr College to study biology. After graduating in 1909, she qualified as a secretary and taught stenography and bookkeeping to US Indians in Carlisle. When, in 1918, her brother became a chaplain in the navy, Marianne and her mother followed him to New York, renting a basement in Greenwich Village before moving in 1929 (for the rest of their lives) to a fifth floor apartment on Cumberland Street in Brooklyn.

The poet's literary career began, in fact, before she moved to New York, when Hilda *Doolittle (H. D.), a former Bryn Mawr classmate, then married to the English imagist Richard *Aldington, published Moore's poem 'To Military Progress' in *The Egoist* in 1915. In May of the same year, Harriet Monroe's *Poetry* (Chicago) published five poems by Marianne Moore, attracting praise from Alfred *Kreymborg and Ezra *Pound, both of whom hastened to patronize her 'flaming red hair', her innocence, and her bold, ladylike particularity. By the time H. D. and Winifred Ellerman ('Bryher') brought out Moore's *Poems* in 1921, her reputation already stood high with the avant-garde. Her second collection, *Observations* (1924) won her the *Dial* Award, and led to Moore's appointment as assistant editor of that magazine; she replaced Scofield Thayer as editor in 1926, a position she held until the *Dial's* demise after July 1929.

During and after the Second World War Marianne Moore's reputation as *the* leading American woman poet steadily increased. In 1935 Macmillan in New York and Faber in London published her *Selected Poems*. She won the Shelley Memorial Award in 1940, the Harriet Monroe Award and Contemporary Poetry's Patron Prize in 1944, a Guggenheim Fellowship in 1945, and a joint grant from the American Academy of Arts and Letters and the National Institute of Arts and Letters in 1946. In 1947 she was elected to the National Institute for Arts and Letters. At least four honorary degrees were bestowed on her by US colleges in the 1950s, and in 1952, following the publication of her *Complete Poems*, she won, in one year, the Bollingen Award, the National Book Award, and the Pulitzer Prize. She went on to win the NIAL Gold Medal for Poetry in 1953, and in 1955 she was elected a member of the American Academy. It seemed that Moore's eccentric, zoological, moralistic, syllabic verses offended no one; moreover, everyone who met her delighted in her company.

To Moore's credit, she remained her unspoiled, decisive self throughout this storm of patronage and honours, producing slender new collections (*Like a Bulwork*, 1956, and O *To Be a Dragon*, 1960), a version of *The Fables of La Fontaine* (1954), and a selection of essays called *Predilections* in 1955. By 1961, when Viking published *A Marianne Moore Reader*, she was already defending herself against rumbling criticism in the literary quarterlies: 'Prose: mine [she wrote] will always be "essays" and verse of mine, observations . . .

Why an inordinate interest in animals and athletes? They are subjects for art and exemplars of it, are they not? minding their own business . . . ', and then, quoting from Charles Ives: '"The fabric of existence weaves itself whole. You cannot set art off in a corner and hope for it to have vitality, reality and substance."'

Moore's achievement remains unique within the modernist movement. To have withstood alike sentimentality and self-indulgence, 'literariness' and philistinism, is to have survived the worst intellectual plagues of the post-Romantic period. As spokeswoman for 'literalists of the imagination' and creator of 'imaginary gardens with real toads in them', she is likely to be long celebrated as the founder of a woman's poetry that bears no stigma either of self-aggrandizement or hysteria.

Some of the most celebrated modern poets have been avowed admirers of Moore's verse, from T. S. *Eliot and W. H. *Auden to John *Ashbery and Paul *Muldoon. Her acute, quizzical voice continues to be influential on contemporary poets such as Eric *Ormsby and Kay *Ryan. Famously commenting that 'omissions are not accidents', her own *Complete Poems* in 1967 left out a large part of her published work. The oeuvre has been restored and augmented by *The Poems of Marianne Moore* (Penguin, 2003), ed. Grace Shulman. See also *The Complete Prose of Marianne Moore* (Penguin, 1986), ed. Patricia C. Willis, and *The Selected Letters of Marianne Moore* (Knopf, 1997), ed. Bonnie Costello. For her biography, see Charles Molesworth, *Marianne Moore: A Literary Life* (Atheneum, 1990), and for criticism and context, see *Marianne Moore: Women and Poet* (National Poetry Foundation, 1991), ed. Patricia C. Willis.   AS*

Moore, Merrill (1903–57) Born at Columbia, Tennessee, son of the state librarian. While qualifying in medicine at Vanderbilt University he became a member of the *Fugitive group of poets, specializing in the sonnet, of which he wrote about half-a-million. However, Moore's sonnets did not always contain 14 lines, and seldom rhymed in the Shakespearian or Petrarchan pattern. No one—least of all himself, perhaps—took his conversational and diagnostic poetry, or his 'Sonnetarium', a room containing 100,000 sonnets written and 'treated' by him, with the utmost seriousness; but, for a poetry that exists in such an enormous quantity (the average was thirty-five sonnets per week), his is seldom feeble or wholly without interest. Professionally, Moore was an expert on alcoholism, and perhaps did most good by treating a few worthy poets for this disease; but William Carlos *Williams thought that he had 'gone through the blinding, stupid formality' of the sonnet, and 'gone after the core' of 'the . . . form, the gist of the whole matter'.

See *The Noise that Time Makes* (1929), *M: One Thousand Autobiographical Sonnets* (1938—both Harcourt), and *Verse Diary of a Psychiatrist* (Contemporary Poetry, 1954).   MS-S

Moore, Nicholas (1918–86) Born in Cambridge, England, the son of the philosopher, G. E. Moore. After leaving school he spent a year at St Andrew's University, where he met the poet G. S. Fraser. In 1937 he went up to Trinity College, Cambridge, where he was a contemporary of Alex Comfort and Hamish Henderson. From 1938 to 1940 he edited *Seven*, a magazine which published work of the writers of the *New Apocalypse movement and also that of Lawrence *Durrell, Henry Miller, and Anais Nin.

Between 1941 and 1945 Moore produced five books of poetry under his own name, one anonymously, and one under a pseudonym (Guy Kelly). In addition, he edited anthologies and pamphlets for the Fortune Press and Editions Poetry London, and from 1949 to 1951 he was an associate editor of *Poetry London*. *The Glass Tower* (1946) brought together his better early poetry. It was followed by *Recollections of the Gala* (1950)—perhaps his best book. After that he turned to horticulture and published little poetry until 1970, when *Resolution and Identity* appeared, followed in 1973 by *Spleen: Thirty-one Versions of Baudelaire's 'Je suis comme le roi'*, a work of Protean verve and humour. Towards the

end of his life he was partially blind from diabetes; but in his last year he wrote the poems in *Lacrimae Rerum: Last Poems* (1988), some of which are among his best.

Moore wrote too much in his early years; but his best poetry is fluent, perceptive and witty, and owes more to *Auden than to the Apocalypse poets with whom he was associated. He was interested in jazz and popular song and attempted to integrate some of their effects into his poetry. He may be sampled in *Longings of the Acrobats: Selected Poems* (Carcanet, 1990), which has an afterword by Peter *Riley.   ATT

Moraes, Dom (1938–2004) Born in Bombay (now Mumbai) of Goan and Indian Roman Catholic parents. His father was a famous journalist and man of letters whom he accompanied on his travels abroad. When Moraes was seven his mother became mentally ill and had to be institutionalized. Lonely, often uprooted, brought up around books, Moraes early became interested in poetry. His youth is recalled in *My Son's Father: A Poet's Autobiography* (1968).

He went to England in 1954. While still a student at Jesus College, Oxford, he was awarded the Hawthornden Prize for *A Beginning* (1957). He was its youngest recipient. His sensitivity towards language, rhythm, and sound, use of traditional verse forms, the dreaminess and romantic diction (products of a bookish youth and reading of Spenser, Keats, and Verlaine), made him appear the successor of his friends David *Gascoyne, W. S. *Graham, and George *Barker. Famous, handsome, witty, exotic, he was for a time the darling of London's artistic circles. A love affair with a famous actress is the subject of the Cavalier lyrics in *Poems* (1960) and the verse included in *Gone Away* (1960), a maliciously witty travel-book about India. *John Nobody* (1965) alludes, in a more plain, *Audenesque style, to the pains of exile, failed love, and time wasted. He became aware of political issues, especially human rights. *Beldam* (1966) introduces fantasy, surreal perspectives, unappealing personae, the grotesque, and obliqueness.

Moraes supported himself as an international journalist and editor, eventually settling uneasily in India where he married the actress Leela Naidu. The privately published *Absences* (1983) was followed by a renewal of creativity in his *Collected Poems: 1957–87* (1987) and *Serendip* (1990). He became a more difficult poet, disillusioned, worldly wise, masking his emotions and reflections in elliptical, highly crafted dramatic monologues. There is extreme loneliness—an emotional world centred on Leela, himself, and his past—as if he were in unending exile. Multi-layered, at times hermetical, conscious of death, sometimes overwrought, the later poems are concerned with the pains, fears, and art that have gone into their making. In 1994, he published another volume of autobiography, *Never at Home* (1994—all Penguin). Moraes' later books were published in India, with the exception of *In Cinnamon Shade: New and Selected Poems* (Carcanet, 2001). A second *Collected Poems 1954-2004* appeared the year that he died. See also the partly autobiographical travel book, written with Sarayu Srivatsa, *The Long Strider: How Thomas Coryate Walked from England to India in the Year 1613* (Penguin, 2003).

A new *Selected Poems*, edited by Ranjit *Hoskote, appeared from Penguin India in 2012. See also *Three Indian Poets: Ezekiel, Ramanujan and Moraes*, ed. Bruce King (Oxford University Press, 1991; 2nd edn., 2008). BK

Morgan, Edwin (1920–2010) Born in Glasgow. Military service in the Royal Army Medical Corps (1940–6) interrupted Morgan's university education, which he completed 1946–7. From then until 1980 he taught in the English department of the University of Glasgow, retiring as titular professor. As professor emeritus, he retained his connection with the university of his native city.

Against the background of an academic career, and for three decades afterwards, Morgan produced a venturesome poetry. Often experimental, it is also defined at times by traditional forms such as the sonnet, which he used with studied, virtuosic enthusiasm. His versification is often a form of serious play. Even an early poem in couplets, 'The Vision of Cathkin Braes' (1952), has a pronounced ludic element which he sustained with one or another kind of high-spiritedness. Comedy is a noticeable part of his poetic temperament. So, too, is a self-aware employment of literary artifice, evident in the early work but emphasized in *Glasgow Sonnets* (1972), 'New Year Sonnets', *Sonnets from Scotland* (1984), and 'Byron at Sixty-five'. It would therefore be unwise to detach the skills of his formal verse from the ingenuity and word-play of the several experimental modes which he also used. 'Canedolia', 'First Men on Mercury', 'Shaker Shaken', and 'The Computer's First Dialect Poems', for example, could hardly be possible without an inventive, deliberated philology which, when identified with the self-conscious, manipulative versification of his sonnets, reveal Morgan as a poet of finely calculated risks, at least much of the time.

In the 1960s Morgan's talent began to pull together the various interests, concerns, and styles of which it is composed. As well as concrete and science-fiction poetry, he wrote a substantial body of free-verse poems set in Glasgow. 'King Billy', 'In the Snack Bar', 'Glasgow Green', and others virtually added a new place to the map of modern poetry. Significantly, the book was called *The Second Life* (1968). It announced the arrival of a writer known until then chiefly through small-press publications, magazine appearances, and translations (especially his *Beowulf*, 1952; repr. Carcanet, 2002). Many collections followed, often in small-press editions first, as well as translations (*Rites of Passage*, 1976), sometimes into *Scots (e.g. Mayakovsky, *Wi the Haill Voice*, 1972), essays and reviews (*Essays*, 1974; *Crossing the Border*, 1990), libretti, and considerable editorial work. He is among the finest verse translators of his time, and was the most consistently interesting critic of new Scottish writing.

Edwin Morgan received the Queen's Gold Medal for Poetry in 2000, and in 2004 was appointed as the first Scots Makar, having been first Poet Laureate of Glasgow in 1999. *Collected Poems* (1990; new edn. 1996) and *Collected Translations* (1996) were followed by *A. D.*, a 'trilogy of plays on the life of Jesus' (2000), *Cathures* (2002), *The Play of Gilgamesh* (2005), a translation of the Sumerian epic, and *A Book of Lives* (2007—all Carcanet), which includes his poem for the opening of the Scottish Parliament in 2004. See also *Love and a Life* (2003) and *Dreams and Other Nightmares: New and Uncollected Poems 1954–2009* (2010—both Mariscat). As well as critical essays about his work, there is a bibliography in R. Crawford and H. Whyte (eds.), *About Edwin Morgan* (Edinburgh University Press, 1990). Interviews, articles, lectures, etc. are collected in H. Whyte (ed.), *Nothing Not Giving Messages* (Polygon, 1990), in which Morgan first spoke publically about his homosexuality. See also Colin Nicholson, *Edwin Morgan: Inventions of Modernity* (Manchester University Press, 2002), the first full-length study of his work, and James McGonigal, *Beyond the Last Dragon: A Life of Edwin Morgan* (Sandstone, 2010), the first biography.   DED*

Morgan, Esther (1970–   ) Born in Kidderminster, Morgan studied English literature at Cambridge University, and creative writing at the University of East Anglia, where she was taught by Andrew *Motion. In 1998 she received an Eric Gregory Award. She works as a creative-writing tutor and is Historic Recordings Manager at the Poetry Archive. *Beyond Calling Distance* (2001) won the Aldeburgh Poetry Festival First Collection Prize. Morgan is a poet of delicate domestic perceptions and still-life histories, who sees the 'patina of burnt lace' on a milk pan and 'plates scraped clean | of painted flowers' ('After Life'). Her second collection, *The Silence Living in Houses* (2005), reflects time spent as the caretaker of an unrenovated Edwardian house. *Grace* (2011—all Bloodaxe) was shortlisted for the T. S. Eliot Prize.   JNT

Morgan, (George) Frederick (1922–2004) Born in New York City, the only child of well-to-do parents. Attending private schools, he had a sheltered childhood and spent much time alone reading. His father, a soap manufacturer, had enrolled him at birth in Princeton where the young Morgan began studying in 1939. At Prince-

ton he met the newly-arrived instructor, Allen *Tate, who proved a decisive influence in shaping Morgan's literary interests. Graduating in 1943, Morgan served in the US Army's Tank Destroyer Corps. In 1947 he co-founded the *Hudson Review*, which quickly became one of the most influential American literary quarterlies. Early issues of *Hudson Review* featured Ezra *Pound and Wallace *Stevens; later on, poets such as A. R. *Ammons, W. S. *Merwin, Louis *Simpson, Anne *Sexton, and William *Stafford appeared first—or early in their careers—in the magazine. In one of his infrequent editorials, Morgan once alluded to forces in society 'that would pervert art and stifle responsible criticism'. Thus it was all the more necessary 'for an independent literary review to exercise its lonely prerogatives: of remaining accessible to the new and unexpected, of joining no coterie . . . and of maintaining the cleansing function of criticism as the revealer and scourge of fraud'.

He published a few early poems, but gradually abandoned verse for editorial responsibilities. Then in 1968 the suicide of his son, John, shocked Morgan back into poetry. His first collection, *A Book of Changes* (1972), published when the author was 50, met with wide approval. But it was not until *Poems of the Two Worlds* (1977), *Death Mother* (1979), and *Northbook* (1982) that critics realized the scope and originality of his poetic talent.

While most members of his generation developed an understated *confessional style, Morgan's poetry is bold, rhetorical, and philosophical. He also worked in a range of prosodic forms, from fixed stanzas to free verse. Unafraid of grand themes, he writes unabashedly about love, death, redemption, and despair, but while his poetry frequently contains autobiographical elements, it always strives for universal significance. His reach occasionally exceeds his grasp, but his most characteristic work—like the ambitious sequences 'Orpheus to Eurydice' and 'Northbook'—effectively combines classical clarity with direct emotionalism. With each new volume the religious character of his work grew more apparent. Free of any denominational allegiances, his poetry—like that of Lucretius and Blake, two of his models—seeks to explore primary existential questions.

Poems: New and Selected (University of Illinois Press, 1987) remains the most complete collection of his work. Peter Brazeau's 'Interview with Frederick Morgan', *New England Review* (Spring 1979) is a useful source of biographical information. *Poems for Paula* (1995) was a widely-admired collection of his love poems to his wife and *Hudson Review* co-editor, Paula Dietz. Morgan's last volume was *The One Abiding* (2003—both Story Line).   DG/WHP*

Morgan, Robert (1944–) Grew up in a small town in the Blue Ridge Mountains of North Carolina. He attended the University of North Carolina at both Chapel Hill and Greensboro, where he studied with the poet Fred *Chappell. After working as a salesman, house-painter, and farmer, he joined the faculty of Cornell University, where he is Kappa Alpha Professor of English.

Both descriptively and musically, Morgan's poetry is wonderfully tactile; his writing has the consonantal roughness and density of Hopkins, a quality which makes it seem to partake of the natural textures it evokes. His poems form an extended portrait of the region in which he grew up, its ways of life, its dedication to labour and the earth. Despite this deliberate restriction of subject-matter, Morgan is able to move effortlessly when he wants to from particular events and objects to the universals they embody. The real strength and originality of his work, however, comes from his refusal to universalize too quickly or too often; from his insistence on the value of story-telling for its own sake, and on the virtues of simple, physical experience untethered to abstractions. It is perhaps not surprising, then, that he has turned increasingly to the short story as a medium, while continuing to produce his concrete, strongly crafted poems as well. See *The Balm of the Gilead Tree: New and Selected Stories* (Gnomon, 1999). He is also now well-known as a novelist: *Gap Creek* (Alonquin, 1999) was a *New York Times* bestseller. *Green River: New and Selected Poems*

(University of New England Press, 1991) has now been superseded by *The Strange Attractor: New and Selected Poems* (Louisiana State University Press, 2004).   RG

Moritz, A. F. (Albert Frank) (1947–) Born in Ohio, Moritz studied at Marquette University in Wisconsin. In 1974 he moved to Toronto, and is now a Canadian citizen. He has worked in journalism, publishing, and advertising, and currently teaches at Victoria College at the University of Toronto. He has also published translations and non-fiction, and has been the recipient of a Guggenheim Fellowship.

The measured, *Ashberian music and darkly classical surrealism of Moritz's early poetry was an American volume undoubtedly serious in its intention to enter 'the tradition' (as he titled from 1986). Poetry here is a vehicle of *Eliotic prophecy against the inhumanities of an industrialized world: see *Rest on the Flight to Egypt* (Brick, 1999). More recently he has written that the hardest vision is 'the sense that life, with all its good and bad, taken together is somehow good, not bad, not neutral', and his later verse also celebrates "infinite erotic civilization" in its unwinding descriptions of decline. *Early Poems* (Insomniac, 2002) reprints his first four volumes, from *Here* (1975) to *The Visitation* (1983). *The Sentinel* (2008) won the 2009 Griffin Poetry Prize. See also *Night Street Repairs* (2004) and *The New Measures* (2012—all Anansi).   JNT

Morley, David (1964–) Born in Lancashire, Morley studied zoology at Bristol University, where he was also taught by Charles *Tomlinson. In 1996 he co-founded the writing programme at the University of Warwick, and has been a professor there since 2007.

After university, Morley conducted research on acid rain, and met Simon *Armitage in a poetry-writing group run by Peter Sansom. In 1993, he co-edited *The New Poetry* (Bloodaxe), an influential anthology. He also edited the British and Irish poetry list for Arc, his first publisher: see *Releasing Stone* (1989) and *Mandelstam Variations* (1991).

Morley's *Scientific Papers* (2002) contains poems written over the course of the next decade. Its declared ambition is to combine 'the practice of writing science and poetry [as] a single discussion of perception'. *The Invisible Kings* (2007) foregrounded the poet's part-Romany heritage in a macaronic narrative sequence, 'Kings'. *Enchantment* (2010—all Carcanet) concluded this ambitious, Les *Murray-esque trilogy of intertwined histories and landscapes.

Pedagogy, ecology, and public art are important aspects of Morley's work. He has placed poems in natural settings, edited an anthology of new writing for the National Health Service in Britain, and recorded popular creative-writing podcasts. He has also written *The Cambridge Introduction to Creative Writing* (Cambridge University Press, 2007). JNT

Morris, John N. (John Nelson Morris) (1931–97) Educated at the Augusta Military Academy, Hamilton College, and Columbia University. He was the recipient of a Guggenheim Fellowship and an Award in Letters from the Academy and Institute of Arts and Letters, and taught eighteenth-century literature at Washington University in St Louis. He published four volumes of poetry—*Green Business* (1970), *The Life Beside This One* (1975), *The Glass Houses* (1980), and *A Schedule of Benefits* (1987—all Atheneum).

Morris' scholarly study *Versions of the Self: Studies in English Autobiography* (Basic, 1966) seems to have provided an inspiration for his poetry, which explores the same issues of consciousness, memory, and the relationship between the subjective 'I' and the outside world that are characteristic concerns of the eighteenth-century writers whom he analyses and admires. The title-poem of *The Life Beside This One* is indicative as a poem of loss and disappointment, written in a style of low-strung emotional intensity reminiscent of Philip *Larkin. Morris' subject-matter is often redolent of a cloistered life spent amongst books, but particularly in *A Schedule of Benefits* he also shows himself absorbed in the quest to make sense of his own family history and, through it, the history of America. His wilfully short lines sometimes result in a rigidity of form and tone, but his honest,

straightforward poetry is always personal, if not intense. See the posthumous *Selected Poems* and *Then: Essays in Reconstruction*, an unfinished memoir (both Washington University, 2002). IES

Morris, Mervyn (1937–) Born in Kingston, Jamaica. He was educated at Munro College, the University College of the West Indies, and, as a Rhodes Scholar, at St Edmund Hall, Oxford. Based in the department of English at the Mona campus of the University of the West Indies, he is emeritus professor in West Indian Literature and Creative Writing. In his day he was also a tennis player of international standing.

He is a supreme ironist, eschewing direct statement and political rhetoric in favour of poetry that yields its full meaning only after repeated reading. He also believes that poetry imposes on the poet a logic of its own, which he must follow wherever it leads. As he put it: 'In talking to people who are trying to write, I tend to stress that respect for the original impulse can be an obstacle if it prevents the "author" from seeing what the poem wants to be.' This, and other observations on the craft of poetry, are to be found in Morris' introduction to a selection of his poems in *Hinterland: Caribbean Poetry from the West Indies and Britain*, ed. E. A. Markham (Bloodaxe, 1989). 'Stripper' wittily sums up his views about poetry as a process of revelation, for both poet and reader.

Fierce irony pervades poems like 'Literary Evening, Jamaica', which attacks both militant political posturing and the poems of Philip *Larkin; 'The Early Rebels', about the corruption of political idealism; and 'The House Slave', a comment on compromise. A great admirer of Louise *Bennett, he too shows a mastery of vernacular and dialect. 'Valley Prince' is in vernacular mode, a powerful elegy on a trombone player, and is full of pent-up, explosive energy. Collections include *The Pond* (1973), *Shadowboxing* (1979), and *Examination Centre* (1992—all New Beacon). See *I been there, sort of: New and Selected Poems* (Carcanet, 2006). In 2009 Mervyn Morris received the Jamaican Order of Merit. MR

Morrison, Blake (1950–) Born in Yorkshire and graduated from Nottingham University. He worked in London as a literary editor and is now Professor of Creative and Life Writing at Goldsmiths College. His first book, *The Movement: English Poetry and Fiction of the 1950s* (Oxford University Press, 1980) was a detailed critical history of the trends in the new writing of that decade associated with Philip *Larkin, Kingsley *Amis, Thom *Gunn, Elizabeth *Jennings, and others. Introducing a first volume of his own poems, *Dark Glasses* (1984, reissued with additional work in 1989), Morrison stated his belief that poetry 'must always be a contemplation or unravelling of mysteries'. One half of the book is a single long poem, 'The Inquisitor', which takes as its themes 'secrecy and trust' and employs cryptically handled material relating to the Falklands War, the early life of Lech Walesa, and the death of the Italian banker Roberto Calvi. The shorter poems are usually brief, enigmatic narratives, some suggesting personal memories ('Grange Boy', 'Metamorphoses of Childhood') or aspects of his domestic life in the present ('Pine', 'A Child in Winter'). The title-poem of his second book, *The Ballad of the Yorkshire Ripper* (1987—both Chatto & Windus) is a monologue, in quatrains, in the accents of the notorious murderer. Like other, more oblique poems, on subjects like environmental pollution and the nuclear threat ('On Sizewell Beach', 'Havens'), it implicitly opposes a concerned humanist decency and responsibility to the forces of cruelty and waste. Morrison has also edited, with Andrew *Motion, the *Penguin Book of Contemporary British Poetry* (1982) and published a study of *Seamus Heaney* (Methuen, 1982). He has since written non-fiction, including the memoir *And When Did You Last See Your Father?* (1993), and three novels. See *Selected Poems* (1999—both Granta). AB

Morrissey, Sinéad (1972–) Morrissey was born in Portadown and read English and German at Trinity College, Dublin. She currently teaches Creative Writing at Queen's University, Belfast.

Morrissey won an Eric Gregory Award for the manuscript of her first collection, *There Was a Fire in Vancouver* (1996). Her second collection, *Between Here and There* (2002), is divided between poems set in Ireland and Japan, where she lived and taught for two years. *The State of the Prisons* (2005) uses historical personae to great effect, particularly in the title sequence, which is spoken by John Howard, the eighteenth-century prison reformer. *Through the Square Window* (2009—all Carcanet) is concerned with the anxieties and discoveries attendant on the birth and early infancy of her son. Morrissey is equally at home using traditional forms, free verse, or inventing her own formal challenges. Her work is characterized by its daring use of the extended line.

At the age of eighteen Morrissey received the Patrick Kavanagh award. She has also won the Rupert and Eithne Strong Award, and the Michael Hartnett Poetry Award. Her three most recent books were shortlisted for the T. S. Eliot Prize, and in 2007 she received a Lannan Literary Fellowship.   PBa

Moss, Howard (1922–87) Born in New York City, the only son of a prosperous importer and manufacturer. He was a sickly infant, and for his health Moss' parents moved to nearby Rockaway Beach, Long Island, where he spent his childhood and adolescence. He entered the University of Michigan but was expelled after one year for participating in a dormitory workers' labour protest. Upon graduating from the University of Wisconsin in 1943 he worked for the War Information Office. After the war he took various editorial jobs and taught one year at Vassar College before joining *The New Yorker* as a fiction editor in 1948. Two years later he became the magazine's first full-time poetry editor, a position he held for nearly four decades until his death.

Before Moss' tenure, *The New Yorker* was not a prestigious venue for poetry and was best known for light verse. Under his discriminating leadership it became an important showcase for new poetry in America. As an editor, Moss often published sophisticated, polished, intellectually demanding poetry, but his taste was remarkably diverse. He championed many poets early in their careers and helped establish the reputations of *Roethke, *Bishop, *Sexton, *Plath, *Strand, *Dickey, *Merrill, *Kinnell, *Ashbery, *Merwin, *Justice, *Clampitt, and others.

Moss' fame as an editor often obscured his substantial achievements as a poet. Maturing early, he wrote prolifically, and his published poetry spans forty years and twelve major collections. His early work—influenced by *Auden, *Yeats, and *Stevens—was tight, formal, and lucid, but it did not share the ironic intellectuality or emotional detachment that characterized the verse of his 1950s contemporaries like *Nemerov or *Hecht. Moss' best early poems, like 'Burning Love Letters' or 'Elegy for My Father', frequently talked about love and loss in colloquial but musically precise language. Moss later experimented with free verse, often writing compressed psychological narratives, but the lyric and elegy remained his most characteristic forms. Moss' first *Selected Poems* (Atheneum, 1972) won the National Book Award.

In addition to his poetry, Moss was a diversely talented man of letters. He wrote two plays, *The Folding Green* (for the Cambridge, Mass., Poet's Theatre in 1958) and *The Palace at 4 a.m.* (1964). He collaborated with the artist Edward Gorey on *Instant Lives* (1974), a sophisticated literary satire. He edited several anthologies, most notably *New York: Poems* (1980) which celebrated his native city. He was also an active critic, but because of his influential position at *The New Yorker*, he eventually refused to review the work of living poets (a rule he broke each time Elizabeth Bishop published a new volume). His best criticism is collected in *Minor Monuments: Selected Essays* (Ecco, 1986). *New Selected Poems* (Atheneum, 1985) remains the definitive collection of his verse.   DG

Motion, Sir Andrew (1952–) Born in London and educated at Radley College. He attended University College, Oxford, where he won the Newdigate Prize, and in 1975 he received an Eric Gregory Award. In the 1980s he was editor of *Poetry Review* and poetry editor at Chatto and Windus. He has since been a professor of creative writing at the universities of East Anglia and Royal Holloway, London.

Motion's first full collection, *The Pleasure Steamers* (Carcanet, 1978) was greeted with critical acclaim. It exhibits all of his mannerisms in a forceful, concentrated form: an elusive metre, which cannot conceal the ghost of the iamb; a reticent but memorable phrasing; a plangency deriving partly from the attitude of the narrator, partly from a melancholy subject-matter. It is clear that he has learnt from two poets he much admires, Edward *Thomas and Philip *Larkin (he has written studies of both and was Larkin's authorized biographer); but he has refined the quietness of the former, and substituted sadness for the despair of the latter. He does not share the taste for rhyme of either. Nor is he as constantly observant as they, choosing his moment for precise perceptions.

Despite its similarity to a conventional collection of short lyrics, *The Pleasure Steamers* was already striking out in a direction Motion was to pursue in subsequent collections: towards narrative writing, with the use of a narrator. This is particularly clear in the sequence called 'Inland', which conveys moments in the story of a fenland village whose livelihood is threatened equally by flooding and enclosures. In *Independence* (1981) Motion evokes the atmosphere of the twilight of the Raj while telling the story of a brief marriage curtailed by the death in childbirth of the narrator's young bride. *Secret Narratives* (1983—both Salamander), is, as the title suggests, more mysterious, in the sense that though the short poems it contains tell stories through the medium of a narrator, the general context remains unclear.

Love in a Life (Faber, 1991), shows a new simplicity and directness of language, along with an exactness that is sometimes startling. Although an interest in narrative fragments is still present, the reader is given more clues as to how to put these together, though never in such a way as to encourage faith in a complete, objective story. His subsequent collections, including *Selected Poems* (1998), have all been published by Faber and Faber.

In 1999, Motion succeeded Ted *Hughes as Poet Laureate of Great Britain. Previously a life honour, his was the first appointment to be fixed for a period of ten years. *Public Property* (2003) included commissions for the Salvation Army and the Trades Union Congress, but, unlike Hughes, Motion has not collected his poems on royal occasions. In 2009, the year of his knighthood, he spoke of the inhibiting effect of the post on his own poetry, an experience reflected by the slightness of *The Cinder Path* (2009). Motion nevertheless managed to redefine the laureateship as a platform for social commentary. *Laurels and Donkeys* (Clutag, 2010) is a short sequence on modern warfare, a recurrent theme. He has also written biographies and novels, including one of each about John Keats: *Keats* (1997) and *The Invention of Dr. Cake* (2003). See also the title poem of *Salt Water* (1997—all Faber). ETL*

Mouré, Erin (1955–) Born and raised in Calgary, moving to Vancouver in 1974, where she worked for the Canadian National Railway and then for VIA Rail. In 1984 she moved to Montreal, where she has worked as a freelance editor, translator, teacher, and communications specialist.

Beginning with *Empire, York Street* (1979), Mouré has drawn on ordinary communal and individual experience—working lives in Canada, sexuality and the politics of relationships, the allure of alcohol, the transformations within families over time—but has increasingly reflected on the powers of language to create reality. 'The Acts', the final section of *Furious* (1988—both Anansi), Mouré's fifth book, is a sequence of prose poems about the ways in which the surfaces and the depths of language create our forms of thought. Mouré proposes that language actively structures reality, rather than simply reflecting or referring to it. In her most recent writing, these thoughts on language have developed in conjunction with a more sustained focusing on the experience of women—their apprehension of language and power in relation to their own bodies and voices, and their experience of male versions and embodiments of language and power. See her correspondence with Bronwen *Wallace, *Two Women Talking* (Feminist Caucus of the League of Canadian Poets, 1993).

Mouré's collections since *The Green Word: Selected Poems 1973–1992* (Oxford University Press) include the trilogy *Search Procedures* (1996), *A Frame of the Book* (1999), and *O Cidadán* (2002), *Little Theatres* (2005), which won the A. M. Klein Prize for Poetry, *O Cadoiro* (2007), *O Resplandor* (2010), and the deliberately miswritten *The Unmemntioable* (2012—all Anansi). She has translated the work of the Galician poet Chus Pato and the French Canadian Nicole Brossard. NB

Moxley, Jennifer (1964–) Born in San Diego, California, Moxley now lives and works in Maine, teaching poetry and poetics at the University of Maine.

She is author of *Imagination Verses* (Tender Buttons, 1996) and *The Sense Record* (Edge, 2002)—both published in the UK by Salt in 2003; *Often Capital* (Flood, 2005); *The Line* (Post-Apollo, 2007); *The Middle Room* (Subpress, 2008); *Clampdown* (Flood, 2009), and several chapbooks. She has translated a book of essays and one of poems by the French poet and scholar Jacqueline Risset and poetry by Anne Portugal. Moxley founded and edited *The Impercipient* magazine in Providence (1992–5) and, following this, *The Impercipient Lecture Series* with her long-term partner, Steve Evans. She has also been poetry editor for *The Baffler* and *The Poker* magazines.

Moxley's oeuvre displays a quite unusual stylistic variety, from traditional forms such as sonnets, ballads, and villanelles, occasionally (and unusually amongst experimental writers) using end-rhyme, as well as prose poetry and even narrative. Communication is obviously important to this writer. Indeed, a cool, *New York School-esque lyricism sometimes masks the poetry's rather weightier and more anxious subject matter, much of which is about Moxley's life, or writing *per se*, but almost always politically and philosophically charged. Alice *Notley has described *The Line* as embodying 'the search for the line of time and the poet's immortality'.   ECr

Mtshali, Oswald (Joseph) Mbuyiseni (1940–) Born at Vryheid, in rural Natal, coming to Johannesburg only after completing his schooling. Unable to gain entry to Witwatersrand University, and unwilling to attend a 'tribal college', he chose to work as a messenger. He later studied at Columbia University in New York. His first collection of poems, *Sounds of a Cowhide Drum*, published in Johannesburg by Lionel *Abraham's Renoster Books in 1971, with a preface by Nadine Gordimer, sold 16,000 copies within a year, and remains his most popular collection. It was reprinted by Oxford University Press in 1972. During and after the Soweto uprising of 1976, Mtshali aligned himself increasingly with the Black Consciousness movement, and his second collection, *Fireflames* (Shuter & Shooter, 1980), was banned by the authorities. He later worked as a journalist, the vice-principal of a Soweto school (see *Give Us A Break*, Skotaville, 1988), and as an adjunct professor at New York City College of Technology. He writes both in Zulu and English.

Mtshali's poems give a vivid picture of urban South Africa. His spontaneous-sounding free verse evokes the frustrations of migrant workers, the humiliations of the pass laws, and the violence of Soweto shebeens. Unlike his fellow 'township poets', *Sepamla and *Serote, he has strong roots in rural tradition, contrasting its human warmth with the brittle stylishness of city life. Mtshali argued that his message was too urgent to be lost in ornate and lofty poetry, and objected that white people who claimed to 'enjoy' his poems were in fact enjoying his suffering. His style is marked by simple alliterations, straightforward syntax, and a mixed, everyday vocabulary. His images are instantaneously amusing or shocking: the sun setting like a coin falling into a parking-meter slot, a convict's head shaved smooth as a potato, dogs fighting over a dead baby on a rubbish heap.   JB

Mudie, Ian (Mayelston) (1911–76) Born in Hawthorn, South Australia, and spent most of his life in that state working as a freelance writer, editor, and lecturer. Influenced by the *Jindyworobak movement, Mudie's early poetry contains many references to Aborigines and their beliefs, as well as a deep concern for the changes wrought on the Australian landscape and its inhabitants by European migration. Mudie was a passionate nationalist, and expressed in his poetry a vision of a potent future for Australia and its recent immigrants, but an equal distaste for the shallowness of contemporary life. His best-known poems celebrate the myth of the pioneer and the bushman, and use the vernacular freely. He wrote for a wide audience and out of a conviction that in bush life there were traditional Australian values which could be transplanted into the city. His style could be both prosaically colloquial and rhetorically ambitious. He was at his best describing landscapes and suburban living, and at his most approachable in articulating the 'bush mystique' of the mid-twentieth century. He published six books of poetry between 1940 and 1970, and a selection, containing previously uncollected poems, *Selected Poems 1934–1976* (Nelson, 1976), appeared in the year of his death in London.   JCr

Mudrooroo See JOHNSON, COLIN.

Muhammad, Haji Salleh (1942–) One of Malaysia's foremost poets. In 1991 he won the highest literary honour in Malaysia, the Anugerah Sastera Negara (National Literature Award).

He began to write poetry in both English and Malay when he was undergoing teacher-training in England during the early 1960s. The poems of his apprenticeship show the fructifying influence of English poetry, and his later work evinces an intellectual quality not seen in conventional Malay poetry. He read English in the University of Singapore under D. J. *Enright, and also studied at the universities of

Malaya and Michigan. His published thesis, *Tradition and Change in Contemporary Malay-Indonesian Poetry* (1977), is perhaps the best book on the subject.

Although Muhammad's last collection in English was in 1979 he continues to be an active verse translator. *Time and Its People*, published in Kuala Lumpur (Heinemann, 1978) is the only volume of his poetry to have been originally written in English. *The Travel Journals of Si Tenggang II* (1979) and *Rowing Down Two Rivers* (2000) are his own selections and translations from many volumes written in Malay.   LCS

Muir, Edwin (1887–1959) Poet and translator, was born on his father's rented farm on Deerness, Orkney; two years later the family moved to the neighbouring island of Wyre. His peaceful childhood gained symbolic significance through contrast with his youth in Glasgow, where the family moved in 1901, and where Muir had jobs in offices, in a beer-bottling factory, and in a factory at Fairport for reducing bones to charcoal. The sequence of personal tragedies that blighted his time in the city (both parents and two brothers dying within two years) and his horror at its slum life are recorded in *An Autobiography* (1954). In this environment Muir turned successively to evangelicalism, socialism, and the philosophy of Nietzsche, none of which could heal his injured psyche, and began to write essays and reviews for journals.

In 1919 he married Willa Anderson, setting up home in Bloomsbury and working as A. R. Orage's assistant on *The New Age*. It was at this time that he underwent psychoanalysis involving the recording of his dreams, with important consequences for his writing: he describes how his analyst warned him that his unconscious 'was far too near the surface for comfort and safety, and that I should hurry to put something soundly substantial between me and it'.

In 1921 the Muirs left for Europe. It was in Dresden that Muir began to write poetry, at the age of 35, 'too old', as he put it, 'to submit to contemporary influences'. *First Poems* was published in 1925, the year in which the Muirs began their collaborative translations from German (most notably of

Kafka). After the Second World War, Muir held British Council posts in Prague and in Rome, where he became a practising Christian. He gave the 1955–6 Norton Lectures at Harvard on 'The Estate of Poetry', which allowed him to buy the Cambridgeshire cottage where he spent his last years.

Form, for Muir, was simply inherited; he set out, he observed, with 'the rhythms of English poetry on the one hand, the images in my mind on the other'. (To those English rhythms may be added the ballads he heard in his childhood—his early poems include ballads in Scots—which contributed to his instinct for narrative.) Michael Roberts excluded him from his *Faber Book of Modern Verse* on the grounds of unquestioningly traditional technique. Similarly, very little in Muir's language or imagery would seem out of place in, say, Tennyson's 'Ulysses'; he relies on a narrow stock of archetypal properties: the road, the stronghold, the labyrinth. His characters undergo psychological and political tests and traumas, often transplanted from Muir's own dreams but (despite his admiration for Wordsworth) invariably mythologized: Odysseus, Oedipus, Orpheus, Achilles, and Prometheus are among his agents. Poems are titled plainly—'The Voyage', 'The Escape', and 'The Journey Back', and are unafraid to recall literary precursors on the road: one sonnet tells how Milton 'to the dark tower came', though the horror he confronts there is distinctly Glaswegian ('the steely clamour known too well | On Saturday nights in every street in Hell'). The same sonnet uses the word 'Paradise' four times, suggesting how obsessively Muir returned to the myth of Eden and the Fall that his own early life had enacted.

Most readers of Muir's stately *Collected Poems* will feel a want of variety that a greater realism would have supplied, and regret that the heraldic atmosphere is not more often relieved by the personal tone of which Muir was a diffident master: see the elegy 'For Ann Scott-Moncrieff', the lyric sweetness of 'The Bird' and 'A Birthday', and the discursive ease of 'Reading in Wartime'. Instead, he will likeliest be remembered for the series of poems inventing atomic aftermaths: 'The Horses', 'The Shortage', and others, in which his patient pessimism is most dramatically universalized.

The best book about Muir is his *Autobiography* (1954); see also P. H. Butter, *Edwin Muir: Man and Poet* (Oliver & Boyd, 1966) and Willa Muir, *Belonging: A Memoir* (Hogarth, 1968). *The Collected Poems*, ed. W. Muir and J. C. Hall (Faber, 1960 and 1963, new edn. 1984), omits much early work, which was restored in 1991 by *The Complete Poems*, ed. Peter Butter (Association for Scottish Literary Studies). In 2008, Mick *Imlah made a new selection of Muir's poems for Faber and Faber. See also *Edwin Muir: Centenary Assessments*, ed. C. T. H. MacLachlan and D. S. Robb (Association for Scottish Literary Studies, 1990).   MI

Muldoon, Paul (1951–) Born in Portadown, Co. Armagh, Northern Ireland, and brought up near a village called The Moy which figures prominently in a number of his poems. His mother was a schoolteacher and his father a farm labourer and market gardener. After studying at Queen's University, Belfast, where Seamus *Heaney was a tutor and where he met other poets such as Michael *Longley as part of the Belfast 'Group' (*See* HOBSBAUM, PHILIP), he published his first book, *New Weather* (Faber) in 1972, when he was only 21. He worked as a producer for the BBC in Belfast until, in the mid-1980s, he gave up his job to become a freelance writer and moved to the United States. In 1988 he edited *The Faber Book of Contemporary Irish Verse*. He is Howard G. B. Clark '21 Professor in the Humanities at Princeton University and has been poetry editor of *The New Yorker* since 2007.

'The Mixed Marriage', in his second collection, *Mules* (1977), concerns the opposed educational and class backgrounds of his parents: his mother's cosmopolitan literariness and his father's rural knowledge and Republican sympathies. His poetry, which frequently returns to his parents (particularly his father), itself conducts mixed marriages of various kinds. It brings his own family and rural background into a strangely dislocating relationship with an astonishing range of sophisticated literary, historical, and cultural allusion; it crosses contemporary Irish experience with Amerindian Trickster mythology; it joins early Irish legend to the thrillers of Raymond Chandler; it performs some radical formal experiments with that most traditional of poetic means, the sonnet, and is notable for its ingenious dedication to pararhyme (e.g. 'interim'/'Antrim'). Wily and mischievous, these conjunctions are energetic displays of a subtle, learned, and ironic intelligence, placing the reader in a constant state of interpretative alertness and insecurity. In his influential longer poems, such as 'Immram' in *Why Brownlee Left* (1980) and 'The More a Man Has the More a Man Wants' in *Quoof* (1983), he employs oblique, intermittent narratives of conspiracy, quest, and pursuit whose slippery air of giving nothing away, at once cajoling and unaccommodating, gracefully testifies to that most bedrock marriage of all in his work: that of a Northern Irish Catholic sensibility and the English poetic tradition.

Muldoon's move to America was marked by two longer poems on trans-Atlantic literary crossings. '7, Middagh Street', from *Meeting the British* (1987), retells W. H. *Auden's move to New York in 1939, while *Madoc: A Mystery* (1990) imagines Samuel Taylor Coleridge and Robert Southey pursuing a utopian scheme in the New World. A new phase in Muldoon's work began with *The Annals of Chile* (1994), which brought his interest in complex narrative structures to bear on the autobiographical material previously only treated in shorter lyrics. 'Incantata', a Yeatsian elegy for a former lover, Mary Farl Powers, introduces 'Yarrow', a long fantasia on the poet's childhood written in 'intercut, exploded sestinas'. It won the T. S. Eliot Prize. Both poems repeat the same ninety rhyme sounds, a device which has continued to underpin long poems in subsequent volumes, from *Hay* (1998) to *Maggot* (2010). The result is a unique experiment in the extended poetic sequence.

Muldoon is also a virtuoso miniaturist, often in nature poems which reveal his admiration for the pastoralism of Edward *Thomas and Robert *Frost (see 'Hopewell Haiku'). A collected volume, *Poems*

1968–1998, was followed by *Moy Sand and Gravel* (2002), which won both the Pulitzer Prize and the Griffin International Poetry Prize. All Muldoon's major volumes have been published by Faber in the UK. In the US he was published first by Wake Forest University Press (from *Mules* to *Meeting the British*) and, subsequently, Farrar, Straus and Giroux.

In a review of *Meeting the British*, the British critic and academic John Carey attacked Muldoon's work as 'arcane, allusive' and 'packed to the gunwales with higher education'. But much of its show of learning is self-deprecating and even parodic, and its down-to-earth wit and realism have proved equally influential on younger poets. His fascination with etymologies and the associative processes of composition are explored in *The End of the Poem* (2006, Faber/Farrar, Straus), which collects his lectures as the Oxford Professor of Poetry from 1999 to 2004. For criticism see Clair Wills, *Reading Paul Muldoon* (Bloodaxe, 1998) and *Paul Muldoon: Critical Essays* (Liverpool University Press, 2004), ed. Tim Kendall and Peter McDonald.   NC*

Mulford, Wendy (1941–) Born in Wales, Mulford studied English at Cambridge University. She has worked as an editor, university lecturer, and freelance writer. In 1972, she founded the small press Street Editions, which later merged with Ken Edwards' Reality Studios to become Reality Street. She lives in Suffolk.

and suddenly, supposing (etruscan books, 2002) selects from three decades of writing. Mulford's first volume, *Bravo to Girls & Heroes* (Street Editions, 1977), established a quick-moving voice which, like her peers among those she has called the '*Cambridge [England, that is] poets*', brought a new American lightness to the post-war British quotidian. She has written of her passionate 'absorption' in Barbara *Guest's *The Blue Stairs* (1968), an influence which shows in her painterly deployment of colour. The title poem of *The ABC of Writing and Other Poems* (Torque, 1985) is an extended autobiographical sequence.

Mulford's early work articulates her feminism: see her anonymized collaboration with Denise *Riley, *No Fee* (Street Editions, 1978). She has written a study of women saints, a biography of Sylvia Townsend *Warner and Valentine Ackland, and edited *The Virago Book of Love Poetry* (1991), an anthology of women's lyric writing. She has also translated the German poet, Sarah Kirsch. *The Land Between* (Reality Street, 2009) collects recent work, including 'I CHINA AM'.   JNT

Mullen, Harryette (1953–) Born in Florence, Alabama and raised in Fort Worth, Texas, Mullen currently teaches African-American literature and creative writing at the University of California, Los Angeles. She received major acclaim in 2002 with the publication of *Sleeping with the Dictionary,* which was a finalist for the National Book Critics Circle Award, the National Book Award, and the *Los Angeles Times* Book Award in poetry. In 2006, Graywolf Press released *Recyclopedia*, which collected three of her early experimental works in one volume: *Trimmings* (1991), *S*PeRM**K*T* (1992), and *Muse & Drudge* (1995). It received the PEN Beyond Margins award that year.

Mullen's unique contribution to American letters 'mongrelizes' two traditions: linguistic experimentalism in the vein of Gertrude *Stein, *Language poetry, and *Oulipo; and the tradition of African-American literature from the *Harlem Renaissance to the *Black Arts movement. She foregrounds the language of the poem using parataxis, puns, heteroglossia, and formal constraints to comment on race and gender, in a signal turn from a previous generation that had emphasized storytelling as a vehicle for civil-rights awareness.

Other honours include an Academy of American Poets Fellowship in 2009, artist grants from the Texas Institute of Letters and the Helene Wurlitzer Foundation of New Mexico, the Gertrude Stein Award in Innovative American Poetry, and a Rockefeller Fellowship from the Susan B. Anthony Institute for Women's Studies at the University of Rochester.   AMl

Murphy, Richard (1927–) Born in the west of Ireland but spent part of his early childhood in Ceylon. He attended Magdalen College, Oxford, and the Sorbonne. Then, for some years, he ran a fishing boat in County Galway—this is the 'hooker' of 'The Last Galway Hooker'. He restored the boat himself: a revealing enterprise, suggesting as it does that concern for the objective recovery of the Irish past which is so much a feature of his verse. His cosmopolitan, colonial Anglo-Irish background fitted him to explore his Irish inheritance from a position combining intimacy with a measure of detachment: an astute stance which makes itself evident both in his manner and in his subject-matter. As a lyric poet, Murphy's gift is for quiet, precise, musical phrasing but this is not his only talent. He is equally notable—indeed unusual—for his skill in narrative poems, as in 'Sailing to an Island' or 'The Woman of the House', which, though it describes itself as an elegy for his grandmother, Lucy May Ormsby, is predominantly a narrative created from memory, and one which vividly succeeds in evoking the lost world of the Ascendancy. Such poems are often written in a rhythmic, four-stress, accentual metre, with some alliteration and the use of half-rhyme: they seem, appropriately enough, indebted both to Saxon and Gaelic models. In *The Battle of Aughrim* (Knopf/Faber, 1968), Murphy examines the consequences of one of the most decisive events in Irish history. 'Aughrim's dread disaster' (1691) was the final defeat for the Catholic forces arrayed against the Williamites. It was followed by the Treaty of Limerick, and the penal period. Murphy's series was broadcast in 1968, with Ted *Hughes and Cecil *Day Lewis among the readers. It seeks to trace some of the roots of present troubles: 'Names in the rival churches are written on plaques.' But Murphy's forebears, he seems guiltily aware, are implicated in some of the wrongs committed since then. His collected poems were published by the Gallery Press in 2000 and Wake Forest University Press in 2001. *The Kick* (Granta, 2002) is a memoir of his 'life among writers'.

See also *New Selected Poems* (Faber, 1989), and Maurice Harmon (ed.), *Richard Murphy, Poet of Two Traditions* (Wolfhound, 1978). ETL

Murray, Les(lie Allan) (1938–) Born in the village of Nabiac on the remote north coast of New South Wales. An only child, he grew up on his father's dairy farm at Bunyah nearby, before attending Sydney University where he read modern languages. He worked with the translation unit at the Australian National University, 1963–7, but since 1971 he has made his living from literature. (Murray is a forceful advocate of state funding for the arts.) In 1986 he left Sydney—a city whose fashionable priorities and 'imported idiocies' he has long satirized—and returned to buy a forty-acre farm in Bunyah.

His first book *The Ilex Tree* (Australian National University Press), co-written with his friend Geoffrey *Lehmann, came out in 1965, and he has since written prolifically, employing an unusually wide range of subject-matter and treatment. Since his conversion to Roman Catholicism, all his volumes have been dedicated 'to the glory of God'. The novel-in-verse *The Boys Who Stole the Funeral* was first published in 1980. Technically, its 140 deftly varied fourteen-line units, a mosaic of different kinds of writing, are a triumphant solution to the problem of how to square the demands of a prolonged narrative with the reverberating stops of lyric and meditative verse; they also keep Murray's habitual garrulousness in check. Its plot, however, a fable at the service of Murray's Roman Catholic beliefs and masculine and agrarian prejudices, is calculated to antagonize. Uncompromising views on war, abortion, and the sexes are aired between scenes of instructive violence: in one, a deplored feminist is retributively 'baptised' by scalding and disfiguring her face.

The novel reminds us of Murray's *Jindyworobak claim that white Australians should partake of the Aboriginal affinity with the environment—see also poems like 'The Buladelah-Taree Holiday Song Cycle' from *Ethnic Radio* (1977). But for all its marvellous facility, it suggests a poet out of his place; and Murray's return to the country in the mid-Eighties had a measurable effect on his verse, restoring a serene non-fiction to the fore. The personality of the later poems is genial and mostly tolerant, the address muted and the technique subdued, their concerns as large and impersonal as the continent behind them. Murray has identified the distinguishing mark of Australian poetry as 'the endless detailed rehearsal...of Australian peculiarities that goes into it'; and neutral detail is the stuff of many spacious poems. The long piece which opens *The Daylight Moon* (1987—all Angus & Robertson), for example, a voyage through flood-plains, ends on the exact and tranquil note of an 'unhurt' crocodile's 'pineapple abdomen'. A distinguishable class of poem is content to perform quiet variations on themes of home, farm and farm machinery, family, landscape, and provincial history.

Murray was also increasingly preoccupied with telling stories, which, as he explains sarcastically for urban readers, are 'a kind of spoken video'; his refinements of the fireside yarn allow him virtuoso re-creations of a range of voices, and to convey choice scraps of local non-fiction. A second verse-novel, *Fredy Neptune* (Carcanet/Duffy & Snellgrove, 1998), narrates the picaresque adventures of a German-Australian hero through the first half of the twentieth-century, with a consciously epic 'quality of sprawl' (also the subject of one of his best-known shorter poems). As restlessly curious about the possibilities of vocabulary as the later *Auden, there is no single Les Murray style, as subsequent collections from *Conscious and Verbal* (Duffy & Snellgrove, 1999) to *Taller When Prone* (Black Inc., 2010) have continued to demonstrate. Nor is there a consistent quality: as William *Logan has put it, 'poets of such intelligence can seldom be quoted so plainly against themselves'. He takes a persistent delight in provocative squibs, such as 'The Beneficiaries' (*Subhuman Redneck Poems*, Duffy & Snellgrove, 1996).

Murray's somewhat forbidding critical prose is selected in *A Working Forest* (Duffy & Snellgrove, 1997); his essay on his earlier poetics, 'The Human Hair-Thread', appeared in the journal *Meanjin* in 1977. From 1973 to 1979, Murray was the editor of *Poetry Australia*. He has also edited *The New Oxford Book of Australian Verse* (revd. edn., Oxford University Press, 1999), the *Anthology of Australian Religious Poetry* (Collins Dove, 1986) and a selection of the poems of A. B. *Paterson. *New Collected Poems* appeared in 2002 and *Learning Human: New Selected Poems* in 2003 (both Duffy & Snellgrove). Murray now has a worldwide readership: in the UK, his work is published by Carcanet, and in the States by Farrar, Straus, and Giroux. See also a later *New Selected Poems* (Black Inc., 2007; Carcanet, 2012). For biography, see Peter Alexander, *Les Murray: A Life in Progress* (Oxford University Press, 2000), and for criticism, *The Poetry of Les Murray*, ed. Laurie Hergenhan and Bruce Clunies Ross (University of Queensland Press, 2001).   MI*

Musgrave, Susan (1951–) Born in Santa Cruz, California, of Canadian parents. She left school at 14 and has travelled widely. For long periods she has lived in the wilderness of the Queen Charlotte Islands off the coast of British Columbia, alongside the Native Indians. She regards this area as her spiritual home. She teaches at the University of British Columbia.

Musgrave gained recognition with her first collection, *Songs of the Sea Witch* (Sono Nis, 1970), in which she projects the anarchic impulses of the authentic self seeking freedom. Written in short lines, the poems refer to blood, absence, and dismemberment. Typically, Musgrave speaks as an animistic force located between the spirit of the air and the spirit of the sea; she enacts the struggle of an unformed self to realize itself in its own unique form. Much of the imagery stems from the Pacific Northwest. Musgrave has also written a number of poems through the eyes of the Canadian native peoples to suggest that the desecration of the land and the spirit derive from the same impulse towards absolute control. When writing about the contemporary urban world, Musgrave often employs a cold, detached voice to parody what she sees as its death-in-life quality. Her first selected poems, *Tarts and Muggers* (McClelland &

Stewart, 1982), opens with the statement: 'the embalmer's art is poetry', signalling her rejection of art that does not bring new forms into being, but rests content with embalming the dead. *Cocktails at the Mausoleum* (McClelland & Stewart, 1985; revd. edn. Beach Holme, 1992), was more conversational in tone; here she reflects with wit and intelligence on the place of love and the 'shamelessness of the body' in a violent world.

Musgrave's later volumes include *Forcing the Narcissus* (1994) and *Things That Keep and Do Not Change* (1999—both McClelland & Stewart). In 2000 Porcepic Books published her pre-1990s volumes as *What the Small Day Cannot Hold. When the World Is Not Our Home: Selected Poems 1985-2000* (Thistledown) appeared in 2009. It has been followed by *Origami Dove* (McClelland & Stewart, 2011). She has also published novels, books for children, and collections of autobiographical non-fiction: see *You're in Canada, Now Motherfucker . . . A Memoir of Sorts* (Thistledown Press, 2005). For discussion of Musgrave's early work, see Dennis Brown's 'Susan Musgrave: The Self and the Other', *Canadian Literature*, 79 (Winter 1978).   RBH

Muske(-Dukes), Carol (1945–   ) Lives in Los Angeles, California, and is a professor of English and creative writing at the University of Southern California. Formerly known as Carol Muske, she was married to the actor David Dukes who died in 2000. Los Angeles figures in Muske-Dukes' work as a trope for the seduction of appearances; reality crosses from the Wallace *Stevens notion of the sun, 'hovering in its guise of impatient tribunal' ('The Red Trousseau') to a director's reshooting of a tarnished sunset, so that 'the scene, infinite, rebegins' ('Unsent Letter'). Muske-Dukes works in primary colours: red, blue, and yellow dominate, serving to link such disparate things as a soundstage's fake *prie-dieu*, a precinct-station map of gang activity, and a schoolgirl's model of the planets, all of which take on the red of Salem burnings, the self-immolation of a political dissident in Prague, and Eros itself, moving like a red shadow over the body in love. Muske-Dukes' work derives much of its spiralling energy from Marianne *Moore. Much like Moore's paper nautilus, first protective then, freed of its fragile cargo, becoming the beautifully empty form of itself, Muske-Dukes' Hollywood spirals around its version of reality, infinitely re-beginning, until it becomes wholly the form.

Carol Muske-Dukes' poetry books include *Camouflage* (University of Pittsburgh Press, 1975), *Skylight* (Doubleday, 1981), *Wyndmere* (1985), *Applause* (1989—both University of Pittsburgh Press), *The Red Trousseau* (Viking, 1993), *Sparrow* (Random House, 2003), and *Twin Cities* (Penguin, 2011). See *An Octave Above Thunder: New and Selected Poems* (Penguin, 1997). Her novels include *Dear Digby* (1989) and *Channelling Mark Twain* (2007). See also her collection of essays *Women and Poetry: Truth, Autobiography, and the Shape of the Self* (University of Michigan Press, 1997) and a memoir, *Married to the Ice Pick Killer: A Poet in Hollywood* (Random House, 2002). In 2008 she became Poet Laureate of California.   LMCM

Nabokov, Vladimir (Vladimirovich) (1899–1977) Born in St Petersburg, the eldest son of cosmopolitan aristocrats. Mastering both French and English in childhood, Nabokov demonstrated precocious literary gifts, publishing two collections of verse while still in his teens. When his family fled revolutionary Russia in 1919, Nabokov entered Trinity College, Cambridge, where he published his first English verse. After his father, a liberal politician, was assassinated by Russian reactionaries in 1922, Nabokov moved to Berlin where he married Vera Slonim, and established himself as a leading emigré writer, usually using the pseudonym, V. Sirin. Moving to Paris in 1937 to avoid the Nazi threat, Nabokov began writing in English, and in 1940 the Nabokovs and their son Dimitri (later his father's translator), emigrated to America where he obtained university positions in literature and lepidopterology, eventually accepting a professorship at Cornell. The international success of *Lolita* following its American publication in 1958 allowed Nabokov to retire from teaching in 1959 and move to Switzerland to be near his son. Although Nabokov, an American citizen, claimed his European residency would be temporary, he died in Montreux.

Nabokov maintained that there was no generic difference between poetry and 'artistic prose', and his own verse displays the same conspicuous virtues of his fiction—playful musicality, dark wit, and narrative ingenuity. He published only a few mature poems in English, but they are uniformly strong and strikingly original. The long monologue, 'An Evening of Russian Poetry', which is spoken by an imaginary lecturer visiting a women's college, begins as gentle academic satire but builds into an exile's extravagant elegy for his lost Russia. Nabokov's finest poems, like 'The Ballad of Longwood Glen' and 'The Literary Dinner', often employ black comedy but use that savage and sophisticated humour to protect their essential innocence. Nabokov's most ambitious poem in English (or Russian) was 'Pale Fire', which formed the centre-piece of his masterful 1961 experimental novel of the same title. Purportedly written by John Shade (whom Nabokov convincingly called 'the greatest of invented poets'), this 999-line poem in heroic couplets provides the mysterious and eccentric critic, Charles Kinbote, the opportunity to project his autobiography into 200 pages of hilarious and heart-breaking footnotes. A masterful performance, *Pale Fire* became an influential model to postmodern novelists. Nabokov's poetry, however, has had little direct influence.

Nabokov also made significant contributions to verse translation and prosody. After having done many literary translations of Russian poetry, he eventually became a ferocious champion of 'honest and clumsy' literalism. His massively annotated translation of Pushkin's *Eugene Onegin* (Bollingen Foundation, 1964) demonstrates scholarship and pedantry in equal measure. His book-length appendix on Pushkin's metre (later published separately as *Notes on Prosody*), which brilliantly compares English and Russian iambic tetrameter, remains a magisterial study of versification. The fullest collection that Nabokov made of his verse was *Poems and Problems* (McGraw-Hill, 1970). The poem 'Pale Fire' has been published separately in an illustrated boxed edition, with commentary by Brian Boyd and R. S. *Gwynn (Gingko, 2011). *Selected Poems* (Knopf/Penguin,

2012), ed. Thomas Karshan, draws on six decades of Nabokov's verse and contains new translations of Russian poems by his son, Dmitri Nabokov.   DG

Nair, Chandran (1945–   ) Born in India but his family moved to Singapore when he was still a child. He was trained as a marine biologist, but his literary interests took him into the world of publishing where he remained for many years, eventually taking up an appointment as consultant with UNESCO.

In Nair's first volume of poems, *Once the Horseman and Other Poems* (Singapore University Education Press, 1972), there is a recourse to Hindu myths and legends as sources of comfort and spiritual nourishment, but in his second book, *After the Hard Hours this Rain* (Woodrose, 1974), there is a shift away from Hindu themes; love is the central preoccupation. A later volume, *Reaching for Stones* (Ethos, 2010), collects Nair's poems from over four decades. See *idea to ideal: 12 singapore poets on the writing of their poems*, ed. Felix Cheong (firstfruits, 2004).   KS

Nair, Rukmini Bhaya (1952–   ) Born in Vishakhapatnam, Nair studied English at the University of Calcutta, and then did doctoral work in linguistics at the University of Cambridge. She is Professor of Linguistics and English at the Indian Institute of Technology, Delhi, and has been a visiting professor at Stanford University. Her academic works include *Narrative Gravity: Conversation, Cognition, Culture* (Routledge, 2003).

Nair has said that her work poetry has the same motivation as her work in linguistics: 'to discover the limits of language'. It has been widely admired by other poets and critics for its postmodern approach to lyrical meaning and feminine identity in Indian English: 'I am obscure as a sibyl. | The hailstone syllables | Clatter | And melt.' Her three collections, all published by Penguin India, are *The Hyoid Bone* (1992), *The Ayodha Cantos* (1999), and *Yellow Hibiscus: New and Selected Poems* (2004). Nair's work is featured in *The Bloodaxe Book of*

Contemporary Indian Poets (2008), ed. Jeet Thayil.   JNT

Nash, Ogden (1902–71) Born in Rye, New York, the son of wealthy parents. After one year at Harvard, 1920–1—'it was my idea to leave, not the Dean's, and I have affidavits to prove it'—he taught, was a bond salesman, wrote streetcar ads, and (1925–31) worked in the publicity and editorial departments of first Doubleday and then Rinehart. In 1929 he joined the staff of *The New Yorker*, his preferred venue, though he also contributed to more than thirty journals. In 1931 he married and published *Hard Lines* and *Free Wheeling*. His lyrics for Broadway musicals include those for Kurt Weill's *One Touch of Venus* (1943), and for Bette Davis in *Two's Company* (music by Vernon Duke, 1962). Tall, bespectacled, elegantly suited, with fair curling hair and an intelligent, toothy smile, he was an urbane public reader of his verse and also produced Thurberish illustrations.

Though Nash belongs to entertainment, he deploys poetic resources. The inordinately lengthy, short, or alternating lines stumble along in a mix of anapaests and iambs, culminating, with expert timing, in elaborately improbable couplet-rhymes; clowning and witty by turn, his punning, ironic medleys of the sophisticated and *faux-naif* can also be epigrammatic or occasionally lyrical. Constantly revising, he crafted an instantly identifiable match for his insights—touching on sore points from family life's sex- and generation-wars, through lying, money, drink, and Englishness, to God—without which his games could and sometimes did become facetious formulas.

At his best Nash belongs with playful haters of dullness like Carroll, Lear, and W. S. Gilbert, often read when more distinguished names are mere names.

I Wouldn't Have Missed It (Little, Brown, 1975; Deutsch, 1983), selected by his two daughters, Linell Smith and Isabel Eberstadt, represents all fourteen volumes, with dates, .and was republished as a paperback, *Candy Is Dandy: The Best of Ogden Nash* (Deutsch, 1985).   HL

Neilson, (John) Shaw (1872–1942)
Born in Penola, South Australia, of Scottish
parents. When he was 9 his family moved
to Minimay, Victoria, and eventually settled
near Nhill, in the Horsham district. Neilson
received scarcely two-and-a-half years'
schooling and acquired much of his educa-
tion from his parents: his father was a com-
petent provincial poet who imbued his son
with a great respect for Scottish poetry; his
mother, a passionate Free Church Presby-
terian, educated the boy through the Bible,
focusing on the Old Testament and the
letters of St Paul. In 1906 Neilson began a
literary relationship with the critic A. G.
Stephens, who was to become his mentor
and major publisher until Stephens' death
in 1933. *Heart of Spring* appeared in 1919,
Ballads and Lyrical Poems in 1923, and
New Poems in 1927. A *Collected Poems*
was published in 1934, and was followed
by *Beauty Imposes* (1938). See *Selected
Poems* ed. Robert Gray (Angus & Robert-
son, 1992).

Neilson's work has received a range of
critical response. Until quite recently he
was regarded as a bush innocent with little
education or knowledge of the world; a 'sim-
ple singer', or rough, uneducated navvy who
wrote without thinking. Douglas *Stewart
saw him as a rustic figure born with a 'gift
from the sky', who only had to 'take down
the words as they arrive'. Neilson indeed
lived in the bush for most of his life, but his
poetry bore little resemblance to his simple
rustic image, and he has suffered from a
critical approach that has been unable or
unwilling to see past his background. Far
from being a simpleton, he was a well-
educated writer with a good working knowl-
edge of English and Australian literature.

See: *Poet of the Colours* (1988), a biogra-
phy by John Phillips, and Cliff Hanna (ed.),
John Shaw Neilson (1991), which has a
selection of Neilson's writings including
the poet's 'Autobiography'. Hanna has
also published a critical book on Neilson,
The Folly of Spring (1990).   CHa

Nelson (Waniek), Marilyn (1946–)
Born in Cleveland, Ohio, Nelson's father
was one of the first African-Americans to
be an airman in the US Army (see her poem

'Tuskegee Airfield'). She studied at the uni-
versities of California, Pennsylvania, and
Minnesota. From 1978 she taught English
at the University of Connecticut, where she
is now emeritus professor. She was Poet
Laureate of the State of Connecticut from
2001 to 2006.

Praised for her lyrical, storytelling voice,
three collections of Nelson's poetry have
been nominated for the National Book
Award: *The Homeplace* (1990), *The Fields
of Praise: New and Selected Poems* (1997—
both Louisiana State University Press), and
Carver: A Life in Poems (Front Street, 2001),
a poetic biography of the African-American
botanist, George Washington Carver. Her
latest collection is *The Cachoeira Tales, and
Other Poems* (Louisiana State University
Press, 2005). She has also written for chil-
dren and young adults. In 2012 she was
awarded the Robert Frost Medal for lifetime
achievement by the Poetry Society of Amer-
ica.   JNT

Nemerov, Howard Stanley (1920–91)
Born and brought up in New York City,
graduated at Harvard, and served in the
Canadian and American Air Forces during
the Second World War. His subsequent ca-
reer as poet, teacher, novelist, editor, and
critic took him to many of America's most
prestigious universities, and won him
many of its most distinguished literary
awards, culminating in the American poet
laureateship (1988–90).

Nemerov's first books establish, to a
large extent, the breadth of his concerns
and the shapes of his expression. Relaxed
and ruminative pentameters would always
serve him well, whether in contemplation
or celebration, satire or lament, but his
relatively narrow formal horizons contrast
throughout his career with the remarkable
range of his interest and observation. From
the outset his reach is both global and spe-
cific, ancient and contemporary, domestic
and mystical. Some of the most successful
early pieces (many from 1955's *The Salt
Garden*) combine lyrical description of the
natural with some special human detail,
elevating image into parable or myth.
Brief visions—of soldiers on the move, a
child drowned in a pond, the flight of

seagulls—crystallize and illuminate back and forth through time. *Mirrors and Windows* (1958) evinces further development of Nemerov's skills in description and dialogue, as his high-rhetorical strain makes way for the kind of low-pitched, colloquial swing one associates with the later *Frost, a poet he resembles in other ways: two measured voices ranging far and wide from a sane, stoical centre; public citizens with an abiding faith in form and reason; artists capable of great expansion and intense compression.

The Blue Swallows (1967) displays a further range, as America's accelerating, double-speaking, jargon-spouting democracy sparks against Nemerov's ever-wider and warier muse. Nemerov is one of the first poets to reflect on the status and predicament of that fast-multiplying species: the poet as college professor. His next books are more epigrammatic, noting and speculating, peering at words themselves, at creativity itself with the eyes of painters, composers, novelists, or nagging at the powerful and pretentious. Nemerov becomes a wisecracker just off the public stage, blending jauntiness and wry observation into a highly accessible modern commentary, though his facility with the pentameter at times loosens its effectiveness.

In his last book, *War Stories* (1987), he rediscovers a distinct focus. The self-examination of an American in wartime, at the heart of this century, recollected with the sharpness of maturity, carries a potent charge of meaning.

Some fine, chiefly occasional poems are included in the posthumously published *Trying Conclusions: New and Selected Poems* 1961–91 (1991). *The Collected Poems of Howard Nemerov* (1977—both University of Chicago Press) won both the National Book Award and the Pulitzer Prize of 1978. A new *Selected Poems*, ed. Daniel Anderson, with a foreword by Wyatt Prunty, appeared in 2003 (Ohio University Press).

See also *The Critical Reception of Howard Nemerov: A Selection of Essays and a Bibliography*, ed. Bowie Duncan (Scarecrow, 1971); *The Stillness in Moving Things: The World of Howard Nemerov*, by William Mills (Memphis State University Press, 1975), and *Howard Nemerov*, by Ross Labrie (Twayne, 1980).   GM

Newlove, John (1938–2003) Born in Regina and lived for a number of years in nearby farming communities in eastern Saskatchewan, where his mother taught school. He worked in Vancouver, Toronto, and Ottawa as a warehouseman, a technical writer, and publisher's editor, and was a writer-in-residence at several Canadian universities, but his most formative and lasting influence was the prairies, where the rigours of climate and terrain as well as the mixture of dispossessed natives and competing ethnic minorities created such a fascinating social and political milieu.

Newlove's earliest work focuses on derelicts, misfits, and wanderers who inhabit the margins of society; it also dramatizes the plight of the poet as outsider in a disintegrating world, finding grace in fleeting encounters and small epiphanies. The stance in these lyrics is *confessional, but the tone is more often ironic than self-indulgent; and the style, which is spare, halting, and disjunctive, is remarkable for its playfulness and its acknowledgement of the limits of language and the poetic process. There is a jazz-like, improvisational quality in Newlove's best verse that is entirely original: see, for example, 'Ride Off Any Horizon', a poem that moves from image to image by way of a repetitive structure and associational logic which allows the poet to draw into a unified whole a wide range of personal and historical materials.

Newlove's most celebrated work is 'The Pride', a longish poem that employs various levels of poetic discourse, including lyrical fragments, quasi-documentary prose pieces, and direct statement, asking the perennial Canadian question about 'the knowledge of | our origins, and where | we are in truth, | whose land this is | and is to be'. Like a cultural anthropologist, Newlove calls up the ghosts, of great moments and great Indian leaders, that must be remembered and given the permanence of art; he finds the 'roots | and rooted words', 'the pride, the grand poem | of our land, of the earth itself'. And in so doing, he accomplishes what can only be described as a poetics of recall.

Newlove's major publications are *Moving in Alone* (1965), *Black Night Window* (1968), *The Cave* (1970), *The Fat Man* (1977), and *The Night the Dog Smiled* (1986). *A Long Continual Argument: The Selected Poems of John Newlove*, ed. Robert MacTavish, with an afterword by Jeff Derksen (Chaudiere, 2008), includes all of his later poetry. See Douglas Barbour, *John Newlove and His Works* (ECW, 1992). GG

Nichol, bp (Barrie Phillip) (1944–88) Born into a railroad family, Nichol was brought up in various Canadian cities, most of them in the west. He trained as an elementary-school teacher, but abandoned that profession quickly to make a career as a writer and therapist.

For Nichol writing involved all the arts. He was Canada's best-known concrete poet and sound poet. He wrote children's books and children's television. He composed opera and pop musicals, fiction, cartoons, theory and lyric verse. He and three other Toronto poets formed The Four Horsemen, a sound-poetry performance group that gained international attention over nearly two decades.

Nichol did not recognize a line between living and art. He was an editor who encouraged and taught scores of younger writers. He turned literature into outdoor sculpture and wore clothing made of visual poems. He scored performance pieces based on French semiotic theory. He was immensely popular with other poets, and his early death occasioned ceremonies across the country.

As a poet he worked on forms derived from the examples of Gertrude *Stein and the Dadaists. A Nichol poem insists on its materiality, and the play of signifiers gives rise to much of its meaning. The most important of these poems is *The Martyrology*, which has been published in seven volumes since 1972 (Coach House). Characterized as a 'Life-poem', it is an exhaustive, cabalistic, and witty exploration of language as the writer's creed and environment.

The Martyrology is the subject of an anthology of essays, *Tracing the Paths* (Talonbooks, 1988), ed. Roy Miki. Nichol's work was also the subject of another anthology, *Read the Way he Writes* (Davey, 1986) ed. Paul Dutton and Steven Smith. A useful monograph is Stephen Scobie's *What History Teaches* (Talonbooks, 1985). See *An H in the Heart: A Reader*, ed. George Bowering and Michael Ondaatje (McClelland & Stewart, 1994). GHB

(⊕) SEE WEB LINKS
• Visit the bp Nichol online archive.

Nichols, Grace (1950–) Born in Guyana and educated at the University of Guyana. In Guyana Nichols worked as a teacher and journalist. She declared, in her brief autobiographical essay 'Home Truth', that it was 'only after coming to England in 1977 that poetry began to play a bigger and bigger part in my life'. Her poetry is characterized by sensitivity to the experience of women, a sensuous apprehension of mundane reality, and a piquant wit. 'Shopping', for instance, with its playful echoes of T. S. *Eliot's 'The Hollow Men', subtly hints at a domestic rift between the shopper, who is the 'voice' of the poem, and her 'old man', to make a telling point about consumer values.

Her debut collection, *i is a long memoried woman* (Karnak House, 1983; repr. 1990), won the Commonwealth Poetry Prize, and was later made into a radio drama and a film for television. The humorously defiant persona of *The Fat Black Woman's Poems* (1984) and *Lazy Thoughts of a Lazy Woman* (1989— both Virago) gives voice to some of her best-known work. She has also published children's books, including *No Hickory, No Dickory, No Dock: A Collection of Caribbean Nursery Rhymes*, with her husband, John *Agard (Viking, 1991), and a novel, *Whole of a Morning Sky* (Virago, 1986), which is set in Guyana. *Startling the Flying Fish* (Virago, 2006) is a mythological history of the Caribbean. Nichols' most recent collections are *Picasso, I Want My Face Back* (2009) and *I Have Crossed an Ocean: Selected Poems* (2010—both Bloodaxe). MR*

Nicholson, Norman (1910–87) Born at Millom, Cumberland, educated locally, and stayed all his life in the same house. In the moving poem which closes his last collection (*Sea to the West*, 1981) he describes how his father saw Halley's Comet in 1910 and wonders whether he himself will live to see its return in 1986. What is significant about this characteristically anecdotal poem is Nicholson's awareness that if he does see the comet he will do so from the same spot, sharing his father's 'long-ago Edwardian surprise'. Place, the local habitation of the Lake District with all its continuity and change, is of the essence in Nicholson's work, although he achieved what *Auden described as 'the poet's hope' (quoted as an epigraph to *Sea to the West*) to be, like some valley cheese, local but prized elsewhere.

Nicholson wrote several prose works about the Lake District—its literary figures, inhabitants and landscape—including *The Lakers* (1955) and his autobiography *Wednesday Early Closing* (1975)—but it was in his poetry, which can be seen to become increasingly confident in the handling of blank verse and syllabic metre after beginning (*Five Rivers*, 1944) with a much more conventional lyricism, that he addressed most directly the forces of change he observed around him. The magnificent, gravelly 'On the Dismantling of Millom Ironworks', with its ironically lofty Wordsworthian title and its passionately meticulous itemizing of natural beauty and industrial waste, shows him at his very best, while such poems as 'Comprehending it Not' (from *Sea to the West*), 'The Whisperer' (from *A Local Habitation*, 1972), and 'Rising Five' (from *The Pot Geranium*, 1954) show how successful he could be in dealing, unsentimentally, with intimate personal reminiscence and building on the proverbial idiom of local dialect. His sequence of poems about Black Combe, first published as a handsome illustrated pamphlet, *The Shadow of Black Combe*, in 1978, is particularly distinctive in its blending of topography with anecdote. Nicholson also wrote two novels and four verse plays of somewhat lesser interest.

See *Selected Poems 1940–1982* (1982) and *Collected Poems*, ed. Neil Curry (1994—both Faber). JM

Niedecker, Lorine (1903–70) Born and died in Fort Atkinson, Wisconsin, living much of her adult life in a small cabin on Black Hawk Island on Lake Koshkonong, Wisconsin. An active correspondent with numerous poets such as Louis *Zukofsky, Cid *Corman, and William Carlos *Williams, all of whom both influenced and praised her work, she lived an essentially isolated life, one which appealed to both her affinity for nature and her innate shyness. From her earliest work on, Zukofsky was an encouraging mentor, and his notions of objectivity and sincerity as elaborated in his essay 'An Objective' in *Poetry* magazine (1931), were extremely important to her. A keen reader, her interests lay in history, the natural sciences, and pre-Socratic philosophy, subjects full of resonance for her, which informed both the content and shape of her poetry.

Niedecker is an American miniaturist; in this, her work bears some comparison with the short poems of Robert *Creeley or the terseness of J. V. *Cunningham. Her natural register is the epigrammatic mode, one which renders a life or a landscape as though it were composed of a series of small, intense moments. Her mode of construction, something she obviously took from Zukofsky, aims for fidelity to the musical phrase, the leading of sound syllables, and the sense of closure afforded by rhyme-schemes and metrical attentiveness. By such a method she invests with a satisfying density and self-containment what might ordinarily escape into ephemerality. The consequent musical completeness and condensation in the poems transforms what could easily have become effusions into something like the workings of a scientist or botanist. Whether commenting on the life of Audubon or Thomas Jefferson or on the often deeply painful events of her own life, she exhibits a rigorous detachment, all the more moving for its precision and lack of self-indulgence.

See *The Granite Pail: The Selected Poems of Lorine Niedecker*, ed. Cid Corman (North Point, 1985). Jenny Penberthy has edited the *Collected Works* for University of California Press (2002) and written a study of

Niedecker's correspondence with Zukofsky (Cambridge University Press, 1993). The first full biography is Margot Peters, *Lorine Niedecker: A Poet's Life* (University of Wisconsin Press, 2011). MH

Nims, John Frederick (1913–99) Born in Muskegon, Michigan, to a Catholic family, and educated at DePaul University and Notre Dame. By 1945, when he earned a PhD in comparative literature from the University of Chicago, he had already distinguished himself as a poet and critic: his contributions to *Five Young American Poets* (1944) display the formal acuity and urban settings characteristic of his poetry, and his 1945 review of early books by Robert *Lowell and *Merton contains prescient observations about their work. In 1947 Nims married Bonnie Larkin. They had five children, one of whom died at an early age. Nims taught in Milan, Florence, and Madrid, as well as at several American universities; he taught at the University of Illinois at Chicago Circle from 1965 until his retirement.

In America Nims is best known for his powerful impact as editor of *Poetry* from 1978 to 1984, and as the author of an important textbook, *Western Wind* (2nd edn., 1983). In both capacities he fostered the use of traditional forms evident in his own work. Though perhaps too cold and densely written, Nims' early poems show a talent for satire. His second full-length collection, *A Fountain in Kentucky* (1950), is more assured and emotionally profound, particularly in 'The Masque of Blackness', a sonnet-sequence touching on the death of his son George. Throughout his career Nims was preoccupied with love and death in their most ironic correspondences, but in 'The Evergreen', from *Knowledge of the Evening* (1960), he discards ironic distance to create a moving elegy. The epigrams in *Of Flesh and Bone* (1967) are reminiscent of J. V. *Cunningham's.

Some of Nims' best work was done as a translator and essayist. He made important versions of the poems of St John of the Cross and Euripedes' *Andromache*. *Sappho to Valéry* (1971; revd. edn., 1990) contains not only an impressive number of translations from half-a-dozen languages, but also an introductory essay calling on translators to be poets, to make new English poems rather than versions of the originals that are merely accurate and lifeless. His lecture 'The Topless Muse' argues persuasively for reticence and restraint as ways of increasing the imaginative impact of poetry. Essays on Golding's Ovid and other subjects prove, by their lightly-worn erudition, that Nims is an important post-war American critic.

Sixteen of Nims' essays and introductions are collected in *A Local Habitation* (University of Michigan Press, 1985). See *The Powers of Heaven and Earth: New and Selected Poems* (Louisiana State University Press, 2002). DM

Noonuccal, Oodgeroo (formerly Kath Walker) (1920–93) Born on North Stradbroke Island, Queensland, the home of the Noonuccal tribe. She changed her name in 1988, the bicentennial year of the European invasion of her country. Awarded the MBE in 1971 in recognition of her efforts on behalf of her people, from 1961 she was a leader in Aboriginal activist movements, and a frequent speaker, reader, and lecturer, both in Australia and overseas.

Her book *We Are Going* (1964) was the first volume of poems by an Aboriginal writer and has been one of the most successful verse publications in Australia, selling many thousands of copies. It was succeeded by *The Dawn Is at Hand* (1966) and a collected edition of her writings, *My People* (1970—all Jacaranda). She also published a charming prose book about her childhood and her Noonuccal heritage, *Stradbroke Dreamtime* (1972; repr. Vulgar Press, 2006), and a volume of her artwork, *Quandamooka: The Art of Kath Walker*, was edited by Ulli Beier (Robert Brown, 1985).

Her poetry—direct, impassioned, and deeply committed to declaring the basic rights of her race—has its origins in the ballad tradition as much as in her search for an Aboriginal inflection through the English language. Her success in the latter aim has had a profound influence on the later striking development of Aboriginal writing in the 1980s. *Oodgeroo*, a biographical tribute written and edited by her friend Kathie Cochrane, includes an appreciation of the poetry by Judith *Wright (University of Queensland Press, 1994).   TWS

Norris, Leslie (1921–2006) Born in Merthyr Tydfil, Glamorgan. Formerly a teacher, he earned his living from 1974 as a full-time writer and lecturer, mostly in the USA. From 1985 he was humanities professor of creative writing at Brigham Young University, Utah.

His principal volumes of poetry are *Finding Gold* (1967), *Ransoms* (1970), *Mountains, Polecats, Pheasants* (1974), *Water Voices* (1980), and *A Sea in the Desert* (1989). He also published two collections of short stories, *Sliding* (1978) and *The Girl from Cardigan* (1988), and with Alan Keele he translated Rilke's *The Sonnets to Orpheus* (1989).

The emotional basis of Leslie Norris' writing was in his experience as a child in Merthyr, an industrial town which continuously exercised a powerful influence on his imagination and creative skills. His poems and stories abound with the colourful characters of the place and with the rich wildlife of its rural hinterland. The energy and meticulous craftsmanship of his verse produce a wealth of images and much verbal ingenuity, and his poems usually have an impact which arises from a deep melancholy and poignancy, especially in the eclogues for childhood and youth, in which his sense of loss is most apparent.

His years in America made his poetry more diffuse and technically more sophisticated, but his main preoccupations with place, time, and personal relationships are still firmly rooted in the Merthyr of his early years.

The Complete Poems (Seren, 2008), ed. Meic Stephens, with an introduction by Patrick McGuinness, includes Norris' translations from the Welsh of Dafydd ap Gwilym. A monograph on his work has been written by James A. Davies for the Writers of Wales series (Cardiff, 1991).   MS

Nortje, Arthur (1942–70) Born in Oudtshoorn (Cape Province), South Africa. His early education was in the segregated schools of Port Elizabeth. He graduated from the segregated University College of the Western Cape and taught English in South Africa until 1965 when he went to Jesus College, Oxford, to read English. He taught in Hope, British Columbia, and Toronto from 1967 until 1970 when he returned to Oxford to work for a doctoral degree. He died from an overdose of barbiturates in 1970 whilst in Oxford.

His poems first appeared in *Black Orpheus* in 1961 and he was awarded an Mbari Poetry Prize. Two collections of his poems were published posthumously: *Lonely Against the Light* (Institute for the Study of English in Africa, 1973) and *Dead Roots* (Heinemann, 1973). Nortje's early poems were directly concerned with the emotional consequences of living within the inhumane structures of South Africa. The poems which he wrote whilst in England are some of the most poignant, exploring the isolation and loneliness of the exile. He was a double exile; of mixed race, he was rejected by white South Africa. This and his distance from the everyday realities of his country of birth gave emotional impetus to his best work. His later poems documented the gradual disintegration of his personality; even here his poetry was elegant, coherent, and purposeful. *Anatomy of Dark: Collected Poems of Arthur Nortje* (University of South Africa Press, 2000), ed. Dirk Klopper, presents Nortje's decade of maturity chronologically.   FO

Notley, Alice (1945–) Notley was born in Arizona and grew up in California. She studied at Barnard College and the Iowa Writers' Workshop. In 1972 she married Ted *Berrigan, with whom she had two sons, the poets Anselm and Edmund Berrigan. She and Berrigan were active in the Chicago poetry scene before moving to New York where they became prominent members of the second-generation *New York School. After Berrigan's death, Notley married British poet Douglas *Oliver. They moved to Paris in 1992 where she has remained, visiting the USA frequently to teach and give readings.

Notley's poetry maintains a *New-York-style balance between lyricism and formal experimentation. Modernist influences such as Gertrude *Stein and William Carlos *Williams are notable too. She has published over twenty-five books of poetry, a play, a book of essays, an autobiography, and experiments with visual art. Her work has received numerous honours and prizes, including an Academy Award from the American Academy of Arts and Letters. Notley describes her early work as presenting the voice of 'the new wife, and the new mother'. The themes of gender and cultural politics can be traced across her oeuvre, though her later style is more concerned with transcribing the movement of thought itself ('Whose mind are you? All of those I say.... | When your baby's on the cooling board. Yes I've seen that too.') See *Grave of Light: New and Selected Poems 1970–2005* (2006) and *Songs of Stories of the Ghouls* (2011—both Wesleyan University Press).   ECr

Nowlan, Alden

Nowlan, Alden (1933–83) Born in Stanley, a small community near Windsor, Nova Scotia. At the age of 12 he left school and worked for several years as lumber-man, millhand, and farmhand. At 19 he moved to Hartland, New Brunswick, and worked for the *Hartland Observer*. Later he became editor of the Saint John *Telegraph-Journal*. He published *The Rose and the Puritan*, his first volume of poems, in 1958, and *Bread, Wine and Salt* in 1967. In 1969 he was appointed writer-in-residence at the University of New Brunswick, a position he held until his death.

Many of Nowlan's poems are based on anecdotes from personal experience and are used to point up some moral. The emotions that inform his lyrics arise from his memories of growing up in a family and community that were both economically and imaginatively impoverished. His realistic imagery, conversational speech, and controlled irony allow him to avoid the sentimentality and bombast to which his subject-matter is susceptible.

Both the natural goodness of life and the evils inflicted upon us by failed institutions are central to Nowlan's poetry. He decries puritanical attitudes and moral hypocrisy in 'All Down the Morning' and 'Beginnings'. In 'Warren Pryor', he shows how economic depression prompted well-intentioned parents to force their son into a career that crippled his spirit. He condemns anything that denies life, as, for example, in 'God Sour the Milk', or diminishes the dignity of any creature, as in 'The Bull Moose'. He is tolerant of anything that creates even the illusion of happiness and hope, as in 'Marian at the Pentecostal Meeting'.

Among his twelve volumes of poetry are: *The Rose and the Puritan* (University of New Brunswick, 1958); *Bread, Wine and Salt* (Clarke, Irwin, 1967), *Playing the Jesus Game: Selected Poems* (The Crossing Press, 1970); *Between Tears and Laughter* (1971); *I'm a Stranger Here Myself* (1974); *Smoked Glass* (1977); *I Might Not Tell Everybody This* (1982—all Clarke, Irwin); *Early Poems* (Fiddlehead, 1983); and *An Exchange of Gifts* (Irwin, 1985), edited and introduced by Robert Gibbs. A selected volume, also titled *Between Tears and Laughter* (2004), has been published in the Bloodaxe World Poets series.   DRB

Ntiru, Richard

Ntiru, Richard (1946–) Born near Kisoro, Uganda, and educated at Ntare school, Nbarara, and Makerere University, where he acquired precocious standing as an editor, as organizer of the 1969 Arts Festival, radio playwright, short-story writer, and poet. The verse in his book *Tensions* (1971) dates from these student years. Its great promise was recognized by the inclusion of eleven items in Wole *Soyinka's *Poems of Black Africa* (Heinemann, 1975). But Ntiru fell silent after he took his first-class degree. Following a spell with the East African Publishing House in Nairobi, he remained in that city as part of the tragic Ugandan diaspora of the Amin-Obote years, working for international organizations.

In *Tensions*, admirable control of syntax and a sound ear for free-verse rhythm support an unusually wide vocabulary, displayed with evident relish. Original intelligence plays over themes of alienation and social satire characteristic of work by young African poets of the time, with some influence from the post-Poundian sequences of Christopher *Okigbo.

Ntiru is also represented in David Cook and David Rubadiri (eds.), *Poems from East Africa* (Heinemann, 1971), and is discussed by Adrian Roscoe in *Uhuru's Fire: African Literature East to South* (Cambridge University Press, 1977).   ALRC

Nurkse, D. (Dennis) (1949–) Son of the Estonian economist Ragnar Nurkse, his work is marked by his experience as the child of refugees and exiles. Educated at Harvard, he was a factory worker throughout the 1970s, before working for human-rights organizations and teaching in the Riker's Island Correctional Facility. He lives in New York and teaches writing at Sarah Lawrence College. As Dennis Nurkse, he has written on human rights, and currently serves on the American board of directors for Amnesty International.

In the United States, Nurkse has published ten collections: *Isolation in Action* (State Street, 1987), *Shadow Wars* (Hanging Loose, 1988), *Staggered Lights* (Owl Creek, 1990), *Voices over Water* (Graywolf/Four Way,1996), *Leaving Xaia* (2000), *The Rules of Paradise* (2001—both Four Way), *The Fall* (2003), *Burnt Island* (2006), *The Border Kingdom* (2008), and *A Night in Brooklyn* (2012—all Knopf). *Voices over Water* was republished in the UK in 2011, by Charles *Boyle's CB Editions, and shortlisted for the Forward Prize. Nurkse writes spare poems in free verse, often sequentially linked, especially attentive to small details and the sense of place. Resonance often comes (see 'Albi' or 'Cat's Eye') from scenes of horror or pain being calmly and tenderly described.   GR

Nwankwo, Chimalum (1945–) Nwankwo was born in Eastern Nigeria and educated in Nigeria and the USA. He holds a PhD in English from the University of Texas Austin and is Professor of English at North Carolina State University, Raleigh.

He has held a senior Fulbright fellowship, spending 2010–11 at Nnamdi Azikiwe University Awka Nigeria.

Nwankwo has published five poetry collections: *Feet of the Limping Dancers* (ABIC, 1987), *Towards the Aerial Zone* (Spearpoint, 1988), which won the Association of Nigerian Authors prize, *Voices from Deep Water* (Malthouse, 1997), *The Womb in the Heart* (2002), which also won the Association of Nigerian Authors prize, and *Of the Deepest Shadows and the Prisons of Fire* (2009—both African Heritage). He is also author of a critical study of Ngugi wa Thiongo, *Toward the Kingdom of Man and Woman: The Works of Ngugi wa Thiongo* (1992), and of a play, *The Trumpet Parable* (1988). Nwankwo's poetry is often said to be influenced by Christopher *Okigbo in its derivation from Igbo rhythmic chanting and its commitment to a mystical cosmogony. However, this is only part of the story, for Nwankwo's sensibility is also attuned to the corruption and infelicities of contemporary Nigeria.   FO

Nye, Naomi Shihab (1952–) Born in St Louis, Missouri and holds a BA in English and World Religions. She lives in San Antonio with her family. Best known as a writer of children's fiction, the Arab-American Nye has written verse and prose for children and adults. In 1988 she was selected by W. S. *Merwin for the Lavan Award, and in 2012 was elected a Chancellor of the Academy of American Poets.

Influenced by Gary *Snyder, Wallace *Stevens, and her early mentor William *Stafford (whose posthumous poems she edited), Nye's conversational free verse focuses on the importance of the everyday as an anchor in the face of changing place, language, and culture, and—like the poet's own humanitarian work—aims to promote cultural understanding through art.

From her first full-length volume, *Different Ways to Pray* (Breitenbush, 1980), Nye's poetry has used different voices to articulate cultural difference. *Red Suitcase* (Consortium, 1994) is set in Palestine, and *Fuel*

(BOA, 1998) in Nye's hometown, San Antonio. *19 Variations of Gazelle: Poems of the Middle East* (HarperCollins, 2002), written in reaction to 9/11 to raise awareness of Arab voices in America, was nominated the International Reading Association Notable Book for a Global Society. Nye has edited various volumes of world poetry, including *This Same Sky* (1996) and *The Tree is Older than You Are* (1995). See *Tender Spot: Selected Poems* (2008), published in the Bloodaxe World Poets Series. HY

Nye, Robert (1939–) Born in London. He is best known for his novels and for his poetry reviews; but he also has a reputation as a poet. Like Robert *Graves, to whose poetry he has a debt, he has subjected his poems to a process of continuous revision, so that pieces which first appeared in *Juvenilia 1* (1961) or *Juvenilia 2* (1963), have resurfaced in often-drastically revised form in successive collections: *Darker Ends* (1969), *Divisions on a Ground* (1976), and *A Collection of Poems 1955–1988* (London, 1989). The last collects all his work. Early poems were largely inchoate, and littered with phrases from his own favourite poets (*de la Mare as well as Graves); but they were always deeply felt. Many have survived into *A Collection of Poems*, purged of most of the echoes but sometimes less energetic. His direction has always been towards clarity and perfection of form. His main themes are love—which he approaches as a distinctly Celtic phenomenon—and guilt. He has written narrative poems, such as 'Crowson', in which his own voice is much more in evidence.

Nye's latest collection is *The Rain and the Glass: 99 Poems New and Selected* (Greenwich Exchange, 2004). POM*

Nyezwa, Mxolisi (1967–) Born in Port Elizabeth, Mxolisi Nyezwa has published three collections of poetry and is the editor of the South African literary magazine, *Kotaz*. He lives in the Eastern Cape where he works on literacy projects with rural and township communities.

The South Africa in which Mxolisi Nyezwa's *Song Trials* (Gecko, 2000) and *New Country* (University of Natal Press, 2008) is rooted seems more spiritual than that of his contemporaries. Throughout his work, a bright, casual, and spare language, combined with an unflinchingly neutral tone, muffles an underlying weariness (and sometimes despair). The poems are full of strange images which are progressively distorted through associative leaps or disjointedly strung together, as in 'i am smitten, | i have ridden a lame horse | like a matador in snow' from the poem 'no longer'. This surreal tendency, and the repetition of parts of sentences, shows the influence of Spanish poets. The poetic voice, however, represents itself authentically—the speaking self is never undermined by stylistic devices. The poet avoids making statements or representing ideas, even when dealing with political or social subjects. *Malikhanye* (Deep South, 2011) is concerned with the death of the poet's infant son (after whom the book is named), related in a plainer and more direct style than his previous books. KK

O'Brien, Gregory (1961–) Born in Matamata, O'Brien worked as a journalist before studying at Auckland University. Poet, art critic, editor, and painter, he curates the City Gallery in Wellington, and is married to Jenny *Bornholdt, with whom he co-edited *An Anthology of New Zealand Poetry in English* (Oxford University Press, 1997). A major figure in contemporary New Zealand culture, his work has also been published in Australia and Britain.

O'Brien's many books begin with *Location of the Least Person* (University of Auckland Press, 1987), a volume of his verse and visual art. The verbal tracing of a scene or a landscape is a characteristic procedure of this imagistic poetry, which ranges from haiku-like lyrics to verse letters, love poems, and historical narratives. Later collections include *Days beside Water* (Auckland University Press, 1993; Carcanet, 1994), *Winter I Was* (1999), and *Afternoon of an Evening Train* (2005—both Victoria University Press), which includes his 'Ode to the chair', a lightly moving meditation on modern art, poetry, and domesticity.

He has written a novel, *Diesel Mystic* (1989), and a verse novella, *Malachi* (1993). See also his prose memoir of France, *News of the Swimmer Reaches Shore* (Victoria University Press/Carcanet, 2007), and the essays on New Zealand art and poetry in *After Bathing at Baxter's* (Victoria University Press, 2002). O'Brien's latest book of poems is *Beauties of the Octagonal Pool* (Auckland University Press, 2012), an eight-part collection set around Waitemata Harbour.   JNT

O'Brien, John *See* HARTIGAN, P. J.

O'Brien, Sean (1952–) Born in London and grew up in Hull. He took degrees in English at Cambridge and Birmingham,

returned to the University of Hull for three years, and from 1981 to 1989 taught at a secondary school in East Sussex. He was a fellow in Creative Writing at Dundee University from 1989 to 1990, taught at Sheffield Hallam University between 1998 and 2006, and is now Professor of Creative Writing at Newcastle University.

O'Brien's movements about 1980s Britain have been reflected in the poetry he has written. His experience of Hull both as a place to live and as a landscape much mined by Douglas *Dunn and Philip *Larkin infected his own first collection, *The Indoor Park* (1983). But O'Brien is both a more extravagant fabulist and a more overtly political writer than these two; while he shares with Larkin a determination to record the details of ordinary urban lives, the rhythmical and rhetorical effects his poems create are jauntier, more self-consciously rhetorical. There is also anger at the inflexibility of British social institutions. *The Frighteners* (1987—both Bloodaxe) developed this sense of anger in an inventive, historically informed group of poems, 'In a Military Archive'; but it also included a northerner's satirical reactions to the complacency of an emphatically contemporary Thatcherite south-east. In *H.M.S. Glasshouse* (Oxford University Press, 1991) both the satire and the historical overviews continue; more revealing, however, are strange poems such as 'Hatred of Libraries', in which O'Brien comes to terms with his own involvement in the tradition he both loves and distrusts.

In 1998 he published two influential books: an anthology of British and Irish poetry since 1945, *The Firebox* (Picador), which begins with Basil *Bunting and ends at the *New Generation; and a critical study, *The Deregulated Muse* (Bloodaxe), which offers a complementary history of the post-Larkin landscape. A widely published literary reviewer in Britain, with relatively eclectic tastes, as a poet O'Brien has consolidated the vision of his early work rather than developing it through significant experiment. The nostalgic fascination of industrial England in decline 'after the age of the train' is a recurring theme of later books, which typically employ a flexible blank verse line as the measure of a deadpan manner (of a railway buffet sandwich he writes, 'Stay here too long and it may speak your name'). He has also been drawn to Dantesque sequences which fantasize a dark satirical country inhabited by the living and the dead, and has translated the *Inferno* (2006). *Ghost Train* (Oxford University Press, 1995) and *Downriver* (2001) both won the Forward Prize for Best Collection, as did *November* (2011), making O'Brien the only poet to have the won the award three times. *The Drowned Book* (2007) won the T. S. Eliot Prize. *Cousin Coat* is a selected poems (2002—all Picador). He has also translated Aristophanes' *The Birds* (2002) and published a novel, *Afterlife* (2008).   MRW*

O'Callaghan, Conor (1968–) Born in Newry, Co. Down, but grew up across the border in Dundalk. He has taught in Dublin and North Carolina and currently lives in Manchester. His debut, *A History of Rain* (1994), was awarded the Patrick Kavanagh Prize, and juxtaposes atmospheric domestic interiors with longer historical vistas. Derek *Mahon is an important precursor, not least in O'Callaghan's ability to mine the banal for mythic resonances.

Far removed from Dublin and the Atlantic west coast, O'Callaghan's Dundalk, explored in *Seatown* (1999), is a zone of run-down passions and rained-on urban decay. While 'East' and 'Sublet' strike a *Larkinesque note, O'Callaghan displays a Mediterranean sensuality too, with Eugenio Montale a notable influence. A vein of caustic wit might appear laddish, but serves a deeper and far-reaching critique of the self. The O'Callaghan persona is typically somewhere between self and other: there will always be 'some faceless other', announces the speaker of 'Landscape with Canal', 'who'll call in the murk ahead, "Who goes there?" | and call once more when you don't quite answer'.

Formally, the careful stanzas of his debut have evolved in unexpected and unusual directions. *Fiction* (2005—all Gallery) shows the loosening effects on O'Callaghan's style of life in America. He has also written a non-fiction prose book, *Red Mist: Roy Keane and the Football Civil War* (2004), and was awarded the Bess Hokin Prize by *Poetry* in 2007.   DW

O'Connor, Mark (1945–) Born in Melbourne and educated at the University of Melbourne. He has worked at various jobs—editing the journal *Canberra Poetry*, 1973–5, minding houses in Europe, gardening on a Barrier Reef resort island, being for a time writer-in-residence for the New South Wales National Parks Service. Believing that in Australia there are 'thousands of different nature-feelings evoked by natural places and all requiring different words to capture them', he has assumed in his poetry the naming task of an antipodean Adam. From his first collection, *Reef Poems* (University of Queensland Press, 1976)—which led Les *Murray to write of him as 'the man with a Muse a thousand miles long'— O'Connor has tried to describe with exquisite precision the flora and fauna of environments that he intimately knows. In this vein were *Poetry of the Mountains* (Second Back Row, 1988) and *The Great Forest* (Hale & Iremonger, 1989), illustrated with photographs of the Blue Mountains and of the tropical rain-forests of Australia and Papua New Guinea respectively. For all the delights of this distinctive and scrupulous poetry, its educative function—together with the author's temperament—encourages a lack of humour, while the poems do not always transcend their descriptive particulars. The human dimension is polemically absent, for O'Connor finds that in the real world 'humans are in plague proportions'. He has also written a book in favour of phonetically accurate spelling. See *Fire-Stick Farming: Selected Poems 1972–90* and *The Olive Tree: Collected Poems 1972–2000* (both Hale & Iremonger). Recent books include a volume of prose and verse on the Pilbara region in Western Australia (Leonard, 2009) and, with William Lines, an environmental polemic, *Overloading Australia* (2009). PP

O'Connor, Philip (1916–98) Born in Leighton Buzzard, Buckinghamshire. O'Connor describes his unconventional upbringing and early bohemian life-style in his autobiography, *Memoirs of a Public Baby* (Faber, 1958). As well as his collections of verse, *Selected Poems 1936–1966* (Cape, 1968) and *Arias of Water* (Sidgwick & Jackson, 1981), O'Connor's varied and eccentric corpus of work includes sociology (*Vagrancy*, Penguin, 1963), personal reminiscence (*The Lower View*, Faber, 1960), and an autobiographical novel, *Steiner's Tour* (Olympia, 1960). He died in France.

O'Connor's work was first published in *New Verse* during the 1930s, and the early poems vary in style from the out-and-out surrealism of 'Blue Bugs in Liquid Silk' to the *Auden-influenced Marxist and Freudian expostulations of 'Useful Letter' and 'Poem'. His later poems are ironic and angry in tone and still deploy the associative techniques of *surrealism. Viewed as a whole his work amounts to a proclamation of uncompromising individualism.

A selection of his early work can be found in Robin Skelton (ed.), *Poetry of the Thirties* (Penguin, 1964).

O'Donoghue, Bernard (1945–) Born in Co. Cork, Ireland, O'Donoghue went to school in Manchester at the age of sixteen, and has spent his adult life in England. He is a Fellow in English at Wadham College, Oxford, where he teaches medieval literature.

An early pamphlet of O'Donoghue's poems, *Razorblades and Pencils*, appeared from John *Fuller's Sycamore Press in 1984. *Poaching Rights* followed in Ireland in 1987 from The Gallery Press. *Selected Poems* (Faber, 2008), however, begins with O'Donoghue's first full-length volume, *The Weakness* (Chatto & Windus, 1991), which includes a number of earlier poems. The impulse to poetry is itself implicitly a kind of 'weakness' in this reticent, clear-eyed

writing. O'Donoghue has spoken of his mistrust of the *Confessional mode, and cites instead the anonymous 'elegies' of Anglo-Saxon literature as the perfect form of lyric. His own poetry repeatedly returns to the North Cork world of his childhood in nostalgic meditation, tempered by the long view of later wisdom: characteristically, his translation of the Old English 'The Wanderer' recalls 'the old days, | listening to whatever was on the radio'.

O'Donoghue's later collections are: *Gunpowder* (1995), *Here Nor There* (1999), *Outliving* (2003—all Chatto & Windus), and *Farmers Cross* (Faber, 2011). He has also edited an anthology of medieval European lyrics, *The Courtly Love Tradition* (Manchester University Press, 1982), written a critical study, *Seamus Heaney and the Language of Poetry* (Prentice Hall, 1995), and made a fine translation of *Sir Gawain and the Green Knight* (Penguin, 2006). JNT

O'Driscoll, Denis (1954–2012) Born in Thurles, O'Driscoll studied Law at University College Dublin, and served as a civil servant for forty years until retirement in 2010. O'Driscoll was a prolific essayist and incisive reviewer, and a former editor of *Poetry Ireland Review*. He was a member of Aosdána and was awarded an honorary doctorate by University College, Dublin in 2009.

O'Driscoll's poetry is highly formal; he wrote that 'form and rhythm...can somehow confer higher destiny and density on even the most workaday words'. A concern with mortality is an undercurrent to the work, yet a strong sense of irony dispels any possibility of sentimentality. *The Bottom Line* (Dedalus, 1994) is a curtal sonnet sequence which wryly addresses the aesthetic cost of the banalities of office life in 'Celtic Tiger' Dublin. Yet O'Driscoll sits well within a wider European context. George *Szirtes has commented on the influence of writers such as Zbigniew Herbert, Miroslav Holub, and Czesław Miłosz on O'Driscoll's work, calling him 'a poet of European temperament. His terrain is...without borders'.

Stepping Stones (Faber, 2008) collects O'Driscoll's interviews with Seamus

*Heaney. See *New and Selected Poems* (Anvil, 2004) and *Troubled Thoughts, Majestic Dreams* (Gallery, 2001) for his essays. His ninth collection was *Dear Life* (Anvil, 2012).   HY

Ofeimun, Odia (1947–) Grew up in Western Nigeria. As well as having been a journalist and an academic, Ofeimun was for several years the personal secretary of Chief Obafemi Awolowo, one time premier of the western region of Nigeria.

The scandal that led to the withdrawal of the original edition of his first collection, *The Poet Lied* (Longman, 1981)—when J. P. *Clark Bekederomo decided that the title-poem pointed a finger too uncomfortably at him and threatened to sue the publishers—ensured that Odia Ofeimun's name would be well remembered. His second collection, *A Handle for the Flutist* (1986) attracted wide critical applause and quickly sold out. A new edition of *The Poet Lied* (1990—both Update Communications) was effectively a provisional 'collected poems', including both of his previous books, many uncollected poems, and a long interview with Ofeimun by Onwuchekwu Jemi. Ofeimun cites Quasimodo, Rilke, and Martin *Carter among his formative influences, and his work acknowledges a notion of 'poetry' that transcends regional and even cultural boundaries.

A Feast of Return Under African Skies collects his poems for dance drama in the 1990s. In 2000 Ofeimun published two collections, *London Letter* and *Dreams at Work*. Three others have appeared since, and he has edited an anthology of poems about the city that fascinates him, *Lagos of the Poets* (2009—all Hornbill House).   SB

O'Grady, Desmond (1935–) Born in Limerick, and educated by the Jesuits and Cistercians; he later studied at Harvard. O'Grady spent time in Paris and Rome in the 1950s and became a friend and secretary to Ezra *Pound. He lived for many years on the Greek island of Paros.

O'Grady's limpid lyricism in his first collection, *Chords and Orchestrations* (1956), soon gave way to a more blustering rhetoric under the influence of Pound—*The*

Dying Gaul (1968), for example, is a Poundian mélange of myth and history. *His Skaldcrane's Nest* (1979), however, contains some fine, subtle lyric verse, reminiscent of the work of O'Grady's friend Thomas *Kinsella. O'Grady's best work, which deserves much wider recognition, is his translations, ranging from versions of Armenian courtly love poems in *Off Licence* (1968) to his long free-verse rendering of Aneirin's heroic Middle Welsh epic *The Gododdin* (1977—both Dolmen).

See *The Road Taken: Poems 1956–1996* (1996) and *Trawling Tradition: Translations 1954–1994* (1994). An interview can be found in *The Wide World: A Desmond O'Grady Casebook* (2003—all Poetry Salzburg). *The Wandering Celt* (2001; repr. 2008) is a poetic history of Celtic cultural influence. O'Grady's translations of Cavafy appeared in 1999. His latest collection is *On My Way* (2006—both Dedalus Press).   IES*

O'Hara, Frank (1926–66) Born in Baltimore, Maryland, but grew up in Grafton, Massachusetts. He served in the US Navy, 1944–6, and from 1946 to 1950 he attended Harvard College, where he majored in music. After graduate school at Ann Arbor, he moved in 1951 to New York, where he was employed by the Museum of Modern Art. For the rest of his life O'Hara was deeply involved in the New York art scene, particularly with the work of abstract expressionist painters such as Willem De Kooning, Jackson Pollock, and Franz Kline. Between 1953 and 1955 he worked as editorial associate for *Art News*, for which his poet friends John *Ashbery and James *Schuyler also wrote. In 1955 he rejoined the staff of MOMA, where he was appointed assistant curator in 1960. In the early morning of 24 July 1966 he was struck and gravely injured by a beach-buggy on the beach of Fire Island, and died the following day. He is buried in Springs Cemetery on Long Island.

O'Hara's poems are a heady mixture of Whitmanian enthusiasm and explosive *surrealism. For O'Hara, as for the abstract expressionists, art is process, and many of his poems can be seen as chronicles of their own coming-into-being. His airy poetic structures are full of the random clutter of metropolitan living and casually dropped details of O'Hara's own life, his love-affairs, friendships, his responses to paintings, movies, and literature. His conception of poetry is perhaps best conveyed by a line in his mock-poetic manifesto, 'Personism': 'You just go on your nerve.'

O'Hara is best known for his I-do-this, I-do-that poems, such as 'A Step Away From Them', 'Why I am Not a Painter', and 'The Day Lady Died' (an elegy for Billie Holliday), but some of his later longer poems, in particular 'In Memory of My Feelings' and 'Biotherm (for Bill *Berkson)' are equally effective, and have proved influential on a host of younger poets. Donald Allen edited his *Collected Poems* (1971) and also a *Selected Poems* (1974—both Knopf).

See also *Frank O'Hara: Poet Among Painters* (Braziller, 1977; new edn., University of Chicago Press, 1998) by Marjorie Perloff; *City Poet: The Life and Times of Frank O'Hara*, by Brad Gooch (Knopf, 1993); *Frank O'Hara: Poetics of Coterie* by Lytle Shaw (University of Iowa Press, 2006); and *Frank O'Hara Now: New Essays on the New York Poet*, ed. Robert Hampson and Will Montgomery (Liverpool University Press, 2010). The *Collected Poems* was reprinted by University of California Press in 1995. O'Hara's plays appeared in 1997 under the title *Amorous Nightmares of Delay* (Johns Hopkins University Press). The most recent selections of O'Hara's poetry are both by Mark Ford: a pocket UK volume in 2004 (Faber) and a longer US selection in 2008 (Knopf).   MF*

Ojaide, Moses Tanure (1948–) Born in the Delta Province of what is now Nigeria's Midwestern State. He was educated at Federal Government College, Warri, and at the University of Ibadan, graduating in 1971. He worked for a time as a schoolteacher, and was senior lecturer at the University of Maiduguri, where he taught African poetry, oral and written African literature, and creative writing. He is now a professor of Africana studies at the University of Carolina.

Like *Okigbo, whose poetry he admires, Ojaide fuses the gnomic, riddling quality of African oral poetry with the allusiveness and fragmentation of European modernism. His language is flavoured with West Africanisms: boldly mixed registers ('correlation', 'pep'), inventively 'incorrect' vocabulary ('fecundive', 'postcede'), and polysyllabic sonorities ('Reverberations ... resuscitated ... interspaces ... evanescent'). Some of his poems are symbolic accounts of his personal love history, others focus on the beliefs and rituals of his Urhobo people. 'Where Everybody is King' is a witty satire on the unwillingness of Nigerians to accept the indignity of menial labour. 'The Fate of Vultures' expresses moral indignation at the corruption of Nigerian society, while in 'Song of My Land' the poet addresses a nation tainted by tribal antagonisms which mock his love for her.

Ojaide has published many collections of poetry. *Invoking the Warrior Spirit: New and Selected Poems* (1999) was followed by *In the Kingdom of Songs: Poems 1995–2000* (2002—both Africa World Press). *The Tale of the Harmattan*, his fifteenth volume, appeared in 2007 from Kwela/Snailpress in South Africa. He has also published three novels, two collections of short fiction, a memoir of his childhood, and a number of critical studies on African poetry and poets, including Wole *Soyinka.   JB

Okai, John Atukwei (1941–) Born in Accra and was educated in Ghana and in the Soviet Union, where he studied at the Gorky Institute in Moscow and received an MA in 1967. Since returning home Okai has taught Russian and literature at the University of Legon near Accra. He has also been involved in the organization of the Ghana Association of Writers as well as the Pan-African Writers Association.

Okai's style is that of public performance using dance, drumming, and chants. His concerns are the social and political issues of his country, his people, and of Africa in general. He has performed his poetry in North America, Europe, and in different countries of Africa. His collections include *Flowerfall* (Writers Forum, 1969), *The Oath of Fontomfrom and Other Poems* (Simon and Schuster, 1971), *Lorgorli Logarithms* (1974), *Freedom Symphony: Selected and New Love Poems* (2008); and *Mandela The Spear* (2008—all Ghana Publishing). He has also written verses and chants for children. For an extended discussion of Okai's work drawing on interviews with the poet, see Pietro Deandrea, *Fertile Crossings: Metamorphoses of Genre in Anglophone West African Literature* (Rodopi, 2002). KO

Okara, Gabriel Imomotimi Gbaingbain (1921–2011) Born at Bumoundi in the Niger Delta, and educated at Government College, Umuahia, and at Yaba Higher College. After wartime service in the RAF he became a professional bookbinder, working for the Government Press in Enugu. In the late 1950s he studied journalism in the United States before becoming information officer for the Eastern Nigerian Government. His poetry first appeared in magazines, including the first issue of *Black Orpheus* (1957). *The Voice*, a poetic novella, appeared in London in 1964 (Africana, 1970). During the Civil War Okara was director of cultural affairs for the Biafran Ministry of Information, and in 1969 he toured the United States with Chinua *Achebe to promote the Biafran cause. After the war he became head of the Rivers State Cultural Centre.

The two roots of Okara's poetry are the folklore and imagery of his Ijaw background, and his self-directed reading in Wordsworth, Keats, Hopkins, and Dylan *Thomas. In some poems Ijaw spiritual concepts are boldly transposed direct into English ('shadow', 'inside', 'Front', 'Back'). But his lyrical free verse is by no means obscure to non-Ijaw readers; indeed, it is distinguished by its assured idiom and lucid musicality. His themes are at the same time African and universal: the conflict between tradition and modernity, homesickness, the sufferings of war. Primary images are employed with quiet conviction: the river of life flowing to the sea of death; migrating storks symbolizing the restless soul; pure stars beyond the reach of human yearning.

During the Civil War many of Okara's manuscripts were lost, and his long-awaited collection, *The Fisherman's Invocation* (Heinemann, 1978) contained only thirty-three poems. He later published books for children. See also *West African Poetry* (Cambridge University Press, 1986), by Robert Fraser. JB

Okigbo, Christopher (1932–67) Born in Ojoto in the Igbo-speaking region of Nigeria. Intended from birth for the priesthood of the riverain goddess Idoto, he instead followed an academic career at Government College, Umuahia, and at the University of Ibadan, where he graduated in classics. Whilst teaching at Fiditi Grammar School his commitment to poetry emerged in a series of translations from the classics (notably from Virgil), followed by a spate of lyrics of increasing originality and power. For short periods he worked as a representative for the Cambridge University Press and as university librarian, but abandoned everything in 1966 to fight for the Biafran side in the Nigerian Civil War, dying in action in August of the following year. He left behind a clutch of lyrics which gained him a reputation as the most distinguished English-language poet in Africa. Indeed, the manner of his death, the liveliness of his conversation, and the precarious devotedness of his craft have since established him as a sort of African Sir Philip Sidney, and have given rise both to a wide following and to copious imitation. His style is characterized by lyric terseness, cries from the deep wrung out of an agony both personal and archetypal. His eclecticism has attracted criticism from parochially minded critics, but on a wider view his claim to pre-eminence can be sustained.

Okigbo's major work is the interconnected sequence *Labyrinths* (1971), comprising the subsequences *Heavensgate* (1962), *Limits* (1964) and *Silences* (1965). The hortative sequence *Path of Thunder: Poems Prophesying War*, written after the first Nigerian coup of 1966, appeared for the first time in volume form in 1971. A *Collected Poems*, ed. Maja Adewale-Pearce, was published by Heinemann in 1986. A detailed analysis of his poetry is to be found in Robert Fraser's *West African Poetry: A Critical History* (Cambridge University Press, 1986). Obi Nwakanma's biography, *Christopher Okigbo 1930-67* (Currey, 2010), places the poems in the context of his life. RF

((⊕)) SEE WEB LINKS
• More information can be found at The Christopher Okigbo Foundation website.

Olds, Sharon (1942–) Raised in California, but has lived most of her adult life in New York City, where she teaches creative writing at New York University, and was the State Poet Laureate from 1998 to 2000. She has won many awards: her first book, *Satan Says* (University of Pittsburgh Press, 1980), was chosen for the San Francisco Poetry Center Award; her second, *The Dead and the Living* (1984), was a Lamont Poetry Selection; and her third, *The Gold Cell* (1987), won the National Book Critics Circle Award for Poetry. Her fourth, *The Father* (1992—all Knopf), was published also in London (Secker & Warburg, 1993). She writes an emotionally charged verse, centring her negative feelings on abusive members of her childhood family and on cruel figures drawn from political history. Against these Olds sets the power of love, directed primarily towards her adult family (particularly her two children), but also towards the physical world: 'I am | paying attention to small beauties, | whatever I have—as if it were our duty to | find things to love, to bind ourselves to this world.'

Though her poems seem literally expressed when first encountered—because of their clarity and directness—in fact they are carefully designed and cunningly figurative. One poem speaks of a broken elbow as a 'fine joint that | used to be thin and elegant as | something made with Tinkertoy, then it | swelled to a hard black anvil, | softened to a bruised yellow fruit'. Though Olds is sometimes seen by critics as a shriller Sylvia *Plath who deals with less important subjects, she really does not take herself so seriously. Her poems have the saving grace of humour: 'When I take my girl to the swimming party | I set her down among the boys. They tower and | bristle, she stands there smooth and sleek, | her math scores unfolding in the air around her.' *Strike Sparks* (2004) selects from all her books to 2002. It has been followed by *One Secret Thing* (2008). Since *The Wellspring* (1996—all Knopf) Olds has also been published in the UK by Cape.   PS

Oliver, Douglas (1937–2000) Born in Hampshire to Scottish parents, Oliver left school at sixteen and worked as a journalist in Coventry, Cambridge, and Paris. He later attended the University of Essex, and taught at the British Institute in Paris.

His first book, *Oppo Hectic* (1969), published by Andrew *Crozier's Ferry Press, established his place among the poets of the *Cambridge School. *The Harmless Building*, a novel, followed (Ferry/Grosseteste, 1973). *In the Cave of Suicession* (Street Editions, 1974) records an experiment in oracular consciousness, conducted with a typewriter in a cave in Derbyshire. The death of Oliver's young son, born with Down's Syndrome, is a recurring theme from this period. *The Diagram Poems* (Ferry, 1979) imagines 'Tom' haunting the night shift at Agence France-Presse, providing a moral touchstone as his father tracks reports of the Tupamaro guerrillas in Uruguay.

Later sequences became explicitly political in address, risking didacticism in the hope of provoking public response. *The Infant and the Pearl* (1985) is a rewriting of the intricately rhymed medieval dream poem for (that is, against) Margaret Thatcher's Britain. It was reprinted in *three variations on the theme of harm* (Paladin, 1990). *Penniless Politics* (Hoarse Commerce, 1991) a vision of underclass America, by a poet now living in New York. *A Salvo For Africa* (Bloodaxe, 2000) appeared shortly before his death. A hybrid memoir, *Whisper 'Louise'* (Reality Street, 2005), was completed by his second wife, the American poet Alice *Notley. *Poetry and Narrative in Performance* outlines Oliver's original theory of prosody (Macmillan/St Martins, 1989).   JNT

Oliver, Mary (1935–) Born in Ohio and attended Ohio State University and Vassar College; she has taught at Case Western Reserve. Her first four collections—*No Voyage and Other Poems* (1965), *The River Styx and Other Poems* (1972), *The Night Traveler* (1978), and *Sleeping in the Forest* (1979)—revealed a poet in full command of considerable technical resources who delighted in odd line-breaks and varying rhyme placements. Her work has been compared to that of Theodore *Roethke, James *Wright, and Emily Dickinson, although it is the former's intense identification with nature's remorseless processes that most strikingly characterizes her lyric approach. Unlike

Roethke, however, she exhibits a didactic tendency which sometimes attenuates her keen, empathetic observations.

Oliver's fifth collection, *American Primitive* (Little, Brown, 1983), earned her a Pulitzer Prize. *New and Selected Poems* (1992, Beacon Press), won a National Book Award, and has become one of the best-selling volumes of poetry in America. It was followed by a second volume in 2004.

Since the turn of the century, Oliver has been prolific, publishing poems, prose, and spoken-word CDs. She is a popular reader of her own work and has received several honorary doctorates. She is also the author of two books on writing poetry: *A Poetry Handbook* (Harcourt, 1994) and *Rules for the Dance* (Houghton, 1999). *Our World* (2007) is a tribute in words and pictures to her partner, the photographer Molly Malone Cook.   EB*

Olson, Charles (1910–70) Born and raised in Worcester, Massachusetts, and educated at Wesleyan University and Harvard, where he studied American civilization. During the Second World War he worked for the Democratic Party and for the Office of War Information as assistant chief of the Foreign Language Division. His first two books, *Call Me Ishmael* (1947), a study of Melville's *Moby-Dick*, and *The Mayan Letters* (1953), written to Robert *Creeley from Mexico where he was studying Mayan hieroglyphics, cover a range of subjects—mythology, anthropology, language, and cultural history—and use the fervent informal style that was to distinguish all his discursive prose. Olson's influential manifesto, *Projective Verse*, was published in pamphlet form in 1950 and then quoted generously in William Carlos *Williams' *Autobiography* (1951). In the 'projective', or 'open', verse it recommends, which aims to transfer energy from the world to the reader without artificial interference, syntax is shaped by sound, not sense; sense is conveyed by direct movement from one perception to another, not rational argument; and the reader's rendition directed by freely varied spacing between words and lines on the page. For Olson two factors are crucial in allowing the poet to translate the moment-by-moment process of composition into language. One is the poet's own breathing, which Olson insists must generate the poem's shape and rhythms; the other is the typewriter (Olson assumes that modern poets compose on it), which allows for a precise mechanical registering of 'the intervals of its composition'.

Olson himself had started writing poetry in the late 1940s, and 'The Kingfishers', the longest poem in his first collection, *In Cold Hell, In Thicket* (1953), remains his most striking demonstration of projective verse. *The Distances* (1960), his second collection, is less formally innovative but more ambitious in treating personal dreams and universal myths. In 1951 Olson succeeded the artist Josef Albers as rector of *Black Mountain College, North Carolina, and remained there until it closed in 1956. He taught again—at the State University of New York, Buffalo (1963–5)—but, settling in Gloucester, Massachusetts, devoted most of his time and energy in subsequent years to *The Maximus Poems*, his most substantial work.

Begun in 1950 as a sequence of verse letters to his friend Vincent Ferrini, and modelled formally on *Pound's *Cantos*, *The Maximus Poems* is, in Olson's words, 'a poem of a person and a place'. In the first volume, *The Maximus Poems* (1960), Maximus (named after an itinerant Phoenician mystic of the fourth century, but referring also to Olson, who was six feet eight inches tall), dismayed by the culture of contemporary Gloucester, examines its origins in the European settlement of America. In the second volume, *The Maximus Poems, IV, V, VI* (1968), his interest widens to embrace ancient myths and religious texts, and narrows to scrutinize certain documentary details of Gloucester's past. The unfinished final volume, *The Maximus Poems, Volume Three* (1975), imagines a new Gloucester in which material and commercial values have been abandoned and spiritual and communal values restored. The complete work, *The Maximus Poems* (1983), and the rest of Olson's verse, *The Collected Poems of Charles Olson* (1987), have both been edited by George F. Butterick. *Collected Prose* (1997), eds. Donald Allen and Benjamin

Friedlander, has an introduction by Robert Creeley, who also edited a *Selected Poems* (1997). See also *Selected Letters*, ed. Ralph Maud (2001—all University of California Press), *Muthologos: Lectures and Interviews*, ed. Ralph Maud (revd. and expanded edn., Talonbooks, 2010), and *The Poetry of Charles Olson: A Primer*, by Thomas F. Merrill (University of Delaware Press, 1982). There are biographies by Ralph Maud and Tom *Clark.   NE/RG*

Olson, Elder (1909–92) A member of the Neo-Aristotelians, so named by Kenneth *Burke, a group of critics based at the University of Chicago, where Olson taught from 1942 to 1977. He was by no means exclusively an Aristotelian, however, and a great range of theoretical positions are adopted in his well-regarded critical works, which include *Tragedy and the Theory of Drama* (Wayne State University Press, 1961), *The Theory of Comedy* (Indiana University Press, 1968), and *On Value Judgment in the Arts, and Other Essays* (University of Chicago Press, 1976).

As a poet, Olson was by no means a programmatic Aristotelian either. He is perhaps best known as a dramatic lyricist, but his work resists easy categorization and ranges from meditative poems to comic verse. An exceedingly demanding precisionist and craftsman, he worked slowly, and in a prefatory note to *Last Poems* (University of Chicago Press, 1984), wrote that the book was so named 'not because I think I shall write no more, but because—considering my rate of production—I think it unlikely that I shall make another collection'.

Olson was also a playwright and a pianist, who once considered a professional career as a musician.

His *Collected Poems* (1963) was followed by *Olson's Penny Arcade* (1975—both University of Chicago Press, 1975) and *Last Poems*. See Thomas E. Lucas, *Elder Olson* (Twayne, 1972), and James L. Battersby, *Elder Olson: An Annotated Bibliography* (Garland, 1983).   EHF

Ondaatje, Michael (1943–   ) Born in Sri Lanka, where he lived for eleven years. He was educated at Dulwich College in England, before emigrating to Canada, where he studied at Bishop's University, University of Toronto, and Queen's University, completing an MA thesis on Edwin *Muir. Ondaatje has lived in Toronto for many years and has taught intermittently at Glendon College at York University. He has been involved in the staging of some of his work and has long been interested in film-making, producing a film about bp *Nichol called *Sons of Captain Poetry* and a documentary about Theatre Passe Muraille's 'The Farm Show', called *The Clinton Special*. Ondaatje's writings are numerous and have been enthusiastically received. The poems include *The Dainty Monsters* (Coach House, 1967), *The Collected Works of Billy the Kid* (Anansi, 1970; repr. with an afterword, Knopf, 2008), *There's A Trick With A Knife I'm Learning to Do* (McClelland & Stewart/Norton, 1979), and *Secular Love* (Coach House, 1984; Norton 1985). His prose works include *Coming Through Slaughter* (1976), *Running in the Family* (1982), *In the Skin of a Lion* (1987), and *The English Patient* (1992), which was joint-winner of the 1992 Booker Prize, and was later made into an award-winning film.

There is a startling intimacy, or physicality, in Ondaatje's work, that derives from an imagination closely attuned to the body and its processes. The personae in his poems notice the movement of bones in a wrist, the archaeology of scars, and the politics of personal space. His method is that of the cinematic close-up or the image that conjures the inscape of a human or animal figure.

If Ondaatje is a subtle student of human behaviour, he is also a dramatist of disaster; charting transformations in the personal fortunes of his characters as they spiral towards madness. His short narratives, including 'Peter', 'Elisabeth', and *The Man With Seven Toes* (1969), move with the slow-motion quality one associates with the dream state, where violence is all the more powerful because it is indirect or understated. And the figures of Buddy Bolden in *Coming Through Slaughter* and Pat Garrett in *The Collected Works of Billy the Kid*, who is described as a sane assassin, embody the full measure of the irrational energy that underscores Ondaatje's situations and characters. See *The Cinammon Peeler: Selected Poems* (Picador, 1989; Knopf, 1991). *Handwriting: Poems* (McClelland & Stewart, 1998; Knopf, 1999) and *Anil's Ghost* (2000), a novel, return to the Sri Lanka of his childhood.   GG

Oppen, George (1908–84) Born in Alsace-Lorraine and grew up in San Francisco. Oppen had a small income from a trust fund on which he and his wife Mary could live. In the Fifties the Oppens lived in Mexico, where George ran a small carpenter's shop. His first book, *Discrete Series*, appeared in 1934.

Though associated with William Carlos *Williams and the '*Objectivists', Carl *Rakosi, Charles *Reznikoff, and Louis *Zukofsky, Oppen felt a greater kinship with the anonymous poet of 'O Western Wind' and Blake than with poets who kept their eye on the object. He was interested in images which retain a trace of the sacred. His poems have an intensity of vision that he took from the *Imagists—seeing, as Blake prescribed, '*through*' the eye.

Oppen wrote no poetry for twenty-eight years after *Discrete Series*, and while he always tended to explain the hiatus in terms of other commitments and concerns, he acceded to Hugh Kenner when Kenner interrupted his narrative of lost time in an interview to say, 'in other words, it took you twenty-eight years to write the next poem'. After that his work rapidly gathered velocity and momentum: he wrote like a man reborn. *The Materials* appeared in 1962 and *This In Which* in 1965, but only with *Of Being Numerous* (1968) does Oppen begin doing his best work.

Oppen is a modernist with a populist streak, and a conscience. There is a sense in his work that every increment of the poem has meaning, that the placement of each word, each line-break, is of primary importance. There is no appeasing flow in Oppen, no narrative. Everything about him bespeaks a certain spareness, an obsession with the 'unearthly bonds | Of the singular | Which is the bright light of shipwreck' ('Of Being Numerous'). A poem, for Oppen, is a realm of pure attention. His goal is always 'to somehow see the one thing'.

In the 1970s Oppen returned to San Francisco and just as he had captured New York and 'a language, therefore, of New York' in *Of Being Numerous*, in *Seascape: Needle's Eye* he grasps San Francisco and the feel of the late Sixties from an interested, engaged, yet sceptical perspective.

He did not want 'things themselves' but 'to construct a method of thought from the imagist technique of poetry—from the imagist intensity of vision'. Oppen's work is notable for what it leaves out: it abounds in gaps, white space.

Oppen's main collections are: *Discrete Series* (1932–4), *The Materials* (1962), *This In Which* (1965), *Of Being Numerous* (1968), *Seascape: Needle's Eye* (1972), *Myth of the Blaze* (1972–5), *Primitive* (1978). *The Collected Poems of George Oppen 1929–1975* appeared in New York and London in 1975. *New Collected Poems*, ed. Michael Davidson, and a *Selected Poems*, ed. Robert *Creeley, appeared from New Directions in 2002 and 2003 respectively. See also: *Meaning a Life*, by Mary Oppen (Black Sparrow, 1978), *The Selected Letters of George Oppen*, ed. Rachel Blau DuPlessis (Duke University Press, 1990), and *Selected Prose, Daybooks, and Papers*, ed. Stephen Cope (University of California Press, 2008). There is a growing body of criticism around Oppen's work. Two recent studies are Peter Nicholls' *George Oppen and the Fate of Modernism* (Oxford University Press, 2007) and Michael Heller's *Speaking the Estranged: Essays on the Work of George Oppen* (Salt, 2008; expanded edn., Shearsman, 2012).   MRU

Oppenheimer, Joel (1930–88) One of the principal members of the 'second generation' of *Black Mountain poets. A student at Black Mountain College for three years, where his mentors included Charles *Olson and Paul Goodman, he became professionally a printer and later a teacher. He was also the first director of the *Saint Mark's Church Poetry Project in New York (1966–8), a columnist for the *Village Voice*, a playwright, a fiction writer, and the author of popular books on baseball and Marilyn Monroe. He is best known for his deeply personal poetry, in which the 'I' (or 'i' as he prints it) is central. Oppenheimer's poetics are grounded in Jungian psychology, however, and the personal in his poems can often be read as a manifestation of the archetypal. Like Robert *Creeley's work, Oppenheimer's tends to be written in short, abrupt lines, but it is generally less conflicted and jagged in its rhythms.

Poetry, the Ecology of the Soul (White Pine, 1983), ed. David Landrey and Dennis Maloney, includes several talks and a selection of the poetry. David Thibodaux's *Joel Oppenheimer: An Introduction* (Camden House, 1986) is a useful critical study. See Lyman Gilmore, *Don't Touch the Poet: The Life and Times of Joel Oppenheimer* (Talisman House, 1998).   EHF

Ormond, John (1923–90) Born at Dunvant in Swansea and educated at the University College in that town. He joined the staff of *Picture Post* in 1945.

His early verse (written under the name Ormond Thomas) appeared in the volume *Indications* with that of James *Kirkup and John Bayliss in 1943, but on the advice of Vernon *Watkins he wrote little more until the mid-1960s, when he began contributing to the magazine *Poetry Wales*. By that time he had had a distinguished career with BBC Wales as a maker of documentary films about Welsh painters and writers, including Ceri Richards, Dylan *Thomas, Alun *Lewis, and R. S. *Thomas.

The volume *Requiem and Celebration* (1969) collects work written over a period of twenty-five years; it is uneven in quality but provided evidence of his struggle to find his own voice. It was followed by *Definition of a Waterfall* (1973) which consolidated his reputation as one of the best Welsh poets of his generation.

There is a brilliance and eloquence about John Osmond's poems that are recognizably Welsh. Many are rooted in Swansea: local and elegiac they may sometimes be, and wryly affectionate for the people who made him—family, neighbours, and village characters—but they also tackle more complex themes such as personal identity, communal loyalty, the natural world, and love between men and women, confronting the numinous with an attractive wit and fortitude. His best poems are unsentimental but emotionally effective, and they are usually meticulously crafted.

John Ormond's best work appeared in his *Selected Poems* (Poetry Wales, 1987); another selection is to be found in *Penguin Modern Poets, 27* (1978). There is an autobiographical essay by the poet in *Artists in Wales*, ed. Meic Stephens (Gomer, 1973); see also *In Place of Empty Heaven*, a study of Wallace *Stevens (the W. D. Thomas Memorial Lecture at University College, Swansea, 1982).   MS

Ormsby, Eric (1941–) Born in Atlanta, Georgia, and raised in Miami, Ormsby studied at the universities of Pennsylvania and Princeton. A professor at McGill University in Montreal for many years, and latterly at the Institute of Ismaili Studies in London, he has had a distinguished career as a scholar of Islamic thought.

Ormsby's delight in flamboyant description has often seen him compared to Wallace *Stevens. But the dandyish opening of an anthology piece such as 'Flamingos' is really a parodic 'quarrel' with Stevens for preferring a 'fatal petal | tint' over the ruder reality of the 'rubicund'. The 'words acting in concert' of Ormsby's intricately composed poems—on animals, landscapes, and family life—reveal themselves to be more concerned with the empirical than the imaginary, after the example of Marianne *Moore, who would also take 'satisfaction in the prompt | pinnacle of waves . . . | . . . that sense | Precision amid pandemonium | Provides' ('Gazing at Waves'). *Time's Covenant: New and Selected Poems* (Biblioasis, 2007) appeared in Canada, and draws on five previous collections, beginning with *Bavarian Shrine* (ECW, 1990). A later selected poems, *The Baboons of Hada* (2011), has been published in the UK by Carcanet. See also his two collections of critical prose: *Facsimiles of Time: Essays on Poetry and Translation* (2001), and *Fine Incisions: Essays on Poetry and Place* (2010—both Porcupine's Quill).   JNT

Ormsby, Frank (1947–) Born in Enniskillen, Co. Fermanagh, and has stayed in

Northern Ireland. Educated at Queen's University, Belfast, he began editing *Honest Ulsterman* magazine as a student, and remained its editor until 1989. From 1971 he taught English at the Royal Belfast Academical Institution, and has consistently championed the work of other Ulster poets. He has edited several anthologies, including *A Rage for Order: Poetry of the Northern Ireland Troubles* (Blackstaff Press, 1992), and the *Collected Poems* of John *Hewitt (1992). Ormsby won an Eric Gregory Award for his own poetry in 1974.

His first full collection, *A Store of Candles* (Oxford University Press, 1977), concentrates with a defiant exactness of phrase and observation on the life existing behind and around the headlines that make the province's public history. His poems resemble 'The Practical Farms' with which the book starts: making use of detail, asserting a faith in form which survives violent, off-stage eruptions almost intact. Unobtrusive half-rhymes suggest equivalences that work against or above political allegiances, and allow for surprisingly tender explorations of a family's movements through the Troubles. The impressive sequence which provides the title of Ormsby's next collection, *A Northern Spring* (Secker & Warburg/Gallery, 1986), complicates these despatches from 'My Careful Life' by adopting personae and different voices to relive his family's experiences of the two world wars as retailed in their journals. He has continued to publish at the rate of a collection a decade, each quietly registering changing personal and historical circumstances: see *The Ghost Train* (Gallery, 1995) and *Fireflies* (Carcanet, 2009), which travels in America, nodding to Robert *Frost and others.   MRW*

Orr, Bob (Robert) (1949–) Born in Hamilton, Orr grew up in rural Waikato, and has spent much of his working life as a boatman on Waitemata Harbour, Auckland. The early poems of *Blue Footpaths* (Amphedesma, 1971) testify to the influence of the *Beat poets on New Zealand poets published in *Freed* magazine ('belting out | crazy meditations | on a plastic typewriter' ('Baudelaire's Scarf')). *Poems for Moira*

(Hawk, 1979) saw him refine this style towards the momentary itemizing of delicate emotion, with a hesitancy reminiscent of Robert *Creeley (see 'Love Poem', from *Cargo* (Voice, 1983)). Drawn to urban life, travel, and seascapes, his later collections are *Red Trees* (1985), *Breeze* (1991), *Valparaiso* (2002), and *Calypso* (2008—all Auckland University Press).   JNT

Orr, Gregory (1947–) Born in Albany, New York, the son of a physician. He attended Hamilton College from 1964 to 1966 but completed his BA at Antioch College in 1969 and his MFA at Columbia University in 1972. He teaches at the University of Virginia in Charlottesville.

Burning the Nests Empty (1973), his widely praised first collection, was followed by *Gathering the Bones Together* (1975) and *The Red House* (1980). In 1985 he published *Stanley *Kunitz: An Introduction to the Poetry* in the Columbia University series on twentieth-century American poetry, and a fourth book of his own poems, *We Must Make a Kingdom*, the next year. His spare poetry often seems a *Deep Image-esque mixture of Charles *Simic, James *Tate, and David *Ignatow in its use of small personal anecdotes to link together a chain of surreal associations and juxtapositions, often grotesque or morbid in content.

Since *City of Salt* (University of Pittsburgh Press, 1995) Orr has been published by Copper Canyon Press, who issued a new and selected poems, *The Caged Owl*, in 2002. Two later books—*Concerning the Book That Is the Body of the Beloved* (2005) and *How Beautiful the Beloved* (2009)—see Orr developing a mode of lyric mysticism.

His writings on poetry have been collected in *Richer Entanglements* (University of Michigan Press, 1993) and *Poetry as Survival* (University of Georgia Press, 2002). *The Blessing* (Council Oak, 2002) is an acclaimed memoir of a childhood overshadowed by a hunting accident in which he shot and killed his brother.   EB*

O'Sullivan, Maggie (1951–) Born in Lincolnshire to Irish parents. In the 1970s and 1980s O'Sullivan worked for the BBC, where she was involved in making arts documentaries. Since 1988 she has lived in Yorkshire, and taught writing at a wide range of institutions.

O'Sullivan's intensely lexical and visually dramatic work looks to 'outsider' modernists in Britain and *Language poetry in America. *Body of Work* (Reality Street, 2006) gathers and selects O'Sullivan's early small-press publications, from *Concerning Spheres* (Broken Ground, 1982) to *Unofficial Word* (Galloping Dog, 1988). Charles *Bernstein speaks of the 'medleyed consciousness' of these mosaic, neologizing poems, whose 'colliderings' (*Palace of Reptiles* (The Gig, 2003)) perform a poetics of incantation through expressively patterned typography.

Live performance is an important part of O'Sullivan's work. *her/story:eye* (STEM recordings, 2004) is a reading of two later 'bookworks', *red shifts* and *WATERFALLS* (etruscan, 2001 and 2009). Her central vision is of art as a mediation between the natural and the spiritual world, a form of social magic that reveals a suppressed collectivity: see *In the House of the Shaman* (Reality Street, 1993—the title alludes to a drawing by Joseph Beuys). O'Sullivan also published several titles through Bob *Cobbing's Writers Forum press, including a collaboration with Bruce *Andrews, *eXcLa* (1993). In 1996 she edited *out of everywhere* (Reality Street), an anthology of linguistically innovative poetry by women in North America and the UK.   JNT

O'Sullivan, Vincent (1937–) Born in Auckland, New Zealand. He graduated from Auckland University (1959) and Oxford (1962), where he was a Commonwealth Scholar at Lincoln College. After lecturing at the universities of Victoria, Wellington (1963–6) and Waikato (1968–78), he became literary editor of the *New Zealand Listener* (1978–80). This was followed by freelance writing and (from 1981) literary and research fellowships in New Zealand and Australia. He was appointed to a chair in the English department at the University of Victoria, Wellington, in 1987, where he is now emeritus professor.

O'Sullivan's works include plays, two novels, a critical monograph, four volumes of short stories, the five-volume Letters of

Katherine Mansfield (co-editor), a biography of John Mulgan, and anthologies of New Zealand literature.

O'Sullivan's first two volumes of poetry, *Our Burning Time* (1965) and *Revenants* (1969—both Prometheus), make revealing reading. Though introspective and convoluted, they contain lines of force that anticipate the satirical poems to come, and they provided early literary exercises in the tense and sinewy compressions that characterize his later work.

Bearings (Oxford University Press, 1973) was followed by *From the Indian Funeral* (McIndoe, 1976). Here the poems deal with personal observation, experience and feeling, and the themes that illuminate his mature poetry can be detected.

His later volumes include: *Butcher and Co.* (Oxford University Press, 1977); *Brother Jonathan, Brother Kafka* (McIndoe, 1978); *The Butcher Papers* (Oxford University Press, 1982); *The Rose Ballroom and Other Poems* (McIndoe, 1982); *The Pilate Tapes* (1986); and *Selected Poems* (1992—both Oxford University Press).

Further Convictions Pending: Poems 1998–2008 collects poems from collections published between *Seeing You Asked* (1998) to *Blame Vermeer* (2007—all Victoria University Press), two of which won the Poetry category in the Montana New Zealand Book Awards. In 2000, O'Sullivan was made a Distinguished Companion of the New Zealand Order of Merit, and in 2006 received a Prime Minister's Award for Literary Achievement.   KI

Osundare, Niyi (1947–) Osundare lectured at the University of Ibadan and since 1997 has been Professor of English at the University of New Orleans. He is a leading figure among English-language poets in Nigeria. He might be described as a committed poet, as a self-consciously political writer, for his work deals with profoundly serious and topical themes. But this could be misleading. His collection *The Eye of the Earth* (Heinemann, 1986) is as much a celebration of the natural world and the peasant traditions of his Ikere people as it is a political critique. Osundare seems always conscious of the priorities of his craft; his poetry is by turns lyrical and declamatory, carefully structured and full of vivid, original imagery. His other collections include *Moonsongs* (Spectrum Books, 1988), *Waiting Laughters* (Niyi Osundare, 1989), which won the Noma Award for Publishing in Africa, and *Midlife* (Heinemann, 1993).

Pages from the Book of the Sun (2002) was a new and selected volume, and *Thread in the Loom* (2002) a collection of essays on African literature and culture (both Africa World Press). *Tender Moments: Love Poems* (University Press, Nigeria, 2006) reflects on the devastation of the poet's life in America after Hurricane Katrina in 2005.   SB

Oswald, Alice (1966–) Born in Reading, Oswald read Classics at Oxford University, and then worked as a gardener. She is married to the playwright, Peter Oswald, and lives in Devon.

The Thing in the Gap-Stone Stile (Oxford University Press, 1996) won the Forward Prize for Best First Collection, and reflects Oswald's grounding in traditional forms (the Shakespearean sonnet 'Wedding' has become a popular reading at ceremonies). The natural world is often a source of metaphor in her work, but its concerns are never far from the life of the mind observing it. Her second book, *Dart* (2002), was a polyphonic 'map poem' which channels, in appropriately fluid verse, three years of talking with people met along the River Dart in Devon. *A Sleepwalk on the Severn* (2009—both Faber), commissioned for performance, similarly explores Britain's longest river.

Woods etc. (2005) returned to the lyric modes of her debut with a new swiftness of perception. In the same year she edited an ecopoetic anthology, *The Thunder Mutters*. *Weeds and Wild Flowers* (2009), a collaboration with the artist Jessica Greenman, recalls Ted *Hughes' illustrated volumes, and draws on her horticultural expertise in lighter verse about 'rootless misfits'. The importance of Hughes' example to Oswald is evident in the oral formalism and chthonic imagery of *Memorial* (2011—all Faber), her 'excavation' of the dead in *The Iliad* ('Grief is black it is made of earth'). She has also made a selection of Sir Thomas Wyatt's verse.   JNT

Owen, Jan (1940–) Born in Adelaide, South Australia, of Australian and Hungar-

ian ancestry. She is married with three children. Her first book, *Boy With A Telescope* appeared in 1986, and her second, *Fingerprints on Light* (1990—both Angus & Robertson) confirmed the range of her subject-matter, which includes character-studies, historical vignettes, and an extended impressionistic series of monologues based on the 1780s French expedition to explore the Pacific, commanded by La Perouse.

Owen's verse holds an easy equilibrium between a contemporary use of traditional forms and the breath-related experiments of projective-verse composition initiated by Charles *Olson. Her awareness of a distinctively Australian pace holds a poise between laconicism and enthusiasm. *Poems: 1980–2008* (Leonard, 2008) selects from five volumes and also contains a new collection, *Laughing in Greek*, also the title of a spoken-word CD from River Road Press. It was widely admired for the subtlety with which Owen has developed her thinking about science, art, and the metaphorical description of experience (see the witty, wide-ranging quatrains of 'Travelling Towards the Evidence').   JRO*

Owen, Wilfred (Edward Salter) (1893–1917) Born in Oswestry. His parents were then living in a comfortable house owned by his grandfather, Edward Shaw. At his death two years later this former mayor of the city was found to be almost bankrupt, and Tom Owen was obliged to move with his wife and son to lodgings in the back-streets of Birkenhead. They carried with them vivid memories of their vanished prosperity, and Susan Owen resolved that her adored son Wilfred should in time restore the family to its rightful gentility. She was a devout woman, and under her influence Wilfred grew into a serious and slightly priggish boy. At school in Birkenhead and later in Shrewsbury—where Tom Owen was appointed assistant superintendent of the Joint Railways in 1906—he worked hard and successfully, especially at literature and botany.

Leaving school in 1911, Owen took up a post as lay assistant to the vicar of Dunsden in Oxfordshire. Removed from his mother's influence, he became less enamoured of evangelical religion and more critical of the role of the Church—as represented by the vicar—in society. His letters and poems of this period show an increasing awareness of the sufferings of the poor and the first stirrings of the compassion that was to characterize his later poems about the Western Front. He attended botany classes at Reading University and was encouraged by the professor of English to read and write more poetry. In February 1913, on the verge of a nervous breakdown, he left Dunsden and, when he had recovered, crossed to France where he taught at the Berlitz School of Languages in Bordeaux.

He was in the Pyrenees, acting as tutor in a cultivated French household, when war was declared. A visit to a hospital for the wounded soon opened his eyes to the true nature of war, but it was not until September 1915 that he finally decided to return to England and enlist. Commissioned into the Manchester Regiment, Owen crossed the Channel on 30 December 1916 and, in the first days of 1917, joined the 2nd Manchesters on the Somme near Beaumont Hamel. In March he fell into a cellar and suffered concussion, and some weeks later, after fierce fighting near St Quentin, was invalided home with shell-shock. At Craiglockhart War Hospital, on the outskirts of Edinburgh, he met Siegfried *Sassoon. Discharged in October, he was posted successively to Scarborough and Ripon, where many of his finest poems were written. At the end of August, he was certified 'fit to proceed overseas' and, a month later, was again in action. He was awarded the Military Cross for his part in a successful attack on the Beaurevoir-Fonsomme Line and, before sunrise on the morning of 4 November, led his platoon to the west bank of the Sambre and Oise Canal. They came under fire from German machine-guns behind the parapet of the east bank, and at the height of the ensuing battle Owen was hit and killed.

He had begun writing poems when he was 10 or 11 and soon fell under the influence of Keats, who was to remain the principal influence on his work, at least until at Dunsden he discovered the more political Shelley and, later, the Romantics' successors, the English and French poets of the Nineties. In a poem of 1912 Owen sees himself as 'a meteor, fast, eccentric, lone', moving through darkness; a prophecy to be

fulfilled when—in the words of his sonnet '1914'—'War broke: and now the Winter of the world | With perishing great darkness closed in.' Having survived his first exposure to that murderous darkness, he met Sassoon, whose 'war poems' had just been collected in *The Old Huntsman and Other Poems* (1917). This introduced him to a colloquial language (to which Sassoon had himself been introduced by *Hardy) suitable for rendering the experience of battle. Under Sassoon's influence, and with his sympathetic encouragement, Owen purged his style of archaism and poetic diction to find a voice of his own. At Craiglockhart, probably in August 1917, he read the anonymous 'Prefatory Note' to an anthology, *Poems of Today* (1916), that spoke of one contributor who had 'gone singing to lay down his life for his country's cause', and ended with the statement that the poets' themes 'mingle and interpenetrate throughout, to the music of Pan's flute, and of Love's viol, and the bugle-call of Endeavour and the passing bell of Death'. It is not difficult to imagine Owen responding to this euphemistic rubbish with his 'Anthem for Doomed Youth', beginning: 'What passing bells for these who die as cattle?' There is no time to give them the trappings of a Christian funeral that Owen remembers from his Dunsden days; instead, they receive a brutal parody of such a service ('demented choirs of wailing shells'), and bitterly but obliquely he assigns responsibility for their deaths. The manuscript of this poem shows Owen and Sassoon working on it together, but although one can detect Sassoon's influence in the target of its protest—the *old* men of the Army, Church, and Government who send *young* men to their deaths—its metaphorical and musical texture is more complex than anything Sassoon had so far achieved: for example, the word-play in Owen's line, 'The pallor of girls' brows shall be their pall'. This device was to find its fullest expression in the system of pararhyming that would prove his major contribution to the technique of English poetry. The second pararhyme of a pair would usually be lower in pitch than the first ('escaped/scooped', 'grained/groaned'), which gives the musical movement of a poem like 'Strange Meeting' a dying fall that underscores the tragic unfulfilment that is its theme.

'Anthem for Doomed Youth' is only one of a number of Owen's poems triggered by an indignant response to a prior text. 'Dulce et Decorum Est' is another, prompted by Horace's Latin sentence and the jingoistic verse of Jessie Pope, to whom Owen's manuscripts reveal the poem was originally dedicated. Sassoon showed his young friend how to articulate and direct his indignation, and the intensity of Owen's compassion for suffering boys probably owes something to the homosexual orientation that he must latterly have recognized but may have resisted. It is clear that a principal cause of his distress at Craiglockhart was to prove a principal factor in the liberation and organization of his poems: the recurrent dreams that are a symptom of shellshock. The realities of battle, banished from his waking mind, now erupt into his dreams and into his poems: dreams and poems alike are often haunted by tormented eyes (as in 'Dulce et Decorum Est')—those, perhaps, of the sentry he saw blinded in January 1917, the subject of his late poem 'The Sentry'. The dream-like intensity of this, and the dreamscapes of 'Strange Meeting' and 'The Show', contribute to the mythic power of Owen's best work and set him in a tradition that extends back to Dante, Virgil, Homer, and beyond. His vision of a subterranean Hell, its mouth agape, can be traced through these and other poems of his brief maturity and adolescence to the Calvinist Hell of which he heard at his mother's knee. Owen's descents into the Underworld have a curious common denominator: in each case the earth is described in terms of the human body (mouth, throat, womb), and usually with a marked sense of physical revulsion. This is the more strange and tragic since his early poems abound in lyrical descriptions of beautiful bodies and celebrations of the natural world.

Owen may have repudiated the Church of England in which his mother hoped he would make his career, but he never wavered in his belief in the person and teachings of Christ. This left him on the battlefield, as he said, 'a Conscientious Objector with a very seared conscience'. In his celebrated draft Preface for the book of poems he was never to see in print, he wrote: 'All a poet can do today is warn. That is why the true Poets must be truthful. It sounds easy, but it is not easy to tell the truth in a poem, especially a truth from which the memory recoils.' He tells the truth when he says in 'The Sentry': 'I try not to remember these things now.' But, when he tries to forget them, 'Eyeballs, huge-bulged like squids' | Watch my dreams still'. In those dreams the horror is reborn, the reality of battle reshaped to the dimensions of the poem; poems to which we, his readers, owe—more than to any others—our vision of the reality of the Western Front, of Hell on earth.

The most recent and comprehensive edition of Owen's poetry is *The Complete Poems and Fragments*, ed. Jon Stallworthy (Chatto & Windus 1983; Norton, 1984). He also edited the paperback *Poems of Wilfred Owen* (Chatto & Windus, 1985), and wrote the standard biography, *Wilfred Owen* (Oxford University Press, 1974). See also *Owen the Poet*, by Dominic Hibberd (Macmillan, 1986).   JHS

Oyebode, Femi (1954–) Grew up in Lagos and studied medicine in Ibadan before going to England to study psychiatry. He has lived and practised as a psychiatrist in Birmingham since 1980. His first collection of poems, *Naked to Your Softness and Other Dreams* (1988), was much admired by reviewers in both Britain and Nigeria. His second, *Wednesday is a Colour* (1990—both Ijala), is similar in style: constructed of five sequences that seem—but are not directly—linked, charting a personal effort to understand the experience of exile. Oyebode's manner is a distinctive combination of the imagistic lyric and the densely referential prosaic. There is a narrative unfolding in the sequences but it is hardly linear or transparent. There is a surreal edge to Oyebode's work, but its 'difficulty' evolves as much from his absorption in Yoruba mythology and the ideas of contemporary psychology. See *Selected Poems* (Kraft Books, 1998; repr. 2001), edited with an introduction by Onookome Okome. Oyebode has also edited and contributed to a volume of essays on literature and psychiatry, *Mindreadings* (Royal College of Psychiatrists, 2009).   SB

Padel, Ruth (1946–) A great-great-grandchild of Charles Darwin, born in London and educated at the University of Oxford, where she later taught Classics. Her publication career began with scholarly works on Greek tragedy: *In and Out of the Mind: Greek Images of the Tragic Self* (1992) and *Whom Gods Destroy: Elements of Greek and Tragic Madness* (1995), both from Princeton University Press.

She emerged as a poet substantially in the 1990s, beginning with the collection *Angel* (Bloodaxe, 1993) and continuing with increasing assurance and originality through *Fusewire* (1996) and the groundbreaking rhythmic triumph of *Rembrandt Would Have Loved You* (1998). Padel's structures are frequently influenced by the choral patterns found in Greek tragedy, producing coiled springs of stanzas whose energy and agility are sometimes reminiscent of Hopkins. Further collections are *Voodoo Shop* (2002), *The Soho Leopard* (2004), *Darwin: A Life in Poems* (2009), and *The Mara Crossing* (2012—all Chatto & Windus). The latter, a prosimetrum, ranges over genre and discipline: ornithology, zoology, memoir, history, and travel-writing combine thrillingly, particularly in the prose essays.

Padel's other non-fiction prose works range from *I'm a Man: Sex, Gods and Rock 'n' Roll* (Faber, 2000) to *The Poem and the Journey, and Sixty Poems to Read Along the Way* (Chatto & Windus, 2007). The titles alone are indicative of her informal, broadstroked, imaginative pedagogy. She has also written a novel, *Where the Serpent Lives* (Little, Brown, 2010). Padel was elected the first woman Oxford Professor of Poetry in 2009 although she resigned the post without giving a lecture. CAR

Padgett, Ron (1942–) Born in Tulsa, Oklahoma, and attended Columbia University. He is married and lives in New York City, where he was a member of the Teachers and Writers Collaborative, a project that introduces school-children to poetry. Although he resists the label, he is generally viewed as a second-generation member of the *New York School, following in the footsteps of Frank *O'Hara, John *Ashbery, and Kenneth *Koch. In Padgett's case the seminal influence is probably that of Koch, with whom he studied at Columbia. Padgett's poems lack both the thematic complexity and depth of Ashbery and the documentary texture of O'Hara; their appeal lies chiefly in their bright, zany sense of humour and their cartoon imagery. Like Koch, Padgett cultivates a childlike sensibility. Convention, artifice, and cliché provide the primary stuff of his imagination, together with a fluid, discontinuous sense of form inherited from French *Surrealism.

A number of books have been produced in collaboration with other writers, like Ted *Berrigan, and with artists like Jim Dine and Joe Brainard: see the seminal *Bean Spasms* (1967), reprinted by Granary Books in 2012. In addition to his poetry, Padgett has translated the French poets Apollinaire, Larbaud, and Cendrars. His books of poems include *Tulsa Kid* (Z Press, 1979), and *Triangles in the Afternoon* (SUN, 1980).

Since *New and Selected Poems* in 1995 (Godine), he has published three collections with Coffee House Press: *You Never Know* (2002), *How to Be Perfect* (2008), and *How Long* (2011). In 2004, Padgett wrote a memoir of Brainard, *Joe* (Coffee House), and later edited his collected writings for the Library of America. See also: *The Straight Line: Writings on Poetry and Poets*

(University of Michigan Press, 2000) and *Oklahoma Tough: My Father, King of the Tulsa Bootleggers* (University of Oklahoma Press, 2003).   RG

Page, Geoff(rey Donald) (1940–)

Born in Grafton, New South Wales, and educated in Canberra, where he taught English and history until his retirement.

His interest in history is evident throughout his verse, and in the anthology he edited, *Shadows from the Wire: Poems and Photographs of Australians in the Great War* (1983), and is voiced too in the novels *Benton's Conviction* (1985) and *Winter Vision* (1989), and in the short prose pieces of *Invisible Histories* (1990). Influenced by Les *Murray, Page's linguistic range is, however, narrower than Murray's, his subject-matter and its handling more conservative, even nostalgic. Music, especially jazz, is another continuing interest, informing a range of formal experiments. These are most notable in *Footwork* (Angus & Robertson, 1988), which is Page at his most metrically and linguistically innovative. More typically, in volumes such as *Small-town Memorials* (University of Queensland Press, 1975), *Cassandra Paddocks* (1980), and *Collected Lives* (1986), his poetry is spare, almost reticent, though flashes of vivid imagery often fix a poem's image of the historic past with a modern tone or gesture. *Selected Poems* (1991) gives Page's own choice of the best from his previous eight volumes—a distillation of the careful voice of a craftsman poet. It was followed by *Gravel Corners* (1992—all Angus & Robertson) and *Human Interest* (Heinemann, 1994).

Since his fifteenth collection, *Darker and Lighter* in 2001 (Five Islands Press), he has published two verse novels—*Drumming on Water* (2003) and *Freehold* (2005—both Brandl & Schlesinger), as well as a 'movie in verse', *Lawrie and Shirley: The Final Cadenza* (Pandanus, 2006). See also *Seriatim* (Salt, 2007). Page has received both the Patrick White and Christopher Brennan awards, and is a well-known poetry reviewer and anthologist: see *A Reader's Guide to Contemporary Australian Poetry* (University of Queensland Press, 1995).   JD

Page, P. K. (Patricia Kathleen) (1916–2010)

Born in Swanage, England, but raised on the Canadian prairies by parents who migrated to Canada in 1919. After attending St Hilda's School in Calgary, she was employed initially as a shop assistant and radio actress in Saint John, New Brunswick, and worked later as a researcher and scriptwriter in Montreal at the National Film Board. From 1942 to 1945 she was associated with F. R. *Scott, A. M. *Klein, and Patrick *Anderson on the editorial board of *Preview*, an avant-garde literary magazine, and she published *As Ten as Twenty*, her first collection of poems, in 1946. In 1950 she married W. A. Irwin, who was then commissioner of the National Film Board and later Canada's ambassador to Australia, Brazil, and Mexico. It was while living abroad that she took up drawing and painting (exhibiting as P. K. Irwin). In 1954 she published *The Metal and the Flower*, and followed this with *Cry Ararat* (1967—both McClelland & Stewart), illustrated with her drawings, *Poems: Selected and New* (Anansi, 1974), and *Evening Dance of the Grey Flies* (Oxford University Press, 1981), which contains one of her stories, 'Unless the Eye Catch Fire'. Page was made a member of the Order of Canada in 1977 and lived in Victoria.

Page's earlier work is written, mostly, in a modernist, 'metaphysical' mode, and is characterized by density of metaphor, extraordinary juxtapositions, and attitudes that range from the whimsical to the ironic. Some of her later work is in a plainer style and expresses her symbolic search for a sense of unity of being. Several of her verses, like her drawings, are rich in images of plant life. Among her best-known poems is the frequently anthologized 'The Stenographers'.

Page continued to publish into her eighties and nineties. In 1997 her poems were collected in two volumes as *The Hidden Room*, and in 2004 she received the British Columbia Lieutenant Governor's Award for Literary Excellence. Her last book, *Coal and Roses* (2010), was a sequence of formal 'glosas' elaborating four-line quotations from a range of modern poets, including Ted *Hughes, Wallace *Stevens, and Dionne *Brand. It was posthumously shortlisted for the Griffin Poetry Prize. See *Planet Earth: Poems Selected and New*, ed. Eric Ormsby (2002) and *The Essential P. K. Page* (2008—all Porcupine's Quill). JST

Palmer, Michael (1943–) Born in New York City and educated at Harvard. Since 1969 he has lived in San Francisco with his wife, the architect Cathy Simon, and daughter. Palmer teaches intermittently but, unlike most poets of his generation, has not pursued a teaching career. He translates from the French, has collaborated on books with the painters Irving Petlin and Sandro Chia, and on dance with the Margaret Jenkins Dance Company.

Beginning with *Blake's Newton* (Black Sparrow) in 1972, ten full-length books of poetry have appeared—each a more radical exploration of his poetics than the last. Often grouped with the *Language poets and considered one of their precursors, Palmer's poems are an original synthesis of Louis *Zukofsky, *Surrealism, reading in philosophy and linguistic theory, *Beckett, Jack *Spicer, and Paul Celan. For all his daunting range of reference, Palmer's work has a sense of humour based on deadpan assertion and a use of misheard and misspoken speech. He builds his books around serial poems. Three of his most accomplished—*Notes for Echo Lake* (1981), *First Figure* (1984), and *Sun* (1988—all North Point)—have been collected by New Directions as *Codes Appearing* (2001). Constantly subverting their own lyric impulse, intelligent, and somewhat dry, yet supple in their inclusiveness, Palmer's poems speak in many voices at once.

His later books are *At Passages* (1995), *The Promises of Glass* (2000), *Company of Moths* (2005), and *Thread* (2011), as well as a selected poems, *The Lion Bridge* (1995—all New Directions). In 2006 the judges of the Poetry Society of America's Wallace Stevens Award called him 'the foremost experimental poet of his generation'. A useful introduction to his method and interests is Palmer's anthology *Code of Signals: Recent Writings in Poetics* (NorthAtlantic, 1983). WC

Pang, Alvin (1972–) Born in Singapore, Pang read English at the University of York. He has worked as a teacher, a civil servant, a journalist, a freelance editor, and an anthologist.

His first volume of poems, *Testing the Silence* (1997), was at the forefront of a new wave of poetry that was unabashedly contemporary and urban, throwing aside the academic slant of previous Singapore poetry, yet in Pang's case not without a sense of the provisional in his style. *City of Rain* (2003—both Ethos), Pang's second volume of poetry, establishes a voice that is playfully sardonic yet confident to the point of assertive, along with subject matter that at once embraces the increasing cultural diversity of the city and laments its limitations. Among these is a sense of Singapore as a small market for poetry, motivating Pang to seek overseas exposure, for instance through co-editing with John *Kinsella an anthology of Singaporean and Australian poetry, *Over There* (2008). His third volume, *When the Barbarians Arrive* (Arc, 2012), is a new and selected volume for an international audience. THM

Pankey, Eric (1959–) Born in Kansas City and educated at the University of Missouri and the University of Iowa. He was a member of the Iowa Writers' Workshop and is presently a professor of English at George Mason University, in Washington, DC. His first volume, *For the New Year* (1984), won the Walt Whitman Award of the Academy of American Poets.

Pankey's first three volumes, from the first, *For the New Year*, through *Heartwood* (1988—both Atheneum), and on to *Apocrypha* (Knopf, 1991), showed a development from an innocent, intelligent lyric poetry influenced by Robert *Frost towards a more complex poetry of argument dealing with difficult philosophical subject-matter. What have remained constant are Pankey's sharp observational skills, careful structural formality, and religious sensibility. The shift may be seen by comparing the too-easily won satisfactions of the early poem

'Elegy' with the later poem 'Prayer', which not only admits the possibilities of pain and suffering but actually performs a struggle with them. In *Apocrypha*, which is split into six sections with names like 'Depositions', 'Arguments', and 'Reconstructions', Pankey's whimsy has matured into a poetry of methodical wisdom that is reminiscent of *Eliot. Like Eliot's later work, however, the privilege of this increase in dialectical intensity has been the sacrifice of tonal variety and ambiguity. *The Pear as One Example: New and Selected Poems 1984–2008* draws on four further volumes, including *Reliquaries* (Ausable, 2005), a meditative landscape sequence.   IES

Parker, Dorothy (1893–1978)

Born in New York, was famous in her heyday (the Twenties and Thirties) as the foremost American wit and as a writer of short prose pieces for *The New Yorker*. Her light verse is excellent ('Byron and Shelley and Keats | Were a trio of lyrical treats', etc.), but the more 'serious' poems, mainly love poems, can be mawkish ('Oh, gallant was the first love, and glittering and fine'), full of much unresolved romanticism. Constantly 'betrayed' by unsatisfactory and unreliable lovers, Parker fought back in sharp epigrammatic verse, critical of men—particularly of the highbrows and Bohemians who were her usual companions: 'Oh, hard is the struggle, and sparse is | The gain of the one at the top, | For art is a form of catharsis, | And love is a permanent flop.' She published several books of verse, but the easiest way to find the poems now is to consult *The Collected Dorothy Parker* (Penguin, 2007), which has the best prose pieces too.   GE

Parsons, Clere (Trevor James Herbert)

(1908–31) Born in India, where his father worked in the Indian Civil Service. He was educated at St Paul's School and Christ Church, Oxford. He suffered from a severe form of diabetes, which brought about his early death.

While at Oxford he was active in undergraduate poetry circles, founding a poetry society with the help of *MacNeice, *Spender, Bernard *Spencer, and others, editing issues of *Oxford Poetry* and *The Oxford Outlook*, and contributing poems, essays, and reviews to them; he was also involved in the publication of a short-lived avant-garde magazine, *Sir Galahad*. Faber published a slim volume containing eighteen of his poems in 1932.

Although, according to MacNeice in *The Strings Are False* (Faber, 1965), Parsons had 'an invalid's fanaticism' in politics, his poetry is radically unlike that of most of his generation's at Oxford, since it is unconcerned with the great events of the day and draws on French and American models: Mallarmé is invoked in the fine poem 'Introduction', and the example of E. E. *Cummings was at one time important. There is apparent in Parsons' best poems an extreme and wholly individual sensitivity to what Parsons called the 'melody of words', a sensitivity which makes his poems, once read, hard to forget. Had he lived, our view of the poetry of this century might have been different.

There is an excellent selection of the poems, *The Air Between: Poems of Clere Parsons*, ed. T. W. Sutherland (Cloud, 1989). Four poems are included in Keith Tuma's *Anthology of Twentieth-Century British and Irish Poetry* (Oxford University Press, 2001). For brief and sympathetic accounts of the poetry, see C. H. Sisson's *English Poetry 1900–1950: An Assessment* (Hart-Davis, 1971) and the same author's *The Avoidance of Literature* (Carcanet, 1978), as well as *Recollections* by Geoffrey Grigson (Chatto & Windus, 1984).   TJGH

Parthasarathy, Rajagopal (1934–)

Born in Tirupparaiturai, Tamil Nadu, and educated in Bombay (now Mumbai). Between 1959 and 1971 he taught English in various colleges in Bombay and Madras (now Chennai), joining Oxford University Press in Madras as regional editor. Latterly he has lived in the United States, where he taught at Skidmore College until his retirement.

Though Parthasarathy's earliest published poems date from 1956, it was another twenty years before he brought out *Rough Passage* (1977; revd. edn. 1980), his first and so far only book of original verse.

Its individual poems are of varying length but written in the same three-line stanza, and the whole is divided in three parts, 'Exile', 'Trial', and 'Homecoming'. In a preface, Parthasarathy says *Rough Passage* should be read as one poem. It begins in a basement flat in London where, in his thirtieth year, after a taste of exile, he learns 'roots are deep', and ends fifteen years later, when he tries to initiate a dialogue between himself and his 'Tamil past'. Disappointingly, the Tamil past turns out to be 'an unrecognizable carcass', and the poet reconciles himself to going 'through life | with the small change of uncertainties'. Indian readers of Parthasarathy's generation, especially those who spent their youth 'whoring | after English gods', are particularly responsive to the poem, while the younger generation are less sympathetic.

Parthasarathy is also the editor of *Ten Twentieth-Century Indian Poets* (1976), a widely used anthology of Indian verse in English. For a discussion of his work, see *Modern Indian Poetry in English* by Bruce King (1987; revd. edn., 2001—all Oxford University Press). His translation of the Tamil epic *The Tale of an Anklet* (Columbia University Press, 1993) won several awards. AKM

Pastan, Linda (1932–) Raised in New York City but has lived for most of her life in Potomoc, Maryland, a suburb of Washington, DC. The problems her work deals with are familiar ones—loneliness and death—and in her early books Pastan's control of her images was now and then uncertain, as in this lament at her inability to prevent her father's death: 'my father [is] running out upstairs, and me without a nickel | for the meter.' Later she became more successful at harmonizing her metaphors. Though known as a 'domestic' poet who is fond of recording everyday happenings, she is at her best when writing elegiacally. *PM/AM: New and Selected Poems* (1982) reprinted what Pastan wishes to save from her first four volumes; it was followed by *A Fraction of Darkness* (1985) and *The Imperfect Paradise* (1988). Since *Carnival Evening: New and Selected Poems: 1968–1998* she has published three further volumes: *The Last*

Uncle (1998), *Queen of a Rainy Country* (2006), and *Traveling Light* (2011—all Norton). Between 1991 and 1995 she was Poet Laureate of Maryland, and in 2003 received the Ruth Lilly Poetry Prize for lifetime achievement. PS

Patchen, Kenneth (1911–72) Born in Niles, Ohio. After a short education at Alexander Meiklejohn's Experimental University of Wisconsin, where he distinguished himself as an athlete, Patchen did a variety of menial jobs, until Random House published his first collection of poems, *Before the Brave* (1936), after which he was taken up as a leftist and rebel. He thereafter wrote poetry prolifically, but never managed to gain any real control over his work, which was 'furious', sometimes powerful, and increasingly prophetic in tone, in the manner of the poet who most influenced him, William Blake. Critics deplored his 'carelessness', which was always evident, and also the contempt with which he seemed to regard his own lyrical gifts. But Henry Miller and others (including, latterly, Jonathan *Williams) admired and excused him, and funds were raised for him by people as eminent as T. S. *Eliot and W. H. *Auden, who regarded him as worth supporting. He was for a long period incapacitated by a spinal illness, although the extent of this has recently been questioned. A few critics saw him as one of 'America's great poet-prophets', but a more moderate view applauded flashes of real power and cherished, rather, the prose memoir, *Memoirs of a Shy Pornographer* (New Directions, 1945; Grey Walls, 1948). See: *Collected Poems* (New Directions, 1969) and *Kenneth Patchen: A Centennial Selection*, ed. Jonathan Clark (Kelly's Cove, 2011). MS-S

Patel, Essop (1943–2007) Born in Germiston but grew up in Ladysmith, Natal, and spent seven years in London from 1962, working and studying law. He gained his LLB at the University of the Witwatersrand and practised as an advocate in Johannesburg. He was later a high-court judge in Pretoria. He edited the work of the *Drum* writers Nat Nakasa and Can

Themba and, with Tim Couzens, an anthology of black South African poetry, *The Return of the Amasi Bird* (1982). His poems were published in literary magazines such as *Staffrider* and *The Classic* before the appearance of his first volume, *They Came at Dawn* (BLAC, 1980).

His poems exhibit characteristics of what has become known as 'Soweto poetry': an aesthetics of resistance, shot through with a strongly imaged black consciousness. But they gain a poignancy from their tenderness towards all victims of dispossession: Patel calls them love poems because, in their contempt for the oppressor, they affirm love for the oppressed. The poems in his later volume, *The Bullet and the Bronze Lady* (Skotaville, 1987), experiment with formal techniques, word-play, and satire. Some are the poems of a Muslim revolutionary, revealing his solidarity with all who fight against oppressive regimes.   CWO

Patel, Gieve (1940–   ) Born in Bombay (now Mumbai), and educated there at St Xavier's College and Grant Medical College. After working for two years (1969–71) as a medical officer in rural Gujarat, he returned to Bombay where he ran his own clinic. His first book, *Poems*, appeared in 1966, and in 1971 his first play, *Princes*, was produced. See also *Mister Behram and Other Plays* (Seagull, 2008). He is now better known as a painter.

Patel's preoccupation is with the human body, which he views with objectivity, bemusement, and, at times, exasperation. 'I am continuum with the century's skin', he writes, and his poems explore both the body's and the world's vulnerability and resilience. Like *Daruwalla and *Jussawalla, Gieve Patel is a Parsi. This fact, together with the wryness and detachment of much of his work, is reflected in the title of one of his best-known poems, 'The Ambiguous Fate of Gieve Patel, He Being Neither Muslim Nor Hindu in India'.

Patel's second collection of poems, *How Do You Withstand, Body* (Clearing House, 1976), was followed by *Mirrored, Mirroring* (Oxford University Press, 1991). For a discussion of his work, see *Modern Indian Poetry in English* by Bruce King (Oxford University Press, 1987; revd. edn., 2001).   AKM

Paterson, A. B. (Andrew Barton; known as 'Banjo' Paterson) (1864–1941) Born near Orange, New South Wales. Due to financial and rural misfortune, his family moved to Illalong Station, close to Yass, when Paterson was 6. He was educated at the Sydney Grammar School, and later became a solicitor.

In 1889 Paterson began to publish, under the pseudonym 'The Banjo', with the *Bulletin*. 'Clancy of the Overflow' and 'The Man from Snowy River' were immediately popular, and in the following years Paterson conducted a poetic 'debate' with Henry *Lawson, championing his heroic and romantic vision of the bush against Lawson's battling vision of flies and dust and floods. These poems were collected in *The Man from Snowy River and Other Verses* (1895), which has remained one of the biggest-selling books of verse in Australia. This was followed by *Rio Grande's Last Race and Other Verses* (1902) and *Salt Bush Bill J. P. and Other Verses* (1917). All three volumes are contained in the *Collected Verse of A. B. Paterson* (1923), which is regularly reprinted.

See also *Selected Poems* (1992—both Angus & Robertson). Paterson edited the first collection of Australian bush ballads (1905), and wrote three books of fiction: *An Outback Marriage* (1906), *Three Elephant Power and Other Stories* (1917), and *The Shearer's Colt* (1934). He covered the Boer War as a correspondent, served in the Remount Service during the First World War, and edited various Sydney journals.

Paterson's popularity rests on his ability to create characters which capture cultural stereotypes. His best ballads are told with sturdy galloping rhythms and cavalier rhymes, generating the humour of the tall bush story, or the pathos or glory of the sporting hero. He is credited with the composition of Australia's unofficial national anthem, 'Waltzing Matilda'.

Clement Semmler's *The Banjo of the Bush: The Work, Life and Times of A. B. Paterson* (2nd edn., University of Queensland Press,

1974) gives a good account of the cultural importance of Paterson's poetry.   AU

Paterson, Don (1963–) Born in Dundee, Paterson is Professor of Creative Writing at the University of St Andrews, and also a jazz musician. In 1993 he won the Arvon Foundation International Poetry Competition, shortly before the publication of his first collection, *Nil Nil*. As poetry editor at Picador since 1997, he has built up a prize-winning list of British poets, including Sean *O'Brien, Robin *Robertson, and John *Stammers. Twice a winner of the T. S. Eliot Prize, he was awarded an OBE in 2008 and the Queen's Gold Medal for Poetry in 2010.

Paterson's early collections cultivate a darkly masculine persona, reminiscent on occasion of Paul *Muldoon. *Nil Nil*'s broodingly humorous examination of the poet's working-class childhood and faltering adulthood continued in *God's Gift to Women* (1997). *Landing Light* (2003) introduced paternity into Paterson's emotional concerns, and *Rain* (2009) elaborated the negative mysticism that shadows his *noir*-ish nihilism (the blank pages of 'Unfold' pay tribute to an origami artist). 'Phantom' is an elegy for his friend Michael *Donaghy.

Paterson's philosophical inclinations are evident in his translations of Machado (*The Eyes*, 1999) and Rilke (*Orpheus*, 2006), his two books of aphorisms, and his long Borgesian poem, 'The Alexandrian Library'. A skilful practitioner of traditional modes such as *Scots, the ballad quatrain, and the sonnet—about which he has written at length in *Reading Shakespeare's Sonnets* (2010)—he is nevertheless attracted to ingenious set pieces in postmodern moulds: shape poems, prose poems, and fictive translations. See *Selected Poems* (2012—all Faber).   JNT

Patten, Brian (1946–) Born and brought up in Sefton Park, a working-class area of Liverpool, Patten left school at fifteen. He met Roger *McGough and Adrian Henri while working as a local music journalist. He published them in his magazine,

Underdog, and the group later became famous as the Liverpool Poets.

Patten's most enduringly popular work is his direct, imagistic love poetry, which echoes the unabashed romanticism of D. H. *Lawrence and Pablo Neruda, as well as the lighter side of the *Beat poets. It also contains an admixture of wry English realism (a couple have sex after a party among 'the woodbines and guinness stains'), and he has said that his first experience of irony was growing up on an urban street called Wavetree Vale.

For such qualities he was included by Philip *Larkin in the *Oxford Book of Twentieth-Century English Verse* (1973). The pop-surrealist title poem of his first collection, *Little Johnny's Confession* (Allen & Unwin, 1967), also established his talent as a writer of poetry for children: see *Gargling with Jelly* (Kestrel, 1985). *Love Poems* (Allen & Unwin, 1981), in print for many years, has been succeeded by *Collected Love Poems* (Harper, 2007). Individual volumes give a better sense of Patten's range as a writer, from satirist to elegist. For both moods, see 'The Brackets', which concludes his eighth collection, *Armada* (Harper, 1996). *Selected Poems* was published by Penguin in 2007. For criticism and background, see Linda Cookson, *Brian Patten* (Northcote House, 1997).   JNT

Paulin, Tom (1949–) Born in Leeds but brought up after 1953 in Belfast. Educated at the universities of Hull and Oxford, he lectured in English literature at the University of Nottingham and is now a Fellow of Hertford College, Oxford. An acerbic commentator on both literature and politics, he has collected his critical work in *Ireland and the English Crisis* (1984), *Minotaur* (1992), *Writing to the Moment* (1996), and *Crusoe's Secret* (2005), and edited the *Faber Book of Political Verse* (1986). Since his first volume, *A State of Justice* (1977), his poetry has been continuous with this prose effort, engaging the political and cultural realities of Northern Ireland in a variety of forms and from a flexible position in which the secular, non-sectarian republicanism of the eighteenth century is a point of frequent recourse. The commentary has also been pursued in a number of plays, including a version of Sophocles' *Antigone* (1985). The play was first performed by the Field Day Theatre Company, of which Paulin has been a director together with Seamus *Heaney, Brian Friel, and others.

Paulin's is not, however, a politicized poetry in any simple or single sense. Particularly since *Liberty Tree* (1983), when his style altered radically from an earlier tight-lipped, rather dour formalism towards a greater suppleness and musicality, he appears to have been emulating the James *Joyce whom he admiringly describes as a 'politicized aesthete'. He takes a playful, lingering delight in the world's surfaces and textures, implying a politics through the sensuous apprehension and fragmentary evocation of ordinary moments and episodes, as in the sequence 'The Book of Juniper', where a utopian desire for a 'sweet | equal republic' is conjured out of a series of vivid evocations (religious, historical, and even culinary) of the juniper plant. Where *Liberty Tree* is by turns luxuriant and ascetic, *Fivemiletown* (1987) is more desolately the latter, paring Paulin's natural eloquence back to the bone. In thin, disconsolate poems combining a wide range of dictions (including Belfast dialect), Paulin writes abrupt narratives of joyless sexuality and political oppression, creating insinuating vignettes of the Northern Protestant condition.

With *Walking a Line* (1994) and *The Wind Dog* (1999) Paulin's associative, insistent verse became more expansive again: the title poem of the latter is a bravura autobiographical cento. As with Tony *Harrison, however, the lower limit of Paulin's vernacular poetics is doggerel. In 2001, the *Observer* newspaper published 'Killed in the Crossfire', a squib that crudely equated the Israeli military with Nazism ('the Zionist SS'). *The Invasion Handbook* (2002) was the first part of a projected epic on the Second World War. Paulin has also published a study of William Hazlitt's prose, *The Day-Star of Liberty* (1998), a collection of translations, *The Road to Inver* (2004), and *The Secret Life of Poems* (2008), a 'primer' of close-reading

which emphasizes sound pattern. His most recent collection of poetry, *Love's Bonfire* (2012—all Faber), includes translations of the Palestinian poet Walid Khazendar.   NC*

p'Bitek, Okot (1931–82) One of the most significant voices in African literature in English. As a poet he drew his inspiration, and adapted his techniques, from the Acoli oral tradition that was his particular cultural heritage. Born in Gulu in Northern Uganda, he became a scholar of distinction, finally taking a B.Litt. at Oxford. He returned to Uganda as director of the National Cultural Centre, but after independence his outspoken criticism of politicians in *Song of Lawino* (1966) led to his dismissal. He took up a post at the University of Nairobi and was only able to return to Uganda, as professor of creative writing at Makerere University, in 1982. He died just a few months later.

Lawino, in *Song of Lawino*, is a 'traditional' Acoli woman who laments her displacement in the affections of her husband, Ocol, by an educated, westernized Christian girl who 'aspires' | to look like a white woman'. But Lawino is expressing more than jealousy; she is, as it were, defending indigenous African ways of thought and behaviour against the insidious corruption of those values by the alien forces of colonialism and Christianity. Ocol, who once admired her for the very qualities he now despises, has changed only since he was exposed to those 'civilizing' forces. *Song of Ocol* (1970) allows Ocol to reply to the criticisms Lawino has made, though in the process he concedes and confirms many of her points. The issues these poems raise were, and indeed still are, of great importance in Uganda and across the whole of Africa, but it is the music and humour of the poetry which speaks to all readers. *Song of Lawino and Song of Ocol* were published as one volume in the Heinemann African Writers Series (1984).

Two other long poems by p'Bitek, in a similar style, 'Song of a Prisoner' and 'Song of Malaya', were published in one volume as *Two Songs* by the East African Publishing House in Nairobi in 1971. He also published a collection of translations from Acoli oral poetry, *Horn of My Love* (1974), and a collection of folk-tales, *Hare and Hornbill* (1978—both Heinemann). Taban *Lo Liyong has published a new translation of p'Bitek's original Acoli poem, *Wer pa Lawino*, as *The Defence of Lawino* (Fountain, 2001). SB

Peacock, Molly (1947–) Born in Buffalo, New York and graduated from the State University of New York at Binghamton in 1969. From 1970 to 1976 she held administrative posts at the college, then earned her MA at Johns Hopkins University in 1977 as an honorary fellow. After moving to Manhattan, she became a learning specialist at Friends Seminary and was elected president of the Poetry Society of America in 1988. She lives and works in Canada and the USA.

Peacock's first two poetry collections, *And Live Apart* (University of Missouri Press, 1980) and *Raw Heaven* (1984), displayed a virtuoso gift for using formalist means in a fluid fashion to scan the psychological dilemmas of contemporary life, often lightened by humour or ironic distance. Her third volume, *Take Heart* (1989), is more intimate and intense than its predecessors, more willing to confront confessional themes, such as the lingering impact of an abusive father.

Cornucopia: New and Selected Poems 1975–2002 draws on a fourth, *Original Love* (1995—all Norton). Her latest volume is *The Second Blush* (Norton, 2008; McClelland & Stewart, 2009). Peacock has sought to widen the audience for poetry through her public appearances and readings. See also *How To Read A Poem & Start A Poetry Circle* (Riverhead Penguin, 1998; McClelland & Stewart, 1999) and, as co-editor, *Poetry in Motion: One Hundred Poems from the Subways and Buses* (Norton, 1996), a project initiated at the Poetry Society of America. She has also performed a one-woman show, *The Shimmering Verge*, and published a literary memoir, *Paradise, Piece by Piece* (Riverhead Penguin/McClelland & Stewart, 1998). EB*

Peacocke, Meg (M. R.) (1930–) Born in London; her father was a writer for children, and her mother a musician and composer; her younger brother is the composer Richard Rodney Bennett. She was educated at Cheltenham Ladies' College and at St Anne's College, Oxford, where she read English. Following some teaching abroad, she married and had children. In 1980, she trained as a counsellor, and worked for four years in the children's cancer unit at Addenbrooke's Hospital in Cambridge. In 1985 she moved alone to a hill farm in Cumbria, which she worked as a smallholding until 2001.

With a move to Cumbria came a new dedication to her life-long practice of writing poetry. After success in competitions, she found a publisher in Peterloo Poets, with whom she published four volumes: *Marginal Land* (1988), *Selves* (1995), *Speaking of the Dead* (2003), and *In Praise of Aunts* (2008). In 2011, Shoestring Press issued *Caliban Dancing*. Her poetry combines unsentimental detail with melancholy understatement; her subject is often Cumbrian rural life, but her influences are as much American as English. Largely unrhyming, and occasionally experimental (see 'Goose Hymn'), her work consistently answers the challenge in 'A Glass of Water': 'How to be naked enough | to attend to a thing in its presence'. Critics typically find Peacocke vivid and memorable, and reviews invariably end with the wish that her work should be more widely known. GR

Peake, Mervyn (Lawrence) (1911–68) Born at Kuling in China, the son of a medical missionary. He came to England aged 11, was educated at Eltham College, and trained as an artist. He was invalided out of the army in 1943 after a nervous breakdown, but later (as a war artist) visited Belsen. He was by then at work on a novel, *Titus Groan* (1946), the first of the Gothic trilogy for which he is best known, though he also earned renown as an illustrator (of his own work and others'). He suffered latterly from what was eventually diagnosed as Parkinson's disease.

Peake's first published work was poetry (*Sights and Sounds*, 1941) and he produced three further volumes of verse: *The Glass-blowers* (1950); *The Rhyme of the Flying Bomb* (1962), a ballad of the blitz; and *A Reverie of Bone* (1967); but his oeuvre is not substantial. The products of mental distress, most of the poems exist to give vent to violence of expression ('Thunder the Christ of it...') or monstrousness of image. Not many refer to the external world, as 'London, 1941' does; and the standard length is eight or ten jagged lines. The creative energy of Peake the novelist is glimpsed in 'Reverie of Bone', whose length (thirty-eight six-line stanzas), as well as its subject, may reflect his experience of mass graves; the poem is covered with striking phrases ('arctic filigree of feet', 'the dumb bullion of the shrouding clay') but itself lacks a skeleton.

A re-evaluation of Peake's verse is offered by *Collected Poems*, ed. Robert Warner Maslen (2008), a third of which was previously unpublished. See also *Complete Nonsense* (2011—both Carcanet).   MI

Peck, John (Frederick) (1941–) Born in Pittsburgh, Pennsylvania. He studied at Allegheny College and, under Yvor *Winters, at Stanford University, where he wrote a doctoral thesis on *Pound. He has lectured in English at several universities and now works as a Jungian analyst and a freelance editor. He has published nine collections of poetry, running from *Shagbark* (Bobbs-Merrill, 1972) to *Contradance* (University of Chicago Press, 2011). *Collected Shorter Poems* (Carcanet, 1999) includes a substantial selection from his first six books.

Peck's poetry draws consciously on two seemingly incompatible models: Pound and Winters. A subtle practitioner of standard metres, he now writes mainly in free or syllabic verse with a musical sensitivity to relative degrees of stress that only a student of Pound could hope to achieve. From Pound, too, he has learnt to value the integrity of the line and the firmly defined sensuous particular, but he rejects the associated fragmentation of syntax, assuming with Winters that poetry belongs to a necessary human order defended against the

vegetable flux of nature. The consequent preoccupation with the space between consciousness and 'the stout weave | Of what is' accounts for the fascination of his work, but also for some regrettable obscurity.   CW

Peeradina, Saleem (1944–) Born in Bombay (now Mumbai), and educated at St Xavier's College, Bombay, and Wake Forest University in the United States. During the Seventies and Eighties he taught English in various colleges in Bombay, and he has also worked as reviews editor of *Express Magazine*, and as advertising copywriter. He now lives in the United States, where he teaches.

Peeradina's first book, *First Offence* (Newground, 1980), opens with poems that look at Bombay's suburbs and shanty towns, its Hindu, Muslim, and Christian places of worship, and its streets and crowds. Peeradina is not particularly observant, however, and offers only a generalized picture, sometimes satirical, of life in the metropolis. *First Offence* ends with 'Wife's Touch', a poem whose title prefigures the theme of his next collection, *Group Portrait* (Oxford University Press, 1992). In it Peeradina celebrates domestic bliss, and if his concerns have narrowed, the writing is far more assured. Whether describing a family scene or expressing parental anxiety, Peeradina goes about his business in a brisk, straightforward manner.

Peeradina also edited *Contemporary Indian Poetry in English: An Assessment and Selection* (Macmillan, 1972). This early anthology is important both for its critical assessments, made by diverse hands, and its discriminating selection of poets. His later collections of poetry are *Meditations on Desire* (2003) and *Slow Dance* (2010—both Ridgeway). See *The Ocean in My Yard*, a memoir of his Bombay childhood (Penguin, 2005).   AKM

Perelman, Bob (Robert) (1947–) Born in Youngstown, Ohio, Perelman studied music and classics at the Universities of Rochester and Michigan, and went on to the Iowa Writers' Workshop. In 1990 he received a PhD from the University of

California, Berkeley, and teaches English at the University of Pennsylvania.

Perelman's first book, *Braille* (Ithaca House, 1975), appeared shortly before he moved to the San Francisco Bay Area. Here he continued to edit *Hills*, an important *Language poetry magazine. He also organized the Talks series: see *Writing/Talks* (Southern Illinois University Press, 1985). The early poetry is characterized by Perelman's use of improvisatory procedures to foster linguistic disjunction. 'China', from *a.k.a.* (The Figures, 1984), a series of dissociative sentences responding to a book of photographs, was famously cited by the critic Fredric Jameson as an illustration of the 'schizophrenia' of postmodernist art. In the same year, however, with *To the Reader* (Tuumba), Perelman's writing turned to a more discursive mode, a change he has attributed to the experience of having children.

Drawing on his classical education, the later work exhibits his satirical political wit, and his critical engagement with the ambitions of modernism (see *The Trouble with Genius* (University of California Press, 1994)). *The Marginalization of Poetry* (Princeton University Press, 1996) is a collection of essays, including the verse essay of the title. *Ten to One: Selected Poems* (Wesleyan University Press) appeared in 1999 and *IFLIFE* (Roof) in 2006. *Playing Bodies* is a collaboration with his wife, the artist Francie Shaw (Granary, 2003).   JNT

Peters, Lenrie (1932–2009) Grew up in the Gambia and Sierra Leone, studied medicine at Trinity College, Cambridge, and worked as a doctor in the English Midlands for several years. He settled back in the Gambia, where he practised as a surgeon in Banjul. He was also the chairman of the West Africa Examinations Council.

Peters published one novel, *The Second Round* (1965), but is best known as a poet; the appearance of his *Selected Poems* (1981—both Heinemann) was a major event in African poetry. In some ways Peters is an untypical African poet; his verse is measured and articulated in the traditions of European poetry, and he is a man of the world who draws on the mythologies of the whole planet as his

legitimate cultural heritage. But the heart of Peters' poetry is his commitment to Africa, and in particular to the people of the Gambia. *Selected Poems* collects work written over twenty years, including selections from *Poems* (Mbari, 1964), *Satellites* (1967), and *Katchikali* (1971—both Heinemann), as well as a selection of previously uncollected poems. The title-poem of *Katchikali* is in many ways characteristic of his work as a whole: a lament for the desecration of an ancient Gambian holy place by developers and tourists, it offers a vigorous critique of a society that can sell out its shrines to 'hide-hunters'. What happened to the crocodile pool at Katchikali seems to the poet a metaphor for what is happening to spiritual values across the continent. Such a sensitivity to the conflict between an apparent short-term good and the values that would promote real, long-term development underpins much of Peters' poetry.   SB

Petersen, Donald (1928–2005) Born in Minneapolis, Minnesota, and educated at the Sorbonne and at Carleton College. Subsequently he did graduate work at Indiana University and the University of Iowa. Petersen began his teaching career at Iowa, but in 1956 he moved to the State University of New York College at Oneonta.

Petersen's reputation as a poet rests almost entirely upon one book, *The Spectral Boy* (Wesleyan University Press, 1964). A strict and traditionally formal poet, Petersen published poems and criticism occasionally in some of the literary periodicals in the United States, particularly the *New Criterion*—generally at the request of editors, for Petersen did not take the initiative to submit his work, though he circulated a manuscript, 'Later Poems' (*c.*1988), among his friends. In a brief forenote for the collection he wrote that, for reasons such as 'scope', the 'often intractable' materials, and the 'variable, refractory tone', he had to keep the poems private, but in fact it is not apparent that Petersen's problems are much different from those of any other poet. The later poems are as well-written and as worthy of publication as any of those to be found in his first book. *Early and Late: Selected Poems* (Ivan R. Dee, 2001) won the inaugural *New Criterion* poetry prize.   LT

Petit, Pascale (1953–) Born in Paris, Petit grew up in France and Wales, and studied sculpture at the Royal College of Art in London, where she now lives. Formerly a visual artist, between 1989 and 2005 she edited *Poetry London*, and was a co-founder, with Mimi *Khalvati, of the Poetry School.

Petit's debut, *Heart of a Deer* (Enitharmon, 1998), reflected her experience of travelling down the Venezuelan Amazon. Her second collection, *The Zoo Father* (Seren, 2001), was admired by Les *Murray among others, and won several awards. The central subject of caring for an abusive father, now dying, makes it *Confessional in tenor. But the first poem, 'The Strait-Jackets', on a suitcase of hummingbirds, introduces the bold magical realism that brings figurative complication to autobiographical fact. Among her peers, Petit's poetic psychodrama is perhaps closest to the satirical fantasies of Selima *Hill. An equivalent in visual art might be the painting of Frida Kahlo, about which Petit has written a series of poems, *What the Water Gave Me* (Seren, 2010), published in the USA by Black Lawrence Press. *The Huntress* (2005) reimagines a mentally ill mother in a number of mythopoetic ways, while *The Treekeeper's Tale* (2008—both Seren) explores her range as a traveller and ecopoetic writer.   JNT

Philip, Marlene Nourbese (1947–) Born in Tobago, Philip grew up in Trinidad. She read economics at the University of the West Indies before moving to Canada, where she studied law and political science at the University of Western Ontario. In the 1970s she practised law in Toronto, becoming a full-time writer after the publication of her first two collections, *Thorns* (1980) and *Salmon Courage* (1983). *She Tries Her Tongue, Her Silence Softly Breaks* (Ragweed, 1988; repr. Poui, 2006) won the Casa de las Américas Prize. She has also written

plays, fiction, and collections of essays articulating her position as a black Canadian woman writer: see *Frontiers: Essays and Writings on Racism and Culture* (1993) and *Genealogy of Resistance and Other Essays* (1997—both Mercury). Concerned from the first with 'fluttering lives | among shuffled papers', her most recent work is *Zong!* (Wesleyan University Press, 2008), which searches the legal text relating to the African slave-ship massacre of 1781 for its lost voices.   JNT

Phillips, Carl (1959–) Born into a military family, Phillips was educated in Massachusetts. He studied classics at Harvard University, taught Greek and Latin to high-school students, and took an MFA at Boston University (where he was taught by Geoffrey *Hill). He is now a professor of English and African-American studies at Washington University in St Louis.

Since his 1992 debut *In the Blood* (Northeastern University Press) was chosen by Rachel *Hadas for the Samuel French Morse Poetry Prize, Phillips has been a prolific and high-profile poet. Shortlisted four times for the National Book Award, he won the Kingsley Tufts Poetry Award for *The Tether* (2001), and the Theodore Roethke Memorial Foundation Prize and the Thom Gunn Award for Gay Male Poetry for *The Rest of Love* (2004—both Farrar, Straus).

Phillips has translated Sophocles' *Philoctetes* (Oxford University Press, 2003), and spoken of the importance of the classics to his own writing. Like Anne *Carson, his free verse inhabits classical models in order to formalize the impressionistic privacy of love, as in the title poem of *Cortège* (Graywolf, 1995), a short choric sequence on 'the dreaming' of desire. In 2006 Phillips received a Fellowship from the Academy of American Poets. *Quiver of Arrows: Selected Poems* appeared in 2007. His eleventh collection is *Double Shadow* (2011—both Farrar, Straus). See also *Coin of the Realm: Essays on the Art and Life of Poetry* (Graywolf, 2004).   JNT

Phillips, Robert (1938–) Born and grew up in rural Laurel, Delaware, and attended the local public schools. He received both BA and MA degrees in English from Syracuse University, where he edited *Syracuse 10*, the literary magazine where he published his own early work as well as that of classmates Joyce Carol Oates and Dick *Allen. In 1965 he left Syracuse and academia to pursue an advertising career in Manhattan, and moved shortly thereafter to Westchester County. He is a professor of English at the University of Houston.

The poems in his first book, *Inner Weather* (Golden Quill, 1966), are juvenilia but they confirm his strong grounding in traditional poetic metre, as well as establishing his affinity for the elegy and the pastoral and his interest in music and art as poetic subjects. His poetic development was significantly advanced both by his collection of stories set in Delaware, *The Land of Lost Content* (Vanguard, 1970), and by his critical book, *The Confessional Poets* (Southern Illinois University Press, 1973). His examination of *Roethke, Robert *Lowell, *Plath, *Sexton, and others enabled him to view his own life as a legitimate poetic subject, though his autobiographical poems eschew the sensational subjects of the most extreme *confessional poets. Instead, the persona that emerges in his work is that of a congenial, sensitive individual who has survived a somewhat less-than-idyllic Southern boyhood to achieve a precarious middle-aged stability in suburbia. This persona evolved in three volumes of poetry published in the Seventies and reached its fruition in his definitive volume, *Personal Accounts: New and Selected Poems 1966–1986* (Ontario Review, 1986). His sequence 'Middle Age Nocturnes' contains many affecting poems on how natural and domestic details reflect the condition of marriage, as in 'Middle Age: A Nocturne' and 'Autumn Crocuses'. Another sequence, 'Ninety Miles from Nowhere', by contrast, portrays the poet's Southern childhood; in 'Once' he celebrates the single occasion his father took the family to the nearby beach, while in 'Running on Empty' he equates driving on an empty gas tank with creating

poetry despite his father's withheld love. As literary executor, he has edited numerous posthumous volumes of Delmore *Schwartz's work. *Now & Then: New & Selected Poems* (Ashland Poetry, 2009) draws on ten collections, including *Breakdown Lane* (1994), *Spinach Days* (2000), and *Circumstances Beyond Our Control* (2006—all Johns Hopkins University Press). *The Madness of Art* (Syracuse University Press, 2003) includes his *Paris Review* interviews with Philip *Larkin and Karl *Shapiro.   RMCP

Pickard, Tom (1946–) Born in Newcastle upon Tyne. He was co-founder, with Basil *Bunting, of the poetry centre, the Morden Book Tower, and managed it (1963–73). Pickard was one of the more interesting of those British poets to base their procedures on the *Black Mountain school: he attracted the attention of Bunting because, instead of merely imitating them, he tried to remain true to his locale (which was that of the elder poet). Bunting wrote a preface to his first collection, *High on the Walls* (Fulcrum, 1967), and praised the 'music' of its Carlos *Williams-like short lines, which were touchingly evocative of the Northumberland landscape, and of adolescent love. Bunting hoped he would develop to learn 'to sing with a longer breath'; but Pickard's talent developed in other directions, notably that of documentary film, several of which he scripted or directed for television. The best of his Seventies' work is to be found in the poems contained in radio and television documentaries such as *The Jarrow March* (1976). His early work was analysed in depth by Eric Mottram in *Poetry Information, 18* (1978).

In 1994, *Tiepin Eros: New & Selected Poems* appeared in the UK from Bloodaxe, who also published *Shedding Her Skirts* (1985). Pickard's first new book of poetry after this was *Fuckwind* (Etruscan, 1999)—an archaic name for the kestrel—which has an introduction by Paul McCartney. *Hole in the Wall* (2002), a new and selected volume published in the States, with collages by Tom *Raworth, has been followed by two books inspired by the British border ballads: *The Dark Months of May* (2004) and

The Ballad of Jamie Allan (2007—all Flood). See also *More Pricks Than Prizes*, a prose memoir (Pressed Wafer, 2010).   MS-S*

Piercy, Marge (1936–) Born in Detroit, Michigan, attended the University of Michigan on a scholarship, and now lives with her husband, writer Ira Wood, on Cape Cod. Well known as both novelist and poet, Piercy has published seventeen novels and eighteen volumes of poetry. Among her best novels are the utopian feminist *Woman on the Edge of Time* (1976) and the autobiographical *Braided Lives* (1982).

Her poetry, from *Breaking Camp* (1968) to *Mars and Her Children* (1992), reflects the influence of Whitman and *Ginsberg, as well as her own Jewish-Welsh working-class background. Long seen as a political poet, the ardent Marxist, feminist, and environmentalist argues for race- and class-equality, decries traditional male-female roles and relationships, and explores tensions between nature and technology. Sometimes criticized as a propagandist, Piercy nevertheless achieves a successful balance of ideology and aesthetics, particularly in *My Mother's Body* (1985) and *Available Light* (1988).

The Hunger Moon: New and Selected Poems, 1980-2010 (2011) samples her later work and *Ways of Knowing: Essays on Marge Piercy* (Negative Capability, 1991), ed. Sue Walker and Eugenie Hamner, contains useful critical commentary. See also *Early Grrrl: The Early Poems of Marge Piercy* (1999), published by her own Leapfrog Press, and three later volumes: *The Art of Blessing the Day* (1999), a collection of her Jewish liturgical poems, *Colors Passing Through Us* (2003), and *The Crooked Inheritance* (2006—all Knopf).   EDF

Pinkerton, Helen (1927–) Born in Butte, Montana. She received her BA and MA from Stanford University and her PhD in 1966 from Harvard. At Stanford she became a member of the Yvor *Winters circle and published seven poems in Winters' anthology *Poets of the Pacific: Second Series* (Stanford University Press, 1949). She continues to live in California, where she

has engaged in teaching, writing poetry, studying and translating her favourite Greek poet, Pindar, and in researching her favourite American writer, Herman Melville.

Her carefully crafted poetry is profoundly philosophical and religious. Her subject-matter is the metaphysical problems of the nature of reality, evil, divinity, and self, together with the possibility of Christian or theistic belief in the twentieth century. Her style is austere and conventional. Among her notable poems are 'Indecision', 'Good Friday', 'The Gift', and two 'Holy Sonnets', all of a religious nature. Latterly she has turned to the arts for her inspiration, as in *The Harvesters and Other Poems on Works of Art* (R. L. Barth, 1984).

Taken in Faith (Ohio University Press, 2002) was the first widely available edition of her poems. Her basic metaphysical views are discussed in her article (published, like her other prose, under her married name Helen Trimpi) 'Contexts for "Being", and "Self" in Valéry and Edgar Bowers', *The Southern Review, 13* (1977). Among her prose works are *Melville's Confidence Men and American Politics* (Archon, 1987).   DS

Pinsky, Robert (1940–) Born in New Jersey and educated at Rutgers University and afterwards at Stanford under Yvor *Winters. He has taught at various American universities, including Wellesley College, the University of California at Berkeley, and Boston University. Complimented by Robert *Lowell for belonging 'to that rarest category of talents, a poet-critic', Pinsky published an outstanding critical book, *The Situation of Poetry*, in 1976, and he has also been poetry editor of *New Republic*. His first volume was *Sadness and Happiness* (1975), followed by *An Explanation of America* (1979—all Princeton University Press) and *History of My Heart* (Ecco, 1984). He has also, with Robert *Hass, translated some of the poems of the Polish poet Czesław Miłosz.

Pinsky's work aims very deliberately at a return, after the various forms of modernism and confessionalism, to a new discursiveness in American poetry, a rationality and temperateness in which the objects and feelings of the ordinary suburban world may be given their due. Decisively rejecting the Poundian advice to 'go in fear of abstractions', Pinsky positively welcomes them, in poems which approach the reader in the tone of civilized, slightly earnest conversation. In the long poem *An Explanation of America*, for instance, the Vietnam War is absorbed into the ratiocinative texture: 'I think it made our country older, forever. | I don't mean better or not better, but merely | As though a person should come to a certain place | And have his hair turn gray, that very night.' Such discursiveness may, of course, turn lax or prolix, reminding the reader of nothing so much as a slow, funereal, late-Wordsworthian chunter; but Pinsky has absorbed the lessons of the moderns too, and this long passage on Vietnam concludes with a memorably well-focused figure which proposes that the war will be taken into the American 'family' like 'A new syllable buried in their name'. If it was ever his poet-critic's intention, Pinsky has probably failed in any attempt to establish a 'New Discursive' school of American poets; but his own work, measured and scrupulous, makes a proper case for itself.

In 1994, he made a widely praised translation of Dante's *Inferno*, an epic complement of the prophetic voice that sounds in the title lyric of his new and collected poems, *The Figured Wheel* (1996). He has since published two further volumes: *Jersey Rain* (2000) and *Gulf Music* (2007). *Selected Poems* (2012) foregrounds the more fragmentary poetics of his later work. As the US Poet Laureate from 1997 to 2000, Pinsky initiated the Favourite Poem project, a Library of Congress archive of Americans reading verse aloud, which has resulted in several popular anthologies. See also *The Sounds of Poetry* (1998—all Farrar, Straus). *The Figured Wheel* was published in the UK by Carcanet.   NC*

Pinter, Harold (1930–2008) Born in London. It is usual to consider that the playwright Pinter's command of rhythm and nuance makes his drama poetic, although his poems, which were not collected until the 1970s, have tended to be overshadowed by his other writings. The poems contain shifts of register familiar from the plays (as in 'Message': 'I was well acquainted with the pong myself, | I told him, and I counselled calm. | Don't let the fuckers get you down.'), as well as the characteristic air of menace. While the earliest poems ('New Year in the Midlands', 'I Shall Tear Off My Terrible Cap') are clearly touched by Dylan *Thomas, the most striking influence is the William *Empson of 'Missing Dates', 'Success', and 'Let it Go': 'It is the test they set that will not go, | The failing of the doing so, | Ungainly legacy that they bestow' ('The Doing So'). Latterly, Pinter wrote stripped-down dramatic lyrics ('Before They Fall'), and 'Partners', an outburst of political fury paralleled in his later writing for the stage. He was awarded the Nobel Prize for Literature in 2005. See *Various Voices: Prose, Poetry, Politics 1948–2008* (Faber, 2009).   SO'B

Pitter, Ruth (1897–1992) Born in Ilford, Essex, a suburb of London. Her parents, artisans and East End school-teachers, reared their daughters to love the countryside and to that end rented a cottage in the Essex forest where Ruth spent the happiest hours of her childhood. During the First World War she worked as a clerk in the War Office. After the war she earned her living in London as a painter and decorator of tea-trays and pots. She set up a gift shop with her companion Kate O'Hara which was twice bombed in the Second World War. She then engaged in war work again. By 1952 she had established her reputation as a poet, and she and Kate were able to buy a house in the country where Ruth could indulge her passion for gardening.

She started writing verse at the age of 5 and achieved her first publication in 1912, in *The New Age* edited by A. R. Orage, who became a dominant influence on her. Her earliest book of poems was *First Poems* (Palmer, 1920) but it was not until *A Mad Lady's Garland* (Cresset, 1934; Macmillan, 1935) that she received substantial attention from reviewers, partly because her friend Hilaire *Belloc wrote the preface.

Pitter's poetry, usually but not always written in conventional prosody, is classical and traditionalist. Her subject-matter reflects her wide-ranging response to a variety of experiences, ranging from the pleasures of gardening, in *The Rude Potato* (1941), to transcendental religious experience, as in 'Six Dreams and a Vision' in *The Ermine: Poems, 1942–1952* (1953—both Cresset) written after her conversion in the 1940s to Anglicanism under the influence of C. S. Lewis.

See *Collected Poems* (Enitharmon, 1996), with an introduction by Elizabeth *Jennings. Helpful biographical information and critical evaluation will be found in Arthur Russell (ed.), *Ruth Pitter: Homage to a Poet* (Dufour, 1969).   DS

Pitt-Kethley, Fiona (1954–) Born in Middlesex. She trained as a painter at Chelsea College of Art, and, after many years in Sussex, now lives in Spain. Her most recent collection, *Selected Poems* (Salt, 2008) draws on three earlier volumes, all from Chatto & Windus: *Sky Ray Lolly* (1986), *Private Parts* (1987), and *The Perfect Man* (1989). Her travel writing includes *Journeys to the Underworld* (Chatto, 1989) and *Red Light Districts of the World* (Tamworth, 2000).

Fiona Pitt-Kethley's work is unflinchingly anti-romantic. Once banned by the Poetry Society for her use of four-letter words, Pitt-Kethley might be seen as a moral and even a didactic writer, though it could also be argued that the erotic frankness for which she is best known is an outcome of the social sexual hypocrisy it defies. She has edited two collections of prose and verse, *The Literary Companion to Sex* (1994) and *The Literary Companion to Low Life* (1995—both Sinclair Stevenson).   CAR

Place, Vanessa (1968–) Born in Stratford, South Dakota, Place lives in Los Angeles, California where she writes, co-directs Les Figures Press, and is a criminal defence attorney.

Place is author of eight books of poetry and conceptual writing, including *Dies: A Sentence* (Les Figures, 2006), a 50,000-word, one-sentence novel in verse; *La Medusa* (Fiction Collective 2, 2008); *The Guilt Project: Rape, Morality and Law* (Other, 2010), an analysis of the prosecution of sexual offenders, and *Statement of Facts* (Blanc, 2010), the first volume of her trilogy *Tragodía*, which cites legal prosecution and defence documents verbatim. She is also co-author with Robert Fitterman of *Notes on *Conceptualisms* (Ugly Duckling Presse, 2009), and writes articles, lectures, and performs around the world.

Her use of the records of sex offenders and their victims' court testimonies do not make for easy reading or listening. Place sees her work as 'challenging the idea of what poetry is'. That work is highly intertextual: mingling high and low culture, 'fact' as well as 'fiction', in a bid to question dividing lines. Her engagement with postmodern philosophy is a serious one: Place has said of her work, 'Authorship doesn't matter. Content doesn't matter. Form doesn't matter. Meter doesn't matter. All that matters is the trace of poetry.'   ECr

Plath, Sylvia (1932–63) Born in Boston, Massachusetts, on 27 October (she shared a birthday with Dylan *Thomas), and spent her childhood in Winthrop. When she was eight her German father, a professor at Boston University, died of diabetes. Two years later her mother moved the family inland to Wellesley, where she struggled to give Sylvia and her younger brother every advantage of a superior education. Self-consciousness and anxiety about status and money during adolescence contributed to the profound insecurity Plath concealed all her life beneath a façade of brassy energy and brilliant achievement.

Plath discovered that writing was her vocation very early. By the time she was at Smith College in the early 1950s she had published precocious poems in newspapers and written over fifty short stories, some of which won prizes from ladies' magazines. At Smith she went on winning prizes, but after a third year of feverish overwork, she broke down and attempted suicide. Six months in a private hospital set her on her feet again, but in reality she never recovered.

After she had graduated, *summa cum laude*, from Smith in 1955, she went to

Cambridge University on a Fulbright scholarship, and there she met the poet Ted *Hughes. They were married in London in June 1956. The marriage was for six years a strong union of supremely dedicated writers. Sylvia's wholehearted enthusiasm for Hughes' work, which she sent off to the competition that won him fame, was balanced by his steadfast belief in her exceptional gift. They lived in Massachusetts (Cambridge, Northampton—where Sylvia taught for a year at Smith—and Boston), then in London and Devon. A daughter, Frieda, was born in April 1960, and a son, Nicholas, in January 1962.

Sylvia Plath's early poems—already drenched in typical imagery of glass, moon, blood, hospitals, foetuses, and skulls—were mainly 'exercises' or pastiches of work by poets she admired: Dylan Thomas, W. B. *Yeats, Marianne *Moore. Late in 1959, when she and her husband were at Yaddo, the writers' colony in New York State, she produced the seven-part 'Poem for a Birthday', which owes its form to Theodore *Roethke's 'Lost Son' sequence, though its theme is her own traumatic breakdown and suicide attempt at 21. After 1960 her poems increasingly explored the surreal landscape of her imprisoned psyche under the looming shadow of a dead father and a mother on whom she was resentfully dependent.

A fanatical preoccupation with death and rebirth informs her sad, cynical novel, *The Bell Jar*, as it does her first book of poems, *The Colossus*, published in London by Heinemann in October 1960, and by Knopf in New York, in 1962. Plath's mature poetry, too exalted to be merely '*confessional', frequently treats of this resurrection theme, together with a related one which attempts to redeem meaningless life through art. Lines like 'I am lost, I am lost, in the robes of all this light' ('Witch Burning'), and 'On Fridays the little children come | To trade their hooks for hands' ('The Stones') foreshadow the powerful, wholly convincing voice of poems like 'The Hanging Man', published posthumously in *Ariel*: 'By the roots of my hair some god got hold of me. | I sizzled in his blue volts like a desert prophet.'

Ted Hughes has described how Sylvia Plath underwent a searing, 'curiously independent process of gestation' during the spring of 1962, when, two months after giving birth to a son, she produced a powerful radio drama, 'Three Women'. The first deathly Ariel Poems appeared soon afterwards with 'The Moon and Yew Tree', 'Little Fugue', 'Elm', 'Event', 'Berck-Plage', and others. During the summer of 1962 her marriage to Hughes began to buckle; she was devastated when she learned that he had been unfaithful to her. Although she and Hughes travelled to Ireland together in September, the marriage was by then in ruins, and in October she asked her husband to leave for good.

It was after Hughes' departure that Plath produced, in less than two months, the forty poems of rage, despair, love, and vengeance that have chiefly been responsible for her immense posthumous fame. Throughout October and November of 1962 she rose every day at dawn to take down, as from dictation, line after miraculous line of poems like 'The Bee Meeting', 'Stings', 'Daddy', 'Lady Lazarus', 'Ariel', and 'Death & Company', as well as those heart-breaking poems to her baby son: 'Nick and the Candlestick' and 'The Night Dances'.

In December 1962 she moved with her children from Devon to London. What she recognized as the 'genius' of her poetry temporarily restored her self-confidence, but in January 1963, after the publication of *The Bell Jar*, and during the coldest winter of the century, she descended into a deep, clinical depression, and in the early morning of 11 February, she gassed herself.

In the half-century following her suicide Sylvia Plath has become a heroine and martyr of the feminist movement. In fact, she was a martyr mainly to the recurrent psychodrama that staged itself within the bell jar of her tragically wounded personality. Twelve final poems, written shortly before her death, define a nihilistic metaphysic from which death provided the only dignified escape. Hughes included these in the first edition of *Ariel* (1965), and published other poems in *Crossing the Water* and *Winter Trees* (1971—both Faber).

Sylvia Plath's *Collected Poems* were published in London and New York in 1981 (Faber/Harper). There are biographies by Lindsay Wagner-Martin (1987) and Anne Stevenson (1989). Both are discussed by Janet Malcolm in *The Silent Woman* (Knopf, 1994), a history of the writing of Plath's memory. Hughes' poetic account of his life with Plath was published as *Birthday Letters* (1997). See also the correspondence in *Letters Home* (Harper, 1965; Faber, 1966), edited by her mother, Aurelia Plath, and *The Journals of Sylvia Plath*, ed. Karen V. Kukil (2000, Faber; published in the States by Anchor as *The Unabridged Journals of Sylvia Plath*). In 2004, a restored edition of *Ariel* appeared, presenting the poems in the sequence that Plath indicated, with a foreword by Frieda Hughes (Harper/Faber). Carol Ann *Duffy made a new selection of Plath's poems for Faber and Faber in 2012.   AS*

Plomer, William (Charles Franklyn) (1903–73) Born in Pietersberg, South Africa, founded the satirical magazine *Voorslag* (Whiplash) in 1926 with Roy *Campbell, the venture being joined later by Laurens van der Post. In 1926 Leonard Woolf published at the Hogarth Press *Turbott Wolfe*, a novel about South Africa. After spending two years teaching in Japan Plomer published two further novels, *Paper Houses* (1929) and *Sado* (1931). In 1929 he emigrated to England, where he was welcomed by Bloomsbury and by Bohemian literary London. His first collection of verse, *The Fivefold Screen* (1932), contained poems whose visual clarity, musical resonance, and atmospheric intensity he never recaptured, perhaps because after 1932 his memories of his native land lost their freshness and poignancy. In 1937 Plomer became chief reader to Jonathan Cape, a task he performed with skill and assiduity. He at once recognized the unique quality of the diary kept from 1870 to 1879 by Francis Kilvert, curate of a parish on the Welsh borders, and edited a three-volume selection between 1938 and 1944.

Plomer wrote a number of satirical poems and ballads in the late 1930s and early 1940s. Some portray the sleazier aspects of sexual transactions in London. We meet Mews-Flat Mona; French Lisette and Dublin Dan fleecing a client in a Maida Vale flat; and D'Arcy Honeybunn, 'A rose-red sissy half as old as time'. The wartime ballads recount incidents as grotesque as the cruel surrealistic comedy of Dali and Buñuel. In 'The Flying Bum', a bomb plants on the dining-room table of a vegetarian guesthouse 'A lightly roasted rump of horse'. Such poems and those that dwell lovingly on a severed human thigh, or on the strangling of a girl with a stocking, may reflect Plomer's forays into the dangerous underworld of homosexual promiscuity that marked his conduct from the late 1920s until the mid-1940s.

After the war Plomer brought out some highly successful works of prose fiction and embarked on a career as one of Benjamin Britten's librettists, happily subduing his own artistic inclinations to the composer's imperative demands. His post-war verse became more benign and wider in its human sympathies. 'Mrs Middleditch' concerns an elderly woman who is suddenly overcome, while shopping in a supermarket, by a vision of the poor and hungry of the world. It is a far cry from Mews-Flat Mona and French Lisette. 'A Young Jackdaw' sounds a note of lyricism, less sharp-edged and ironical than in his early poems, but with a new tenderness. During the last years of his life Plomer made a tentative return to the Anglicanism of his devout mother. In 'The Bungalows', surveying the drab uniformity of suburban houses, he envisages the birth of a Saviour as once in Bethlehem: 'It may be born, it may be born.'

See *Collected Poems* (Cape, 1973) and Peter F. Alexander's *William Plomer* (Oxford University Press, 1989).   JPr

Plumly, Stanley (1939–   ) Born in Barnesville, Ohio, and grew up in the lumber and farming regions of Virginia and Ohio. His father was a lumberjack and welder. He was educated at Wilmington College, a Quaker school in Ohio, and Ohio University. He is a professor of English at the University of Maryland. His first collection, *In the Outer Dark* (Louisiana State University Press, 1970), won the Delmore Schwartz Memorial Award; his third, *Out-of-the-Body Travel*

(Ecco, 1978), was nominated for the National Book Critics Circle Award, and his most recent, *Old Heart* (Norton, 2007), was nominated for the National Book Award and received the Los Angeles Times Book Prize.

For his Keatsian eye to nature, Plumly has been called the most English of American poets, and his quiet poems are unmistakable. His more autobiographical work, often depicting a working-class rural childhood, suggests that he may have inherited the mantle of James *Wright, his fellow Ohioan. But the reader is more astonished by the garden found there than by the resolute bleakness of the life. Plumly writes compact, descriptive lyrics and more prosaic narrative poems. Both genres are rooted in nature and both assert themselves melodically. In his earlier books, Plumly used his mother and father as dual-axes for his poetry, but over time the machinery has enlarged, rotating history, family, and nature. In addition to the volumes named earlier, Plumly has published six later collections of poetry, including *Now That My Father Lies Down Beside Me: New & Selected Poems, 1970–2000* (Ecco, 2000). He has also published *Posthumous Keats: A Personal Biography* (Norton, 2008), a moving study of the poet's work and legend.   HC

Plutzik, Hyam (1911–62) Born in Brooklyn, the son of Jewish immigrants from Russia. He grew up in the countryside near Southbury, Connecticut, and did not speak English until he was 7. He studied English at Trinity College in Hartford and, after two years of graduate study at Yale at the beginning of the Depression, worked as a reporter for several newspapers (including Walt Whitman's *Brooklyn Eagle*). In 1936–7 Plutzik spent a crucial year of Thoreauvian solitude near Quaker Farms, Connecticut, meditating on his purposes as a writer, and then returned to Yale, earning an MA in English in 1940. In 1942 he enlisted in the US Army; he was commissioned in 1943, and married Tanya Roth of Brooklyn, before being posted to duty as an ordnance officer with the 44th Heavy Bomb Group of the Eighth Air Force, in Norfolk. Discharged at the end of 1945, Plutzik joined the English faculty of the University of Rochester (New York), becoming Deane Professor of Poetry and Rhetoric in 1961. He died of cancer in 1962, leaving his wife and two sons and two daughters.

Plutzik's first collection, *Aspects of Proteus* (Harper, 1949) marked him as a seasoned poet already, lyrically inclined but sturdily independent of the pieties of postwar formalism. He found his main themes early—the tragic meanings of the war, the interplay of science and the imagination, the ways ordinary private lives attain to myth, the enigmatic witnessing of nature to human life and death—and in his second book, *Apples from Shinar* (Wesleyan University Press, 1959), these themes took on a new depth and resonance, infused with Jewish mysticism and a distinctive phenomenological awareness, as in 'Jim Desterland', 'For My Daughter', and 'The Bass'. His third book, *Horatio* (Atheneum, 1961) is something of a surprise: a long and absorbing narrative account of what happens to Hamlet's friend after he promises to represent Hamlet faithfully to the world.

The last lines of one of Plutzik's last, unpublished poems read: 'Out of my life I fashioned a fistfull of words. | When I opened my hand, they flew away.' The durability of his achievement is manifested by generous selections of his work in recent British and American anthologies and by the publication of a sumptuous *Collected Poems*, including previously uncollected and unpublished work, with commentary by Anthony Hecht and Ted Hughes (BOA, 1987).   JRa

Porter, Dorothy (Featherstone) (1954–2008) Born and educated in Sydney, where she was taught by David *Malouf. She later lived in Melbourne.

Porter's early verse, beginning with *Little Hoodlum* (Poetry Society of Australia, 1975), showed the influence of American poets such as William Carlos *Williams and Frank *O'Hara. Her style is immediate, humorous, erotic and energetic, and her subject matter eclectic, from the semimythical Australian bird of *The Night Parrot* (Black Lightning, 1984) to Antarctic exploration in *Driving Too Fast* (University of Queensland Press, 1989). She spoke disparagingly of 'looking-out-the-window' verse, as well as poetry's 'modernist fatigue'.

In 1992 Porter wrote her first verse novel, *Akhenaten* (University of Queensland Press), about a King of ancient Egypt who attempted to impose a personal monotheism of the sun. Her second, *The Monkey's Mask* (Hyland, 1994), was a crime thriller woven around a lesbian love affair, which observes 'I never knew poetry | could be | as sticky as sex'. It won multiple awards and became one of the fastest-selling books of poetry ever published in Australia. Three more verse novels followed: *What a Piece of Work* (1999), *Wild Surmise* (2002), and *El Dorado* (2007—all Picador).

Porter's later collections of lyric poetry included *Crete* (Hyland, 1996)—also a bestseller—and, posthumously, *The Bee Hut* (Black Inc., 2009). She wrote several libretti as well as fiction for young adults. Her attitude to poetry was summed up by the title of a book of prose, *On Passion* (Melbourne University Press, 2009).   JNT

Porter, Peter (1929–2010) Born in Brisbane. He came to England in 1951 and, apart from short periods as writer-in-residence at English, Scottish, and Australian universities, lived in London. In the 1950s he was associated with the *Group, and felt a particular affinity for the work of Martin *Bell (whose *Complete Poems*, edited by Porter, appeared in 1988). For some years in the 1960s Porter worked in an advertising agency—fellow employees included Peter *Redgrove and Gavin *Ewart—but after 1968 he earned his living as a freelance writer and broadcaster, and was for many years a regular poetry critic for the *Observer*. He had two daughters by his marriage to Jannice Henry, who died in 1974.

Porter was a prolific poet, and an uneven one. He regarded fecundity as a virtue (as did *Auden, who was an important influence), and one suspects that obscure or awkward passages, the occasional impression of impatience or carelessness, particularly in his handling of rhyming, stanzaic forms, are prices he was willing to pay for a substantial and varied oeuvre. Critics were quick to cast him—on the strength of a few muscular, overwrought poems in his first book which parade their author's queasy fascination with the London 'scene', consumer goods, and casual sex—as a privileged outsider, the satirist of a new Elizabethan age. In fact some of the poems are strikingly Elizabethan in a different sense—steeped in corruption, plucking anatomies of decay from the fashionable decadence; while others energetically recall an Australian background shadowed by illness, loneliness, and childhood fears (Porter's mother died when he was 9). A fruitful sense of unbelonging, and scathing irony at the expense of what 'belonging' might mean, inform Porter's satirical verse, which at its best (as in the pointed 'recreations' of Martial) is witty and scabrous, full of what one commentator has called 'the provincial's sour relish for attacking the vices and absurdities of the world he has entered'. With hindsight, though, the targets (fatuous officialdom, artistic pretension, sexual greed) seem softer than they might once have seemed, the attack too nearly tailored to the demands of the poetry reading. The real fulfilment of Porter's early promise was in his mature persona: that of an elegiac moralist, stoical, compassionate, sardonic, preoccupied with mortality and 'the sadness of the creatures', and most memorable when confessing more than hopeless lust or moral torpor—notably in the tender, self-accusing poems that followed his wife's suicide.

Porter said that his poetry deals with 'the art and life of the past, the everyday life of the present'. This is true as far as it goes, but it drastically understates the intellectual richness and the—sometimes impenetrable—allusiveness of his manner. In Australia 'alienated', as his compatriot Clive *James wrote, by his 'European sensibility', suspicious of his homeland's 'dreadful health' (though prepared in more recent poems to celebrate its natural glories), Porter set about imaginatively possessing Europe with determination and an impressive range of cultural and historical reference. Baroque music, opera, Renaissance painting, and the Italian landscape are regularly invoked as consolations for the vanity and imperfection of the world, while 'God' and 'the gods' also recur frequently as the origins both of injustice and mysterious benediction. In all this the poet's voice is pained, urbane, sententiously aphoristic or stately, oracular, lapidary, and discursive.

The volumes published after his first *Collected Poems* showed the increasing influence of Wallace *Stevens and John *Ashbery—a marked interest in dreams, in the opulence and irrational punning vitalism of words, and in varieties of ironic parable—though not to the point where Porter was prepared to relinquish his customary, controlled eloquence (a matter of phrasing more than formal or musical properties) for, say, Ashbery's colloquialism and 'directionless drift'. Warily noting the decline of civilization in an age of nuclear threat and literary theory, Porter as warily (and controversially) recognized the limitations of his own art, continuing to find a role for the poet as self-deprecating scourge.

Porter was awarded the Duff Cooper Memorial Prize for his *Collected Poems* (1983), which contained virtually all the poems published in nine volumes up to and including *English Subtitles* (1981). A later edition added the several volumes up to *Both Ends Against the Middle* (both 1999—all Oxford University Press). From *Max Is Missing* (2001), which won the Forward Prize, Porter's later poetry was published by Picador. He also made a selection of Lawrence *Durrell's poetry for Faber in 2006. His last collection was *Better Than God* (2009). *The Rest on the Flight: Selected Poems* (2010) appeared posthumously. Porter received the Queen's Gold Medal for Poetry in 2002.

See also Bruce Bennett, *Spirit in Exile: Peter Porter and his Poetry* (1991), and Peter Steele, *Peter Porter* (1992—both Oxford University Press).   AJ

Pound, Ezra (Loomis) (1885–1972) Born in Hailey, Idaho, but grew up and was educated mainly in Pennsylvania. In 1908, when a projected academic career was cut short, he set sail for Europe, spending several months in Venice and finally settling in London, where he was befriended by his hero, W. B. *Yeats. Between 1908 and 1911 he published six collections of verse, most of it dominated by a passion for Provençal

and early Italian poetry. This is filtered through the medievalizing manner of Browning and the Pre-Raphaelites. Under the influence of Ford Madox *Ford and T. E. *Hulme he modernized his style, and in 1912 launched the Imagist movement, advocating concreteness, economy, and free verse. The oriental delicacy of his brief Imagist lyrics (e.g. 'In a Station of the Metro') soon gave way to the more dynamically avant-garde manner of Vorticism. Association with Vorticist visual artists (e.g. Henri Gaudier-Brzeska and Wyndham *Lewis) helped him to see how poems could be made up, like post-Cubist sculptures, of juxtaposed masses and planes. These lessons were reinforced by his work on Ernest Fenollosa's literal versions of classical Chinese poems, which he turned into the beautiful free-verse lyrics of *Cathay* (1915). Fenollosa had argued that Chinese written characters were ideograms—compressed and abstracted visual metaphors. In this interplay of concrete signs Pound saw the model for a new kind of poetry, dynamic and economical, which juxtaposed not only images but diverse 'facts'—allusions, quotations, fragments of narrative. Such a method, soon to be tried out in his major work *The Cantos* (on which he tentatively embarked in 1915), would permit the use of quotations from other languages and even gobbets of prose.

The range and brilliance of Pound's contacts in all the arts convinced him that London was to be the centre of a new Renaissance. He cast himself in the role of impresario, editor, and advocate, contributing to Yeats' mature style, discovering and promoting *Joyce and *Eliot, advising an American businessman on the modern works of art to buy in London. But his hopes foundered in the waste of the First World War, and the consequent disappointment was to colour the rest of his life's work. In the short term it provoked his first major poems, 'Homage to Sextus Propertius' (1919) and *Hugh Selwyn Mauberley* (1921). These two ironic sequences represent a contrast. The free-verse 'Homage', an ironic persona poem based on the lyrics of the first-century Roman poet, is a defence of the private and erotic in poetry against the imperialistic jingoism promoted by war. *Mauberley*, in tautly rhymed satirical stanzas, depicts the war as the *Götterdammerung* of an emasculated and philistine culture, condemned by the limitation of its own horizons. The poem is also evidence of Pound's close working relationship with Eliot, whose taste it reflects (cf. the 'Sweeney' poems of the same period). The relationship was to culminate in the crucial part played by Pound in cutting *The Waste Land* (1922).

Mauberley has been described as Pound's farewell to London. In 1920 he left, spending four years in Paris then moving on to Italy, where he settled in Rapallo in 1924. He was now concentrating on *The Cantos*, his 'poem including history', and the first section was published in 1925.

As *The Cantos* shows, he was now preoccupied with economics. The war, as he saw it, had been caused by the rivalries of international capitalists. He thought he had found a solution to the evils of unchecked capitalism, one especially favourable to the arts, in the Social Credit theory of Major C. H. Douglas, who argued that a system of state credit could increase purchasing power in the population at large, thus promoting creativity and removing power from bankers and financiers. Attracted to Mussolini by his energy and his promises of monetary reform, Pound naïvely assumed that the Italian leader could be persuaded to put Douglas' theory into practice. At first, the main target of Pound's attacks is 'usury', which he depicts (e.g. in Canto 45) as an unnatural force that pollutes the creative instinct in humanity. By about 1930 the usurers he condemns are usually Jews, and his language is vitiated by virulent anti-Semitism.

A Draft of XXX Cantos (1930) presents the poet as wandering Odysseus, travelling among the dead. Through juxtaposition, he uncovers repeated patterns in history and experiences moments when the world of time is transfigured by the eternal world of the gods. The mainly Mediterranean emphasis of the first thirty Cantos then gives way (in Cantos 31–70, published 1934–40) to the economic policies of early US presidents and the governance of ancient China.

Despite an increase in prosy didacticism and much consequent turgidity, these sections contain some of Pound's finest poetry (e.g. Cantos 36, 45, 47, and 49).

In the later 1930s Pound devoted much of his energy to defending fascism and trying to avert war. When war broke out, he embarked on a series of fanatical addresses to American troops, which were broadcast on Rome Radio. As a result, he was arrested by partisans in 1945 and handed over to the US forces, who held him for six months at a Disciplinary Training Centre near Pisa, pending trial on a treason charge. It seems likely that the inhuman conditions he endured there for the first three weeks accelerated the breakdown in rationality already to be glimpsed in his writings. Repatriated to the United States to stand trial, he was found unfit to plead on grounds of insanity and incarcerated in St Elizabeths Hospital, Washington DC, from 1946 to 1958.

His imprisonment brought about an artistic recovery. *The Pisan Cantos* (1948), drafted in the DTC, are the most directly personal poems he wrote. In adversity, and conscious of the tragedy of Europe, he contemplates his own past in that context, especially the watershed years of the modern movement. Suffering and retrospection induce a new humility, exemplified in his care for the life around him—the insects, the animals, the camp guards. In St Elizabeths he completed two rather more cryptic sections of the poem—*Section: Rock-Drill* (1955) and *Thrones* (1959)—as well as a programme of translations from the Confucian classics.

On his release he returned to Italy, dying in Venice in 1972. Despite moments of defiance, his last years were overshadowed by self-doubt and consciousness of his 'errors and wrecks'. In rare public utterances he condemned *The Cantos* as a failure, a view he seems not consistently to have held; but the poem was never completed. In 1969 he concluded its publication with *Drafts and Fragments of Cantos CX–CXVII*: thirty-two pages of verse, mostly serene but poignant in its fragmentation.

Pound was the central figure in the modern movement, personally responsible for the renewal of English poetry in the 1910s.

Yet he remains a controversial figure. His brutal politics have been damaging to his lofty view of the artist and civilization; he is also condemned as an élitist, an obscurantist, and a charlatan—a man deficient in self-knowledge, with no real understanding of the modern world despite his avant-gardiste posturing. None of these charges quite shakes the substance of his achievement, which is fundamentally a matter of technical accomplishment to a point where refinement of skill becomes a moral quality. Such is the sensitivity of his verse movement that it seems to release independent life and otherness in his subjects, as if it had discovered them by chance. This is so whether he seeks to evoke the movement of olive leaves in the wind or the character of a Renaissance *condottiere*. The same quality lies behind his genius for translation, an art he has been said to have invented for our time: uncannily, he creates a language for each author which registers the remoteness of the author from our world while at the same time making his work available to us. If Pound is obscure, it is largely because of his wide frame of reference; he was also an educator, who used poetry to introduce his readers to works and ideas he had discovered for himself. It is hardly his fault that his syllabus has never been adopted.

Pound's poetry is collected in two main volumes: the Library of America's *Poems and Translations* (New York, 2004) and his great work *The Cantos of Ezra Pound* (New Directions, 1972; Faber, 1981). *Selected Poems and Translations of Ezra Pound 1908-1969*, ed. Richard Sieburth (Faber, 2011) provides a substantial and annotated introduction to this complex body of work. Sieburth has also produced an annotated edition of *The Pisan Cantos* (New Directions, 2003). *The Literary Essays of Ezra Pound*, ed. T. S. Eliot (Faber, 1954), suggests the scope of his criticism, while *Selected Prose, 1909-1965*, ed. William Cookson (Faber, 1973), includes much of his polemical writing as well. Earlier biographies are now being superseded by A. David Moody's *Ezra Pound, Poet: A Portrait of the Man and his Work*, the first volume of which is *The Young Genius* (Oxford University Press, 2007). There is a vast critical literature, from which two classics emerge: Donald Davie, *Ezra Pound: Poet as Sculptor*, now reprinted in *Studies in Ezra Pound* (Carcanet, 1991), and Hugh Kenner, *The Pound Era: The Age of Ezra Pound, T. S. Eliot, James Joyce and Wyndham Lewis* (University of California Press, 1971).   CW

Powell, Craig (1940–   ) Born in Wollongong, New South Wales, graduated in medicine from Sydney University in 1965, and went on to qualify as a psychiatrist. In 1972 he left Australia and spent ten years in Manitoba and Ontario, Canada. He returned to Sydney in 1982, where he practises psychiatry.

Powell won the Australian *Poetry Magazine* Award in 1964 and two years later published *A Different Kind of Breathing*, his first collection of poetry. Later volumes include *I Learn by Going* (1968), *A Country without Exiles* (1972), *Rehearsal for Dancers* (1978), and *A Face in Your Hands* (1984). In 1983 he was awarded the Mattara Poetry Prize.

Powell's poetry, influenced by the ideas of the Chicago analyst Heinz Kohut, expresses a tragic view of existence. Many of his poems develop around people he has come to know in his profession as a psychiatrist. The central section of *A Country without Exiles* consists of compassionate portraits of the inmates of a mental hospital. Powell has also written a number of poems to fellow poets, including Francis *Webb, reflecting on the emotional and spiritual sources of poetry. His accounts of personal experience and that of the characters he recreates balance the imperfections of human nature against an affirmation of shared humanity.

Since *Minga Street: New and Selected Poems* (Hale & Iremonger, 1993) he has published another collection, *Music and Women's Bodies* (Five Islands, 2002), and two chapbooks: *The Poem as a Place* (2004) and *Poems for a Marriage* (2008—both Picaro).

For criticism, see 'The Language of the Poem', *The Phoenix Review*, 3 (1988), an interview, 'Tenderness Towards Existence', *Poetry Australia, 107/108* (1986), and an essay, 'The Nameless Father in the Poetry and Life of Francis Webb', reprinted by Picaro Press in 2004.   PK

Powell, D. A. (1963–   ) Born in Albany, Georgia, Powell attended Sonoma State University in California, and then the Writers' Workshop at the University of Iowa. He has been Briggs-Copeland Lecturer in Poetry at Harvard University and now teaches at the University of San Francisco. From 1995 to 2008 he edited *Electronic Poetry Review*.

The untitled poems of *Tea* (1998) initiated an autobiographical trilogy about growing up as a gay man in America during the AIDS era. *Lunch* (2000—both Wesleyan University Press) included earlier work, as well as poems on Powell's HIV-positive diagnosis. *Cocktails* (2004) cast his experience in the mythological contexts of Hollywood and the Bible. It was nominated for a National Book Critics Circle Award, as was *Chronic* (2009), which won the Kingsley Tufts Poetry Award. His fifth collection is *Useless Landscape, or A Guide for Boys* (2012—all Graywolf). See also his experimental collaborative memoir, *By Myself: An Autobiography*, with David Trinidad (Turtle Point, 2009).

Powell's work is characterized by its deployment of quicksilver imagery and diction in a long line that embraces the slangy, the sensual, and the sombre ('we slip and slop and spill our soup—pop our rocks—droop and droplet flung over the back of the sofa: limp as a cashmere coverlet. damp as a bloodclot'). As the critic Stephen Burt has written, 'what has made Powell stand out in other poets' eyes is not his set of affecting subjects but his invention of an original style' (*Close Calls With Nonsense* (Graywolf, 2009)).   JNT

Pratt, E. J. (Edwin John) (1882–1964) Born in Western Bay, Newfoundland. He was an ordained Methodist minister and long-serving member of the English department at Victoria College in the University of Toronto, from which he retired in 1953. Educated in schools in Newfoundland, Pratt attended the University of Toronto from which he received a BA and

MA, and a PhD. He also held a degree in divinity.

A self-described 'writer of tragic situations relating to the sea', Pratt established a reputation as a poet of strong conventional rhythms which lent themselves readily to the telling of his 'story-poems'. A convivial yarn-spinner and friendly presence on the poetry scene in Canada in the first half of the twentieth century, Pratt exerted considerable influence on fellow writers, publishers, and magazine editors of this period. He was founding editor (1936–43) of the *Canadian Poetry Magazine*, and a prominent member of the Canadian Authors' Association, and he was awarded many medals, distinctions, and honorary degrees for his services to Canadian writing in his role as chronicler of the heroics and the history of the raw Canadian experience.

Newfoundland Verse (1923), Pratt's first collection, gives evidence of the essentially traditional approach of this poet to his art. It was followed by *The Witches Brew* (1925) which, in style and content, announces Pratt's whimsical interest in primordial creatures and conflict on an epic scale. The behaviour of man in heroic and self-sacrificing conflict with forces of nature, ideology, or history greater than himself became the substance of much of his work from the 1930s onwards. *The Roosevelt and the Antinoe* (1930) deals with rescue at sea; *The Fable of the Goats and Other Poems* (1932) frames that bellicose decade; while *The Titanic* (1935) is a study in the hubristic arrogance of technological man. In 1940 Pratt published *Brébeuf and his Brethren*, a narrative concerned with the clash of Christianity and Amerindian culture. During the war and immediately thereafter Pratt produced four collections of verse—*Dunkirk* (1941), *Still Life and Other Verse* (1943), *They Are Returning* (1945), *Behind the Log* (1947)—which were overtly patriotic and celebratory of the allied war effort, as well as his first *Collected Poems* which appeared in 1944. In 1952 Pratt published *Towards the Last Spike*, aptly described in the subtitle as a verse panorama of the struggle to build the first Canadian transcontinental railway. 1958 saw the publication of *The Collected*

Poems of E. J. Pratt (Macmillan), with an introduction by Northrop Frye who had been one of Pratt's students.

In spite of his reliance on traditional verse-patterns and rhythms, his tendency to see life in terms of a slightly dated equation of struggle and redemption, and his predisposition to robust story-telling in his poems, Pratt remains a compelling and influential figure in twentieth-century Canadian poetry. The annotated *Selected Poems* (University of Toronto Press, 2000) is also available online.   MG

Presley, Frances (1952–) Born in Chesterfield, Derbyshire, of English and Dutch-Indonesian parents, Presley studied literature at the universities of East Anglia and Sussex. She wrote an MA thesis on 'the convergence of art and poetry' in Apollinaire and *Pound, and an M.Phil. thesis on Yves Bonnefoy. Of her ten full collections of poetry, three consist of collaborations with other poets—Elizabeth James, Irma Irsara, and Tilla Brading—and one with an artist, Ian Robinson.

Her first full collection was *The Sex of Art* (North and South, 1988). Most recently she has published *Paravane: New and Selected Poems 1996–2003* (Salt, 2004), *Myne: New and Selected Poems and Prose 1976–2005* (2006), *Lines of Sight* (2009—both Shearsman), and, with Brading, *Stone Settings* (Odyssey, 2010). Writing in a fragmented free verse, Presley treats the page as an open field, breaking words across and over lines as well as placing passages in varying places and formats. Words devolve into their parts and/or related sounds, as when 'sempstress' becomes, over the next few lines, 'sem stress', 'semper and simper', then 'sempre forte' (from *Paravane*). Numerous poems, especially those in prose, interweave multiple threads of thought. While her work consistently conflates the personal and the political, over time it has increasingly engaged with the English countryside, most particularly the Neolithic stone monuments on Exmoor. Recent appearances in the anthologies *Infinite Difference* (2010) and *The Ground Aslant* (2011—both

Shearsman), have brought her writing to wider critical appreciation.   CE

Press, Karen (1956–) Born in Cape Town. Press has worked as a teacher and editor, and has written educational textbooks, as well as children's fiction and a film script. She is a founder and associate of The Writer's Network, an advice and support service in South Africa.

Karen Press began to publish her work in small magazines in the mid-1980s. In 1985, she collaborated with Ingrid *de Kok on a collection of found examples of apartheid's 'absurd' language, *Emergency Declarations*. *This Winter Coming* (Cinammon Crocodile), her first volume of poetry, appeared in 1986. In 1987, she co-founded Buchu Books, a publishing collective through which her volume *Bird Heart Stoning the Sea* appeared in 1990.

In interview, Press has criticized the 'rather dated British model of good poetry' in South Africa: 'poetry that's talking about the tree in my garden, and how I feel about the tree in my garden'. Her own values plain, forceful statement, and reflects directly on the ever-present 'reality of material poverty' in the country, as in 'Dispossessed Words', a collage drawn from social-research interviews. It can also be vividly descriptive. In 2000, Press published her first collection with Carcanet in Britain, *Home. The Canary's Songbook* (2005) and *Slowly, As If* (2012—both Carcanet) followed. She has also written two books of verse which take the form of a visitor's guide to aspects of South African life: *Echo Location* (Gecko, 1998) and *The Little Museum of Working Life* (University of KwaZulu-Natal Press, 2004).   JNT

Prewett, Frank (James 'Toronto') (1893–1962) Born in Kenilworth, near Mount Forest, Ontario, on his maternal grandfather's pioneer farm. He was raised in Toronto and educated at the University of Toronto, and later at Christ Church, Oxford. During the First World War he was transferred from the Canadian Expeditionary Force to the Royal Artillery, wounded and shell-shocked in April 1918, and sent to Lennels near Coldstream, Scotland, where he was placed under the care of the psychologist/anthropologist W. H. R. Rivers. There Prewett met Siegfried *Sassoon who introduced him to the literary figures and circles associated with both war-writing and the later *Georgian poetry, including Robert *Graves, Edmund *Blunden, Wilfred *Owen, and Lady Ottoline Morrell and the Garsington circle.

Prewett stands apart from other 'Georgian' poets in two respects: that he was the only Canadian to participate in the stylistic movement (Edward Marsh included eight of Prewett's poems in *Georgian Poetry* 1920–2); and that his images are shaped not by the gentility of English nature but by the exacting harshness of the Canadian environment and the war.

Prewett's first volume, *Poems* (1920), handset by Virginia Woolf and published by the Hogarth Press, contains many of the poet's finest trench verses, such as 'Voices of Women', 'The Somme Valley, 1917', and 'Burial Stones', interspersed with more truly 'Georgian' poems of bucolic landscapes observed during his recuperation. A second volume, *The Rural Scene* (1924), continued many of the themes of love, death, and nature that Prewett had explored in his previous collection.

Prewett died in poverty and obscurity in 1962 and was buried in Inverness.

See *Collected Poems of Frank Prewett* (Cassell, 1964), ed. Robert Graves; *The Selected Poems of Frank Prewett*, ed. Bruce Meyer and Barry Callaghan (1987); Bruce Meyer, *Profiles in Canadian Literature: Frank Prewett* (1991); Andrew Coppolino, 'A Canadian in the Garsington Circle: Frank Prewett's Literary Friendships', *Studies in Canadian Literature*, 12:2 (1987).   BM

Price, Richard (1966–) Born in Reading and grew up in Renfrewshire, Price studied journalism in Edinburgh and English and librarianship at Strathclyde University, where he wrote a PhD thesis on Neil M. Gunn. He works at the British Library and writes fiction as R. J. Price.

Price was the youngest poet associated with the *Informationist group. He co-founded Vennel Press, and with W. N.

*Herbert edited the anthology *Contraflow on the Super Highway* (Southfields, 1994). Since 2001, he has edited the small magazine *Painted, spoken*. He has also co-authored a bibliography of twentieth-century British poetry magazines, and a collection of essays on Basil *Bunting (*The Star You Steer By* (Rodopi, 2000)).

Price's interest in the diverse modernities of British poetry is evident in his own light-footed lyricism, which employs a wide range of modes—from pop songs to experimental translations—and is often arranged in sequences. *Marks & Sparks* (Akros, 1995), a series of love poems, and *Hand Held* (1997), a diary of early parenthood, are reprinted in *Lucky Day* (2005). *Greenfields* (2007—both Carcanet) contains poems from Price's earliest publications in 1993: *Sense and a Minor Fever* (Vennel) and *Tube Shelter Perspective* (Southfields). It develops the imaginative rewriting of a 'half-rural, half-urban' Renfrewshire which is also the landscape of his fiction: See *A Boy in Summer* (2002) and *The Island* (2010). *Rays* (2009) was praised by David *Wheatley as the work of 'the best Scottish poet in recent years'. His fourth collection is *Small World* (2012— both Carcanet).   JNT

Prince, F. T. (Frank Templeton) (1912–2003) Born in South Africa. He was educated there and at Oxford and Princeton universities. During the Second World War he served in Army Intelligence. From 1957 to 1974 he was professor of English at Southampton University. In 1973 he gave the Clark Lectures at Cambridge. His critical works include *The Italian Element in Milton's Verse* (1954) and *William Shakespeare: The Poems* (1963).

Prince's best-known single poem is probably the personal and deeply Christian 'Soldiers Bathing', which was first collected in the volume of that title in 1954. By the year of publication (1963) of his *The Doors of Stone*, the good Prince poem is readily definable. It is well made; it tends to be long; the poet projects his imagination into the realities of named people (e.g. Edmund Burke, the Zulu king Chaka, Michelangelo); the clarity and subtlety of perception challenges the reader's attentiveness and willingness to think, albeit within a familiar context of mainstream ideas and attitudes.

Beginning in 1970, Prince published us a succession of long poems, each amounting to several hundred lines. Much of this later work confirms the trends already indicated. Some of the pieces are informed with a remarkable idealism, a concern with the possibility and fact of self-transcendence, which is traditional in that its roots are in Plato, Shelley, Judaism, and Christianity, but original in its personal presence, its particular statements and fervour. The derivation and overt subject-matter of such writings might be pre-judged as bookish (cf. the titles *Drypoints of the Hasidim* and *Afterword on Rupert Brooke*), but in fact the poetry impinges urgently on ethical, moral, and religious aspects of daily reality. Yet it is not didactic: it is concerned with spiritual work in progress, not with the exposition of finalized wisdom.

Prince is an outstanding craftsman, as can be seen from even cursory attention to his prosody. This includes free verse of exemplary precision in the placing and relative emphasis of stressed syllables, lively but 'natural' iambics, and syllabics (based on *Bridges) whose arithmetical count does not prejudice the verve of English speech.

The *Collected Poems* of 1979 was revised and brought up to date in 1993 (Sheep Meadow/Carcanet; repr. Carcanet, 2012). Two later poems appeared in 1995 in *PN Review*, issues 102 ('The Little Gidding Seminar') and 106 ('Keats Country'). The magazine also published a tribute to Prince by other poets, including John *Ashbery and Geoffrey *Hill, in issue 147 (September-October 2002).   WGS

Prynne, J. H. (Jeremy Halvard) (1936–   ) Born in Kent, Prynne did National Service in Germany before reading English at the University of Cambridge. He subsequently taught there until his retirement in 2005. He is a Life Fellow and former Librarian of Gonville and Caius College, an Honorary Professor at the University of Sussex, and a Visiting Professor at Sun Yat-sen University in China.

The most prominent and influential member of the *Cambridge School, Prynne has been called 'Britain's leading late modernist poet'. Having studied Ezra *Pound at Cambridge with Donald *Davie, he went to Harvard University as a Frank Knox Fellow in 1960, and began formative friendships with the American poets Charles *Olson and Ed *Dorn. His first collection was *Force of Circumstance* (Routledge & Kegan Paul, 1962), a measured volume recalling the more austere poems of the *Movement (and the early work of Charles *Tomlinson) in its concern with calibrating 'the place' of man in the world. It has not been reprinted in any later edition of Prynne's poetry, which all begin with 'The Numbers' from *Kitchen Poems* (Cape Goliard, 1968): 'The whole thing it is, the difficult | matter, to shrink the confines | down'. This restates the dominant idea of his debut, now enlarged by the Olsonian exhortations to 'dig one thing' and (in 'Projective Verse') to follow 'the whole business' of thought 'as fast as you can'. Writing 'knowledge | back to the springs' has been Prynne's project as a poet ever since. Thus, 'The Glacial Question, Unsolved' from *The White Stones* (Grosseteste, 1969), like W. H. *Auden in the 1930s, explores the geological history of Britain as an allegory of modernity ('what we hope to call land'). The presiding discipline of the oeuvre, however, is philology. As Donald Davie noted in *Thomas Hardy and British Poetry* (1973), 'The structuring principle of this poetry, which makes it difficult (sometimes too difficult), is the unemphasized but radical demands it makes upon English etymologies.'

Few would disagree that Prynne's verse has become ever more resistant to paraphrase. The first book-length critical introduction, *Nearly Too Much: The Poetry of J. H. Prynne* (Liverpool University Press, 1996) by N. H. Reeve and Richard Kerridge, took its title from a characteristically sardonic sentiment expressed in *Down where changed* (Ferry, 1979): 'Nearly too much | is, well, nowhere near enough'. The discursive verse-essays of *Kitchen Poems*, the ode-like meditations of *The White Stones*, and the delicate lyrics of *Day Light Songs* (R Books, 1968) gave way in *Brass* (Ferry, 1971) to the dialectic encounter of these modes in language culled from every kind of contemporary register. 'No | poetic gabble will survive which fails | to collide head-on with the unwitty circus' ('L'Extase de M. Poher') might be the new motto of the poetry that followed. What has drawn readers to the demands it makes is the intellectual urgency and aesthetic intensity that animates Prynne's reinvention of traditional lyric subjectivity in a world governed by market forces and scientific empiricism. In sequences such as *The Oval Window* (privately printed, 1983), *Her Weasels Wild Returning* (Equipage, 1993), *Red D Gypsum* (Barque, 1998), *Unanswering Rational Shore* (Object Permanence, 2001), and *Sub Songs* (Barque, 2010), the result, as Marjorie *Welish has put it, is 'a stratified field of rich linguistic construction'.

Prynne has remained a prolific poet for four decades, publishing new work through small presses. Since the 1990s his characteristic form has been the symmetrical stanzaic block or grid, but there are notable exceptions to this, such as the ballad-like quatrains of *Pearls That Were* (privately printed, 1999) and the ragged, mock-reportage of *Triodes* (Barque, 1999), which engages with the geo-political panoramas of younger Cambridge poets such as Keston *Sutherland and John *Wilkinson (see also 'Refuse Collection' (2004), written in response to the torture of prisoners by American soldiers at Abu Ghraib prison in Iraq). *Kazoo Dreamboats, or, On What There Is* (Critical Documents, 2011), a rhapsodic verse-essay composed around quotations from Maoist philosophy, theoretical physics, and archaeology, offers an artistic testament, while remaining hyper-responsive to the historical moment of its writing.

Prynne's *Poems* were first published by Allardyce, Barnett in a collected edition in 1982. An expanded and corrected edition was prepared by Fremantle Arts Centre Press/Folio in Australia, and published in Britain by Bloodaxe in 1999, with a further expanded edition in 2005. Selections have been translated into French, German, Norwegian, and Chinese. See also, in America, *Furtherance* (The Figures, 2004), which collects the sequences from 1998–2001.

As with T. S. *Eliot, Prynne's formidably analytical and rhetorical criticism has been influential in the reception of his work, but there is not yet a collected edition of his prose. This would include the extended scholarly commentaries he has published on lyric poems by Shakespeare, Wordsworth, and George Herbert. Other important items are the early statements reprinted in *Certain Prose of the English Intelligencer* (Mountain, 2012), ed. Neil Pattison, Reitha Pattison, and Luke Roberts; published letters to Andrew *Crozier, Steve *McCaffery, and Allen *Fisher; an essay on Chinese poetry and metonymy, printed in *New Songs from a Jade Terrace*, trans. Anne Birrell (Penguin, 1986); and the lectures 'English Poetry and Emphatical Language' (*Proceedings of the British Academy*, 74 (1988)), *Stars, Tigers, and the Shape of Words* (Birkbeck College, 1993), and 'Mental Ears and Poetic Work' (*Chicago Review*, 55:1 (Winter 2010)). A succinct outline of Prynne's own understanding of modernist poetics may be found in 'Difficulties in the Translation of "Difficult" Poems' (*Cambridge Literary Review*, 1:3 (Easter 2010)).

Critical commentary in recent years has proliferated online and in journals. The best general introduction remains Reeve and Kerridge (see above). There are illuminating discussions in Veronica *Forrest-Thomson, *Poetic Artifice* (Manchester University Press, 1978), Andrew Duncan, *The Failure of Conservatism in Modern British Poetry* (Salt, 2003), and Jon Clay, *Sensation, Contemporary Poetry and Deleuze* (Continuum, 2010). See also the essays in *A Manner of Utterance: The Poetry of J. H. Prynne* (Shearsman, 2009), ed. Ian Brinton. For a contrarian view of Prynne's achievement, see Ben Watson, *Blake in Cambridge* (Unkant, 2012).   JNT

Pugh, Sheenah (1950–) Born in Birmingham, Pugh studied Russian and German at the University of Bristol, and lived and worked in Wales for many years as a lecturer at the University of Glamorgan. She now lives in Shetland.

Pugh began to publish in the late 1970s. *Selected Poems* (1990) draws on her first four collections, and includes her popular anthology piece 'Sometimes', a short, understated hymn of optimism. She has since repudiated the poem as unrepresentative of 'the kind of poet I want to be'—which is undoubtedly a poet of plain language and familiar things, but also an ironic observer of human survival, in verse narratives of world history and ecology. *Later Selected Poems* (2009) is taken from the half-dozen collections she has published since 1990: *Sing for the Taxman* (1993), *Id's Hospit* (1997), *Stonelight* (1999), which won the Wales Book of the Year Award, *The Beautiful Lie* (2002), *The Movement of Bodies* (2005), and *Long-Haul Travellers* (2008—all Seren). She has also published translations of German poetry, two novels, and a study of fan fiction, *The Democratic Genre* (2005—see also her sequence 'Fanfic'). JNT

Purcell, Sally (Anne Jane) (1944–98) Read Medieval French at Lady Margaret Hall, Oxford. Later she published a translation of Dante's *De vulgari eloquentia* (*Literature in the Vernacular*, 1981) and an edition of *The Poems of Charles of Orleans* (1973—both Carcanet). Her versions of Provençal troubadour poems appeared in 1969, and her own poetry depended closely on the classical and medieval legends she grew up studying. Precise, stylized evocations of Queen Proserpina or Merlin dominated her work from *The Devil's Dancing Hour* (1968) and *The Holly Queen* (1972—both Anvil) to *By the Clear Fountain* (Mammon, 1980), *Guenever and the Looking Glass* (Greville, 1984), and *Lake and Labyrinth* (TAXVS, 1985); while her poems always exploited the superstition inherent in their subjects, they also increasingly emphasized intricate, occasionally precious patterns of reflection operating between the landscapes of her poems and the characters who inhabit them. Her lyrics have been criticized as a little too ethereal, and for their avoidance of the earthier physical realities of the situations they conjure; if one of her *Four Poems* (Other Branch, 1985) is to be believed, however, Purcell prefers to see 'God's pattern | linking all

the gardens'. Her *Collected Poems* (Anvil, 2002) was edited by Peter Jay, with a foreword by Marina Warner.   MRW

Purdy, Al(fred Wellington) (1918–2000) Born at Wooler, Ontario, a hamlet near Lake Ontario. His father, a farmer of United Empire Loyalist stock, died when Purdy was 2; the boy was then raised by his religious mother in the nearby city of Trenton. After leaving school, Purdy worked at a variety of jobs in Trenton, Belleville, Vancouver, and Montreal. He also served in the Royal Canadian Air Force from 1940 to 1944. In later years, he lived at Roblin Lake, near Trenton. Although he brought out his first book of poems in 1944, his reputation as a poet was not securely established until the publication of *The Cariboo Horses* (1965). He was the recipient of several Canada Council grants and was appointed a writer-in-residence at a number of Canadian universities.

While Purdy's poetic world includes places as remote as the Cariboo country of central British Columbia, villages in the Canadian Arctic, and the 'long road' to Newfoundland, the rural landscape around Trenton figures most significantly in his verse. Much of the charm of his poetry lies in the variety and extravagance of its descriptive detail, its somewhat folksy similes, and its sudden turns of thought. He typically subordinates his poetic lines to the casual, emergent syntax of colloquial speech. In many of his poems, a past and a present state of affairs are contrasted nostalgically.

His many publications included his edition of a collection of statements by Canadians on their attitudes towards the United States, *The New Romans* (St Martin's, 1968); a collection of semi-autobiographical essays, *No Other Country* (1977); an historical novel, *A Splinter in the Heart* (1990—both McClelland & Stewart); and over thirty volumes of poetry. An autobiography, *Reaching for the Beaufort Sea*, appeared in 1993. *Rooms for Rent in the Outer Planets: Selected Poems 1962–1996* was followed by *To Paris Never Again* (1997). *Starting from Ameliasburgh* (1995), his collected prose, gathers essays in travel writing, memoir, and criticism.

At the time of his death, Purdy was considered one of the greatest Canadian writers. *Beyond Remembering: Collected Poems*, ed. Sam Solecki, appeared in 2000, with forewords by Margaret *Atwood and Michael *Ondaatje, and a collected letters, *Yours, Al*, in 2004 (all Harbour), which included his correspondence with Charles *Bukowski.   JST*

Putnam, H. Phelps (1894–1948) Born and raised near Boston, Massachusetts. After graduating from Yale he worked as a miner in Colorado, as a bureaucrat in Washington, and as an advertising copywriter in Boston, and travelled in Europe during the heady years following the First World War, before publishing *Trinc* (Doran, 1927), a collection notable for several haunting short stories in verse, one of which, 'Ballad of a Strange Thing', a retelling of the fable of Pan and Syrinx set in the Massachusetts countryside, is perhaps his single most accomplished poem. When *Trinc* came out he was planning an epic of modern life to be modelled on Dante, and his next book, *The Five Seasons* (Scribner's, 1931), introduces the protagonist, a wanderer named Bill Williams, and his Virgilian *alter ego*, Hasbrouck. But the poem never went any further, in part because Putnam seems to have been overwhelmed by his own ambition, and in part because of his worsening health. Asthmatic from an early age, he spent much of the Twenties and Thirties in the south-western United States, but the asthma eventually weakened his heart and he died of a stroke after seventeen years of writing little and publishing less.

See *The Collected Poems of H. Phelps Putnam*, ed. Charles L. Walker (Farrar, Straus, 1971).   RH

Quinn, Justin (1968–) Born in Dublin and studied at Trinity College there. With fellow student David *Wheatley he was a founding editor of *Metre* magazine. Since 1992 he has lived in Prague, where he teaches American and English Literature at Charles University. Quinn's first book, *The 'O'o'a'a' Bird*, appeared in 1995. It was immediately noticed for its European outlook and inventive formalism, and was followed by *Privacy* in 1999 (both Carcanet).

Wallace *Stevens is a presiding spirit of the way that Quinn suspends and elaborates his perception of a scene: like Stevens' 'jar in Tennessee', the songbird of his debut's title denotes a 'pristine' poetic space around and against which reality gathers. Stevens was also the subject of his first critical monograph, *Gathered Beneath the Storm: Wallace Stevens, Nature and Community* (University College Dublin Press, 2002). But his ingeniously colloquial rhymes have absorbed Irish models such as *Mahon and *Muldoon too—see his *Introduction to Modern Irish Poetry, 1800–2000* (Cambridge University Press, 2008).

Fuselage (2002) was praised by Peter *Manson for its 'Mallarméan sinuousness' of construction, and Quinn's standing among his peers has continued to grow with each new collection: *Waves and Trees* in 2006 and *Close Quarters* in 2011 (all Gallery Press). These books have also reflected his growing involvement with Czech poetry. Quinn's selected translations of his contemporary, Petr Borkovec (*From the Interior*) appeared from Seren in 2008. JNT

Rafat, Taufiq (1927–98) Born in Sialkot and educated in Lahore. His first collection, *Arrival of the Monsoon* (Vanguard), appeared only in 1985. He also translated two Punjabi folk poets, Bulleh Shah (1680–1758) and Qadir Yar (1802–50).

Rafat was not prolific—*Arrival of the Monsoon* has 116 poems written over thirty years (1947–78)—but he had an easy, entertaining way of describing local customs, rituals, and seasonal festivities: see 'Eve of Eid-ul-Azha', 'The Kite-flyers', 'Sacrifice', and 'Arrival of the Monsoon'. In these the craftsmanship is deft and the line is generally uncluttered and colloquial. Rafat wrote mainly in the narrative-descriptive mode, but sometimes lapsed into abstract moralizing. The social facts in 'Sialkot Bombed', 'Kitchens', 'Circumcision', and 'Divorce' are familiar, and the anti-Western sneers are comfortably populist: 'Their divorce is final | but they still meet by appointment | and are helpful and friendly to each other. | They call it civilized behaviour.' See also *A Selection* (1997), published by Oxford University Press. Rafat stopped writing after a stroke in 1984. When *Half Moon*, a collection of his poems written between 1979 and 1983, appeared in 2009, he was described as the 'Ezra *Pound of Pakistan' for his pioneering development of a Pakistani idiom in English-language poetry.   sbinH

Rahim, Jennifer (1963–) Born in Trinidad, where she teaches in the Liberal Arts Department at the University of the West Indies. Her first collection, *Mothers Are Not the Only Linguists* (New Voices, 1992), with its glance at Jeanette Winterson's semi-autobiographical novel, *Oranges Are Not the Only Fruit* (1985), announced Rahim's self-conscious play with the tropes of *confessional writing. Her poems also evince a wider concern for community life in Trinidad, as in the ecological stories of *Between the Fence and the Forest* (2002). 'Lady Lazarus in the Sun', from her third collection, *Approaching Sabbaths* (2009), resurrects Sylvia *Plath's speaker as a Caribbean woman rising from history, 'learning to take back my sun again | becoming the dark past brown'. She has also published a book of short stories, *Songster* (2007—all Peepal Tree).   JNT

Raine, Craig (1944–) Born at Shildon, Co. Durham. His father, Norman Edward Raine, appears in the prose centre-piece of the 1984 collection *Rich* as a one-time boxer who once beat Olympic featherweight champion Otto Kästner, and latterly as a jack-of-all-trades, raconteur, spiritualist and faith-healer. His mother, Olive Marie Raine, is portrayed as an intense, Lawrentian woman; poems in *A Martian Sends a Postcard Home* describe her dressmaking or at Roman Catholic mass.

Raine attended Barnard Castle School and Exeter College, Oxford. Subsequently he obtained a B.Phil. at Oxford (1968) and read for a D.Phil. on Coleridge (abandoned in 1973). From 1971 to 1981 Raine combined periods of teaching at Oxford colleges with work on the *New Review, Quarto,* and the *New Statesman*. Critical work dating from that time is collected with essays of the 1980s in *Haydn and the Valve Trumpet* (1990). From 1981 to 1991 Raine was poetry editor at Faber & Faber and is now a fellow of New College, Oxford. In 1972 he married Ann Pasternak Slater.

Raine's first two collections of poems, *The Onion, Memory* (1978) and *A Martian Sends a Postcard Home* (1979—both Oxford University Press), accompanied competition successes and attracted a great deal of attention. His hallmark in both books was vitality in metaphor and simile. Some critics complained of an over-reliance on ostentatious effects; others defended the plurality and vigour of Raine's imagination. James *Fenton and others saw Raine as the founder of the *Martian school, which took a fresh, transforming look at the everyday. *A Free Translation* (Salamander, 1981) and *Rich* (Faber, 1984) were as strikingly inventive (and tender, even sentimental) as the debut volumes. They also demonstrated once again Raine's affinity with the modernist writers he has repeatedly written on (*Eliot, *Joyce, *Stevens). See *Haydn and the Valve Trumpet* (Faber, 1990).

Raine's own allusive homage to *The Waste Land*—via Eliot's notion of the 'mythical method' in Joyce's *Ulysses*—took the form of a verse-novel written over the next decade. *History the Home Movie* (Penguin, 1994) is a fictional twentieth-century saga of the Raine and Pasternak families told in unrhymed, photorealist tercets full of wordplay. Raine's most characteristic later mode, the elegy, emerged in the lyric poems that he wrote during the same period, and collected in *Clay: Whereabouts Unknown* (Penguin, 2006). *A la recherche du temps perdu* (Picador, 2000), a book-length memorial to a former lover who died of AIDS, was controversial for its revelation of intimate personal history. But Raine has successfully continued in this *confessional manner, with its colloquial, *Muldoonish couplets: see 'I Remember My Mother Dying' from *How Snow Falls* (Atlantic, 2010).

In 1999 Raine launched *Areté*, a literary magazine modelled on those of previous eras such as *The Criterion* and *The New Review*. A second volume of his clever and combative critical essays, *In Defence of T. S. Eliot* (Picador), appeared in 2000. A later study of Eliot was published by Oxford University Press in 2007. Raine has also written adaptations for the stage— *The Electrification of the Soviet Union* (1986), an opera libretto after a novella by Pasternak, *1953* (1990—both Faber), and a version of Racine's *Andromaque*—and two novels: *Heartbreak* (2010) and *The Divine Comedy* (2012—both Atlantic). See 'Interview with Craig Raine', *Thumbscrew*, 20–21 (2002).   MHU*

Raine, Kathleen (1908–2003) Born in Ilford, Essex, but spent much of her childhood in Northumberland. She took her MA in Natural Sciences at Girton College, at a time when the Thirties generation of Cambridge poets, including *Empson, *Bottrall, and Charles *Madge (who became her second husband), was beginning to make its mark. Cambridge, however, was not a formative influence on her work, and she felt she had to break free of its analytic and scientific ethos before finding her own poetic voice. During a long and prolific career she produced ten volumes of poetry, the first two, *Stone and Flower* (1943) and *Living in Time* (1945), appearing under Tambimuttu's *Poetry London* imprint. Her poetry criticism includes volumes on Coleridge, Hopkins, and Yeats, and she was particularly noted for her Blake scholarship. From 1981, she was a founder, and, later, the sole editor of the *Temenos Review*.

Influenced by Swedenborg and the Neo-Platonists, Kathleen Raine was interested in archetypal forms of being. Her work is in many ways the polar opposite of *Imagism and the notion of 'no ideas but in things'. Though the natural world is important to her, 'things' for Raine are only the beginning. The appeal to the big, abstract ideas of time, eternity, and so on, and the constantly elevated tone produce a somewhat amorphous effect, more sacred text than life-study. *Selected Poems* (Golgonooza, 1989) covers her career fairly generously, if less fully than the *Collected Poems* (Counterpoint, 2001), which spans her work from the mid-1930s to the late 1990s. She produced four volumes of autobiography, and the authorized biography by Philippa Bernard, *No End to Snowdrops*, was published by Shepheard-Walwin in 2009.   CAR

Raji, Remi (1961–) Born Aderemi Raji-Oyelade, Raji studied English at University of Ibadan where he is now Professor of Literature and Creative Writing. He has been visiting professor at Southern Illinois University, University of California at Riverside and Irvine, University of Cape Town, and Cambridge University, and von Humboldt scholar at Humboldt University Berlin.

Raji's first collection of poetry, *A Harvest of Laughters* (Kraft, 1997), was joint winner of the Association of Nigerian Authors/ Cadbury poetry prize and winner of the Association of West African Young Writers' VOCA award for best first published book. He has published four other volumes since then: *Webs of Remembrance* (Kraftgriots, 2001), *Shuttlesongs America: a poetic guided tour* (2001), *Lovesong for my Wasteland* (2005—both Bookcraft), and *Gather my Blood Rivers of Song* (Diktaris, 2009). Raji's poetry has evolved from an abstract, enigmatic, and highly symbolic use of language after Christopher *Okigbo's style to a more direct narrative engagement with the world. His language is now more open and transparent and the images startling and powerful. For example, in 'Flakes' he writes: 'The flaky white dust | The battering male wind | The skin-deep stings | Icicles of rain without water | Embodied and whitened storms | This is my first story of snow...' In this, Raji has achieved his own remarkably recognizable voice and it is a lyrical and contemplative voice.   FO

Rakosi, Carl (name legally changed to Callman Rawley) (1903–2004)

The son of Hungarian nationals, Rakosi was born in Berlin and went to the United States in 1910. His family settled in Wisconsin, where he was raised. He majored in social work at the University of Wisconsin at Madison, which led to a lifelong career in the social-welfare field.

While still a student Rakosi had begun writing poetry, and by the late 1920s *Pound was taking his poems for the *Exile* and the *Literary Review*. *Zukofsky, recognizing Rakosi's clear, distinctive voice, championed his work and included him in the important '*Objectivist' issue of *Poetry* magazine and the subsequent *An 'Objectivists' Anthology*. After having published actively throughout the late Thirties Rakosi, like many politically left-wing American writers of the period, became disillusioned with writing and gave up poetry. In 1965, at the urgings of the young British poet Andrew *Crozier, Rakosi took up poetry again, producing the vast bulk of his work,

including much aphoristic prose and autobiography, by which he is known.

Rakosi's poetry, marked by clarity and a quiet, yet compelling intensity, is a form of American plainsong. His work, broad in scope, ranges from poems of deep, meditational seriousness, like 'Association with a View from the House' or 'Yaddo', to the probing, often hilarious social commentary of his 'Americana' series, a sustained poetic rendering of American mores, politics, and polyvocalisms.

The fullest editions of Rakosi's work are *The Collected Poems of Carl Rakosi* (1986) and *The Collected Prose of Carl Rakosi* (1983—both National Poetry Foundation, University of Maine). *Poems 1923–1941*, ed. Andrew Crozier (Sun & Moon, 1995), won a PEN award. Two later volumes were published in the UK by Etruscan Books: *The Earth Suite* (1997) and *The Old Poet's Tale* (1999), which includes old and new poems, as well as an essay.

See also *Conviction's Net of Branches: Essays on the Objectivist Poets and Poetry* (Southern Illinois University Press, 1985), by Michael Heller.   MH

Ramakrishnan, E. V. (1950–)

Born in Kannur, Kerala, Ramarkrishnan has had a distinguished career as a critic, editor, and translator. He writes in both English and Malayalam, and is Professor of Comparative Literature at the Central University of Gujarat. Among his academic publications are a study of American *Confessional poetry, and *Making It New: Modernisms in Malayalam, Marathi and Hindi Poetry* (Indian Institute of Advanced Study, 1999).

Praised by Keki N. *Daruwalla for its 'striking images' and 'unique perspectives', Ramakrishnan's poetry has appeared in three volumes: *Being Elsewhere in Myself* (Writers Workshop, 1980), *A Python in Snake Park* (Rupa, 1994), and *Terms of Seeing: New and Selected Poems* (Konark, 2006). The title of the latter points to his central theme of revelation at the margins of Indian society, where 'Stray Cats' are 'Ill-omens to those who cannot | see beyond what they see'. He has also edited an anthology of Indian poetry in translation,

The Tree of Tongues (Indian Institute of Advanced Study, 1999).   JNT

Ramanujan, A. K. (Attipat Krishnaswami) (1929–93) Born and educated in Mysore, was a fellow of Deccan College, 1958–9, and Fulbright Scholar at Indiana University, 1960–2. From 1962 he was at the University of Chicago, where he was William E. Colvin Professor in the departments of South Asian Languages and Civilizations, and Linguistics. Besides being a distinguished translator of poetry and prose in Tamil and Kannada—notable, especially, are his translations from classical Tamil verse, *The Interior Landscape* (Indiana University Press, 1967) and *Poems of Love and War* (Columbia University Press, 1985)—he is one of the most consistently rewarding of the Indian poets who have written in English. Though his output was relatively small, he seems to have created, in his three books of poems, *The Striders* (1966), *Relations* (1971), and *Second Sight* (1986—all Oxford University Press), a recognizably 'Ramanujanesque' world from the dailyness of South Indian small-town life, populated with relations and Hindu gods.

There is a sense of rootedness in Ramanujan's poetry, which often exists in tension with the curious and anxious sense of cultural displacement an educated postcolonial Indian sometimes feels. His involvement with Indian culture is, in all senses of the word, intimate: both deeply knowledgeable and loving; it is an involvement he allows to filter into, and enrich, his English verse. By his own definition, two general 'realms' can be distinguished in South Indian classical poetry and folklore: *akam* consists of narratives or songs performed by women inside the house, usually describing familial relationships; *puram* genres are performed in public by men, and describe battles, and historical and communal events. If we extend this distinction to his poetry, we find that Ramanujan is an *akam* poet, and that his best poems—such as 'Small-scale Reflections on a Great House', 'Still Another for Mother', 'History'—deal with domestic interiors and the fabric of family life; it is also perhaps no accident that many of the protagonists of his poems are women—mothers, grandmothers, cousins, and aunts. The tone of his poetry is tolerantly humorous, ostensibly unambitious, but fastidiously accurate in evoking surface-texture and detail; a seemingly innocent detail in an anecdote—a grain of rice on a kitchen floor, the noise of his father slapping soap on his back during a bath—might set off intangible echoes and resonances.

The Collected Poems of A. K. Ramanujan appeared from Oxford University Press in 1995, and *Poems and a Novella*, a translated volume of his writing in Kannada, in 2006. See also *The Flowering Tree and Other Oral Tales from India* (University of California Press, 1997), which represents three decades of work as a scholar and translator of folklore, and *The Collected Essays of A. K. Ramanujan*, eds. Vinay Dharwadker and Stuart H. Blackburn (Oxford University Press, 1999; 2nd edn. 2004).   AC*

Ramke, Bin (1947–) Born in Port Neches, Texas. Educated at Ohio University, Ramke has taught at Columbus College in Georgia and the University of Denver in Colorado. He edits *Denver Quarterly* magazine and from 1984 to 2005 also edited the Contemporary Poetry Series for the University of Georgia Press.

Ramke is a regionalist: his scenarios—domestic, romantic, and sexual—are generally set in the southern and southwestern United States. Concentrating on this segment of American society, Ramke's responses are intelligent and humane. He relies upon imagery to carry meaning; he rarely editorializes. When he does allow himself the luxury of comment, he usually means it as just that—comment, not pronouncement.

Ramke's books are *The Difference Between Night and Day* (Yale University Press, 1978), *White Monkeys* (University of Georgia Press, 1981), *The Language Student* (Louisiana State University Press, 1986), *The Erotic Light of Gardens* (Wesleyan University Press, 1989), *Massacre of the Innocents* (1995), *Wake* (1999), *Airs, Waters, Places* (2001), *Matter* (2004—all University of Iowa Press), and *Tendril* (Omnidawn, 2007).   RS

Rampolokeng, Lesego (1965–   ) Born in Soweto, Johannesburg, Rampolokeng began as a law student at the University of North, but did not complete his degree. Influenced by rap and *dub as well as Sesotho oral tradition, he began to perform his poetry in the 1980s, and was active in opposing apartheid. His first two collections, *Horns for Hondo* (1990) and *Talking Rain* (1993), were published by the Congress of South African Writers. His debut includes fifty 'raps' in emphatic rhyming metre, introduced by Andries Oliphant as 'the subversive voice of a poet-preacher'. But the contrarian Rampolokeng has been wary from the start of labels ('i'm called subversive | when i'm only creative'), including 'poetry', 'a word I've often grappled with and always lost against'. His later work has divided opinion with its surreal and scabrous intensification of his early political critique: see *Head on Fire: Rants / Notes / Poems* (Deep South, 2012). Rampolokeng has also written novels and a satirical post-liberation play in homage to Frantz Fanon, one of his most important literary influences.   JNT

Ranasinghe,   Anne(liese   Katz) (1925–   ) Born of a German-speaking Jewish family in Essen, left Germany for England in January 1939. Her parents and most of her family circle died in Nazi concentration camps. Her education, begun in Cologne, was completed at Parkstone Girls' Grammar School in Britain.

Ranasinghe trained as a nurse in London, studied journalism, and speaks five languages. Settling in Colombo following her marriage in 1949 to a Sri Lankan physician, she began writing poetry in 1968 and published her first poems in 1971. Her experience of the Nazi holocaust helped her to write of Sri Lanka's 1971 insurrection in powerful poems that have imparted a new strength to Sri Lankan poetry, especially that written by women. Until her retirement in 1990 she worked for Amnesty International.

Writing articles about Hitler's Germany for a Sri Lankan newspaper, Ranasinghe began a journey back into her past which culminated in a return to Essen in 1983 that has profoundly influenced her subsequent writing. She has won several awards and prizes, including the Sri Lanka Arts Council Prize for Poetry (1985). Her publications, all printed in Colombo, include *Poems* (1971), *With Words We Write Our Lives Past Present Future* (1972), *Plead Mercy* (1976), *Love, Sex and Parenthood* (1977), *Of Charred-Wood Midnight-Fear* (1983), *Against Eternity and Darkness* (1985), *Not Even Shadows* (1989), *At What Dark Point* (1991), *Desire and Other Stories* (1994), and *Mascot and Symbol* (2002). Her work has been translated into four languages, and is included in Y. Goonerate (ed.), *Poems From India, Sri Lanka, Malaysia and Singapore* (Heinemann, 1979) and Hilda Schiff (ed.), *Holocaust Poetry* (St Martin's, 1995). See also Le Roy Robinson, 'An Interview with Anne Ranasinghe', *Annual Review of Economics*, 6 (1990). A recording of Ranasinghe reading and speaking about her poetry for the South Asian Literary Recordings Project is available through the Library of Congress website.   YG

Rankin, Jennifer (1941–79) Born Jennifer Mary Haynes in Sydney, grew up there and at a small property near Mittagong. She graduated from Sydney University, where she had been a fringe-member of the Downtown Push, a loose group of artists, bohemians, and libertarians which included Clive *James and Germaine Greer.

With her first husband, John Roberts, she lived in Adelaide and later Canberra. She then lived briefly with the novelist Frank Moorhouse before marrying David Rankin, an artist, in 1969. Her earliest poems, fostered by friendships with Robert *Adamson, John *Tranter, and others of the '*Generation of 68', date from this period, although her first collection, *Ritual Shift*, did not appear until 1976.

Although her later poetry shows traces of Ted *Hughes, Margaret *Atwood, and Galway *Kinnell, she had already a distinctive style. *Earth Hold* was published in London in 1978. At the time of her death from cancer a third collection, *The Mud Hut*, had just appeared in *Exile* in Canada.

Her short career and the dispersed nature of her publication has retarded the growth of Rankin's reputation. Her *Collected Poems* (University of Queensland Press, 1990), however, was hailed as revealing one of the most significant Australian poets of the 1970s.   DBr

Rankine, Claudia (1963–) Born in Kingston, Jamaica, Rankine moved to America as a child, and studied at Williams College and Columbia University, where she received an MFA in poetry. Having taught at the University of Houston, she is now Henry G. Lee Professor of Poetry at Pomona College. Her collections are: *Nothing in Nature Is Private* (Cleveland State University Press, 1994), *The End of the Alphabet* (1998), and *Plot* (2001—both Grove). Rankine's work is interested in the fragmentation of narratives. *Don't Let Me Be Lonely: An American Lyric* (Graywolf, 2004) develops a documentary poetics, juxtaposing television stills and photographs with diaristic writing on the poet's personal life, politics, and reading. In 2005 she received a Fellowship from the Academy of American Poets. Rankine has co-edited two critical anthologies of new experimental American poets for Wesleyan University Press: *American Women Poets in the 21st Century: Where Lyric Meets Language* (2002), with Juliana *Spahr, and *American Poets in the 21st Century: The New Poetics* (2007), with Lisa Sewell.   JNT

Ransom, John Crowe (1888–1974) Associated with the American South, Ransom was an early member of the group of writers known as *Fugitives, many of whom met at Vanderbilt University in the period after the First World War (in which he served as a lieutenant). Born in Pulaski, Tennessee, Ransom received his AB from Vanderbilt in 1909; he was afterwards a Rhodes Scholar at Christ Church, Oxford, from which he took another degree in 1913. In his poem, 'Philomela' he describes how unimpressed he was with the famous song of the nightingale while walking with some Oxford students in Bagley Wood.

Ransom's reaction against the nightingale is typical of his anti-Romantic, neoclassical stance as a poet—a stance he shared with T. S. *Eliot and other modernists.

Unlike Eliot, however, Ransom was deeply committed to his native region, and he returned to his home state of Tennessee to teach at Vanderbilt, where he remained until 1937 and where he met Robert Penn *Warren, Allen *Tate, Donald *Davidson, and Randall *Jarrell, all of whom considered him a friend and mentor.

The Fugitives had much in common with T. S. Eliot, though Ransom personally disliked his poetry. Eliot declared himself a classicist, a Catholic, and a royalist, and there are echoes of this in Ransom's self-description: 'In manners, aristocratic; in religion, ritualistic; in art, traditional.' In his first critical work, *God Without Thunder* (1930), Ransom urged the return to religious values, suggesting that a belief in the supernatural was necessary if one wished to 'represent the fullness of the natural'. In returning to religion, Ransom stressed the importance of orthodoxy, advocating 'a virile and concrete God', also described as 'the Demigod who came to do honour to the God'. The son of a minister, Ransom seemed very like a typical Southern fundamentalist in this early prose work; he modified this view somewhat in *The World's Body* (1938), where he was less prescriptive and, in the tradition of Matthew Arnold, saw poetry as taking on many of the tasks formerly performed by religion. In another important book of prose essays, *The New Criticism* (1941), Ransom argued for an 'ontological critic' who could show the ways in which the logical structure of poetry embodied the world by summoning creation in all its variegated detail and natural, organic form.

This organic theory of poetry was illustrated perfectly by the poems. As Robert Penn Warren once noted, Ransom is a critic whose theories of poetry and poems uniquely mirror each other. There is, in fact, a decidedly academic, if not archaic, quality apparent in Ransom's poetry. Critics have, variously, described his poems as 'metaphysical' and 'formalist', both terms which fit rather well, although there is an unruly energy in Ransom's finest poems, such as 'Janet Waking', 'The Equilibrists', or 'Bells for John Whiteside's Daughter'.

Ransom was not a prolific poet. He published three relatively slim books of verse between 1919 and 1927; after that he turned his attention largely to criticism and to editing the *Kenyon Review*, which he founded at Kenyon College, Ohio, where he taught from 1937 until his retirement in 1959. Ransom himself credited Roberta Teale Swartz, a poet who was married to Kenyon president Gordon K. Chalmers, as the driving force behind its inception. The first issue featured two of Robert *Lowell's earliest poems, Randall Jarrell's 'A Winter's Tale', John Peale Bishop's 'The Sorrows of Thomas Wolfe', and reviews by R. P. *Blackmur and Yvor *Winters. Subsequent issues in the first volume included poetry by John *Berryman, Dylan *Thomas, Muriel *Rukeyser, and Allen Tate. During the *Kenyon Review's* first twenty-five years, poets as diverse as John *Ashbery, James *Dickey, Anthony *Hecht, James *Merrill, Theodore *Roethke, Wallace *Stevens, and William Carlos *Williams appeared there.

Under Ransom's editorship, the *Kenyon Review* became the leading organ of the New Criticism, publishing important articles on poetry by Tate, Cleanth Brooks, Robert Penn Warren, William *Empson, and Ransom himself, who contributed to virtually every issue during the magazine's first decade. Of this great period Lowell once remarked that 'when a good critical essay came out it had the excitement of a new imaginative work'. With Ransom's retirement the editorship was offered to Jarrell, who declined. *The Kenyon Critics*, edited by Ransom in 1951, collected important essays and book reviews.

Ransom's poetry has consistently attracted interest for its poise, its idiosyncratic language, its cultivated obliquity, and its wry humour. The inevitability and pity of human failure and the evanescence of life are primary subjects for Ransom, and the elegy is his most natural form, as in 'Here Lies a Lady', which begins: 'Here lies a lady of beauty and high degree, | Of chills and fever she died, of fever and chills, | The delight of her husband, an aunt, an infant of three | And medicos marveling sweetly on her ills.' In 'Blue Girls' Ransom describes the pampered young students of a seminary for girls, advising them: 'Practise your beauty, blue girls, before it fail.' The poem ends with a typical Ransom twist: 'For I could tell you a story which is true; | I know a woman with a terrible tongue, | Blue eyes fallen from blue, | All her perfections tarnished—yet it is not long | Since she was lovelier than any of you.'

Summing up the work of Ransom, Robert Penn Warren said that his old teacher's prose and poetry together amounted to 'a celebration of life, as manifested in the virtues of charity and endurance, tenderness and gaiety'. These deeply human values shine through Ransom's small but luminous body of writing. For selections, see Ransom's *Selected Poems* (Knopf, 1963) and *Selected Essays* (Louisiana State University Press, 1984). A *Selected Poems* was published by Carcanet in 1991. There is a good biography of Ransom, *Gentleman in a Dustcoat*, by Thomas Daniel Young (Louisiana State University Press, 1976). For criticism, see Miller Williams, *The Poetry of John Crowe Ransom* (Rutgers University Press, 1972) and Thornton H. Parsons, *John Crowe Ransom* (Twayne, 1969).   JP/RSG*

Rao, Mani (1965–) Born in India, Rao moved to Hong Kong in 1993, where she published six of her eight books of poetry. More recently she has pursued doctoral studies in Sanskrit and religion while dividing her time between the USA and India. Neither personal biography nor geopolitical location is prominent in her poems, which are almost all short, no more than a page. She often works in frequently end-stopped, staccato lines of variable length, with a line not necessarily connecting to its predecessor, and with unstable pronouns and gender ambiguity confounding any notion of a discrete, confessional self—although there are traces of narrative.

Among the early collections, *The Last Beach* (Asia 2000, 1999), is perhaps the strongest. *Echolocation* (2003), which appears to recollect a love affair echoed against the sound of the sea and the radio, switches visually to prose, with each isolated sentence also becoming the measure of the line. *100 Poems, 1985–2005* (2006) excerpts from six previous books. *Ghostmasters* (2010—all Chameleon) ramps up her linguistic playfulness. Rao's version of the *Bhagavad Gita* (Autumn Hill, 2010; Penguin, 2011) unpacks the original Sanskrit with a range of avant-garde techniques—in prosody, diction, mise-en-page, and lineation—rendering a new translation of the well-known philosophical text unlike any before it. Her most recent poetry continues her erotic themes but makes more explicit reference to stories and characters drawn from Indian and Western classical sources.   VN

Rattenbury, Arnold (1921–2007) Born in China, where his father served as a Wesleyan minister. He was educated at Kingswood School, and while there became friendly with such kindred spirits as E. P. Thompson and Geoffrey Matthews. He then proceeded to Cambridge University. However, the outbreak of the Second World War put an end to his formal education. War service came to a premature end in 1943, and in the following years Rattenbury was first an editor at *Our Time* and *Theatre Today* and then an exhibition designer. He lived in north Wales.

Rattenbury's first volume of poems, *Second Causes* (Chatto, 1969), is notable for its close weave of social satire and political vision. Like many of his generation Rattenbury had early become a Marxist but he never reneged on his ideals or thought it appropriate to apologize for them. His poems are often prompted by an angry contempt for social arrangements that commit the majority of people to thwarted lives; but his wit and relish for the things that make up the observable world keep his work well clear of didacticism. This is apparent in his second collection *Man Thinking* (Byron, 1972), with its epigraph taken from a letter of Gorky's to Chekhov: 'I'm a very rough, clumsy man and my soul is incurably sick. Incidentally, this is how the soul of a thinking man should be.' A similar vein of hard-edged wit can be discerned in *Dull-Weather Dance* (Peterloo, 1981). His later volumes included *Living Here* (Katabasis, 1996) and *Mr. Dick's Kite*

(Shoestring, 2005). See also *Several Forms of Speech: New, Early, Escaped and Last Poems* (Smokestack, 2008).   JL

Raworth, Tom (Thomas Moore) (1938–) Born in London, Raworth left school at sixteen 'out of boredom', and worked in various jobs. He later attended the University of Essex, and in the 1970s lived and worked in North America and Mexico, teaching at various universities. In 1977 he was poet-in-residence at King's College, Cambridge, and in 1991 he was the first European writer for thirty years to be invited to teach at the University of Cape Town. He now lives in Brighton, Sussex.

A prolific experimental poet, Raworth is the author of more than forty books, mainly brought out by various small presses. He himself published a number of the better-known contemporary avant-garde poets at the Goliard Press, which he helped to found. His own first book, *The Relation Ship*, was published by Goliard in 1966. He appeared in Michael *Horovitz's *Children of Albion* anthology (1969) and in *Penguin Modern Poets*, 19 (1971), where his work stood alongside selections from Lee *Harwood and John *Ashbery. The company he kept there is instructive about his own work which, like theirs, often attempts to transcribe the immediate present. But various tricks can be played with this idea. One may treat the moment as subjective, or try to be objective, concentrating on sense-perception, or pay attention to the creation of the text. Raworth uses all these approaches, sometimes within the space of one poem. This can be illustrated from 'Stag Skull Mounted', a series of poems each of which is given a date and time of day. In '9.30 p.m. May 13th 1970' Raworth, letting his thoughts flow, announces: 'i am a ping pong ball from face to face | idea to idea and what i do | is a disservice.' But in '8:00 p.m. May 5th 1970' we are treated to a more objective view: 'each evening a girl with a twisted spine | passes my window as the weather warms | her dresses thin and shorten.' But at any moment we may be reminded that the poet is making artefacts out of his stray perceptions: the brief entry for '11:08 a.m. May 7th 1970' ends 'found poem'. This last emphasis, on poem as object, has produced some adventurous work in his *Logbook* series, written in England in 1970, and published in the United States by Poltroon Press in 1976, with illustrations by Frances Butler. The conceit of this is that we are given the few remaining pages of the logbook of what appears, at first, to be a voyage. But our construction of a chronology is deliberately hindered, so that we cannot identify the text with the reflection of reality.

The odd juxtapositions in some Raworth poems have led critics to use the word 'surrealism'. But while this is an undoubted influence—as are the *Beat, the *Black Mountain, and the *New York poets—it is idle to pin labels to his work. Trained, like Clark *Coolidge, as a jazz musician, Raworth improvises. This informal approach is mirrored in his language. For whatever licence he permits himself in subject-matter, his diction and rhetoric are the opposite of bardic. He has no special poetic register other than contemporary idiom, quizzically picked up.

The sustained associative style of *Ace* (1974; repr. Edge, 2001), with its short staccato lines ('the energy | gaps again'), introduced the cross-cutting lyricism of Raworth's later work, and its fascination with the speed of media and communications technology (see also the title poem of *Caller* (Edge, 2007)). Major sequences in this mode such as *Writing* (The Figures, 1982) and *Eternal Sections* (Sun & Moon, 1993) have won him admirers among the American *Language poets. It is characteristic of Raworth's go-on-your-nerve attitude that his compendious *Collected Poems* (Carcanet, 2003) was not complete. *There Are Few People Who Put on Any Clothes (starring it)*, a prose poem from the same period as *Logbook*, was first published by Equipage in 2009, and *Windmills in Flames: Old and New Poems* (Carcanet, 2010) contained the rediscovered text of *Pleasant Butter* (1971), a sardonic *ars poetica*. See also the prose works collected in *Earn Your Milk* (Salt, 2008), which include *A Serial Biography* (1969).

Raworth's work remains relatively neglected in the UK, but is esteemed in the USA and Europe, where he regularly gives readings and has also exhibited his visual collages. In 2002, he was presented with the Philip Whalen Memorial Award, and in 2007 the Antonio Delfini Prize for Lifetime Achievement. His rapid-fire reading style may be heard on the Rockdrill CD *Writing: Poems 1980–2003* (2005). For criticism, see the essays collected in *Removed for Further Study: The Poetry of Tom Raworth* (The Gig, 2003), and John Muckle, 'How Radio Works: Tom Raworth—Time, Identity and Tradition', an extended essay in four parts, which appeared in *PN Review*, issues 173-76 (2007).   ETL*

Ray, David (1932–) Born in Oklahoma. He is professor emeritus of English at the University of Missouri. His poetry, usually in unrhymed but regular lines, is for the most part personal, dealing with his family and his domestic experiences, although he has written some political poems—for example, protests at American involvement in Vietnam, and at treatment of minority groups. His most poignant work is to be found in *Sam's Book* (Wesleyan University Press, 1987), dealing in a direct manner with the death of his young son. His output as a whole is liberal in spirit and deeply felt, and its content, personal and detailed, is remarkably free from stridency or pretentiousness. He has been influenced by his experiences in India as an Indo-US Fellow (1981-2) in the poems of *Elysium in the Halls of Hell* (Nirala, 1986); and he has edited, with Amritjit Singh, *India: An Anthology of Contemporary Writing* (Ohio University Press, 1983). He is a generous and useful critic of the work of other poets.

Wool Highways (Helicon Nine, 1994), a book of poems on New Zealand, won Ray his second William Carlos Williams Award (the first was for *The Tramp's Cup* (1979)). *The Death of Sardanapalus* (2004) contained poems 'of the Iraq wars' (Howling Dog, 2004). See *Music of Time: New and Selected Poems* (Backwaters, 2006). *After Tagore: Poems inspired by Rabindranath Tagore* (Nirala) appeared in India in 2008. *The Endless Search* (Soft Skull,

2003) is a memoir of his impoverished youth. MS-S*

Rayaprol, Srinivas (1925–98) Rayaprol was the son of one of the most influential Telugu poets of the early twentieth century, Rayaprolu Subbarao, who is credited with starting *Bhaavakavitvam*—a neo-romantic and nationalist poetic movement—in the Telugu language. The younger Rayaprol, however, was given what he called a 'strictly British' formal education and then went to study engineering at Stanford University in America. There he frequented writing circles in Berkeley, befriended Kenneth *Patchen, Yvor *Winters, and others, and began, in English, to write a very different kind of poetry from that of his father, as interested in things and desires as Subbarao was interested in morals, mellifluousness, and Platonic love. He later said he owed America not only his education but his 'personal emancipation'.

In the early 1950s, Rayaprol published in magazines like *Poetry* (Chicago) and the *Atlantic Monthly*, and began a long, intimate, and fascinating correspondence with William Carlos *Williams (three letters are included in Williams' *Selected Letters*). To Williams, Rayaprol spoke of his anger at being misunderstood by his father, a generational conflict that was also a conflict of poetics; to Rayaprol, sympathetically positioned between Britain and the United States, Williams could complain about the British and his frustration at not being understood in England.

Returning to Secunderabad, Rayaprol started a seminal magazine, *East and West*, that published Indians alongside American and world writers. The magazine folded after thirteen issues in 1961, but Rayaprol went on to publish his first book of poems, *Bones and Distances* (1968) in India—a vibrant collection, most of it written in the USA, full of references to painting, the bohemian life, and the British and American poets he admired. After this, although Rayaprol became a successful civil engineer for the government, married, and had children, he also seems to have become increasingly lonely and isolated—as reflected in the gloomy tone of his much slimmer second collection, *Married Love & Other Poems* (1972). He then fell into obscurity until a *Selected Poems* (1995—all Writers Workshop) three years before his death. The new poems in this last collection hint at reconciliation—including with his father—but also at remorse. VN

Read, Sir Herbert (Edward) (1893–1968) Born in rural Yorkshire and educated (after years of struggle) at Leeds University. He fought in the First World War—winning the DSO and MC—and attracted some attention as a minor war poet. He became very influential as a champion of modernism in art and poetry, and as a pioneer of Jungian depth-psychology in criticism. A lifelong anarchist, he was knighted in 1953. Of all his imaginative work, the allegorical novel *The Green Child* (Grey Walls, 1935) attracted the most praise; but he seldom achieved a comparable synthesis of thought and feeling in his poetry. This, although respected and published by his friend T. S. *Eliot at Faber, has fallen into near oblivion. Read was a determined modernist; but the modernist procedures did not come as easily or as naturally to him in poetry as in criticism. As a result of meeting *Pound and others while a serving soldier, he began to write in the manner of the *Imagists (*Songs of Chaos*, Mathews, 1915). But Robert *Bridges always seemed as strong an influence as any other poet—and this he acknowledged. He was closely connected with the magazine *Arts and Letters* (1917–20), and contributed to No. 3 an article offering 'definitions towards a modern theory of poetry' that made cautious moves in the direction of free verse, suggesting that 'rhyme, metre, cadence, alliteration, are various decorative devices to be used as the vision demands'. Vision was defined as 'the recognition of emotions possessing an aesthetic value'. Aesthetic value remained undefined, but Read's conclusion was that the poet's 'duty and joy' was to 'express the exquisite among his perceptions'.

His war poetry was admirably laconic and lacking in heroics, but somewhat flat. However, *The End of a War* (Faber, 1933), a long poem, remains his most notable achievement. See *Collected Poems* (Faber, 1966), and *Herbert Read* (Longman, 1961), by Francis Berry.   MS-S/JGS*

Reading, Peter (1946–2011) Born in Liverpool, he worked as a teacher, lecturer in art history, and as a weighbridge operator. His strongly anti-romantic, disenchanted, and usually satirical verse began to attract attention—and some reprobation—with *For the Municipality's Elderly* (1974). Reading's often mechanically ironic verse deliberately assaults 'good taste' for its hypocrisy. In *C* (1984—both Secker & Warburg), 100 prose poems of 100 words each are supposed to be composed by a man dying of cancer. Yet Reading, in his relentless pursuit of shocking subject-matter, is often clever or funny in his presentation of it, putting parodic emphases where news items do not, and vice versa.

The elegiac mood of Reading's paradoxically prolific later work revealed an austere attraction to classical, Chinese, and Anglo-Saxon poetry, translated or imitated in lyrical fragments, as in the early work of *Ezra Pound. *Ob.* (1998) featured his own death mask on the cover. Personal feeling entered strongly too: see the elegies for his friends and poetic mentors, George *Macbeth and Gavin *Ewart. The ecological sequences *Faunal* (Bloodaxe, 2002) and *–273.15* (2005) displayed his talent for precise observation of other endangered species. He won the Lannan Literary Award twice, in 1990 and 2004, and in 1998–9 held the first Lannan Literary Residency, resulting in the Texan small-town sequence of *Marfan* (2000). Reading's last volume was *Vendange Tardive* (2010). His *Collected Poems* appeared in three volumes, up to 2003, and there is a critical study by Isabel Martin, *Reading Peter Reading* (2000—all Bloodaxe).   MS-S*

Reaney, James (1926–2008) Born on a farm near Stratford, Ontario, and was educated at the University of Toronto—his thesis title was 'The Influence of Spenser on Yeats'. Like Jay *Macpherson, Reaney is one of the Canadian 'mythopoetic' poets influenced by Northrop Frye (who supervised his thesis). From 1960 he taught in the English department of the University of Western Ontario, London. The poems he published as a student and the forty-two lyrics in *The Red Heart* (McClelland & Stewart, 1949) announced a striking and original new voice in Canadian poetry: childlike, playful, witty, steeped in knowledge, given to wayward fantasy, technically assured, and coloured by a childhood in southern Ontario. This region is also the background of *A Suit of Nettles* (Macmillan, 1958; new edn. Porcupine's Quill, 2010), a series of twelve eclogues modelled on Spenser's *Shepheardes Calender*, though the intention is satirical: the dialogues are between learned geese, and the twelve-month cycle ends in ritual slaughter. Exuberantly, and sometimes comically, in a virtuoso display of verse forms the poet treats a variety of subjects that include sterility and fertility, education, religion, and Canadian history. By contrast, *Twelve Letters to a Small Town* (Ryerson, 1962) is quiet and charming—recollections of a childhood in Stratford, Ontario, in the form of lyrics, dialogues, and prose poems, written as a libretto that was set to the music of Canadian composer John Beckwith and broadcast in July 1961. Both collections won the Governor General's Award. This same voice is also heard in the quatrains that make up most of *The Dance of Death in London, Ontario* (Alphabet, 1963), illustrated by the late Jack Chambers. From the 1960s Reaney concentrated on playwriting. His poetry was first collected in *Poems: James Reaney*, ed. with an introduction, by Germaine Warkentin (New Press, 1972), who also edited his *Selected Shorter Poems* (1975) and *Selected Longer Poems* (1976—both Porcepic). *Scripts: Librettos for Operas and Other Musical Works*, ed. John Beckwith, was published by Coach House Books in 1994. See *The Essential James Reaney*, ed. Brian Bartlett (Porcupine's Quill, 2009).   WT

Redgrove, Peter (1932–2003) Redgrove described himself as a 'poet and analytical psychologist'. His poetry was central to a crusading and controversial body of work that also included novels, short stories, radio and television plays, and volumes of psychology and sociology.

Born into an English middle-class family and educated at a public school, Redgrove's first breach of convention was painful and involuntary. Conscripted into the army at eighteen, he suffered a mental breakdown and was given insulin-shock treatment, an experience that underlies the first of his narrative poems, 'Lazarus and the Sea'. At Cambridge, where he read natural sciences, he was a contemporary of Ted *Hughes, with whom he had strong affinities. In London, where he worked as a scientific journalist and copy-writer, he was a member of the *Group and was particularly influenced by Martin *Bell, who encouraged him to give his poems narrative and dramatic form.

Redgrove's work made an immediate impact. He became visiting poet at Buffalo University, Gregory Fellow in Poetry at Leeds University, O'Connor Professor of Literature at Colgate University, and resident author at Falmouth School of Art, an association that lasted from 1966 to 1983. But the early books, culminating in *The Force* (Routledge & Kegan Paul, 1966), have an unfocused energy.

Redgrove might be termed a scientific visionary. The more idiosyncratic he allowed himself to become, the clearer the work became. In *Dr Faust's Sea-Spiral Spirit* (Routledge & Kegan Paul, 1972), confirmed by his studies with the Jungian analyst, John Layard, and by a close working relationship with his second wife, Penelope *Shuttle, he began to fashion the concentrated, expository style that became his hallmark. He deploys a range of techniques that may appear surreal, but all proceed from a consistent vision of the universe as a living entity in which the human species plays only a small part. Typical is his acceleration and deceleration of time, so that trees 'Lope away over the red-hot fence | Or stand for a three-hundred-year moment'.

Never arbitrary, his inventive visual images are really links in a chain of argument. He drew on scientific data, dream images, the arcana of myth and magic, whatever would serve as a metaphor for the 'intense wholenesses' he wanted to convey. In the course of this impassioned pleading, he developed an extraordinary range of tones,

humorous, erotic and ecstatic—often within the same poem. He was a prolific poet and, once the procedures become familiar, the poems can seem formulaic. At their best, though, they have an undeniable transforming power.

Peter Redgrove received the Queen's Gold Medal for Poetry in 1996. His *Collected Poems* were edited by Neil Roberts, who has also written a sympathetic but searching biography, *A Lucid Dreamer: The Life of Peter Redgrove* (both Cape, 2012). Eight essays on Redgrove's work are to be found in a special issue of *Poetry Review*, 71:2/3 (1981), and there is an extended interview with Philip Fried in *The Manhattan Review*, 3:1 (1983).   RGa

Reed, Henry (1914–86) Born in Birmingham and educated at King Edward VI School and Birmingham University, where he studied language and literature and wrote an MA thesis on *Hardy. He worked as a teacher and freelance journalist, 1937–41. After a short period in the army he was transferred to the Foreign Office to work in Naval Intelligence, 1942–5. Thereafter Reed made his career in radio as a journalist, broadcaster, and playwright. The BBC's Third Programme was inaugurated in October 1946, and he became a member of the legendary group of writers—including Louis *MacNeice, Dylan *Thomas, Terence Tiller, P. H. Newby, Patric *Dickinson, W. R. *Rodgers, and Rayner Heppenstall—who were attached to the network during its golden period. Later he was a visiting professor and associate professor of English at the University of Washington, Seattle.

Reed published only one book of poems, *A Map of Verona* (Cape, 1946), which in turn is famous chiefly for one poem, 'Lessons of the War'. It is probably the most celebrated English poem, and certainly the most popular, to emerge from the Second World War. Part I in particular, 'Naming of Parts', has entered the collective folk-memory. Reed told the poet Vernon *Scannell that the poem began as a comic monologue recited for the amusement of his fellow recruits. Its good-natured humour, broad sexual innuendo, and lyrical evocations of nature make it instantly memorable. By juxtaposing dry and faintly absurd technical language about the cleaning of guns with the immemorial goings-on of flowers and bees in spring Reed dramatizes both the ridiculousness and boredom of war—time out of time, as it were—and its relationship to the awkward, unbalanced lives of the individuals haplessly caught up in it.

The other two sections, 'Judging Distances' and 'Unarmed Combat', employ the same strategy of juxtaposing military jargon with the ordinary-language meaning of such terms as 'proper issue' and 'dead ground'. Part of the poem's success is bound up in its formal rhythmic brilliance, which cleverly mixes prosaic and lyric modes of speech and versification.

The volume's other success is the famous parody of *Eliot, 'Chard Whitlow' ('As we get older we do not get any younger'), which Eliot himself commended for its accuracy. Elsewhere in the book Eliot proves rather more of a hindrance than a help, for example in the title-poem, whose wistful sensitivities ('underground whispers of music', 'shifting crowds in the causeways . . . discerned through the dusk') recall the perplexities of Prufrock and *The Waste Land. Lessons of the War* (Clover Hill, 1970) reprints Reed's most famous poem and adds two new sections to it, 'Movement of Bodies' and 'Returning of Issue'.

Reed worked for many years on a biography of Hardy, which he never finished. Much of this research went into his first 'Hilda Tablet' radio play, *A Very Great Man Indeed* (see *Hilda Tablet and Others: Four Pieces for Radio*, BBC, 1971). Others of his many radio plays include an adaptation of *Moby-Dick* (Cape, 1947), several versions of plays by the Italian playwright Ugo Betti, and *The Streets of Pompeii and Other Plays for Radio* (BBC, 1971), some of which are based on incidents in the life of Leopardi. The plays belong partly to BBC radio's period of achievement and experimentation, under the producer Douglas Cleverdon, and partly to the general attempt to revive verse drama of the 1940s and 1950s, led by Eliot and Christopher Fry. Outside literature Reed's main interest was in music,

especially opera. *A Collected Poems*, ed. Jon Stallworthy, was published in 1991 by Oxford University Press (repr. Carcanet, 2007). ws

Reed, Jeremy (1951–) Born in Jersey. Deprecated by some for his Firbank-like, *poète maudit* persona, Reed has been much admired by a minority, including David *Gascoyne and Kathleen *Raine (who saw him as lone inheritor, respectively, of the English *surrealist and the Neo-Platonic traditions). He has continued to be able to write in the formal manner which characterized his first substantial collection, *By the Fisheries* (Cape, 1984). Here such poems as 'John Clare's Journal' show him to be a potentially rich and capable, if somewhat over-sonorous and derivative nature-poet, writing under the influences of 'mad' poets such as Smart, as well as of Eugenio Montale, whom he has translated in *The Coastguard's House* (Bloodaxe, 1990). His glances towards more fashionable themes such as AIDS, cross-dressing, and pop- and drug-culture in general were judged by most critics not of his coterie as a distraction from his real capabilities as a poet writing—if only intermittently—in the British surrealist tradition of Scarfe, Roger Roughton, and, above all, his mentor Gascoyne. See *Selected Poems* (Penguin, 1987).

Red-Haired Android (Harper, 1992) was a substantial volume on these themes and more, which begins unapologetically with epigraphs from William Blake and David Bowie. Reed's later oeuvre includes book-length poems on Billie Holiday (*Saint Billie* (Enitharmon, 2000)) and Elvis Presley (*Heartbreak Hotel* (Orion, 2002)), and a collection of elegies, *This Is How You Disappear* (Enitharmon, 2007). He is a popular performer of his work, and his admirers have included the singer Björk and the novelist J. G. Ballard. Since the 1990s, he has been a prolific author of novels, non-fiction, and biographies of singer-songwriters such as Lou Reed, Scott Walker, and Marc Almond, with whom he collaborated on *Piccadilly Bongo* (Enitharmon, 2010). See also *Madness: The Price of Poetry* (Owen, 1990). MS-S*

Reese, Lizette (Woodworth) (1856–1935) Grew up in a rural Maryland village and became a teacher of English at Western High School in Baltimore, where she would remain until her retirement in 1921. Although an admirer of the seventeenth century and of the entire English pastoral tradition, her first two collections, *A Branch of May* (1887) and *A Handful of Lavender* (1891), were surprisingly modern in their supple directness and lack of excessive sentiment. A later volume, *A Wayside Lute* (1909), contains her best-known poem, the sonnet 'Tears', and in many ways—high polish, sharp observations, concise clarity of images—her verses invite comparison with the more original work of Emily Dickinson and seem to anticipate the terse lyricism of *Millay, *Wylie, and the later *Teasdale, despite lingering traces of a Victorian sensibility. *Pastures* (1933) was her tenth and final collection.

A generous selection of her poems is scattered throughout *The Home Book of Modern Verse*, ed. Burton Egbert Stevenson (Holt, 1963), but the smaller group in *Modern American Poetry*, ed. Louis Untermeyer (Harcourt, 1969), which includes 'Tears' and the equally effective 'A Puritan Lady', is better chosen.   EB

Rees-Jones, Deryn (1968–   ) Born and brought up in Liverpool, Rees-Jones spent formative stretches of her childhood on visits to a family home in Eglwysbach in North Wales. After studying English literature at the University of Wales, Bangor, she wrote her doctoral thesis at Birkbeck College, University of London, involving research which would later form the basis of her critical study *Consorting With Angels: Essays on Modern Women Poets* (Bloodaxe, 2004).

Rees-Jones received an Eric Gregory Award in 1993, and her debut book of poems, *The Memory Tray* (1994), devoted to themes of gender and identity cut with wit and poignancy, was shortlisted for the Forward Prize for Best First Collection. Further critical success for a more intensely personal second collection, *Signs Round a Dead Body* (1998), and a book-length verse murder-mystery, *Quiver*

(2004—all Seren), helped secure her a spot on the Poetry Book Society's Next Generation Poets list when it was announced in 2004. What holds Rees-Jones work together is its fascination with memory and 'how we "become"'. In addition to her own poems, she has published a monograph on Carol Ann *Duffy (Northcote House, 1999) and is the editor of the anthology *Modern Women Poets* (Bloodaxe, 2005).   KGr

Reeves, Gareth (1947–   ) Read English at Oxford and was a postgraduate at Stanford University, California, where he held a Wallace Stegner Writing Fellowship from 1973 to 1974. He lectures in English at the University of Durham, and is a co-founder and editor of *Poetry Durham*. Reeves has fashioned a style that is idiomatic, often ironic, and yet capable of a terse lyricism. *Real Stories* (1984), his first collection, is divided into three sections. Several elegies appear in the first. Given the fineness of these elegies and of others—especially about Reeves' father, the poet James *Reeves—published subsequently in *Listening In* (1993—both Carcanet), it is unsurprising that in *T. S. Eliot: A Virgilian Poet* (Macmillan/St Martin's, 1989) Gareth Reeves writes well about the 'Hades of memory'. The first section of *Real Stories* also touches wryly on the poet's 'English' schooling: the plaited comedy of 'Can We Interest You in God?' is an example. The second section includes poems set in America; they show a vigorous relish for the 'alien' and the 'random'. The final section's mainly domestic pieces number some of the best poems in a precisely observed and emotionally mature collection. Poems from both books are included in *To Hell With Paradise: New and Selected Poems* (Carcanet, 2012).   MO'N

Reeves, James (1909–78) Born in Middlesex and educated at Stowe and Jesus College, Cambridge. Thereafter, he held various school-teaching and lecturing jobs until 1952, when he turned to full-time writing and editing. He was responsible for over forty titles, several as general editor of the Heinemann 'Poetry Bookshelf' series, whose selections of English poets were widely used in schools. His varied output included four books of verse for children and collections of folk-song texts.

He was not, however, a prolific or assertive poet. His first volume, *The Natural Need*, was published in 1936 by Robert *Graves and Laura *Riding's Seizin Press; in the same year, Graves tells us, *Yeats excluded him from the *Oxford Book of Modern Verse* as 'too reasonable, too truthful', since the Muses prefer 'gay, warty lads'. (From this early connection Reeves has frequently been conscripted into a Graves 'school'.) Reeves' five subsequent volumes are full of well-proportioned poems, many in tuneful quatrains, but there is a general lack of passion or even character, despite the privacy of the subject-matter. In the introduction to his first *Collected Poems* (1960) he explains why none of the momentous events of his times had got into his writing: 'To me poetry is rooted in the particular and the immediate.' The smooth, inhibited lyricism is, however, varied by the angry local satire of such poems as 'Greenhallows', 'Planning Permission', and 'Converting the Vicarage'.

Reeves' *Collected Poems 1929–1974* (1974) supplanted the earlier volume, and presents a debate on his own limitations. Some poems stand up for timidity: one of them prefers his 'backwater' to a mainstream fouled with ambition, another condemns the noisy egos of the Dylan *Thomas era, 'where every other poet is a megaphone'. But the verdict of 'Voices Loud and Low' is ambiguous, and later poems like 'The Solvers' and 'A Stoical Robin' ridicule their author's procedure. His alert self-doubt is encapsulated in the foreword to *Subsong* (1969—all Heinemann); 'subsong' is explained as the quietest form of birdsong, performed for the sole benefit of the performer; but at times it can sound as if the bird 'is prevented from singing normally by being strangled'. MI

Reid, Alastair (1926–) Born in Whithorn, Scotland. His mother was a physician, his father a minister in the Church of Scotland. Reid's studies at the University of St Andrews were interrupted by the Second World War, in which he served in the Pacific with the Royal Navy. Returning to St Andrews after the war, he graduated with a degree in classics. He soon migrated to America, where he took a position in classics at Sarah Lawrence College.

It was during this period that he began writing poems, many of which were published in *The New Yorker*, a magazine with which Reid has had a continuing association for over three decades as a staff writer. Reid's first book of poems, *To Lighten My House* (1953), was influenced by Dylan *Thomas and Gerard Manley Hopkins, though his particular voice—intensely musical, alliterative—was present even in his apprentice work.

In the mid-Fifties Reid began to spend part of each year in Majorca, where he befriended Robert *Graves, with whom he translated Suetonius. Graves has been an abiding influence on Reid's poetry. Reid's work as a translator, especially of Spanish poetry, began in the late Fifties, though it was during the Sixties and Seventies that he did his much-admired translations from Pablo Neruda, Jorge Luis Borges, and other Latin American writers. *Oddments, Inklings, Omens, Moments* appeared in 1959.

Reid is primarily a poet of awe, gazing at the world with a childlike vision, registering its bright surfaces in melodic language and arresting phrases. There is wistfulness in his work, too: a sense that in this post-Edenic world one can hope for little except the chance occurrences of love or good weather. The landscapes of his verse—North American, Mediterranean, Scottish—are deeply inward places, often sunswept, occasionally drenched by rain.

Reid, who married twice, has one son, Jasper. For many years he and his son wandered from country to country, with Reid's only permanent address being *The New Yorker*. Later, he divided his time evenly between New York and a rustic, self-built house in the Dominican Republic. *Weatherings* (Canongate/Dutton, 1978) contained most of his published verse. See also *Passwords* (Little, Brown, 1964), a collection of poems and essays, and *Whereabouts* (North Point, 1987), a book of essays.

Reid has also written several books for children. See *An Alastair Reid Reader* (University of New England Press, 1994) and *Oases: Poems and Prose* (Canon gate, 1997). Reid's prose and poetry have now been published in two volumes: *Inside Out: Selected Poetry and Translations*, with an introduction by Douglas *Dunn, and *Outside In: Selected Prose*, with an introduction by Andrew O'Hagan (Polygon, 2008).　　JP

Reid, Christopher (1949–　) Born in Hong Kong but educated in England. At Exeter College, Oxford, he was taught for a term by Craig *Raine, the *Martian poet with whom he is often associated. Yet, for all their shared interest in metaphor, butchers, children, and couplets, they are quite different poets. Raine's poetic presence is exuberant, edgy, vigorous; Reid's is droll, self-contained, cool. Raine's love poems are erotic, Reid's affectionate. Raine admires Picasso's bold distortions; Reid invokes the intimate interiors of Vermeer and Vuillard. Raine's finest poems are capable of a surprisingly raw directness; Reid's best work is elegantly oblique.

In Reid's attractive first collection, *Arcadia* (1979), a close, if partial, reading of Wallace *Stevens shows in the finicky diction and the ring of certain titles: 'A Holiday from Strict Reality', 'Big Ideas with Loose Connections', 'The Meaning of Morning'. The dandy in Stevens offers a model for the way Reid advertises the artifice of his language, usually to witty effect. In 'From an Idea by Toulouse-Lautrec', associations mingle as Reid depicts preparations for a meal: if the eucharist is brought to mind, so too is St Laurence's martyrdom. The more formally compacted poems in *Pea Soup* (1982—both Oxford University Press) sustain the ingenuity and graceful good humour of *Arcadia*, but they reveal, too, greater tonal range; their span includes reflections on fictiveness, poker-faced confrontations between chaos and a wish for order, and affectingly wry love poems (such as the *Nabokovian 'At the Wrong Door'). The writing's comic poise never lapses, yet an awareness of poetry as a ritual that keeps suffering at arm's length is rarely absent.

Reid's interest in personae and parody shapes his third collection, *Katerina Brac* (1985), where he assumes the role of an invented female poet, and mimics the intonations of Eastern European poetry in translation, employing a suppler, lower-key style than in previous volumes. Skirting bathos and banality, the book contrives quirky, half-serious variations on serious themes, especially the relation between history and poetry, experience and representation. *Auden's 'poetry makes nothing happen' appears to lie behind the volume's deadpan uses of 'happen'.

Reid's early poetry was discussed in Alan Robinson, *Instabilities in Contemporary British Poetry* (Macmillan, 1988). The phonetically misspelled sequence 'Memres of Alfred Stoker' from *In the Echoey Tunnel* (1991) continued his interest in *naïf* perceptions and voices, while *Expanding Universes* (1996) evinced the influence of Paul *Muldoon in its formal variety. 'Two Dogs on a Pub Roof', which rhymes persistently on onomatopoeic, bark-like monosyllables, discovers an *Oulipian vein of fantastical satire, later continued in the alliterative, *Larkinesque 'Bollockshire'.

In the 1990s, Reid succeeded Raine as poetry editor at Faber and Faber, publishing Simon *Armitage among others. *For and After* (2003—all Faber) contains poems for Ian *Hamilton, Seamus *Heaney, and Ted *Hughes (whose letters he edited). He was lates Professor of Creative writing at Hull. Reid has also published poems for children through his own Ondt & Gracehoper press. *A Scattering* (Areté, 2009), a collection of elegies for his late wife, the actress Lucinda Gane, won the Costa Book Award and was shortlisted for the T. S. Eliot Prize and the Forward Prize. *The Song of Lunch* (CB Editions, 2009; repr. Faber, 2010), a nostalgic poem looking back on literary London, was made into a television film by the BBC.　　MO'N*

Retallack, Joan (1941–) Avant-garde poet, performer, critic, biographer, and teacher, Joan Retallack was educated at the University of Illinois Urbana-Champaign and Georgetown University. She is John D. and Catherine T. MacArthur Professor of Humanities at Bard College and the author of seven books of poetry as well as critical works on Gertrude *Stein and John *Cage. She lives in New York.

Through its polytextual, polymorphic, and polylingual play, Retallack's poetry refuses easy access. *Errata 5uite* (Edge, 1993) relishes the multiplicity and complexity of language, toying with the materiality of the text; it won the Gertrude Stein Award for Innovative Poetry, and led Charles *Bernstein to describe Retallack's poetic language as one of 'pure substitution, substantiation, surfeit'. *A F T E R R I M A G E S* (Wesleyan University Press, 1995) was described by Marjorie Perloff as a 'stunning example of "language graphics"'. *How To Do Things With Words* (Sun & Moon, 1998), a collage of information from different media, furthers this project of performative and provocative defamiliarization. *PROCEDURAL ELEGIES / WESTERN CIV CONT'D /* (Roof, 2010) collects work written between 1980 and 2010. The essay 'What is Experimental Poetry and Why Do We Need It?' (2007) addresses the relationship of science and art; in the manner of her mentor Cage, Retallack states 'we must somehow find | make patterns among contingencies'.   HY

Rexroth, Kenneth (1905–82) Born in South Bend, Indiana, but lived in San Francisco from 1927, and was thereafter associated with all its literary manifestations, eventually as a kind of elder statesman. He encouraged successive 'movements', especially the *Beat poets, but tended to lose patience with each one and abandon it as a misguided job. He always hoped for a total change in humanity. He was on the board of *Black Mountain Review* (see *Black Mountain Poets), but resigned early on (1954) because he felt a critic had been 'unfair' to *Roethke. He did not approve of adverse criticism of anyone except officials and politicians. His voice, exemplified at its least enduring in such lines as 'Never | Give up this savage religion | For the blood-drenched civilized | Abstraction of the rascals | Who live by killing you and me', was frequently raucous and careless. His best poems, all in the tradition of the *Imagists and *Objectivists, were written despite

his politics, although very occasionally the rhetoric of the political verse takes on an impassioned and bitter tone which has verbal, if not intellectual, power. Thus, when in 'Thou Shalt Not Kill: A Lament for Dylan Thomas', Rexroth laments that the poet was murdered by politicians, lawyers, publishers, and 'bosses', rather than by unwise ingestive habits, he does it with such sincerity that he temporarily persuades the reader. But the best work is about nature, and much of it is in the manner of his translations from the Chinese and Japanese. This kind of poem is, surprisingly, precise, carefully worked out, and above all, quiet.

See *Complete Collected Shorter Poems* (1967); *The Collected Longer Poems* (1968); *Selected Poems* (1984); *World Outside the Window* (selected essays, 1987—all New Directions); and *Complete Poems* (Copper Canyon, 2003), eds. Sam Hamill and Bradford Morrow.   MS-S

Reynolds, Oliver (1957–) Born in Cardiff into a Quaker family. After leaving school he spent a year as a porter at Whitchurch Mental Hospital before going on to study drama at the University of Hull, 1977–80. Since then he has worked intermittently in the theatre, and has been Judith E. Wilson Junior Fellow in creative writing at Cambridge University and a writer-in-residence at the universities of Glasgow and Strathclyde. Reynolds was initially a prolific and restless poet whose first three books seemed far from settling into a single voice or style. *Skevington's Daughter* (1985), *The Player Queen's Wife* (1987), and *The Oslo Tram* (1991—all Faber) variously contain love lyrics, sequences on photography and Wales, contemporary urban vignettes, and brief monologues spoken by other artists, actors, or musicians; but his strongest work is in a vein of oblique or fragmentary historical narrative, in which (often horrific) details of violent death or suffering are treated with extreme detachment, and the poem derives power from the indirection it employs in circling towards a centre of bizarrerie or cruelty. Some of Reynolds' most memorable poems deal with madness and the institutionalized lives of mental patients; his approach is that of the compassionate observer. Reviewers have pointed, not always approvingly, to Reynolds' 'cleverness' and facility; he is a witty poet, with a predilection for mock-learned word-play, for punning both linguistically (where playfulness is used to make political points, in particular about the Welsh language) and visually. He has produced elegant versions of poems by Baudelaire and Rilke, and these, like some of his more consciously light-verse pieces, gain from the use of regular (if flexible) rhyme and metre. His later collections are *Almost* (1999—all Faber) and *Hodge* (Areté, 2010), written while he worked as an usher at the Royal Opera House.   AJ

Reznikoff, Charles (1894–1976) Born in Brooklyn, New York, and educated at New York University's School of Law. Except for an abortive year at journalism school in Missouri when he was 16 and a year working in Hollywood in the 1930s—the source of some of his most mordant and witty poetry—Reznikoff was a lifelong resident of New York City. He briefly practised law, then worked at a number of writing and editing jobs, including one for an encyclopaedia of law for lawyers. A tireless walker, covering five or six miles of the city every day until the end of his life, he found his natural subject-matter in the life of the streets, the ethnic neighbourhoods, and the urban poor. Influenced by the example of *Pound and other early modernists, he had begun writing poetry when he was a teenager. In the Twenties his work came to the attention of Louis *Zukofsky, who saw in it *the* prime example of '*objectivist' poetics. Reznikoff's work was neglected by editors and critics alike until the mid-Fifties, when his association with Zukofsky and other poets such as *Oppen and *Rakosi brought him to the attention of a younger generation. Since the Seventies all of his previous work, much of it self-published, has been reprinted, and his reputation as one of the foremost poets of his generation is now well established.

Reznikoff's poetry, precise, authoritative, and subtle, has its roots in the modern free-verse revolution of the early part of the century, in particular the *Imagist programme of Pound and *Hulme. Equally, Reznikoff's preference for a poetry of statement rather than metaphor, for observation and image over interiority, is deeply related both to his legal training, with its emphasis on unambiguous clarity, and to his sense of the Jewish poet as an objective moral witness, one whose relation to language is traditionally held as sacred.

Reznikoff's work ranges widely from short, darkly sarcastic, epigrammatic jottings to long autobiographical and historical poems and verse dramas which make use of biblical parallelism and a tonal 'recitative' close to colloquial prose rhythms. Shunning rhetorical flourish, the poems achieve, through reticence and understatement, an almost documentary or photographic effect, which contributes to their felt solidity and sense of 'truthfulness.' These effects are particularly pronounced in Reznikoff's masterpiece, 'Autobiography of a Writer', and in the historical volumes *Holocaust* and *Testimony*, works which rely mainly on the use of edited court-room material. Throughout all of his work one is aware of Reznikoff's probing historical vision as it renders the effect of history's impersonal forces on the individual. Such a vision powerfully animates the city poetry with its vignettes of immigrant life, of petty hopes and failure, which seem finally illuminated not only by the poet's attentive eye but also by the light of time itself.

The most complete edition of Reznikoff's work is *Poems 1918–1975: The Complete Poems of Charles Reznikoff*, ed. Seamus Cooney (Black Sparrow, 1989). See also *Holocaust* (Black Sparrow, 1975), *Testimony* (New Directions, 1965), and *The Manner Music*, a novel, with introduction by Robert Creeley (Black Sparrow, 1976); and for criticism, *Charles Reznikoff*, by Milton Hindus (Black Sparrow, 1977), *Charles Reznikoff: Man and Poet* (National Poetry Foundation, 1984), ed. Milton Hindus, *Conviction's Net of Branches: Essays on the Objectivist Poets and Poetry*, by Michael Heller (Southern Illinois

University Press, 1985), and Stephen Fredman, *A Menorah for Athena: Charles Reznikoff and the Jewish Dilemmas of Objectivist Poetry* (University of Chicago Press, 2000). *Holocaust* was reprinted in the UK by Five Leaves Press in 2010, with an introduction by George Szirtes.   MH

Rich, Adrienne (1929–2012) Born in Baltimore, Maryland. The elder of two sisters, Rich grew up in an upper-middle-class environment and was educated at Radcliffe College, from which she graduated in 1951. She won the Yale Series of Younger Poets Award that same year. Her book, *A Change of World*, was selected by W. H. *Auden, who wrote in his preface: 'The poems a reader will encounter in this book are neatly and modestly dressed, speak quietly but do not mumble, respect their elders but are not cowed by them, and do not tell fibs.'

Rich married in her early twenties and bore three children before her thirtieth birthday; she also published *The Diamond Cutters* (1955), a graceful, neatly crafted book much in the vein of her first volume. It was not until the mid-Sixties, when she and her husband began to work actively to end the war in Vietnam, that her poetry acquired the tense, angry voice that was characteristic of her mature work. *Necessities of Life* (1966) was a breakthrough work for Rich, followed quickly by *Leaflets* (1969), *The Will to Change* (1971), and *Diving into the Wreck* (1973). The poems of this middle period are those of a poet who has happily shed the conventions of formal poetry. Images gather like bright shards: phrases from letters, public speech, intimate moments from the poet's past and present. Among the significant poems of this period are 'Face to Face', 'Orion', 'Leaflets', 'I Dream I'm the Death of Orpheus', and 'Waking in the Dark', all written with a fierce new urgency.

Rich's later work came directly out of her experience as an early leader in the feminist movement. Her essays were seminal in the redefinition of patriarchy and motherhood, pointing a way towards a non-sexist future. In poetry and prose, Rich's work of the Seventies and Eighties examines the connections between the literary imagination and history, between ethics and action; she writes in a deeply autobiographical vein about the experience of being white, Jewish, and lesbian in America. The struggle of the individual for freedom is seen, by Rich, as coincident with wider struggles for freedom. The major collection of her middle years was *The Dream of a Common Language* (1978), a book in which she explores the 'technology of silence' as well as 'these words, these whispers, conversations | from which time after time the truth breaks moist and green'. In *Time's Power* (1989), she wrestles with time itself, with the contradictions of memory, with the meaning of human responsibility in the face of change and death (she dated all her later poems by year). Her work is, always, grounded in a radically liberal political perspective. Her main volumes in the 1990s were *Dark Fields of the Republic* (1995) and *Midnight Salvage* (1999). Following a revised edition of her selected poems from five decades, *The Fact of a Doorframe* (2001), Rich published several further collections concerned directly and obliquely with American life during the 'war on terror': *The School Among the Ruins* (2004)—which won the National Book Critics Circle Award—*Telephone Ringing in the Labyrinth* (2007), and *Tonight No Poetry Will Serve* (2011—all Norton).

In 1997, Rich publically declined the National Medal of Arts in protest at the 'racial and economic injustice' of government arts funding. She received many later honours, including the Bollingen Prize in 2003 and the Griffin Lifetime Recognition Award in 2010. Her death was reported on the front page of the *New York Times*. See *Later Poems Selected and New 1971–2012* (2012), her final volume, and also *Adrienne Rich's Poetry and Prose* (1993), eds. Barbara C. Gelpi and Albert Gelpi, a critical edition. Collections of her prose include *Blood, Bread, and Poetry* (1986), *What Is Found There: Notebooks on Poetry and Politics* (1993), and *Arts of the Possible: Essays and Conversations* (2002—all Norton).

For criticism, see Alice Templeton, *The Dream and the Dialogue: Adrienne Rich's*

Feminist Poetics (University of Tennessee Press, 1994).   JP*

Richards, I. A. (Ivor Armstrong) (1893–1979) Educated at Clifton and Magdalene College, Cambridge, where he became a fellow. Famous as the author of *Principles of Literary Criticism* (1925) and *Practical Criticism* (1929), and as the inventor, with C. K. Ogden, of Basic English, Richards was one of this century's best literary critics. His poems, because of this, are often considered side-efforts. Yet, although they do not have the imagination and beauty to be found in the verse of his brilliant pupil William *Empson, they still have many virtues. This is a dense lyrical 'metaphysical' verse, tightly constructed and rhymed, punning ('fain' and 'feign'), with occasional old-fashioned inversion of word-order ('What a word means who'ld say | Will new words choose and use') and quibbling play with words. Complicated argument is attempted, and in every way these poems are thoughtful. Although nothing romantic or exotic is aimed at, some of the philosophy can remind us of Fitzgerald's *Omar Khayyam*: 'Am I not the original Ball | Tossed into Court to call | The players to their Game. | Those tireless Players who | Do what they have to do | That's never twice the same?' It's nice to see 'TV'd' rhymed with 'need'; but sometimes, in the forest of rhymes, the thread can be lost.

Richards' collections are *Goodbye Earth and Other Poems* (Harcourt, 1958; Routledge, 1959), *The Screens and Other Poems* (Harcourt, 1960; Routledge, 1961), and *Internal Colloquies: Poems and Plays* (Harcourt, 1972). *I. A. Richards: New and Selected Poems* came out in 1978 (Carcanet).   GE

Rickword, Edgell (1898–1982) Born in Colchester, Essex, into an educated, middle-class family. He joined the Artists' Rifles in 1916, as soon as he was of an age to enlist, lost an eye in the war, and was invalided out of service. He was awarded the MC. After the war Rickword went up to Oxford to read French, but did not complete the degree. He became a reviewer for the *Times Literary Supplement* and the *New Statesman* (writing one of the few perceptive early reviews of *The Waste Land* in 1923) and published a study of the poet Rimbaud in 1924. He edited the short-lived but influential *Calendar of Modern Letters* (1925–7) and two volumes of *Scrutinies* (1928, 1931), and published three volumes of poetry, *Behind the Eyes* (1921), *Invocations to Angels* (1928), and *Twittingpan* (1931) before he all but gave up the writing of verse. After that time his increasing involvement in Marxist politics turned his energies to political activism. In the Thirties and Forties he was an important member of the British Marxist intelligentsia, founded and edited *Left Review* (1934–8) and *Our Time* (1944–7), and was instrumental in the formation of the Left Book Club. As a poet, writing in the Twenties, he reacted strongly against the insipidity he perceived in the work of his contemporaries and strove to develop an aesthetic of 'negative emotions', deriving his use of form and symbol from the poets he specially admired, the French Symbolists and English metaphysical poets. In these tastes, and in his outstanding ability as an essayist and editor, he has more in common with *Eliot than any other of his contemporaries. Rickword's poetry is trenchant, skilful, and capable of encompassing a wide range of styles, from powerful satire to unusual and lyrical love poems. In metre and diction, as well as politically, he prefigures the *Auden generation of poets, but unlike them wrote in an atmosphere of self-determined isolation. Even in the period of his greatest political involvement, Rickword was a lone figure, pursuing his own way.

In 1933 F. R. Leavis, introducing a selection from the critical work in the *Calendar of Modern Letters*, said the approach could 'fairly be held up as a model for a critical journal'. Frank Kermode, reviewing a reissue of the journal many years later, called it a paradigm. Their praise does not seem exaggerated.

The *Calendar* lasted for no more than two-and-a-half years. It first appeared in March 1925 as a monthly, became a quarterly in April 1926, and closed its doors in July of the following year with 'A Valediction Forbidding Mourning', asserting the validity, not necessarily of all the work printed, but of the attitude behind the editorial choice: 'The value of a review must be judged by its attitude to the living literature of the time (which includes such works of the past as can be absorbed by the contemporary sensibility) and there should naturally be some homogeneity of view among the more regular contributors.'

Such homogeneity, more easily recognized than described, certainly marked the approach of the editors, Rickword and Douglas Garman, and their chief coadjutor Bertram *Higgins. It showed in an approach to imaginative writing that adopted no particular social or political stance, yet was aware that to consider any literary work outside the context of its time must leave a yawning gap of interpretation and some inadequacies of understanding. Both in their sympathies and their sharpness, the editors and their principal reviewers produced critical views of the best writing in the period that remain interesting and valid. What was something like corporate criticism can be seen at its finest in the 'Scrutinies' of established reputations that began to appear from the first number with Rickword on Barrie, and were later embodied in the two volumes of *Scrutinies* that gave Leavis a title for his periodical, *Scrutiny*.

For Rickword's own writing, see *Behind the Eyes: Selected Poems and Translations* (1976) and *Collected Poems* (1991—both Carcanet); also two prose collections: *Essays and Opinions 1921–1931* and *Literature in Society 1931–1978*, both ed. A. Young (Carcanet, 1974 and 1978).   CPH/JGS*

Riddell, Elizabeth (1910–98) Born in New Zealand but moved to Australia immediately she left school to work as a journalist, invited by a Sydney editor on the strength of some schoolgirl verses she had published. She became one of Australia's most respected newspaper-women, and continued to work as a book reviewer for a television programme.

Riddell's four collections of poetry, from *The Untrammelled* (Viking, 1940) to *From the Midnight Courtyard* (1989), were represented in her *Selected Poems* (1992—both Angus & Robertson), which won the Kenneth Slessor Prize. Her fifth, *The Difficult Island* (Molonglo) appeared in 1994, and in 1995 she received the Patrick White Award for long-standing literary achievement. She remarked that her work was strongly influenced, in both style and content, by her career as a journalist, and she did have an admirable readability, a sureness at finding the emotive centre in a seemingly ordinary subject, lightness of touch, and concision. There is also a very unjournalistic aestheticism about her poetry, in tension with its spareness, which seems influenced by Kenneth *Slessor. Her early work is rhymed, her later is less formal; it is lightly but skilfully affecting in either mode.   RGr

Riding Laura (1901–91) Born Laura Reichenthal in New York. The daughter of an Austrian emigré and his second wife, a New Yorker, she was educated at high school in Brooklyn. While at Cornell University she began to write poetry and married a teaching assistant in history, Louis Gottschalk, though the marriage was dissolved in 1925 shortly after she had abandoned her studies and moved with him to the University of Louisville.

At this time she became involved with the *Fugitive Group and with John Crowe *Ransom and Allen *Tate in particular, both of whom were struck by the intensity and commitment with which she had dedicated herself to poetic truth. 'Her intelligence is pervasive,' Tate wrote in 1924. 'It is in every inflexion of her voice, every gesture . . . But always you get the conviction that the Devil and all Pandemonium couldn't dissuade her of her tendency'. This ambivalence has tended to characterize all subsequent critical and personal response, and is inseparable from the often rancorous and partisan assessments of her turbulent and productive literary association with Robert *Graves.

Following the publication of her first collection of poetry, *The Close Chaplet* (1926), in the same year that she took the name Riding, a correspondence with Graves who particularly admired her poem 'The Quids' led to her coming to England and to the beginning of a productive partnership. This produced such seminal works as their joint *A Survey of Modernist Poetry* (1926) and, after their move to Majorca, the founding of the Seizin Press 'to print necessary books by various particular people' and the occasional miscellany *Epilogue*, the aim of which was to 'clarify a standard of reality'. During this time both Graves and Riding supported themselves very largely through 'pot-boiling' writing projects for which he showed more aptitude and enthusiasm than she did.

Riding's complex devotion to 'truth' and linguistic purity resulted in her abandonment of poetry in 1938. She returned to the USA, married Schuyler Jackson, of *Time*, who had written admiringly of her work, and with him devoted herself to a long work on language-study, *Rational Meaning: A New Foundation for the Definition of Words*. This was unfinished at the time of his death in 1968 but has been completed subsequently.

Despite her rejection of poetry for a polemical voice which, for all its undeniable brilliance, is determinedly unattractive and combative, *The Poems of Laura Riding* (Carcanet, 1980; repr. 2005) is a remarkable book. Often, as a poet, dismissed as austere, Riding delights in the play of abstraction, and the more she races over the switchback of her paradoxes the more engrossing her poetry becomes. From the nursery-rhyme rhythms of 'Forgotten Girlhood' to much longer and involved meditations such as 'Laura and Francisca' what Graves, in a poem, referred to as her 'bladed mind' is always evident. In danger of being relegated by reputation to the ranks of the unreadable, Riding's poetry deserves to be come to afresh, freed from its author's denigration and the strictures of the lengthy apologia which she insists on printing as preface and appendices.

Laura Riding's *Progress of Stories* is available in a companion edition (Carcanet, 1982; revd. edn., Persea, 1994), and a study of her life-work, *Riding's Pursuit of Truth*, by T. P. Wexler, was published (Ohio University Press) in 1977. Since her death in 1991, the importance of Riding's example to the post-war American avant-garde has become increasingly apparent.

Robert *Nye edited a selection of her poetry for Carcanet in 1994; Charles *Bernstein wrote an introduction to the 1997 University of Virginia Press edition of *Rational Meaning*, ed. William Harmon; and John *Ashbery discussed his early admiration for her verse in *Other Traditions* (Harvard University Press, 2000). A new edition of Riding's modernist manifesto *Anarchism Is Not Enough* (1928) was published in 2001 by University of California Press, edited with an introduction by Lisa *Samuels, and *A Survey of Modernist Poetry* was reprinted with *A Pamphlet Against Anthologies* by Carcanet in 2002, edited by Patrick McGuinness and Charles Mundye. *The Failure of Poetry, The Promise of Language* (University of Michigan Press, 2007), ed. John Nolan, is a collection of her critical writings on poetry. See *The Laura (Riding) Jackson Reader*, ed. Elizabeth Friedman (Persea, 2005).   JM

Ridler, Anne (1912–2001) Born in Rugby and educated at King's College, London. Married with four children, she worked on the editorial staff of Faber and Faber for a number of years. Her first book, *Poems*, was published in 1939, and she produced ten further collections and pamphlets. She also published a number of translations of opera libretti, including Monteverdi's *Orfeo*, and her verse-plays (*Cain, The Shadow Factory*, etc.) were performed in London and Oxford.

Her poetic development owes something to Wyatt and *Auden, as well as *Eliot, 'who first made me despair of becoming a poet'. Her dramatic work shows more of Eliot's influence, perhaps, than her poetry, in which even her freer verse has a formal, cadenced air. An Elizabethan quality of musical grace pervades her most metrical stanzas. She is a Christian poet and there is a vein of erotic mysticism in her work. However, it is via the calm, dry observation of everyday matters that she moves towards her moments of vision and 'the Third Eye, which sees where sense is dark'. Despite the Latinate elegance, the consoling cadences, and the occasional archaism or inversion, the tone is modern in its 'less-deceived' and searching honesty.

Anne Ridler's *Collected Poems* appeared from Carcanet in 1994. Enitharmon Press published her short memoir, *Working for T. S. Eliot: A Personal Reminiscence*, in 2000.   CAR

Riley, Denise (1948–   ) Born in Carlisle, England, and studied at the universities of Oxford and Cambridge. She has been a writer-in-residence at the Tate Gallery, London, Professor of Literature with Philosophy at the University of East Anglia, and a visiting fellow at various American universities.

Denise Riley's intertwining career as a poet and critical thinker has produced a small but significant oeuvre. Beginning with *Marxism for Infants* (Street Editions, 1977), her elliptical forms and analytical concern with the 'attitudinizing' politics of everyday and poetic language evince her engagement with the Anglo-American avant-garde tradition from a feminist perspective. Riley's way of drawing her philosophical voice into poetic argument has been described by the critic Stephen Burt as 'the song of theory'. It can be heard mingling in deliberate impurity with popular music, travel writing, art criticism, and autobiography throughout *Selected Poems* (Reality Street, 2000). As in the work of W. S. *Graham, whom she admires, the reality and veracity of 'the lyric person' is constantly questioned by Riley's verse ('this isn't me, it's just my motor running') with a scepticism that seems reflected by its infrequent appearance.

Her prose books include *War in the Nursery* (Virago, 1983), *'Am I That Name?'* (Macmillan, 1988), and *Impersonal Passion: Language as Affect* (Duke University Press, 2005). She also edited *Poets on Writing: Britain 1970–1991* (Macmillan, 1992). 'A Part Song', an elegy for her son, won the Forward Prize for Best Single Poem in 2012. See also *Time Lived, Without Its Flow* (Capsule, 2012).   JNT

Riley, John (1937–78) Born in Leeds. He read English at Cambridge, becoming part of the group known as the *Cambridge School of poets, and forming a close association with Tim Longville, with whom he translated Hölderlin, wrote several books, and founded Grosseteste Press and *Grosseteste Review*. After nine years teaching in secondary schools, he returned to Leeds to write full-time and was killed there by muggers in 1978.

Although Riley shared some characteristics with the Cambridge poets—the influence of *Pound and Charles *Olson, a structuralist concentration on language—he was distinguished by his response to the Russian tradition, particularly to Mandelstam, whose 'Octets' and 'Stalin Ode' sequence he translated. Riley was received into the Russian Orthodox Church in 1977. His long poem 'Czargrad' is an impressive fusion of these influences, Byzantium being glimpsed, not in changeless metal, but in the movement of consciousness.

The Collected Works (Grosseteste, 1980) contains poetry, prose, and translations. *Selected Poems* (1995) traces his development as a poet and he is represented as a translator in *What I Own: Versions of Hölderlin and Mandelshtam* (1998—both Carcanet). Critical essays appear in a memorial volume, *For John Riley* (Grosseteste, 1979), and in *Poetry Review, 71:1* (1981). There is a useful discussion of 'Czargrad' by Douglas *Oliver in *PN Review, 20* (1981).   RGa

Riley, Peter (1940–   ) Born in Stockport, England, and studied at the universities of Cambridge, Keele, and Sussex. Since 1975 he has been a freelance English teacher, bookseller, and writer.

A prolific poet who has published through many small presses, Riley is a leading—and often dissenting—member of the first-generation of *Cambridge poets. With Andrew *Crozier he edited the influential 'worksheet' *The English Intelligencer* from 1966 to 1968. As a critic, editor, and publisher, he has drawn attention to a number of neglected post-war poets, from Nicholas *Moore to 'Grace Lake' (Anna Mendelssohn). He has also translated the French-Romanian poet, Lorand Gaspar, and written on musical improvisation.

Passing Measures (Carcanet, 2000), a selected poems arranged under times and places, offers a lyrical autobiography.

Alstonefield (Carcanet, 2003) is a book-length meditation around a Peak District village. *Excavations* (Reality Street, 2004) collected a sequence of prose poems based on fragments of nineteenth-century reports into prehistoric burial mounds. At the heart of Riley's poetry is a passionate concern with culture in its quietest forms as a sign 'that people | find life worth having'. *The Dance at Moicu* (2003) is a book of prose writing about the village music and customs of Transylvania. See also *The Day's Final Balance: Uncollected Writings 1965-2006* (2007—both Shearsman). *The Glacial Stairway* (Carcanet, 2011) contains poems written since 2003, including the Pyrenean title sequence. *The Gig, 4/5* (2000) was a special issue dedicated to Riley's work. In 2012 he received a Cholmondeley Award from the Society of Authors.   JNT

Riordan, Maurice (1953–) Born in Lisgoold and educated at University College, Cork, Riordan now lives in London and teaches creative writing at Sheffield Hallam University. He has edited several anthologies, including the science-themed *A Quark for Mister Mark* (Faber, 2000) and *Wild Reckoning*, an anthology of ecological poetry inspired by Rachel Carson's *Silent Spring*. From 2005 to 2009 he edited *Poetry London*.

Many of the poems in Riordan's debut collection, *A Word from the Loki* (1995), tell stories about characters whose lives are transformed by quirks of fate or by their own impulsive behaviour. While the subject matter is predominantly domestic and urban, Riordan deploys unusual perspectives and time-frames, and draws on an eclectic range of reference points, from classical philosophy to contemporary science. These elements are further developed in *Floods* (2000), particularly in Riordan's free translation of Ferenc Juhasz's long visionary poem 'The Boy Turned into a Stag'. In *The Holy Land* (2007—all Faber), Riordan returns to more familiar territory: the book's centrepiece, 'The Idylls', is a sequence of prose poems depicting rural Cork in the 1950s. Riordan has been shortlisted for the T. S. Eliot Prize and the

Whitbread Poetry Award, and has won the Michael Hartnett Poetry Award.   PBa

Roach, Eric (1915-74) Born in Mt Pleasant, Tobago, Roach was educated at Bishop's High School. During World War II he did military service in Trinidad. Later he worked in the civil service and as a teacher and journalist.

In the 1930s Roach began publishing in local periodicals, notably the *Trinidad Guardian*, and from 1949 the BBC's *Caribbean Voices* broadcasted Roach's poems across the West Indies. In the 1950s he appeared regularly in regional journals like *BIM*, *Kyk-Over-Al*, and *Caribbean Quarterly*. A strong regionalist, Roach was disappointed by the collapse of the Federation of the West Indies in 1962, and published no new poems for nearly a decade. Three of his plays were produced during this time: *Belle Fanto* (1967), *Letter from Leonora* (1968), and *A Calabash of Blood* (1971), winning him a new reputation. When he resumed publishing poems in 1970, his new work engaged with post-independence political questions. In April 1974, Roach swam out to sea at Trinidad's Quinam Bay, committing suicide by drowning.

Though Roach's poems were widely admired and anthologized in the Caribbean, they were not collected until *The Flowering Rock* (Peepal Tree, 1992). 'Immortelles' and 'Homestead' are anthems for the new Caribbean nation Roach imagined in the hopeful decade of the 1950s. His brief late phase expresses disillusion and even despair, as in 'At Quinam Bay', prefiguring his end. Dismissed by some younger writers in the 1970s as formally too conservative, Roach is now widely accepted as a seminal Caribbean poet, precursor of Derek *Walcott, Martin *Carter, and Kamau *Brathwaite.   NL

Roberts, Lynette (1909–95) Born Evelyn Beatrice Roberts in Buenos Aires, Roberts' family was originally from Wales. She studied art and design in London in the 1930s and moved to Wales in 1939 with her husband, the editor and poet Keidrych Rhys, remaining there for the rest of her life. The couple had two children in the mid-1940s, but divorced in 1949. Roberts wrote almost all of her surviving poetry during this period. In the 1950s, she became a Jehovah's Witness and repudiated her writing. She suffered from schizophrenia for many years.

Roberts' two books of poetry were published by T. S. *Eliot at Faber and Faber. *Poems* (1944) explored a variety of lyric forms and styles, from the simple and plaintive to the highly wrought. *Gods with Stainless Ears* (1951) made a bolder claim. Subtitled 'A Heroic Poem', it presents the story of a young married couple from rural Wales, separated by the war, in jangling stanzas that experiment with cinematic montage and esoteric vocabulary.

Roberts' work was admired by Edith *Sitwell, and, in 1948, Robert *Graves dedicated his study of poetic inspiration and Celtic myth, *The White Goddess*, to her. Nevertheless, her poetry was largely forgotten for fifty years. *Collected Poems*, ed. Patrick McGuinness (Carcanet, 2005) has revived interest in Roberts' late modernist vision, which combines natural observation with a technological imagination. *Diaries, Letters and Recollections* (Carcanet, 2008) is a vivid companion volume. See John *Wilkinson, 'The Brain's Tent', in *The Lyric Touch* (Salt, 2007).   JNT

Roberts, Michael (William Edward)

(1902–48) Born in Bournemouth and brought up on a farm in the New Forest. He read chemistry at King's College, London, mathematics at Cambridge, and held a succession of senior teaching posts in Newcastle and London. During the war he worked for the BBC's European Service and later became principal of a teacher-training college. He died of leukaemia in 1948. Roberts was a left-wing humanist, scientist, poet, mountaineer, and perhaps the best interpreter of contemporary poetry of his generation, a successor to T. E. *Hulme, of whom he wrote a critical study in 1938. He edited *New Signatures* and *New Country* in the early 1930s, ushering in the *Auden generation of poets, and wrote an influential *Critique of Poetry* in 1934. His two philosophical books, *The Modern Mind* (1937)

and *The Recovery of the West* (1941), reveal his deep concern about the fate of the earth, but his most enduring work was as editor of the *Faber Book of Modern Verse* (1936), a guide to the poetry enjoyed by intellectuals at the time of publication. The editor's introduction proved to be a piece of criticism as prescriptive as the *Poetics* of Aristotle. Henceforward, poetry would use intricate ideas, condense and compress metaphors, and deploy words in modes which were deliberately fantastic. Exemplars that were put forward included T. S. *Eliot, W. H. Auden, William *Empson, Edith *Sitwell, and Laura *Riding. All were strongly represented in the first edition of the anthology.

As important as what Roberts put in was what he left out. He said in the introduction that he recognized the merit of Walter *de la Mare, Edmund *Blunden, and Edwin *Muir, but he had decided to exclude these poets because they made no notable development in poetic technique. He did not even mention *Hardy, Edward *Thomas, and Robert *Frost, substantial figures conspicuous by their absence.

His poems, published in *These Our Matins* (1930), *Poems* (1936), and *Orion Marches* (1939), are generally meditative and undramatic, reflecting his love and understanding of the natural world. His control of form is perhaps too great to allow much scope to his poetry, but what he does, he does with insight, intelligence, and a great deal of poetic skill. His work is directly spoken and full of a sort of spiritual integrity, often self-effacing and always well made. Roberts' *Selected Poems and Prose*, ed. F. Grubb, was published by Carcanet in 1980.   CPH/PDH*

Robertson, Lisa

(1961–) Born in Toronto. In 1979 Robertson moved to Vancouver, where she studied at Simon Fraser University, and was involved in the *Kootenay School of Writing, an interdisciplinary writer's collective. She has worked as a bookseller, editor, astrologer, and teacher, and has been writer-in-residence at several universities. She has also written art criticism.

Research in the widest sense is fundamental to Robertson's poetry, which has taken the form of a series of book-length sequences in verse and prose. 'The necessity of women's tactical intervention in the official genres' has been a motivating concern since *XEclogue* (Tsunami, 1993). The epigraph from Mina *Loy to *Debbie: An Epic* (1997) sums up the roaming spirit of Robertson's experimentalism: 'Make the world your salon'.

The Weather (2001—both New Star/ Reality Street) was written after a six-month residency at Cambridge University as Judith E. Wilson Fellow. Eclectic enquiry into 'the rhetorical structure of English meteorological description'—from the BBC shipping forecast to James Thomson's *The Seasons*—resulted in a set of *Stein-esque prose choruses for the days of the week ('Now we persons are breaking open'), interleaved with diaristic lyrics. Robertson's interest in the poetics of civic space has also found expression in flaneurial essays issued by 'The Office for Soft Architecture'. Recent books of poetry include *The Men: A Lyric Book* (Book Thug, 2006) and *Lisa Robertson's Magenta Soul Whip* (Coach House, 2009). See also *Nilling: Prose* (Book Thug, 2012).   JNT

Robertson, Robin (1955–) Born in Scone, Scotland. He has worked as a publisher in London for most of his adult life, and did not produce a poetry collection until past the age of forty. The austere and accomplished debut, *A Painted Field* (Picador, 1997), won the Forward Prize for Best First Collection

He has since published *Slow Air* (2002), *Swithering* (2006), and *The Wrecking Light* (2010—all Picador). *Swithering* won the Forward Prize for Best Collection in 2006, and the poem, 'At Roane Head' subsequently published in *The Wrecking Light*, won the Forward Prize for Best Single Poem in 2009. A re-imagining of the Orcadian legend of the Silkie, it has a characteristic sensuousness transfused with subtle violence. Despatching his hybrid children, the drunken father ' . . . went along the line | relaxing them | one after another | with a small knife'. Robertson often seems to be urging the lyric poem to self-harm in his pursuit of the less-deceived epiphany.

Even his admirers may find little tonally to challenge the stereotype of the dour Scot. But Robertson is a rigorous and clear-eyed writer, fruitfully influenced by Northern Irish poets such as Michael *Longley and Paul *Muldoon. He can be witty as well as terse, although postmodern linguistic play is not an overwhelming interest. He has translated the *Medea* of Euripides (Free Press, 2008) and, in *The Deleted World* (Enitharmon, 2008), poetry by the Nobel-Prize-winning Swedish poet, Tomas Tranströmer.   CAR

Robinson, Edwin Arlington (1869– 1935) Born in Head Tide, Maine, and raised nearby in Gardiner which, as 'Tilbury Town', became the setting for many of his poems. He enrolled at Harvard in 1891 but had to leave after only two years when the family's finances collapsed shortly after his father's death. On his return to Gardiner he decided to become a professional poet and for the next decade endured poverty—and sometimes almost dereliction—to fulfil this ambition. His first collection, *The Torrent and the Night Before* (1896), privately printed, and an expanded version, *The Children of the Night* (1897), were barely noticed when they appeared, though they contain several lyrics, such as 'Luke Havergal' and 'Richard Cory', which later became his most popular. Robinson settled in New York City in 1899 and held various jobs— including subway-construction inspector— until 1904, when President Roosevelt, who admired his work, arranged a virtual sinecure for him in the New York Customs House. From 1910 Robinson devoted himself entirely to writing, spending summers at the MacDowell colony in New Hampshire and winters in New York. With *The Town Down the River* (1910) and *The Man Against the Sky* (1916) he emerged from obscurity to become, in the 1920s, the most highly regarded and widely read poet of his generation: the *Collected Poems* (1921, Pulitzer Prize) finally relieved him of dependence on friends and patrons; and *Tristram* (1927, Pulitzer Prize)—the third, after *Merlin* (1917) and *Lancelot* (1920), of his Arthurian trilogy—was a bestseller.

Robinson's is a poetry of ideas and characters presented in traditional forms. Once his reputation was secure, he turned more frequently from short lyric forms to long blank-verse narratives (completing thirteen book-length poems—from *Merlin* to *King Jasper* (1935)—in the second half of his career), which enabled him to indulge expansively in characterization and social and metaphysical discussion. The title-poem of *The Man Against the Sky*, which came, he said, 'as near as anything to representing my poetic vision', considers a variety of philosophical attitudes, eventually stripping them away to reveal the certain need beneath all philosophies for endurance in the face of adversity. This Hardy-esque stoicism, fortified by an Emersonian celebration of the individual, is repeatedly expressed by the many learned and eccentric old failures depicted in his work, 'Miniver Cheevy' and *The Man Who Died Twice* (1924) among them. Indirectness is the most persistent device in Robinson's poetry and accounts both for its best and its worst effects. The cool, cryptic reporting of tragic events has earned shorter poems like 'The Mill' a permanent place in anthologies. The more diffuse verse novels (*Roman Bartholow*, 1923, and *Cavender's House*, 1925), however, which fail to root their Jamesian subtleties in a sufficiently clear context, are now largely neglected. The *Collected Poems of Edwin Arlington Robinson* (Macmillan, 1937) is still the standard edition of his work; *Edwin Arlington Robinson*, by Emery Neff (Methuen/Sloane, 1948), is the most thorough early biography; and *Edwin Arlington Robinson: A Critical Study*, by Ellsworth Barnard (Macmillan, 1952; repr. 1969) is the best critical introduction. See *Selected Poems* (Penguin, 1997), ed. Robert Faggen and Scott Donaldson, and *Edward Arlington Robinson: A Poet's Life* (Columbia University Press, 2007), which draws on unpublished letters. NE

Robinson, Peter (1953–) Born in Salford, Lancashire, Robinson grew up in Liverpool and studied at the universities of York and Cambridge, where he co-edited the magazines *Perfect Bound* and *Numbers*. He taught English at universities in Japan for many years, and is now Professor of English and American Literature at the University of Reading.

An independent figure in contemporary English verse, Robinson has published critical appreciations of a wide range of modern British poets and translated from Italian poetry: see, respectively, *Twentieth Century Poetry: Selves and Situations* (Oxford University Press, 2005) and *Poetry & Translation: The Art of the Impossible* (Liverpool University Press, 2010). He has also edited the poems of Bernard *Spencer.

From his first volumes in the 1980s and 1990s, represented in *Selected Poems* (Carcanet, 2001), to the later prose poems of *Untitled Deeds* (Salt, 2004), Robinson's writing relates autobiography to wider social landscapes with an exacting naturalism. Roy *Fisher, an important exemplar, has admired 'the smoothly-articulated densities of observation and mental event and the careful placing of the figure representing the empirical Peter Robinson'. The *Look of Goodbye* (Shearsman, 2008) contains poems from his final years in Japan. He has published two collections since his return to England: *English Nettles* (Two Rivers, 2010) and *The Returning Sky* (2012). *Talk About Poetry* (2007—both Shearsman) is a book of interviews. See also *The Salt Companion to Peter Robinson* (2007), ed. Adam Piette and Katy Price. JNT

Robinson, Roland (1912–92) Born in Ireland of English parents, went to Australia when he was 9, began working as a houseboy on a sheep station when he was 14, and was later a boundary rider, horse-trainer, jockey, fencer, dam builder, factory worker, railway fettler, cleaner, art-school model, member of a ballet company, gardener, assistant to a collector of crocodiles and snakes for a menagerie, and the greenkeeper of a golf course in Sydney. He was the first white poet to collect the anecdotes and oral traditions of the Aborigines, both the tribal people of the Northern Territory and the detribalized people of the south coast of New South Wales, and he set these down alongside his own work in verse and prose.

Robinson wrote eight small volumes of poetry, five prose works on Aboriginal myths and legends, and three volumes of autobiography. These last reveal an extremely emotional, driven nature. They record how he regularly fled to the bush to escape routine or the complications and demands of his relationships with women. In his old age he lived on the coast near Newcastle, New South Wales, leonine and impassioned as ever, with the last of his companions. He received the Patrick White Award.

The poetry of Edward *Thomas was Robinson's ideal, for its purity. His own work is more vehement and vivid, though less original and subtle, than his master's. Its real achievement is the assimilation of its unique setting—Robinson's best poetry burns and gleams with the colours of the outback, and suggests all the sweep of the coastal bush and heathland within its simple lyric forms. His work is narrow in its range and repetitious, and it lacks any intellectual scheme, but its intensity does much to justify these limits. There is a very slim, judicious *Selected Poems* (Angus & Robertson, 1989).   RGr

Rodefer, Stephen (1940–) Born in Bellaire, Ohio. Rodefer studied Art History and Literature at Amherst College, and went on to SUNY Buffalo, where he was taught by Charles *Olson, and San Francisco State University, where he began a thesis on Robert *Creeley. He has held fellowships and taught at universities in the United States, Britain, and France. He lives in Paris.

Rodefer has been active in a number of modes. In 1965, the year of his debut publication from Island Press, *The Knife*, he was involved in the eclectic *Magazine of Further Studies* with other members of Olson's class, including John *Wieners and Fred *Wah. In the 1970s, he was a founding member of the Poets Theater in San Francisco. His plays include *Tennyson* (1983). He is also a visual artist, whose 'LANGUAGE PICTURES' series has been widely exhibited, and an innovative translator: see (as 'Jean Calais') *Villon* (Pick Pocket, 1976).

The stylistic range of Rodefer's contrarian oeuvre makes it a meeting point for a trans-Atlantic avant-garde of *Beat, *Black Mountain, *New York, *Language, and *Cambridge poetries. *Four Lectures* (The Figures, 1982) employs a long verse line to self-parodically didactic effect, recalling *Eliot's *Four Quartets* via the wise bathos of *Ashbery. *Call It Thought* (Carcanet, 2008), a selected volume with an introduction by Rod Mengham, includes his ongoing translation of Baudelaire, *Fever Flowers: les fleurs du val*, as well as the early satirical squibs, 'Lies of the Artists' ('I dreamt Gary *Snyder ate a pregnant lizard').   JNT

Rodgers, W. R. (William Robert) (1909–69) Generally and affectionately known as Bertie Rodgers. Educated in his native Belfast, he graduated from Queen's University in 1931 and was ordained to the Presbyterian ministry in 1935. He was installed as minister to the rural parish of Loughgall, Co. Armagh, and for his non-sectarianism became known locally as 'the Catholic Presbyterian'.

He began writing poetry in 1939. *Awake!* appeared in 1941, and this first collection borrowed a pre-war idiom of wit and dread, reworking it lyrically and inventively to probe and value everyday living. In 1946 his wife moved to Edinburgh to train as a psychoanalyst and he relinquished the ministry, taking an appointment as producer at the BBC in London offered him by Louis *MacNeice. Following the death of G. B. Shaw, Rodgers was elected to his place in the Irish Academy of Letters in 1951. He remarried in 1953.

Europa and the Bull (1952) was his second collection, and it harnessed Christian and classical mythologies alike to a frank and joyful assertion of sexual exuberance—'Lent' and 'The Net' are outstanding and widely anthologized. At the BBC Rodgers wrote a radio play evoking Belfast—'The Return Room' (1955)—but little poetry. For his broadcast series of *Irish Literary Portraits* (published London, 1972)—among which are intimate and mischievous accounts of *Yeats and *Joyce from their friends and contemporaries—Rodgers became known as oral historian of the Irish literary movement.

In 1966 he moved to California and held fellowships in creative writing. He died in Los Angeles in 1969, and is buried in Loughgall churchyard. *Collected Poems*, ed. Dan Davin (Oxford University Press, 1971), includes the pithy 'Home Thoughts From Abroad' and a terse elegy on Mac-Neice. Darcy O'Brien's biographical study (Bucknell University Press, 1970) draws with sensitivity on unpublished dream-notebooks and other uncollected writings. A later edition of his poems, edited with an introduction by Michael *Longley, appeared from The Gallery Press in 1993. *The Return Room* was published by The Blackstaff Press in 2010, with a CD of the original production, and a foreword by Paul *Muldoon, who describes Rodgers' drama as 'one of the most important Irish poems of the twentieth century'.   PL

Rodriguez, Judith (1936–) Although Born in Perth, Western Australia, she grew up in Queensland, where she first published under her maiden name, Green, in a joint volume, *Four Poets* (Cheshire, 1962). She has travelled widely, especially in the Americas, her first marriage being to a Colombian academic. She later married Thomas *Shapcott, taught creative writing in Melbourne, edited the Penguin Australian Poetry Series, as well as the *Collected Poems* of Jennifer *Rankin (University of Queensland Press, 1990).

New and Selected Poems (1988) draws on six earlier collections, including the PEN Award winner, *Mudcrab at Gambaro's* (1980—all University of Queensland Press). Like previous volumes, it is illustrated by her accomplished linocuts, which reflect, in their boldness and flowing lines, poems that are substantial and sensual. She is particularly successful in the celebratory mode, combining generosity of spirit with sharp observation and a robust wit and intelligence applied alike to domestic existence, literary occasions, and international politics and places. In 1994 she was made a Member of the Order of Australia and received the Christopher Brennan Award. She has also written a musical play, *Poor Johanna*, and

an opera libretto, *Lindy*. *Manatee* (2007) is a chapbook from Picaro Press.   JS

Roethke, Theodore (1908–63) Born in Saginaw, Michigan. He was the son of Otto Roethke, of Prussian extraction, who owned a large greenhouse that figured as a central image in many of Roethke's finest poems. Roethke graduated from the University of Michigan and later took courses at Harvard. He taught English literature and creative writing at Lafayette College, at Penn State University, and at Bennington College before moving permanently to the University of Washington in Seattle in 1948, where he was poet-in-residence.

Roethke's first book, *Open House* (1942), was composed of short, tightly rhyming poems, much influenced by Stanley *Kunitz, Louise *Bogan, and W. H. *Auden, with all of whom he had close personal ties. Roethke's breakthrough as a poetic stylist occurred with *The Lost Son* in 1948, a book which re-created the poet's lost youth among the flowers of the greenhouse. A major lyric sequence in the book contained brief, vividly concrete poems in which flowers—carnations, roses, chrysanthemums—took on an almost spiritual life. 'Cuttings', 'Flower Dump', 'Child on Top of a Greenhouse', 'Big Wind', and 'My Papa's Waltz'—all from this volume—are among the permanent achievements of modern American poetry, as is the title-sequence, 'The Lost Son', an autobiographical poem that is highly innovative in technique.

During the early Fifties Roethke experimented with oblique autobiographical poems that made use of nursery rhymes and Freudian psychology. These were gathered in *The Waking* (1953). In the mid-Fifties he returned to formal poetry, often echoing *Yeats, whom he deeply admired: 'I take this cadence from a man named Yeats', he wrote in 'Four for Sir John Davies'—'I take it, and I give it back again.' One also sees the influence of Dylan *Thomas, Hopkins, and the Elizabethan lyricists in the exuberant love poems of this period, many of which were written for his young wife, Beatrice Heath O'Connell, who had been a student at Bennington when he taught there. Among these is

'Words for the Wind', the title-poem of Roethke's first *Selected Poems* (1958). There is a great deal of metaphysical wit in these poems, too, as in 'I Knew A Woman', where he writes: 'She was the sickle; I, poor I, the rake, | Coming behind her for her pretty sake | (But what prodigious mowing we did make).' Another important poem of the Fifties was 'The Waking', a haunting villanelle.

A consistent strain of Emersonian romanticism runs through Roethke's work from the beginning, with its emphasis on the emblemmatic aspects of the natural world. Roethke was a latter-day Transcendentalist, finding spiritual correspondences in physical things. In his deeply inward symbolism, 'wind' is synonymous with 'spirit'. The poet, in works such as 'In a Dark Time', broods on the natural world, pursuing an intensely subjective *via negativa*: 'In a dark time, the eye begins to see.' Arriving at the end of this negative path, the poet emerges into an almost ecstatic, mystical vision, in which 'The mind enters itself, and God the mind, | And one is One, free in the tearing wind.'

Like so many poets of his generation— *Plath, *Berryman, *Lowell—Roethke suffered bouts of mental illness. He was briefly institutionalized several times. 'This shaking keeps me steady', he wrote in 'The Waking', and he did indeed view his periodic breakdowns as spiritual crises. He liked, in fact, to identify himself with such 'mad' poets of the past as William Blake and Christopher Smart.

The primary influence on Roethke's final work was clearly Walt Whitman, whose spirit presides over *The Far Field*, published posthumously in 1964. Roethke broke free of the formal constraints of the Fifties and began writing long free-verse poem-sequences in sprawling lines reminiscent of *Leaves of Grass*. This last volume contains many of Roethke's most memorable poems, including 'The Far Field', 'Meditation at Oyster River', 'Journey to the Interior', and 'The Rose'. These exquisite nature poems are deeply spiritual, depicting fiercely private journeys from blindness to vision in sensuous, musical, highly concrete language. One of the most effective techniques of these poems is the use of Whitmanian catalogues, which included detailed lists of natural flora and fauna.

Roethke died of a heart attack while swimming at the age of 55. His influence has been profound on many poets, including Sylvia Plath, James *Dickey, James *Wright, Ted *Hughes, and Seamus *Heaney.

See his *Collected Poems* (Doubleday, 1966; Faber, 1968 and 1985; repr. Doubleday, 2011). See also, *On the Poet and His Craft: Selected Prose of Theodore Roethke*, ed. Ralph J. Mills, Jr. (University of Washington Press, 1965; new edn. *On Poetry & Craft*, with a foreword by Carolyn *Kizer, Copper Canyon, 2001), *Selected Letters of Theodore Roethke* (University of Washington Press, 1968; Faber, 1970), and *Straw for the Fire: From the Notebooks of Theodore Roethke*, ed. David Wagoner (Doubleday, 1972; repr. Copper Canyon, 2006). Edward *Hirsch made a selection of Roethke's poems for the Library of America's American Poets Series in 2005.

For biography, see Allan Seager, *The Glass House* (McGraw-Hill, 1968). For criticism, see *Theodore Roethke: Essays on the Poetry*, ed. Arnold Stein (University of Washington Press, 1965) and Jay Parini, *Theodore Roethke: An American Romantic* (University of Massachusetts Press, 1979). JP

Rogers, Pattiann (1940–   ) Born in Joplin, Missouri. She married John Rogers, a geophysicist, in 1960 while she was an undergraduate at the University of Missouri, from where she graduated in 1961. She moved with her family to Texas where she received an MA in creative writing from the University of Houston in 1981. Soon after this Rogers published her first book of poems, *Expectations of Light* (1981). She currently lives with her husband in Castle Rock, Colorado.

Rogers has studied zoology, and her poetry is based firmly in the subjects and images found in the natural sciences. She uses the things of this natural world as conceits to explain and understand the human condition. It has become a signature technique of her poetry to select a particular metaphor and then extend and examine it throughout the poem from every possible angle and point of view. This methodology is used in the title-poem of Rogers' second book, *The Tattooed Lady in the Garden* (1986), in which the poet is symbolized as a woman in a lush garden who is covered with tattoos of the images of nature that surround her. By the poem's conclusion it is impossible to tell where the lady ends and the garden begins. Rogers has also used this technique successfully in her writing of love poems.

Her third collection was *Splitting and Binding* (1989—all Wesleyan University Press). A revised edition of *Firekeeper: New and Selected Poems* (Milkweed, 1994) appeared in 2005. *Song of the World Becoming: New and Selected Poems* (Milkweed, 2001) was followed by *Generations* (2005) and *Wayfare* (2008—both Penguin), which continue her scientifically curious exploration of the creative mind. See also *The Dream of the Marsh Wren: Writing as Reciprocal Creation* (Milkweed, 1999).   LS*

Rohrer, Matthew (1970–) Born in Anne Arbor, Michigan and raised in Oklahoma, Rohrer received his MFA in poetry from the University of Iowa. He is the author of *A Hummock in the Malookas* (Norton, 1995), which was selected by Mary *Oliver for the National Poetry Series in 1994; *Satellite* (Verse, 2001); *A Green Light* (Verse, 2004), *Rise Up* (Wave, 2007); *They All Seemed Asleep* (Octopus, 2008); *A Plate of Chicken* (Ugly Duckling, 2009); he also co-authored *Nice Hat. Thanks* (Verse, 2002) with Joshua Beckman, and was the poetry editor of *Fence* magazine. Of *A Green Light*, shortlisted for the 2005 International Griffin Poetry Prize, the judges commented that Rohrer's self-conscious, funny, and tender poems 'lay bare an anxiety of influence, social and linguistic, and present us the sideways view of the world of a young American not able to assume the mantle of hero'. Shelley's 'Ode to the West Wind' is only the most obvious influence on his recent collection *Destroyer and Preserver* (Wave, 2011); he has also cited William

Carlos *Williams' 'democratic' spirit, and younger poet Jon Woodward's elegiac volume *Rain* (Wave, 2006). Recipient of a Pushcart Prize, Rohrer lives in Brooklyn and teaches at New York University.   SR

Rolls, Eric (Charles) (1923–2007) Born in Grenfell, New South Wales, he was for many years a farmer. He is best known for two prose works, *They All Ran Wild* (1969) about the destructiveness of introduced flora and fauna in Australia, and *A Million Wild Acres* (1981), a natural and social history of the Pilliga scrub in New South Wales, which received major awards. Rolls, however, first gained wide literary acclaim for a poem written when he was 15: 'Death Song of the Mad Bush Shepherd', which was eventually included in his first verse collection, *Sheaf Tosser* (Angus & Robertson, 1967).

Rolls' poetry maintained a vigorous link with the tradition of Border ballads in its wry lyricism and sometimes macabre playfulness. His first collection is dominated by pastoral subject-matter and earthy humour. *The Green Mosaic* (Nelson, 1977) uses his New Guinea experiences during the Second World War to explore similarly sensuous and observant lyrical accounts of human, animal, and vegetable quiddities. His collection of children's rhymes, *Miss Strawberry Verses* (1978) is not for the faint hearted; it is a pity none of these amiable ferocities is included in his *Selected Poems* (1990—both Angus & Robertson), which did, however, restore to circulation the work of a verbally resourceful and playful poet whose essential concerns are summed up in the title of another of his best-selling prose works, *Celebration of the Senses* (1984). His two-volume *Australia: A Biography* appeared in 2000 and 2003.   TWS

Romer, Stephen (1957–) Born in Hertfordshire and educated at Cambridge. *Idols* (1986), his first collection of poems, is marked by an assured stylishness: influences (notably Corbière and Geoffrey *Hill) have been creatively absorbed. The poems in the first half are written in off-rhyming couplets, a form put to elegant yet expressively jittery use. Here Romer's main concerns are love, poetry, and their attendant complications: narcissism, 'the mind', art's dubious triumphs over experience. The pervasive mood is one of dandified, if heartfelt, irony. Romer's lines move with a finicky grace, yet they remain open to what 'Higher Things' calls 'the sublime'. He trains a quasi-philosophical eye on his emotions and explores fictive parallels with a mixture of wit and anguish. Composed in a variety of forms (including blank verse and off-rhyming tercets), the poems in the second half have a less guarded feel, and yet the better pieces (such as 'How Things Continue') retain stylistic control while striking affirmative, even visionary, notes. *Plato's Ladder* (1992) continued in a similar vein, but also includes a sequence about post-Communist Poland, where Romer taught for a year.

His third collection was *Tributes* (1998—all Oxford University Press). A decade later, *Yellow Studio* (Carcanet/Oxford Poets, 2008) saw the poet extending his emotional range in middle age: the collection culminates in a sequence on the death of his father, which also explores family history *à la* Hugo *Williams. Since 1981, Romer has lived in France, where he teaches in the English department at Tours University. He has edited an anthology of twentieth-century French poems for Faber, and is also a critic and translator: see, with Jennie Feldman, *Into the Deep Street: Seven Modern French Poets 1938–2008* (Anvil, 2009).   MO'N*

Root, William Pitt (1941–   ) Born in Austin, Minnesota, and attended the universities of Washington at Seattle and North Carolina.

Among figures he most admires, Root has included W. C. *Williams, *Frost, Whitman, Lorca, and Blake, confessing a special regard for Theodore *Roethke's 'Greenhouse' and 'North American' series. His first two collections, *The Storm and Other Poems* (Atheneum, 1969; repr. Carnegie Mellon University Press, 2005) and *Striking the Dark Air for Music* (Atheneum, 1973), both of which revolve obsessively around the early death of his father, reflect a steady shift from Williams to Blake and Roethke,

from direct statements and concrete scenes to a more introspective quest for allegory and mystical resolutions in nature. His willingness to take risks, to expose the close relationship between narrator and poem-making self, does not always save his work from a tunnel lexicon and focus.

See *Trace Elements from a Recurring Kingdom: The First Five Books* (Confluence, 1994).   EB

Rose, Peter (1955–   ) Born and grew up in Wangaratta, Victoria. He worked as commissioning editor for Oxford University Press in Melbourne before becoming editor of the *Australian Book Review* in 2001. *The House of Vitriol* (1990) established his style distinctly; it was soon followed by *The Catullan Rag* (1993—both Picador), the shapes and quirks of which are clearly the products of the same sensibility.

Rose's is a post-realist poetry which enjoys the modernist habit of incorporating a diversity of cultural materials and proper names. It offers collages without easy signposts, events without manifest conclusions: one of his trade-marks is the strategically weak ending.

The poems in Rose's second collection tend to be larger and more assured than those in *The House of Vitriol*, pointing beyond the operatic or historical materials which bedeck them to the occasions of flat-life in the days and nights of inner suburbia. The persona tends to be mercurial, evasive, and ruefully hedonistic. There is also a suite of fourteen poems spoken by a modern Catullus. Swagged with adjectives, Rose's busy poems refuse the well-made turn and counter-turn. Although obscure at times, they are crammed with the stuff of colourful dailyness.

The dream-like title poem of *Donatello in Wangaratta* (Hale & Iremonger, 1998) draws on childhood memories of his father, the football player and coach, Bob Rose, about whom he has also written in a memoir, *Rose Boys* (Allen & Unwin, 2001—his brother, Robert, was also a footballer). See *Rattus Rattus: New and Selected Poems* (Salt, 2005).   CW-C*

Rosenberg, Isaac (1890–1918) Born in Bristol, the son of poor Jewish immigrants from Eastern Europe. The family moved to the East End of London when Rosenberg was seven. He showed early talent as a graphic artist, and on leaving school at the age of fifteen was apprenticed to a firm of engravers. Private and institutional charity from Jewish sources subsequently enabled him to attend the Slade School of Art. During his time there he exhibited a few pictures in various galleries, without much success, and printed and published, with no success whatever, his first small collection of poems, *Night and Day* (1912). The outbreak of the First World War found him in Cape Town, where he had gone in hope of being cured of a serious pulmonary illness. He returned to England early in 1915, enlisted towards the end of that year (he was posted initially to a special unit for undersized recruits, the 'Bantam' battalion of the Suffolk Regiment), and was sent to France six months later. He was killed in action on 1 April 1918.

Throughout his life Rosenberg was undecided as to whether he should devote himself chiefly to his painting or his poetry. Once he had joined the army, the matter was effectively settled for him: it became impossible for him to continue painting, but even in the front line, or just behind it, he could and did go on writing. Today he is best known as a 'war poet'; his name and reputation are indissolubly linked with those of *Sassoon and *Owen; he is seen as one who tried to write realistically, as they did, about life (and death) in the trenches. In fact his mode of writing is as different from theirs as they are from each other. What Sassoon and Owen do have in common is that they are poets of disillusionment; their subject is not just the horrors of trench warfare, but the falsity of the patriotic emotions and the ideas of military glory which, they felt, had made such horrors possible.

Rosenberg, by contrast, appears never to have had any interest in these ideas and emotions, or any illusions about them. As a civilian he had scarcely known anything but penury, isolation, and illness; even the extreme rigours of army and trench life seem, therefore, to have been for him merely a continuation of peace by other means (to adapt von Clausewitz's famous

maxim). As a result he was able to write about his experiences in France with a stoic sensitivity, a mixture of sardonic poise and passionate fellow-feeling, that is distinctively his own. Indeed, something strangely resembling a note of relish is to be found in the handful of poems which keep his name alive today: 'Break of Day in the Trenches', 'Returning, We Hear the Larks', 'Dead Man's Dump', 'The Burning of the Temple', and perhaps a few others. These poems are as bleak and sombre as any to have emerged from the trenches; but the muscularity of their diction and the energy of their vision reveal how much appetite and ambition there was in his nature. At the same time, and no less importantly, they reveal also how great was his capacity for self-detachment.

Isaac Rosenberg (Oxford University Press, 2009), ed. Vivien Noakes, contains all the surviving writings and a selection of paintings and drawings. See also *Selected Poems and Letters*, ed. Jean Liddiard (Enitharmon, 2003).

For biography see *Journey to the Trenches: The Life of Isaac Rosenberg*, by Joseph Cohen (Robson, 1975), *Isaac Rosenberg: the Half Used Life*, by Jean Liddiard (Gollancz, 1975), and *Isaac Rosenberg: The Making of A Great War Poet*, by Jean Moorcroft Wilson (Northwestern University Press, 2009). DJ

🌐 **SEE WEB LINKS**

- A collection of Rosenberg's writing and related documentary material is available online at The First World War Digital Poetry Archive.

Rosenblatt, Joe (Joseph) (1933–)

Born in Toronto, where he grew up in the Kensington Market district and attended Central Technical School. He moved to British Columbia in 1967 and now lives on Vancouver Island. Since 1969 he has edited the literary magazine *Jewish Dialog*.

Launching his career in 1963 with *The Voyage of the Mood*, Rosenblatt has fashioned a distinctive body of work that draws on sound poetry and experiments in typography related to the work of bp *Nichol and bill *bissett. But Rosenblatt's vision is unique in Canadian poetry in its evocations of a unified, eroticized cosmos in which animal life unabashedly celebrates its being. Rosenblatt is also an accomplished artist; his quirky humour is complemented by the delicate line drawings with which he illustrates his work.

The opening section of one of his best known books, *Bumblebee Dithyramb* (1972), re-creates in passionate detail the rituals of a broad range of animal and natural life, including bees, spiders, toads, mantises, fish, cockroaches, a mushroom, a venus flytrap, and various flowers. Drawing resourcefully on typographical experiment and repetition, Rosenblatt's poems about bumblebees are powerful enactments of the bees' sound and sense.

Top Soil (1976—both Porcepic), a selection from several earlier books, won the Governor General's Award and *Poetry Hotel: Selected Poems* (McClelland & Stewart, 1985) won the Dorothy Livesay Poetry Prize. His most recent selected volume is *The Rosenblatt Reader* (Exile, 1995). *The Voluptuous Gardener* (Beach Holme, 1996) includes later poems and examples of his drawings, and *The Lunatic Muse* (Exile, 2007), ed. David Berry, contains his critical prose. See also the autobiographical *Escape from the Glue Factory* (1985) and *The Kissing Goldfish of Siam* (1989—both Exile).   NB

Ross, Alan (1922–2001) Born in Calcutta (now Kolkata) and educated at Haileybury and at St John's College, Oxford. He served in the Royal Navy from 1942 to 1947, his final post being interpreter to the British Naval C-in-C, Germany. After working for the British Council from 1947 to 1950 he was on the staff of the *Observer* from 1950 to 1971, reporting international cricket tours of South Africa, Australia, and the West Indies.

Many of the poems in *The Derelict Day* (Lehmann, 1947) and *Something of the Sea: Poems 1942–1952* (Verschoyle, 1954; Houghton, 1955) reflect Ross' experience of war. The subtitle of the first volume, *Poems from Germany*, points to its theme— the drab, dispirited, and sleazy world of post-war Germany, defeated and occupied. Various poems in the second collection convey with remarkable power every aspect of

life on a warship in the Arctic. 'J. W. 51B A Convoy', while shirking nothing of the pain and horror of a naval battle, celebrates the heroism and the exhilaration that combat at sea may generate. It is unsurpassed by any narrative poem of the Second World War.

In 1961 Ross took over from John *Lehmann the *London Magazine* and, while maintaining its literary standards, gave more space than before to the other arts. In 1986 he edited a selection of the verse and prose from the years of his editorship. Under Ross the magazine was to change from being 'a review of literature' to 'a review of the arts'. Painting, sculpture, music, film, photography, and theatre would all be considered; and it would be designed to have a more noticeable visual effect. 'Gravity...but never solemnity. Astringency but not malice. And at all costs experiment, the hopefulness that the best, even most melancholy art, always must generate, even in despite of itself'—these were what Ross aimed for.

Ross followed his early volumes with *To Whom it may Concern* (Hamilton, 1958), *North from Sicily* (1965), and the substantial *Poems 1942–67* (1968—both Eyre & Spottiswoode). Later collections include *Tropical Ice* (Covent Garden, 1972), *The Taj Express: Poems 1967–73* (1973), *Open Sea* (1975), and *Death Valley* (1980—all London Magazine), a grim evocation of an oppressive landscape. Much of his work displays the immediacy of impressionistic journalism, and of snapshots on a Mediterranean cruise; his best poems attain a fine solidity and depth, especially when they are concerned with people, places, and erotic encounters. His achievements as poet, writer on cricket and travel, editor, and anthologist were recognized by the award of the CBE in 1972.

His four volumes of autobiography were *Blindfold Games* (1986), *The Coastwise Lights* (1988), *Winter Sea* (1997), and *Reflections on Blue Water* (1999). See the posthumous selected volume, *Poems*, ed. David Hughes (2005—all Harvill).   JPr/CKS*

Ross, W. W. E. (William Wrightson Eustace) (1894–1966) Canadian poet and geophysicist, born in Peterborough,

Ontario, and educated at the University of Toronto. Deliberately aloof from the mainstream of Canadian literary life, Ross developed a self-contained and highly private version of a modernist sensibility. His tightly wound, Giacommeti-like *imagist verse began to appear in *Poetry* (Chicago) in 1923 and in the *Dial*. Not a prolific writer, Ross published privately his first collection, *Laconics*, in 1930. This was followed by *Sonnets* (1932), a collection less concentrated in its imagism. For most of his life Ross was content to immerse himself in his work as a scientist at the Dominion Magnetic Observatory, and he distanced himself successfully from his fellow poets until Raymond *Souster published a modestly mimeographed booklet, *Experiment 1923–1929* (1956). The appearance of this crudely produced pamphlet helped to draw attention to the unique quality of Ross' style. He was recognized as a pioneer who had jettisoned the conventional baggage of European literary modernism, and had constructed a poetry of the sparest contemporary forms into which he had worked the sharp images and the frequently lonely echoes of his native land. In 1968, in a collaborative effort, Raymond Souster and J. R. Colombo edited a representative collection of Ross' poetry entitled *Shapes and Sounds: The Poems of W. W. E. Ross* (Longmans), for which Barry Callaghan wrote a 'Memoir'. Callaghan has also edited a later volume for Exile Editions, *Irrealities, Sonnets & Laconics* (2003). *Modern Canadian Poets* (Carcanet, 2010), ed. Evan Jones and Todd Swift, begins with a selection of Ross' work.   MG

Rothenberg, Jerome (1931–) Born in New York City, and educated at City College of New York and the University of Michigan. From 1959 to 1970 he taught in New York, where he was associated with the poet Robert *Kelly; since 1976 he has taught chiefly at the University of California, San Diego, where he is Professor of Visual Arts and Literature.

Rothenberg follows in the footsteps of such figures as *Pound, *Olson, and *Bly as a teacher, anthologizer, and consolidator of an alternative poetic tradition with its own eccentric genealogy, and his work in these roles has tended to overshadow his own poetry. The literary canon that Rothenberg has been developing over the past five decades is a diverse blend of so-called 'primitive' or oral poetries from many cultures, especially the Native American tribes; the twentieth-century literary avant-garde, especially Dadaism and its tributaries; and the entire Jewish tradition from ancient times to the present, Rothenberg's own primary inheritance. In each of these areas he has produced large anthologies that are particularly noteworthy for their innovative presentations of unfamiliar materials. Latterly Rothenberg has been exploring the larger implications of what he terms 'ethnopoetics', investigating ways in which contemporary poetry can draw on the resources of oral and tribal cultures.

Rothenberg's own poetry freely makes use of all these traditions in varying combinations and proportions. His *New Selected Poems 1970–1985* (1986) gathers work from his moving volume *Poland/1931* (1974), devoted to the experience and culture of European Jews; from *A Seneca Journal* (1978), written while Rothenberg was an honorary member of an Indian tribe in upstate New York; and from *That Dada Strain* (1983), a volume that pays homage to the literary experiments of an earlier generation. Yet while each of these books emphasizes a single tradition, each contains elements of the others as well, producing a heady and unpredictable mix of stylistic and thematic ingredients. One of Rothenberg's most interesting formal inventions, derived from his ethnopoetic research, is the 'event' poem, which takes the form of a set of instructions for performing some ritual procedure; he includes a number of these in *Poland/1931*, characteristically adapting a tribal form to Jewish concerns and sensibility.

A Book of Witness: Spells and Gris-Gris (2003) comprised one-hundred first-person poems written at the turn of the century. *Triptych* (2007—all New Directions), introduced by Charles *Bernstein, reprints *Poland/1931* with *Khurbn* (1989), a volume on Rothenberg's family's experience of the

Holocaust, and a new sequence, *The Burning Babe*. With Pierre Joris, he edited the major international anthology of twentieth-century experimentalism, *Poems for the Millennium, vols. 1 and 2* (University of California Press, 1995 and 1998). See also *Writing Through: Translations and Variations* (Wesleyan University Press, 2004), which includes his versions of Paul Celan, Federico Garcia Lorca, and Kurt Schwitters, among others.   RG*

Rowbotham, David (Harold)

(1924–) Born in Toowoomba, Queensland, and served in the RAAF in the Pacific in the Second World War. His first poems appeared in Australian journals in the immediate post-war years and drew attention to a regional poet of lyric talent. Although he published two prose collections (*Town and City: Tales and Sketches*, 1956, and *The Man in the Jungle*, a novel, 1964), it is as a poet that Rowbotham has established himself. His sixth collection, *The Pen of Feathers* (1971), was second prize-winner in the Cook Bicentenary literary competition, and in 1991 he was awarded an Order of Australia. He has also been made an emeritus fellow of the Australia Council in the form of a life pension.

Rowbotham's literary career has been centred in Queensland, where for many years he was literary editor, arts editor, and theatre critic for the *Courier Mail* newspaper. He retired in 1987. Although there is a strong vein of regional colour and tone in his poetry, an overview reveals that Rowbotham has developed a continuing interest in the fields of science, technology, and other aspects of late twentieth-century civilization. Although his writing reveals the metrically conservative influence of his literary precursors in Australia, notably Douglas *Stewart and R. D. *FitzGerald, Rowbotham has become something of a loner, with a doggedly individual if non-flamboyant tone: his characteristic later poetry teases out meanings and resonances from some initial image or 'pretext'. Although sometimes witty and even biting, the poetry maintains an essential seriousness of purpose which refuses to compromise with postmodernist 'play'. It is this very unfashionableness which may in the long term reveal Rowbotham's best poems as enduring and original.

A critical book on his early work by John Stungnell, *Focus on David Rowbotham* (University of Queensland Press) was published in 1969. Since *New and Selected Poems* (Penguin, 1994) his publications include *The Ebony Gates: New and Wayside Poems* (Central Queensland University Press, 1996), *The Cave in the Sky: Poems at Eighty* (2005), and *Rogue Moons* (2007—both Picaro).   TWS

Rowland, J. R. (John Russell) (1925–96)

Born at Armidale, New South Wales, and after joining the Australian Department of Foreign Affairs in 1944, served in London, Washington, Saigon, Malaysia, Paris, Moscow, and other East European countries. He was ambassador in Moscow (1965–8) and Paris (1979–82).

Not surprisingly, Rowland's wide experience during his diplomatic career contributed to the subject-matter of his poetry, much of which is concerned with reflections and observations of the public world that was his daily life for so many years. His poems of family life and personal concerns complement those of the controlled observer, and such poems as 'Canberra in April' and 'At Noosa' have been frequently anthologized.

In the best sense, his are 'occasional' poems which reflect an urbane and sensitive response to a wider range of contacts and experiences than are experienced by many, reflecting a conservative but caring sensibility. His best-known collections are *The Feast of Ancestors* (1965), *The Clock Inside* (1979), and *Sixty* (1989—all Angus & Robertson).   TWS

Ruark, Gibbons (1941–)

Born in Raleigh, North Carolina, the son of a Methodist minister. Ruark was educated at the University of North Carolina and the University of Massachusetts, and since 1968 has taught at the University of Delaware. His first collection, *A Program for Survival* (University Press of Virginia), was a National Arts Council selection in 1971. Subsequent books include *Reeds* (Texas

Tech Press, 1978), *Keeping Company* (Johns Hopkins University Press, 1983), and *Rescue the Perishing* (Louisiana State University Press, 1991). Fred *Chappell has praised Ruark's elegies and love lyrics, noting his 'insistence on the virtues of quietness and simplicity...in noisy and chaotic times'. While the poet has usually favoured subjects drawn from locale and autobiography, he has also written powerful poems of social protest, like 'Nightmare Inspection Tour for American Generals'. The surrealistic title-piece of his first collection describes a close encounter between a UFO and a ring of copulating men and women: 'Let us admire ourselves in the mirroring surface | While the machine is gentled and admires us all'. Travel in Italy, England, and Ireland has provided Ruark with material for poems like 'Basil', 'Miles from Newgrange at the Winter Solstice', and 'North Towards Armagh', which alludes to an IRA terror bombing, the details of which the poet is told are 'no use in my peaceable poems'. Unlike most of his contemporaries, Ruark has successfully experimented with a number of traditional verse-forms, among them the sonnet, *terza rima*, and Sapphics. See also *Passing Through Customs: New and Selected Poems* (Louisiana State University Press, 1999) and *Staying Blue* (Lost Hills, 2008).   RSG

Rubadiri, David (1930–) Born in Malawi (formerly Nyasaland), but educated at King's College, Budo, and Makerere University, both in Uganda. After a period of detention by the British for his opposition to Central African Federation, he spent two years (1960–2) at King's College, Cambridge. Publishing widely, he could already be clearly seen as a pioneer of verse in English by black Africans and was represented as such in the early anthologies of Moore and Beier (1963) and Reed and Wake (1964).

He had other striking gifts, pedagogic and political. In 1964, after Malawi became independent, he was the country's first ambassador to the United States and United Nations. However, his leader, Banda, turned against the young men who had brought him to power and Rubadiri soon began a life as university teacher in exile— back at Makerere, then in Nairobi, with spells in the USA and Nigeria. His warm encouragement of student drama and of younger writers made him a well-loved figure. Eventually, in the Eighties, he found a niche as professor of education at the University of Botswana. After the end of Banda's presidency in the 1990s, Rubadiri returned to his role as UN ambassador, and later became vice-chancellor of the University of Malawi in Zomba.

Rubadiri has published little new creative work since the 1960s. His novel, *No Bride Price* (1967), has attracted critical attention, and his verse is found in many anthologies, including *Poems from East Africa* (1971), which he co-edited with David Cook, and his own selection for secondary schools, *Growing Up With Poetry* (1989— both Heinemann). Such poems as 'African Thunderstorm' achieved wide currency because they show with taste and clarity how English free verse can be applied to African material. Typically, as in this case, Rubadiri confronts a strong subject with symbolic overtones in a posture ultimately derived from the Romantics, though in 'Stanley Meets Mutesa' the echoes are from *Eliot's 'Journey of the Magi'. See *African Thunderstorm and Other Poems* (East African Educational, 2004), with a foreword by the author.   ALRC

Rudman, Mark (1948–) Born in New York City, Rudman returned there to study after a childhood spent in various parts of the United States. He teaches on the Creative Writing Program at New York University.

One of the more experimental poets associated with the *New Narrative movement, Rudman won the National Book Critics Circle Award for *Rider* (1994). Four further books followed in 'The Rider Quintet': *The Millennium Hotel* (1996), *Provoked in Venice* (1999), *The Couple* (2002), and *Sundays on the Phone* (2005— all Wesleyan University Press). Praised for its hybridity of forms, the sequence encompasses lyricism, prose, and dialogue, and extends the *Confessional mode into epic territory (the first book addresses the poet's relationship with his father, the last with his mother). A widely published essayist, he has also translated Boris Pasternark and written a study of Robert *Lowell. See *The Motel En Route to Life Out There: Selections from the Rider Quintet* (Salt, 2007) and *The Book of Samuel: Essays on Poetry and Imagination* (Northwestern University Press, 2009).   JNT

Ruefle, Mary (1952–   ) Born in Pennsylvania into a military family, Ruefle grew up in the United States and Europe. She attended Bennington College, Vermont, and now teaches at Vermont College and Iowa Writer's Workshop.

Since *Memling's Veil* (University of Alberta Press, 1982), Ruefle has published over a dozen books, many with Carnegie Mellon University Press. Also a visual artist who works through the erasure of found texts (see *A Little White Shadow* (2006)), she is fascinated by the variety of desire induced by the material world and its attendant comedy. 'Naked Ladies' lists a miscellany of 'wants', from Wallace *Stevens' wish for 'a crate from Ceylon full of jam' to 'brazen sex at the barbecue party'. Beneath the humour, however, lies a melancholy, as in 'The World As I Left It'. *Selected Poems* (2010) won the William Carlos Williams Award. See also *The Most of It* (2008), a book of prose stories and essays, and *Madness, Rack, and Honey* (2012—all Wave), a collection of lectures.   JNT

Rukeyser, Muriel (1913–80) Born and raised in New York City. She was educated at Vassar College (where her fellow students included Elizabeth *Bishop and Mary McCarthy) and Columbia University, and taught at Sarah Lawrence College. Her non-literary involvements were unusually eclectic, encompassing aviation, science, photography, and above all political activism. In addition to poetry and translations, Rukeyser wrote biographies and children's books.

Rukeyser's work provides a crucial bridge between the politically engaged poetry of the 1930s and the 1960s in America. Like many intellectuals during the Depression, she was strongly involved in left-wing political causes, including the socialist and labour movements and the resistance to fascism in Spain. Her poetry during this period reflects the influence of 'engaged' poets like Horace *Gregory and, especially, W. H. *Auden, whose intricate formal techniques and eccentric diction offered Rukeyser a way to avoid the heavy-handedness of much social protest poetry. Her first book, *Theory of Flight* (Yale University Press, 1935), derived in part from her experience as a novice pilot, received the Yale Younger Poets Award. Subsequent books show a gradual loosening of technique; Whitman begins to replace Auden as a formal model, until by the Sixties she is writing a sweeping, eclectic free verse that inspired younger women like Adrienne *Rich and Anne *Sexton, both of whom acknowledge their debt to Rukeyser. Rukeyser's voice in her late poetry also becomes less mediated, more open and direct in its assumption of responsibility to lessen the world's suffering; in a famous line that has been taken up as a rallying cry for feminist poets, she announced: 'No more masks!' If few of Rukeyser's poems have become anthology pieces, she nevertheless is a key figure in the transformation of women's poetry over the last eighty years.

See *A Muriel Rukeyser Reader* (Norton, 1994), ed. Jan Heller Levi, and *The Collected Poems of Muriel Rukeyser* (University of Pittsburgh Press, 2005), eds. Anne F. Herzog and Janet E. Kaufman, with Jan Heller Levi, which includes unpublished poems as well as her pioneering translations of Octavio Paz. In 2004, Adrienne Rich made a selection of Rukeyser's poetry for the Library of America's American Poets Series. For a range of responses to her work, see *'How Shall We Tell Each Other of the Poet?': The Life and Writing of Muriel Rukeyser* (St Martin's, 1999; repr. Palgrave, 2001), ed. Anne F. Herzog and Janet E. Kaufman.   RG*

Rumens, Carol(-Ann) (1944–   ) Born in London and attended Bedford College, University of London. After working in publicity and advertising she became a freelance writer and poetry editor of *Quarto* and the *Literary Review* (London). She was creative-writing fellow at Kent University,

Canterbury, 1983–5, and Northern Arts Literary Fellow (Newcastle), 1988–90. In 1991 she took up an appointment at Queen's University, Belfast, and has since been Professor of creative writing at the universities of Hull and Bangor.

From the outset (*A Strange Girl in Bright Colours*, Quartet, 1973) Rumens has insisted on the fusion of the personal and the political. Her feminist-socialist perspective has combined with formal versatility to produce work of considerable variety and scope. *Unplayed Music* (1981) and *Star Whisper* (1983—both Secker & Warburg) contain vivid, melancholy, lyrical, and dramatic poems of love and domestic life, with a firm sense of social and political context, while hinting at the theme of exile and atrocity which emerge fully in *Direct Dialling* (Chatto & Windus, 1985). Here Rumens addresses large historical themes ('Revolutionary Women', 'A Jewish Cemetery', 'Outside Osweicim'), and strikes the international note which characterizes her later work. That she has for the most part avoided the pitfalls of this approach—moralizing, abstraction— is due partly to a developing dramatic imagination and also to the sensual particularity which has often distinguished her poems. A visit to Russia produced *The Greening of Snow Beach* (Bloodaxe, 1988), containing some of her most impressive work ('A Moscow Wife, Waiting', 'The Fire Fighter's Widow on her First Memorial Day Outing'). *From Berlin to Heaven* (Chatto & Windus, 1989) charts further travels, while also marking an intriguing and estranged return to English themes.

She has published a novel, *Plato Park* (Chatto & Windus, 1987), and has edited *Making for the Open: The Chatto Book of Post-Feminist Poetry* (new edn., 1988), *New Women Poets* (1990), and the poems of Elizabeth Bartlett (1995). *Selected Poems* (2004) draws on all her collections up to *Hex* (2002), including *Best China Sky* (1995—all Bloodaxe). Two later collections, both from Seren, are *Blind Spots* (2008) and *De Chirico's Threads* (2010). See also *Writing Poetry* (Routledge, 2006) and *Self Into Song* (Bloodaxe, 2007), a series of lectures on con-temporary poets. Since 2007, she has written a popular 'Poem of the Week' column for the *Guardian* newspaper website.   SO'B

Rutsala, Vern (1934–) Born in McCall, Idaho, and educated at Reed College in Portland, Oregon, where he took his BA in 1956. Subsequently he served as an enlisted man in the US Army for two years, then attended the Iowa Writers' Workshop, where he earned an MFA in 1960. Rutsala has spent his entire academic career at Lewis and Clark College in Portland, except for visiting appointments at the University of Minnesota and Minneapolis and Bowling Green State University in Ohio. He is now retired.

With his first book, *The Window* (1964), Rutsala had already developed the style that has continued to run through all his work, even the book of prose (but not prosaic) poems titled *Paragraphs* (1978—both Wesleyan University Press). Characteristic elements include: statements laid out in prose lines; images that might best be described as 'a surrealism of the everyday'; an existential stolidity in the face of the incursions of time and the world upon our minds and bodies; a sense of the idiocy of it all, of self-satire.

Small Songs (Stone Wall, 1969), a sequence of epigrams, *The Harmful State* (Best Cellar, 1971), and *The New Life* (Trask, 1978) were all chapbooks. Rutsala continued, in *Laments* (New Rivers, 1975), *The Journey Begins* (University of Georgia Press, 1976), and *Walking Home from the Icehouse* (Carnegie Mellon University Press, 1981) to force the reader to see himself clearly, but the poet's sadistic good humour took the edge off the pain. In 1985 Rutsala published two collections, a book, *Backtracking* (Story Line), and a chapbook, *The Mystery of Lost Shoes* (Lynx House). *Selected Poems*, published by Story Line Press in 1991, was followed by *Little-Known Sports* (University of Massachusetts Press, 1994). In 2004, he published *The Moment's Equation* (Ashland), which was nominated for a National Book Award, and *A Handbook for Writers: New and Selected Prose Poems* (White Pine).   LT

Ryan, Gig (Elizabeth) (1956–) Born in Melbourne, Australia. From 1978 she lived mainly in Sydney, where she was instrumental in forming a band, Disband, whose album *Six Goodbyes* was released in 1988. She now lives in Melbourne again, where she completed a BA in classical languages, sings in the band Driving Past, and is poetry editor of *The Age*.

Her first book of poems, *The Division of Anger* (Transit, 1981), established her as an abrasive and vivid new writer. Her subsequent verse collections, *Manners of an Astronaut* (Hale & Iremonger, 1984) and *Excavation* (Picador, 1990) have been equally commanding, and disturbing. The poet and critic Martin *Johnston early on described her writing as 'hallucinatory', but it is also concerned with an increasingly sophisticated manipulation of heard speech, especially the staccato and disjointed speech of inner cities and the environment of rock bands and the drug culture. The politics of sex, power, and the victim mentality remain her chief concerns, though her most recent work gives hints of an abiding lyrical impulse beneath the habitual stance of aggressive, hurt bravado.

Ryan's poetry is widely studied in schools and universities in Australia. *Pure and Applied* (Paper Bark, 1998) won the C. J. Dennis Prize for Poetry. *New and Selected Poems* (Giramondo, 2011; Bloodaxe, 2012) draws on six collections, including *Research* (Salt, 1998) and *Heroic Money* (Brandl & Schlesinger, 2001).   TWS

Ryan, Kay (1945–) Born in San Jose, California, Ryan studied at the University of California and began, but did not finish, a PhD. She has lived in Marin County since 1971, where she taught remedial English at a community college for many years. She served as the United States Poet Laureate from 2008 to 2010.

Ryan has said that she decided to become a poet during a four-thousand-mile bicycle trip in 1976. Her first collection, *Dragon Acts to Dragon Ends* (Taylor Street, 1983), was self-published. Her second, *Strangely Marked Metal*, appeared from Copper Beech Press in 1985. It was another decade before her work began to

be noticed nationally. *Flamingo Watching* (Copper Beech, 1994) received prize nominations, and has been followed by three collections with Grove Press.

Ryan's brief, compact poems make pointed use of short lines and internal rhyme, which she calls 'recombinant rhyme'. The effect is described and performed by 'Bait Goat': 'there is a | distance where | words attract. | Set one out | like a bait goat | and wait'. Her quizzical formalism and patiently extended metaphors have been compared to Emily Dickinson and Marianne *Moore. There is a wise-cracking wit and populist oddity to her imagery as well (see 'Sharks' Teeth') which testifies to her early use of *Ripley's Believe It or Not!* as a source of inspiration. *The Best of It: New and Selected Poems* (Grove, 2010) won the 2011 Pulitzer Prize for Poetry. See also, in the UK, *Odd Blocks: Selected and New Poems* (Carcanet, 2011).   JNT

Ryan, Michael (1945–) Born in St Louis, Missouri. He studied at Notre Dame University and Claremont Graduate School, and gained an MFA and PhD from the University of Iowa. Ryan's first volume, *Threats Instead of Trees* (Yale University Press, 1974), won the Yale Series of Younger Poets Award. He has since published two volumes of poetry, *In Winter* (Holt, 1981, selected by Louise Glück for the National Poetry Series) and *God Hunger* (Penguin, 1989). He has received numerous prizes for poetry, including fellowships from the National Endowment for the Arts and the Guggenheim Foundation. Ryan has also supported himself by teaching at such institutions as the University of Iowa (where he was an editor of *The Iowa Review*), Southern Methodist University, Goddard College (where he directed the writing programme in 1978–9), Warren Wilson College, and the University of California, Irvine. A practitioner of the meditation-inverse and the self-presentational lyric, Ryan attempts to infuse the commonplace with mystery and drama through conversational free verse and, on occasion, traditional forms. See also *New and Selected Poems* (Houghton, 2004), which won the Kingsley Tufts Poetry Award, *A Difficult Grace: On*

Poets, Poetry, and Writing (University of Georgia Press, 2000), a book of essays, and *Secret Life* (Pantheon, 1995), an autobiography.   RMCD

Ryan, Tracy (1964–   ) Born in Perth, Western Australia, and attended Curtin University and the University of Western Australia. She is a poet, novelist, editor, and translator. She has lived in the UK and in Ohio, USA, as well as Western Australia. At UWA she studied European languages, an interest which has continued in her poetry translations, especially from the French. With her husband, the poet John *Kinsella, she collaborated on editing *Salt* magazine and the development of the international publishing imprint Folio/Salt (now Salt Publishing). She was editor of the Fremantle Arts Review from 1993 to 1996.

Critic Tim Allen describes her poems as 'tightly packed vibrations of spiky conceits. They have a restless intelligence which seems to suspect everything they touch; the references are scholarly and the contention is feminist but the result is polychromatic'. Her first collection, *Killing Delilah* (Fremantle), appeared in 1994, and she has since published nine further collections, winning several prizes, including the Australian Book Review Poetry Prize in 2009 and the 2000 Western Australian Premier's Book Awards Prize for Poetry. Ryan has also published three novels, *Vamp* (1997), *Jazz Tango* (2002), and *Sweet* (2008—all Fremantle), and a collection of short stories, *Conspiracies* (Salt, 2003).   ACr

Sacks, Peter (1950–) Born in Port Elizabeth, South Africa and grew up in Durban. Previously a professor at Johns Hopkins University, he now teaches English and writing at Harvard University, and is married to the poet Jorie *Graham.

Sacks writes a strong, clear-sighted poetry that is deeply rooted in place. But if the poems begin in particular locales, the poet's meditative intelligence soon brings the moral topography into view. In his first collection, *In These Mountains* (Macmillan, 1985), Sacks manifested his characteristic concerns—with romantic love, memory, political accountability, and the spiritual impulse—but managed to sustain a subdued lyricism throughout. The title-poem, an imaginative re-creation of the lives of the Bushmen of the Kalahari, summons up the void left behind after their all-but total eradication, but does so in an elegiac manner. The poet hears: 'no bird cry, | no river sound, no spirits travelling quickly | with their quivers under the cold drift of stars, | their bone-chip rattles and their voices | streaming in the darkness and the wind.'

Promised Lands (Viking/Penguin, 1990), Sacks' second collection, reveals a perceptibly more stringent vision. While the majority of the poems are bound to locale—notably the sequence 'States' which surveys the American terrain—Sacks is more inclined than before to historical, mythic, and religious speculation. The result is that the sensuous particulars encountered in the first book recede to make place for more emblematic treatment of subject. Place is not so much seen for itself as seen *through*. A starkly beautiful natural world is also a place for moral and spiritual self-reckoning. In his powerful long poem 'Alaska', Sacks concludes: 'Between destruction and redemption | we who know nothing of purity except the word, | move through the waters, | move into the fire no breath can name, | the fire that will not say *it is enough* | until we breathe again.' His later collections are: *Natal Command* (Chicago University Press, 1998), *O Wheel* (Georgia University Press, 2000), and *Necessity* (Norton, 2002).

Sacks is also the author of *The English Elegy: Studies in the Genre from Spenser to Yeats* (1985). SPB

Sackville-West, Vita (Victoria Mary Sackville-West) (1892–1962) Born into a wealthy and aristocratic family and brought up at Knole, the ancestral home of the Sackville family. She became a prolific novelist and biographer, but never shook off the air of a dilettante and is best remembered for her literary friendships (notably with Virginia Woolf), her well-documented marriage to writer and diplomat Harold Nicolson, and her expertise as a creative gardener. The garden she made with Nicolson at their home, Sissinghurst Castle, became the subject for many gardening books in the later years of her life. Her reputation as a poet rests on *The Land*, a popular success ever since its publication in 1926, which relates at length (2,500 lines) and in the first-person the cycle of a farming year in Kent. The poem was deliberately anti-modernist and provincial, using regular iambic lines and archaic diction, but was not deliberately modelled on Virgil's *Georgics*, of which the author was ignorant. A better poem, started soon after publication of *The Land* but not finished until 1946, is *The Garden*, also a long poem, but by no means so artificial. It was in effect a treatise on gardening, and also a meditation, written in time of war and expressive of an inner landscape as well as a realized, physical one. Sackville-West published several volumes of verse privately, and *King's Daughter* (1929) with the Hogarth Press. *Collected Poems* (*vol. 1*) appeared in 1933 and *Selected Poems* in 1941 (both Hogarth). There was no second volume of *Collected Poems*.

See also Victoria Glendinning, *Vita, The Life of Vita Sackville-West* (Weidenfeld & Nicolson, 1983) and *Selected Writings* (Palgrave, 2002), ed. Mary Ann Caws.   CPH

Sadoff, Ira (1945–) Born in Brooklyn, New York. His father abandoned the family when Sadoff was thirteen. Sadoff attended Cornell University and did postgraduate work at the University of Oregon. He served as the founding editor of the literary magazine, the *Seneca Review*, and poetry editor of the *Antioch Review* during the 1970s. He is currently professor of English at Colby College in Maine. Although his first book of poems, *Settling Down* (1975), was positively received, Sadoff's initial style now seems dated. Influenced by the *Deep Image style popularized in the early Seventies, Sadoff's early work emphasized a mix of the transcendental and absurdist functions of surrealism. By the time of his second book, *Palm Reading in Winter* (1978—both Houghton Mifflin), however, Sadoff's work had changed, and was characterized by its discursive intelligence, as well as its responsiveness to the demands of personal history and memory. The same can be said of *Emotional Traffic* (1991) published by Godine.

Family life and the frailty and complexity of family roles and relationships were among Sadoff's most prominent subjects and themes during this middle period. Many poems, including 'Meditation' and 'The Vacation in Miami: July, 1954', explored confusion, guilt, and anger from the point of view of a boy abandoned by his father. Sadoff's poems drift between dream-like uncertainties and moments of absolute, often terrifying clarity as his adolescent speakers come into self-consciousness.

In the later work, Sadoff's poems become simultaneously more social and formally adventurous, making use of long Whitmanesque lines, collage, and other postmodern techniques to extend his long-term interest in American politics and culture. In both *Grazing* (1998) and *Barter* (2003—both University of Illinois Press), Sadoff serves as a political witness of poetry, and he continues to critique class structure (often in ironic or humorous tones), the irony being especially pointed towards the socially privileged. His later work dramatizes the poem as journey and discovery, emphasizing flux and the instability of the self; wide-ranging shifts of diction and tone often occur within the body of a single poem.

He published a critical book on aesthetics and culture, *History Matters: Contemporary Poetry on the Margins of American Culture*, with the University of Iowa Press in 2009; a new collection of poems, *True Faith*, geared towards a sceptical metaphysics, was published by BOA Editions in 2012.   TSW

Sail, Lawrence (1942–) Born in London. He read French and German at St John's College, Oxford, and taught in Kenya for five years before moving to Exeter, where he taught until 1991. He edited the magazine *South West Review* for nearly five years, and compiled the anthology *First and Always: Poems for Great Ormond Street Children's Hospital* (Faber, 1988). He has been chairman of the Arvon Foundation and was programme director of the Cheltenham Festival of Literature in 1991.

Sail is a taut and sinewy poet, drawn to the epiphanies of nature, particularly the sea, and the sacraments of personal life. There is a development from the poems in *Opposite Views* (Dent, 1974), which attempt, often successfully, to catch the voice of the times—titles such as 'Consumer Poems', 'Curriculum Vitae', 'Report from the Planet Proteus' give the flavour—to the more intense, sometimes religious, poems of *Devotions* (1987). His second book was *The Kingdom of Atlas* (1980—both Secker & Warburg). *Waking Dreams: New and Selected Poems* (2010) draws on three collections since *Out of Land: New and Selected Poems* in 1992: *Building Into Air* (1995), *The World*

Returning (2002), and *Eye-Baby* (2006—all Bloodaxe).

Sail's poems are usually short to medium-length. His descriptions are pithy, crisp, sometimes witty in the *Martian manner. In his mature work even the secular occasions are sacramental: 'Snooker Players' celebrates the Newtonian simplicity and perfection of the game, counterpointing the murkiness of the fallen world beyond the illuminated table; 'Allotments' are seen as the 'last real estate of common prayer'. See also *Cross-currents* (Enitharmon, 2005), a collection of essays, and *Sift* (Impress, 2010), a childhood memoir.   PF

St John, David (1949–) Born in California. He has taught in the writing seminars of Johns Hopkins University and now teaches at the University of Southern California. In St John's lyrics there is a fusion of *confessional, meditative, epistolary, and narrative elements. In 'Dolls' and 'You', from *Hush* (1976), the over-valued desire for individuality is posed against the desire for romantic communion; as the two desires violate one another, each lover has the choice of betraying either one's self or one's mate. This conflict is further explored in St John's later, more ambitious books.

Lyrical and extravagantly emblematic, 'Of the Remembered', a long poem from *The Shore* (1980), is a postmodern reply to *Eliot's *Four Quartets*; it is an effort to find a redemption through memory and language. A prismatic sequence of related dramatic monologues and cinematic vignettes, *No Heaven* (1985—all Houghton) is a powerful presentation of a more fragmented and troubled spirituality, confronting the seductive delusions of godless desire, and finding that antique faiths may be absurd, or impossible to embrace. 'The Man with the Yellow Gloves' is a parable of how the self may become disfigured by appropriating obsolete ancestral spirits.

Study for the World's Body: New and Selected Poems (HarperCollins, 1994) was a finalist for the National Book Award. St John's later collections include *The Red Leaves of Night* (1999), *The Face: A Novella in Verse* (2004), and *The Auroras* (2012—all HarperCollins). See also *Where the Angels*

Come Towards Us (White Pine, 1995), a collection of interviews and essays on contemporary figures such as Jorie *Graham and Charles *Wright. With Cole *Swensen, he edited the *American Hybrid* anthology (Norton, 2009).   DWF

Salkey, Andrew (1928–95) Born in Colón, Panama, of Jamaican parents. He was educated at St George's College and Munro College in Jamaica, and at the University of London, and was an associate professor of writing at Hampshire College, Amherst, Massachusetts.

Though better known for his novels, Salkey published much poetry until his death. Political commitment, very much from a leftist perspective, dominates his poems, but they rise above purely ideological rhetoric. They accentuate personal allegiances, avoid tendentiousness, and are generally tough-minded. Consequently many are occasional in nature, addressed or dedicated to friends. His 'postcard' poems, particularly, make the primacy of the personal clearly evident, 'sent', as their titles indicate, from such developing countries as Mexico, Brazil, and Uganda, and each is precisely dated. Other poems express considerable unease at his comfortable 'exile'. 'I Never Left', for instance, ends with 'I left the island | I never left'.

His books of poems include *Jamaica* (Hutchinson, 1973), a long, historical work in verse, *In the Hills Where Her Dreams Live* (Casa de las Américas, 1979), and *Away* (Allison & Busby, 1980). Two of his best novels are *A Quality of Violence* (1959) and *The Late Emancipation of Jerry Stover* (1968).   MR

Sallah, Tijan Momodou (1958–) Born in Sere Kunda, Gambia. Sallah studied Business Management and Economics at Berea College, Kentucky, USA and graduated with a PhD from Virginia Polytechnic Institute. He joined the World Bank in 1989 and is currently manager of the Capacity Development and Partnerships Unit of the African region.

Sallah has published four volumes of poetry and edited two anthologies of African poetry: *When Africa was a Young*

Woman (Writers Workshop, 1980), *Kora Land: Poems from West Africa* (Three Continents, 1989), *Dreams of Dusty Roads* (Rienner, 1993), *Dream Kingdom: New and Selected Poems* (Africa World Press, 2007), *New Poets of West Africa* (Malthouse, 1995), and *The New African Poetry* (Rienner, 2000).

Sallah's poems have a deep sense of place and time, for they are located in the Gambia and often refer to an earlier time. Even when he is writing about the USA or Britain it is as if he has his feet planted there and his eyes looking elsewhere. In 'Meditation on America' and 'The Evaded Mood' he comments on American manners and culture but as an alien, the Other, who is eavesdropping. This quality of alienation, perhaps also of regret, pervades his writing about Africa too.   FO

Salom, Philip (1950–) Born near Perth and grew up on a dairy farm at Brunswick Junction in the south-west of Western Australia. After graduating from an agricultural college he worked in New Zealand, before returning to Western Australia to study, and later teach, creative writing.

Salom has won Commonwealth poetry awards for his first book, *The Silent Piano* (1980) and his third, *Sky Poems* (1987). The environment of the dairy farm and its 'natural' activities links Salom's first book with those of other Australian rural poets such as Les *Murray and David *Campbell. But Salom's imagination is not restricted to observed detail and ranges very widely: the title-poem of his first volume tells how a prisoner 'escapes' his confinement by making a silent piano from old bits of wood.

Salom's second volume, *The Projectionist* (1983—all Fremantle Arts Centre) develops the character of a country-town projectionist, using the device for a variety of cinematic effects. In the *livre composé*, *Sky Poems*, the poetic self is very mobile, displaying an audacious range of imagery and speculation, questioning settled notions of subject and object. In *The Barbecue of the Primitives* (University of Queensland Press, 1989) a wide-ranging, original intelligence at times recalls Peter *Porter's poetry.

Feeding the Ghost (1993) and *The Rome Air Naked* (1996—both Penguin) were fol-

lowed by a *New and Selected Poems* (1998) from Fremantle Arts Centre Press. See also *A Cretive Live*, a book of poems about art and memory inspired by a misprint, and *The Well-Mouth* (2005—both Fremantle Arts Centre), a 'verse-novel of sorts'. Salom has also written two novels: *Playback* (1991) and *Toccata & Rain* (2004). In 2003 he received the Christopher Brennan Award for lifetime achievement.   BB

Salter, Mary Jo (1954–) Born in Grand Rapids, Michigan, and grew up in Baltimore, Maryland. She was educated at Harvard and has two daughters, Emily and Hilary. Salter lived for several years in Kyoto, then in Rome, London, Reykjavik, and Paris. She is now a professor in the writing seminars at Johns Hopkins University.

Like her teacher Elizabeth *Bishop, Salter values craftsmanship and is known for her rhymed lyric poems. Her poems colour a world of 'Order gloved as Beauty', while constantly subverting elements we count on most as safe and innocent: home, family, and even art. To think of Salter as a placid or comfortable poet is to misunderstand her. Though her range may exclude anger, there is frustration and joy, gratitude and grief. Her subjects range from family life to grittier world topics with fluency. Since *Henry Purcell in Japan* (1985), Salter has published five further collections of poetry, most recently *A Phone Call to the Future: New and Selected Poems* (2008). She has also written a children's book, *The Moon Comes Home* (1989—all Knopf), is co-editor of *The Norton Anthology of Poetry*, and has edited a selection of the poems of Amy *Clampitt (Knopf, 2010).   HC

Sampson, Fiona (1968–) Born in London. She studied at the Royal Academy of Music and, after a short career as a concert violinist, the University of Oxford. Her literary interests are diverse but spring from the same core of commitment to poetry as the fundamental form of imaginative and intellectual discourse. Besides pioneering the uses of creative writing in health-care, she was founder-editor of the journal of contemporary European writing, *Orient*

Express, and edited *Poetry Review* from 2005 to 2012. Her fifteen published volumes include literary criticism, studies of creative-writing theory and practice, and translations of poetry by Jaan Kaplinsky and Amir.Or. Her significant volumes of original poetry are *Folding the Real* (2001), *The Distance Between Us* (2005—both Seren), *Common Prayer* (2007), and *Rough Music* (2010—both Carcanet). The latter two collections were shortlisted for the T. S. Eliot Prize.

Sampson's interest in metaphysics is a unifying feature of all her collections. Her philosophical intelligence is mediated both by her curiosity about the world and by her musicality, resulting in poetry which is finely nuanced, but grounded and wide-ranging. Her poetic strategy seems increasingly concerned with notating the fractured and delicate harmonies made by the duet of language and silence.   CAR

Samuels, Lisa (1963–) Born in Boston, Massachusetts, and educated at the universities of North Carolina and Virginia, where she wrote a PhD on Wallace *Stevens and Laura *Riding. Samuels describes herself as an internationalist poet, having lived in various parts of the world, including the United States, the Middle East, Sweden, and latterly New Zealand, where she teaches literature and creative writing at the University of Auckland. Her published works include six books of poetry, among them *The Invention of Culture* (2008), *Tomorrowland* (2009), *Gender City* (2011), and *Wild Dialectics* (2012—all Shearsman).

As their titles suggest, these works are often charged with an energy born of itinerancy; her poems approach horizons of understanding through critical experiments with lyric voice, keeping meaning in constant motion: 'The object of my nature is triumvirate | circumscribed by anxious latitudes.' Samuels also edited Riding's *Anarchism Is Not Enough* (1928) for the University of California Press in 2001, and has spoken admiringly of Riding's 'rigor, absolutism, hunger, present-ness-of-voice-as-not-a-social-self, anger,

adamance, [and] energetic eschatology (rather than broken-hearted cultural despair)'.   NH

Sanchez, Sonia (1934–) Born in Birmingham, Alabama, and educated at Hunter College, New York. Graduate work in poetry with Louise *Bogan at New York University was followed by growing involvement in the civil-rights and *Black Arts movements. Her first collection, *Home-coming* (Broadside, 1969), was notable for its political militancy, its commitment to the black community and scorn for 'white America', and for its daring use of African-American rhythms and language. Combining political activism with an energetic career as writer and teacher, Sanchez has taught at many universities, including Rutgers, Pennsylvania, and Temple, where she was Laura Carnell Professor of English and Women's Studies. Her interest in developing an understanding of their African inheritance among young black people is reflected in her several books for children, among them *It's A New Day* (1971) and *A Sound Investment* (1986); while she has also produced significant autobiographical work, most notably the prose-poem collection *homegirls & handgrenades* (Thunder's Mouth, 1984; new edn., White Pine, 2007).

In her poetry of the last five decades Sanchez has restructured conventional grammatical forms in order to dramatize black speech rhythms: *We a BaddDDD People* (Broadside, 1970) best illustrates her experiments with sound, idiom, and grammar. *Love Poems* (Third Press, 1973) records some of the more intimate details of the poet's life as woman, lover, and mother. In 1972 Sanchez joined the Nation of Islam and, although she resigned three years later, her 1973 volume, *A Blues Book for Blue Black Magical Women* openly supports that movement while offering a statement on the historical condition of black women. *I've Been A Woman: New and Selected Poems* (Black Scholar, 1981) is a useful selection of her work. Information on her life and writing may be found in *Black Women Writers (1950–1980): A Critical Evaluation*, ed. Mari Evans (Anchor/Doubleday, 1984). Sanchez has received many honours for her work, including the Langston Hughes Award and the Robert Frost Medal. Since 1995 her poetry has been published by Beacon Press: see *Shake Loose My Skin: New and Selected Poems* (1999) and *Morning Haiku*. In 2012 she became Poet Laureate of Philadelphia.   RJG

Sandburg, Carl (1878–1967) Born in Galesburg, Illinois, and lived mostly in Chicago. He is now best remembered for his monumental biography of Abraham Lincoln, but there was a period in the early 1920s when his reputation as a poet was extensive in America and growing in England. The young Rebecca West was one of his early admirers and introduced a selection of his work for Jonathan Cape. Nevertheless, with a brief revival during the period of the *Beat generation (with whom he had little in common), Sandburg has largely dropped from sight.

This is a pity. Sandburg's poetry retains two claims on our attention. As Daniel *Hoffman pointed out, Sandburg was the first important American writer to grow up in a household where English was the second language—the first was Swedish—and this gives his approach to rhythm and diction something more than idiosyncrasy. William Carlos *Williams broke the grip of the iambic line with more subtlety, but Sandburg smashed it open with greater naturalness. Poems like 'Skyscraper' and 'Cool Tombs' offer the paragraph as a verse unit in a way that no one had quite done before, not even Whitman.

The rhythms of Sandburg, refined by his wide experience as a reader of his own verse in public, have still to be fully assimilated, though they echo in poets like C. K. *Williams and Philip *Levine. But the subject-matter of his large opus is perhaps more important. In the age of Dreiser and Sinclair Lewis, Sandburg was the only poet who offered a full portrait of the industrial scene, managing some sort of challenge in verse to the sweep and range of the Zola-esque novel. What Sandburg often catches is the tacky bravura and breezy sentimentality of his midwest subjects, a sense of pulsating energy still unsure of itself and sometimes lapsing into the maudlin, the vicious, or the grotesque. Poems like 'Mag', 'Grass', and 'Fog' illustrate the sketchbook vitality of this kind of work.

The Complete Poems of Carl Sandburg (Harcourt, Brace, 1950) won him a Pulitzer Prize. A revised and expanded edition from 1970 was reprinted in 2003. There is, alas, no selection in print in England; but see *Carl Sandburg: His Life and Works*, by North Callahan (Pennsylvania State University Press, 1987). Those visiting Chicago should seek out the Carl Sandburg Village, a memorial sequence of skyscrapers on the site of the St Valentine's Day Massacre.   GMacB

Sant, Andrew (1950–   ) Born in London and educated in both England and Australia. Although he has frequently returned to England for extended visits, Sant has spent much of his early life in Hobart, Tasmania, where until 1990 he co-edited the literary magazine *Island*. He has worked in a number of occupations, including the management of a hostel for juvenile delinquents, labouring for the Forestry Commission, and teaching. In 1989 he was made a member of the literature board of the Australia Council, and has held university writing residencies in England and China.

Sant's poetry is notable for its quizzical and analytic teasing out of resonances from initial (and graphic) evocations of such universal endeavours as bee-keeping, apple-growing, kelp-harvesting, and wine-making. His earlier work was to a certain extent indebted to such English models as *Hughes and *Larkin, but the stimulus of the Tasmanian environment led him to hone his spare and contemplative style to a new precision, though underlying his close attention to detail is a sophisticated poet's 'raid on reality' in order to bring back multiple possibilities and a continuing search for clarification.

His major collections include *The Caught Sky* (1982), *The Flower Industry* (1985—both Angus & Robertson), *Brushing the Dark* (Heinemann, 1989), *Album of Domestic Exiles* (1997), and *Russian Ink* (2001). In 2004 he published *Tremors: New and Selected Poems* (all Black Pepper) in Australia and *The Unmapped Page: Selected Poems*

(Arc) in the UK. See also *Speed & Other Liberties* (Salt, 2008).   TWS

Sarah, Robyn (1949–   ) Born in New York City, Sarah grew up in Montreal. She studied at Conservatoire de Musique du Québec and McGill University, taught English for many years, and is now a freelance writer and editor. She lives in Quebec.

Sarah has said that her poems, in both free and formal verse, usually begin with 'tinder words'—moments of everyday language that develop into meditations. 'Make much of something small', as she says in 'Bounty'. The first of eight collections of poetry, *Shadowplay* (1978), appeared from Fiddlehead Poetry Books in 1978. In 1992, Anansi Press published a new and selected volume, *The Touchstone*. See also *Questions About the Stars* (Brick, 1998), *A Day's Grace: Poems 1997–2002* (Porcupine's Quill, 2003), and *Pause for Breath* (2009). She has also written two collections of short stories and a book of 'thoughts on poetry', *Little Eurekas* (2007—both Biblioasis).   JNT

Saroyan, Aram (1943–   ) Born in New York City to writer William Saroyan and actress Carol Grace.

Between 1964 and 1965, Saroyan edited the periodical *Lines*, which included contributions from Ian Hamilton *Finlay, Bernadette *Mayer, Lorine *Niedecker, Robert *Grenier, as well as Saroyan's own 'minimal' poems, recently collected in *The Complete Minimal Poems* (Ugly Duckling, 2007).

Although the bent of Saroyan's early poems shows the influence of Robert *Creeley and Finlay, he claims that his typewriter, 'an obsolete red-top Royal Portable,' is the biggest influence on this work: 'The red hood hold[s] the mood, keeps my eye happy. The type-face is a standard pica; if it were another style I'd write (subtly) different poems.' His one-word poem 'lighght' caused considerable controversy after being chosen for a National Endowment for the Arts Poetry Award by Robert *Duncan in 1968.

Saroyan's involvement with the writers' community in Bolinas in the 1970s and 1980s comprises the subject of the largely autobiographical poems collected in *Day and Night: Bolinas Poems* (Black Sparrow, 2001). Their unaffected style shows Saroyan's increasing interest in prose, which is represented by a number of books, including *The Street: An Autobiographical Novel* (Bookstore, 1974), *Genesis Angels: The Saga of Lew Welch and the Beat Generation* (1979), *Last Rites* (1982—both Morrow), and *Door to the River: Essays and Reviews from the 1960s into the Digital Age* (Black Sparrow, 2010).   ROH

Sarton, (Eleanor) May (1912–95) Born in Belgium and taken to America in 1916; after a partly Belgian education she was naturalized as an American in 1924. She won a readership less for her technical skill than for her (as she put it) 'unbuttoned ego'. Apart from many love poems, she wrote observantly (and most successfully) on nature, on paintings and artists, and writers (her novel about F. O. Matthiessen, *Faithful Are the Wounds*, is regarded as one of her most notable achievements). Her greatest debt is to *Millay, in whose tradition she wrote; but she lacked Millay's bite and ability to end a poem. Her verse none the less gives pleasure at a certain level, was awarded many prizes, and sounds an authentic emotional note.

Collected Poems 1930–1993 (Norton, 1993) was followed by *Coming Into Eighty* (1994—both Norton). She also published many novels and selections from her journals. Her selected letters, edited by Susan Sherman, have appeared in two volumes. See also *A House of Gathering: Poets on May Sarton's Poetry* (University of Tennessee Press, 1993), ed. Marilyn Kallett, and Margot Peters, *May Sarton: A Biography* (Knopf, 1997). Mark K. Fulk, *Understanding May Sarton* (University of South Carolina Press, 2001) evaluates her pioneering importance as a feminist and lesbian writer.   MS-S*

Sassoon, Siegfried (Loraine) (1886–1967) The son of a rich Jewish father and an Anglican mother, he was educated at Marlborough and at Clare College, Cambridge, where he failed to take a degree. In the years before 1914 he enjoyed hunting, golf, and cricket, read widely, and issued privately a number of small verse collections, of which the most accomplished was *The Daffodil Murderer* (1913), published under the pseudonym of Saul Kain. Begun as a parody of *Masefield's *The Everlasting Mercy*, it developed into a serious poem in which, Sassoon remarked, 'I was at last writing physically'.

Sassoon, who had joined up on the first day of the war, won the MC during the Somme offensive of July 1916. But by then he had begun to write what he called real trench poems; and in July 1917, having thrown his MC into the Mersey, he protested publicly against the continuation of the war. He was persuaded by Robert *Graves to enter the Military Hospital at Craiglockhart, where he became friends with his fellow-patient Wilfred *Owen. He was discharged, returned to active service, received a head wound, but survived the war.

Sassoon's war poems were published in *The Old Huntsman* (1917) and *Counter-Attack* (1918). Some describe with horrifying detail the nature of trench-warfare: the filth, the stench of decomposing corpses, the rats, the moral degradation. Others satirize the brass-hats and their apparent indifference to the futility of their military operations. The most ferocious lash civilians in Britain who delude themselves with jokes and slogans about the war.

In 1919 Sassoon became literary editor of the socialist *Daily Herald*, and in 1923 his *Satirical Poems* attacked conservative politicians and plutocracy. But 'At the Grave of Henry Vaughan', written in 1924, points in a new direction: 'And this lowly grave tells Heaven's tranquillity | And here stand I, a suppliant at the door.' For years afterwards Sassoon's poetry mirrors his spiritual desolation and his search for the peace that he found at last in the Roman Catholic faith to which he was converted in 1957, and which inspired a number of unpublished devotional poems.

In 1928 Sassoon published *Memoirs of a Fox-Hunting Man*, the first of six prose autobiographies of which the last, *Siegfried's Journey* (1945), carried the story to 1920. His study of Meredith was published in 1948.

Sassoon valued his later poems more highly than his war poems, which were, he said, 'improvised by an impulsive, intolerant, immature young creature under the extreme stress of experience'. Nevertheless, they are the poems by which he is most likely to be remembered and honoured.

Rupert Hart-Davis has edited three volumes of Sassoon's diaries covering the years 1915 to 1925, *Letters to Max Beerbohm* (1986), and *War Poems* (1983—all Faber), which includes seven poems from periodicals and thirteen from manuscripts.

See also *Collected Poems* 1908–56 (Faber, 1961, 1984); Michael Thorpe, *Siegfried Sassoon: A Critical Study* (Oxford University Press 1961); Dame Felicity Corrigan, *Siegfried Sassoon: A Poet's Pilgrimage* (Gollancz, 1973); and Jean Moorcroft Wilson's two-volume biography, *Siegfried Sassoon: The Making of a War Poet* (Taylor & Francis, 2005).   JPr

Scalapino, Leslie (1947–2010) Leslie Scalapino's father founded Berkeley's Institute of East Asian Studies, and as a child, she travelled around the world with her family. Travel and Buddhism are themes in her writing which draw out its sympathies with *Beat poetry, although she was more often associated with the *Language poets. After studying at Reed College and University of California, Berkeley, she taught writing for many years, including sixteen years at Bard College. She wrote poetry, prose, and plays, and was a founding member of the charitable group, Poets in Need, as well as the editor of O Books, publishing nearly a hundred titles. She also edited the poems of Philip *Whalen.

Scalapino's first collection was *O and Other Poems* (Sand Dollar, 1976). She described the motivation of her work as a 'continual conceptual rebellion'. The characteristically disrupted flow of sequence in such volumes as *that they were at the beach—aeolotropic series* (1985), *way* (1988—both North Point), and *Crowd and not evening or light* (O Books, 1992) expresses a reflexive restlessness in the narrative act. *The Return of Painting, The Pearl, and Orion* (North Point, 1991) is a trilogy of experimental novels; *Sight* (Edge, 1999) a collaboration with Lyn *Hejinian; and *R-hu* (Atelos, 2000) recounts a journey across the Gobi desert.

Scalapino's selected poems, *It's go in horizontal*, was published by University of California Press in 2008. An expanded edition of her essays and plays, *How Phenomena Appear to Unfold*, appeared in 2011 from Litmus Press.   JNT

Scammell, William (1939–2000) Born in Hythe, Hampshire, but most commonly associated with Cumbria. He had little early formal education and soon dropped out of school, working at a number of odd jobs, including a spell as a photographer on Cunard liners. He took a degree in English literature from Bristol University as a mature student in 1967, then worked in adult education in Gloucester and Cumbria until early retirement in 1991.

Given the Cumbrian association, it is no surprise that Scammell's poems, including *Yes & No* (1979), *A Second Life* (1982), *Jouissance* (1985), *Eldorado* (1987), and *Bleeding Heart Yard* (1992), all published by Peterloo Poets in Cornwall, show the influence not only of Wordsworth but also of Norman *Nicholson; an admirer and friend of the latter, Scammell edited a Festschrift in his honour (*Between Comets: for Norman Nicholson at 70*, Taxus, 1984). The Wordsworthian legacy is particularly displayed in Scammell's emotive descriptions of landscape, showing not only its affective power on the human subject but also the ravages of industrialization. Though his usual mode is robust, that of the earthy provincial outsider, Scammell can nevertheless be whimsically metropolitan, as in *The Game: Tennis Poems* (Peterloo, 1992), a set of verse parodies describing famous tennis players.

In addition to poems, he published a critical book (*Keith Douglas: A Study*, Faber, 1988) and edited an anthology of *The New Lake Poets* (Bloodaxe, 1991). He also edited a selection of Ted *Hughes' critical prose, *Winter Pollen* (1994), and was well known as a reviewer. Two later collections appeared from Flambard Press: *All Set to Fall Off the Edge of the World* (1998) and

Black and White (2002), published posthumously. See also *Nightwatch* (Shoestring, 2008), a selection of his criticism.   GF

Scannell, Vernon (1922–2007) Born in Lincolnshire, studied at Leeds University, served in the 51st division of the Gordon Highlanders, and was—among various short-term occupations—a professional boxer and a prep-school teacher; in his autobiography *The Tiger and the Rose* (1971) he provided a fascinating account of the colourful early life which shaped his subsequent career.

A freelance writer and broadcaster who published a further autobiography about his wartime experience, several novels with a boxing background, anthologies, and a variety of highly professional occasional criticism as well as many volumes of poetry, Scannell always valued 'a concern with style, an unfussy elegance, wit and intelligence . . . a real involvement with living experience'. A quick glance at the titles of some of his collections—*A Sense of Danger* (1962), *Walking Wounded* (1965), *The Loving Game* (1975), and *Funeral Games* (1987)—immediately suggests what, in fact, distinguished his best work; a fascination with risk-taking, and a resilient, compassionate concern for ordinary human life, in which tenderness is qualified by a kind of brusque disenchantment.

Whether his settings are the battlefield (about which he writes in his prose account *Argument of Kings*, 1987), or the homefront of domesticity, Scannell's sympathies are for the casualties, the 'walking wounded'. While often expressing both the exhilaration and abandon of combat, knowing at first hand how 'a fighter can't pack pity with his gear', he is equally skilful in suggesting the depths of guilt and remorse, perhaps most dramatically in what is probably his most anthologized poem 'A Case of Murder'. Scannell's work, however raw its subject-matter, is always carefully written, and it is a clear indication of his concerns that one of his books for younger readers is entitled *Mastering the Craft* (1970).

Vernon Scannell was granted a Civil List Pension in 1981 for services to literature. His *Collected Poems* were published by

Robson Books, his long-term publisher, in 1993. See also *Of Love and War: New and Selected Poems* (Robson, 2002).   JM

Schmidt, Michael (1947–) Born in Mexico. He studied at Harvard and at Wadham College, Oxford, where he edited the magazine *Carcanet* and went on to found Carcanet Press. This began with small pamphlets but rapidly progressed to the production of full-size books when it moved, with Schmidt, to Manchester. It has become one of the most important poetry presses in Britain. Schmidt also founded the magazine *Poetry Nation*, with C. B. Cox, professor of English at Manchester University, initially as co-editor. Schmidt, strongly influenced by the example of Octavio Paz's magazine *Plural*, pursued a policy of oppositional openness, and was concerned to attack the intellectual orthodoxies of the day rather than to take political positions. In 1976 the hardback *Poetry Nation* was superseded by the A4-format *PN Review* (the form in which the magazine still continues), and C. H. *Sisson and Donald *Davie joined Schmidt as editors (remaining until Issue 37 in 1984). Issue 36, an anthology of contemporary British and Irish poetry, was conceived as a response to the *Penguin Book of Contemporary British Poetry*. Issue 100 in 1994 was an eclectic 'calendar of modern poetry', and issue 200, in 2011, included a tribute to Charles *Tomlinson, the first poet published by the magazine. Schmidt has also edited many anthologies, including *The Harvill Book of Twentieth-Century Poetry in English* (1999), and written a witty and compendious *Lives of the Poets* (Weidenfeld & Nicolson, 1998).

Schmidt's first phase as a poet is strongly marked by his American connection: by the influence of Elizabeth *Bishop, W. C. *Williams, and of Melville's prose. There are no grand gestures, and the occasion of the poem may seem unremarkable, but the phrasing is often memorable: a tough, quiet music pervades his free-verse lines. Lineation is often significant, though sometimes awkwardly handled. A good book from which to gauge Schmidt's first style is *Bedlam and the Oak Wood* (Carcanet, 1970).

In the Eighties he moved towards lines that are rhythmically looser and emotionally more straightforward and personal, as in *The Love of Strangers* (Hutchinson, 1989), though he retains a careful, dry approach to diction. See *Selected Poems 1972–1997* (1997) and *The Resurrection of the Body* (2007—both Smith/Doorstop).   MHU/ETL*

Schnackenberg, Gjertrud (1953–) Born of second-generation Norwegian Lutheran parents in Tacoma, Washington, where she attended local public schools. She began writing poetry as a student at Mount Holyoke College, from which she graduated in 1975, and received an honorary doctorate in 1985. As an undergraduate she earned a reputation as a poetic prodigy, twice winning the Glascock Award for Poetry, as well as the admiration of Harvard classicist and poet Robert *Fitzgerald.

Her first two books of poetry, *Portraits and Elegies* (Godine, 1982; revd. edn., Farrar Straus, 1986) and *The Lamplit Answer* (1985), marked by her fluency with metre and rhyme, have established her as one of the strongest of the *New Formalists and confirmed her early promise. Much of her poetry is related to the death of her father, a history professor, in 1973. This includes a graceful sequence of elegies in the first book, 'Laughing with One Eye', about her shared past with him and her subsequent feeling of loss, and, from the second, 'Supernatural Love', a *tour de force* in rhymed tercets which recalls a childhood scene in her father's study where an inquiry into the roots of the word 'carnation' becomes at once a meditation on Christ's crucifixion and on her own poetic origins. 'Darwin in 1881', published in both books, is an ambitious narrative poem on Charles Darwin's melancholy final year, while 'Heavenly Feast', from the second, is a contemporary prayer, a powerful rendering of Simone Weil's self-starvation. The second volume contains less successful narrative poems based on Sleeping Beauty and the life of Chopin which seem overly academic. Stronger is a sequence addressed to an absent lover which, if too self-conscious, also uses rhyme and wit playfully to balance the at-times desperate mood of the persona.

Schnackenberg's third book, *A Gilded Lapse in Time* (1992), which features a Dantean sequence on travelling to Ravenna, was praised by William *Logan as 'difficult and moving'. *Supernatural Love: Poems 1978–1992* (2000) draws on her first three collections. A UK edition, published by Bloodaxe, also incorporates *The Throne of Labdacus* (2001—all Farrar, Straus), a fragmentary book-length history of the Oedipus myth. The elegiac *Heavenly Questions* (Farrar, Straus, 2010; Bloodaxe, 2011) won the Griffin International Poetry Prize.   RMCP

Schubert, David (1913–46) Born in New York City of Russian parents. His father, severe, restless, with artistic inclinations, left the family in Schubert's childhood, and not long after he found his mother hanged. Living with relatives, Schubert displayed a brilliance at school that brought him early to Amherst College. Robert *Frost, befriending him, did his best to keep Schubert there; but his absorption in writing left no time for studies. Encountering him in New York, Frost offered financial help. A little later he married Judith Ehre, a support in every way. After several near-misses with publishers, New Directions printed him in its *Five Young American Poets* (1941). His difficulties mounting, he fled his home, required hospitalization, and died in 1946.

At the end he tried to destroy all his work. Judith Schubert salvaged what she could, and in 1961 Macmillan published his *Initial A*. Finally, in 1983, the *Quarterly Review of Literature* brought out *David Schubert: Works and Days*, a volume including all his poems, a biography Renée Karol Weiss composed of letters, interviews, and memoirs, and articles by James *Wright, John *Ashbery, David *Ignatow, and others. William Carlos *Williams had already declared Schubert 'a nova in the sky', and on reading the volume Ashbery judged Schubert one of America's great poets. His work was hailed at home and abroad.

Immediately perceptible is the poetry's bulk of colour, action, mercuriality. Not that it is blind to human havoc. On the contrary, Schubert worked constantly within that havoc. But even desperation takes on a sombre gaiety, a more-than-melancholy amusement of the kind that Charlie Chaplin embodied. In Schubert's own words: 'What I see as poetry is a sample of the human scene, its incurably acute melancholia redeemed only by affection.' For a later discussion, see John Ashbery, *Other Traditions* (Harvard University Press, 2000).   TW

Schulman, Grace (1935–   ) Born Grace Waldman in New York City, the only child of a Polish-Jewish immigrant father and a seventh-generation American mother. In 1959 she married Jerome L. Schulman, a research virologist. She has served as Poetry Editor of the *Nation* (1972–2006) and director of the Poetry Center of the 92nd Street Y (1973–85). She is a professor of English at Baruch College, New York City.

Although at the age of fourteen Schulman was introduced to Marianne *Moore, who would become a friend and artistic mentor until her death, Schulman's poems were not influenced by this association. They are not hewn or fabulist, but choose instead a vatic style that is clear and intelligent. The poems range from unabashed love lyrics to prayer-like blessings.

Schulman has published six volumes of poetry, including *Days of Wonder: New and Selected Poems* (2002) and *The Broken String* (2007—both Houghton Mifflin), in addition to a critical appreciation of Moore (1986). She has also published translations from Hebrew and Spanish.   HC

Schuyler, James (1923–91) Born in Chicago but grew up in Washington, DC, and in western New York State. He lived in Italy for several years in the Fifties, staying for a while with W. H. *Auden at his summer retreat at Ischia. A fine elegy for the older poet is included in Schuyler's 1980 collection, *The Morning of the Poem* (Farrar, Straus). Like fellow New York poet and friend Frank *O'Hara, Schuyler worked on the staff of both the Museum of Modern Art and of the magazine *Art News*. In 1959 he commented: 'New York poets, except I suppose the colour blind, are affected most by the floods of paint in whose crashing surf we all scramble.'

While some of Schuyler's early poems experiment with surreal imagery and avant-garde narrative techniques, his later work is conversational and direct. In long poems such as 'The Morning of the Poem' and 'Hymn to Life' (1974) Schuyler meditates fluently on the random happenings of successive days, eschewing grand climaxes and keeping close to the arbitrary flow of his mental processes. Many of his poems are urbane and witty responses to the changing seasons. Schuyler evokes the natural world with a cool, elegant precision that suggests the influence of Elizabeth *Bishop, though his free verse is looser and more ramblingly open to the contingent than Bishop's ever is. Schuyler's love poems are also characterized by a colloquial intimacy and straightforwardness, but these often rear dangerously close to the mawkish. His best-known poem is his restrained and moving elegy for Frank O'Hara called 'Buried at Springs', included in his collection *Freely Espousing* (Doubleday, 1969). His *Selected Poems* was published in New York by Farrar, Straus and Giroux (1988) and Manchester by Carcanet (1990). See also *Collected Poems* (1993) and *Other Flowers: Uncollected Poems* (2010—both Farrar, Straus), ed. James Meetze and Simon Pettet.

Schuyler wrote three novels: *Alfred and Guinevere* (Harcourt 1958), *A Nest of Ninnies* (with John *Ashbery) (Dutton, 1969; Carcanet, 1987), and *What's for Dinner* (Black Sparrow, 1978). All three are amusing comedies of manners, and reflect his immersion in the works of Ronald Firbank, Ivy Compton-Burnett, and E. F. Benson. Posthumously, Black Sparrow Press has published *The Diary of James Schuyler* (1997), ed. Nathalie Kernan, and *Selected Art Writings* (1998), ed. Simon Pettet. See also *Just the Thing* (Turtle Point, 2004), a selection of his letters, edited by William Corbett.   MF

Schwartz, Delmore (1913–66) Born in Brooklyn, New York, where he spent his childhood. Schwartz's highly autobiographical stories often depict the milieu of the middle-class Jewish families who had recently emigrated to America (Schwartz's family had Romanian roots), and of the generation of young intellectuals born of those families; he came to be regarded as their most incisive chronicler. Schwartz's own family suffered the difficulties of his parents' failing marriage; when Delmore was 9 his father left the family for good. The repercussions can be felt most memorably in Schwartz's famous story, 'In Dreams Begin Responsibilities'.

After attending the University of Wisconsin, Schwartz graduated in 1935 from New York University; he then attended Harvard Graduate School in philosophy. At 24 he published *In Dreams Begin Responsibilities* (1938), a volume of poems and stories, which brought high praise from *Eliot, *Pound, W. C. *Williams, Wallace *Stevens, John Crowe *Ransom, and Allen *Tate, who called it 'the first real innovation we've had since Eliot and Pound'. In the words of Schwartz's biographer James Atlas, it was 'heralded as the flowering of a new generation'. Two of Schwartz's best-known poems, 'In the Naked Bed, in Plato's Cave' and 'The Heavy Bear Who Goes With Me', appeared in this volume.

Schwartz became a prominent figure of New York intellectual life. Handsome, a witty and brilliant talker, Schwartz developed a reputation as a compelling presence in his person as well as his poetry. His cultural commentaries and literary essays received widespread praise and continue to be regarded as important documents of the period ('The Isolation of Modern Poetry' and 'The Vocation of the Poet in the Modern World' are considered seminal essays). In his stories, Schwartz's wry portraits of New York intellectuals of the Thirties and Forties are without equal.

Schwartz taught somewhat dissatisfiedly at several universities: Harvard, Kenyon College, Princeton (with friends John *Berryman, Randall *Jarrell, and Saul Bellow), and Syracuse. Literary friendships were essential to Schwartz; also of note include those with R. P. *Blackmur, Robert *Lowell, James Agee, William Barrett, and Dwight Macdonald. Of Schwartz, Lowell said, 'I've never met anyone who has somehow as much seeped into me'. Berryman considered him the century's 'most underrated poet'. Bellow used Schwartz as the model for the brilliant and tortured poet Von Humboldt Fleisher in his novel *Humboldt's Gift*.

Schwartz published *Summer Knowledge* (1959), a selection of poems, to high acclaim. It received the prestigious Bollingen Prize in a year that also saw the publication of Robert Lowell's *Life Studies*. Schwartz's poems resonate with philosophical inquiry; they often consider the conflicts of the self (and its imperatives) with the external world—including those social, cultural, and political demands illuminated by an individual conscience. Late in his life Schwartz looked to nature for the healing premises that might assuage the agony of those philosophical conflicts detailed in his work. Irving Howe called Schwartz 'the poet of the historical moment quite as Auden was in England'.

Schwartz was married twice: to Gertrude Buckman in 1938, and to Elizabeth Pollet in 1949. He spent the last dozen years of his life struggling against mental illness. His paranoid denunciations of even his closest friends left Schwartz alone at the end. He died of a heart attack in July 1966 in a Times Square hotel.

Major works include: *In Dreams Begin Responsibilities* (New Directions, 1938, 1978), *Selected Poems: Summer Knowledge* (Doubleday, 1959), and *Selected Essays* (University of Chicago Press, 1970). New Directions have published a selected volume, *Screeno: Stories and Poems* (2004), with an introduction by Cynthia Ozick, and a new edition of *In Dreams Begin Responsibilities* (2012—both New Directions) with a foreword by the singer-songwriter Lou Reed, who was Schwartz's student at Syracuse.

See also *Delmore Schwartz: The Life of an American Poet*, by James Atlas (Farrar, Straus, 1977; Faber, 1979; repr. Welcome Rain, 2000).   DSTJ

Schwartzman, Adam (1973–) Born in Johannesburg, Schwartzman has degrees in English literature and development studies from Oxford University and has worked for the South African National Treasury, the World Bank, and the International Finance Corporation. He has written three collections of poetry and a novel, *Eddie Signwriter* (Random House, 2011), and is also the editor of the anthology *Ten South African Poets* (Carcanet, 1999). He lives in Istanbul, Turkey.

Schwartzman's three collections, written from within South Africa and abroad, chart the poet's changing impressions of the country's history and culture. His first book, *The Good Life, The Dirty Life and Other Stories* (1995), draws on Schwartzman's experiences of growing up in the final years of apartheid as well as his own identity as a white, Jewish South African (a less-represented section of society in South African poetry). The poems in *Merrie Afrika* (1997) refocus Schwartzman's socio-political interests through the lens of an imagined 'Afrika'—not quite Africa—whose fictional origins are the book's subject. Schwartzman's writing continues to be informed by a social and historical awareness in *The Book of Stones* (2003—all Carcanet) although this volume is less narrative-driven than the earlier books, characterized instead by formal experimentation, repetition, and word patterning. *The Book of Stones* seems energized by an impulse for change—in poems like 'Throw up your arms as if you'd pluck bullets from the air' objects have a tendency to break from their usual mode of existence and become, or merge with, something else.   KK

Scott, David (1947–) Born in Cambridge, studied theology at Durham, and, after an urban curacy and a spell as school chaplain, became vicar of the Cumbrian parishes of Torpenhow and Allhallows in 1980. Now retired, he is an Honorary Canon of Winchester Cathedral. Scott's gentle, contemplative intelligence can be found at work in his quiet but firm poems which invest the parochial and the domestic with a sense of mystery, so that seemingly routine activities take his reader by surprise with the accuracy of their detail. In his best work a small-scale but vivid itemizing is charged with unsentimental affection and often wryly humorous relish.

A number of the poems, such as 'Quodlibet' and 'Hopkins Enters the Roman Catholic Church', celebrate the life of dedicated scholarship and discreet conduct, and if there is sometimes a slight air of sententious piety about them it is usually given an edge by his characteristic wit. Like Andrew *Young, another parson-poet whom in some ways he resembles, he has a keen eye for the natural world and for figures in a landscape. As if to declare his witness to the tradition to which he belongs, he has also attempted free-verse translations of George Herbert's Latin Poems.

David Scott has collaborated with Jeremy James Taylor on several plays for the National Youth Music Theatre, and has written a book of poems for young children, *How Does It Feel?* (Blackie, 1989). His main collections are *A Quiet Gathering* (1984), which won the Geoffrey Faber Memorial Prize, *Playing for England* (1989), *Selected Poems* (1998), and *Piecing Together* (2005—all Bloodaxe). He has also written several prose works on Anglican spirituality.   JM

Scott, Dennis (1939–91) Born in Kingston, and educated at Jamaica College, and the University of the West Indies at Mona. He was principal of the Jamaica School of Drama, associate professor of directing at Yale University, and editor of *Caribbean Quarterly*.

Dennis Scott's poetry is notable for its dramatic personae, and its densely archetypal symbolism. His occasional use of dialect goes beyond the vernacular to delve into the psyche. 'Uncle Time', for instance, seems traditional in its linking of time with foreshadowed death, but it becomes very West Indian in the way he approaches the subject. Not only is the poem in dialect, but Scott also relates the personification of Time to the folkloric figure of Anancy, the cunning spider-man. Other poems about time, 'Time Piece' and 'Time-slip', are in standard English, but equally powerful in suggesting corrosion of life and expectations.

Scott's later poems, particularly in *Dreadwalk* (New Beacon, 1982), appear to construct an aesthetic based on Rastafarian beliefs. Poems like 'Dread-walk' and 'Apocalypse Dub' are immersed in fluid, surrealistic imagery, and suggest increasingly complex personae. His search for archetypal imagery, from whatever source, produced a verse adaptation of *Sir Gawain and the Green Knight* (Anchorage, 1978).

See also *Uncle Time* (University of Pittsburgh Press, 1973). Scott's play, *An Echo in the Bone*, was published in *Plays for Today*, ed. Errol Hill (Longman, 1985). Mervyn *Morris edited a posthumous volume from Scott's unpublished manuscripts, *Afterimage* (Peepal Tree, 2008).   MR

Scott, F. R. (Francis Reginald) (1899–1981) Born in Quebec City and educated at Bishop's College School and University in Lennoxville, Quebec, and at Oxford University, where he was a Rhodes Scholar. Returning to Canada, Scott schoolmastered briefly before entering the law faculty at McGill University, where he obtained his BCL in 1926, was called to the bar in 1927, and became a member of faculty in 1928, ending his career as dean of law, 1961–4.

As a result of his exposure to Fabianism at Oxford, and following upon the Great Depression, Scott became active in left-wing politics and was a founding member of the League for Social Reconstruction (1932), which led to the formation of a socialist political party, the Co-operative Commonwealth Federation, now the New Democratic Party of Canada. He served the United Nations in Burma in 1952, and was a member of the Royal Commission on Bilingualism and Biculturalism from 1963 to 1971.

The poet in Scott was manifested in 1921 when he began to publish light verse of a decidedly *Georgian flavour. At McGill he fell in with A. J. M. *Smith and other budding modernists who were instrumental in publishing a university-based, avant-garde literary paper called *The McGill Fortnightly Review* (1925–7). This initial experience led to a series of involvements with reviews, little magazines, and publishing ventures, most of which had a significant impact on the development of modernism in Canadian poetry. In 1936 he edited *New Provinces: Poems of Several Authors*, the first

S

modernist anthology of Canadian verse. Scott was late in publishing his own first book. *Overture* appeared in 1945, but from then on he had a steady, if measured, output with *Events and Signals* (1954), a collection of satirical poems called *The Eye of the Needle* (1957), and *Signature* (1964). His poetry embraces a wide variety of subjects and forms—nature poems, poems of social, political, and humanitarian dedication, metaphysical and love poems, 'found poems', and translations of French-Canadian verse; but he is best known as a social critic whose cutting satires about hypocrisy, stupidity, and injustice express a deep indignation.

Scott's *Selected Poems* appeared in 1966, to be followed by *The Dance Is One* (1973), and *The Collected Poems* (1981—all McClelland & Stewart). An anglophone native of Quebec, Scott was passionately committed to the building of bridges between Canada's two premier European founding cultures. This dedication is evidenced in his translations of the poetry of such leading French-Canadian poets as Saint-Denys Garneau and Anne Hébert.

See Sandra Djwa, *The Politics of the Imagination: A Life of F. R. Scott* (McClelland & Stewart, 1987).   MG

Scott, John A. (John Alan) (1948–) Born in Littlehampton, Sussex, and emigrated to Melbourne in 1959. In the late Sixties he co-organized the Monash University poetry readings with Alan *Wearne and Laurie *Duggan. He has lectured on media and creative writing in Melbourne, Canberra, and Wollongong, and now lives in Trentham, Victoria.

The *surrealism and *symbolisme* of *The Barbarous Sideshow* (1975) challenged social-realist conceptions of Australian poetry. In *From the Flooded City* (1981—both Makar) and *Smoking* (Scripsi, 1983) Scott developed his own style of poetic narrative from French prose poetry and English sonnet sequences. *The Quarrel with Ourselves; and Confession* (Rigmarole, 1984) includes fragments of a sexual odyssey, a science-fiction apocalypse, and a static murder mystery, these experiments being fully realized in the three verse novels of *St Clair* (1986). Scott assembled his short poems in *Singles* (1989—both University of Queensland Press), and his longer imitations, homages, and revisitations in *Translation* (Picador, 1990), but by the time his *Selected Poems* (University of Queensland Press, 1995) appeared, he had forsaken poetry for the novel. Scott has included his best verse in *Selected Poems* and in *Before I Wake* (Penguin, 1996) has written his most impressive novel to date.   CP

Scott, Margaret (1934–2005) Born in Bristol, read English at Cambridge, and emigrated to Australia in 1959. From 1966 until her retirement in 1990 she taught at the University of Tasmania and published principally in the field of Renaissance drama. Her first volumes of verse, *Tricks of Memory* (1980) and *Visited* (1983), show a robust attentiveness to familiar landscapes allied with a rueful sense of the figure that she cuts within them. Editor, with Vivian *Smith, of an anthology of Tasmanian poetry, *Effects of Light* (1985), and an associate editor of the *Oxford Literary Guide to Australia* (1987), Scott's most accomplished and varied verse collection was *The Black Swans* (Angus & Robertson, 1988). Notably extending her previous range, the book begins with a detailed, wryly celebratory sequence on 'Housework' and includes poems that evoke the Tasman Peninsula where she lived, before modulating into the desolately loving 'Elegies' for her late husband, Michael Scott. She also wrote a historical novel, *The Baby-Farmer* (1990), dealing with the Victorian trade in the adoption and murder of unwanted children. See *Collected Poems* (Montpelier, 2000).   PP

Scott, Winfield Townley (1910–68) Born in Newport, Rhode Island. He spent an idyllic childhood in Newport and wrote about it in a memoir, 'The Owl in the Hall', in *Alpha Omega* (Doubleday, 1971). He graduated from Brown University, where he went with the literary crowd. A visit with Edwin Arlington *Robinson, then the most prominent American poet, was influential; but much as he admired his work, Scott spent most of his life trying to avoid writing like Robinson. From 1929 to 1951 he worked for the Providence (Rhode Island) *Journal*, writing book reviews and becoming editor of its weekly book page, considered the best in the United States outside of New York. Handsome, ambitious, yet for a long time lacking in self-confidence, he was a gracious, socially adept, and well-liked member of the New England literary community.

His most successful poems chronicle momentary, surprising personal victories in a normally bleak world, whose meanings are informed chiefly by the agonies of self-doubt, the play of the imagination, and heterosexual love and longing. A plain and direct diction makes his poems accessible, while a consistent colour symbolism involving green, gold, and red expresses romantic passion and projects it on to the natural and human world. Most of his best work can be found in his *Collected Poems 1937–1962* (Macmillan, 1962). Scott Donaldson's *Poet in America: Winfield Townley Scott* (University of Texas Press, 1972) is an excellent biography. Journal entries were published posthumously in *A Dirty Hand* (University of Texas Press, 1969), and his papers reside at Brown University. Recent appraisals include Laurence Goldstein, *War, Literature, and the Arts Journal*, vol. 12, nos. 1–2, pp. 59–77, and David R. Slavitt, *Re-Verse* (Northwestern University Press, 2005), pp. 33–43.   JTFT

Scovell, E. J. (Edith Joy) (1907–99) Born in Sheffield and educated at Casterton School, Westmorland, and Somerville College, Oxford. Regarded by Geoffrey *Grigson as 'the purest of women poets of our time', she published her first volume, *Shadows of Chrysanthemums*, in 1944. The poems in this and two subsequent volumes, *Midsummer Meadows* (1946) and *The River Steamer* (1956), are the work of a strong lyrical intelligence, achieving a delicate air of mystery which arises from close observation of the physical world. Whether meditating on the 'innocent wild head' of a baby, 'the look of utterance on the silent flower', or, minutely, the progress across a sandy yard of leaf-cutting ants 'under their little sails of green', Scovell combines a

naturalist's precision (she was married to the distinguished ecologist Charles Elton) with what she called her betrothal at birth to a sense of otherness which she took for granted.

Perhaps too quiet for the noisy poetic climate of the late 1940s and too numinous for the period which reacted against the *New Apocalypse, Scovell's work did not receive the attention it deserved. Between 1956 and the early 1980s she published few poems and no book. In 1982, however, *The Space Between* collected the work of this interim period, including some of the translations from the Italian of Giovanni Pascoli on which she had begun to work, and confirmed the consistency and continuity of her vision. Although she has been described as a religious poet, she preferred to avoid such labelling—indeed, her poem 'Agnostic' is the closest she came to a declaration—and it would be more accurate to regard her as a poet constantly astonished by the world. By no means confined to her home ground of Oxford, she travelled widely, working with her husband in tropical America, and a number of her poems give as rapt an attention to exotic landscapes as they do to her garden or to the quiet stretches of the river Isis.

E. J. Scovell's *Collected Poems* (1988) contains her complete set of Pascoli translations and a generous selection of later work. There is also a *Selected Poems* (1991—both Carcanet).   JM

Scupham, (John) Peter (1933–   ) Born in Liverpool and brought up in Cambridge. His father was controller of BBC Educational Broadcasting. He graduated from Emmanuel College, Cambridge, where he read English, in 1957, and married in the same year. A schoolteacher for many years, he lives in Norfolk where he has restored an Elizabethan manor house and runs an antiquarian book business. With John *Mole he founded the Mandeville Press. He is a Fellow of the Royal Society of Literature.

Scupham published his first pamphlet, *The Small Containers* (Phoenix Pamphlet Poets, 1972), relatively late, when he was 39, but has produced full-length collections at regular intervals since. His early poems established a continuing tendency towards private rumination: decorous and fragile—like the title of one of them, 'Painted Shells'—they are products of an essentially fugitive (the word is a favourite of Scupham's) temperament. Toys and games are a recurring subject-matter. A fastidious craftsman, he is comfortable with demanding forms: the title-piece of *The Hinterland* (1977) is a Hungarian sonnet-sequence (compare John *Fuller's 'The Labour of Hercules', 1972). His later work is less ornate in manner, and its treatment of autobiographical materials has a firmer cultural and historical grounding. *The Air Show* (1988), a reconstruction of his boyhood experience of the Second World War, was his most successful single work by the time of *Selected Poems* (1990). *Watching the Perseids* (1990), *The Ark* (1994—all Oxford University Press), and *Night Watch* (Anvil, 1999) were followed by a *Collected Poems* in 2002. His latest collection is *Borrowed Landscapes* (2011—both Carcanet).   MI

Seboni, Barolong (1957–) Born in Kanye, Botswana, Seboni went to school for several years in London. He studied at university in Botswana and later took an MA at the University of Wisconsin-Madison. In 1993, he was poet-in-residence at the Scottish Poetry Library. Currently Senior Lecturer in English at the University of Botswana, he is also a newspaper columnist, radio broadcaster, editor, and literary organizer.

Seboni has said that his experimental early work, which began to appear in magazines in the 1970s, was inspired by the 'revolutionary spirit that was then blowing across southern Africa in search of self-determination and self-actualisation': see, for example, the poem 'Punctuation', which promises to 'punch a full stop' to Africa's status in the West as a 'continent of question marks'. *Images of the Sun*, a collection centred on the Kalahari landscape, was published by the African Studies Program at Wisconsin in 1986. *Love Songs* (Morula, 1994) collected his lyrics on that subject, while *Windsongs of the Kgalagadi* (Macmillan, 1995) draws on Tswana oral traditions.

Seboni's uncle was the writer and academic M. O. M. Seboni, whose collection of Botswanan proverbs (such as 'the war of integrity is through the mouth') he has translated from Setswana into English.   JNT

Seidel, Frederick (1936–) Born in St Louis, attended Harvard, and lives in New York City. He has taught English at Rutgers University and served as Paris editor of the *Paris Review*. His second book of poems, *Sunrise* (Viking, 1980), was the Lamont Poetry Selection for 1979, and also won the National Book Critics Circle Award for 1980. Seidel's first book, *Final Solutions* (Random House, 1963), was an unusually powerful debut, remarkable for its combination of an impeccable formal aesthetic with a dark and gritty vision. Seidel's self-revelations and his obsessional personae make the *confessionalism of Robert *Lowell, his most obvious influence, seem tame by comparison. Seidel's early poems revel in their lack of conviction, marking both the modern loss of faith and the poet's abandoned Jewishness. His frankly erotic poems discuss voyeurism and masturbation, and identify the body parts as well as their functions. With *Sunrise*, Seidel's poetry becomes more of a chronicle of the times, a gossipy insider's view of art and politics during the Sixties that finds the poet at an exclusive fund-raiser for Robert Kennedy ('1968'), pub-crawling with Francis Bacon ('Fucking'), attending the Finnish Grand Prix at Imatra ('Men and Woman'), and visiting the set of Antonioni's *Zabriskie Point* ('Death Valley'), a movie that shares the same apocalyptic sensibility as *Sunrise*. Having celebrated the New Frontier and witnessed its sad aftermath, Seidel explores a private emotional realm in *These Days* (1989), though his bitter view of American politics is still present in poems such as 'Our Gods' and 'Empire'. Many of the poems also return to a more controlled style after the open forms of *Sunrise*, and his main subject is the painful memory of a difficult adolescence. Kinky sex still preoccupies Seidel, and he further develops, in some obscure poems, a more symbolic poetic language.

Poems: 1959–1979 (1989—both Knopf) reprints most of *Final Solutions* and all of *Sunrise. Men and Woman* (Chatto & Windus, 1984), an English edition of Seidel's selected poetry, also draws from both volumes and adds some of the poems that appear in *These Days.*

With *My Tokyo* (1993) and *Going Faster* (1998) Seidel entered a prolific later period in which he has pushed the decadent preoccupations and sophisticated jangling of his verse towards a poetry of sweeping prophetic satire—as though T. S. *Eliot's Prufrock had finally dared to do and say everything he felt. The three volumes of *The Cosmos Trilogy* (2003) comprise an inverted *Divine Comedy* which ends in Manhattan with the attacks on the World Trade Center in September 2001 (*Area Code 212* (2002)).

Ooga Booga (2006), which won the *Los Angeles Times* Book Prize and was shortlisted for the Griffin International Poetry Prize, continues the now self-parodic confessionalism of Seidel's louche persona ('I have never been so cheerily suicidal, so sui-Seidel') and its vision of American imperial decline. See also *Evening Man* (2008) and *Collected Poems: 1959–2009* (2009—all Farrar, Straus).   TDeP*

Senior, Olive (1943–) Born in Jamaica, and educated there and in Canada, where she still spends much of her time. She was managing editor of Jamaica Publications Ltd., and editor of *Jamaica Journal*. She was also involved in the Women in the Caribbean Research Project for the University of the West Indies in Barbados.

According to E. A. *Markham, 'Senior must be—apart from *Walcott—our most elegant and graceful poet'. Although she has said in an interview that 'Jamaica is still a society of great spirituality, of great psychic energy', many of her poems are highly sceptical in tone, most notably 'Epitaph'. It commemorates the death of a young child, but ends with the following lines: 'old superstitions | are such lies'. Her poems vividly convey, as do her short stories, village life in Jamaica, but always in an unsentimental and tough-minded fashion.

Olive Senior's poems have been published in *Talking of Trees* (Calabash, 1985), *Gardening in the Tropics* (McClelland & Stewart, 1994; Bloodaxe, 1995), *Over the Roofs of the World* (2005), which was nominated for the Canadian Governor General's Award, and *Shell* (2007—both Insomniac). Her collections of short stories include *Summer Lightning* (1986), *Arrival of the Snake Woman* (1989), and *Discerner of Hearts* (1995). She has received Silver and Gold Musgrave Medals from the Institute of Jamaica for her contributions to literature.   MR

Sepamla, Sipho (Sydney) (1932–2007) Sepamla belonged to the group of 'township poets', including *Mtshali and *Serote, who emerged in South Africa during the 1970s. He was born in Krugersdorp on the Witwatersrand, and trained to be a teacher. In the late 1960s he was stimulated to write by the new-found confidence of younger blacks in their opposition to apartheid. During the mid-1970s he relaunched the journal *The Classic* as *The New Classic*, and was active in organizing poetry readings, conferences, and art exhibitions. He also edited the theatre magazine *S'ketsh*. Both journals were subject to constant censorship, and he also suffered the banning of a novel and a volume of poetry. In 1980 he was given a passport to visit Germany and England, and in 1981–2 he was a fellow at Iowa University.

Having lived almost all his life in Johannesburg, Sepamla asserted an urbanized identity, satirizing the apartheid 'Bantu culture' of mudhuts and primitive agriculture. He wrote only in English: sometimes in urban dialect, sometimes (as in the much-anthologized 'To Whom It May Concern') in a parody of the inhuman officialese of apartheid. Underlying all his poems, even the elegies for children murdered by the police, is a confidence that time was running out for white domination. Sepamla dismissed 'fine points' of literary discrimination, and his verse lacks punctuation, relying for effect on rhythmic parallelism and repetitions. His verse can seem short-winded and idiomatically insecure, but sometimes it achieves a rhetorical power reminiscent of oral praise-song. See *Selected Poems* (Donker, 1984) and *From Goré to Soweto* (Skotaville, 1988). JB

Serote, Mongane (Wally) (1944–)
Belonged to the group of 'township poets', including *Sepamla and *Mtshali, who came to prominence in South Africa during the 1970s. He was born in Sophiatown, Johannesburg, and attended school in Alexandra Township and in Leribe, Lesotho. He became active in the Black Consciousness Movement, and in 1969–70 was imprisoned for nine months in solitary confinement, only to be released without charge. His second volume of verse, *Tsetlo* (1974) was banned on publication. A Fulbright scholarship took Serote to the United States, and in 1979 he completed a fine arts degree at Columbia University, after which he went to work with the Nedu Arts Ensemble in Gaberone, Botswana.

Serote's intense, expressionist poetry gives lyrical voice to the suffering of blacks under apartheid. In passionate addresses to Alexandra or Johannesburg, he dramatizes the grim violence of township life and celebrates black endurance. Serote mastered English only after leaving school, and the linguistic tensions and dislocations of his writing echo the frustrations of his political theme. He breaks lines in mid-phrase or even mid-word, and in one poem subverts 'Whitey's' language to an incoherent babble. Out of Serote's sharp subjectivity, however, grows the collective confidence of black revolt. He celebrates the spiritual strength of blacks who cannot bring themselves to return hatred for hatred, though his patient musings over injustice frequently modulate into the menacing tone of one driven beyond endurance. In the later 1970s Serote turned to longer poems of explicit political commitment, and his latest volume, *A Tough Tale* (Kliptown, 1987), addresses itself primarily to his companions in the struggle.

Serote returned to South Africa in 1990, and since the end of apartheid he has received many honours for his contribution to national literature and culture. His later collections are *Third World Express* (1992), which won the Noma Award, *Come and*

Hope with Me (1994), *Freedom, Lament and Song* (1997—all David Philip), and *History is the Home Address* (Kwela, 2004). He has also written three novels. JB

Seth, Vikram (1952–) Born in Calcutta (now Kolkata) and educated at Oxford, Stanford, and Nanjing universities, training as an economist. His years in India, England, California, and China have given his work a distinctly cosmopolitan flavour; in addition to poetry and fiction he has written a book about his travels in China and Tibet and a family memoir, *Two Lives* (2005).

Seth has published several volumes of elegant, finely crafted formal poetry, including *All You Who Sleep Tonight* (Penguin, 1990; repr. 2012); but as a poet he is best known as the author of *The Golden Gate* (Random House, 1986), a novel in verse modelled on Pushkin's *Eugene Onegin*, tracing the fortunes of a group of young professional Californians as they come to terms with various problems ranging from nascent homosexuality to the nuclear threat. Urbane, inventive, and rigorous in its adherence to Pushkin's sonnet-like tetrameter stanza, the book enjoyed surprising success when it appeared, perhaps because it was deliberately marketed as a novel rather than a poem. Its appearance placed Seth squarely at the crossroads of two allied movements in American poetry loosely referred to as the *New Formalism and the *New Narrative. Whether the feat is one that bears repetition is another matter. Seth's best lyric pieces appear in *The Humble Administrator's Garden* (Carcanet/Viking, 1985; repr. Penguin, 2005) and in *The Oxford India Anthology of Twelve Modern Indian Poets*, ed. A. K. Mehrotra (1992). His novels include *A Suitable Boy* (1993) and *An Equal Music* (1999). RG

Sexton, Anne (née Harvey) (1928–74) Born in Newton, Massachusetts, and went from boarding school to a Boston finishing school in 1947. The next year she eloped with Alfred Muller Sexton II, who later entered his father-in-law's firm. The birth in 1951 of her first daughter helped trigger a series of mental breakdowns, suicide attempts, and consequent hospitalizations that would pattern the rest of her life.

Sexton began writing poetry in 1957, at first as therapy. She then honed her skills in several workshops, including one with Robert *Lowell, where she met Sylvia *Plath. She was also friends with Maxine *Kumin and W. D. *Snodgrass, whom she viewed as a mentor. His candid approach to intense personal material clearly influenced her first collection, *To Bedlam and Part Way Back* (1960), though her intimate female perspective and use of simple rhyme and metre effects to simulate a regressive state were original, as were the extremes to which she pushed her '*confessional' stance. This held true through *All My Pretty Ones* (1962) and *Live or Die* (1967), which won the Pulitzer Prize. In *Live or Die* there is a poem addressed to the dead Sylvia Plath, in which Plath is reproached for having gone alone 'into the death I wanted so badly and so long'. It was only in *Transformations* (1971), ribald, often wryly Freudian or feminist versions of Grimm fairy tales, that Sexton was able to transcend narrow technical and narrative boundaries. At the time of her suicide in October 1974 she was Professor of Creative Writing at Boston University. A posthumous volume, *45 Mercy Street*, appeared in 1976. This book, Sexton had said in 1974, 'is too personal to publish for some time'.

All her verse is in *The Complete Poems* (Houghton Mifflin, 1981). See also *Anne Sexton: A Self-Portrait in Letters*, ed. Linda Gray Sexton and Lois Ames (Houghton Mifflin, 1977), *Anne Sexton* (Twayne, 1989), by H. Caroline King Barnard Hall, and *Anne Sexton: A Biography*, by Diane Wood Middlebrook (Houghton Mifflin, 1991). The Middlebrook biography caused much controversy when it appeared: the biographer made use of 'session tapes' recorded during Sexton's interviews with her psychiatrist.   EB

Seymour, A. J. (Arthur James) (1914–90) Born in British Guiana (now Guyana), and educated at Queen's College. His career as a senior civil servant included a stint as information officer at the central secretariat of the Caribbean Organization in Puerto Rico (1962–4). He was also founder and editor (1945–61) of *Kyk-over-al*, a highly influential literary periodical, which he resumed editing a few years before his death. His poetry-pamphlet series, 'Miniature Poets', featured early work by such writers as the poet Martin *Carter and the novelist Wilson Harris.

Seymour's poems, particularly the early ones, have been criticized as being too tame and overly conventional. The poetry he wrote from *The Guiana Book* (Argosy, 1948) onwards, however, often displays a vivid, complex, and quirky historical imagination. 'For Christopher Columbus', for instance, focuses on the great voyager's perplexities. He ambiguously emerges as a kind of poet: 'as architect of a new age | the solid world would build upon his poem.' See *Collected Poems, 1937–1989* (Blue Parrot, 2000).   MR

Shapcott, Jo (1953–   ) Born in London, Shapcott was educated at Trinity College, Dublin, and St Hilda's College, Oxford, and later won a Harkness Fellowship to Harvard. She has worked as Education Officer at the South Bank Centre, and for the Arts Council Literature Department. Her significant collections include *Electroplating the Baby* (Bloodaxe, 1988), winner of the Commonwealth Prize, *Phrase Book* (Oxford University Press, 1992), *Her Book: Poems 1988–1998* (2000), *Tender Taxes* (2002), consisting of versions and delicate interrogations of Rilke's French poems, and the Costa-Award-winning *Of Mutability* (2010—all Faber). She has also twice won the National Poetry Competition.

Combining often informal structures with a precise but colloquial diction, Shapcott draws on eclectic sources, including popular culture and the sciences. She excels in short narrative forms and the dramatic monologue. A displaced, oblique, linguistically knowing point of view is characteristic, as in 'Phrase-Book,' where the 'Englishwoman' watching live televised war footage finds herself literally lost in a foreign city. A not-unusual critique of modern warfare becomes memorably spiked with the strange, staccato sentences the speaker has learnt from her phrase-book: 'Where | can I find? What have I done? I have done | nothing . . . ' For Shapcott, as for a number of younger English women poets (e.g. Lavinia *Greenlaw), Elizabeth *Bishop has proved an enabling influence. Shapcott often works in a similarly retrained register, avoiding personal revelation even when her subject-matter is painfully personal, and exploring the balances of power—sexual, political, human-versus-animal—with her own kind of surreal wit.   CAR

Shapcott, Thomas W. (Thomas William) (1935–) Born in Ipswich, Queensland, and maintained an accountancy business there until he chose literature full time in 1978. In that year his *Selected Poems* drew on nine collections. He had influenced perceptions of contemporary poetry through three anthologies: *New Impulses in Australian Poetry* (1968, with Rodney *Hall), *Australian Poetry Now* (1970), and *Contemporary Australian and American Poetry* (1976). He had served (1973–6) on the National Literature Board of which he was to be director, 1983–90.

Also in the future were further verse collections, a substantially extended *Selected Poems* (University of Queensland Press, 1988), and many novels. Of these, *The Search for Galina* (Chatto & Windus, 1989) involved devising poems for the Russian woman poet of its title, while *White Stag of Exile* (Allen Lane, 1984) is structurally dominated by its long concluding poem, 'Canticle'.

Shapcott's early poetic explorations of environment are conventional in evoking the substance of a natural world, but as his literary allegiances realigned towards America a different voice could be heard, self-conscious about form and perception, fracturing syntax and narrative sequence. There remains, however, an alert responsiveness to particularities and to dramatic presences; in short, to the world of substance. He was made an Officer of the Order of Australia in 1989, and later worked as a professor of creative writing at the University of Adelaide until his retirement

in 2005. Later collections include *Chekhov's Mongoose* (2000) and *The City of Empty Rooms* (2006—both Salt). See also: *Biting the Bullet: A Literary Memoir* (Simon & Schuster, 1990).   JS

Shapiro, Alan (1952–) Born in Boston, Massachusetts, and educated at Brandeis University. He has since taught at Stanford University, California, and at the University of North Carolina.

The early poems of *The Courtesy* (1983) explore the need to be a part of the general human experience. In the best of these poems, of which 'Simon, the Barber' is representative, the speaker yearns for acceptance by old friends and family members.

In later poems Shapiro speaks no longer as an outsider but as a willing participant in his extended family of men and women. His love poems celebrate the mundane moments of life. A pregnant wife regards herself in the mirror; a man joins a woman for a swim: casual moments, imbued with stature in Shapiro's poems.

Shapiro's other books include *Happy Hour* (1986), *Covenant* (1991), *Mixed Company* (1996), which won the *Los Angeles Times* Book Award, *The Dead Alive and Busy* (2000—all University of Chicago Press), which won the Kingsley Tufts Award, *Tantalus in Love* (2005), and *Old War* (2008—both Houghton Mifflin). He has also published two memoirs, translations of Aeschylus and Euripides, and a collection of essays, *In Praise of the Impure: Poetry and the Ethical Imagination* (TriQuarterly, 1993)   RS

Shapiro, Harvey (1924–) Born in Chicago and educated at Yale and Columbia universities, has served as an editor with a number of prestigious publications, including *Commentary, The New Yorker*, and the *New York Times Magazine*. Between 1975 and 1983 he was the editor of *The New York Times Book Review*. Shapiro's success as an editor has sometimes obscured his achievement as a poet.

Shapiro's poetry, which owes much stylistically to the work of William Carlos *Williams and Charles *Reznikoff, generally deals with urban experiences, the poet's family, and his identity as a Jew. He is very much a modernist poet of alienation, one at times with nowhere to turn but an inhospitable city: 'The self, humiliated', he says in 'Cityscape', 'has no recourse but to the world'. Perhaps his finest poem is 'National Cold Storage Company', the name of a Brooklyn storage building which becomes for the poet an emblem of the American past, and in which there may be '[a] monstrous birth'.

See *The Sights Along the Harbour: New and Selected Poems* (Wesleyan University Press, 2006). EHF

Shapiro, Karl (1913–2000) Born in Baltimore, Maryland, the grandson of Russian-Jewish immigrants. He was educated at the University of Virginia and Johns Hopkins University, although he never took a degree. Beginning to write while still at high school, his first substantial group of poems appeared in *Five Young American Poets* (1941). His first major collection, *Person, Place, and Thing* (1942), consists of poems that are usually metrically regular with fixed, though untraditional stanza forms and written in a tough, flat idiom. Attentive to the person, place, or incident they describe, they can occasionally move towards satire. Serving in the US Army from 1941 to 1945, Shapiro wrote of his wartime experiences in *V-Letter and Other Poems*, which won him a Pulitzer Prize. Working as poetry consultant to the Library of Congress from 1946 to 1947, and editing both *Poetry* magazine (1950–6) and *The Prairie Schooner* (1956–66), Shapiro also taught at several universities, including Johns Hopkins, Nebraska, and California, and served as a visiting professor in Australia, India, and Japan. An influential figure in contemporary American poetry, he wrote many critical works: among them, *In Defence of Ignorance* (1960), an attack on the influence of T. S. *Eliot and Ezra *Pound, and *The Poetry Wreck: Selected Essays 1950–1970* (1975).

Later collections of Shapiro's poetry show several changes of direction. *Trial of a Poet* (1947) and *Poems of a Jew* (1958), for instance, are frequently ironic in attitude and written in taut, disciplined forms. *The*

Bourgeois Poet (1964) shows Shapiro moving towards a longer, flowing line somewhere between free verse and prose poetry. Intensely personal and virulently anti-authoritarian, the poems of this period offer random celebrations of gaiety and spontaneity. Subsequent collections, however, such as *White-Haired Lover* (1968) and *Adult Bookstore* (1976), mark a return to more traditional forms and a retreat into more conservative values. In 1990 Shapiro completed the second volume of his autobiography, *Reports of my Death.*

See *Collected Poems 1940–1978* (Random House, 1978) and *The Wild Card: Selected Poems, Early and Late* (University of Illinois Press, 1998), ed. Stanley Kunitz and David Ignatow. Robert *Phillips has also edited a selection of Shapiro's essays (*Creative Glut* (Dee, 2004)) and *Coda: Last Poems* (Texas Review, 2008), from unpublished manuscripts. RJG

Shetty, Manohar (1953–) Born in Bombay (now Mumbai) and educated at St Peter's High School, Panchgani, and the University of Bombay. Except for a short period when he worked in a restaurant owned by his family, Shetty has been a journalist since 1974, and at present lives in Goa, where he was formerly editor of *Goa Today.*

Shetty's themes—loneliness, boredom, ennui—are born of the 'daily groove' of living, and make him very much a poet of the city. The poems operate not in wide open spaces but inside enclosed and enclosing ones, observing in great detail the life lived behind shut doors, in the company of domestic creatures (lizards, spiders, cockroaches) and shadowgraphs ('Two flat palms part | and a bored crocodile yawns'). Once in a while, though, he takes in the outside world, looking at it with the same precision, as if through a magnifying glass.

Shetty's early collections of poems, *A Guarded Space* (1981) and *Borrowed Time* (1988), appeared from small presses, and were little noticed except by other poets, among them *Moraes, *Mahapatra, and *Jussawalla (who, in fact, published *Borrowed Time*). For a discussion of his work, see *Modern Indian Poetry in English*, by Bruce King (Oxford University Press, 1987; revd. edn., 2001). *Domestic Creatures* (1994), which appeared from Oxford University Press, brought him to wider attention. He has not been prolific since, but remains an admired poet's poet. His fourth collection is *Personal Effects* (Doosra, 2010). AKM*

Shuttle, Penelope (1947–) Born in Staines, Middlesex, and educated at Staines Grammar School and Matthew Arnold County Secondary School. Her output covers radio drama, fiction, and non-fiction, and includes several books of poetry and prose written in collaboration with her late husband, Peter *Redgrove, notably *The Wise Wound: Menstruation and Everywoman* (Boyars, 1978; 2nd edn. 2005). All her work springs from an essentially poetic imagination. Unusually for a woman poet of her generation, she began publishing while still in her twenties, and won early recognition with the Greenwood Prize (1972) and an Eric Gregory Award (1974). Of her numerous, richly imaginative poetry collections, the most recent are *Taxing the Rain* (1992), *Selected Poems: 1980–1996* (1998—both Oxford University Press), *Redgrove's Wife* (2006), and *Sandgrain and Hourglass* (2010—both Bloodaxe).

Though Sylvia *Plath is an affinity, Shuttle's work expresses a less pressured, more rangily allusive, sensibility. Female experiences and processes are often mythologized in a style that may be inventive and surreal or discursively relaxed. While dreams and archetypes are a prevailing influence, her recent poems of loss are movingly realist elegies. CAR

Silkin, Jon (1930–97) Born in London, the son of a solicitor, and educated at Dulwich College. He worked as a labourer before becoming a magazine editor—he founded the quarterly *Stand*—and teacher.

From 1964 *Stand* was closely associated with Northern House Publishers, Newcastle upon Tyne, also co-founded by Silkin. Tony *Harrison and Ken *Smith joined Silkin as co-editors for the year 1968/9. *Stand* expressed Silkin's own 'stand' as one who mixes 'rationalist agnosticism and dilute Orthodox Judaism', together with, from the time he settled in Newcastle, what has been called 'the voice of the Northumbrian'. However, *Stand* was also notably eclectic in giving space to critics of its left-wing or 'committed' stance on 'responsibilities, community and moral probings': see *Poetry of the Committed Individual: A 'Stand' Anthology* (Penguin, 1973).

Silkin's own early poems in *The Peaceable Kingdom* (1954) and especially in *The Re-ordering of the Stones* (1961) are reminiscent of *Auden in their clipped and unabashed use of abstract terms and ellipsis: 'To hold | In sex and affection, | The adored human creature | Making of both a unit | In love, and procreate.' But unlike Auden's, Silkin's style serves a stringent, thoughtful, and indignant compassion for the suffering and exploited. Sometimes the suffering may be close to the poet, as in the often-anthologized 'Death of a Son'. But in general Silkin's stance implies a wider political attitude. Sometimes his terse style results in a dense and tortuous obscurity, and sometimes the assault on liberal complacency is crude and self-righteous. The recurrent imagery of small animals and birds (vulnerable) and stones (invulnerable) can seem perfunctory and mechanical.

The poems in *Nature with Man* (1965—all Chatto & Windus) represent a change and an advance. There is a closer attention to physical appearance, married to Silkin's gifts with language. The 'Flower Poems' are especially impressive. Daisies 'Look unoriginal | Being numerous. They ask for attention | With that gradated yellow swelling | Of oily stamens. Petals focus them: | The eyelashes grow wide.' The attention to these flowers is made to seem analogous to a considerate attention to humanity. Silkin has learnt something from William Carlos *Williams here, but his language, with its quirky phrasing and inventive diction, is more self-conscious. In *Amana Grass* (Wesleyan University Press, 1971) are a number of poems of place, some about Israel: Silkin now explores the links between the political and the personal (his Jewishness) in a more profound manner.

The style is sometimes reminiscent of Neruda in its capacious lines and exalted meditativeness. Perhaps his most impressive volume was *The Little Time-Keeper* (Carcanet, 1976; Norton, 1977), which fuses public and private, sensuous and abstract, in a rich, authoritative, compact style.

Silkin's critical study, *The Life of Metrical & Free Verse in Twentieth-Century Poetry* (Macmillan/St Martin's) appeared in 1997, shortly before his death. A posthumous volume of new poems, *Making a Republic*, was published by Carcanet in 2002.   ETL/MS-S*

Silko, Leslie Marmon (1948–) Novelist, poet, and essayist Leslie Marmon Silko was born to parents of mixed Laguna Pueblo, Mexican, and Anglo-American heritage, although she identifies as (and is known for her writing on) native American-Indian culture. She took a BA in English from the University of New Mexico, and is currently Professor of English at the University of Arizona, Tucson. Her correspondence with James *Wright has been published in book form (*With the Delicacy and Strength of Lace*, 1986).

Celebrated as a novelist for *Ceremony* (Penguin, 1977), a concern with tradition, story-telling, the feminine, the environment, and cross-cultural relationships informs all of Silko's writing. Her now infamous essay 'An Old-Fashioned Indian Attack in Two Acts' (1978) asserts a cultural possessiveness over American-Indian heritage for American-Indians, accusing Gary *Snyder of profiting from appropriation.

Silko's first volume of poetry, *Laguna Woman* (Greenfield Review 1974), shows her early preoccupation with giving expression to the Laguna experience of the world. It won the Chicago Review Poetry Award. Semi-autobiographical multigenre works such as *Storyteller* (Holt, 1981), *Sacred Water* (1994), and *Rain* (1996—both Flood Plain) have followed. Silko's poetry continues to address environmental issues, identity politics, and power-relations between the sexes through the

framework of Laguna Pueblo myth and folk-tale.   HY

Silliman, Ron (1946–) Born in Pasco, Washington, Silliman grew up in Albany, California, and attended San Francisco State University and University of California, Berkeley, dropping out to become a community organizer. He taught in universities, edited *Socialist Review*, and currently works in the computer industry.

His first book, *Crow* (Ithaca House, 1971), reflected the early influence of William Carlos *Williams. In 1974, he began the lifelong poetic project he has called *Ketjak*, also the title of a 1978 prose poem from This Press. The book-length *Tjanting* (The Figures, 1981 repr. Salt, 2002) developed this mode, arranging sentences into paragraphs that expand according to the Fibonacci sequence.

Silliman's characteristic style juxtaposes quotidian observation and self-reflexive word play ('Tmesis to me is this'). The sheer churn of his writing can seem (intentionally) undiscriminating, and the various forms in which it is cast a secondary consideration. But wit, poignancy, and precision are always to be found among its piecemeal mosaics. In 1979, he began *The Alphabet* (University of Alabama Press, 2008), a twenty-six book sequence. In 2004, he published a prose memoir, *Under Albany* (Salt), expanding the poem 'Albany' from *ABC* (Tuumba, 1983). His later poetry will be part of an even larger project, *Universe*.

As a *Language poet, Silliman has been an important theorist (*The New Sentence* (Roof, 1987)) and anthology editor (*In the American Tree* (National Poetry Foundation, 1986)). In 2002, he began a widely read blog for discussion of what he calls 'post-avant' poetry in America, defined in opposition to a mainstream 'School of Quietude'.   JNT

Simic, Charles (1938–) Born in Belgrade, Yugoslavia (now Serbia), and emigrated with his family to the United States at the age of eleven. Perhaps it is because his formative years were spent in a country occupied by the Nazis that Simic's most persistent thematic concern should be

with the effect of cruel political structures upon ordinary human life. It is this context that explains the series of almost miniaturist poems, on such subjects as 'Fork', 'Spoon', 'Knife', 'Ax', and 'Stone', that Simic included in his first book, *Dismantling the Silence* (1971). Rather than constituting the poet's major achievement, as some critics insist, these poems should be seen as defining momentary stays against confusion. The world of Simic's poems is frightening, mysterious, hostile, dangerous; by focusing on such unimportant, everyday objects, he is able to create, however briefly, some degree of order, comprehension, and control. Elsewhere in his early books Simic presents himself only as a clown, joking the night away; it is this sort of poem that he chose, wisely, not to reprint in his first *Selected Poems: 1963–1983* (1985—both Braziller), which collects from his first six volumes. In his most typical poems, Simic tells stories that are amusing and sinister at the same time: in 'Rough Outline', the 'famous torturer' meets a bride in a wedding-dress, who begs him to spare her beloved. I can't do that, he replies, for he must be tortured tonight, but 'You can come along and help him lament his fate'. The bride declines this invitation, and as the poem ends, 'a dog-like creature' howls 'Down by the slaughterhouse' and 'the snow start[s] to fall again'. As befits the professor of literary theory and creative writing at the University of New Hampshire, the texture of Simic's poems is conceptual and sophisticated; he regularly alludes to a wide range of western thought and literature.

Simic has written a study of the American artist Joseph Cornell, *Dime-Store Alchemy* (Ecco, 1992), an enthusiasm that reflects his own movie-theatre take on *Surrealism. The prose poems of *The World Doesn't End* (Harcourt, 1989) won the Pulitzer Prize. See *The Voice at 3.00 AM: Selected Late and New Poems* (Harcourt, 2003), and *Selected Poems 1963–2003* (Faber, 2004), which won the Griffin International Poetry Prize. In 2007 Simic became Poet Laureate of the United States, and received the Wallace Stevens Award from the Academy of American Poets.

His prose is collected in *The Uncertain Certainty* (1988), *A Fly in the Soup: Memoirs* (2000), and *Metaphysician in the Darkness* (2003—all University of Michigan Press). With Don *Paterson, he edited an anthology of *New British Poetry* (Graywolf, 2004) for an American readership. Also a prolific translator of European literature, his latest collections are *That Little Something* (2008) and *Master of Disguises* (2010). See also the selected volume, *Sixty Poems* (2008—all Harcourt).   PS*

Simmons, James (1933–2001) Born in Derry into a family of singers. He started singing in his father's bar in Portrush, and was popular in Ireland as a singer and songwriter as well as poet, although he did not make a clear division between these activities: several poems in his *Poems 1956–1986* (Bloodaxe, 1986) are also songs. He sought his models in the lyrics of popular music and jazz, and was sometimes overtly hostile to what he saw as the pretensions of high art, especially that of the modern period, as in *No Land is Waste, Dr. Eliot* (Keepsake, 1972): 'What roots? What stony rubbish? What rats? Where? | Visions of horror conjured out of air, | the spiritual D.T.s. The pompous swine . . . | that man's not hollow, he's a mate of mine.' Not surprisingly, he wished his poems to have an appeal outside literary circles. As he said in the first issue of *The Honest Ulsterman*, the literary journal he founded in 1968: 'I hope this magazine gets into the hands of school children and the so-called man in the street, people who think a dull life is inevitable, normal.' Simmons' poems have a wry, bittersweet, ironic flavour. His directness can make his treatment of the Troubles acutely painful, as in 'Claudy', which describes the effects of a car-bomb. His later collections included *Sex, Rectitude and Loneliness* (Lapwing, 1993), *Mainstream* (1995), and *The Company of Children* (1999—both Salmon).   ETL

Simms, Colin (1939–) A professional naturalist who has spent much of his life in the north of England, Simms has published poetry since 1960, mainly through pamphlets and small presses. Shearsman Books has collected many fugitive works from across the decades in *Otters and Martens* (2004), *The American Poems (2005)*, *Gyrfalcon Poems* (2007), and *Poems from Afghanistan* (2012).

Influenced by Basil *Bunting and Charles *Olson's open-field poetics, Simms' work is uncompromising and tautly focused, tracking animal behaviours, human rituals, and reflecting upon the act of observation through repeated returns to the same poem or subject (many carry multiple dates for revisions). In *Otters and Martens* the taxonomic classification of mustelids unifies poems spread across time and space, from the Yukon to the becks of Northumberland. The very title of '(from some Welsh Fieldwork)' acknowledges the poetry's source in the naturalist's labour. Yet there is also wonder here, as the poem begins with pre-cognitive apprehension—'Before I know I'm picking up particular pattern | I'm picking up that pattern of sense and on memory'—and the expanse of waiting is calibrated: 'footfall against leaf fall'. It ends acknowledging the limitations of its own tentative provisionality: 'I mutter as she does, sing under my breath and heart | response no matter how foolish, totter toward its art...' There is a discussion of Simms' work in Andrew Duncan, *Centre and Periphery in Modern British Poetry* (Liverpool University Press, 2005).   LMe

Simpson, Louis (1923–2012) The son of a lawyer of Scottish descent and a Russian mother, was born in Jamaica and emigrated to the United States at the age of 17. He interrupted his studies at Columbia University to serve in the US Army in Europe during the Second World War. Returning to Columbia after the war, Simpson earned a PhD, then taught in California for some years before moving to Long Island, where he lived and taught from 1967.

Simpson is among that group of American poets who made a radical change in style in mid-career. The poems in his early books are tightly written in traditional forms, with careful use of metre and rhyme. Some of these poems—for example 'As Birds Are Fitted to the Boughs'—have been seen by critics as comparable to the great Elizabethan lyrics. The real world also enters Simpson's early work in poems dealing with his war experiences, notably 'Carentan O Carentan' and 'The Runner'. In the early Sixties, however, Simpson began to feel that his forms were distancing his work from real life, and he started to write free-verse poems in which both structure and meaning are created by patterns of imagery. He also at this time became critical of American society, particularly for its warmongering in Vietnam and its lack of cultural seriousness. *At the End of the Open Road* (1963), for which Simpson was awarded the Pulitzer Prize, portrays the United States as a superficial country stalled at a moral dead-end. With *Adventures of the Letter I* (1971), Simpson began writing poems about Russia and his Russian ancestors and about the most ordinary forms of American life, finding his materials for these on the streets or in the shopping-malls and living-rooms of the American suburbs. In 'Quiet Desperation' a nondescript middle-aged man watches a little television, chops a little wood, walks his dog, and broods about his own mortality. In 'The Beaded Pear' a mother goes shopping with her family, converses with them over dinner ('Why don't you get transferred, Dad?'), and later constructs her pear out of styrofoam and sequins.

Collected Poems (Paragon House, 1988) included all the poems that Simpson wanted to preserve from his earlier books. *The Owner of the House: New Collected Poems* (2003) drew on several later volumes, and was nominated for the National Book Award and the Griffin International Poetry Prize. His last collection was *Struggling Times* (2009—both BOA). *Voices in the Distance: Selected Poems* was published in the UK by Bloodaxe in 2010.

Selected Prose (Paragon House, 1989) is supplemented by *Three on the Tower: The Lives and Works of Ezra Pound, T. S. Eliot, and William Carlos Williams* (Morrow, 1975) and *A Revolution in Taste: Studies of Dylan Thomas, Allen Ginsberg, Sylvia Plath, and Robert Lowell* (Macmillan, 1978). He wrote one novel, *Riverside Drive* (1962), an autobiography, *North of Jamaica*

(1972), and a later memoir, *The King My Father's Wreck* (1995). His *Modern Poets of France: A Bilingual Anthology* (Story Line, 1997) won the Harold Morton Landon Translation Award.

See also Hank Lazer (ed.), *On Louis Simpson: Depths Beyond Happiness* (1988), and *Louis Simpson* (1972) by Ronald Moran.   PS

Simpson, R. A. (Ronald Albert) (1929–2002) Born in Melbourne, he studied with the Christian Brothers, then at Melbourne Teachers' College and the Royal Melbourne Institute of Technology. He was an art teacher in various secondary schools until 1968, when he began lecturing in drawing at the Caulfield Institute of Technology, from which he retired in 1987. He travelled frequently to the United States and was poetry editor for the *Melbourne Age*. He combined drawing with the writing of lyric poetry, though he is far better known as a poet.

At once personal, terse, and dispassionate, Simpson assimilated a variety of influences (*Graves, *Ransom, Camus, *Gunn, and William Carlos *Williams) in the process of arriving at his clear, understated poetry of loss and resignation. The early poetry collected in *The Walk along the Beach* (1960) and *This Real Pompeii* (1964) faces annihilation with a *Movement-like concern for lyric shapeliness and measured anticlimax, while the critical sestina. 'All Friends Together' is uncharacteristically hilarious. Simpson's later poetry modulates into free verse, a shorter line, and flattened endings. Affinities might be discerned between this verse and his cubist drawings. It often glumly shows its autobiographical hand.

From his early 'Landscape' to his recent 'The Performer, the Feather and the Dogs', there is a familiar low-toned Simpson world of large fears and small expectations. His work can be found in *The Midday Clock: Selected Poems and Drawings* (Macmillan, 1999). *The Sky's Beach* (Five Islands, 2004) appeared posthumously.

See the critical judgements of Harry Heseltine, 'Poetry, Nature, Counterstatement', *Overland*, 105 (1986).   CW-C

Singer, (James) Burns (1928–64) Born in New York of mixed Polish, Jewish, and Celtic blood. Singer remained an American citizen all his life, though his family left the US for Scotland when he was 4. He began an English degree course at Glasgow University but left to teach mathematics in London, roamed Europe for two years, and returned to Glasgow to read zoology. He made a successful career as a marine biologist while maintaining a separate life as a poet and literary essayist, married psychologist and painter Marie Battle in 1956, and died of a heart-attack in Plymouth, aged 36. As a student he had met and fallen under the influence of W. S. *Graham, and was also an admirer of George *Barker, but his poetry was not significantly like anyone else's, writing as he did in an intellectual register very different from, and almost alien to, the familiar English literary one. His language and rhythms are simple, his arguments complex, rigorously complete, and worked out with acute observation of mental and physical processes. His imagery and themes draw heavily on the scientific world he moved in. His idiosyncratic brand of lyricism is all the more powerful for appearing in an essentially rationalist context. Singer's was the sort of philosophical writing guaranteed not to win a large audience—Hugh *MacDiarmid found him obscure, and Singer's one collection published during his lifetime, *Still and All* (1957), received little attention—yet Singer held strong views on the need for poetry to be open to any sort of reader. His prose writings, which remain uncollected, are illuminating on this and many other points. His *Selected Poems*, ed. Anne Cluysenaar, appeared in 1977 (Carcanet).

Collected Poems (Secker & Warburg, 1970), ed. W. A. S. Keir, contained a memoir by Hugh *MacDiarmid and further biographical information. A later *Collected Poems* (Carcanet, 2001), ed. James Keery, adds further uncollected and unpublished writing to Singer's oeuvre.   CPH

Sirr, Peter (1960–) Born in Waterford and studied at Trinity College, Dublin. He has lived in Holland and Italy, and now works as a freelance writer and translator in Dublin. He was previously editor of *Poetry Ireland Review* and is married to the poet Enda Wyley.

Sirr has published seven volumes with The Gallery Press. His acclaimed debut, *Marginal Zones* (1984), evinced a *Martian influence in its ingenious imagery, and introduced recurring themes of the transitory and the translated, as well as a fascination with dramatized perspectives and historical voices. *Talk, Talk* (1987), *Ways of Falling* (1991), and *The Ledger of Fruitful Exchange* (1995) all followed a pattern of single poems combined with longer sequences such as 'Death of a Travel Writer' and 'A Journal'.

Sirr's inventiveness is not readily pigeon-holed. As a critic, he has praised Irish poets as diverse as Pearse *Hutchinson and Trevor *Joyce, and as a poet he draws on international influences. *Bring Everything* (2000) was called his 'best book to date' by Justin *Quinn. Its renewed focus on contemporary Dublin continues in *Nonetheless* (2004) and *The Thing Is* (2009). A selected poems appeared in Ireland from The Gallery Press in 2004, and in the States from Wake Forest University Press in 2005.   JNT

Sissay, Lemn (1967–) Born in Lancashire, England to Ethiopian parents, Sissay grew up in a white foster family, and then, as a teenager, in care homes. He moved to Manchester and became involved in Cultureword, a centre for black writers in the area. In 2010 he received an MBE for his services to literature, and was the official poet of the London Olympics 2012.

Sissay began to publish poetry in his early twenties, and was included by Fred *D'Aguiar in the revisionary anthology, *the new british poetry* (Paladin, 1988). In the same year he published *Tender Fingers in a Clenched Fist* (Bogle L'Ouverture). By the time of the *Rebel Without Applause* (Bloodaxe, 1992) Sissay was a popular performer on stage, television, and radio. He has also released his own recordings, and in 1995 appeared on *Leftism*, the debut album by British electronic musicians Leftfield.

Sissay's populist style has affinities with that of Benjamin *Zephaniah, often using repetitive and rhyming forms, sometimes influenced by rap, to frame satirical and affirmative poems on black identity. *Rebel Without Applause* was reprinted by Canongate in 2000, who have published Sissay's subsequent books *Morning Breaks in the Elevator* (1999) and *Listener* (2009). He has also written plays, made documentaries, and edited an anthology of contemporary black British poets, *The Fire People* (Payback, 1998).   JNT

Sissman, L. E. (Louis Edward) (1928–76) A precocious only child brought up in Detroit, who at thirteen became national champion in a radio spelling bee, and three years later went to Harvard, already six-foot four and overweight. He was rusticated, readmitted, elected class poet, and graduated *cum laude*. At Harvard, the editor of his collected poems tells us, 'his poetic technique set and was varnished', but it remained unused for more than a decade, during which he became a successful advertising man.

In 1965 Sissman learned that he was suffering from the then-incurable Hodgkin's disease. The knowledge moved him to the writing and publication of poems, written during and between periods of hospitalization and treatment that included chemotherapy. *Dying: An Introduction* (1968) was followed by two other volumes and a collection of essays. His posthumous collected poems, *Hello, Darkness*, appeared in 1978 (both Little, Brown). He was twice married.

The expectation such a life might give of gloomy self-regarding poetry would be wrong. Most of Sissman's poems are written in iambic pentameter, and deal cheerfully or ironically with the universe of things known and seen. He felt more kinship with British than with contemporary American poets, mocked and imitated *Empson, dedicated a poem to Kingsley *Amis and Robert *Conquest, and wrote a tribute to Orwell. His originality rests in working against the poetic grain of almost all the American writing round him, as well as in what John Updike called his 'antic exactitude'. He needed space to achieve his full effects, so that the finest poems are the longer ones, like 'Going Home, 1945' (evidently written much later), 'The Marschallin, Joy Street', 'A Day in the City (Boston-New York)', and the partly autobiographical 'A War Requiem'. He also needed, as it seems at times, reassurance about the existence of the world in which he lived, so that there is much naming of shops, restaurants, and houses. No doubt the need for reassurance was also connected with the death-sentence under which he lived, which is looked at glancingly but courageously in some of the last poems, like 'Cancer: A Dream'.

Sissman's limitation rests in that set, varnished technique. There is little change or variation in his poems, which are chatty, comic, at times rhetorically powerful, but rarely delicate or tender. Yet his achievement was remarkable, nothing less than a hymn to American urban man. See *Night Music* (Houghton Mifflin, 1999), a selection edited by Peter *Davison, with a foreword by Edward *Hirsch.   JGS

Sisson, C. H. (Charles Hubert) (1914–2003) Born in Bristol. He was a higher official in the Ministry of Labour, and as a poet became known late, with *Collected Poems 1943–1983* (1984). Sisson adhered to the position made famous by *Eliot: Anglican, monarchist, Tory; but his Anglicanism, still central to his poetry even though he later refused to attend church on account of the changes in the Prayer Book, was less high-church, and his austere poems in no way resemble Eliot's. The cast of mind of *Hardy is quite as strong an influence; so is French poetry from Malherbe onwards. Sisson believed that the 'truth lies at the bottom of a well of rhythm', and sought to reproduce the rhythms of speech. 'In London' is a characteristic early poem: an ironic note of pastoral is introduced into a squalid urban scene incorporating a shabby erotic encounter; punctuation is light, and treats line-endings as commas or semicolons. A power of feeling of Hardyean intensity is fully acknowledged in Sisson, but expression of it is, more often than not, deliberately denied. The meaninglessness of existence is also acknowledged, countered only tentatively: 'If we have reasons, they lie deep.' Extreme bitterness about contemporary life is most evident in 'The Spectre', a satirical account of a successful modern intellectual going through familiar stages of pseudo-development: Poundian disenchantment sharpened by an uncompromising Augustinian Christianity, from which every consolatory supernatural element has been stripped. This relentless theological position is most fully worked out in 'The Usk'. Sisson has his advocates, but his poetry has not yet entered the mainstream, owing to its persistently exasperated tone and its apparently anti-liberal stance. But it is powerfully representative of what is left of the Christian tradition in English poetry. Following his *Collected Poems* he published *God Bless Karl Marx!* (1988). He also translated Horace, Lucretius, Virgil, Dante, and La Fontaine, among others. His prose works include *The Avoidance of Literature: Collected Essays* (1978) and *Anglican Essays* (1983). In 1993 he was made a Companion of Honour. See *Poems: Selected* (1995), *Collected Translations* (1996), and *Collected Poems* (1998— all Carcanet).   POM

Sitwell, Dame Edith (Louisa) (1887–1964) The eldest child of Sir George and Lady Sitwell of Renishaw Hall, near Scarborough. Lonely and unconventional-looking, she was always to feel that, unlike her younger brothers, Osbert and Sacheverell (to whom she was nonetheless devoted), she had been deprived of her due share of maternal affection. She was educated at Renishaw, from which she was finally rescued by her governess, Helen Rootham. In 1914 they moved to London, and were companions for many years. It was Helen Rootham who introduced Sitwell to the French Symbolists, of whom Rimbaud made the strongest impression on the young writer. She published her first book, *The Mother and Other Poems* (Blackwell, 1915), at her own expense, and went on to edit, with Nancy Cunard, the annual anthology *Wheels*. This ran for six issues and roused controversy by championing literary modernism against the *Georgians.

Famously accused by F. R. Leavis of belonging, with her brothers, 'to the history of publicity rather than that of poetry', Sitwell undoubtedly had an enormously theatrical sense of herself. The famous iconic image of her photos and portraits seems reflected in her poems, with their bright, stately, brocade-like figures. The constant procession of emblems throughout her work—lions, peacocks, roses, gold, blood, bone—sometimes suggests an easy shorthand for symbolic resonance.

Façade, a sequence of poems set to music by William Walton, drew jeers at its first performance in 1922, but later became her most popular work. It is arguably the ideal setting for her nonsense verse, with its concentration on assonance and alliteration. In her own way, Sitwell responded seriously and passionately to public events, and her two wartime collections, *Street Songs* (1942) and *Green Song and Other Poems* (1943), caught the heroic mood of the time, and may have helped instigate the later, neo-romantic school of poets, dubbed the *New Apocalypse.

Whatever her credibility as a poet, Sitwell is undoubtedly an important figure in the literary history of England in the twentieth century. She was a crusading force against the native tendencies to philistinism and conservatism. Though her most sustained loyalty was to the emigré Russian artist Pavel Tchelitchew, she selflessly championed many young and deserving writers. Under constant pressure to earn her living, she almost certainly published too much, not only poetry but also critical pot-boilers and historical works. Her prose is patchy but can be vivid and immediate and, especially in her *Selected Letters* (new edn. Virago, 1998), harshly witty.

The fullest representation of her poetry is in the *Collected Poems* (Duckworth Overlook, 2006). For detailed and sympathetic accounts of her life and work, see Victoria Glendinning, *Edith Sitwell: A Unicorn among the Lions* (Knopf, 1981) and Richard Greene, *Edith Sitwell: Avant Garde Poet, English Genius* (Virago, 2011).   CAR

Skelton, Robin (1925–97) Born in Yorkshire. Educated at Christ's College, Cambridge, and the University of Leeds, Skelton lectured for a time in English literature at the University of Manchester. In 1963 he emigrated to Canada where he taught in the department of English at the University of Victoria, before becoming the university's first chairman of the department of creative writing. In addition to his own creative writing, he published widely on the Irish literary renaissance. He influenced many Canadian writers as a teacher and through his work with the *Malahat Review*, which he co-founded in 1967 and edited until 1983. He also wrote on sorcery and witchcraft.

Skelton wrote in many different poetic styles and voices, and exercised in many forms. Most notably, perhaps, he was influenced by the *Surrealists (he commented that he saw himself as a 'messenger'), and like them he would claim to be in search of the secret world beneath the 'lying intimacies' of everyday life.

Much of Skelton's poetry to 1977 can be found in the two companion volumes *Collected Shorter Poems 1947–1977* (1981) and *Collected Longer Poems 1947–1977* (1985—both Sono Nis). Skelton's own books about poetry include *The Practice of Poetry* (Barnes & Noble, 1971), *The Poet's Calling* (1975), and *Poetic Truth* (1978—both Heinemann). See *In This Poem I Am: Selected Poetry of Robin Skelton* (Dundurn, 2007), ed. Harold Rhenisch.   RH

Skoulding, Zoë (1967–   ) Born in Bradford and spent much of her childhood in Suffolk. She was educated at the universities of Exeter and Bangor, and since 1991 has lived and taught in North Wales.

Skoulding's range of interests includes translation and other collaborative writing, and sound-based vocal performance. Her own work has been widely translated and in technique and subject often reflects a free-ranging European sensibility. She is a meticulous craftswoman, and her skill at subtle destabilizations of line and stanza has developed over her three collections: *Tide Table* (Pantycelyn, 1998), *The Mirror Trade* (2004), and *Remains of a Future City* (2008—both Seren). The latter was shortlisted for the Wales Book of the Year Award.

Skoulding's poetry has featured in various significant anthologies, notably *The Ground Aslant: An Anthology of Radical Landscape Poetry* (Shearsman, 2011), ed. Harriet Tarlo. Since 2008 she has edited the literary journal, *Poetry Wales*.   CAR

Skovron, Alex (1948–) Born in Poland. In 1956 his family moved to Israel, and then in 1958 to Sydney. Since taking degrees in political science at the universities of New South Wales and Sydney, Skovron has worked as an editor for several publishing firms, and was general editor of the *Concise Encyclopedia of Australia*.

In 1976 he married Ruth Paluch, and in 1979 moved to Melbourne. Skovron had begun seriously to write poetry in 1968, but published nothing until 1982. After that he rapidly won recognition and began for the first time to meet other poets and move in literary circles. Nor does he seem before this to have taken an especial interest in any poet more recent than *Eliot.

Where one might expect naïvety, isolation produced in Skovron a brooding complexity of form and imaginative organization. In his first book, the award-winning *The Rearrangement* (Melbourne University Press, 1988), the most striking poems are long and extraordinarily intricate. The title-poem is formally a remarkable *tour-de-force*, done with such cunning that the patterning almost escapes notice; suitably, perhaps, it is a study of obsession. Other poems are more accessible, but most demand an alert reader. *The Rearrangement* was followed by *Sleeve Notes* (Hale & Iremonger, 1992), a musically themed collection. *Infinite City: 100 Sonnetinas* (1999) is written in an invented ten-line form. His later collections include *The Man and the Map* (2003—both Five Islands) and *Autographs: 56 Poems in Prose* (Hybrid, 2008). He has also written a novella, *The Poet* (2005).   EJ

Skrzynecki, Peter (1945–) Born in Germany of Polish/Ukrainian parents. He emigrated to Australia in 1949 and grew up in Sydney, where he gained degrees from Sydney University and the University of New England. He is a teacher. His poems

have been translated and published in Polish and in 1990 he received from the Polish government the medal of *L'ordre du Mérite culturel* for his contribution to Polish culture in Australia.

Skrzynecki was one of the first writers in Australia of his generation to articulate the contours of the post-war migrations in the 1950s, and his anthology *Joseph's Coat* (Hale & Iremonger, 1985) was one of the major collections to cover the increasingly multicultural nature of the evolving Australian society.

Although he has published two notable collections of short stories and two novels (*The Beloved Mountain* (Hale & Iremonger, 1988) and *The Cry of the Goldfinch* (Transworld, 1996)), it is as a poet that Skrzynecki has made his mark. He has published eight collections, including *Immigrant Chronicle* (University of Queensland Press, 1975), *The Polish Immigrant* (Phoenix, 1983), *Night Swim: Poems 1978–1988* (Hale & Iremonger, 1989), and *Time's Revenge* (Brandl & Schlesinger, 1999). He has won a number of literary awards.

Skrzynecki's poetry is imbued with a sense of introspection and a European sensibility. Although he frequently writes about direct experience and the natural environment of Australia, his best work has a driven, worrying quality that reflects both an autobiographical obsession and a deep-seated alienation. He received the Medal of the Order of Australia in 2002. See *Old/New World: New and Selected Poems* (University of Queensland Press, 2007).   TWS

Sleigh, Tom (1953–) Born in Mount Pleasant, Texas. He attended the California Institute of Arts and Johns Hopkins University, and has lived in Cambridge, Massachusetts from the early 1980s. He now directs the Creative Writing MFA programme at Hunter College in New York.

Sleigh's poetry, while anchored at every point to concrete particulars, can also be read as an exploration of Simone Weil's polar terms—'gravity' and 'grace'. Gravity recognizes suffering and the often-harsh exactions of circumstance, and Sleigh probes these in a number of unflinching poems about the lives of family members and his own encounter with illness. Grace, in Sleigh's vision, may not be God-given, but it brings the redemptive recognition of beauty and, at rare moments, a near-mystical surety of connection to a deeper ground of being.

'Ending', Sleigh's most ambitious early work, brings the terms of the opposition into high relief. The poem, chronicling his struggle with illness, is harrowing in its particulars, and shows to full advantage the poet's supple and rhythmic idiom. Sleigh's collections include *After One* (Houghton Mifflin, 1983), *Waking* (1990), *The Chain* (1996), *The Dreamhouse* (1999—all University of Chicago Press), *Far Side of the Earth* (2003), and *Space Walk* (2007—both Houghton Mifflin), which won the Kingsley Tufts Poetry Award. See also *Interview with a Ghost* (2006), a collection of critical essays, and *Army Cats* (2011—both Graywolf).   SB

Slessor, Kenneth (1901–71) Slessor is widely held to be Australia's first modern poet as well as one of its finest. His writing career was comparatively short. He published his first volume in 1924 and the last of his hundred-odd poems appeared in the mid-1940s. Yet, with the possible exception of his contemporary R. D. *FitzGerald, it was Slessor who did more than anyone to propel Australian poetry into the twentieth century and help it shake off the 'colonial' tag. Commentators on his first mature poems were quick to find in them evidence of the influence of T. S. *Eliot. Slessor himself always claimed Tennyson as an early master. It has been suggested that his poems mingle Eliot's edgy toughness with Tennyson's tender fantasy and feeling. However, any attentive reader of such characteristic poems as 'Heine in Paris', 'Captain Dobbin', and above all 'Five Bells', will recognize the originality of Slessor's ample rhetoric and of his technical assurance. This is not to say he is free of influences. But while these exist they are well absorbed into work which represents a blend of the ironic, poised tone of such French poets as Corbière and Laforgue together with the sumptuous cadences of *Yeats and, just possibly, the Wallace *Stevens of *Harmonium.*

Slessor's poetry is entirely professional. Its polish is the result of hard work. It is also dense with the actualities of Australian life, and in this Slessor seems to be the source for much of Les *Murray's poetry. The second edition of his *Poems* was published in 1957 and *Selected Poems* in 1975 (both Angus & Robertson). Dennis Haskell made a selection from Slessor's poetry and prose for University of Queensland Press in 1991, and an annotated *Collected Poems* appeared in 1994 (Angus & Robertson), ed. Haskell and Geoffrey Dutton. There are biographies by Dutton (Penguin, 1991) and Adrian Caesar (Oxford University Press, 1995).   JL

Smith, A. J. M. (Arthur James Marshall) (1902–80) Born in Montreal and educated at McGill University and the University of Edinburgh. Smith developed a taste for the new poetry as a young browser in Harold *Monro's bookshop in London where he lived from 1918 to 1920. At McGill University he teamed up with F. R. *Scott, recently returned from Oxford, to launch a literary supplement to the student newspaper. This was followed by a more mature effort in the form of the *McGill Fortnightly Review* (1925–27). The effect of Smith's enterprise both as a practising poet and a budding critic was to draw like-minded and aspiring young writers into a circle which became known as the 'McGill Movement'. They read *Eliot, *Yeats, the Symbolists, and followed the literary currents of international modernism in the avant-garde periodicals of the times. Smith himself published in the *Measure* and the *Dial* in the middle Twenties, and would go on to win the Harriet Monroe Memorial Prize from *Poetry* (Chicago) in 1943. All of this helped to solidify his strong anti-parochialism, and to turn Smith into a sophisticated and witty internationalist in his literary outlook. After his return from Edinburgh, Smith drifted to the United States where he eventually settled into a long and distinguished career at Michigan State University as professor of English and poet-in-residence. In 1936 he collaborated with F. R. Scott in assembling *New Provinces: Poems of Several Authors*, a milestone anthology of modernist Canadian verse. A meticulous craftsman, Smith took a long time to produce his first book, *News of the Phoenix and Other Poems* (1943). This was followed eleven years later by *A Sort of Ecstasy: Poems New and Selected* (1954) which offered twenty new poems. This pattern of worrying, polishing, and reworking material became a hallmark of Smith's method, and has meant that the sum total of his life's published work stands at some 200 poems. In spite of this, Smith managed to produce poems in a great variety of modes. A versatile and playful stylist, his poetry ranges from the stark image and the simple lyric to the allusive conceits of a literary imagination schooled in Donne and the metaphysical poets. Smith's *Collected Poems* came out in 1962, and was followed by *Poems New and Collected* (1967—both Oxford University Press) and *The Classic Shade: Selected Poems* (McClelland & Stewart, 1978).

In addition to his poetry, Smith carved out a prominent role for himself as an anthologist and influential critic. He edited *The Book of Canadian Poetry* (Gage, 1943, 1948, 1957) and the *Oxford Book of Canadian Verse in English and French* (Oxford University Press, 1960). His critical writings can be found in *Towards a View of Canadian Letters: Selected Critical Essays 1928–1971* (University of British Columbia Press, 1973).

See also Michael E. Darling, *A. J. M. Smith: An Annotated Bibliography* (Véhicule, 1981), *Selected Writings* (Dundurn, 2006), ed. Michael Gnarowski, and *The Complete Poems*, ed. Brian Trehearne (Canadian Poetry, 2007).   MG

Smith, Dave (David Jeddie) (1942–) Born in Portsmouth,Virginia. He attended local schools and graduated from the University of Virginia. He served in the US Air Force and, later, studied in the graduate schools of Southern Illinois University and Ohio University. He is now Elliot Coleman Professor of Poetry at Johns Hopkins University.

The author of over a dozen books of poetry, Smith has been widely praised for his lyricism and narrative powers, both of which are brought forcefully to bear in poems which are often set in the rural south. His talent for the gradual release of narrative details gives his longer poems, such as 'Night Fishing for Blues' or 'In the House of the Judge', a sustained drive. As in 'Goshawk, Antelope', Smith regularly invokes a 'country of blue sedge' populated by wild animals and birds that, in this poet's hands, become powerful natural symbols. His poetic stage is crammed with workers: fishermen, oystermen, clamdiggers; the natural landscape of the poems is frequently a backdrop to country revels at sundown, to old railroad roundhouses, racial fights, and dusty roads—a landscape reminiscent of Robert Penn *Warren, whose poetry has had a profound influence on Smith.

As in 'The Roundhouse Voices', Smith is primarily a poet of memory, summoning his own childhood and family in haunting ways. He can vividly recall a childhood swimming-hole in 'Hole, Where Once in Passion We Swam', an old family heirloom in 'The Spinning Wheel in the Attic', a lost cousin in 'De Soto', or the discovery of an old chest filled with pornographic photos in 'The Pornography Box', one of many poems that invoke the poet's father. Helen Vendler has called Smith 'a distinguished allegorist of human experience', describing his poems as 'solemn, harsh, driven, obdurate, hungry for some guarantees—which he wants as much to create as to experience—of promises kept, love exchanged, hope confirmed'. Smith has said that 'Poetry is the knight doing psychic combat for us', and his poems frequently aspire to an almost heroic stance, with the acts of memory and vision viewed as something akin to restitution and recovery.

See *The Wick of Memory: New and Selected Poems* (2000) and *Little Boats, Unsalvaged* (2006). His sixteenth collection was *Hawks on Wires* (2011—all Louisiana State University Press).

He has also written a novel, *Onliness* (1981), a book of stories, and two collections of critical essays on American poetry, *Local Assays* (University of Illinois Press, 1985) and *Hunting Men* (Louisiana State University Press, 2006).   JP

Smith, Iain Crichton (1928–98) Born in Glasgow, Smith was taken as an infant to the island of Lewis where he remained until entering the University of Aberdeen in 1945. After National Service he taught in various schools in the west of Scotland. He was a freelance writer from 1977.

Smith was prolific in both English and Gaelic (of which he was a native speaker). As well as poetry he published novels, collections of stories, plays, essays, and reviews. His major themes are the contest of the individual with repressive religious, social, and political forces which result in the displacement of the poet; the offensiveness of a superficial, consumerist society; and the vulnerability of the Gaelic language and its culture in the face of corrosive modern pressures. The first and third of these themes originate in his upbringing on Lewis where the power of the Presbyterian United Free Church (the 'Wee Frees') is evoked as personally and culturally negative. Smith's term for this 'patriarchal' sway is Law, which he counters with Grace, the values of which he takes from poetry, art, classical mythology, and the 'endlessly various, real, human | world which is no new era, shining dawn', as he writes in 'Lenin', where he tackles a political version of straitjacketing denial.

Much of Smith's poetry in English is stanzaic, iambic, and uses rhyme. The much-anthologized 'Old Woman', and 'At the Sale', are good examples. Other work, perhaps his best—'The Clearances', 'Poem in March', 'Chinese Poem', and a good deal in his later collections—is usually freer. Ostensibly casual forms permit the release of often eccentric imagery. He refers widely to literature, art, history, and philosophy, but also introduces vivid observations of contemporary life ('By the Sea'). Many influences are detectable—*Auden, *Lowell, and *Stevens among them—but there are others which appear momentarily and suggest that Smith was a restless and perhaps uncertain writer for whom the issues raised by a bilingual poetic endeavour were not always fruitful. However, they also help to identify Smith as an eclectic poet who was willing to take stylistic and emotional

risks. His sense of humour is evident in 'Chinese Poem' and especially in his satirical poems in Gaelic (which he translated himself), such as 'The TV' and 'Gaelic Stories'.

Smith published fifteen major separate collections in English and/or Gaelic. *Selected Poems* (1985) offers a cross-section of his generous productivity to that date. His last collection, *A Country for Old Men*, appeared posthumously in 2000. There is now a *New Collected Poems* (2011—all Carcanet), ed. Matthew McGuire, which enlarges the original 1992 edition. *Towards the Human: Selected Essays* appeared in 1986 (MacDonald). There is a full bibliography by G. F. Wilson (1990), and see *Iain Crichton Smith: New Critical Essays*, ed. C. Nicholson (Edinburgh University Press, 1991) and Carol Gow, *Mirror and Marble* (Saltire Society, 1992).   DED

Smith, Ken(neth John) (1938–2003) Born in Yorkshire, the son of an itinerant farm labourer. He read English at Leeds during the University's literary flowering in the early Sixties, when G. Wilson Knight and Geoffrey *Hill were on the teaching staff and Jon *Silkin and Peter *Redgrove were Gregory Fellows in poetry. *The Pity* (Cape, 1967) shows the social commitment associated with *Stand*, of which he was co-editor from 1963 until he moved to America in 1969.

That move precipitated a change, not simply in his style, but in his conception of poetry. Influenced by the work of James *Wright and Robert *Bly, and even more by the primitive poetry collected in *Technicians of the Sacred* (Doubleday, 1968), he became impatient with an art of framed observations. *Work, distances/poems* (Swallow, 1972) marked the beginning of what was really one lifelong poem, an intermittent narrative that fluctuated from lyrics and epigrams to extended sequences. He developed myths and discovered personae, telling stories in order to understand his own story, finding 'a language to speak to myself'.

Such a project was not widely understood in England. He returned in 1973 but did not re-establish his reputation until *The Poet Reclining* appeared in 1982, bringing together ten years' work that had been published only in fugitive pamphlets. The poems had immediate virtues—rhythmic vitality, clarity of image—but their importance lay in their cumulative power, in the way they seemed to grow from a sustained and necessary activity.

A writer's residency at Wormwood Scrubs prison (1985–7) led to the poems of *Wormwood* (1987—both Bloodaxe) and to the prose of *Inside Time* (Harrap, 1989), co-written with David Wait. He travelled widely, making a series of programmes for the BBC that merged poetry and speech with music and sounds recorded on location, and these fed into another prose book, *Berlin: Coming in from the Cold* (Hamilton, 1990) and into the poems collected in *Shed: Poems 1980–2001* (2003). In 2003 he returned from Cuba with Legionnaire's Disease and was taken into intensive care, only to die of an infection contracted in the hospital.

Ken Smith received a Lannan Award in 1997 and a Cholmondeley Award in 1998. His last poems were published in *You Again* (2004—both Bloodaxe), together with a selection of his prose pieces, two critical essays on his work, and tributes from other poets.   RGa

Smith, Michael (1954–83) Born in Kingston, Jamaica. Working-class in origin (his father was a mason, and his mother a factory worker) he enrolled at the Jamaica School of Drama, and by the time he graduated in 1980, he was one of the most popular *dub performance poets in Jamaica. In 1982 he toured Britain and Europe with great success. His life, however, was tragically cut short when four hired thugs stoned him to death during the Jamaican general-election campaign of 1983. When challenged, he had reputedly said: 'I-man free to walk anywhere in this land.'

Michael Smith's most famous poem, 'Me Cyaan Believe It', is a sardonic protest against any limits which hedge the lives of ordinary people, and his Rastafarian contempt for the merely political bares its teeth in the following lines from 'I an I Alone':

'Hey, lady, yuh believe in Socialism?' | 'No, sah, me believe in social livin.'

It a Come (Race Today, 1986), his only book of poetry, was edited by Mervyn *Morris, and received a Poetry Book Society Recommendation. It was reissued in 1989 by City Lights in San Francisco. The Island LP record, *Me Cyaan Believe It* (1982) records his style of public performance, and was produced by fellow dub poet Linton Kwesi *Johnson.   MR

Smith, Simon (1961–) Born in Cornwall, Smith studied English and American Literature at the University of Kent, where he is now a lecturer in creative writing. He was formerly the librarian of the Saison Poetry Library in London and poetry editor of *Angel Exhaust* magazine.

After university, Smith lived for two years in the United States, and admirers have often noted the American influence on his characteristic quickfire manner. After several small-press publications in the 1990s, his first book was *Fifteen Exits* (Waterloo, 2001), which took its epigraph from Jack *Spicer ('Things do not connect; they correspond') and, in a gesture of *O'Hara-esque sociability, dedicated its poems to friends and fellow writers.

Reverdy Road (2003) and *Mercury* (2006) are book-length sequences of short lyrics which pick up and redistribute the language and life-world of modern London with a *Raworthian lightness. *London Bridge* (2010—all Salt) saw Smith experiment with a collection of formally discrete pieces, interspersed with his own translations of Martial, Propertius, Rilke, and Apollinaire. He has also published translations of Reverdy and Catullus, and 'found' sonnets from the letters of Robert and Elizabeth Barrett Browning: see *Telegraph Cottage* (Mindmade, 2007) and *Browning Variations* (Landfill, 2009).   JNT

Smith, Stevie (Florence Margaret) (1902–71) Born in Hull, but from the age of three lived in a north London suburb, Palmers Green. Until 1953 she worked as a secretary, mainly in a publishing company. Most of her adult life she lived with an aunt. She never married.

She first came to prominence as the author of a novel, *Novel on Yellow Paper* (1936), a book which shares some qualities with her poetry: quirky, sardonic, disconcerting in its varying tones of voice. Her first book of poems, *A Good Time Was Had By All* (1937), established from the beginning several of her characteristics: quick changes of tone, abrupt veerings between comic and tragic, absurd and solemn, and a range of lyrical, satirical, discursive, and flippant modes.

'I can't make up my mind', she wrote, 'if God is good, impotent or unkind.' She scratched obsessively at the Christian Church and the Christian faith, as if they were sores which would not quite heal. Her lectures to university societies ('The Necessity of Not Believing' at Cambridge, 'Some Impediments to Christian Commitment' at Oxford) are variations on the themes of many poems: 'There is a god in whom I do not believe | Yet to this god my love stretches | This god whom I do not believe in is | My whole life, my life and I am his.'

Throughout the entire period of her writing life, and since her death (when, incidentally, she was at the height of her fame and popularity), Stevie Smith's 'seriousness' and 'importance' have been frequently questioned. Was she naïve, or *faux-naïf*? Childlike or childish? Ingenuous or disingenuous? To some, she was William Blake rewritten by Ogden *Nash. The drawings that accompanied many of her poems, and the curious combination of ceremony and levity she brought to the reading aloud of her work, have been called in question. In the best full-length book so far written about her (*Stevie Smith: A Critical Biography*, Faber, 1988), Frances Spalding convincingly argues for her importance without abandoning her acclaimed role as an idiosyncratic and often very funny entertainer.

In her lifetime, she produced seven books of poems, including a *Selected Poems* (Longmans/New Directions, 1964). If any distinction can be made between poems written at different periods, it is that the theme of death increasingly preoccupied her in her later work, often seen in a whimsical and even sprightly way, as if

death were almost someone to be comfortably welcomed, like a neighbour. She drew on many invented voices, controlling a range of personae unequalled since *Eliot, and possibly Browning, but always recognizably issuing from the same tormented, lyrical, hymn-haunted, Poe-addicted, teasing, inconsequential, truth-telling mouth.

After her death, her *Collected Poems* was edited by her literary executor, James MacGibbon (Allen Lane, 1975; Oxford University Press, 1976). There is a miscellaneous collection of her prose pieces and several otherwise unpublished or uncollected poems, *Me Again* (Virago, 1981; Farrar, Straus, 1982). See also *A Very Pleasant Evening With Stevie Smith: Selected Short Prose* (New Directions, 1995).   AST

Smith, Sydney Goodsir (1915–75) For a poet who wrote in vigorous *Scots, it is remarkable that Smith was born in New Zealand, settled in Edinburgh only in his late teens, and was educated in English public schools and at Oxford (having failed first-year medicine at Edinburgh). His work draws from the spirit of the Scottish poetry of the fifteenth and sixteenth centuries more than the epoch of Fergusson and Burns. Not having lived a childhood in Scotland, he was perhaps sufficiently free of the latter-day class associations of the Scots language to appropriate it for his poetry with what can seem a mixture of instinctive, sentient scholarship on the one hand, and recklessness on the other. While Hugh *MacDiarmid was his master, and MacDiarmid's poetry of the 1920s his enabling exemplum, Smith shares with other outstanding writers in Scots (Robert *Garioch, William *Soutar) a distinctive idiom that differs from MacDiarmid's.

In very general terms, Smith's work is of two kinds. 'The Grace of God and the Meth-Drinker', 'Gowdspink in Reekie' (i.e. Oliver Goldsmith in Edinburgh), 'Kynd Kittick's Land', or 'Slugabed' (Part V of 'Under the Eildon Tree'), present a rumbustious humour with directness, bravura, and speed. He distrusted passages of figurative imagery (the mainstay of much English and other poetry), and, indeed, anything other than incidental metaphor can be seen as unusual in poetry in Scots until this century. The wilder side of Smith's poetic temper found expression in prose too, in *Carotid Cornucopius* (1947, repr. 1964), which owes something to Rabelais, Urquhart, Jarry, and *Joyce, but more to an individual release of inspired linguistic lunacy.

Smith's other main line of work is lyrical, passionate, and controlled. Lyrics like 'Aa my Life' and 'Time be Brief' exclude that fanciful, supercharged prolixity to which Scots diction can be prone, achieving instead the chaste quality of timeless song. Despite passages where his language can feel more artificial than it need be, Smith's work as a whole reaches for a classic Scottish imbalance of daftness and common sense, broad comedy and seriousness.

Smith also wrote *The Wallace* (1960), a verse drama on the Scottish hero, a good deal of criticism, and undertook editing— for example, (with J. Barke) Burns' *The Merry Muses of Caledonia* (1959) and *A Choice of Burns' Poems and Songs* (1966). Almost all his collections were published in Edinburgh, with the exception of *Collected Poems* (Calder, 1975), which was published in London. *For Sydney Goodsir Smith* (MacDonald, 1975) contains essays on his poetry, poems, a checklist and memoirs of a writer still remembered by his nickname, 'The Auk'. He was also an artist and cartoonist.   DED

Smith, Vivian (1933–   ) Born in Hobart, and in the 1960s was associated with *Harwood and *McAuley as establishing a Tasmanian regional school of meditative landscape lyrics. While objects of the natural world are evoked (and celebrated) in the present as they 'dance a meaning for the mind', his human figures are often treated elegiacally. Summoned up 'At an Exhibition of Historical Paintings, Hobart', they demonstrate the 'pathos of the past, the human creature'; their presence haunts such places as a 'Deserted Bandstand, Kingston Beach' or declares itself in the things they have left behind ('Old Men are Facts', 'In the Colonial Museum').

He also writes of Paris, Tuscany, and Sydney, to which he moved as reader in English at Sydney University, changing fields from French literature, although this interest is pursued in the closing section of *Selected Poems* (Angus & Robertson, 1985) where the 'Translations and Variations' series is drawn from a number of modern European poets, notably Paul Celan.

His combination of intelligence and feeling and the subtle musicality of his traditional verse-forms have commanded critical respect. Apart from editing of several anthologies, his substantial contribution to Australian literary criticism includes authorship of the poetry section of the *Oxford History of Australian Literature* (1981). From 1975 to 1990, he was also the literary editor of *Quadrant*. See *New Selected Poems* (Angus & Robertson, 1995) and, for later poems, *Along the Line* (Salt, 2006).   JS

Smith, William Jay (1918–   ) Born in Winnfield, Louisiana. Soon after his birth, Smith's father, an unsuccessful farmer, re-enlisted to become a clarinettist in the US Army band. In 1921 the family moved to Jefferson Barracks near St Louis, where Smith spent his entire youth—memorably recounted in his elegant memoir, *Army Brat* (Persea, 1980). He took a BA and MA in French from Washington University. During the Second World War he served in the US Navy as liaison officer on board a French frigate in both the Atlantic and Pacific theatres of operation. After the war he taught briefly before winning a Rhodes scholarship in 1947 to study at Wadham College, Oxford. That year he also married the poet Barbara *Howes. This marriage ended in divorce in 1964. Two years later he married Sonja Haussman of Paris. Smith's career has been remarkably diverse. He taught at several colleges and universities as well as serving two years in the Vermont House of Representatives. In 1968–70 he worked as poetry consultant to the Library of Congress. A pre-eminent translator of modern poetry, he has also lectured abroad, especially in Eastern Europe. He currently divides his time between New York, Paris, and Cummington (Massachusetts).

Smith has been a prolific writer, publishing over forty books of poetry, translation, children's verse, literary criticism, and

memoirs in addition to editing several in-
fluential anthologies. His best poems are
unlike anything else in contemporary
American literature. His early lyric poetry
is as close as any verse by the French Sym-
bolists to the unattainable ideal of *poésie
pure*. Although often based on realistic sit-
uations, Smith's compressed, formal lyrics
develop language musically in a way which
summons an intricate, dreamlike set of im-
ages and associations. The poems some-
times use simple syntax and diction—as in
'American Primitive' or 'The Closing of the
Rodeo'—to create dark and ambiguous ef-
fects. Smith likewise uses tight formal pat-
terns—as in 'Galileo Galilei' or 'Miserere'—
to present nightmarish scenes which defy
rational explanation. Without abandoning
formal verse, Smith also explored a unique
brand of free verse in later volumes like *The
Tin Can* (Delacorte, 1966). Written in long,
powerfully rhythmic lines reminiscent of St
John Perse's *versets*, these poems avoid the
pseudo-Biblical sound of the Whitmanian
tradition but none the less grant Smith
the expansive freedom of unmetred verse.
Although Smith is often grouped with the
formalist poets of his generation (*Wilbur,
*Nemerov, *Hollander, etc.), his work re-
mains original and distinctly personal, ulti-
mately bearing as much relation to French
as to American literature.

Collected Poems: 1939–1989 (Scribner,
1990), remains the most comprehensive
edition of Smith's poetry. *The World
Below the Window: Poems 1937–1997*
(Johns Hopkins University Press, 1998;
repr. 2001) is an extensive selection. *Laugh-
ing Time: Collected Nonsense* (Farrar,
Straus, 1990) is the best gathering of his
polished light verse. A substantial selection
of his literary criticism can be found in *The
Streaks of the Tulip* (Delacorte, 1972). For a
sampling of his voluminous translations,
see *Collected Translations* (New Rivers,
1985).   DG

Smither, Elizabeth (1941–) Born in
New Plymouth, New Zealand, Smither has
lived there most of her life, and formerly
worked part-time as a librarian.

She has published prolifically since 1975,
producing over a dozen substantial collec-
tions of poetry and several lighter booklets,
as well as novels and short stories. Her
poetry, conservative in form, is distinguished
by, for the most part, epigrammatic brevity, a
dry wit, and a pleasure in syntactic complex-
ity to the point of ambiguity. In a period
when many New Zealand poets adopted
American models of poetry, fraught with
local reference, she has preferred a more
British idiom of restrained, cosmopolitan in-
tellectualism, with an occasional personal
poem: there is a perpetual re-negotiation of
the boundaries between the poet's life, art,
and mythology. Typical are her book-titles,
such as *You're Very Seductive William Carlos
Williams* (McIndoe, 1978), *Casanova's Ankle*
(Oxford University Press, 1981), *The Legend
of Marcello Mastroianni's Wife* (1981), and
Professor Musgrove's Canary (1986).

A Pattern of Marching (1989) won the
1990 New Zealand Book Award for poetry.
The Tudor Style: New and Selected Poems
(all Auckland University Press) appeared in
1993. In 2002, Smither was named New
Zealand Poet Laureate. *A Question of Grav-
ity: Selected Poems* (Arc, 2004) appeared in
the UK at the end of her two-year term, and
draws on two later collections, *The Lark
Quartet* (Auckland University Press, 1999)
and *Red Shoes* (Godwit, 2003). See also *The
Year of Adverbs* (2007) and *The Common-
place Book: A Writer's Journey Through
Quotations* (2011—both Auckland Univer-
sity Press). In 2008 Smither received the
Prime Minister's Award for Literary
Achievement in Poetry.   KJ

Smithyman, Kendrick (1922–95) Born
in Te Kopura, Northland, New Zealand. He
moved to Auckland as a child and lived
there ever after. In 1946 he married the
poet Mary Stanley and remarried following
her death in 1980. In 1963 he joined the
teaching staff of Auckland University, retir-
ing in 1987. His first significant collection,
The Blind Mountain, was published by the
Caxton Press in 1950. Like James K. *Baxter
and Louis *Johnson, Smithyman is a major
middle-generation New Zealand poet who
turned away from the overt 'nationalism' of
a previous generation (*Curnow, *Brasch,
*Fairburn) in order to create a densely de-
tailed syntax which explores relationships

between language and locality. If Johnson's post-war contribution to New Zealand poetry was to widen subject-matter, and Baxter's to humanize the life of the spirit, then Smithyman's equally significant gift was in his persistent struggle to get away from 'the English line'. Turning to the early American modernists for inspiration (particularly *Ransom, Marianne *Moore, and Robert Penn *Warren), he was probably the first New Zealand poet to cultivate a highly developed personal language on purely modernist terms. His early collections are sometimes dominated by 'poetic' considerations but, following an extended visit to England and Canada in 1969, his poetry relaxed, and in *The Seal in the Dolphin Pool* (1974), *Dwarf with a Billiard Cue* (1978), *Stories About Wooden Keyboards* (1985), and his *Selected Poems* (1989—all Auckland University Press), a tendency to garrulousness is more than compensated for by the increasing wit, irony, and sheer weight of knowledge that his poems have learned to carry. He published a collection of essays on New Zealand poetry, *A Way of Saying*, in 1965, and in 1987 he edited a selection of stories by the New-Zealand-domiciled English writer Greville Texidor. Essays on Smithyman's poetry can be found in *Landfall, 168*, and in the excellent introduction to his *Selected Poems* (1989) by Peter Simpson. *Atua Wera* (1997), a long poem about Papahurihia, the nineteenth-century Nga Puhi religious leader, on which he had worked for a decade, appeared posthumously, as did *Imperial Vistas Family Fictions* (2002—all Auckland University Press), a collection written in the 1980s. PB

( ) SEE WEB LINKS

• Visit *Smithyman Online: Collected Poems 1943–1995*, an open-access website edited with notes by Margaret Edgcumbe and Peter Simpson.

Snodgrass, W. D. (William De Witt) (1926–2009) Born in Wilkinsburg, Pennsylvania. He attended Geneva College before he enlisted in the US Navy, where he served in the Pacific. On his return from military service he became a student at the University of Iowa Writers' Workshop, spending seven years there. He subsequently taught at various universities, including Cornell, Wayne State, Syracuse, and the University of Delaware.

Snodgrass' first collection, *Heart's Needle*, came out in 1959 and brought him widespread notice and a Pulitzer Prize. It was evidence of a copious and restless talent. It included some very funny, self-deprecating light verse ('April Inventory'), alongside exercises, only just this side of laborious, in Donneish metaphysical conceits ('Riddle', 'These Trees Stand'), poems on heroic classical themes ('Orpheus'), poems about music that are themselves unusually musical in tone and form, and a sequence of poems about his recent divorce and his separation from his baby daughter.

In any other year *Heart's Needle* would have been noteworthy for its wide-ranging, sometimes hit-and-miss experimentalism and for its orthodox technical facility: Snodgrass rhymed and scanned—and appeared to rhyme and scan about everything in sight. But 1959–60 was a year that saw the publication of Robert *Lowell's *Life Studies*, Anne *Sexton's *To Bedlam and Part Way Back*, and Sylvia *Plath's *The Colossus*, and on the strength of his poems about his divorce, Snodgrass was press-ganged as a '*Confessional Poet'.

Much later, reviewers were prone to describe Snodgrass as an imitator of Lowell—which was utterly untrue of his plangent and oblique private poems, although some of his historical-metaphysical verse does recall the Lowell of the 1940s. Lowell himself once nicely distanced Snodgrass, with due respect, calling him 'the American Philip Larkin'.

The poem 'Heart's Needle' is long, intricate, tender, and formal in its verse manners; a world away from the stripped-to-the-bone technique of *Life Studies*. It is—in an almost Victorian way—unafraid of sentiment, a solemn threnody lightened by continuous, skilful changes of landscape and metrical pattern. It speaks of deep distress, but does so in a tone of triumphant virtuosity.

In subsequent collections Snodgrass continued to widen his already impressively wide range, zigzagging between 'public' and 'private' themes with an ambitious series of poems about paintings, exuberant poems for children, and pained, exact, sometimes lacerating poems about his family. 'A Flat One' (collected in *After Experience*, 1967) represents Snodgrass at his finest: it combines a jolting emotional frankness with confident technical mastery. Addressed by a hospital nurse to an old man, a veteran of the First World War, who has just died in the nurse's care, the poem has the pungent detail, the recessed narrative, and the unabashed feeling of a nineteenth-century genre painting.

Snodgrass' major project from 1977 was an epic verse cycle, designed for dramatic delivery, titled *The Fuehrer Bunker*. It consists of a series of monologues by Hitler, Eva Braun, Himmler, Goebbels, Goering, and other leading Nazi figures in the spring of 1945 during the Allied capture of Berlin. From the first appearance of these poems critical opinion has been violently divided over their merits. Reviewing the 1977 collection, Hugh Kenner wrote (in the *New York Times Book Review*) that it was a mystery why 'Snodgrass should be wasting his gifts on attempts to outdo "the banality of evil"'—a sentiment that was echoed by the many reviewers who referred to Snodgrass' 'wasting' of his talent on this theme. However, Harold Bloom (in the *New Republic*) admired the sequence: 'Granted the immense difficulties he has taken on, Snodgrass demonstrates something of the power of a contemporary equivalent of Jacobean drama at its darkest.' Snodgrass' reputation went into eclipse after *The Fuehrer Bunker*, although he continued to publish poems unrelated to his Nazi epic (including a quantity of high-spirited light verse), and enjoyed a revival of interest in his work from the mid-1990s: see *Tuned and Under Tension: The Recent Poetry of W. D. Snodgrass* (University of Delaware Press, 1998), ed. Philip Raisor.

Snodgrass collections included *Heart's Needle* (Knopf, 1959); *After Experience* (Harper, 1967); *If Birds Build With Your Hair* (Nadja, 1979); *The Boy Made of Meat* (1982); *A Locked House* (1986—both Ewert); and *The Death of Cock Robin* (University of Delaware Press, 1989). The 'com-plete cycle' of *The Fuehrer Bunker* appeared from BOA Editions in 1995. There are two volumes of his lectures and essays on poetry: *In Radical Pursuit* (Harper & Row, 1975) and *To Sound Like Yourself* (2003). See *Selected Translations* (1998) and *Not for Specialists: New and Selected Poems* (2006—all BOA).   JR*

Snyder, Gary (1930–) Born in San Francisco, and brought up in Oregon and Washington State. He received his BA in anthropology at Reed College, Portland, in 1951. His subsequent career has been a remarkable combination of the academic and the contemplative, spiritual study and physical labour. Between working as a logger, a trail-crew member, and a seaman on a Pacific tanker, he studied Oriental languages at Berkeley (1953–6), was associated with *Beat writers such as *Ginsberg and *Kerouac, lived in Japan (1956–64), later studied Buddhism there, and won numerous literary prizes, including a Guggenheim fellowship (1968) and the Pulitzer Prize (1975). He later taught literature and 'wilderness thought' at the University of California at Davis.

The shapes and strengths of Gary Snyder's craft were established at the outset of his career. His first book, *Riprap* (1959), first published by Origin Press in Japan, demonstrates the clarity of his seeing, his desire to crystallize moments, his striking ability to convey the physical nature of an instant: 'I cannot remember things I once read | A few friends, but they are in cities. | Drinking cold snow-water from a tin cup | Looking down for miles | Through high still air' ('Mid-August at Sourdough Mountain Lookout'). Simplicity, distance, accuracy of atmosphere: these are hallmarks of the work throughout. The laid-back, jotted-down tone masks an acute sensitivity to rhythm and, in particular, assonance. Though his formal spectrum is narrow, from terse, rhythmic observation with a resonant conclusion ('I feel ancient, as though I had | Lived many lives', 'An Autumn Morning in Shokoku-ji') to lengthy, free-associative odysseys through the American 'back country', his territory is vast, and his resources of phrase and juxtaposition seemingly endless. Such a ranging strategy does not always pan gold from the water, but when it does Snyder comes face to face with a wide, gladdening openness, or touches wellsprings of healing profundity.

Snyder's poetry blends America's native past with the grandeur and detail of nature, and the mental disciplines of Zen Buddhism: his long apprenticeship in the latter has harvested a tough simplicity and freshness of expression (at its best in *Cold Mountain Poems*, the translations of Han Shan first published with a reprinting of *Riprap* in 1965), a trust in the way words lead him, the faith of a traveller through an interior, whether continental or psychological. He writes in the first person, as individual in the wilderness, but the beauty and glory of the wilderness allows that individual the status of common man. He tells no tales: what he says is what he heard or saw; imagination is not for invention, but for finding the forms of expression that most perfectly mirror the world outside. For Snyder, symbol and metaphor cause a distancing from the thing itself: as *Pound suggested, the thing itself is at least enough.

Love and respect for the primitive tribe, honour accorded the Earth, the escape from city and industry into both the past and the possible, contemplation, the communal, peace, and the ascetic: what came to fruition and influence in the Beat waves of the Fifties and Sixties has stood the test of the cynical decades that followed. Though Snyder's later work has not surpassed his early, his 'green' philosophy seems as deep-rooted and prophetic as his best work has remained fresh and unique: 'There is not much wilderness left to destroy, and the nature in the mind is being logged and burned off. Industrial-urban society is not "evil" but there is no progress either . . . A gas turbine or an electric motor is a finely-crafted flint knife in the hand. It is useful and full of wonder, but it is not our whole life . . . I try to hold both history and the wilderness in mind, that my poems may approach the true measure of things and stand against the unbalance and ignorance of our times' (quoted in David Kherdian, *Six San Francisco Poets*, (Giligia,

1969)). See *The Practice of the Wild: Essays* (1990).

Snyder's epic poem *Mountains and Rivers Without End* (1996—both Counterpoint), written over four decades, was widely praised, and won the Bollingen Prize. Among his other collections are *Turtle Island* (New Directions, 1974), *Axe Handles* (North Point, 1983), *Left Out in the Rain: New Poems 1947–1985* (North Point, 1986; repr. Shoemaker & Hoard, 2005), and *Danger on Peaks* (Shoemaker & Hoard, 2004). See *The Gary Snyder Reader: Prose, Poetry, and Translations* (Counterpoint, 1999) and *Look Out* (New Directions, 2002), a selection made by the poet.   GM

Sobin, Gustaf (1935–2007) Born in Boston, Massachusetts, and graduated from Brown University in 1957. Meeting René Char in Paris in 1962 led Sobin to visit Char's home region of Vaucluse, Provence where he lived for the rest of his life.

Sobin's is 'a poetry of great distinction,' according to Robert *Duncan, 'awakening the spirit to a world of errant clarities renewed.' The poetry is characterized by a terse minimalism and a discerning use of the linguistic fragment, the verbal shard, aphorism, and enjambment. As well as reflecting Sobin's principal influence, Char, the poetry uniquely develops the American examples of George *Oppen and Louis *Zukofsky.

Sobin perceived the Provence landscape as 'a textus, a woven fabric,' which is reflected in the exacting notations of process in his poetry ('gather | branches, bear | stones, || bulbs, | fleece... | that they || be brought, set | vibrant, in | sound') and in the settings of his novels, *Dark Mirrors* (Bloomsbury, 1992) and *The Fly-Truffler* (Norton, 1999). His fascination with the revelatory fragment also informs his essays on the prehistory, antiquity, and medieval vestiges of Provence and Langue-doc, collected in *Luminous Debris* (University of California Press, 1999), *Aura* (Counterpath, 2008), and *Ladder of Shadows* (University of California Press, 2009).

Sobin translated Char's books *The Brittle Age* and *Returning Upland* (Counterpath, 2009) and Henri Michaux's *Ideograms in China* (New Directions, 2002). *Collected*

Poems was published by Talisman House in 2010.   ROH

Sole, Kelwyn (1951–) Born in Johannesburg, Sole was educated at the University of the Witwatersrand as well as the University of London's School of Oriental and African Studies. He worked in Botswana and Namibia and is currently a professor of English at the University of Cape Town, where he lives.

Sole has published six collections of poetry alongside an extensive body of criticism, focused mainly on South African and postcolonial literature. A political activist in the 1980s and 1990s, Sole's first two collections, *The Blood of Our Silence* (1987) and *Projections in the Past Tense* (1992— both Ravan), responded to South Africa's political struggle and established his reputation as a provocative, independent political commentator. (Fellow South African poet, Rustum Kozain, recently called Sole 'the conscience of the nation'.) Influenced by Charles *Olson amongst others, his forms range from traditional to playful, including a collection of prose poems, *Land Dreaming* (University of KwaZulu-Natal Press, 1996). Although the unpretentious style and often bathetic tone which characterize Sole's earlier work—from erotic poems to satires on white liberals—gives way to a more sincere and tender voice in newer books like *Absent Tongues* (Modjaji, 2012), the poems remain underpinned by a political commitment.   KK

Solie, Karen (1966–) Born in Moose Jaw, Solie grew up in southern Saskatchewan, and now lives in Toronto. She has worked as a truck driver, held writing residencies, and taught creative writing at several institutions.

Like her contemporary Ken *Babstock, Solie's first three collections have seen her rise to prominence among the Canadian poets of her generation. *Short Haul Engine* (2001) won the Dorothy Livesay Poetry Prize and was shortlisted for several others, while *Modern and Normal* (2005—both Brick) was shortlisted for the Trillium Award. *Pigeon* (Anansi, 2009), won the Trillium, the Griffin Poetry Prize, and the Pat Lowther Award. Described as a 'singer of

existential bewilderment', Solie's poems draw on memories of her prairie-farm and small-town youth with a restless verbal energy and dark wit, declaring 'Any resemblance | to the woman I was is purely | agricultural' ('Cardio Room, Young Women's Christian Association').   JNT

Solway, David (1941–) Born in Montreal, Solway studied English and philosophy at McGill University. He taught English for many years, and has spent much time in Greece, about which he wrote a travel book, *The Anatomy of Arcadia* (1992). Between 1999 and 2000 he was poet-in-residence at Concordia University.

Although not as acclaimed as some poets of his generation, Solway has nevertheless been called 'one of the best things ever to happen to English Canadian poetry'. Associated early on with the romantic lyricism popularized by Leonard *Cohen, Solway emerged in the 1970s as a more studiously formal poet, notable for the extended metaphors and arguments of his verse. See *Selected Poetry* (1982), *Modern Marriage* (1987—both Véhicule), and *Chess Pieces* (1999). His long poem *Franklin's Passage* (2004—both McGill-Queen's University Press) was the first English-language work to win the Grand Prix du Livre de Montréal. He has latterly received acclaim for his fictive 'translations', including *Reaching for Clear: The Poetry of Rhys Savarin* (Véhicule, 2007), which won the A. M. Klein Prize.

An influential critic, Solway has written on culture, education, and literature: see *Random Walks: Essays in Elective Criticism* (McGill-Queen's University Press, 1997). *The Big Lie* (Lester, Mason, 2007), reflects on the ideology of the 'war on terror' and his own Jewish identity. For criticism, see *David Solway: Essays on His Works* (Guernica, 2001), ed. Carmine Starnino.   JNT

Song, Cathy (1955–) Born in Hawaii to a Chinese mother and Korean father, Cathy Song took a BA in English literature at Wellesley College and an MA in creative writing from Boston University. An early poetic mentor was poet and Hart *Crane biographer, John Unterecker. She is the author of five volumes of poetry and teaches creative writing at the University of Hawaii, where she lives with her husband and three children.

Picture Bride (Yale University Press, 1983) established Song's poetic voice as one of a quiet, unforced lyricism. It was nominated for the National Book Critics Circle award and was selected by Richard *Hugo for the Yale Series of Younger Poets. A concern with the female experience is seen in her editorship of a book of fiction and poetry by women, *Sister Stew* (Bamboo Ridge, 1991). Song's poetry explores aspects of the immigrant experience, her heritage, and ideas of family, selfhood, inheritance, and the environment. *Frameless Window, Squares of Light* (Norton, 1988), *School Figures* (1994), and *The Land of Bliss* (2001) show Song honing her characteristically vivid metaphors, which often catalyse shifts between personal and universal. *Cloud Moving Hands* (2007—all University of Pittsburgh Press), takes its title from a T'ai Chi movement and extends the poet's concern with the relation of self to world through the influence of Buddhism.   HY

Sorley, Charles Hamilton (1895–1915) Born in Aberdeen, of Lowland Scottish descent on both sides. In 1908 he gained an open scholarship to Marlborough College where, in his father's words, 'he abounded in the mysteries of its etiquette and slang' and distinguished himself as a member of the school literary society to which, among other contributions, he presented 'John Masefield and the Twentieth Century Renaissance'. The whole of this paper can be found in the posthumous edition of Sorley's letters, edited by his father and published by the Cambridge University Press in 1919. Appreciative, incisive, convinced that 'one of the worst traits of modern literature, as of modern conversation, is its inability to call a spade a spade', it is an invigorating performance. Sorley's literary promise was clearly outstanding, and although his output as a poet was small it is an indication of the impact his work made on the keenest poetic intelligences among his contemporaries that, on learning of his death at Loos in 1915, Robert *Graves should have

written in one of his own letters home 'what waste!'

At the outbreak of war—before, as he hoped, taking up an Oxford scholarship—Sorley was studying and travelling in Germany, and the poems he later wrote while an officer on active service are characterized by a refusal to endorse the jingoism prevalent in the early stages of the war. Openly critical of what he considered Rupert *Brooke's adoption of 'the sentimental attitude', and attacking Thomas *Hardy's 'Victory crowns the just' as the worst line he ever wrote, Sorley's position was passionately clear-sighted. His sonnet 'To Germany' describes the opposing sides as 'gropers both through fields confined' who 'stumble' and 'do not understand'.

Perhaps inevitably Sorley's juvenilia outweigh his achieved successes, and not surprisingly in a writer neither ambitious for publication nor benefiting (as did *Owen, Graves, and *Sassoon) from mutual criticism amongst peers, he is often self-consciously romantic and stilted in his diction, but at least one poem—'All the hills and vales along'—is a small masterpiece and his achievement remains considerable. His poems are available in *Collected Poems*, ed. Jean Moorcroft Wilson (1985), who has also written *Charles Hamilton Sorley: A Biography* (1985—both Woolf); and Hilda Spear has edited *Poems and Selected Letters* (Blackness, 1978).   JM

Soto, Gary (1952–) A leading presence in Chicano poetry, Soto grew up in a *campesino* family in California, the memory of whose landscape and field-hands underwrites nearly all his verse from *The Elements of San Joaquin* (University of Pittsburgh Press, 1977) to *Who Will Know Us?* (Chronicle, 1991). His appeal lies in the sparenesses of his language and imagery, and a respect—usually within a frame of Californian locale and history—for the insistent particularity of experience. An early poem like 'October' makes the point. A field-worker sees animals readying themselves for the change of seasons: sparrows from 'a bare sycamore', 'an owl shuffled into a nest | Of old leaves and cotton', and a coyote 'squatted behind granite, | His ears tilting | Towards a rustle, eyes dark | with the winter to come'. This same quiet, vivid alertness, and Soto's command of measure, runs variously through a magic-realist composition like 'The Space', in *The Tale of Sunlight* (1978), a compassionate worker poem like 'Mission Tire Factory, 1969', in *Where Sparrows Work Hard* (1981), or the title-poem of *Black Hair* (1985—all University of Pittsburgh Press), which calls up Soto's own Chicano, yet wholly self-particular, childhood in describing its narrator as 'Mexican, | a stick | Of brown light'. Since *New and Selected Poems* (1995) he has published several later collections with Chronicle Books in San Francisco, three novels with University of New Mexico Press, and many books for children and young adults. See *The Effects of Knut Hamsun on a Fresno Boy: Recollections and Short Essays* (Persea, 2000).   ARL

Souster, Raymond Holmes (1921–2012) Born in Toronto where he was educated at the University of Toronto schools and Humberside Collegiate Institute, and where, except for wartime service in the RCAF, he lived and worked in banking all his life. Souster's literary activities began in the 1940s when he became involved in editing two avant-garde periodicals, *Direction* (1943–6) and *Enterprise* (1948), which led to involvement with a group of Montreal poets who were first associated with First Statement Press in that city. Souster went on to edit two other important literary periodicals, *Contact* (1952–4) and *Combustion* (1957–60), thus establishing himself firmly at the heart of mid-century poetry in Canada. Introduced in the anthology *Unit of Five* (1944), Souster had his first independent collection, *When We Are Young*, in 1946, followed by *Go to Sleep World* (1947). Of the Canadian poets of his generation Souster was the one most overtly interested in, and influenced by, American contemporaries. He was first attracted to Henry Miller, and later entered into lasting friendships and correspondence with Robert *Creeley and Cid *Corman. Souster's *Selected Poems* were published in 1956 and brought him his first serious critical attention. In the decade of the 1960s

Souster entered upon a prolific and distinguished period in his creative life. His collected poems, *The Colour of the Times* (McGraw-Hill) appeared in 1964. He was one of the founders of The League of Canadian Poets, serving as its president, 1968–9.

Very much a cautious modernist, Souster was involved in the quiet promotion of young talent, both through the agency of a poets' cooperative publishing venture called Contact Press, which he co-founded with Louis *Dudek and Irving *Layton in 1952, and by editing *Poets '56* and *New Wave Canada: The New Explosion in Canadian Poetry* (1966). In the late 1960s he embarked on the revision of his early poetry with a view to its reissue. *Selected Poems* (Oberon, 1972) was the result of that process, and served to lead up to a multi-volume *Collected Poems*, also from Oberon Press, which began to appear in 1980 and confirmed a strong colloquial tone in a poetry of urban images informed by the modest emotions of a middle-class nostalgia.

Souster also wrote fiction, publishing *The Winter of Time* (1949) and *On Target* (1972) under the pseudonym of R. and J. Holmes, and co-authored *From Hell to Breakfast* (1980) with Douglas Alcorn. He made much use of his experiences in the RCAF in his fiction. Souster collaborated, as well, in the compiling of several school anthologies. Often considered the unofficial Poet Laureate of Toronto, in 1995 Souster received the Order of Canada. See *Of Time and Toronto* (Oberon, 2000).   MG

Soutar, William (1898–1943) Soutar went to school in his native Perth. After First World War service in the Royal Navy, from which he was invalided out with the disease that led to his relatively early death, he attended the University of Edinburgh. His first poems in *Scots coincided with the momentum generated by Hugh *MacDiarmid, but a devotion to the fifteenth- and sixteenth-century Makars and balladry was closer to Soutar's inspiration than the modernism expounded by MacDiarmid.

Spondylitis led to seven years as a semi-invalid from 1923, after which Soutar was bedridden until his death. He published ten collections in his lifetime and there was a posthumous volume in 1944. Only two of these are in Scots, but there were many uncollected poems and it is for his Scots poetry that he is chiefly remembered. Some of his lyrics are pure and haunting ('The Tryst', 'Sang'), as are several of his ballads. A vigorous, grotesque poem like 'The Hungry Mauchs' (maggots) shows him at his best and working close to the taproot of the Scottish imagination—fantastic, earthy, folkish, and direct.

In English, his anti-war satires ('The Guns') and poems attacking unemployment, privilege, rank, and other ills of the times rise occasionally to forcefulness. His epigrams, of which he wrote many, suffer from a lack of the necessary malice.

It was Soutar's conviction that a long-lasting and authentic revival of poetry in Scots (or Doric as he called it) depended on impressing the young with the worth of the native language. 'If the Doric is to come back alive, it will come first on a cock-horse.' His Scots verse for children ('bairn rhymes') is among his best work and still enjoys a degree of currency.

Collected Poems (Dakers, 1948) was edited by Hugh MacDiarmid. There is a biography by Alexander Scott, *Still Life* (1958), who also edited a selection from Soutar's diaries, *Diaries of a Dying Man* (1954; repr. 1991). See *Poems of William Soutar: A New Selection*, ed. W. R. Aitken (Scottish Academic, 1988).   DED

Soyinka, Wole (Oluwole Akinwande) (1934–) Born in Ijebu Isara, Nigeria. He grew up in Abeokuta, where his father was a schoolteacher. He was educated at Abeokuta Grammar School and Government College, Ibadan. He studied at University College, Ibadan (1952–4) and then at Leeds University (1954–7), where he graduated with an honours degree in English. He has been at various times on the academic staff of the universities of Lagos, Ibadan, and at Ife, where he was professor of comparative literature and dramatic arts. Between 1973 and 1974 he was overseas fellow at Churchill College, Cambridge, and visiting professor at the University of Sheffield. More recently, Soyinka has been professor at a number of American universities including Cornell University, Emory University, University of Nevada, and Loyola Marymount University. He is currently emeritus professor at Obafemi Awolowo University Ile-Ife, Nigeria. He was awarded the Nobel Prize for Literature in 1986.

Soyinka's influence and impact in Africa is evident in drama, poetry, fiction, and autobiography. In addition to his poetical works, he has published two novels, four volumes of autobiographical writing, critical essays, and several plays. He has also edited an impressive anthology, *Poems of Black Africa* (Secker & Warburg, 1975). As a consequence of his political activities during the Nigerian Civil War he was detained from August 1967 until October 1969 by the Federal Military Government of Nigeria.

The early poems which were included in his first volume, *Idanre and Other Poems* (Methuen, 1967), were often self-consciously impenetrable. The images were startling but remote. *A Shuttle in the Crypt* (Collings, 1972) emerged from Soyinka's prison experience. It is a companion volume to *The Man Died* (Harper & Row, 1972; repr. Random House, 2004) in which he gave an account of his prison experience in prose. The poems served several different functions; some were 'animystic spells' designed to modulate his thinking processes, whereas others were descriptive of his environment and his internal awareness of his predicament. *Ogun Abibiman* (Collings, 1976), a narrative poem, was written to celebrate Mozambique's declaration of war against the white regime in erstwhile Rhodesia. It was regarded by observers as Soyinka's first explicit avowal of a wider political vision. This and his latest volumes, *Mandela's Earth and Other Poems* (Deutsch, 1989) and *Samarkand and Other Markets I Have Known* (Methuen, 2002), mark a structural departure for Soyinka; the old opacity is less evident and there is a more natural correspondence of language and meaning. Soyinka's poetry is characterized by his capacity to see in a particular and ordinary situation the opportunity for poetic imagery that transcends its merely local and parochial existence. The most recent poems have an immediacy that is both urgent and impatient, as if time is running out for the poet.

The Writing of Wole Soyinka (1973), by Eldred D. Jones, *Critical Perspectives on Wole Soyinka* (1980—both Heinemann), ed. James Gibbs, and Yemi D. Ogunyemi, *The Literary/Political Philosophy of Wole Soyinka* (PublishAmerica, 2009) give a critical background to Soyinka's writings.   FO

Spahr, Juliana (1966–) Born in Chillicothe, Ohio, Spahr received a BA from Bard College and a PhD from University at Buffalo, State University of New York. She lives in Berkeley, California.

The experimental style of Spahr's post-*Language writing frequently employs repetition over the course of long lyric sequences. She also incorporates found text such as news clippings within her poetry, in particular information pertaining to war, politics, and the environment. Her expansive poetic representation of national consciousness has often been compared to that of Walt Whitman.

Spahr is also an active editor and critic. With the poet Jena Osman, she co-edits the journal *Chain*, and has edited several anthologies of poetry and criticism. In 2001, she published a critical study, *Everyone's Autonomy: Connective Reading and Collective Identity* (University of Alabama Press), which deals with the relationship between experimental poetry and identity politics.

Her first collection of poetry, *Response* (Sun & Moon, 1996), won the National Poetry Series Award. Other publications include *Fuck You—Aloha—I Love You* (Wesleyan University Press, 2001), *Things of Each Possible Relation Hashing Against One Another* (Palm, 2003), *This Connection of Everyone With Lungs* (University of California Press, 2005), *The Transformation* (Atelos, 2007), and *Well Then There Now* (Black Sparrow, 2011).   SRO

Spark, Muriel (Sarah) (née Camberg) (1918–2006) Born in Edinburgh to a Jewish father and English mother. She was educated at James Gillespie's School for Girls in Edinburgh, which she left at the age of 18 to live in Rhodesia where, in 1937, she was married (she is divorced, with one son); returning to England in 1944, she worked for the Intelligence Service in a department producing anti-Nazi propaganda. Between the end of the war and her early successes as a novelist she worked at a variety of jobs connected with publishing; she became secretary of the Poetry Society in 1947, and in 1948–9 was editor of *Poetry Review*. In the early 1950s she wrote or edited, in collaboration with Derek Stanford, a critical biography of Emily Brontë, a selection of Brontë's poems, and selections from the letters of Mary Shelley, the Brontës, and John Henry Newman. She also published biographical studies of Mary Shelley and John *Masefield, and a volume of poems. In 1954 Spark became a Roman Catholic. Her first novel, *The Comforters*, appeared in 1957, and was followed by eighteen further novels to date, for which Spark was awarded numerous prizes and honours; she also published short stories and radio plays. From 1962 to 1966 she lived in New York, but later made her home in Italy.

Though there is nothing in it to match the quality and originality of her achievement in fiction (which sets a high standard), the little poetry Spark wrote was important to her, and is not negligible. Those characters in her fiction to whom Spark extends a (rare) indulgence tend to write metrical verse, quote the English classics, translate from the Latin. In her own verse there is a fair sprinkling of neat, consciously archaic forms (ballads, roundels, villanelles, jaunty quatrains and couplets), and, correspondingly, of epigrammatic neatness of statement, as well as riddling narrative (parables and cautionary tales), plangent lyricism, heavy-handed satire, and Stevie *Smith-like whimsy. She said that important early influences were the Old Testament and the border ballads; the visionary extravagance and strong emotions of such sources take on a whiff of Nineties-ish decadence in 'The Ballad of the Fanfarlo', an ambitious 'recreation' from Baudelaire on themes of atonement, death, damnation, and salvation, and in those poems which explore the workings of religious mystery in a 'Kensington of dreadful night'. See *All the Poems* (New Directions/Carcanet, 2004).   AJ

Sparshott, Francis (1926–) Born in Chatham, England. He served with the

Intelligence Corps, attended Oxford University, and in 1950 joined the faculty at the University of Toronto, where he is now professor emeritus of philosophy. Sparshott is an accomplished satirist, elegant or rough as the occasion demands. At ease with a large number of forms, he is especially striking in his command of rhyming effects. His poetic voice and range of subject-matter are reminiscent of some of the classical lyric poets. His collections of poetry are: *A Divided Voice* (Oxford University Press, 1965), *A Cardboard Garage* (Clarke, Irwin, 1969), *The Rainy Hills* (privately printed, 1979), *The Naming of the Beasts* (Black Moss, 1979), *The Cave of Trophonius* (Brick, 1983); then, published by Childe Thursday Press, *The Hanging Gardens of Etobicoke* (1983), *Storms and Screens* (1986), *Sculling to Byzantium* (1989), *Views from the Zucchini Gazebo* (1994), *Home from the Air* (1997), *The City Dwellers* (2000), and *Scoring in Injury Time* (Wolsak and Wynn, 2006). EC

Spear, Charles (1910–85) Born in Owaka, South Otago, New Zealand, and educated at Canterbury and Otago universities. He worked as a journalist and teacher, and then as a lecturer in Middle English at the University of Canterbury until his retirement in 1976. He spent the last decade of his life in London. His reputation as a poet rests on a single slim volume, *Twopence Coloured* (Caxton, 1951), from which substantial selections have been made by every significant anthologist of New Zealand verse. Spear's 'muse' is, as he himself claimed in 'Remark', 'Studiously minor, yet attuned to doom'. It is as though an 1890s aesthete had been infected by a post-war malaise. Spear is a miniaturist, compressing into his neatly rhymed stanzas a phantasmagoria of the fictional and the historical. Spear also wrote, with L. A. Baigent, the novel *Rearguard Actions* (1936). MacDJ

Spence, Lewis (1874–1955) Although he wrote little, Spence's position in modern Scottish poetry rests on his introduction of a richer *Scots idiom than the rural dialect of his contemporaries prior to Hugh *MacDiarmid's more sweeping innovations. His best-known poem is 'The Prows O'Reekie',

an impassioned, proud, excitable, and memorable piece about Edinburgh, and 'Great Tay of the Waves', 'The Siller Bullet', and 'Kinrick' are not without their exhilarations. 'The Stown Bairn' and 'The Ferlie' draw from his interest in fairy lore, mythology, and the occult, in which subjects Spence was a scholar, publishing many books, some of them possibly crazed— *Will Europe Follow Atlantis?*, for example.

Spence shared with MacDiarmid the distinction of being a founder of the National Party of Scotland; indeed, he was the first to stand for a parliamentary seat in the party's cause.

His poems in English are more backward-tending in style than his work in Scots, although there, too, his modernity is probably marginal, if sometimes original and gripping. *Collected Poems* appeared in 1953 (Serif). DED

Spencer, Bernard (1909–63) Born in Madras (now Chennai), son of a high-court judge, and was educated at Marlborough College and Corpus Christi College, Oxford, where he took a degree in Greats. From 1932 to 1940 he was, in turn, a preparatory schoolmaster, an advertising copy-writer, and a script-writer in a film company. After that, and until his apparently accidental but certainly mysterious death (he was found dead by a railway track in Vienna), he worked for the British Council in Greece, Egypt, Italy, Spain, Greece again, Turkey, and Austria.

Spencer began, and to some extent continued, in the shadow of those Oxford contemporaries who quickly achieved a reputation: *Auden, *MacNeice (who was his senior at Marlborough), and *Spender. He was co-editor of *Oxford Poetry* 1930 and 1931. The first poem by which he can clearly be distinguished is 'Allotments: April', which Geoffrey *Grigson published in *New Verse* in 1936: it has a pertinacious sensuousness which was his own, to be seen later in more exotic settings in his Mediterranean poems of the 1940s and 1950s.

A central characteristic of Spencer's poems is a sense of loneliness, of being someone apart. Living most of his working life in non-English-speaking communities, professionally having to do the work of a bonhomous British Council officer, Spencer seems almost to have cultivated a kind of gregarious isolation. He became, quite consciously, 'a stranger here', a man fixing and defining modes of unease.

But equally there are those moments which signal 'things amazingly connected'. Spencer, early and late, was good in an unexpected way at memorializing moments of precarious happiness, with 'an importance of beauty' (from a poem written in celebration of his first wife in 1937) or, in one of his last poems in 1963, a moment of hilarity on 'that fine particular day' ('Traffic in April').

Spencer's rhythms were very personal, sometimes uncertain, tantalizing, full of indirections; but increasingly they carried his own individual voice, his own quizzical view of things. Sometimes he wrote with a strong sense of the living past: in an interview he commented that: 'The fact of being in some sort of continuity with earlier civilisations does have an exciting effect on me.' He collaborated with Nanos Valaoritis and Lawrence *Durrell in producing versions of the modern Greek poet George Seferis, *The King of Asine*, which reflect such archaeological excitement.

In his lifetime Spencer published *Aegean Islands and Other Poems* (1946), *The Twist in the Plotting* (1960), and *With Luck Lasting* (1963). After his death, Alan Ross edited a *Collected Poems* (1965). *Collected Poems* (Oxford University Press, 1981), ed. Roger Bowen, has been expanded by *Complete Poetry, Translations and Selected Prose* (Bloodaxe, 2011), ed. Peter Robinson.   AST

Spender, Sir Stephen (Harold) (1909–95)

Born in London, and educated at University College School, Hampstead, and Oxford (University College), where he was a contemporary and friend of *Auden, Isherwood and *MacNeice. Thus began a famous association with other writers who developed social and political themes from a left-wing standpoint; though his political affiliation (with the Communist Party) was brief. He visited Spain during the Civil War (1936–9), assisting the Republican cause with propaganda activity. During the Second World War he served in the National Fire Service in London, and was for two years co-editor, with Cyril Connolly, of literary monthly *Horizon*. His contribution to the volume of essays *The God that Failed* (1951), and his reversal of the critical position he adopted in *The Destructive Element* (1935) with the publication of *The Creative Element* (1953), establish his rejection of Communism in favour of a liberal individualism. In the latter year he became inaugural co-editor of *Encounter*, an anti-Communist political and literary monthly supported initially by the US Central Intelligence Agency. By this time his main period of creativity as a poet had virtually ended, though his work as a critic, and as a translator of Spanish and German (and later, Greek) poetry and drama continued and expanded.

Spender's early verse (in books such as *Poems*, 1933, and *The Still Centre*, 1939) catches movingly the alarm and confusion in the atmosphere of 1930s Europe, and affirms, in poems like 'The Funeral' and 'An Elementary School Classroom in a Slum', the political values he then held (a very personal, humanistic socialism). It also deliberately substitutes for the traditional English poet's devotion to nature a celebration of technological achievement ('The Express' and 'The Pylons'). At this time he displays at his best an eloquent Romantic pity for the poor and the oppressed, and a gift for rendering scenes of wartime suffering and destruction (in Spain, and in London during the air-raids) with photographic accuracy, even if the images sometimes remain somewhat unfocused. These prominent features of his poetry diverted attention at first from the presence of a deeply self-questioning personality, unsure how to match poetry to either external events or his own feelings. How he should, or could, commit himself emotionally is a recurrent theme; reassessment and revision of the poems is a constant habit. He is only too aware of a heritage of daunting greatness (in Beethoven, say, or Hölderlin) which transcends his untidy and violent modern experience.

There is more emotional directness in the poems of love and tribute to be found in *Ruins and Visions* (1942) and *Poems of Dedication* (1947); notably in 'Elegy for

Margaret', a dead sister-in-law. As before, he attempts rhetorical effects, but it is rarely his best vein, the poems becoming turgid and overreaching; though the rhetoric of 'Returning to Vienna, 1947' produces one of his finest sustained passages. A calmer, even informal, style employed in later poems of a retrospective kind, in *The Generous Days* (1971) and the second *Collected Poems* of 1985, shows a more relaxed side to his talent; the tributes to Auden and MacNeice are entertaining as well as moving. Spender's ultimate reputation may depend on how future readers will assess the appropriateness of his nakedly Romantic approach to the stresses of twentieth-century life. The most original poems deserve to remain famous. But the characteristic quality of undisguised vulnerability, tenderness, and even gaucheness in the endeavour to be truthful, may have the more enduring appeal.

His *Collected Poems 1928–53* (1955) presents a highly selective and substantially revised body of work from the individual books published up to that point; his development as a poet may be traced in much closer detail in those. This volume in turn was revised and re-ordered, with further poems added, for its reissue as *Collected Poems 1928–1985* (1985—both Faber/Random House). *World Within World* (Hamilton/Harcourt, Brace, 1951) is a work of candid autobiography. A volume of memoirs, *The Thirties and After* (Macmillan/Random House) appeared in 1978, and his *Journals 1939–83*, ed. John Goldsmith (Faber/Random House), were published in 1985. Spender's last volume of poetry was *Dolphins* (1994). See *New Collected Poems* (2004), ed. Michael Brett, *Selected Poems*, ed. Grey Gowrie (2009), and *New Selected Journals* (2012—all Faber), ed. Lara Feigel and John Sutherland, with Natasha Spender.   AB

Spicer, Jack (1925–65) Born in Hollywood, he attended the University of California, Berkeley, where he met Robert *Duncan and Robin *Blaser, and was deeply impressed by the poetry of *Yeats, though Duncan and Charles *Olson would have the most impact on his own verses. He became a professional linguist with a strong interest in semiotics, philosophy, and cosmology. A leading member of the so-called *San Francisco Renaissance, and convenor of the legendary 'Poetry as Magic' workshop, his poetry favoured open, serial forms, especially after 1961. *Billy the Kid* (Enkidu Surrogate, 1959) is among his most impressive performances, using the outlaw as an admittedly romanticized culture hero who engages in archetypal mythic rituals and pursues a Neo-Platonic line of thought. A similar, lyrical anti-narrative disrupts the medievalism of *The Holy Grail* (1962). *Language* (1965), its title scrawled over the cover of the journal of the Linguistic Society of America, opens with the sequence 'Thing Language', which declares 'No | One listens to poetry'. A poet of many voices, from the passionate to the sardonic ('the poet is a counterpunching radio'), Spicer's last collection was *Book of Magazine Verse* (1966), dedicated to various American publications that had rejected his work. See also the critical letters and 'translations' of *After Lorca* (1957—all White Rabbit).

Robin Blaser edited *The Collected Books of Jack Spicer* (Black Sparrow, 1975). *My Vocabulary Did This To Me: The Collected Poetry of Jack Spicer* (2008), ed. Peter *Gizzi and Kevin Killian, confirmed Spicer as an important figure for the post-*Language generation (the title alludes to his legendary last words). Gizzi also edited the transcripts of four lectures that Spicer gave shortly before his death, in which he advises young poets to 'stay absolutely loose, and don't accept any offers whatsoever' (*The House That Jack Built* (1998)). For criticism, see *After Spicer*, ed. John Emil Vincent (2011—all Wesleyan University Press).   EB*

Spires, Elizabeth (1952–) Born in Lancaster, Ohio. She was raised in nearby Circleville and attended Vassar College and Johns Hopkins University. She married the novelist Madison Bell in 1985, and their daughter Celia was born in 1991. Spires lives in Baltimore, Maryland, and she has taught at Goucher College since 1982.

The poems of Spires are notable for both their secular and spiritual subjects. Like Elizabeth *Bishop (whom Spires interviewed in the *Paris Review* series), Spires is a poet attentive to the physical world; yet while relishing description, she approaches pain and ecstasy more immediately than Bishop. Though for many years a lapsed Catholic, Spires often meditates on human suffering and annunciations of good and evil. Other poems suggest a kind of allegorical autobiography through archetypal Jungian terms instead of conventional '*confessional' details.

Spires has published six volumes of poetry, *Globe* (Wesleyan, 1981), *Swan's Island* (Holt, Rinehart, 1985), *Annonciade* (Viking, 1989), *Worldling* (1995), *Now the Green Blade Rises* (2002), and *The Wave-Maker* (2008—all Norton). She is also an accomplished children's book author.   HC

Sprackland, Jean (1962–) Born in Burton upon Trent, Sprackland studied English and philosophy at the University of Kent, Canterbury. In 2004 she was named a Poetry Book Society Next Generation Poet. She is currently a senior lecturer in creative writing at Manchester Metropolitan University, Education Director for the Poetry Archive, and a tutor for the Arvon Foundation.

Tattoos for Mother's Day (Spike, 1997) and *Hard Water* (2003) established Sprackland's poetic concern with exploring cross-generational relationships and finding mystery in the quotidian. They were admired by Vicki *Feaver and Carol Ann *Duffy. *Tattoos* was shortlisted for the Forward Prize, and *Hard Water* for the T. S. Eliot Prize and the Whitbread Award, as well as being recommended by the Poetry Book Society. *Tilt* (2007) won the Costa Poetry Prize, the poem 'The Birkdale Nightingale' also being shortlisted for the Forward Prize for Best Single Poem.

Hard Water demonstrates the influence of regional speech and landscape on Sprackland's poetry, in particular the place of her upbringing, Burton upon Trent, and coastal areas between Manchester, Liverpool, and Blackpool, where she has lived. Concerns with regional and environmental issues, as well as watery liminality, are extended in *Tilt*, and a book of non-fiction, *Strands* (2012—all Cape).   HY

Squire, Sir John (Collings) (1884–1958) Born in Plymouth and educated at Blundell's School, Tiverton, and St John's College, Cambridge. From 1913 he was literary editor of the *New Statesman*, for which he wrote under the pseudonym 'Solomon Eagle'; in 1919 he founded the monthly *London Mercury*, which he edited until 1934, and used to combat the 'anarchical cleverness' of modernism. As chief literary critic of the *Observer* he had further opportunity to promote those writers who shared his Edwardian tastes and values, derisively dubbed 'the Squirearchy' by the *Sitwell family. He was knighted in 1933.

Squire was a talented parodist, and his *Collected Parodies* (1921) may oddly capture more of his own character than his poems do. His assimilative sensibility gives a derivative taste to much of his serious verse, which began with *Three Hills* (1913); and Squire's low regard for originality in general can be gauged from his Second World War poem, 'Arnhem by Zutphen': 'We are waging the old warfare where Sir Philip Sidney died.' To an age which increasingly prized difficulty and precision, Squire offered poems which were not only easy to read but seemingly easy to write. Some pieces carry the impression of haste, as if, surmised John *Betjeman, 'they have been finished off after some interruption in a busy editor's life had diminished the force of the original inspiration'.

Two of Squire's efforts are more sustained than the rest: 'The Stockyard', a sickened response to a visit to the slaughterhouses of Chicago; and, in a different mood, 'The Rugger Match', a comprehensive account of a Twenties Varsity game. There are a handful of other notable poems. In the brightly coloured sonnet 'Discovery', an Indian trembles as Columbus' 'doom-burdened caravels' nudge his shore. His best work gives simple expression to his keen sense of mortality: 'Winter Nightfall', a surprisingly tough elegy for a retired colonel; another elegy, 'To a Roman' (Catullus); and 'Meditation in Lamplight', in which a contemporary reviewer saw a characteristic mixture of 'tragedy and chat'.

The posthumous *Collected Poems* (Macmillan, 1959) was edited by Betjeman. Squire also wrote short stories and an autobiography, *The Honeysuckle and the Bee* (1937).   MI

Stafford, William (1914–93) Raised in various small towns in rural Kansas, then earned bachelor's and master's degrees at the University of Kansas. During the Second World War he was a conscientious objector, an experience later described in his prose memoir, *Down in My Heart* (1947). After the war Stafford earned a PhD at the newly formed Iowa Writers' Workshop. In 1948 he moved to the West Coast, and from 1956 to 1979 was professor of English at Lewis and Clark College in Portland, Oregon. His poetry is generally seen as emerging intimately from the landscape of the Pacific Northwest, though he wrote at least as many poems with homey, Midwestern settings. Stafford started writing poems as a child and began accumulating mature work and publishing it in magazines in approximately 1948. His first book, *West of Your City*, did not come out until 1960, however—simply because no publisher asked until then, according to the poet. Stafford had a good many poems stockpiled, as it were, and his procedure for most of his books was to select a group of poems written over a long period of time, rather than just gather his most recent work together. Critics have often commented on the consistency in his work in terms of theme, style, and content, meaning to imply a lack of development. James *Dickey commented, however, that Stafford never wrote a bad poem, that lyric poetry seemed to spring almost spontaneously from his pen. Stafford's first five books were collected into *Stories That Could Be True* (Harper & Row, 1977), which also contained several new poems.

Stafford was fond of counselling young writers not to be critics of their own work; the key to writing good poetry was not to censor what wanted to come out. His own writing process was to get up early in the morning, before anyone else, recline on his couch with a pad of paper and a pen, and let the words flow. He did not revise heavily, preferring only to correct obvious mistakes and harmonize his rhythms.

Thematically, Stafford celebrated familiar human virtues and had great respect for quiet, contemplation, and hidden significances. Thus, in his most characteristic poems he seeks a place in the wilderness, an almost sacred location untouched by man, where an answer to the ultimate mysteries of the universe might be approached. The process of the search, along with its implications, was enough for him.

A collection of late chapbooks, *Even in Quiet Places* (1995), appeared posthumously from Confluence Press. See *The Way It Is: New and Selected Poems* (1998) and *Another World Instead: The Early Poems of William Stafford, 1937–1947* (2008—both Graywolf). Stafford's critical prose is collected in *Writing the Australian Crawl* (University of Michigan Press, 1978).

See also Jonathan Holden, *The Mark to Turn: A Reading of William Stafford's Poetry* (University Press of Kansas, 1976); *On William Stafford: The Worth of Local Things* (University of Michigan Press, 1995), ed. Tom Andrews; and the memoir by his son, Kim Stafford, *Early Morning* (Graywolf, 2002).   PS

Stainer, Pauline (1941–) Read English at St Anne's College, Oxford, and gained an M.Phil from Southampton University. She has worked in a mental hospital, pub, and library. Married, with four children, she has lived in Essex, Suffolk, and the Orkney Islands. She has won a variety of prizes in poetry competitions and festivals and, in 1987, was awarded a Hawthornden Fellowship. Her first three collections were Poetry Book Society Recommendations.

Stainer's poems juxtapose elemental ice, glass, and stones with fibre-tip pens, hang-gliders, and the red-light district of Bangkok. Artists, musicians, archetypal figures, angels, and virgins are blended into Christianity, chemistry, optics, and medicine. Reminiscent of pre-Raphaelite paintings, her poems are coloured predominantly by blacks, whites, and reds, usually blood red, as they move smoothly from the sacramental and mystical to the sexually implied and explicit.

Her first collection, *Honeycomb* was published in 1989 and her second, *Sighting The Slave Ship*, in 1992. Stainer was selected as one of the *New Generation poets in 1994, the year that saw the publication of her third collection, *The Ice-Pilot Speaks*. *The Lady & the Hare: New and Selected Poems* (2003) draws on two more: *The*

Wound-Dresser's Dream (1996) and *Parable Island* (1999), which includes the sequences 'Salt Over Skara Brae' and 'Little Egypt', the latter first published as a pamphlet by Smith/Doorstop in 1987. See also *Crossing the Snowline* (2008—all Bloodaxe). PMCC

Stallworthy, Jon (Howie) (1935–) Born in London. He worked for many years as poetry editor of Oxford University Press before taking up a teaching post at Cornell which he held for a decade. He is now professor emeritus of English Literature at Wolfson College, Oxford and co-editor of *The Norton Anthology of Poetry*. Well known for his meticulous edition of the poems of Wilfred *Owen, whose biography he wrote, and for his work with *Yeats' manuscripts, Stallworthy is a graceful, fastidious, and emotive poet who has been content, for the most part, to work in conventional forms. His poems are much concerned with 'family, England and "good form"', although the last-named quality is often dealt with in an ironic and impatient manner. His sequence *A Familiar Tree* (Oxford University Press, 1978), about the history of his own family, provides a British and well-bred counterpart to similar poems by Americans such as *Lowell, but is in no way less sophisticated. Stallworthy has also written a biography of Louis *MacNeice, edited the poems of Henry *Reed, and written a memoir of his own 'poetic apprenticeship', *Singing School: The Making of a Poet* (Murray, 1998), which appeared with his collected poems, *Rounding the Horn* (1998). See also *Body Language* (2004—both Carcanet). MS-S

Stammers, John (1954–) Born in Islington, Stammers studied philosophy at King's College London. From 2002 to 2003 he was Judith E. Wilson Fellow in Poetry at the University of Cambridge. He now teaches creative writing.

Stammers began to write poetry in the 1990s as a member of a writing group run by Michael *Donaghy. His debut, *Panoramic Lounge-Bar* (2001), won the Forward Prize for Best First Collection. Stammers describes himself as a 'post-postmodern' love poet. Critics tend to agree that his wry, cinematic vignettes are most satisfying when they address this subject: see 'On Love' and 'Closure' from his second collection, *Stolen Love Behaviour* (2005). His urban lyricism has been compared to that of Frank *O'Hara, but it is not so breezy, cultivating an English melancholy under cover of its stylized realism. (The covers of his first three books are paintings by the British pop artist, Patrick Caulfield.) In *Interior Night* (2010), London serves as a dark stage for a variety of dramatic monologues. He has edited *The Picador Book of Love Poetry* (2012), which pairs contemporaries such as Roddy *Lumsden and Don *Paterson with canonical poets. JNT

Stanford, Ann (1916–87) Born in LaHabra in southern California, a beautiful farming area with orange, lemon, and walnut groves and a view of the distant coastal range of mountains, a landscape frequently described in her poetry. At Stanford University, from which she was graduated in 1938, she became a member of the Yvor *Winters circle, and was the youngest poet to contribute to his anthology *Twelve Poets of the Pacific* (New Directions, 1937). In 1942 she married the architect Ronald White, who built her a study near their home in the Santa Monica mountains where she worked daily, writing in longhand her highly personal, luminescent, lyrical poetry, as well as two volumes of dramatic poetry, a translation of the *Bhagavad Gita* (Herder, 1970), and a critical biography of Anne Bradstreet (Franklin, 1974). She also found time to obtain a doctor's degree at UCLA, to raise a family, and to teach English literature at California State University at Northridge. She died in Los Angeles.

Of her eight volumes of poetry, the best-known are *The Weathercock* (1966), *The Descent* (1970), and *In Mediterranean Air* (1977), all published by Viking. There is an interview with her by Karla M. Hammond in the *Southern Review*, 18 (April 1982). See *Holding Our Own: The Selected Poems of Ann Stanford* (Copper Canyon, 2001). DES

S

Stanford, Frank (1948–78) Born in Mississippi and raised by adoptive parents in Memphis and north central Arkansas. After his stepfather died in 1963, Stanford was sent to a Benedictine monastery and academy in Subiaco, Arkansas, where he spent his last three years of high school. He entered the University of Arkansas in 1967, and in 1969 enrolled in the graduate poetry workshop there. From this time until his death ten years later Stanford dedicated his life to the writing of poetry. He left the University of Arkansas in 1971 without a degree, and for most of the next seven years earned his living as a land-surveyor in north-west Arkansas. At the time of his death at the age of 29 Stanford had published seven volumes of poetry. Most significant among these are his first book, *The Singing Knives* (1972), and a five-hundred page epic poem entitled *The Battlefield Where the Moon Says I Love You* (1977). Two posthumous volumes, *You* (1979) and *Crib Death* (1979), were also published.

Stanford embodied in his work those themes and attributes that are usually associated with the literature of the southern United States. Pre-occupations with the elegiac, the past as personal history, narrative, the natural world, and a sense of Gothic romanticism, permeate his poetry much as they do the works of William Faulkner, Carson McCullers, and James *Dickey. Stanford's early work centred on narrative creations of a mythic lost world of childhood in rural Arkansas. The prolific outpouring of these poems about his childhood was an attempt to deny time and mutability, and to create a past on the poet's own terms. Stanford's last poems, however, are direct confrontations with death. This theme becomes so obsessive in the late work that Death occasionally appears as a character in his narratives and lyrics of this period. Stanford died in Fayetteville, Arkansas, from self-inflicted gunshot wounds. The fullest collection of his work is *The Light the Dead See: The Selected Poems of Frank Stanford* (University of Arkansas Press, 1991). Lost Roads, the small press Stanford founded in 1976, and now co-edited by the poets C. D. *Wright and Forrest *Gander, has reprinted several of his original volumes.   LS

Starbuck, George (Edwin) (1931–96) Born in Columbus, Ohio, and graduated from the California Institute of Technology in Pasadena, majoring in mathematics. A distinguished university career was interrupted only by two years in the army and three in publishing.

An early poem, 'Named Individual' (from *Bone Thoughts*, Yale University Press, 1960) shows Starbuck in characteristic pose, as citizen menaced or circled by shapeless inhuman forces, whether Government, the Bomb, or the Universe itself. He is equipped, however, with a veritable arsenal of strategies against the darkness, and the very qualities that make his work seem at first wilfully odd—ceaseless formal exploration, Byronic ingenuity in rhyme, and playful linguistic whimsy—proclaim his strength and sanity, while at the same time dramatizing the idiocy of what he opposes.

Throughout the Sixties and Seventies America's wars, leaders, laws, and broadcasters are caught in the roving spotlights of his craft, either in short, comic diplodactyls and clerihews, or in long, zigzagging rambles, culminating in *Talkin' B. A. Blues* (Pym-Randall, 1980), a Dylanesque satire on higher education. But the poet's own practice does not escape: in 'Tuolomne' (from *Desperate Measures* (Godine, 1978) he apologizes to heaven for his tangential habits ('I scribble sidenotes to the fall of nations'), displaying, alongside his self-awareness, signposts to a couple of roads he might have taken: descriptive lyric, and ruminations on 'serious' matters in 'serious' metres. That he continued instead to experiment at the edges of formal possibility, while delighting in America's Absurd, demonstrates his intelligence about what truly constitutes poetic 'seriousness': knowledge of the powers and limits of words themselves, and awareness that to don a joker's mask is merely one of the oldest and swiftest ways into the palace. The best of his unique work has been posthumously collected in *The Works: Poems Selected from Five Decades* (University of Alabama Press, 2003), with a foreword by Anthony *Hecht.   GM

Stead, C. K. (Christian Karlson) (1932–) Born in Auckland, New Zealand. In his essays on New Zealand literature, *In the Glass Case* (Auckland University Press, 1981), Stead writes of his excitement at moving from the suburbs to the University of Auckland in 1951. His association with that university as student, lecturer, and professor of English was to last until he retired in 1986 in order to write full time. At the university he quickly became part of a talented older generation of Auckland-based writers and academics, including Allen *Curnow, Robert Chapman, Frank Sargeson, Rex *Fairburn, Maurice Duggan, Keith Sinclair, and Kendrick *Smithyman. This early discovery of New Zealand voices that were 'distinct and in which each believed he had a subject-matter ready to hand', gave him an immediate sense of belonging and a considerable critical zeal. He is probably New Zealand's most influential literary critic and an early advocate of modernism in that country. His book *The New Poetic: Yeats to Eliot* (Hutchinson, 1964) was an international success, and in 1986 he published a further critical study of *Pound and the modernist movement. His poem 'Pictures in an Undersea Gallery' (1958) was voted the most popular poem ever printed in the quarterly *Landfall*. Strongly influenced by Pound, Stead's poetry is notable for its linguistic elegance and exotic appeal. It has a literary sophistication often somewhat at odds with the day-to-day realities of the New Zealand scene, but in *Walking Westward* (The Shed, 1979) and, particularly, *Between* (Oxford University Press, 1988), a growing interest in the invention of personae and dramatized voices gave his poetry a sharper contemporary edge.

This may have something to do with his parallel development as a novelist. His early novel, *Smith's Dream*, was followed by *All Visitors Ashore* (1984), *The Death of the Body* (1986), and *The End of the Century at the End of the World* (1992), and he is now best known for his fiction, which also includes *The Secret History of Modernism* (2001) and *Mansfield* (2004). He has been awarded the CBE for his services to New Zealand literature, and in 2007 was made a Member of the Order of New Zealand. *Collected Poems 1951–2006* (Auckland University Press/Carcanet, 2009) draws on several later volumes, including *The Red Tram* (2004) and *The Black River* (2007—both Auckland University Press). It won the 2009 Montana Book Award for Reference and Anthology. In the same year, Stead received the Prime Minister's Award for Achievement in Literary Fiction. See also the essays collected in *The Writer At Work* (Otago University Press, 2000), *Book Self* (2008), and *South West of Eden: A Memoir, 1932–1956* (2010—both Auckland University Press).   PB

Steele, Peter (1939–2012) Born in Perth, Western Australia, and educated at the University of Melbourne, graduating BA in 1966, MA in 1968, and PhD in 1976. He taught at the University of Melbourne from 1966 and was later Reader in English. From 1973 to 1977 Steele was rector of Campion College, Melbourne, and from 1985 to 1991 was provincial superior of the Society of Jesus in Australia.

Steele's first important work was his magisterial *Jonathan Swift: Preacher and Jester* (Clarendon Press, 1978), in which he emerges not only as an acute critic of Swift but also as a remarkable prose stylist in his own right. His next critical work was *Expatriates: Reflections on Modern Poetry* (Paul & Company, 1985), in which it becomes clear that Steele is better approached as an essayist than as a literary critic in any narrow sense. In prose that dazzles as it informs, Steele's essays often trace eccentric orbits around their topics, combining close analysis with aphoristic energy. An abiding interest in the self and its disguises is embodied in *The Autobiographical Passion* (Melbourne University Press, 1989). A host of uncollected and fugitive papers explore a rich variety of religious and literary themes.

Steele's prose and verse are of a piece in terms of their absorption with play, imagination, and the quest for meaning. Yet the poems adopt and work with a plainer style than the essays. The title of his first collection, *Word from Lilliput* (Hawthorn, 1973), reminds us that Swift remains a guiding spirit; while a fellow-feeling with the *Auden of 'In Praise of Limestone' is apparent in *Marching on Paradise* (Longman Cheshire, 1984). Perfectly at home in a variety of formal modes, Steele writes as wittily and sharply about modern manners as he does about age-old moral and spiritual perplexities. He also published two volumes of ekphrastic verse, subtitled 'art into poetry': *Plenty* (2003) and *The Whispering Gallery* (2006—both Macmillan). *White Knight with Beebox: New and Selected Poems* appeared from John Leonard Press in 2009. See also *Braiding the Voices: Essays in Poetry* (Leonard, 2012).   KH

Steele, Timothy (1948–) Born in Burlington, Vermont, where he attended the local public schools. He was educated at Stanford and received his PhD from Brandeis, where he was strongly influenced by his teacher J. V. *Cunningham (whose poems he has edited). He returned to Stanford as a Wallace Stegner fellow, and has lived in California through the Seventies and Eighties, teaching at Stanford and UCLA. He currently lives in Los Angeles and teaches at that campus of California State University.

Among the most notable of the *New Formalists, he is also the poet who most successfully embodies the tenets associated with Cunningham and *Winters (whose legacy at Stanford was still strong long after his death in 1968), which include strict adherence to traditional, usually iambic, metre and to the plain style of Ben Jonson, with an emphasis upon paraphrasable intellectual argument and on reason controlling emotion. In his first two books of poetry, *Uncertainties and Rest* (Louisiana State University Press, 1979) and *Sapphics Against Anger* (Random House, 1986), he writes with quiet authority, passion, and wit about the landscapes of Vermont ('Incident on a Picnic', 'Learning to Skate', 'The Sheets') and California ('California Street, 1975–76', 'Near Olympic', 'Will Rogers Beach'), as well as about such abstractions as culture, faith, and friendship. Both books contain a sequence of epigrams in the tradition of Cunningham and *Auden, as well as classically restrained yet delicately sensual love lyrics, including 'Last Night as You Slept', 'An Aubade', and 'Love Poem'. His belief that poetic form should reflect the reasoned balance of strong passions is concisely stated in 'Sapphics Against Anger'.

His critique of modernism, *Missing Measures: Modern Poetry and the Revolt Against Meter* (University of Arkansas Press, 1990), is a carefully argued and lucidly written work of scholarship as well as being the strongest defence yet of the New Formalists' return to metred verse. See also *All the Fun's in How You Say a Thing: An Explanation of Meter and Versification* (Ohio University Press, 1999). His first two collections, reprinted as *Sapphics and Uncertainties: Poems 1970–1986* (University of Arkansas Press, 1995), have been followed by two more: *The Color Wheel* (Johns Hopkins University Press, 1994) and *Toward the Winter Solstice* (Ohio University Press, 2006).   RMCP

Stefans, Brian Kim (1969–) Born in Rutherford, New Jersey, Stefans has been an innovator in digital poetry, frequently using flash animation and film to create multimedia and interactive texts. He is author of the books *Gulf* (Object, 1998), *Angry Penguins* (Harry Tankoos, 2000), *What Is Said to the Poet Concerning Flowers* (Factory School, 2006), and *Free Space Comix* (Roof, 1998), which is also the name of his long-running blog, now in its third incarnation. He is the creator of arras.net, a site devoted to new-media poetics, where much of his own work can be found, and the editor of the */ubu* series of e-books at www.ubu.com. *Kluge: A Meditation* (2006) is a digital poetry piece including video, animation, essays, and repurposed poetic texts. For his criticism, see the volumes *Before Starting Over: Selected Writings and Interviews 1994–2005* (Salt, 2006) and *Fashionable Noise: On Digital Poetics* (Atelos, 2003). He has also edited a downloadable collection of new work by contemporary Southern California writers and text-artists, *The L.A. Telephone Book, vol. 1 2011–2012*. Stefans studied Literature at Bard College and received his MFA in Electronic Literature from Brown University in 2006. He is Assistant Professor of English at the University of California, Los Angeles.   SR

Stein, Gertrude (1874–1946) Born in Allegheny, Pennsylvania and educated at Radcliffe College and Johns Hopkins University, Stein was an American modernist writer of novels, essays, plays, poetry, and libretti. In 1902, she moved to Paris, France, where she spent the rest her life with her partner Alice Toklas. A collector, with her brother Leo, of avant-garde painting, and an influential talker, she held salons at her home attended by many famous figures, including Pablo Picasso (of whom she wrote an early 'portrait'), Georges Braque, Ernest Hemingway, and Guillaume Apollinaire. She gave her own account of this world in *The Autobiography of Alice B. Toklas* (1933).

Stein's poetic writing has been described as 'verbal cubism'. Just as cubist paintings broke objects down into smaller units and abandoned a singular point of view or perspective, Stein's poems work with associative rather than cumulative phrasing, in a manner akin to collage. Her poetry is characterized by a playful approach to language, an emphasis on the malleability of nouns, a minimalist attitude to punctuation, and a rejection of fixed meaning. Repetition is also a distinctive feature of its gnomic and meditative manner, which aspires to make the familiar new through 'losing refusing and pleasing and betraying and caressing nouns' ('Poetry and Grammar'). In her often-quoted line 'a rose is a rose is a rose', Stein said, 'the rose is red for the first time in a hundred years'.

Stein's attitude to language, and her practice as a writer, were influenced by her education, in particular her studies with the philosopher and psychologist William James. Her practice of 'automatic' or, in James' phrase, 'stream-of-consciousness' writing is evident in *Tender Buttons* (1914), Stein's best-known and most controversial work. Divided into three sections—'Objects', 'Food', and 'Rooms'—the text consists of a series of prose poems which abstract everyday domesticity in associative sentences that unfix their subjects from the usual field of referents. Thus, 'Red Roses' reads in full: 'A cool red rose and a pink cut pink, a collapse and a sold hole, a little less hot.' Of her writing process in *Tender Buttons*, Stein said: 'I used to take objects on a table, like a tumbler or any kind of object and try to get the picture of it clear and separate in my mind and create a word relationship

between the word and the things seen' ('A Transatlantic Interview', 1946). This statement illuminates Stein's practice more generally: her poetics investigate how connections made in language construct how we see the world.

Stein's work has been increasingly influential on poetry in the avant-garde tradition. Early admirers included Mina *Loy and Edith *Sitwell. John *Ashbery has praised the long, posthumously published *Stanzas in Meditation* (1956) as a 'poem about the world, about "them" . . . Like people, Miss Stein's lines are comforting or annoying or brilliant or tedious. Like people, they sometimes make no sense and sometimes make perfect sense'. Latterly, Stein's experimental approach to writing has been one of the chief influences on the *Language poets, and especially their development of a disjunctive prose poetry. Analysis and discussion of Stein's work featured heavily in the L=A=N=G=U=A=G=E magazine edited by Bruce *Andrews and Charles *Bernstein, which ran from 1978 to 1982. As with other modernist innovators, however, the contrast between Stein's progressive aesthetics and conservative politics remains a controversial question for the post-war appreciation of her work: see 'Stein's War Years: Setting the Record Straight', a 'dossier' on her survival as a Jewish lesbian in Vichy France, edited by Bernstein for the online magazine *Jacket 2*, in response to Barbara Will's book *Unlikely Collaboration* (Columbia University Press, 2011).

The American poet Harryette *Mullen has notably revisited Stein's *Tender Buttons* in her books *Trimmings* (1991) and S*PeRM**K*T (1992). These texts take the same associative, sound-driven approach as Stein and apply them to objects associated with womanhood and supermarkets. Mullen politicizes Stein's writing practice by creating rhythmic prose poems around questions of femininity, capitalism, and race. Whilst Stein's legacy as a cultural icon of lesbianism has sometimes led to reductive, biographical readings of her work (ironically, considering Stein's dismissal of her sexuality as an important feature of either her biography or her writing), a poem such as 'Lifting Belly' (1917), widely discussed as a representation of the lesbian body, has become an influential part of the queer canon of contemporary literature.

A two-volume edition of Stein's *Writings* was published by the Library of America in 1998. *Look at Me Now and Here I Am: Selected Works 1911–1945* (Penguin, 1971) ed. Patricia Meyerowitz, remains a useful introduction. A more recent selection has been made by Joan *Retallack for the University of California Press. See also *Stanzas in Meditation: The Corrected Edition* (Yale University Press, 2012), ed. Susannah Hollister and Emily Setina. For a biography of Stein, see Janet Malcolm, *Two Lives: Gertrude and Alice* (Yale University Press, 2007). For criticism, see Marjorie Perloff, *The Poetics of Indeterminacy* (Northwestern University Press, 1981), Lisa Ruddick, *Reading Gertrude Stein: Body, Text, Gnosis* (Cornell University Press, 1991), and Ulla E. Dydo with William Rice, *Gertrude Stein: The Language That Rises* (Northwestern University Press, 2003), a study of Stein's writing life between 1923 and 1934.   SRO

Stephens, James (1880–1950) Born in Dublin. Recognized as important in the Irish Revival, he is now a neglected figure. *Joyce at one point thought him the only man capable of completing the composition of *Finnegans Wake*. Stephens was a poet of great prosodic ability, whose work, firmly rooted in Irish lore, changed little from *Insurrection* (Maunsel, 1909), his first collection, to *Kings and the Moon* (Macmillan, 1938), his last. He possessed simplicity, but his frequently nonchalant manner concealed a profound melancholy. His robust enjoyment of life was always jostled by a metaphysical and religious unease. This blend of feelings comes across as brilliantly anecdotal in his best poems, such as 'What Thomas an Buille Said in a Pub'. He kept his verse, if not consistently light in tone, then at least only briefly tragic, as in the famous 'The Snare'. His work cries out for judicious selection, only partly fulfilled in *Collected Poems* (1954) or in *James Stephens: A Selection* (1962—both Macmillan), ed. Lloyd Frankenberg. It is in his novel *The Crock of Gold* (Macmillan, 1912) that his comic genius is most substantial.

See *Stephens* (Routledge & Kegan Paul, 1965), by Hilary Pyle, and *The Writings of James Stephens* (Macmillan, 1979), by Patricia McFate.   MS-S

Stern, Gerald (1925–) Born in Pittsburgh, and studied at the University of Pittsburgh and Columbia. After serving in the Air Corps he taught at many colleges and universities, for the longest period at Somerset County College in New Jersey. He taught at the University of Iowa Writers' Workshop for many years.

To say that Stern's distinctive and endearing voice combines the bluster of Allen *Ginsberg with the tenderness of James *Wright may seem unhistorical, given that Stern is in fact a year or two older than those poets. Yet while Wright and Ginsberg published their first books in the mid-Fifties, Stern did not make his debut until 1971, when *The Pineys* appeared. Even then he received little attention until the publication of *Lucky Life* in 1977. Thereafter he has come to be recognized as a major poet of celebration, indeed one of the few writing today who has been able to sustain the Whitmanian note convincingly. Together with the characteristic sense of plenitude reflected in his fondness for parataxis, catalogue, and anaphora, Stern's poetry displays an avowedly Jewish attitude towards suffering (see his poem 'Behaving Like a Jew', in which he refuses to be consoled for the death of an opossum on the highway); the amalgamation of these two strains, the Whitmanian and the Judaic, produces a bitter-sweet music unlike any other in contemporary poetry. Stern's focus on his solitary experience, his comically narcissistic portrayals of his own epiphanies and ecstasies, make him in many ways an old-fashioned poet, limited in the range of contemporary reality he can encompass. Yet by the same token he demonstrates the continued viability of a poetic mode that may well nourish the psyches of its readers more than other, less solipsistic modes can. His early work may be sampled in *Leaving Another Kingdom: Selected Poems* (Harper, 1990).

This Time: New and Selected Poems (1998) won the National Book Award. Stern's later books, which have been admired for their lyrical ardency and formal expansiveness, include *American Sonnets* (2002), *Everything Is Burning* (2005), *Save the Last Dance* (2008), and *In Beauty Bright* (2012). *Early Collected Poems 1965–1992* was published in 2010. From 2000 to 2002 Stern was Poet Laureate of New Jersey, and in 2005 received the Wallace Stevens Award from the Academy of American Poets. See also *What I Can't Bear Losing: Notes from a Life* (2004—all Norton).   RG

Stevens, Wallace (1879–1955) Born in Reading, Pennsylvania, and grew up in a comfortable, upper-middle-class family. He attended Harvard from 1897 to 1900, where he studied French and German and became friendly with George Santayana, the philosopher, to whom he would later address one of his finest poems, 'To an Old Philosopher in Rome'. At Harvard, Stevens was editor of the college literary magazine, *The Advocate*.

After leaving Harvard, Stevens planned to become a journalist; he worked briefly with the *New York Herald Tribune*, but he did not like the daily routines of journalism. Following advice from his father, he left his job at the paper to enter New York Law School in 1901. In 1904 he was admitted to the New York bar. For several years he practised law with mediocre success, moving from firm to firm while, at the same time, reading and writing poetry. In 1908 he began working for the legal department of an insurance company, a shift of emphasis that led to his ultimate appointment with the Hartford Accident and Indemnity Company, of which he became vice-president in 1934. 'It gives a man character to have this daily contact with a job', he would later say, dividing his life sharply between his literary and business lives.

Stevens married Elsie Moll in 1908, a woman whom he had met five years earlier in Reading. They had one child, a daughter, Holly, and lived a secluded, upper-middle-class life in Hartford, Connecticut. Stevens did not travel, though he relished postcards from friends abroad, and he delighted in fine wines, French cheeses, paintings, and flowers. He acquired an impressive collection of classical recordings and spent a good deal of time gardening. He continued to work at the insurance company until his death, often composing poems on his way to the office and revising them while there.

Though Stevens began publishing in magazines such as *Poetry* as early as 1914, he did not actually publish a book until 1923, when he was 44 years old. That book, *Harmonium*, is a landmark volume in modern American poetry. It contains many of Stevens' best-known poems, such as 'Earthy Anecdote', 'The Snow Man', 'Ploughing on Sunday', 'Sunday Morning', 'Tea at the Palace of Hoon', 'Peter Quince at the Clavier', and 'Thirteen Ways of Looking at a Blackbird'. These poems exhibit a dandified, almost baroque quality of language typical of Stevens' early work, which is much in contrast to the later, barer style. *Harmonium* suggests that Stevens had been closely reading the English Romantics—especially Keats—as well as the French Symbolists. The poems of this period are marked by high spirits, a fascination with sensual experience, and a fine sense of parody and pastiche. The influence of *Imagism can be seen throughout, with sharply defined images everywhere. The linguistic medium itself is brought to the fore, with a huge emphasis on the musicality of the line. In contrast to the brightness so pervasive in this volume, there is a sombre tone that occasionally enters the work, as in 'The Snow Man', wherein the poet, like the snowman of the poem, 'beholds | Nothing that is not there and the nothing that is'.

'The poet's subject is his sense of the world', Stevens once wrote. His principal, almost obsessive, subject was in fact the interplay between reality and the imagination. Like the great Romantics he admired, he believed in the ultimate value of imagination, in the ability of the imagination to transform reality. In this, Stevens echoes Coleridge and Nietzsche, Bergson and Santayana, all of whom he read avidly. One long poem of his middle period, 'The Man with a Blue Guitar' (1936), is a brilliant sequence of couplets that explores the meaning and complex figural workings of imaginative vision, represented here by the colour blue. Green, here as elsewhere, represents 'reality' in Stevens' developing symbology, which is remarkably consistent throughout his work. This polarity is similarly represented by north and south, wind and stone, and other oppositional terms.

There is a consistent anti-clerical, atheistical strain in Stevens, who is none the less a deeply 'religious' writer in a sense. 'Poetry', he writes in 'Blue Guitar', '. . . must take the place | Of empty heaven and its hymns.' But the music of imagination, in Stevens, is not supernatural. Later in life, in an essay called 'Imagination as Value', he remarks that 'the great poems of heaven and earth have been written and the great poem of the earth remains to be written'. Thus, Stevens set out to write what, in a poem called 'Of Modern Poetry', stands as something of a credo: 'The poem of the mind in the act of finding | What will suffice.' The poet's job in an age of disbelief is, he suggests elsewhere, to supply the 'satisfactions of belief, in his measure and in his style'. This quasi-religious quest became, increasingly, his central preoccupation as he explored the dialectic of reality and the imagination throughout the Thirties, Forties, and early Fifties.

Transport to Summer appeared in 1947, and it contained the major poem of Stevens' later period, 'Notes Toward a Supreme Fiction', a poem which examines the notion of 'fiction' and its relation to 'fact'. Stevens declares: 'The poem refreshes life so that we share, | For a moment, the first idea.' That is, poetry takes us back to an 'immaculate beginning'. It quickens our sense of the world we inhabit. Stevens celebrates the 'war between the mind | And sky, between thought and day and night'. He finds endless new ways to provide 'the bread of faithful speech'. In a remarkable book of essays, *The Necessary Angel* (1951), Stevens explained his concept of the poet's role: 'What makes the poet the potent figure that he is, or was, or ought to be, is that he creates the world to which we turn incessantly and without knowing it and that he gives to life the supreme fictions without which we are unable to conceive of it.'

Stevens' last book (apart from his *Collected Poems* of 1954, which included the famous sequence 'The Rock'), was *The Auroras of Autumn* (1954), a book markedly different in texture from *Harmonium*, though one sees the same fundamental preoccupations. Stevens in his later work wrote poetry very much in opposition to Ezra *Pound's version of Imagism. Increasingly, blank verse became his medium, with its regularity of rhythm, though he also cultivated highly idiosyncratic forms of abstraction and narrative indirection that have strongly influenced many contemporary poets.

Typical of the later Stevens is the fine meditative sequence, 'An Ordinary Evening in New Haven', where he argues that 'The poem is the cry of its occasion, | Part of the res itself and not about it'. With characteristic obliquity and wit, the poet searches out 'the inner men | Behind the outer shields', contemplating the objective world from a supremely subjective viewpoint.

One observes throughout Stevens career a deepening sense of duality; indeed, the life of the successful insurance company executive and the life of the great modernist poet never coincided, except in the most superficial ways. The outer shields that Stevens wore correspond in some ways to the famous masks of W. B. *Yeats; they were projections meant to aid the poet in his antithetical quest. This quest, for Stevens, is a holy one, and the poet is regarded as a vatic philosopher in the ancient Roman sense: a high priest of the imagination. 'If one no longer believes in God (as truth)', Stevens says in a letter, 'it is not possible merely to disbelieve; it becomes necessary to believe in something else.' That 'something else' is, of course, poetry itself, seen as a self-defining quest for meaning, an attempt to conjure a world of bright, hard things that, in the Emersonian sense, become inner objects. The final unity towards which all poetry leans is a blending of subject and object, of self and other.

In 'To an Old Philosopher in Rome', a very late poem, Stevens invokes his old Harvard teacher and friend, George Santayana, celebrating 'a kind of total grandeur at the end'. In this total grandeur the physical objects of the world are all 'enlarged'. Yet they remain themselves, too: 'No more than a bed, a chair and moving nuns.'

Santayana is seen to pause upon the threshold of death with a sudden waft of understanding: 'He stops upon this threshold, | As if the design of all his words takes form | And frame from thinking and is realized.' This realization is a form of embodiment that Stevens sought perpetually through his life as a poet. It is what he called in 'Not Ideas About the Thing But the Thing Itself' a 'new knowledge of reality'. This is the knowledge, the transmogrification, that Stevens looked for and, often enough in the poetry itself, found.

The Collected Poems of Wallace Stevens (Knopf, 1954; Faber, 1955 and 1984) remains the standard volume. In addition, there is Opus Posthumous (Knopf, 1957, expanded edn., 1989; Faber, 1959 and 1990), a collection of posthumous poems, plays, and prose, originally edited by Samuel French Morse. The Letters of Wallace Stevens (Knopf, 1966; Faber, 1967) was edited by his daughter, Holly Stevens.

See also Stevens' The Necessary Angel (Knopf, 1951; Faber, 1960). A one-volume Collected Poetry and Prose, ed. Frank Kermode and Joan Richardson, containing new selections from his journals, notebooks, and letters, was published by the Library of America in 1997.

Among innumerable critical works of note are Frank Kermode, Wallace Stevens (Oliver & Boyd, 1969, revd. edn., Faber, 1989); Helen Vendler, Wallace Stevens: Words Chosen out of Desire (University of Tennessee Press, 1984); Harold Bloom, Wallace Stevens: The Poems of our Climate (Cornell University Press, 1977); Milton Bates, Wallace Stevens: A Mythology of the Self (University of California Press, 1985); James Longenbach, Wallace Stevens: The Plain Sense of Things (Oxford University Press, 1991); Alan Filreis, Modernism from Right to Left: Wallace Stevens, the Thirties and Literary Radicalism (Cambridge University Press, 1994); Simon Critchley, Things Merely Are: Philosophy in the Poetry of Wallace Stevens (Routledge, 2005); Tim Morris, Wallace Stevens: Poetry and Criticism (Salt, 2006); and Edward Ragg, Wallace Stevens and the Aesthetics of Abstraction (Cambridge University Press, 2010). See also Eleanor Cook, A Reader's Guide to Wallace Stevens

(Princeton University Press, 2007). For biographical studies, see Peter Brazeau, Parts of a World: Wallace Stevens Remembered (Random House, 1983); Holly Stevens, Souvenirs and Prophecies: The Young Wallace Stevens (journals) (Knopf, 1977); and Joan Richardson's two-volume life, Wallace Stevens: The Early Years, 1879–1923 (1986) and Wallace Stevens: The Later Years, 1923–1955 (1988—both Beech Tree).   JP

Stevenson, Anne (1933–) Born of American parents in Cambridge, England, and educated in the USA at the University of Michigan. She began to write poetry in response to her research on the breakdown of puritanism as a moral force. This concern is reflected in her 1974 volume Correspondences (Wesleyan University Press/ Oxford University Press, 1974), a warm and vividly colloquial sequence of verse-letters, fictional but inspired by her family archive. In 1954 she settled in England, where she was a founder of the Poetry Bookshop in Hay-on-Wye. She currently lives in Durham and North Wales. Anne Stevenson combines technical mastery with exceptional musicality. She writes expressively about landscape and the natural world, but seems at her best as a chronicler of human behaviour and concerns. She has written critical studies, including Five Looks at Elizabeth Bishop (Bloodaxe, 2006) and a biography of Sylvia *Plath (Bitter Fame, Viking/Houghton, 1989). Her latest collections are Poems 1955–2005 (Bloodaxe, 2005), A Lament for the Makers (Clutag, 2006), Stone Milk (2007), and Astonishment (2012—both Bloodaxe). A Selected Poems, with an introduction by Andrew *Motion, was published by the Library of America in 2008, and a collection of essays on her work, Voyages Over Voices, ed. Angela Leighton, appeared in 2010 from Liverpool University Press. In 2007, she won the Lannan Award for a Lifetime's Achievement in Poetry and the Poetry Foundation of America's Neglected Masters Award.   CAR

Stewart, Douglas (1913–85) Born at Eltham, Taranaki Province, New Zealand, and moved to Sydney in 1938 to work on the Bulletin, becoming literary editor of the

Red Page in 1940. In 1961, when the *Bulletin* changed ownership, he became literary editor with the publishers Angus & Robertson until he retired in 1971.

Editor, dramatist, poet, and anthologist, Stewart was one of the most influential literary figures in the Australia of his time. He first made his reputation with the verse plays *Ned Kelly* (1943), *The Fire on the Snow* and *The Golden Lover* (both 1944), and *Shipwreck* (1947), explorations of the meaning of heroism and the struggle of passionate feeling against convention. Stewart also wrote short stories, belles-lettres, and reminiscence, and edited fifteen volumes of poetry and prose, most notably the collections *Australian Bush Ballads* (1955), *Old Bush Songs and Rhymes of Colonial Times* (1957), and *The Pacific Book of Bush Ballads* (1967), all in collaboration with Nancy *Keesing. His reputation as a poet rests on thirteen volumes of poetry. After his move to Sydney his early New Zealand landscape poetry was followed by a series of attempts to come to terms with Australian nature, history, and landscape, and to write poems that combined popular and traditional Australian elements. He was much influenced by the Australian landscape and nature poetry of the 1940s, which he fostered in the *Bulletin*, and in *Sun Orchids and Other Poems* (1952) and *The Birdsville Track and Other Poems* (1955) found his own voice in a poetry of sparse, meticulous, and often humorous observation. The search for the meaning of heroism continued in *Rutherford and Other Poems* (1962), where his earlier concern with historical exploration led to poems about scientific discovery. Stewart became more and more aware of the fragility of civilized values in a world of increasing violence and fanaticism, and some of his finest poems like 'B Flat', 'Silkworms', the elegy for Kenneth *Slessor, and 'Terra Australis' celebrate the virtues of wise passivity, and the acceptance of the inevitable restrictions of life.

See *Collected Poems 1936–67* (1967); *Selected Poems* (1992—both Angus & Robertson).   vs

Stewart, Susan (1952–) Born in York, Pennsylvania, Stewart currently teaches the history of poetry and poetics at Princeton University. She is the author of five collections of poetry, among them *The Forest* (1995), *Columbarium* (2003), which received the National Book Critics Circle Award that year, and *Red Rover* (2008—all University of Chicago Press). She is also the author of numerous books of criticism, including *Poetry and the Fate of the Senses* (2002), which won the 2002 Christian Gauss Award for Literary Criticism from Phi Beta Kappa and the 2004 Truman Capote Award in Literary Criticism. Her most recent book on the theory of poetics, *The Poet's Freedom: A Notebook on Making*, was published by University of Chicago in 2011.

Stewart's principal investigations in her poetry and scholarship centre on changing accounts of personhood, the development of the senses, and the expression of consciousness through history as reflected in Western poetry. She has translated from Italian, including the selected poems of Alda Merini (*Love Lessons* (Princeton University Press, 2009)), and with Wesley D. Smith she has translated Euripides' *Andromache* (Oxford University Press, 2001). In 2010 she received an Academy Award in Literature from the American Academy of Arts and Letters.   AMl

Stone, Ruth (1915–2011) Born in Roanoke, Virginia, and attended the University of Illinois. The mother of three daughters, Stone taught creative writing at many institutions, including Indiana and Brandeis universities, and State University New York at Binghamton.

One of the more neglected poets of her generation until the last decade of her long life, Stone published thirteen books. What many readers first notice in her poetry is its humour, which ranges from delicate whimsy to verbal slapstick ('Then I picked at the tiling | And the house fell down'). It quickly becomes apparent, however, that Stone's comic energies are placed in the service of a humane and tender vision that gives a special place to the experience of ordinary women. While many of her poems are autobiographical lyrics, other lives, however dimly known, exert a powerful claim on her imagination: in one poem she summons up an android composed of the particles left by all the past occupants of a particular hotel room; another poem depicts the speaker passing a crowd on a train platform, ending with the line: 'I feel their entire histories ravish me.' Elsewhere Stone explores individual histories, giving them the circumstantial weight of fiction while still maintaining the light-footed poise of her language, with its quick puns, quirks of diction, and startling metaphors. Her poetry balances the immediate life of the self with the inferential life that surrounds it, with results that are both funny and affecting.

Stone's first collection, *In an Iridescent Time*, appeared in 1959. Her second husband, the writer Walter Stone, committed suicide the same year, a loss which haunted her later verse: see *Who Is the Widow's Muse?* (1991). *Second Hand Coat: New and Selected Poems* (1987—both Yellow Moon) drew on four collections. *In the Next Galaxy* (2002), with its acute reflections on ageing, won the National Book Award. Stone received many further accolades in recognition of her achievement, including the Wallace Stevens Award from the Academy of American Poets. *In the Dark* (2004—both Copper Canyon) addressed the subject of her failing sight. In 2007, Stone became State Poet Laureate of Vermont, where she lived from the 1950s. *What Loves Come To: New and Selected Poems* (Copper Canyon, 2008; Bloodaxe, 2009) has an introduction by Sharon *Olds and was nominated for the Pulitzer Prize.   RG*

Stow, Randolph (1935–2010) Born into a long-established pastoralist family in Geraldton, Western Australia, and had published a volume of poetry and two novels by the time he graduated from university in Perth. He worked first as a storeman at an isolated mission station in the Kimberley Ranges, then as a cadet patrol officer in New Guinea. While on duty in the Trobriand Islands he contracted a severe form of malaria and was invalided home with a suicidal depression. For three years he was in London, being treated at a hospital for tropical diseases, then lived in Malta and the United States, writing fiction. Having settled in East Anglia, from where his forebears had emigrated, Stow left off the writing of his seventh (and best) novel, *Visitants*, for ten years, partly because of an addiction to the drug Mandrax which had been prescribed for him after a car accident. When eventually finished, this book, which draws on his painful experiences in the Trobriands, helped him to win the Patrick White Award. In his lost years Stow lived in complete obscurity in a farm cottage, on a trickle of royalties and working at a village pub for the price of his drinks. He later had a small terrace house in Old Harwich, where he lived alone, frugally and self-effacingly. Once among the most recognizably Australian poets and novelists, he remained in England because of the greater social and linguistic complexity in that country, which he felt his work needed.

Stow's poetry is impressive but there is little of it. *Act One* (1957) contained his accomplished juvenilia; *Outrider* (1962—both MacDonald), his main book of verse, was illustrated with paintings especially done for it by Sidney Nolan; *A Counterfeit Silence* (Angus & Robertson, 1969) is a slim selected volume; and there were nine new poems in the anthology *Randolph Stow* (University of Queensland Press, 1990).

The main theme of both Stow's poetry and prose is isolation, a sense of 'otherness', within nature and society. His poetry is introspective and quiet, but there is a *frisson* of neuroticism about it. His imagery is subjective, and his lines are usually loose and lapsing, arranged in couplets or short stanzas. The manner is feverish, piercing, and yet frail. There is patrician reserve and anguish together.

Stow was influenced, he said, by Rimbaud, Whitman, and St John Perse, but perhaps just as important to him was the Australian poet Francis *Webb (who also spent time in East Anglia). The best of his fiction, including *Tourmaline* (1963), is as effective as his verse.   RGr

Strand, Mark (1934–   ) Born in Canada on Prince Edward Island. He studied at Antioch College, where he took a BA. He also received a BFA from Yale, where he studied painting. At the University of Iowa, he worked closely with poet Donald *Justice, completing an MA in 1962. He spent a year in Italy on a Fulbright scholarship, and later taught at Iowa for three years. In 1965 he spent a year as Fulbright Lecturer at the University of Brazil, where he was deeply influenced by contemporary Latin American poets (especially the Brazilian poet Carlos Drummond de Andrade). Strand has moved around a good deal, teaching at many American universities, including Columbia, Princeton, Harvard, Johns Hopkins, and the University of Utah. Between 1990 and 1991 he was Poet Laureate of the United States.

Strand's poetry is known for a clarity reminiscent of the paintings of Edward Hopper, of which he wrote a study, and for a deeply inward sense of language. Many of the poems aspire to the condition of dreams, shot through with images possessing a strangely haunting vividness, as in 'The Ghost Ship', which summons a mysterious ship that floats 'Through the crowded streets... | Its vague | tonnage like wind'. He frequently invokes everyday images, as in 'The Mailman', where a wraith-like mailman visits the narrator at midnight to deliver 'terrible personal news'. In 'The Last Bus' the poet imagines Rio de Janeiro, calling the sea 'a dream' in which the city 'dies and is reborn'. The poem is surreal in a manner that combines the dreamlike quality of Pablo Neruda with aspects of nightmare that recall such European expressionists as Georg Trakl.

Strand's first book, *Sleeping with One Eye Open* was published in 1964 by Stone Wall Press. His second, *Reasons for Moving* (1968), attracted widespread attention from critics; it includes 'Eating Poetry' which begins: 'Ink runs from the corners of my mouth. | There is no happiness like mine. | I have been eating poetry.' This antic surrealism also animates poems like 'Moontan', 'The Man in the Tree', and 'The Marriage'. *Darker* (1970) was an obliquely autobiographical volume, containing such poems as 'My Life' and 'My Death'. These poems are full of a quiet, ironically pictured anguish as the poet teeters on the brink of self-consciousness in pursuit of his *via negativa*. In 1973 Strand published *The Story of Our Lives*, more explicitly autobiographical than anything he had written before. It includes a striking elegy for the poet's father.

The Late Hour (1978) is among the strongest of Strand's early books, containing poems for the poet's son and daughter, and a number of poems (such as 'The Late Hour', 'Snowfall', and 'The Garden') that possess a deeply elegiac quality. In this book, Strand began writing with a freshness and simplicity that recall the poetry of ancient China.

As the Mexican poet Octavio Paz has written: 'Mark Strand has chosen the negative path, with loss as the first step towards fullness: it is also the opening to a transparent verbal perfection.' Strand's *Selected Poems* (1980—all Atheneum) adds to previously published work a number of beautifully realized autobiographical poems, including 'Shooting Whales' and 'Nights in Hackett's Cove'. He did not publish another volume until *The Continuous Life* in 1990. Later volumes include *Dark Harbour* (1993), a book-length sequence, and *Blizzard of One* (1998), which won the Pulitzer Prize. In 2004, Strand received the Wallace Stevens Award from the Academy of American Poets. See also *Man and Camel* (2006), his eleventh collection, and *New Selected Poems* (2007—all Knopf). Strand has also published short stories, several translations from European and Latin American poets, and anthologies of contemporary poetry. With Eavan *Boland, he edited *The Making of a Poem: A Norton Anthology of Poetic Forms* (2000). See also *Weather of Words: Poetic Invention* (Knopf, 2000).   JP

Strang, Catriona (1966–) After a childhood in Vancouver, Strang studied at Simon Fraser University and the *Kootenay School of Writing with Robin *Blaser and George *Bowering, and later with Fred *Wah and Peter Quartermain. She lives in Vancouver, where she is a founding member of the Institute for Domestic Research, and active in the home-schooling community.

Much of Strang's poetic work has been collaborative: her books *Busted* (Coach House, 2001) and *Light Sweet Crude*

(Linebooks, 2007) are co-authored by the late poet and scholar Nancy Shaw, with whom she also published a number of chapbooks. Her collaborations with the clarinettist François Houle, including the audio recording *The Clamourous Alphabet* (Periplum, 1999), explore the sometimes antagonistic relationship between language and music, and form part of Strang's ongoing attention to musical gestures in speech. Strang also co-edited the feminist press Barscheit with Lisa *Robertson and Christine Stewart, with whom her work shares an openly polemical feminist stance in questioning historically masculine forms of hierarchy and governance. In *Low Fancy* (ECW, 1993), opulent and sensual language suggestively underlines its own materiality and political cadences.   ADA

Strauss, Jennifer (née Wallace) (1933–) Born at Heywood, Victoria, Australia, and graduated from Melbourne University. Married in Scotland to fellow-expatriate Werner Strauss, she has studied and taught in England, Germany, the USA, and Canada. From 1964 she lectured, specializing in medieval English literature, at Monash University in Melbourne, where she is now an Honorary Research Fellow. She has published four collections: *Children and other Strangers* (Nelson, 1975), *Winter Driving* (Sisters, 1981), *Labour Ward* (1988), and *Tierra del Fuego: new and selected poems* (1997—both Pariah), and edited the *Oxford Book of Australian Love Poems* (1993). Strauss provides sharply focused insights into injustice, especially the oppression of women, from literature ('Wife to Horatio') and legend ('Bluebeard Re-Scripted'), as well as history ('The Anabaptist Cages, Munster', 'Ignaz Semmelweis Enters the Vienna Insane Asylum, 1865'). She has also edited the poems of Mary *Gilmore, and written studies of Judith *Wright and Gwen *Harwood. In 2007 she was made a Member of the Order of Australia.   JRO

Stryk, Lucien (1924–) Born in Poland and taught at the Northern Illinois University at DeKalb. A deliberately 'minor' poet, wishing in his own words 'to avoid the hateful evidence of our will to impress',

Stryk has been decisively influenced by Zen poetry, some of which he has translated (e.g. *Triumph of the Sparrow: Zen Poems of Shinkichi Takahashi*, University of Illinois Press, 1986; repr. Grove, 2000). His first substantial book, published by the Fantasy Press in Oxford, *The Trespasser* (1956), was *Pound-influenced and artificial, but full of ably and conscientiously made poems of a generally *imagist variety. Fear of 'impressing' may well have robbed his later work of impact, for its subject-matter is frequently far from that of Zen Buddhism, covering both his war and domestic experience. He has even been described as a 'tourist poet', because of his vivid snapshots of people (usually deprived) and places all over the world. Like many American poets, Stryk is suspicious of rhetoric and linguistic excitement; but he seldom declines into the prosaic. His highest achievement lies in his successful adaptation of Japanese procedures into English.

See *Zen, Poetry, The Art of Lucien Stryk* (1993), ed. Susan Porterfield, and *And Still Birds Sing: New and Collected Poems* (1998—both Ohio University Press).   MS-S

Stuart, Dabney (1937–) Born in Richmond, Virginia. He was educated at Davidson College and Harvard University and teaches at Washington and Lee University in Lexington, Virginia, where from 1988 he edited the literary quarterly *Shenandoah*. Stuart's first book, *The Diving Bell* (Knopf, 1966), was widely praised by reviewers for its formal polish and its inventiveness with autobiographical subject-matter, particularly in poems about the poet's extended Southern family. His early work is indebted to the *confessional poets, especially Robert *Lowell and *Snodgrass, but over a dozen published collections he displays a wide variety of other formal modes, from *surrealism in *The Other Hand* (1974), to the songs and ballads of *Yeats and *Muir in *Round and Round: A Triptych* (1977). Stuart writes personal poetry of unusual honesty, and many of his love poems are marked by their directness and absence of false sentiment. His later collections—*Common Ground* (1982), *Don't Look Back* (1987), and *Narcissus Dreaming* (1990)—reveal

S

the poet's familiarity with contemporary psychoanalytical literature, particularly in poems which rework and further develop family material. These books also contain poems of lyric meditation, occasional pieces of social and literary satire, and serious examples of acrostic verse. Stuart has also written a critical study of Vladimir *Nabokov and a book of children's verse, *Friends of Yours, Friends of Mine. Light Years: New and Selected Poems* (1994) has been followed by *Long Gone* (1997), *Settlers* (1999), *The Man Who Loves Cezanne* (2003—all Louisiana State University Press), and *Family Preserve* (University of Virginia Press, 2005).   RSG

Suknaski, Andrew (1942–2012) Born in Wood Mountain, Saskatchewan, to immigrant parents. Exposed only to Polish-laced Ukrainian in his early childhood, his first contact with English was not until he turned 6. Suknaski ran away from home at 16 and spent seventeen years travelling the world, working at various jobs. He attended Simon Fraser University and the University of British Columbia, as well as the Kootenay School of Fine Arts and the Montreal Museum School of Art and Design. He published four substantial collections: *Leaving* (1974); his most celebrated book, *Wood Mountain Poems* (1976); *the ghosts call you poor* (1978), and *In the Name of Narid* (1981), as well as numerous chapbooks and collections of concrete poetry.

Suknaski's poems are simultaneously a personal search for identity and self, and an attempt to define Canada's multicultural dimension. When asked which ethnic group he identified with, Suknaski allied himself with the eclectic nationalities of Wood Mountain, ranging from Romanian and Metis to Irish and Dutch. Dialect, heavily-accented pidgin English, and beer-parlour slang are all rendered on the page in their phonetic simplicity. Influenced by the immigrant's heritage, the dialect is neither English nor the language which infiltrates it; the poems depend on the vividness of the anecdote for their analogies.

The National Film Board of Canada produced an informative film, *Wood Mountain Poems* (1982), on Suknaski, his heritage, and his poems, directed by Harvey Spak.

His poetry collections were all published by small, independent presses (some of which he also ran) with the exception of *Wood Mountain Poems* and *the ghosts call you poor*, published in Toronto by Macmillan of Canada. See *There is No Mountain: Selected Poems of Andrew Suknaski* (Chaudiere, 2010), ed. Rob McLennan.   MQA

Sullivan, Robert (1967–) Of Ngā Puhi and Irish descent, Sullivan studied with Michele *Leggott at Auckland University, where he later worked as a librarian. He now lives in Honolulu and teaches creative writing at Manukau Institute of Technology. With Albert *Wendt and Reina Whaitiri he has co-edited two anthologies of Polynesian poetry. He also edits the online journal *trout*.

Jazz Waiata (Auckland University Press, 1990), won the PEN Award for Best First Book of Poetry, and introduced an energetic voice sharpened by satirical anger about Maori poverty in contemporary Auckland as well as the prevailing conventions of New Zealand poetry (Hone *Tuwhare and James K. *Baxter were two important early influences). It ends with an extended personal sequence, 'Tai Tokerau Poems'. Subsequent work has developed his interest in Maori language and story-telling traditions: see *Weaving Earth and Sky: Myths and Legends of Aotearoa*, (Random House, 2003). His later collections include *Piki Ake!* (1993), *Star Waka* (1999), *Captain Cook in the Underworld* (2002)—a rhyming libretto on colonial adventure which combines European and Polynesian myth—and *Voice Carried My Family* (2005—all Auckland University Press). With *Shout Ha! To the Sky* (Salt, 2010) Sullivan confirmed his reputation as one of the leading voices of the Pacific region, in sequences that address Maori history and culture, as well as contemporary his own postmodern politics his own postmodern and poetics (see 'Lunch with Frank *O'Hara', which exclaims, tongue-in-cheek, 'I've never read him but people have said | we're alike!').   JNT

Surendran, C.P. (1959–) Born in Ottapalam, North Kerala, into a family of writers and left-wing intellectuals, Surendran studied English Literature at university in Delhi, where he is now a journalist on the *Times of India*, having previously lived and worked in Mumbai. After receiving early encouragement from Dom *Moraes, he published four collections of poetry, including *Posthumous Poems* (Penguin, 1999) and *Portraits of the Space We Occupy* (Harper-Collins, 2007), and two novels. His poems offer ironic vignettes of urban life and modern love in short lines that keep emotion reined in by realism ('Milk Still Boils'). A sharp critic of contemporary Indian culture ('poetry is dead because normal-looking people killed it with their shopping') he has said that he stopped writing verse in 2006.   JNT

Sutherland, Keston (1976–) Born in Bristol, Sutherland grew up in Berkshire and studied at Cambridge University, where he wrote his doctoral thesis on the poetry of J. H. *Prynne. He is now Reader in English at the University of Sussex.

A leading figure to a younger generation of avant-garde poets, Sutherland's poetry is notable for its Marxist critique of daily life, which subjects the lyric 'I' to intense abjection as it pursues a revolutionary— and increasingly psychoanalytic—concern with 'the significance of love'. The surreal combinations of language that characterize his diction can recall the anti-capitalist collage of a *Language poet such as Bruce *Andrews ('shut in in the flaming Nestlé beach hut'). But these poems, often denominated 'odes', are also strongly structured as arguments, in the tradition of Prynne and other *Cambridge poets. Narrative threads, both personal and satirical, run across longer works.

As a student, Sutherland founded Barque Press with Andrea *Brady, and has printed much of his own work in pamphlet form. *Antifreeze* (2002) is a selected volume of early verse. Since *Neutrality* (2004) and *Neocosis* (2005), Sutherland has published two extended dream-like sequences, which turn from Bush-era America to capitalist China: *Hot White Andy* (2007) and *Stress Position* (2009—all Barque), his most formally complex poem yet. He also edits the magazine *Quid*. See the critical essays collected in *Stupefaction* (University of Chicago Press, 2011).   JNT

Sweeney, Matthew (1952–) Born in Co. Donegal, Ireland. He moved to England in 1973 and studied German and English at the Polytechnic of North London and the University of Freiburg, 1975–9. Since then he has made a profession of creative writing, doing many readings and school visits, and holding writing residencies in Ireland, England, and abroad. He has also lived in Germany and Romania, and been translated into several languages.

Sweeney's first volume, *A Dream of Maps*, was published in 1981 with his name inauspiciously misspelt on the title-page. In subsequent books—*A Round House* (1983), *The Lame Waltzer* (1985—all Raven Arts), and *Blue Shoes* (Secker & Warburg, 1989)—he developed an economical, naïve style of narration for his lugubrious fables, in which domestic rituals are intruded on, and sometimes overtaken, by the surreal. Contemporary landscapes, whose features include the golf courses, lighthouses, and cold seas of Donegal, are peopled by eccentrics and solitaries, when not with mysterious pronouns. His chief concern is mortality; there are deaths (especially by drowning) and resurrections, but it is in the mixed realm of the moribund—as when he charts the functionless survival of his character the Lame Waltzer—that his imagination has probed most distinctively.

Sweeney's later collections include *Cacti* (Secker & Warburg, 1992), *The Bridal Suite* (1997), *A Smell of Fish* (2000), *Sanctuary* (2004), and *Black Moon* (2007—all Cape), which was nominated for the T. S. Eliot Prize. He has also written for children, and edited several anthologies including, with Jo *Shapcott, *Emergency Kit: Poems for Strange Times* (Faber, 1996) and, with Ken *Smith, *Beyond Bedlam: Poems Written Out of Mental Distress* (Anvil, 1997). With John Hartley *Williams, he has co-written a guide to *Writing Poetry* (Hodder & Stoughton, 1996). See *The Night Post: A New Selection* (Salt, 2010).   MI

Swensen, Cole (1955–) Professor of Literary Arts at Brown University, Swensen received her BA and MA from San Francisco State University, and her PhD from the University of California. She now divides her time between Paris and Providence, Rhode Island.

Swensen's poetry blends the experimental attitude to composition of the *Language poets with a more traditional lyric style. She is known for collections which explore a specific and intensively researched theme. *The Book of a Hundred Hands* (University of Iowa Press, 2005), for example, consists of a hundred poems on the subject of the human hand, from its physiology to its symbolism. Swensen's work is also frequently ekphrastic, dealing in language with other modes such as visual art and architecture.

Swensen has translated several contemporary French-language poets into English, including Olivier Cadiot, Jean Tortel, and Pierre Alferi. She is also the founder of La Presse, which publishes French poetry in English translation. Her original collections include *New Math* (Morrow, 1987), *Park* (Floating Island, 1991), *Numen* (Burning Deck, 1995), *Noon* (Sun & Moon, 1997), *Oh* (Apogee, 2000), *Such Rich Hour* (University of Iowa Press, 2001), *Goest* (Alice James, 2004), and *Ours* (University of California Press, 2008). With David *St John, she edited the *American Hybrid* anthology (Norton, 2009).   SRO

Swenson, May (1919–89) Born in Logan, Utah and educated at Utah State University. She moved to New York during the 1930s and worked for the Writer's Project (a part of the Works Progress Administration). During those years Swenson practised and refined her craft; many of the poems that first made her reputation were published in *The New Yorker*, beginning in the 1940s.

Swenson was a poet of strong formal instinct who was drawn to the particulars of her natural and domestic surroundings. In her early publications—as in the book *Another Animal* (Scribner, 1954)—formal considerations guided most of her choices of subject and presentation. Nevertheless, from the start Swenson showed herself capable of keenly registering the sensuous, and was willing to let sounds and rhythms inscribe a confined world.

Swenson's poems published in the 1960s suggest a struggle in her art. She essayed a number of ambitious visual effects; many of her 'iconographs' incorporated a vertical split in the text. Later, she brought more of her own experience forward as subject-matter. Her poems took on a new kineticism; they seemed less concerned with stilling an object or animal in the amber of pure perception. The surface is altogether friendlier and more inviting.

In 1980 Swenson succeeded Elizabeth *Bishop as chancellor of the Academy of American Poets; in 1981 she was awarded the Bollingen Prize for Poetry; and in 1987, just two years before her death, she received a fellowship from the MacArthur Foundation. Swenson's books include: *A Cage of Spines* (Rinehart, 1958), *To Mix With Time: New and Selected Poems* (1963), *Half Sun Half Sleep* (1967—both Scribner); *New and Selected Things Taking Place* (Little, Brown, 1978); and her last volume, *In Other Words* (Knopf, 1987). *Nature: Poems Old and New* (1994; repr. 2000) appeared posthumously. *The Complete Love Poems* (1991—both Houghton Mifflin) was reprinted in 2003 with an introduction by Maxine *Kumin. Swenson's *Collected Poems* is forthcoming from the Library of America. For criticism, see Kirstin Hotelling Zona, *Marianne Moore, Elizabeth Bishop and May Swenson: The Feminist Poetics of Self-Restraint* (University of Michigan Press, 2002).   SPB

Swift, Todd (1966–   ) Born in Montreal, Canada and moved to Europe in 1997. Having lived in Budapest and Paris, he now resides in London, where he teaches at Kingston University. Active in both the Canadian and UK poetry scenes as a critic, editor, and anthologist, he has a PhD in Creative and Critical Writing from the University of East Anglia. His collections include *Budavox* (1999), *Rue du Regard* (2004), *Winter Tennis* (2007), and *England Is Mine* (2011—all DC Books). Swift's norm as a poet is an approachable lyric mode, pitched between the elegiac and the whimsical or wry (see 'Evening on Putney Avenue'). But he also experiments with postmodern forms, drawing on subjects from both classical and pop culture, and has said he tries 'to write and edit poems with a cinematic eye'. His anthologies include *100 Poets Against The War* (nth position, 2003), *Modern Canadian Poets* (Carcanet, 2010), with Evan Jones, and *Lung Jazz: Young British Poets for Oxfam* (Cinnamon Press, 2011), with Kim Lockwood. He also writes a widely read blog, *Eyewear*. See *Seaway: New and Selected Poems* (Salmon, 2008).   NH

Swingler, Randall (1909–67) Educated at Winchester and Oxford. In 1934 he joined the Communist Party and in 1937 became editor of *Left Review*. During the Second World War he served in North Africa and Italy and was awarded the MM. After the war he lived by lecturing and editing. He left the Communist Party in 1952.

His first books, *Poems* (1932) and *Reconstruction* (1933), were followed by *Difficult Morning* (1933), which had an impressive fluency. However, its tone of loosely focused aspiration and its conventional imagery belied an appearance of modernity largely confined to a rejection of puritanical restrictions. This liberal, middle-class ambience seemed more congenial to Swingler than the call for change of the party with which he aligned himself; and in his best poem, 'Sussex in Winter', he responds movingly to the conflict.

The Years of Struggle (1946) was presented as an account of the inner development of one involved in the struggle to prevent war and then build a new society. His last collection, *The God in the Cave* (1950), consists of two short sequences that deal with the struggle to accept the forces of life and change—a theme common to all Swingler's poetry. A great deal of his poetry remained uncollected, including words for the music of Alan Rawsthorne, Benjamin Britten, and others.

Swingler wrote two novels, *No Escape* (1937) and *To Town* (1939). A memoir and a selection of his poetry can be found in *The 1930s: A Challenge to Orthodoxy*, ed. J. Lucas (Harvester, 1978). *Selected Poems* (Trent, 2000) was edited by Andy Croft, who has also written a biography, *Comrade Heart* (Manchester University Press, 2003)   ATT

Sykes, Roberta (Bobbi) (1943–2010) Born in Townsville, Queensland, the eldest of three daughters. An Aborigine, she spent much of her early life combating racist taunts. Forced to leave school at 14 because of her colour, she experienced a succession of 'life-or-perish' situations as a dishwasher, floor-scrubber, factory-worker, and trainee nurse. She left Townsville for Sydney in the early 1970s, ultimately working with a range of urban Aboriginal organizations. Sykes became a recognizable public figure when arrested in mid-1972 as the secretary of the Aboriginal (tent) Embassy, erected on the lawns of Parliament House, Canberra, as a symbol of indigenous pride and defiance.

Encouraged by the black American scientist, Professor Chester Pierce, she obtained an Ed.M (Harvard, 1981) and an Ed.D (1984), and later turned her doctoral thesis into the Sydney University Press publication *Incentive, Achievement and Community* (1986)—an analysis of black viewpoints on Aboriginal education. *Black Majority*, an analysis of the first twenty-one years (1967–88) of black Australian citizenship, was published in 1989 to much critical acclaim. She was a lecturer in the department of English, Macquarie University.

Sykes' first volume of poems, *Love Poems and Other Revolutionary Actions* (Saturday Centre, 1979; repr. University of Queensland Press, 1988), is divided into three sections—'The Revolution', 'For Love', and 'Of People'. *Love Poems* catalogues the poet's confusions, joy, sense of communal pain, and political intentions in verse stylistically reminiscent of much African-American poetry of the Sixties and Seventies. Powerful poems such as 'Counselling', 'Ambrose', and 'Black Women' depict the stark realities of being black in Australia in the second half of the twentieth century. Sykes wrote in order to publicize revolutionary ideas about race, women's issues, and the political system. Her second volume, *Eclipse* (University of Queensland Press, 1996), has a foreword by Colin *Johnson (Mudrooroo) and an introduction by Sykes, in which she discusses the 'contradiction' she experienced as an author of both public reports and the 'soul-poetry' of personal experience, which she published under the informal name 'Bobbi'.

The best source on Sykes is Sykes herself, in works such as *Black Power in Australia* (1975), the biography *Mumshirl* (1981), *Incentive, Achievement and Community* (1986), *Black Majority* (1989), and *Connections—Essays on Black Literatures* (1988), ed. Emmanuel S. Nelson. Her award-winning three-volume autobiography, *Snake Dreaming*, was published by Allen & Unwin between 1997 and 2001. DH*

Symmons Roberts, Michael (1963–) Born in Preston, Lancashire, Symmons Roberts read Philosophy and Theology at the University of Oxford, an experience formative in his transition from atheistic rationalism to Roman Catholicism.

His work in all media has consistently garnered awards. He began his career as a radio-writer and went on to make film-documentaries. He has written two novels, *Patrick's Alphabet* (2006) and *Breath* (2008), besides libretti for opera, oratorio, and song-cycle, frequently collaborating with the composer James MacMillan. With Paul *Farley, he wrote the post-pastoral non-fiction work, *Edgelands : Journeys into England's True Wilderness* (2012), winner of the Foyles Best Book of Ideas Award, 2012.

These diverse talents and preoccupations coalesce in his poetry. In his two most recent collections, *Corpus* (2004) and *The Half-Healed* (2008—all Cape), the poems are linked in a manner both song-like and polyphonic. Interesting and effective use is made of recapitulation. At times showing the influence of Robin *Robertson, his work has a fierce moral intelligence, and the mood has become increasingly apocalyptic. *The Half-Healed* stretches the lyric in encounters with modern warfare and consumerist waste and chaos. Even in a poem concerned with transcendence, the symbol is 'The Sharpest Knife in the World'. CAR

Sze, Arthur Jiazhang (1950–) Second-generation Chinese-American poet, translator, and editor, Arthur Sze was born in New York City. He studied at the University of California, Berkeley, and has published

eight volumes of poetry. With John Brandi, he is editor of Tooth of Time Books. He was the first Poet Laureate of Santa Fe, and in 2012 was elected a Chancellor of the Academy of American Poetry, alongside Jane *Hirshfield and Toi *Derricotte. Speaking on this occasion, Naomi Shihab *Nye noted the 'exquisitely shaped and weighted lines' and 'deep attunement and lyrical precision' of his poetry. Sze lives in New Mexico and is emeritus professor at the Institute of American Indian Arts.

Sze has translated Chinese poetry from the T'ang dynasty to the present day (collected in *The Silk Dragon* (Copper Canyon, 2001)), and edited *Chinese Writers on Writing* (Trinity University Press, 2010). Besides ancient and modern Chinese poets, the greatest influence on his poetics is William Carlos *Williams. Sze's poetry employs unusual combinations of image and idea to generate a terse complexity balanced between positions of seeing and not-seeing, knowing and not knowing, leading Jackson *Mac Low to characterize it as a poetry of 'clarity and compassion'. *The Redshifting Web* (1998) collects poetry from 1970 to 1998. In *The Gingko Light* (2009—both Copper Canyon) Sze reaches new levels of formal accomplishment, extending his poetic concern with the image and the multiplex simultaneity of language and being. HY

Szirtes, George (1948–) Born in Hungary and came to England with his parents, following the uprising in Budapest in 1956. His education and formative experiences have all been in England, but he has never lost sight of his Central European origins. In the Eighties he returned to Hungary on extended visits, and major poem-sequences have had Hungarian subjects and settings. His discovery of his Jewish background, as much as the thawing of relations between the Communist world and the West, have led him to revalue the experience of his family, and to pioneer a coming-together of English and European identity.

One further important agent in Szirtes' poetry is his training in art, particularly as an etcher, painter, and graphic artist. It was while he was studying for his diploma that he met Martin *Bell, then teaching liberal studies at Leeds Art School. Bell, with his affection for French poetry and Italian opera, saw in Szirtes an ideal amalgam of English individualism and European culture. Szirtes has fulfilled Bell's confidence. His first collection, *The Slant Door* (1979), though sometimes stiff in its devotion to formality, has much of the surrealist charm and eccentricity of his own painting and etching. From this book onwards Szirtes has grown in confidence, raiding the great store of European myth, fairy-tale, legend, and history, to produce a poetry where proverbial charm joins hands with *Audenesque wisdom. Szirtes has never abandoned his English models: behind his pictures of Central European persecution (see especially his sequence 'Courtyards') there lies the moral clarity of Marvell or Herbert. Later collections include *Short Wave* (1983), *The Photographer in Winter* (1986—all Secker & Warburg), *Metro* (1988), *Blind Field* (1994), and *Selected Poems* (1996—all Oxford University Press).

The Budapest File (2000) draws on Hungarian-themed poems from across Szirtes oeuvre, including the title sequence of *Portrait of My Father in an English Landscape* (1998), a double 'crown' of sonnets in which the fifteenth poem comprises lines that link the previous fourteen (also known as a 'Hungarian sonnet'). The long title poem of *An English Apocalypse* (2001), a selection of poems about the poet's adopted country, is written in *terza rima*, a form continued to cinematic effect in the first half of *Reel* (2004), which won the T. S. Eliot Prize. *New and Collected Poems* (2008) has been followed by *The Burning of the Books and other poems* (2009). See also *Fortinbras at the Fishhouses* (2010—all Bloodaxe), an extended essay on poetry and politics during the Cold War period, written under the aegis of Elizabeth *Bishop's ironic notion of 'historical' knowledge. Now Reader in Creative Writing at the University of East Anglia, Szirtes is also a prolific translator of Hungarian literature: see *The Colonnade of Teeth: Twentieth Century Hungarian Poetry* (1996) and *The Night of Akhenaton: Selected Poems of Ágnes Nemes Nagy* (2004—both Bloodaxe).   PNFP*

Szumigalski, Anne (1922–99) Born in London. Raised in a family that loved language, she began composing poems as a young girl, feeling that this would be her lifelong vocation. She was educated privately in languages and literature.

Szumigalski emigrated to Canada in 1951, moving to Saskatoon, Saskatchewan, in 1956, where she established herself as a force in Canadian poetry written on the prairies. She was a founding member of the Saskatchewan Writers' Guild, a founding editor of the literary magazine *Grain*, and a co-founder of the Saskatchewan Writers' Colony, and worked as a teacher, editor, writer-in-residence, and translator. In addition to poetry she also wrote prize-winning short fiction, and several works in collaboration with Saskatoon writer Terrence Heath, including *Journey/Journée* (Red Deer College Press, 1988).

Szumigalski's first book, *Woman Reading in Bath* (Doubleday, 1974), while powerfully evoking the cycles of natural, mortal, and passionate life, frequently intermingles the surreal or the holy in the domestic and mundane scenes she re-creates. Her other books include: *Doctrine of Signatures* (1983) and *Instar: Poems and Stories* (1985). *Rapture of the Deep* (1991) shows her abiding skill with narrative forms. *Voice* (1995), a collaboration with artist Marie Elyse St George, won the Governor General's Award. *Z: A Meditation on Oppression, Desire, and Freedom*, her play about the Holocaust, appeared the same year.

The fullest selection of Szumigalski's work to appear in her lifetime was *On Glassy Wings: Poems, New and Selected* (1997—all Coteau). *When Earth Leaps Up*, a posthumous collection, was published by Brick Books in 2006. Mark Abley has edited a short selection, *A Peeled Wand* (Signature, 2010), with an introduction by the poet Elizabeth Phillips, and a later career-spanning selection from all of Szumigalski's writing, *A Woman Clothed in Words* (Coteau, 2012). See also Szumigalski's autobiographical work, *The Word, The Voice, The Text: The Life of a Writer* (Fifth House, 1990).

The journal *Arc* devoted a special issue to Szumigalski in Fall, 1989.   NB

Taggard, Genevieve (1894–1948) Born in Waitsburg, Washington to teacher parents who took her to Hawaii to live when she was two. Due to her father's lung problems the family shifted back and forth several times before 1914, when Taggard entered Berkeley, where she was encouraged in her writing by Witter *Bynner. In 1920 she moved to Manhattan, worked for an avant-garde publisher, and helped found *Measure: A Magazine of Verse* a year later, the same year she married novelist Robert Wolf.

The marriage was marred by several clashes before its dissolution in 1934. Taggard's poetry, first gathered in *For Eager Lovers* (1922), *Hawaiian Hilltop* (1923), and *Travelling Standing Still* (1928), was highly polished, occasionally touching, backed by sure erudition, as was her study, *The Life and Mind of Emily Dickinson* (1930). She also taught at Mount Holyoke and Sarah Lawrence. Her taste for the metaphysical vied with an equally intense commitment to leftist politics, evident in the protest poetry of *Calling Western Union* (1936), and her editing both *May Days: An Anthology of Verse from Masses-Liberator* (1925) and *Circumference, Varieties of Metaphysical Verse, 1456–1928* (1929). She married an American representative of *Tass* in 1935. Her last volumes, *Long View* (1942) and *Slow Music* (1946) returned to a metaphysical mode. Her daughter, Marcia D. Liles, edited *To the Natural World* (Ahsahta, 1980), a generous selection of her work with bibliographical notes.　EB

Tate, Allen (1899–1979) Born in Winchester, Kentucky. At Vanderbilt University he joined John Crowe *Ransom's literary discussion group (his friend Robert Penn *Warren was also a member), and co-founded and edited its journal, *The Fugitive*, thus beginning a lasting alliance with the *Agrarian group of Southern writers. In 1924 he married the novelist Caroline Gordon, and over the next ten years, living variously in West Virginia, New York, Paris, and Tennessee, published biographies of Stonewall Jackson (1928) and Jefferson Davis (1929), and made his name as a poet with *Mr. Pope and Other Poems* (1928), *Three Poems* (1930), and *Poems, 1928–31* (1932). During the 1930s he took up his first teaching post, in Tennessee (1934–6), and published his first book of criticism, *Reactionary Essays on Poetry and Ideas* (1936); like much of his poetry, his only novel, *The Fathers* (1938), set in antebellum Virginia, is an attempt to understand his regional and cultural origins. Tate was poet-in-residence at Princeton in the early 1940s. Then, as editor of the *Sewanee Review* (1944–6), he encouraged and influenced writing on Old Southern and New Critical issues alike. His version of New Criticism, most forcefully defended and practised in *Reason in Madness* (1941) and *On the Limits of Poetry* (1948), holds that poetry is not a vehicle for imprecise feeling but an autonomous structure, an objective frame for a tension between themes. His commentaries, however, are usually as alert to a poem's intellectual, cultural, and biographical context as to its formal qualities. From 1951 Tate was professor of English at the University of Minnesota, making frequent trips elsewhere to lecture, and continuing to publish volumes of well crafted poems: *Poems* (Scribner, 1960), *The Swimmers* (Oxford University Press, 1970; Scribner, 1971). His first marriage, always troubled (he and Gordon had divorced and remarried in 1946), was finally annulled in 1959; and Tate was married again twice.

Tate's poetry is marked by classical erudition, strong and carefully worked metrical effects, and an elevated tone—a baroque manner which has been traced to the rhetoric of the preachers and politicians of the Old South. Present in all his work are the preoccupations he identified in his most celebrated poem, 'Ode to the Confederate Dead': the tension between '"active faith" which has decayed, and the "fragmentary cosmos" which surrounds us'; and 'heroism in the grand style, elevating even death from mere physical dissolution into a formal ritual'. Tate's conversion to Catholicism in 1950, then, was not surprising, and is reflected in his later work: throughout *The Forlorn Demon* (critical essays, 1953) he draws on Catholic doctrine to organize his perceptions; and 'The Swimmers' and 'The Buried Lake', late poems in Dante's *terza rima*, find in Christian rather than classical tradition a religio-moral context for assessing Southern experience. Tate was in a sense a poet's poet: his advice was crucial in guiding poets— as diverse as Hart *Crane and Robert *Lowell—whose work is more likely to endure than his.

See *Collected Poems, 1919–1976* (Louisiana State University Press, 1977) and *Collected Essays* (Swallow, 1959).   NE

Tate, James (1943–) Born in Kansas City, Missouri, attended the University of Missouri and Kansas State College, and took an MFA at the Iowa Writers' Workshop in 1967, the same year in which he won the Yale Younger Poets competition for his book *The Lost Pilot*. He has taught at the University of California, Berkeley, and Columbia University; he now teaches at the University of Massachusetts.

Tate is the funniest and most prolific of the group of young American surrealists who emerged in the late Sixties, a group which included *Simic, *Strand, Bill *Knott, and Charles *Wright. While much of this poetry aims for a bare, primitive quality that involves a restricted palette of images, Tate from the start has opted for a more wide-ranging, quirky, idiosyncratic brand of imagery less concerned with purity of effect than with surprise and bewilderment. His lines are often clotted with colourful nouns that release energy through their clashing associations, as in the title of his early poem 'The Wheelchair Butterfly'. Tate also makes brilliant use of folksy Midwestern idioms, which bring a casual, demotic air to his derangements of reality. His most memorable poems are those which temper his surrealist manner with a recognizable sense of subject or occasion; he writes wonderfully of the suburbs, of formal events like weddings and funerals, and of other areas of life in which his verbal anarchy can wreak havoc on the routine complacency it encounters. Tate is more than a poetic Marx brother, however; his sense of fun is inextricably bound up with darker emotions like fear, anxiety, and repulsion. These flit about the edges of his landscapes, deepening their shadows and revealing a kind of desperation as the primary motive for his manic play, as hinted by the title of his early book *The Oblivion Ha-Ha*.

Tate's *Selected Poems* (Wesleyan University Press, 1991) won the Pulitzer Prize, and the following volume, *Worshipful Company of Fletchers* (1994) won the National Book Award. Tate's later work has tended towards prose poetry; his poems in this mode have been selected in *The Eternal Ones of the Dream* (2012—both Ecco). Essays, interviews, and short stories may be found in *The Route as Briefed* (University of Michigan, 1999), and a later interview (with Charles Simic) in the *Paris Review*, 177 (Summer 2006). See also *On James Tate*, ed. Brian Henry (University of Michigan Press, 2004).   RG

Taylor, Andrew (1940–) Born in the fishing port of Warrnambool, Victoria. He studied at Scotch College, at the University of Melbourne, and in Italy. For much of his adult life he has taught at the University of Adelaide, and he is now emeritus professor at Edith Cowan University in Perth. His second wife being German, he has spent a good deal of time in Germany and this has had its effect on his poetry, which has moved away from much of its early zest and jauntiness into a plangency which has slippery, dark affinities with European modernism. He was at his liveliest in an early sequence, 'The Cat's Chin and Ears: A Bestiary' but the dominant tone of his writing was signalled by the titles of his first two books, *The Cool Change* (1971) and *Ice Fishing* (1973); it is a poetry of cool spaces, of silence, of dividing waters, and of absences. He has also practised that disconcerting form, the prose poem.

Taylor's poetry may be read in *Selected Poems* (1982, revd., 1988). He published little poetry in the 1980s but would seem to have devoted his energies to the theory-driven study, *Reading Australian Poetry* (1987—all University of Queensland Press), a book which throws much light on his own poetic concerns.

Taylor became more prolific again in the 1990s, and *Collected Poems* (Salt, 2004) contains three further volumes, including *Sandstone* (University of Queensland Press, 1995), which won the Western Australia Premier's Prize for Poetry, as well as new work. *The Unhaunting* (Salt, 2009) features a sequence of translations from Montale, written during a residency in Rome.   CW-C

Taylor, Eleanor Ross (1920–2011) Born in South Carolina and educated at the Women's College of the University of North Carolina at Greensboro. In 1943 she married the fiction writer Peter Taylor. Her first book, *Wilderness of Ladies* (McDowell, Obolensky), appeared in 1960 with a fulsome introduction by Randall *Jarrell—so fulsome, indeed, that some commentators wondered if it might not somewhat impede Taylor's development. In 1972, though, she published *Welcome Eumenides* (Braziller)— a book notable for the fieriness and economy of its lyrics and for two resourceful narratives: 'A Few Days in the South', which has been described by Richard *Howard as 'the best poem since Whitman about the War Between the States', and the title-poem, a dramatic work done in the voice of Florence Nightingale. Taylor's first *New and Selected Poems* (Wright) appeared in 1983. A later volume, *Captive Voices* (Louisiana State University Press,

2009), with a foreword by Ellen Bryant *Voigt, selected from two further collections: *Days Going/Days Coming Back* (University of Utah Press, 1991) and *Late Leisure* (Louisiana State University Press, 1999). Taylor received many American poetry awards and honours in later life, including, in 2010, the Ruth Lilley Poetry Prize for lifetime achievement.   POM

Taylor, Henry (1942–) Born to Quaker parents and grew up in Lincoln, Virginia in the farm country west of Washington, DC, attending local public schools through the ninth grade. His father was a dairy farmer and he himself a trainer of jumping horses which he began to ride at horse-shows at an early age. He spent his last three years of high school at the Quaker George School in Pennsylvania before going on to the University of Virginia where he began writing poetry, eventually under the tutelage of George *Garrett. He graduated from the writing programme at Hollins College in 1967. Though he spent three years teaching at the University of Utah, he never overcame the feeling of being a displaced Southerner—a situation wittily captured in 'Buildings and Grounds'—and returned to Virginia in 1971 when he began teaching at American University in DC, in 1977 building a house on his family farm in Lincoln. It is not surprising then that the majority of the poems in his first three collections, *The Horse Show at Midnight* (Louisiana State University Press, 1966), *An Afternoon of Pocket Billiards* (University of Utah Press, 1975), and *The Flying Change* (Louisiana State University Press, 1985)—which won the Pulitzer Prize—grow out of his experience in this pastoral setting. He captures the visual texture and the rhythm of the changing seasons as well as the subtle tensions and continuities of relationships within families and between generations, the latter most poignantly in 'At the Swings', centred on his interactions with his sons as his wife's mother is dying of cancer. His poetry is notable for its wit, as in his parodies of *Bly, James *Dickey, and others in his first volume, and his epigraph 'Divorce'; for the chilling detail with which he captures the violence inherent in farm life, as in 'Barbed Wire', on the death of a frightened horse; and for finding metaphors from farming and horse-training which embody the elements of craft and grace that characterize the writing of poems, as in 'The Flying Change'.

His later books are *Understanding Fiction: Poems 1986–1996* (1996) and *Crooked Run* (2006). He has also worked as a translator, and published a study of recent American poets, *Compulsory Figures* (1992), and a collection of clerihews, *Brief Candles* (2000—all Louisiana State University Press).   RMCP

Teasdale, Sara (1884–1933) Born in St Louis, Missouri. The child of elderly, over-protective parents, the delicate Teasdale was raised in an atmosphere of Victorian constraint. She moved to New York, and in 1914 married businessman Ernst Felsinger whom she divorced in 1929. Her poetic output declined during the 1920s and she became increasingly depressed and reclusive until, in 1933, she committed suicide.

Influenced by the work of Sappho, Christina Rossetti, Dickinson, and later *Yeats, but curiously unaffected by contemporary movements, Teasdale developed as a skilled lyricist. Her fragile, musical verse, usually in rhymed quatrains, originally dealt with idealized love and beauty, but later focused on death. *Love Songs* (1917) brought her international recognition and a Columbia (now Pulitzer) Poetry Prize. Poems in *Flame and Shadow* (1920), *Dark of the Moon* (1926), and the posthumously published *Strange Victory* (1933) illustrate Teasdale's artistic maturity and growing fascination with death.

The Collected Poems of Sara Teasdale (1937) remains widely available; *Mirror of the Heart: Poems of Sara Teasdale* (1984—both Macmillan) includes nearly seventy previously uncollected or unpublished poems. See also Margaret Haley Carpenter's *Sara Teasdale: A Biography* (Schulte, 1960), William Drake's *Sara Teasdale: Woman and Poet* (Harper & Row, 1979), and Carol B. Schoen's critical study, *Sara Teasdale* (Twayne, 1986).   EDF

Tessimond, A. S. J. (Arthur Seymour John) (1902–62) Born in Birkenhead, an only child. Educated at Charterhouse, he refused to re-attend at the age of 16, running away to London—to return home in a fortnight. A year later he went to Liverpool University, after which he moved to London, working in bookshops then settling down as an advertising copy-writer. During the Second World War, deciding he would be a useless soldier, dangerous to the cause, he went into hiding, only to find later that he was unfit to fight. Inheriting £4,000 from his father in 1945, he spent half on various psychoanalysts, the rest on his night-life. In later years he underwent shock treatment, which may have contributed to the brain haemorrhage from which he died.

The early influence of *Imagism, and, for all his depressive tendencies, an exhilaration with form, give his work a honed and memorable succinctness and clarity—which produces some delightful humour, as in 'Pets'. Night-lifer, loner, *flâneur*, Tessimond is an excellent recorder of the general, of the stereotypes of the city. His 'Man in the Bowler Hat', 'The British', and 'Cats: II' are justly in many anthologies. He also has a genre of conversation-poems, such as the fine 'Middle-aged Conversation', that capture succinctly his sense of the melancholy of existence.

Three volumes were published during his life: *The Walls of Glass* (Methuen, 1934): *Voices in a Giant City* (Heinemann, 1947), and *Selection* (Putnam, 1958). Three posthumous collections, ed. Hubert Nicholson, have appeared: *Not Love Perhaps . . .* (1978), *Morning Meeting* (1980—both Autolycus), and finally *The Collected Poems*, with translations from Jacques Prévert (Whiteknights, 1985; repr. Bloodaxe, 2010), containing previously uncollected poems.   PD

Thayil, Jeet (1959–) The son of a peripatetic writer, editor, and journalist, Thayil was born in Kerala but spent a significant part of his childhood in Hong Kong and New York. In the late Seventies, he arrived in Bombay (now Mumbai) to attend college; influenced by Baudelaire as a model, he was drawn into the city's heroin dens and became an addict—an experience that was later to become one of his signature themes. Thayil's first significant publication was shared with Vijay Nambisan in the series *Gemini* (Penguin, 1992). *Apocalypso* (Aark Arts, 1997), his first full-length collection, casts Bombay in a hallucinatory light but also dwells on the tragic deaths of American poets—John *Berryman, Delmore *Schwartz, and Hart *Crane. *English* (Penguin/Rattapallax, 2003), completed after Thayil's return to New York in the late 1990s, continues these textures, blending autobiography and fictional personae to sing the lives and dilemmas of immigrants. *These Errors Are Correct* (Tranquebar, 2008), his most formally adventurous collection, is divided between poems of drug rehabilitation, return to India, and intimations of death and loss.

More recently, Thayil has worked in a range of other genres. He released a music album as part of the band Sridhar/Thayil, authored a libretto for the composer Edward Rushton and published a novel of Bombay in the 1970s and 1980s, *Narcopolis* (Faber, 2012), which was shortlisted for the 2012 Booker Prize.   VN

Thesen, Sharon (1946–) Born in Saskatchewan and went to school in Prince George, British Columbia, a northern pulp-mill town curiously full of poets. She studied poetry with Robin *Blaser at Simon Fraser University, and spent some years teaching at a community college in North Vancouver. She is now a professor of creative writing at the University of British Columbia, Okanagan.

Thesen published four books in the 1980s, and was hailed as a bright lyric poet. Her voice is sweet and ironic at the same time: a poem is likely to allude to classical literature or recent philosophy, but also to offer the energy of colloquial quips. A singular book is the sequence called *Confabulations: Poems for Malcolm Lowry* (Oolichan, 1984). Thesen lets the poem range from Lowry's Vancouver home, forward to England, back to Mexico, the pronouns sliding through all persons as she exhibits the struggle between the talent to compose and the urge towards drunkenness. It is an ambitious poem, and like those of Lowry, sometimes more intelligent than beautiful.

More successful are Thesen's poems about being a woman in the late twentieth century. They are filled with rueful delight and wisdom's pain; not overtly feminist, their images present a woman's life in writing, including its political necessities. In 1982 she edited the selected poems of Phyllis *Webb. Her first selected poems, *The Pangs of Sunday* (McClelland & Stewart), was published in 1990, and a later volume, *News and Smoke*, in 1999 (Talonbooks). Her ninth collection of poems is *Oyama Pink Shale* (Anansi, 2011).   GHB

Thomas, D. M. (Donald Michael) (1935–) Born in Redruth, Cornwall, and educated at New College, Oxford. He was senior lecturer in English at Hereford College of Education (1964–78).

D. M. Thomas' obsessions are plain: love, death, and place. From his earliest work sexual fantasy is to the fore, sometimes in a violent context. Greater tenderness is apparent in poems of familial love—'The Journey' (*Love and Other Deaths*, Elek, 1975) addresses the poet's mother: 'we are water and moor | And far journeyers together. Whatever else we are'—and in dealing with his Cornish inheritance in 'For Doll Pentreath', an elegy for the last native Cornish speaker. There is a strong narrative element in his work, incorporating dream and myth (as in 'Diary of a Myth Boy' and 'The Dream Game' from *The Honeymoon Voyage*, Secker & Warburg, 1978). In recent years much of Thomas' energy has been applied to fiction (though he disputes the separation of forms) and translation.

The Puberty Tree: New and Selected Poems appeared in 1992 (Bloodaxe), and an autobiography, *Memories and Hallucinations* in 1989 (Gollancz). Thomas' novels include *The White Hotel* (1981) and *Ararat* (1983). His latest collection of poems is *Flight and Smoke* (Boutle, 2010).   SO'B

Thomas, Dylan (1914–53) Born in Swansea. He worked for a short time as a junior reporter on the *South Wales Evening Post*, then moved to London to embark on a literary career. His first book of poems, *Eighteen Poems*, was published in 1934. Thomas' poetry, although it has attracted admiration and adulation—increased in some of his hearers to a state of worship by the booming bardic readings he gave in public—has also seemed to some formless, incoherent, and over-wordy. When the poems are analysed, however, it is clear that the charge of formlessness must be dropped. He worked out his stanzas very carefully, with exact syllable-counts for the lines so that they correspond in each stanza. Likewise, the rhymes are scrupulously observed—though they are very unusual rhymes. Some rely on assonance ('Heaven/pheasants'), some are 'vowel-rhymes' ('kind/night'), and some are assonantal vowel-rhymes ('planets/valley'), while in the same poem comparatively conventional rhymes can occur ('fires/friars'). Since the rhymes are usually separated from one another by intervening lines, they are seldom obvious. His habit of declaiming the poems non-stop, running on from line to line and stanza to stanza, increased the impression of formlessness.

Of course the poems are rhetorical, and can sometimes sound like a preacher in full flow—it has been suggested that Thomas' remembrances of chapel sermons played their part—but they also have originality and beauty, which his marvellous readings displayed to advantage. The main impetus came from Thomas' romanticized, idealized childhood; 'Fern Hill', one of his greatest poems, is entirely about this, a rustic idyll that has nothing to do with the respectabilities of lower-middle-class Swansea (his father was a schoolmaster) but everything to do with summer holidays in the country. 'The ball I threw while playing in the park | Has not yet reached the ground', as he wrote in 'Should lanterns shine'. In other words, his childhood was present to him at all times, a 'land of lost content'.

Thomas could also write much tighter, more conventional, verse. 'In my craft or sullen art' is a good example of this, and so is the famous villanelle on the death of his father, 'Do not go gentle into that good night'. These poems are exceptional, as they contain none of the theatricality and posturing that one finds in the more flamboyant pieces. The effort that went into the longer poems is legendary—there are supposed to be more than 300 drafts of 'Fern Hill'—and this is even more remarkable when one considers his life-style, which was that of an alcoholic, a talkative and witty one, but irreclaimable.

Thomas did not produce a huge body of work; there are only ninety-nine poems in his *Collected Poems*, two of them added posthumously by the editors. There is also the radio play *Under Milk Wood* (New York and London, 1954). He died, though, just before he was 40, and a lot of his time was taken up by his work for the BBC (freelance and as a member of the staff), by writing short stories and other prose pieces, and by the never-ending drunkenness.

Thomas' poems are full, not so much of 'the most heterogeneous ideas yoked by violence together' (Dr Johnson's description of metaphysical verse), but of heterogeneous *images*, from books as well as from life. He also used clichés ('animals thick as thieves') and unexpected metonymy ('tangled with chirrup and fruit'). Some epithets seem to be there for surprise value only—'the religious wind'. There is lurking Blake—'worms' are everywhere—and the repetitive key-words can be wearisome—'green', 'bones', 'marrow', 'thighs', etc. Although Thomas makes great use of the countryside and its creatures he was, as he confessed, unmoved by such things. In the poems, however, they work well (like the heron below Sir John's Hill). In the first two books there are good lines ('I see the boys of summer in their ruin'—paunchy, middle-aged men lying on the beach, as he later explained) and some good poems; mostly the more straightforward ones ('The force that through the green fuse', 'The hand that signed the paper'), but also some that are more Dionysiac ('If I were tickled by the rub of love', 'Especially when the October wind', and 'Light breaks where no sun shines'). But he could also, at all stages of his career, write extremely bad individual lines ('His mother's womb had a tongue that lapped up blood').

The later poems include some that are undistinguished—and one long failure, 'The ballad of the long-legged bait'—but they also include some that could be called great, by most standards: 'Fern Hill', 'Over Sir John's Hill', 'In my craft or sullen art', 'Do not go gentle into that good night', 'Poem in October', 'In the White Giant's Thigh', and 'Elegy'. Just a few are untypical but rewarding: 'Now', 'Paper and stick'. In general, the later verse is less compact and dramatic, easier to get on with, and a good deal more moving in human terms.

See *The Poems of Dylan Thomas*, ed. Daniel Jones (Dent/New Directions, 1971); also Paul Ferris' biography (Hodder & Stoughton, 1977) and Constantine Fitz-Gibbon's edition of the Letters (Dent, 1966). John Ackerman edited *A Dylan Thomas Companion* (Macmillan, 1991) and an edition of Thomas film-scripts (Dent, 1995), and also wrote a biographical study, *Welsh Dylan* (Jones, 1979; repr. Seren, 1998). A collection of new critical essays on Thomas was edited by John *Goodby and Chris Wigginton for Palgrave in 2001. Thomas own *Collected Poems* from 1952 was reprinted by New Directions in 2010, with an introduction by Paul *Muldoon. *Dylan Thomas at the BBC* (2003) is a double CD of archive recordings.   GE

Thomas, Edward (1878–1917) Edward Thomas wrote all his poems in the last two-and-a-half years of his life. In the previous sixteen years he had published thirty volumes of topography, biography, criticism, and belles-lettres, compiled sixteen editions and anthologies, and produced over a million-and-a-half words of reviews. The poetry came in a burst of creative activity; the prose was soul-destroying. It kept him, he said, 'so confoundedly busy I feel as if the back of my head would come out'.

Relatively little of the prose has stood the test of time. Although some titles (the best of them is *The South Country*, most recently reprinted in 2009) were carried back into print on the wave of interest in turn-of-the-century rural writers which broke across popular taste in the 1970s, the majority are too deeply bogged down in antiquated locutions and attitudes to attract more than specialist interest. What they represent is generally cherished and admired: stable country values in the moment before they were destroyed by the First World War; but in substance and detail their pastoralism seems not so much remote as fusty.

Thomas' poems, on the other hand, embody similar virtues but manage to wrestle them free from late Victorian encumbrances—and in the years since Philip *Larkin and other writers associated with the *Movement began to espouse a specifically English poetic line, their stock has risen steadily. For all their occasional lapses (they were written hurriedly) and traces of an earlier idiom (inverted syntax, sweetly sentimental ruralism), they are now clearly and rightly established as part of the tradition of English pastoral lyricism which runs forward from Wordsworth through *Hardy and *Housman to Larkin himself.

The strength of Thomas' poems lies in their ability to enact with great subtlety and discretion the emergence of a recognizably modern sensibility. More profoundly than his contemporary *Georgians (whom he resembles in many superficial respects), more often and more steadily than Ivor *Gurney, his poems function as a hinge between old and new worlds. Their account of country things (in 'Lob', for instance) itemizes particular idioms as well as particular ways of life, but their reflections on time and its passing describe how these things are destroyed; their intelligent shyness charts the growth of a familiar self-consciousness; and their skilful testing of time-honoured forms—notably their use of long, pensive sentences to conduct the rhythm of a thinking voice through the whole length of a poem—challenges received technical conventions and looks forward to the more radical experiments of the modernists.

The material for Thomas' lyrics and little dramas of displacement came directly from his own experience. Born in Lambeth, south London, he was the eldest son of 'mainly Welsh' parents whose principal adult sense of their homeland was nostalgia. As a town-boy Thomas was nostalgic for the nearer country of southern England too, and by the time he came to the end of his career at Saint Paul's school in Hammersmith he had begun writing essays and articles celebrating his rural walks and expeditions. His first collection of these pieces, *The Woodland Life*, appeared when he was 19.

Before taking his degree at Oxford (in 1900) he had married Helen, the daughter of his early mentor James Ashcroft Noble, had a son, and resolved to live by his pen. The decision brought him freedom of a desperately restricted kind, and he spent most of the next fourteen years on a treadmill of hack-work, increasingly prone to depression, occasionally contemplating suicide, and painfully aware that he had 'lost his way'. Various Georgian friends (W. H. *Davies, Walter *de la Mare) suggested that he try writing poems, but Thomas was too far gone in self-doubt to make the attempt. When he did, it was only by force of accident, as well as intervention. Robert *Frost, whose *North of Boston* Thomas had reviewed enthusiastically, urged him to try his hand at precisely the same time as war broke out, and this advice from a poet he respected more than most others living, combined with the sense of danger which suddenly clouded everything he valued, finally persuaded him.

Thomas wrote his first poem in December 1914 and his last—his one hundred and forty-third—shortly before he was killed at Arras on 9 April 1917, when he was 39. In a sense they are all war poems, and not only because they were all written after the outbreak of war. Sometimes openly—in the Frost-like dramatic dialogue 'As the Team's Head-brass'—they chronicle the impact of the fighting in France on the Home Front; sometimes obliquely—in 'The Green Roads'—they sketch the unique tenuousness of life in wartime; sometimes with delicate lyric yearning—in 'Lights Out'—they record the hope and fear of an individual soldier expecting to die. Whatever their form, their tone is strikingly consistent. When Thomas began writing poems his voice was already fully mature, and although for many years after his death he was regarded as a 'poet's poet', the careful scrutiny of his gaze, the tact of his rhythms, and the deftness with which he assimilates large social and political issues into a delicate lyric framework, have meant that he has gradually become one of the most generally admired, as well as one of the most influential English poets of the century.

See *The Collected Poems of Edward Thomas*, ed. and introduced by R. George Thomas (Oxford University Press, 1978; repr. Faber, 2004). In 2008, an annotated edition was published by Bloodaxe, ed. Edna Longley. There is a biography by R. George Thomas (Clarendon, 1985) and interesting memoirs by Helen Thomas (*As It Was*, Heinemann, 1926; *World Without End*, Heinemann, 1935) and Eleanor Farjeon (*Edward Thomas: The Last Four Years*, Oxford University Press, 1958). The Helen Thomas memoirs can be had in a combined edition, *Under Storm's Wing* (1988). See also *Letters to Helen*, ed. R. George Thomas (2000). *Edward Thomas' Poets*, ed. Judy Kendall, contextualizes Thomas period of poetic output with extracts from his reading and correspondence (2007—all Carcanet). Matthew Hollis biography *Now All Roads Lead to France* (Faber, 2011) traces the final five years.   AM

Thomas, R. S. (Ronald Stuart) (1913–2000) Born in Cardiff and brought up and educated in Holyhead. His parents were not Welsh-speaking, though it is probable that his father had some Welsh as a child but lost it after being sent to sea as an apprentice at 16. However, through chance encounters while a classics student at the University College of North Wales, Bangor, Thomas learnt that his father's mother was Welsh-speaking, and this discovery encouraged what had already become his own intention to learn the language. The intention became a commitment which developed while he trained in theology at St Michael's College, Llandaff.

Thomas' relationship to the language and the Welsh literary tradition is central to an understanding of his growth as a poet. Although it was important for him to speak Welsh in order to communicate, as an Anglican priest, with his first parishioners—in Denbighshire and Flintshire between 1936 and 1942—the ability to do so enabled him to fulfil what he had come to regard as 'the necessary qualifications of a truly Anglo-Welsh writer, namely that he should steep himself in all things Welsh to justify the hyphen'. That hyphen—a contentious mark of unease, ambivalence, and intense, agitated enquiry—in many ways proved to be the mainspring of Thomas' poetic career, in that for him it never entirely disappeared. Although much of his prose, including the autobiography *Neb* (no-one/ anyone) and his lecture on the spiritual Good Place 'Abercuawg', was written in Welsh, he was only able to write poetry in his mother tongue, since it required a naturalness and instinctiveness he realized he could not achieve in a second language. This dilemma had a profound effect on his work as a whole.

Thomas' first collection from an English publisher, *Song at the Year's Turning*, was published in 1955, the year after his move to the parish of Eglwysfach. It contained poems selected from his first two volumes privately printed in Wales—*The Stones of the Field* (1946) and *An Acre of Land* (1952)—as well as *The Minister* (1953), a long radio poem for several voices. With this work Thomas achieved a reputation for addressing the harsh realities of the depopulated hill country in a verse which is uncompromisingly austere and rooted in an unforgiving landscape. The scenic emptiness and arid conditions are matched by an appalled sense of mental vacancy and emotional impoverishment in the inhabitants. 'A Peasant', the first poem to introduce the archetypal peasant farmer Iago Prytherch, sets the tone of what is to come although its stately, almost Yeatsian, rhetoric and sonorous closing couplet are soon to be replaced in Thomas' stronger poems by harsher cadences, more arbitrary line-breaks, and a conspicuous absence of consoling rhymes. In these 'bleak litanies' (to borrow a title from a later poem) lives and landscapes become a focus of Thomas' entirely unsentimental compassion for the individual and his often bitter scorn and resentment of the dehumanizing social conditions which have cut a community off from the tradition which would have given its life meaning. The abiding issue remains implicit in the priest's understanding of the bald question asked in 'Here'— 'Does no God hear when I pray?'—while the last line of 'Kneeling' offers the provisional, loaded answer which recurs in all Thomas' poetry, with varying degrees of patience, up to the present: 'The meaning is in the waiting.'

In the period between 1955 and 1968 Thomas continued to work at these themes, though with increasing evidence of metaphysical speculation and inner debate developing alongside the more earthbound poems of character and place. The main volumes of this period are *Poetry for Supper* (1958), *Tares* (1961), *The Bread of Truth* (1963), *Pieta* (1966), and *Not that he Brought Flowers* (1968).

In 1967 Thomas moved to the parish of Aberdaron on the Lleyn Peninsula, and in the work which followed there was a distinct change of style. This was evident at first in the watershed volume *H'm* (1972) with its resonant abstraction, occasionally apocalyptic imagery not a little reminiscent of Ted *Hughes' *Crow*, and its experimentation with indented lines under the conscious influence of William Carlos *Williams. In *Laboratories of the Spirit* (1975) and *Frequencies* (1978), with a vocabulary often drawn from mechanics, physics, and biology, he continues to contend with 'the disposer of the issues | of life', exploring interior worlds of private doubt in the search for consolation. As in the earlier work, he remains waiting 'somewhere between faith and doubt | for the echoes of arrival', while often, even in the same poem, pursuing a protean *deus absconditus*. There was much debate at the time about this development. Some saw him as having abandoned the rocky acres for a nebulous cosmos, and a firm footing in metaphor for an inconclusive and often prosaic space-walking. Others regarded his later work as his finest, as an enlargement of his concerns and a refinement of his technique. What is certainly interesting is that, as the poetry moved away from its precise Welsh location, and with his retirement from the Church in 1978, Thomas became increasingly active as a public figure in nationalist politics. It was as if direct political involvement eased the tension between his imagination and his conscience, and resulted in the achievement of a greater poise, a more resonant austerity.

Collected Poems 1945–1990 (Dent) was published to coincide with his eightieth birthday in 1993; *Collected Later Poems* (Bloodaxe, 2004) contains his last five collections, from *The Echoes Return Slow* (Macmillan, 1988) to the posthumous *Residues* (Bloodaxe, 2002) An extensive and revealing interview, conducted by Ned Thomas, appeared in the Welsh Internationalist magazine *Planet, 80* (1990). Byron Rogers *The Man Who Went Into the West* (Aurum, 2006) is an improbably lively life. For criticism, see *Echoes to the Amen*, ed. Damian Walford Davies (University of Wales Press, 2003). A biography by Jason Wintle, *Furious Interiors: R. S. Thomas and God*, appeared in 1996, and the poet's *Autobiographies* in Welsh were translated by Jason Walford Davies in 1997.   JM*

Thompson, John (Michael) (1938–76) Born in Manchester, England. His father died during the Second World War. His mother remarried and moved to Australia. Thompson was educated at Manchester Grammar School and the University of Sheffield. After completing compulsory military service in 1960, he became a graduate student at Michigan State University. He obtained a PhD in comparative literature in 1966, with a thesis on the recent poetry of René Char. Among those on his guidance committee was A. J. M. *Smith.

Between 1966 and 1976 Thompson taught English and American literature and creative-writing classes at Mount Allison University, Sackville, New Brunswick. During the three years following publication of *At the Edge of the Chopping There Are No Secrets* (1973), Thompson's marriage ended in separation, he experienced depression and mental instability, began drinking heavily, and suffered the loss through fire of his old farmhouse on the Tantramar Marshes. Early in 1976 he died in a coma judged to have been accidentally induced by medication and alcohol. *Stilt Jack* (both Anansi), a collection of thirty-eight ghazals which Thompson completed just before his death, was published in 1978.

Thompson is considered one of the most important Canadian poets of the 1970s. *Atwood, Phyllis *Webb, D. G. *Jones, and Douglas *Lochhead have all written poems alluding to him, as have numbers of other Canadian poets. Thompson's first book, written in free verse, with frequent stepped lines, is stylistically related to the poems of Denise *Levertov. Like Char, Thompson's intent was to make language synonymous with the natural existence of such things as stones, birds, and fish, transforming all into a state of archetypal perfection. *Stilt Jack* persists in this ambition, but also phrases those recoils, lapses, and imperfections inevitably attendant upon it. The apparent obscurity of *Stilt Jack* and its radical parataxis are the result of the collection's extraordinary allusiveness. *Yeats, Char, *Roethke, Wallace *Stevens, and Emily Dickinson are among the poets engaged. *Hamlet* and *King Lear* are the sources of several defining lines. One of the poet's personae is Orestes. *Stilt Jack* may be read as the record of a Jungian quest for individuation and as an attempt to recover and personally integrate one interpretation of western poetic tradition.

See *Collected Poems and Translations*, ed. Peter Sanger (Goose Lane, 1995)   PMS

Thorpe, Adam (1956–) Born in Paris, and brought up in Beirut, Calcutta (now Kolkata), Cameroon, and the south of England. After graduating from Magdalen College, Oxford, in 1979, he founded Equinox Travelling Theatre, touring villages with actors, puppets, and mime. In 1984 he won the Time Out Mime Street Entertainer of the Year Award, and he taught in London from 1983 until moving to France to complete his first novel, *Ulverton* (1992), a widely praised postmodernist chronicle of an English village.

Thorpe's first full-length verse collection, *Mornings in the Baltic* (1988), reflects a wide range of subjects presented through a series of first-person voices, both autobiographical and historical. His best poems bring together very different types of experience with something of a Flaubertian attention to detail and sensitivity to illusion. His second volume, *Meeting Montaigne* (1990—all Secker & Warburg), is shorter, more sombre and restrained, gesturing towards Dante's *Inferno* as a model for London life, while, at the same time, looking to the family and the artistic traditions of France as sources of consolation. Thorpe is now better known as a novelist, but four further volumes of verse have continued to demonstrate his anecdotal, *Heaney-esque eye for unnoticed histories: *From the Neanderthal* (1999), *Nine Lessons from the Dark* (2003), *Birds with a Broken Wing* (2007), and *Voluntary* (2012—all Cape).   CLB*

Thumboo, Edwin (Nadason) (1933–)
Born in Singapore, he read English at the University of Malaya. In 1967 he joined the University of Singapore (now the National University of Singapore), where he was head of the department of English language and literature. He took his PhD there, and rose to become a full professor in 1979, serving also as dean of the faculty of arts and social sciences until late 1991. He is now emeritus professor.

His three volumes of poetry have established him as the Republic's unofficial poet laureate. Since the early 1970s Thumboo has had more influence over the course of Singapore writing than any other individual. *Rib Of Earth* (Fernando, 1956), *Gods Can Die* (1977), and *Ulysses By The Merlion* (1979—both Heinemann) are marked by courageous social and political statement. Thumboo's verse has a strong sense of the nascent history of an emerging nation struggling to find new roots out of the soil of colonialism and a diverse multiracial immigrant culture. *Gods* and *Ulysses* won the National Book Development Council of Singapore Award for poetry in 1978 and 1980, as did his new and selected volume, *A Third Map* (Singapore University Press, 1993). *Bring the Sun* (Ethos Books, 2008) is a later selected poems. There is an online interview with Thumboo in *Quarterly Literary Review Singapore*, 5:1 (October 2005).   KBS*

Thwaite, Anthony (Simon) (1930–)
Born in Chester, the son of a bank employee, and spent his childhood in Yorkshire. After four wartime years in the USA he finished at Kingswood School and did his national service, going up to Christ Church, Oxford, in 1952. From the time of his first lectureship at Tokyo University (1955–7), Thwaite combined periods of academic life with literary and media work. He was a producer with the BBC from 1957 to 1962, literary editor of the *Listener* (1962–5) and of the *New Statesman* (1968–72),

and co-editor of *Encounter* from 1973 till 1985; in the intervals he was assistant professor of English at the University of Libya (1965–7) and visiting professor at the University of Kuwait (1974), and in 1985 returned to Tokyo University for a year as Japan Foundation Fellow.

His first two collections of poetry, *Home Truths* (1957) and *The Owl in the Tree* (1963), shared the *Empsonian tone, common sense, and emotional empiricism of the *Movement writers, particularly *Larkin ('Death of a Rat', 'Mr Cooper', 'Manhood End'). Thwaite's archaeological and cultural interests were broad, though, and in *The Stones of Emptiness* (1967), *Inscriptions* (1973), and *New Confessions* (1974) he developed a resourceful historical imagination ('The Letters of Synesius', 'Monologue in the Valley of the Kings').

The mastery of the dramatic monologue which Thwaite demonstrated in these volumes was suspended in the more anecdotal *A Portion for Foxes* (1977) but persuasively displayed once again in *Victorian Voices* (1980). In the 1980s two collected editions followed—*Poems 1953–1983* (Secker & Warburg, 1984) and *Poems 1953–1988* (Hutchinson, 1989)—with *Letter from Tokyo* (Hutchinson, 1987) renewing Thwaite's engaging tussle with Japan.

The qualities of civil accessibility, curiosity, and even-handedness which distinguish Thwaite's poetry have also been characteristic of his work as critic, reviewer, editor, travel writer, and broadcaster. He edited Philip Larkin's *Collected Poems* in 1988 and his *Selected Letters* in 1992. His wife Ann is a well-known biographer and children's writer. See *Selected Poems* (1997) and *Collected Poems* (2007—both Enitharmon). In 1999, Between the Lines published an extended interview with Thwaite by Peter *Dale and Ian *Hamilton.   MHU

Tillinghast, Richard (1940–) Born in Memphis, Tennessee, and educated at the University of the South (Sewanee) and at Harvard, where he studied with Robert *Lowell. The author of three books of poems, Tillinghast has taught at Harvard and Berkeley and directed the writing programme at the University of Michigan at

Ann Arbor. He lived in rural Ireland for many years, and has worked as a reviewer, travel writer and translator.

The early poems in Tillinghast's first volume, *Sleep Watch* (1969) reflect both the poet's Southern roots and the influence of such poets as Allen *Tate, but the most characteristic work in this book is more casual: evocative phrases float in a loose syntax. Tillinghast's later volumes, *The Knife and Other Poems* (1980) and *Our Flag Was Still There* (1984—all Wesleyan University Press), venture beyond the contingencies of self and towards history, but a wistful, elegiac, and tentative tone remains. Poems bear witness to both the Vietnam War and the Civil War, through the vicarious filter of the poet's life. 'Sewanee in Ruins', perhaps this poet's most ambitious sequence, traces the fortunes of the Sewanee campus from 1860 to the present (1983). See *Selected Poems* (Dedalus Press, 2009), with an introduction by Dennis *O'Driscoll. His memoir of Lowell, *Damaged Grandeur* (University of Michigan Press), appeared in 1995.   RHa

Tipping, Richard (Kelly) (1949–) While still an undergraduate in his native Adelaide, Tipping edited *Mok*, a little magazine of the *Generation of '68. He went on to co-found the Friendly Street readings and edit the Adelaide group's first anthology in 1997, then moved to Sydney. Since 1989 has lectured in communications at the University of Newcastle, New South Wales. A sculptor and photographer, video- and film-maker, he has produced video interviews with a range of Australian writers, but his own work keeps faith with the countercultural programme of the Sixties.

Tipping's three volumes of poetry for the page and ear, *Soft Riots* (1972), *Domestic Hardcore* (1975), and *Nearer by Far* (1986), were published by University of Queensland Press. The better verse from Tipping's first two collections consists of minimalist, haiku-like *aperçus* concatenated with gentle wordplays. Overtly political attempts to sing himself and his times now sound portentous. If *Nearer by Far* (1986) gainsays his early acclaim as a 'revolutionary' poet, this substantial volume nevertheless includes

engaging poems on the bizarreries of the moment. At its best Tipping's work is more overheard than overworked, more found than made.

Signs of Australia (Penguin, 1982) illustrates his devotion to visual puns and found poems, still apparent in the visual poetry of *Subvert i sing: Subvertising and Other Verse* (Red Fox, 2008). The later gathering takes its title from photoshopped mutations of branded products, logos, and advertising slogans. Much of Tipping's later work has been exhibited rather than published. *Notes Towards Employment: Some Uncollected Poems* (Picaro, 2006) reprints twenty-eight conventional and nine concrete poems, all of which, at David *Malouf's suggestion, were omitted from *Soft Riots*. In the preface to the 2006 collection Tipping records that from the early Seventies his interest in negative space, disjunctive film cuts, and conceptual art and music was pointing him away from conventional poetry.   CP

Toh, Hsien Min (1975–) Born in Singapore, Toh Hsien Min read English Literature at Oxford University. He is the founding editor of the *Quarterly Literary Review Singapore*, an online literary journal, and works in financial analysis and risk management.

Mentored by the Singaporean poets *Lee Tzu Pheng and Arthur *Yap, Toh's first collection, *Iambus* (1994), appeared under the UniPress imprint of the National University of Singapore. His second, *The Enclosure of Love* (2001), showcased the work of an observant traveller and inventive formalist, adept at casual rhyme, colloquial phrasing, and poignant structural returns (see 'Grandmother Thng'). *Means to an End* (2008—both Landmark), which was shortlisted for the Singapore Literature Prize, broke forcefully out of this mould in flowing *O'Haraesque verse paragraphs reflecting on the enmeshed existence of the poet as a global consumer ('Oil'). In 2010 he won the Young Artist Award from the National Arts Council of Singapore.   JNT

Tolson, Melvin B. (1898?–1966) Born in Moberley, Missouri. He attended Fisk University, took a BA with honours from

Lincoln University in Pennsylvania in 1923, and an MA from Columbia University in New York City in 1940. He began his working life as a manual labourer, but became an academic when he taught at Wiley College in Marshall, Texas, from 1924 to 1947. He continued his career at Langston University, in Langston, Oklahoma, from 1947 to 1965, where he was mayor of the city from 1952 to 1958. His last post was at Tuskegee Institute during the final two years of his life.

Tolson's first book was *Rendezvous with America* (1944) which contained protean and technically various poems, including some written in traditional forms and others in experimental prose patterns. It was ignored by the critics. *Libretto for the Republic of Liberia* (Twayne/Collier, 1953) got considerably more notice and resulted in Tolson's being appointed poet laureate of the Republic of Liberia. *Harlem Gallery: Book One, The Curator* (1965) had been planned as an epic in five parts, but the poet's premature death intervened. This book was a fusion of Tolson's earlier formal style with a more idiomatic expression derived from the world of jazz.

A Gallery of Harlem (Twayne/Macmillan, 1979) was made up of earlier and, some maintain, livelier versions of the poems in *Harlem Gallery*. In the late 1930s and early 1940s Tolson wrote a column for the Washington *Tribune*; these pieces were gathered posthumously as *Caviar and Cabbages* in 1984. A critical work by Mariann Russell, *Melvin B. Tolson's Harlem Gallery*, appeared in 1980, and in 1984 Robert M. Farnsworth published *Melvin B. Tolson: Plain Talk and Poetic Prophecy*.   LT

Tomlinson, Charles (1927–) Born in Stoke-on-Trent and went to Queens' College, Cambridge, where he studied with Donald *Davie. His reputation was first established in the USA, where his collection *Seeing Is Believing* appeared in 1958, two years before the British edition. He taught at the University of Bristol from 1957 to his retirement, and was made Professor of English Literature in 1982.

Tomlinson's work has been somewhat against the tide of contemporary British poetry. His 1961 essay 'Poetry Today' took issue with the 1950s poetry of the *Movement, and argued instead for poets such as Basil *Bunting and Hugh *MacDiarmid. His own early verse was influenced by the prosody of poets such as the Italian Giuseppe Ungaretti and the Americans Wallace *Stevens and William Carlos *Williams. However, his debt to modern American, Italian, or French poetry has been rather overestimated. His essential sense of the 'otherness' of things in the visible world is nearest in spirit to the native English meditative tradition of Wordsworth and Coleridge. He has written: 'In both graphic and poetic art, I like something lucid surrounded by something mysterious'. His poetry accommodates both the exotic and the local and this has led him to be described variously as both Augustan and modernist, the latter through his co-authorship of the multilingual *Renga: A Chain of Poems* (Penguin, 1979) with Octavio Paz, Jacques Roubaud, Edoardo Sanguineti.

Tomlinson's *Collected Poems* provides evidence of his range: from poems linking chance encounters between things seen in his local Gloucestershire landscape, to descriptive pieces about travels in the United States, France, Mexico, and Italy. Tomlinson also writes on music, historical situations, and, in *The Way In* (1974), on his youth in the Potteries. His poems after *Collected Poems* (1985), gathered in *The Return* (1987), *Annunciations* (1989), and *The Door in the Wall* (1992—all Oxford University Press) show a deepening religious sense.

Tomlinson is also an artist and has written poems on painters, including Cézanne and Constable. His own graphic works are executed in surrealist decalcomania, consisting of black gouache pressed between two sheets. An Arts Council touring exhibition of his work was launched at the Hayward Gallery in 1978, later published as *Eden*.

Tomlinson has also written critical prose and edited the *Oxford Book of Verse in English Translation* (1980). He has translated poets, including Tyutchev, Machado, Vallejo, Paz, and Ungaretti, collected in *Translations* (Oxford University Press, 1983). *New Collected Poems* (2009) contains five further collections. The most recent, *Cracks* *in the Universe* (2006—both Carcanet) offers Tomlinson's characteristic range of observational and conversational verse on art, travel, friendship, and the imaginative interplay between the mythological and the human: as both volumes conclude, 'It was man | made Eden'.   JDB*

Tonks, Rosemary (1932–) Born in London and educated at Wentworth School, from which she was expelled at the age of sixteen. In the same year she published her first book, a children's story, *On Wooden Wings: The Adventure of Webster* (John Murray, 1948). She married at nineteen and worked for a time as poetry reviewer for the BBC European Service. She has written three novels, the most recent being *The Halt During the Chase* (Bodley Head, 1972), and two collections of poems, *Notes on Cafés and Bedrooms* (Putnam, 1963) and *Iliad of Broken Sentences* (Bodley Head, 1967).

Reflecting her early travels in Europe and the Middle East, her usual poetic territory is the seedy underworld of the modern city, with its shifting, nomadic population of survivors. The angle of vision is that of the *flâneur*, Baudelairean but more good-humoured than splenetic. If there is a youthful naïveté about her celebrations of the louche and derelict, she can also be attractively self-mocking. Her imagery, often near-surreal, is accessible and vivid. Since converting to evangelical Christianity in the early Seventies, she has ceased to publish, although her poetry has continued to attract interest and to be represented in anthologies, e.g. *Modern Women Poets*, ed. Deryn Rees-Jones (Bloodaxe, 2005).   CAR

Toomer, Jean (Eugene) (1894–1986) Born in Washington, DC, and raised there by his divorced mother in the home of his maternal grandfather, P. B. S. Pinchback, who was the primary influence on the poet's early life. Although the Pinchbacks were light enough in skin colour to pass as Caucasians, and lived in what was essentially a white middle-class neighbourhood, the grandfather insisted that Eugene attend a school for black children outside the neighbourhood. In 1907 his mother remarried

and moved, first to Brooklyn and then to New Rochelle, a suburb of New York City. Here, in the public library, Toomer expanded his early interest in literature. When his mother died in 1909 he moved back to Washington, and from 1914 to 1919 shunted back and forth between there and New York, attending various colleges but never earning a degree. In the latter year he decided to cast his lot as a professional writer.

His first book was a collection of poems and stories, *Cane* (1923), and his reputation rests almost exclusively on this one volume, although in 1921 and 1922 he wrote two plays, *Balo* and *Natalie Mann*, a drama satirizing black middle-class Washington society. He had little luck publishing other works during his lifetime, but in 1988, two years after his death, Darwin T. Turner edited *The Wayward Seeking*, a collection of writings by Toomer, and in the same year *The Collected Poems of Jean Toomer* appeared, ed. Robert B. Jones and Margery Toomer Latimer (University of North Carolina Press).

Toomer was not a part of the *Harlem Renaissance, and despite the Afro-American themes of *Cane*, his relationships with both whites and blacks remained ambivalent. The only substantial study to appear in Toomer's lifetime was Brian Joseph Benson's and Mabel Mayle Dillard's *Jean Toomer* (1980). See also *The Lives of Jean Toomer: A Hunger for Wholeness* (1987), by Cynthia Earl Kerman and Richard Eldridge, and *Jean Toomer: Selected Essays and Literary Criticism*, ed. Robert B. Jones (University of Tennessee Press, 1996).   LT

Torrance, Chris (1941–) Born in Edinburgh, Torrance grew up in South London. He has taught creative writing and been a member of poetry performance groups. Torrance moved to the Upper Neath Valley in Wales in 1970, where he has lived ever since.

As in the work of Michael *Haslam, Torrance's writing of life on the rural fringes of modern Britain discovers a daily overlapping of the practical and the mystical, with a freedom that reflects *Black Mountain influences (see 'It is Difficult to Exaggerate the Importance of Mushrooms as Food').

Early collections include *Aries Under Saturn and Beyond* (Ferry, 1969) and *Acrospirical Meanderings in a Tongue of the Time* (Albion Village, 1973). His major ongoing sequence, *The Magic Door*, begun in 1975, has been described by Billy Mills as 'one of those very interesting works that have been quite systematically written out of the official view of contemporary British poetry'. A selection from this work was printed in *The Tempers of Hazzard* (Paladin, 1993), alongside work by Barry *MacSweeney and Thomas A. *Clark. See William Rowe, *Three Lyric Poets: Harwood, Torrance, MacSweeney* (Northcote House, 2009).   JNT

Torrence, Ridgely (1875–1950) Born in Florida, spent two years at Miami University before going on to Princeton for his degree. He moved to New York City, where he married Olive Howard Dunbar, also a writer, was befriended by Edwin Arlington *Robinson, and worked for six years at the New York Public Library. After a stint as an editor at *Cosmopolitan*, he served as the *New Republic's* poetry editor from 1920 to 1933. His own small body of verse was marked by a wide diversity of content and styles, extending from 'The Bird and the Tree', a ballad about a lynching, to the city-scape explored in 'Three O'Clock', often exhibiting a Pre-Raphaelite dreaminess that flowed easily into cosmic allegory.

Fascinated by both the theatre and black life, Torrence wrote for the Negro Theatre in the 1910s, producing verse plays in 1914 and 1917, and in 1939 began the National Survey of the Negro Theatre for the Rockefeller Foundation. A year later he edited *Selected Letters of Edwin Arlington Robinson*; his *Poems* (Macmillan) appeared in 1941.   EB

Tranter, John (1943–) Born at Cooma in the south-east of New South Wales. He read English at Sydney University but did not pursue an academic career. He has worked in printing and publishing and as a radio producer. In the Sixties he travelled to the East and to Europe, though he was never tempted to become an expatriate. He began to publish early. His first four books, *Parallax, Red Movie, The Blast Area*, and

The Alphabet Murders were in print by 1976, and show a poet attempting to find an equivalent in verse to the urban discontents of the age. The young Rimbaud has always been Tranter's ideal, and there is a calculated *deréglement du sens* about his early work. A key book in his development is his sequence of 100 sonnets, *Crying in Early Infancy* (1977). Here a near *confessional abruptness meets the ludic language-centred poetry of the *New York School. It is characteristic of both Tranter and his age that often the hero of his poetry is the poem itself. Tranter sealed his importance in contemporary Australian letters with his influential anthology *The New Australian Poetry* (1979—both Makar). *Under Berlin* (1988), his richest collection yet, reveals the unexpected influence of *Auden in its fondness for surveying multiple historical vistas, and its witty psychological dramatizing.

The award-winning *Urban Myths: 210 Poems New and Selected* (2006—both University of Queensland Press) draws on several collections published in Australia and the UK since the narratives of *The Floor of Heaven* (Angus & Robertson, 1992). *The Salt Companion to John Tranter* (Salt, 2010), ed. Rod Mengham, contains critical essays and an interview with John *Kinsella. From 1997 to 2010 Tranter edited the international online poetry magazine *Jacket*. Tranter's example has been decisive among Australian poets of his generation, those who began writing in the Sixties and during the Vietnam War. Tranter's revolution may be expressed simply as an orientation of Australian sympathies away from the 'bush' tradition of Australian verse, which was still being promulgated in journals such as the *Bulletin and Meanjin* when he was growing up, but also away from Britain and any decorous or academic style. The models to hand were American—more West Coast aestheticism (Robert *Duncan) than *Beat or *Black Mountain. Young Australian poets looked to Tranter as their stylistic mentor, not so much for his polemical force as for his practical example. He has never been a strenuous theorist of poetry, but always a brilliant strategist. Whether poets in Sydney and Melbourne tuned in to New York or followed notions from Parisian theorists mattered less to him than that they should devote themselves to creating a new Australian poetry which could take its place unapologetically on the world stage.   PNFP

Treece, Henry (1912–66) Born in the West Midlands of (he claimed) 'Welsh extraction originally'. He took a degree at Birmingham University, and until the war was a schoolmaster. He served in the RAF, and then wrote radio scripts for adults (including the trilogy *The Dark Island, The End of a World*, and *The Tragedy of Tristram*) and children. As a poet, he found his first mentor in Michael *Roberts. With J. F. *Hendry, and encouraged by Herbert *Read, he founded the *New Apocalypse movement. He was a close friend of Stefan Schimanksi (killed in an air crash on his way to Korea in 1950), and with him edited the magazine *Kingdom Come* and the biyearly *Transformation*. Treece's verse arose from his and the New Apocalyptic belief in the priestly role of the poet; T. S. *Eliot published *Invitation and Warning* (Faber, 1942), but after the war he was better known as a historical novelist. There is a selection and discussion of Treece's verse by Andrew *Crozier in *Conductors of Chaos*, ed. Iain Sinclair (Picador, 1994).   MS-S*

Trevelyan, R. C. (Robert Calverly) (1872–1951) Born in Weybridge, the son of Sir George Otto Trevelyan, and brought up in London and in Wallington Hall, Northumberland. He attended Trinity College, Cambridge, 1891–5, where he was an Apostle. He travelled frequently in Europe, especially Italy, where he paid annual visits to Bernard Berenson at I Tatti. After his marriage to Elizabeth des Amorie van der Hoeven, he settled in The Shiffolds near Dorking where he and his Dutch wife (a violinist) entertained a constant flow of musicians, painters, and poets.

His prolific original verse, from his first book, *Mallow and Asphodel* (1898), to his last, *From the Shiffolds* (1947), was written usually in conventional metres, although he occasionally experimented within the bounds of a formulable prosody. His prose tract *Thamyris* (1925) is an attack on the *vers libre* movement. He frequently made use of Greek and Latin mythologies, yet just as frequently indulged in descriptions of the beauties of rural England. He was steeped in Greek and Latin literature and he was an indefatigable translator. Especially noteworthy is the *De Rerum Natura* of Lucretius translated into English verse. Of his many verse plays, *The Bride of Dionysus* (1912), made into an opera by Sir Donald Tovey and produced in Edinburgh in 1929 and 1932, and *The New Parsifal* (1914) are the most readable today. Trevelyan's collected works are in two volumes (Longmans, 1939).   DES

Trethewey, Natasha (1966–) Born in Mississippi to mixed-race parents, Trethewey studied at the universities of Georgia, Hollins, and Massachusetts. She is Charles Howard Candler Professor of English and Creative Writing at Emory University and in 2012 became Poet Laureate of the United States.

Her first book, *Domestic Work* (2000), was chosen by Rita *Dove for the 1999 Cave Canem Prize. Dove's introduction praises Trethewey's formal variety, from sonnets to free verse and blues, and her presentation of working-class African-Americans in a way that 'resists the lure of autobiography and . . . narrow identification' in favour of a historical 'tapestry of ancestors'. *Bellocq's Ophelia* (2002—both Graywolf) concerned the life of a prostitute in turn-of-the-century New Orleans. In her third collection, *Native Guard* (Houghton, 2006), which won the Pulitzer Prize, two sequences on the poet's parents and childhood in the Deep South are arranged around a long poem on the Louisiana Native Guard, one of the first black regiments in the Civil War. See also *Beyond Katrina: A Meditation on the Mississippi Gulf Coast* (University of Georgia Press, 2010), a family memoir.   JNT

Trimpi, Helen. *See* PINKERTON, HELEN.

Tripp, John (1927–86) Brought up in Whitchurch, a suburb of Cardiff, and worked as a journalist in London until

1969, when he returned to Wales and lived thereafter as a freelance writer, often precariously. His early poems, contributed to *Poetry Wales* and subsequently published in the booklet *Diesel to Yesterday* (1966), were mostly concerned with aspects of Welsh history, often from a nationalist point of view. An English-speaking Welshman with left-wing and pacifist convictions, he felt compelled to write about what he saw as the shoddy materialism afflicting the Welsh people and the decay of the community's traditional values, as in the volumes *The Loss of Ancestry* (1969), *The Province of Belief* (1971), and *The Inheritance File* (1973).

His view grew more bitter after the failure of the devolution referendum in 1979, but he then turned to more contemporary subjects such as the social dereliction of south Wales. The sequence of poems entitled 'Life under Thatcher' is perhaps the most typical of his later mode, turning a laconic eye not only on social deprivation but on himself as poet-observer. But he was also capable of humour, compassion, and anger, as in the volume *Passing Through* (1984). These qualities were widely appreciated at the many public readings which the poet gave during his last years. He was also passionately engaged in Welsh literary affairs, first as a member of the editorial board of *Planet* between 1973 and 1979 and later with the Welsh Academy and the Welsh Union of Writers.

A selection of John Tripp's work (with that of John *Ormond and Emyr *Humphreys) appeared in the *Penguin Modern Poets* series (1978). A posthumous volume of his *Selected Poems* (Seren, 1989) was edited by John Ormond. A monograph on the poet's life and work was contributed to the Writers of Wales series (University of Wales Press, 1989), by Nigel Jenkins. Since 1988, his example as a performer has been honoured by the John Tripp Award for Spoken Poetry. MS

Tsaloumas, Dimitris (1921–) Born on the Greek island of Leros and later met Lawrence *Durrell on Rhodes. Among poets who are not native speakers of English (such as *Skrzynecki and *Kefala), he is distinctive in having arrived in Australia in 1952 with an established poetic reputation in his original language, and he continues to publish in Athens.

His first two Australian-published collections were in Greek, translated by Philip Grundy. *The Observatory* (1983) won a National Book Council Award and the 100 pithily concentrated short poems of *The Book of Epigrams* (1985) received an enthusiastic critical reception. Editing the anthology *Contemporary Australian Poetry* (1986), he prepared the translations for the dual-language Greek edition.

Falcon Drinking (1988) was his first collection 'conceived and written in English'. The qualities of his Greek poetry—intense and densely metaphoric lyricism and sardonic observation of the self and its surrounding world—persist, and the Australian poems, even when not specifically linked to Greece, as in 'Note with Interlude from the Banks of the Brisbane in September', are perhaps most interesting when they suggest palimpsests, cultural inscriptions written over a shadow text of memory and attitudes. Tsaloumas has received many awards in honour of his contribution to Australian literature. *New and Selected Poems* appeared in 2000, followed by a new volume, *Helen of Troy and Other Poems*, in 2007 (all University of Queensland Press). JS

Turnbull, Gael (Lundin) (1928–2004) Born in Edinburgh and worked as a medical practitioner in England before emigrating to Canada in the 1950s. He became a Canadian citizen before returning permanently to Great Britain, where—in his magazine *Migrant*—he was active as the publisher of many lesser known, often avant-garde, poets such as Roy *Fisher and Ed *Dorn. Although Turnbull was associated with *Origin*, his work does not in fact much resemble that of the *Black Mountain poets, except that it is resolutely low-key and suspicious of rhetoric, in the tradition of William Carlos *Williams, whom he admired. *Twenty Words, Twenty Days* (Migrant, 1966) is characteristic: he takes a word randomly from the dictionary for each of twenty days, and builds an autobiographical poem around it. This reads inconsequentially to some, but as a set of remarkably truthful impressions to others (Edwin *Morgan praised the 'glancing insights and humanities of his work'). See *There Are Words . . . Collected Poems* (2006) and also *More Words—Gael Turnbull on Poets & Poetry* (2012—both Shearsman), ed. Jill Turnbull and Hamish Whyte. See also Richard Price, 'Migrant the Magnificent', *PN Review*, *174* (March–April 2007).   MS-S*

Turner, Brian (1944–) Born in Dunedin, has been a publisher's editor, freelance writer, playwright, and university writer-in-residence. Having come from a background of sport (he represented New Zealand at hockey, and his father and two brothers have competed internationally in their sports), he came rather late to poetry. However, with his first book, *Ladders of Rain* (McIndoe, 1978) he established a personal style which was identifiably local. The subjects are rooted in his own territory of Dunedin and the South Island of New Zealand. Turner rejects travel as dislocating and refuses the influences of imported trends in poetry. Unlike many New Zealand poets of the Seventies and Eighties he does not look to American poetry, preferring a more conservative British model while citing the particular influence of W. S. *Merwin and Ian *Hamilton. *Beyond* (McIndoe, 1992) won the New Zealand Book Award for Poetry. Later books include *Taking Off* (2001) and *Just This* (2009—both Victoria University Press). In 2003, Turner became the fourth New Zealand Poet Laureate. *Timeless Land* (Longacre, 1995), his collaborative celebration of the Central Otago landscape with Owen Marshall and Graeme Sydney, reached a fourth edition in 2010.   RB

Turner, Frederick (1943–) Born in Northamptonshire, he grew up in England and Africa, and was educated at Oxford. He is presently Founders Professor of Arts and Humanities at the University of Texas at Dallas. His first book, *Between Two Lives* (Wesleyan University Press, 1972), consists of lyrics in various stages of metamorphosis as they try to become narrative poems. *The New World* (Princeton University Press, 1985) recounts the adventures of a rather chivalric science-fiction hero around whom a fascinating cosmos of good and evil, wisdom and folly, springs up. *Paradise: Selected Poems 1990–2003* was published in 2004, and *The Prayers of Dallas* in 2006 (both Word Tech).

The sources of Turner's story-telling lie on the one hand in the great epics (Greek, Christian, Indian, Welsh, Nordic), and on the other in the detail of modern scientific theory and the magical, dangerous technology to which it has given rise. (As a scholar, he has written extensively on both modern cosmology and the epic.) His characters are warriors who fight with intelligent swords guided by solar-powered microprocessors; in Turner's exuberant, epigenetic Lamarckian materialism, the right configuration of chemicals is as good as a soul. His people create themselves bodily as well as culturally, choosing beauty for generation after generation in the midst of tragic conflict. Their adventures lead them always further into trouble, which however teaches them 'that we cannot fall back on the comfort of despair | but are bound to build the world in the human image, | and cleanse ourselves only with fluids of past pollutions'. The new world is thus never a return to innocence, but a surprising new twist, lovely and threatening, in the traffic of angels up and down nucleic acid's symbolic ladder.   EG

Turner, W. J. (Walter James) (1884–1946) Born and educated in Melbourne, Australia. In 1907 he went to London to become a writer. His first success came with satirical sketches which Orage published in *The New Age*. He earned his living from music criticism (principally for the *New Statesman*) and literary editing.

Sir Edward Marsh first brought Turner's poetry to prominence when he included it in his *Georgian poetry anthology for 1916–17. Influenced by *de la Mare, Turner was committed to rhythm, music, sensibility, and imagination, but his early work also shows the inspiration of the Australian landscape and his interest in anthropological study and what it revealed about the relationship between art and religious yearning. In 1922 Turner refused to be included in the fifth Georgian anthology, which did not, he later argued, include 'the most complex art of the age'. Turner's enthusiasms for Symbolist poetry, Plato, Kierkegaard, and 'philosophical-religious explanations of human life' distinguish his poems. *Yeats included a generous selection of Turner's poems in the *Oxford Book of Modern Verse* (1936). He confessed himself 'lost in admiration and astonishment' at Turner's 'majestic song', but also praised his modernity, 'strange philosophical poems', and intellectual subtlety.

The only recent edition of Turner's poetry is *W. J. Turner: Selected Poetry*, ed. Wayne McKenna (New South Wales University Press, 1990), but see *Selected Poems* (Oxford University Press, 1939) and *Fossils of a Future Time?* (1946). See also McKenna's *W. J. Turner: Poet and Music Critic* (Smythe, 1990).   WMCK

Tuwhare, Hone (1922–2008) Born in Kaikohe, New Zealand. His mother died when he was young, and he was brought up by his father, who worked on market gardens. Tuwhare remembered lying awake at night, hearing his father chant in Maori or tell ghost stories. His father also introduced him to the King James Bible, a lasting influence on his work.

In 1939 Tuwhare joined the Railway Workshops at Otahuhu and served his apprenticeship as a boilermaker tradesman. He became a Marxist, read a range of left-wing writers, and met the poet R. A. K. *Mason. After the Soviet invasion of Hungary in 1956 he left the Communist Party and at about the same time began writing poetry seriously. *No Ordinary Sun* (1964) was welcomed as the first book of verse in English by a Maori poet and became one of New Zealand's best-selling poetry collections.

Tuwhare's poetry can be anecdotal, political, and sometimes—as in 'Rain'—effortlessly lyrical. His earliest poems adopted a high, rhetorical, formal manner; later work is more conversational, open to the vernacular. Often a Tuwhare poem is a piece of direct address—to a friend, to the spirits of the dead, to a Maori meeting house. Tuwhare writes usually in a flexible English (in the space of a few lines he can sound as if he is both in church and at the pub), but

the oral and oratorical elements in his work, along with a ground-note of lament and an informing animism, have their roots in Maori spirituality.

His collected poems, *Deep River Talk*, were published by the University of Hawaii Press in 1993. In 1999, Tuwhare became the second Poet Laureate of New Zealand, and in 2003 received a Prime Minister's Award for Literary Achievement. His last collection was *Oooooo......!!!* (Steele Roberts, 2005). See Janet Hunt, *Hone Tuwhare: A Biography* (Godwit, 1998).   WM

Twichell, Chase (1950–   ) Received a BA from Trinity College and an MFA from the University of Iowa. For years she lived in Florence, Massachusetts, and worked there for a small press as an editor and typesetter while also doing freelance editorial work. Her first book of poems, *Northern Spy* (1981), was one of the first collections by poets of her generation to integrate poetry's traditional field of experience and the language and subjects of contemporary science. Her second book, *The Odds* (1986—both University of Pittsburgh Press), expands this effort and adds to the poet's spare, crisp execution of line and rhythm and anecdotal narrative impulse. Notable in this collection are two long poems, 'My Ruby of Lasting Sadness', which looks back with bitter-sweet precision on a youthful romance, and 'A Suckling Pig', an ambitious rendering of psychological torment and physical excesses among an artistic, Yuppie set of New England friends. *Perdido* appeared from Farrar, Straus in 1991.

Twichell taught at the University of Alabama and received fellowships in poetry from the Artists' Foundation (Boston), the Guggenheim Foundation, and the National Endowment for the Arts. She lives in New York with her husband, the American fiction writer Russell Banks. Twichell's later poetry continues to reflect her study of Zen Buddhism. *Horses Where the Answers Should Have Been: New and Selected Poems* (Copper Canyon, 2010) won the Kingsley Tufts Poetry Award. She has also translated the poetry of Rabindranath Tagore and co-edited a book of writing exercises, *The Practice of Poetry* (Harper-Collins, 1992).   RMCD

Untermeyer, Louis (1885–1978) Born in New York. As a famous and at one time influential anthologist Untermeyer attracted praise from Allen *Tate (his anthologies of American poetry were the 'best available') and rude dispraise from E. E. *Cummings ('Mr u will not be missed | who as an anthologist | sold the many on the few | not excluding mr u'). Tate was right about the quality of the anthologies: as works for the general reader they are admirably eclectic, and they give useful representative selections from interesting poets otherwise difficult of access. Untermeyer's knowledge of modern poetry was extensive. The best of his own poetry consists of enjoyably sharp parodies (*Collected Parodies*, 1926), in which poets such as *Yeats, Poe, Vachel *Lindsay, and *Masefield tell Mother Goose tales: their excesses as well as virtues are amusingly brought out. The rest of his poetic output, which is competent, is most of all influenced by Heine, of whose poems he made many translations. It is pallid, since he seemed to need the parody form to bring out his undoubted wit. But Edwin *Muir praised his 'opulence'. *From Another World* (1939), is valuable for its anecdotes of the large number of poets he knew.

See *Selected Poems and Parodies* (1935) and *Long Feud: Selected Poems* (1962—all Harcourt, Brace). MS-S

Urdang, Constance (1922–96) Born in New York City, Urdang graduated from Smith College and the University of Iowa. Married to the poet Donald *Finkel, she divided her time between St Louis, Missouri (her home for many years) and San Miguel de Allende, Mexico.

All three geographical locations figure in her first works of fiction, *Natural History* (1969), *Lucha* (1986), and *American Earthquakes* (1988) and her novellas, *The Woman who Read Novels* and *Peacetime* (1990). Her five volumes of poetry, from *Charades and Celebrations* (October House, 1965) to *Alternative Lives* (University of Pittsburgh Press, 1990), use a similar geography to explore the multiple roles of women and changing sense of self.

Urdang's poetry, while intensely private and introspective, transcends the merely personal. Her ironic humour and clarity of detail, particularly in *The Picnic in the Cemetery* (Braziller, 1975) and *The Lone Woman and Others* (Pittsburgh, 1980), allow her to explore self-alienation with an objective compassion. EDF

Valentine, Jean (1934–   ) Born in Chicago, and educated at Radcliffe College. In 1965 she won the Yale Younger Poets Award for her book *Dream Barker*. She has taught at several colleges and universities, including Sarah Lawrence College. In 2008 she became State Poet of New York.

Jean Valentine writes a deeply personal poetry that seems to withhold its secrets from us, yet in doing so opens itself to a different kind of attention. Her poems make frequent references to family, lovers, and events that remain obscure, unnarrated; but these bits of experience furnish germs for Valentine's extraordinary, incantatory spells of language. Syntax in her work often seems to dissolve into a series of nouns or namings, as though summoning the presences she desires. Like other poets who came of age in the Fifties, Valentine moved from a carefully worked, somewhat brittle style to a freer, less rational mode, in her case perhaps influenced by Mandelstam, whom she has translated. Her poems can be virtually opaque in the way they pass from image to image; at their best, however, a lucid dream logic makes itself felt in the absence of story or argument.

Door in the Mountain: New and Collected Poems (Wesleyan University Press, 2004) won the National Book Award. *Break the Glass* (Copper Canyon, 2010), was her eleventh collection. *Jean Valentine: This-World Company* (University of Michigan Press, 2012), ed. Kazim Ali and John Hoppenthaler, collects essays in appreciation by critics and poets including Fanny *Howe and Mark *Doty.   RG

Van Doren, Mark (1894–1972) Born in Hope, Illinois, grew up there and in Urbana, Illinois, and was educated at the University of Illinois and Columbia University. He taught at Columbia, 1920–59, where he was considered an outstanding educator.

Van Doren, who owned a farm and farmhouse in Connecticut, is best known for his poetry about the people of New England who are depicted with sympathy and understanding, usually in a rural setting which is described with sharp-eyed, loving detail. He was well aware, however, that New England culture was in a state of decline, and hence much of his poetry was elegiac in tone. He wrote in conventional prosody in carefully crafted lines and stanzas and in a style that has been described as autumnal and dry. In his foreword to *Good Morning: Last Poems by Mark Van Doren* (1973), Richard *Howard placed him in the tradition of E. A. *Robinson and *Frost.

Van Doren published more than a thousand poems. Among those praised by critics are 'Most Difficult', 'Private Worship', 'Return to Ritual', 'This Amber Sunstream', and 'Young Woman at a Window'. A long verse narrative of note is *The Mayfield Deer* (1941), derived from an historical account of a nineteenth-century Illinois hunter and his tame deer. *Collected and New Poems 1924–1963* (1963—all Hill & Wang) is a substantial compilation of his shorter poems. *The Autobiography of Mark Van Doren* (Harcourt, 1958) supplies details of his life up to 1957.   DES

Van Duyn, Mona (1921–2004) Born in Waterloo, Iowa, and earned a BA from the University of Northern Iowa in 1942, followed by an MA from the University of Iowa in 1943, the same year she married Jarvis Thurston. From 1944 she taught at various universities and (beginning in 1947) edited *Perspective: A Quarterly of Literature* with her husband.

From the start of her writing career Van Duyn enjoyed unusual critical acceptance. The traditional nature of her lyric gift, which often involves complex rhyme-schemes, in tandem with her sensitivity to the web-fine nuances of ordinary experiences have made her popular with prize-awarding juries. On the basis of only two undramatic but impressive collections, *Valentines to the Wide World: Poems* (Cummington, 1959) and *A Time of Bees* (University of North Carolina Press, 1964), she won the Bollingen Prize in 1970, and her third volume, *To See, To Take: Poems* (Atheneum, 1970), received a National Book Award a year later.

In 1992 Van Duyn published her collected poems, *If It Be Not I*, and a new volume of 'minimalist sonnets', *Firefall*, and began her one-year term as Poet Laureate of the United States. See also her *Selected Poems* (2002—all Knopf).   EB

Van Wyk, Christopher (1957–) Born in Johannesburg, where he has worked as a clerk, an educational writer for the independent South African Council for Higher Education, and also as the editor of *Staffrider* magazine, a literary journal which was particularly influential in South Africa in the 1980s.

Van Wyk showed early promise, his first and only collection having been published when he was barely out of his teens. Entitled *It Is Time To Go Home* (Donker, 1979), it at once placed him among the several protest poets who emerged in South Africa in the 1970s. Written largely in the years immediately after the Soweto Revolt of 1976, it dealt with the poet's initiation into the oppressive South African reality of that time. Many of the best poems in the volume establish a link between the poet's coming of age and his growing awareness of the fraudulence of apartheid. Other poems included are an impressive demonstration of Van Wyk's satirical gifts. Although many South African poets have drawn attention to the evils of racism, few before Van Wyk focused with a more bitter wit on the grotesque distortions of language for which apartheid was responsible. This is the subject of his 'In Detention', still

his best-known and most widely anthologized poem. He has since published fiction for young adults and a memoir of his childhood, *Shirley, Goodness and Mercy* (Picador, 2004).   SW

Vidiikas, Vicki (1948–98) Born and grew up in Sydney. She dropped out of school, and published her first poem at nineteen in the magazine *Poetry Australia*. She was a notable part of the Sydney counter-culture of the 1970s, where she became a well-known part of the male-dominated literary scene around Balmain. She travelled extensively in Asia, living in India for more than ten years, experiences which were recurrent themes in her poems. Much of her work anticipates the later *confessional poetry of women writers in Australia, concerning itself with raw experience; as Pam *Brown points out, it is concerned with the darker side of female experience, but this is never analysed in any formal feminist sense.

During her life Vidiikas published three collections of poems: *Condition Red* (University of Queensland Press, 1973), *Knäbel* (Wild & Woolley, 1978), and *India Ink* (Hale & Iremonger, 1984), as well as a collection of prose pieces, *Wrappings* (Wild & Woolley, 1974). Her later life was increasingly dominated by heroin addiction, and she published no more books in the fourteen years before her premature death. A posthumous selection, *Vicki Vidiikas: New and Rediscovered*, ed. Barry Scott, was published by Transit Lounge in 2010.   ACr

Viereck, Peter (Robert Edwin) (1916–2006) Born in New York. He taught history at Mount Holyoke College, Massachusetts. His first collection, *Terror and Decorum: Poems 1940–1948* (Scribner, 1948) won the Pulitzer Prize. This and its successors contained tricksy poems, many of them parodic, which risked everything on a rather trite, or folksy, humour: undoubtedly serious themes were juxtaposed with deliberately absurd expositions of them, so that the impression conveyed was either of banality or cleverness. Thus, a comment on Keats' odes, 'To A Sinister Potato', began: 'O vast earth-apple, waiting to be fried.' This kind of nervous zest prevented Viereck, despite a certain proportion of lyrical successes in his earlier work, from being accepted into the mainstream. *Archer in the Marrow: The Applewood Cycles 1967–1987* (Norton, 1987), a long poem with a huge *apparatus criticus*, has its moments, but is similarly flawed by a not-quite-coherent zaniness, as if the poet had given up on his audience. See *Tide and Continuities: Last and First Poems, 1995–1938* (University of Arkansas Press, 1995). Viereck also wrote several books on the history of political conservatism. MS-S

Violi, Paul (1944–2011) Born in Brooklyn, New York, Violi was the author of thirteen books of poetry, including *The Curious Builder* (Hanging Loose, 1993) and *Breakers: Selected Longer Poems* (Coffee House, 2000). He also published a volume of prose, *Selected Accidents, Pointless Anecdotes* (Hanging Loose, 2002) and was widely anthologized, appearing four times in the *Best American Poetry* series and also in *The Oxford Book of American Poetry*.

Violi's poetry is characterized by a vivid, colloquial voice and a sharp wit. One of his best-known poems is 'Counterman', which features a dialogue between a customer and a sandwich-maker at a deli, that metamorphoses into an architectural aria. Violi was closely associated with the *New York School of Poets, counting Kenneth *Koch, Tony Towle, and Charles North among his friends and colleagues.

Violi received two awards from the National Endowment for the Arts, the John Ciardi Lifetime Achievement Award in Poetry, the American Academy of Arts and Letters Morton Dauwen Zabel Award, as well as several grants. He was teaching at Columbia University and New School University prior to his death from pancreatic and liver cancer in Cortlandt Manor, New York. AMl

Voigt, Ellen Bryant (1943–) Born in Danville, Virginia, in the Piedmont South and raised on a farm owned by her father. The rural world of her childhood—and of her adult years in Vermont—is one of the major forces in her poetry. Ten years after earning an MFA at the Iowa Writers' Workshop she published her first collection of poems, *Claiming Kin* (Wesleyan University Press, 1976). The book's title attests to the importance of family memories and family relationships throughout Voigt's poetry. Though candid and intensely personal at times, her poems also embrace a human community beyond the self. Her attention to nature aligns her with the pastoral tradition, but Voigt rejects any consoling equation between the human and natural worlds, as 'Liebesgedicht' and the ironically titled 'Pastoral' of her second collection, *The Forces of Plenty* (1983), indicate. For Voigt nature is both beautiful and terrifying, nurturing and flatly indifferent.

All of Voigt's poetry, including *The Lotus Flowers* (1987—both Norton), is marked by her sense of human vulnerability. The forces of plenty contend against the forces of loss. Yet she has become a poet of survival as well as of evanescence. Moving with ease from narrative to descriptive to meditative poems, alert to the music of her language and to the moral implications of the experiences and emotions she records, Voigt creates elegant and accessible poems of quiet authority, particularly in 'The Spire', 'Year's End', 'At the Movie: Virginia, 1956', and 'The Farmer'. Voigt teaches on the low-residency MFA programme at Warren Wilson College. Her essays on the practice of writing have been published as *The Flexible Lyric* (University of Georgia Press, 1996). From 1999 to 2003 she was Vermont State Poet. See *Messenger: Selected Poems 1976–2006* (Norton, 2007). JLa

Volkman, Karen (1967–) Born in Miami, Florida, Volkman received a BA from New College, Sarasota, and an MA from Syracuse University. She taught at New York University and the New School while living in Brooklyn, and currently lives in Missoula, where she teaches in the MFA writing program at the University of Montana.

Volkman has published three full collections. Her first collection, *Crash's Law,* appeared from Norton in 1996 and was selected for the National Poetry Series by Heather McHugh. *Spar* (University of Iowa

Press, 2002), her second book, won the James Laughlin Award from the Academy of American Poets, along with the Iowa Poetry Prize. In 2006 she received the PIP Gertrude Stein Award for Innovative Poetry in English. Her experiments in lyric form range from free verse and prose poetry to fully rhymed Petrarchan sonnets: see *Nomina*, her third collection, published in 2008 by BOA Editions. Acknowledging Sylvia *Plath and Rosmarie *Waldrop among her influences, Volkman's poems eschew narrative, instead 'edgelessly' questioning the world in disjunctive representations of a modern consciousness struggling for psychic orientation ('Tell the boys we're leaving—wind as red | event left at the altar—the bride is fled').   NH

Waddington, Miriam (1917–2004) Born Miriam Dworkin, the daughter of Jewish-Russian immigrants, in Winnipeg, Manitoba. In 1931 her family moved to Ottawa. Waddington received her BA from the University of Toronto in 1939, the year she married journalist Patrick Waddington; they had two sons. During the Second World War she published poems, stories, and reviews while studying social work at the universities of Toronto and Pennsylvania. She moved to Montreal in 1945, taught at McGill's School of Social Work, and was later a case-worker for various social organizations. In 1960 she separated from her husband and returned to Toronto, where she continued her social work and, in 1964, joined the English department of York University, where she was professor emeritus and senior scholar.

Spare and deceptively simple, and often lyrical, joyous, and humorous, the poems in Waddington's thirteen volumes—from her first collection, *Green World* (1945), to *The Last Landscape* (1992)—explore her prairie childhood, her social concerns, landscape, people, Jewish folklore, love and loss, memory and isolation, ageing and death.

Waddington paid homage to A. M. *Klein in her 1970 monograph on him and in her edition of *The Collected Poems of A. M. Klein* (1974). Her own *Collected Poems* (Oxford University Press, 1986) is complemented by selections from her short fiction in *Summer at Lonely Beach and Other Stories* (Mosaic, 1982), and from her memoirs and essays in *Apartment Seven* (Oxford University Press, 1989).   DS

Wagner, Catherine (1969–) Born in Rangoon, Burma, Wagner lived in Asia and the Middle East until 1977, when her family moved to Baltimore, Maryland. Wagner obtained her BA in English from the University of Tennessee at Chattanooga, her MFA in poetry at the University of Iowa Writers' Workshop, and her PhD in English with a creative dissertation at the University of Utah. Presently she is an associate professor at Miami University of Ohio, where she has taught since 2006. She has published four collections: *Miss America* (2001), *Macular Hole* (2004), *My New Job* (2009—all Fence), and *Nervous Device* (City Lights, 2012). She also edited, with Rebecca Wolff, the anthology, *Not for Mothers Only: Contemporary Poems on Child-Getting and Child-Rearing* (Fence, 2007).

Miss America established Wagner as a distinctive new voice in her juxtaposition of multiple registers to evoke as well as address personal and social tensions. The title aptly suggests the way the book's many voices comprise one decidedly American one. Throughout her work, poems make unexpected and often abrupt connections between disparate ideas as they interweave the speaker's train of thought and physical experience. As Wagner writes in 'Exercise 1 (11/28/00 PM)' from *My New Job*, 'What would be in my chest to hurt me? A leaf crumpled to the window | I lean forward on a nerve ebullient | my sweet alive and roasting in a current.'   CE

Wagoner, David (1926–) Born in Massillon, Ohio. At Pennsylvania State University he studied under Theodore *Roethke and received his BA in 1947. Two years later he took an MA from Indiana University and subsequently taught at DePauw University for a year, 1949–50, and at Pennsylvania State for four years, 1950–4. In the latter year he went to the University of Washington in Seattle, which he has ever since maintained as his home-base and where, for many years, he edited *Poetry Northwest*, a highly regarded quarterly.

A 1950s competence was the main feature of Wagoner's first book, *Dry Sun, Dry Wind* (1953). *A Place to Stand* (1958) went in two directions simultaneously: there was greater formality of structure, but a loosening of language giving, in certain poems, an almost jazz-like effect. The most engaging aspect of the poems in *The Nesting Ground* (1963) was their colloquial music. That remained true of *Staying Alive* (1966), and particularly of the title-poem, simultaneously a handbook about surviving in the woods and a parable about how to stay human in the process. *New and Selected Poems* (1969) sampled the best of these volumes.

The outdoors of the Pacific Northwest figures prominently in Wagoner's work, as in *Riverbed* (1972), but manifesting itself at times in poems having to do with Native Americans and their lore, such as 'Seven Songs for an Old Voice' which concludes *Sleeping in the Woods* (1974). In *Who Shall Be the Sun* (1978—all Indiana University Press) Wagoner personified natural forces and gave them Indian names in his retelling of the myths of the tribes. The poems of *First Light* (Little, Brown, 1983) were crisp, the imagery evocative, the sensibility contemplative; they exhibited a keen sense of narrative, an insight into character, an eye for composition, and a feeling for atmosphere, light, and colour.

Wagoner has also written ten novels. In 1991 he received the Ruth Lilly Prize for Poetry. A prolific later period as a poet began with *Walt Whitman Bathing* (University of Illinois Press, 1997). Since *Traveling Light: Collected and New Poems* (1999) he has published three further volumes with the University of Illinois Press—*The House of Song* (2002), *Good Morning and Good Night* (2005), and *A Map of Night* (2008)—and, with Copper Canyon Press, *After the Point of No Return* (2012).   LT

Wah, Fred (1939–   ) Born in Swift Current, Saskatchewan, and grew up in the West Kootenay mountains of south-eastern British Columbia. He entered the University of British Columbia as a music student, but became interested in poetry there, where he was one of the founders of the poetry newsletter *Tish*. He pursued his education at the universities of New Mexico and Buffalo, studying with Robert *Creeley and Charles *Olson. He returned to the Kootenays to teach writing at colleges for two decades, and was a founding member of the *Kootenay School of Writing. In 1990 he took a post at the University of Calgary, where he is now professor emeritus. In 2011, he became Canada's fifth Parliamentary Poet Laureate.

Wah has always been active as an editor, founding and co-editing numerous magazines and books. He is on the editorial board of *Open Letter*, a journal of postmodern theory and criticism. He is also a fervent talent-scout, and has helped launch the careers of many younger poets, often during writer-in-residencies at western universities and retreats.

His early experience in music (including his jazz trumpet playing) shows in his poetry, where sound and improvisation are more important than syntax. In recent years he has explored his own childhood and the early life of his half-Chinese father, who was born in Canada and raised in China. He has also, since a trip to China and Japan, been finding verse-forms which will accommodate Asian and Native North American practices.

Waiting for Saskatchewan (Turnstone, 1985) won the Governor General's Award. Since *Diamond Grill* (1996), an autobiographical 'biotext about racial anger', there has been a growing body of criticism on the political significance of Wah's experimentalism: see Jeff Derksen, 'Making Race Opaque: Fred Wah's Poetics of Opposition and Differentiation', *West Coast Line*, 18, Winter 1995–1996. *Faking It: Poetics and Hybridity* (2000—both NeWest) collects his own critical writing on this subject from the 1980s and 1990s. A selected poems, *The False Laws of Narrative*, ed. Louis Cabri, appeared in 2009 (Wilfrid Laurier University Press). *is a door* (Talonbooks, 2009) won the Dorothy Livesay Poetry Prize.   GHB*

w

- All of his work is currently being made available at The Fred Wah Digital Archive.

Wain, John (Barrington) (1925–94) Born in Stoke-on-Trent, Staffordshire, and educated at the High School, Newcastle-under-Lyme. A damaged eye kept him out of military service, and he became a wartime undergraduate at St John's College, Oxford, where he was taught by C. S. Lewis (see his early volume of autobiography, *Sprightly Running*, 1962). In 1947 he was appointed lecturer in English at Reading University; but after the success of his first novel, *Hurry on Down* (1953), a picaresque account of a lower-middle-class life after college, he gave up teaching to live as a full-time writer. As well as eleven novels, he published volumes of literary criticism and a biographical study of Samuel Johnson, but he continued to regard his poems as 'the best things I have done'. He was Professor of Poetry at Oxford, 1973–8.

His career as a poet had two clear phases. The poems he wrote in the 1950s, some of which Robert *Conquest published in *New Lines*, are archetypal *Movement pieces: they aim at discipline, a chilly sort of wit, measured understatement; favoured forms include villanelle and *terza rima*; the prevailing influence is *Empson. The last of Wain's poems in this style are gathered in *Weep Before God* (Macmillan/St Martin's, 1961); among them is 'Au Jardin Des Plantes', whose gorilla suffers the 'prodigal idleness' of unemployment, a subject to which Wain's occasional habit of superfluous restatement is well suited. This and several other pieces put the world scathingly to rights.

A radical break is marked by the publication in 1965 of *Wildtrack* (Macmillan/Viking), a long philosophical poem whose opening barrage—'BAM BAM WHEE CRUMP'—blows away all traces of Empsonian restraint. Wain took up Anthony Hartley's challenge to the maturing Movement poet to 'let it rip' and 'risk making a fool of himself'. Subsequent volumes confirmed his belated commitment to modernist principles; the best of them is *Feng* (Macmillan/Viking, 1975), a sequence of poems dealing with the Hamlet story.

Poems 1949–1979 (Macmillan, 1981) is highly selective, tending to suppress the compact earlier work. It shows Wain's preference for 'short-long' poems of between 75 and 150 lines, the length (he said) 'in which Pound was a master in his early days'. MI

Wainwright, Jeffrey (1944–) Born in Stoke-on-Trent, Staffordshire, read English at Leeds University, and was Professor in English at Manchester Metropolitan University until 2008.

Wainwright has been bracketed with Douglas *Dunn and Tony *Harrison as a working-class poet, but in output and method his work is markedly different from theirs. The brief *Selected Poems* (1985) reveals a political poet who aims at an intensity usually thought of as religious. His best-known poem, 'Thomas Muntzer', is a series of dramatic lyrics in which the sixteenth-century Protestant reformer meditates on his visions and eventual defeat; elsewhere, in dealing with his central themes of power and love, Wainwright offers a sense of the commonwealth of human life as—in the absence of another adequate term—sacred ('Transitive').

Whilst Wainwright's poems continually imply the scope of imperial history, they derive their force from regard for people—the drowned girl and the dead of Waterloo in '1815', a drowned sailor in 'The War with Japan'. The poems are characterized by extreme economy and clarity, and Wainwright moves deftly between terseness and full-throated feeling. Because he dramatizes (rather than merely asserting) the field of force binding private and public concerns, the love poems and the more evidently historical-political poems show themselves as part of a single endeavour.

Wainwright's most recent poems are the playfully philosophical sequences of his fifth collection, *Clarity or Death!* (2008), and the quibbling meditations of *The Reasoner* (2012—all Carcanet), which evince the influence of Geoffrey *Hill's later manner. He is also the author of a handbook, *Poetry: The Basics* (Routledge, 2nd edn., 2011) and a collection of essays on Hill, *Acceptable Words* (Manchester University Press, 2005). SO'B*

Wakoski, Diane (1937–) Born in Whittier, California, and in 1960 earned a BA from the University of California at Berkeley. She taught English in a Manhattan junior high from 1963 to 1966, and was granted a Guggenheim fellowship in 1972. Twice married and divorced, she supported herself for many years by giving workshops and readings around the country, and is now Distinguished Professor at Michigan State University.

Wakoski is often associated with the '*Deep Image' poets, such as Robert *Bly and James *Wright, although her concern for plumbing archetypal depths has always exhibited strong surreal and *confessional drives as well, leading to comparisons with Sylvia *Plath. Her first collection was *Coins and Coffins* (1962), but *The George Washington Poems* (1967), which cleverly uses the first president as an avatar for various male roles, *Inside the Blood Factory* (1968), *The Magellanic Clouds* (1970), and *The Motorcycle Betrayal Poems* (1971) are disturbing books that confirmed her reputation.

Wakoski's *The Collected Greed* (Black Sparrow, 1984) completes a sequence begun in the 1960s, and her critical prose can be found in *Towards a New Poetry* (University of Michigan Press, 1979). Her most recent selected poems is *The Butcher's Apron* (Black Sparrow, 2000), which includes a later section of *The Collected Greed*.   EB

Walcott, Derek (1930–) Born in St Lucia, Walcott studied at the University of the West Indies in Jamaica, and in 1953 moved to Trinidad, where he founded the Trinidad Theatre Workshop. He has been publishing poetry and plays for over six decades, starting with *25 Poems* in 1948. He apprenticed himself early on to the English tradition and has never strayed far from the declamatory lyrical line. His mentors include the Elizabethans and Jacobeans, Wordsworth, Tennyson, *Yeats, *Hardy, and Robert *Lowell (who himself sought to incorporate that tradition into his work). Reverberating against this diction one hears the local influences, the dialect phrases and constructions of the Caribbean. The whole heritage is there, but it is quickened and jazzed.

Walcott gradually discarded his early ambition to be a painter, devoting himself instead to poetry and drama. From the time of his first departure for the United States in the 1950s, he has shuttled back and forth between Boston, New York, and St Lucia. The work manifests the contrasts, collisions, and convergences of urban American and West Indian cultures.

In the crisis-ridden decades of the 1950s and 1960s, when poets took up various cudgels—for free verse, projective verse, *Beat prosody, *confessionalism, and so on—Walcott's work was little heeded. He was always to one side of the current excitement. From the 1980s, however, he moved forward to claim his rightful place.

His first collection of poems to appear outside the Caribbean was *In a Green Night* (1962), published by Jonathan Cape in London. Walcott's breakthrough volume, so far as his own development was concerned, was probably *Another Life* (1973), a book-length lyrical saga in which the poet, modulating between first and third persons, dramatized the artistic struggles that finally led him to leave the Caribbean. The staging of episodes reveals something of the playwright's instinct, while the lines themselves manifest an unquenchable lyricism.

Walcott's next collections, *Sea Grapes* (1976), *The Star Apple Kingdom* (1979—all Farrar, Straus/Cape), and *The Fortunate Traveller* (Farrar, Straus, 1981; Faber, 1982) show the poet taking firm control of his idiom—fusing the diction of his masters with his own particularly sensory drives. *Midsummer* (1984), a fifty-four-poem sequence, delights throughout in the freedom that arrives when form and craft become second-nature: 'My palms have been sliced by the twine | Of the craft I have pulled at for more than forty years. | My Ionia is the smell of burnt grass, the scorched handle | of a cistern in August squeaking to rusty islands; | the lines I love have all their knots left in' (from 'XXV').

In 1990, he published the ambitiously epical *Omeros* (both Farrar, Straus/Faber), in which he not only reinterpreted but fundamentally reimagined the core Western

W

legends of the *Iliad* and the *Odyssey*. The work, widely praised—indeed, deemed by many to be Walcott's crowning achievement—can be read as the poet's bid to gather the many strands of Caribbean culture into an emblematic statement that can be read alongside, as well as against, the canonical Homeric text.

Walcott's *Collected Poems* (Farrar, Straus) was published in 1986 (Faber, 1990). He taught for many years at Boston University and travels frequently to give readings or in connection with performances of his many plays. He spends part of every year on St Lucia. In 1992 he was awarded the Nobel Prize for Literature and received the Order of the Caribbean Community. He is also an OBE.

In 1998, Walcott published a collection of essays, *What the Twilight Says*, which includes his contribution to *Homage to Robert Frost* (1996), written with fellow Nobel laureates Seamus *Heaney and Joseph *Brodsky. Two further volumes—*Tiepolo's Hound* (2000), a personal homage to the painter Camille Pisarro featuring the poet's own watercolours, and *The Prodigal* (2005)—were followed by a *Selected Poems* (2007), edited by Edward *Baugh. In his introduction, Baugh comments on the 'self-scrutinising awareness' of Walcott's later poetry. These prolifically metaphorical poems (a fluency that some critics have felt Walcott overuses, to dilution) conjure memories of a travelling life that return repeatedly to the Caribbean. As he comments in *The Prodigal*, an autobiographical odyssey written in dialogue with *Another Life*, 'I should have known that I would wind up beached | as I began'.

In 2009, Walcott's candidacy for the Oxford Professorship of Poetry was withdrawn after the revival in the British media of sexual harassment allegations made against him in America in the 1980s. In 2010 he became Professor of Poetry at the University of Essex. *White Egrets* (2011—all Farrar, Straus/Faber), which won the T. S. Eliot Prize and the OCM Bocas Prize for Caribbean Literature, continues to find inspiration in the seascapes of St Lucia (a former British colony) and looks back on a life during which 'there was no more

Empire all of a sudden'. This poem, 'The Lost Empire', suggests Walcott's affinity as a postcolonial poet with the Irish experience in the same period. Surveying his island home, he observes, 'I'm content as Kavanagh with his few acres', a reference to Patrick *Kavanagh's sonnet, 'Epic' (1951), and its claim that Homer 'made the Iliad from such | A local row'.

With Colbert Nepaulsingh, Baugh has also published a fully annotated critical edition of *Another Life* (Rienner, 2004). *The Haitian Trilogy* (Farrar, Straus, 2002) collects Walcott's plays on the history of the West Indies. For criticism and context, see *Conversations with Derek Walcott* (University Press of Mississippi, 1996), ed. William Baer; Bruce King, *Derek Walcott: A Caribbean Life* (Oxford University Press, 2000); Paul Breslin, *Nobody's Nation: Reading Derek Walcott* (University of Chicago Press, 2001); and Edward Baugh, *Derek Walcott* (Cambridge University Press, 2006; repr. 2012). SPB*

Waldman, Anne (1945–) Born in New Jersey and grew up in Manhattan. She attended Bennington College, where she wrote a study of Theodore *Roethke and was taught by Howard *Nemerov. In the late 1960s, under the influence of *Beat poetry, she started the influential *Angel Hair* magazine and press, and became the director of the *Saint Mark's Church Poetry Project in New York. In 1974, Waldman and Allen *Ginsberg founded the Jack Kerouac School of Disembodied Poetics at the Naropa Institute, Boulder, Colorado, where she is now Distinguished Professor of Poetics.

Waldman was poet-in-residence on Bob Dylan's Rolling Thunder Revue tour of 1975-6, and has frequently collaborated with artists in other modes. She is also renowned for the dramatic readings she gives of her poems, such as 'skin Meat BONES (chant)', where the words of the title are intoned across an octave. The title poem of *Fast Speaking Woman and Other Chants* (City Lights, 1975; revd. ed. 1978) is a long incantation composed on the model of a Mazatec shaman priestess chant. Her emphasis on the poetics of immediate experience reflects both her Buddhist beliefs and her performative feminism.

Waldman's poems have been selected in two overlapping volumes: *Helping the Dreamer* (1966–88) and *In the Room of Never Grieve* (1985–2003). *The Iovis Trilogy: Colors in the Mechanism of Concealment* collects the books of an epic poem in progress since the 1980s (2011—all Coffee House).   JNT

Waldrop, Rosmarie (1935–) Waldrop spent her first twenty three years in Germany, before moving to the United States in 1958 where she earned a PhD from the University of Michigan. She started publishing her poetry in English and translating others' work from French and German in the 1960s. In 1961 she and her husband, the poet Keith Waldrop, began *Burning Deck Magazine*, now Burning Deck Press, an important publisher of innovative poetry and translations.

Waldrop has received numerous awards and fellowships and in 2006 was elected to the American Academy of Arts and Sciences. She is the author of approximately fifty books of poetry, prose, criticism, and translation. Her work shows the influence of some of those she has translated, especially Edmond Jabès' poetry of exile; her own 'transnational' condition; critical examinations of political power—particularly regarding gender, religion, and colonization; linguistic philosophy (above all, Ludwig Wittgenstein); the German/Austrian avant garde; the Vienna Group; and the *Language writing movement, with which she is often associated.

Waldrop's oeuvre is based on a dialogue between philosophic inquiry and the personal aspects of quotidian life, which highlights the dangers of separating the two. Technically, her work shows a general move from highly 'vertical' verse experiment to more spacious and philosophic prose poetry. Her best known work is perhaps her prose-poem trilogy—*The Reproduction of Profiles* (1987), *Lawn of Excluded Middle* (1993), and *Reluctant Gravities* (1999)—collected in one volume, *Curves to the Apple*, in 2006 (New Directions).   ECr

Walker, Kath. *See* NOONUCCAL, OODGEROO.

Walker, Ted (Edward Joseph Walker) (1934–2004) Born in Sussex and educated at St John's College, Cambridge. He was professor of creative writing at New England College, Arundel, Sussex. His prize-winning collections *Fox on a Barn Door* (1965) and *Solitaries* (1967) consisted for the most part of nature poems reflecting the landscape of West Sussex. The chief, and slightly obtrusive, influence upon these was Ted *Hughes; but Walker's technique was more conventional. Personal themes were expressed through observations of landscape in a manner reminiscent of *Hardy. *Gloves for the Hangman* (1975), which marked an advance, cast off the earlier influences and attempted a more direct approach with some success; but the book met with less attention.

Walker was also an accomplished translator of European poetry—see *The Night Bathers* (1970). *The Last of England* (1992—all Cape) was an autobiographical prose volume. After a long silence *Mangoes on the Moon* (London Magazine, 1999) collected Walker's late poems of love and loss. *Minting the Sun* (2010), a posthumous selection edited by Diana Barsham and Ross Hair, was published by the University of Chichester, which also holds his archive.   MS-S*

Wallace, Bronwen (1945–89) Born and lived most of her life in Kingston, Ontario, where she worked in a centre for battered women and children and taught part-time at Queen's University. In addition to freelance writing and editing, she collaborated with Chris Whynot on two films: *All You Have To Do* (1982) and *That's Why I'm Talking* (1987).

Wallace claimed to be concerned with the 'hidden lives' of people and the 'unexpected rituals' by which these hidden lives may be revealed. Thus her fascination with narrative and 'how we tell the story of our lives', which consists of 'detours and double-backs, leaps' of ordinary story-telling. The digression, or lateral shift, which she uses so cleverly, has the effect of increasing the reader's attention and bringing new and unexpected ideas into play. While her poetry, recorded conversations, and interviews reveal the influence of poets such as Al *Purdy and Galway *Kinnell, Wallace's social and domestic parables owe their largest debt to what she calls 'kitchen-table conversation', the nitty-gritty of confession, self-deception, and denial that can be involved in our attempts to communicate.

Her publications include *Signs of the Former Tenant* (1983), *Common Magic* (1985—both Oberon Press), and *The Stubborn Particulars of Grace* (1987). Her first collection of short stories, *People You'd Trust Your Life To* (both McClelland & Stewart), was published posthumously in 1990 (new edn., 2001). See also *Keep That Candle Burning Bright and Other Poems* (Coach House, 1991).   GG

Wallace-Crabbe, Chris(topher) (1934–) Born in Melbourne and Professor Emeritus in the Australian Centre at Melbourne University. Periods in America include a Harkness fellowship (1965–7) and a visiting professorship of Australian Studies at Harvard (1987–8).

His early advocacy of American poets (Robert *Lowell, Wallace *Stevens) demonstrated the sharp eye for shifts in poetic preoccupations which has been a feature of critical work such as his influential essay 'The Habit of Irony: Australian Poets of the Fifties,' in *Meanjin*, *20* (1961); *Melbourne or the Bush* (Angus & Robertson, 1974), which examines different cultural values; *Toil and Spin* (Hutchinson, 1980), which considers different modes of poetic creativity; and *Falling into Language* (Oxford University Press, 1990), which deals with postmodernist issues like 'The Textual Self', or 'Struggling with an Imperial Language'.

In poetry which is equally at home in Melbourne's suburbs (the setting of his 1981 novel *Splinters*) and the great international cities, an interest in complexities and ambiguities of tone, in slippages of language, has been consistent throughout a prolific and protean performance. This began in coolly stoic and intelligent formalism; its most recent manifestations sometimes confuse a prevailing Australian taste for straightforward melancholy by

mixing both sombreness and a jauntily epigrammatic despair with wittily sensuous celebrations of worldly pleasures and glimpses of Gothic nightmares.

For discussion of his work, see *Stop Laughing! This is Serious: Three Studies in Wit and Seriousness in Contemporary Australian Poetry*, by Jennifer Strauss (Foundation for Australian Literature Studies, 1990). *Selected Poems* (1973) drew on five collections; three more preceded *The Amorous Cannibal* (1985), *I'm Deadly Serious* (1988), *For Crying Out Loud* (1990), *Rungs of Time* (1993), and *Selected Poems 1956–94* (1995), all in the Oxford Poets series (Oxford University Press). Later volumes include *Whirling* (Oxford University Press, 1998), *By and Large* (2001), *Next* (2005— both Brandl & Schlesinger), and *Telling a Hawk from a Handsaw* (Oxford Poets/ Carcanet, 2008). *Read It Again* (Salt, 2005) is a wide-ranging study of contemporary poetry from an Australian perspective. In 2011, Wallace-Crabbe was made a Member of the Order of Australia.   JS

Walsh, Catherine (1964–) Born in Dublin, Walsh grew up in the city and rural Wexford. She later lived and taught in Barcelona. With the poet Billy Mills, she runs hardPressed Poetry, which has published and distributed a number of experimental Irish-born poets such as Maurice Scully and Brian *Coffey.

Walsh has spoken in interview of her resistance to an 'ongoing linear tradition' which celebrates 'Irishness' above all. Her own work typically projects fragments of language in sequences that map multiple voices—lyrical, narrative, overheard—in a self-consciously textual landscape: *Short Stories* (North & South, 1989) ends with the words 'an absurd white formality' in the middle of an otherwise empty page. Her early small-press sequences include *Pitch* (1994), published in Durham by Pig Press, and *Idir Eatortha & Making Tents* (1997), published in London by Invisible Books. Her later Dublin sequence, *City West* (2005), has been collected in one volume by Shearsman, who also published *Optic Verve* (2009). Her latest book is

Astonished Birds Cara, Jane, Bob and James (hardPressed, 2012). There is a discussion of Walsh's work in Sarah Broom, *Contemporary British and Irish Poetry* (Palgrave, 2005).   JNT

Wangusa, Timothy (1942–) Born in Bugisu, Uganda. A student at Makerere University, he returned after postgraduate work at Leeds to teach there, becoming full professor in 1981. He was one of the few leading academics, and the only widely published creative writer, to live in Uganda throughout the dictatorship of Amin and Obote's horrific second term. In 1985–6 he was briefly minister of education in the cabinet of a transitional government: in 1989 he was elected MP for Bubulo County, Mbale. He has since acted as literary advisor to the head of state and Vice Chancellor of Kumi University in eastern Uganda.

His novel *Upon This Mountain* (Heinemann, 1989) deals with the conflicts experienced by a village boy educated under colonialism. His verse is charged with a strong sense of African mythologies and speech forms. It confronts a wide range of themes, from the mysteries of Christian faith to topicalities. An ambitious, uneven sequence, 'Anthem for Africa', sets the evils of Amin's Uganda in the context of the entire continent's history. Traces of Shakespeare, Milton, and *Eliot flavour a diction which is at times Parnassian but which at its best is straightforwardly eloquent. His book *Salutations* was published in Nairobi (1977). Wangusa's selected poems, *A Pattern of Dust* (Fountain), appeared in 1994. His later work has been published in *Africa's New Brood: Poems 1985–2005* (Bow & Arrow, 2006).   ALRC

Wantling, William (1933–80) Born in Peoria, Illinois, and after leaving high school at 16 enlisted in the US Marine Corps. Volunteering for combat duty he fought in the Korean War until discharged in 1955. Having experienced morphine in Korea (following an injury), he quickly became addicted to hard drugs on his return to the USA. A failed marriage, and continued use of narcotics, eventually led to his imprisonment in 1958. After release on parole in 1960 Wantling was soon back in San Quentin prison.

Psychic and addiction problems, plus a long list of briefly held jobs, gave Wantling the drifter's aura of an 'on the road' poet typical of the Fifties. His poetic output was small but what was published indicated a vibrant, fresh talent allied to great sensitivity. His highly colloquial poems, often unstructured, dealt with experiences (prison life; addiction; violence) well outside the usual subject-matter for poetry.

The Awakening (1967) contains poetry of pain and despair in brutal urban situations. The love poems are especially poignant and resonant. A British edition of *The Awakening* appeared in 1968, and Wantling was included in *Penguin Modern Poets 12* in the same year. *10,000 r.p.m. and diggin' it, yeah* (1970) and *San Quentin Blues* (1973) offered further outlets for his distinctive work, but like his earlier collections both booklets are now out of print. A selection of Wantling's work was republished in two limited-edition volumes by Tangerine Press: *Only in the Sun* (2008) and *The Fix* (2009).   WM

Warner, Sylvia Townsend (1893–1978) Born and brought up at Harrow School, where her father was a history master. She trained as a composer and musicologist before turning to writing in the mid-1920s. In 1930 she left a busy London literary life and moved to Dorset with the woman poet Valentine Ackland in what turned out to be a lifelong commitment. Warner was a successful novelist in the Twenties, with her early books (especially *Lolly Willowes*, 1926) in the fantastic mode popularized by her friends David Garnett and T. F. Powys, and later she became well known for her short stories, many of which appeared in *The New Yorker*. Warner joined the Communist Party in 1935 and was a prominent political activist, travelling to Spain twice during the Civil War. Her poetry, which was the least public face of a varied writing career, is characterized by sharp wit, rich vocabulary, and a deliberately ambiguous tone. Using mostly traditional forms, domestic themes, and blessed with a gift for lyricism, her work can at first seem an odd off-shoot of the *Georgian school, but the subversive vision and mischievous humour of even her earliest volumes, *The Espalier* (1925) and *Time Importuned* (1928), are determinedly counter-Georgian. A disparate body of work published, often obscurely, over a period of fifty years is distinguished by linguistic and syntactical verve. A significant quantity of her poetry was not published until after her death (*Collected Poems*, 1982). *New Collected Poems*, ed. Claire Harman, was published in 2008 (both Carcanet). Warner wrote seven novels, ten volumes of stories, a biography of T. H. White, and translations from the French. Her *Letters* were published in 1982 (Chatto).

See also Claire Harman, *Sylvia Townsend Warner: A Biography* (1989; new edn., Minerva, 1991) and Wendy *Mulford's biographical study of Warner and Ackland, *This Narrow Place* (Pandora, 1988).   CPH

Warren, Robert Penn (1905–88) Born in Guthrie, Kentucky, and came in at the tail-end of the Southern renaissance, whose main luminaries included William Faulkner, Cleanth Brooks, and John Crowe *Ransom. Warren shared something of the gifts of all three. He collaborated with Cleanth Brooks on the seminal studies *Understanding Poetry* and *Understanding Fiction*, and his own *Selected Essays* reveal insights into a variety of topics in verse and prose. His fiction ran to a long list of novels and two books of short stories; his most famous novel, *All The King's Men* (Harcourt, 1946; Eyre & Spottiswoode, 1948), a study of small-town and state politics based on the career of the Louisiana governor Huey Long, was made into a successful film in the 1940s.

But the central thrust of Warren's literary career lay in the field of poetry, though it was not until late in his career—after the age of 50 in effect—that his best work and his major acclaim were to come. The bridge work between his early and later verse career is the narrative poem—or verse novel—*Brother To Dragons*, which draws on an actual set of events, the murderous Oedipal fixation of Lilburn Lewis, a nephew

of Thomas Jefferson. The brooding violence and Southern guilt of this poem surface increasingly in Warren's later verse, though here they may owe something to the extended narratives of Robinson *Jeffers. Indeed, the controlled ruggedness of Jeffers' free verse may be an important contributor to the formation of Warren's distinctive later style. The shift in this between autobiographical anecdote and meditation and a repeated interest in exploring objective narratives with a moral to them may be seen as the special polarity of Warren's career, something which marks a comparison with the verse of Thomas *Hardy, another poet whose rough-hewn individual style was only perfected in older age.

Poems like 'Star-Fall' and 'The Mission' illustrate how Warren increasingly worked. An everyday incident is clearly described, the human elements are outlined against the vast unyielding continuity of the universe, and a gloomy or inspiring moral is drawn. This is a crude analysis, and fails to unveil the grandeur and huge emotion Warren can deploy through these bare frameworks; but the frameworks themselves, prosaic and humble, enable the vast sensations to stoop to an earthy dimension, and the poems avoid—almost always—the airy emptiness which ventures of this kind so often drift into. There is much of the honesty of *Frost in Warren, but none of his cracker-barrel flippancy. On the other hand, there is rarely Frost's sense of balance, at line level, between a rigid metre and a varying rhythm, and when Warren attempts rhyming and metrical poems he is not often at his best.

John Burt edited the *Collected Poems* in 1998 and a *Selected Poems* in 2001, both for Louisiana State University Press.   GMacB

Warren, Rosanna (1953–) The daughter of Robert Penn *Warren and Eleanor Clark, Warren was born in Fairfield, Connecticut, and educated at Yale and at Johns Hopkins universities. She teaches at Boston University.

She developed an early interest in Latin and French poetry and an apprehension of or sense of poetic form when required to memorize French poems in her *lycée*. Her father encouraged her to read the poetry of Donne, Blake, *Hardy, and *Ransom. Of these, Hardy has remained an abiding influence together with Baudelaire, whom she read earlier, in addition to her more recent study of Greek lyric poetry, especially Sappho.

In her undergraduate years at Yale she was introduced to the poetry and painting of Max Jacob, whose work she especially admires. Some of her best poems are inspired by or are about painting and about the relationship of art to nature, but her subjects also include domestic life, love, war, and death. One of her most moving poems is on the Civil War Battle of Antietam Creek. All of her poetry is written in carefully crafted free verse combining strong cadences with freshly perceived particulars, and creating a density of style reminiscent of Greek sculpture, as in 'Painting a Madonna' and 'A Cypress'.

Warren's first chapbook, *Snow Day* (Palaemon, 1981), was incorporated into *Each Leaf Shines Separate* (1984). Warren has published three further collections—*Stained Glass* (1993), *Departure* (2003), and *Ghost in a Red Hat* (2011)—and a personal study of lyric poetry from Sappho to Louise *Glück, *Fables of the Self* (2008—all Norton). She has also edited William *Arrowsmith's translations of Montale.   DES

Watkins, Vernon (Phillips) (1906–67) Born in Maesteg in Wales and educated at Repton and at Magdalene College, Cambridge, where he was a contemporary of William *Empson and Kathleen *Raine. Out of sympathy with the prevailing positivism at Cambridge, he left without taking a degree. In 1927 he had a breakdown, following a vision that he had conquered time. After he recovered he went to work at Lloyds Bank in Swansea, where he remained for the rest of his life, refusing promotion to devote himself to poetry. He died of a heart attack while playing tennis in Seattle, where he had gone as a visiting professor.

Watkins wrote steadily throughout his career, and by the time he met Dylan *Thomas in 1934 he had written a thousand poems and published none. Encouraged by Thomas, he allowed his poems to appear in *Wales* and *Life and Letters Today*; but his first book, *The Ballad of the Mari Lwyd*, did not appear until 1941 when he was 35.

Watkins was a great admirer of *Yeats, a visit to whom in 1938 was the occasion of a long poem, 'Yeats in Dublin'. However, Watkins' serene simplicity had little in common with Yeats' rhetorical grandeur. Another important formative influence was his friendship with Dylan Thomas; and their correspondence, published as *Dylan Thomas: Letters to Vernon Watkins* (1957) and later as *Letters to Vernon Watkins* (1988) and *Letters to Dylan Thomas* (1988), constitutes an important poetic document.

Watkins said that he could never write a poem dominated by time: constancy within change he recognized as the theme that engaged his imagination. His poetry draws on and attempts to create myth, because he saw myth as a redemptive process constantly re-enacted. For all his insistence on simplicity of impulse, Watkins was a learned poet: he translated Heine's *The North Sea* (1957), and his *Selected Verse Translations* appeared in 1977.

His *Collected Poems* were published in 1986 (Golgonooza). *New Selected Poems* (Carcanet), ed. Richard Ramsbotham, appeared in 2006, with a foreword by Rowan Williams. See also *Vernon Watkins*, by R. Mathias (University of Wales Press, 1974) and *Portrait of a Friend* by Gwen Watkins (Gomer, 1983; also as *Dylan Thomas: Portrait of a Friendship*, University of Washington Press, 1985).   ATT

Watson, Stephen (1954–2011) Born and educated in Cape Town, Watson was a poet, scholar and critic. He was professor in the English Department of University of Cape Town and director of the university's Centre for Creative Writing. He wrote nine collections of poetry and three books of non-fiction as well as editing books including *A City Imagined: Cape Town and the Meanings of a Place* (Penguin, 2006).

Through *Poems: 1977–1982* (Bateleur, 1982), *In This City* (David Philip, 1986), and *Cape Town Days* (Skotnes & Clarke's

Bookshop, 1989), Watson emerged as a lyrical poet writing extensively about Cape Town. Sceptical of an increasingly politicized South African poetry, the motifs which pervade Watson's poetry—desire, solitude, and the harsh beauty of the Cape landscape—engaged with politics obliquely, if at all, which drew criticism from some of his contemporaries. *Return of the Moon: Versions from the /Xam* (Carrefour, 1991) is a poetic reworking of the linguist Wilhelm Bleek's records of Cape Bushman myths and legends. More recently, in *The Other City: Selected Poems 1977–1999* (David Philip, 2000) and *The Light Echo And Other Poems* (Penguin, 2007), Watson's characteristic long-lined poems with their accumulating phrases reveal landscapes and intimate relationships through which (as in the phenomenon of a light echo) something hoped for, or lost, is perceived. Frequently drawing from the twentieth-century European poetic tradition, Watson nodded to Miłosz, Herbert, and others in both his poems and his collection of essays, *The Music of Ice* (Penguin, 2010).   KK

Watten, Barrett (1948–) Born in California, Watten studied at the Massachusetts Institute of Technology, University of California, Berkeley (where he read biochemistry), and the Iowa Writers' Workshop. He teaches at Wayne State University in Detroit, and is married to the poet Carla *Harryman. At Berkeley, Watten met Ron *Silliman and Robert *Grenier, friendships that would become central to the *Language poetry movement. In 1971, he and Grenier started the magazine *This*. Watten became sole editor in 1974, the same year that he began This Press. From 1982, he edited *Poetics Journal* with Lyn *Hejinian.

In its formal resistance to discursive continuity, and its juxtaposition of geopolitical and quotidian registers, Watten's mode of Language writing seems closest to the political critique of Bruce *Andrews. Works such as *Progress* (Roof, 1985; repr. with *Under Erasure*, Green Integer, 2004), however—Watten's commentary in broken quatrains on Reagan-era America—also point to his admiration for the lyrical collage of John *Ashbery and Clark *Coolidge

('Shadow, | fog. Collapses self, | And invading enemy wins'). *Frame* (Sun & Moon, 1997) collects the poetry of two decades, from 1971 to 1990 (his first pamphlet was *Radio Day in Soma City* (privately printed, 1971)). *Bad History* (Atelos, 1998; repr. 2002) is a prose poem 'counter-epic' of the first Gulf War. Watten has published two volumes of criticism, *Total Syntax* (Southern Illinois University Press, 1985) and *The Constructivist Moment: From Material Text to Cultural Poetics* (Wesleyan University Press, 2003).   JNT

Wayman, Tom (Thomas Ethan Wayman) (1945–) Born in Hawkesbury, Ontario. He took his BA at the University of British Columbia and his MFA at the University of California, Irvine. In the late 1960s he became involved with the radical left on a number of American campuses. On his return to Vancouver he experienced difficulty in finding a teaching job and worked for a time as a building labourer.

Wayman's first book, *Waiting for Wayman* (McClelland & Stewart, 1973), records his discovery that all human relations, even the most intimate, are distorted by the economic forces of capitalism. Influenced by Pablo Neruda, he places everyday North American events within an international context. His later collections continue this vein but emphasize the lives of average workers, explaining how the economic system impoverishes their lives. In *Inside Job: Essays on the New Work Writing* (1983), he argues that poetry needs to express the actual moment in which we live, and that since work takes up a large part of our lives, poetry must similarly be about work. *In A Small House on the Outskirts of Heaven* (1989), a collection of poetry, also contains a prose Afterword entitled 'Work, Money, Authenticity'. In his accounts of the workplace and the treatment of workers, Wayman writes in the narrative mode and in free verse. He employs a hard-hitting vernacular, is often anecdotal, and expresses anger at particular people and institutions; his poetry also contains much wit and quiet irony about his own place as a poet and worker in society. A selected poems, *Did I Miss Anything?*, appeared in 1993.

In 2001 he edited *The Dominion of Love*, an anthology of Canadian love poems. *My Father's Cup* (2002) was shortlisted for the Governor General's Award for Poetry. Since 2002, Wayman has taught at the University of Calgary. *High Speed Through Shoaling Water* (2007) reflects on his life in the mountain valleys of south-eastern British Columbia, while *Dirty Snow* addresses the war in Afghanistan (2012—all Harbour).   RBH

Wearne, Alan (1948–) Grew up in the east Melbourne suburb of Blackburn. He joined with John A. *Scott and Laurie *Duggan in the Monash University poetry readings, and in the 1979 Victorian elections stood as the Labor candidate for Nunawading. He has lived in most major Australian cities, and the verse novels that centre his poetic achievement are focused on their (to him) endlessly various suburbs, their subcultures and sublanguages.

The pamphlet *Public Relations* (Makar, 1972) is memorable for off-key monologues like 'St Bartholomew Remembers Jesus Christ as an Athlete'. *New Devil, New Parish* (University of Queensland Press, 1976) includes the verse novella 'Out Here', a Browning-esque monologue wheel in which relatives and teachers puzzle over a teenager's self-mutilation in the school toilets. In *The Nightmarkets* (Penguin, 1986) Wearne adopted a final strategy of Browning's—length. The monologues in this 11,000-line verse novel began as a journalist's investigation of political corruption, broadened into a study of prostitution and sexual obsession, feminism and political charisma, and at last became a *Ulysses*-like paean to Melbourne's cultural and linguistic diversity. *The Lovemakers* is a still more prodigious, 750-page verse novel, broken into two instalments: in *Saying All the Great Sexy Things* (Penguin, 2001), the erotic motives of a weave of Sydney and Melbourne suburbanites are tracked from their school and university days through a range of professional and commercial adventurism; the second instalment, *Money and Nothing* (ABC, 2004), numbers in its cast the arch-criminals and plutocrats of the Nineties, drug-runners operating out of Thailand and investment tycoons bantering about

their Manets and Monets. Monologues are composed in villanelles or sestinas, limericks or *ottava rima*, their diction teetering on the edge of the inane and sublime.

Wearne has written a comic detective novel on Australian Rules football, *Kicking in Danger* (Black Pepper, 1997). His *Australian Song Book* (Giramondo, 2008), which he modelled on Manuel de Falla's *Popular Spanish Songs*, taps as well into popular Australian tradition. An entry on Wearne in the *Dictionary of Literary Biography: Australian Writers, 1975–2000*, ed. Selina Samuels (2006), refers to important publications on his writing.   CP

Weaver, Afaa M. (Afaa Michael) (1951–) Born and grew up in Baltimore, Maryland. Weaver studied at the university there for two years, served in the US Army Reserve, and worked in Baltimore factories and as a freelance journalist and small-press editor. Formerly known as Michael S. Weaver, he adopted the Igbo name 'Afaa' in 1997. He now teaches and directs the Zora Neale Hurston Literary Center at Simmons College in Massachusetts.

Weaver's first volume of poems, *Water Song* (University Press of Virginia), appeared in 1985. In the same year that he received a fellowship from the National Endowment for the Arts, and began postgraduate study at Brown University, where he wrote a play for his MA thesis. *The Plum Flower Dance: Poems 1985–2005* (University of Pittsburgh Press, 2007) surveys two decades of work during which he has become increasingly interested in Chinese poetry and philosophy. Weaver is a widely admired figure in contemporary African-American literature, and was named the first elder of the *Cave Canem group. He has also published short fiction and edited an anthology of writing on black family life, *These Hands I Know* (Sarabande, 2002).   JNT

Webb, Francis (1925–73) Born Francis Webb-Wagg in Adelaide and raised in North Sydney by his paternal grandparents after his mother died and father suffered a breakdown when he was two. He was

w

educated by the Christian Brothers, then joined the Royal Australian Air Force in the Second World War and trained in Canada as a wireless air-gunner, although he never saw combat.

The Webb-Wagg family's love of music, art, hiking, and sailing influenced the young prodigy profoundly, from his first poem around age seven, 'The Hero of the Plain', to his first attempts at the Hopkins-esque epic in 'Disaster Bay' (1946–47) and the dramatic monologues of 'A Drum for Ben Boyd' (1948). While in high school, he was published by Douglas *Stewart in *The Bulletin*, shortening his surname to Webb. Stewart also arranged for Angus and Robertson to publish Webb's first collection, *A Drum for Ben Boyd*, in 1948 (with illustrations by another mentor-to-be, Norman Lindsay). He commented later: 'It was major poetry. For Webb to have written it at the age of twenty-two is an extraordinary achievement; without parallel, I imagine, considering its maturity and merits, in Australian literature.'

By this stage, Webb had returned to Canada; this period from 1947–9, complete with jaunts to Buffalo, Boston, and Nantucket, exposed him to international views on the Holocaust and Cold War as well as the Americans Hart *Crane and Robert *Lowell, who inspired Webb to write more openly about himself and his 'strict, if not puritanical' Catholicism (as he later put it). *Leichhardt in Theatre* (1952), with its title poem pre-dating Patrick White's interpretation of the same explorer-narrative in *Voss* (1957), demonstrates the tug-of-war the poet felt at the time between the secular, heroic tastes of his Sydney mentors and his increasing fascination with modernist, confessional, and Christian mystical poetics.

In Montreal in 1949, Webb fell out with Lindsay (forty-six years his senior) over the latter's anti-Semitism and perceived accusations of 'corruption' and 'abstraction'. En route to England shortly thereafter, Webb had a personal crisis about his future direction and the guilt he felt for not challenging Lindsay earlier. He threw Lindsay's initial sketches for *Leichhardt in Theatre* into the Atlantic and on arrival at his aunt's house in Epsom suffered a breakdown which resulted in his initial experience of institutionalization (though he had visited his father at a young age, an experience explored in 'Palace of Dreams' and 'Hospital Night'). Apart from three years back in Australia, Webb would remain institutionalized or in short-term accommodation in a variety of punitive and restorative settings, under equally transitory diagnoses including 'persecution mania', temporary epilepsy, and ultimately chronic schizophrenia. He spent 1950–3 living in Sydney, Melbourne, and Adelaide and visiting Perth. Finally able to write with impunity, he self-published and hand-sold his majestic third collection *Birthday* (1953), which featured an extended sequence on St Francis, a radio play about Hitler's last days, and social perspectives on the mistreatment of migrants and Aborigines. Upon return to England he was again institutionalized, but found solace in the Norfolk region of his ancestors, engaging with its landscape, history, and art in his sequence 'Around Costessey'.

Webb returned to Australia in 1960 with help from his poet friends David *Campbell, Rosemary *Dobson, Nan MacDonald, Vincent *Buckley, and others, who would continue to support him despite the frustrations of an illness that was either innately degenerative or made so by years of confinement, medication, and electric-shock treatment. *Socrates and Other Poems* (1961), *The Ghost of the Cock* (1964, featuring a radio play in the shadow of the Cuban Missile Crisis), and *Collected Poems* (1969) suggested to *Generation of '68 poets such as Bruce *Beaver, Robert *Adamson and Thomas *Shapcott that this post-war prodigy, still only in his forties, truly belonged to them (though others, such as Rodney *Hall, found his work too Catholic-oriented and scornful of the body). Webb's dense, ambitious, metaphor-laden style means that, like his favourite composers Mahler and Bruckner, he can confound readers new to his work but also reward the dedicated. In 2011 an expanded and annotated edition of *Collected Poems* was published by University of Western Australia, ed. Toby Davidson. See also the biography by Michael Griffiths, *God's Fool* (Angus & Robertson, 1991).   TD

Webb, Harri (1920–94) Born in Swansea into a family whose roots were in Gower, and educated at Magdalen College, Oxford, where he read Romance languages. After serving in the Second World War as an interpreter with the British Naval Mission to the French Provisional Government, he worked with Keidrych Rhys at the Druid Press in Carmarthen, and eventually as a librarian, first at Dowlais in Merthyr Tydfil and later at Mountain Ash in Glamorgan. He entered politics in the ranks of the Welsh Republican Movement, but from 1959 was active on behalf of Plaid Cymru (the Welsh nationalist party), editing the party's newspaper. In 1965, while living in Merthyr Tydfil, he was associated with Meic Stephens in the launching of the magazine *Poetry Wales*, and they collaborated in the writing of political ballads.

His early poems appeared in the magazine *Wales* during the 1940s and (with those of Meic Stephens and Peter Griffith) in the volume *Triad* (1963), but he found his mature voice as a contributor to the early numbers of *Poetry Wales*. Most of the poems in his first collection, *The Green Desert* (1969), are about the history and social condition of the Welsh people. They are witty, erudite, and iconoclastic, and although sometimes propagandist, they are never crude or hectoring. His reputation as a poet of the Welsh nationalist cause was consolidated by his second volume, *A Crown for Branwen* (1974—both Gomer), which included one of his few poems in Welsh, 'Colli Iaith' (Losing a Language), which achieved the status of a folk-song.

During the 1970s Harri Webb began writing scripts for television, and his work was frequently to be heard on the BBC programme *Poems and Pints*. Thereafter his verse aimed at a wider audience: he still wrote about Welsh historical characters but more often in a light-hearted or satirical way.

In 1993, University of Wales Press published a book-length study of Webb's life and work by Brian Morris. Meic Stephens has edited Webb's *Collected Poems* (Gomer, 1995), as well as volumes of his political and literary journalism (*No Half-way House* (Y Lolfa, 1997) and *Militant Muse* (Seren, 1998)), and *Looking Up England's Arsehole* (Y Lolfa, 2000), a collection of nationalist lyrics and 'boozy ballads'.   MS

Webb, Phyllis (1927–) Born in Victoria, British Columbia. She has lived and worked all over Canada, and has in recent years settled on Saltspring Island off Canada's west coast. She has been a politician, secretary, radio producer, and university lecturer. Notorious for her long silences, she has nevertheless produced a considerable body of lyrical poems and is an influence on writers of two generations.

Her third book, *Naked Poems* (Periwinkle, 1965), has become a key text in contemporary Canadian literature. It is a suite of intimate stanzas often cited as the source for what many critics call the characteristic Canadian invention—the lyric become a long poem.

Her subject is often suicide or other deaths. The territory is variously the personal psyche, world politics, or other literatures. The poetry itself is the means by which one may avoid despair and seek beauty, a tactic for survival. Webb's persona often seems highly strung, given to a music whose source is next to pain. It often celebrates heroes who have been to the edge of death—Jacobo Timmerman, the Old Testament's Daniel, Dostoyevsky. In recent years it has named other women poets and their need to be heard.

Webb's work before 1980 can be found in *The Vision Tree: Selected Poems* (Talonbooks, 1982), which won the Governor General's Award. Her important 1980 volume, *Wilson's Bowl*, had not been nominated for this award, provoking a group of poets including Margaret *Atwood and bp *Nichol to send her an alternative cash prize as a gesture of recognition and esteem. *Hanging Fire* (both Coach House) appeared in 1990. In 1992, Webb was made an Officer of the Order of Canada. *Nothing but Brush Strokes* is a volume of selected prose (NeWest, 1995). See Pauline Butling, *Seeing in the Dark: the Poetry of Phyllis Webb* (Wilfrid Laurier University Press, 1997) and Stephen Collis, *Phyllis Webb and the Common Good: Poetry/Anarchy/Abstraction* (Talonbooks, 2010).   GHB*

W

Wedde, Ian (1946–) Born in Blenheim, New Zealand. After early years spent largely overseas, Wedde returned to New Zealand for university study, gaining an MA from Auckland in 1968. He began publishing poetry in 1966. After travelling through Asia, Europe, and North Africa, Wedde worked in Jordan and Syria, and then in England, where he was poetry critic for the *London Magazine*. A poem sequence, *Homage to Matisse* (Amphedesma, 1971), was published in London. The years of travel inform Wedde's New-Zealand-published first collection, *Made Over* (Chan, 1974). The book made clear his interest in the poetics of William Carlos *Williams.

Returning to New Zealand, Wedde settled in Otago, 1972–5. The birth of his first son in 1972 inspired *Earthly: Sonnets for Carlos* (Amphedesma, 1975), a highly reticulated sequence of sixty free-form sonnets embodying Wedde's ambition to connect domestic and political landscapes. Outside the sonnets, Wedde explored other 'worlds within worlds' and diverse notions of responsibility ('the ability to respond'). The long poem *Pathway to the Sea* (1975), from Hawk Press, denounced the proposed siting of an aluminium smelter near a local bird sanctuary. A second collection, *Spells For Coming Out* (Auckland University Press, 1977), also belongs to the Otago period.

In 1975 Wedde moved to Wellington, where his literary activities ranged from script-writing for experimental theatre to co-editing the tabloid *Spleen*. A first novel, *Dick Seddon's Great Dive*, was published in 1976, and Wedde began the research on Pacific whaling that became crucial to his poetry and fiction from 1976 on.

Longer forms and a darker vision characterize the poems of *Castaly* (1980) and *Tales of Gotham City* (1984—both Auckland University Press). *Georgicon* (Victoria University Press, 1984) proposes new uses for the elements of irony and affectionate parody which are strongly developed in Wedde's writing. Other projects of the 1980s included publication of *The Shirt Factory and Other Stories* (1981) and co-editing the *Penguin Book of Contemporary New Zealand Verse* (1985, revd. edn., 1989).

In 1986 Wedde published an epic novel, *Symmes Hole*, and in 1987 assembled a selected poems, *Driving into the Storm* (Oxford University Press). A comic novel, *Survival Arts*, followed in 1988. The most recent collection of poems, his fourteenth, is *Good Business* (Auckland University Press, 2009). Between 1994 and 2004, Wedde was head of art and visual culture at Museum of New Zealand Te Papa Tongarewa. He was made an ONZM in 2010, and Poet Laureate of New Zealand 2011–13. ML

Weiner, Hannah (1928–97) Born in Providence, Rhode Island, and attended Radcliffe College. She then settled in New York, where she participated in performance-art happenings and began writing poetry.

Weiner's work is often associated with the *Language poets, an avant-garde group who emerged in the late 1960s and 1970s. *Clairvoyant Journal* (Angel Hair, 1973), her best-known publication, is a series of experimental poems that she claimed were partially composed of words she saw on various surfaces. As Weiner writes in an epigraph to the book, 'I SEE words on my forehead IN THE AIR on other people on the typewriter on the page.' This 'clairvoyant' method of composition became a defining feature of subsequent work. Much of it is characterized by its use of multiple speakers, often indicated through typographical differences: capital letters and italics interrupt a regular font to indicate polyvocality. Weiner suffered from schizophrenia, a factor many consider to be connected to her methods of composition. But her inclusion of multiple voices, and the resulting destabilization of the lyric self within her poetry, is also characteristic of Language poetry more generally: it makes clear the postmodern move away from authenticity and self-expression, and towards a more conceptual investigation of language itself.

Weiner's publications include *Magritte Poems* (Poetry Newsletter, 1970), *Spoke* (Sun & Moon, 1984), and *We Speak Silent* (Roof, 1997). See also the selected volume

Hannah Weiner's Open House (Kenning, 2007), ed. Patrick F. Durgin.   SRO

Weiss, Theodore (1916–2003) Born in Reading, Pennsylvania, and educated at Muhlenberg College and Columbia University. He married Renée Karol in 1941; in 1943 the Weisses founded an influential literary magazine, the *Quarterly Review*. The recipient of many honours, including a Guggenheim fellowship, Weiss was the subject of a documentary film, *A Year in the Life of a Poem* (1988). He taught at Yale, Bard, Washington University, the Massachusetts Institute of Technology, and, for over twenty years, at Princeton. Weiss lived in Princeton and continued to edit the *Quarterly Review* together with his wife.

Weiss was a prolific essayist and critic as well as poet. His criticism includes a selection of the notebooks of Gerard Manley Hopkins (1945) and *The Breath of Clowns and Kings: Shakespeare's Early Comedies and Histories* (1971). He was the author of twelve volumes of poetry, including *From Princeton One Autumn Afternoon: Collected Poems* (New York, 1989).

Weiss' poetry, while not at all inaccessible, is perhaps best summed up as quirky in style. A tone of jocular alertness informs poems which take bird-like hops down or across the page: short lines often seem to articulate brief arcs of somewhat fragmented thoughts. Weiss' poetry evokes the visible world of nature and cities, domestic interiors and artefacts, but it is also constantly pulled toward the kind of abstract questions posed in the title-poem of *From Princeton One Autumn Afternoon*, an epistolary meditation on language, fame, and mortality. Weiss' work manages to combine a serene sense of the absurd with an anxious awareness of the clutter and detritus of a crowded century, a chaotic culture. A *Selected Poems* (TriQuarterly Books/ Northwestern University Press) appeared in 1995.   RHa

Welish, Marjorie (1944–) Born and grew up in New York City. Welish studied Art History at Columbia University, and taught for many years at the Pratt Institute. She has held visiting posts in poetry at the universities of Brown and Cambridge, and is now Distinguished Lecturer in Literature at Brooklyn College. She is also a painter and an art critic.

The originality of Welish's 'destabilized or folded poetry' (David Shapiro) has been widely admired by her avant-garde peers in Britain and America. As she has said of Barbara *Guest, her writing, like her painting, 'decomposes reference' to inhabit a *Steinian space between image and abstraction, contemplating 'the matted | information' of the page as a surface 'smeared with process'. As in Stein and Guest, too, wit and lyricism gesture towards the subject so abstracted: 'the excited jets surrounding these inquiries'.

The Annotated 'Here' and Selected Poems (Coffee House, 2000) includes work from Welish's first four books: *Handwritten* (SUN Press, 1979), *Two Poems* (Z Press, 1981), *The Windows Flew Open* (Burning Deck, 1991), and *Casting Sequences* (University of Georgia Press, 1993). Three later volumes have appeared from Coffee House Press: *Word Group* (2004), *Isle of the Signatories* (2008), and *In the Futurity Lounge / Asylum for Indeterminacy* (2012). Welish's art criticism has been selected in *Signifying Art: Essays on Art after 1960* (Cambridge University Press, 1999). *Of the Diagram: The Work of Marjorie Welish* (Slought, 2003) collects conference papers on her writing and art.   JNT

Wellesley, Dorothy (Violet), Duchess of Wellington (1889–1956) Born in Berkshire. Her father died young; her mother married the Earl of Scarborough in 1899, thus introducing Dorothy to a world in which her own subsequent marriage to Gerald, seventh Duke of Wellington, in 1914, firmly established her.

Wellesley liked to experiment with an erudition never quite suited to her romantic impulsiveness; her first book, *Poems* (1920), betrayed this mixture of languor and aspiration. Not until 1934, and her *Poems of Ten Years*, did she benefit from any critical reassessment: she was praised for the detail with which she observed natural objects, and for the vigorous, if melodramatic, intensity of her laments over the suppression of the natural world by the commercial. But it was only when W. B. *Yeats read her poem 'Horses', which he included in his *Oxford Book of Modern Verse* (1936), that Wellesley found an influential champion. He wrote his *Letters on Poetry* (1940) to her, and enthusiastically introduced a new selection of her work in 1936. 'Matrix', which Yeats proclaimed one of the most moving philosophical poems of the age, is a strange, visionary assertion of the womb as the origin of the masculine soul; 'Fire' exhibits Wellesley's 'frenzied grandeur', as Yeats termed it, as well as her recurrent preoccupation with the elements, and the sequence 'Deserted House' is a luminous, if grotesque, revisitation of childhood.

Wellesley collected her poems in *Early Light* (Hart-Davis, 1955). See also her autobiography, *Far Have I Travelled* (Barrie, 1952).   MRW

Wells, Robert (1947–   ) Born in Oxford. He read classics and English at King's College, Cambridge, has lived in Iran, and farmed in England and Italy.

His farming experience is closely associated with a prevalent theme in his poetry—love of the earth and the spiritual benefit of labouring in the fields, of establishing a union and communion with the earth, as expressed in his poems 'The Winter's Task' and 'Further on Down' in his first volume of verse, *The Winter's Task* (1977). It naturally followed that the poem chosen for his first major translation would be Virgil's *Georgics* (1982), a poem that he says demonstrates the value of cultivating the land with one's own hands. In his next translation, *The Idylls of Theocritus* (1988), he explains in his introduction his endeavour to reveal the poems as they truly are, unobscured by the pastoral tradition they stimulated. Both translations, written in unrhymed lines of five accents, succeed in conveying the sense and tone of the original text without being exactly literal. See *Collected Poems and Translations* (2009—all Carcanet).   DES

Wendt, Albert (1939–) Born in Apia, Samoa, Wendt's fiction, poetry, criticism, and editorial work has made him an important figure in New Zealand and Pacific literature. He studied history at Victoria University in Wellington, and subsequently taught in Samoa, Fiji, where he was pro-vice-chancellor at the University of the South Pacific, Hawaii, and Auckland, where he is emeritus professor. In 2001, Wendt was made a Companion of the Order of New Zealand.

Wendt's first book was a novel, *Sons for the Return Home* (1973), and he continues to be best known as a writer of fiction. But his poetry, which begins with Inside *Us the Dead: Poems 1961–1974* (Longman, 1976), is also significant for its experimentation between Samoan oral tradition and postmodern poetics. The volume's vividly descriptive title poem is an autobiographical sequence on the poet's family and colonized history of Polynesia. *Shaman of Visions* (Auckland University Press/Oxford University Press, 1984) includes the comic-philosophical sequence 'Where the Mind Is, or, a Conversation With My Mind'. His later books include *Photographs* (1995) and *The Book of the Black Star* (2002—both Auckland University Press), a sequence in words and pictures, each page a hand-drawn poster-poem concerning the mysterious force of the title. *The Adventures of Vela* (HUIA, 2009), a mythological novel in verse, won a Commonwealth Writer's Prize. See Paul Sherrad, *Albert Wendt and Pacific Literature: Circling the Void* (Manchester University Press, 2003).   JNT

Wevill, David (Anthony) (1935–   ) A Canadian citizen, he was born in Japan, educated in Canada and Cambridge, England, and now teaches at the University of Texas. His early poems, particularly those collected in *A Christ of the Ice-Floes* (Macmillan, 1966), gained attention in England owing to his association with the *Group and with Peter *Redgrove. The chief influences on his work have remained the psychological theories of Jung, and such Spanish-language poets as Paz, Neruda and Lorca. The Jungian 'search', an admittedly circular one, is Wevill's main theme, and so his is a poetry that needs to be read in its entirety to be fully appreciated. Moreover, in later work, such as that collected in *Figure of Eight* (Exile, 1984; Shearsman, 1988), a somewhat more epigrammatic quality became apparent, even though the mage-like narrator continued to be present. Wevill translated, with Edwin *Morgan, *Selected Poems* by the Hungarians Sandor Weöres and Ferenc Juhász. See *Departures: Selected Poems* (Shearsman, 2003) and *To Build My Shadow A Fire: The Poetry and Translations of David Wevill*, ed. Michael McGriff (Truman State University Press, 2010).   MS-S*

Whalen, Philip (1923–2002) Born in Portland, Oregon, and educated there at Reed College, where he roomed with the poets Lew Welch and Gary *Snyder. He served in the US Air Force during the Second World War. His growing involvement with Zen Buddhism culminated in 1973 with his ordination as a priest. He then lived on a Buddhist commune in San Francisco.

Whalen was an eccentric but respected figure in recent American poetry, with strong links to the *Beat movement and the *San Francisco group. His spiritual authority as a Buddhist priest consorts oddly with his garrulous, quirky manner; many of his poems are long, free-associative meditations that snake their way among references to food, politics, classical music, science, Greek literature, and similarly eclectic topics. Whalen is fond of various visual tricks involving typography and spacing, and he occasionally even incorporated little drawings and diagrams in his poems. At times his later poems move towards the contemplative quietness associated with Zen, but for the most part he attempts to wed his spiritual concerns with a restless, self-consciously rhetorical sensibility that is more American than Japanese.

A selected poems, *Overtime*, appeared in 1999 (Penguin) and a *Collected Poems* in 2007 (Wesleyan University Press), both edited by Michael Rothenberg. A foreword by Snyder and an introduction by Leslie *Scalapino attest to Whalen's high reputation among his contemporaries. As Tom *Raworth has written: 'For more than forty years Philip Whalen's books have been among the very few my hand reaches for

from the shelf to open at random and read: I have never been disappointed.'   RG*

Wheatley, David (1970–) Born in Dublin and grew up in Bray, Co. Wicklow. Wheatley studied at Trinity College, Dublin where he wrote a doctoral thesis on Samuel *Beckett and began *Metre* magazine with Justin *Quinn. He taught for many years at the University of Hull, and is now a senior lecturer in English at Aberdeen.

Wheatley has translated poems from Irish, edited the verse of Beckett and James Clarence Mangan, and is also a widely published critic who has promoted alternative canons of poetry in Britain and Ireland. His own books, all published by The Gallery Press and beginning with *Thirst* (1997), reflect the spread of his admirations, as well as a life lived between two countries: from the meditative formalism of the Dublin sonnet sequence dedicated to Mangan in *Misery Hill* (2000) to the *Cobbing-esque sonnet of dead-end two-syllable phrases in *Mocker* (2006), a collection centred on the estuarial landscapes of Hull.

Like Peter *Reading, whom he has praised, Wheatley's coolly ironic imagination is attracted both to the dehumanized oddities of urban life and the otherworld of ornithology. *A Nest on the Waves* (2010), his fourth collection, also brought out his range as a traveller in other languages and cultures, as in the expansive 'Lament for Ali Farka Touré', the African blues musician.   JNT

Wheeler, Susan (1955–) Wheeler is the author of five books of poetry, including a selected volume (*Assorted Poems,* Farrar, Strauss, 2009), and *Record Palace*, a novel (Graywolf, 2005). Her first book of poems, *Bag o'Diamonds* (University of Georgia Press, 1993), was chosen by James *Tate for the Norma Farber First Book Award. Since then, she has been awarded the Witter Bynner Prize for Poetry from the American Academy of Arts & Letters, and fellowships from the John Simon Guggenheim Foundation and the New York Foundation for the Arts. Wheeler's collagist poetics are derived from the *New York School, particularly John *Ashbery's inventive formalism. While alluding to a broad range of cultural and pop references, Wheeler maintains a semantic disjunctiveness; her impersonal monologues create the illusion of natural speech but are undercut by digressions, interjections, and eruptions of traditional form (see 'Benny the Beaver'). Raised in Minnesota and New England, Wheeler now teaches creative writing at Princeton University.   AMI

Wheelwright, John (Brooks) (1897–1940) Born in Milton, Massachusetts, the descendant of two state governors and a Puritan divine expelled from Boston in 1637 for his non-conformist views. Religion and politics played as prominent a part in Wheelwright's life and poetry as they had played in his family's past. After graduating from Harvard he toured expatriate Europe, then returned to Boston and settled into a superficially eccentric life made possible by inheritances. Publication of his verse in the 1920s was confined for the most part to circulation among friends, perhaps because of an intuition that his Anglo-Catholic poems, despite their heresies, were unlikely to find a wider audience among the extravagances of the Jazz Age; but shortly after the stockmarket crash in October 1929 he joined the Socialist Labor Party, and he published his first book, *Rock and Shell* (1933), at a time when similarities between the sacrament of Communion and the ritual of the breadline, and between the persecution of a new faith and government-sanctioned strike-breaking, would be apparent even to readers who weren't steeped in Marxist doctrine and the history of primitive Christianity. It was, however, his less tendentious poems, crisply phrased and scrupulously fanciful, that made the deepest impression on his contemporaries and on later advocates such as John *Ashbery and Frank *O'Hara. Two more collections followed, and a fourth manuscript was ready for print when he was killed by a drunken driver while crossing a street. Thirty years passed before the publication of his *Collected Poems*, ed. Alvin H. Rosenfeld (New Directions, 1972).   RH

Whigham, Peter (1925–87) Born in England, lived for some years in Italy and in 1966 took up a teaching post in Santa Barbara. A classicist and translator, he found inspiration for his own poetry in his impressively eclectic reading. The title of the first, slight, collection he published with Denis Goacher, *Clear Lake Comes from Enjoyment* (1959), suggests an ideal of limpidity resulting from immersion in a pure source, and the epigrammatic style he continued to favour proved both imitation and homage to the manner of unimpeachable models. His translations of *The Poems of Catullus* appeared in 1966, and he later edited and contributed to *Epigrams of Martial Englished by Divers Hands* (1987). He also translated two books by the traveller and anthropologist Boris de Rachewiltz, *Black Eros* (1964) and *Introduction to African Travel* (1966). The poems collected in Whigham's next two volumes, *The Ingathering of Love* (1967) and *The Blue Winged Bee* (1969), somewhat uneasily blended Catullan questioning and self-deprecation with a tribute to the less stylized poetry of the Dalai Lama, whose work 'suggested' several of the poems. Whigham was keen to roughen the metrical pattern of his poetry, and repeatedly attempted to inject into it a colloquial register—*Astropovo* (1970) contains a number of experiments in musical and metrical form. But he remained a student of the classics. Poems about natural subjects repeatedly hinge on allusions to his masters; what he called the 'Honey of memory' is the dominant influence and note in *Things Common, Properly: Selected Poems 1942–1982* (Anvil, 1984).   MRW

White, Kenneth (1936–) Born in Glasgow and educated at the universities of Glasgow, Munich, and Paris. He was a lecturer in French at Glasgow in the mid-1960s, but since 1967 has lived in France. From 1983 he was professor of twentieth-century poetics at the Sorbonne. He is now a freelance writer and academic.

Two early collections appeared in France, *Wild Coal* (1963) and *En toute candeur* (1964). Two others then appeared in London, *The Cold Wind of Dawn* (Cape, 1966) and *The Most Difficult Area* (Cape Goliard, 1968). Almost ten years were to pass before White's poetry began to appear again, this time in France in bilingual editions. One consequence of this was that his work was relatively little known among English-language readers until 1989 and the appearance simultaneously of *The Bird Path: Collected Longer Poems* and the prose work *Travels in the Drifting Dawn* (both reissued by Penguin Books in 1990). See also *Handbook for the Diamond Country: Collected Shorter Poems 1960–1990* (Mainstream, 1990). As his publishing history suggests, White was well known in his adopted country, France—enough for him to be hailed as 'the foremost English-language poet'—and hardly known at all in his native Scotland until 1989, where, however, his work has now received considerable critical attention and attracted a number of followers.

White's poetry is founded on a need to replace what Thoreau called a 'desponding creed' with attempts and beliefs that might contribute to 'chances of wholeness' otherwise confounded by technological and materialist society. In questing after 'something else', White's poetry proposes a shift from history to geography. He has written about what he calls 'geopoetics', assuming the stance of an 'intellectual nomad' (the idea is originally Norman Douglas') and a 'laughing anarchist'. The objective is to win through to 'the space won at the end of the personal journey'. See the lectures collected in *On the Atlantic Edge* (Sandstone, 2006).

*MacDiarmid, *Pound, *Snyder, *Olson, Chinese and Japanese poetry, are among White's sources and influences, although the biggest impact on his work could have been the places where he has travelled. A satisfyingly outdoors poetry (often with much naming of places) is made to co-exist with more bookish, philosophical impulses. Its best effect is one of wind-swept contemplation in remote places. A genuinely meditative, sometimes mystical, beauty, can be the result.

On Scottish Ground: Selected Essays (1998) and *Open World: The Collected Poems 1960–2000* (2003) both appeared from Polygon in Edinburgh. See Gavin Bowd, Charles Forsdick, and Norman Bissell (eds.), *Grounding a World; Essays on the Work of Kenneth White* (Alba, 2005).   DED

Whitworth, John (1945–) Born in India to English parents, Whitworth grew up in Scotland, studied at Oxford University, and lives in Canterbury.

Whitworth's nimbly rhyming poems began to appear in the 1980s, when he published three volumes with Secker & Warburg: *Unhistorical Fragments* (1980), *Poor Butterflies* (1982), and *Lovely Day for a Wedding* (1985). The title of his first volume with Peterloo Poets, *Tennis and Sex and Death* (1989), suggests the *Betjemanian range of his interests, which shade into the darker satire of Gavin *Ewart and Philip *Larkin (whom he considers the greatest poet of the post-war period). *Landscape with Small Humans* (1993), a study of his Fifties childhood, was widely admired. His deftly sardonic *Sonnet History of Modern Poetry* was serialized by Peter Forbes in *Poetry Review* in the 1990s, and published with caricatures by Gerald Mangan in 1999. Overlooked in comparison to Sophie *Hannah and Wendy *Cope, his female peers in light verse, Whitworth's admirers have included Les *Murray and Peter *Reading. Later volumes include *The Whitworth Gun* (2002), *Being the Bad Guy* (2007—all Peterloo), and *Girlie Gangs* (Enitharmon, 2012). See also his handbook, *Writing Poetry* (Black, 2001; revd. edn., 2006).   JNT

Wickham, Anna (1884–1947) Born in 1884 in Wimbledon, where her father kept a music shop. She was taken to Queensland, Australia, as a small child, and returned to England at the age of 20 to train as a singer. An unhappy marriage frustrated this ambition, and she increasingly turned to poetry. Her first poems were printed by Harold and Alida Monro of the Poetry Bookshop, and she went on to produce many collections, beginning with the privately printed *Songs of John Oland* (1911), under the pseudonym John Oland. Despite her literary successes, Anna Wickham hanged herself in London in 1947.

She wrote in both free and rhymed forms, and though her distinctive, forthright voice is always audible, what she called her 'free rhythms' can sound rather inert and unsure. Her short, formal pieces are often more successful, with a crispness that enhances the social observation of, for example, men 'of the Croydon class' and women 'passionate about pins and pence and soap'. *The Writings of Anna Wickham: Free Woman and Poet*, ed. R. D. Smith (Virago, 1984), contains her essays and a substantial quantity of poems. A biography by Jennifer Vaughan Jones, *Anna Wickham: A Poet's Daring Life*, was published by Madison Press in 2003. CAR

Wicks, Susan (1947–) Born and raised in Kent, England, Wicks studied French at the universities of Hull and Sussex, and has taught at universities in France, England, and Ireland.

Citing Louise *Glück and Fleur *Adcock among her influences, Wicks' early poetry presents the world of the family as an enclosed place of intense perceptions. Her first collection, *Singing Underwater* (1992), was followed by *Open Diagnosis* in 1994, which saw her promoted as one of the *New Generation poets. *The Clever Daughter* (1996) continued in verse her memoir of life after the death of her mother, *Driving My Father* (1995—all Faber). After a decade in which she only published *Night Toad: New and Selected Poems* (2003), Wicks returned to poetry with *De-iced* (2007), which includes a long North American sonnet sequence, 'MacDowell Winter'. Her latest collection is *House of Tongues* (2011—all Bloodaxe).

Wicks has also published two novels, *The Key* (1997) and *Little Thing* (1998). Her translation of the contemporary French poet Valérie Rouzeau, *Cold Spring in Winter* (Arc, 2009), was shortlisted for the 2010

Griffin International Poetry Prize and the Weidenfeld Translation Prize. JNT

Wieners, John (1934–2002) Born in Milton, Massachusetts, the son of working-class parents of Irish descent. After graduating from Boston College he studied at *Black Mountain College with Charles *Olson, Robert *Duncan, and Robert *Creeley, and at the age of 24 published *The Hotel Wentley Poems* (Auerhahn, 1958), in which he writes about his experiences with drugs, his homosexual love-affairs, and his bouts of mental illness in powerful unmetred verse influenced by Forties jazz and Abstract Expressionist painting. In subsequent collections he widened his thematic scope to include explorations of feminine psychology and imaginings of moneyed leisure, and the end of this intensely lyrical period was marked by the publication of his first *Selected Poems* (Grossman, 1972). His next book, *Behind the State Capitol or Cincinnati Pike* (Good Gay Poets, 1975), is one of the strangest in the history of American poetry. Poems of civic protest alternate with harrowing fantasies about movie stars, socialites, and kingpins of organized crime, and the media-obsessed subject-matter is reflected in radically distorted syntax and bizarre physical properties: letters are capitalized wilfully, often in the middle of a word; words are hyphenated mid-syllable, sometimes at the end of a line; and lines and sentences begin and end without warning. Wieners fell silent until the appearance of *Selected Poems 1958–1984*, ed. Raymond Foye (1985), which closes with a group of new and more accessible poems.

See also *Cultural Affairs in Boston: Poetry and Prose 1956–1985*, ed. Raymond Foye (1988—both Black Sparrow), with a preface by Creeley. Three more volumes edited from his notebooks have appeared: *The Journal of John Wieners is to be called 707 Scott Street for Billie Holiday, 1959* (Sun & Moon, 1996), *Kidnap Notes Next: Selected Notebook Entries 1988–1999*, ed. Jim Dunn (Pressed Wafer, 2002), and *Book of Prophecies*, ed. Michael Carr (Bootstrap Press,

2007). For a discussion of Wieners' poetry, see John Wilkinson, 'Chamber Attitudes', in *The Lyric Touch* (Salt, 2007).   RH*

Wikkramasinha, Lakdasa (1941–78) Educated at St Thomas' College, Mount Lavinia, Sri Lanka, and studied law before becoming an English teacher. His interest in Sinhala literature led him to experiment with methods of fusing the Western and Oriental traditions creatively in his own writing.

A bilingual poet, whose career ended prematurely with his death by drowning, Wikkramasinha's first book of verse, *Lustre. Poems* (Ariya, 1965), was written entirely in English in the contrary spirit of one who, finding himself constrained by his education to write in the language of 'the most despicable people on earth', had set himself to write as anarchically as possible. This mood did not last. His work appeared in *Madrona, Eastern Horizon, New Ceylon Writing, Outposts, University of Chicago Review*, and other local and international journals, and was published privately by him in *Janakiharana and Other Poems* (1967), *Fifteen Poems* (1970), and *Nossa Senhora dos Chingalas* (1973), *O Regal Blood* (1975), and *The Grasshopper Gleaming* (1976). In honour of a Sri Lankan artist of a previous generation, Wikkramasinha edited and privately published *Twelve Poems to Justin Daraniyagala 1903-67* (1971).

See also Y. Gooneratne (ed.), *Poems From India, Sri Lanka, Malaysia and Singapore* (Heinemann, 1979), and *New Ceylon Writing*, 4 (1979), which include Wikkramasinha's work; the latter also contains biographical information and critical assessments of his poetry by several hands.   YG

Wilbur, Richard (1921–) Born in New York and educated at Amherst College and Harvard University. He began writing poetry while serving in the United States Army during the Second World War and later explained this as his way of attempting to restore order to a world gone mad. His first book, *The Beautiful Changes and Other Poems* (1947), was published shortly after the war and only one year after Robert

*Lowell's *Lord Weary's Castle* (1946). There were many more similarities than differences in the work of the two young writers, but when Lowell turned to a '*confessional' subject-matter with his *Life Studies* in 1959—leading the turn towards the personal that has dominated American poetry ever since—Wilbur did not follow. He thus stands apart from his literary age in at least three ways: he exhibits a classic, objective sensibility in a romantic, subjective time; he is a formalist in the midst of a relentless informality; and he is a relative optimist among absolute pessimists.

Wilbur has never stopped writing in the carefully metred and rhymed forms with which he began; he is the only contemporary poet to whom the term 'elegant' has regularly, and appropriately, been applied. But though Wilbur's consistency of form has allowed him to develop his skills and earn praise, it has also opened him to the charge that his work lacks development. His second book, *Ceremony and Other Poems* (1950), was followed by *Things of This World* (1956), generally thought by critics to be his best volume. *Advice to a Prophet and Other Poems* (1961), Wilbur's fourth volume, is his least attractive because in it he essentially abandons the positive quest for spirituality that underlies his best poems. Here he adopts a negative stance and satirically condemns modern mankind for its materialism and lack of depth. However, for his next volume, *Walking to Sleep: New Poems and Translations* (1969), Wilbur was awarded the Bollingen Prize for poetry, indicating that his reputation had not fallen excessively far. Interestingly, Wilbur had already been awarded the Bollingen Prize for translation in 1963, in honour of his rendering of Molière's *Tartuffe* (his version of *The Misanthrope* was performed in 1955). He has also written two books for children, and his literary essays are collected in *Responses: Prose Pieces, 1953-1976* (Harcourt, 1976; expanded edn., Story Line, 2000). *The Mind-Reader* (1976), contains a few unrhymed poems, but nothing that could truly be called informal (regular metres are retained). In 1987 Wilbur was named the second poet laureate of the United States, succeeding Robert Penn *Warren.

As he indicated in his lecture 'The Bottles Become New Too', Wilbur has a deep regard for the physical world: 'poets can't afford to forget that there is a reality of things which survives all orders great and small . . . No poetry can have any strength unless it continually bashes itself against the reality of things.' This sense of regard is balanced, both in his view of the world and in his work, by an equally strong sense that an unseen power of spirituality underlies that physical realm. As Wilbur said during an interview with Peter Stitt: 'To put it simply, I feel that the universe is full of glorious energy, that the energy tends to take pattern and shape, and that the ultimate character of things is comely and good.' It would seem to be the ultimate goal of Wilbur's poetry to praise both of these aspects of reality and to show their inherent union.

It is through the power of the imagination to create metaphor that Wilbur attempts to unite these two realms, as he himself has indicated: 'the imagination . . . when in best health neither slights the world of fact nor stops with it, but seeks the invisible through the visible.' Metaphor allows Wilbur to point out a close physical resemblance (between wings and leaves, for example), to transform one thing into another (ferns into ocean waves), or to suggest the presence of the unseen within the seen (Arcadia within an ordinary grove of trees). It is thus through metaphor that Wilbur's poetry accomplishes technically what he has conceived as true of the world in a philosophical sense. Motion seems always an aspect of his most effective metaphors, reflecting Wilbur's high regard for the concept of *grace*, which combines beautiful movement with a sense of benediction. His conception of God would seem similarly dual, something that exists both within the poet—as creative intelligence, an aspect of the imagination—and outside him. These two facets work in consort in a Wilbur poem: for the spirituality that exists within the universe to be both recognized and expressed, what is required is a perceiving creative intelligence within the observer that can somehow faintly match that of God.

Wilbur's work is gathered in *Collected Poems: 1943–2004* (Harcourt, 2004) and *Anterooms: New Poems and Translations* (Houghton, 2010; Waywiser, 2011). See also Donald Hill, *Richard Wilbur* (Twayne, 1967); Wendy Salinger (ed.), *Richard Wilbur's Creation* (University of Michigan Press, 1983); and *Richard Wilbur in Conversation with Peter Dale* (Between the Lines, 2000).   PS

Wilkinson, Anne (1910–61) Born Anne Gibbons in Toronto. Through her mother she was related to the prominent Osler family and enjoyed a privileged upbringing; she was educated by private tutors and at progressive schools in England, France, and the United States. In 1932 she married Frederick Robert Wilkinson, a Toronto surgeon, and they had five children, two of whom died in infancy; their marriage ended in divorce in 1953. After a long battle with cancer, Wilkinson died in Toronto.

Encouraged by E. J. *Pratt and Alan Crawley, editor of *Contemporary Verse*, Wilkinson published two poetry collections, *Counterpoint to Sleep* (1951) and *The Hangman Ties the Holly* (1955), that revealed an extraordinary imagination and poetic gift—combining light and lively diction, and elegance and wit—in poems that explored her sensuous identification with nature and love, and life itself, including its pain and the omnipresence of death. A founding editor and patron of *The Tamarack Review*, Wilkinson also wrote *Lions in the Way* (1956), a history of the Osler family, and *Swann and Daphne* (1960), a fantasy for children.

See also *The Tightrope Walker: Autobiographical Writings of Anne Wilkinson* (University of Toronto Press, 1992), ed. Joan Coldwell. *Heresies: The Complete Poems of Anne Wilkinson*, ed. Dean Irvine (Véhicule), appeared in 2003.   DS

Wilkinson, John (1953–) Born in London and grew up in Cornwall and Devon. Wilkinson studied English at Jesus College, Cambridge, and researched the poetry of John *Wieners at Harvard University. He trained as a psychiatric nurse and worked in mental-health services for many years, before moving to the States to teach at the universities of Notre Dame and Chicago.

A prolific poet who has said 'if I were to stop I would be struck dumb,' Wilkinson began publishing in the 1970s through small presses in London and Cambridge: see *Oort's Cloud: Earlier Poems* (Barque/ subpress, 1999). The book-length *Proud Flesh* appeared in 1986 (Equifinality/ Délires; repr. Salt, 2005). *Flung Clear: Poems in Six Books* (Parataxis, 1994; repr. Salt, 2010) collects pamphlets from the late 1980s and early 1990s.

Like other poets associated with the *Cambridge School, Wilkinson's characteristic mode is the extended lyric sequence (he has called *Proud Flesh* the 'repeated' failure to write a short love poem), played out against a wide geopolitical horizon. *The Nile* (1992) surveys the late capitalist landscape from Cairo, and *Sarn Helen* (1997— both Equipage), dedicated to Lynette *Roberts, from Wales. The later American sequences of *Lake Shore Drive* (2006) and *Down to Earth* (2008) loosen densely sensual, language with a new declarative fluency. As a critic, Wilkinson has been an eloquent advocate of the work of J. H. *Prynne, and has also written appreciatively on the *New York poets: see *The Lyric Touch* (2007—all Salt). JNT

Williams, C. K. (Charles Kenneth)

(1936–) Born in Newark, New Jersey, and now lives in Paris, but spends part of each year teaching at Princeton University. In 1975 he married Catherine Mauger; they have a son, and Williams also has a daughter by a previous marriage. He has been contributing editor to *American Poetry Review* (Philadelphia) since 1972. An exalted—though often comic or rueful— sense of the ties of marriage, family, and friendship, and an acute sympathy for 'flesh and blood'—in both senses—exposed to cruelty or indignity, colour Williams' uncompromising and distinctive poems. He is, as one reviewer has pointed out, 'almost synonymous' with the very long, unrhymed line that seems to owe something to Whitman and the Psalms; and he shows a novel-ist's or short-story writer's absorption in the matter of neglected, humble, or humiliated lives and places. His run-down urban settings are inhabited by the vulnerable and the walking wounded: hobos, misfits, war-veterans, invalids, lovers, and especially children and the old; a tendency to voyeurism inherent in Williams' meditative luxuriance is mostly transcended, and harsh or squalid subjects are invested with raw urgency, sombre tenderness, even reverence.

Williams has been publishing for almost thirty years, but his first books seem as misjudged in their bid for originality as his later ones seem confident and unerring. His work of the 1960s and early 1970s is crippled by its wilful commitment to extremes—an extreme horror and outrage, an equally extreme, anguished compassion, expressed in a poetic idiom that is, for the most part, unpunctuated, unfocused, and full of inarticulate ferocity. With his third book appeared the longer, more relaxed line, the spacious, clause-rich syntax (all patient modification and qualification), and the engagement with a populous, impressively detailed reality. This is the vein which—with occasional lapses into bathos or a garrulous self-fascination—Williams has worked to greatest effect ever since.

Poems 1963–1983 (1988) contains a generous selection from Williams' first two books, and his subsequent three volumes in their entirety; *Flesh and Blood* (1988) won the National Book Critics Circle Award; it was followed by *A Dream of Mind* (1992). *Repair* (1999) won the Pulitzer Prize for Poetry. *Collected Poems* appeared in 2006, and a new volume, *Wait*, in 2010 (all Farrar, Straus/Bloodaxe). *Misgivings: My Mother, My Father, Myself* (Farrar, Straus, 2000) is a memoir. Williams has also published translations of Sophocles's *Women of Trachis* (with Gregory Dickerson), *The Bacchae of Euripides*, Adam Zagajewski, and Francis Ponge. AJ

Williams, Charles (1886–1945) Born in

London and for most of his life worked for the Oxford University Press. Williams' personal influence exceeded his general literary reputation, even though his novels, effective supernatural thrillers, were popular. T. S. *Eliot believed him to be a 'man who was always able to live in the material and spiritual world at once', and W. H. *Auden, when he first met him in 1936, said that in his presence he felt 'for the first time in my life in the presence of personal sanctity...I felt transformed into a person who was incapable of doing anything base or unloving'. Williams had also a profound influence upon the life and work of C. S. Lewis, who admired his poetry. This poetry has received little attention outside a circle which included Eliot, Lewis (of whose group, the Inklings, Williams was a member) and, more recently, John *Heath-Stubbs. After beginning with somewhat pallid and more or less *Georgian lyrics in such volumes as *The Silver Stair* (Herbert & Daniel, 1912) and *Windows of Night* (1924), he published a long series of poems on Arthurian themes, *Taliessin Through Logres* (1938). It is this volume, and its successor *The Region of the Summer Stars* (1944), that attracted the attention of his fellow Anglicans. Lewis' *Arthurian Torso* (1948) contains a posthumous fragment by Williams called 'The Figure of Arthur' and a full commentary. This body of work has struck more than one reader uninitiated into higher Anglicanism as resembling the agnostic *Bridges of *The Testament of Beauty* crossed with the Eliot of *Murder in the Cathedral:* well and carefully wrought, meticulous, somewhat self-consciously 'beautiful'.

See John Heath-Stubbs' introduction to *Collected Plays* (1963—all Oxford University Press), and his *Charles Williams* (Longmans, 1955); *Further Papers on Dante* (Methuen, 1957), by Dorothy L. Sayers; and the article 'The Mathematics of the Soul' (*Poetry London*, 11, 1947), by M. Diggle.   MS-S

Williams, Hugo (1942–) Born at Windsor. His father, the actor Hugh Williams, is portrayed in *Writing Home* (1985) as 'handsome', 'masterful', a man who was once 'on Famous Film Star | Cigarette Cards' but later had little work and less money. Stylish in his thirties before the war, a soldier in Tunisia during it, Hugh

Williams was glamorously unknowable for his young son, and 'Death of an Actor', for all its affection, remembers the remoteness of a 'stiff theatrical man'.

Hugo Williams was educated at Eton College (1955–60) and then spent two years as editorial assistant to Alan *Ross on the *London Magazine* before leaving to spend twenty months travelling around the world. Those travels were recorded in *All the Time in the World* (1966), which appeared the year after Williams' first book of poems, *Symptoms of Loss*. In 1965 Williams married, and soon went back to work on the *London Magazine*, where he remained until 1970, the year in which his second collection of poems, *Sugar Daddy*, was published.

These early years, which brought him an Eric Gregory Award (1966) and Cholmondeley Award (1971), also saw the beginnings of Williams' association with Ian *Hamilton's *Review*. The brevity and restraint of poems in *Sugar Daddy* and *Some Sweet Day* (1975) linked Williams to other *Review* poets, including Hamilton himself and David *Harsent; but poems in *Love-Life* (1979) showed him opening out towards a more relaxed, anecdotal and (auto)biographical style. With further awards and a reading tour of the USA (recorded in his frank *No Particular Place to Go*, 1981), Williams finally emerged from the 'record-breaking dole-run' which he described as the 'real background story' of his 1970s. *Writing Home* (1985) and *Self-Portrait with a Slide* (1990), together with a 1989 *Selected Poems* (all Oxford University Press), established Williams as a poet of candour, irony, and brio.

With *Dock Leaves* (1994) Williams moved to Faber and Faber, who published his T.S. Eliot Prize-winning *Billy's Rain*—the story of a love affair—in 1999, and a *Collected Poems* in 2002. In *Dear Room* (2006) and *West End Final* (2009) Williams continues to write about his life in London with an unpretentious openness that has been influential on younger poets. *Freelancing* (1995—all Faber) selects from his urbane autobiographical column in the *Times Literary Supplement*.   MHu*

Williams, John Hartley (1944–) Born in Cheshire, grew up in North London, and was educated at William Ellis School and the universities of Nottingham and London. He has lived and worked in France, Francophone Africa, and Yugoslavia, and, since 1976, in Berlin where he teaches English at the Free University. His first collection, *Hidden Identities* (Chatto & Windus, 1982), showed the influence of American modernism—particularly *Cummings—but was also notable for its interest in narrative and its presentation of English poetry as part of a wider European experience. *Bright River Yonder* (1987) expanded the fictionalizing aspect into a sequence of poems set in a Wild West frontier town which assembled a story from a variety of differing voices and perspectives. *Cornerless People* (1990) collected restless poems of journeying and cultural dislocation set against the background of capitalist Europe. His translations of the Romanian poet Martin Sorescu appeared as *Censored Poems* (2000—all Bloodaxe).

Ignoble Sentiments (Arc, 1995) is a prose work, part memoir and part fiction, and *Mystery in Spiderville* (Cape, 2002; repr. Vintage, 2003) a book of prose poems. *Blues* (Cape, 2004), shortlisted for the T. S. Eliot Prize, includes an elegy for Ken *Smith. *The Ship* (Salt, 2007) selects from largely unpublished work between the late 1950s and early 1980s. Surreal reflections from Williams' time as poet-in-residence at Wordsworth's Dove Cottage can be found in *Café des Artistes* (Cape, 2009). See also *Teach Yourself Writing Poetry* (revd. edn., Hodder, 2004), with Matthew Sweeney.   DK*

Williams, Jonathan (Chamberlain) (1929–2008) Born in Asheville, North Carolina. He was educated at various institutions, including Princeton and, from 1951 to 1956, Black Mountain College where he encountered Charles *Olson. From 1969, Williams divided his time between Highlands, North Carolina and Dentdale, Cumbria, establishing strong links with American and British poets and artists.

Although labelled a *Black Mountain poet, Williams disliked the term. Influences include Olson, Robert *Duncan, Edith *Sitwell, Charles Ives, William Bartram, and Edward Dahlberg. Williams launched his press The Jargon Society in San Francisco in 1951, publishing a range of modern writers, including Olson, Lorine *Niedecker, Paul Metcalf, and Ian Hamilton *Finlay.

Key books include *An Ear in Bartram: Selected Poems, 1957–1967* (University of North Carolina Press, 1969); *In England's Green & (A Garland & Clyster)* (Auerhahn, 1962), Williams' celebration of the British visionary tradition of William Blake and Samuel Palmer; *Mahler* (Marlborough Fine Arts, 1967), a suite of poems responding to Mahler's symphonies; and *Blues & Roots/Rue & Bluets: A Garland for the Appalachian* (Grossman, 1972), whose assembly of found poems, reported speech, and visual texts depict the poet as 'an autochthonous mindless recording mechanism established ecologically within a mountain region'.

A penchant for the laconic, ludic, and satiric, as well as the erotic and priapic, characterizes much of the work. Examples of Williams' own form, the 'meta-four', are included in *Jubilant Thicket: New & Selected Poems* (Copper Canyon, 2005). His photography was published in *A Palpable Elysium: Portraits of Genius and Solitude* (Godine, 2002).   ROH

Williams, Miller (1930–) Born in Hoxie, Arkansas. After holding a number of academic appointments and other positions, he has taught since 1970 at the University of Arkansas, where he is emeritus professor of literature. He also directed the University of Arkansas Press for two decades, developing it into a leading literary publisher. His books include critical studies of *Ransom and Ciardi; translations of Nicanor Parra, Pablo Neruda, and G. G. Belli; and several anthologies.

A prolific poet as well, Williams has published since 1964 a dozen full collections, and two volumes of new and selected poems. His work is uneven; many poems are more clever in inspiration than they are satisfying in execution. But he has always been capable of powerful and concentrated work ('Late Show'), and has written a number of impressive poems—including 'Original Sin', 'And When in Scenes of Glory . . .', 'In Your Own Words . . .', 'Getting Experience', and 'Wiedersehen'—about his Southern boyhood and adolescence. His poetry has grown in depth and sureness from book to book; his latest full collection, *Imperfect Love* (1986), is his best. 'In Extremis in Hardy, Arkansas' is an especially effective blend of his strengths: wit, colloquialism, technical fluency, and a wry tenderness concerning the complexities of the human heart.

Living on the Surface: New and Selected Poems (1989—both Louisiana State University Press) is a severe and judicious selection from all his published work. Michael Burns has edited *A Habitation and a Name: Essays on the Poetry of Miller Williams* (University of Missouri Press, 1991). In 1997, Williams read his poem 'Of History and Hope' at President Clinton's second inauguration ceremony. Since *Some Jazz a While: Collected Poems* (University of Illinois Press, 1999), he has published *Making a Poem: Some Thoughts About Poetry and the People Who Write It* (2006) and *Time and the Tilting Earth: Poems* (2008—both Louisiana State University Press).   MP

Williams, William Carlos (1883–1963) Williams was a medical student at the University of Pennsylvania, where he began his lifelong friendship with *Pound (a 'special student' there) and H. D. (Hilda *Doolittle), the daughter of an astronomer whose observatory was associated with the university. Williams had a serious medical career. He studied advanced pediatrics in Germany after his internship, set up private practice in Rutherford, New Jersey (his native town), and eventually became head pediatrician of the General Hospital in the nearby city of Paterson.

Meanwhile, he played an active role in the avant-garde poetic movements centred in New York City and was also constantly in touch with Pound's literary activities and associates in Europe. His major difference with Pound (apart from Williams' acutely responsive and realistic presentations of women and his revulsion against fascism; see especially *Paterson III-V*) lay in his desire to create a specifically American

poetics based on the rhythms and colorations of American speech, thought, and experience. His little prose work *In the American Grain* (1925) is a highly original and intense effort to present—in a sense, to create—the key events and figures of what Horace *Gregory, in his introduction to the 1939 reprint, called America's 'mythical history'. Without being so intended, it is something of a companion volume to D. H. *Lawrence's *Studies in Classic American Literature* (1923). The two books complement one another, and in fact Lawrence reviewed Williams' book with respectful interest. The reciprocal preoccupations of these two dynamic intelligences is one demonstration among many that Williams, like Whitman, was not a provincial despite his passionate search for a truly American poetry. His art and his larger interests were ultimately cosmopolitan.

His *Autobiography* (1951) is partly devoted to the medical side of his life and its crucial relation to his poetry—which, like his fiction, draws heavily on his experience as a doctor. His working-class patients, especially the women whose babies he delivered and whose hardy courage he vastly admired, absorbed his sympathetic if sometimes irritated attention much as Chekhov's peasant patients did his. They were of a different order of ethnic and class background, often, from the essentially middle-class world of Rutherford where he had spent his childhood and where he settled after his marriage to Florence Herman, the 'Floss' of his poems, who also appears in his plays and is the central figure of his novel *White Mule* (1937)—the first in a trilogy based on the lives of her Swedish mother and German father as immigrants in America.

Williams has gradually emerged as one of the great forces in twentieth-century American verse. His experiments, though striking, may have lacked the brilliance of Pound's and *Eliot's at their best, and they may lack the elegance of Wallace *Stevens in *Harmonium* or *The Auroras of Autumn*. But Williams' work is more expressive of American sensibility, and more saturated with American speech and its rhythms, than any poet's since Whitman. For these reasons he has entered the bloodstream of later American poetry: Allen *Ginsberg, Robert *Lowell, Paul *Blackburn, and many others—including a number of *Language poets—show strong traces of his influence. (And indeed his poetry has also cast a net of 'Americanization' overseas, in the form of some poets' stylistic reorientation. We find writers like Charles *Tomlinson and John *Montague, for example, reflecting this influence while adapting it to their own countries' colloquial turns and poetic traditions.)

Robert *Frost, of course, rivals Williams in his use of the native idiom—his poems are true to the speech and the trapped psyches of the New England country-people he knew; the dark elegiac and tragic strains running through so much of what he wrote carry it far beyond mere pastoral charm. Williams, however, expresses the whole nation's character, and especially its urban volatility: its multiracial and immigrant streams of speech and behaviour, its violence and exuberance, its ignorance of its own general and regional history. His important sequence *Paterson*, published serially between 1946 and 1961 in five 'Books' and part of a sixth, is an exploration of all these matters. It is presented as a search for the elements of a 'common language': a shared cultural and historical awareness to counteract the fragmentation of American society. Williams saw this fragmentation as a pressure for 'divorce' (i.e., inability to connect or communicate), not only between the sexes but among the people at large.

Williams' *Selected Essays* (1954) are most useful as clues to his artistic and intellectual affinities. *Joyce, Pound, Gertrude *Stein, Marianne *Moore, and Kenneth *Burke loom large in this respect, together with Alfred Stieglitz and certain painters: Brueghel, Matisse, Tchelitchew, Sheeler. Williams had far more of a painter's eye than do most poets; see, for instance, his *Pictures from Brueghel* (1962). His famous, somewhat baffling, yet nevertheless valuable concept of the 'variable foot' (each 'foot'—or line-fragment—a held moment or unit of measure within an unfolding apperception) gives the typographical movement of his later poems

something of the character of animated abstract painting. It is clear that he felt a compelling convergence of visual and aural patterns as he wrote.

At the same time, his poems project a sensuous and associative immediacy of extraordinary vivacity. Their aura of spontaneous improvisation has misled many younger poets into overlooking his artistry. ('Rigor of beauty is the quest,' he wrote at the start of the 'Preface' to *Paterson*.) Perhaps it was his apparently relaxed colloquialism—often coupled, however, with startling shifts of focus and with eloquent passages of beautifully controlled rhythm and phrasing—that delayed recognition of his achievement even in the United States.

Since his first published book, *The Tempers* (1913), Williams' poems have appeared in numerous individual volumes and collected editions. Except for *Paterson*, they have now been gathered together in chronological order, and with scrupulous scholarly care, in the two-volume *The Collected Poems of William Carlos Williams* (New Directions, 1986 and 1988; Carcanet, 1987 and 1989), ed. A. Walton Litz and Christopher MacGowan. M. L. Rosenthal brought out *The William Carlos Williams Reader* (New Directions, 1966), and Charles Tomlinson edited a *Selected Poems* (Penguin, 1976). More recently, Robert *Pinsky has edited a selected volume for the American Poets Project (Library of America, 2004).

See the biographies by Paul Mariani, *William Carlos Williams: A New World Naked* (McGraw-Hill, 1981; repr. Norton, 1990), and Herbert Leibowitz, *'Something Urgent I Have to Say to You': The Life and Works of William Carlos Williams* (Farrar, Straus, 2011) See also Emily Mitchell Wallace, *A Bibliography of William Carlos Williams* (Wesleyan University Press, 1968).

James *Laughlin's New Directions was an important supporter of Williams from the 1930s onwards, and has continued to issue new and revised volumes, including *Paterson*, ed. Christopher MacGowan (1992); *The Collected Stories of William Carlos Williams* (1996); editions of Williams' letters to *Pound (1996) and Denise *Levertov (1998); a facsimile first edition of *Spring *and All*, with introduction by C. D. *Wright; and *By Word of Mouth: Poems from the Spanish, 1916–1959*, ed. Jonathan Cohen (both 2011).   MLR*

Willis, Elizabeth (1961–) Born in Bahrain, Willis grew up in the United States and studied at the University of Wisconsin and SUNY Buffalo, where she completed a doctoral thesis on Pre-Raphaelite aesthetics. She has held residencies and fellowships across America, and now teaches at Wesleyan University. Her first book was *Second Law* (Avenue B, 1993), followed by *The Human Abstract* (Penguin, 1994), which was chosen for the National Poetry Series. The title alludes to William Blake, and points to Willis' imaginative fascination with the art and culture of eighteenth- and nineteenth-century Britain. One of a post-*Language generation of poets for whom 'textual labour' is an important part of the writing process, Willis' next collection *Turneresque* (Burning Deck, 2003) meditates on the history of painting and cinema, while *Meteoric Flowers* (Wesleyan University Press, 2006) explores the botanical writing of Erasmus Darwin. In both volumes the prose poem becomes a vehicle for moving between research and response. She has also edited a collection of essays on Lorine *Niedecker, *Radical Vernacular* (University of Iowa Press, 2006). Her latest collection is *Address* (Wesleyan University Press, 2011). In 2012 she received a Guggenheim Fellowship.   JNT

Wilmer, Clive (1945–) Born in Harrogate, Yorkshire, grew up in London, and was educated at King's College, Cambridge. He has lived in Florence and Padua and has taught at the University of California at Santa Barbara. He lives in Cambridge, where he was a founder-editor of the periodical *Numbers*, and is a Fellow of Sidney Sussex College. He was the presenter of the BBC programme 'Poet of the Month'.

His poetry at times has affinities with the '*Stanford School' founded by Yvor *Winters in its employment of the plain style and substantial rational subject-matter, and it frequently reflects his long-standing admiration for George Herbert. A careful craftsman, he aims at what he calls 'exactness of form', with each poem having its own distinctive structure. He frequently expresses a religious feeling derived from his Anglican upbringing and social and aesthetic thought as represented by the works of John Ruskin and William Morris, both of whom he has edited.

Wilmer's poems are in *The Dwelling Place* (1977); *Devotions* (1982); *Of Earthly Paradise* (1992); and *The Mystery of Things* (2006—all Carcanet). *The Falls* (2000) appeared from Worple Press. See *New and Collected Poems* (Carcanet, 2012), which includes a selection of his many translations from Hungarian. He has edited John Ruskin's *Unto this Last and Other Writings* (Penguin, 1985) and the essays of Donald *Davie and Thom *Gunn.   DES

Wilmot, Frank (1881–1942) Born in Melbourne, subject of his most significant work, *Melbourne Odes* (Lothian, 1934), published under the pseudonym 'Furnley Maurice'. In representations of depression life such as 'Upon a Row of Old Boots and Shoes in a Pawnbroker's Window', these expressed the radicalism which had led him to attack Australian involvement in the First World War: 'To God from the Weary [later 'Warring'] Nations', published in 1916, became the centrepiece of the anti-war *Eyes of Vigilance* (Endacott, 1920).

However, *Melbourne Odes* also celebrated the city as a place of social dreams and vivid activity, challenging the dominance of nature poetry such as Wilmot himself had written in *The Gully and Other Poems* (Melbourne University Press, 1929). And in their formal experimentation, they put into practice his conviction that Australian writers should look to American modernism for methods to develop the 'National Poetry' he advocated in the essay collected in *Romance* (Endacott, 1922).

Wilmot, who managed Melbourne University Press, remained active in literary life but published little after *Melbourne Odes*. E. Morris Miller's account in *Australian Literature 1795–1938* (Melbourne University Press, 1940; facsimile Sydney University Press, 1973) compares interestingly with David Headon's 'Frank Wilmot: The First Australian Modernist', *Meanjin*, 41:4 (1982).   JS

Wiman, Christian (1966–) Born in West Texas, Wiman studied at Washington Lee University and has taught at a number of universities in the United States, including Stanford, and the Prague School of Economics. He now lives in Chicago, where he edits *Poetry* magazine with Don Share: see their centennial anthology, *The Open Door* (University of Chicago Press, 2012).

Ambition and Survival: Becoming a Poet (Copper Canyon, 2007) combines criticism on Basil *Bunting and Robert *Lowell, among others, with autobiographical essays. The concluding piece describes the poet's marriage, diagnosis with a rare cancer, and discovery of religious faith, life-changes reflected in his third collection, *Every Riven Thing* (Farrar, Straus, 2010). Often compared to Robert *Frost for his commitment to a lyricism of unsentimental, spoken observation (as revived by the *New Narrative movement) Wiman's other collections are *The Long Home* (Story Line, 1998; repr. Copper Canyon, 2007) and *Hard Night* (Copper Canyon, 2005). He has also translated Osip Mandelstam (*Stolen Air*, Ecco, 2012).   JNT

Wingfield, Sheila (1906–92) Born in Hampshire and attended Roedean School. In her childhood she was obliged to hide her literary interests from her parents, and later came a ban 'on meeting literary personalities' from her husband, the Viscount of Powerscourt. History and mythology became compelling objects of study for her in her isolation, interests reflected in her richly allusive writing. Her early poems were praised by *Yeats. She went on to produce a further six volumes, including the symphonic meditation, 2,000 lines long, on war and love, *Beat Drum, Beat Heart* (1946). She also wrote two volumes of memoirs, *Real People* (1952—both Cresset) and *Sun Too Fast* (Bles, 1974).

Her early work is often imagistic in style. The sonorous, dignified tone and intellectual range she later achieved are suggestive of Geoffrey *Hill. Her most philosophical flights are always tempered by precise observation. The fullest selection of work by this underrated poet may be found in her *Collected Poems* (Enitharmon, 1983). The biography by Penny Perrick, *Something to Hide: The Life of Sheila Wingfield, Viscountess Powerscourt* (Lilliput, 2007), includes a selection of her poems as an appendix.   CAR

Winters, Yvor (1900–68) Born in Chicago. His father, who had a nervous and physical breakdown before Winters was 4, took the family to Los Angeles and Seattle and, in 1914, back to Chicago in search of secure and lucrative employment. Winters spent one year at the University of Chicago, three years in bed in Santa Fe, New Mexico, with tuberculosis, and two more as a school teacher in the coal camps of Madrid and Cerillo, south of Santa Fe. He took an MA in Romance languages from the University of Colorado in 1925, and taught French and Spanish at the University of Idaho (1925–7). In 1926 he married Janet *Lewis, and the following year was enrolled as a graduate student at Stanford University, where he stayed for the rest of his working life, becoming professor of English in 1949.

Winters' poetry falls clearly into two phases. His first three volumes (thought by many to be his best), *The Immobile Wind* (1921), *The Magpie's Shadow* (1922), and *The Bare Hills* (1927), all collected in *The Early Poems: 1920–28* (1966), were written under the technical influence of *Pound, William Carlos *Williams, Marianne *Moore, H. D. (Hilda *Doolittle), and other modernists. Their imagistic free verse is emotionally charged, vividly evocative of the New Mexican landscape, and—as Winters himself later observed—redolent of his youthful solipsistic and deterministic philosophy. In the late 1920s and early 1930s Winters tired of modernist innovations and found inspiration in the conventional prosody of Dryden, Pope, *Hardy, E. A. *Robinson, and others. *The Proof* (1930) begins with *imagist poems but ends with traditional metres; and all eight poems in *The Journey* (1931) use heroic couplets. As Western editor of *Hound & Horn* during its last two years (1932–4), and in his first three critical books, collected as *In Defense of Reason* (1947), Winters gave trenchant and dogmatic expression to his revised opinions; he believed that poetry should be a clear statement using traditional metres (since they alone could exploit the full emotional potential of language) to convey feeling informed by understanding. Not only, he felt, were *Bridges and T. Sturge Moore better poets than *Eliot and Pound; free verse and imagism were themselves temporary aberrations from the Anglo-American poetic tradition. These views involved Winters in some bitter critical disputes. Meanwhile, he continued publishing his neoclassical poems, in *Before Disaster* (1934), *Poems* (1940), which he printed on his own press, *The Giant Weapon* (1943), and *Three Poems* (1950); 'Sir Gawaine and the Greene Knight' and 'A Summer Commentary', in particular, succeed in combining effective use of imagery with ordered and precise statement. In *The Function of Criticism* (1957) and *Forms of Discovery* (1967), Winters sustained and developed his anti-modernist polemic, championing the 'post-symbolist' style of poetry which made 'no sacrifice of rational intelligence'. His poetic output diminished towards the end of his life, but his *Collected Poems* (1952; revd. and enlarged, Swallow, 1960; Carcanet, 1978; repr., Ohio University Press, 1980) won a Bollingen Prize in 1960.

See also *In Defense of Reason* (1947; repr., Swallow, 1986) and *An Introduction to the Poetry of Yvor Winters*, by Elizabeth Isaacs (Swallow, 1981). Two selected volumes, of poems (1999) and letters (2000), edited by R. L. Barth, were published by Swallow Press/Ohio University Press. Thom *Gunn's selection of Winters' work appeared as part of the Library of America American Poets Project (2003).   NE

Wojahn, David (1953–) Born in St Paul, Minnesota, and lived in the Twin Cities until earning a BA in English from the University of Minnesota in 1977. He next completed an MFA at the University of Arizona and has since taught at five universities, currently at Indiana. In 1981, Richard *Hugo selected *Icehouse Lights* (Yale University Press, 1982) for the Yale Younger Poet Award. He teaches at Virginia Commonwealth University and Vermont College.

Both *Icehouse Lights* and Wojahn's second book, *Glassworks* (1987), repeatedly pursue the theme of memory as a source of endurance rather than loss. In brief narratives such as 'The Astral Body' and 'Porch Lights' Wojahn creates purely personal juxtapositions of past and present. But in some longer poems like 'Cold Glow: Icehouses' and 'Steam' he blends personal memory and present context with historical analogues, such as the origins of a resort town's defunct mineral baths. Besides first-person narratives, Wojahn sometimes writes dramatic monologues; 'Song of Burning' adopts the voice of rock-singer Jim Morrison. Along the same lines, *Mystery Train* (Pittsburgh, 1990) contains a series of imaginative character-sketches about rock musicians from Elvis Presley to Bob Marley. Wojahn has published five further volumes, including the Pulitzer-shortlisted *Interrogation Palace: New and Selected Poems 1982–2004* (all University of Pittsburgh Press), and a volume of essays on contemporary American poetry, *Strange Good Fortune* (University of Arkansas Press, 2001). He has also edited the *Collected Poems* of his late wife, Lynda Hull, for Graywolf Press.   MCB

Wong, Cyril (1977–) Born in Singapore, Wong studied English Literature at the National University of Singapore, eventually finishing with a doctoral degree in 2012. In between formal education, he has also worked in arts administration.

With nine collections of poetry, Wong is acknowledged as the most prolific of the post-1995 generation of Singapore poets. His first collection, *squatting quietly* (2000), was tentatively received, but *the end of his orbit* (2001) and *below: absence* (2002) established him as a poet to watch. He has been most often labelled a *confessional poet on the basis of the brutally candid sexuality in his poetry, along with a barely submerged anxiety over the fragility of human connection and a relentless self-querying; but the label understates Wong's constant evolution. With *tilting our plates to catch the light* (2007—all Firstfruits), Wong signals his departure from the personal lyric for a poetry of more ambitious scope, and that trajectory has led to *Satori Blues* (Softblow, 2011), a sustained meditation that recalls turn-of-the-century Geoffrey *Hill in its intricately patterned probing.   THM

Wong, Phui Nam (1935–) Born in Kuala Lumpur. English was the main medium of his education, but as a schoolboy he also attended Chinese school in the afternoon for some years and later studied Chinese classical poetry under a tutor. Between 1955 and 1959 he studied in the University of Malaya (then in Singapore), majoring in economics but also studying philosophy and English. He has worked mainly in development and merchant-banking and finance, and as an investment consultant.

Wong started writing verse as an undergraduate. His mature poems are among the best Malaysian poems in English, unsurpassed in their eloquence and linguistic richness. Most of them are contemplative or introspective and draw their images from the Malaysian landscape. In his introduction to the collection *How the Hills are Distant* (University of Malaya, 1968), Wong expresses the need to naturalize English, his adopted language, for his poetic purposes, just as a Malaysian of immigrant ancestry like himself would have to be naturalized to the culture of the country his forefathers have adopted.

His second collection of poems was *Remembering Grandma and Other Rumours* (National University of Singapore, 1989). Wong's collected poems, *An Acre of Day's Glass*, appeared in 2006, the same year that he published a verse drama, *Anike*, a version of *Antigone* (both Maya Press).   FA

Woodcock, George (1912–95) Born in Winnipeg, Manitoba. His parents returned to England when he was five months old, and he was educated there. During the 1930s Woodcock worked as a railway clerk and began contributing poems to Julian Symons' *Twentieth Century Verse*. His first collection, *Six Poems*, was published in 1938. He founded the magazine *Now* in 1940, and under the influence of Herbert *Read became an anarchist. In 1949 he married the artist Ingeborg Linzer and they emigrated to Canada. A man of letters, Woodcock wrote on many subjects, including anarchism, and wrote biographies of Godwin, Gandhi, and

Orwell. He also published extensively on the social history of Canada. As well, in 1959 he became the first editor of *Canadian Literature*, and for the next eighteen years worked closely with Canada's writers and critics.

In his *Collected Poems* (Sono Nis, 1983), Woodcock notes that he virtually stopped writing poetry when he left England in 1949 and began again only in the late 1960s. His early poetry owes much to the *Imagists: brief, suggestive renderings of landscape which intimate a coming storm. He was influenced also by *Eliot and *Auden: many of his poems re-create an abstract landscape, a world of innocence which might extend to humanity, except that mankind's rapacity and greed intrude. His poems often employ mythic figures, in particular an Odysseus figure who returns from his wanderings and finds himself unable to prevent civilization from destroying itself. Woodcock's later poetry, in which he draws on Canada's west-coast imagery, tends to be more affirmative. The emphasis falls on metamorphosis, the power to change 'the eternal dark to light'.

Woodcock's two volumes of autobiography, *Letter to the Past* (1982) and *Beyond the Blue Mountains* (1987—both Fitzhenry & Whiteside), contain valuable insights into his development as a poet. The only biography is George Fetherling, *The Gentle Anarchist: A Life of George Woodcock* (Douglas & McIntyre, 1998; Subway, 2005).   RH

(⊕) SEE WEB LINKS
• For more information see the George Woodcock Lifetime Achievement Award website and the George Woodcock Research Centre website.

Wright, C. D. (Carolyn) (1949–) Born in Mountain Home, Arkansas, in the Ozark Mountains, she was educated at Memphis State University and the University of Arkansas. In 1983 she married the poet Forrest *Gander, and they have a son, Brecht. Wright has lived in Providence, Rhode Island, since 1983 and is on the faculty at Brown University.

Her poems have a strong sense of narrative in a rural Southern idiom. They are colloquial in diction, and their subjects are 'half pulled out of earth and rivers'. Wright has written of herself: 'I am, irrevocably, a purebred hill person.' And of her work: 'My poems are about desire, conflict, the dearth of justice for all. About persons of small means.'

Wright has published more than a dozen books, most recently *Steal Away: New and Selected Poems* (2002), *Rising, Falling, Hovering* (2009), which received the International Griffin Poetry Prize, and *One with Others* (2010—all Copper Canyon), which received the National Book Critics Circle Prize. In 2004 she received a MacArthur Fellowship (nicknamed the Genius Award) for her 'originality, insight, and potential'. *Like Something Flying Backwards* (Bloodaxe, 2007) is an expanded edition of the 2002 selected volume, which includes a new title sequence and the complete book-length poem *Deepstep Come Shining* (Copper Canyon, 1998).   HC

Wright, Charles (1935–   ) Born in Pickwick Dam, Tennessee. Educated at Davidson College and the University of Iowa, he began writing poems while stationed in Verona, Italy, with the Army Intelligence Unit between 1957 and 1961. He has since taught at the University of Padua as a Fulbright lecturer and studied in Rome. During his early years in Italy he came under the poetic spell of Ezra *Pound, whom he addresses as 'Cold-blooded father of light' in one of his finest early poems, 'Homage to Ezra Pound', in *Hard Freight* (1973). Wright has also been deeply influenced by Dante and such modern Italian poets as Eugenio Montale and Cesare Pavese, both of whom he has translated. Wright's translation of Montale's *The Storm and Other Things* won a PEN translation award in 1979.

Before taking his current post as professor of English at the University of Virginia, Wright taught for many years at the University of California at Irvine. The various landscapes of Wright's life—the South, California, Italy—have inevitably found their way into his poems, but his landscapes are deeply interior, often surreal. His poems, from *The Grave of the Right Hand* (1970) to *Zone Journals* (1988), are austere and difficult of access. As Helen Vendler has

said 'they defy exposition. They cluster, aggregate, radiate; they add layers, like pearls.'

Wright is fundamentally a religious poet, his poems subverting the traditional imagery of eastern (*China Trace*, 1977) and western (*The Southern Cross*, 1981) spiritual traditions in unusual ways. His densely imagistic poems, with their inescapable rhythms and insistent musicality, explore possibilities for a spiritual life in a world overwhelmed by concrete objects. He often, as in *Bloodlines* (1975), works in obliquely autobiographical poem-sequences. More recently, as in *Zone Journals*, he has adapted the journal form to his own uses, creating complex meditations on the mysteries of memory and creation.

Wright's selected volume of early poems, *Country Music* (Wesleyan University Press, 1982), and two later retrospectives, *The World of the Ten Thousand Things* (1990) and *Negative Blue* (2000), each draw on three major books—Wright has spoken of them as 'three trilogies'. The long sequences of the latter volumes have developed a ruminating late style, using a long, stepped verse line, that is still imagistic and musical but less sonorously conclusive than the early work. *Black Zodiac* (1997) won the Pulitzer Prize and the National Book Critics Circle Award. Since the turn of the century, Wright has been prolific, publishing seven volumes in a decade, and meditating on transience and mortality. *Scar Tissue* (2006—all Farrar, Straus) won the International Griffin Poetry Prize. For an interview with Wright, see the *Paris Review*, 113 (Winter 1989).   JP*

Wright, David (1920–94) Born in Johannesburg. He became deaf in childhood and, at the age of 14 was brought to England to attend the Northampton School for the Deaf. He graduated from Oriel College, Oxford, in 1942. His first collection, *Poems*, was published by *Poetry London* in 1949 (though it had been in the publisher's hands since 1943); his second collection, *Moral Stories* (1954), showed a strong reaction against his earlier manner. From 1959 to 1962 he edited, with the painter Patrick Swift, the quarterly review *X* (see

An Anthology from X, ed. Wright, Oxford University Press, 1988). Also with Patrick Swift, he wrote three books about Portugal. There is an autobiographical work, *Deafness: A Personal Account* (1969), and one critical work about a fellow South African, Roy *Campbell (1961). As an anthologist, Wright edited a number of excellent volumes, among them *Longer Contemporary Poems* (1966), the *Penguin Book of English Romantic Verse* (1968), and the *Penguin Book of Everyday Verse* (1976). He lived in the Lake District.

His poetry is remarkable for its quiet intelligence and humour, and the integrity of its style. The tone is conversational, though not in the sense of reproducing a factitious chattiness; rather, it creates the lively curve of an eminently humane mind's thinking and speaking. The perceptions are romantic, elegiac, exact. The subjects are various: there are recollections of childhood and of friends; poems about places and things observed, as well as on his deafness; some attractive poems about animals and birds; and noble elegies to Patrick *Kavanagh, Patrick Swift, Jean Murray Wright, and Philippa Reid.

After To the Gods the Shades: New and Collected Poems (1976) appeared, Wright published two collections: *Metrical Observations* (1980—both Carcanet) and *Elegies* (Greville, 1990). There is also a *Selected Poems* (1988). A warmly appreciative essay on Wright's work can be found in *In Two Minds: Guesses at Other Writers*, by C. H. Sisson (1990—both Carcanet).   TJGH

Wright, Franz (1953–) Born in Vienna, Austria, Wright grew up in the United States. His father was the poet James *Wright. He has taught in universities and worked in mental health, and lives in Massachusetts.

A prolific poet since the 1990s, *Ill Lit: Selected and New Poems* (Oberlin College Press, 1998) draws on Wright's first four full-length volumes. See also *Earlier Poems* (2007). *Walking to Martha's Vineyard* (2004) won the Pulitzer Prize. A post-*Confessional poet who writes openly about his struggle with alcoholism, depression, and religious faith as 'one of the

patients of God, | one of the orphans of light', Wright has also translated the poetry of René Char and Rainer Maria Rilke, whom he cites as an important influence. See also *God's Silence* (2006), *Wheeling Motel* (2009), and *Kindertotenwald*, a volume of prose poems (2011—all Knopf).   JNT

Wright, James (1927–80) Born into the family of an Ohio steelworker and educated in that state. After military service Wright went to Kenyon College where he studied under *Ransom, later completing his university training in Seattle with Theodore *Roethke. He taught for many years in the University of Minnesota and was attached to other academic institutions, latterly to Hunter College, New York.

There is a paradox at the heart of Wright's poetry: this most finely tuned of stylists, this clear delineator of language's own needs, is able to appeal directly to the feelings of his readers as few other American poets of his generation can. It is customary to speak of Wright's shifts of allegiance from formal versification to open-ended composition as a conversion to populism, but a Wright poem from any period will have a high emotional tension fitted to striking directness of utterance. When he came into prominence in the late Fifties and early Sixties, Wright seemed a cuckoo in each partisan's nest—a formalist (by Roethke out of *Yeats) in the age of the *Beats, a 'Minnesotan-Peruvian' (see *Deep Image) among the *Confessionals, and a master translator eschewing the academy in favour of Whitmanesque vernacular.

Such stylistic ambiguity sprang from Wright's impassioned identification with poor and unrepresented minorities in the United States, fused with an equally characteristic American fondness for the pressures of high art. Martin's Ferry, the mining town in Ohio where Wright grew up, recurs in his poetry like a tocsin of doom. It is both the source of many of his most terrible stories of poverty and wretchedness and the focus of his pantheism. Early in his career, he stated: 'I try to say how I love my country and how I despise the way it is treated. I try to speak of the beauty and again of the ugliness in the lives of the poor and neglected.'

Perhaps the most significant of early influences on Wright's work were two great European expressionist masters, Trakl and Rilke: indeed, if any one stylistic term might be applied to every stage of his development it would be expressionism. Wright's most celebrated conversion, immediately visible in the progression from *Saint Judas* (1959) to *The Branch Will Not Break* (1963), was seen at the time as deriving from the influence of his friend Robert *Bly, who championed the objective lyricism of Spanish-American poetry against the prevailing 'Confessional' mode of *Lowell and his followers. Finely stitched impacted stanzas, usually rhymed, were replaced by lyrical statements of an *Imagist sort. The language of these poems is direct and addresses personal and emotional concerns in a manner almost *en plein air*.

Wright's affection for and critical esteem of Vallejo and other South American poets, however, does not fully account for his stylistic shift; nor can his practice be held to resemble Bly's. Wright's originality has always shone more brightly when he appears to be imitating some prevailing mode. The poems from *The Branch Will Not Break* and *Shall We Gather at the River* (1968) show Wright experimenting with an open language appropriate to the increasing desperation of life in the USA. While Vallejo's poetry challenges political injustice in authoritarian regimes, Trakl's is wrought from the internal drama of the Central European mind, and Wright's, in turn, follows Trakl's tendency. From the beginning Wright was concerned with extremes of mental suffering, with poverty of hope as well as material poverty, and with murderers, hobos, and dispossessed American Indians. 'At the Executed Murderer's Grave' is one of the most powerful of his earlier poems.

The Branch Will Not Break reprinted one of his most notorious works, a poem which exemplified his changed style and which was so conspicuously misunderstood it became a rallying point for those suspicious of Wright—'Lying in a Hammock at William Duffy's Farm in Pine Island, Minnesota'. Long and facetiously elaborate titles, occasionally exceeding the body of the poem in length, are a feature of his work in the Sixties, and in this case a short passage of natural observation culminates in the line: 'I have wasted my life.' Years afterwards, Wright explained reasonably that this was a statement of mood, not an Augustinian confession. At the time it seemed a veritable polemic in favour of poetic detachment.

Wright travelled widely and often, and some of the most moving among his later poems are set in Italy. Whether he is rescuing a bee from a suicidal orgy in a ripe pear, 'among the gasworks at the edge of Mantua', watching the fast-flowing Adige river at Verona, or pausing at Leonardo's and Michelangelo's town of Aghiara, Wright finds occasion for many exquisite sorties into Latin elegy, and ties them to a specifically American *lacrimae rerum* from his Ohio childhood. The Italian poems are central to his book *To a Blossoming Pear Tree* (Farrar, Straus, 1977). Before this Wright had published a *Collected Poems* (Wesleyan University Press, 1971). He died in 1980. *Above The River: The Complete Poems* (Farrar, Straus/Bloodaxe, 1992) contains also some prose pieces and translations. Two selected volumes, of letters (*A Wild Perfection*) and poems (with an introduction by Robert Bly), appeared from Farrar, Straus and Giroux in 2005.   PNFP

Wright, Jay (1934–) Born in Albuquerque, New Mexico, Wright is the author of numerous books of poetry, including the two-volume *The Guide Signs* (2007) and *Transfigurations: Collected Poems* (2000— both Louisiana State University Press). He is also a playwright and essayist.

Wright is considered the most erudite and difficult African-American poet of his generation. He has found a champion in the critic Harold Bloom, but he has courted a small and devoted readership with dense lyrics that allude to esoteric, spiritualist, or occult themes from Western and non-Western sources like the west African griot tradition and Native American shamanism. Before attaining a master's degree in literature from Rutgers University, Wright studied chemistry at the University of New Mexico, spent a year at Union Theological Seminary, served three years in the Medical Corps of the United States Army, and played professional baseball with the San Diego Padres. His first collection was *The Homecoming Singer* (Corinth, 1971).

Wright has received awards from the Lannan, Guggenheim, MacArthur, and Ingram Merrill Foundations, the American Academy and Institute of Arts and Letters, and the National Endowment for the Arts. In 2005 he won the Bollingen Prize. He has taught at many universities over the years, including Yale. He makes his home in Bradford, Vermont.   AMl

Wright, Judith (1915–2000) Born and brought up in the New England area of New South Wales. For many years she made her home at Mount Tambourine, Queensland, but later returned to New South Wales and settled in Braidwood. With the publication of her first volume *The Moving Image* (Meanjin, 1946) Wright established herself as a poet of the first rank, and subsequent volumes brought her a well-deserved international reputation. She published work other than poetry, including criticism, short stories, and studies of conservation and of Australian history. Nevertheless, it is the poetry which counts for most.

Her range is wide. She is technically adroit over a variety of forms, and in all her volumes the poems, meditative, lyrical, and combative by turns, move easily from the personal to the social, and from the world of nature to the world of politics. Through them all, however, runs a tough connecting thread, a conviction that the created world and its inhabitants have been touched by a grace they repeatedly deny. Over the years her poems became darker. Yet the conviction survived. In her early poetry she tended to concentrate on the intensely personal, as in the beautiful 'The Company of Lovers', 'Woman to Man', and 'Our Love Is so Natural'; and even the much-anthologized 'Bullocky', a deftly constructed fable at whose heart is the archetypal figure of the ploughman, can be read as a poem which gathers together the possibilities of several kinds of fruition, including the personal. Going with these poems are others about Australia's native flora and fauna, and some of these

were gathered together in the delightful volume *Birds*, first published in 1962 and then reprinted in 1967, this time with some unfussy illustrations by the Australian artist Annette Macarthy Onslow.

With the publication of *The Other Half* (1966) it is possible to detect a change, not so much of direction as of tone. There had been poems of social awareness in previous volumes, but when Wright turns to such matters in the new collection the poems have about them a distinctively sharpened note of displeasure at the despoiling of 'green earth'. The volume's final poem, called 'Turning Fifty', ends with her raising her cup to the 'new sun', but there is nothing bland or absolving about the gesture. The poem is taut with anger. It may be that this is at least one reason why she said in a late poem, 'Skins', that she no longer wished to read the poems she wrote in her thirties. 'They dropped off several incarnations back.' That poem comes from *Phantom Dwelling* (1985). Her earlier work may be most conveniently consulted in the *Collected Poems* (1971—all Angus and Robertson). She was awarded the Queen's Gold Medal for Poetry in 1992.

See also *A Human Pattern: Selected Poems* (Angus & Robertson, 1990; new edn., with an introduction by John *Kinsella, Carcanet, 2010).   JL

Wright, Kit (1944–   ) Born in Kent, and educated at Oxford. He has lectured in Canada, was fellow-commoner in creative art at Cambridge, 1977–9; from 1970–75 he was education secretary at the Poetry Society. He now lives in London, where he works as a freelance writer, broadcaster, and editor, and is a well-known figure on the poetry-workshop scene. Both the Home Counties background and unfashionable urban life elicit Wright's lyricism, and his poetry is profoundly English in its combining of jaunty rhythms, comic rhymes, a detached or impersonal air, with subject-matter that is frequently bleak, blackly funny, and grimly personal. Bereavement, breakdown, failure (particularly in love), the 'tears and terror' or the quiet desperation beneath the surfaces of ordinary English life, a recurring note of grief or

w

sympathy for victims and underdogs—and a persistent strain of remorse and self-reproach, often connected with drinking: these are fairly constant in Wright's work, but so are the metrical ingenuity, the levity, and verbal panache. He has not been prolific since *Short Afternoons* (Hutchinson, 1989), but his verse remains admired by other British formalists such as Sophie *Hannah and Carol Ann *Duffy. It has been collected under the *Hardy-esque title, *Hoping It Might Be So: Poems 1974–2000* (Leviathan, 2000). He is also the author of several books for children, which have been collected in *The Magic Box* (Macmillan, 2009).   AJ*

Wylie, Elinor (Morton Hoyt) (1885–1928) Born in New Jersey and grew up in Philadelphia and Washington, DC. Married at 20 to socialite Philip Hichborn, she eloped five years later with Horace Wylie, with whom she lived, partly in England, from 1911 to 1915. Divorced from Wylie in 1923, she married William Rose Benét, a man of letters and brother of the poet Stephen Vincent Benét. She lived in Greenwich Village from 1922 until her death from a stroke in 1928.

Elinor Wylie's first book of poems was privately printed in London in 1912 and was followed in 1921 by *Nets to Catch the Wind*; three more collections, and four novels, followed in quick succession.

During and immediately after Wylie's lifetime her striking beauty combined with a social persona both aristocratic and artistic to cast an adulatory spell. Edmund Wilson, no gusher as a rule, called Wylie in an essay after her death 'master of a divine language' and 'a free spirit as few Bohemians are'. This aura has dissipated, and Wylie is now regarded as a minor poet. Her novels, precious period pieces, are now hardly read; but some poems, particularly from the earlier collections, retain both force and charm. With firmly chiselled lines and colourful images, lyrics like 'August', 'Wild Peaches', or 'Bronze Trumpets and Sea-Water' stand out from the *Imagist practices of the period. More closely resembling the traditionally shaped lyric intensities of Edna St Vincent *Millay, Wylie's best poems have a distinctively worldly voice, as they ruefully limn the tensions between experience and idealism. Wylie's burnished diction and supple rhymes influenced the poetry of the young James *Merrill.

Wylie's work is to be found in *Collected Poems of Elinor Wylie* (1932), *Collected Prose of Elinor Wylie* (1933), and *Last Poems* (1943—all Knopf). See also *Elinor Wylie*, a largely hostile study of the work by Thomas A. Gray (Twayne, 1969); *Elinor Wylie: A Life Apart* by Stanley Olson (Dial, 1979); and *The Life and Art of Elinor Wylie* by Judith Farr (Louisiana State University Press, 1983).   RHa

W

Yap, Arthur (1943–2006) Born in Singapore, and educated locally, at Leeds University, and at the National University of Singapore, where he was a senior lecturer.

His poems are original, but can also be demanding: elliptical, dense, dry, sometimes droll. At their best, they shuttle between playfulness and sobriety and are alert to the rhythms and contours of the natural and the peopled landscape, seasoning insight with compassion.

Yap's stories can be sampled from *Singapore Short Stories: Volume 1*, ed. Robert Yeo (Heinemann, 1978). He was also an abstract painter. His poetry collections (all published in Singapore) are: *Only Lines* (Federal Publications, 1971); *Commonplace* (1977); *Down the Line* (1980); and *Man Snake Apple* (1986—all Heinemann). Some later poems appeared in *The Space of City Trees: Selected Poems* (Skoob, 2000). *Collected Poems*, edited by Jenny Yap, were published by the National University of Singapore Press in 2012. See 'Arthur Yap: Uniquely Singaporean?' by Thow Xin Wei in the online journal *Quarterly Literary Review Singapore* (July 2006). RPa

Yau, John (1950–) Born in Lynn, Massachusetts to a Chinese mother and English-Chinese father. Yau took a BA from Bard College, an MFA from Brooklyn College, and currently teaches art criticism at Mason Cross School of the Arts, Rutgers University. He has published over fifty monographs and collaborative books spanning poetry, novels, art criticism, and artists' books, and edits Black Square Editions. His work has won numerous awards, and in 2002 he was appointed a *Chevalier de l'ordre des arts et des lettres*.

Citing Robert *Kelly as a formative influence, in his poetry Yau works against 'the structures of languages—the accepted narratives, their little boxes'. Language is a tool which creates a multi-textured polyvocal poetry which probing Yau's dual cultural heritages—as Chinese and American, as a poet and an artist. His poetry and short stories practise an abstract urbanism set against the backdrop of New York City. *Corpse and Mirror* (Holt, Rinehart, 1983) saw Yau receive an Academy of American Poets Lavan Award, and was selected for the National Poetry Series by John *Ashbery. *Ing Grish*, a collaboration with painter Thomas Nozowski, led Robert *Creeley to commend the 'complexly articulate play' and 'wildly divergent thought' of his poetics. HY

Yeats, W. B. (William Butler) (1865–1939) Born in Dublin, son of the painter John Butler Yeats and Susan Pollexfen. His family moved to London when he was 2, and back to Dublin when he was 16. His childhood holidays were spent in Co. Sligo, which came to share with Lady Gregory's Coole Park the central place in his poetry's imaginative geography. After it was decided that he would not go to Trinity College, Dublin (where his father's friend Edward Dowden was professor of English), he studied at the Dublin Metropolitan School of Art from 1884 to 1886. His first published poems appeared in the *Dublin University Review* in 1885; his first volume of poems, *The Wanderings of Oisin and Other Poems* (1889), already suggests the three major preoccupations of his writings: Ireland, spiritualism, and love—unsurprising concerns in the context of both English and Irish poetry of his time. The preponderance of one or other of these depended on who Yeats was currently influenced by (though

Conor Cruise O'Brien argues in his essay 'Passion and Cunning' that the poet's declared passions were always controlled by his determination to be a significant poet). He was a founder-member of the Irish National Literary Society in 1892.

The first major influence was Yeats' father, whom he both revered and reacted against. But as early as the mid-1880s he was reading Sinnett's *Esoteric Buddhism*; in 1890 he joined the Hermetic Order of the Golden Dawn, and in 1892 he wrote to John O'Leary that his interest in the occult was, after his poetry, the most important pursuit of his life. His interest in Irish affairs was fanned by meeting O'Leary, the exiled Fenian leader who returned to Dublin from Paris in 1885; Yeats first encountered him in the exclusive, Trinity-based Contemporary Club to which he was introduced by his father. O'Leary was in turn responsible for Yeats' first meeting with Maud Gonne in London in January 1889: an event which he described in the Dantesque phrase 'the troubling of my life'. As a passionate Irish nationalist of great beauty, she represented the poet's ideal, and his largely (though not entirely) unrequited love for her obsessed him for the next quarter-century. The volumes of poems up to *The Green Helmet* (1910) are dominated by Yeats' love for her and the despair caused by her marriage to John MacBride in 1903, culminating in the love-lament 'No Second Troy'.

In this period Yeats was by no means a prolific poet. His friend (and later enemy) George Moore testifies that his poetic career was thought to have largely ended in the early years of the new century, something which is partly corroborated by the appearance of an eight-volume *Collected Works* in 1908. In that period Yeats was most active in the successful attempt to set up an Irish National Theatre, started in 1899 in collaboration with Augusta, Lady Gregory, and Edward Martyn. He found in writing for the theatre a literary way of combining through mythology his interests in Irish nationalism and the mysterious, and it also afforded acting parts for Maud Gonne. In 1902 Maud played the title-role in the nationalistic play *Cathleen Ni Houlihan* (of which Yeats wondered in his late poem

'The Man And The Echo', 'Did that play of mine send out | Certain men the English shot?'—Stephen Gwynn said it did have an emotionally rousing impact). But strangely, despite his energetic involvement with the theatre throughout his life, Yeats' plays lack a natural sense of the theatrical; though they have moments and subjects of high drama, they are often defeated by their brevity and by verging on the ludicrous. He was, though, a very effective promoter of other playwrights, most importantly Synge, whom he encouraged to return to Ireland from Paris in the 1890s. Whether or not Yeats has the principal responsibility for Synge's inspiring sojourns in the Aran Islands from 1899 to 1902, there is no doubting his defence of Synge's *The Playboy of the Western World* (1907) against what he saw as the small-minded prudery and nationalism of the protesting audience in his Abbey Theatre in Dublin. The occasion was the first of many when Yeats accused the new Irish (and indeed English) middle classes of debased materialism—though it must be said that it was a charge which had general fashionable currency in literary circles long before, and after, Yeats.

From *Responsibilities* (1914) onwards, Yeats' poetry develops great dramatic power and scope. As public events in Ireland became more crucial, his poetry becomes correspondingly more public, beginning with the disillusioned but rhetorical 'September 1913': 'Romantic Ireland's dead and gone, | It's with O'Leary in the grave.' These poems of Yeats' 'middle period' combine to great effect a declamatory voice with a diction which is more spare than in his earlier, 'Celtic twilight' verse. 'Easter 1916' notes the new 'terrible beauty' that the rebellion represents, and Yeats traces with horror the growing violence of the period, through 'Nineteen Hundred And Nineteen' on to 'Meditations in Time of Civil War' (both published in *The Tower*, 1928). Outside his poetry, he was practically active in the public sphere, and he was nominated to the Senate, the Upper House of the new Free State, in 1922. He made some historically significant speeches there, many arguing the Anglo-Irish Protestant interest which he felt was insufficiently represented in the new state: something which led to increasing political disillusion and disengagement on his part. But by the 1920s, under the pressure of political events around him, Yeats had become an important public poet.

There were major developments in Yeats' private and intellectual life in the middle period too. In 1917, after Maud Gonne's daughter Iseult had also refused him, he married Georgie Hyde Lees whom he met in 1911. The marriage was very happy and they had two children. A week after the wedding, George (Yeats' name for her) started to produce automatic writing which greatly excited her husband. Her communications were the basis of Yeats' pseudo-philosophical, mystical book *A Vision* (1925); more importantly, they provided material for several powerful visionary poems, such as 'The Second Coming' (published 1921) and 'Leda and the Swan' (in *The Tower*). A further literary stimulus was Yeats' introduction by Ezra *Pound to the Japanese Noh plays. This led to the production in 1916 of *At the Hawk's Well*, the first of Yeats' *Four Plays for Dancers*, plays which used masks, which Yeats saw as shifting the emphasis from the actor to the language. Like the thought of *A Vision*, the notion of the mask extended into Yeats' poetry to salutary effect.

Perhaps the most important aspect of Yeats' poetry in this period was the development of his theory of symbolism as mediating between life and art, a dichotomy which was to be the principal concern of his poetry for the rest of his life. To represent this concern, he refined the symbols which he had used throughout his writing (the swan and the rose, for example), in a process which is brilliantly traced in Frank Kermode's *Romantic Image* (1957). To those he added some new symbols, derived from his own life, particularly the tower which was Thoor Ballylee, near Gort, Co. Galway, not far from Coole Park. Yeats bought it in 1917 and, though he lived in it only very briefly, it afforded an important artistic domicile for him. Many critics (C. K. *Stead, for example) have felt that his greatest achievement was this development of a symbolic language to express an equilibrium

between the conflicting demands on the poet of the outside world and his art: what he called in a late poem, 'The Choice', the intellect's dilemma of choosing between 'Perfection of the life, or of the work'. This theme is central to the two volumes which are often thought to be Yeats' best, *The Tower* (1928) and *The Winding Stair* (1933). The maintenance of this equilibrium is the subject of the complementary Byzantium poems; 'Sailing to Byzantium' (1927) declares the physical world to be 'no country for old men', and takes the poet to the holy, artistic city of Byzantium (as extolled by the Nineties aesthetes) where, 'out of bodily form', the soul can sing. In 'Byzantium' (1930), the objective has ostensibly been reached, as 'the unpurged images of day recede'. But the tension is sustained by the use of sexual language (the images in Byzantium *beget*, for instance) to keep the demands of the physical world in contention.

Yeats remained unreconciled to growing old (at least in his poetry; Louis *MacNeice reported that in reality Yeats viewed approaching death with surprising equanimity), and one of the principal subjects of his *Last Poems* is the raging against old age which is the central issue in the poem 'The Tower' (1926). But it is by no means the only topic in Yeats' later work; there is a development in the language of his masterly reverie poems, in 'Among School Children' (1926), 'In Memory of Eva Gore-Booth and Con Markiewicz' (1927), 'Coole Park, 1929' and 'Coole Park and Ballylee, 1931', for example. His health—physical, and to some extent mental—came under increasing strain as he attempted to 'hammer his thoughts into unity' and to make his complete poems represent that unity. His prose writing, which was voluminous throughout his life, becomes increasingly central to his work in later years. Yeats was not a good critic of other people's writing, but he was a compelling commentator on his own and a vitally important analyst of the poet in action. His self-commentary and his manuscripts have been used very effectively by Curtis Bradford and Jon *Stallworthy to trace the evolution of his poetry.

In his last years he shared with *Eliot the undisputed central place in English poetry (*Hardy was drafted in later to provide a more English and less complex alternative); he was awarded the Nobel Prize for Literature in 1923. In 1936 he edited the *Oxford Book of Modern Verse 1892–1935* (eccentrically—he represented *Auden minimally and his own friends generously), and he spent part of his later years in France, where he died in January 1939, prompting a great elegy by Auden. His body was returned to Ireland in 1948 and buried, as he had wished, in Drumcliffe churchyard, Co. Sligo (where his paternal grandfather had been rector), under the epitaph from the end of his 'Under Ben Bulben': 'Cast a cold eye | On life, on death. | Horseman, pass by!'

Yeats' *Last Poems* (1939) present serious problems of editing and interpretation. The standard one-volume edition (the 1952 extended 2nd edition of the 1933 *Collected*) ended in a fine climax with 'Under Ben Bulben'. But all the major editions (which are seriously divided on other issues) agree that Yeats' intention—left unfulfilled at his death—was that that volume should be left divided as first published, with *New Poems* (1938) ending with 'Are You Content?' and the separate volume called *Last Poems* beginning with 'Under Ben Bulben'. As a result, these *Last Poems*, beginning with this epitaph poem, become a voice from the grave: something which suits the theme of many of them ('Cuchulainn Comforted', for instance). Whatever form of *Last Poems* is preferred, there is no doubt that they are a remarkable and powerful swan-song, some written within a week of the poet's death and all in the face of illness. Perhaps the poems which make the best epitaph for his work (as distinct from his life) are two describing the enduring discontent with his achievement that gives his poetry such unflagging energy, 'What Then?' (from *New Poems*) and 'The Circus Animals' Desertion' (from *Last Poems*).

The critical evaluation of Yeats will always be problematical because of controversy over his political views (Irish nationalist or right-wing eugenicist in the 1930s) or the seriousness with which he took the occult (which Yvor *Winters said reduced his poetry to nonsense). But there is no disputing his influence. As Eliot prophesied, he created a poetic language for the twentieth century, as is evident throughout the writing of poets such as *Larkin and *Heaney.

No fully definitive version of Yeats' poems is possible, for reasons which are evident in the *Variorum Edition*, ed. P. Allt and R. K. Alspach (1957). The fiftieth anniversary of Yeats' death in 1989 saw several new editions of the poems, but there are two major contenders, representing two separate traditions: *W. B. Yeats: The Poems Revised*, ed. R. J. Finneran (1989) which ultimately derives (with important changes) from the one-volume *Collected Poems*; and *Yeats' Poems*, ed. A. N. Jeffares (1989) which derives from the limited edition *The Poems of W. B. Yeats* (1949—all Macmillan), overseen by the poet's widow George, the publisher Harold Macmillan, and the publisher's reader Thomas Mark. The Jeffares edition has an appendix by Warwick Gould, the editor of the *Yeats Review*, arguing the case for regarding this as nearly the definitive edition. The most obvious difference between the editions is that the longer pieces, headed 'Narrative and Dramatic' in the *Collected Poems* are kept as a separate category at the end by Finneran but incorporated chronologically into the whole corpus by Jeffares, following the 1949 edition. Pending the publication of the Longman Annotated edition by Peter *McDonald, the most convenient one-volume edition is now Daniel Albright, *W. B. Yeats: The Poems* (Dent, 1990) which has particularly interesting notes.

Perhaps inevitably in the case of a poet as public as Yeats, the most prominent work on him has tended to be scholarly-historical rather than critical, as is evident from the volumes of the valuable *Yeats Review*. Of this work the most important is John Kelly's monumental edition of the *Letters*, the first volume of which appeared in 1986, and which is now also available in an electronic edition, alongside all the extant unannotated letters. The letters of Yeats and his wife have been edited in a separate volume by Ann Saddlemyer. R. F. Foster's 'official' biography appeared in two volumes from Oxford University Press: *The Apprentice Mage* (1997) and *The Arch-Poet* (2003). The most important editorial project is the Cornell University Press multi-volume editions of the complete works, of which *The Tower* (ed. R. J. Finneran with Jared Curtis and Ann Saddlemyer) completed the poetic manuscripts in 2007. Finneran's edition of the poems was the first volume of this new standard edition of the complete works; in the meantime most of his writings exist in a series of lightly edited Macmillan volumes: *A Vision* (2nd edn., 1937); *Collected Plays* (2nd edn., 1952); *Autobiographies* (1955); *Mythologies* (1959); *Essays and Introductions* (1961); *Explorations* (1962). More fully edited are a series of volumes of various prose writings: *The Senate Speeches of W. B. Yeats*, ed. D. R. Pearce (1960); *Uncollected Prose by W. B. Yeats, vol. 1*, ed. J. P. Frayne (1970) and *vol. 2*, ed. J. P. Frayne and C. Johnson (1975); *Memoirs*, ed. D. Donoghue (1972). See also Finneran (ed.), *The Yeats Reader* (Palgrave/Scribner, 1997; revd. edn., 2002). Of criticism on the poetry, the pioneering works by Richard Ellmann, *Yeats: The Man and the Masks* (1949) and *The Identity of Yeats* (1954—both Macmillan) have not been superseded. But there is a huge volume of writing on Yeats; for further guidance, see the extensive bibliographies in the volumes of the *Yeats Review*.   BO'D

Yong, Shu Hoong (1966–) Born in Singapore, Yong grew up speaking English and Chinese. He studied Computer Science at the National University and received an MBA from Texas A&M University at College Station. His first volume, *Isaac* (1997), which grew out of a manuscript of poems begun in America, was shortlisted for the Singapore Literature Prize. It established the characteristic themes of family and travel, and includes verse in both English and Mandarin. A revised edition, *Isaac Revisited*, appeared from Ethos Books in 2001. Yong's more experimental second collection, *dowhile* (2002), draws on his experience of working in the 'dotcom' economy ('do' and 'while' are 'used to execute instructions repeatedly while a given condition holds true'). *Frottage* (2005) responds to the painting of Max Ernst and travels in Australia. It shared the 2006 Singapore Literature Prize with Cyril *Wong's *unmarked treasure*. His latest collection is *From within the marrow* (2010—all firstfruits).   JNT

Young, Andrew (John) (1885–1971) Born at Elgin, Morayshire, where his father was station-master. The family later moved to Edinburgh and he attended the Royal High School there and Edinburgh University. Taking an arts degree in 1907, he seemed set on a career in the law, but after a brief period spent studying art and ecclesiastical architecture in Paris he entered New College, Edinburgh, to prepare himself for the Presbyterian ministry. During the First World War he served at an army rest-camp near Boulogne. In 1920 he was appointed minister of the Presbyterian church at Hove, Sussex, but in 1939 he joined the Anglican communion and was made vicar of Stonegate, Sussex, later becoming a canon of Chichester Cathedral.

His first collection of poems, *Songs of the Night*, was published in 1910, while he was still a student at New College. Despite a steady output in the years that followed, it was not until his eighth book, significantly entitled *Winter Harvest* (1933), that he felt satisfied he had found his true voice. This was also the first volume in which he showed his practice of reworking old material in his new manner, the ultimate fruits of which were displayed in his radically selective *Collected Poems* of 1950.

Young's earliest poems betray something of the influence of Swinburne and his Decadent disciples, and he later passed through a phase that might be classified as *Georgian. His mature style, however, is quite distinctive, and while the occasional line may be coloured by the influence of one of the poets he continued to admire—*Hardy perhaps above all—the discovery of a personal voice, sturdily independent of fashion and at the exclusive service of a highly idiosyncratic vision, is at the very heart of his achievement.

What connects Young with the Georgians is his abiding interest in landscape, flora, and fauna as poetic subjects; what differentiates him from them is the use he made of those subjects. His extensive knowledge of wild flowers and intimacy with the places where they grew give his descriptive writing a rare authority. Employing traditional lyric forms, terse in utterance and argument, pointed with simile and paradox in a manner that recalls the work of Herbert, Marvell, and other metaphysical poets, constantly upsetting preconceptions and seeking to accommodate the profoundest mysteries within the smallest span of words, his finest poems are to be read as meditations on death and the impermanence of worldly attachments. A pawky humour and relish of the tricks played by the perceiving mind are also characteristic of his stance. Young continued his investigation of favourite themes in two long, blank-verse poems, 'Into Hades' and 'A Traveller in Time', which purport to recount otherworldly journeys made by the poet himself and which were published in 1958 under the joint title, *Out of the World and Back.*

Because Young revised or rejected so much of his early work, the establishment of a canonic text has been no simple matter. After the poet's own 1950 edition, a *Collected Poems* edited by Leonard Clark was published in 1960, and this was followed in 1974 by a *Complete Poems*, also edited by Clark. The most satisfactory text, however, is provided by *The Poetical Works of Andrew Young* (Secker & Warburg, 1985), ed. Edward Lowbury and Alison Young. This includes early poems thought to have been worth rescuing, as well as a number of verse plays. Young's essays on wild flowers, topography, architecture, and kindred matters give a strong impression of his wit and breadth of learning, and are to be found in such volumes as *A Prospect of Flowers* (1945), *A Prospect of Britain* (1956), and *The New Poly-Olbion* (1967).   CJR

Young, Dean (1955–) Born in Columbia, Pennsylvania. He is the author of numerous books of poetry, including *Skid* (2002), which was a finalist for the Lenore Marshall Prize; *Elegy on Toy Piano* (2005),

which was a finalist for the Pulitzer Prize; and *Primitive Mentor* (2008—all University of Pittsburgh Press), which was a finalist for the 2009 International Griffin Poetry Prize. His book of prose, *The Art of Recklessness: Poetry as Assertive Force and Contradiction*, was published by Graywolf Press in 2010.

Young is a poet of both passion and comedy, combining the two modes in imagistic, freewheeling, urgently voiced monologues. While clearly influenced by *New York School poets like Kenneth *Koch and Frank *O'Hara, Young has written of his debt to the French *Surrealists, particularly André Breton. He is a proponent of exuberance and anti-rationalism: 'Whatever you start out as | you end up as something else, | the process lurches, jumps, stalls | but maybe there's balance in the ravage, | the invisible origins of music' ('Dragonfly').

Young's prizes include an Academy Award in Literature from the American Academy of Arts and Sciences, a Stegner Fellowship, residence at the Fine Arts Work Center in Provincetown, and awards from the National Endowment for the Arts and the Guggenheim Foundation. He is the William Livingston Chair of Poetry at the University of Texas, Austin.   AMl

Young, Douglas (1913–73) Born in Tayport, Fife, and spent some of his younger years near Calcutta (now Kolkata) where his father worked in the jute trade. He took degrees in classics from the universities of St Andrews and Oxford, and taught Latin and Greek at the universities of Aberdeen, University College Dundee, St Andrews, McMaster (Ontario), and North Carolina, where he died.

A lifelong Scottish nationalist, Young's academic career was interrupted during the Second World War by controversy and imprisonment arising from his conscientious objection to the right of the British parliament to conscript Scots into the armed forces. His first poems appeared around this time as *Auntran Blads* (1943), followed by *A Braird o Thristles* (1947), and a brief *Selected Poems* (1950).

At its best Young's use of *Scots is stark, lyrical and philologically astute as well as affecting—see 'Thonder They Ligg', 'For a Wife in Jizzen', and 'The Shepherd's Dochter'. He translated Aristophanes' *The Frogs* into Scots as *The Puddocks* (1957) and *The Birds* as *The Burdies* (1959). In 1968 he translated (into English verse) Euripides' *Hippolytus* (as *Venus with a Vengeance*, McMaster University Press, 1968) and *The Oresteia* of Aeschylus (University of Oklahoma Press, 1974). Other books include *Chasing an Ancient Greek* (Hollis & Carter, 1950), *St. Andrews* (Cassell, 1969), and *Scotland* (Cassell, 1971). He also edited Theognis for the Bibliotecha Teubneriana. His anthology *Scottish Verse: 1851–1951* (Nelson, 1952) is still a valuable survey of its period. *A Clear Voice: Douglas Young, Poet and Polymath*, ed. C. Young and D. Murison (Macdonald, 1976) contains a memoir and selections from Young's work in verse and prose.   DED

Young, Kevin (1970–) Born in Lincoln, Nebraska, Young studied with Seamus *Heaney and Lucie *Brock-Broido at Harvard University. While a student at Harvard, he also became a member of the Dark Room Collective, a community of African-American writers founded by Thomas Sayers Ellis and Sharan Strange. He received his MFA in creative writing from Brown University in 1996. His first book, *Most Way Home* (Zoland, 1998), was winner of the Zacharis First Books Award from *Ploughshares*, and was selected for the National Poetry Series by Lucille *Clifton. Young's following three collections form what he calls 'an American trilogy', each with a central theme: *To Repel Ghosts* (Zoland, 2002) explores the paintings of Jean-Michel Basquiat; *Jelly Roll* (2003)—a finalist for the James Laughlin Award—investigates the blues form; while *Black Maria* (2005) is styled as a film noir. He has published three further books of poetry since then: *For the Confederate Dead* (2007); *Dear Darkness* (2008—all Knopf); and *Ardency* (Random House, 2011). Young has also edited a number of anthologies, including *Giant Steps: The New Generation of African American Writers* (Harper, 2000); *Blues Poems* (2003); *Jazz Poems* (Everyman, 2006); and a selection of John *Berryman's poems (Library of America, 2004). He includes Berryman among the foremost influences on his poetry, as well as Langston *Hughes and Emily Dickinson. Young has taught at the universities of Georgia and Indiana, and lives in Boston and Atlanta.   SR

Yu, Ouyang (1955–) Born in Huangzhou, China, Yu took a BA in English and American Literature at Wuhan University, and an MA in English and Australian Literature at East China Normal University. He emigrated to Australia in 1991, undertaking a PhD in Sino-Australian Literature at La Trobe University, and gained Australian citizenship in 1998. In 1996 he co-founded *Otherland* (Yuanxiang), Australia's first Chinese-language literary journal.

Yu has authored and edited over fifty books of poetry, fiction, non-fiction, translation, and criticism in both English and Chinese; the English-language *Foreign Matter* (Otherland, 2003) won the 2003 Fast Books Prize, and the Chinese-language *Report on Australia* (2009) won an Award for Excellence from the Federation of Overseas Chinese Associations. A novel, *The Eastern Slope Chronicle* (Pluto, 2002), was shortlisted for the 2003 NSW Premier Award. Yu has also translated the work of David *Malouf, Hanif Kureishi, and Germaine Greer, amongst others.

Yu's poetry deals with the frustrations of the migrant experience, interrogating cultural identity and diversity in Australia with a 'tongue held | between two languages like a vice' (*Moon over Melbourne* (Papyrus, 1995)). In his taut, lyrical free verse, introspection and self-criticism are balanced with criticism of social and cultural establishments: poetry is one of the freest means of political commentary in China, and his work in both languages is shot through with a concern for his native country, and for the Chinese in Australia.   HY

y

Zamora, Bernice (1938–) Born and raised in Colorado, Zamora won an extensive reputation largely on the basis of a single volume, *Restless Serpents* (Diseños Literarios, 1976), a collection both of her own poems and those of José Antonio Burciaga. Her poetry has been notable, in both Spanish and English, for its subtlety of idiom, her command, often colloquial, of a distinctively crafted *chicana* speaking voice. Even so, Robinson *Jeffers and Theodore *Roethke have been prime influences. Her versatility shows through on a number of related fronts: as a poet of feminine sexuality and consciousness ('Gata Poem', 'Notes From a Chicana "Coed"' or 'When We Are Able'), of childhood ('Angelita's Utility'), of eroticism ('Pueblo 1950', 'Bearded Lady', and 'And All Flows Past'), of Chicano linguistic and cultural tradition ('Let the Giants Cackle'), of landscape and place (the Jeffers-like 'California'), and of creativity itself (the impressively wrought title-poem 'Restless Serpents', alongside 'Without Bark' or 'Metaphor and Reality'). Long a critic of 'Anglo' oppression and insensitivity to cultural difference, she none the less avoids all polemical calls to arms or self-pity. She especially parodies stereotypes, both cultural and sexual. In 1994, Zamora selected her early poems alongside new work in *Releasing Serpents* (Bilingual Press).

See *Flor y Canto IV and V: An Anthology of Chicano Literature*, ed. Bernice Zamora and José Armas (Pajarito, 1980); and *Contemporary Chicana Poetry: A Critical Approach to an Emerging Literature*, by Marta Ester Sánchez (University of California Press, 1985). ARL

Zapruder, Matthew (1967–) Born in Washington, D.C., Zapruder is the cofounder and editor of Wave Books (formerly Verse Press), an independent poetry press based in Seattle and publisher of some of the most notable contemporary American poets to emerge in recent years, including Mary *Ruefle and Dorothea Lasky. He is the author of the collections *American Linden* (Tupelo, 2002) and *The Pajamaist* (Copper Canyon, 2006), which was selected by Tony *Hoagland as the winner of the William Carlos Williams Award; he is also co-translator of *Secret Weapon* by Romanian poet Eugen Jebeleanu (Coffee House, 2007). His most recent book, *Come on All You Ghosts* (Copper Canyon, 2010), garnered praise for Zapruder's development of his meandering, spontaneous style—indebted as much to the *Beat poets as to James *Schuyler and John *Ashbery—into poems that encompass moments of grace and stillness while retaining the ardour and quirkiness of his earlier work (e.g. his irreverent yet heartfelt take on Wordsworth, 'The Prelude'). Zapruder studied at Amherst and Berkeley, and currently teaches at the University of California. He lives in San Francisco. SR

Zaturenska, Marya (Alexandrovna) (1902–82) Born in Kiev, Ukraine (then part of Russia), Zaturenska's mother's family was Polish, and worked for generations for the Radziwill family. Her father served in the Russian Army during the Russo-Japanese War and the Boxer Rebellion. As a little girl Zaturenska loved Polish and Russian folk-songs, and before she could read or write, created lyrics for the tunes. In 1909, when she was eight, the family moved to America, residing on Henry Street in New York City near the Settlement House. She was educated in public schools, but had to drop out. She attended high school at night, worked in a factory by day—and wrote poetry. Her first published poems appeared in national magazines, including *Poetry*, when she was still in her teens, and she won the John Reed Memorial Award in 1922, when she was 20. She graduated from the University of Wisconsin Library School in 1925. That same year she married the poet and critic Horace *Gregory, of a patrician Milwaukee family. They later collaborated on anthologies and *A History of American Poetry, 1900–40* (New York, 1946).

Threshold and Hearth, her first collection, appeared in 1934. It received the Shelley Memorial Award. But it was her second book, *Cold Morning Sky*, which put her on the literary map. Published in 1937—a year which saw new collections by *Bogan, H. D. (Hilda *Doolittle), *Jeffers, *Millay, *Pound, *Stevens, and *Tate, among others—it was awarded the Pulitzer Prize. It was reprinted twice the following year.

Her greatest influence was the English Decadent school, particularly Christina Rossetti, of whom she wrote a biography. Zaturenska's meditative and mystical lyrics are admired for their delicacy, mastery of metre and rhyme, and her ability to make something fresh out of lyric conventions. As late as 1974, when she published her eighth and last collection, *The Hidden Waterfall*, she had not altered her style or subjects to make them more fashionable. Mention should also be made of her fine translations from the Italian, including works by Monti, Stampa, and Tasso.

The largest edition is *Collected Poems of Marya Zaturenska* (Viking Press 1965). *New Selected Poems*, ed. Robert Phillips, appeared from Syracuse University Press in 2001, as did her diaries for 1938–44, with an introduction and notes by her son, Patrick Gregory.   RSP

Zephaniah, Benjamin (1958–) Born in Birmingham, but brought up in Jamaica. He spent his early teens at various approved schools in England, and also had a spell in prison. In his late teens he made his way as an impersonator of famous stars, eventually branching out as a very popular performance poet.

Arguably a cruder kind of *dub poet than Linton Kwesi *Johnson or John *Agard, the very rawness of Zephaniah's verse is true to the emotions and attitudes of dispossessed people submerged even within the Afro-Caribbean community in Britain. His poetry also displays the prophetic vein of a Rastafarian, and ranges from pure rhetoric to visionary rapture. At its best, it is full of ambivalent tension between these two poles. He can also be refreshingly down-to-earth. In 'Just Like David' he makes it clear that the function of the poet is to smite oppressive Goliaths everywhere.

The institutional racism that Zephaniah encountered during his early career included, in 1987, an editorial in the *Sun* newspaper on his nomination to a creative arts fellowship at Trinity College, Cambridge, which asked 'Would You Let This Man Near Your Daughter?'. *The Dread Affair* (Arena, 1985) collected his early poems. Since the early 1990s, Zephaniah has published three collections with Bloodaxe: *City Psalms* (1992), *Propa Propaganda* (1996), and *Too Black Too Strong* (2001). He has also written plays, verse for children, and fiction for teenagers. In 2003, he declined an OBE; in 2009, he was voted third in a BBC poll of favourite poets; and in 2011 he became Professor of Creative Writing at Brunel University. *To Do Wid Me* (2012) is a film portrait of Zephaniah as a performer. See *Benjamin Zephaniah: My Story* (Collins, 2011).   MR*

Zieroth, David (Dale) (1946–) Born in Neepawa, Manitoba, the son of a farming couple. Before settling in North Vancouver, where he teaches creative writing at Douglas College, he worked as a park ranger in the Banff-Kootenay region, a problematic 'wilderness' experience which forms the basis for his second collection of poems, *Mid-River* (Anansi, 1981). Zieroth has taught at the Banff Centre for the Fine Arts, holds an MA from Simon Fraser University, British Columbia, and edited the literary magazine *event* for over a decade.

Zieroth's first book, *Clearing: Poems from a Journey*, appeared in 1973. His third collection, *When the Stones Fly Up* (1985— both Anansi) moves in and out of past and present, memory and dream, with impressive fluidity, exploring the configurations of urban living and domestic interrelations, and also the haunting lacunae inherited from his German family's experience of immigration. Previously known as Dale Zieroth, in the 1990s he began to publish under his given first name, David. Zieroth's later books of poems include *The Weight of My Raggedy Skin* (Polestar, 1991); *How I Joined Humanity at Last* (1998); *The Village of Sliding Time* (2006), a long autobiographical poem; and *The Fly in Autumn* (2009—all Harbour), which won the Governor General's Award for Poetry. *The Education of Mr. Whippoorwill: A Country Boyhood* (Macfarlane Walter & Ross, 2002) is a prose memoir.   JKK

Zimunya, Musaemura (1949–) Born in Mutare, Zimbabwe (then Rhodesia), and studied at the University of Kent. He has been a lecturer in English at the University of Zimbabwe, and also a visiting professor in the United States.

Much of Zimunya's poetry is concerned with the war of liberation and its aftermath. It is a poetry of disillusion. The poet sees little sign that the move from Rhodesia to Zimbabwe has effected any profound transformation in the society: 'Bulawayo was a place of killing again | to remind us that our peace was a hasty marriage . . .'. He has published a book of criticism, *Those Years of Drought and Hunger: The Birth of African Fiction in English* (Mambo, 1982) and has co-edited a number of anthologies.

He has published four collections of poetry: *Zimbabwe Ruins* (Poetry Society of Rhodesia, 1979); *Thought Tracks* (1982); *Kingfisher, Jikinya, and Other Poems* (1982); and *Country Dawns and City Lights* (1985). His 1995 *Selected Poems* confirmed him as one of Zimbabwe's leading poets. *Nightshift*, a book of short stories, appeared in 1993 (all Longman).   AM-P

Zolf, Rachel (1968–) A founding editor of *The Walrus* magazine, Zolf has worked as a media documentary researcher and communications consultant. Originally from Toronto, she now lives in New York.

Zolf began writing after attending a workshop run by Di *Brandt. Like other experimental female poets of her generation in North America, her writing has taken the form of *conceptual book-length sequences, mixing original writing with found text. *Her Absence, this Wanderer* (Buschek, 1999) was followed by *Masque* (Mercury, 2004), a multi-vocal collage on modern ideas of family life. *Human Resources* (2007), which won the Trillium Book Award for Poetry, subjects the poet and her language to the dehumanized imperatives of corporate office-work. It includes a list of tips on 'How to Write for the Internet': '1. Write for skimmers | 2. Write for peckers | . . . | 8. Tell your visitor where to go'. See also *Neighbour Procedure* (2010—both Coach House).   JNT

Zukofsky, Louis (1904–78) Born in New York City, the son of Yiddish-speaking immigrant parents. Educated at Columbia University, he lived and worked mainly in New York. By his early twenties he was already an accomplished poet and critic, earning the respect and admiration of *Pound, William Carlos *Williams, and *Eliot. Williams, especially, came to rely on Zukofsky as an important adviser and editor for his own poetry, and as something of a guide amidst the highly politicized literary community before the Second World War. Pound constantly promoted Zukofsky as both editor and critic, seeing in him an exceptional advocate of the new poetry. Not yet 30, Zukofsky, through Pound's efforts, was asked to edit and to write a manifesto for the now-famous 1931 *'Objectivist' issue of *Poetry* magazine, in effect creating a poetic movement whose influence is more widely felt today than ever. Zukofsky's own career in the late Thirties and Forties seemed to be in eclipse while critical interest focused on poets influenced by the *New Criticism. In the early Fifties, however, Zukofsky's work was rediscovered by such poets as *Duncan, *Creeley, and *Corman. Today, Zukofsky's reputation as a poet and theorist is at its highest, especially among younger poets who see him as one of the founding figures of modernist poetry.

Two traits, a sensitivity to the sound-forms of the language and a high degree of intellection, mark all of Zukofsky's poetry and other writings. If he is one of the most musical poets of the modern era, he is also one of the most intellectually difficult. Varied in tone and subject-matter, as in the comic ode beginning 'To my wash-stand', or in the long travel-poem, 'Barely and Widely', his works can be gems of sonic counterpoint and verbal compression. Typically, as in the complex sestina 'Mantis' with its moving coda, '"Mantis", An Interpretation', he skilfully weaves social commentary and philosophy into an ongoing *ars poetica*, and in '*A*', a poem of twenty-four movements composed throughout his life, he creates an epic collage of autobiography, history, and reflection, replete with theatre pieces, music, word-play, and punning. An act of intense attentiveness to the associative power of word and thought, '*A*' is, like Pound's *Cantos*, profoundly serious, prolix, and irreducible to easy exegesis.

Of equal note among Zukofsky's works is his massive study, *Bottom: On Shakespeare*, which invokes much of Western literature and philosophy as it elaborates a highly original reading of the key tropes of the Shakespearian canon. Zukofsky's essays, including studies of Henry Adams, Pound, *Stevens, and Williams, and appreciations of such diverse figures as William Blake and Charlie Chaplin, are important documents in our understanding of modernist art and literature.

The most complete editions of Zukofsky's work are '*A*' (new edn., 1993) and *Complete Short Poetry*, with a foreword by Robert Creeley (1991—both Johns Hopkins University Press). His critical textbook, *A Test of Poetry* (1948), was republished in 2000, inaugurating the Wesleyan University Press Centennial Edition of Zukofsky's critical writings. The series includes *Prepositions+: The Collected Critical Essays* (2000) and *Bottom: On Shakespeare* (2002). In 2006, Charles *Bernstein edited a *Selected Poems* for the Library of America. *Collected Fiction* was published by Dalkey Archive Press in 1990. The first critical biography is Mark Scroggins, *The Poem of a Life* (Counterpoint, 2007).

See also *Louis Zukofsky: Man and Poet*, ed. Carroll F. Terrell (National Poetry Foundation, 1979); Michael Heller, *Conviction's Net of Branches: Essays On The Objectivist Poets and Poetry* (Southern Illinois University Press, 1985; repr. 2002); Sandra Kumamoto Stanley, *Louis Zukofsky and the Transformation of Modern American Poetics* (University of California Press, 1994); and *Upper Limit Music: The Writing of Louis Zukofsky*, ed. Mark Scroggins (University of Alabama Press, 1997).   MH

Zwicky, Fay (1933–) Born in Melbourne to an old-established Jewish family (Rosefield). She has been successively a concert pianist, an academic, and a full-time writer of poetry, short stories (*Hostages*, Fremantle Arts Centre, 1983), and literary criticism. *The Lyre in the Pawnshop: Essays on Literature and Survival 1974-1984* (University of Western Australia Press, 1986) illuminates Zwicky's poetics by its defence of humanist values and seriousness of mind and by its commitment to the power of language to integrate both social fabric and individual consciousness.

Zwicky's poetic truth-telling can be fierce, celebratory, witty, compassionate—sometimes all combined. Neither in style nor content does she slot easily into any poetic group, including the 'feminist', although much of her work can be seen as challenging the definition of Australian identity as strong, silent, and masculine. While her argument with her personal and cultural heritage, with the love that she can deny neither to her Jewish father nor to traditional European culture, may be most vividly present in the title poem of *Kaddish and Other Poems* (University of Queensland Press, 1982), similar preoccupations occur in *Isaac Babel's Fiddle* (Maximus, 1975) and *Ask Me* (University of Queensland Press, 1989). They are also dramatized in her revisions of traditional representations of figures such as Mrs Noah, Penelope, or Devi. A selected *Poems, 1970-1992* came out from University of Queensland Press in 1993. *The Gatekeeper's Wife* (Brandl & Schlesinger, 1997) saw Zwicky win the Western Australian Premier's Poetry Award for the third time. In 2004 she was declared a State Living Treasure. See also *Afloat and Other Poems* (Picaro, 2006) and *Picnic* (Giramondo, 2006).   JS

Zwicky, Jan (1955–) Born in Northern Alberta, Canada, Zwicky studied at the universities of Calgary and Toronto, where she wrote her PhD on 'A Theory of Ineffability'. She has taught at various universities in North America, and now lives on Quadra Island, British Columbia, where she works as an editor for Brick Books in Ontario.

Like her contemporary Tim *Lilburn, Zwicky is a philosophical poet with ecological concerns. She is also an accomplished violinist. *Forge* (Gaspereau, 2011), shortlisted for the Griffin Poetry Prize, contains a number of poems that respond thematically and formally to 'the absence | music is', including 'The Art of Fugue', which meditates on the familiar scene of 'A room, a table, and four chairs'. Earlier collections published by Brick Books include *Where Have We Been* (1982), *Songs for Relinquishing the Earth* (1998), which won the Governor General's Award, and *Robinson's Crossing* (2004), which won the Dorothy Livesay Poetry Prize. See also *Plato as Artist* (Gaspereau, 2009), and two earlier prose works, *Lyric Philosophy* (1992) and *Wisdom & Metaphor* (2003), reissued by Gaspereau Press. For criticism and context, see *Lyric Ecology: Essays in Honour of Jan Zwicky* (Cormorant, 2010), ed. Mark Dickinson and Clare Goulet. JNT

Groups and Movements

Agrarianism A movement among men of letters in the American South of the late 1920s and 1930s to defend its traditional agricultural way of life against the industrialization and urbanization that were fast overwhelming it. The 'Twelve Southerners' who contributed essays to the most substantial Agrarian publication, *I'll Take My Stand: The South and the Agrarian Tradition* (1930), were Donald *Davidson, John Gould *Fletcher, Henry Blue Kline, Lyle Lanier, Andrew Lytle, H. C. Nixon, Frank Lawrence Owsley, John Crowe *Ransom, Allen *Tate, John Donald Wade, Robert Penn *Warren, and Stark Young. As Agrarians they had no formal affiliation with Vanderbilt University, although ten of them had either taught or studied there. The book urged southerners not to adopt the industrial ideal, its essays variously pointing out the adverse effects of industrialism (on attitudes to labour, religion, and the fine arts) and the exemplary and civilized qualities of a society, like that of the Old South, which refuses to deify technological improvement and material prosperity. As its critics quickly realized, the volume failed to show how Agrarianism could be properly implemented, let alone compete with industrialism. So, in the following decade, in several public debates and many articles, the Agrarians attempted to justify its practicability. Contemporary attacks on Agrarian writing accused it of being a romantic apology for slavery and a nostalgic dream of restoring plantation life. Later attacks see it as a Utopian exercise which ignored the more vexing realities of southern history and experience. Certainly it did not succeed in its explicit objectives: after the Depression the South was rapidly urbanized and industrialized. Tate, however, later thought the movement had been successful, if only in convincingly demonstrating that the dehumanizing results of modern industrialism could—and should—be tempered by religious humanism.

Like Tate, the other Agrarian poets, Ransom, Davidson, and Warren, had all originally become interested in defending the South in 1925 in response to the northern ridicule poured on the Tennessee Anti-Evolution Bill (which had prohibited the teaching of Darwin's evolutionary theory in all public schools and universities). But ultimately only Davidson was committed to the South above all else. For the others, as Louis D. Rubin shows in *The Wary Fugitives: Four Poets and the South* (Louisiana State University Press, 1978), Agrarianism had actually been an expression of other—religious, social, and aesthetic—imperatives.

See also, for a mixture of group biography and intellectual history, *The Southern Agrarians*, by Paul K. Conkin (University of Tennessee Press, 1988).   NE

Beat Generation A group of poets and writers who rose to prominence during the 1950s and exerted considerable influence on literary fashions over the subsequent ten or fifteen years. The key members of this group were Allen *Ginsberg, Jack *Kerouac, William Burroughs, and Gregory *Corso; other poets more loosely associated with the Beats, particularly during their sojourn on the West Coast, were Gary *Snyder, Michael *McClure, Lawrence *Ferlinghetti, Diane *di Prima, and others involved in the *San Francisco poetry renaissance (though the latter is usually considered a distinct movement extending well beyond the Beats).

In its purest form Beat writing is characterized by a distinctive blending of comic exuberance and prophetic aspirations. Neither as wholly playful as the work of New York poets like Frank *O'Hara, nor as earnestly visionary as the poetry of San Franciscans like Robert *Duncan, Beat poetry tries, and at its best is able, to walk a narrow line between camp and mysticism, comedy and apocalypse. The very term 'Beat', a rare instance of a self-bestowed label, captures some of this precarious doubleness, combining as it does a colloquial sense (as in 'beat up', 'beaten down', raffish and socially outcast) with an almost religious sense ('beatific', angelic)—perhaps with overtones also of jazz rhythm, a significant influence on Beat poetics. The key event in the emergence of the Beats (as poets rather than fiction writers) was probably the famous group reading at the Six Gallery in San Francisco, at which Ginsberg gave the first public performance of *Howl*. Thanks to the rather bemused attention of magazines like *Time* and *Life*, and the publicity generated by the obscenity trial over the publication of *Howl*, the Beats quickly became notorious figures, literary versions of James Dean, Marlon Brando, and other popular embodiments of rebellious youth. With their disdain for bourgeois values and their readiness to shock middle-class sensibilities, the Beat writers opened the way for the much broader counter-culture of the 1960s. See *The Portable Beat Reader* (Penguin, 1992), ed. Ann Charters, and *The Beat Book* (Random House, 1996), ed. Anne Waldman.

The Beat legacy remains a living presence in contemporary American poetry. Poets such as Clark *Coolidge and Leslie *Scalapino have acknowledged the its liberating influence, and the Jack Kerouac School of Disembodied Poetics writing programme at Naropa University—founded by Ginsberg and Waldman in 1974—continues to associate the movement with contemporary experimental practice. Less well-known figures such as Lew Welch, meanwhile, have been rediscovered: see *Ring of Bone: Collected Poems* (City Lights, 2012).

Beat Writers at Work (Random House, 1999), ed. Rick Moody, collects interviews with several leading figures. See also Jonah Raskin, *American Scream: Allen Ginsberg's* Howl *and the Making of the Beat Generation* (University of California Press, 2004).   RG*

Black Arts Movement A movement based in Harlem in the 1960s which called for the assertion of African-American identity in the arts, in parallel with the Black Power movement. The leading spokesperson, and leading poet, was Amiri *Baraka, who, as LeRoi Jones, had previously been associated with the *Beats. Theatre was a focusing collaborative activity, and performance was often an important aspect of Black Arts poetry, notably in the work of Gil Scott-Heron ('The Godfather of Rap'). Other poets associated with the movement included Gwendolyn *Brooks, Nikki *Giovanni, Etheridge *Knight, Clarence *Major, Keorapetse *Kgositsile (then in exile from South Africa), Haki R. *Madhubuti, and Sonia *Sanchez. Some contemporaries such as June *Jordan, however, criticized its essentialism, which extended to gender attitudes.

Continuing the aims of the *Harlem Renaissance into the civil-rights era, the Black Arts legacy is evident in later organizations such as *Cave Canem, and the work of individual poets such as Harryette *Mullen. See *Furious Flower: African American Poetry from the Black Arts Movement to the Present* (University of Virginia Press, 2004), ed. Joanne V. Gabbin, and James Edward Smethurst, *The Black Arts Movement: Literary Nationalism in the 1960s and 1970s* (University of North Carolina Press, 2005).   JNT

Black Mountain Poets, The The poets associated with Black Mountain College, a small, experimental, democratically run college in North Carolina, in the late 1940s and early 1950s. Charles *Olson was its rector, Robert *Creeley and Robert *Duncan were members of staff, and Edward *Dorn, Joel *Oppenheimer, John *Wieners, and Jonathan *Williams studied there. Paul *Blackburn, Paul Carroll, Larry *Eigner, and Denise *Levertov never attended the college but their work was also given its first significant American publication in *Origin* (1951–7) and *The Black Mountain Review* (edited by Creeley, 1954–7), and later included in Donald Allen's influential anthology, *The New American Poetry* (1960), which first recognized the poets as a group.

Like many other American poets who emerged in the 1950s, the Black Mountain poets reacted against the poetic 'closure' and compression advocated by the New Criticism. Their models were not the seventeenth-century 'metaphysical' poets and *Eliot, but Blake, Whitman, *Lawrence and, above all, *Pound and William Carlos *Williams, whose work they found exemplary of what they called 'open' or 'organic' form. In fact the word 'open' described their ideal not only for a poem's form but also for its substance and even for the process of its composition. The speaker of an open poem, according to Olson, is neither a fictional persona nor the poet's autobiographical personality but the part of the poet's self, beyond his ego, that provides an open channel through which impersonal nature can speak. It followed that grammatical and poetic conventions (including ordinary lineation, straight left-hand margins, and regular metres) should be discarded so that a poem's form could spontaneously adapt to its substance as it progressed. The resulting poems are open because provisional in form and spirit: art, said Duncan, is not an 'achievement' but an 'adventure'.

The Black Mountain poets were much more united in theory, however, than in practice. Each responded to different qualities in Pound and Williams. Olson wanted to revise Pound's historiography, Duncan to emulate his 'sublime and ecstatic' poetry. Creeley turned to the more 'sincere' style of Williams, and Levertov also wrote variations on the Williams lyric. None of the others, except perhaps Dorn, has been as widely read, though Blackburn, Jonathan Williams, and Oppenheimer deserve mention as the most engaging, accessible, and humorous of the group.

All seven issues of *The Black Mountain Review* have been collected in three volumes (AMS, 1969), but *The New American Poetry: 1945-1960*, ed. Donald Allen (Grove, 1960), is still the best short selection of the group's early work. *Black Mountain: An Exploration in Community*, by Martin Duberman (Northwestern University Press, 1972; repr. 2009), is a comprehensive history of the college.   NE

Cambridge School, The Individual poets and informal movements of writers emerge continuously from Oxford and Cambridge, but the term 'Cambridge School' refers to a particular grouping who began writing in the later 1960s, some of whom studied or worked in the city. J. H. *Prynne is a central figure, together with Andrew *Crozier, John *James, Wendy *Mulford, Douglas *Oliver, and Peter *Riley. These poets initially used self-publication as a means of encouraging an active interchange of poetry and ideas within a diffuse network of writers and readers. *The English Intelligencer* (1967-8) was the circulating worksheet which provided the forum for this exchange. The term 'school', applied to this loose association of individuals, is only a retrospective category, as is so often the case.

Self-publication was partly dictated by the singularity of their aims and of the poems which they wrote. The group drew on a wide range of American and European influences, reacting against the state of poetry then prevailing in Britain. Their poetry at its best articulates a new sense of subjectivity in relation to the world as if freshly received, and combines lyric intensities with ethical concerns. The Ferry Press, edited by Andrew Crozier, published collections of poems in striking format and to a very high standard. Tim Longville and John *Riley edited the *Grosseteste Review* and Press (1966-75) with similar energy. *A Various Art* (Carcanet, 1987), edited by Crozier and Longville, offers a representative selection of the poetry. *Poets on Writing. Britain, 1970-1991* (Macmillan, 1992), edited by Denise *Riley, collects statements from writers involved in the initial activity, and also from poets subsequently influenced by their work. See also *Certain Prose of the English Intelligencer*, ed. Neil Pattison, Reitha Pattison, and Luke Roberts (Mountain, 2012).

The avant-garde of the 1960s and 1970s extended well beyond the city limits of one university town to London, Scotland, Wales, and the North of England, and to other important figures, such as Bob *Cobbing and Tom *Raworth. Hence Eric Mottram's proposal of a wider term, the 'British Poetry Revival'. The ongoing concentration of activity in Cambridge, however, makes it a central point on any map.

As with the *New York School, it is now possible to speak of a 'second generation' of Cambridge poets, who from the late 1970s engaged with the *Language poets in America, just as the earlier generation had looked to the *Black Mountain poets. As critics, teachers, and editors, they have advocated an ongoing modernist tradition, both native and international. The most influential work of second-generation Cambridge School criticism may be Veronica *Forrest-Thomson's *Poetic Artifice* (Manchester University Press, 1978), which looks back to *Pound and *Empson. The most important small press has been Rod Mengham's Equipage. A major anthology, *Conductors of Chaos* (Picador, 1996), ed. Iain Sinclair, includes work by Andrew Duncan, Michael *Haslam, Tony *Lopez, Grace Lake, Rod Mengham, Drew *Milne, Ian Patterson, Denise *Riley and John *Wilkinson.   NW*

Cave Canem A non-profit organization founded in New York by Toi *Derricotte and Cornelius *Eady to foster and promote the work of African-American poets. Its first formal gathering, in 1996, was a writer's retreat with Elizabeth *Alexander and Afaa M. *Weaver, the first 'Elder' of the group (who on another retreat invented the three-stanza 'bop' form). Cave Canem's activities now encompass poetry prizes, workshops, readings, publications, and two interview series: Legacy Conversations and Poets and Craft. Current faculty members include Thomas Sayers Ellis, C.S. *Giscombe, Harryette *Mullen, and Natasha *Trethewey. Younger poets who have won the Cave Canem Poetry Prize include Major Jackson and Tracey K. Smith. In 2011 a series of biennial anthologies was launched. See *Gathering Ground: A Reader Celebrating Cave Canem's First Decade* (University of Michigan Press, 2006), ed. Derricotte and Eady, and *The Ringing Ear: Black Poets Lean South* (University of Georgia Press, 2007), ed. Nikky Finney.   JNT

Conceptualism 'Conceptual poetry' or 'conceptual writing' has its origins in the conceptual art of the twentieth century, as well as the avant-gardism of Dada, *Oulipo, and *Language writing. But it has only been recognized and promoted as a distinctive form of (North American) poetry in the twenty-first century. In works such as *Day* (2003), a continuous transcription of a complete edition of the *New York Times*, the leading practitioner, Kenneth *Goldsmith, performs what he calls 'uncreative writing'. Goldsmith argues that in the Internet age the poet's function is not to produce new writing but rather to reveal the language environment. Similarly, Craig Dworkin argues for a 'non-expressive poetry', in which 'the substitutions at the heart of metaphor and image [are] replaced by the direct presentation of language itself'. The critic Marjorie Perloff has been an important advocate of Conceptualism's attempt to 'absorb, recharge, and redistribute' text. But it also has its detractors, such as Kent *Johnson, who in 2009 republished *Day* under his own name, effectively satirizing the theory of authorial appropriation. The web-based genre of Flarf poetry arguably has Conceptual aims, while embracing a kitsch aesthetic (see Benjamin Friedlander, *Citizen Cain* (Salt, 2011)). Other poets associated with the movement include Christian *Bök and Vanessa *Place. See *Against Expression: An Anthology of Conceptual Writing* (Northwestern University Press, 2011), ed. Dworkin and Goldsmith, and *I'll Drown My Book: Conceptual Writing by Women* (Les Figues, 2012), ed. Caroline Bergvall, Laynie Browne, Teresa Carmody, and Place.   NH

Confessional Poetry Verse in which the author describes parts of his or her life which would not ordinarily be in the public domain. The prime characteristic is the reduction of the distance between the persona and the author.

Confessional poetry derives from the Romantics, from such poems as Wordsworth's 'Nutting' and Coleridge's 'Dejection: An Ode'. More immediately, it relates to Ezra *Pound's 'Hugh Selwyn Mauberley' and 'Pisan Cantos', where intimate references to friends are worked into the verse.

The term 'confessional verse' was first made current in a review of Robert *Lowell's *Life Studies* by M. L. Rosenthal (*The Nation*, 19 Sept. 1959, revised version repr. in M. L. Rosenthal, *The New Poets* (Oxford University Press, 1967)). Rosenthal points out that Lowell's speaker in his poems is unequivocally himself. When that speaker attacks his father for lack of manhood, or refers to his breaking marriage, we are in no doubt that it is Lowell's own father who is under attack and Lowell's own marriage that is in reference. Other poets of the Confessional school are John *Berryman, Anne *Sexton, W. D. *Snodgrass, and Sylvia *Plath.

At its worst, Confessional poetry is a kind of therapy that thrusts private experience upon an unwilling reader. At its best, as in Lowell's *Life Studies*, it is a way of creating character so as to inform the trauma of the past with understanding and, sometimes, compassion. Plath's symbolic dramatization of female sexuality has also been widely influential. Confessionalism remains an important mode in America and elsewhere, although later proponents such as Sharon *Olds and Mark *Doty have been wryly conscious of its critics. From a longer perspective, the Confessional poets' affinity with other pioneers of lyric autobiography from the same period, such as Allen *Ginsberg and Frank *O'Hara, becomes more apparent. See Stephen Burt, *Forms of Youth: Twentieth-Century Poetry and Adolescence* (Columbia University Press, 2007) and Dan Chiasson, *One Kind of Everything: Poem and Person in Contemporary America* (University of Chicago Press, 2007).   PDF*

Deep Image A term that came to be associated with certain American poets, above all Robert *Bly and James *Wright, who practise a variety of image-based verse that emphasizes not the empirical and the concrete, as in Objectivism, but the connections between images and the unconscious. Strongly influenced by Carl Jung's thought on archetypes, Bly has been the most polemical spokesman for such poetry, in various essays published in his journal *The Fifties*, *The Sixties*, and *The Seventies*. Bly calls for American poets to abandon rational, discursive thinking and to cultivate the associational modes of imagery found in poets like Lorca, Trakl, Neruda, and Transtrӧmer. Other poets loosely associated with this mode include Galway *Kinnell, Louis *Simpson, Donald *Hall, Jerome *Rothenberg, and Robert *Kelly, who coined the term 'deep image'; its influence among younger American poets has been widespread, particularly during the 1970s.   RG

Desert Poets During the Second World War a surprisingly large and heterodox number of British writers found themselves, for a variety of reasons, in the Middle East. Not all were combatants, and these included R. D. Smith, Olivia Manning, Robert Liddell, Bernard *Spencer, and Lawrence *Durrell. Together with Robin Fedden, the latter two founded the Cairo-based poetry magazine *Personal Landscape*, whose first number appeared in January, 1942. Among the magazine's regular contributors were most of the writers already mentioned, together with George Seferis, Terence Tiller, and Keith *Douglas.

See *Return to Oasis: War Poems and Recollections from the Middle East, 1940–1946* ed. Victor Selwyn, Erik de Mauny, Ian Fletcher, G. S. Fraser, and John Waller, with an introduction by Lawrence Durrell (Shepheard-Walwyn, 1980), and Roger Bowen, *'Many Histories Deep': The Personal Landscape Poets in Egypt 1940–1945* (Fairleigh Dickinson University Press, 1995). Other army-based periodicals of the Middle East included *Citadel* (edited by David Hicks from the Anglo-Egyptian Institute) and *Parade*, to both of which Douglas contributed.   JL

Dub Poetry A style of poetry which is performed to bass-heavy reggae accompaniment (the words are 'dubbed' over the music). It originated from the Jamaica School of Drama in the 1970s, and was influenced by Edward Kamau *Brathwaite's call for an Afro-Caribbean 'nation language' poetry. The term was coined by Linton Kwesi *Johnson, the leading figure associated with dub poetry in Britain, where it emerged as an important mode of black social protest. Some of the original dub poets, such as Oku Onuora and Mutabaruka, remain best known as performers and recording artists, but others, such as Johnson, also have a significant output in print. In the 1980s, Mervyn *Morris edited early collections by Jean 'Binta' *Breeze and Michael *Smith, and Benjamin *Zephaniah popularized dub to the growing audience for performance poetry. See Christian Habekost, *Verbal Riddim: The Politics and Aesthetics of Afro-Caribbean Dub Poetry* (Rodopi, 1993). JNT

Fugitives, The *The Fugitive* was a poetry magazine, nineteen issues of which were published in Nashville, Tennessee, from April 1922 to December 1925. It was edited jointly by the self-designated Fugitives who had been meeting weekly for several years to read and discuss each other's poems. The original Fugitives were Walter Clyde Curry, Donald *Davidson, William Yandell Elliott, James Frank, William Frierson, Sidney Hirsch, Stanley Johnson, John Crowe *Ransom, Alec B. Stevenson, and Allen *Tate. They were later joined by Merrill *Moore, Laura *Riding (Gottschalk), Alfred Starr, Robert Penn *Warren, and Jesse and Ridley Wills. All but Hirsch, Frank, Riding, and Stevenson were either students or teachers at Vanderbilt University, which would not, however, support the magazine. Not until the fourth issue were its pages opened to outside contributors. Thereafter the most notable of these were Hart *Crane, John Gould *Fletcher, and Robert *Graves.

The Fugitives were committed to no particular programme but did agree on some basic points: that poetry should avoid the sentimentality and 'local colour' of the standard Southern literature of the time, and be intellectual and demanding as well as emotional: 'not the act of a child', as Ransom later said, 'but the act of an adult mind'. The magazine's poetry received much enthusiastic, and some adverse, criticism both for its dense and intricate verse and for its gloomy vision of modernity. Ransom, Davidson, and Tate always stood out from the rest of the group as ambitious, professional literary men. They conducted critical debates about modernism (to which most of the others were not sympathetic) in the magazine, developing what would later become the tenets of the New Criticism; they went on to enjoy successful literary careers; and for them, as well as for Warren (the youngest Fugitive), *Fugitives: An Anthology*

(edited by Davidson, 1928) marked the watershed between their involvement as Fugitive poets and as *Agrarian Southerners. *The Fugitive Group: A Literary History*, by Louise Cowan (1959), is the best account of its history, while *The Wary Fugitives: Four Poets and the South*, by Louis D. Rubin (1978—both Louisiana State University Press) is a more detailed study of Ransom, Davidson, Tate, and Warren. NE

Generation of '68 A term now largely accepted as applying to a radical shift of poetic perspectives in Australia, stimulated by official government commitment to the Vietnam War. This released strong protest movements among young Australians (and many of their elders), and coincided with the beginnings of the 'drug culture'. The emerging poets bypassed normal channels to produce their own publications, inspired by American models. They were first given prominence in the anthology *Australian Poetry Now*, edited by Thomas *Shapcott in 1970. Roger McDonald, editor of the Paperback Poets series at the University of Queensland Press from 1969 to 1976, was also an important supporter. As a poetic movement, the 'Generation of '68' served to challenge existing conventions of poetic style and form and had a profound influence on major older poets, such as John *Blight and David *Campbell, as well as creating a wide audience for the young poets involved. Although John *Tranter in his 1979 anthology *The New Australian Poetry* assumed the role of spokesman (male poets predominated), two talented poets who died young—Michael *Dransfield and Charles *Buckmaster—perhaps best exemplify the freshness and vulnerability of the period. What is of particular importance, however, is that many poets whose writing first found its focus in the specific politics of the time were to continue to develop as writers (e.g. Robert *Adamson, Alan *Wearne, John Tranter) and now occupy a central position in Australian poetry. David McCooey has proposed a second-wave 'generation of '79', centred around Tranter, and including Laurie *Duggan, Alan Wearne, and the late John *Forbes. Their example has in turn been important to the innovative Australian poets who emerged in the 1990s, such as John *Kinsella, M. T. C. *Cronin, Alison *Croggon, and Peter *Minter, a period when the male dominance of Australian poetry also began to wane, and female poets from the 1970s such as Pam *Brown received greater recognition. At the same time, Tranter and Brown's online magazine, *Jacket*, and Kinsella's journal and press, Salt, continued the independent editorial ethos of '68, becoming forums for postmodern poetic exchange between North America, Australia, and Britain. TWS*

Georgian Poetry A term coined by Edward Marsh in 1911 to signal a reaction against the expansive sententiousness of the Victorians and to proclaim his belief that 'English poetry is now once again putting on new strength and beauty', as he said in his preface to *Georgian Poetry 1911–1912*. This anthology, published by Harold *Monro in 1912, was followed by four further volumes, the last of which appeared shortly before *The Waste Land* in 1922, a chronological misfortune which partly explains the common perception of 'Georgian Poetry' as a species of lightweight, sentimental lyricism catapulted into deserved oblivion by modernism; furthermore, attention lavished on the 'war poets' in general, and on Wilfred *Owen in particular, has prevented many readers from noticing the other poets who were writing in the second decade of the century. Yet the Georgians were considered daring and indeed revolutionary in the literary context of their time: the anthologies included poets as controversial as D. H. *Lawrence and as considerable as Robert *Graves, who later vigorously denounced the movement; other contributors included Edmund *Blunden, Rupert *Brooke, W. H. *Davies, Walter *de la Mare, John *Masefield, and Siegfried *Sassoon. In his Penguin anthology *Georgian Poetry* (Penguin, 1960), James *Reeves argued plausibly for the exclusion of Lawrence and for the inclusion of Owen and Edward *Thomas, thus defining Georgianism in terms of style rather than as a label for anyone who appeared in the anthologies: this strategy, by extending the range of subject-matter and by emphasizing the poets' formal qualities, presented the

movement in its most coherent and persuasive light. See also Peter Howarth, *British Poetry in the Age of Modernism* (Cambridge University Press, 2005).   NP

Group, The A deliberately antithetical response to the supposedly tame, formalist poetics of the *Movement, which were exemplified in the anthology *New Lines*. However, unlike the Movement, whose members never assembled in any organized way, the Group was from the start a tightly knit, even local affair, originating in Cambridge in 1952 when a number of poets connected with the magazine *Delta* began holding regular meetings to read and critically analyse each other's recent work. Subsequently the focus moved to London, where poets met at the homes of Philip *Hobsbaum and, later, Edward *Lucie-Smith. After the Group disintegrated as a formal entity during the 1960s, it was resurrected as Poets' Workshop, and its members remained influential in organizations such as the Poetry Society.

The Group may have been socially more coherent but it was poetically more diverse than the Movement: perhaps its most widely shared characteristics were an interest in natural and violent imagery, and a corresponding suspicion of gentle irony and closed forms. Among the poets who have been associated with it at different times are Alan *Brownjohn, Philip Hobsbaum, Ted *Hughes, Edward Lucie-Smith, George *MacBeth, Peter *Porter, and Peter *Redgrove, most of whom would have broadly supported the 'anti-gentility' stance of A. *Alvarez in his Introduction to *The New Poetry* (1962). *A Group Anthology*, edited by Hobsbaum and Lucie-Smith, appeared in 1963 (Oxford University Press). Between 1963 and 1966, Hobsbaum ran a second 'Group' in Belfast, whose members included Seamus *Heaney and Michael *Longley.   NP*

Harlem Renaissance, The During the 1920s, black American writers and artists converged in a district which was already fashionable among the white smart set as the music-and-entertainment capital of New York. The early years of the century had seen the publication of works such as W. E. B. DuBois's *The Souls of Black Folk* and Booker T. Washington's *Up From*

Slavery, indicating the future role of black people in America. In 1925, Alain Locke, a professor at Howard University, brought together a collection of short stories, poems, and prose by divers hands, under the title *The New Negro*. As the abstraction was held to characterize the 'spiritual Coming of Age' of the black race, so the volume itself could be seen as a mark of its cultural maturity.

Major figures in the Harlem Renaissance were Langston *Hughes, Arna Bontemps, James Weldon *Johnson, Nella Larsen, Countee *Cullen, Claude *McKay, Jean *Toomer, and Zora Neale Hurston, many of whom treated the themes of black life in a way that felt modern, while borrowing elements from the folk literature of black tradition. Visual artists of the Renaissance, including Aaron Douglas and William H. Johnson, incorporated African and primitive motifs into their work. Among the magazines founded at the time which devoted themselves to 'Negro studies' were *Crisis* (edited by DuBois), *Opportunity*, and the *Messenger*.

These magazines were not exclusively literary, but the significance of the Harlem Renaissance did not lie solely in its literary impact. Although much that was produced from Harlem in the 1920s is of greater historical than artistic importance, the Renaissance made white America aware for the first time of the modern art of a people it had not long before kept in slavery.

For an account of this development see *Harlem Renaissance*, by Nathan Irvin Huggins (Oxford University Press, 1971; revd. edn., 2007). *When Harlem Was in Vogue*, by David Levering Lewis (Knopf, 1981), is a study of broader scope, with less emphasis on the literary life of the 1920s. Lewis also edited *The Portable Harlem Renaissance Reader* (Viking, 1994). In recent years, the contribution of women writers to the Harlem movement, such as Angelina Weld Grimké and Georgina Douglas Johnson, has increasingly been recognized. See *Shadowed Dreams: Women's Poetry of the Harlem Renaissance* (Rutgers University Press, 1989; revd. edn., 2006), ed. Maureen Honey.   JC*

Imagism A poetical movement instigated by American poets in London, roughly coterminous with the First World War. There were four numbers of an annual anthology, 1914–17. Its main associates were the Americans Ezra *Pound, H. D. (Hilda *Doolittle), John Gould *Fletcher, and Amy *Lowell, and the Britons Richard *Aldington (who for a time edited the movement's chief organ, the *Egoist*) and F. S. *Flint.

T. E. *Hulme was a seminal figure. Flint describes meetings in 1909 where Hulme, he, and some others discussed how contemporary poetry might be revivified by *vers libre*, by the influence of the *Symbolistes*, and by forms derived from the Japanese tanka and haiku. Among Hulme's circle was Pound, newly arrived from America. Two years later Pound's former fiancée H. D. also came to London, and with her future husband Richard Aldington began to sculpt poems whose severity Pound admired ('Straight talk, straight as the Greek!'). In 1912 Pound told these two that they were 'Imagistes', and sent their work to Harriet Monroe's *Poetry*. The word *Imagiste* first occurred in print in Pound's prefatory note to the poems of Hulme; and the first statements of an evolving programme appeared in *Poetry* for March 1913: 'Imagisme', printed over Flint's signature and purporting to be an interview with an Imagiste (in fact all contrived by Pound); and 'A Few Don'ts by an Imagiste' signed by Pound himself. The first enumerated the cardinal rules of the movement as '1. Direct treatment of the "thing" . . . 2. To use absolutely no word that did not contribute to the presentation. 3. . . . to compose in sequence of the musical phrase, not in sequence of the metronome'; 'A Few Don'ts', meanwhile, proscribed superfluous words, abstractions, and iambs.

Pound edited the first anthology, *Des Imagistes*, published in March 1914 with poems by himself, Aldington, H. D., and Flint, and one each from Skipwith Cannell, John Cournos, Ford Madox Hueffer (see Ford), James *Joyce, Amy Lowell, Allen Upward, and William Carlos *Williams, not all of whom would have subscribed in full to Pound's principles. These received a further exposition (by now using the English form 'Imagist') in his essay on 'Vorticism' in the *Fortnightly Review*, September 1914, with its useful distinction between image and symbol: 'The symbolist's *symbols* have a fixed value, like numbers in arithmetic, like 1, 2 and 7. The imagist's images have a variable significance like the signs *a*, *b* and *x* in algebra... the author must use his *image* because he sees it or feels it, *not* because he thinks he can use it to back up some creed or some system of ethics or economics.'

But Pound was already chafing at his partners. He and Flint had fallen out when Amy Lowell arrived from America to put her promotional energy and financial backing at the group's disposal. Pound refused to contribute to the anthologies on her democratic terms, so it was she who oversaw the volumes *Some Imagist Poets* for 1915–17. Her first volume's 'Preface' contains a six-point credo derived from Pound and Hulme, but Pound thought what he called 'Amy-gism' a debasement of his own ideas, and it is true that she had a broader policy of promoting *vers libre* of all sorts. (Fletcher credited her with pioneering one variety—'Polyphonic Prose'—in which he himself experimented.) She was able, for instance, to convince D. H. *Lawrence that he was an Imagist.

By 1917 the movement was felt to have served its purpose. (A nostalgic fifth 'Imagist Anthology', with new work by most of the original contributors, was edited by Aldington on a whim in 1930.) Its limitations are perhaps suggested by the fact that the same pair of miniatures—H. D.'s 'Oread' and Pound's 'In a Station of the Métro'—are invariably cited to represent its achievement; and even of these Harold *Monro's contemporary objection is arguable: 'It is petty poetry... such images should appear by the dozen in poetry.' Equally valid, however, is a *Times Literary Supplement* review of 1917 which suggests that 'even when it is not very good in itself, it seems to promise a form in which very good poetry could be written'; and the fulfilment of the Imagist promise may best be located in Pound's *Cantos*, Eliot's *The Waste Land*, and H. D.'s *War Trilogy*, works which absorb certain elements of Imagist practice into effective larger structures. At the very least, Imagism introduced several of the prominent features of modernist poetics—organic form, elimination of personality, rejection of public themes—to the élite audience it sought for itself. *Imagist Poetry*, ed. Peter Jones (Penguin, 1972), has an authoritative introduction and useful appendices. See also William Pratt, *The Imagist Poem: Modern Poetry in Miniature* (Dutton, 1963; revd. edn., Story Line, 2001) and Helen Carr, *The Verse Revolutionaries: Ezra Pound, H. D. and the Imagists* (Cape, 2009).   MI

Informationism A term used to describe the technologically inspired writing of a young group of Scottish poets in the 1990s, coined by one its main proponents and publishers, Richard *Price. In 1989, with W. N. *Herbert, Price founded *Gairfish* magazine, and in 1991, with Leona Medlin, started Vennel Press. Together these outlets promoted a new postmodern poetry from Scotland, after the example of earlier pioneers such as Hugh *MacDiarmid and Edwin *Morgan. One vision of Informationism is encapsulated by Robert *Crawford's 'Scotland', which sees fields as 'epitaxies of tweed'. A *Martian influence might be discerned in such metaphorical play, but Informationism also included formally experimental work such as Peter McCarey's computer-generated poem *The Syllabary*, ongoing at www.thesyllabary.com. Other poets associated with the group include David Kinloch and Alan Riach. The defining anthology, edited by Price and Herbert, was *Contraflow on the Super Highway* (Southfields, 1994).   JNT

Jindyworobak Movement An Australian poetic development named after the Jindyworobak Club, founded by Rex *Ingamells in Adelaide (1938) with his prose statement *Conditional Culture*. The movement sought to incorporate an Aboriginal sense of 'place' within the developing English-language culture of the time. Its preoccupations ran counter to currents of international modernism, and the last vestiges of the Bush Ballad tradition still evident in the national weekly the *Bulletin*. The Jindyworobaks sometimes incorporated Aboriginal words into their poems, and this led to charges of primitivism. The wealth and spiritual wholeness of Aboriginal culture was not to be widely appreciated for another forty years. If, in retrospect, only a few of the poets involved produced outstanding work (e.g. Roland *Robinson), they were prescient in seeking intellectual and cultural nourishment from within rather than from without. Later movements of the 1950s (A. D. *Hope and the academic claimants of poetry) and the late 1960s (post-Vietnam internationalism) continued to sneer at the Jindyworobaks, who produced annual anthologies from 1938 to 1953. The 1980s, more environmentally self-conscious and responsive to Aboriginal heritage, began to recognize in the Jindyworobak Movement important predecessors, not only in these areas but in the movement's more general identification with a laconic 'Australian' speech cadence (e.g. in poems by Ian *Mudie) that anticipated the acknowledged breakthrough of later poems by Bruce *Dawe and Les *Murray.   TWS

Kootenay School of Writing The KSW collective, as it is often known, is a writer-run centre based in Vancouver, Canada. It was formed in 1984, following the enforced closure of the David Thompson University Centre in 1983, a liberal arts college in the Kootenay mountain region of British Columbia. During the 1980s the non-profit collective offered courses in writing, editing, and publishing, and produced the influential *Writing* magazine. Later, the focus shifted towards the School's reading series, talks, and writing workshops.

The original members of the KSW included Tom *Wayman and Jeff *Derksen. Emerging from DTUC, where the influence of the *San Francisco Renaissance and *Black Mountain poets had been strongly felt, the aesthetics and politics of early KSW

writing were also influenced by its strong relationship with labour movements (formed partly in response to the Social Credit Party's policy of 'restraint', which had led to the closure of DTUC). But the 1985 New Poetics Colloquium in Vancouver may be seen as the marker of a decisive turn away from straightforward 'protest-' or 'work-writing' and towards *Language writing, as characterized by Ron *Silliman's essays on 'the new sentence'. As Derksen wrote in the Canadian poetics journal *Open Letter*, much of the work at this time aimed 'to articulate links across discourses and fields in a dialogism that is aware of ideology and its effects'.

The KSW was also quickly expanding, however, to involve a number of writers whose poetics were at variance with, or even opposed to, these aesthetics. Catriona *Strang, Nancy Shaw, Lisa *Robertson, and Christine Stewart, for example, began publishing *Barscheit Magazine* as part of a project aimed at developing distinct feminist writing practices through the strategic use of 'dissensual language'.

See *Writing Class: The Kootenay School of Writing Anthology* (New Star, 1999), ed. Michael Barnholden and Andrew Klobucar, and *The Only Poetry That Matters: Reading the Kootenay School of Writing* (Arsenal Pulp, 2011). Other writers later involved with or influenced by the KSW include Stephen *Collis, Kevin *Davies, Deanna Ferguson, Dorothy Trujillo Lusk, and Lissa Wolsak.   ADA

Language Poetry A dominant movement in postmodernist American poetry since the 1970s, named after the magazine $L=A=N=G=U=A=G=E$ (1978–81) which united two geographically separate groups of writers on the East and West coasts. The editors of the magazine, Bruce *Andrews and Charles *Bernstein, were based in New York, while leading figures in San Francisco included Carla *Harryman, Lyn *Hejinian, Kit Robinson, Ron *Silliman, and Barrett *Watten.

Also known as 'Language writing' for its tendency to hybridize verse and prose, Language poetry positioned itself in relation to an American avant-garde tradition from Gertrude *Stein and Louis *Zukofsky to the *Black Mountain poets and the *New York School. Contemporary with the rise of post-structuralist and Marxist theory in literary criticism, Language poetry made explicit the politics of literary form and the textual nature of identity, narrative, and 'voice', often through procedural methods of composition. Fredric Jameson's analysis of Bob *Perelman's disjunctive poem 'China' in *Postmodernism, or, the Cultural Logic of Late Capitalism* (1991) is well known, although the most nuanced critical accounts of this writing are by the poets themselves: see Bernstein, *Content's Dream* (Sun & Moon, 1986; repr. Northwestern University Press, 2001); Silliman, *The New Sentence* (Roof, 1987); Perelman, *The Marginalization of Poetry* (Princeton University Press, 1996); and Hejinian, *The Language of Inquiry* (University of California Press, 2001).

As a literary movement, Language poetry is notable for the prominence of its female exponents, including Rae *Armantrout, Susan *Howe, and Leslie *Scalapino. Sometimes wrongly supposed to have prohibited the autobiographical or lyric 'I', the Language poets have in fact produced distinctly individual oeuvres. The San Francisco group have even undertaken an 'experiment in collective autobiography', named after their formative reading series, *The Grand Piano*.

It is no longer feasible to characterize Language as a 'renegade' literary movement in contrast to the New *Formalism, given that 'some of [its] members write very much for | a if not the public' (Bob Perelman). Perelman's own later verse has turned towards the discursive; Bernstein has experimented with deliberately simple forms and voices; and Silliman has maintained a widely read blog on 'post-avant' poetry. The election of Hejinian as a Chancellor of the Academy of American Poets in 2006 and the award of the Pulitzer Prize for Poetry to Armantrout's *Versed* (2009) confirmed Language poetry's acceptance by the literary establishment. See *The Language Book* (Southern Illinois University Press, 1984), ed. Bernstein and

Andrews, and *In the American Tree* (National Poetry Foundation, 1986; new edn., 2002), ed. Silliman.   JNT

Martian Poetry Craig *Raine's poem 'A Martian Sends a Postcard Home' prompted James *Fenton, to hail the new 'Martian School' (*New Statesman*, 20 Oct. 1978). Raine's poem is strikingly inventive. Misunderstanding the ignition and rear-view mirror in a car, Raine's alien declares that 'a key is turned to free the world | for movement, so quick there is a film | to watch for anything missed'. Riddling wit of this kind was partly inspired by William Golding's novel *The Inheritors* (according to Raine himself, quoted in *The Observer*, 2 Mar. 1980) and partly by similar effects in fellow-Oxonian John *Fuller's collection of poems *The Mountain in the Sea* (1975). The riddling was married in Martian poetry to the wit of 'outrageous simile', as a way of 'viewing the commonplace with wonder and innocence' (Blake *Morrison and Andrew *Motion, in their introduction to the 1982 *Penguin Book of Contemporary British Poetry*). Seven collections constitute the core of Martian poetry: Craig Raine's *The Onion, Memory* (1978), *A Martian Sends a Postcard Home* (1979), *A Free Translation* (1981), and *Rich* (1984); Christopher *Reid's *Arcadia* (1979) and *Pea Soup* (1982); and David Sweetman's *Looking into the Deep End* (1981).

The Martian poets were widely imitated, and for a while were influential, but journalistic talk of a school was misleading. Critics complained that the reliance on visual imagery was both ostentatious and limiting, but detected affinities with the work of the Metaphysicals and of the *Imagists, and with the aesthetics of Coleridge and of the high modernists. In *Katerina Brac* (1985), a set of poems voiced for an imaginary East European poet, Christopher Reid was the first of the Martians to choose an entirely new approach.

As poetry editors at the London publishing house Faber and Faber in the 1980s and 1990s, Raine and Reid continued to promote the metaphorical defamiliarization that has become a norm of post-war British poetry, from Ted *Hughes to Simon

*Armitage. Their own later work includes two elegiac sequences—Raine's *À la recherche du temps perdu* (Picador, 2000) and Reid's *A Scattering* (Areté, 2009)—in which the pathos implicit in Martianism's misrecognitions emerges to moving effect.   MHu*

Movement, The A new grouping in British literature identified by an anonymous article, 'In the Movement', which appeared in the *Spectator* on 1 October 1954. The article (in fact written by the paper's literary editor, J. D. Scott) suggested that Movement writers admired Leavis, *Empson, Orwell, and *Graves; that they were 'bored by the despair of the Forties, not much interested in suffering, and extremely impatient of poetic sensibility'; and that they were 'sceptical, robust, ironic'. Five writers were named; the publication of *Poets of the 1950s* (1955, ed. D. J. *Enright) and the *New Lines* anthology (1956, ed. Robert *Conquest) settled the list at nine: Kingsley *Amis, Robert Conquest, Donald *Davie, Enright, Thom *Gunn, John *Holloway, Elizabeth *Jennings, Philip *Larkin, and John *Wain. The anthology has become almost as celebrated for its artfully self-effacing introduction as for the poems it contains. While its editor modestly argued that the poets had in common 'little more than a negative determination to avoid bad principles', it was clear that these principles—and corresponding good ones—had been pretty thoroughly aired over the preceding years. By guardedly invoking *Yeats, *Graves, *Auden, and Edwin *Muir in the final section of his introduction, Conquest claimed for his poets a greater significance than his gently diplomatic tone implied.

The poetry of these writers, particularly in the 1950s, and the novels *Lucky Jim* (1954) and *That Uncertain Feeling* (1955) by Amis and *Hurry on Down* (1953) by Wain, together with Davie's critical study *Purity of Diction in English Verse* (1952), are now widely accepted as the core Movement texts, while a none-too-easily-defined Movement tone is often detected both in post-1950s work by these writers and in the poetry of others not originally associated with the group (Alan

*Brownjohn, George *MacBeth, Anthony *Thwaite). This tone is generally felt to be one of middlebrow scepticism, conformist disrespect, and ironical common sense: Larkin's poem 'Church Going' epitomizes the Movement's tone and stance. The consensus on the definition of the Movement is less secure; some have even suggested that the putative group was merely a journalistic invention.

Central and influential though the Movement writers became in post-war British literature, some critics, beginning with Charles *Tomlinson in 'The Middlebrow Muse', *Essays in Criticism*, 7 (1957), have felt parochialism, philistinism, and narrow-mindedness to be the foremost characteristics of their work. The Movement's rejection of Romantic excess links it to the post-war wave of ironical, level-headed sobriety which Chris *Wallace-Crabbe was to complain of in Australia and Robert *Lowell to react against in the USA as the 1960s began. The best survey, placing the Movement in its societal, political, and aesthetic contexts, is Blake Morrison, *The Movement* (Oxford University Press, 1980). See also *The Movement Reconsidered: Essays on Larkin, Amis, Gunn, Davie and Their Contemporaries* (Oxford University Press, 2009), ed. Zachary Leader.   MHu/NP

New Apocalypse, The A movement founded by J. F. *Hendry, Henry *Treece, and Dorian Cooke at a meeting in Leeds in August, 1938. In 1939 Hendry and Treece produced *The New Apocalypse*, with contributions by Hendry, Treece, Cooke, Norman McCaig (later *MacCaig), Nicholas *Moore, Philip O'Connor, Dylan *Thomas, and Robert Melville. Dylan Thomas was a decidedly unwilling recruit; and Hendry, Treece, Cooke, and McCaig were the core group.

In his introductory essay, 'Writers and Apocalypse', Hendry wrote of the problem of writing organically and of finding a living synthesis of man and the exterior world. This, as he explained in the slightly later 'Myth and Social Integration', was to be through personal myth—the aura within which a man grows and which he makes his own.

Henry Treece had contributed an essay, 'An Apocalyptic Writer and the Surrealists';

and Apocalypse, like *Surrealism, was concerned with the relation of art to the unconscious. G. S. *Fraser called it a dialectical development of Surrealism in his essay 'Apocalypse in Poetry', which appeared in the second anthology, *The White Horseman*, in 1941. Fraser was a friend of Nicholas Moore, in whose periodical *Seven* (which ran from summer 1938 to spring 1940) several of the Apocalypse writers had first appeared, though the urbane writing of Moore and Fraser had little in common with that of Apocalypse. A third anthology, *The Crown and the Sickle*, appeared in 1943 and marked the end of the movement. Of the earlier contributors there remained only Hendry, Treece, and Cooke, all of whom were away on war service; and shortly thereafter the movement faded into what Herbert *Read named the New Romanticism, of which Treece was to be a leading figure.

The poetry of the movement did not measure up to its aspirations, and Hendry's essays were the best things to come out of it. Hendry, Cooke, and McCaig wrote a prophetic poetry with a surrealist tone that was uncontrolled and often violent in its imagery. Treece leaned to the banal and sentimental. McCaig, Moore, and Fraser wrote good poems in the decade, but not in the Apocalypse manner. Apocalypse and its successor, the New Romanticism, fostered much of the looseness and pretentiousness that were the vices of the worst poetry of the Forties.

Apocalypse is discussed in *The Poetry of the Thirties* (Gollancz, 1975) and *The Poetry of the Forties* (Manchester University Press, 1985), both by A. T. Tolley, and in *Poets of the Apocalypse*, by A. E. Salmon (Twayne, 1983). *Conductors of Chaos* (Picador, 1994) ed. Iain Sinclair, includes a selection of Hendry's poetry by Andrew *Crozier. For the wartime context of Apocalyptic poetics, see Leo Mellor, *Reading the Ruins: Modernism, Bombsites and British Culture* (Cambridge University Press, 2011). ATT

New Formalism and New Narrative

New Formalism is the name commonly given to the resurgence of metred and rhymed poetry among younger American poets during the 1980s. These poets came of age during the 1960s and 1970s, when the free-verse revolution instigated by *Pound, *Eliot, and William Carlos *Williams had become the accepted orthodoxy within the American university writing workshops. The New Formalists—many of whom studied English metrics with poet and classicist Robert *Fitzgerald at Harvard, or were influenced at Stanford by the Yvor *Winters formalist aesthetic, emphasizing iambics, the plain style of Ben Jonson, and paraphrasable intellectual argument, that remained a strong presence through the Seventies—returned to traditional metres and forms and to narrative in order to give back to American poetry a clarity, a music, and an objectivity which might make it accessible to a general audience.

While there is some continuity between this generation of formalists in the United States and previous ones, there are also distinct differences between it and the academic formalism that emerged out of the New Criticism in the 1950s. While the former eschewed emotion in favour of irony, used elevated poetic diction and inverted syntax, and frequently looked to European culture for its subject, the New Formalists, by contrast, are more direct in their depiction of emotion, more colloquial in their diction, and more at ease with American popular culture as a source for formal poems (hence the later term 'Expansive Poetry'). These qualities are best exemplified in Dana *Gioia's lyrics on the landscapes of California and suburban New York; in Gjertrud *Schnackenberg's elegies to her father; in Timothy *Steele's direct yet classically restrained love lyrics.

The related work of the New Narrative movement is characterized by clear storylines in both fixed and open forms. Christopher Clausen's *The Place of Poetry* (1981) established a historical context for the return to narrative in verse. The same year saw publication of Frederick Feirstein's *Manhattan Carnival*, a long poem in rhymed couplets. Other book-length poems include Vikram *Seth's *The Golden Gate* (1986) and Frederick *Turner's science-fiction epics *The New World* (1985) and *Genesis*

(1988). Robert *McDowell's *Quiet Money* (1987) and Mark *Jarman's *The Black Riviera* (1990) contain shorter narratives.

New Narrative poets have been called reactionary for their return to traditional techniques, but they are also credited with helping to revitalize American poetry. They have written eloquently about E. A. *Robinson, *Frost, and *Jeffers as literary forebears, and have praised poets like Louis *Simpson for writing narratives of ordinary life when it was unfashionable to do so. Rita *Dove's sequence of short narrative poems, *Thomas and Beulah* (1986), may have given momentum to the movement by winning the Pulitzer Prize.

Expansive Poetry: Essays on the New Narrative and the New Formalism, ed. Frederick Feirstein (1989) collected critical essays by a number of these writers. *New Expansive Poetry: Theory, Criticism, History* (1999—both Story Line), ed. R. S. Gwynn, claimed the movement as 'the most compelling ... in American poetry ... since the *Beats'. But narrative verse did not capture the popular imagination like *Ginsberg's *Howl*, and the title essay of Gioia's *Can Poetry Matter?* (Graywolf, 1992; new edn. 2002) now marks the high point of New Formalism's influence.   RMCP/DM*

New Generation A promotional label applied by the Poetry Society in 1994 to twenty British poets who had recently published collections: Moniza *Alvi, Simon *Armitage, John *Burnside, Robert *Crawford, David *Dabydeen, Michael *Donaghy, Carol Ann *Duffy, Ian *Duhig, Elizabeth Garrett, Lavinia *Greenlaw, W. N. *Herbert, Michael *Hofmann, Mick *Imlah, Kathleen *Jamie, Jamie *McKendrick, Sarah *Maguire, Glyn *Maxwell, Don *Paterson, Pauline *Stainer, and Susan *Wicks. The selection panel included Vicki *Feaver and Michael *Longley, the critic James Wood, and the broadcaster Melvyn Bragg.

As a media campaign, the New Generation successfully associated poetry with a mid-90s mood of quasi-rebellious cultural renewal, which had also identified new generations in visual art (the Young British Artists) and music (Britpop). As with those movements, formative associations already existed between the leading participants, and they have since become influential figures in their own right as editors, teachers, and judges.

Anticipated by *The New Poetry* (Bloodaxe) in 1993, the New Generation's claim to canonical status was made by two 1998 anthologies: *The Penguin Book of Poetry from Britain and Ireland since 1945*, ed. Armitage and Crawford, and *The Firebox* (Picador), ed. Sean *O'Brien. Both presented a devolved history of post-war poetry, characterized by equality of opportunity and pluralism of identity. (Scottish poets were strongly represented in the New Generation, although it was noted there were no Welsh poets.) Daljit Nagra (b.1966) has written that the presence of Alvi in the group 'inspired me to think it was possible for someone to write about "Asians" and be successful in poetry'.

Selected as individuals, the group never articulated a collective poetics. Nevertheless, a number of poets had affinities with the *New Formalism in America; many approached the poetic anecdote with the colloquial knowingness of Elizabeth *Bishop or Paul *Muldoon; and the majority may be said to have continued the 'empirical lyricism' identified by Andrew *Crozier as the dominant British mode from the *Movement to *Martianism, in which 'the authoritative self ... depends on its employment of metaphor and simile for poetic vitality'. See *New Generation Poets – A Poetry Review Special Issue*, 84:1 (Spring 1994), ed. Peter Forbes.   JNT

New Narrative See NEW FORMALISM.

New York School, The A term used since the 1960s to refer to a group of American poets who emerged in the 1950s, when the New York School of painting dominated the art world with which most of them were closely linked. Frank *O'Hara, John *Ashbery, and Kenneth *Koch had been classmates at Harvard; in New York they met painters and wrote about them for art magazines, and O'Hara worked at the Museum of Modern Art, as did James *Schuyler. Rounding out the group were Barbara *Guest, Kenward *Elmslie, and Harry *Mathews. Besides their friendship and the affinities of their verse with twentieth-century vanguard art generally, and with Abstract Expressionism in particular, these poets shared a relationship to the poetry of the immediate past that was unique at the time: thoroughly familiar with *Yeats, *Pound, *Eliot, *Stevens, Hart *Crane, and *Auden, they were influenced no less by French poetry from Baudelaire through to the *Surrealists, and by translations of the Russian poets Mayakovsky and Pasternak; and their familiarity with the French and Russian modernist traditions, as well as their appreciation of maverick English and American poets such as Laura *Riding, John *Wheelwright, F. T. *Prince, David *Schubert, and Edwin *Denby, cleared the way for a common interest in what might be called the intense urbane, expressed in language that is witty, abstract, and colloquial by turns. One section of Donald Allen's anthology, *The New American Poetry 1945–1960* (1960), was devoted to Ashbery, Guest, Koch, O'Hara, and Schuyler, and the work of all seven poets was influential during the following decade, in America especially but in England as well. After reaching its zenith with the publication of O'Hara's *Collected Poems*, also edited by Allen, six years after O'Hara was fatally injured by a beach taxi in 1966, this collective influence declined somewhat, though Ashbery, O'Hara, Schuyler, and Koch were read more widely than ever during the Seventies and Eighties. Other poets associated with the New York School include Bill *Berkson, Ted *Berrigan, Ron *Padgett, Joseph *Ceravolo, Lee *Harwood, Clark *Coolidge, and Bernadette *Mayer. The artist Joe Brainard, who collaborated with many of these writers, has also emerged as an honorary member for his experimental prose memoir *I Remember* (Angel Hair, 1970; repr. Granary, 2001).

See David Lehman, *The Last Avant Garde: The Making of the New York School of Poets* (Doubleday, 1998) and *The Angel Hair Anthology* (Granary, 2001), ed. Anne Waldman and Lewis Warsh. *The Poets of the New York School*, ed. John Bernard Myers (University of Pennsylvania, 1969), and *An Anthology of New York Poets*, ed. Ron Padgett and David Shapiro (Random

House, 1970), were influential early anthologies. Mark *Ford has edited two later selections: *The New York Poets* (2004) and, with Trevor Winkfield, *The New York Poets II* (2006—both Carcanet). RH*

Objectivism A movement associated with the work of William Carlos *Williams, George *Oppen, Louis *Zukofsky, and Charles *Reznikoff. In February 1931, *Poetry* (Chicago) brought out a special Objectivist issue edited by Zukofsky who specified as required reading Williams's *Spring and All*, T. S. *Eliot's *The Waste Land* and 'Marina', E. E. *Cummings's *Is 5*, Marianne *Moore's *Observations*, Wallace *Stevens's *Harmonium*, and Ezra *Pound's *XXX Cantos*. A press was established in New York financed by Oppen, and in 1932 under the name 'To Publishers' it brought out *An Objectivists' Anthology*. Edited by Zukofsky, this included work by Williams, Oppen, Reznikoff, Carl *Rakosi, and Kenneth *Rexroth. Pound and Eliot were also represented. Shortly after this, 'To Publishers' became the Objectivist Press, under the editorship of Zukofsky and Williams.

Recalling Objectivism in his *Autobiography* (1951), Williams described it as a rejection of *Imagism: but, in fact, many of its priorities were similar. Like the Imagists, the Objectivists were concerned with precision, with dramatized experience rather than statement, and with rhythms and cadences that were the necessary products of a particular moment and voice. 'The poem' Williams argued, 'is an object'; and 'the poem being an object', he continued, 'it must be the purpose of the poet to make of his words a new form: to invent, that is, an object consonant with his day.' Of course there are differences between Objectivism and Imagism: there is a greater emphasis on the formal structure of the poem in Objectivist writing, and a more intense interest in the musical properties of poetry. But it seems fair to see Objectivism as a movement that grew dialectically out of Imagism, not in opposition to it but in fruitful tension with it.

See *The Objectivists* (Bloodaxe, 1996), ed. Andrew McAllister and *The Objectivist

Nexus (University of Alabama Press, 1999), ed. Rachel Blau DuPlessis and Peter Quartermain.   RJG

Oulipo The acronym of a group of writers and mathematicians convened in France in 1960 by Raymond Queneau and Francois Le Lionna as 'Ouvroir de littérature potentialle'. The name indicated their interest in inventing abstract methods for literary production. Oulipo's influence on postmodern Anglophone poetry, like that of *Surrealism, has been indirect but wide-ranging. The troubadour sestina, for example, was recognized by Oulipo (and its only American member, Harry *Mathews) as a lyric mode led by 'the successive powers of a permutation' (Queneau). The aleatory potential of such fixed forms has been developed in the practice of John *Ashbery and Paul *Muldoon among others. The Oulipian ideal of 'discovering' literature in other texts also informs some *Conceptual writing as well as mixed-media works such as Tom Phillips' *A Humument* (1970), and computer-generated poetry such as the algorithmic 'Pentametron'. See *Oulipo Compendium* (Atlas, 1998), ed. Mathews and Alistair Brotchie.   JNT

Saint Mark's Poetry Project, The The Poetry Project at Saint Mark's Church-in-the-Bowery, located on the north-east corner of Second Avenue and East 10th Street in New York City, has played a vital part in the development and dissemination of new American poetry since 1966, when it was started with the help of the Episcopalian church's rector, Father J. C. Michael Allen, and with money from a federal grant for the social rehabilitation of New York's lower East Side. The Project's first director, poet Joel *Oppenheimer, initiated a roster of activities which remains basically unchanged: open readings on Monday nights, invitational readings on Wednesday nights, weekly workshops conducted by neighbourhood poets, and the irregular publication of a poetry magazine, *The World*. During the tenure of the Project's second director, poet Anne *Waldman, the church became the unofficial campus of the *New York School of poetry, though both the

Project and its publications have always been hospitable to a wide range of poets, and the church has been the site of memorable readings not only by poets associated with the New York School, but also by Robert *Lowell, Allen *Ginsberg, Adrienne *Rich, John *Cage, Amiri *Baraka, John *Wieners, and many others. Father Allen was succeeded as rector by the equally co-operative Father David Garcia, and since Waldman the Project's poet-directors have included Ron *Padgett, Bernadette *Mayer, Eileen Myles, Ed Friedman, and Anselm Berrigan. See Anne Waldman (ed.), *Out of This World: An Anthology of the St. Mark's Poetry Project 1966–1991* (Crown, 1991) and Daniel Kane, *All Poets Welcome: A History of the Lower East Side Poetry Scene in the 1960s* (University of California Press, 2003).   RH

San Francisco Renaissance, The A group which grew out of a poetry reading held in 1955 at the Six Gallery, a small cooperative arts centre located in the Marina district of San Francisco and run by painters associated with the San Francisco Art Institute. The reading, recorded by Jack Kerouac in his novel *The Dharma Bums* (1958), brought together Allen *Ginsberg, Gary *Snyder, Michael *McClure, Philip *Whalen, and Philip *Lamantia, each of whom was introduced by Kenneth *Rexroth, a San Francisco poet from an earlier generation. Further readings at different venues, including the City Lights bookshop run by Lawrence *Ferlinghetti, helped to promote what came to be known as the San Francisco Renaissance. Among other poets associated at one time or another with this movement were Robert *Duncan, William *Everson, Jack *Spicer, Robin *Blaser, and Lew Welch. Although it was predominantly a white, male group, a few black writers, like Bob Kaufman, and some women writers, such as Helen Adam, Madeline Gleason, Joanne Kyger, and Diane *di Prima, were actively involved.

The movement was more notable for its spirit of camaraderie than its unanimity of purpose: it in fact incorporated a variety of styles, among them prophetic rapture, *imagist precision, *surrealism, satire, and personal confession. Also, several writers associated with the group were equally, if not more, involved with the activities of the *Black Mountain movement and the *Beat generation. If there was a common objective uniting the San Francisco writers, however, it was summed up by Ferlinghetti, who declared in 1955 that the kind of poetry that was 'making most noise' in his city was 'what should be called street poetry'. 'It amounts,' he said, 'to getting poetry back into the street where it once was, out of the classroom . . . and—in fact—off the printed page.' Believing that 'the printed word has made poetry so silent', the San Francisco poets aimed at a language and line shaped by the *voice*, an oral poetry frequently accompanied by jazz. Their experimental approach to the representation of voice on the page has also been influential in American verse. See Michael Davidson, *The San Francisco Poets: Poetics and Community at Mid-Century* (Cambridge University Press, 1989), and Lewis Ellingham and Kevin Killian, *Poet Be Like God: Jack Spicer and the San Francisco Renaissance* (Wesleyan University Press, 1998).   RJG*

Scots Other names for the language of Lowland Scotland have included Lallans, Braid Scots, the Scots Vernacular, Aggrandized Scots, Synthetic Scots, and Plastic Scots. Doric, now seldom used, properly applies to the dialect of north-east Scotland, especially Aberdeenshire.

After the revival of poetry in Scots in the eighteenth-century, by Allan Ramsay, Robert Fergusson, Alexander Ross, and Robert Burns, poetry continued to be written in Lallans, or Lallan as it was called by R. L. Stevenson, who can be credited with lending the term a new currency. Much of this subsequent verse rarely aspired to a level above that of dialect and the districts associated with it. Supernatural themes were especially common, in, for example, the poetry of Violet Jacob (1863-1946). Lewis *Spence (1874-1955) introduced a diction with more historical resonance, harking back to the Scotland of the sixteenth century. More successful, however, were Sir Alexander *Gray's (1882-1967) translations into Scots from Heine (*Songs and Ballads, Chiefly from Heine*, 1920).

Christopher Murray Grieve, better known as Hugh *MacDiarmid, published his first Scots lyrics in his collection *Sangschaw* in 1925. In such poems as 'The Bonnie Broukit Bairn', 'The Watergaw', and 'The Eemis Stane', he produced a startling modernity in terms of imagery and psychology together with a strongly ancestral note conveyed by Scots diction. In editorials in his magazine *The Scottish Chapbook* (15 issues, 1922-3), MacDiarmid justified Scots in terms of modernity, psychology, and indigenousness. Equally important to him was the extent to which its 'speculative and imaginative tendencies' were superior to those of English, especially as used by 'Anglicized Scots'.

MacDiarmid's Scots, and that of writers after him, has been called Synthetic Scots. To some extent the phrase is an attempt to escape the belittling associations of dialect, but what it describes is the practice of using in the same poem words which originate from two or more districts. In recovering a language in which, MacDiarmid noted, there was embedded 'a vast unutilized mass of lapsed observation', dictionaries were, and continue to be, indispensable. Philological acumen is peculiarly important to any poet attempting to write Scots verse. Indeed, it should be apparent that it is by now a literary or poetic language. Its relationship to contemporary Scottish speech is ideal, tangential, and retrospective, rather than a reflection of how Scottish people actually speak.

Poetry in Scots can be seen as an attempt to preserve a linguistic and poetic tradition of very considerable antiquity. Political as well as literary factors enter the picture. The Scots language is associated by many with political independence, as well as with perhaps the greatest period of Scots poetry, that of the 'Makars', Henryson, Dunbar, Douglas, and Lindsay. However, there are specific qualities to Scots which underline its distinctiveness. Especially in native stanzas, such as Standard Habbie (or the Burns stanza), or that of the old poem 'Christis Kirk on the Grene', or the elaborate stanza of Montgomerie's 'The Cherry and the Slae' (*c.*1597), it lends itself to a remarkable directness, precision, and fast tempo. Qualities such as these can be seen in the plainer measures of Mac-Diarmid's long poem *A Drunk Man Looks at the Thistle* (1926). They come through strongly in Robert *Garioch's artfully stanzaic verse, as well as his sonnets, especially those translated from Belli. Satirical and comic effects suit Scots well, too, as does tenderness, which can hardly be surprising in a tradition which includes the songmaker Robert Burns. Good examples are William *Soutar's 'The Tryst' and Sydney Goodsir *Smith's 'Aa My Life'.

Others who have used Scots include Douglas *Young, Maurice Lindsay, George Bruce, Alasdair *Mackie, Alexander Scott, and Tom Scott. Edwin *Morgan used Scots in his translations (see, especially, his versions of Mayakovsky). It is used by William Neill (b.1922), Raymond Vettese (b.1950), Robert *Crawford (b.1959), and by W. N. *Herbert (b.1961), whose tonal base is Dundonian speech, to which he adds an extraordinary diction gleaned from lexicons. Contemporaries for whom Scots is an occasional alternative to standard English include Kathleen *Jamie, Don *Paterson, and Jackie *Kay. While the literary perpetuation of Scots (or Lallans) seems more or less secure, a language's detachment from the actual speech of a country remains a problem with potentially serious consequences. It has no standardized orthography.   DED

Stanford School, The The name sometimes given to the writers associated with Yvor *Winters during his career (1927–66) at Stanford University, California. Between May 1929 and February 1930, Winters, his wife Janet *Lewis, and the poet Howard *Baker published four issues of a magazine, the *Gyroscope*, which included work by themselves, Caroline Gordon, and Katherine Anne Porter. In the course of the 1930s, Winters's dissatisfaction with the forms and ideas of modernism hardened into the systematic reaction expressed in his criticism, notably in the short books later collected as *In Defense of Reason* (1947) and in the manifesto-foreword to *Before Disaster* (1934), a pamphlet of his poems. His ideas were also forcefully expressed in

his verse-writing classes, which led in time to two anthologies: *Twelve Poets of the Pacific* (New Directions, 1937) and *Poets of the Pacific: Second Series* (Stanford University Press, 1949). Among the poets included were, in the former, J. V. *Cunningham, and in the latter, Edgar *Bowers. Among other poets who attended the writing classes were Thom *Gunn, Donald *Hall, Philip *Levine, and Robert *Pinsky.   CW

Surrealism Surrealism had its origins in France. It was concerned with the resolution of the two seemingly contradictory states of dream and reality in an absolute 'Surreality', by means of which freedom from the shackles of reality would be attained. The Surrealists advocated an art that was free of control by reason; and Freud's theories concerning the unconscious had great importance for them. The movement originated in the group that directed the review *Littérature* from 1919 to 1924—Louis Aragon, André Breton, and Phillipe Soupault—and in 1924 Breton produced *La Manifeste du Surréalisme* (the First Surrealist Manifesto).

Surrealism came to public attention in England with the International Surrealist Exhibition at the New Burlington Galleries in June 1936, which was accompanied by the publication of *Surrealism*, edited by Herbert *Read. An earlier account had been *A Short Survey of Surrealism* (1935) by the 19-year-old David *Gascoyne, one of the young poets who were to be seen in David Archer's bookshop in Parton Street, at once a home for Surrealism and for left-wing ideas. It was among certain writers born between 1911 and 1915 that Surrealism had its impact on English poetry: David Gascoyne; Charles *Madge; Kenneth *Allott; Lawrence *Durrell; Francis Scarfe; Philip *O'Connor; and Dylan *Thomas (in his stories); though the older Hugh Sykes-Davies and Humphrey Jennings also espoused it.

The most notable British organ of Surrealist literature was *Contemporary Poetry and Prose*, which ran from May 1936 to autumn 1937 and was edited from Parton Street by Roger Roughton, then 19.

The impact of Surrealism on literature in England was much less than it was on the visual arts. However, cultural manifestations as various as the *New Apocalypse movement and Mass-Observation owed a great deal imaginatively to Surrealism. Many of the younger writers associated with the movement stopped writing at an early age, perhaps because the coming of the Second World War destroyed the adventurous climate in which Surrealism thrived. *The Poetry of the Thirties*, by A. T. Tolley (Gollancz, 1975), discusses Surrealism and British poetry. The later influence of Surrealism on post-war American poetry, through groups such as the *Beats and *New York School (and in particular, the work of John *Ashbery), is a potentially vast subject. For an outline, see Andrew Joron, *Neo-Surrealism, or The Sun at Night: Transformations of Surrealism in American Poetry, 1966-1999* (Black Square, 2004; revd. edn., Kolourmeim, 2010).   ATT*

Wellington Group, The The term refers to a loose association of New Zealand poets in Wellington in the years between 1950 and 1965. New Zealand poetry after the Second World War tended to polarize around debate on the precepts that Allen *Curnow had outlined in his *A Book of New Zealand Verse 1923-1945*. What Curnow sensed as a 'common problem of the imagination' seemed to some of the younger poets to have become a prescription for thematic concerns, and Curnow's editorial practice became the subject of ongoing controversy.

The Wellington group saw themselves as establishing poetic practices that differed from those of Curnow as anthologist and, to a lesser degree, of Charles *Brasch as *Landfall*'s editor. Controversy flared over the withholding of permission for some work that Curnow wished to include in the *Penguin Book of New Zealand Verse* in 1960, and over the editorial introduc-

tion and practice when that anthology appeared. Yet seen retrospectively, the idea of a 'Wellington group' is more a term of geographical convenience than of poetic identity.

Certainly James K. *Baxter and Louis *Johnson, both Wellington residents during the period, seemed to draw a number of poets around them: Alastair *Campbell, for example, and the immigrants Peter *Bland and Charles Doyle. Yet Baxter was a poet less at odds with Curnow than the rhetoric of his criticisms might have suggested. Only Louis Johnson, the editor of *Poetry Yearbook*, which published ten issues between 1951 and 1964, might be argued to have been at the centre of a school. The identification of a Wellington presence occurs in a paper Baxter gave to the 1951 Writers' Conference, and it underpins the ongoing critical rhetoric of the next decade. The issues in contention became those of the 'universal', as opposed to regional, concerns of local poetry, the primacy of 'content' as opposed to notions of academic formalism, and an increasing focus upon the suburban, the domestic, and the personal in much of the new work.

It is arguable that the sense of community asserted by the Wellington group was based less on poetic practice than on literary politics, in which a century of antipathy between the cities of Auckland and Wellington simply found a new focus. The notion of a 'group' and the polemics associated with it seem to have disappeared by about 1966.

For further information, see Kendrick Smithyman, 'Wellington and the Fifties,' in *Essays on New Zealand Literature*, ed. Wystan Curnow (Heinemann, 1973). The anthology *Big Smoke: New Zealand Poems 1960-1975* (Auckland University Press, 2000), ed. Alan Brunton, Murray *Edmond, and Michele *Leggott charts the wider reaction against Curnow's localism after the Wellington group.   WSB*

Lists of Prizes and Prizewinners

United States of America: Pulitzer Prize for Poetry

1922 Edwin Arlington Robinson, *Collected Poems*
1923 Edna St Vincent Millay, *The Ballad of the Harp-Weaver*
1924 Robert Frost, *New Hampshire*
1925 Edwin Arlington Robinson, *The Man Who Died Twice*
1926 Amy Lowell, *What's O'Clock*
1927 Leonora Speyer, *Fiddler's Farewell*
1928 Edwin Arlington Robinson, *Tristram*
1929 Stephen Vincent Benét, *John Brown's Body*
1930 Conrad Aiken, *Selected Poems*
1931 Robert Frost, *Collected Poems*
1932 George Dillon, *The Flowering Stone*
1933 Archibald MacLeish, *Conquistador*
1934 Robert Hillyer, *Collected Verse*
1935 Audrey Wurdemann, *Bright Ambush*
1936 Robert P. Tristram Coffin, *Strange Holiness*
1937 Robert Frost, *A Further Range*
1938 Marya Zaturenska, *Cold Morning Sky*
1939 John Gould Fletcher, *Selected Poems*
1940 Mark Van Doren, *Collected Poems*
1941 Leonard Bacon, *Sunderland Capture*
1942 William Rose Benét, *The Dust Which Is God*
1943 Robert Frost, *A Witness Tree*
1944 Stephen Vincent Benét, *Western Star*
1945 Karl Shapiro, *V-Letter and Other Poems*
1946 [No Award]
1947 Robert Lowell, *Lord Weary's Castle*
1948 W. H. Auden, *The Age of Anxiety*
1949 Peter Viereck, *Terror and Decorum*
1950 Gwendolyn Brooks, *Annie Allen*
1951 Carl Sandburg, *Complete Poems*
1952 Marianne Moore, *Collected Poems*
1953 Archibald MacLeish, *Collected Poems 1917–1952*
1954 Theodore Roethke, *The Waking*
1955 Wallace Stevens, *Collected Poems*
1956 Elizabeth Bishop, *Poems: North & South*
1957 Richard Wilbur, *Things of This World*
1958 Robert Penn, *Promises: Poems 1954–1956*
1959 Stanley Kunitz, *Selected Poems 1928–1958*
1960 W. D. Snodgrass, *Heart's Needle*
1961 Phyllis McGinley, *Times Three: Selected Verse From Three Decades*
1962 Alan Dugan, *Poems*
1963 William Carlos Williams, *Pictures from Brueghel*
1964 Louis Simpson, *At The End Of The Open Road*
1965 John Berryman, *77 Dream Songs*
1966 Richard Eberhart, *Selected Poems*
1967 Anne Sexton, *Live or Die*
1968 Anthony Hecht, *The Hard Hours*
1969 George Oppen, *Of Being Numerous*
1970 Richard Howard, *Untitled Subjects*
1971 W. S. Merwin, *The Carrier of Ladders*
1972 James Wright, *Collected Poems*
1973 Maxine Kumin, *Up Country*
1974 Robert Lowell, *The Dolphin*
1975 Gary Snyder, *Turtle Island*
1976 John Ashbery, *Self-Portrait in a Convex Mirror*
1977 James Merrill, *Divine Comedies*
1978 Howard Nemerov, *Collected Poems*
1979 Robert Penn Warren, *Now and Then*
1980 Donald Justice, *Selected Poems*
1981 James Schuyler, *The Morning of the Poem*
1982 Sylvia Plath, *The Collected Poems*
1983 Galway Kinnell, *Selected Poems*
1984 Mary Oliver, *American Primitive*
1985 Carolyn Kizer, *Yin*
1986 Henry Taylor, *The Flying Change*
1987 Rita Dove, *Thomas and Beulah*
1988 William Meredith, *Partial Accounts: New and Selected Poems*
1989 Richard Wilbur, *New and Collected Poems*
1990 Charles Simic, *The World Doesn't End*
1991 Mona Van Duyn, *Near Changes*
1992 James Tate, *Selected Poems*
1993 Louise Glück, *The Wild Iris*

1994 Yusef Komunyakaa, *Neon Vernacular: New and Selected Poems*
1995 Philip Levine, *The Simple Truth*
1996 Jorie Graham, *The Dream of the Unified Field*
1997 Lisel Mueller, *Alive Together: New and Selected Poems*
1998 Charles Wright, *Black Zodiac*
1999 Mark Strand, *Blizzard of One*
2000 C. K. Williams, *Repair*
2001 Stephen Dunn, *Different Hours*
2002 Carl Dennis, *Practical Gods*
2003 Paul Muldoon, *Moy Sand and Gravel*
2004 Franz Wright, *Walking to Martha's Vineyard*
2005 Ted Kooser, *Delights & Shadows*
2006 Claudia Emerson, *Late Wife*
2007 Natasha Trethewey, *Native Guard*
2008 Philip Schultz, *Failure*
2008 Robert Hass, *Time and Materials*
2009 W. S. Merwin, *The Shadow of Sirius*
2010 Rae Armantrout, *Versed*
2011 Kay Ryan, *The Best of It: New and Selected Poems*
2012 Tracy K. Smith, *Life on Mars*

Canada: Governor General's Literary Award for Poetry (Governor General's Literary Award for Poetry and Drama until 1980)

1937 E. J. Pratt, *The Fable of the Goats*
1938 Kenneth Leslie, *By Stubborn Stars*
1939 Arthur S. Bourinot, *Under the Sun*
1940 E. J. Pratt, *Brebeuf and his Brethren*
1941 Anne Marriott, *Calling Adventurers*
1942 Earle Birney, *David and Other Poems*
1943 A. J. M. Smith, *News of the Phoenix*
1944 Dorothy Livesay, *Day and Night*
1945 Earle Birney, *Now Is Time*
1946 Robert Finch, *Poems*
1947 Dorothy Livesay, *Poems for People*
1948 A. M. Klein, *The Rocking Chair and Other Poems*
1949 James Reaney, *The Red Heart*
1950 James Wreford Watson, *Of Time and the Lover*
1951 Charles Bruce, *The Mulgrave Road*
1952 E. J. Pratt, *Towards the Last Spike*
1953 Douglas LePan, *The Net and the Sword*
1954 P. K. Page, *The Metal and the Flower*
1955 Wilfred Watson, *Friday's Child*

1956 Robert A. D. Ford, *A Window on the North*
1957 Jay Macpherson, *The Boatman*
1958 James Reaney, *A Suit of Nettles*
1959 Irving Layton, *Red Carpet for the Sun*
1960 Margaret Avison, *Winter Sun*
1961 Robert Finch, *Acis in Oxford*
1962 James Reaney, *Twelve Letters to a Small Town and The Killdeer and Other Plays*
1963 [No award]
1964 Raymond Souster, *The Colour of the Times*
1965 Alfred Purdy, *The Cariboo Horses*
1966 Margaret Atwood, *The Circle Game*
1967 Eli Mandel, *An Idiot Joy*
    Alden Nowlan, *Bread, Wine and Salt*
1968 Leonard Cohen, *Selected Poems 1956–1968*
1969 George Bowering, *Rocky Mountain Foot and The Gangs of Kosmos*
    Gwendolyn MacEwen, *The Shadow-Maker*
1970 bp Nichol, *Still Water / The True Eventual Story of Billy the Kid / Beach Head / The cosmic chef: an evening of concrete*
    Michael Ondaatje, *The Collected Works of Billy the Kid*
1971 John Glassco, *Selected Poems*
1972 Dennis Lee, *Civil Elegies and Other Poems*
1973 Miriam Mandel, *Lions at her Face*
1974 Ralph Gustafson, *Fire on Stone*
1975 Milton Acorn, *The Island Means Minago*
1976 Joe Rosenblatt, *Top Soil*
1977 D. G. Jones, *Under the Thunder the Flowers Light up the Earth*
1978 Patrick Lane, *Poems New and Selected*
1979 Michael Ondaatje, *There's a Trick with a Knife I'm Learning to Do*
1980 Stephen Scobie, *McAlmon's Chinese Opera*
1981 F. R. Scott, *The Collected Poems of F. R. Scott*
1982 Phyllis Webb, *The Vision Tree: Selected Poems*
1983 David Donnell, *Settlements*
1984 Paulette Jiles, *Celestial Navigation*
1985 Fred Wah, *Waiting for Saskatchewan*
1986 Al Purdy, *The Collected Poems of Al Purdy*
1987 Gwendolyn MacEwan, *Afterworlds*

1988 Erin Mouré, *Furious*
1989 Heather Spears, *The Word for Sand*
1990 Margaret Avison, *No Time*
1991 Don McKay, *Night Field*
1992 Lorna Crozier, *Inventing the Hawk*
1993 Don Coles, *Forests of the Medieval World*
1994 Robert Hilles, *Cantos from a Small Room*
1995 Anne Szumigalski, *Voice*
1996 E. D. Blodgett, *Apostrophes: Woman at a Piano*
1997 Dionne Brand, *Land to Light On*
1998 Stephanie Bolster, *White Stone: The Alice Poems*
1999 Jan Zwicky, *Songs for Relinquishing the Earth*
2000 Don McKay, *Another Gravity*
2001 George Elliott Clarke, *Execution Poems*
2002 Roy Miki, *Surrender*
2003 Tim Lilburn, *Kill-site*
2004 Roo Borson, *Short Journey Upriver Toward Ōishida*
2005 Anne Compton, *Processional*
2006 John Pass, *Stumbling in the Bloom*
2007 Don Domanski, *All Our Wonder Unavenged*
2008 Jacob Scheier, *More to Keep Us Warm*
2009 David Zieroth, *The Fly in Autumn*
2010 Richard Greene, *Boxing the Compass*
2011 Phil Hall, *Killdeer*
2012 Julie Bruck, *Monkey Ranch*

New Zealand Post Book Awards (New Zealand Book Award for Poetry until 1996, Montana New Zealand Book Award for Poetry until 2010)

1976 Louis Johnson, *Fires and Patterns*
 C. K. Stead, *Quesada*
1977 Ruth Dallas, *Walking in the Snow*
 Alan Loney, *Dear Mondrian*
1978 Bill Manhire, *How to Take Your Clothes Off at the Picnic*
 Ian Wedde, *Spells for Coming Out*
1979 Kevin Ireland, *Literary Cartoons*
1980 Allen Curnow, *An Incorrigible Music*
1981 Michael Jackson, *Wall*
1982 Alistair Campbell, *Collected Poems*
1983 Allen Curnow, *You Will Know When You Get There*
 Cilla McQueen, *Homing In*

1984 Fleur Adcock, *Selected Poems*
1985 Bill Manhire, *Zoetropes*
1986 Kendrick Smithyman, *Stories About Wooden Keyboards*
1987 Allen Curnow, *The Loop in Lone Kauri Road*
 Elizabeth Nannestad, *Jump*
1988 Anne French, *All Cretans are Liars*
1989 Cilla McQueen, *Benzina*
1990 Elizabeth Smither, *A Pattern of Marching*
1991 Cilla McQueen, *Berlin Diary*
1992 Bill Manhire, *Milky Way Bar*
1993 Brian Turner, *Beyond*
1994 Andrew Johnston, *How to Talk*
1995 Michele Leggott, *Dia*
1996 Bill Manhire, *My Sunshine*
1997 Jenny Bornholdt, Gregory O'Brien, and Mark Williams, *An Anthology of New Zealand Poetry in English*
1998 Hone Tuwhare, *Shape-Shifter*
1999 Vincent O'Sullivan, *Seeing You Asked*
2000 Elizabeth Smither, *The Lark Quartet*
2001 Allen Curnow, *The Bells of Saint Babels*
2002 Hone Tuwhare, *Piggy-back Moon*
2003 Glenn Colquhon, *Playing God*
2004 Anne Kennedy, *Sing-Song*
2005 Vincent O'Sullivan, *Nice morning for it, Adam*
2006 Bill Manhire, *Lifted*
2007 Janet Frame, *The Goose Bath*
2008 Janet Charman, *Cold Snack*
2009 Jenny Bornholdt, *The Rocky Shore*
2010 Brian Turner, *Just This*
2011 Kate Camp, *The Mirror of Simple Annihilated Souls*
2012 Rhian Gallagher, *Shift*

Australia: The Kenneth Slessor Prize for Poetry (New South Wales Premier's Literary Awards)

1980 David Campbell, *Man in the Honeysuckle*
1981 Alan Gould, *Astral Sea*
1982 Fay Zwicky, *Kaddish and Other Poems*
1983 Vivian Smith, *Tide Country*
1984 Les Murray, *The People's Other World*
1985 Kevin Hart, *Your Shadow*
1986 Robert Gray, *Selected Poems 1963–83*
1987 Philip Hodgins, *Blood and Bone*

1988 Judith Beveridge, *The Domesticity of Giraffes*
1989 John Tranter, *Under Berlin*
1990 Robert Adamson, *The Clean Dark*
1991 Jennifer Maiden, *The Winter Baby*
1992 Elizabeth Riddell, *Selected Poems*
1993 Les Murray, *Translations from the Natural World*
1994 Barry Hill, *Ghosting William Buckley*
1995 Peter Boyle, *Coming Home From the World*
1996 Eric Beach, *Weeping for Lost Babylon*
    J. S. Harry, *Selected Poems*
1997 Anthony Lawrence, *The Viewfinder*
1999 Lee Cataldi, *Race Against Time*
2000 Jennifer Maiden, *Mines*
2001 Ken Taylor, *Africa*
2002 Alan Wearne, *The Lovemaker*
2003 Jill Jones, *Screen Jets Heaven*
2004 Pam Brown, *Dear Deliria: New and Selected Poems*
2005 Samuel Wagan Watson, *Smoke Encrypted Whispers*
2006 Jaya Savige, *Latecomers*
2007 John Tranter, *Urban Myths*
2008 Kathryn Lomer, *Two Kinds of Silence*
2009 L. K. Holt, *Man Wolf Man*
2010 Jordie Albiston, *The Sonnet According to 'M'*
2011 Jennifer Maiden, *Pirate Rain*
2012 Gig Ryan, *New and Selected Poems*

Great Britain and Ireland: Costa Poetry Award (Whitbread Poetry Award until 2006)

1985 Douglas Dunn, *Elegies*
1986 Peter Reading, *Stet*
1987 Seamus Heaney, *The Haw Lantern*
1988 Peter Porter, *The Automatic Oracle*
1989 Michael Donaghy, *Shibboleth*
1990 Paul Durcan, *Daddy, Daddy*
1991 Michael Longley, *Gorse Fires*
1992 Tony Harrison, *The Gaze of the Gorgon*
1993 Carol Ann Duffy, *Mean Time*
1994 James Fenton, *Out of Danger*
1995 Bernard O'Donoghue, *Gunpowder*
1996 Seamus Heaney, *The Spirit Level*
1997 Ted Hughes, *Tales from Ovid*
1998 Ted Hughes, *Birthday Letters*
1999 Seamus Heaney, *Beowulf*
2000 John Burnside, *The Asylum Dance*
2001 Selima Hill, *Bunny*
2002 Paul Farley, *The Ice Age*
2003 Don Paterson, *Landing Light*
2004 Michael Symmons Roberts, *Corpus*
2005 Christopher Logue, *Cold Calls*
2006 John Haynes, *Letter to Patience*
2007 Jean Sprackland, *Tilt*
2008 Adam Foulds, *The Broken World*
2009 Christopher Reid, *A Scattering*
2010 Jo Shapcott, *Of Mutability*
2011 Carol Ann Duffy, *The Bees*
2012 Kathleen Jamie, *The Overhaul*

General Web Links

Academy of American Poets
- Biographies of many modern American poets with sample poems.

Archive of the Now
- Audio archive of British innovative poetry at Queen Mary, University of London.

Australian Poetry Library
- Extensive collection of complete volumes by contemporary Australian poets.

Best New Zealand Poems
- Online annual poetry anthology with audio clips.

British Council Literature
- Critical biographies and bibliographies of living British poets.

Canadian Poetry Online
- Biographies, bibliographies, and poems by 19th- and 20th-century Canadian poets.

Canadian Women Poets
- Bibliographic guide to female Canadian poets.

The Caribbean Poetry Project
- Cambridge University website to promote Caribbean poetry in education.

Electronic Poetry Center
- Guide to American experimental poets at SUNY Buffalo.

First World War Poetry Digital Archive
- Resource of texts and contexts for British war poets.

Internet Poetry Archive
- Selected poems by international contemporary poets.

Irish Writers Online
- Bibliographic database of living Irish writers.

Kootenay School of Writing
- Archive of the experimental Canadian writing collective.

The League of Canadian Poets
- Guide to members of the professional organization for Canadian poetry.

The Modernist Journals Project
- Digitized archive of literary magazines from 1890 to 1922.

Naropa Poetics Archive
- Audio archive of readings from the Jack Kerouac School of Disembodied Poetics.

New Zealand Book Council: Writers Files
- New and updated biographies from *Oxford Companion to New Zealand Literature* (1998).

New Zealand Electronic Poetry Centre
- Guide to contemporary poets from New Zealand and the Pacific region.

Penn Sound
- American audio archive of modernist and contemporary poets.

The PIP (Project for Innovative Poetry) Blog
- Anthologies and biographies of innovative poets from Green Integer Press.

Poems Out Loud
- Audio and news website for American poets sponsored by W. W. Norton.

Poetry Africa Festival
- Biographies of festival participants from the University of KwaZulu-Natal.

Poetry Archive
- British audio archive of modern poets from around the world.

Poetry Foundation
- American guide to Anglophone poets at the Poetry Foundation, Chicago.

Poetry International
- Biographies and poems from the Poetry International Festival, Rotterdam.

Poetry Magazines
- Digitized archive of UK poetry magazines maintained by the Saison Poetry Library, London.

Representative Poetry Online
- Web anthology of poems from all periods of Anglophone literature.

Sackner Archive of Visual and Concrete Poetry
- Digitized catalogue of experimental print poetry.

The South Asian Literary Recordings Project
- Audio archive of contemporary writers from the Indian subcontinent.

Ubu Web
- Extensive digital archive of avant-garde poetics.